MW00450777

THE CRB COMMODITY YEARBOOK 1999

BRIDGE Commodity Research Bureau

John Wiley & Sons, Inc.
New York • Chichester • Weinheim • Brisbane • Singapore • Toronto

Published by John Wiley & Sons, Inc.

ISBN 0-471-32704-2

Printed in the United States of America
10 9 8 7 6 5 4 3 2 1

Bridge Commodity Research Bureau
30 South Wacker Drive, Suite 1810
Chicago IL 60606
312-454-1801
800-621-5271
http://www.crbindex.com
Email: crbinfo@bridge.com

TABLE OF CONTENTS

PAGE 4T Acknowledgments
8T The Commodity Price Trend
22T The Threat of Inflation
34T Understanding Electronic Trading
40T The Bridge/CRB Total Return Index
46T Futures Volume Highlights, U.S.
55T Futures Volume Highlights, Worldwide
66T Conversion Factors

PAGE 1 Aluminum
5 Antimony
6 Apples
7 Arsenic
8 Barley
11 Bauxite
12 Bismuth
13 Broilers
14 Butter
16 Cadmium
17 Canola (Rapeseed)
20 Cassava
21 Castor Beans
22 Cattle and Calves
29 Cement
30 Cheese
32 Chromium
33 Coal
36 Cobalt
37 Cocoa
42 Coconut Oil and Copra
44 Coffee
49 Coke
50 Copper
56 Corn
63 Corn Oil
64 Cotton
73 Cottonseed and Products
75 CRB Futures Index
79 Currencies
87 Diamonds
88 Eggs
92 Electric Power
94 Fertilizers (Nitrogen, Phosphate & Potash)
96 Fish
99 Flaxseed and Linseed Oil
103 Fruits
105 Gas
108 Gasoline
112 Gold
117 Grain Sorghum
119 Hay
120 Heating Oil
124 Hides and Leather
127 Hogs
132 Honey
133 Interest Rates, U.S.
144 Interest Rates, Worldwide
150 Iron and Steel
155 Lard
157 Lead
161 Lumber and Plywood
166 Magnesium
167 Manganese
169 Meats
173 Mercury
175 Milk
177 Molasses
179 Molybdenum
180 Nickel
181 Oats
185 Olive Oil
186 Onions
187 Oranges and Orange Juice
190 Palm Oil
191 Paper
193 Peanuts and Peanut Oil
197 Pepper
199 Petroleum
204 Plastics
206 Platinum-Group Metals
211 Pork Bellies
215 Potatoes
219 Rayon and Other Synthetic Fibers
221 Rice
224 Rubber
229 Rye
232 Salt
233 Sheep and Lambs
235 Silk
236 Silver
241 Soybean Meal
245 Soybean Oil
250 Soybeans
256 Stock Index Futures, U.S.
264 Stock Index Futures, Worldwide
268 Sugar
274 Sulfur
275 Sunflowerseed and Oil
276 Tall Oil
277 Tallow and Greases
279 Tea
280 Tin
284 Titanium
286 Tobacco
289 Tung Oil
290 Tungsten
291 Turkeys
294 Uranium
296 Vanadium
297 Vegetables
300 Wheat and Flour
311 Wool
314 Zinc

ACKNOWLEDGMENTS

The editors wish to thank the following for source material:

Agricultural Marketing Service (AMS)
Agricultural Research Service (ARS)
American Bureau of Metal Statistics, Inc. (ABMS)
American Forest & Paper Association (AF & PA)
The American Gas Association (AGA)
American Iron and Steel Institute (AISI)
American Metal Market (AMM)
Bureau of the Census
Bureau of Economic Analysis (BEA)
Bureau of Labor Statistics (BLS)
Chicago Board of Trade (CBT)
Chicago Mercantile Exchange (CME / IMM / IOM)
Coffee, Sugar & Cocoa Exchange (CSCE)
Commodity Credit Corporation (CCC)
Commodity Futures Trading Commision (CFTC)
The Conference Board
Economic Research Service (ERS)
Edison Electric Institute (EEI)
E D & F Man Cocoa Ltd
Farm Service Agency (FSA)
Federal Reserve Bank of St. Louis
Fiber Economics Bureau, Inc.
Florida Department of Citrus
Food and Agriculture Organization of the United Nations (FAO)
Foreign Agricultural Service (FAS)
Futures Industry Association (FIA)
International Cotton Advisory Committee (ICAC)
International Rubber Study Group (IRSG)
Johnson Matthey
Kansas City Board of Trade (KCBT)
Leather Industries of America
MidAmerica Commodity Exchange (MidAm)
Minneapolis Grain Exchange (MGE)
National Agricultural Statistics Service (NASS)
National Coffee Association of U.S.A., Inc. (NCA)
New York Cotton Exchange (NYCE / NYFE / FINEX)
New York Mercantile Exchange (NYMEX)
Commodity Exchange, Inc. (COMEX)
Oil World
The Organisation for Economic Co-Operation and Development (OECD)
Random Lengths
The Silver Institute
The Society of the Plastics Industry, Inc. (SPI)
United Nations (UN)
United States Department of Agriculture (USDA)
United States Geological Survey (USGS)
Wall Street Journal (WSJ)
Winnipeg Commodity Exchange (WCE)

THE COMMODITY PRICE TREND

In 1998, the Bridge Commodity Research Bureau's Futures Price Index declined for the third consecutive year and closed at the lowest end-of-year level since 1975. The December 31, 1998 closing value of 191.22 was 37.92 lower, or 16.55 percent below the December 31, 1997 closing level of 229.14. The yearly percentage loss was the second largest since the Index was created in 1957, trailing only the 1981 decline of 17.37 percent.

For the year, all six of the Bridge/CRB Futures Price Index sub-indices fell led by the 28.23 percent decline in the energy group. The best performing group was the precious metals which only declined 6.04 percent.

Energy

The energy subindex fell 28.23 percent in 1998 led by declines for the second consecutive year in excess of 31 percent in both crude oil and heating oil. Natural gas prices fell by 14 percent from their year earlier level compared to an 18 percent loss in 1997.

Crude oil trended lower throughout the year with the high price reached in January at just above $18.00 per barrel, and the low price of the year set in December at $10.56. In 1997, crude oil began the year near $26.00 per barrel.

High global crude oil stock levels, especially in the Atlantic Basin, combined with declining worldwide demand to keep prices under pressure throughout the year. These bearish factors outweighed publicized O.P.E.C. production cuts of 2.65 million barrels per day.

Grains

The grains index was the third weakest subindex in 1998, declining 17.96 percent for the year after a virtually unchanged performance in 1997. Both soybean and corn prices declined in excess of 19 percent while wheat prices fell over 15 percent for the year.

The decline in demand for grain imports that shook the markets due to the currency crisis in late 1997 continued unabated during 1998. The result has been a buildup in world grain stocks to levels not seen in recent years.

Industrials

Although the industrial index was the second strongest CRB subindex in 1998 it still declined 12.14 percent for the year. This followed 1997's decline of 22.2 percent. The group's two components, copper and cotton, declined 14 percent and 10 percent, respectively, from their 1997 closing values.

Copper prices reached 11-year lows in 1998 at a level of 64.5 cents per pound due to growing global stock levels resulting from slack demand. Cotton prices declined for the year in spite of a 28 percent reduction in the size of the U.S. cotton crop as compared to 1997.

Livestock

The 21.59 percent decline in the livestock index was the second largest drop among all of the subindices and came as a direct result of a 43 percent drop in lean hog prices. This followed a 27 percent decline in hog prices in 1997. Live cattle, the other livestock index component, also fell but at a much more manageable rate of 9 percent.

The pork industry got caught gearing up for robust international export growth at exactly the same time that those target market economies suffered currency collapses and reduced internal economic growth. Herd production increases continued unabated in the U.S. throughout all of 1998, driving the price of a whole hog to a lower value than the price of a single ham.

Precious Metals

The precious metals sub-index fell 6.04 percent for the year, the smallest decline of any subindex in 1998. The decline is almost solely attributable to the 16 percent decline in silver prices as gold finished the year unchanged and platinum was off by less than 2 percent.

Increased supplies and selling from European central banks pushed gold prices to 19-year lows of $273.00 per ounce in mid-1998 but prices recovered to end the year unchanged. Weak demand for silver from India and Pacific Rim countries contributed to silver's decline to lows of $4.50 per ounce.

Softs

The softs index fell by 15.64 percent in 1998 as three of the four components declined. Sugar fell 36 percent, coffee fell 29 percent and cocoa fell 16 percent. The only Bridge/CRB Futures Price Index component to register a gain in 1998 was orange juice, up 24 percent for the year.

The depressed economies in Asian countries contributed to the weakness in the sugar market as they had led the world in per-capita consumption increases prior to 1998. A 50 percent increase in Brazilian production compared to 1997 accounted for the weakness in coffee prices. Cocoa drifted lower in response to declining demand due to economic weakness. Orange Juice bucked general commodity price weakness due to a 22 percent decline in the Florida orange crop vs. 1997.

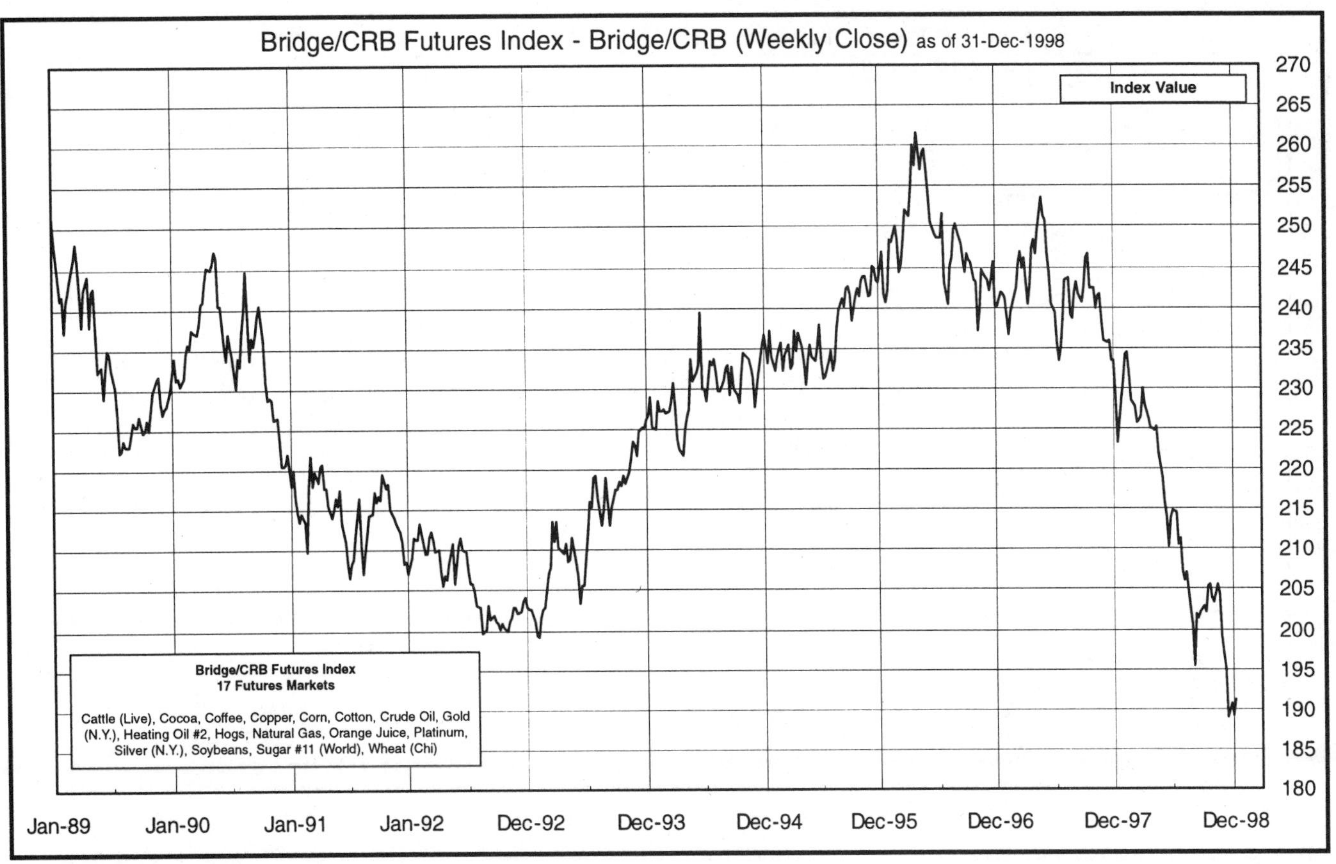

Monthly Bridge/CRB Futures Index High, Low and Close 1967 = 100

Year		Jan.	Feb.	Mar.	Apr.	May	June	July	Aug.	Sept.	Oct.	Nov.	Dec.	Range
1989	High	251.6	243.3	248.1	244.6	242.8	235.4	237.0	225.5	226.8	228.1	231.7	229.9	251.6
	Low	241.1	236.6	241.7	237.7	229.4	227.9	221.2	221.5	222.9	223.0	226.0	225.6	221.2
	Close	242.4	243.2	242.1	238.0	229.4	234.4	221.2	225.5	226.8	225.7	228.8	229.9	------
1990	High	235.1	236.3	239.0	245.8	247.8	241.2	240.0	244.7	239.8	242.0	231.1	223.8	247.8
	Low	228.8	229.9	234.2	238.4	241.5	233.8	230.3	233.1	234.9	228.6	223.2	220.1	220.1
	Close	229.9	234.6	238.2	245.8	241.5	236.9	235.0	233.7	239.2	229.8	223.3	222.6	------
1991	High	222.8	215.6	221.8	222.2	217.0	217.7	214.1	216.5	217.6	219.8	218.6	213.9	222.8
	Low	214.1	209.7	217.3	216.2	214.1	208.4	205.9	204.7	211.9	216.2	213.3	207.2	204.7
	Close	214.1	215.6	218.5	216.2	215.4	208.4	214.1	211.8	215.6	218.2	213.3	208.1	------
1992	High	212.2	215.3	212.9	210.3	211.7	212.9	209.1	204.9	203.5	202.9	203.6	204.3	215.3
	Low	206.9	207.2	208.6	204.5	204.9	208.0	203.0	198.2	199.3	199.1	199.2	201.2	198.2
	Close	211.2	209.6	209.8	204.8	208.0	209.3	203.1	201.0	200.4	199.9	203.1	202.8	------
1993	High	203.2	204.9	214.3	213.9	211.8	210.0	219.7	223.5	217.8	220.6	223.8	226.8	226.8
	Low	199.3	198.4	203.4	207.8	207.4	202.6	207.2	212.1	211.9	216.6	217.4	218.4	198.4
	Close	199.5	202.9	212.5	210.9	208.7	207.1	219.3	217.2	216.1	218.4	218.0	226.3	------
1994	High	229.8	229.2	231.0	227.8	239.2	239.7	234.7	235.4	234.4	235.2	234.7	237.2	239.7
	Low	226.2	225.7	227.4	227.8	225.2	235.9	230.4	228.0	228.6	227.0	228.8	227.0	225.2
	Close	225.6	227.6	227.7	225.0	235.5	230.4	233.7	231.9	229.9	233.3	229.2	236.6	------
1995	High	238.0	236.2	236.9	237.7	237.1	238.0	235.9	240.3	245.8	242.7	244.5	246.5	246.5
	Low	232.6	231.0	231.1	233.2	229.6	232.2	229.3	231.7	239.4	238.3	240.9	240.9	229.3
	Close	232.8	234.3	232.9	235.3	232.7	233.4	233.2	240.0	241.7	242.2	241.8	243.2	------
1996	High	247.6	251.2	253.5	263.8	261.2	252.9	251.9	252.0	250.4	249.6	247.1	246.9	263.8
	Low	238.6	245.6	242.7	250.2	251.8	246.6	240.1	242.8	243.1	237.8	236.0	238.1	236.0
	Close	247.5	248.8	251.4	256.1	254.1	248.7	242.0	249.5	245.6	237.8	243.4	239.6	------
1997	High	244.3	243.9	248.0	249.0	254.8	250.0	243.4	245.3	244.5	247.6	243.5	238.4	254.8
	Low	238.9	236.1	241.6	237.6	245.5	238.5	232.0	236.7	240.0	238.3	235.3	228.8	228.8
	Close	239.0	242.4	245.2	248.3	251.0	239.4	242.8	242.0	243.1	240.0	235.9	229.1	------
1998	High	235.4	236.1	231.7	229.1	226.7	216.8	216.8	207.5	205.0	206.6	206.7	197.3	236.1
	Low	221.6	224.0	223.0	223.4	214.0	208.4	206.0	195.2	196.3	201.3	195.2	187.9	187.9
	Close	234.3	227.7	228.9	224.0	215.9	214.6	206.0	195.7	203.3	203.3	195.4	191.2	------

Source: Bridge Commodity Research Bureau (CRB)

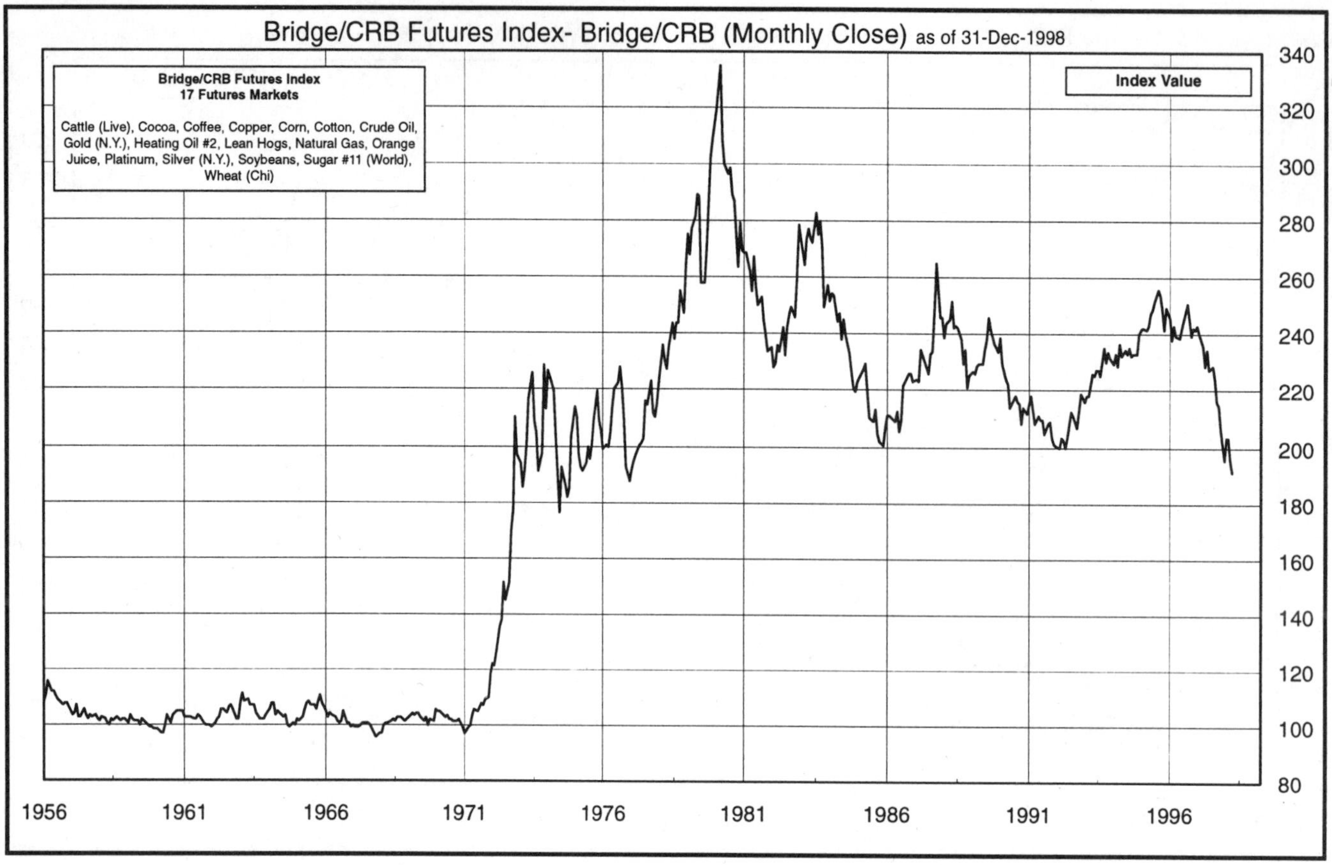

Bridge/CRB Futures Index- Bridge/CRB (Monthly Close) as of 31-Dec-1998

Bridge/CRB Futures Index
17 Futures Markets

Cattle (Live), Cocoa, Coffee, Copper, Corn, Cotton, Crude Oil, Gold (N.Y.), Heating Oil #2, Lean Hogs, Natural Gas, Orange Juice, Platinum, Silver (N.Y.), Soybeans, Sugar #11 (World), Wheat (Chi)

Index Value

340 320 300 280 260 240 220 200 180 160 140 120 100 80

1956 1961 1966 1971 1976 1981 1986 1991 1996

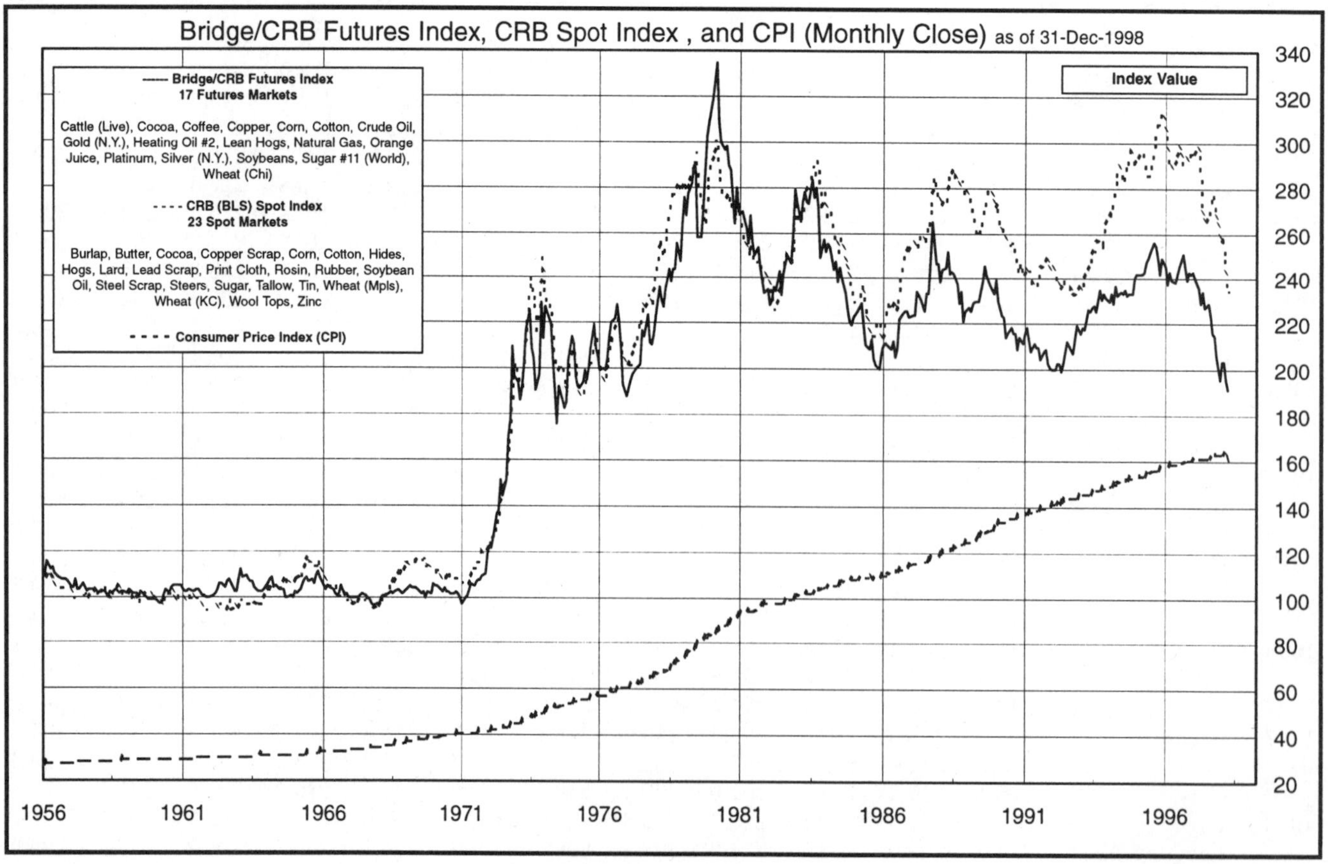

Bridge/CRB Futures Index, CRB Spot Index , and CPI (Monthly Close) as of 31-Dec-1998

—— **Bridge/CRB Futures Index**
17 Futures Markets

Cattle (Live), Cocoa, Coffee, Copper, Corn, Cotton, Crude Oil, Gold (N.Y.), Heating Oil #2, Lean Hogs, Natural Gas, Orange Juice, Platinum, Silver (N.Y.), Soybeans, Sugar #11 (World), Wheat (Chi)

- - - - **CRB (BLS) Spot Index**
23 Spot Markets

Burlap, Butter, Cocoa, Copper Scrap, Corn, Cotton, Hides, Hogs, Lard, Lead Scrap, Print Cloth, Rosin, Rubber, Soybean Oil, Steel Scrap, Steers, Sugar, Tallow, Tin, Wheat (Mpls), Wheat (KC), Wool Tops, Zinc

- - - - **Consumer Price Index (CPI)**

Index Value

340 320 300 280 260 240 220 200 180 160 140 120 100 80 60 40 20

1956 1961 1966 1971 1976 1981 1986 1991 1996

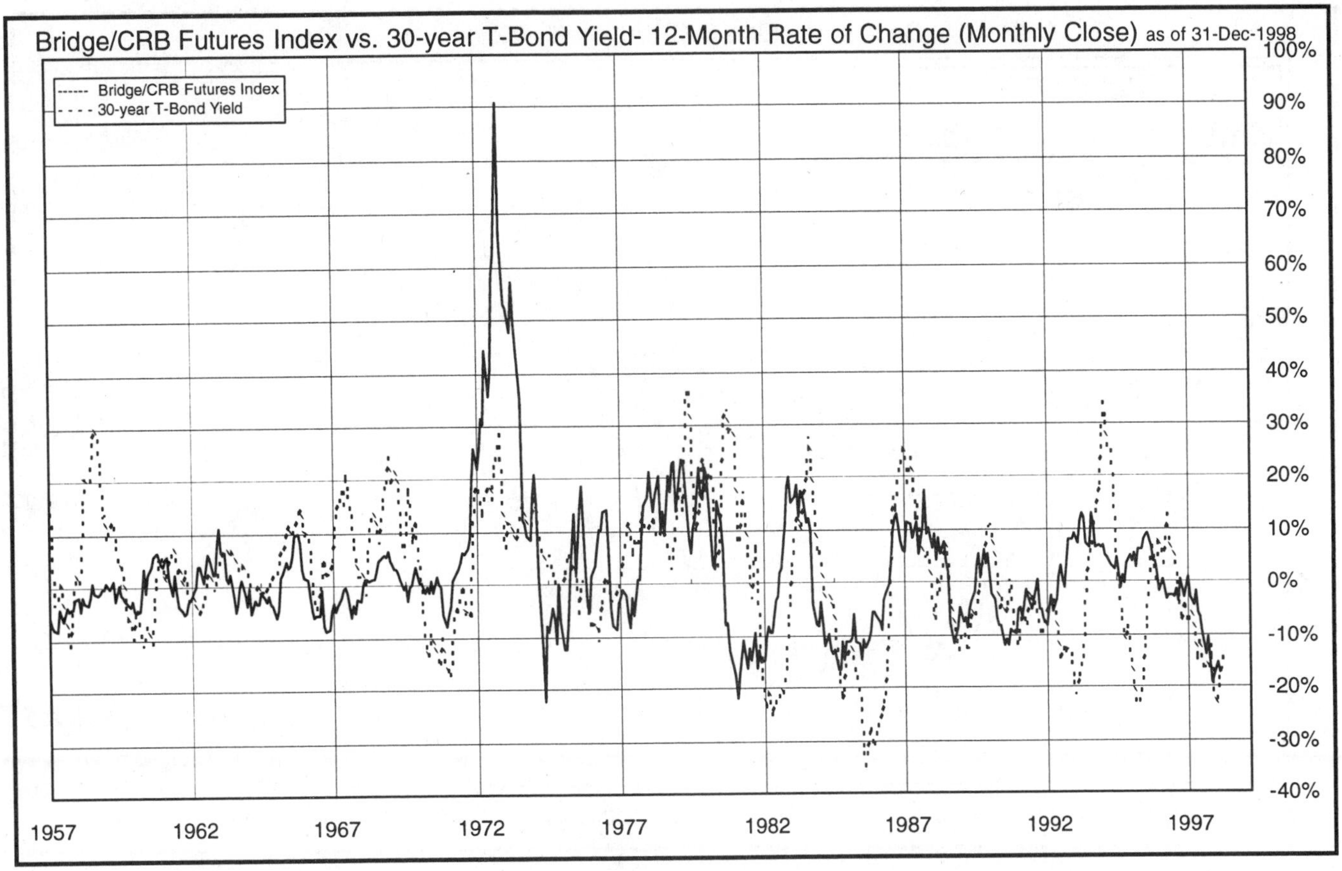

Bridge/CRB Futures Index vs. 30-year T-Bond Yield- 12-Month Rate of Change (Monthly Close) as of 31-Dec-1998

------ Bridge/CRB Futures Index
- - - - 30-year T-Bond Yield

100%
90%
80%
70%
60%
50%
40%
30%
20%
10%
0%
-10%
-20%
-30%
-40%

1957 1962 1967 1972 1977 1982 1987 1992 1997

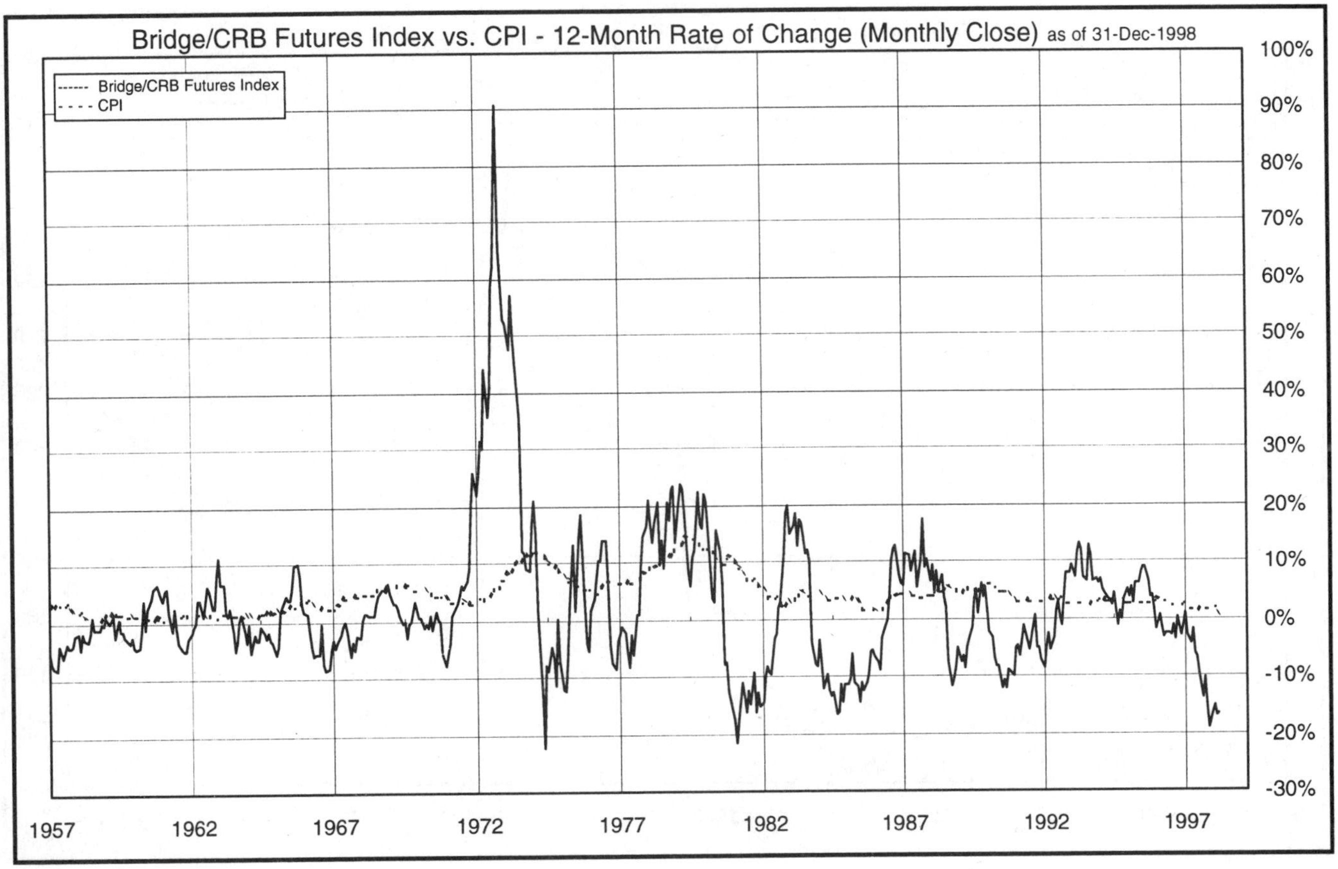

Bridge/CRB Futures Index vs. CPI - 12-Month Rate of Change (Monthly Close) as of 31-Dec-1998

------ Bridge/CRB Futures Index
- - - - CPI

100%
90%
80%
70%
60%
50%
40%
30%
20%
10%
0%
-10%
-20%
-30%

1957 1962 1967 1972 1977 1982 1987 1992 1997

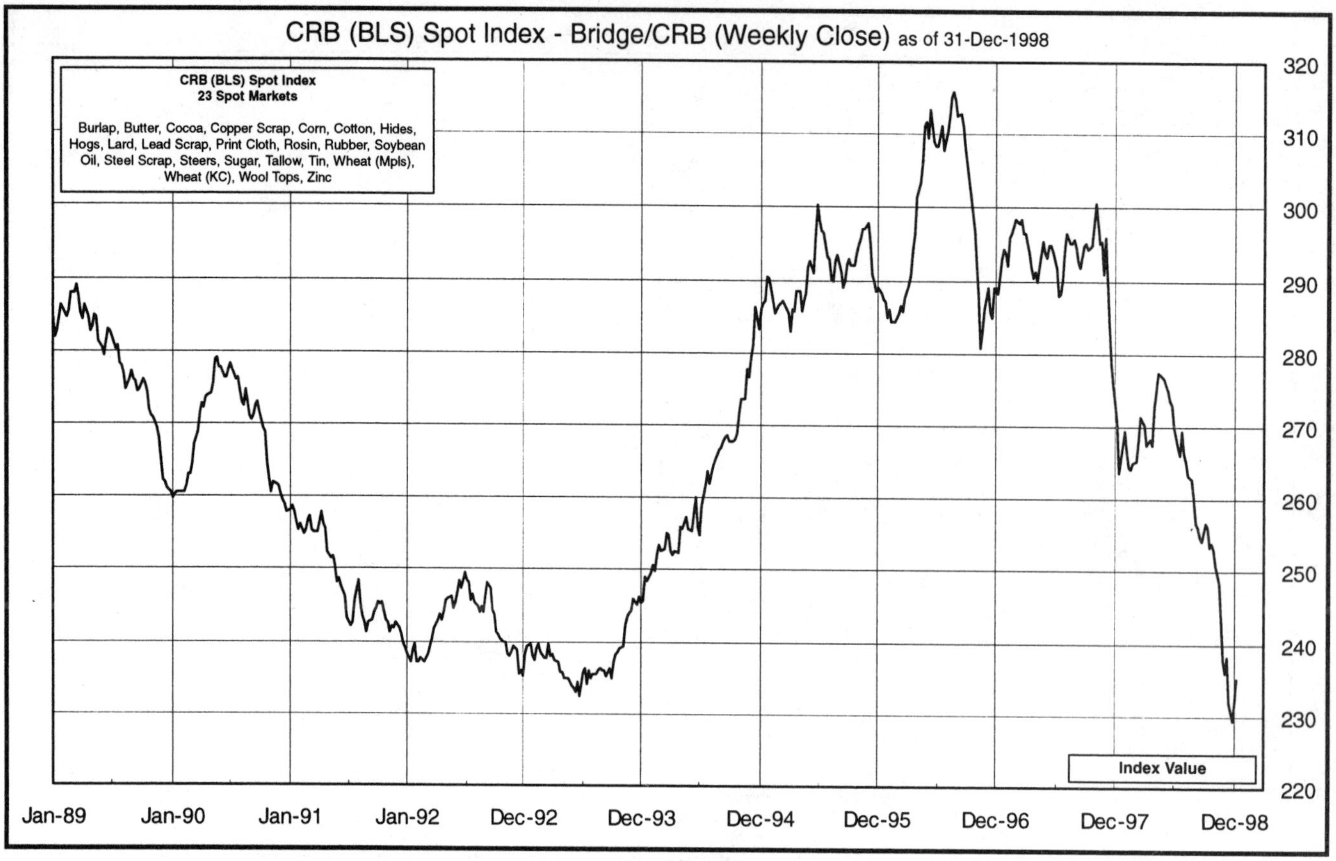

CRB (BLS) Spot Index - Bridge/CRB (Weekly Close) as of 31-Dec-1998
CRB (BLS) Spot Index
23 Spot Markets
Burlap, Butter, Cocoa, Copper Scrap, Corn, Cotton, Hides, Hogs, Lard, Lead Scrap, Print Cloth, Rosin, Rubber, Soybean Oil, Steel Scrap, Steers, Sugar, Tallow, Tin, Wheat (Mpls), Wheat (KC), Wool Tops, Zinc
Index Value
320
310
300
290
280
270
260
250
240
230
220
Jan-89
Jan-90
Jan-91
Jan-92
Dec-92
Dec-93
Dec-94
Dec-95
Dec-96
Dec-97
Dec-98

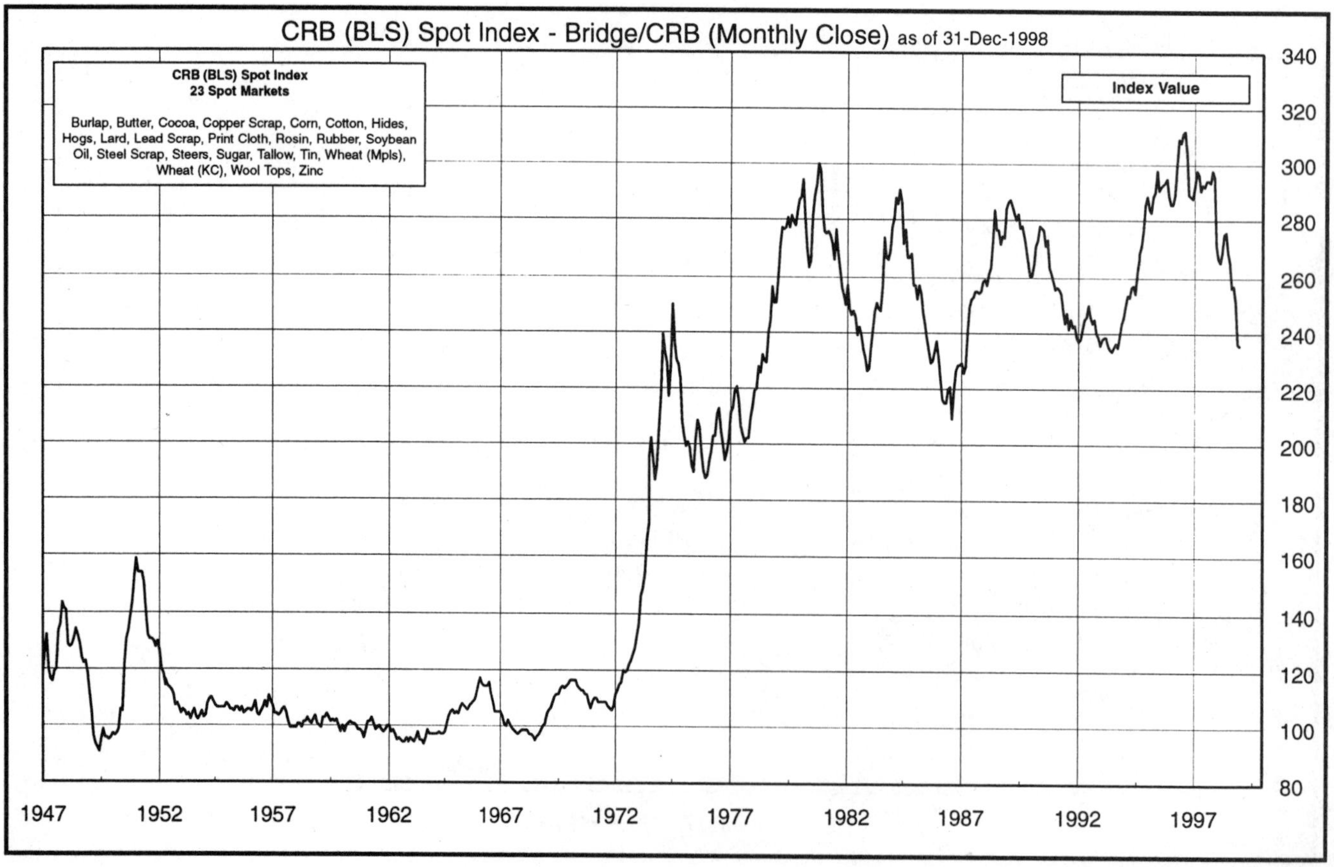

CRB (BLS) Spot Index - Bridge/CRB (Monthly Close) as of 31-Dec-1998
CRB (BLS) Spot Index
23 Spot Markets
Burlap, Butter, Cocoa, Copper Scrap, Corn, Cotton, Hides, Hogs, Lard, Lead Scrap, Print Cloth, Rosin, Rubber, Soybean Oil, Steel Scrap, Steers, Sugar, Tallow, Tin, Wheat (Mpls), Wheat (KC), Wool Tops, Zinc
Index Value
340
320
300
280
260
240
220
200
180
160
140
120
100
80
1947
1952
1957
1962
1967
1972
1977
1982
1987
1992
1997

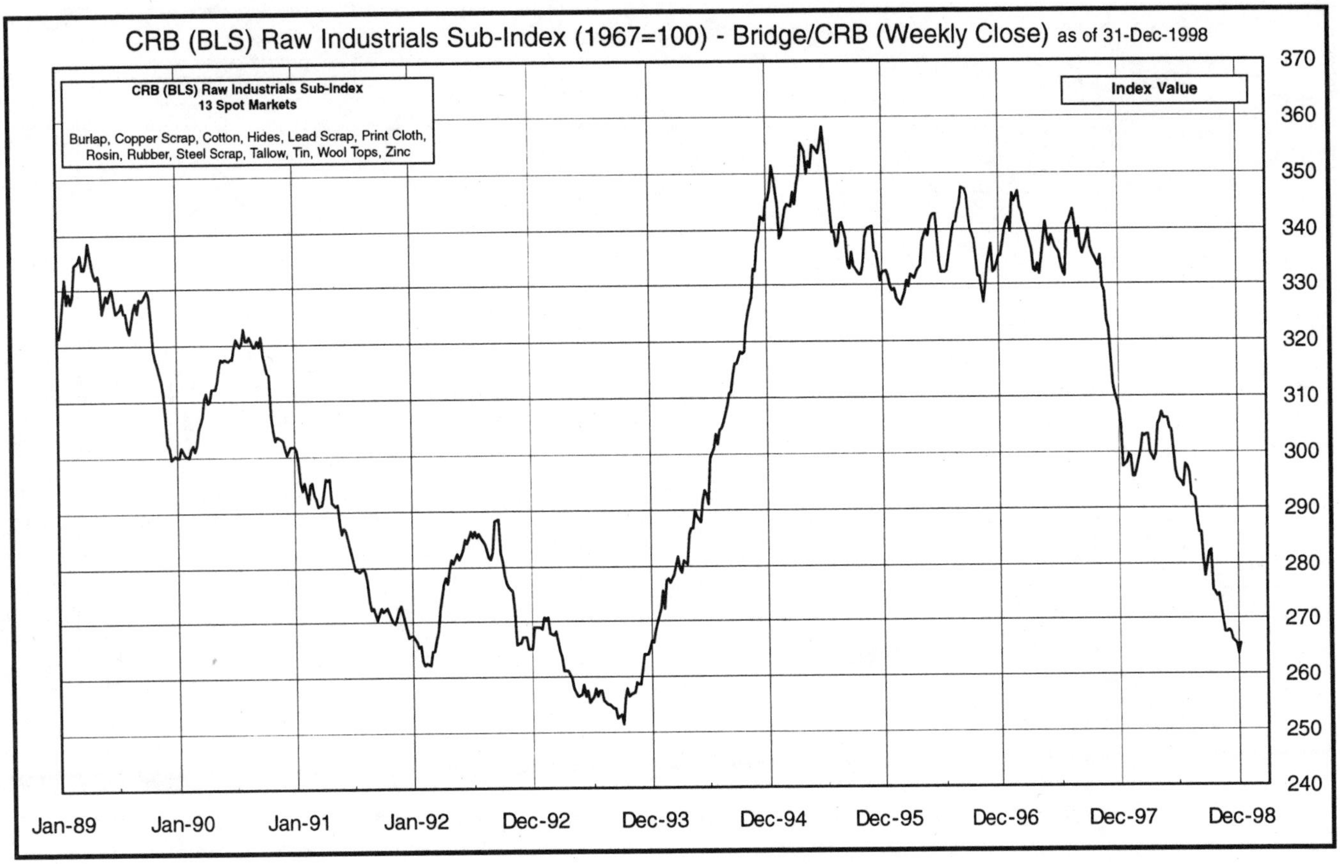

CRB (BLS) Raw Industrials Sub-Index (1967=100) - Bridge/CRB (Weekly Close) as of 31-Dec-1998

CRB (BLS) Raw Industrials Sub-Index (1967=100) - Bridge/CRB (Monthly Close) as of 31-Dec-1998

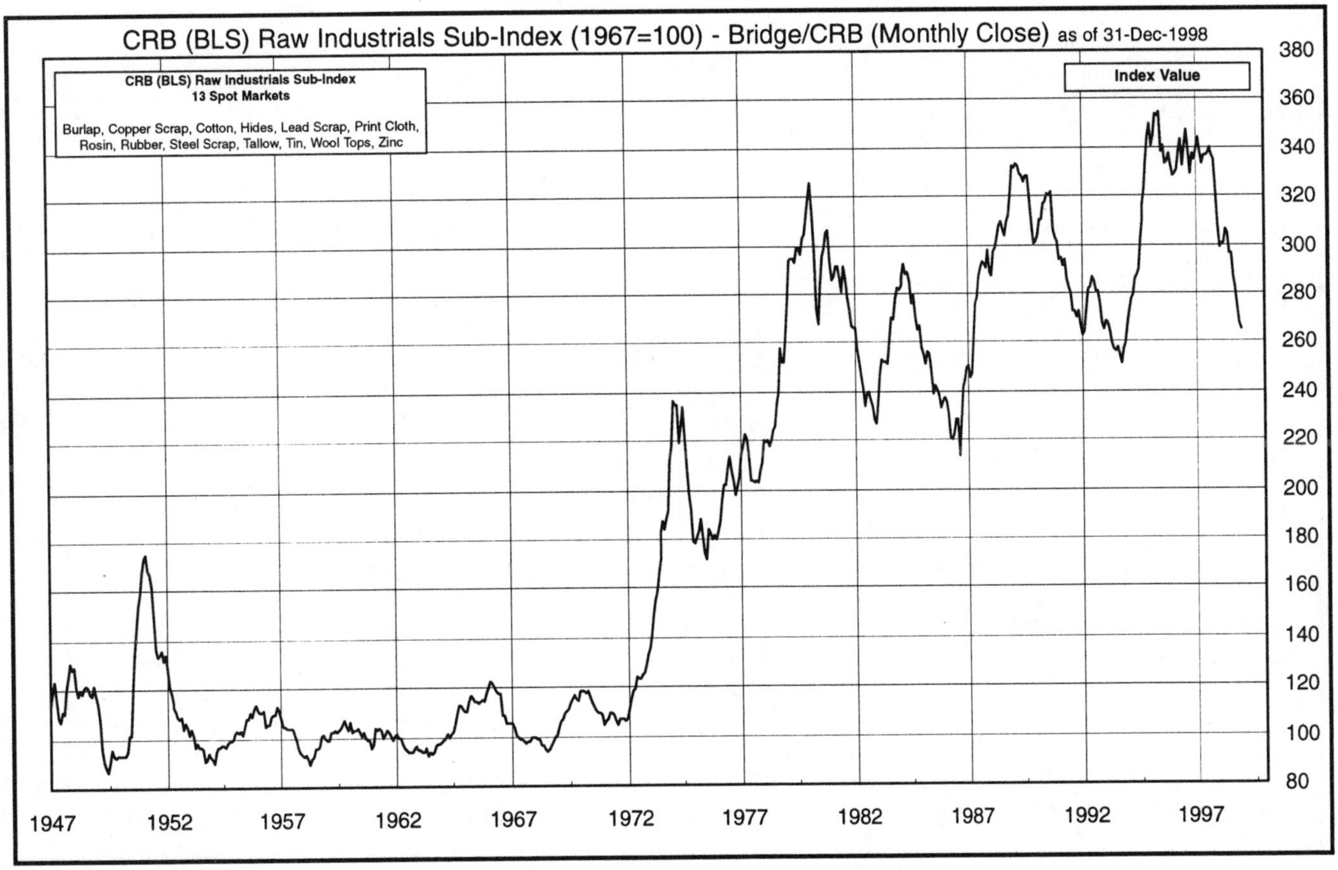

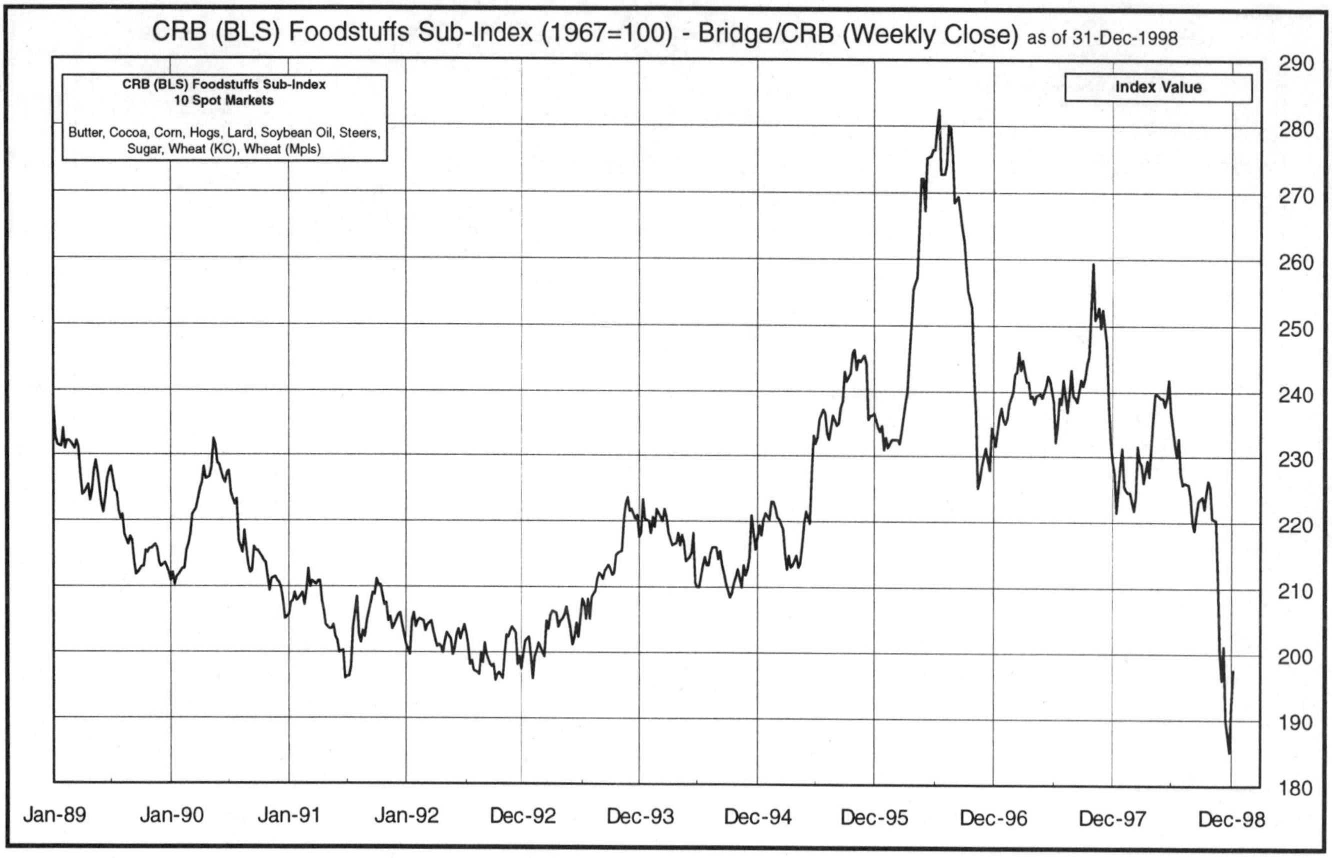

CRB (BLS) Foodstuffs Sub-Index (1967=100) - Bridge/CRB (Weekly Close) as of 31-Dec-1998

CRB (BLS) Foodstuffs Sub-Index (1967=100) - Bridge/CRB (Monthly Close) as of 31-Dec-1998

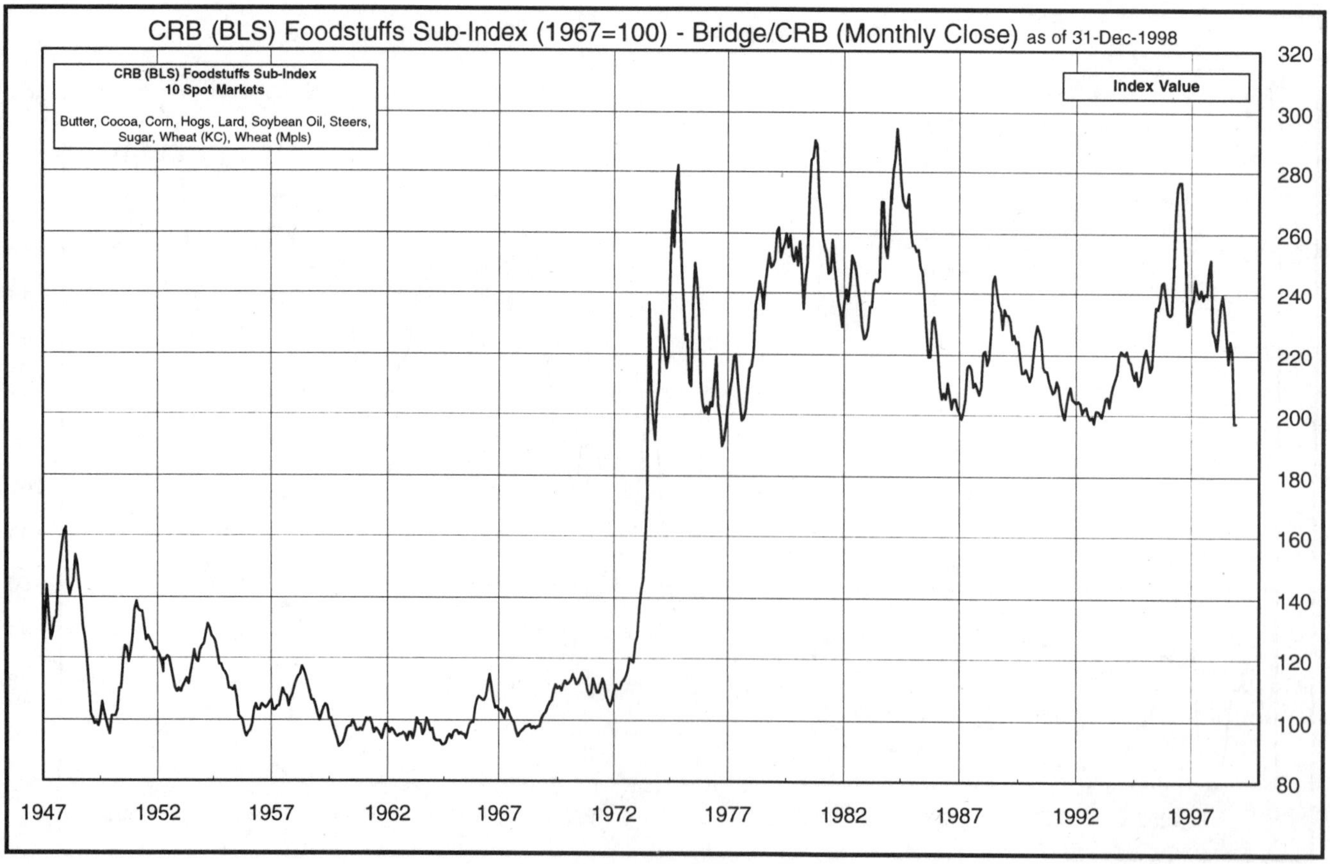

CRB Softs Sub-Index (1967=100) - Bridge/CRB (Weekly Close) as of 31-Dec-1998

CRB Softs Sub-Index
4 Futures Markets
Cocoa, Coffee, Orange Juice, Sugar #11 (World)

Index Value

460
440
420
400
380
360
340
320
300
280
260
240
220
200

Jan-89 Jan-90 Jan-91 Jan-92 Dec-92 Dec-93 Dec-94 Dec-95 Dec-96 Dec-97 Dec-98

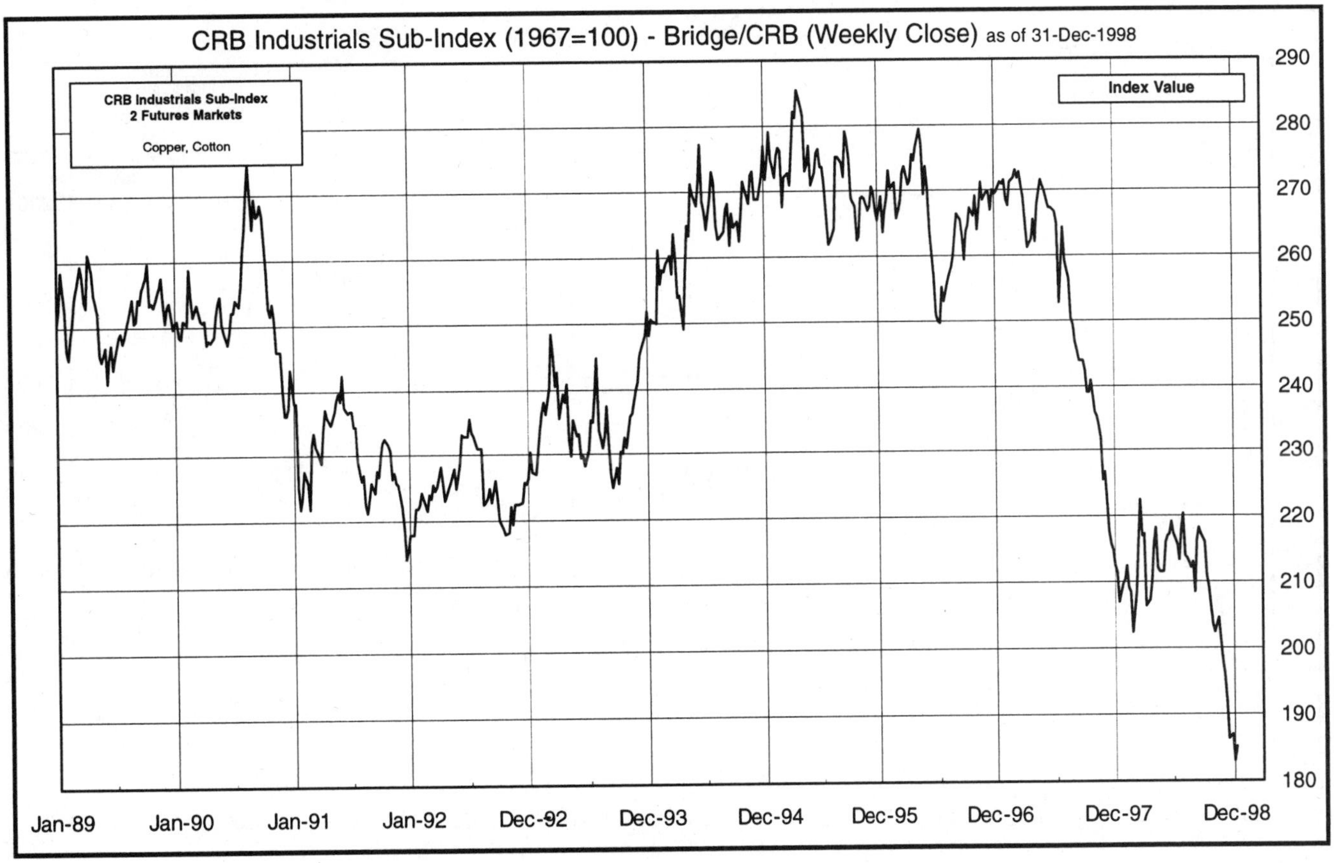

CRB Industrials Sub-Index (1967=100) - Bridge/CRB (Weekly Close) as of 31-Dec-1998

CRB Industrials Sub-Index
2 Futures Markets
Copper, Cotton

Index Value

290
280
270
260
250
240
230
220
210
200
190
180

Jan-89 Jan-90 Jan-91 Jan-92 Dec-92 Dec-93 Dec-94 Dec-95 Dec-96 Dec-97 Dec-98

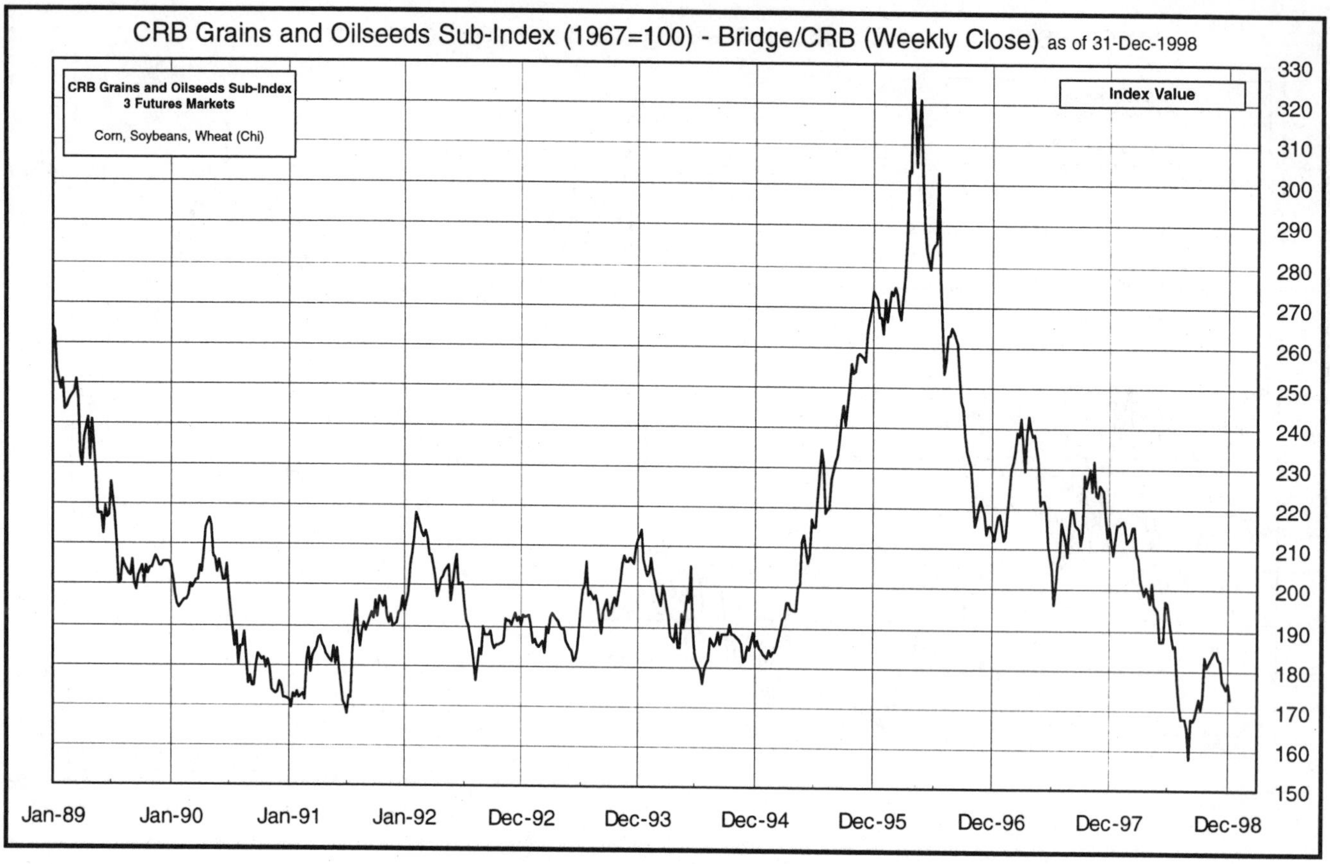

CRB Grains and Oilseeds Sub-Index (1967=100) - Bridge/CRB (Weekly Close) as of 31-Dec-1998

CRB Grains and Oilseeds Sub-Index
3 Futures Markets

Corn, Soybeans, Wheat (Chi)

Index Value

330
320
310
300
290
280
270
260
250
240
230
220
210
200
190
180
170
160
150

Jan-89 Jan-90 Jan-91 Jan-92 Dec-92 Dec-93 Dec-94 Dec-95 Dec-96 Dec-97 Dec-98

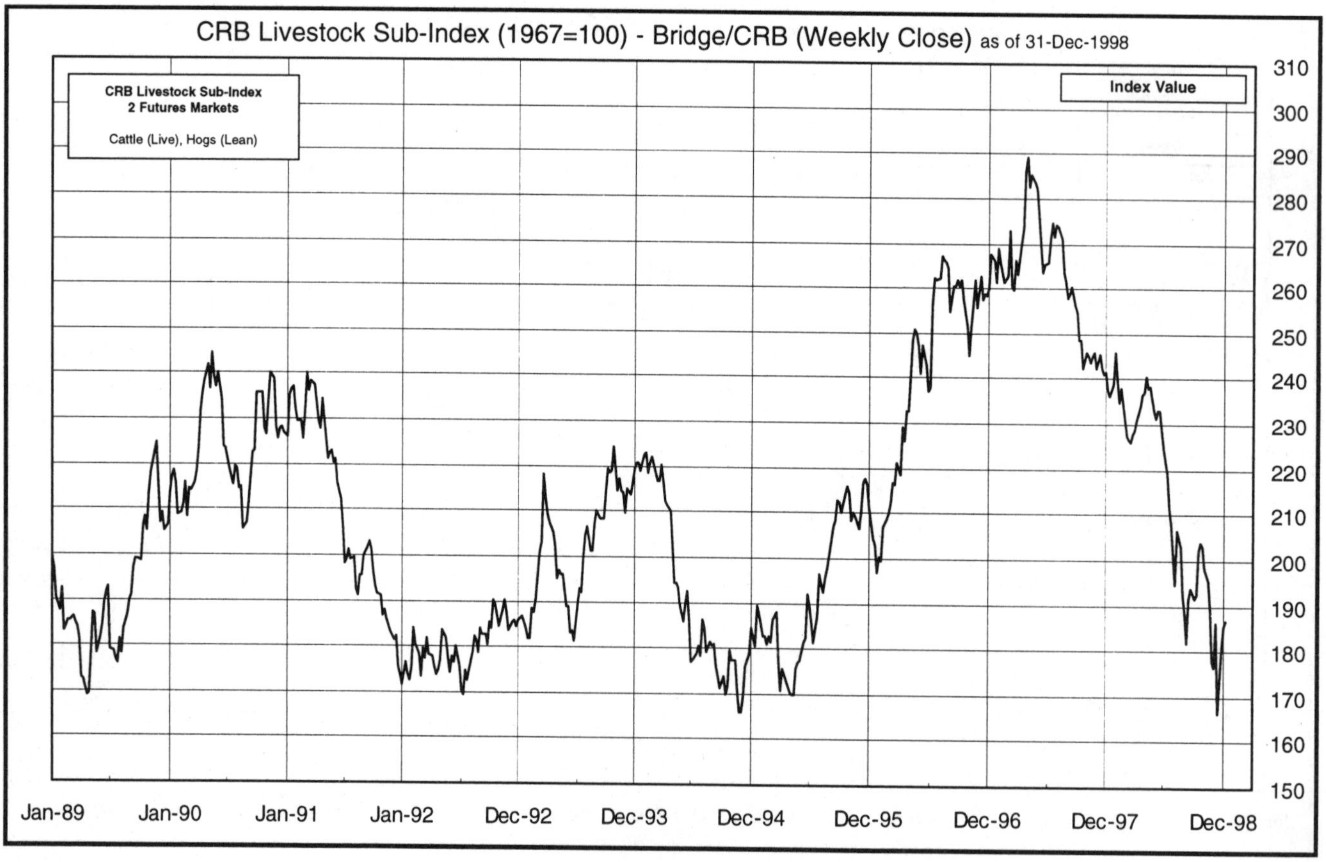

CRB Livestock Sub-Index (1967=100) - Bridge/CRB (Weekly Close) as of 31-Dec-1998

CRB Livestock Sub-Index
2 Futures Markets

Cattle (Live), Hogs (Lean)

Index Value

310
300
290
280
270
260
250
240
230
220
210
200
190
180
170
160
150

Jan-89 Jan-90 Jan-91 Jan-92 Dec-92 Dec-93 Dec-94 Dec-95 Dec-96 Dec-97 Dec-98

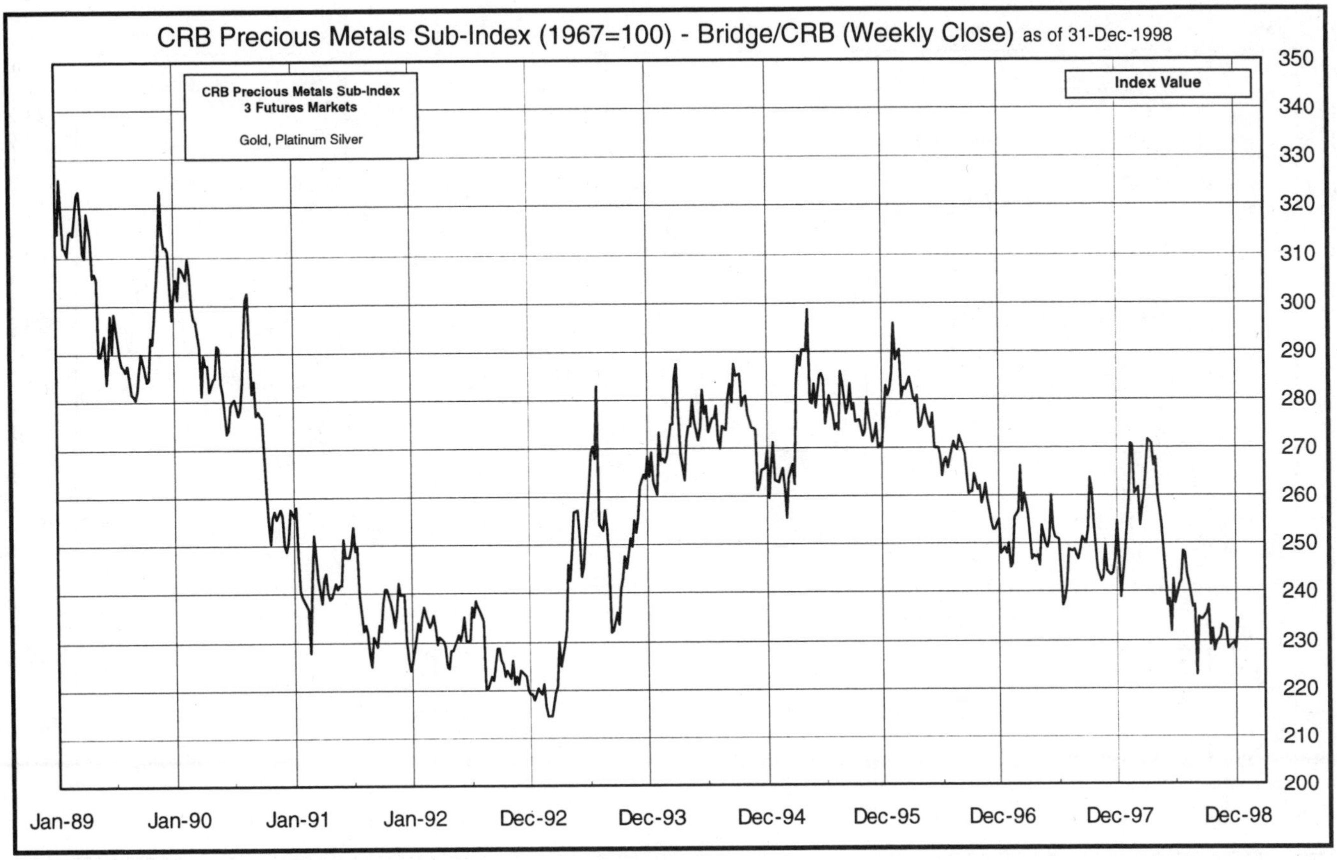

CRB Precious Metals Sub-Index (1967=100) - Bridge/CRB (Weekly Close) as of 31-Dec-1998

CRB Precious Metals Sub-Index
3 Futures Markets

Gold, Platinum Silver

Index Value

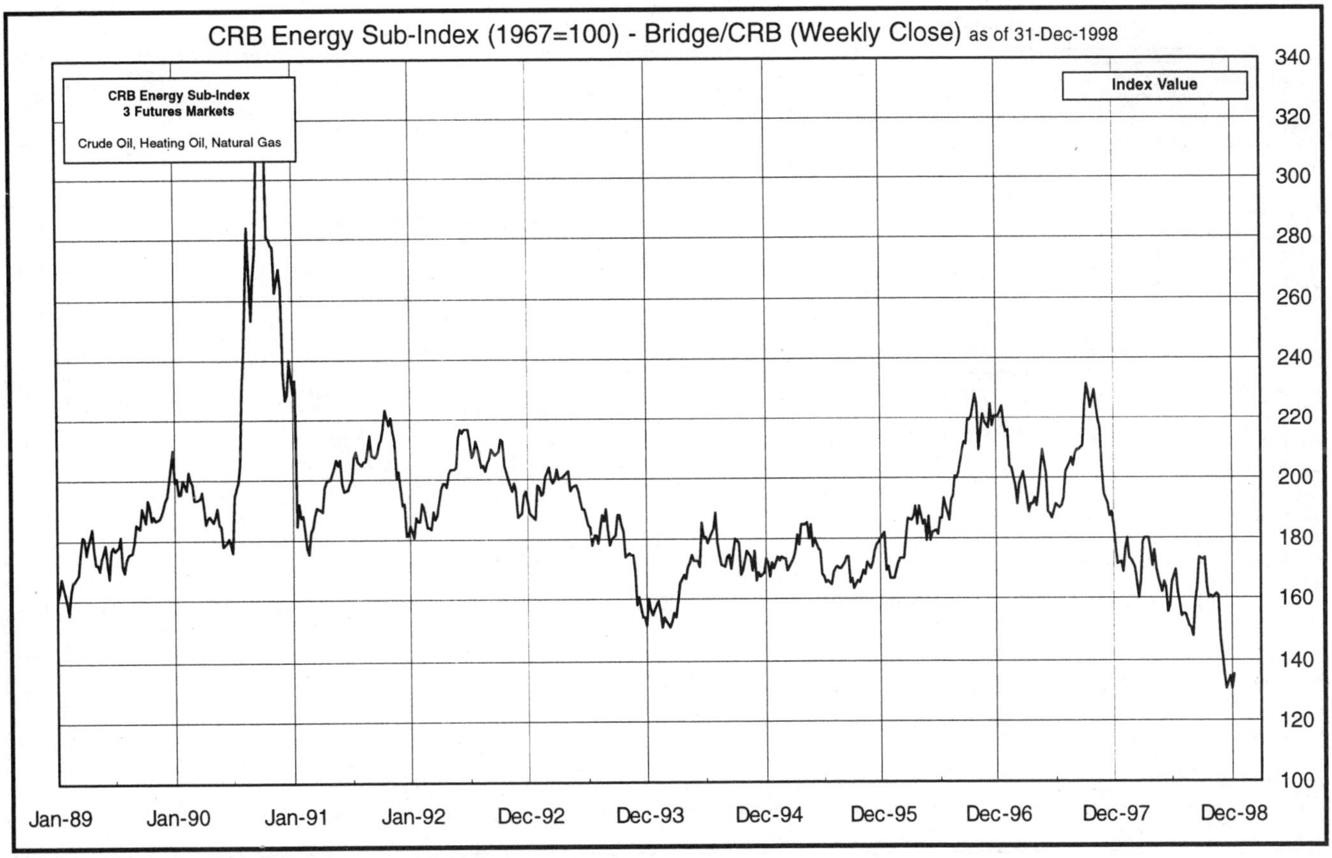

CRB Energy Sub-Index (1967=100) - Bridge/CRB (Weekly Close) as of 31-Dec-1998

CRB Energy Sub-Index
3 Futures Markets

Crude Oil, Heating Oil, Natural Gas

Index Value

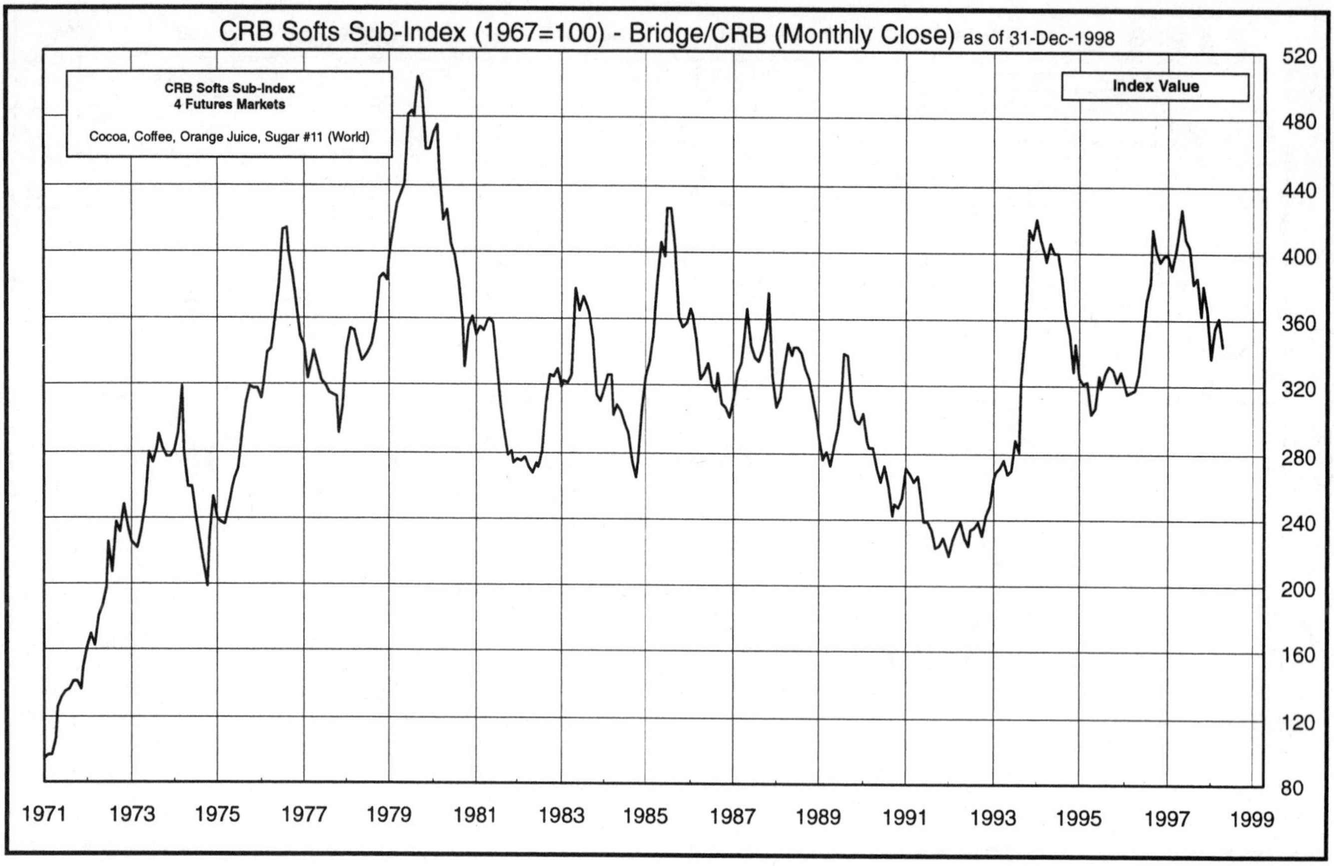
CRB Softs Sub-Index (1967=100) - Bridge/CRB (Monthly Close) as of 31-Dec-1998
CRB Softs Sub-Index
4 Futures Markets
Cocoa, Coffee, Orange Juice, Sugar #11 (World)
Index Value
520
480
440
400
360
320
280
240
200
160
120
80
1971
1973
1975
1977
1979
1981
1983
1985
1987
1989
1991
1993
1995
1997
1999

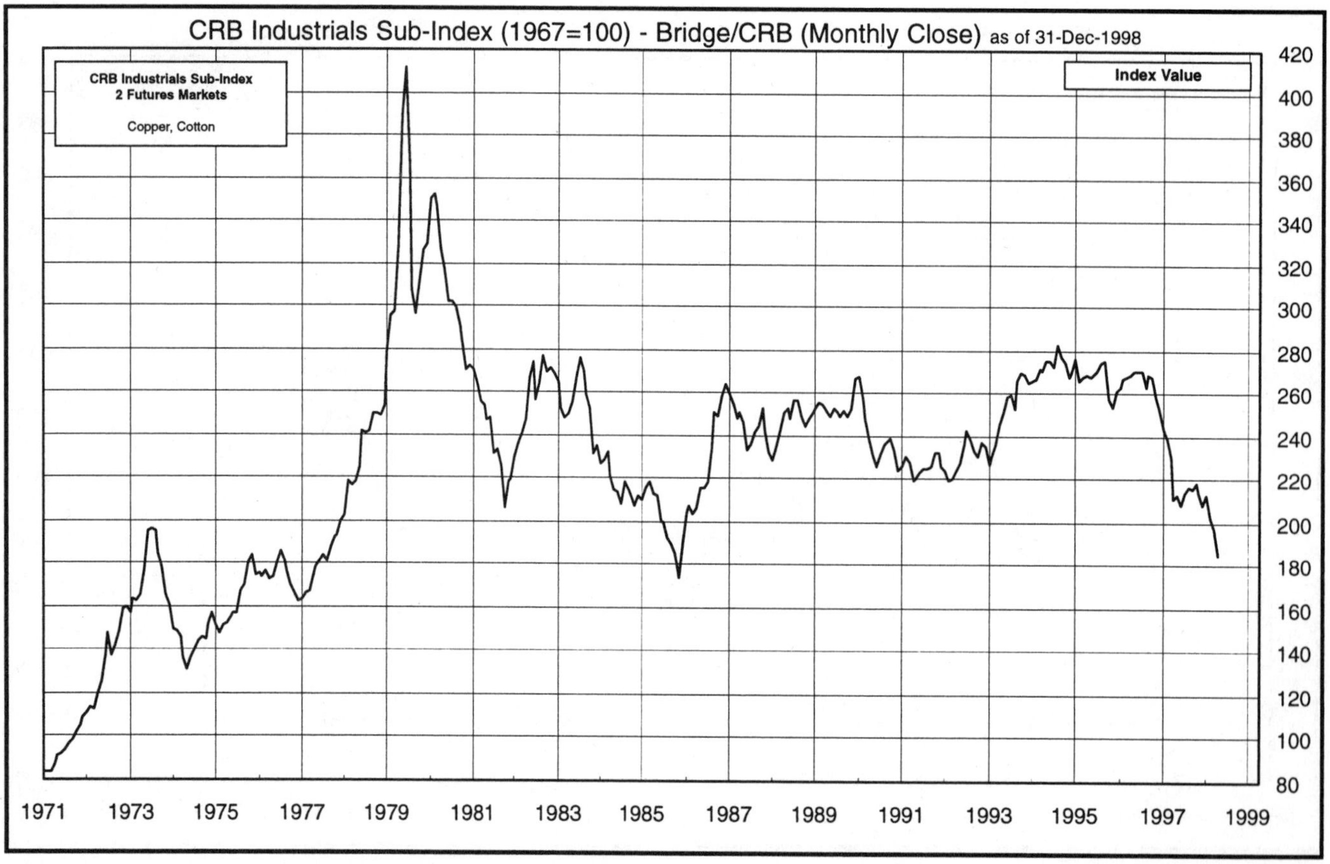
CRB Industrials Sub-Index (1967=100) - Bridge/CRB (Monthly Close) as of 31-Dec-1998
CRB Industrials Sub-Index
2 Futures Markets
Copper, Cotton
Index Value
420
400
380
360
340
320
300
280
260
240
220
200
180
160
140
120
100
80
1971
1973
1975
1977
1979
1981
1983
1985
1987
1989
1991
1993
1995
1997
1999

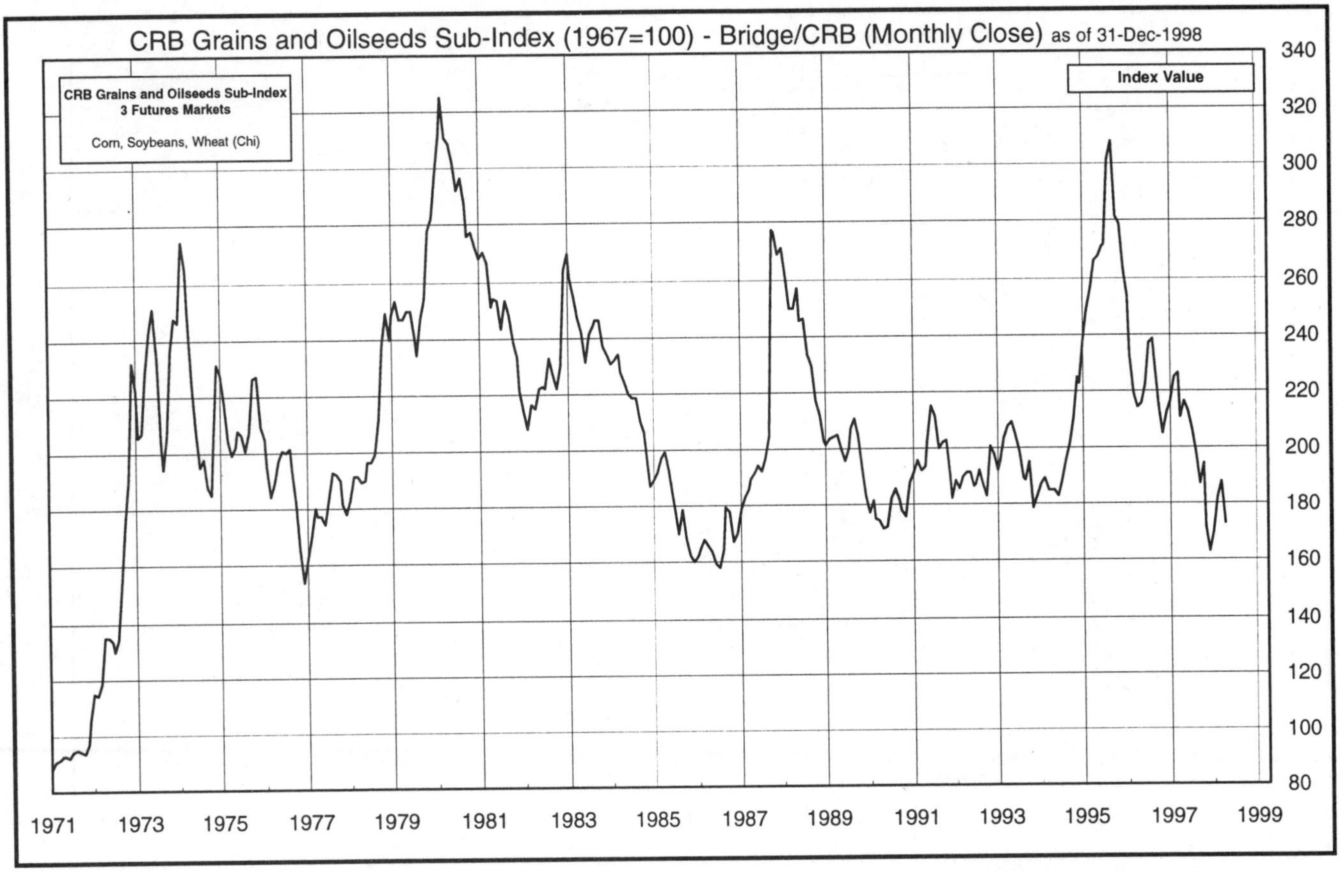
CRB Grains and Oilseeds Sub-Index (1967=100) - Bridge/CRB (Monthly Close) as of 31-Dec-1998
CRB Grains and Oilseeds Sub-Index
3 Futures Markets
Corn, Soybeans, Wheat (Chi)
Index Value
340
320
300
280
260
240
220
200
180
160
140
120
100
80
1971
1973
1975
1977
1979
1981
1983
1985
1987
1989
1991
1993
1995
1997
1999

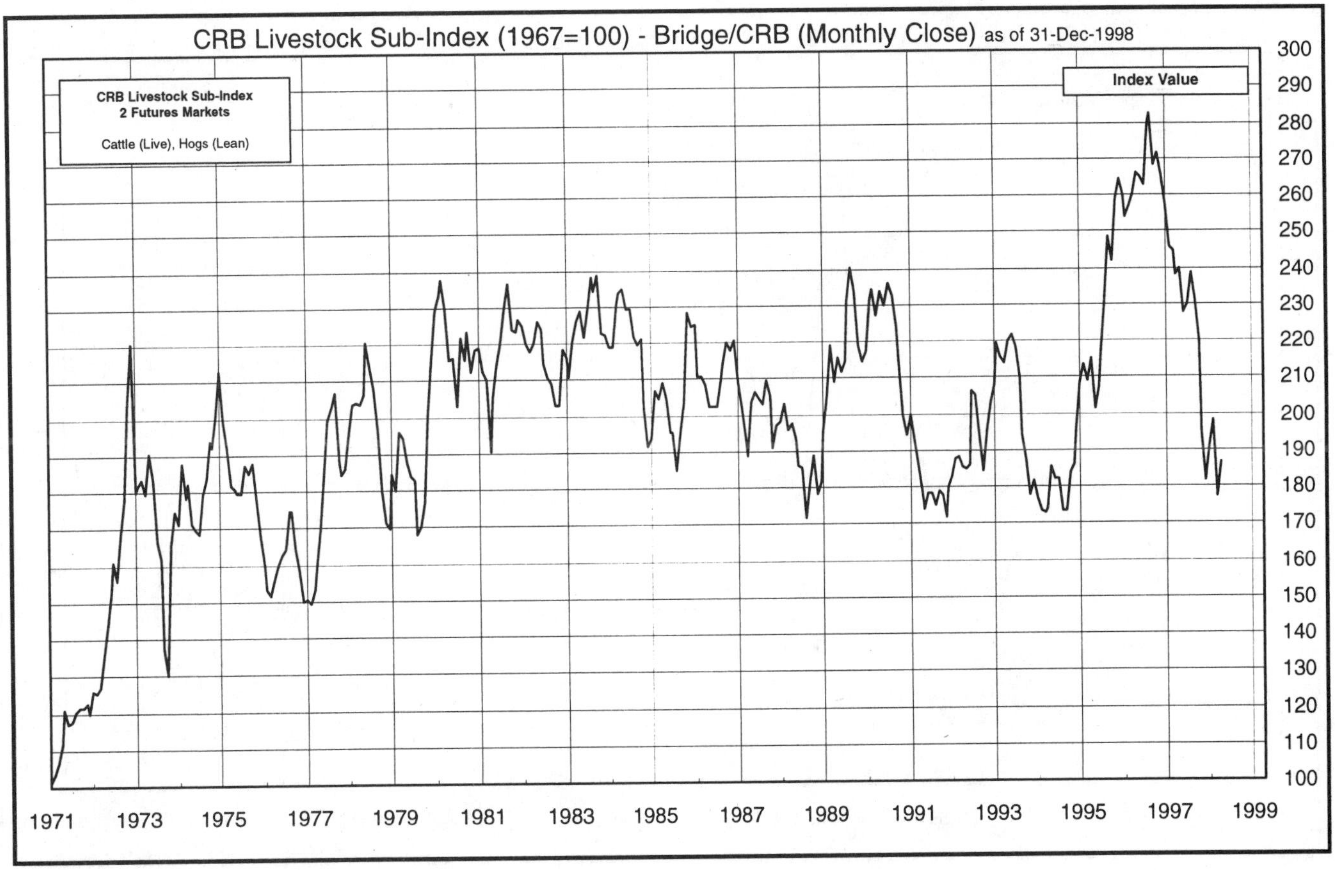
CRB Livestock Sub-Index (1967=100) - Bridge/CRB (Monthly Close) as of 31-Dec-1998
CRB Livestock Sub-Index
2 Futures Markets
Cattle (Live), Hogs (Lean)
Index Value
300
290
280
270
260
250
240
230
220
210
200
190
180
170
160
150
140
130
120
110
100
1971
1973
1975
1977
1979
1981
1983
1985
1987
1989
1991
1993
1995
1997
1999

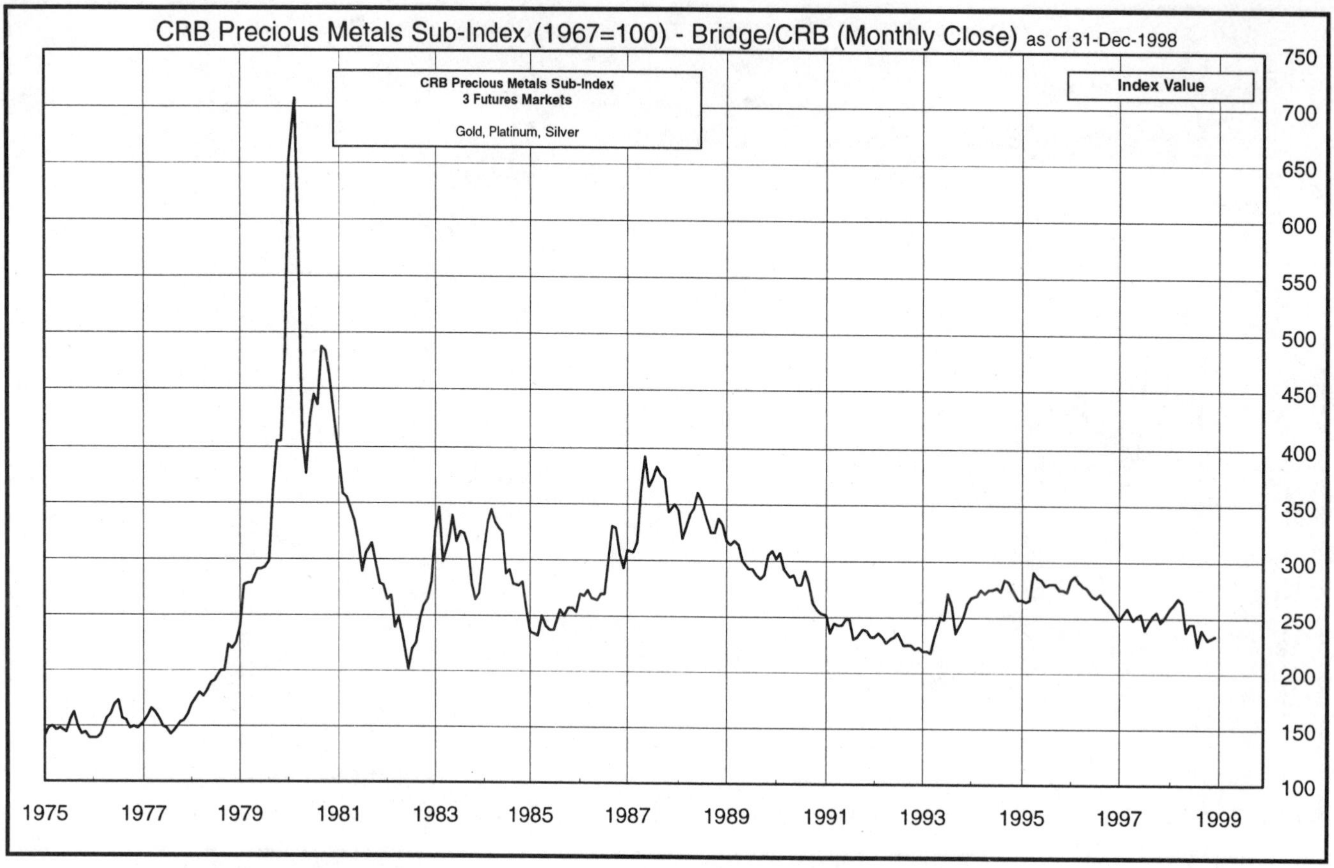

CRB Precious Metals Sub-Index (1967=100) - Bridge/CRB (Monthly Close) as of 31-Dec-1998
CRB Precious Metals Sub-Index
3 Futures Markets
Gold, Platinum, Silver
Index Value
750
700
650
600
550
500
450
400
350
300
250
200
150
100
1975
1977
1979
1981
1983
1985
1987
1989
1991
1993
1995
1997
1999

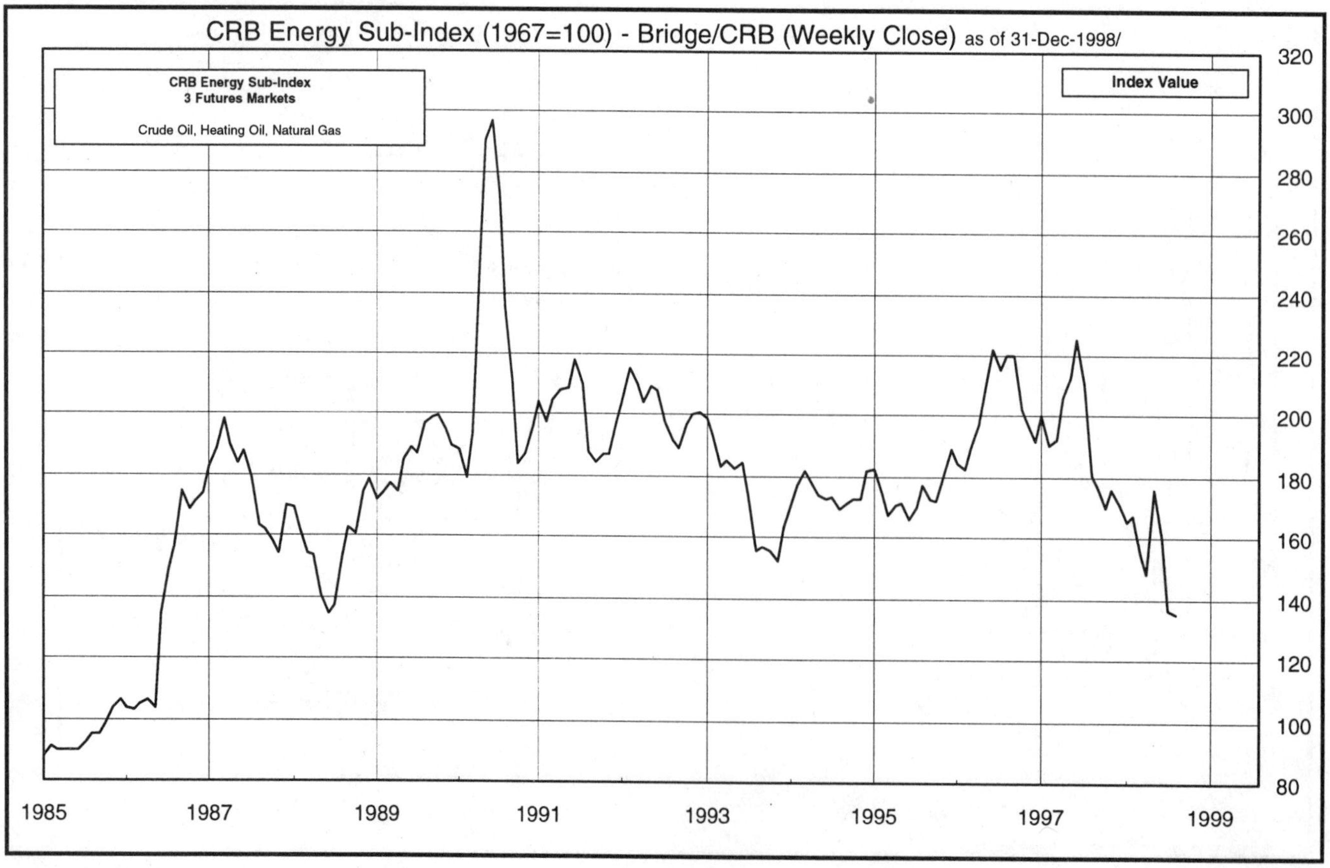

CRB Energy Sub-Index (1967=100) - Bridge/CRB (Weekly Close) as of 31-Dec-1998/
CRB Energy Sub-Index
3 Futures Markets
Crude Oil, Heating Oil, Natural Gas
Index Value
320
300
280
260
240
220
200
180
160
140
120
100
80
1985
1987
1989
1991
1993
1995
1997
1999

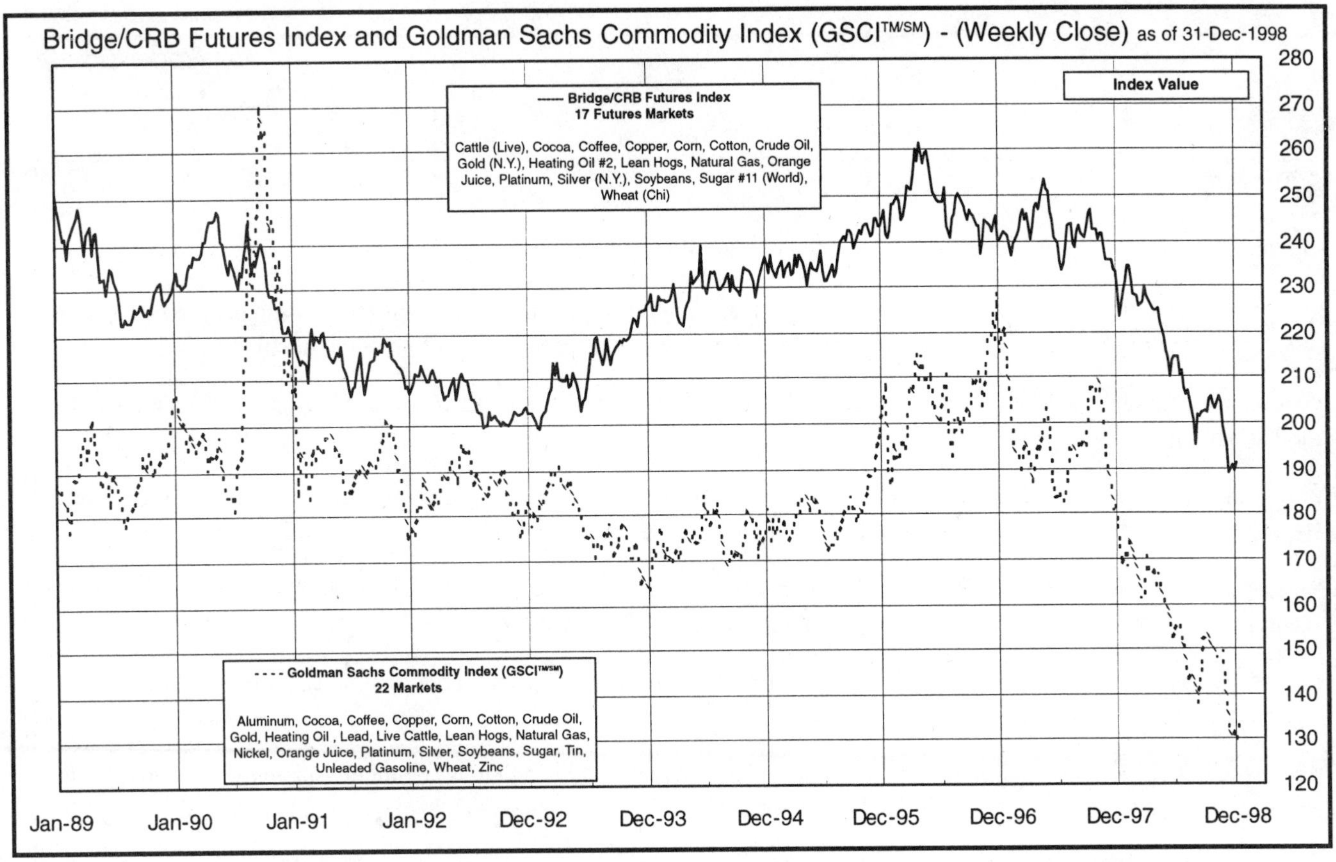

Bridge/CRB Futures Index and Goldman Sachs Commodity Index (GSCI™/SM) - (Weekly Close) as of 31-Dec-1998

—— Bridge/CRB Futures Index
17 Futures Markets

Cattle (Live), Cocoa, Coffee, Copper, Corn, Cotton, Crude Oil, Gold (N.Y.), Heating Oil #2, Lean Hogs, Natural Gas, Orange Juice, Platinum, Silver (N.Y.), Soybeans, Sugar #11 (World), Wheat (Chi)

Index Value

280 270 260 250 240 230 220 210 200 190 180 170 160 150 140 130 120

- - - - Goldman Sachs Commodity Index (GSCI™/SM)
22 Markets

Aluminum, Cocoa, Coffee, Copper, Corn, Cotton, Crude Oil, Gold, Heating Oil, Lead, Live Cattle, Lean Hogs, Natural Gas, Nickel, Orange Juice, Platinum, Silver, Soybeans, Sugar, Tin, Unleaded Gasoline, Wheat, Zinc

Jan-89 Jan-90 Jan-91 Jan-92 Dec-92 Dec-93 Dec-94 Dec-95 Dec-96 Dec-97 Dec-98

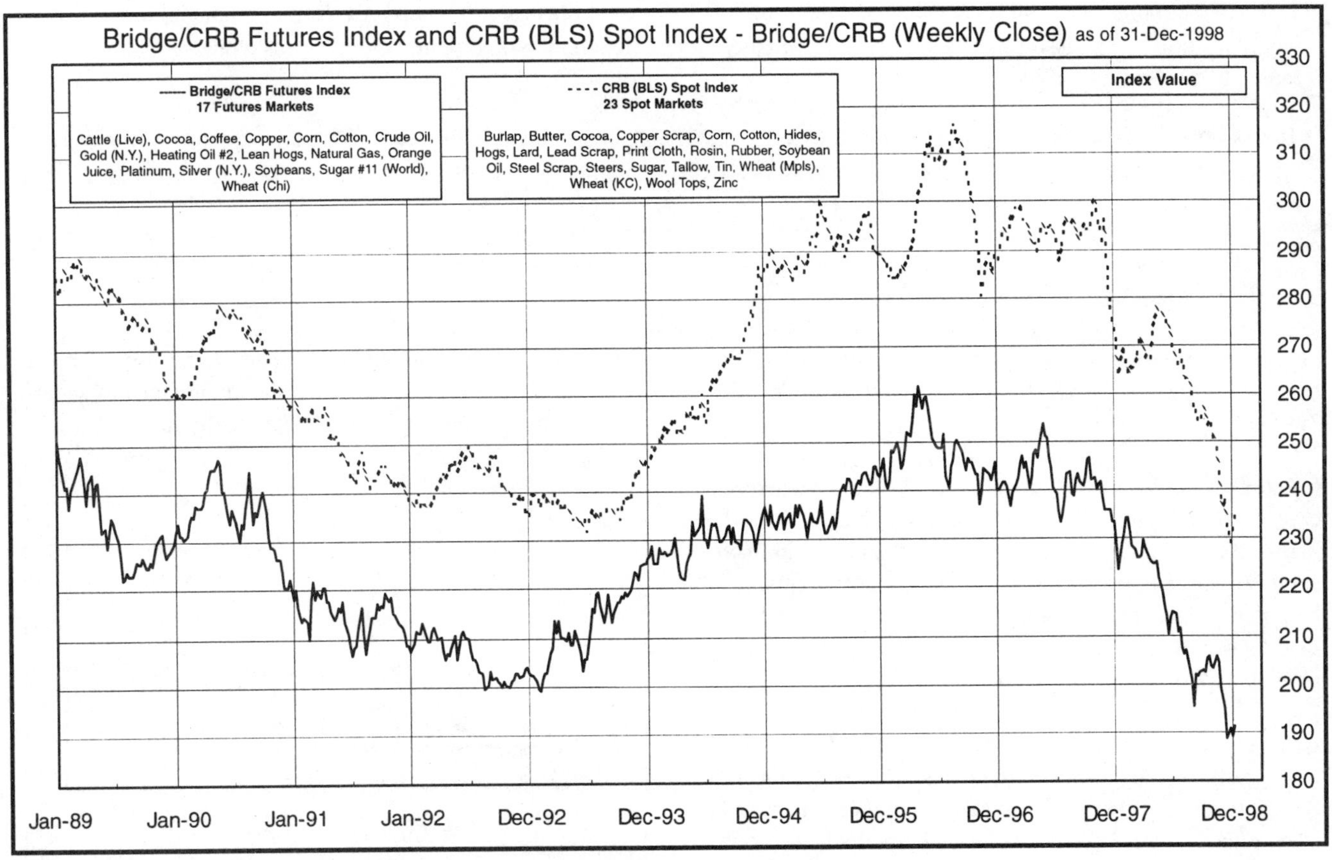

Bridge/CRB Futures Index and CRB (BLS) Spot Index - Bridge/CRB (Weekly Close) as of 31-Dec-1998

—— Bridge/CRB Futures Index
17 Futures Markets

Cattle (Live), Cocoa, Coffee, Copper, Corn, Cotton, Crude Oil, Gold (N.Y.), Heating Oil #2, Lean Hogs, Natural Gas, Orange Juice, Platinum, Silver (N.Y.), Soybeans, Sugar #11 (World), Wheat (Chi)

- - - - CRB (BLS) Spot Index
23 Spot Markets

Burlap, Butter, Cocoa, Copper Scrap, Corn, Cotton, Hides, Hogs, Lard, Lead Scrap, Print Cloth, Rosin, Rubber, Soybean Oil, Steel Scrap, Steers, Sugar, Tallow, Tin, Wheat (Mpls), Wheat (KC), Wool Tops, Zinc

Index Value

330 320 310 300 290 280 270 260 250 240 230 220 210 200 190 180

Jan-89 Jan-90 Jan-91 Jan-92 Dec-92 Dec-93 Dec-94 Dec-95 Dec-96 Dec-97 Dec-98

THE THREAT OF DEFLATION

by Roger Bootle

Summary

- In large parts of the world, the emerging danger is not inflation, but deflation.
- Before World War II, intermittent deflation was a normal occurrence, alternating with inflation. Although markets remain concerned about inflation, it is possible that the world is on the brink of returning to something like this regime.
- Consumer inflation is low nearly everywhere, while wholesale prices and some asset markets are already showing marked deflationary trends.
- Meanwhile, consumer prices are much more flexible than previously, so that if aggregate demand were to weaken severely, then it is now more likely that the overall level of consumer prices would fall.
- It might be thought that central banks would lower interest rates sharply at the first sign of falling prices but their innate conservatism, and continued paranoia about inflation, may stand in the way.
- Moreover, as realized inflation rates fall, central banks' objectives may become more ambitious. Targeting "price stability", and meaning exactly that, is a serious possibility.
- In any case, central banks' ability to stop deflation is much more constrained than is commonly supposed. In particular, the printing and distribution of notes may still fall foul of perceived restrictions on the level of the public deficit.
- Not that price deflation would necessarily be bad for the economy - once the system had adjusted to it.
- In current circumstances, however, the emergence of deflation could presage a financial revolution. Financial market risk would be radically re-assessed. The yields on top quality government debt would plummet but bonds would be sharply differentiated by credit quality.
- But if we experience deflation in the near future, it is likely to be associated with weak aggregate demand. Accordingly, equities would face a blast not only from reduced production volumes but also from an intense squeeze on margins and doubts about the robustness of balance sheets.

The Threat of Deflation

(This article was originally published in an HSBC Economics and Investment Strategy newsletter on July 20, 1998.

Inflation has fallen to very low levels nearly everywhere. In core Europe it has settled at 1-2 percent. Even previously high inflation countries such as Italy and Spain have achieved low inflation status. In Asia, Japan remains a chronically low inflation country, while China, which not that long ago had inflation of more than 20 percent, is already experiencing falling prices. (See Chart 1.)

In the United States, inflation is not *extremely* low, although it is pretty low by its own standards. Moreover, the US economy has enjoyed a long expansion and the unemployment rate is several notches below the level which economists had thought was likely to trigger higher inflation. In fact, though, the inflation rate has shown no signs of accelerating. On the contrary, last year it actually fell.

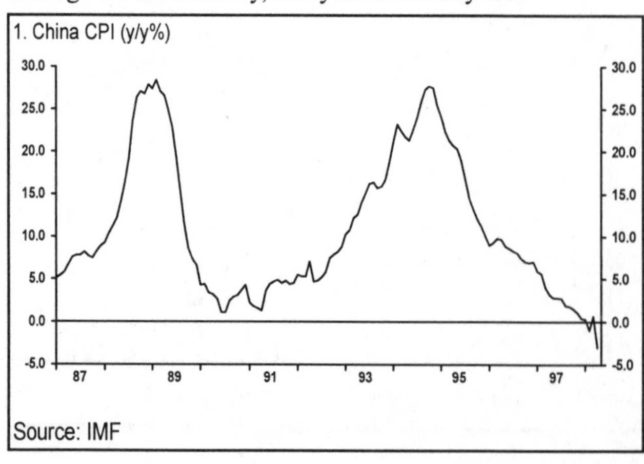

So the evidence is piling up that we have entered a new regime of low inflation. Although discussion continues about how long this is likely to last, and while short-term inflationary risks continue in some countries (e.g. Britain), for the most part, low inflation is now accepted as the new order. The debate is now largely about what has caused this change and about the scope for *deflation.*

Our views about inflation are by now fairly well-known. The economic research team at what was then Midland Montagu first forecast that the 1990s would be a decade of low inflation in October 1990, and several documents pursuing this theme were published subsequently. In April 1996, the book, *"The Death of Inflation"*[1], appeared in print. We have argued that although in many countries the primary role in the reduction in inflation has been played by the monetary authorities' adoption of tough policies, there have in addition been a series of structural changes which have altered price and wage behavior. As inflation rates have fallen to low levels, these structural changes have taken on increased importance.

We do not propose to rehearse those arguments here. Rather, despite current parochial British worries about the resuscitation of inflation, our focus in this paper is explicitly on *deflation.* A year ago, it would have seemed bizarre to consider such a subject, except as an academic exercise or a peep into the history books. But now it should no longer seem outlandish for economists and investors to take this topic seriously, particularly in the light of recent events in Asia.

We start by looking briefly at the current signs of emerging deflation in the world economy. We then go on to consider the forces which could turn these incipient signs into deflation proper, and to ask how easy it would be for monetary authorities to stop it. Finally, we briefly examine the consequences of deflation and the implications for financial markets. In the Appendix we review some of the historical evidence on deflation.

Is Deflation Here Already?

The term deflation is used at different times to mean quite different things. Sometimes, it can mean a fall in asset prices, sometimes a fall in demand and output, sometimes falls in wholesale prices. But the generally accepted definition is a fall in the general level of consumer prices.

On these other definitions, you could argue that deflation is here already. In most western countries, of course, asset prices are caught up in a decided boom, but in Japan, prices of just about every sort of asset (apart from bonds) have been falling for most of the decade. (See Chart 2.) Periods of falling prices have been far from unusual for commodity prices. Chart 3 shows the history of the Bridge/CRB index over the last quarter century. Recently, prices seem to have entered one of their periodic downturns.

2. Japanese Asset Prices, 1980-1998

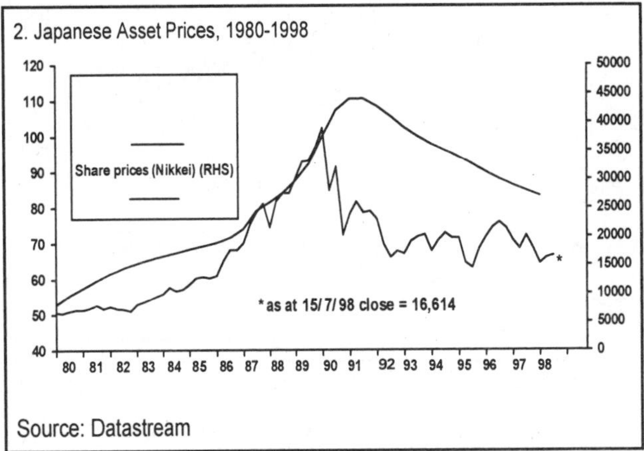

Source: Datastream

3. Bridge/CRB Futures Price Index

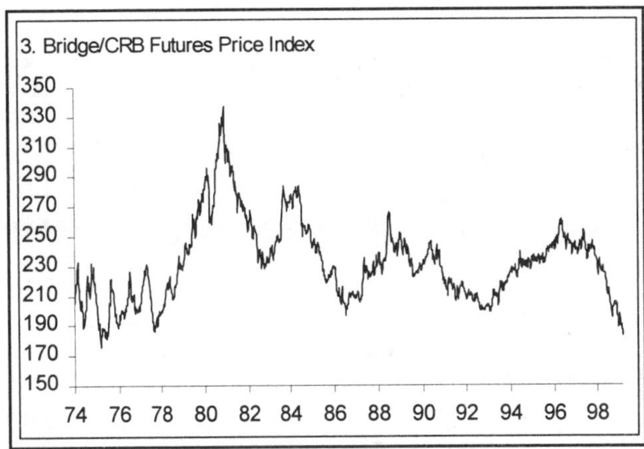

Moreover, two major commodities of particular interest to investment markets, namely oil and gold, are also no strangers to periods of falling prices and both have experienced weakness recently. (See Charts 4 and 5.) Meanwhile, not only in Japan, but also in a number of other countries, wholesale input prices have already been declining, while output prices are not far off. (See Charts 6, 7 and 8.)

4. Brent Crude Oil Price ($/Barrel), 1982-98

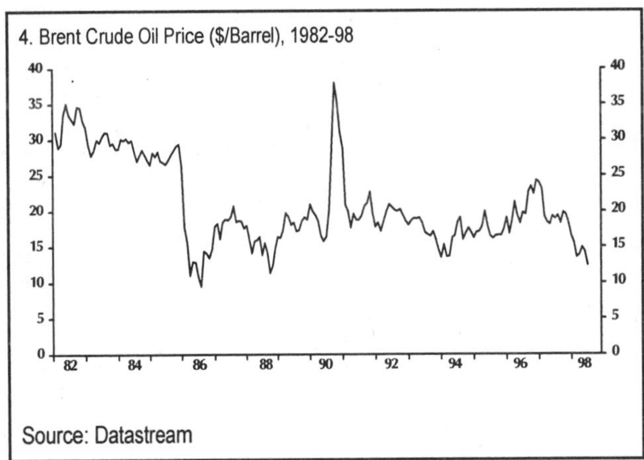

Source: Datastream

---

[1] "The Death of Inflation - Surviving and Thriving in the Zero Era", by Roger Bootle, published by Nicholas Brealey, London, 1996.

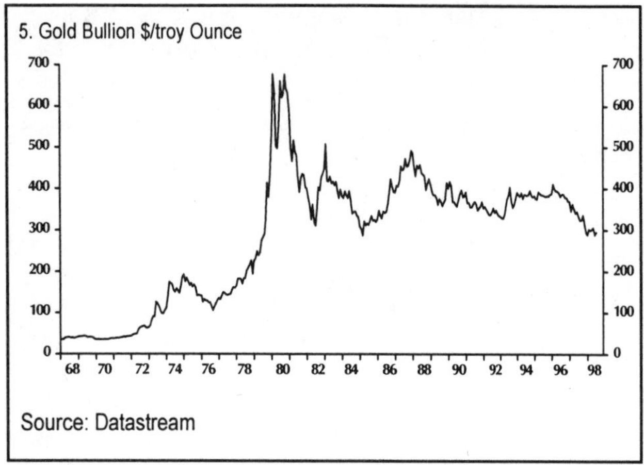

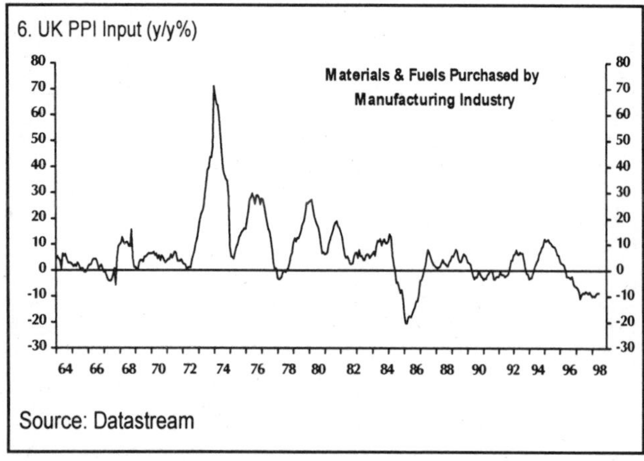

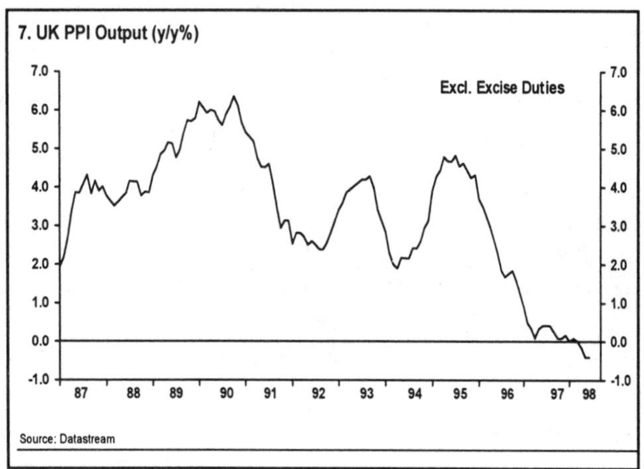

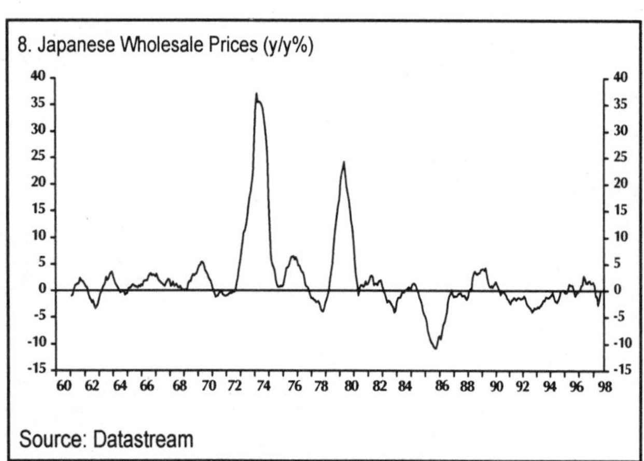

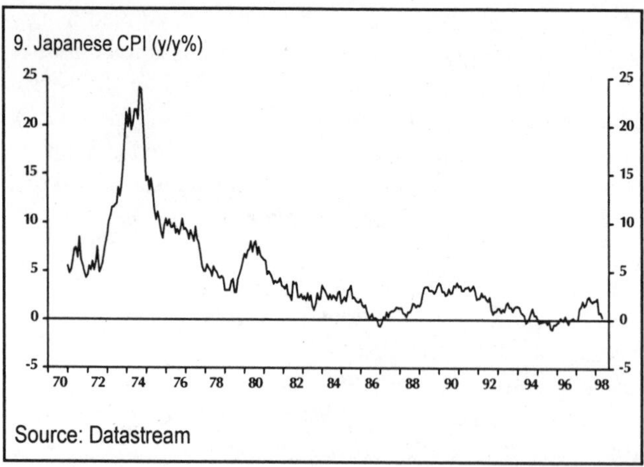

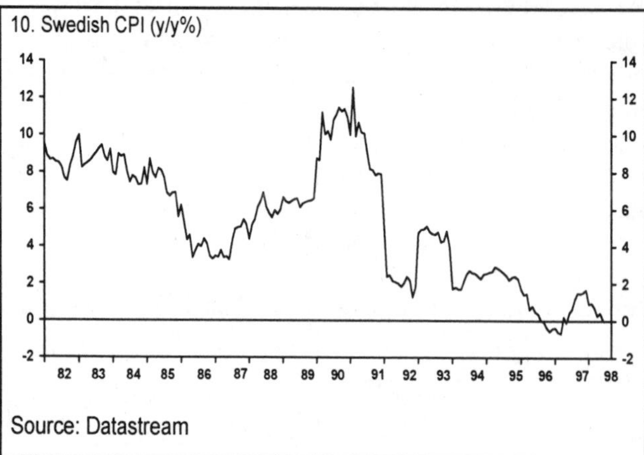

But with regard to consumer prices, deflation has hardly been experienced since the 1930s. There are, however, some minor exceptions. Japan experienced negative official inflation in 1995, and Sweden also had a brief period in 1996. (See charts 9 and 10.) Germany had experienced brief periods of falling consumer prices in 1959 and 1986, and the US in the mid-fifties, but they were very short-lived.

What Makes Deflation Possible Now?

Given that we experienced prolonged low inflation in the 50s and 60s without any break into deflation, what is it that makes deflation a serious possibility now? Why shouldn't the world simply carry on with a very low rate of inflation?

For a start, there has been a sharp change in the priorities of policy-makers. The monetary authorities are now paranoid about inflation. The result is that they aim for very low rates of inflation, and are inclined to be aggressive in raising interest rates at the first sign of trouble on the horizon.

The markets are also super-sensitive to the danger of inflation and accordingly set long interest rates at a level which imposes high real interest rates on borrowers.

Moreover, prices are now more downwardly flexible than they were, so that weak aggregate demand will now more readily result in falling prices. Lighter regulation, a more competitive and more unstable business environment, the growth of variable pricing practices, including discounting and special offers, have all contributed to a situation in which prices can now more readily fall across wide sections of the economy.

It is now more conceivable that even wages could fall. In the United States and Britain, but also increasingly elsewhere, a larger proportion of pay is now made up of variable components such as bonus and performance awards and profit-related elements. Even if "the rate for the job" is still sacrosanct, these variable elements mean that total earnings can now fall - even in nominal terms, if there should be an adverse shock to aggregate demand.

Furthermore, whereas during the 1950s and 60s there was no really serious adverse demand shock, now the world confronts several factors which could conceivably cause such a shock, including the fragility of Japan and the weakness of the whole Far East, and the high level of the equity market, particularly in the US.

For all these reasons, it is now possible to imagine a break into negative inflation, whereas until recently this would have been unthinkable. But still most people are inclined to be skeptical. The prevailing view among economists and market operators is that in the end we get the inflation rate that central banks choose. In that case, what really matters is what they, the central banks, want.

What Do Central Banks Want?

Central banks' inflation objectives are critical to the possibility of deflation in the modern world because of the way that, in contrast to the pure Gold Standard, monetary policy is *managed.* Indeed, at least until recently, it has been common to dismiss the possibility of deflation on the grounds that no government or central bank is aiming for it, nor is ever likely to. The underlying assumption has been that even if the economy was ever in danger of sliding into a deflationary phase, which was itself the subject of some dispute, central banks would see the danger coming and take appropriate offsetting action.

This is naive. After all, the world's central banks did not see the Great Depression coming, nor the Great Inflation of the 1970s. Nor, despite all the propaganda, are their tools so finely honed and effective that they can be relied upon to take exactly offsetting action when they do see a major shock coming.

In our view, certain features of the current situation make a slip into deflation distinctly possible. Firstly, the starting level of inflation is extremely low - sub 2 percent in many countries and sub 1 percent in some. Moreover, this is the level of inflation most central banks are now aiming at.

Because of the history of high inflation over the last thirty years, and more or less continuous inflation over the last sixty years, central banks are paranoid about their reputation as inflation fighters. Perhaps the US Fed might be classed as an honorable exception, but whereas central banks are inclined to see inflationary risks very clearly, they readily play down the chances of deflation. Accordingly, there is likely to be a marked asymmetry in their policy responses. As and when western central banks are confronted by emerging deflation, they are likely to be slow to reduce interest rates, and the pace of reductions is likely to lag behind the pace of the deflationary process, which is usually characterized by falling confidence and a collapse of credit availability, against which minor reductions in interest rates may be next to useless.

Moreover, it is far from obvious that all central banks would stand resolutely against a small rate of deflation. After all, the history of inflation fighting since the battle was first joined in earnest at the end of the 1970s is that the objectives have become more demanding as central banks have enjoyed more success. Far from relaxing as they succeeded in reaching their objectives, central banks have become more ambitious. At the moment, 1-2 percent is presented as the ultimate prize. But it is by no means clear that we have reached the final destination.

After all, what is the justification for an inflation objective of 1-2 percent? One answer is that a little bit of inflation does you good. This is the doctrine which was widely advanced in the 1950s and 60s to justify rather higher rates of inflation and there has recently been a bold attempt to rehabilitate it on the grounds of downward inflexibility of nominal wages and prices[2]. But this is precisely the reasoning which central banks have stood steadfastly against on the grounds that opting for a little bit of inflation is like opting to be a little bit pregnant. They are likely to be highly resistant to this line of reasoning.

The second justification is more acceptable, namely that official indices overstate true inflation and that measured inflation of 1-2 percent really corresponds to price stability properly measured. But in that case, properly measured *deflation* is closer than the official numbers suggest.

Indeed, any lapse into lower measured inflation than currently recorded would take the economy into deflation properly measured. Moreover, across the world there will probably be a trend towards adjusting inflation indices so that they are a better reflection of reality. The ultimate destination may well be to aim for an inflation rate of zero.

---

[2] See Akerlof, Dickens and Perry, " The Macroeconomics of Low Inflation", Brookings Papers on Economic Activity, 1, 1996.

Even if the inflation objective remains 1-2 percent, unless there is substantial downward price rigidity, there is a significant chance of inflation falling below zero simply as a result of the normal process of economic fluctuation. The chance of a flip over into negative territory is all the greater, of course, if the central banks start by aiming for zero.

Talk of zero inflation raises an important issue, namely what rate of inflation should be the objective after a period when the inflation rate has departed from zero. Suppose, for instance, that in a country where the inflation objective is zero, the outturn one year is 5 percent. Should the objective in the "next period" be zero or minus 5 percent? The answer zero means that the price level will always be subject to upward creep and there will always be an upward risk to both the price level and the rate of inflation. This is bound to have an effect on both financial and real economy behavior which may not be helpful to stabilizing inflation and which may have substantial real costs.

By contrast, if central banks adopt the medium-term objective of stabilizing the price level, thereby saying that a period of 5 percent inflation must be offset by a period of *minus* 5 percent inflation, they will be accepting that aiming for falling prices will become a central part of the policy framework. In this case, so far from deflation being the unintended result of things slipping out of central banks' control, it would sometimes be their deliberate intent, as a result of *inflation* temporarily slipping out of their control. No central bank is yet at the point of adopting this objective, but once a period of falling prices has been experienced, the aim of price stability, properly defined, may seem both more achievable and more acceptable.

How Easily Can Deflation Be Stopped?

This still leaves, though, the question of how effective the central banks' tools would be for stopping and reversing the deflationary process once it had begun by accident, or once the rate of price fall had exceeded what central banks thought acceptable. Until recently, at least, the widespread presumption has been that whereas *inflation* might on occasions be difficult to stop, deflation would be easy. The authorities had a powerful armory at their disposal. First in line was interest rates. If a deflationary threat were to merge, all the authorities supposedly have to do is reduce interest rates to sufficiently low levels and this will increase demand and stop deflation in its tracks.

Putting aside the question of whether concerns about credibility would limit the speed at which central banks reduced interest rates, it is important to recognize the limits to the efficacy of reductions in rates in deflationary conditions. When confidence is collapsing, interest rate reductions may do little good. In our view, recent years have seen an excessive emphasis on the ability of changes in short-term interest rates, often of very small proportions, to fine tune the path of nominal aggregate demand. For real efficacy, monetary policy has always relied upon either very large movements in rates, or the ability to deliver some sort of shock which affects expectations or the supply of credit. Changes of ¼ percent or ½ percent, which have recently become the norm in the industrialized west, may have next to no effect.

Moreover, there is a definite lower limit to the level of interest rates, namely zero[3]. Accordingly, once interest rates have fallen to zero, not only is there no chance of further reductions in nominal rates but real rates will rise as the inflation rate continues to fall, and when it falls through zero, then the real rate will turn from negative to positive, and rising, thereby tightening monetary policy at just the time that it is supposed to be becoming "looser" in order to boost demand. Indeed, since there is no absolute lower limit to the rate at which prices can fall, nor to the rate at which they can be expected to fall, in theory at least, it is possible to imagine real rates rising uncontrollably, thereby increasing the rate of deflation, which would raise real rates of interest still further. In this way, it is possible to imagine a deflationary spiral developing, mirroring the inflationary spiral of conventional experience.

Such a possibility has attracted very little attention principally because, to the best of our knowledge, nothing closely resembling this situation has ever occurred, and nothing *remotely* like it has occurred for the last sixty years. In the more distant past, of course, there have been umpteen deflationary episodes, as we stressed at the beginning, and in some cases the annual rates of deflation have reached high levels. In 1922 in the UK, for instance, the consumer price index fell by 18 percent.

---

[3] Three qualifications must be acknowledged. First, there are some historical examples of negative interest rates, although they occurred for specific reasons with next to no general applicability. In 1978, for instance, operating a system of tight exchange controls, Switzerland imposed negative interest rates on foreigners depositing in Swiss francs in order to deter speculative buying of the franc.

Second, even without exchange controls, it might be possible for banks to charge depositors a negative interest rate for "safe-keeping" of money. But this would have to be very low, probably no larger than ½ percent p.a. Otherwise, people would surely prefer to hold their money in hoards of notes.

Third, the root reason for the "impossibility" of negative interest rates is the option to hold notes which pay (and charge) zero interest. In this case, the "solution" is to issue dated notes, whose value declines with time, i.e. they do carry a negative rate of interest. With a negative interest rate on notes, it would then be possible for banks to impose negative interest rates on deposits. This idea has played a definite role in the theoretical literature, but to the best of our knowledge, no examples of it exist in practice - and for a very good reason. It is difficult to see how a monetary economy would function effectively if the value of notes was time-dependent.

But large falls of this sort tended to be reversed fairly quickly, while persistent falls lasting several years were limited to small annual rates of decline. So there was never really the experience of deflation running out of control in the way that there have been countless examples of *inflation* running out of control.

It is perhaps worth asking why this is. The theoreticians' answer would be that as prices fall, the real value of the *outside* money stock rises and this increases real wealth, which tends to boost consumption. Accordingly, there is an automatic stabilizer at work. (By the "outside" money stock, economists mean monetary assets which are not liabilities of the private sector. This disqualifies bank deposits, which count as "inside" money. The reason is that with inside money, the increased real value of the monetary asset to its holder is matched and offset by an increase in its real value as a liability. For this reason, only notes and coin count as outside money, the assumption being that the public sector, acting in the long-run public interest, can be indifferent to movements in the real value of its monetary liabilities.)

Whether this mechanism, known to the theoreticians as the "real balance effect", is in practice what has held deflation in check is open to dispute, although this is a question beyond the scope of this paper. But there are other forces which we suspect may have been stronger. Reacting to the experiences of the 1920s, Keynes wrote in 1930:[4]

> *"I believe that the resistances to a severe Income Deflation, which is not merely a reaction from a recent inflation, have always been very great. But in the modern world of organized Trade Unions and a proletarian electorate they are overwhelmingly strong."*

The frictions and imperfections which are usually blamed for the "downward inflexibility" of wages and the resulting inefficiencies may actually have had strong stabilizing effects when the economy confronted deflationary dangers.

A further stabilizing force may have developed from the behavior of consumers. When people had experienced fluctuations in the price level over many years, they may have developed a sense of "normal" prices, so that their own behavior tended to operate in a stabilizing fashion even without any influence from the real value of outside money holdings.

Even if conventional monetary policy - or, to call a spade a spade, interest rate policy - does not do the trick, then there is a widespread belief that other policies would. Since Keynes, prime among these "other policies" has been fiscal policy. When deflation looms, or once it has begun and threatens to become established, according to the conventional view, all that has to happen is for the government to launch an expansionary fiscal policy involving cuts in taxes, increases in spending or both. This was the prevailing and deeply ingrained wisdom of the Keynesian age, and it is not to be lightly discarded. It remains the case that in slump conditions, a substantial and sustained fiscal expansion may offer a plausible way out of the problem. But during the Keynesian age, which lasted, perhaps, to the end of the 1970s, limits to this policy were barely acknowledged.

Things do not look quite the same now. In many countries, decades of profligate borrowing have left governments feeling uncomfortably close to the point where, under pressure of rising debt interest payments, government debt spirals out of control. When a government reaches this position, or thinks it has, then ordinary fiscal expansion has also reached its limits. Indeed, it is possible to imagine a fiscal expansion having such negative effects on confidence that the overall effect on aggregate demand was zero or even negative.

Japan is in something like this position. The precise seriousness of the Japanese long-term fiscal situation is open to dispute. The US Treasury and a host of respected economists have tried to persuade the Japanese authorities that they do have room for a conventional Keynesian stimulus. But the important thing is that the Japanese government has thought that its long-term fiscal situation is serious. As a result, the several fiscal packages which have been launched to try to bolster the economy have been disappointing with regard to both size and content. Most importantly, the government has been reluctant to announce substantial *permanent* tax cuts. Instead, it has announced temporary cuts which, precisely because they are perceived as temporary, have had very little apparent impact on demand.

But the Japanese situation is not unique. Other governments face serious fiscal constraints. Italy and Belgium have gross public debt to GDP ratios of over 120 percent, while in Canada the ratio is over 90 percent, and in Sweden over 70 percent. All these governments have reached the point where fiscal expansion is dangerous.

Even in those countries in Europe where, on the face of it, the debt to GDP ratio does not look so troubling, once you take into account off balance-sheet items such as unfunded pension liabilities, the position is a good deal worse.

Moreover, in the European case, the freedom of government to use expansionary fiscal policy is now circumscribed by the Stability Pact which limits the size of the government deficit in relation to GDP, and lays down penalty fines if the limits are breached. (There are important exceptions to this which should allow scope for fiscal action to moderate a severe recession. But, at the very least, the existence of the Pact may serve to delay effective action.)

[4] J.M. Keynes, "A Treatise on Money", Vol. II, ch 30, Macmillan, London, 1960 (1930), p 184.

Expanding the Money Supply

Where governments are, or consider themselves to be, fiscally constrained, the answer, so the textbooks say, is to "print money". That way the economy can enjoy the same boost to demand that the real balance effect unleashes after a period of deflation - but without having to go through the pain in the first place. If the solution is a higher ratio of money to output or expenditure then the easy way out is for the central bank simply to print it.

Indeed, it seems so very easy. Unfortunately, this is one of those things which is repeated by economists without careful attention to what is actually meant. What does "printing money" mean? Encouraging increased lending activity by commercial banks does not qualify.

What the advocates of "printing money" have in mind is an increase in the supply of "outside money", that is to say the monetary liabilities of the public sector. But how can this be achieved? The central bank can buy assets in the market, crediting the sellers with deposits at itself, thereby expanding its balance sheet. That has the effect of increasing the supply of outside money. But it will not directly increase the total size of private wealth holdings. For the private sector will have given up assets in exchange for deposits at the central bank. Unless the central bank has bought these assets at inflated prices, as in the case when it buys dud loans at full face value, even though their true market worth is minimal, (which raises other difficulties), there is no direct effect on private wealth.

Nevertheless, there could be indirect effects. The purchase of assets will tend to drive up their price and reduce their yield, which would ordinarily encourage increased spending. But a policy of lower interest rates is precisely what we said above may not have much effect in deflationary conditions. Once interest rates have fallen to very low levels, an economy may find itself in a "liquidity trap."

Strictly interpreted, even Japan is not in the liquidity trap as envisaged by Keynes. He wrote about a condition where interest rates were so low that wealth holders were convinced that the next move in rates was up and so interest rates could not be forced any lower through cash purchases of securities by the central bank. In fact, as the Japanese experience indicates, it has been possible to drive bond yields down to levels which were thought unimaginable even a few months ago, and accordingly, there is not an overwhelming view in the market that bond yields necessarily have to rise. Indeed it is possible that a massive program of official stock purchases would drive bond yields below 1 percent.

But in a deeper sense Japan *is* in a liquidity trap. For given that zero constitutes an absolute limit for bond yields, once they have fallen to nearly 1 percent , as they have in Japan today, they have only a maximum of 1 percent or so to fall. Yet a 1 percent drop in funding costs may be neither here nor there when confidence is collapsing and consumer prices are thought likely to fall. **For a country in this trap, the scope for further interest rate falls is close to its minimum at precisely the point that the response to interest rate falls is minimal.**

Yet there is another channel through which, superficially at least, asset purchases by the central bank looks different, and potentially more powerful, namely the effect on banks' liquidity. When the central bank buys securities, the cash lands up at the commercial banks, held in the form of deposits at the central bank. According to the textbook models, banks seek to keep their cash holdings to a minimum, constrained by legal requirements, topped up only marginally by prudential considerations - not least because in most countries they earn next to nothing on these deposits, and in many cases literally nothing.

Accordingly, when they are rendered flush with cash by a policy of central bank buying of securities, they seek to replace their idle and unproductive cash at the central bank with interest-earning assets, including loans. Moreover, the effect is compounded because, when they disburse this cash, it merely lands back in the banks, thereby starting the whole process all over again. It will only come to an end when bank balance sheets have expanded sufficiently to make the banks willing and necessary holders of the newly expanded cash supply.

But in deflationary conditions, why should the banks wish to do this? The interest rate on government credits will be next to nothing, for the reasons given above. Meanwhile, the risks attaching to ordinary commercial lending will appear to be severe. Any assets used as security for loans will be liable to fall in value. Similarly, projected cash flows will be judged extremely risky, even if the borrowing institution maintains its business volumes and manages to survive. In practice, the conditions we are discussing will be ones where the real business climate is grim and where corporate bankruptcies are at a high level. What this amounts to is a case for keeping assets in the form of deposits at the central bank even though they pay no interest. At least they will not lose the bank money, and in real terms they may actually yield a decent return.

Probably the most that could be hoped for is aggressive bank buying of government paper which drives the yield lower. But, as we argued above, when rates are already close to 1 percent and the interest sensitivity of consumer and corporate spending is extremely low, this may achieve next to no beneficial result, while blowing up the size of commercial bank balance sheets and probably reducing their rate of return on capital. In other words, when deflation has already taken hold, simply making the banks flush with cash does not clearly provide a way of avoiding the limitations on the effectiveness of interest rate reductions. On the contrary, it may fail for analogous reasons.

Admittedly, it could be argued that in that case, the authorities should simply carry on buying assets and increasing cash, and carry on doing it until the banks do respond by lending more. But in practice, other considerations are likely to limit this policy - not least concerns about the size of the central bank's balance sheet and about banks being pushed into yet more "dodgy" lending which, if it ultimately proves to be unsound, will actually worsen the underlying problem. **If general confidence in the economy has collapsed because of a perception that the banking system has been severely weakened by indiscriminate lending, it is unlikely to be boosted by the knowledge that the banks are being prodded to lend more when their own inclinations may be to lend less.**

Let the Printing Press Take the Strain

So now we come to the real *coup de grâce*. If all else fails, the government should simply "print money" - literally. Instead of asking the central bank to provide extra money by taking something back in exchange - namely the securities it purchases with the cash - the government should simply distribute the extra money without asking for anything back. That way, private wealth will increase and at some point this must encourage increased spending. This is the remedy advocated by Keynes when he suggested burying bottles stuffed with pound notes and employing men to dig them up. It is also effectively the way of increasing the money supply assumed by Milton Friedman in one of his theoretical models, namely the distribution of dollar bills by helicopter.

Yet to the best of our knowledge, there are no examples of notes being buried in the ground, nor of helicopters distributing notes at random. And for good reason. Quite apart from anything else, it would hardly be politically acceptable for some people to gain massively at the expense of others purely as the result of the turn of a spade or a gust of wind.

So what is the practical equivalent of flying a helicopter over Tokyo dropping trillions of yen notes? It is a temporary tax cut. In a modern financial system, the money would accrue to individuals in the form of increased bank deposits, rather than bundles of notes, but no matter. Analytically, provided that the tax cuts are financed by a bond or bill issue bought by the central bank, these come to the same thing. (And if the public prefers to hold its increase in money holdings in the form of notes rather than bank deposits, then it can choose to withdraw the funds and hold them in the form of extra notes.) The result is that people find themselves with increased money in the bank, and banks find themselves with increased deposits at the central bank.

But this means that, far from constituting a completely different way of alleviating the deflationary predicament, "printing money" in fact ends up as exactly the same as a mixture of two of the policies which are likely to, in current conditions, have only limited chances of success, that is to say, a temporary tax cut and an open market purchase by the central bank of bonds for cash.

Perhaps the answer is for the government to declare that the "helicopter" will disperse this extra money every year - that is to say, that the tax cuts are permanent - and that the central bank will carry on buying the paper. In theory, at some point, this ought to prompt increased spending. But the key point is that far from being a separate solution altogether, "printing money" is simply an amalgam of two rather more conventional solutions, to which there are objections, or apparent limitations.

The most important point is that when a government thinks it is debt constrained, then even "printing money" is no easy option. If the government sent out the helicopter to distribute notes, how would such largess be classified in the accounts? It would surely count as government expenditure, even though nothing was being bought with the money. If you like, it would be expenditure on charitable donations. Accordingly, it would lead to a larger deficit and involve increasing the stock of debt, albeit that (at least if you net across the public sector as a whole) the extra debt would be in non-interest-bearing form, namely notes.

In this regard, it is worth noting that in the great inflations of the past, when governments have financed themselves by printing money, they have had no inhibitions about levels of the deficit or accumulated debt. Sometimes the lack of effectively functioning capital markets has meant that sales of debt to the central bank, or in extreme cases, simply the outright printing of notes, has been the only way of financing a gap between revenue and expenditure. In these circumstances, "monetary" and "fiscal" expansions are indistinguishable.

In this respect, it is also worth noting the European dimension. The European Central Bank is explicitly forbidden from lending directly to governments with precisely the objective of preventing the printing of money. Article 21 of the Protocols to the Maastricht Treaty states:

> *"In accordance with Article 104 of this Treaty, overdrafts or any other type of credit facility with the ECB or with the national central banks in favor of Community Institutions or bodies, central governments, regional, local or other public authorities, other bodies governed by public law, or public undertakings of Member States shall be prohibited, as shall the purchase directly from them by the ECB or national central banks of debt instruments."*

Meanwhile, the Stability Pact restricts the scope of European governments to indulge in discretionary fiscal loosening to head off or limit the emergence of deflationary forces. Accordingly, if Euroland were ever to find itself in deflationary conditions, official policy would have to rely mainly on reductions in official interest rates, which lands us back with the problems discussed above.

Moreover, the actions of the ECB are likely to be closely circumscribed. It will surely feel that it has to try to establish its credibility. With the weight of the past behind it, doubtless it will feel that this is not consistent with cutting rates to very low levels very quickly. Accordingly, it is likely that policy relaxation would lag behind any deterioration in sentiment in the economy. In any case, with official Euro rates likely to start in the 3-4 percent range, while Euroland will not be in the Japanese position, there would nevertheless not be enormous scope to use rate reductions for stimulatory purposes. Accordingly, the ECB might feel the need to be sparing in its use of the interest rate weapon for fear of using up the last few shots in the locker.

Deflation: Fear or Fantasy?

So is there a realistic prospect of deflation? In the US and UK it is not in the cards in the immediate future. The starting level of inflation is relatively high and economic growth is still too strong. Indeed, the immediate risk appears to be of higher inflation. But even in these countries, deflation is a realistic prospect on the horizon. In particular, it is striking that the US has enjoyed a fall in inflation to about 2 percent in the seventh year of economic recovery. If this is what inflation runs at in the context of strong demand, what will it get to as and when the economy slows considerably? We think the answer is that it will fall much further - and there is nothing sacrosanct about the number zero. Provided that the US maintains roughly the current rate of inflation during this continued phase of strong growth, then it is just one recession away from price stability, meaning a regime which will encompass periods of falling prices. Elsewhere, deflation is much closer. Japan risks slipping back into falling prices by the end of the year, while Chinese retail prices are already falling. And in core Europe, the disinflationary forces unleashed by the advent of the euro, combined with more intense competition from eastern Europe, will bring inflation even lower. A slip into negative territory is perfectly plausible in the next couple of years, despite what may be a fairly robust cyclical recovery.

Why Worry About Deflation?

So inflation may be about to turn negative. So what? It is possible to regard the emergence of deflation as largely irrelevant for real values. A fall in inflation from plus 2 percent to minus 2 percent may be regarded as the same as a fall from an inflation rate of 6 percent to an inflation rate of 2 percent. The change of sign is of no significance. Indeed, if everything is free to adjust equally, then provided that every part of the system sees what is going on and adjusts, no adverse effects need follow. Moreover, there is some historical support for this conclusion. In the nineteenth century an extended period of economic growth coincided with falling prices in both the United States and Britain. Yet this is remarkably like the argument that inflation has no ill effects provided that it is perfectly anticipated. In current circumstances, when deflation is not widely regarded as a realistic possibility, not all parts of the system would see it coming and not all parts of it would be free to adjust if they did. In particular, the real value of contracts fixed in money terms would be increased, just as inflation reduces them.

Even where contracts are not necessarily fixed for the long term, it may be more difficult for some prices to be varied than for others. In particular, wages and salaries are likely to be more downwardly sticky than prices. Accordingly, profit margins are likely to come under pressure. The combination of falling product and asset prices, squeezed profit margins and major changes in balance sheet quality, may induce considerable financial instability.

Moreover, in our view, the emergence of even a small rate of deflation would have considerable significance for bond markets. Most importantly, the realization that in the new world, the level of consumer prices can go down as well as up would erode the asymmetry in the risk position facing bond investors and thereby serve greatly to reduce the risk premium built into bond yields. Without this risk premium, bond yields could fall to the much lower levels common in the past. If it becomes widely believed that we are in a period of "price stability", with the possibility that prices will from time to time fall, then in the light of past experience in both the US and the UK, 4 percent seems a perfectly reasonable level for bond yields, and even 3 percent should not be ruled out in crisis conditions. (See charts 11 and 12.)

11. UK 2.5% consol yields, annual average %, 1756-1997

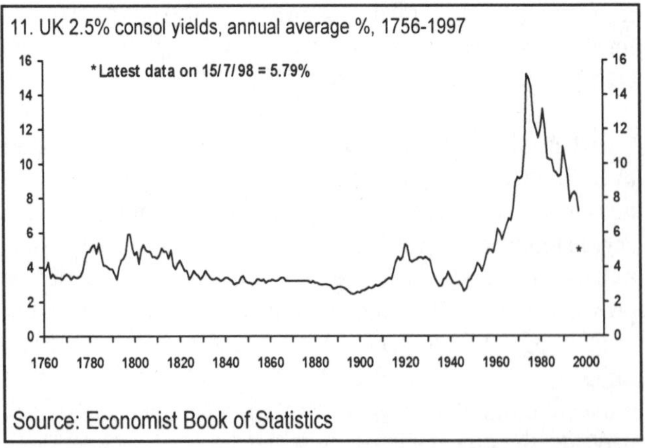

Source: Economist Book of Statistics

Needless to say, however, in conditions of deflation, it is not true that any old bond will do provided that it is long. On the contrary, the quality of the bond would take on added significance. There would probably be a sharp divergence between prime and low quality bonds. In general, this could

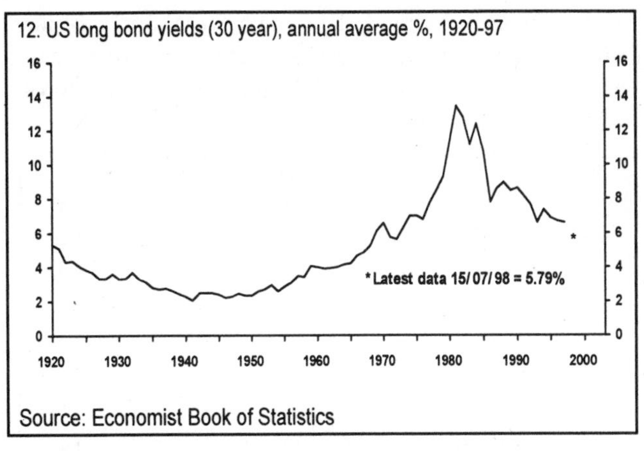

12. US long bond yields (30 year), annual average %, 1920-97

Source: Economist Book of Statistics

be taken to favor government over corporate bonds, but things are unlikely to be quite this simple. In particular, governments with a high ratio of debt to GDP would be distinctly out of favor.

How would deflation affect equity markets? It is possible to imagine circumstances where equities did well against a background of falling prices - provided that the rate of decline were not very great. But because deflation is unfamiliar and because the system is not adapted to it this is unlikely to be the initial effect.

Moreover, for anything other than low rates of deflation, there could be seriously adverse financial effects. There is no reason why interest rates could not get close to zero, as they did in the US in the late 1930s. (See Chart 13.) But the point about short term interest rates not being able to go negative is extremely important. Rising real short rates would be decidedly bad news for equities. If real bond yields fell in response to the change in the inflation climate that would be good news, but it is not clear that real bond yields would fall. It is possible that the fall in nominal yields would lag behind the fall of inflation into negative territory. Indeed, once bond yields have fallen to zero, they can fall no further. At that point, any acceleration in the rate of deflation would cause real bond yields to rise. Even if real bond yields did fall significantly from current levels, if this merely reflected a change in risk premium, it would not necessarily help equities.

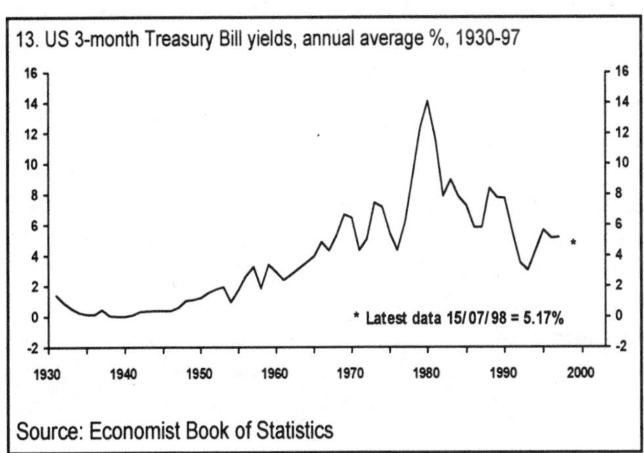

13. US 3-month Treasury Bill yields, annual average %, 1930-97

Source: Economist Book of Statistics

But over and above this, equities stand to be major casualties of the squeeze on profit margins which we argued above, is likely to be the result of the slip into deflation. Moreover, we should avoid thinking of deflation merely arithmetically. In current circumstances, if deflation emerges, it is likely to be in the context of very weak aggregate demand. Thus, earnings are likely to suffer an adverse effect from volumes as well as profit margins. Furthermore, if it is true that the world has become much more competitive, then in the context of weaker demand, the degree of price competition may be greater than previously. Accordingly, prices and hence margins may be under even more intense pressure. The emergence of deflation could readily be the factor which finally bursts the equity bubble.

Conclusion

The world economy is in an intensely dangerous phase. Deflationary trends are evident in both Japan and China, while the recovery of the smaller Asian countries after last year's crisis will be heavily dependent upon the growth of net exports to the west. This is bound to put intense pressure on western prices.

Meanwhile, a cyclical slowdown is likely in the US and UK. Euroland should be accelerating, but disinflationary forces are so strong there that inflation will stay subdued, even if the widely touted stronger growth does emerge. A slip into deflation in core Europe is a distinct possibility.

If price deflation were to appear in the west, and especially in the United States, the consequences for financial markets would be momentous, with interest rates and bond yields moving lower but equities under severe threat.

In conclusion, far from being an arcane subject which can be left to historians and academics, deflation is very much with us in the here and now. The possibility that the western world will enter a deflationary phase is something which both economists and financial analysts should take very seriously indeed.

The end of the Second World War was so momentous in so many more important respects that its economic and financial impact can easily be listed well down the ledger. But looking back, it marked the beginning of the Age of Inflation. Does the end of the Cold War mark the re-emergence of Deflation as part of our normal experience?

Appendix: The Historical Experience

The long run historical experience is not one of continual inflation but rather of periods of inflation and deflation alternating, with the result that over long spans of time there was no continual upward drift of the price level. In fact, for an extended period in the nineteenth century, the price level in both Britain and the US trended downwards. Charts 14 and 15 show the record for the United States going back to 1800. Chart 14 shows the US price level: Chart 3 shows the annual rate of inflation. They clearly reveal this alternating pattern of inflation and deflation lasting right up to the Second World War.

14. The US Price Level from 1800 to 1997 (1800=100)

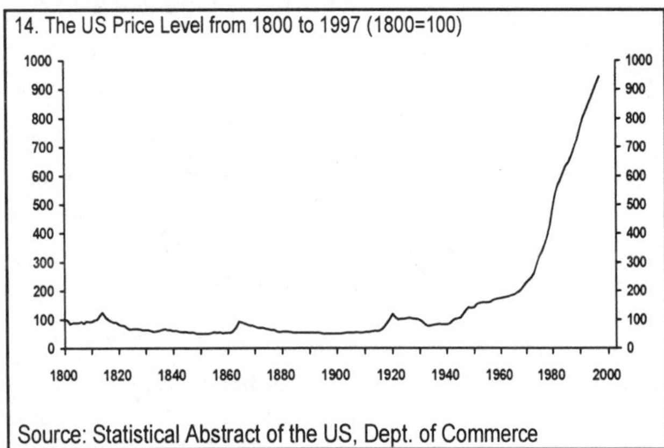

Source: Statistical Abstract of the US, Dept. of Commerce

15. US Inflation (1800-1997) (y/y%)

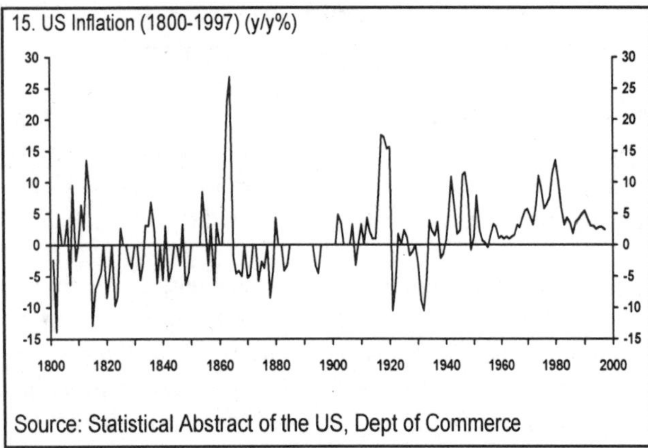

Source: Statistical Abstract of the US, Dept of Commerce

In Britain, with a little imagination and some heroic use of data, we can show an even longer record of the same thing - going back to 1264, although it is fair to say that the record suggests that not much at all was going on for a few hundred years. (See Chart 16.) If we concentrate on the last three hundred years and look at annual rates of change of the price level, however, as shown in Chart 17, then the picture is clear - inflation and deflation alternating right up to the Second World War.

Against the background of this history, you can readily see how something which our generation takes for granted - namely the continual upward march of prices - came as such a surprise to people in the late 1940s and early 50s. But now, of course, there are some signs of profound change. Even the sage and august Chairman of the Federal Reserve, Mr. Alan Greenspan, apparently takes seriously the idea of the "new paradigm" or "new era", and, according to the evidence of a recent speech, he thinks that deflation is a topic worthy of serious consideration.

16. The British Price Level 1264 to 1997 (1264=100)

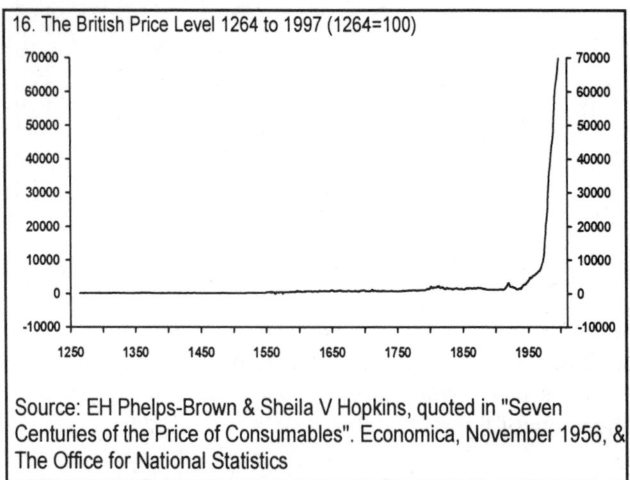

Source: EH Phelps-Brown & Sheila V Hopkins, quoted in "Seven Centuries of the Price of Consumables". Economica, November 1956, & The Office for National Statistics

17. British Inflation (y/y%), 1700-1997

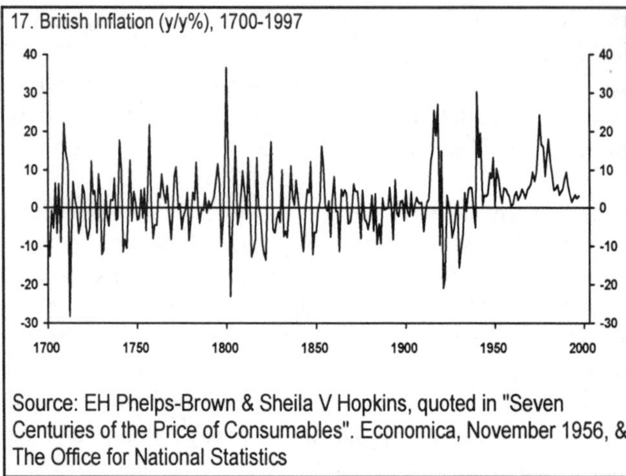

Source: EH Phelps-Brown & Sheila V Hopkins, quoted in "Seven Centuries of the Price of Consumables". Economica, November 1956, & The Office for National Statistics

Misinterpreting the Gold Standard

Nevertheless, many commentators and investors still believe that even if we are set for a prolonged period of low inflation, *deflation* in the modern world is somehow impossible. It is something which belongs to the history books alone. Partly this view derives from a misinterpretation of history - specifically the history of the Gold Standard.

It is possible to dismiss the experience of deflation in the past on the grounds that it all occurred during a period when the world's money was metallic. Indeed, in the later part of the period, the developed world was on the system known as the Gold Standard. In this regime, deflation occurred when there was a shortage of the precious metal in relation to the demand for it. Moreover, there was no opportunity for a country to avoid or escape from the ravages of deflation because it had no control over the supply of gold. This experience, it can be argued, is of no relevance in an era of paper money when the money supply can be expanded at will.

But in our view, this is much too simplistic an interpretation of the Gold Standard experience (as well as too simplistic an interpretation of the situation confronting modern policy-makers, as we argue below). In fact, in the earlier part of the nineteenth century, several countries did not adopt the Gold Standard for fear that gold discoveries would induce inflation[5]. In the event, these fears were misplaced but for those countries which did adopt the Gold Standard, the interesting (and important) question is why countries stuck to it and endured the restraints imposed by the attachment to a precious metal. It certainly was not because they knew of no alternative. Debasement of the coinage had occurred intermittently since ancient times. Moreover, there had been bursts of sharp inflation associated with the large scale printing of notes in the early stages of the French Revolution, the American War of Independence, and in the American Civil War. Furthermore, the country at the centre of the Gold Standard, Britain, twice suspended it - during the Napoleonic wars and during the First World War - and twice decided to go back to it.

Why did Britain twice go back to the Gold Standard? The answer speaks volumes about why the system apparently succeeded and about its relevance for today's world. Britain twice returned to the Gold Standard because it believed that it worked, and that its alternative did not. It was this belief which underpinned the self-discipline needed to sustain the Standard.

So one thing should be clear. The essential change from the world of precious metal to the world of paper money was not a technological one - the sudden discovery of paper money and the realization that society could be free from tutelage to the "barbarous relic." It was not the sudden discovery of the technique of using paper rather than precious metal and thereby of the power to create money simply by printing it. This much had been clear for centuries.

Accordingly, because there was an alternative, the operation of the Gold Standard required discipline and restraint. This carries the clue to its eventual abandonment. The system was abandoned when it was no longer believed that such discipline and restraint was necessary/desirable.

Psycho-social theorists might associate this change of beliefs with the wider kicking over of the traces which followed the First World War and the widespread atmosphere of experiment and license in the world of the arts and personal morality - associated in Britain with the Bloomsbury Group, whose members, of course, included Keynes himself. Economists might instead concentrate more narrowly on changed economic behavior, and specifically on the evidence that prices and wages were now highly inflexible downwards so that sticking to the Gold Standard discipline would involve a massive loss of output.

Wherever the balance lies between these two (not necessarily competing) explanations, one thing is clear: the essential change from the world of the Gold Standard to the world of paper money was psychological and intellectual. It was all about the acceptance of discipline, about its costs and benefits.

This is not so far from today's world as first appears. Indeed, the new conventional wisdom is precisely about the importance of sticking to monetary disciplines - and being seen to do so. Credibility is now regarded as critical. Would today's generation of central bankers have argued, with Keynes, against the restoration of the Gold Standard at the old parity? In the all-important intellectual aspects, today's world shares much in common with the Gold Standard era. Indeed, it is tempting to say that given the same discipline and restraint, it is now possible to achieve similarly low inflation, or "price stability" - if that is what central banks (and others) want.

[5] See Eichengreen and Flandreau, "The Gold Standard in Theory and History", 2nd edn., Routledge, 1997, London, pp 7-8.

*   *   *

Roger Bootle is the author of the best-selling book **"The Death of Inflation"** *published in 1996 by Nicholas Brealey, and now translated into seven languages. Roger Bootle recently resigned as Chief Economist of HSBC to set up his own independent consultancy, based in London, called* **"Capital Economics."**
Telephone-- 44-171-486-3871; E-mail-- business@capitaleconomics.com

UNDERSTANDING ELECTRONIC TRADING

by Joseph H. Zoller

Introduction

Over six million U.S. households made their first purchase on the Internet in 1998, a 40 percent increase over the previous year. With this growth in Internet usage for the purchase of goods and services, it seemed only a matter time before Futures Commission Merchants (FCMs), institutional traders, and the general public would expect the same keyboard access enabling them to execute futures and options trades.

The major exchanges recognized at least 15 years ago the need to institute new forms of technology to reduce costs, improve reliability, meet regulatory requirements, and continue to attract and hold business.

Electronic order entry attracted the initial attention of exchanges and brokerage offices. The objectives were to speed the flow of orders to the floor and send price information back, improve the accuracy of orders, and provide an improved audit trail.

Today the mantra of users of the derivatives and futures markets appears to be "Electronic Trading." This catchall phrase has gained currency among the Internet-savvy public, exchange members, institutional customers, FCMs, and the media.

In reality, the term "electronic trading" describes a variety of situations. To some it means totally electronic trading of futures and options, without human interaction. It is straight through processing of orders from an individual's PC via a user-friendly screen for order entry, matching, reporting and clearance, and settlement. To others, it means electronic transmission of orders to a firm's booth or into the pits, where they are executed by traditional methods. And of course, many participants believe that the transmission to a broker from their PC's via the Internet or dedicated line constitutes electronic trading.

Concept

Today futures and derivatives trading is clearly a global enterprise. Wheat, metals, energy and financials are now traded around the world and in many different contracts. In addition, exchanges have developed mutual offset that allows for continuous trading and settlement across many time zones.

Global electronic entry systems such as the original Globex and the new Globex2, Project A©, and others allow traders the opportunity to deal in contracts after the close of open outcry sessions. In fact, they can speculate or hedge positions virtually 24 hours a day. In addition, automated trading platforms have been developed that match bid and offer orders automatically and report information directly to clearinghouses.

Without question, the concept of electronic trading is gaining ground and is perceived by many as the method of the future. Even those who embrace open outcry believe that eventually electronic trading will be the dominant system for many contracts. The biggest unknown is the timing of the movement.

Many traders and customers alike fully believe that open outcry is the best trading system available. The ability of floor traders standing face-to-face to quickly execute orders and provide the fills that customers need can be persuasively argued. In addition, this environment creates the deep and very liquid markets preferred by users.

But even the most ardent proponents of open outcry fully accept the electronic enhancements that speed orders to and from of the floor, automatically time stamp them, and help eliminate the cumbersome writing of order tickets. In one form or another, a variety of these systems are now in place at all major exchanges.

FCMs have been at the forefront in promoting electronic order entry systems. They not only desire the faster order flow but also the automatic transmission of trade information for exchange reporting and clearinghouse matching. This contemporaneous status of all trades within minutes of execution creates faster and more accurate backroom processing.

In a short time, many traders have found order entry via the Internet to be a new and user-friendly way of participating in the futures market. Whether initiated to e-commerce through the purchase of books, airline tickets, CDs, or a host of other products, retail customers have discovered that the move to Internet trading can be the equivalent of a small leap.

Most retail online trading simply replaces the telephone call to the broker with an online order. To these traders, online order entry is less intimidating than a phone call. Instead of struggling with a harried, impatient order taker, the customer simply fills out an online form and then clicks "okay." Depending on the broker, the exchange, and the contract, in most cases the order is transmitted to the floor electronically, then into the pit via floor runners, or by flash signals.

Electronic Exchange Tools

Order Routing Systems

One system that is used by all major U.S. exchanges is the Trade Order Processing System (TOPS) route. An electronic link between broker firms and the floor booths, TOPS was developed jointly by the Chicago Board of Trade (CBOT) and the Chicago Mercantile Exchange (CME). It is the standard electronic order entry and fill reporting system. TOPS sends information directly from the FCM to the floor, where all of the relevant information required to maintain an order book, advise the clearing house, and confirm execution customer orders is maintained. This entire process can be accomplished within just a few minutes--or less.

Firms also have additional means of shortening the trading process. An Internet interface with a database incorporating customer information, such as credit worthiness and margin available, can be connected directly to the TOPS route, without the need for intervention by anyone in the broker's office.

Depending on the contract and timing, the order can be transmitted directly to the exchange order matching system (CUBS/GLOBEX2 at the CME, or Project A at the CBOT). As of this writing, the CME's Mini S&P 500 ("e-mini") is the only contract in the United States that is being traded wholly electronically. The CME membership recently voted to allow Eurodollar futures to be traded side by side with the traditional open outcry system as of June 1999. The CBOT offers side-by-side trading (along with open outcry) on 30-year Treasury Bonds, and ten-year, five-year and two-year Treasury Notes. Additionally, most CBOT and CME contracts are traded electronically after regular trading hours.

Consolidation and Alliances

The momentum toward electronic trading was initiated by European exchanges that have enhanced electronic trading platforms. Ironically, the Globex model that was available to European traders during their work hours helped inspire the shift to an electronic trading platform. MATIF, the French futures exchange, was one of the early adopters of Globex and its members constituted a large portion of trading volume. After the MATIF was purchased by Societe des Bourse Francaises (SBF), there was a strong motivation to improve technological capabilities.

Recently the SBF (including its two subsidiaries MATIF SA and MONEP SA) announced the first global alliance with the CME and the Singapore International Monetary Exchange (SIMEX). In addition to having a common trading engine that is accessible from a single terminal, the alliance provides for a Mutual Offset System (MOS), which allows members to establish positions on one exchange and offset them with subsequent trades on another.

The February 1999 agreement between the CME, SBF, and the SIMEX established a common trading platform for futures and options that is open almost continuously over the Asian, European, and U.S. trading periods.

The CME claims that the pact establishes the French NSC trading platform as a world standard and allows the CME and other exchanges to trim their own development costs. Likewise, the French will adopt CLEARING 21, developed by the CME and the New York Merçantile Exchange (NYMEX). The networks of each exchange will be connected through a common interface, also known as the HUB Application Program Interface (API). Its routing and managing technology will give exchange members direct access to a broad range of electronically traded futures and options. Orders will then be routed to the appropriate trading engine for matching and confirmation to the member. As a result of the HUB API, independent software vendors will be able to efficiently connect their front-end systems to the separate platforms for each exchange.

Chicago Board of Trade

The CBOT has spent considerable development time and money to establish Project A©. Although the membership rejected an alliance with EUREX and the use of the EUREX trading platform, the CBOT is committed to advanced technology and has several electronic systems in place. The TOPS system (developed in conjunction with the CME) simplifies the delivery of customer orders directly to the participating FCMs booth on the floor. Several FCMs have developed interfaces that allow customers to directly input their orders through dedicated lines, specific dial-up numbers, and most recently, via the Internet.

COMET, a booth-based system facilitating computerized order entry, tracking, and management. works with the CBOT's Electronic Clerk (EC) to efficiently deliver and receive information into and out of the pit. EC is a pit-based order receiving and deck management system.

Project A is an electronic trading system available on the CBOT's Agricultural and Financial Treasury products. Originally designed as an after-hours venue, the membership recently voted to allow side-by-side Project A and open outcry trading. Although Project A trading has increased handily over the past year, 98 percent of Project A volume was conducted between 5:30am and 7:19am, when open outcry was closed. By January 1999, over 560 terminals had been installed in the U.S. and in London. Currently, the CBOT plans to increase Project A into a full-featured, enhanced electronic trading system with capacity to meet all of the Board's anticipated volume requirements.

Chicago Mercantile Exchange

Globex was introduced by the CME in 1992 as an after-hours, interactive trading platform. The French futures exchange, MATIF, was an initial participant in the system and the relationship continues with the development of newer, more enhanced systems. In late 1998, Globex2 superseded the original Globex, with 21 additional features including execution of a greater variety of order types. The CME acquired the software for Globex2 in a technology swap with the French options, stock, and futures exchanges for the CME's CLEARING 21 system. In return, the French trading platform, the Nouveau Systeme de Cotation (NSC) was adopted by the CME. An additional 12 exchanges worldwide also adopted the NSC platform.

The Chicago Mercantile Exchange Universal Broker Station (CUBS) delivers orders from FCMs directly into the trading pit or to Globex2 for execution. The CUBS system can also be interfaced with member firms' order entry systems, and if so configured can be accessed directly from a customer's PC, via the Internet. But despite its promise, CUBS has been plagued with shutdowns and capacity problems, to the extent that many firms who want to use CUBS have been forced to maintain a backup staff on the floor. Unfortunately, this negates the economies so desperately desired. In January 1999, much of the original software was replaced in anticipation of the introduction of CUBS2. The hope is that these revisions and enhancements will minimize the computer problems experienced by FCMs with the earlier incarnation.

London International Financial Futures (and Options) Exchange (LIFFE)

After the Deutsche Terminbörse (DTB) electronic trading floor acquired the greatest share of the German Bund futures volume from the LIFFE's open outcry system, LIFFE shifted its orientation to electronic trading. LIFFE CONNECT is an electronic platform for the trading of derivative products. Using cutting-edge technology, it facilitates customization of trading front ends and meets members' trading requirements. Currently LIFFE CONNECT is trading individual equity options and the FTSE 100 Index. Additional futures and options are expected to begin trading in late spring, 1999.

EUREX

The high development costs of a fully electronic trading platform have led many exchanges to seek alliances or consolidation with other exchanges. One of the more notable joint efforts was the creation of the EUREX by the Deutsche Terminbörse (DTB) and the Swiss Options and Financial Futures Exchange (SOFFEX) in late 1998. Together they have developed a market with opportunities for additional partners to join the alliance.

Until a membership vote to the contrary in January 1999, the Chicago Board of Trade was scheduled to join with EUREX in utilizing its electronic trading platform. In spite of the rejection, EUREX had a trading volume in January exceeding that of all other exchanges, including the CBOT. The consolidation of the DTB and SOFFEX has led to a joint, cross-border futures market. Their fully automatic trading platform offers participants decentralized, standardized, and global access to a worldwide network.

New York Mercantile Exchange

NYMEX ACCESS trading was developed to extend the trading day for the NYMEX's metals and energy contracts. NYMEX and SIMEX signed an agreement in January 1999 allowing NYMEX ACCESS in Singapore. This trading system already is operational in London, Hong Kong, and Sydney, and provides for trading in NYMEX contracts in these markets after U.S. trading hours The NYMEX has not announced any plans for totally electronic trading.

Sydney Futures Exchange

The Sydney Futures Exchange (SFE) has made a commitment to screen trading. The SFE anticipates that SYCOM© IV (the SFE's latest version of its screen trading program) will be operational during the third quarter of 1999. This system is based on a Windows NT platform making it easily accessible to third party vendors

The implementation of SYCOM IV is in anticipation of a shift from open outcry to electronic, screen based trading. In addition to the order routing system, an Automated Order Entry Interface (AOEI) will allow members to trade globally or input orders directly from the members' proprietary or third party order routing systems.

New York Stock Exchange

The New York Stock Exchange (NYSE) initiated many of the technological changes later copied or modified by other exchanges. Its Super Designated Order Turnaround System (Super DOT) is widely acknowledged to be one of the most reliable electronic trading aids. However, it is still constructed around the Exchange's market-maker system. Even with Internet-accessible brokerage systems, a specialist executes the orders as soon as market interest and activity permit. Although it is possible for a broker-dealer to communicate instantly with the trading post, a market-maker is still required to complete the transaction.

NASDAQ

NASDAQ is the largest screen-based stock market. In fact, many people consider NASDAQ to be synonymous with electronic trading. Although it has no trading floor with broker stations, it still depends on assigned specialists to make the market on its listed securities. NASDAQ recently signed with OptiMark™ Technologies to provide NASD members with a trading "facility" that will eventually act as an order matching system across a range of prices.

Other initiatives by NASDAQ included a proposal to implement an integrated order delivery and execution system and a voluntary consolidated limit order file. The exchange is also pilot testing methods for conducting trades over the Internet. Currently, investors can request trades via the Internet to brokers, but the actual trading is still done over dedicated links between the broker and the exchange.

Chicago Board Options Exchange

The Chicago Board Options Exchange (CBOE) has emerged as a leader of technological change in the trading process in the securities industry. The CBOE's order handling, routing, and execution systems have been developed to speed the order flow from the customer to the floor and back. Many futures exchanges have looked at the CBOE's systems with an eye toward modifying them for futures trading.

The backbone of the exchange is the CBOE Order Routing System, the means by which 80 percent of public orders are handled on the floor. Because the CBOE is still a market-maker system, the types of execution techniques among the floor traders range from the traditional trading cards to hand-held computers that automatically relay customer orders.

In addition, the CBOE developed a Retail Automatic Execution System (RAES) to provide smaller retail customers with fast executions. Orders that fall within designated premium levels, contract size, and series parameters are guaranteed fills at the current bid and offer. Approximately 25 percent of public orders are executed through RAES. The traditional trading system still provides the price discovery while actual fills are handled by market makers who agree to participate in the system.

Another CBOE system is the Public Automated Routing (PAR) system, a PC-based, touch screen, order routing and execution system used by floor brokers. PAR increases the speed at which a public order is represented, executed, and filled.

In addition to these systems, the CBOE utilizes the Electronic Book (Ebook), which automatically opens, sorts, and files orders in price and time sequence. Most orders received prior to the opening of the market are routed to Ebook.

The Market Maker hand-held terminal (MMT) brings personalized computer trading support to market-makers on the trading floor. Currently more than 500 market makers use the 19-ounce, hand-held MMT unit and other hand-held computers to execute over 60 percent of all trades floor-wide. The MMT has a variety of features built in to assist the market maker. Probably the best of these is the ability to interface with the exchange's other automated systems. Public access to the trading floor via the Internet or direct dial-up accounts is still subject to the preferences and abilities of the customer's brokerage firm.

International Securities Exchange

The International Securities Exchange (ISE) is designed to be the first entirely electronic options exchange. The ISE will be the first U.S. market that will combine the efficiencies of electronic trading within an open auction market environment. An auction market is one in which open bids and offers meet directly with transaction prices determined by the current supply and demand.

The stated ISE philosophy is that the investing public should have the highest priority. Customer orders will always be executed before professional orders, the price will be the best price of any U.S. options exchange, and a complete, detailed electronic record (audit trail) of all transactions, time-stamped to the nearest 1/1000th of a second, will be immediately available for surveillance purposes.

Scheduled to begin trading in January 2000, the ISE is based on the OM Click Exchange System. Currently 13 exchanges around the world have acquired this system, including the Australian Stock Exchange, the Hong Kong Futures Exchange, and the Milan Stock Exchange. The ISE has specified major enhancements to the system to meet specific exchange requirements. The trading platform will be built on an open and flexible client/server architecture that will allow members a wide range of trading tools.

The importance of the ISE is that it represents the first all-electronic exchange in the U.S. If successful, it will apply even more pressure on the major U.S. trading floors to embrace the electronic technology in favor of the broker based open outcry system.

Cantor Financial Futures Exchange (CFFE)

After much fanfare, and over the protests of the CBOT, Cantor Fitzgerald Securities gained approval from the CFTC for a computer-based trading system in U.S. Treasury bonds, and 10-year, five-year, and two-year U.S. Treasury note futures contracts. The CFFE was formed as part of an agreement between the New York Cotton Exchange (NYCE) and Cantor Fitzgerald.

The new screen-based exchange opened in September 1998 with 200 contracts being traded daily and slipped from there. Although many advocates of open outcry took this as evidence that the country was not ready for electronic trading, insiders said the problem was based more on the structure of the market. Screen traders could only relay orders via telephone to a CFFE Terminal Operator who was a Cantor Fitzgerald employee. The terminal operator had to enter the order into the CFFE system, where it was matched based on time and price, according to a trade-matching algorithm.

The CFFE expects to introduce an improved system, which will include more features, in mid 1999.

Timber Hill Group

Some proprietary trading systems have been developed by individual firms as a means of accelerating the use of electronics. Timber Hill Group is a notable example. It has developed a unique screen-based order routing system that utilizes a high-speed communications network linking floor brokers. Orders are electronically routed to an executing broker using a wireless hand-held computer in the traditional open outcry trading pits. The computer maintains up-to-the-second market information which traders can access directly. Orders are instantly communicated to these computers where they are executed, and fills are confirmed in a matter of seconds. The system holds all of the trading information and no paper is generated. Timber Hill has been approved by the CFTC for its system, since it trades only for its own account. The system also interfaces directly with the CME's "E-Mini" contract as well as several other electronically traded contracts around the world.

The system is also available to other FCM's through the firm's Interactive Brokers. Initially it was available as a hard-wired service, utilizing Timber Hill's own Interactive Trader Workstation (ITW). In 1998, however, the firm added the Internet to its existing proprietary network, allowing an expanded client base to take advantage of its unique system. Clientele is limited to FCMs who either trade for themselves or maintain full responsibility for the integrity of their customer orders, margins, and disclosures. Several firms offer their own interactive brokerage, based on this system, to qualified clients. By utilizing the Internet, Interactive Brokers can offer its system to customers globally, 24 hours a day, without the need to develop an infrastructure in countries that could not support it.

The ability of the Timber Hill system to continue its growth will be an indicator of how institutional traders view the electronic markets.

Clearing Considerations

All futures and options exchanges have clearinghouses that are critical to their operation. Most notably, a futures clearinghouse facilitates trades among strangers by eliminating counterparty risk and guaranteeing the integrity of trades. Historically, each exchange has had its own clearing operation. Recently, however, exchanges have explored common forms of clearing. In December 1998, the Chicago Board of Trade Clearing Corporation and the CME clearing operation agreed to work towards common banking and cross-margining.

When trade data can be transmitted electronically, concurrent with the execution, it speeds up the trade matching process and allows the status of the trades to be transmitted to the member firms for print-out or online viewing.

Because of the rapidly changing nature of the futures and options business, including new products, systems, and strategic alliances, clearinghouse technology must be extremely adaptable, scalable, and open.

Regulatory Environment

The regulatory agencies have been cooperative in allowing the introduction of new technologies. In December 1998 the U.S. Securities and Exchange Commission (SEC) approved new rules that will allow electronic trading systems to register as full-fledged exchanges.

The SEC also adopted new guidelines that subject electronic systems to more stringent fair access and security requirements.

"Technology is fundamentally changing our marketplace," said SEC Chairman Arthur Levitt. "It has caused us, as regulators, to rethink the way we do our jobs."

The Commodity Futures Trading Commission (CFTC) has not formally issued broad sweeping rules. They have approved many specific requests involving electronic trading systems including the request, in August 1998, by the Board of Trade of the City of New York, Inc. to begin trading on its affiliate, the Cantor Financial Futures Exchange. They have also looked favorably on many other electronically enhanced systems and have informally given encouragement to several planned systems.

Security Considerations

After some initial trepidation, the question of security with Internet transactions has been addressed. Technically, the Secure Sockets Layer (SSL) protocol, which was created by Netscape and also implemented by Microsoft, addresses all of the necessary security issues. SSL authenticates the server so customers know they are dealing with the intended Web commerce site. It encrypts sensitive information before sending it across the wire, and provides a way to verify that the transmission has not been altered en route. Optionally, it can even authenticate the client to the server, a feature important to banks, e-commerce sites, and other institutional customers.

The Arguments

Advocates of the time tested open outcry system of trading believe that no electronic system is as efficient as that which currently exists at the CBOT or CME. They argue that while there is a lot of conversation regarding electronic trading, most major customers are only concerned with their fill. One plausible argument in their favor is that large customers (institutions, banks, large commercial traders, etc.) maintain open telephone lines to the order desks on the floors where the most important contracts are traded. his direct link allows the trader to immediately convey his or her orders to the desk. Then, in a single movement, the order is flashed to the pit where it can be confirmed in seconds. The trader of stock indexes, interest rate, and foreign exchange contracts can readily take advantage of these deep, highly efficient markets in this manner. However, even some traders concede that electronic trading may work better in those contracts with lower volume.

Since futures markets are known to be highly volatile there is concern about whether the electronic systems described here can handle massive surges in volume. The experience of the online Internet securities brokers in January 1999 when day traders on the NASDAQ choked the existing networks is pointed to as a reason for maintaining a system that is not so susceptible to computer breakdowns. Today, many online futures brokers that have the capability to interface directly with exchange order-entry systems maintain a backup staff to step in when the computer "hiccups" or goes down.

Proponents of electronic trading in the futures markets claim that the existing electronic order routing and trading systems were built specifically to supplement, rather than replace, the traditional open outcry systems. They claim that the new technology being developed for that purpose has the capabilities and reliability required by the FCMs. Many members of domestic exchanges, particularly in Chicago, are concerned that the switch to electronic trading by European and Asian exchanges will cut deeply into their volume. Growth of the Internet and e-commerce across the board will make it easier for traders to shift to electronic systems.

Epilogue

Clearly, there is a movement towards increased use of electronic technology by all exchanges and all firms. This technology, which will improve efficiency, reduce errors, and ultimately add to profits appears to be an inevitable result of unstoppable pressures. Just as the telegraph made it possible to communicate market prices great distances from the trading floors, and the telephone enabled customers to deal with brokers in a timely manner, electronic trading seems destined to change the markets. The only questions are in what way and according to what timetable.

* * *

Joseph H. Zoller, is president of The Zoller Organization, a marketing/communications firm specializing in marketing, creative, and communications services for the futures and financial services industry since 1981. Mr. Zoller's clients have included major futures and options exchanges, as well as leading FCMs, IBs, and CTAs. The Zoller Organization offers clients a broad range of communication services, including sales materials, advertising, trade show management, and editorial assistance. Additionally, Zoller consults with management of various firms regarding marketing and communications situations. Mr. Zoller can be contacted at The Zoller Organization, 1861 Old Briar Road, Highland Park, Illinois 60035, 847-831-4788, (FAX, 847-831-9082), or at zollernet@compuserve.com.

THE BRIDGE/CRB TOTAL RETURN INDEX

by Raymond T. Murphy

Commodities as an Asset Class

As the world markets continue their evolution toward one global marketplace, the advent of financial futures trading has had much to do with that unification. The popularity of financial futures has removed some of the stigmas and fears that were associated with the perceived rough and tumble world of commodities. Previously, commodity futures were considered too risky for investors looking for the stability associated with a traditionally diversified portfolio. But now, with money managers searching the globe for additional investment opportunities, commodities have fallen under the spotlight. The advantages of asset diversification have uncovered this area of investment as the newest tool which will enable investors to better evaluate their long term exposure to the up and down movements inherent in today's markets. By allocating a portion of their investment dollars to commodities, investors are better able to obtain desirable long term results while at the same time lowering the volatility of their portfolio.

Diversification into commodities allows the portfolio to attain a more balanced inventory of assets. Whether or not high levels of inflation resurface, the allocation of a percentage of investable funds into an asset that will successfully lower the overall volatility of a portfolio, while improving the annual performance, is every investors goal. The counter-cyclic nature of commodities to financial assets makes commodities an ideal asset class to incorporate into a portfolio to achieve a more desirable return scenario. Should inflation remain under control, the commodity portion of a properly allocated portfolio may lag other asset classes, but that lag normally indicates that the other non-commodity assets performed well. This is historically true because low to moderate inflationary periods allow for the stable environment in which traditional financial assets have performed well. In such a case, the commodity allocation would have served its purpose as a counter-cyclic asset to the rest of the portfolio. They also provide a hedge against political instability and natural disasters which may adversely affect existing supply/demand alliances.

The Bridge/Commodity Research Bureau Index (CRB) and the Goldman Sachs Commodity Index (GSCI) are currently the only two commodity indices which have exchange listed futures contracts. The newly formed New York Board of Trade (NYBOT), in conjunction with Bridge/CRB and RTM Management, have recently produced a total return calculation based upon the Bridge/CRB Futures Price Index that is directly related to the New York listed CRB futures contract. This calculation is referred to as the Bridge/CRB Total Return Index (CRB-TR). Previously any analysis of the CRB Index could only be done on the level of commodity prices. The information now available will allow investors to analyze the return characteristics of the CRB Index as well.

A New Total Return Measurement for Commodities

The Bridge/CRB Futures Price Index, developed in 1956, is the most well known indicator of overall commodity prices in the world. Its original design had weighted the index heavily towards agricultural commodities. Over the past ten years changes have been made so that the CRB today is more equally representative of a broad range of commodity prices. Currently, the index is geometrically weighted evenly among 17 arithmetically averaged component commodities. CRB future and option contracts have been traded on the New York Futures Exchange (a division of the New York Board of Trade) since June 1986. The CRB futures contract has 6 expiration months per year (Jan-Feb-Apr-Jun-Aug-Nov). All futures and options expire to cash on the same date. One CRB contract is worth $500 times the price of the index.

As the recognized benchmark for commodity prices, the CRB plays an important role in the investment strategies of funds both large and small. In the past, fund managers based their commodity allocation investment decisions on commodity index prices instead of actual realized returns. It would be hard to fault them on this since overall commodity return information was practically nonexistent. The very nature of commodity future contracts requires them to regularly expire. When this occurs, an existing position needs to be continually rolled forward. This is rarely done at the same price. Storage, interest charges, and short-term supply/demand anomalies are some (certainly not all) of the factors attributing to the difference in price between the near term futures price and a more deferred one.

An example would be carrying a Gold futures position. Gold is a market which trades almost exclusively in contango, which means that near term future contracts trade at a lower price than more deferred future contracts. (Backwardation is the term used when the opposite price structure is present). Let's say you own one April Gold 1999 futures contract at a price of $300.00. This means you control 100 ounces of gold at $300.00 per ounce. The April contract will "expire" on a particular day in April of 1999. In order to maintain your desired position of being long 100 ounces of gold, you decide to roll your futures position forward to a December contract. To do this you need to sell your April contract and buy a December contract. At the time you do this the December future is priced $8.00 above the April future. You now have the same position as before but your price is now $8.00 higher. This $8.00 is not a profit but the carrying cost of maintaining a Gold position that far out into the future. A total return index of holding a passive Gold futures position over time would measure only the dollar return associated with the price movement of Gold. The price of Gold has always been an important factor in many macro economic models, but it is the real dollar return which is the true measure of its utility as an investment.

The CRB Futures Price Index is based on the average price of individual commodities over a six month period of time. When a commodity expired it was simply deleted from the index and whatever effect this may have had on the index was simply reflected in the price the following day. This is why many times you may see the CRB Futures Price Index moving significantly from its closing price the day before, to the next day, before any of its components have opened for trading. This is the effect of actual component future contracts being added or deleted to the index. This properly reflects price levels for its component commodities and is therefore useful in gauging commodity price strength or weakness against historical periods. What it does not show are the returns which would have been achieved by a passively held investment using the CRB. By calculating this return characteristic investment professionals are now able to accurately assess the usability of commodities in their overall investment program. A total return index allows commodities to be examined on an even playing field with other traditional asset classes.

Total Rate of Return

The nature of commodity futures make it difficult to determine the actual long term returns associated with a passive position over long periods of time. A passive long term position needs to be continually rolled in order to avoid expiring contracts. A total return measures the actual dollar return associated with a passive commodity position plus the interest earned on a fully collateralized position. The total rate of return for both the CRB and the GSCI is determined by three factors: spot yield, roll level, and the collateral yield.

The spot yield is the return associated with the price performance of the index.

The roll yield is the return associated with the continuous rolling of near term commodity contracts to more deferred ones. The levels of these rolls will either involve rolling into a lower priced contract (backwardation) or a more expensive one (contango). The roll yield may be either positive or negative, depending on the prices present during the roll period. The combination of the spot yield and the roll yield make up the continuous contract (GSCI literature refers to this calculation as the "excess return"). The continuous contract is a measurement of the realized return of a passive investment in any commodity based on price movement alone. Adjustments are made to account for the rolling of contracts to more deferred contract months without affecting the actual dollar return of the instrument.

The collateral yield is the interest rate component derived from an unleveraged commodity investment. The total return index for both the CRB and GSCI is the continuous contract plus interest earned from the uncollateralized position. Each index uses 90 day T-Bill rates for this component of their respective total return results.

Passive opportunities in the Bridge/CRB-TR

As Table A below clearly shows, the CRB-TR is an excellent vehicle for diversifying into commodities. The return and volatility characteristics allow it to serve as an ideal benchmark for institutions looking to take advantage of this asset class. And while the CRB-TR has impressive credentials, other factors make it even more attractive for real world investors.

One of the key features of the CRB is its method of calculation. Because the CRB is geometrically averaged, the listed CRB future contracts almost always trade at a discount to their fair value. This is due to the fact that arbitrageurs are able to manage a short CRB futures position against an equal weighted long component position which is arithmetically weighted. As time passes, and depending upon the volatility of the component commodities, the arbitrageurs long component position will outperform the short CRB position. This mathematical certainty allows the arbitrageurs to sell CRB futures contracts at a slight discount to their daily calculated value. Informed investors may regularly obtain this price anomaly and therefore increase their overall return by the level of the discount captured. A large institutional investor may find this aspect of using the CRB particularly attractive. Along with the size of a CRB futures contract ($100,000 per contract with the index at 200.00), using CRB futures contracts may seem the most useful of the current commodity benchmarks currently available.

Many investors looking to commodities as a hedge against other held assets are not so much concerned with commodity prices rising but with commodities prices rising quickly. Large upward spikes in commodity prices may send investors scrambling to insulate their portfolio against the possible inflationary ramifications associated with such a move. The comparatively low volatility of the CRB make using CRB options a reasonably priced insurance policy.

An institutional investor thinking about using commodities now has a benchmark linked to the premier commodity indicator in the world. A trader willing to spend the required time learning the subtleties of the index will be able to find numerous trading opportunities. Both groups will find the following summary page provided by Bridge to be invaluable in their decision making.

The Bridge/CRB Summary Page

In its continuing effort to provide both traders and investor professionals the most complete and usable information on commodities, Bridge/CRB has provided on its web site (www.crbindex.com) a summary page of all the pertinent data required to make informed decisions regarding the CRB and CRB Total Return Indices. An example of the summary page as of the close of trading on December 4, 1998 is shown below with accompanying commentary on how one might use the information.

CRB / Bridge Index Price Page

Results from trade date 4-Dec-98

Index of summary page

Section I : Component futures daily net changes effect on each CRB cash / futures fair value.
Section II : CRB cash and futures settlements. CRB fair values and premium/discount versus settlements.
Section III : CRB futures time spreads settlements and fair values.
Section IV : CRB Total Return Index daily performance.
Section V : Next day changes to the CRB cash index with associated values due to expiring/added contracts.
Section VI : CRB Futures Contract windows.

Section I

Commodity	Exchange	CRB Cash Index Averages	Net change $ effect on CRB Cash	CRB Jan Contract Averages	Net change $ effect on CRB Jan	CRB Feb Contract Averages	Net change $ effect on CRB Feb	Trading Hours Eastern Standard Time
Wheat	CBOT	291.13	+0.04	295.92	+0.06	295.92	+0.06	10:30am to 2:15pm
Corn	CBOT	227.00	- 0.08	230.42	- 0.07	230.42	- 0.07	10:30am to 2:15pm
Beans	CBOT	590.33	+0.01	598.67	+0.00	600.94	+0.00	10:30am to 2:15pm
Live Cattle	CME	63.228	+0.05	63.470	+0.05	63.897	+0.03	10:05am to 2:00pm
Lean Hogs	CME	38.903	- 0.11	45.060	- 0.04	46.418	- 0.04	10:10am to 2:00pm
H.G. Copper	NYMEX	69.03	- 0.03	69.38	- 0.04	69.38	- 0.04	8:10am to 2:00pm
Gold	NYMEX	296.13	+0.02	296.13	+0.02	297.90	+0.02	8:20am to 2:30pm
Silver	NYMEX	480.20	- 0.01	481.57	- 0.01	481.57	- 0.01	8:25am to 2:25pm
Platinum	NYMEX	349.00	+0.03	350.20	+0.03	350.20	+0.03	8:25am to 2:25pm
Cocoa	NYBOT	1479.50	- 0.12	1491.00	- 0.12	1491.00	- 0.13	9:00am to 2:00pm
Sugar #11	NYBOT	8.28	- 0.06	8.31	- 0.05	8.31	- 0.05	9:30am to 1:20pm
Coffee	NYBOT	111.08	- 0.16	111.43	- 0.16	111.43	- 0.16	9:15am to 1:35pm
Cotton	NYBOT	63.97	+0.09	64.29	+0.09	64.29	+0.09	10:30am to 2:40pm
Orange Juice	NYBOT	119.50	+0.02	121.28	+0.01	121.28	+0.01	10:15am to 2:15pm
Crude Oil	NYMEX	11.88	- 0.04	12.22	- 0.05	12.54	- 0.05	9:45am to 3:10pm
Heating Oil	NYMEX	0.3408	- 0.04	0.3488	- 0.04	0.3555	- 0.05	9:50am to 3:10pm
Natural Gas	NYMEX	2.0102	+0.12	2.0196	+0.11	2.0208	+0.09	10:00am to 3:10pm
CRB Index	NYBOT	195.05	-	198.51	-	199.58	-	9:40am to 2:45pm

Section II

CRB FUTURES CONTRACTS	Settlement	Daily Real Change	Fair Values	Fair Value Daily Change	Fair Value Premium/ Discount to Futures
CRB Cash Index	195.05	- 0.24	-	- 0.28	-
CRB January 99	198.25	- 0.40	198.51	- 0.23	- 0.26
CRB February 99	199.00	- 0.40	199.58	- 0.27	- 0.58
CRB April 99	201.50	- 0.40	203.17	- 0.35	- 1.67
CRB June 99	204.50	- 0.40	207.01	- 0.35	- 2.51

The CRB Jan 99 contract is worth	+ 3.45	to CRB cash at settlement of last trading day.
The CRB Jan 99 contract will be	+ 3.45	to CRB cash at settlement on the next trade day

Section III

Calander Spreads	Settlement	Fair Value	Fair Value Premium/ Discount
CRB Feb - Jan	0.75	1.07	- 0.32
CRB Apr - Jan	3.25	4.67	- 1.42
CRB Jun - Jan	6.25	8.50	- 2.25
CRB Apr -Feb	2.50	3.60	- 1.10
CRB Jun -Feb	5.50	7.43	- 1.93
CRB Jun -Apr	3.00	3.83	- 0.83

Section IV

	Current	Daily Change	One Week Ago	Index on 01-Jan-98	Y-T-D % Change	I Year Ago Value	52 Week % Change
CRB Total Return Index	182.33	- 0.19	185.88	223.11	- 18.28%	229.78	- 20.65%

Section V

CRB / Bridge calendar of expiring / newly listed contracts for the month of DECEMBER

Commodity	Contract Month	Last Day in Index	New Listed Month	First Day in Index
Wheat	-	-	-	-
Corn	-	-	-	-
Soybeans	Jan-99	28-Dec	-	-
Live Cattle	Dec-98	7-Dec	-	-
Lean Hogs	-	-	-	-
HG Copper	-	-	-	-
Gold	-	-	-	-
Silver	-	-	-	-
Platinum	-	-	-	-
Cocoa	-	-	-	-
Sugar #11	-	-	-	-
Coffee	-	-	-	-
Cotton	-	-	-	-
Orange Juice	-	-	-	-
Crude Oil	Jan-99	17-Dec	Jun-99	18-Dec
Heating Oil	Jan-99	31-Dec	Jun-99	4-Jan
Natural Gas	Jan-99	22-Dec	Jun-99	23-Dec

Section VI

CRB Futures Contract Windows

Commodity	January	February	April	June	August	November
Wheat	H K N	H K N	K N U	N U Z	U Z	Z H K
Corn	H K N	H K N	K N U	N U Z	U Z	Z H K
Soybeans	H K N	H K N Q	K N Q	N Q X	X F	F H K
Live Cattle	G J M	J M Q	M Q V	Q V Z	V Z G	Z G J
Lean Hogs	G J M N	G J M N Q	J M N Q V	M N Q V Z	Q V Z G	Z G J
HG Copper	H K N	H K N	K N U	N U Z	U Z	Z H K
Gold	G J M	J M Q	M Q	Q Z	Z G	Z G J
Silver	H K N	H K N	K N U	N U Z	U Z	Z H K
Platinum	J N	J N	N V	N V	V F	F J
Cocoa	H K N	H K N	K N U	N U Z	U Z	Z H K
Sugar #11	H K N	H K N	K N V	N V	V H	H K
Coffee	H K N	H K N	K N U	N U Z	U Z	Z H K
Cotton	H K N	H K N	K N	N Z	Z H	Z H K
Orange Juice	H K N	H K N	K N U	N U X	U X F	F H K
Crude Oil	G H J K M	H J K M N	K M N Q U	N Q U V X	U V X Z F	Z F G H J
Heating Oil	G H J K M	H J K M N	K M N Q U	N Q U V X	U V X Z F	Z F G H J
Natural Gas	G H J K M	H J K M N	K M N Q U	N Q U V X	U V X Z F	Z F G H J

Month Codes

F - January
G - February
H - March
J - April
K - May
M - June
N - July
Q - August
U - September
V - October
X - November
Z - December

Section I

This section of the summary page contains the daily information showing each components contribution to the overall index price move. This is particularly useful on days when one or two commodities move the index drastically up or down while other components may have moved little. Someone looking only at the CRB price movement on days like this may miss the overall price picture of commodities as a whole. For longer term traders this may help them decide to stay in a trade instead of exiting a position prematurely based on the price behavior of a small group of commodities when the overall trend of the remaining commodities is still positive for their position.

An important part of this section shows not only the price effects of each commodity on the cash index but also on the differing listed futures windows also. Followers of the index will find the associated futures windows information useful throughout the summary sheet since these numbers are directly related to the CRB listed futures contracts which trade in New York.

The opening and closing times for each of the component commodities are shown and allow readers to determine when all of the component commodities are open. This may seem like a small point but it is best to trade the CRB futures contract during those times which all of the component commodities are open because it allows arbitrageurs in the trading pit to provide the most competitive prices. After component commodities begin to close the associated risk to the arbitrageurs may cause bid/ask spreads to widen to reflect the increased risk associated with taking, in effect, overnight positions in the closed components.

Section II

This section is probably the most useful to traders of the index. It shows the real net change of each of the five CRB windows (cash index and the four listed future contracts). It also shows the fair value of each of the component CRB future contracts compared to the cash index. In this manner a trader or investor can determine at what level to enter a long or short position depending on their own criteria.

Section III

Simply shows the numbers from Section II in a spread format. Watching these numbers can be very informational. When deferred CRB future contracts are valued at a premium to the nearer term contracts, it normally reflects a bearish outlook since it means that commodities overall are trading in contango. When these spreads begin to close or expand it may mean the beginning of a trend change.

Section IV

This section shows the daily CRB total return performance for the day. The CRB total return is directly related to the performance of the front month CRB futures contract fair value plus the daily 90 T-Bill rate for one day. For long-term investors this number represents the actual dollar return for the given trading day. It also shows the CRB-TR performance over the last week, year to date, and last 52 weeks.

Section V

Indicates the current months calendar of when commodities will be deleted and added to the index.

Section VI

This section shows the component commodity future contracts active in each of the CRB future contract windows. The CRB is defined as the geometric average of 17 arithmetically averaged component commodities. Each component commodity is averaged using any of its listed future contracts expiring over the six months from the first business day of the current month. There are certain exceptions to this rule and for simplicity sake a table is presented.

* * *

Raymond T Murphy is the President of RTM Management, Inc., a Commodity Trading Advisor and consulting company for institutional investors. RTM Management specializes in commodity investing and arbitrage strategies involving both the Bridge/CRB Futures Price Index and the Goldman Sachs Commodity Index, and has developed commodity allocation programs for diversifying large institutional portfolios. Mr. Murphy has done extensive work with Bridge/CRB and The New York Board of Trade in developing a total return measurement for the Bridge/CRB Commodity Index. He is a member of the New York Futures Exchange, a subsidiary of the New York Board of Trade, and has traded the CRB since it was listed on the Exchange in June of 1986.

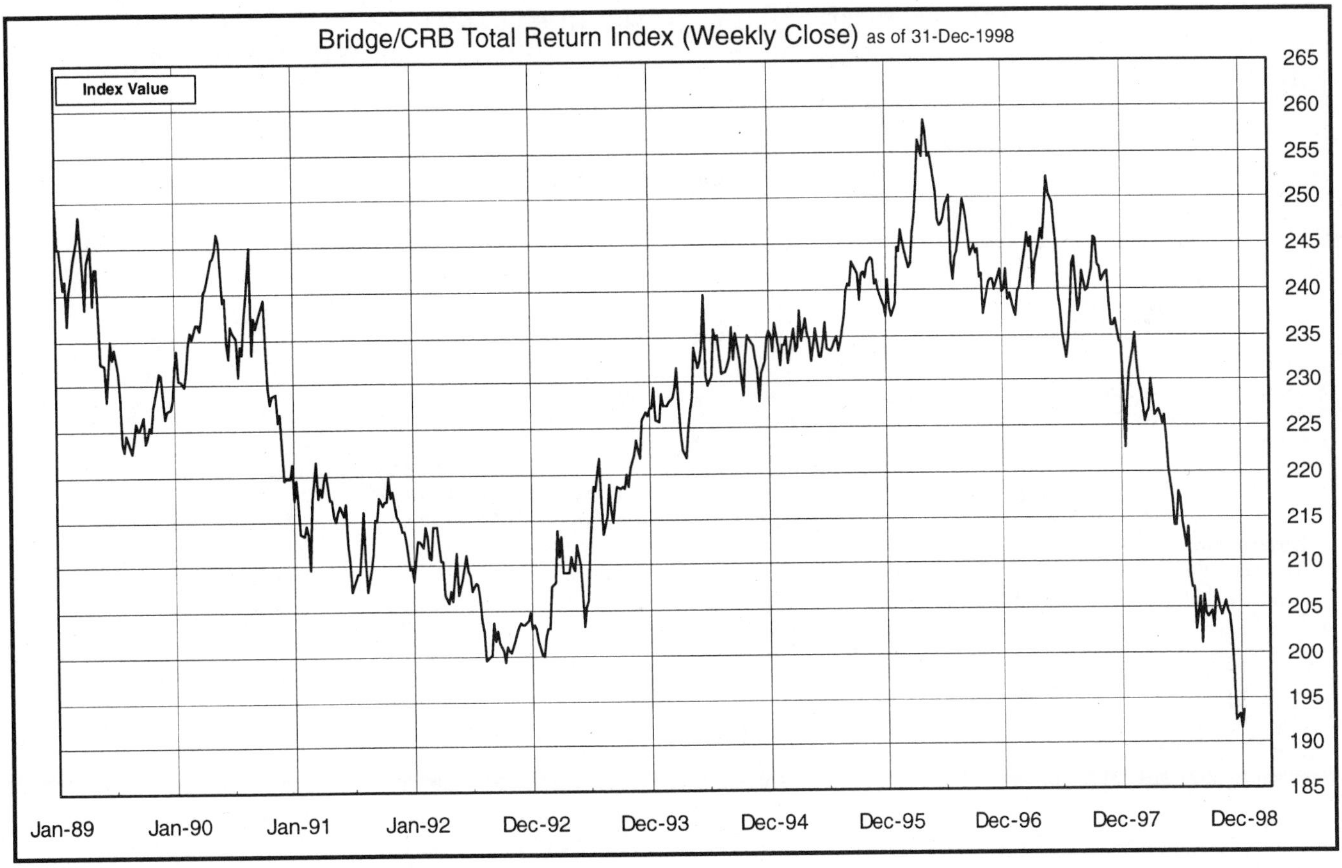
Bridge/CRB Total Return Index (Weekly Close) as of 31-Dec-1998
Index Value
265
260
255
250
245
240
235
230
225
220
215
210
205
200
195
190
185
Jan-89
Jan-90
Jan-91
Jan-92
Dec-92
Dec-93
Dec-94
Dec-95
Dec-96
Dec-97
Dec-98

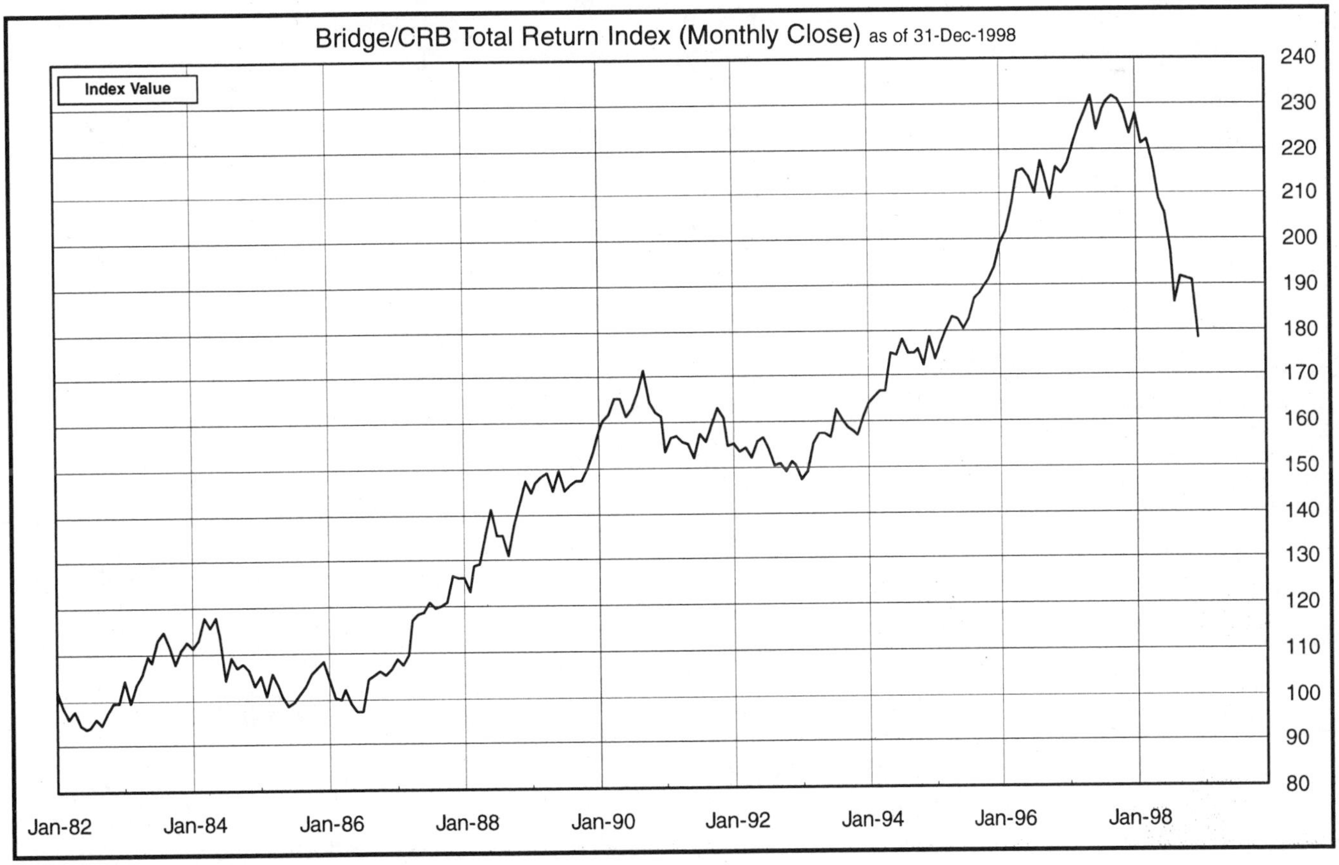
Bridge/CRB Total Return Index (Monthly Close) as of 31-Dec-1998
Index Value
240
230
220
210
200
190
180
170
160
150
140
130
120
110
100
90
80
Jan-82
Jan-84
Jan-86
Jan-88
Jan-90
Jan-92
Jan-94
Jan-96
Jan-98

Volume U.S.

U.S. FUTURES VOLUME HIGHLIGHTS

1998 in Comparison with 1997

1998 Rank	Top 50 Contracts Traded in 1998	1998 Contracts	1998 %	1997 Contracts	1997 %	1997 Rank
1	T-Bonds, CBT	112,224,081	22.30%	99,827,659	21.32%	1
2	Eurodollar, CME	109,472,507	21.76%	99,770,237	22.37%	2
3	T-Notes (10 Year), CBT	32,482,576	6.46%	23,961,819	5.52%	4
4	S&P 500 Index, CME	31,430,523	6.25%	21,294,584	5.01%	5
5	Crude Oil, NYMEX	30,495,647	6.06%	24,771,375	5.91%	3
6	T-Notes (5 Year), CBT	18,060,048	3.59%	13,488,725	2.88%	8
7	Natural Gas, NYMEX	15,978,286	3.18%	11,923,628	2.22%	9
8	Corn, CBT	15,795,493	3.14%	16,984,951	4.94%	6
9	Soybeans, CBT	12,431,156	2.47%	14,539,766	3.58%	7
10	Gold (100 oz.), COMEX Div. of NYMEX	8,990,094	1.79%	9,541,904	2.24%	10
11	#2 Heating Oil, NYMEX	8,863,764	1.76%	8,370,964	2.10%	11
12	Unleaded Regular Gas, NYMEX	7,992,269	1.59%	7,475,145	1.59%	12
13	Japanese Yen, CME	7,065,266	1.40%	6,034,565	1.28%	15
14	Deutsche Mark, CME	6,884,026	1.37%	7,044,783	1.50%	13
15	Soybean Meal, CBT	6,553,846	1.30%	6,424,945	1.50%	14
16	Soybean Oil, CBT	6,498,263	1.29%	5,284,994	1.25%	16
17	Wheat, CBT	5,681,569	1.13%	5,058,645	1.36%	18
18	Sugar #11, CSC	5,524,111	1.10%	5,284,971	1.20%	17
19	E Mini S&P, CME	4,466,032	0.89%	885,825		41
20	Live Cattle, CME	4,216,506	0.84%	3,919,642	0.99%	21
21	Silver (5,000 oz), COMEX Div. of NYMEX	4,094,616	0.81%	4,893,520	1.23%	19
22	Swiss Franc, CME	3,974,163	0.79%	4,222,268	0.99%	20
23	Dow Jones Industrial Index, CBOT	3,567,512	0.71%	755,476		45
24	Cotton, NYCE	3,200,830	0.64%	2,837,280	0.60%	22
25	British Pound, CME	2,645,017	0.53%	2,664,401	0.75%	23
26	High Grade Copper, COMEX Div. of NYMEX	2,483,610	0.49%	2,356,170	0.58%	25
27	Canadian Dollar, CME	2,396,300	0.48%	2,542,102	0.49%	24
28	Lean Hogs, CME	2,136,282	0.42%	2,100,909		28
29	Coffee "C", CSC	2,095,030	0.42%	2,294,181	0.51%	26
30	Wheat, KCBT	2,006,779	0.40%	1,937,140	0.46%	29
31	Cocoa, CSC	1,810,580	0.36%	2,274,509	0.53%	27
32	T-Bonds, MIDAM	1,537,286	0.31%	1,513,925	0.32%	31
33	Mexican Peso, CME	1,353,867	0.27%	1,707,706	0.21%	30
34	T-Notes (2 Year), CBT	1,347,575	0.27%	1,018,545	0.16%	37
35	One Month LIBOR, CME	1,108,454	0.22%	1,504,230	0.30%	32
36	Wheat, MGE	1,092,964	0.22%	1,024,523	0.25%	36
37	NASDAQ 100, CME	1,063,328	0.21%	807,604	0.10%	43
38	Municipal Bond Index, CBT	1,002,075	0.20%	983,877	0.22%	38
39	Euroyen, CME	962,574	0.19%	1,119,827	0.13%	33
40	Orange Juice (Frozen Conc.), NYCE	914,614	0.18%	1,029,861	0.16%	34
41	Goldman Sachs Commodity Index, CME	854,264	0.17%	773,088	0.11%	44
42	30 Day Federal Funds, CBT	844,408	0.17%	910,747	0.15%	40
43	Soybeans, MIDAM	767,858	0.15%	1,026,830	0.25%	35
44	Feeder Cattle, CME	738,567	0.15%	837,165	0.19%	42
45	Australian Dollar, CME	664,563	0.13%	595,573	0.12%	47
46	NYSE Composite Index, NYCE	590,327	0.12%	916,716	0.20%	39
47	Platinum, NYMEX	528,269	0.10%	698,597	0.20%	46
48	Pork Bellies, CME	481,252	0.10%	595,319	0.15%	48
49	Nikkei, CME	479,248	0.10%	432,461		
50	U.S. Dollar Index, NYCE	469,291	0.09%	485,481	0.13%	49
	Top 50 Contracts	498,317,566		438,316,424 *		
	Contracts Below the Top 50	4,883,879	0.97%	5,337,333	1.20%	
	TOTAL	**503,201,445**	**100.00%**	**443,653,757**	**100.00%**	

* For 1997 Top 50 contracts totaled 438,748,885 including 1 contract that is not among 1998's Top 50.

U.S. FUTURES VOLUME HIGHLIGHTS

1998 in Comparison with 1997

1998 RANK	EXCHANGE	1998 CONTRACTS	1998 %	1997 CONTRACTS	1997 %	1997 RANK
1	Chicago Board of Trade (CBT)	217,138,928	43.15%	190,056,287	42.84%	1
2	Chicago Mercantile Exchange (CME)	183,627,443	36.49%	159,975,955	36.06%	2
3	New York Mercantile Exchange (NYMEX) *	80,011,517	15.90%	70,634,699	15.92%	3
4	Coffee, Sugar & Cocoa Exchange (CSCE)	9,593,944	1.91%	10,022,427	2.26%	4
5	New York Cotton Exchange (NYCE) **	6,455,707	1.28%	6,201,235	1.40%	5
6	MidAmerica Commodity Exchange	3,081,181	0.61%	3,500,791	0.79%	6
7	Kansas City Board of Trade (KCBT)	2,164,959	0.43%	2,192,694	0.49%	7
8	Minneapolis Grain Exchange (MGE)	1,125,194	0.22%	1,040,594	0.23%	8
9	Philadelphia Board of Trade (PBOT)	2,572	0.00%	29,075	0.01%	9
	TOTAL	**443,653,757**	**100.00%**	**397,402,153**	**100.00%**	

* Includes Comex Division.

** Includes the New York Futures Exchange.

U.S. FUTURES VOLUME 1994 - 1998

CHICAGO BOARD OF TRADE (CBT)

FUTURE	CONTRACT UNIT	1998	1997	1996	1995	1994
Wheat	5,000 bu	5,681,569	5,058,645	5,385,967	4,955,067	3,620,631
Corn	5,000 bu	15,795,493	16,984,951	19,620,188	15,105,147	11,529,884
Oats	5,000 bu	397,332	397,332	501,858	475,538	492,504
Soybeans	5,000 bu	12,431,156	14,539,766	14,236,295	10,611,534	10,749,109
Soybean Oil	60,000 lbs	6,498,263	5,284,994	4,980,277	4,611,336	5,063,188
Soybean Meal	100 tons	6,553,846	6,424,945	5,955,977	5,601,242	4,593,814
Rice	200,000 lbs	157,764	171,973	119,900	121,914	16,693
Crop Yield	Crop yield est. X 10	337	1,472	1,343	3,123	
Diammonium Phosphate	100 tons		144	3,935	6,755	15,588
Anhydrous Ammonia	100 tons		19	351	1,060	2,811
Edible Oil Index	100 tons				21	298
Structural Panel Index	100,000 sq. ft.				885	7,033
National Catastrophe Insurance	Loss/EP x $25,000					4
Com Ed Hub Electricity	1,680 mwh	88				
TVA Hub Electricity	1,680 mwh	184				
Silver	5,000 oz	7	61	110	8,617	10,278
Silver	1,000 oz	35,505	30,771	41,575	76,667	88,663
Gold	100 oz	204	138	335	647	984
Gold	Kilo	13,363	13,620	17,687	20,245	22,712
T-Bonds	$100,000	112,224,081	99,827,659	84,725,128	86,375,916	99,959,881
T-Notes (6 1/2-10 Year)	$100,000	32,482,576	23,961,819	21,939,725	22,445,356	24,077,828
T-Notes (5 Year)	$100,000	18,060,048	13,488,725	11,463,640	12,637,054	12,462,838
T-Notes (2 Year)	$200,000	1,347,575	1,018,545	643,845	744,866	939,043
30-Day Federal Funds	$5,000,000	844,408	910,474	608,308	643,717	416,200
German Bund	250000		200,588			
Municipal Bond Index	$1,000 x Index	1,002,075	983,877	883,901	1,169,470	1,600,533
Treasury Note Inflation Indices	$100,000		22			
Canadian Government Bonds	$100,000 CAD					27,163
Dow Jones Industrial Index	$10 x Index	3,567,512	755,476			
Brady Bond Index	$1,000 x Index			69		
Yield Curve Spread	$25,000 x 100YC		271	3,771		
Total		**142,241,377**	**190,056,287**	**171,134,185**	**165,616,177**	**175,697,680**

Volume U.S.

CHICAGO MERCANTILE EXCHANGE (CME)

FUTURE	CONTRACT UNIT	1998	1997	1996	1995	1994
Live Hogs	40,000 lbs			1,784,564	1,669,680	1,554,022
Lean Hogs	40,000 lbs	2,136,282	2,100,909	311,347	984	
Pork Bellies, Frozen	40,000 lbs	481,252	595,319	612,649	561,913	633,646
Pork Bellies, Fresh	40,000 lbs	4,922				
Boneless Beef	200,000 lbs 90% lean	3,433	4,245			
Boneless Beef Trimmings	200,000 lbs 50% lean	1,239	4,876			
Butter	40,000 lbs	667	2,805	273		
Cheddar Cheese	40,000 lbs	1,540	533			
Fluid Milk	50,000 lbs	30,734	4,188	2,336		
Live Cattle	40,000 lbs	4,216,506	3,919,642	3,926,192	3,257,105	3,580,896
Stocker Cattle	25,000 lbs.	411				
Feeder Cattle	44,000 lbs	738,567	837,165	772,222	511,895	446,639
Lumber	160,000 bd ft			26,293	179,538	172,963
Orient Strand Board Lumber	100,000 bd ft	505	1,115	235		
Random Lumber	80,000 bd ft	249,847	260,318	277,781	3,148	
T-Bills (90-day)	$1,000,000	104,180	199,084	251,353	620,223	1,020,491
T-Bills (1 Year)	$500,000					586
Eurodollar (3-month)	$1,000,000	109,472,507	99,770,237	88,883,119	95,730,019	104,823,245
Euroyen	$1,000,000,000 xy	962,574	1,119,827	503,104		
Euromark (3-month)	$1,000,000					566
Federal Funds Rate	$3,000,000		2,790	47,495	52,412	
Federal Funds Turn	$45,000,000	370				
One Month LIBOR	$3,000,000	1,108,454	1,504,230	1,190,652	1,707,062	1,911,184
Argentine FRB Bond	$1,000 X Bond	5	1,553	9,610		
Brazilian C Bond	$500 x Bond		2,995	10,198		
Brazilian EL Bond	$500 x Bond	3,150		253		
Mexican PAR Bond	$500 x Bond		366	1,926		
Mexican CETES	2,000,000	343	8,598			
Mexican TIIE	6,000,000		1,897			
BP/DM Crossrate	125,000 GBP	109	127			
JY/DM Crossrate	250,000 DEM	3	180			
DM/JY Cross (New)	125,000 x dm/jy X				106	
British Pound	62,500	2,645,017	2,664,401	2,961,782	2,610,510	3,562,865
Brazilian Real	100,000	79,509	49,092	87,323	20,364	
Canadian Dollar	100,000	2,396,300	2,542,102	1,932,729	1,756,569	1,740,205
Deutschemark	125,000	6,884,026	7,044,783	5,979,464	7,186,476	10,956,479
ECU	125,000	17				
Euro Canada	1,000,000	12,311				
Japanese Yen	12,500,000	7,065,266	6,034,565	5,101,819	5,630,053	6,612,993
Mexican Peso	500,000	1,353,867	1,707,706	850,040	133,791	
Swiss Franc	125,000	3,974,163	4,222,268	3,929,225	4,399,932	5,217,236
Australian Dollar	100,000	664,563	595,573	461,084	346,823	355,183
French Franc	250,000	72,562	112,520	67,835	48,621	49,005
New Zealand Dollar	100,000	16,580	3,506			
South African Rand	500,000	12,766	6,287			
Russian Ruble	500,000	21,766				
Deutschemark Forward	$250,000				38,582	46,979
Japanese Yen Forward	$250,000				16,898	
Japanese Yen Rolling Spot	$250,000				15,310	
Deutschemark Rolling Spot	$250,000				44,013	126,994
Nikkei 225	$5 x Index	479,248	417,541	502,072	609,720	548,233
Mexican IPC Index	$25 x Index		88	4,481		
E-Mini S&P	$50 x S&P Index	4,466,032	885,825			
S&P 500 Index	$500 x 500 Index	31,430,523	21,294,584	19,899,999	18,852,149	18,708,599
S&P 500 Barra Growth Index	$500 x 500 Index	9,816	6,196	3,400	1,240	
S&P 500 Barra Value Index	$500 x 500 Index	21,245	11,203	7,531	1,478	
S&P MidCap 400 Index	$500 x 400 Index	310,008	262,017	289,989	253,741	285,962
Major Market	$500 x Index	4	732	4,592	58,048	150,308
NASDAQ 100 Index	$500 x Index	1,063,328	807,604	380,963		
Dow Jones Taiwan Stock Index	$250 x Index		8,558			
Russell 2000	$500 x Index	276,662	182,717	78,353	43,857	36,239
Goldman Sachs Commodity Index	$250 x GSCI	854,264	773,088	446,186	270,504	154,511
Total		**183,627,443**	**159,975,955**	**141,600,469**	**146,662,764**	**162,696,029**

COFFEE, SUGAR & COCOA EXCHANGE (CSCE)

FUTURE	CONTRACT UNIT	1998	1997	1996	1995	1994
Coffee "C"	37,500 lbs	2,095,030	2,294,181	2,039,576	2,003,014	2,658,073
Sugar #11	112,000 lbs	5,524,111	5,284,971	4,751,852	4,711,082	4,719,218
Sugar #14	112,000 lbs	157,987	158,431	182,393	119,508	150,472
White Sugar	50 metric tons		10	333		
Cocoa	10 metric tons	1,810,580	2,274,509	2,121,576	2,090,098	2,417,006
Cheddar Cheese	40,000 lbs	4	289	980	977	1,366
Non Fat Dry Milk	44,000 lbs	7	559	282	90	905
Butter	10,000 lbs.		1,482	93		
BFP Milk		6,222	7,084			
Milk	50,000 lbs	3	911	4,944	436	
Total		**9,593,944**	**10,022,427**	**9,102,029**	**8,925,205**	**9,947,040**

KANSAS CITY BOARD OF TRADE (KCBT)

FUTURE	CONTRACT UNIT	1998	1997	1996	1995	1994
Wheat	5,000 bu	2,006,779	1,937,140	1,830,276	1,560,538	1,502,348
Western Natural Gas	10,000 MMBtu	77,350	86,723	89,706	77,595	
Value Line Index	$500 x Index	4,485	14,047	28,663	35,185	50,259
Mini Value Line	$100 x Index	76,345	154,784	135,848	74,346	51,901
Total		**2,164,959**	**2,192,694**	**2,084,493**	**1,747,664**	**1,604,508**

MIDAMERICA COMMODITY EXCHANGE (MidAm)

FUTURE	CONTRACT UNIT	1998	1997	1996	1995	1994
Wheat	1,000 bu	13,200	130,968	151,755	137,573	102,145
Corn	1,000 bu	314,815	432,461	462,318	305,347	232,855
Oats	1,000 bu	5,451	4,916	8,449	5,846	5,208
Soybeans	1,000 bu	767,858	1,026,830	976,134	868,577	797,803
Soybean Meal New	20 tons	18,371	23,773	11,638	4,060	3,757
Soybean Oil	30,000 lbs	27,923	37,962	14,248	6,658	
Live Cattle	20,000 lbs	18,883	16,316	20,983	18,811	15,895
Lean Hogs	20,000 lbs	18,597	1,312			
Live Hogs	20,000 lbs	1,354	4,152	21,118	24,059	19,614
Rice, Rough New	200,000 lbs					68,379
New York Silver	1,000 oz	14,999	8,928	8,398	13,320	17,170
New York Gold	33.2 oz	14,060	15,161	15,876	18,964	24,926
Platinum	25 oz	1,582	4,248	6,949	3,055	2,841
T-Bonds	$50,000	1,537,286	1,513,925	1,281,967	1,341,877	1,385,904
T-Bills	$500,000	315	461	753	754	826
T-Notes (10 Year)	$50,000	39,458	49,700	41,849	38,494	35,303
T-Notes (5 Year)	$50,000	96	479	383	37	4
Eurodollars	$500,000	5,347	5,997	8,893	23,550	8,987
Australian Dollar	50,000	1,205	585	266	221	
British Pound	12,500	23,929	28,094	21,424	23,620	66,162
Swiss Franc	62,500	33,599	47,504	48,027	50,201	64,501
Deutschemark	62,500	36,674	84,344	79,093	95,775	113,166
Japanese Yen	6,250,000	47,821	48,585	42,085	55,213	67,641
Canadian Dollar	50,000	18,358	14,090	7,104	11,970	9,522
Total		**3,081,181**	**3,500,791**	**3,229,710**	**3,047,982**	**3,042,609**

MINNEAPOLIS GRAIN EXCHANGE (MGE)

FUTURE	CONTRACT UNIT	1998	1997	1996	1995	1994
Wheat	5,000 bu	1,092,964	1,024,523	996,780	914,882	737,089
White Wheat	5,000 bu	15,209	14,284	14,602	20,411	27,446
Durum Wheat	5,000 bu	15,997				
Barley	180,000 lbs.		452	631		
White Shrimp	5,000 lbs	679	737	56	336	854
Black Tiger Shrimp	5,000 lbs	291	598	529	387	119
Twin Cities Electricity - On Peak	736 mhw	54				
Total		**1,125,194**	**1,040,594**	**1,012,598**	**936,016**	**765,508**

Volume U.S.

NEW YORK COTTON EXCHANGE (NYCE)*

FUTURE	CONTRACT UNIT	1998	1997	1996	1995	1994
Cotton #2	50,000 lbs	3,200,830	2,837,280	2,373,855	2,525,434	2,289,998
Potato	85,000 lbs.	70	540	744		
Cotlook World Cotton	50,000 lbs X CWC					79
Orange Juice Frozen Concentrate	15,000 lbs	914,614	1,029,861	654,937	688,932	653,824
Deutsche Mark / British Pound	125,000 GBP	123,043	86,166	87,757	32,804	12,351
Deutsche Mark / Spanish Peseta	250,000 DEM	11,869	754			
Deutsche Mark / French Franc	500,000 DEM	71,290	158,740	77,263	36,649	10,295
Deutsche Mark / Japanese Yen	125,000 DEM	301,555	172,612	167,093	66,405	30,566
Deutsche Mark / Italian Lira	250,000 DEM	119,667	137,077	74,997	31,604	3,572
Deutsche Mark / Swiss Franc	125,000 DEM	220,117	121,303	37,566	1,209	
Deutsche Mark / Swedish Krona	125,000 DEM	121,203	63,685	8,378		
British Pound / Swiss Franc	125,000 GBP	29,902	5,699			
British Pound / Japanese Yen	125,000 GBP	46,584	9,629			
Swiss Franc / Japanese Yen	200,000 CHF	6				
U.S. Dollar / Deutsche Mark	125,000 USD	43,331	33,917	32,441	29,441	30,385
U.S. Dollar / Canadian Dollar	200,000 USD	3,726	830			
U.S. Dollar / Swiss Franc	200,000 USD	18,224	4,282	4,098	1,586	10
U.S. Dollar / Japanese Yen	200,000 USD	23,828	9,060	9,037	4,943	2
U.S. Dollar / British Pound	125,000 GBP	7,795	6,375	2,290	3,021	2
U.S. Dollar / South African Rand	100,000 USD	3,165	4,683			
U.S. Dollar / Australian Dollar	$200,000 AUD	7,310	5,393			
U.S. Dollar / New Zealand Dollar	$200,000 NZD	30,622	9,499			
U.S. Dollar / Indian Rupiah	$500,000,000 RUD		2			
U.S. Dollar / Malaysian Ringgit	$500,000 RIN	70	228			
U.S. Dollar / Thai Baht	$5,000,000 BAH		2			
ECU		1,574				
ECU (EURO)		1,325				
Euro / Japanese Yen	100,000 EUR	356				
Euro / Swedish Krona	100,000 EUR	89				
Euro / British Pound	100,000 EUR	50				
Euro / Swiss Franc	100,000 EUR	199				
U.S. Dollar Index	$1,000 x Index	469,291	485,481	509,067	456,859	558,439
Emerging Markets Debt Index	$1,000 x Index		261	341	732	
T-Note (5 Year)	$100,000	13,088	18,040	45,064	44,959	69,858
T-Note (2 Year)	$200,000	830	1,790	1,147	11,072	3,233
NYSE Composite Index	$500 x Index	590,327	916,716	791,325	685,922	729,231
NYSE Utility Index	$500 x Index					11
PSE Tech 100	$500 x Index	9,814	9,848	8,663		
PSE Tech 100	$100 x Index	10,950				
Commodity Research Bureau Index	$500 x Index	58,993	71,482	81,113	81,413	109,986
Total*		**6,455,707**	**6,201,235**	**4,967,176**	**4,702,985**	**4,501,842**

NEW YORK MERCANTILE EXCHANGE (NYMEX)**

COMEX DIVISION

FUTURE	CONTRACT UNIT	1998	1997	1996	1995	1994
High Grade Copper	25,000 lbs	2,483,610	2,356,170	2,311,919	2,519,414	2,737,967
Silver	5,000 oz	4,094,616	4,893,520	4,870,808	5,183,236	5,994,345
Gold	100 oz	8,990,094	9,541,904	8,902,179	7,781,596	8,503,366
Eurotop 100 Index	$100 x Price	50,619	47,427	38,925	49,328	62,231
Total		**15,618,939**	**16,839,021**	**16,123,831**	**15,533,574**	**17,297,909**

NYMEX DIVISION

FUTURE	CONTRACT UNIT	1998	1997	1996	1995	1994
Palladium	100 oz	131,250	238,716	205,610	166,713	143,773
Platinum	50 oz	528,269	698,597	802,468	846,693	895,805
No. 2 Heating Oil, NY	1,000 bbl	8,863,764	8,370,964	8,341,877	8,266,783	8,986,835
Unleaded Gasoline, NY	1,000 bbl	7,992,269	7,475,145	6,312,339	7,071,787	7,470,836
Natural Gas	10,000 MMBTU	15,978,286	11,923,628	8,813,867	8,086,718	6,357,560
Gulf Coast Unleaded Gas	42,000 gal				252	300
Alberta Natural Gas	10,000 MMBTU		110	2,876		
Palo Verde Electricity	736 Mwh	139,738	155,977	17,548		
California Oregon Border Electricity	736 Mwh	128,423	120,896	52,340		
Cinergy Electricity	736 Mwh	48,483				

NYMEX DIVISION (continued)

FUTURE	CONTRACT UNIT	1998	1997	1996	1995	1994
Entergy Electricity	736 Mwh	42,580				
Permian Basin Natural Gas	10,000 MMBTU		15	8,811		
Propane	42,000 gal	43,868	40,255	53,903	49,532	45,100
Sour Crude Oil	1,000 bbl	1				
Crude Oil	1,000 bbl	30,495,647	24,771,375	23,487,821	23,613,994	26,812,262
Total		**64,392,578**	**53,795,678**	**48,099,460**	**48,102,472**	**50,712,471**
Total**		**80,011,517**	**70,634,699**	**64,223,291**	**63,636,046**	**68,010,380**

PHILADELPHIA BOARD OF TRADE (PBOT)

FUTURE	CONTRACT UNIT	1998	1997	1996	1995	1994
Australian Dollar	100,000	148	1,270	2,532	1,716	265
British Pound	62,500	235	2,543	1,761	4,147	2,485
Canadian Dollar	100,000		80	91	208	639
ECU	125,000		158	616		1,768
Deutschemark	125,000	909	12,510	23,904	17,121	21,661
Swiss Franc	125,000	445	3,913	4,723	3,915	3,038
French Franc	500,000	101	3,489	3,704	4,162	7,167
Japanese Yen	12,500,000	734	5,112	10,871	7,372	5,323
Total		**2,572**	**29,075**	**48,202**	**38,641**	**42,346**

	1998	1997	1996	1995	1994
TOTAL FUTURES	**503,201,445**	**443,653,757**	**397,402,153**	**395,313,480**	**426,307,942**
PERCENT CHANGE	**13.42%**	**11.64%**	**0.53%**	**-7.27%**	**25.73%**

* The New York Cotton Exchange volume now includes the New York Futures Exchange.
** In August 1994, the Commodity Exchange and the New York Mercantile Exchange merged and is now listed as one exchange.

OPTIONS TRADED ON U.S. FUTURES EXCHANGES VOLUME HIGHLIGHTS

1998 in Comparison with 1997

1998 RANK	EXCHANGE	1998 CONTRACTS	1998 %	1997 CONTRACTS	1997 %	1997 RANK
1	Chicago Board of Trade (CBT)	64,050,508	50.24%	52,642,632	47.40%	1
2	Chicago Mercantile Exchange (CME)	42,991,388	33.72%	40,738,473	36.68%	2
3	New York Mercantile Exchange (NYMEX) *	15,007,168	11.77%	13,216,647	11.90%	3
4	Coffee, Sugar & Cocoa Exchange (CSCE)	3,436,403	2.70%	3,043,615	2.74%	4
5	New York Cotton Exchange (NYCE) **	1,815,885	1.42%	1,232,052	1.11%	5
6	Kansas City Board of Trade (KCBT)	114,542	0.09%	103,879	0.09%	6
7	Minneapolis Grain Exchange (MGE)	44,339	0.03%	47,710	0.04%	7
8	MidAmerica Commodity Exchange (MidAm)	25,728	0.02%	34,337	0.30%	8
	TOTAL	**127,485,961**	**100.00%**	**111,059,345**	**100.00%**	

* Includes Comex Division.
** Includes the New York Futures Exchange.

OPTIONS VOLUME ON U.S. FUTURES EXCHANGES 1994 - 1998

CHICAGO BOARD OF TRADE (CBT)

OPTION	CONTRACT UNIT	1998	1997	1996	1995	1994
Corn	5000 bu	4,267,274	4,963,603	6,602,010	3,783,446	2,144,461
Soybeans	5000 bu	3,845,804	5,339,936	5,135,124	3,149,635	2,710,656
Oats	5000 bu	51,852	21,654	45,037	35,250	20,495
Wheat	5000 bu	1,346,272	1,698,969	1,886,909	1,243,567	827,930
Soybean Oil	60,000 lbs	752,627	381,193	285,274	232,635	287,905
Soybean Meal	100 tons	889,462	716,079	593,165	304,835	263,734

Volume U.S.

CHICAGO BOARD OF TRADE (CBT) (continued)

OPTION	CONTRACT UNIT	1998	1997	1996	1995	1994
Rice	200,000 lbs	33,602	37,769	14,658	14,336	1,750
Diammonium Phosphate	100 tons			50		
Crop Yield	Crop yield est. X 10	841	165	1,061	3,519	
Silver	1,000 oz	154	68	515	1,476	5,952
Eastern Catastrophe Insurance	Loss/EP x 25,000 USD			66	3,274	7,742
Midwest Catastrophe Insurance	Loss/EP x 25,000 USD				50	44
National Catastrophe Insurance	Loss/EP x 25,000 USD					1,590
Westerm Insurance-Annual	Loss/EP x 25,000 USD					44
PCS Castastrophe Insurance		7,753	15,706	14,688	1,064	
T-Bonds	100,000 USD	39,941,672	30,805,885	25,930,661	25,639,950	28,142,549
T-Notes (10 Year)	100,000 USD	9,296,742	6,032,088	7,907,650	6,887,102	6,437,215
T-Notes (5 Year)	100,000 USD	3,184,609	2,105,792	2,723,525	3,619,462	2,675,097
T-Notes (2 Year)	200,000 USD	2,780	4,268	2,806	13,189	12,862
German Bund	250,000 USD		15,620			
Muni Bonds	1,000 USD x Index	100,739	210,990	43,219	13,018	24,772
Brady Bond Index	1,000 USD x Index			440		
Yield Curve Spread	25,000 USD x 100 YCS		360	3,284		
Canadian Government Bonds	100,000 CAD					1,385
Flexible U.S. T-Bonds		68,043	118,895	94,453	59,804	174,295
Flexible T-Notes (10 Year)		10,520	15,910	12,735	36,425	46,606
Flexible T-Notes (5 Year)		4,364	1,350	6,990	14,730	19,060
Flexible T-Notes (2 Year)			200		100	250
Dow Jones Industrial Index	10 USD x Index	245,398	156,132			
Total		**64,050,508**	**52,642,632**	**51,304,320**	**45,056,867**	**43,806,394**

CHICAGO MERCANTILE EXCHANGE (CME)

OPTION	CONTRACT UNIT	1998	1997	1996	1995	1994
Live Hogs	40,000 lbs			169,214	137,435	109,448
Lean Hogs	40,000 lbs	206,014	210,429	35,831		
Live Cattle	40,000 lbs	685,606	540,804	539,523	463,455	519,813
Fluid Milk	40,000 lbs			307		
Boneless Beef	20,000 lbs 90% lean	425	997			
Boneless Beef Trimmings	20,000 lbs 50% lean	134	1,054			
Butter	50,000 lbs	595	479	92		
Cheddar Cheese	40,000 lbs	168	54			
Fluid Milk	200,000 lbs	16,680	4,078			
Mini BFP Milk	50,000 lbs	304				
Pork Bellies, Frozen	40,000 lbs	21,545	29,324	52,040	21,156	24,173
Pork Bellies, Fresh	40,000 lbs	19				
Feeder Cattle	44,000 lbs	170,857	161,100	174,518	109,096	95,845
Lumber	160,000 bd ft			1,753	14,433	17,603
Orient Strand Board	100,000 bd ft	40	489	86		
Random Lumber	80,000 bd ft	18,928	19,826	26,922	491	
One Month LIBOR	3,000,000 USD	5,541	28,809	16,031	54,219	79,172
Brazilian C Bond	500 USD x Index			30		
Mexican PAR Bond	500 USD x Index			130		
Mexican TIIE	6,000,000	35	110			
Eurodollar (3-month)	1,000,000 USD	33,147,148	29,595,246	22,234,888	22,363,853	28,145,929
Eurodollar 5-year Bundle		64				
Euroyen	100,000,000 JPY	38,208	41,577			
T-Bill (90-day)	1,000,000 USD			80	3,594	5,269
British Pound	62,500	241,720	986,950	2,886,041	1,668,624	920,109
Brazilian Real	100,000	14,397	114,464	74,106	3,700	
Deutschemark	125,000	734,678	1,411,110	1,822,649	2,642,904	4,793,639
Euro Canada	1,000,000	2,109				
Mexican Peso	500,000	25,948	186,594	13,466	1,114	
Swiss Franc	125,000	281,354	591,509	753,418	630,016	767,583
Japanese Yen	12,500,000	1,942,417	1,661,417	1,734,186	2,141,043	2,946,432
Canadian Dollar	100,000	278,730	253,075	197,741	259,857	185,652
New Zealand Dollar	100000	46	32			
Australian Dollar	100,000	9,133	25,465	5,785	9,892	7,800
French Franc	250,000	38	1,884	2,149	4,935	1,064
Nikkei 225	5 USD x Index	7,725	7,834	5,722	8,986	7,982
Mexican IPC Index	25 USD x Index			75		
S&P 500 Index	500 USD x Index	4,986,687	4,734,950	4,636,236	4,568,232	3,820,893
E-Mini S&P	50 USD x Index	20,629	8,661			

CHICAGO MERCANTILE EXCHANGE (CME) (continued)

OPTION	CONTRACT UNIT	1998	1997	1996	1995	1994
S&P 500 Barra Value Index	500 USD x Index	40	1,791	4,765	30	
S&P 500 Barra Growth Index	500 USD x Index	82	962	2,960		
S&P MidCap 400 Index	500 USD x Index	1,899	3,272	2,201	5,435	3,622
Major Market	500 USD x Index		20	729	289	804
NASDAQ 100 Index	500 USD x Index	127,532	108,922	23,992		
Dow Jones Taiwan Index	250 USD x Index		146			
Russell 2000	500 USD x Index	2,656	2,849	2,089	1,532	2,793
Goldman Sachs Commodity Index	250 USD x GSCI	1,257	2,190	1,971	28,028	33,949
Total		**42,991,388**	**40,738,473**	**35,421,726**	**35,142,349**	**42,489,574**

COFFEE, SUGAR & COCOA EXCHANGE (CSCE)

OPTION	CONTRACT UNIT	1998	1997	1996	1995	1994
Sugar	112,000 lbs	2,113,369	1,369,465	1,094,879	1,203,779	1,166,748
Flexible Sugar		9,930	155			
Coffee	37,500 lbs	974,690	1,272,767	856,710	867,303	1,208,925
Cocoa	10 metric tons	326,221	399,408	335,173	319,513	341,131
Cheddar Cheese	40,000 lbs			4	76	150
Non Fat Dry Milk	44,000 lbs			21		58
BFP Milk		12,193	1,364			
Butter	10,000 lbs		77			
Milk	50,000 lbs		379	963	103	
Total		**3,436,403**	**3,043,615**	**2,287,750**	**2,390,774**	**2,717,012**

NEW YORK MERCANTILE EXCHANGE (NYMEX)*

COMEX DIVISION

OPTION	CONTRACT UNIT	1998	1997	1996	1995	1994
Gold	100 oz	1,945,366	2,064,883	2,079,663	2,006,695	1,589,065
5 Day Gold	100 oz			150	688	911
Silver	5,000 oz	818,053	842,923	949,239	1,146,513	1,316,650
5 Day Silver	5,000 oz			96	221	368
High Grade Copper	25,000 lbs	153,332	133,603	150,339	134,212	184,125
5 Day Copper	25,000 lbs				34	41
Total			**3,041,409**	**3,179,487**	**3,288,363**	**3,091,160**

NYMEX DIVISION

OPTION	CONTRACT UNIT	1998	1997	1996	1995	1994
No. 2 Heating Oil	42,000 gal	669,725	1,147,034	1,108,935	703,388	699,325
Crude Oil	1,000 bbl	7,448,095	5,790,333	5,271,456	3,975,611	5,675,072
Unleaded Gasoline	1,000 bbl	730,421	1,033,778	655,965	766,557	573,502
Natural Gas	10,000 MMBTU	3,115,765	2,079,607	1,234,691	921,520	493,491
Alberta Natural Gas	10,000 MMBTU			15		
Gas-Crude Oil Spread	1,000 bbl	22,575	41,867	31,743	64,285	13,932
Heating Oil-Crude Oil Spread	1,000 bbl	36,615	18,657	45,920	72,969	13,965
Palo Verde Electricity	736 Mwh	28,597	19,328	3,964		
California Oregon Border Electricity	736 Mwh	19,989	13,495	7,650		
Cintergy Electricity	736 Mwh	2,597				
Entergy Electricity	736 Mwh	1,855				
Platinum	50 oz	14,183	31,139	36,175	43,601	90,556
Total		**12,090,417**	**10,175,238**	**8,396,514**	**6,547,931**	**7,559,843**
Total*		**15,007,168**	**13,216,647**	**11,576,001**	**9,836,294**	**10,651,003**

Volume U.S.

KANSAS CITY BOARD OF TRADE (KCBT)

OPTION	CONTRACT UNIT	1998	1997	1996	1995	1994
Wheat	5,000 bu	112,825	99,092	65,190	75,849	89,960
Western Natural Gas	10,000 MMBtu	55	240	1,850	2,546	
Mini Value Line	100 USD x Index	1,662	4,547	1,439	3,014	3,404
Total		**114,542**	**103,879**	**68,479**	**81,409**	**93,364**

MIDAMERICA COMMODITY EXCHANGE (MidAm)

OPTION	CONTRACT UNIT	1998	1997	1996	1995	1994
Soybeans	1,000 bu	44,603	19,594	13,689	11,908	13,498
Soybean Oil	30,000 lbs	7	3		5	
Soft Red Winter Wheat	5,000 bu	3,121	4,491	3,422	2,425	3,536
Corn	1,000 bu	8,348	8,904	9,753	7,296	5,765
Rough Rice	200,000 lbs					5,588
T-Bonds	50,000 USD	2,646	1,282	530	721	3,149
Gold	33.2 oz	3	63	137	772	417
Total		**25,728**	**34,337**	**27,531**	**23,127**	**31,953**

MINNEAPOLIS GRAIN EXCHANGE (MGE)

OPTION	CONTRACT UNIT	1998	1997	1996	1995	1994
American Spring Wheat	5,000 bu	41,702	40,383	21,126	26,893	26,441
European Spring Wheat	5,000 bu	153	88	44	184	284
White Wheat	5,000 bu	1,772	6,320	5,175	5,333	13,556
Barley	180,000 lbs			8		
White Shrimp	5,000 lbs	337	180	7	118	102
Black Tiger Shrimp	5,000 lbs	278	739	531	138	28
Total		**44,339**	**47,710**	**26,891**	**32,666**	**40,411**

NEW YORK COTTON EXCHANGE (NYCE)**

OPTION	CONTRACT UNIT	1998	1997	1996	1995	1994
Cotton	50,000 lbs	1,127,326	648,154	816,550	1,416,054	816,031
Orange Juice Frozen Concentrate	15,000 lbs	464,773	457,143	316,469	171,209	159,365
Potato	85,000 lbs		14	26		
U.S. Dollar Index	500 USD x Index	21,575	22,539	50,461	23,987	42,268
Deutsche Mark / British Pound	125,000 GBP	10,687	3,484	9,247	116	
Deutsche Mark / French Franc	500,000 DEM		105	1,473	570	
Deutsche Mark / Japanese Yen	125,000 DEM	884	458	2,010	160	
Deutsche Mark / Swiss Franc	125,000 DEM	6,926	675	7,313	33	
Deutsche Mark / Swedish Krona	125,000 DEM	37				
Deutsche Mark / Italian Lira	250,000 DEM	3,500	1,637	367	354	
British Pound / Japanese Yen	125,000 GBP	20				
New Zealand Dollar / U.S. Dollar	200,000 NZD	2				
U.S. Dollar / Deutsche Mark	125,000 DEM	3,974	912	266		
U.S. Dollar / British Pound	125,000 GBP	6	32	22		
U.S. Dollar / South African Rand	100,000 USD	11				
U.S. Dollar / Japanese Yen	12,500,000 JPY	1,811	1,225	1,209		
NYSE Composite Index	500 USD x Index	93,343	81,038	48,714	26,457	26,636
PSE Tech 100	500 USD x Index	37,339	8,801	2,211		
PSE Tech 100	100 USD x index	37,827				
Bridge/CRB Futures Index	500 USD x Index	5,844	5,835	4,771	6,384	7,495
Total**		**1,815,885**	**1,232,052**	**1,261,109**	**1,645,324**	**1,051,795**

	1998	1997	1996	1995	1994
TOTAL OPTIONS	**127,485,961**	**111,059,345**	**101,973,807**	**94,208,810**	**100,881,506**
PERCENT CHANGE	**14.79%**	**8.91%**	**8.24%**	**-6.61%**	**23.24%**

* In August 1994, the Commodity Exchange and the New York Mercantile Exchange merged and is now listed as one exchange.
** The New York Cotton Exchange volume now includes the New York Futures Exchange volume.

Volume Worldwide

Agricultural Futures Markets (AFM), Netherlands

	1998	1997	1996	1995	1994
Live Hogs	45,705	57,069	49,986	30,877	41,382
Piglets	2,531	2,610	2,529	1,047	3,417
Potatoes	114,601	76,646	75,046	165,313	229,071
Potatoes Options	16,394				
Total	**179,231**	**136,325**	**128,097**	**197,237**	**273,870**

Amsterdam Exchanges (AEX), Netherlands

(formerly European Options Exchange (EOE))	1998	1997	1996	1995	1994
AEX Stock Index (FTI)	3,484,558	2,554,776	2,426,699	1,004,005	1,031,333
Dutch Top 5 Index (FT5)	14,412	58,891	70,873	63,751	61,957
Eurotop 100 Index	2,026	249	31	233	435
Old U.S. Dollar/Guilder (OFUS)	1,818	16,604	7,955	14,663	13,395
US Dollar / Euro (FDE)	4,411	2,987			
Guilder Bond (FTO)	211	6,052	21,368	8,051	14,132
Gold Options	29,562	59,871	89,779	45,283	133,412
Silver Options	4,435	4,320	7,799	5,704	5,100
US Dollar/Guilder (FUS) Options	4,511	408,820	539,799	552,452	482,961
US Dollar / Euro (FDE) Options	273,455	270,088			
Dutch Government Bond Options	208,994	286,808	474,525	406,500	449,511
AEX Stock Index Options	7,864,884	8,232,719	6,039,984	3,681,781	2,851,170
Eurotop 100 Options	33,586	12,127	5,090	5,204	853
0100 Index Options	2,520				
Dutch Top 5 Index Options	86,454	414,956	861,025	561,611	393,584
All Options on Individual Equities	52,741,082	36,340,078	18,754,623		
Total	**61,249,483**	**48,669,669**	**29,299,550**	**6,349,238**	**5,439,406**

Wiener Borse - Derivatives Market of Vienna, Austria

(formerly the Austrian Futures & Options Exchange)	1998	1997	1996	1995	1994
Austrian Government Bond	35,865	107,421	151,633	176,527	124,070
ATX Index	618,358	566,459	412,047	498,234	348,291
CeCe (5 Eastern European Indices)	472,077	464,480			
ATX Index Options	557,463	572,644	960,513	1,748,567	1,252,782
ATX LEOs (Long-term Equity Options)	11,421	4,693	43,990	71,555	9,077
CeCe (5 Eastern European Indices) Options	75,709	43,424			
All Options on Individual Equities	1,201,197	1,346,990	1,266,960		
Total	**2,972,090**	**3,111,523**	**2,841,978**	**2,494,883**	**1,734,220**

Belgian Futures and Options Exchange (BELFOX), Belgium

	1998	1997	1996	1995	1994
Belgian Government Bonds	5,169	200,413	390,013	507,254	687,987
Belgian Medium Term Government Bond (BMB)	20	7,887			
BIBOR 3 Months	45,841	230,714	157,909	175,082	150,238
Bel 20 Index	664,360	551,044	326,542	187,686	154,574
Bel 20 Index Options	978,341	954,238	1,170,948	862,492	561,012
USO (Dollar/Belgian Franc)	81,806	119,251	128,548	108,471	29,546
Gold Index Options	34,611	61,269	82,442	81,897	
All Options on Individual Equities	364,885	402,547	378,034		
Total	**2,175,033**	**2,527,665**	**2,635,945**	**1,927,386**	**1,635,346**

Bolsa Brasileira de Futuros (BBF), Brazil

(Merged with BM&F)	1998	1997	1996	1995	1994
R$/US$ Exchange Rate		5,225	41,130	22,948	
U.S. Denominated Arabica Coffee		570	7,308	6,733	
Stock Price Future Return Index		335,908	189,773		
Average Interest Rate on Interbank Deposits		7,140	58,325	78,662	999,617
R$ (Brazilian Real)/US$ Exchange Rate Options		178,000	1,819,120	89,700	
Average Interest Rate on Interbank Deposits Options		502,820	48,213,690	127,924,464	2,049,380
Total		**1,029,663**	**50,047,438**	**128,734,681**	**3,048,997**

Volume Worldwide

Beijing Commodity Exchange (BCE), China

	1998	1997	1996	1995	1994
Greenbean	549,679	9,275,688	81,081,235	141,662,184	
Total	**549,679**	**9,275,688**	**81,100,110**	**141,664,141**	

Bolsa de Mercadorias & Futuros (BM&F), Brazil

	1998	1997	1996	1995	1994
Arabica Coffee	198,547	114,521	116,071	76,206	79,220
Live Cattle	88,054	109,261	117,395	39,174	5,687
Sugar Crystal	30,080	8,330	6,212	4,301	
Cotton	17,007	13,689	2,339		
Corn	15,949	18,907	3,696		
Soybean Futures	13,489	16,082	20,274	3,750	11
Gold Futures	108,942	195,310	219,567	607,288	132,240
Gold Forward	10				
Gold Spot	132,747	173,752	278,476		
Bovespa Stock Index Futures	9,926,890	14,914,692	15,122,751	15,304,666	10,583,594
Interest Rate	35,150,416	36,466,961	49,541,598	35,152,630	28,474,764
Interest Rate Swap	8,562,215	11,660,972	6,313,852	3,592,277	6,002,555
Interest Rate x Exchange Rate Swap	2,499,084	3,504,600	2,069,329	1,500,685	3,666,097
Interest Rate x Reference Rate Swap	83,256	139,929	161,159	127,796	119,229
Interest Rate x Inflation Index Swap (formerly Inflation)	4,496	10,324	6,486	7,601	
Interest Rate x Basic Financial Rate Swap	16,187				
Interest Rate x Ibovespa Swap	4,113		1		
ID x U.S. Dollar Spread Futures	3,013,081	52,587	99,631		
C-Bond	6,581	296,758	608,798		
El-Bond	703	4,060	1,850		
U.S. Dollar	18,573,100	40,387,111	45,132,135	74,241,367	39,231,744
Exchange Rate Swap	6,333	71,713	58,885	174,177	170,662
Price Index x Exchange Rate	9	773	564		
Gold Options on Actuals	88,932	141,880	363,089	1,882,502	6,772,894
Gold Options Exercise	41,928	81,542	150,144	1,124,792	2,246,674
U.S. $ Denominated Arabica Coffee Options	17,921	3,210	14,767	2,810,322	3,290,667
U.S. $ Denominated Arabica Coffee Options Exercise	1,103	1,256	29,249	1,375,756	1,359,128
Corn Options	122				
Soybean Options	82				
Live Cattle Options	308	392	5,882	34,240	88,428
Bovespa Stock Options	103,860	359,846	201,757	74,469	11,875
Bovespa Stock Options Exercise	2,810	31,971	15,722	1,765	
Interest Rate Options Exercise	57,015	57,390	30,550		
Interbank Deposit Rate Index Options	1,605,106	348,990			
Fexible Bovespa Stock Index Options	333,582	618,424	167,918		
U.S. Dollar Options on Actuals	3,405,413	7,211,258	5,180,578	3,338,020	588,911
U.S. Dollar Options Exercise	86,963	974,381	142,710	403,456	80,703
Flexible Currency Options	2,818,616	3,809,659	7,662,050	6,097,019	
Total	**87,015,050**	**122,179,393**	**134,609,876**	**148,055,778**	**102,981,783**

Budapest Commodity Exchange (BCE), Hungary

	1998	1997	1996	1995	1994
Milling Wheat	35,164	108,431	65,454	18,065	
Corn	37,941	77,992	44,253	16,954	
Euro Wheat	17,254	2,263			
Feed Wheat	858	13,693	6,179	1,790	
Feed Barley	2,139	10,330	5,982	767	
Wheat	2,011				
Black Seed	9,623	4,448	2,580	2,933	
Europe I Live Hogs	198	249	191	150	
Europe II Live Hogs	40	101	322	358	
Deutsche Mark	5,823,625	2,731,592	751,130	697,200	
U.S. Dollar	1,730,165	1,097,502	871,174	357,610	
Japanese Yen	183,118	852,629	916,857	269,826	
British Pound	42,454	201,974	304,872		
Swiss Franc	389,118	849,185	419,885		
Italian Lira	550	83,692	710,455		
3 Month BUBOR	178,684	405,726	22,333		
Corn Options	290				
Milling Wheat Options	360				
Wheat Options	525				
Euro Wheat Options	5				
Total			**5,427,393**	**1,399,143**	

Budapest Stock Exchange (BSE), Hungary

	1998	1997	1996	1995	1994
3 Month Hungarian T-Bills	10	3,409	30,933	6,333	
1 Year Hungarian T-Bills	14,097	8,126			
1 Month BUBOR	97	101	4,585		
3 Month BUBOR	18,031	3,679	161		
Budapest Stock Index (BUX) Futures	1,993,353	1,208,388	136,920	3,207	
DEM/HUF	503,539	183,470	25,429	1,407	
EURO/HUF	1				
CHF/HUF	1,004				
GBP/HUF	1,602				
USD/HUF	144,368	55,116	20,439	940	
ECU/HUF	25,561	2,339	24,299	494	
All Futures on Individual Equities	71,158				
Total	**2,772,821**	**1,464,628**	**242,766**	**12,381**	

EUREX, Frankfurt, Germany

(formerly Deutsche Terminborse (DTB))	1998	1997	1996	1995	1994
DAX	6,937,139	6,623,287	5,452,505	4,788,661	5,140,803
MDAX	58,013	180,668	47,865		
VOLAX	14,737				
DJ Euro STOXX 50	366,435				
DJ STOXX 50	94,771				
BUND	89,877,840	31,337,633	16,496,809	12,525,264	14,160,460
Euro BUND	2				
Medium Term Notional Bond (BOBL)	31,683,256	24,299,906	18,269,169	7,351,783	5,647,859
1-Month Euribor	10,418				
3-Month Euribor	378,420				
1-Month Euro-Libor	1				
3-Month Euro-Libor	400				
1-Month Euromark	36,811	166,936	85,519		
3-Month Euromark	400,168	964,096			
Jumbo-Pfandbrief	177,057				
Euro-BUXL	625				
SCHATZ	10,043,087	4,805,755			
DAX Options	29,948,503	31,521,286	26,042,463	24,299,078	23,499,552
DJ Euro STOXX 50	122,951				
DJ STOXX 50	73,779				
BUND Options	6,827,203	702,882	205,520	194,036	261,110
Euro-BUND Options	5,000				
SCHATZ Options	378,448				
3-Month Euribor Options	900				
3-Month Euromark	169,029				
Medium Term Notional Bond (BOBL) Options	1,077,939	1,640,211	663,502	123,019	46,145
US$/DM Options	14,267	250,783			
All Options on Individual Equities	30,853,782	9,667,248	10,024,170		
Total	**209,550,981**	**112,164,106**	**77,314,480**	**49,407,307**	**49,323,237**

EUREX, Zurich, Switzerland

(formerly SOFFEX)	1998	1997	1996	1995	1994
Swiss Market Index	4,445,396	1,810,698	1,720,053	1,457,108	1,694,260
Swiss Government Bond (CONF)	722,066	638,638	913,466	955,895	949,657
Medium Term Swiss Government Bond (COMI)	1,534	20,055	42,007		
Swiss Market Index Options	3,394,098	8,632,768	8,018,333	6,027,308	6,678,779
Swiss Government Bond Options	3,423	5,289	26,446	35,695	49,749
All Options on Individual Equities*	30,104,988	33,334,251	28,802,225		
Total	**38,671,505**	**40,125,315**	**39,522,530**	**8,476,006**	**9,372,445**

* 1998 data reflects different contract size introduced in July. Not comparable with 1997 data.

Finnish Options Market Exchange (FOM), Finland

	1998	1997	1996	1995	1994
Finnish Government Bond	156,455	374,214	291,658	125,298	
FRA Interest Rate	634,735	1,827,730	1,167,155	4,375	
FRX Currency	5,776	8,940			
STOX Stock Future	811,834	640,268	275,172		
FOX Index	236,220	246,907	203,138	181,428	
FRX Currency Options	7,800	31,125	1,800	9,669	
FOX Index Options	267,959	684,704	404,161	521,008	
All Options on Individual Equities (STOX)	693,310	1,699,591	1,143,787		
Total	**2,814,089**	**5,513,479**	**3,491,471**	**841,778**	

Volume Worldwide

FUTOP Clearing Centre, Denmark

	1998	1997	1996	1995	1994
Danish Government Bonds 8% 2003	9,042	422			
Danish Government Bonds 7% 2007	68,535	49,768			
6% 2026 Mortgage Bonds	38,234	44,395	58,590	54,885	172,239
6% 2029 Mortgage Bonds	15,722				
7% 2029 Mortgage Bonds	977	390			
KFX Stock Index	289,424	252,571	303,856	263,537	429,466
All Futures on Individual Equities	690	39,633	6,625		
Danish Government Bonds 7% 2007 Options	23,170	7,859			
KFX Stock Index Options	4,073	31,638	42,586	51,053	79,952
All Options on Individual Equities	4,152	34,306	44,810		
Total	**454,019**	**681,466**	**747,723**	**653,078**	**1,335,392**

International Petroleum Exchange (IPE), United Kingdom

	1998	1997	1996	1995	1994
Crude Oil	13,861,008	10,301,918	10,675,389	9,773,146	10,082,761
Gasoil	5,013,759	4,031,608	4,361,062	4,491,463	3,779,064
Natural Gas Daily (NBP)	3,320				
Natural Gas Monthly (NBP)	335,045	81,445			
Crude Oil Options	342,388	250,176	374,233	571,308	531,742
Gasoil Options	106,038	68,195	110,226	116,424	136,859
Total	**19,661,558**	**14,733,342**	**15,520,910**	**14,955,371**	**14,534,403**

Italian Derivatives Market of the Italian Stock Exchange, Italy

	1998	1997	1996	1995	1994
MIB 30 Index	5,896,238	4,463,034	2,675,238	1,140,636	
MIDEX	30,072				
MIB 30 Index Options	1,616,635	1,159,059	476,138	12,464	
All Options on Individual Equities	1,296,791	2,444,424			
Total	**8,839,736**	**8,066,517**	**3,151,376**	**1,153,100**	

Korea Stock Exchange (KSE), Korea

	1998	1997	1996	1995	1994
KOPSI 200	17,893,592	3,252,060	715,621		
KOPSI 200 Options	32,310,812	4,528,424			
Total	**50,204,404**	**7,780,484**	**715,621**		

Commodity and Monetary Exchange of Malaysia, Malaysia

(formerly the Kuala Lumpur Commodity Exchange)	1998	1997	1996	1995	1994
Crude Palm Oil	353,545	935,595	498,118	524,665	567,902
Total	**353,545**	**935,595**	**498,118**	**524,665**	**568,132**

Kuala Lumpur Options & Financial Futures Exchange, Malaysia

	1998	1997	1996	1995	1994
KLSE Composite Index	771,244	382,974	71,278		
Total	**771,244**	**382,974**	**71,278**		

London Metal Exchange (LME), United Kingdom

	1998	1997	1996	1995	1994
High Grade Primary Aluminum	20,091,765	22,484,144	14,552,878	14,060,243	14,604,218
Aluminum Alloy	498,839	389,558	292,429	210,787	148,685
Copper - Grade A	15,699,702	15,099,842	18,484,367	17,530,263	17,236,317
Standard Lead	2,420,777	2,352,731	2,202,864	1,758,742	1,942,234
Primary Nickel	4,676,526	4,627,929	3,104,514	3,319,697	3,404,942
Special High Grade Zinc	5,742,948	7,390,436	4,852,942	5,241,931	5,303,060
Tin	1,429,115	1,119,776	1,121,836	1,275,718	1,192,735
High Grade Primary Aluminum Options	909,526	1,659,879	1,030,703	1,241,596	1,231,794
Aluminum Alloy Options	1,031	535	242	96	
Copper - Grade A Options	1,052,239	1,732,509	1,623,575	2,212,821	2,155,587
Standard Lead Options	36,862	34,531	30,992	22,262	45,769
Primary Nickel Options	119,406	60,645	54,646	83,637	142,107
Special High Grade Zinc Options	204,479	285,453	126,094	177,005	253,782
Tin Options	61,132	13,005	8,925	15,532	26,487
Primary Aluminum TAPOS	115,626	47,447			
Copper TAPOS	15,108	74,080			
Total	**53,075,081**	**57,372,500**	**47,487,007**	**47,150,330**	**47,687,717**

London International Financial Futures Exchange (LIFFE), United Kingdom

(LCE merged with LIFFE in 1996)	1998	1997	1996	1995	1994
3-Month Short Sterling	33,750,746	20,370,846	15,793,775	15,314,576	16,603,152
3-Month Euromark	54,559,028	43,326,030	36,231,178	25,737,379	29,312,222
1-Month Euromark	8,908	113,408	48,644		
3-Month Eurolira	15,592,396	14,894,163	6,936,873	4,005,125	3,456,437
3-Month Euroswiss	7,381,809	4,746,234	3,299,058	1,749,774	1,698,736
3-Month ECU	262,997	534,457	602,518	693,526	622,457
3-Month Euribor	1,269				
3-Month Euroyen	39,240	162,686	242,413		
5-Year Deutsche Mark Libor Financial Bond	8,185				
10-Year Deutsche Mark Libor Financial Bond	14,190				
Long Gilt	16,185,316	19,651,565	15,408,010	13,796,555	19,048,097
5-Year Gilt	113,372				
German Government Bund	14,548,537	44,984,029	39,801,928	32,231,210	37,335,437
Medium Term German Government Bond (BOBL)	90,222	731,865			
Italian Government Bond	8,213,552	15,260,072	12,603,754	9,612,899	11,823,741
Japanese Government Bond	692,404	813,241	816,059	845,329	610,925
FTSE 100 Index	6,955,096	3,698,368	3,627,044	3,373,259	4,227,490
FTSE Eurotop 100 Index	42,058				
FTSE Mid 250 Index	65,219	68,280	34,068	35,068	40,674
Barley	11,142	15,325	17,892	18,088	8,072
BIFFEX (Baltic Freight Index)	23,595	45,059	60,577	74,696	47,805
Cocoa	1,786,090	1,857,065	1,688,921	1,653,790	1,600,746
U.S. Dollar Coffee	1,290,049	1,544,193	1,182,528	1,062,744	1,269,477
Potatoes in Bulk	24,697	22,933	21,330	27,268	36,672
Wheat	98,501	128,411	115,869	101,025	84,212
White Sugar	945,896	686,302	579,463	575,734	480,973
3-Month Short Sterling Options	7,348,877	2,662,716	2,213,494	3,348,945	4,057,878
3-Month Sterling Mid-curve Options	35,480				
3-Month Euro Options	4				
3-Month Euromark Options	5,878,551	4,225,874	4,888,942	3,427,376	2,943,936
3-Month Euromark Mid-curve Options	70,123				
3-Month Euroswiss Options	154,477	31,390	45,568	33,781	19,245
3-Month Eurolira Options	2,632,896	2,402,371	953,558	100,129	
3-Month Eurolira Mid-curve Options	100				
Long Gilt Options	1,644,323	1,799,660	1,361,344	1,756,533	2,357,348
German Government Bond Options	5,186,402	10,082,217	8,462,806	6,988,655	8,574,137
Medium Term German Gov't Bond (BOBL) Options	29,507	196,128			
Italian Government Bond Options	564,504	2,544,870	2,456,177	1,130,762	1,030,672
FTSE 100 Index Options (ESX)	3,512,173	7,188,349	6,738,955	4,434,086	4,786,656
FTSE 100 Index Options (SEI)	1,001,428				
FTSE 100 Index FLEX Options	27,855	32,985	65,701	60,699	
Barley Options	40	206	22	103	64
BIFFEX (Baltic Freight Index) Options	1,350	149	728	447	94
Cocoa Options	25,317	27,838	57,094	48,196	87,215
U.S. Dollar Coffee Options	159,557	184,975	129,844	169,130	204,945
Potatoes Options	35	5	35		
Wheat Options	10,784	9,326	8,758	12,907	6,866
White Sugar Options	97,949	21,062	13,268	23,016	8,196
All Options on Individual Equities	3,307,913	4,295,877	4,298,010		
Total	**194,394,159**	**209,425,578**	**170,805,206**	**128,678,388**	**148,726,421**

Volume Worldwide

Marche a Terme International de France (MATIF), France

	1998	1997	1996	1995	1994
CAC 40 Index*	16,443,276	6,461,308	5,853,172	6,549,953	7,464,449
ECU Bond	62,327	357,094	579,493	657,152	618,715
Notional Bond	23,284,475	33,752,483	35,321,843	33,610,221	50,153,150
5-Year Bond	2,825,479	2,100,683			
30-Year Eurobond	3,932				
Long Gilt	1,637				
3-Month Pibor & Euribor	5,305,778	14,417,310	14,133,278	15,488,076	13,176,354
Sugar	86,762	144,849	193,024	305,598	297,940
Sugar 100	1,695	7,086			
Wheat	573	13,673	7,236		
Wheat #2	41,091				
Rapeseed	102,897	74,387	60,148	51,135	7,026
Notional & Euro Notional Bond Options	3,302,799	8,376,474	8,894,196	9,517,932	18,024,502
3-Month Pibor Options	484,057	2,788,126	3,107,113	4,615,434	3,361,277
5-Year Bond Options	91,936	70,416			
Total	**52,038,714**	**68,608,704**	**68,293,238**	**71,090,512**	**93,438,671**

* 1998 data reflects different contract size introduced in July. Not comparable with 1997 data.

MEFF RENTA FIJA (RF), Spain

	1998	1997	1996	1995	1994
90 Day MIBOR Plus	1,886,299	2,462,893	1,275,222	302,681	
360 Day MIBOR Plus	32,523	80,555	61,702	15,403	
German Diff	4,489	17,446	123,311		
3-Year Notional Bond	1,561	4,930	212,933	456	12,112
5-Year Notional Bond	44,893	9,731			
10-Year Notional Bond	15,662,560	21,046,078	18,535,566	13,035,805	13,191,835
30-Year Notional Bond	55,047				
5-Year Notional Bond Options	200				
10 Year Notional Bond Options	1,078,904	2,563,370	3,372,235	1,888,547	2,047,754
90 Day MIBOR Plus Options	150,683	400,311	249,806	58,297	
Total	**18,917,159**	**26,585,419**	**23,931,008**	**19,082,575**	**19,735,329**

MEFF RENTA VARIABLE (RV), Spain

	1998	1997	1996	1995	1994
IBEX 35 Plus	8,627,374	6,053,283			
IBEX 35 Plus Options	1,681,205	1,411,101			
All Options on Individual Equities	2,695,206	1,485,074	951,271		
Total	**13,003,785**	**8,949,458**	**4,739,599**	**3,627,630**	**3,456,244**

MERCADO A TERMINO DE BUENOS AIRES, Argentina

	1998	1997	1996	1995	1994
Wheat	48,502	49,492			
Corn	42,451	42,125			
Sunflowerseed	23,543	19,312			
Soybean	28,996	26,934			
Wheat Options	20,586	24,490			
Corn Options	15,013	20,679			
Sunflowerseed Options	9,965	9,805			
Soybean Options	10,916	9,905			
Total	**199,972**	**202,742**			

Mercato Italiano Futures (MIF), Italy

	1998	1997	1996	1995	1994
10-Year BTP	1,293,408	2,851,585	2,240,085	2,636,161	3,702,802
5-Year BTP	146	28,585	68,697	166,002	667,115
RIBOR	101,839	135,414			
10-Year BTP Options	45,150	140,597	130,307	113,665	
Total	**1,440,543**	**3,156,181**	**2,439,089**	**2,915,828**	**4,369,917**

Marche des Options Negociables de Paris (MONEP), France

	1998	1997	1996	1995	1994
CAC 40 Index (Short Term) Options	5,108,041	6,250,090	2,465,497	2,425,363	2,755,289
CAC 40 Index (Long Term) Options	2,752,536	3,285,383	2,126,001	3,013,926	2,996,181
STOXX 50 Options	144,536				
Euro STOXX 50 Options	106,457				
All Options on Individual Equities*	28,953,142	5,565,057	3,980,856		
Total		**15,100,530**	**8,572,354**	**5,439,289**	**5,751,470**

* 1998 data reflects different contract size introduced in July. Not comparable with 1997 data.

Montreal Exchange (ME), Canada

	1998	1997	1996	1995	1994
3-Month Bankers Acceptance	6,803,028	4,139,777	2,415,563	2,326,709	1,918,976
10-Year Canadian Government Bond	1,836,937	1,272,970	1,072,111	1,026,854	1,496,543
5-Year Canadian Government Bond	45,113	50,944	35,649	63,842	
5-Year Canadian Government Bond Options	2,797	933	703	2,191	6,363
3-Month Bankers Acceptance Options	210,850	155,308	75,224	51,855	29,464
10-Year Canadian Government Bond Options	18,533	23,175	30,159	40,147	51,305
All Options on Individual Equities	1,375,274	1,016,945	660,962		
Total	**10,292,532**	**6,660,052**	**4,290,685**	**3,518,823**	**3,514,823**

New Zealand Futures Exchange (NZFOE), New Zealand

	1998	1997	1996	1995	1994
3-Year Government Stock	18,240	43,967	15,046	26,912	101,229
10-Year Government Stock	9,948	17,265	8,565	8,456	42,541
90 Day Bank Bill	1,236,944	1,019,686	655,270	478,806	608,460
Trade Weighted Index	220	40			
NZSE-10 Captial Share Price Index	2,138	3,037	5,686	2,971	
New Zealand Electricity	3,092	4,596			
90-Day Bank Bill Options	410	1,811	8,845	16,321	6,870
10-Year Government Stock Options	20				
NZSE-10 Captial Share Price Index Options	33	7	23	24	
All Options on Individual Equities	71,847	117,669	144,207		
Total	**1,342,892**	**1,208,079**	**837,672**	**539,839**	**772,783**

OM Stockholm (OMS), Sweden

	1998	1997	1996	1995	1994
Interest Rate	9,356,221	12,704,397	15,642,920	10,949,860	14,123,881
OMX Index	9,265,510	2,163,560	1,625,391	1,593,408	1,706,984
All Futures on Individual Equities	533,508	288,841	272,514		
Interest Rate Options	2,727	5,846	32,825	42,783	86,410
OMX Index Options	4,947,486	3,545,967	5,399,227	6,067,268	5,812,435
All Options on Individual Equities	20,589,273	19,485,816	12,920,145		
Total	**44,694,725**	**38,194,473**	**35,896,860**	**18,653,319**	**21,741,415**

Oslo Stock Exchange (OSE), Norway

	1998	1997	1996	1995	1994
OBr10	36,423	58,518	55,376	52,001	165,443
OBr2	1,000				
OBr5	31,332	33,422	50,673	49,187	43,745
Forwards	57,938	1,630			
OBX	354,602	135,284	36,366	18,615	4,151
OBX Options	828,445	926,646	512,460	481,865	422,430
All Options on Individual Equities	883,045	1,086,171	815,396		
Total	**2,192,785**	**2,241,671**	**1,470,271**	**613,768**	**637,139**

SHANGAI METAL EXCHANGE (SME), China

	1998	1997	1996	1995	1994
Copper	2,772,124	1,299,520			
Aluminum	60,656	73,077			
Nickel	8	74			
Total	**2,832,788**	**1,372,671**			

Volume Worldwide

Singapore International Monetary Exchange (SIMEX), Singapore

	1998	1997	1996	1995	1994
Eurodollar	9,837,115	7,400,058	8,184,887	8,394,933	8,687,969
Deferred Spot US$/JY	3,324	61,468	86,833	58,922	68,605
Deferred Spot US$/DM	2,682	49,264	70,651	109,181	131,210
Nikkei 225 Index	5,537,558	4,844,495	4,887,912	6,456,984	5,801,098
Nikkei 300 Index	95,255	129,695	156,482	174,234	
Dow Jones Thailand Index	721				
MSCI Hong Kong Index	6,124				317
MSCI Singapore Index	27,727				
MSCI Taiwan Index	1,842,977	677,295			
Brent Crude	32,600	33,067	63,535	73,445	
Euroyen	8,757,516	9,624,680	8,162,548	6,549,295	6,820,673
Japanese Government Bond	194,373	132,104	138,471	297,426	443,564
Eurodollar Options	559	7,825	3,319	5,247	13,545
Euroyen Options	661,008	481,138	208,363	128,944	126,280
Japanese Government Bond Options	2,211	11,658	18,709	35,071	39,808
Nikkei 225 Index Options	838,891	628,222	58,660	1,943,096	1,496,922
MSCI Taiwan Index Options	20,521	7,550			
Total	**27,861,162**	**24,090,285**	**22,568,545**	**24,251,339**	**24,060,274**

South African Futures Exchange (SAFEX), Africa

	1998	1997	1996	1995	1994
All Share Index	4,620,298	2,599,489	1,943,973	1,816,846	2,185,672
Industrial Index	2,709,146	1,960,260	1,493,987	1,030,714	920,786
Financial Index (FNDI)	850	3,710	10,080	4,290	
Financial Index (FINI)	80,229				
Mining Index	3,210				
Gold Index	53,033	491,351	603,205	656,696	933,591
3-Month Bank Bill	92	106	1,360	5,154	3,901
R 150	8,376	8,489	37,982	30,472	1,750
R 153	8,394	5,924	101		
R 157	2				
All Share Index Options	7,915,791	4,873,560	3,759,424	2,932,564	2,804,855
Industrial Index Options	713,337	1,282,555	913,342	481,053	377,593
Financial Index (FNDI) Options	400	3,533	11,168		
Financial Index (FINI) Options	56,924				
Gold Index Options	31,978	248,765	1,015,065	195,720	132,230
R 150 Options	5,294	10,467	26,682	29,683	
R 153 Options	5,957	20,085	2,060		
All Options on Individual Equities	152,960	75,360			
Total	**16,366,271**	**11,583,654**	**9,822,581**	**7,218,914**	**7,377,937**

Sydney Futures Exchange (SFE), Australia

	1998	1997	1996	1995	1994
All Ordinaries Share Price Index	3,678,151	3,204,266	2,675,754	2,476,331	2,552,546
90 Day Bank Bills	7,735,231	5,918,447	4,977,945	6,172,512	9,369,008
3 Year Treasury Bonds	10,485,750	10,378,357	9,209,228	8,820,651	9,709,791
10 Year Treasury Bonds	5,640,716	5,819,677	5,315,845	5,740,870	6,814,733
NSW Electricity	6,797	1,191			
VIC Electricity	4,615	1,129			
Wheat	9,692	7,937	6,482		
Fine Wool	2,041				
Broad Wool	496				
Greasy Wool	11,507	10,127	7,554	4,799	
All Futures on Individual Equities	9,026	29,157	54,463		
All Ordinaries Share Price Index Options	847,375	896,340	896,880	652,607	833,667
90 Day Bank Bills Options	770,229	984,363	911,005	712,834	943,749
3-Year Treasury Bond Options	223,842	418,081	457,808	426,836	507,252
Overnight 3 Year Treasury Bond Options	64,394	43,540	42,461	7,443	2,078
10-Year Treasury Bonds Options	354,311	545,359	845,571	580,091	800,263
Overnight 10 Year Treasury Bond Options	90,015	149,817	128,426	24,419	18,656
Wheat Options	2,040	1,740	788		
Greasy Wool Options	47	11	41		
Total	**29,936,275**	**28,409,539**	**25,530,251**	**25,620,614**	**31,556,584**

Toronto Futures Exchange (TFE), Canada

	1998	1997	1996	1995	1994
TSE 35 Index	440,851	317,408	155,652	110,011	104,209
TSE 100 Index	1,690	19,317	8,135	2,963	10,819
TSE 35 Options	388,273	431,623	254,199	337,764	247,482
Total	**846,024**	**768,399**	**418,831**	**459,218**	**384,010**

Winnipeg Commodity Exchange (WCE), Canada

	1998	1997	1996	1995	1994
Wheat	146,713	197,619	206,120	155,699	191,696
Oats	3,970	3,205	3,496	32,761	52,550
Flaxseed	115,552	140,756	99,889	132,525	105,338
Canola (Rapeseed)	1,557,358	1,387,675	1,345,952	1,075,683	1,167,447
Feed Peas	3,286	14,247	17,979	7,802	
Western Barley	238,994	284,614	334,809	172,733	115,376
Wheat Options	537	250	355	734	3,145
Flaxseed Options	1,093	66	466	1,567	1,692
Western Barley Options	553	959	3,166	274	1,716
Canola Options	23,310	31,810	61,233	71,197	82,565
Total	**2,091,366**	**2,061,201**	**2,073,465**	**1,670,037**	**1,759,525**

Hong Kong Futures Exchange (HKFE), Hong Kong

	1998	1997	1996	1995	1994
Hang Seng Index	6,969,708	6,446,696	4,656,084	4,546,613	4,192,574
Hang Seng 100 Index	15,450				
HKFE Taiwan Index	71				
Red-Chip Index	170,385	143,078			
Deutschemark Rolling Forex	2,263	121,173	76,075	12,633	
Japanese Yen Rolling Forex	14,100	109,578	106,888	8,688	
British Pound Rolling Forex	783	20,475	12,392		
1-Month HIBOR	4,405				
3-Month HIBOR	502,982	87,819			
All Futures on Individual Equities	4,082	4,453			
Hang Seng Index Options	798,712	1,147,374	1,093,871	645,538	606,674
Hang Seng 100 Index Options	4,610				
HKFE Taiwan Index Options	56				
Red-Chip Index Options	2,035	1,234			
Total	**8,489,642**	**8,081,880**	**5,945,310**	**5,213,472**	**4,799,738**

Kanmon Commodity Exchange (KCE), Japan

	1998	1997	1996	1995	1994
Red Beans	200,215	95,982	118,438	237,745	492,294
Imported Soybeans	572,570	1,382,063	496,376	130,520	213,271
Refined Sugar	1,433	1,421	1,438	1,449	1,432
Corn	2,951,184	5,069,142	4,346,586	2,890,258	1,709,248
Total	**3,725,402**	**6,548,608**	**4,962,838**	**3,259,972**	**2,416,245**

Kansai Agricultural Commodities Exchange (KANEX), Japan

	1998	1997	1996	1995	1994
Red Beans	450,610	483,330	877,474	1,723,230	2,931,256
Imported Soybeans	1,513,589	4,022,023	2,656,174	1,695,414	1,298,180
Refined Sugar	2,866	2,842	2,876	2,886	2,864
Raw Sugar	558,075	643,742	577,641	730,582	664,683
Raw Silk (formerly at Kobe Raw Silk Exchange)	231,376	327,009	458,243	591,922	695,172
Kansai International Grain Index	60,008				
Raw Sugar Options	70,561	47,189	71,145	79,365	63,789
Total	**2,887,085**	**5,526,135**	**4,643,553**	**4,823,399**	**5,655,944**

Chubu Commodity Exchange (CCE), Japan

(formerly NGSE, NTE, and TDCE)	1998	1997	1996	1995	1994
Red Beans	188,937	241,008	287,220	502,369	919,371
Sweet Potato Starch	35	48	48	48	48
Imported Soybeans	505,345	1,010,201	620,703	307,451	177,513
Refined Sugar	1,433	1,421	1,438	1,449	1,789
Dried Cocoon	277,944	684,141	1,202,536	488,709	488,558
Cotton Yarn (40S)	114,877	126,684	296,455	755,844	1,100,388
Staple Fiber Yarn (Dull)	9,194	9,948	10,001	9,967	13,114
Wool Yarn	33,973	35,315	27,277	53,811	87,240
Total	**1,131,738**	**2,108,766**	**2,445,678**	**2,119,648**	**2,788,021**

Volume Worldwide

Osaka Securities Exchange(OSE), Japan

	1998	1997	1996	1995	1994
Nikkei 225 Index	8,191,130	7,484,182	7,043,977	7,220,900	6,208,754
Nikkei 300 Index	1,531,004	1,526,538	1,872,983	2,318,652	4,184,480
High-Tech Index	3,794				
Financial Index	3,576				
Consumer Index	2,626				
Nikkei 225 Index Options	5,230,046	4,910,359	3,924,543	5,174,571	4,273,641
Nikkei 300 Index Options	2,577	7,798	44,254	122,084	269,067
High-Tech Index Options	57				
Financial Index Options	86				
Consumer Index Options	5				
All Options on Individual Equities	363,901	222,094			
Total	**15,328,802**	**14,150,971**	**12,885,757**	**14,836,207**	**14,935,942**

Osaka Mercantile Exchange (OME), Japan

(formerly KRE and OTE)	1998	1997	1996	1995	1994
Staple Fiber Yarn (Dull)	5,338	4,952	2,928	2,940	2,910
Wool Yarn	15,677	22,589	18,624	64,073	266,974
Cotton Yarn (20S)	583,851	1,245,452	1,109,607	2,151,580	2,000,530
Cotton Yarn (40S)	42,993	147,444	254,828	659,110	833,307
Rubber (RSS3)	2,835,126	1,200,850	2,232,827	3,810,938	2,933,883
Rubber Index	672,582	382,913	373,879	173,409	
Aluminum	1,107,266	160,060			
Total	**5,261,833**	**3,164,947**	**3,995,802**	**6,866,178**	**6,041,111**

Tokyo Commodity Exchange (TOCOM), Japan

	1998	1997	1996	1995	1994
Gold	9,373,909	8,871,965	9,510,941	10,945,134	12,481,095
Silver	1,679,647	792,844	752,995	1,440,297	1,042,185
Platinum	16,944,343	10,839,577	6,895,464	5,975,872	4,551,406
Palladium	5,194,391	3,817,892	434,163	629,034	774,284
Aluminum	305,436	567,175			
Rubber	9,975,520	4,758,390	9,085,709	14,287,783	9,021,881
Cotton Yarn	110,645	524,717	874,052	1,838,448	2,573,963
Woolen Yarn	5,832	5,789	6,830	8,859	36,499
Total	**43,589,723**	**30,178,349**	**27,560,154**	**35,125,427**	**30,481,313**

Tokyo Grain Exchange (TGE), Japan

	1998	1997	1996	1995	1994
American Soybeans	3,820,850	9,966,257	7,120,741	2,699,926	2,559,288
Arabica Coffee	831,163				
Red Beans	1,953,638	2,542,760	2,847,511	3,384,267	5,122,015
Corn	7,267,045	13,840,721	16,034,716	6,899,593	3,053,244
Refined Sugar	2,866	2,842	2,876	2,898	2,864
Robusta Coffee	305,160				
Raw Sugar	189,778	1,279,550	1,045,438	1,291,441	1,220,931
American Soybean Options	97,599	263,990	275,269	206,993	96,505
Corn Options	201,269	44,220			
Raw Sugar Options	143,434	186,698	182,724	158,044	67,636
Total	**15,412,802**	**28,127,038**	**27,509,275**	**14,643,162**	**12,122,483**

Tokyo International Financial Futures Exchange (TIFFE), Japan

	1998	1997	1996	1995	1994
3-Month Euroyen	21,162,012	25,523,583	29,334,830	36,329,959	37,425,846
U.S. Dollar / Japanese Yen	46,949	63,755	44,194	5,037	13,770
Euroyen Options	500,002	535,895	567,793	361,920	570,237
Total	**21,708,963**	**26,123,233**	**29,970,017**	**36,722,216**	**38,034,953**

Tokyo Stock Exchange (TSE), Japan

	1998	1997	1996	1995	1994
5-Year Government Yen Bond	195,207	118,447	220,955		
10-Year Government Yen Bond	10,784,966	11,873,549	12,450,925	14,010,374	12,999,698
20-Year Government Yen Bond	123	2,167	2,242	2,734	3,194
TOPIX Stock Index	2,727,070	3,035,724	2,857,272	2,745,614	2,623,067
Electric Appliance Index	2,671				
Transportation Equipment Index	429				
Bank Index	1,127				
30-Year U.S. T-Bond	2,060	30,650	31,030	102,340	115,750
TOPIX Options	583	9,356	13,444	16,742	20,078
10-Year Government Yen Bond Options	1,848,851	2,002,357	1,975,274	2,017,031	1,691,834
Total	**15,563,087**	**17,072,250**	**17,551,142**	**16,877,804**	**15,761,787**

Yokohama Commodity Exchange, Japan

(formerly Maebashi Dried Cocoon & Yokohama Raw Silk Ex.)	1998	1997	1996	1995	1994
Raw Silk	371,732	658,176	1,083,386	1,256,094	998,686
Dried Cocoon	520,698	565,423	864,703	443,411	475,978
Total	**892,430**	**1,223,599**	**1,948,089**	**1,699,505**	**1,474,664**

	1998	1997	1996	1995	1994
TOTAL FUTURES	**797,771,429**	**750,548,594**	**703,482,637**	**783,168,145**	**637,865,283**
PERCENT CHANGE	**6.29%**	**7.54%**	**-1.68%**	**0.35%**	**48.67%**
TOTAL OPTIONS	**344,877,049**	**275,602,274**	**271,860,316**	**265,921,807**	**141,969,616**
PERCENT CHANGE	**25.14%**	**-1.22%**	**-26.70%**	**87.30%**	**27.21%**
TOTAL	**1,142,648,478**	**1,026,150,868**	**975,342,953**	**1,049,089,952**	**779,834,899**
PERCENT CHANGE	**11.35%**	**5.10%**	**-8.03%**	**16.18%**	**44.29%**

Conversion Factors

Commonly Used Agricultural Weights and Measurements

Bushel Weights:
wheat and soybeans = 60 lbs.
corn, sorghum and rye = 56 lbs.
barley grain = 48 lbs.
barley malt = 34 lbs.
oats = 32 lbs.

Bushels to tonnes:
wheat and soybeans = bushels X 0.027216
barley grain = bushels X 0.021772
corn, sorghum and rye = bushels X 0.0254
oats = bushels X 0.014515

1 tonne (metric ton) equals:
2204.622 lbs.
1,000 kilograms
22.046 hundredweight
10 quintals

1 tonne (metric ton) equals:
36.7437 bushels of wheat or soybeans
39.3679 bushels of corn, sorghum or rye
45.9296 bushels of barley grain
68.8944 bushels of oats
4.5929 cotton bales (the statistical bale used by the USDA and ICAC contains a net weight of 480 pounds of lint)

Area Measurements:
1 acre = 43,560 square feet = 0.040694 hectare
1 hectare = 2.4710 acres = 10,000 square meters
640 acres = 1 square mile = 259 hectares

Yields:
wheat: bushels per acre X 0.6725 = quintals per hectare
rye, corn: bushels per acre X 0.6277 = quintals per hectare
barley grain: bushels per acre X 0.538 = quintals per hectare
oats: bushels per acre X 0.3587 = quintals per hectare

Commonly Used Weights

The troy, avoirdupois and apothecaries' grains are identical in U.S. and British weight systems, equal to 0.0648 gram in the metric system. One avoirdupois ounce equals 437.5 grains. The troy and apothecaries' ounces equal 480 grains, and their pounds contain 12 ounces.

Troy weights and conversions:
24 grains = 1 pennyweight
20 pennyweights = 1 ounce
12 ounces = 1 pound
1 troy ounce = 31.103 grams
1 troy ounce = 0.0311033 kilogram
1 troy pound = 0.37224 kilogram
1 kilogram = 32.1507 troy ounces
1 tonne = 32,151 troy ounces

Avoirdupois weights and conversions:
27 11/32 grains = 1 dram
16 drams = 1 ounce
16 ounces = 1 lb.
1 lb. = 7,000 grains
14 lbs. = 1 stone (British)
100 lbs. = 1 hundredweight (U.S.)
112 lbs. = 8 stone = 1 hundredweight (British)
2,000 lbs. = 1 short ton (U.S. ton)
2,240 lbs. = 1 long ton (British ton)
160 stone = 1 long ton
20 hundredweight = 1 ton
1 lb. = 0.4536 kilogram
1 hundredweight (cwt.) = 45.359 kilograms
1 short ton = 907.18 kilograms
1 long ton = 1,016.05 kilograms

Metric weights and conversions:
1,000 grams = 1 kilogram
100 kilograms = 1 quintal
1 tonne = 1,000 kilograms = 10 quintals
1 kilogram = 2.204622 lbs.
1 quintal = 220.462 lbs.
1 tonne = 2204.6 lbs.
1 tonne = 1.102 short tons
1 tonne = 0.9842 long ton

U.S. dry volumes and conversions:
1 pint = 33.6 cubic inches = 0.5506 liter
2 pints = 1 quart = 1.1012 liters
8 quarts = 1 peck = 8.8098 liters
4 pecks = 1 bushel = 35.2391 liters
1 cubic foot = 28.3169 liters

U.S. liquid volumes and conversions:
1 ounce = 1.8047 cubic inches = 29.6 milliliters
1 cup = 8 ounces = 0.24 liter = 237 milliliters
1 pint = 16 ounces = 0.48 liter = 473 milliliters
1 quart = 2 pints = 0.946 liter = 946 milliliters
1 gallon = 4 quarts = 231 cubic inches = 3.785 liters
1 milliliter = 0.033815 fluid ounce
1 liter = 1.0567 quarts = 1,000 milliliters
1 liter = 33.815 fluid ounces
1 imperial gallon = 277.42 cubic inches = 1.2 U.S. gallons = 4.546 liters

ENERGY CONVERSION FACTORS

U.S. Crude Oll (average gravity)
1 U.S. barrel = 42 U.S. gallons
1 short ton = 6.65 barrels
1 tonne = 7.33 barrels

Barrels per tonne for various origins

Abu Dhabi	7.624
Algeria	7.661
Angola	7.206
Australia	7.775
Bahrain	7.335
Brunei	7.334
Canada	7.428
Dubai	7.295
Ecuador	7.58
Gabon	7.245
Indonesia	7.348
Iran	7.37
Iraq	7.453
Kuwait	7.261
Libya	7.615
Mexico	7.104
Neutral Zone	6.825
Nigeria	7.41
Norway	7.444
Oman	7.39
Qatar	7.573
Romania	7.453
Saudi Arabia	7.338
Trinidad	6.989
Tunisia	7.709
United Arab Emirates	7.522
United Kingdom	7.279
United States	7.418
Former Soviet Union	7.35
Venezuela	7.005
Zaire	7.206

Barrels per tonne of refined products:

aviation gasoline	8.9
motor gasoline	8.5
kerosene	7.75
jet fuel	8
distillate, including diesel	7.46
residual feul oil	6.45
lubricating oil	7
grease	6.3
white spirits	8.5
paraffin oil	7.14
paraffin wax	7.87
petrolatum	7.87
asphalt and road oil	6.06
petroleum coke	5.5
bitumen	6.06
LPG	11.6

(continued above)

Approximate heat content of refined products:
(Million Btu per barrel, 1 British thermal unit is the amount of heat required to raise the temperature of 1 pound of water 1 degree F.)

Petroleum Product	**Heat Content**
asphalt	6.636
aviation gasoline	5.048
butane	4.326
distillate fuel oil	5.825
ethane	3.082
isobutane	3.974
jet fuel, kerosene	5.67
jet fuel, naptha	5.355
kerosene	5.67
lubricants	6.065
motor gasoline	5.253
natural gasoline	4.62
pentanes plus	4.62

Petrochemical feedstocks:

naptha less than 401*F	5.248
other oils equal to or greater than 401*F	5.825
still gas	6
petroleum coke	6.024
plant condensate	5.418
propane	3.836
residual fuel oil	6.287
special napthas	5.248
unfinished oils	5.825
unfractionated steam	5.418
waxes	5.537

Source: U.S. Department of Energy

Natural Gas Conversions

Although there are approximately 1,031 Btu in a cubic foot of gas, for most applications, the following conversions are sufficient:

Cubic Feet					**MMBtu**
1,000	(one thousand cubic feet)	=	1 Mcf	=	1
1,000,000	(one million cubic feet)	=	1 MMcf	=	1,000
10,000,000	(ten million cubic feet)	=	10 MMcf	=	10,000
1,000,000,000	(one billion cubic feet)	=	1 Bcf	=	1,000,000
1,000,000,000,000	(one trillion cubic feet)	=	1 Tcf	=	1,000,000,000

Aluminum

The U.S. Geological Survey reported that domestic primary aluminum production increased slightly in 1997 to just over 3.6 million tonnes. Thirteen companies operated 22 primary aluminum reduction plants and one plant remained closed. Washington, Montana and Oregon accounted for 38 percent of the production; Kentucky, North Carolina, South Carolina and Tennessee produced 21 percent and other states 41 percent. Aluminum recovered from purchased scrap increased to almost 3.7 million tonnes. Of the recovered aluminum, 59 percent came from new manufacturing scrap and 41 percent from old discarded aluminum scrap. Aluminum beverage can scrap accounted for more than one-half of the old scrap consumption in 1997. The transportation, packaging and container industries were the largest domestic markets for aluminum products in 1997.

U.S. imports for consumption of aluminum materials increased in 1997 after having trended lower since 1995. Canada was the largest supplier of aluminum materials to the U.S. Russia was the second largest supplier of crude aluminum metal and alloys.

World inventory levels of aluminum at the end of 1997 declined 130,000 tonnes. Inventories of aluminum at the London Metals Exchange decreased by 300,000 tonnes. Stocks of aluminum metal held by producers increased slightly and U.S. inventories increased slightly. Primary aluminum was produced in 43 countries in 1997. The U.S. was the largest producer followed by Russia and Canada. Global production of aluminum increased by 3 percent in 1997.

U.S. primary aluminum production in July 1998 was 319,000 metric tonnes. That was an increase of almost 5 percent from a year earlier. In the first seven months of 1998, production was 2.15 million tonnes, up nearly 3 percent from the same period of 1997. Secondary recovery of aluminum from new scrap in July 1998 was 148,000 tonnes, down 1 percent from a year ago. In the January-July 1998 period, production was 1.08 million tonnes which was down 8 percent from 1997. Secondary recovery of aluminum from old scrap was 923,000 tonnes, down 1 percent from a year ago. Total aluminum produced from scrap in the first seven months of 1998 was 2.01 million tonnes, down 5 percent from 1997.

U.S. imports for consumption of aluminum crude metals and alloys in June 1998 were 243,000 tonnes. Imports for consumption of aluminum plates, sheets and bars in June 1998 were 54,000 tonnes. Total aluminum stocks, including scrap, at the end of June 1998 were 1.88 million tonnes.

In the January-June 1998 period, U.S. imports for consumption of aluminum crude metals and alloys were 1.26 million tonnes. The major supplier was Canada with 701,000 tonnes while Russia supplied 404,000 tonnes. Other major suppliers were Venezuela, Brazil and Australia. In the first six months of 1998, U.S. imports of aluminum plates, sheets and bars were 324,000 tonnes. The major supplier was Canada with 180,000 tonnes. Other large suppliers were Germany, Russia and Venezuela. Imports of aluminum scrap in the same period were 243,000 tonnes. Canada was the largest supplier with 128,000 tonnes while Mexico supplied 39,700 tonnes. Other large suppliers included Venezuela, Russia, England and France. Total U.S. imports for consumption of aluminum in the first half of 1998 were 1.83 million tonnes. The major supplier was Canada followed by Russia.

Futures Markets

Aluminum futures and options are listed on the London Metals Exchange (LME).

World Production of Primary Aluminum In Thousands of Metric Tons

Year	Australia	Brazil	Canada	China	France	Germany	Norway	Russia[3]	Spain	United Kingdom	United States	Venezuela	World Total
1989	1,244	890	1,555	750	335	796	863	3,300	352	297	4,030	540	19,010
1990	1,230	931	1,570	850	326	740	845	3,523	353	294	4,050	590	19,300
1991	1,228	1,140	1,822	963	286	690	833	3,251	355	294	4,121	601	19,700
1992	1,236	1,193	1,972	1,100	418	603	838	2,700	359	244	4,042	561	19,500
1993	1,381	1,172	2,308	1,220	426	552	887	2,820	356	239	3,695	568	19,800
1994	1,317	1,185	2,255	1,450	437	505	857	2,670	338	231	3,299	585	19,200
1995	1,297	1,188	2,172	1,680	372	575	847	2,724	361	238	3,375	630	19,700
1996[1]	1,372	1,195	2,283	1,770	380	576	863	2,874	362	240	3,577	635	20,800
1997[2]	1,495	1,200	2,327	2,000	390	575	919	2,906	362	240	3,603	640	21,400

[1] Preliminary. [2] Estimate. [3] Formerly part of the U.S.S.R.; data not reported separately until 1992. *Source: U.S. Geological Survey (USGS)*

Production of Primary Aluminum (Domestic and Foreign Ores) in the U.S. In Thousands of Metric Tons

Year	Jan.	Feb.	Mar.	Apr.	May	June	July	Aug.	Sept.	Oct.	Nov.	Dec.	Total
1989	346	312	347	334	347	335	346	341	323	328	328	343	4,030
1990	345	311	345	331	342	330	340	341	332	347	337	347	4,048
1991	349	317	352	340	353	343	354	350	336	347	337	343	4,121
1992	344	320	343	330	342	330	339	340	330	343	335	347	4,043
1993	335	292	323	313	325	315	316	302	291	303	287	294	3,696
1994	292	261	286	269	277	268	275	274	267	277	270	280	3,296
1995	281	253	280	272	285	277	288	286	280	289	285	299	3,375
1996	301	283	303	293	303	293	301	302	292	304	295	305	3,577
1997	305	277	307	295	304	296	305	304	294	307	298	310	3,603
1998[1]	309	280	312	305	316	307	319	318	309	315	307		3,706

[1] Preliminary. *Source: U.S. Geological Survey (USGS)*

ALUMINUM

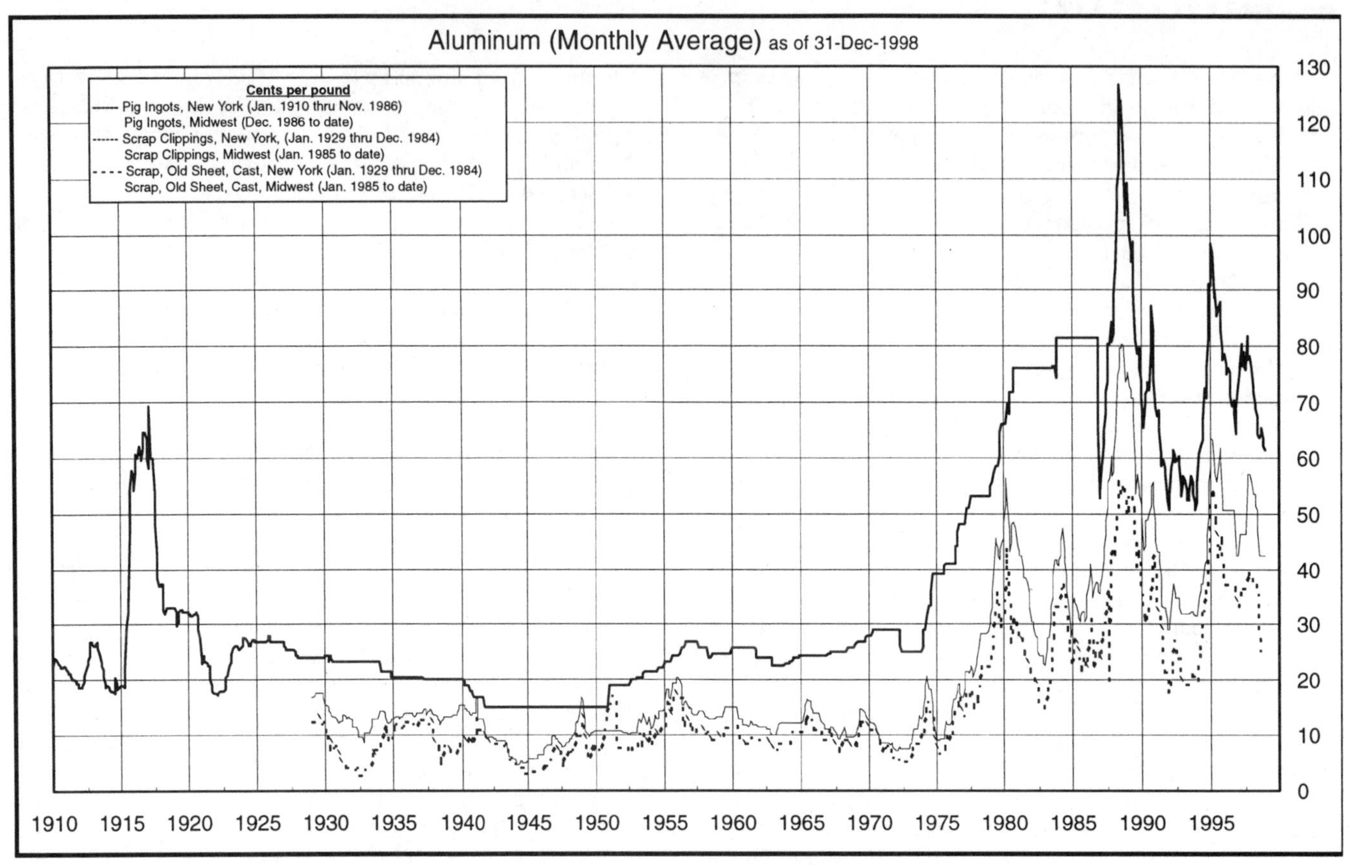

Salient Statistics of Aluminum in the United States In Thousands of Metric Tons

	Net Import Reliance as a % of Apparent	--- Production ---		Primary Ship-	Recovery from ----- Scrap -------		Apparent Con-	Net Shipments[5] by Producers --- Wrought Products ---				--- Castings ---				Total All Net Ship-
Year	Consumption	Primary	Second-ary	ments[2]	Old	New	sumption	Plate Sheet, Foil	Rolled Structural Shapes[3]	Ex-truded Shapes[4]	All	Perma-nent Mold	Die	Sand	All	ments
1988	7	3,944	2,122	6,851	1,045	1,077	5,373	3,787	343	1,341	5,589	201	700	115	1,055	6,621
1989	E	4,030	2,054	6,751	1,011	1,043	4,957	3,900	339	1,280	5,633	210	740	110	1,096	6,728
1990	E	4,048	2,390	6,590	1,360	1,030	5,260	3,799	301	1,211	5,425	208	620	103	968	6,393
1991	E	4,121	2,290	6,400	1,320	969	5,040	3,787	311	1,096	5,300	168	575	97	864	6,156
1992	1	4,042	2,760	6,810	1,610	1,140	5,730	4,097	303	1,186	5,691	198	595	99	804	6,609
1993	19	3,695	2,940	7,300	1,630	1,310	6,600	4,030	297	1,300	5,770	225	645	103	994	6,770
1994	30	3,299	3,090	8,160	1,500	1,580	6,880	4,810	296	1,420	6,690	247	551	208	1,050	7,740
1995	23	3,375	3,190	8,260	1,510	1,680	6,320	4,900	526	1,540	7,130	442	627	207	1,440	8,580
1996	22	3,577	3,310	8,330	1,580	1,730	6,600	4,430	350	1,540	6,480	473	612	180	1,390	7,860
1997[1]	23	3,603	3,690	8,880	1,530	2,160	6,690	4,640	366	1,710	6,870	NA	NA	NA	NA	NA

[1] Preliminary. [2] To domestic industry. [3] Also rod, bar & wire. [4] Also rod, bar, tube blooms & tubing. [5] Consists of total shipments less shipments to other mills for further fabrication. NA = Not available. E = Net exporter. *Source: U.S. Geological Survey (USGS)*

Supply and Distribution of Aluminum in the United States In Thousands of Metric Tons

	Apparent Con-	---- Production ----	From			Inventories -- December 31 --	Govern-		Apparent Con-	---- Production ----	From			Inventories -- December 31 --	Govern-
Year	sumption	Primary	Old Scrap	Imports	Exports	Private	ment[3]	Year	sumption	Primary	Old Scrap	Imports	Exports	Private	ment[3]
1986	5,143	3,037	784	1,967	753	2,235	2	1992	5,730	4,042	1,610	1,725	1,453	1,880	57
1987	5,469	3,343	852	1,850	917	2,000	2	1993	6,600	3,695	1,630	2,540	1,210	1,980	57
1988	5,373	3,944	1,045	1,620	1,247	1,883	2	1994	6,880	3,299	1,500	3,380	1,370	2,070	57
1989	4,957	4,030	1,011	1,470	1,615	1,822	2	1995	6,320	3,375	1,510	2,980	1,610	2,000	57
1990	5,260	4,048	1,360	1,514	1,659	1,820	2	1996[1]	6,600	3,577	1,580	2,810	1,500	1,860	57
1991	5,040	4,121	1,320	1,490	1,762	1,780	2	1997[2]	6,690	3,603	1,530	3,080	1,570	1,880	[4]

[1] Preliminary. [2] Estimate. [3] National Defense Stockpile. [4] Less than 1/2 unit. *Source: U.S. Geological Survey (USGS)*

Aluminum Products Distribution of End-Use Shipments in the United States In Thousands of Metric Tons

Year	Building & Construction	Consumer Durables	Containers & Packaging	Electrical	Exports	Machinery & Equipment	Trans-portation	Other	Total
1988	1,316	588	2,036	671	787	435	1,536	269	7,638
1989	1,294	544	2,112	663	1,060	436	1,448	264	7,821
1990	1,208	509	2,157	594	1,131	452	1,388	261	7,700
1991	1,052	472	2,210	579	1,357	426	1,414	241	7,752
1992	1,144	523	2,259	587	1,236	448	1,591	256	8,045
1993	1,240	563	2,180	609	1,090	477	1,970	259	8,390
1994	1,400	647	2,270	682	1,200	572	2,310	276	9,360
1995	1,220	621	2,310	657	1,310	570	2,610	279	9,570
1996	1,330	655	2,180	671	1,290	569	2,640	291	9,610
1997[1]	1,320	694	2,220	708	1,360	626	2,990	318	10,200

[1] Preliminary. *Source: U.S. Geological Survey (USGS)*

World Consumption of Primary Aluminum In Thousands of Metric Tons

Year	Brazil	Canada	China	France	Ger-many	India	Italy	Japan	Rep. of Korea	Russia	United Kingdom	United States	World Total
1988	324.2	437.1	658.0	660.6	1,232.6	327.0	581.0	2,123.2	268.0	2,900.0	427.4	4,601.9	18,877.9
1989	420.1	450.2	920.0	685.5	1,289.1	420.0	607.0	2,211.6	287.6	2,700.0	454.7	4,381.4	19,281.1
1990	341.2	387.2	861.0	720.9	1,295.4	433.3	652.0	2,415.2	368.9	2,790.0	453.7	4,330.4	19,275.4
1991	354.2	408.2	938.0	734.2	1,360.9	430.2	670.0	2,431.6	383.5	2,409.0	412.4	4,137.2	18,778.2
1992	377.1	420.4	1,253.8	722.8	1,457.1	414.3	660.0	2,271.6	397.0	1,352.0	483.3	4,616.9	18,475.4
1993	378.9	486.6	1,318.0	665.0	1,300.0	475.3	554.0	2,138.3	524.8	767.0	475.0	4,877.1	18,278.7
1994	414.1	565.1	1,484.0	747.5	1,370.3	475.0	660.0	2,344.8	603.9	470.0	570.0	5,407.1	19,666.8
1995	500.2	611.9	1,874.9	750.0	1,503.9	581.0	631.0	2,335.6	692.6	476.0	620.0	5,054.8	20,436.6
1996	497.0	620.1	2,033.1	693.0	1,394.4	576.4	585.1	2,473.8	697.6	439.6	600.0	5,300.0	20,825.4
1997[1]	479.1	580.8	2,028.0	642.1	1,621.9	576.4	711.7	2,571.2	576.6	418.4	619.1	5,317.5	21,406.4

[1] Preliminary. *Source: American Metal Market (AMM)*

Salient Statistics of Recycling Aluminum in the United States

Year	Percent Recycled	New Scrap[1]	Old Scrap[2]	Recycled Metal[3]	Apparent Supply	New Scrap	Old Scrap	Recycled Metal	Apparent Supply
		In Thousands of Metric Tons				Value in Millions of Dollars			
1988	33	1,077	1,045	2,122	6,450	2,614	2,536	5,150	15,654
1989	34	1,043	1,011	2,054	6,000	2,020	1,958	3,978	11,620
1990	38	1,034	1,359	2,393	6,298	1,688	2,218	3,906	10,280
1991	38	969	1,320	2,290	6,010	1,270	1,730	3,000	7,880
1992	40	1,140	1,610	2,760	6,870	1,450	2,040	3,500	8,710
1993	37	1,310	1,630	2,940	7,920	1,540	1,920	3,460	9,300
1994	36	1,580	1,500	3,090	8,460	2,480	2,360	4,840	13,300
1995	40	1,680	1,510	3,190	8,010	3,190	2,850	6,040	15,200
1996	40	1,730	1,580	3,310	8,330	2,730	2,480	5,200	13,100
1997	42	2,160	1,530	3,690	8,880	3,670	2,590	6,260	15,100

[1] Scrap that results from the manufacturing process. [2] Scrap that results from consumer products. [3] Metal recovered from new plus old scrap.
Source: U.S. Geological Survey (USGS)

Producer Prices for Aluminum Used Beverage Can Scrap In Cents Per Pound

Year	Jan.	Feb.	Mar.	Apr.	May	June	July	Aug.	Sept.	Oct.	Nov.	Dec.	Average
1988	65.80	70.50	72.93	72.50	72.50	72.50	72.50	71.63	66.21	63.92	61.50	64.93	68.95
1989	72.64	73.76	73.15	69.50	71.55	66.59	57.92	55.50	54.68	55.50	54.30	51.50	63.05
1990	48.50	45.50	47.55	50.50	50.77	50.50	49.71	51.13	57.53	52.15	48.00	44.67	49.71
1991	49.00	49.11	48.67	42.09	37.86	37.00	39.79	37.50	37.50	35.76	35.18	34.50	40.33
1992	35.38	38.32	40.73	43.91	44.40	41.50	41.50	41.69	39.93	38.07	38.00	38.68	40.18
1993	41.00	41.00	38.04	36.63	35.00	35.00	37.52	37.59	36.50	34.19	33.60	34.78	36.74
1994	38.45	43.08	42.50	46.60	45.50	48.98	56.40	56.00	56.00	62.64	70.40	71.00	53.13
1995	74.85	72.24	65.00	65.00	65.00	65.00	65.00	67.98	64.80	58.45	57.00	58.50	64.91
1996	57.73	56.00	56.24	58.90	59.00	49.70	47.50	49.25	50.20	48.50	49.03	53.50	52.96
1997	56.98	59.00	59.00	58.27	58.05	58.05	58.32	59.60	59.50	59.13	59.00	57.12	58.50

Source: American Metal Market (AMM)

ALUMINUM

Average Price of Cast Aluminum Scrap (Crank Cases) in Chicago In Cents Per Pound

Year	Jan.	Feb.	Mar.	Apr.	May	June	July	Aug.	Sept.	Oct.	Nov.	Dec.	Average
1991	33.50	32.00	32.00	30.64	28.45	22.40	21.50	21.50	21.13	19.00	18.11	18.00	24.85
1992	18.71	23.00	26.91	27.00	24.45	24.00	24.00	24.00	21.21	19.50	19.50	19.50	22.65
1993	19.50	19.50	19.50	19.50	19.50	19.50	20.79	21.00	20.62	20.00	20.00	20.00	19.95
1994	20.00	25.79	28.33	32.50	32.50	33.18	35.90	36.50	41.07	44.45	50.50	53.50	36.19
1995	53.53	54.08	49.02	48.50	44.41	42.50	43.76	45.80	45.05	39.27	37.50	37.50	45.08
1996	37.50	37.50	37.50	37.50	37.50	37.50	37.50	36.50	35.40	33.80	33.50	33.50	36.27
1997	36.09	36.50	36.50	36.50	36.50	36.50	36.50	39.36	38.60	38.50	38.50	38.07	37.34
1998	37.50	37.50	37.50	35.95	35.50	31.59	25.50	25.50	25.50	25.50	25.50	25.50	30.71

Source: American Metal Market (AMM)

Aluminum Products (Ingot and Mill Products) Shipments[1] in the United States In Million Pounds

Year	Jan.	Feb.	Mar.	Apr.	May	June	July	Aug.	Sept.	Oct.	Nov.	Dec.	Total
1991	1,177	1,087	1,261	1,244	1,313	1,287	1,387	1,389	1,276	1,371	1,265	1,241	15,298
1992	1,324	1,280	1,376	1,298	1,277	1,339	1,330	1,333	1,361	1,453	1,333	1,360	16,081
1993	1,251	1,291	1,486	1,408	1,377	1,440	1,296	1,410	1,382	1,306	1,364	1,284	16,294
1994	1,584	1,620	2,007	1,679	1,895	1,758	1,679	1,934	1,744	1,760	1,868	1,811	20,295
1995	1,632	1,472	1,704	1,594	1,605	1,576	1,368	1,493	1,533	1,571	1,469	1,404	18,422
1996	1,420	1,457	1,555	1,642	1,735	1,564	1,516	1,661	1,510	1,639	1,473	1,451	18,623
1997	1,185	1,165	1,282	1,307	1,313	1,303	1,254	1,288	1,307	1,286	1,147	1,154	14,992
1998[2]	1,245	1,176	1,309	1,302	1,272	1,303	1,302	1,284	1,296	1,367	1,225	1,200	15,282

[1] Mills products & pig & ingot (net shipments). [2] Preliminary. *Source: Bureau of the Census, U.S. Department of Commerce*

Aluminum Inventories of Ingot, Mill Products and Scrap in the U.S., on First of Month In Million Pounds

Year	Jan.	Feb.	Mar.	Apr.	May	June	July	Aug.	Sept.	Oct.	Nov.	Dec.
1991	4,013	4,068	4,169	4,256	4,212	4,135	4,044	3,990	4,028	4,008	3,992	3,923
1992	3,913	4,321	4,346	4,375	4,411	4,486	4,482	4,333	4,376	4,418	4,336	4,263
1993	4,093	4,124	4,179	4,250	4,274	4,327	4,398	4,417	4,387	4,360	4,294	3,020
1994	4,372	4,646	4,758	4,778	4,784	4,790	4,725	4,659	4,637	4,605	4,540	4,551
1995	4,572	4,710	4,845	4,691	4,743	4,745	4,639	4,691	4,594	4,403	4,366	4,346
1996	4,403	4,382	4,481	4,433	4,451	4,327	4,358	4,318	4,216	4,174	4,061	4,030
1997	4,105	4,073	4,071	4,038	4,032	4,007	4,023	3,992	4,051	4,023	4,017	4,074
1998[1]	4,109	4,172	4,157	4,144	4,159	4,174	4,193	4,264	4,150	4,104	4,112	4,124

[1] Preliminary. *Source: Bureau of the Census, U.S. Department of Commerce*

Aluminum Exports of Crude Metal and Alloys from the United States In Cents Per Pound

Year	Jan.	Feb.	Mar.	Apr.	May	June	July	Aug.	Sept.	Oct.	Nov.	Dec.	Total
1991	61.1	54.8	46.7	82.8	56.4	71.3	69.0	80.1	54.6	68.0	80.7	67.3	792.8
1992	50.8	43.8	49.7	38.6	33.6	39.8	50.0	50.3	40.4	82.1	50.5	73.5	603.1
1993	54.8	38.6	41.7	26.3	38.6	30.7	33.9	24.5	27.9	31.7	24.1	27.6	400.4
1994	22.1	18.3	28.3	17.9	37.5	30.5	30.6	38.3	40.3	24.8	26.1	24.1	338.9
1995	26.1	32.7	25.4	31.1	31.4	20.7	26.6	39.2	38.9	33.0	30.4	33.6	369.1
1996	23.1	27.9	31.2	34.3	46.2	54.3	36.3	33.7	30.2	40.3	33.2	26.2	416.9
1997	31.0	25.5	22.5	33.0	24.1	34.9	23.9	33.2	34.4	26.5	33.0	30.0	352.0
1998[1]	21.2	21.4	21.8	17.4	22.6	21.8	20.9	21.5	28.0	23.9			264.6

[1] Preliminary. *Source: U.S. Geological Survey (USGS)*

Aluminum General Imports of Crude Metal and Alloys into the United States In Cents Per Pound

Year	Jan.	Feb.	Mar.	Apr.	May	June	July	Aug.	Sept.	Oct.	Nov.	Dec.	Total
1991	79.5	79.4	84.3	88.2	85.1	75.9	97.3	89.0	86.6	90.4	81.0	88.0	1,024.7
1992	100.7	93.1	97.1	94.6	96.3	87.8	82.4	103.4	94.3	108.4	100.5	96.8	1,155.4
1993	120.8	123.9	165.8	172.0	152.1	152.6	125.1	162.7	173.5	149.4	182.9	155.6	1,836.4
1994	200.2	157.8	282.0	206.9	251.9	179.3	202.8	198.3	160.0	183.4	240.1	222.2	2,484.9
1995	214.0	168.0	204.0	195.0	184.0	172.0	136.0	134.0	117.0	137.0	139.0	133.0	1,933.0
1996	158.0	150.0	148.0	188.0	176.0	169.0	139.0	149.0	136.0	170.0	147.0	180.0	1,910.0
1997	145.0	147.0	209.0	196.0	198.0	167.0	157.0	152.0	150.0	175.0	146.0	222.0	2,060.0
1998[1]	220.0	204.0	202.0	200.0	189.0	243.0	170.0	204.0	198.0	198.0			2,433.6

[1] Preliminary. *Source: U.S. Geological Survey (USGS)*

Antimony

Antimony is primarily a by-product of mining, smelting and refining of other metals, primarily lead and silver-copper ores. It finds use in flame retardants, fabrics, plastics and ammunition. Most antimony is found in Idaho, Nevada, Alaska and Montana.

The U.S. Geological Survey reported that more than one-half of the primary antimony used in the United States in 1997 went into flame retardants; the remainder was used in the transportation industry, in chemicals, in ceramics and in glass and in other uses. Secondary antimony, which is derived from recycled lead-acid batteries, was used to make new batteries.

U.S. production of primary smelter antimony in the second quarter 1998 was 5,420 tonnes (antimony content). That was down 11 percent from the first quarter. For all of 1997, primary smelter production of antimony was 26,700 tonnes. Secondary production of antimony in the second quarter of 1998 was 1,260 tonnes, an increase of almost 12 percent from the first quarter. For all of 1997, secondary production of antimony was 7,550 tonnes.

U.S. imports for consumption of antimony in the second quarter of 1998 were 6,870 tonnes, down 27 percent from the first quarter. For 1997, imports for consumption were 39,300 tonnes. Of the second quarter import total of 6,870 tonnes, some 361 tonnes were ore and concentrate. For 1997, imports were 1,300 tonnes. Metal antimony imports in second quarter 1998 were 3,020 tonnes, down from 4,210 tonnes in the first quarter. For all of 1997, metal imports were 14,800 tonnes. Imports of antimony oxide in the second quarter 1998 were 3,490 tonnes, down from 4,760 tonnes in the first quarter. For 1997, imports were 23,200 tonnes.

Exports of antimony products in the second quarter 1998 were 781 tonnes, down 20 percent from the first quarter. Exports in 1997 were 3,890 tonnes. Metal, alloy and scrap exports in second quarter 1998 were 124 tonnes while oxide exports were 657 tonnes. Consumption of primary antimony in the second quarter 1998 was 3,130 tonnes compared to 3,580 tonnes in the first quarter. For all of 1997, consumption was 13,500 tonnes.

Producer and consumer stocks of antimony at the end of second quarter 1998 were 12,400 tonnes. Metal stocks were 4,020 tonnes, oxide stocks 4,550 tonnes, and other including ore and concentrate 3,800 tonnes.

World Mine Production of Antimony (Content of Ore) In Metric Tons

Year	Australia	Bolivia	Canada	China[2]	Guatemala	Kyrgyzstan[4]	Mexico[5]	Peru[6]	Russia[4]	South Africa	Thailand	Turkey	World Total
1994	1,300	7,050	643	91,000	296	2,000	1,758	460	7,000	4,534	500	75	118,000
1995	900	6,426	684	125,000	665	1,500	1,783	460	6,000	5,537	230	416	151,000
1996[1]	1,800	6,489	1,716	129,000	880	1,200	983	460	6,000	5,137	70	450	156,000
1997[2]	1,900	8,700	652	120,000	880	1,200	1,909	460	6,000	5,000	60	400	149,000

[1] Preliminary. [2] Estimate. [3] Formerly part of Czechoslovakia, data not reported separately until 1993. [4] Formerly part of the USSR; data not reported separately until 1992. [5] Includes antimony content of miscellaneous smelter products. [6] Recoverable W=Withheld proprietary data. *Source: U.S. Geological Survey*

Salient Statistics of Antimony in the United States In Metric Tons

Year	Avg. Price ¢ per lb. CIF U.S. Ports	Production[3]: Primary[2] Mine	Production[3]: Primary[2] Smelter	Production[3]: Secondary (Alloys)[2]	Imports for Consumption: Ore Gross Weight	Imports for Consumption: Ore Antimony Content	Imports for Consumption: Oxide (Gross Weight)	Exports (Oxide)	Industry Stocks, December 31[3]: Metallic	Oxide	Sulfide	Other	Total[4]
1994	177.7	215	25,500	12,200	7,680	5,640	21,300	6,500	2,770	5,000	W	3,170	10,900
1995	227.8	262	23,500	10,500	6,140	4,260	18,600	6,950	2,450	4,450	W	3,680	10,600
1996[1]	146.5	242	25,600	7,780	1,610	1,000	22,100	3,990	3,520	4,420	W	3,060	11,000
1997[2]	97.8	356	26,700	7,550	1,530	1,300	27,900	3,230	3,070	4,300	W	3,240	10,600

[1] Preliminary. [2] Estimate. [3] Antimony content. [4] Including primary antimony residues & slag. W = Withheld proprietary data
Source: U.S. Geological Survey (USGS)

Industrial Consumption of Primary Antimony in the United States In Metric Tons (Antimony Content)

Year	Metal Products: Ammunition	Antimonial Lead	Sheet & Pipe	Bearing Metal & Bearings	Solder	Total All Metal Products	Flame Retardents: Plastics	Flame Retardents: Total	Non-Metal Products: Ceramics & Glass	Pigments	Plastics	Total	Grand Total
1994	W	1,990	W	36	183	3,740	6,690	8,570	980	369	1,030	2,490	14,800
1995	W	2,230	W	53	192	3,760	6,690	7,800	1,080	492	1,090	2,770	14,300
1996	W	1,760	W	44	256	3,110	6,850	7,770	1,030	450	1,080	2,690	13,600
1997[1]	W	1,170	W	45	226	2,600	6,610	7,550	1,080	824	1,220	3,300	13,500

[1] Preliminary. [2] Estimated coverage based on 77% of the industry. W=Withheld proprietary data. *Source: U.S. Geological Survey (USGS)*

Average Price of Antimony[1] in the United States In Cents Per Pound

Year	Jan.	Feb.	Mar.	Apr.	May	June	July	Aug.	Sept.	Oct.	Nov.	Dec.	Average
1995	293.00	293.00	284.00	284.00	201.00	142.00	188.00	240.00	244.00	213.00	170.00	170.00	226.83
1996	153.00	152.50	152.50	150.12	142.50	142.50	132.50	127.50	127.50	127.50	127.50	127.50	138.59
1997	127.50	127.50	115.95	106.50	106.50	106.50	105.27	93.00	94.90	98.00	98.00	86.00	105.47
1998	80.00	80.00	80.00	80.00	74.38	71.25	66.25	61.50	62.50	65.00	65.00	65.00	70.91

[1] Prices are for antimony metal (99.65%) merchants, minimum 18-ton containers, c.i.f. U.S. Ports. *Source: American Metal Market (AMM)*

Apples

The U.S. Department of Agriculture forecasts the 1998 U.S. apple crop to be 11.3 billion pounds, up 9 percent from 1997. If this level of production is obtained, it would be the second largest crop after the 1994 crop of 11.5 billion pounds. Washington state is the largest producer of apples with a 1998 crop forecasted to be 6.1 billion pounds, an increase of 22 percent from the previous year. Washington is the largest producer of both fresh and processed apples. The second largest Western producer is California with the 1998 crop expected to be 915 million pounds, down 5 percent from 1997.

In the Central states, the largest producer is Michigan with a 1998 crop forecast to be 1 billion pounds, down 5 percent from 1997. In the Eastern states, New York is the largest producer with a 1998 crop estimated at 1.04 billion pounds, down 7 percent from the previous year. Pennsylvania's apple crop is forecast to be 430 million pounds, down 20 percent from 1997.

Over half of the U.S. apple crop is sold for the fresh market. Fresh use of apples is likely to increase in 1998 because of the large Washington crop. Over 70 percent of the Washington crop is used in the fresh market.

World Production of Apples[3], Fresh (Dessert & Cooking) In Thousands of Metric Tons

Year	Argentina	Canada	France	Germany	Hungary	Italy	Japan	Netherlands	South Africa	Spain	Turkey	United States	World Total
1987	925	506	1,985	1,077	1,064	2,273	998	340	526	971	1,680	4,873	20,922
1988-9	1,030	501	1,935	2,467	1,131	2,443	1,042	383	534	845	1,950	4,140	22,662
1989-90	1,050	538	1,818	1,727	959	2,162	1,045	417	557	747	1,850	4,519	21,654
1990-1	950	540	1,895	2,222	945	2,102	1,053	431	542	635	1,900	4,398	21,224
1991-2	1,043	513	1,236	1,165	859	1,869	760	223	605	517	1,900	4,413	18,250
1992-3	947	564	2,398	3,228	666	2,394	1,039	640	633	1,095	2,100	4,798	35,443
1993-4	1,006	488	2,079	1,719	819	2,145	1,011	670	638	891	2,080	4,847	36,505
1994-5	1,146	554	2,166	2,080	610	2,153	989	590	577	739	2,095	5,217	37,712
1995-6[1]	1,147	591	2,089	1,373	353	1,889	963	595	703	843	2,100	4,801	38,773
1996-7[2]	1,276	560	2,049	1,776	475	2,100	936	490	675	875	2,100	4,733	42,265

[1] Preliminary. [2] Estimate. [3] Commercial crop. [4] Formerly part of Yugoslavia; data not reported separately until 1992. NA = Not available.
Source: Foreign Agricultural Service, U.S. Department of Agriculture (FAS-USDA)

Salient Statistics of Apples[2] in the United States

Year	Production: Total	Production: Utilized	Growers Prices: Fresh ¢ Lb.	Growers Prices: Processing $ Ton	Utilization: Fresh	Processed[5]: Canned	Processed: Dried	Processed: Frozen	Processed: Juice & Cider	Processed: Other[3]	Avg. Farm Price ¢ Per Lb.	Farm Value Million $	Foreign Trade[4]: Domestic Exports Fresh	Domestic Exports Dried[5]	Imports Fresh & Dried[5]	Fresh Per Capita Consumption Lbs.
	Millions of Pounds												Metric Tons			
1988	9,120	9,070	17.4	123.0	5,230	1,399	285	266	1,824	67	12.7	1,147.8	254.5	12.0	133.0	19.9
1989	9,917	9,871	13.9	107.0	5,822	1,320	282	322	2,068	57	10.4	1,024.6	357.4	23.7	119.7	21.2
1990	9,657	9,618	20.9	144.0	5,515	1,378	270	304	2,077	74	15.1	1,447.7	371.3	55.5	122.0	19.6
1991	9,707	9,637	25.1	171.0	5,447	1,311	299	286	2,194	100	17.9	1,727.0	530.1	44.2	143.9	18.2
1992	10,569	10,463	19.5	130.0	5,767	1,498	324	247	2,472	155	13.6	1,428.0	487.8	22.1	139.3	19.2
1993	10,685	10,574	18.4	107.0	6,124	1,335	366	282	2,382	85	12.9	1,363.9	662.9	19.2	130.9	19.2
1994	11,501	11,331	18.6	114.0	6,366	1,406	415	304	2,707	133	12.9	1,467.1	663.1	25.1	115.8	19.6
1995	10,585	10,390	24.0	159.0	5,843	1,292	334	305	2,538	78	17.0	1,765.6	565.0	24.6	196.1	19.0
1996	10,392	10,340	20.8	171.0	6,215	1,294	317	268	2,185	61	15.9	1,644.2	656.8		182.3	19.0
1997[1]	10,386	10,320	22.2	129.0	5,823	1,509	267	341	2,206	174	15.3	1,688.0				18.5

[1] Preliminary. [2] Commercial crop. [3] Mostly crushed for vinegar, jam, etc. [4] Year beginning July. [5] Fresh weight basis. *Source: Economic Research Service, U.S. Department of Agriculture (ERS-USDA)*

Average Price of Apples Received by Growers (for Fresh Use) in the United States In Cents Per Pound

Year	Jan.	Feb.	Mar.	Apr.	May	June	July	Aug.	Sept.	Oct.	Nov.	Dec.	Average
1989	18.1	17.9	16.5	14.4	13.5	10.8	11.5	15.9	16.7	14.3	13.3	12.1	14.6
1990	12.2	12.4	12.3	12.0	12.6	13.7	20.3	22.3	22.2	19.3	19.6	20.9	16.7
1991	20.1	20.5	20.3	20.2	22.5	23.2	24.6	23.2	26.4	23.8	25.1	25.7	23.0
1992	24.6	24.8	24.3	24.1	25.0	25.2	28.6	33.3	27.1	21.2	19.4	19.9	24.8
1993	18.3	16.7	14.5	14.3	14.9	16.1	17.8	24.4	24.1	21.1	19.3	18.6	18.3
1994	18.7	17.8	16.6	15.5	14.3	13.5	19.4	29.0	20.8	19.2	16.4	19.2	18.4
1995	19.5	18.3	18.2	16.6	15.4	15.6	17.5	24.5	26.0	25.1	23.5	24.0	20.4
1996	25.4	24.2	25.1	22.6	21.9	21.9	23.3	25.2	30.2	24.6	23.2	22.6	24.2
1997	22.5	20.3	17.6	15.6	14.3	13.7	14.6	19.2	25.9	25.3	23.0	23.3	19.6
1998[1]	21.9	21.6	21.3	19.2	18.2	16.3	16.1	19.0	22.7	22.8	17.9	15.2	19.4

[1] Preliminary. *Source: Economic Research Service, U.S. Department of Agriculture (ERS-USDA)*

Arsenic

According to the U.S. Geological Survey, the United States has recorded no domestic production of arsenic since 1985 and the country remains dependent on imports for its supply. Nearly all imports of arsenic were in compound form, primarily as arsenic trioxide, although some arsenic metal was also imported. China has been the principal supplier of arsenic and its compounds to the United States.

World production of arsenic trioxide in 1997 was estimated at 40,600 metric tonnes. That represented a decline of 6 percent from 1996. For 1997, China was by far the largest producer of arsenic trioxide with 15,000 tonnes or some 37 percent of the world total. Over the last five years, Chinese production of arsenic trioxide has averaged 16,600 tonnes. The next largest producer was Chile with 6,000 tonnes, down 6 percent from the previous year. Ghana was the next largest producer with almost 4,600 tonnes, followed by Mexico, Belgium and the Philippines.

There is no data on domestic arsenic consumption in the U.S. but trade data indicates that apparent demand in the U.S. is more than 20,000 tonnes. Although none is locally produced, the U.S. is probably the world's largest consumer of arsenic. It was estimated that about 95 percent of the arsenic consumed domestically was in compound form, primarily arsenic trioxide.

The largest market for arsenic in the U.S. is in the production of arsenical wood preservatives. Demand for arsenic is closely related to the home construction industry. With low interest rates and a robust economy, it can be assumed that the demand for arsenic remains strong. Wooden decks on homes use arsenical preservatives. Due to the toxic nature of arsenic, there will continue to be questions about its future in the construction industry.

One area where arsenic does have a future is in the semiconductor industry. It is here that very high-purity arsenic is finding use in the form of gallium arsenide. One of the important uses of arsenic is in integrated circuits that operate at high speeds or frequencies. Circuits made with gallium arsenide have better signal reception and lower power consumption.

U.S. imports of arsenic metal in 1997 were 909 tonnes (arsenic content). That was a substantial increase from the 252 tonnes imported in 1996. Imports of arsenic compounds in 1997 were 22,800 tonnes, arsenic content, an increase of over 7 percent from the previous year.

Of the total supply of 23,700 tonnes, agricultural chemicals consumed 1,400 tonnes or some 47 percent more than in 1996. Production of glass used some 700 tonnes, unchanged from the previous year. Use in wood preservatives totaled 20,000 tonnes, an increase of 4 percent from the previous year. Nonferrous alloys and electronics took 900 tonnes, a substantial increase from the 250 tonnes used in 1996. Other uses took 300 tonnes.

U.S. imports for consumption of arsenic trioxide in 1997 were 30,000 tonnes, an increase of 7 percent from 1996. The major supplier was China with 15,100 tonnes, followed by Chile. U.S. imports of arsenic acid in 1997 were 117 tonnes as China supplied 106 tonnes. In 1996, one tonne of arsenic acid was imported into the U.S. Imports of arsenic metal were 909 tonnes as China supplied 783 tonnes. In 1996 imports were 252 tonnes.

World Production of White Arsenic (Arsenic Trioxide) In Metric Tons

Year	Belgium	Bolivia	Canada[4]	Chile	China	France	Germany	Mexico	Namibia[3]	Peru	Phillippines	Russia[5]	World Total
1990	3,000	300	485	5,830	9,000	6,480	360	4,810	1,640	500	5,090	7,800	53,400
1991	2,500	463	236	6,820	10,000	2,000	300	4,920	1,800	661	5,000	7,000	46,000
1992	2,000	633	250	6,020	15,000	2,000	300	4,293	2,456	644	5,000	2,500	45,800
1993	2,000	663	250	6,200	14,000	3,000	300	4,447	2,290	391	2,000	2,000	41,700
1994	2,000	341	250	6,300	18,000	6,000	300	4,400	3,047	286	2,000	1,500	51,000
1995	2,000	362	250	6,400	21,000	5,000	250	3,620	1,661	285	2,000	1,500	51,300
1996[1]	2,000	255	250	6,400	15,000	3,000	250	2,942	1,302	285	2,000	1,500	43,200
1997[2]	2,000	260	250	6,000	15,000	2,500	250	3,000	500	285	2,000	1,500	40,600

[1] Preliminary. [2] Estimate. [3] Output of Tsumeb Corp. Ltd. only. [4] Includes low-grade dusts that were exported to the U.S. for further refining. [5] Formerly part of the U.S.S.R.; reported seperately until 1992. *Source: U.S. Geological Survey (USGS)*

Salient Statistics of Arsenic in the United States In Metric Tons (Arsenic Content)

	Supply				Distribution		Estimated Demand Pattern						Average Price			
	Imports												Trioxide	Metal		
Year	Metal	Compounds	Industry Stocks Jan. 1	Total	Apparent Demand	Industry Stocks Dec. 31	Agricultural Chemicals	Glass	Wood Preservatives	Non-Ferrous Alloys & Electric	Other	Total	Mexican ¢ Per Pound	Chinese ¢ Per Pound	Imports Trioxide[3]	Exports
1990	796	19,900	100	20,796	20,500	100	4,200	800	14,400	800	300	20,500	23	180	26,256	149
1991	1,010	20,700	100	21,810	21,600	----	5,000	900	14,300	1,000	400	21,600	25	68	27,142	233
1992	740	23,300	----	24,040	23,900	----	3,900	900	17,900	800	400	23,900	29	56	30,671	94
1993	767	20,900	----	21,667	21,300	----	3,000	900	16,200	800	400	21,300	33	44	27,500	364
1994	1,330	20,300	----	21,630	21,500	----	1,200	700	18,000	1,300	300	21,500	32	40	26,800	79
1995	557	22,100	----	22,657	22,300	----	1,000	700	19,600	600	400	22,300	33	66	29,000	430
1996[1]	252	21,200	----	21,452	21,400	----	950	700	19,200	250	300	21,400	33	40	28,000	36
1997[2]	909	22,800	----	23,709	23,700	----	1,400	700	20,000	900	300	23,700	31	32	30,000	61

[1] Preliminary. [2] Estimate. [3] For Consumption. *Source: U.S. Geological Survey (USGS)*

Barley

World barley production in 1998/99 of 141 million metric tonnes compares with 145 million in 1997/98 and average production in the early 1990's of 165 million tonnes, reconfirming that the steady decline in world production has not yet run its course.

Collectively, the E.U. is the largest producing area with 53 million tonnes in 1998/99, up slightly from 1997/98. Russia, once the world's largest producer, continues to see a steady drop in production, from 27 million tonnes in 1994/95 to 20.8 million by 1997/98 and only 10 million in 1998/99. Canada is now the largest single producer with 13 million tonnes in 1998/99 vs. almost 14 million in 1997/98. In the U.S., barley is the third largest produced feed grain, but on a worldwide basis U.S. production accounts for only 5 percent of the total. World barley usage continues to slip, totaling 141 million tonnes in 1998/99 vs. 146 million in 1997/98, and an average of 165 million early in the 1990's. Ending 1998/99 world carryover of 32.7 million tonnes is unchanged from a year earlier.

The U.S. barley crop year begins June 1. Production peaked in the 1980's and has since declined about a third as producers found returns more favorable from wheat and sunflowers. Barley production in 1998/99 of a record low 358 million bushels compares with the 1997/98 crop of 374 million. The decline reflects planted acreage of only 5.98 million acres, down 7 percent from 1997/98 which more than offset an average yield per acre of 59.9 bushels, up 1.6 bushels. North Dakota is the largest producing state, followed by Montana and Idaho.

U.S. disappearance in 1998/99 of a record low 392 million bushels compares with the year earlier low of 404 million; in 1991/92 usage neared 500 million bushels. Feed and residual use was estimated at 185 million bushels, up 27 million from 1997/98. Industrial use, mostly for beer and alcohol, was forecast as unchanged at 172 million bushels, while exports fell to 35 million vs. 74 million in 1997/98. Imports were estimated at 35 million bushels vs. 40 million in 1997/98 and mostly of malting quality barley from Canada. Carryover stocks on May 31, 1999 of 121 million bushels are about unchanged from a year earlier.

World barley trade was forecast at 14.6 million tonnes in 1998/99 vs. 13.3 million in 1997/98. The European Union exports almost half of the total, and Canada and Australia most of the balance. Importing countries are more numerous, but Saudi Arabia, China and Japan are forecast to take 7.5 million tonnes in 1998/99 vs. 9 million tonnes in 1997/98, with Saudi Arabia accounting for the decline.

U.S. farmers' barley prices were forecast to average between $1.75-2.15 per bushel in 1998/99 vs. $2.38 in 1997/98.

Futures Markets

Barley futures and options are traded on the Winnipeg Commodity Exchange (WCE) and the London Commodity Exchange (LCE). Futures are traded on the Budapest Commodity Exchange.

World Barley Supply and Demand In Thousands of Metric Tons

	Exports						Imports			Utilization			Ending Stocks		
Crop Year	Australia	Canada	EC-12	Total Non-U.S.	U.S.	Total Exports	Saudi Arabia	Unaccounted	Total Imports	Russia[3]	U.S.	Total Utilization	Canada	U.S.	Total Stocks
1989-90	2,447	3,773	7,905	15,905	1,798	17,703	4,146	467	17,703	22,433	8,030	167,440	2,056	3,501	28,789
1990-1	2,683	4,460	7,053	17,016	1,507	18,523	4,342	742	18,523	29,156	8,283	174,898	2,646	2,948	32,317
1991-2	1,951	3,379	9,459	16,929	2,090	19,019	6,873	77	19,019	25,635	8,735	165,833	2,615	2,800	32,471
1992-3	2,600	2,859	5,816	15,084	1,611	16,695	3,917	807	16,695	28,368	7,916	166,065	3,271	3,292	31,923
1993-4	4,232	3,789	6,793	16,986	1,553	18,539	4,497	415	18,539	27,041	9,053	169,633	3,376	3,023	32,252
1994-5	1,356	2,556	5,061	14,197	1,355	15,552	4,303	99	15,552	24,488	8,726	166,107	1,820	2,451	28,498
1995-6	3,375	2,603	2,480	12,043	1,181	13,224	3,668	92	13,224	17,500	7,635	151,565	1,749	2,168	19,794
1996-7	4,020	3,440	6,183	16,093	1,213	17,306	5,479	181	17,306	16,500	8,459	150,078	2,919	2,383	23,484
1997-8[1]	2,832	1,897	3,200	12,018	1,066	13,084	3,250	168	13,084	16,700	6,879	145,462	2,457	2,596	32,774
1998-9[2]	2,500	1,600	7,250	14,255	800	15,055	5,000	139	15,055	12,750	7,773	141,912	1,917	2,497	28,362

[1] Preliminary. [2] Estimate. [3] Formerly part of the U.S.S.R.; data not reported separately until 1989-90.
Source: Foreign Agricultural Service, U.S. Department of Agriculture (FAS-USDA)

World Production of Barley In Thousands of Metric Tons

Year	Australia	Canada	China	Denmark	France	Germany	India	Kazakhstan[3]	Spain	Turkey	United Kingdom	United States	World Total
1989-90	4,044	11,666	6,180	4,982	9,840	9,716	1,721	48,500	9,100	4,900	8,025	8,784	169,680
1990-1	4,184	13,441	3,930	4,990	10,150	13,990	1,490	8,500	9,410	6,600	7,900	9,192	178,056
1991-2	4,606	11,617	3,928	5,041	10,789	14,494	1,640	3,085	9,140	6,800	7,700	10,110	169,136
1992-3	5,460	11,032	4,000	2,974	10,580	12,196	1,700	8,511	6,105	6,500	7,350	9,908	165,767
1993-4	6,956	12,972	4,200	3,369	8,981	11,000	1,510	7,149	9,520	7,300	6,040	8,666	169,962
1994-5	2,913	11,690	4,411	3,450	7,650	10,900	1,310	5,100	7,600	6,500	5,950	8,162	161,246
1995-6	5,823	13,035	4,089	3,860	7,740	11,890	1,730	2,178	5,200	6,900	6,830	7,824	142,861
1996-7	6,809	15,562	4,000	3,950	9,540	12,070	1,510	2,700	9,600	7,200	7,780	8,544	153,768
1997-8[1]	6,427	13,527	4,000	3,890	10,180	13,400	1,440	2,600	8,600	7,300	7,850	7,835	154,752
1998-9[2]	5,300	12,700	3,500	3,550	10,700	12,500	1,700	1,000	11,000	7,600	6,600	7,674	137,500

[1] Preliminary. [2] Estimate. [3] Formerly part of the U.S.S.R.; data not reported separately until 1990-91. *Source: Foreign Agricultural Service, U.S. Department of Agriculture (FAS-USDA)*

Barley Acreage and Prices in the United States

Year Beginning- June 1	Acreage 1,000 Acres: Planted	Acreage 1,000 Acres: Harvested for Grain	Yield Per Harvested Acre -- Bushels --	Received by Farmers[3]	Seasonal Prices: Duluth or Better: Feed (No. 2)	Seasonal Prices: Duluth or Better: Malting (No. 3)	Seasonal Prices: Portland No. 2 Western	Government Price Support Operations: National Average Loan Rate	Target Price	Put Under Support (Mil. Bu.)	% of Production
				Dollars per Bushel							
1990-1	8,221	7,529	56.1	2.14	2.13	2.42	2.65	1.28	2.36	33.8	8.0
1991-2	8,941	8,413	55.2	2.10	2.17	2.38	2.66	1.32	2.36	38.0	8.2
1992-3	7,762	7,285	62.5	2.04	2.11	2.37	2.57	1.40	2.36	42.9	9.4
1993-4	7,786	6,753	58.9	1.99	2.05	2.48	2.40	1.40	2.36	37.7	9.5
1994-5	7,159	6,667	56.2	2.03	2.02	2.75	2.51	1.54	2.36	28.2	7.5
1995-6	6,689	6,279	57.3	2.89	2.67	3.69	3.51	1.54	2.36	14.9	4.1
1996-7[1]	7,144	6,767	58.5	2.74	2.32	3.18	3.07	1.55	NA	28.7	NA
1997-8[2]	6,910	6,425	58.3	2.38	1.86	2.54	2.60	1.57	NA	32.8	NA

[1] Preliminary. [2] Estimate. [3] Excludes support payments. *Source: Economic Research Service, U.S. Department of Agriculture (ERS-USDA)*

Salient Statistics of Barley in the United States In Millions of Bushels

Year Beginning- June 1	Supply: Beginning Stocks	Supply: Production	Supply: Imports	Supply: Total Supply	Disappearance: Domestic Use: Food & Alcohol Beverages	Domestic Use: Seed	Domestic Use: Feed & Residual	Domestic Use: Total	Exports	Total Disappearance	Ending Stocks: Gov't Owned	Ending Stocks: Privately Owned[3]	Ending Stocks: Total Stocks
1991-2	135.4	464.3	24.5	624.2	163.3	12.9	224.9	401.1	94.5	495.6	6.5	122.1	128.6
1992-3	128.6	455.1	11.4	595.1	158.4	13.1	192.1	363.6	80.3	443.9	5.4	145.8	151.2
1993-4	151.2	398.0	71.5	620.7	162.9	11.8	241.1	415.8	66.1	481.8	5.2	133.7	138.9
1994-5	138.9	374.9	65.9	579.6	163.8	11.2	225.8	400.8	66.2	467.0	5.0	107.6	112.6
1995-6	112.6	359.6	40.7	512.9	160.1	11.8	179.0	350.9	62.4	413.3	4.2	95.4	99.6
1996-7	99.6	395.8	36.8	532.1	160.8	11.2	219.8	391.8	30.8	422.7	0	109.5	109.5
1997-8[1]	109.0	374.0	40.0	524.0	172.0	11.6	158.0	341.6	74.0	404.0	0	112.0	112.0
1998-9[2]	120.0	358.0	35.0	513.0	172.0	11.0	185.0	368.0	35.0	392.0	0	120.0	120.0

[1] Preliminary. [2] Estimate. [3] Uncommitted inventory. [4] Includes quantity under loan & farmer-owned reserves. *Source: Economic Research Service, U.S. Department of Agriculture (ERS-USDA)*

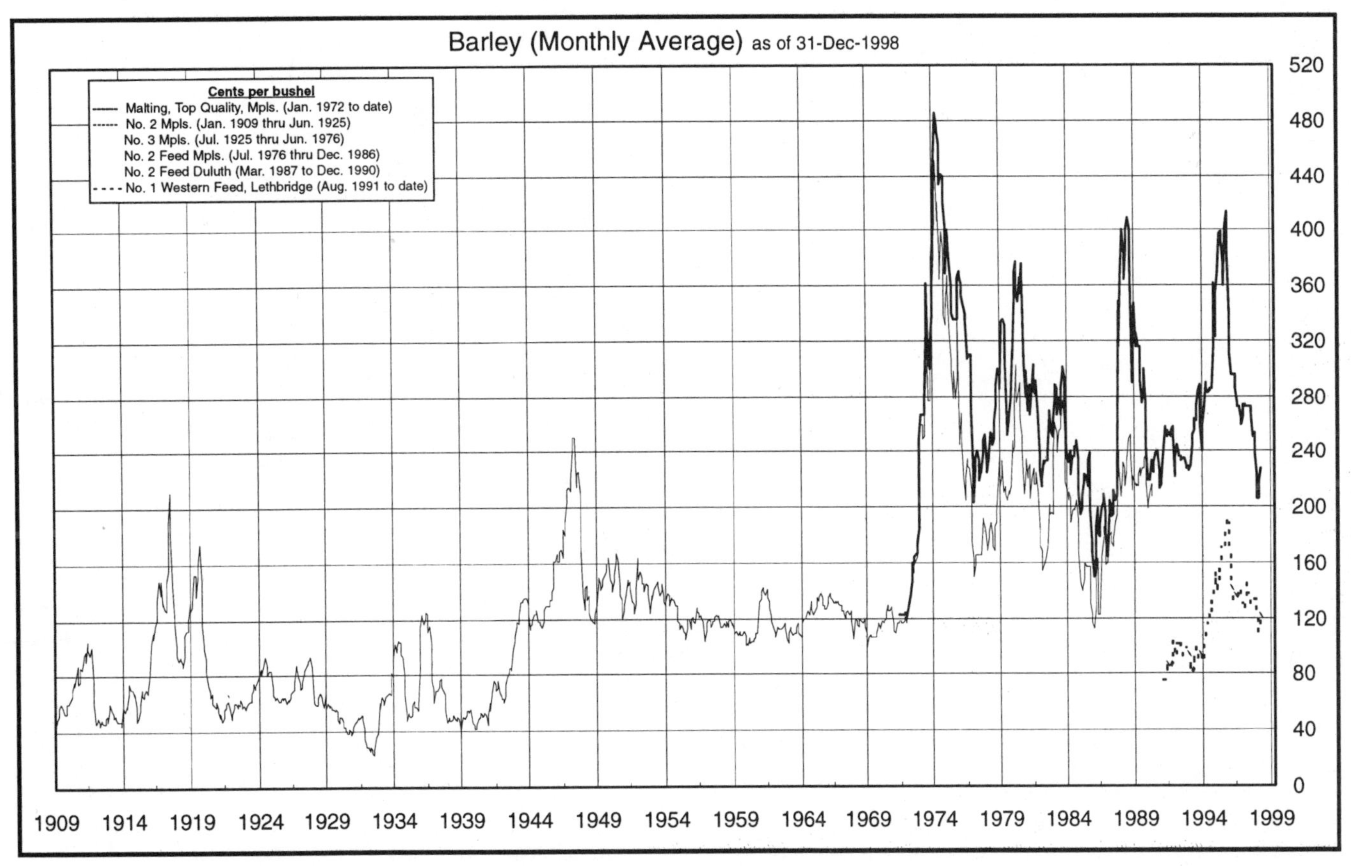

BARLEY

Average Price of No. 2 (or Better) Feed Barley, in Duluth   In Cents Per Bushel

Year	June	July	Aug.	Sept.	Oct.	Nov.	Dec.	Jan.	Feb.	Mar.	Apr.	May	Average
1991-2	202	189	192	208	218	223	218	220	228	230	235	238	217
1992-3	230	215	203	212	211	208	206	206	208	210	212	205	211
1993-4	199	196	189	189	201	216	214	215	216	207	208	211	205
1994-5	205	202	199	204	195	204	200	202	206	202	197	211	202
1995-6	222	225	209	206	258	298	292	294	300	286	299	320	267
1996-7	322	279	260	234	210	190	196	195	201	222	233	245	232
1997-8	231	204	210	229	205	198	166	158	156	151	142	NQ	186
1998-9[1]	NQ	123	NQ	NQ	NQ	NQ							123

[1] Preliminary. NQ = No quote. *Source: Economic Research Service, U.S. Department of Agriculture (ERS-USDA)*

Average Prices Received by Farmers for All Barley in the United States   In Cents Per Bushel

Year	June	July	Aug.	Sept.	Oct.	Nov.	Dec.	Jan.	February	Mar.	Apr.	May	Average
1991-2	190	173	206	206	210	220	224	221	215	212	214	222	209
1992-3	209	226	216	184	192	205	195	207	200	200	209	197	203
1993-4	195	190	202	187	182	201	202	215	207	201	202	206	199
1994-5	191	192	207	193	193	209	199	205	213	213	215	221	204
1995-6	225	241	262	257	288	309	315	315	328	324	324	345	294
1996-7	355	318	299	278	269	265	267	252	244	236	227	231	270
1997-8	226	227	235	238	244	261	243	242	239	242	214	214	235
1998-9[1]	195	201	206	201	186	202	200	199					199

[1] Preliminary. *Source: National Agricultural Statistics Service, U.S. Department of Agriculture (NASS-USDA)*

Average Open Interest of Western Feed Barley Futures in Winnipeg   In Contracts -- 20 Tonnes

Year	Jan.	Feb.	Mar.	Apr.	May	June	July	Aug.	Sept.	Oct.	Nov.	Dec.
1993	1,471	1,000	1,369	2,318	2,818	3,500	2,287	2,016	2,580	3,643	4,743	5,946
1994	7,600	8,164	7,650	8,212	8,153	9,019	8,511	8,558	9,633	12,340	10,802	9,457
1995	8,900	9,295	9,965	8,657	7,279	8,731	9,297	9,770	10,704	12,043	10,324	12,089
1996	13,803	12,979	15,746	18,022	19,045	18,502	15,504	14,190	16,647	20,143	21,233	24,590
1997	22,718	19,290	15,080	14,620	14,385	12,291	10,023	13,641	12,909	13,147	14,473	13,576
1998	15,789	17,337	18,039	14,706	12,666	10,847	9,915	10,384	11,420	11,460	11,338	8,622

Source: Winnipeg Commodity Exchange (WCE)

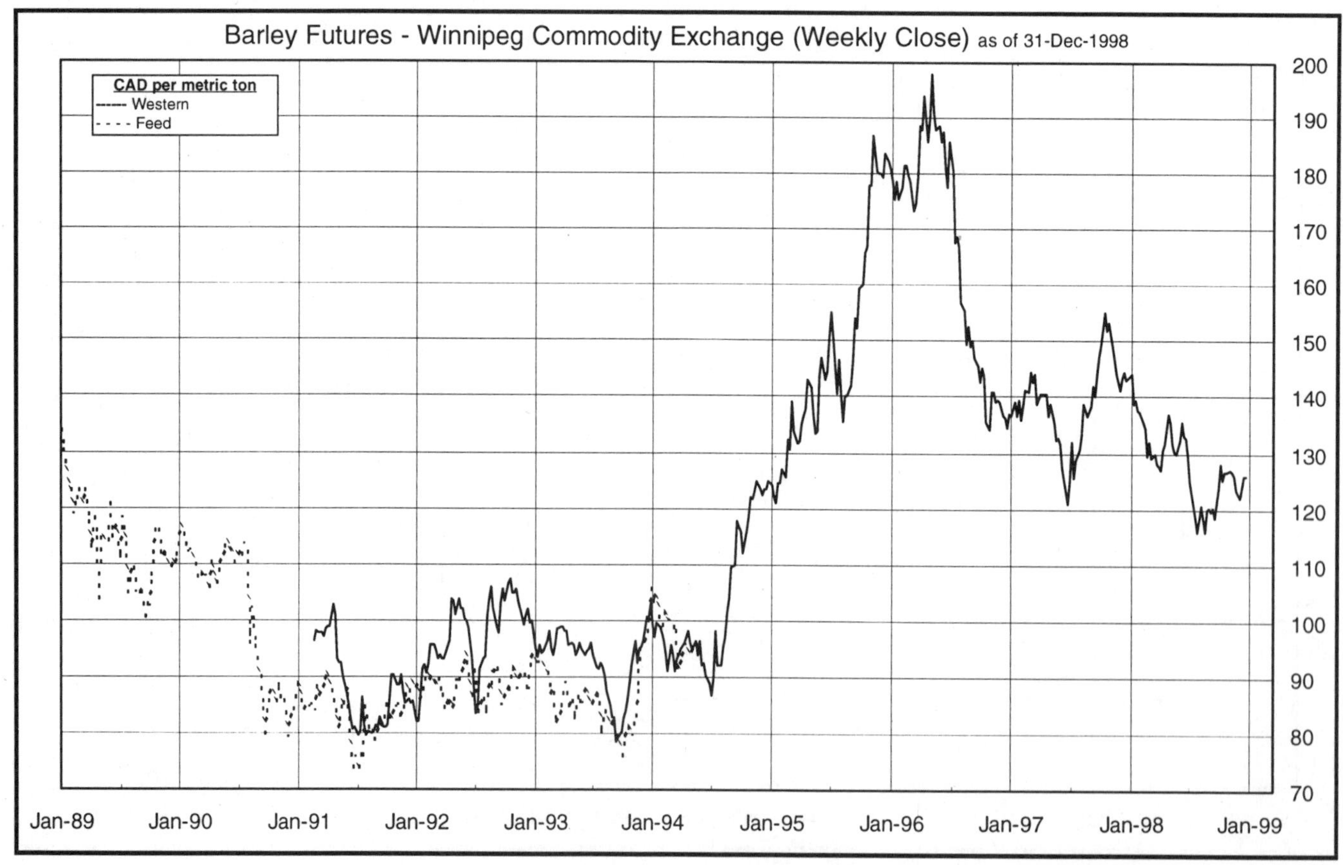

Bauxite

Bauxite is a naturally occurring, heterogeneous material composed primarily of one or more aluminum hydroxide minerals, plus various mixtures of silica, iron oxide, titania, aluminosilicates and other impurities in trace amounts.

Bauxite is the only raw material used in the production of alumina on a commercial scale in the U.S. Bauxites are typically classified according to their intended commercial applications: abrasive, cement, chemical, metallurgical, refractory and others. Of all the bauxite mined, approximately 85 percent is converted to alumina for the production of aluminum metal. Another 10 percent goes to non-metal uses as various forms of specialty alumina with the remaining 5 percent used in nonmetallurgical bauxite applications.

In 1997, according to the U.S. Geological Survey, 24 countries reported bauxite mine production and total world production increased slightly from 1996. The main producers in 1997 were Australia, Brazil, Guinea and Jamaica. Abrasive grade bauxite is produced in Australia, China, Guinea and Guyana, while refractory grade bauxite is produced in Brazil, China and Guyana. Total known world reserves of bauxite are sufficient to meet world primary aluminum metal demand well into the 21st century.

U.S. production of alumina (calcined equivalent) increased by 8 percent in 1997 compared to 1996 due to additional capacity installed at some refineries. An estimated 89 percent of the alumina shipped by U.S. refineries went to domestic primary smelters for aluminum metal production.

U.S. imports (for consumption) of crude and dried bauxite in the first five months of 1998 were 4.16 million tonnes. The major supplier was Jamaica with 1.69 million tonnes followed by Guinea with 1.49 million tonnes. Other large suppliers were Brazil and Guyana. For all of 1997, imports were 10.7 million tonnes. U.S. exports of crude and dried bauxite in the first five months of 1998 were 33,700 tonnes with Canada being the primary destination.

U.S. imports of alumina in the January-May 1998 period were 1.62 million tonnes. The major supplier was Australia with 978,000 tonnes followed by Suriname with 200,000 tonnes and Jamaica with 192,000 tonnes. In 1997, imports were 3.83 million tonnes. U.S. exports of alumina in the first five months of 1998 were 648,000 tonnes while for all of 1997 they were 1.27 million tonnes.

World Production of Bauxite In Thousands of Metric Tons

Year	Australia	Brazil	China	Greece	Guinea	Guyana[2]	Hungary	India	Jamaica[3]	Russia[3/4]	Sierra Leone	Suriname	World Total
1988	36,192	8,083	2,300	2,433	15,624	1,339	2,593	3,961	7,305	5,500	1,403	3,434	103,105
1989	38,584	8,665	2,388	2,550	15,792	1,321	2,644	4,471	9,601	5,500	1,548	3,530	103,722
1990	41,391	9,678	2,400	2,496	15,772	1,424	2,559	4,852	10,921	5,500	1,430	3,283	113,000
1991	40,510	10,365	2,600	2,133	15,466	2,204	2,037	4,735	11,552	5,000	1,288	3,198	111,000
1992	39,746	9,366	2,700	2,078	13,800	2,376	1,721	4,898	11,302	4,578	1,250	3,250	105,000
1993	41,320	9,669	3,500	2,205	14,100	2,130	1,561	5,277	11,391	4,260	1,165	3,412	109,000
1994	41,733	8,673	3,700	2,196	13,300	1,732	836	4,809	11,564	3,000	735	3,772	106,000
1995	42,655	10,214	5,000	2,200	15,800	2,028	1,015	5,240	10,857	3,100	----	3,530	112,000
1996[1]	43,063	12,307	6,200	2,452	16,500	2,485	1,044	5,757	11,863	3,300	----	4,000	120,000
1997[2]	44,065	12,300	8,000	2,211	16,500	2,502	743	5,800	11,875	3,350	----	4,000	123,000

[1] Preliminary. [2] Estimate. [3] Dry Bauxite equivalent of ore processed. [4] Formerly part of the U.S.S.R.; data not reported separetely until 1992.
Source: U.S. Geological Survey (USGS)

Salient Statistics of Bauxite in the United States In Thousands of Metric Tons

Year	Net Import Reliance as a % of Apparent Consumption	Average Price FOB Mine $ per Ton	Consumption by Industry: Total	Alumina	Abrasive	Chemical	Refractory	Dry Equivalent: Imports[3] (for Consumption)	Exports[3]	Consumption	Stocks, December 31: Producers & Consumers	Government	Total
1988	97	13-17	10,074	8,970	274	236	524	9,944	71	10,074	3,021	18,474	21,495
1989	96	15-20	11,810	10,782	275	223	407	10,893	44	11,810	2,891	18,474	21,365
1990	98	15-20	12,042	11,064	276	212	387	12,144	74	12,042	2,318	18,477	20,795
1991	100	15-18	12,204	11,383	204	218	328	11,871	51	12,204	2,620	18,477	21,097
1992	100	15-18	11,873	11,066	223	190	334	10,939	63	11,873	2,319	17,805	20,124
1993	100	15-24	11,917	11,002	203	225	429	11,621	90	12,200	1,590	16,938	18,500
1994	99	15-24	11,200	10,400	197	192	350	10,700	129	11,200	1,560	17,200	18,800
1995	99	15-18	10,900	10,100	133	201	394	10,100	108	10,900	1,730	16,300	18,100
1996[1]	100	15-18	11,000	10,300	117	W	380	10,200	132	11,000	1,930	15,700	17,600
1997[2]	100	15-18	11,500	10,700	98	W	466	10,700	85	11,500	2,260	14,300	16,500

[1] Preliminary. [2] Estimate. [3] Including concentrates. W = Withheld proprietary data. *Source: U.S. Geological Survey (USGS)*

Bismuth

Bismuth finds a wide variety of uses ranging from pharmaceutical compounds to glass ceramics to chemicals and pigments. Bismuth is found in household pharmaceuticals and is used to treat stomach ulcers. There has been interest in using bismuth as a non-toxic substitute for lead in such applications as plumbing fixtures and even ammunitions. Bismuth is substituted for lead in ceramic glazes for china. Bismuth has the advantage of being as durable as lead without being as hazardous.

The U.S. Geological Survey reported that the last U.S. producer of primary bismuth permanently shut down its refinery. In November, the last stocks of bismuth held in the National Defense Stockpile were sold leaving the U.S. completely dependent on foreign suppliers. The largest foreign producers are Mexico, Peru, Belgium and China.

World mine production of bismuth in 1997 was 4,210 tonnes. That represented an increase of almost 17 percent from the previous year. Mexico was the largest producer of mined bismuth with output of 1,642 tonnes in 1997. Peru had production estimated at 1,000 tonnes while China's output was 600 tonnes. World refinery production of bismuth in 1997 was 4,400 tonnes, up 1 percent from the previous year. Mexico was the largest producer of refinery bismuth in 1997 with output of 990 tonnes. Peru produced 940 tonnes while China's production was 800 tonnes, the same as Belgium. Bismuth is produced primarily as a by-product of other metals, mostly lead. Bolivia is the sole producer of primary bismuth.

U.S. consumption of bismuth in second quarter 1998 was 534,000 kilograms. In the first half of 1998, consumption was 970,000 kilograms. For all of 1997, bismuth consumption was 1.53 million kilograms. Of the first half 1998 consumption of 970,000 kilograms, some 465,000 kilograms was used in chemicals. Another 325,000 kilograms was used in bismuth alloys with 163,000 kilograms used in metallurgical additives.

U.S. imports of bismuth metal for consumption in May 1998 were 256,000 kilograms. In the first five months of 1998, imports were 1.26 million kilograms while for all of 1997 they were 2.17 million kilograms. In the first five months of 1998, the major supplier of bismuth metal to the U.S. was Belgium with 413,000 kilograms or 33 percent of the total. The next largest supplier was Mexico with 348,000 kilograms or 28 percent of the total. Other large suppliers were China, the U.K. and Canada. With the ending of domestic bismuth production in the U.S., imports were likely to increase in the coming years.

U.S. exports of bismuth metal, alloys, and waste and scrap in May 1998 were 34,300 kilograms (metal content). In the first five months of 1998, exports were 107,000 kilograms, while for all of 1997 they were 206,000 kilograms. In the January-May 1998 period, the largest export market was Belgium which took 50,700 kilograms or 47 percent of the total. Other large markets include Canada, Germany and the U.K.

World Production of Bismuth In Metric Tons

	Mine Output, Metal Content						Refined Metal						
Year	Canada	China	Japan	Mexico	Peru	Total	Belgium	China	Kazakhstan[3]	Japan	Mexico	Peru	Total
1988	181	750	160	958	363	3,220	795	750	85	524	622	341	3,669
1989	205	850	150	883	687	3,750	800	850	85	502	597	646	3,970
1990	87	1,060	133	733	555	3,440	1,000	1,060	80	442	549	521	4,190
1991	65	1,040	138	651	610	3,230	800	1,260	70	461	500	377	3,820
1992	224	820	159	807	550	2,740	800	1,060	45	530	550	419	3,670
1993	144	740	149	908	1,000	3,220	950	1,050	170	497	650	937	4,360
1994	129	610	152	1,047	1,210	3,340	900	850	84	505	836	877	4,180
1995	187	740	177	995	900	3,400	800	800	166	591	924	581	3,970
1996[1]	150	610	169	1,070	1,000	3,610	800	800	160	562	957	939	4,340
1997[2]	183	600	168	1,642	1,000	4,210	800	800	160	560	990	940	4,400

[1] Preliminary. [2] Estimate. [3] Formerly part of the U.S.S.R.; data not reported separately until 1992. *Source: U.S. Geological Survey (USGS)*

Salient Statistics of Bismuth in the United States In Metric Tons

	Bismuth Consumed, By Uses							Imports of Metallic Bismuth from				
Year	Metallurgical Additives	Other Alloys & Uses	Fusible Alloys	Chemicals[3]	Total Consumption	Consumer Stocks Dec. 31	Exports of Metal & Alloys	Belgium	Mexico	Peru	Total	Dealer Price $ Per Pound
1988	493	27	332	679	1,531	433	147	340.2	448.5	188.9	1,641	5.78
1989	396	25	272	659	1,352	440	122	835.7	390.8	271.4	1,880	5.76
1990	424	24	249	577	1,274	331	122	668.1	404.8	262.7	1,612	3.56
1991	341	26	271	789	1,427	247	75	345.1	535.0	169.8	1,411	3.00
1992	381	33	278	758	1,450	272	90	467.4	550.5	75.7	1,621	2.66
1993	232	59	256	750	1,300	323	70	275.1	479.1	117.2	1,330	2.50
1994	306	26	276	841	1,450	402	160	512.0	665.0	114.9	1,660	3.25
1995	257	27	544	1,320	2,150	390	261	636.0	444.0	10.9	1,450	3.85
1996[1]	231	35	401	855	1,520	122	151	584.0	453.0	19.5	1,490	3.65
1997[2]	252	31	593	655	1,530	213	206	691.0	601.0	163.0	2,170	3.50

[1] Preliminary. [2] Estimate. [3] Includes pharmaceuticals. *Source: U.S. Geological Survey (USGS)*

Broilers

1998 U.S. federally inspected broiler production reached 27.8 billion pounds vs. 27.3 billion in 1997. In the early 1990's production averaged 20 billion pounds. Production of ready-to-cook (RTC) broiler meat in the second half of 1998 of 14 billion pounds compares with 13.9 billion in 1997.

The fractional increase in second half 1998 production, the smallest for the period since a 1 percent rise in 1982, reflected hatchery supply flock problems which limited increases in bird numbers while hot weather slowed growth rates in some leading southern producing areas. A forecasted increase for 1999 partially reflects an increase in broiler-type chicks for future hatchery supply flocks in late 1998. Producer profitability is also expected to improve. Net returns for broiler processors in 1998 were near record highs as broiler prices increased and feed costs were about 20 percent below 1997 levels.

Wholesale whole broiler prices in 1998 peaked in mid-summer, averaging $.69 a pound vs. $.62 a year earlier. The 12-City wholesale price averaged near $.62 per pound in 1998 vs. the 1997 average of $.588. Initial forecasts for 1999 suggest some easing with the year's average near $.59. Retail prices tend to average about $.25 higher than wholesale prices. U.S. per capita broiler consumption in 1998 of 72.4 pounds, retail weight, compares with the previous year's 72.7 pounds. However, a sharp gain is forecast for 1999 with consumption at a record large 75.8 pounds.

A key factor for the steady gains in U.S. broiler production is continued strong foreign demand, reflecting a combination of attractive prices of U.S. broilers, notably leg quarters, and the rapid development of foreign markets. U.S. exports in the first half of 1998 of 2.6 billion pounds compares with 2.2 billion in 1997. Russia was the major importer with over 1 billion pounds in 1998 vs. 868 million pounds the previous year. Hong Kong and Japan are the largest Asian importers, although regional financial turmoil is likely to restrict 1998 totals.

Broiler Supply and Prices in the United States

Year & Quarters	Federally Inspected Slaughter: Number (Millions)	Average Weight (Pounds)	Liveweight Pounds (Mil. Lbs.)	Certified RTC Weight (Mil. Lbs.)	Total Production RTC[3] (Mil. Lbs.)	Per Capita Consumption RTC Basis (Pounds)	Prices: Farm (Cents per Pound)	Georgia Dock[4] (Cents per Pound)
1993	6,681	4.56	30,474	22,178	22,015	77.7	34.40	53.65
1994	7,270	4.64	33,595	23,846	23,666	79.4	35.06	54.40
1995	7,371	4.66	34,348	25,021	24,827	79.2	34.68	54.73
1996	7,546	4.78	36,034	36,336	26,124	81.4	38.67	61.09
1997[1]	7,714	4.81	39,098	27,271	27,041	83.7	37.35	59.96
1998[2]	7,797	4.86	37,923	28,207	27,964	85.1	39.73	61.97
I	1,917	4.86	9,316	6,832	6,773	20.4	34.23	54.89
II	1,948	4.86	9,470	7,125	7,064	22.0	37.90	58.43
III	1,999	4.76	9,550	7,150	7,088	21.7	45.33	68.56
IV	1,932	4.96	9,587	7,100	7,039	21.0	41.47	65.99

[1] Preliminary. [2] Estimate. [3] Total production equals federally inspected slaughter plus other slaughter minus cut-up and futher processing condemnation. [4] Ready-to-cook-basis. *Source: Economic Research Service, U.S. Department of Agriculture (ERS-USDA)*

Salient Statistics of Broilers in the United States

Year	Commercial Production: Number (Millions)	Commercial Production: Liveweight (Mil. Lbs.)	Average Liveweight Per Bird (Pounds)	Average Price (¢/Pound)	Value of Production (Mil. $)	Total Chickens[3] Production: Federally Inspected (Mil. Lbs.)	Other Chickens (Mil. Lbs.)	Total (Mil. Lbs.)	Storage Stocks January 1 (Mil. Lbs.)	Exports (Mil. Lbs.)	Broiler Feed Ratio in Pounds	Consumption: Total (Mil. Lbs.)	Per Capita[4] (in Lbs.)
1992	6,402	28,829	4.51	31.8	9,174	21,052	36	21,088	300	1,489	5.1	19,347	66.57
1993	6,694	30,618	4.56	34.0	10,417	22,178	36	22,015	368	1,966	5.3	20,059	68.50
1994	7,018	32,529	4.64	35.0	11,372	23,846	38	23,666	358	2,876	5.2	20,690	69.50
1995	7,326	34,222	4.66	34.4	11,762	25,021	39	24,827	458	3,894	5.2	20,832	68.80
1996	7,598	36,483	4.80	38.1	13,905	26,336	38	26,124	560	4,420	4.5	21,626	70.80
1997[1]	7,760	37,523	4.84	37.7	14,153	27,281	39	27,055	641	4,664	5.1	22,421	72.70
1998[2]						29,200	42	28,953	607	4,900		24,081	77.40

[1] Preliminary. [2] Estimate. [3] Ready-to-cook. [4] Retail weight basis. *Source: Economic Research Service, U.S. Department of Agriculture (ERS-USDA)*

Average Wholesale Broiler[1] Prices RTC (Ready-to-Cook) In Cents Per Pound

Year	Jan.	Feb.	Mar.	Apr.	May	June	July	Aug.	Sept.	Oct.	Nov.	Dec.	Average
1992	50.14	50.28	50.24	49.45	55.06	52.38	56.04	56.13	51.29	53.67	54.98	51.17	52.57
1993	52.14	53.01	54.02	54.66	57.86	55.04	55.36	57.77	57.59	55.72	55.82	53.17	55.18
1994	52.67	55.22	57.56	57.80	61.39	60.71	57.36	54.65	55.80	54.02	50.50	50.87	55.71
1995	51.14	51.73	52.32	51.51	52.94	55.88	58.76	61.74	61.48	58.79	61.08	58.87	56.35
1996	59.00	55.31	54.31	56.01	61.71	65.52	64.58	64.07	64.01	62.64	64.37	63.50	61.25
1997	61.99	59.53	58.41	59.77	58.53	59.05	63.04	63.25	59.86	55.39	54.62	52.25	58.81
1998[2]	54.66	56.40	58.10	58.52	60.08	64.26	68.53	72.13	70.53	68.04	64.13	60.45	62.99

[1] 12-city composite wholesale price. [1] Preliminary. *Source: Economic Research Service, U.S. Department of Agriculture (ERS-USDA)*

Butter

1998 U.S. butter production fell to a ten-year low continuing the well entrenched downtrend in the domestic milk-cow inventory. The U.S. produced 505,000 metric tonnes in 1998 vs. 522,000 tonnes in 1997 and the 1992 record high of 616,000 tonnes. 1998 U.S. butter consumption of 506,000 tonnes was unchanged from 1997. The 1998 supply/demand balance was the first time since the late 1980's that production failed to top demand.

There is a production seasonality: January is generally the highest producing month and August the lowest. Total U.S. butter stocks, much of which were once government owned when production was subsidized, dropped sharply during the 1990's; from a high at yearend 1991 of 249,000 tonnes to 8,000 at yearend 1995. Annual U.S. per capita butter use has averaged about 4.4 pounds since the mid-1990's, slightly under the late 1980's average.

Butter production is derived directly from milk production. Butter manufacture is the third largest use of milk production, the first being milk as a fluid and then its conversion into cheese. California is the largest producing state with one third of U.S. production, followed by Wisconsin.

World butter production in 1998 of 5.2 million metric tonnes compares with 5.1 million in 1997 and a 1993-97 average of 5.2 million tonnes. A combined Russia and the Ukraine were once the world's largest producers with 1,044,000 tonnes in 1993, but their year-to-year-totals have since dropped sharply with only 360,000 tonnes in 1998 vs. 370,000 in 1997. The U.S. generally produces 10 percent of the world total. India is the largest producer with a record 1.54 million tonnes in 1998 vs. 1.47 million in 1997, but their product is mostly Ghee, a butterlike substance consumed almost entirely in India. Other than India, there are very few countries that have shown any increase in butter production in recent years.

World consumption mirrors production: India is first, Russia and the Ukraine's use of 580,000 tonnes in 1998 is nearly half of their consumption earlier in the 1990's. Germany's usage of 580,000 tonnes in 1998 is their norm of the past few years; consumption in France of 525,000 tonnes compares with less that 500,000 before 1995.

Global foreign trade in butter is small. U.S. imports are generally insignificant, but rose to 10,000 tonnes in 1998, twice that of 1996 and 1997. U.S. exports have been trending down, from 145,000 tonnes in 1993 to only 10,000 tonnes in 1998. New Zealand was 1998's largest exporter with 305,000 tonnes, 41 percent of the world total. Russia was 1998's largest importer with 275,000 tonnes, 58 percent of the world total. World stocks continue to slide, with 418,000 tonnes at yearend 1998 vs. 459,000 tonnes a year earlier, and ending stocks over 800,000 in the early 1990's.

The 1998 price outlook for butterfat (82 percent--unsalted) suggested a well balanced market with firm prices. The reasons were twofold: E.U. exportable supplies were expected to be low and stocks of non-government butter were relatively tight. Butter prices, basis North Europe FOB, rose from $1,750 per ton at the start of 1997 to $2,200 by yearend and averaged $1,900 during the first half of 1998. U.S. wholesale prices also firmed during 1997, from $1,990 per ton (Chicago--AA-salted) to $2,870 at yearend, and soared to $4,563 by July, 1998; equivalent to about $1.11 on a per pound basis, and a retail price of $3.00 per pound; in a price surge reflecting the national shortage of butterfat.

Supply and Distribution of Butter in the United States   In Millions of Pounds

	Supply				Distribution							93 Score AA Wholesale Price	
					Domestic Disapearrance			Department of Agriculture					
Year	Production	Cold Storage Stocks[3] Jan. 1[6]	Imports	Total Supply	Total	Per Capita (Pounds)	Exports	Jan 1. Stocks[5]	Dec. 31 Stocks[5]	Removed by USDA Programs	Total Use	California ($ per Pound)	Chicago ($ per Pound)
1988	1,208	143	5.328	1,359	1,131	4.5	15	96	173	312.6	1,147	1.6097	1.3412
1989	1,295	215	4.621	1,515	1,127	4.4	112	173	223	413.4	1,243	1.5660	1.2951
1990	1,302	256	4.798	1,582	1,039	4.4	126	223	373	400.3	1,167	1.3050	1.0346
1991	1,336	416	4.740	1,759	1,181	4.4	26	373	511	442.8	1,208	1.2856	1.0182
1992	1,365	539	4.153	1,919	1,323	4.4	142	511	430	439.5	1,466	1.1386	.8427
1993	1,315	448	4.374	1,774	1,327	4.7	204	430	229	288.8	1,532	1.0612	.7693
1994	1,296	244	3.340	1,543	1,463	4.8	101	229	67	204.3	1,464	.9581	.7068
1995	1,264	80	1.536	1,340	1,329	4.5	141	67	----	78.5	----	----	.8188
1996[1]	1,174	19	2.205	1,175	1,182	4.3	42	----	----	0	----	----	1.0824
1997[2]	1,152	14	8.818	1,151	112	4.1	51	----	----	1	----	----	1.0710

[1] Preliminary. [2] Estimates. [3] Includes butter equivalent. [4] Includes USDA shipments to territories. [5] Includes butteroil. [6] Includes stocks held by USDA.
Source: Economic Research Service, U.S. Department of Agriculture (ERS-USDA)

Commercial Disappearance of Creamery Butter in the United States   In Millions of Pounds

Year	First Quarter	Second Quarter	Third Quarter	Fourth Quarter	Total	Year	First Quarter	Second Quarter	Third Quarter	Fourth Quarter	Total
1987	222.7	222.1	218.4	239.3	902.5	1993	224.6	231.5	271.9	312.7	1,040.6
1988	194.5	221.6	219.7	274.0	909.8	1994	261.7	254.9	285.0	298.3	1,097.3
1989	188.3	145.6	228.8	291.3	854.1	1995	335.7	269.0	261.2	304.9	1,186.0
1990	197.5	218.1	218.1	281.8	915.2	1996	325.6	301.8	237.5	310.3	1,180.0
1991	186.8	184.0	255.6	276.5	903.5	1997	302.7	250.7	265.8	287.6	1,109.0
1992	214.6	216.6	236.8	276.2	944.3	1998[1]	280.1	269.6	252.0	283.7	1,085.4

[1] Preliminary. *Source: Economic Research Service, U.S. Department of Agriculture (ERS-USDA)*

World (Total) Butter[3] Production In Thousands of Metric Tons

Year	Australia	Canada	France	Germany[4]	India	Ireland	Netherland	New Zealand	Poland	Russia[5]	Ukraine[5]	U.K.	United States
1988	98	105	521	585	850	139	214	276	293	----	1,724	140	547
1989	96	99	525	711	880	156	213	246	325	820	441	130	588
1990	111	100	514	640	970	159	209	276	300	833	444	138	591
1991	111	97	496	555	1,020	146	196	269	220	729	376	132	606
1992	116	86	454	474	1,060	142	191	268	180	762	303	127	619
1993	131	83	444	480	1,110	135	184	276	180	732	312	152	596
1994	147	88	444	461	1,200	136	159	297	160	488	254	154	588
1995	138	93	453	486	1,300	150	132	280	163	419	219	130	573
1996	153	93	462	480	1,400	150	122	309	160	290	163	129	533
1997[1]	147	90	466	462	1,470	148	129	320	178	280	109	134	522
1998[2]	154	86	465	450	1,600	145	140	343	180	300	110	138	480

[1] Preliminary. [2] Forecast. [3] Factory (including creameries and dairies) and farm. [4] Includes the former East Germany after 1988. [5] Formerly part of the U.S.S.R.; data not reported seperately until 1989. *Source: Foreign Agricultural Service, U.S. Department of Agriculture (FAS-USDA)*

Production of Creamery Butter in Factories in the United States In Millions of Pounds

Year	Jan.	Feb.	Mar.	Apr.	May	June	July	Aug.	Sept.	Oct.	Nov.	Dec.	Total
1988	126.1	119.7	115.5	113.8	108.0	90.8	76.3	74.1	83.3	92.3	95.6	112.0	1,207.5
1989	129.0	124.7	135.7	124.7	122.5	95.3	72.2	80.1	81.6	95.1	94.4	107.4	1,262.7
1990	134.0	127.3	136.2	125.6	118.6	96.7	84.6	84.2	83.4	106.7	110.1	112.2	1,319.6
1991	142.1	126.3	131.6	133.7	126.0	98.3	88.9	85.0	84.7	105.2	108.5	130.1	1,360.4
1992	156.0	132.0	129.9	119.7	118.2	103.0	97.8	86.7	96.6	101.6	98.3	119.8	1,365.2
1993	147.3	127.2	131.6	121.8	116.4	102.3	86.2	80.7	86.3	97.8	97.3	120.3	1,315.2
1994	135.3	118.4	118.0	119.4	118.2	99.2	84.2	88.2	91.2	101.8	100.7	121.4	1,295.9
1995	135.6	121.7	127.3	120.6	119.4	98.4	85.0	76.0	80.2	93.5	90.5	112.4	1,260.7
1996	132.4	114.7	111.9	109.3	100.9	72.7	75.2	73.2	80.7	96.6	95.3	111.3	1,174.5
1997[1]	127.6	108.6	105.4	118.3	102.7	82.0	80.0	68.8	79.3	83.3	89.1	106.0	1,151.3
1998[2]	113.5	102.7	100.8	103.0	92.9	72.6	67.1	61.5	67.1	83.2	87.2	101.6	1,053.4

[1] Preliminary. [2] Estimate. *Source: Economic Research Service, U.S. Department of Agriculture (ERS-USDA)*

Cold Storage Holdings of Creamery Butter on First of Month in the United States In Millions of Pounds

Year	Jan.	Feb.	Mar.	Apr.	May	June	July	Aug.	Sept.	Oct.	Nov.	Dec.
1988	143.2	157.3	198.9	221.1	240.4	280.5	293.4	295.8	294.4	253.4	237.3	226.2
1989	214.7	246.6	314.4	341.9	377.2	438.3	464.1	461.3	439.7	407.9	370.6	294.1
1990	256.2	269.7	293.8	335.4	358.8	399.6	420.0	420.8	427.9	412.3	413.6	407.6
1991	416.1	470.8	524.8	555.9	620.5	646.7	662.7	659.8	629.4	597.2	567.1	539.4
1992	539.4	565.4	624.8	645.3	678.7	712.6	747.0	755.8	705.7	608.1	541.7	487.6
1993	447.7	489.1	492.5	515.6	552.7	559.0	569.0	516.4	473.3	395.4	341.1	276.3
1994	234.7	251.0	243.2	253.5	265.7	281.4	275.1	245.9	206.6	163.4	124.6	84.5
1995	79.5	89.9	88.3	74.8	79.1	81.3	79.2	68.3	50.2	32.8	23.6	15.7
1996	18.6	25.5	33.7	48.7	39.8	34.0	29.7	31.7	27.3	21.4	20.5	17.6
1997	13.7	23.2	36.0	50.3	86.8	104.2	93.7	85.6	69.5	43.9	26.6	15.4
1998[1]	20.8	34.2	44.2	55.9	67.4	72.7	60.6	51.0	41.1	34.1	31.2	28.7

[1] Preliminary. *Source: Agricultural Statistics Board, U.S.Department of Agriculture (ASB-USDA)*

Wholesale Price of 92 Score Creamery (Grade A) Butter, Central States[1] In Cents Per Pound

Year	Jan.	Feb.	March	April	May	June	July	Aug.	Sept.	Oct.	Nov.	Dec.	Average
1988	131.9	131.0	131.0	131.0	131.0	133.5	135.9	135.6	134.3	132.0	131.3	131.3	132.5
1989	131.0	131.0	131.0	131.0	131.0	131.0	130.3	132.8	125.1	120.5	120.5	120.0	127.9
1990	110.9	108.3	108.3	106.9	99.0	98.4	100.3	98.9	98.9	98.9	98.9	98.0	102.1
1991	97.3	97.3	97.3	97.3	97.3	98.6	98.9	98.9	100.7	106.3	104.6	98.4	99.3
1992	94.9	86.3	86.3	86.3	83.8	76.6	76.6	76.6	81.7	82.2	80.7	78.6	82.5
1993	75.3	75.3	75.3	75.3	75.3	76.2	73.5	74.6	74.3	74.2	73.6	69.7	74.4
1994	64.0	64.0	65.5	65.5	64.5	65.1	66.9	71.5	71.5	71.5	71.5	67.0	67.4
1995	64.0	65.5	66.5	66.5	66.5	69.9	74.5	79.5	80.9	95.4	103.5	74.4	75.6
1996	75.4	66.4	65.5	69.0	87.8	129.3	145.3	145.5	145.5	128.6	74.1	71.9	100.4
1997	81.9	98.4	106.3	95.6	86.1	105.5	102.7	102.5	101.6	135.3	148.8	120.1	107.1
1998	109.2	139.8	134.1	136.4	153.2	186.7	203.1	216.6	273.1	242.3	187.9	140.8	176.9

[1] Data Prior to June 1998 are for Grade AA in Chicago. *Source: Economic Research Service, U.S. Department of Agriculture (ERS-USDA)*

Cadmium

Cadmium is a rare chemical element that is the by-product of the smelting and refining of zinc ores. It is used primarily for the plating of iron and steel to protect them from corrosion. Due to the cost of waste disposal and assorted problems with its toxicity, the use of electroplating has decreased. Cadmium is highly toxic and its disposal represents a problem for users.

The U.S. Geological Survey reported that in 1997, two companies produced primary cadmium in the United States. These companies recovered cadmium as a by-product of the smelting and refining of zinc concentrates. A third company recovered cadmium from used nickel-cadmium batteries. Cadmium recycling has been practical only from nickel-cadmium batteries, some alloys, and dust from electric-arc furnaces. The estimated consumption pattern in the U.S. is batteries, 67 percent; pigments, 14 percent; coatings and plating, 8 percent; stabilizers for the manufacture of plastics and similar synthetic products, 8 percent; nonferrous alloys, 2 percent; and other, including electro-optics, 1 percent.

The United States was a net importer of cadmium metal in 1997. Over half of total U.S. imports came from Canada followed by Mexico, Germany and Australia. In 1997, the U.S. was a net exporter of cadmium sulfide, most of which went to Canada, Colombia and Australia.

U.S. production of cadmium metal in 1997 was 2,060 metric tonnes (cadmium content). This was 35 percent more than in 1996. 1997 production of cadmium sulfide, including cadmium lithopone and cadmium sulfoselenide, was 113 tonnes, down 5 percent from 1996. 1997 production of other cadmium compounds, including plating salts and oxides, was 607 tonnes, down 16 percent from 1996. Shipments of cadmium metal by producers in 1997 were 1,370 tonnes, up 5 percent from 1996.

U.S. exports of cadmium metal in 1997 were 554 tonnes, an increase of 176 percent from the previous year. The major export destination was Japan with 249 tonnes followed by France with 116 tonnes. U.S. exports of cadmium sulfide (gross weight) in 1997 were 399 tonnes, down 50 percent from the previous year. The major export destination was Canada with 375 tonnes.

U.S. imports for consumption of cadmium metal in 1997 were 790 tonnes, down 6 percent from 1996. The major supplier was Canada with 436 tonnes followed by Mexico with 104 tonnes. Imports for consumption of cadmium sulfide (gross weight) were 40.1 tonnes, substantially above the 13.6 tonnes of 1996. The major supplier was the United Kingdom.

Industry stocks of cadmium metal on December 31, 1997 were 1,090 tonnes. That was 4 percent less than the year before. U.S. apparent consumption of cadmium metal in 1997 was 2,510 tonnes, an increase of almost 12 percent from 1996.

World Refinery Production of Cadmium In Metric Tons

Year	Australia	Belgium	Canada	China	Finland	Germany	Italy	Japan	Kazakhstan[4]	Mexico	United Kingdom	United States[3]	World Total
1988	855	1,836	1,694	750	703	1,186	686	2,614	3,000	1,117	399	1,885	21,869
1989	696	1,764	1,620	800	612	1,234	776	2,694	3,000	976	395	1,550	20,873
1990	638	1,960	1,470	1,100	569	990	691	2,450	2,800	882	438	1,680	20,200
1991	1,076	1,807	1,829	1,200	593	1,048	658	2,889	2,500	688	449	1,680	20,900
1992	1,001	1,550	1,963	1,150	590	961	742	2,986	1,000	602	383	1,620	19,600
1993	951	1,573	1,944	1,160	785	1,056	517	2,832	1,000	797	458	1,090	19,000
1994	910	1,556	2,173	1,280	548	1,145	475	2,629	1,100	646	469	1,010	18,200
1995	838	1,710	2,349	1,450	539	1,150	308	2,652	1,209	689	549	1,270	20,000
1996[1]	639	1,580	2,537	1,570	648	1,150	296	2,343	1,200	784	541	1,530	19,200
1997[2]	632	1,600	1,320	1,600	650	1,140	300	2,460	1,200	800	500	2,060	18,900

[1] Preliminary. [2] Estimate. [3] Primary and secondary metal. [4] Formerly part of the U.S.S.R.; data not reported separately until 1992.
Source: U.S. Geological Survey (USGS)

Salient Statistics of Cadmium in the United States In Metric Tons of Contained Cadmium

Year	Net Import Reliance as a % of Apparent Consumption	Production (Metal)	Producer Shipments	Cadmium Sulfide Production	Production Other Compounds	Imports of Cadmium Metal[3]	Exports[4]	Apparent Consumption	Industry Stocks Dec. 31[5]	N.Y. Dealer Price $ per Pound[6]
1988	59	1,885	2,074	345	1,451	2,482	613	3,620	854	6.91
1989	62	1,550	2,015	267	1,451	2,787	369	4,096	726	6.28
1990	55	1,680	1,860	228	1,144	1,740	385	2,800	653	3.38
1991	58	1,680	1,740	263	1,089	2,040	448	3,080	835	2.01
1992	55	1,620	2,080	270	1,073	1,960	213	3,330	868	.91
1993	64	1,090	1,320	303	731	1,420	38	2,940	579	.45
1994	3	1,010	1,290	170	898	1,110	1,450	1,040	423	1.13
1995	E	1,270	1,280	105	936	848	1,050	1,160	543	1.84
1996[1]	32	1,530	1,310	119	720	843	201	2,250	693	1.24
1997[2]	33	2,060	1,370	113	607	790	554	2,510	990	.51

[1] Preliminary. [2] Estimate. [3] For Consumption. [4] Cadmium Metal, alloys, dross, flue dust. [5] Metallic, Compounds, Distributors (including in compounds from 1985). [6] Sticks and Balls in 1 to 5 short ton lots. E = Net exporter. *Source: U.S. Geological Survey (USGS)*

Canola (Rapeseed)

The steady increase during the 1990's in world canola (rapeseed) production carried to a record high in 1998/99. Canola pushed into second place, besting cottonseed for the first time in crop size. Production, however, remains only 20 percent that of soybeans. An estimated 36.6 million metric tonnes were produced in 1998/99 vs. 34.3 million in 1997/98. In the mid 1980's production averaged 17 million tonnes. On a protein meal basis, rapeseed is the world's second largest crop, production of which totaled 20 million tonnes in 1998/99 vs. 19.1 million in 1997/98; but for oil, rapeseed ranks after soybean and palm with production of 12.3 million tonnes in 1998/99 vs. 11.7 million in 1997/98. Total rapeseed 1998/99 world supplies of 37.4 million tonnes compare with 35.3 million in 1997/98. The estimated world 1998/99 (July/June) crush of a record 33.2 million tonnes compares with the previous year's 31.5 million tonnes.

Projections for the 1998/99 supply reflect strong world prices due to increased demand for vegetable oil. This triggered an 8 percent rise in rapeseed plantings from 1997/98 to a record 25.2 million hectares. Major acreage expansion occurred in Australia, Canada, the E.U. and China.

China produces about a third of total world production, but poor weather trimmed yields in 1998/99, and despite more planted acreage the crop fell to 8.3 million tonnes from the 1997/98 record 9.6 million. Canada and India produced more than 7 and 6 million tonnes, respectively, in 1998/99. Collectively, the European Union (EU-15) was the largest producing area with 9.5 million tonnes in 1998/99 vs. 8.6 million in 1997/98. E.U. rapeseed production, with Germany the largest producer, is now more than twice that of the region's second largest oilseed crop--sunflowerseed. In terms of protein meal consumption E.U. rapeseed usage, at 5.5 million tonnes in 1998/99 vs. 5 million in 1997/98, is about one-fifth that of soybean meal. E.U. rapeseed oil usage, however, tops soybean oil use with 2.7 million tonnes in 1998/99 vs. 1.9 million in 1997/98. Foreign trade in canola is second only to soybeans. World exports totaled 7.4 million tonnes in 1998/99, up from 6.5 million in 1997/98.

U.S. production of canola seed is small but growing steadily. 1.4 billion pounds were produced in 1998/99 (June/May) vs. 914 million in 1997/98. The crop is grown mostly in the Northern Plains states. U.S. production fails to cover disappearance (80 percent is domestic crush), estimated at 1.9 billion pounds in 1998/99 vs. 1.7 billion in 1997/98, and less than 1.1 billion in the early 1990's. Canola seed imports from Canada bridge the domestic shortage. Imports of 606 million pounds in 1998/99 compare with 782 million in 1997/98. The U.S. also exports canola seed.

Production of canola oil in 1998/99 (October/September) was forecast at a record large 561 million pounds vs. the previous record of 485 million in 1997/98. Oil imports, however, mostly from Canada, of a record large 1.3 billion pounds compares with 1.1 billion in 1997/98. At the turn of the 1990's oil production totaled about 50 million pounds and imports about 500 million pounds. Domestic oil demand was forecast at a record high 1.5 billion pounds in 1998/99 vs. 1.3 billion in 1998/98. The oil carryover tends to be small at around 75 million pounds. Canola meal production of 444,000 tonnes in 1998/99 compares with 383,000 tonnes in 1997/98, but imports were a record large 1.5 million tonnes vs. 1.4 million in 1997/98.

Contributing to the sharp gains in U.S. canola supply/demand data since the mid-1980's include (1) government enticements to increase canola acreage, (2) development of low-erucic canola varieties that can be grown in the U.S., and (3) the wider acceptance of canola oil in cooking due to its lower content of saturated fats. Canola oil is said to be about 94 percent saturated fat free, the lowest of any leading vegetable oil. Demand for canola meal has also grown impressively as a livestock feed; domestic usage of meal in 1998/99 of a record high 1.5 million short tonnes compares with 1.3 million in 1997/98.

The U.S. canola oil price was forecast at $.285-.305 per pound in 1998/99 vs. $.286 in 1997/98, while meal's price of $80 to $95 per short ton compares with $126, respectively.

Futures Market

Canola futures and options are traded on the Winnipeg Commodity Exchange (WCE) and quoted in Canadian dollars per ton. Rapeseed futures are traded on the Marche a Terme International de France (MATIF).

World Production of Canola (Rapeseed) In Thousands of Metric Tons

Year	Australia	Canada	China	Czecho-slovakia	France	Germany	India	Pakistan	Poland	Sweden	United Kingdom	former U.S.S.R.	World Total
1987-8	66	3,847	6,605	337	2,645	1,723	3,455	204	1,192	250	1,353	296	23,435
1988-9	58	4,218	5,044	380	2,303	1,642	4,377	249	1,199	250	1,040	420	22,646
1989-90	78	3,209	5,436	387	1,748	1,908	4,125	233	1,586	370	976	424	22,096
1990-1	98	3,266	6,958	380	1,926	2,155	5,152	228	1,206	367	1,258	506	25,321
1991-2	170	4,224	7,436	446	2,270	3,030	5,863	219	1,043	252	1,308	409	28,489
1992-3	179	3,872	7,653	430	1,810	2,617	4,872	207	758	247	1,159	388	25,588
1993-4	294	5,480	6,939	466	1,550	2,848	5,390	215	594	313	1,256	325	27,039
1994-5	309	7,228	7,492	452	1,800	2,896	5,884	312	756	214	1,254	363	30,626
1995-6	584	6,436	9,777	662	2,782	3,103	6,071	385	1,377	216	1,235	415	34,919
1996-7[1]	641	5,062	9,201	531	2,902	2,150	6,300	410	449	143	1,410	214	30,974
1997-8[2]	861	6,393	9,578	561	3,496	2,867	4,800	435	595	132	1,523	236	33,336
1998-9[3]	1,588	7,588	8,200	698	3,736	3,334	6,100		1,075	1,290	1,564	324	36,972

[1] Preliminary. [2] Estimate. [3] Forecast. *Source: The Oil World*

Canola

Volume of Trading of Canola Futures in Winnipeg In Contracts

Year	Jan.	Feb.	Mar.	Apr.	May	June	July	Aug.	Sept.	Oct.	Nov.	Dec.	Total
1989	53,322	62,513	53,926	53,143	80,411	62,378	52,661	51,673	50,701	76,917	76,173	50,947	724,765
1990	52,473	66,423	52,720	55,158	82,685	53,085	51,270	61,642	56,933	57,302	49,450	58,994	698,135
1991	67,489	59,380	64,193	67,572	68,849	59,270	90,575	65,541	76,966	75,457	53,660	66,421	815,373
1992	57,429	54,546	57,174	38,674	87,638	75,018	50,157	72,971	79,034	93,692	99,577	73,805	839,715
1993	73,411	74,362	63,737	73,358	61,996	70,117	94,286	77,325	56,377	73,953	107,485	112,377	938,784
1994	119,691	103,517	85,125	100,923	111,962	79,307	83,903	95,712	54,893	87,350	101,727	96,797	1,120,907
1995	75,068	87,113	86,340	67,937	95,447	85,126	94,576	70,904	94,794	126,210	84,991	107,177	1,075,683
1996	99,542	95,034	76,704	128,169	148,189	103,892	135,652	87,896	108,490	161,894	90,105	110,453	1,346,020
1997	121,433	133,056	131,473	148,647	117,219	116,117	80,867	72,602	93,967	150,065	97,984	124,245	1,387,675
1998	100,926	144,309	110,708	140,789	130,551	121,829	107,816	89,457	121,573	181,002	127,120	181,278	1,557,358

Source: Winnipeg Commodity Exchange (WCE)

Average Open Interest of Canola Futures in Winnipeg In Contracts

Year	Jan.	Feb.	Mar.	Apr.	May	June	July	Aug.	Sept.	Oct.	Nov.	Dec.
1989	22,435	20,889	18,591	22,690	24,587	21,025	22,280	22,027	16,153	21,556	20,981	21,749
1990	18,431	20,340	17,599	19,825	24,718	22,546	23,073	24,353	24,872	25,688	18,706	22,057
1991	22,000	22,829	24,815	26,637	30,072	28,240	28,288	27,547	27,558	29,079	23,880	20,117
1992	15,943	17,556	20,559	21,410	23,727	28,885	26,013	25,674	28,049	32,724	35,693	37,375
1993	34,098	37,658	36,715	38,210	38,231	29,743	39,763	43,844	50,616	55,107	54,998	54,475
1994	50,335	55,280	54,899	58,012	60,567	55,434	54,733	57,044	57,049	54,375	55,045	49,475
1995	47,579	43,662	36,530	32,580	38,361	42,961	43,607	42,828	51,067	57,638	46,640	45,444
1996	42,646	43,808	45,126	47,989	54,228	52,176	49,387	40,619	42,242	52,273	53,121	54,323
1997	48,681	48,281	50,815	50,025	49,212	43,941	35,496	30,039	25,255	36,674	38,702	42,510
1998	35,864	46,678	49,161	48,683	56,163	60,285	57,627	51,462	53,919	56,651	51,426	60,663

Source: Winnipeg Commodity Exchange (WCE)

World Supply and Distribution of Canola and Products In Thousands of Metric Tons

Crop Year	Canola: Production	Canola: Exports	Canola: Imports	Canola: Crush	Canola: Ending Stocks	Canola Meal: Production	Canola Meal: Exports	Canola Meal: Imports	Canola Meal: Consumption	Canola Meal: Ending Stocks	Canola Oil: Production	Canola Oil: Exports	Canola Oil: Imports	Canola Oil: Consumption	Canola Oil: Ending Stocks
1989-90	22,096	2,831	2,891	21,075	3,240	12,709	1,681	1,773	12,721	160	7,944	1,624	1,730	8,000	743
1990-1	25,321	2,433	2,474	23,318	3,130	14,083	1,950	1,877	14,056	114	8,786	1,577	1,550	8,697	781
1991-2	28,489	2,674	2,645	25,111	3,700	15,203	2,527	2,507	15,169	128	9,469	1,529	1,633	9,518	836
1992-3	25,588	3,058	3,003	23,634	780	14,304	2,705	2,626	14,206	147	8,990	1,129	1,134	9,120	742
1993-4	27,039	4,150	4,087	25,270	790	15,151	2,623	2,736	15,287	124	9,726	1,590	1,527	9,532	849
1994-5	30,626	4,506	4,579	27,511	1,040	16,519	2,630	2,558	16,405	167	10,648	2,038	2,052	10,276	1,236
1995-6	34,919	4,270	4,265	30,382	1,120	18,302	3,011	2,999	18,264	192	11,729	1,894	1,938	11,685	1,283
1996-7[1]	30,974	3,725	3,730	29,103		17,905	2,891	2,975	17,942	239	11,482	1,789	1,680	11,591	1,070
1997-8[2]	33,336	4,319	4,300	31,411		19,020	2,860	2,915	19,092	222	12,232	2,084	2,153	12,315	1,057
1998-9[3]	36,972	6,250	6,220	32,942		20,133	3,175	3,145	20,100	225	12,987	2,270	2,300	12,974	1,100

[1] Preliminary. [2] Estimate. [3] Forecast. *Source: The Oil World*

Salient Statistics of Canola and Canola Oil in the United States In Millions of Pounds

Crop Year Beginning June 1	Canola Supply: Stocks June 1	Canola Supply: Production	Canola Supply: Imports	Canola Supply: Total	Canola Disappearance: Crush	Canola Disappearance: Exports	Canola Disappearance: Total[3]	Canola Oil Supply: Stocks June 1	Canola Oil Supply: Production	Canola Oil Supply: Imports	Canola Oil Supply: Total	Canola Oil Disappearance: Domestic	Canola Oil Disappearance: Exports	Canola Oil Disappearance: Total
1989-90	3	95	231	329	298	10	308	20	130	391	541	510	6	516
1990-1	21	97	141	259	195	32	227	24	18	583	625	577	7	584
1991-2	32	191	2	225	109	97	212	41	32	815	888	801	15	816
1992-3	13	144	27	184	59	104	174	71	49	861	981	898	16	914
1993-4	10	252	773	1,036	850	78	941	67	406	902	1,375	1,228	76	1,304
1994-5	95	447	630	1,173	899	227	1,139	137	299	938	1,374	1,165	153	1,318
1995-6	34	548	558	1,140	899	138	1,052	54	355	1,086	1,496	1,270	147	1,417
1996-7	88	479	570	1,137	866	173	1,057	79	341	1,075	1,493	1,136	293	1,429
1997-8[1]	80	914	782	1,776	1,427	277	1,734	66	485	1,088	1,638	1,177	349	1,526
1998-9[2]	42	1,433	606	2,081	1,551	386	1,972	112	561	1,212	1,885	1,400	375	1,775

[1] Preliminary. [2] Estimate. [3] Forecast. *Source: Economic Research Service, U.S. Department of Agriculture (ERS-USDA)*

Wholesale Price of Canola Oil, Refined (Denatured), in Tanks in New York In Cents Per Pound

Year	Jan.	Feb.	Mar.	Apr.	May	June	July	Aug.	Sept.	Oct.	Nov.	Dec.	Average
1989	70.00	70.00	80.25	80.25	80.25	80.75	80.25	80.25	80.25	80.25	80.25	80.25	78.58
1990	81.75	82.25	82.23	82.25	82.25	82.25	82.25	82.25	79.25	77.25	77.25	81.00	81.02
1991	82.25	82.25	82.25	82.25	82.25	82.25	82.25	82.25	82.25	82.25	82.25	82.25	82.25
1992	82.25	82.25	82.25	82.25	82.25	82.25	82.25	82.25	67.25	62.25	62.25	62.25	76.00
1993	62.25	62.25	62.25	62.25	55.88	53.75	53.25	53.00	53.00	52.00	52.50	50.00	56.03
1994	53.75	53.75	53.75	53.75	53.75	53.75	53.75	53.75	53.75	53.75	53.75	53.75	53.75
1995	53.75	53.75	53.75	53.75	53.15	50.75	50.75	50.75	50.75	50.75	50.75	50.75	51.95
1996	50.75	50.75	50.75	50.75	50.75	50.75	50.75	50.75	50.75	60.56	90.00	90.00	58.11
1997	90.00	90.00	90.00	90.00	90.00	90.00	90.00	90.00	90.00	82.00	82.00	82.00	88.00
1998[1]	90.00	90.00	90.00	90.00	90.00	90.00	90.00	90.00	90.00				90.00

[1] Preliminary. *Source: Economic Research Service, U.S. Department of Agriculture (ERS-USDA)*

Average Price of Canola in Vancouver In Canadian Dollars Per Tonne

Year	Jan.	Feb.	Mar.	Apr.	May	June	July	Aug.	Sept.	Oct.	Nov.	Dec.	Average
1988	302.56	303.16	294.22	305.27	336.31	413.98	395.28	381.19	379.83	349.68	333.96	344.35	344.98
1989	329.54	321.64	333.29	331.44	335.18	306.10	300.49	289.44	297.10	293.79	303.10	302.54	311.97
1990	300.01	301.45	311.00	318.78	322.24	303.89	300.83	299.43	292.74	295.23	290.08	290.01	302.14
1991	285.01	280.36	291.50	298.57	293.83	277.25	258.12	269.40	275.00	270.30	262.90	261.60	276.99
1992	264.15	273.35	282.70	276.85	288.08	292.35	272.20	282.26	320.62	302.10	327.22	331.57	292.79
1993	344.22	329.26	328.67	325.06	318.85	319.23	331.29	322.85	311.29	311.66	331.44	366.37	328.35
1994	408.60	413.10	422.23	454.90	481.44	484.95	388.63	382.54	381.70	379.99	401.38	432.35	419.32
1995	431.85	440.41	456.13	425.40	404.27	414.31	426.49	405.94	405.89	413.29	416.03	423.77	421.98
1996	424.07	422.60	417.55	443.94	473.04	469.28	470.38	453.86	453.53	444.01	432.30	439.79	445.36
1997	441.96	441.68	457.95	448.09	446.00	428.47	395.58	400.68	390.38	398.81	419.12	410.21	423.24
1998	416.48	428.88	434.68	441.44	450.56	443.11	404.86	387.05	389.34	400.40	412.17	417.41	418.87

Source: Winnipeg Commodity Exchange (WCE)

Cassava

Cassava, or tapioca root, is used primarily as an animal feed and as a foodstuff in tropical countries. For sometime, cassava has been looked upon as a possible solution to world hunger problems. Technology advances have held forth the promise of increasing yields substantially. New strains of cassava root are being developed in Africa and they could eventually be used in the fight against hunger.

Cassava is grown in countries with mostly tropical climates. Production among countries in fairly well balanced. For 1996, the Food and Agricultural Organization of the United Nations reported that world production of cassava was 162.9 million metric tonnes. That represented a 1 percent decline from the previous year. In the five year period between 1992 and 1996, world production of tapioca root averaged 161.3 million tonnes.

The world's largest producer of cassava in 1996 was Nigeria with production of 31.5 million tonnes, some 19 percent of the world total. Nigerian production in 1997 was about the same as in 1996. Over the five recent years, Nigeria's production averaged 29 million tonnes per year. The next largest producer of tapioca root was Brazil. For 1996, production was 24.6 million tonnes, a decline of 3 percent from the previous year. Between 1992 and 1996, Brazilian cassava production averaged 23.6 million tonnes. The next largest producer of cassava is the Congo (formerly Zaire) with 1996 production of 18 million tonnes, up nearly 3 percent from the previous year. For the most recent five year period, the Congo's production averaged 18.9 million tonnes. Cassava production by Thailand was estimated to be 16 million tonnes in 1996, down 12 percent from the previous year. Thailand's cassava production has been trending lower. In 1992, production was over 20.3 million tonnes while in the 1992-1996 period production averaged 18.8 million tonnes. Indonesia's cassava production in 1996 was 15.4 million tonnes, unchanged from the previous season. Other large producers of cassava are Ghana, Tanzania, India, Mozambique and China.

Most cassava production is consumed in the countries in which it is produced. It is interesting to note that world trade in cassava amounts to 2 percent of production. The largest exporter of cassava is Thailand while the largest importer is the European Community.

World Cassava Production In Thousands of Metric Tons

Year	Brazil	China	Ghana	India	Indonesia	Mozambique	Nigeria	Paraguay	Tanzania	Thailand	Uganda	Zaire	World Total
1991	24,538	3,310	3,600	5,416	15,954	3,690	20,000	2,585	7,460	20,356	3,229	19,500	153,562
1992	21,919	3,357	4,000	5,469	16,516	3,239	21,320	2,591	7,112	20,356	2,896	20,210	153,058
1993	21,837	3,403	4,500	5,413	16,799	3,511	29,900	2,656	6,833	20,203	3,139	20,835	163,002
1994	24,464	3,501	6,025	5,784	15,729	3,352	31,005	2,518	7,209	19,091	2,080	18,051	163,514
1995	25,423	3,501	6,612	5,929	15,442	4,178	31,404	3,054	5,969	17,388	2,224	17,500	165,436
1996	24,584	3,501	7,111	5,979	17,003	4,734	31,418	2,649	5,992	18,084	2,245	18,000	165,650
1997[1]	24,354	3,501	6,800	5,979	16,103	5,337	30,409	3,155	6,444	18,000	2,291	——	164,751

[1] Estimate. *Source: Food and Agricultural Organization of the United Nations (FAO-UN)*

Prices of Tapioca, Hard Pellets, F.O.B. Rotterdam U.S. Dollars Per Metric Ton

Year	Jan.	Feb.	Mar.	Apr.	May	June	July	Aug.	Sept.	Oct.	Nov.	Dec.	Average
1991	187	186	163	160	168	158	158	177	187	187	202	197	178
1992	197	184	179	177	179	181	184	192	195	187	172	170	183
1993	160	150	140	149	145	133	130	131	136	127	120	125	137
1994	122	123	128	133	138	141	147	154	158	161	161	161	144
1995	164	170	180	178	174	176	183	176	178	184	182	178	177
1996	167	160	155	158	163	154	149	154	146	139	140	133	152
1997	133	118	112	108	114	110	100	97	100	102	102	100	108
1998	96	100	98	104	106	104	105	106	112	122	124	109	107

Source: The Oil World

World Trade in Tapioca In Thousands of Metric Tons

	Exports					Imports						
Year	China	Indonesia	Thailand	Viet Nam	Total World Exports	China	EC-12[2]	Japan	Rep. of Korea	United States	Former U.S.S.R.	Total World Imports
1991	410	859	6,187	3	7,571	175	5,692	162	444	127	----	7,353
1992	316	873	8,045	32	9,422	230	6,128	181	876	217	22	8,951
1993	269	936	6,707	29	8,089	149	6,449	151	658	60	8	8,417
1994	77	686	4,703	28	5,642	92	5,441	94	132	18	----	6,076
1995	10	481	3,297	1	3,865	362	2,924	16	140	----	----	3,580
1996	11	389	3,607	1	4,052	69	3,321	22	554	----	----	4,168
1997[1]	11	247	4,155	27	4,480	223	3,482	15	455	----	----	4,521

[1] Estimate. [2] Excluding trade between the EEC members. *Source: The Oil World*

Castor Beans

World production of castorseed beans in the 1997-98 season was estimated by the U.S.D.A. at 1.21 million metric tonnes, up 8 percent from the previous season. Over the last five seasons, global production of castorseed beans has been very steady averaging 1.18 million tonnes. India is by far the largest producer of castor beans with 1997-98 production estimated at 800,000 tonnes, up almost 4 percent from the previous season. India produces nearly three-quarters of the world's castor beans. Castor beans are used to produce castor oil and India is the largest exporter of castor oil. China is the next largest producer of castor beans with 1997-98 production of 220,000 tonnes, the same amount as in 1996-97. Brazil is the world's third largest producer of castor beans with production in 1997-98 estimated at 110,000 tonnes, substantially above the 48,000 tonnes of 1996-97. The other producers of castor oil are responsible for smaller amounts with the 1997-98 crop in Thailand estimated at 15,000 tonnes. Still smaller amounts are produced in Paraguay, the Philippines, Pakistan and Ecuador.

The U.S. is a major importer and user of castor oil. In the period between 1993-94 and 1996-97, imports averaged just over 59 million pounds per year. The U.S.D.A. reported that U.S. castorseed oil imports in August 1998 were 7,894 tonnes, up substantially from the previous month and some 94 percent more than a year earlier. In the October-August 1997-98 period, U.S. imports were 43,548 tonnes, up 51 percent from the comparable period of 1996-97. The value of castorseed oil imports in August 1998 were $5.7 million. In the October-August 1997-98 period the imports were valued at $32.6 million.

World Production of Castorseed Beans In Thousands of Metric Tons

Crop Year	Brazil	China	Ecuador	India	Mexico	Paraguay	Pakistan	Philippines	Sudan	Tanzania	Thailand	Former U.S.S.R.	World Total
1992-3	102	291	12	617	1	20	6	7	8	3	24	20	1,140
1993-4	45	280	13	700	1	15	7	7	6	3	22	4	1,135
1994-5	53	230	7	850	1	10	5	7	4	3	15	8	1,226
1995-6	33	165	5	930	1	9	9	7	2	3	16	3	1,214
1996-7[1]	48	220	2	770	1	8	5	7	1	2	15	3	1,115
1997-8[2]	125	180	4	800	1	9	6	7	1	3	15	3	1,188
1998-9[3]	45	210	4	900		10	7	7			15		1,241

[1] Preliminary. [2] Estimate. [3] Forecast. *Sources: Foreign Agricultural Service, U.S. Department of Agriculture (FAS-USDA); The Oil World*

Castor Oil Consumption[2] in the United States In Thousands of Pounds

Crop Year	Oct.	Nov.	Dec.	Jan.	Feb.	Mar.	Apr.	May	June	July	Aug.	Sept.	Total
1992-3	4,712	3,250	3,100	3,287	4,271	3,924	4,098	3,965	4,496	4,902	5,073	4,400	49,478
1993-4	5,046	5,649	5,092	5,510	4,982	5,766	4,548	6,335	5,258	4,603	4,929	4,543	62,261
1994-5	5,032	4,204	5,092	6,001	5,179	4,911	4,722	3,740	5,067	4,891	6,452	4,834	60,125
1995-6	5,228	5,463	6,232	5,794	6,979	5,545	3,369	5,864	5,469	5,439	4,332	3,818	63,532
1996-7	3,921	4,460	4,555	3,738	4,679	4,256	4,476	4,006	3,851	3,855	3,763	5,050	50,610
1997-8	3,276	4,353	4,367	4,409	3,035	4,389	4,218	3,645	4,651	4,350	3,489	4,210	48,392
1998-9[1]	2,348	3,579											35,562

[1] Preliminary. [2] In inedible products (Resins, Plastics, etc.). *Source: Bureau of the Census, U.S. Department of Commerce*

Castor Oil Stocks in the United States, on First of Month In Thousands of Pounds

Crop Year	Oct.	Nov.	Dec.	Jan.	Feb.	Mar.	Apr.	May	June	July	Aug.	Sept.
1992-3	7,158	5,383	5,364	4,124	10,076	13,154	19,345	14,983	17,094	24,652	20,616	25,070
1993-4	22,981	21,275	23,482	21,132	29,871	9,946	18,394	25,249	22,550	21,795	27,911	20,950
1994-5	21,066	23,484	23,357	21,132	29,245	20,986	10,387	5,492	22,765	33,557	37,542	42,516
1995-6	27,143	35,329	43,189	51,713	45,746	37,210	29,718	36,829	55,687	43,954	37,802	25,535
1996-7	23,831	38,785	41,016	31,755	23,630	15,157	7,200	24,164	14,166	27,754	17,426	20,656
1997-8	25,098	24,188	25,425	17,543	12,736	7,138	2,804	18,897	15,386	24,682	16,586	29,862
1998-9[1]	40,018	46,809	36,881									

[1] Preliminary. *Source: Bureau of the Census, U.S. Department of Commerce*

Average Wholesale Prices of Castor Oil No. 1, Brazilian Tanks in New York In Cents Per Pound

Year	Jan.	Feb.	Mar.	Apr.	May	June	July	Aug.	Sept.	Oct.	Nov.	Dec.	Average
1992	37.50	37.50	37.50	36.00	34.50	34.50	34.50	34.50	34.50	34.00	34.00	34.00	35.21
1993	34.00	32.00	32.00	32.00	37.00	37.00	37.00	37.00	38.50	41.50	44.00	44.00	37.17
1994	44.00	41.75	41.00	41.00	46.00	45.00	45.00	45.00	45.00	45.00	45.00	45.00	44.06
1995	45.00	45.00	45.00	45.00	45.00	45.00	45.00	45.00	45.00	45.00	45.00	45.00	45.00
1996	43.50	41.50	41.50	41.50	41.50	41.50	41.50	41.50	41.50	41.50	41.50	41.50	41.67
1997	41.50	41.50	41.50	41.50	41.50	41.50	41.50	41.50	41.50	41.50	41.50	41.50	41.50
1998	41.50	41.50	41.50	41.50	41.50	48.00	48.00	48.00	48.00				44.39

Source: Foreign Agricultural Service, U.S.Department of Agriculture (FAS-USDA)

Cattle and Calves

The world cattle inventory has held about unchanged during the past decade, although with a slight downward bias. The January 1, 1998 total of 1,033 million head compares with 1,038 million a year earlier and the low so far in the 1990's of 1,031 million in 1993. However, some large changes have occurred in selected areas, notably the decline in cattle numbers in the former U.S.S.R. and the increase in China. Russia's and the Ukraine's cattle inventory in early 1998 was estimated at 51 million head vs. 57 million in 1997 and 84 million in 1993. China's January 1, 1998 inventory of a record high 147 million head compares with 140 million a year earlier and around 123 million in the mid 1990's, suggesting a faster than expected year-to-year expansion. India, who holds about 25% of the world's total cattle inventory--about 278 million head--has shown little change in cattle numbers in recent years.

The U.S. cattle mid-1998 inventory of 107 million head compares with 109 million a year earlier and the lowest midyear total since 1991. As of late 1998 there was little sign that the cyclical contraction had run its course, especially since cattle prices towards yearend were running about $.05 a pound under the first half of the year. The three largest cattle inventory states are generally Texas, Kansas and Nebraska.

Despite the passing of the "mad cow" disease threat during 1998, the lingering effects of which had disrupted European trade and beef usage in 1997, the improvement in global usage in 1998 proved somewhat routine; consumption was estimated at 48.9 million tons vs. 48.1 million in 1997. European Union use in 1998 increased to 7.1 million tons from 7.0 million in 1997, and in China to 5.8 million tons from 5.3 million, respectively. However, in the former U.S.S.R., consumption fell to 4.1 million tons from 4.3 million and an annual average near 6 million tons earlier in the 1990's.

U.S. commercial cattle slaughter in 1998 (through July) of 23.9 million head compares with 21.4 million in the like 1997 period. Fed cattle slaughter in 1998 followed a fairly normal seasonal pattern, peaking in the second and third quarters. However, while 1998 witnessed record beef supplies from herd liquidation and record slaughter weights, 1999 is expected to see sharply curtailed feeder cattle supplies and lower beef production. Dressed slaughter weights in mid-1997 averaged around 700 pounds and in mid-1998 a record large 732 pounds. U.S. beef production in 1999 is forecast at 23.8 billion pounds vs. 25.8 billion in 1998 and 25.4 billion in 1997. U.S. per capita beef consumption has shown little growth in recent years as consumers opt for less red meat in their diet; per capita use in 1998 of 68.5 pounds (retail weight) compares with 66.9 pounds in 1997 and a 1999 estimate of 63.2 pounds.

U.S. beef (and veal) exports in 1998 of 2.1 billion pounds were a shade under 1997 and compare with forecasts of 2.2 billion in 1999. Typically, Japan has been the largest market for U.S. beef, but Mexico has been the most rapidly growing market recently. The economic crisis in Japan did not appear to dampen that nation's demand for U.S. beef, quite the contrary, imports were up 10% in the first five months of 1998. U.S. beef imports in 1998 of 2.6 billion pounds compare with 2.3 billion in 1997 and 2.8 billion estimated for 1999; Australia, New Zealand and Canada are the largest beef suppliers to the U.S. Live cattle are also imported from Canada and Mexico.

1998 choice steer prices, basis Nebraska, averaged $61-$65 per cwt. vs. $66.32 in 1997. Prices are forecast between $71-$76/cwt. in 1999. On the retail level, choice beef prices in mid-1998 averaged around $2.79/lb., about unchanged from a year earlier. Despite lower beef production in 1999 and predicted higher cattle prices, large supplies of competing meats will likely prevent any viable strength from taking hold in retail beef prices.

Futures Markets

Live cattle futures and options are traded on the Chicago Mercantile Exchange (CME), the Bolsa de Mercadorias & Futuros (BM&F), and the MidAmerica Commodity Exchange (MidAm). Feeder cattle futures are traded on the CME and the BM&F, and feeder cattle options are traded on the CME.

World Cattle and Buffalo Numbers as of January 1 In Thousands of Head

Year	Argentina	Australia	Brazil	China	Colombia	France	Germany	India	Mexico	Russia[3]	Ukraine[3]	United States	World Total (Mil Head)
1989	56,482	23,938	130,500	97,948	17,627	21,340	20,369	268,470	34,999	59,300	25,621	98,065	1,037
1990	56,482	24,673	140,400	100,752	16,835	21,394	20,287	270,070	31,747	58,800	25,195	95,816	1,035
1991	56,982	25,026	142,900	102,884	16,225	21,446	19,488	272,300	29,847	57,000	24,623	96,393	1,036
1992	55,229	25,857	141,800	104,592	16,008	20,970	17,134	271,200	30,232	54,677	23,728	97,556	1,032
1993	55,577	25,182	143,700	107,840	16,391	20,383	16,207	271,255	30,649	52,226	22,457	99,176	1,032
1994	54,875	25,758	144,900	113,157	16,614	20,112	15,897	272,655	30,702	48,914	21,607	100,988	1,036
1995	54,207	25,736	149,315	123,317	16,725	20,524	15,962	274,155	30,191	43,296	19,580	102,755	1,033
1996	53,569	26,500	149,228	132,058	16,768	20,662	15,890	296,462	28,140	39,700	17,526	103,487	1,065
1997	51,696	26,354	146,110	140,010	18,455	20,557	15,760	299,802	26,822	35,100	15,295	101,460	1,062
1998[1]	50,138	25,500	144,670	147,052	18,631	20,040	15,227	303,030	25,612	31,700	13,500	99,501	1,057
1999[2]	50,873	25,300	142,965		18,807	19,850	14,950	306,967	24,636	38,430	12,100	97,549	

[1] Preliminary. [2] Forecast. [3] Formerly part of the U.S.S.R.; country data not shown seperately prior to 1989. *Source: Foreign Agricultural Service, U.S. Department of Agriculture (FAS-USDA)*

Cattle Supply and Distribution in the United States In Thousands of Head

					Livestock Slaughter - Cattle and Calves							
					Commercial							
Year	Cattle & Calves on Farms January 1	Imports	Calves Born	Total Supply	Federally Inspected	Other[3]	All Commercial	Farm	Total Slaughter	Deaths on Farms	Exports	Total Disappearance
1989	96,740	1,459	38,817	139,626	35,110	980	36,089	240	36,329	4,361	169	40,859
1990	95,816	2,135	38,613	139,546	34,133	800	35,032	245	35,277	4,327	120	39,724
1991	96,393	1,939	38,583	139,861	33,285	841	34,126	242	34,368	4,247	311	38,927
1992	97,556	2,255	38,933	141,104	33,428	817	34,245	244	34,489	4,366	322	39,177
1993	99,176	2,499	39,448	142,750	33,752	767	34,519	227	34,746	4,630	153	39,529
1994	100,988	2,083	40,059	143,799	34,719	745	35,465	227	35,700	4,268	231	40,190
1995	102,755	2,694	40,264	145,713	36,128	785	36,913	387	37,300	4,400	88	41,800
1996	103,548	1,965	39,823	145,336	35,718	863	36,583	2,017	38,600	4,600	174	43,300
1997[1]	101,656	2,046	38,961	142,663	35,567	767	36,332	1,768	38,100	4,800	282	43,100
1998[2]	99,744	2,037			34,787	684	35,471				271	

[1] Preliminary. [2] Estimate. [3] Wholesale and retail. *Source: Economic Research Service, U.S. Department of Agriculture (ERS-USDA)*

Beef Supply and Utilization in the United States

		Production							Per Capita Disappearance	
Year/Quarter	Beginning Stocks	Commercial	Total	Imports	Total Supply	Exports	Ending Stocks	Total Disappearance	Carcass Weight	Retail Weight
	Million Pounds								Pounds	
1995	548	25,115	25,222	2,104	27,874	1,821	519	25,534	97.0	67.4
I	548	5,888	5,925	572	7,045	368	514	6,163	23.5	16.3
II	514	6,325	6,341	540	7,395	452	471	6,472	24.6	17.1
III	471	6,625	6,641	539	7,651	499	464	6,688	25.4	17.6
IV	464	6,277	6,315	453	7,232	502	519	6,211	23.5	16.4
1996	519	25,419	25,525	2,073	28,117	1,877	377	25,863	97.4	67.7
I	519	6,302	6,340	508	7,367	452	461	6,454	24.4	17.0
II	461	6,642	6,658	526	7,645	544	406	6,695	25.2	17.5
III	406	6,390	6,406	555	7,367	436	414	6,517	24.5	17.0
IV	414	6,084	6,121	484	7,019	445	377	6,197	23.2	16.2
1997	377	25,384	25,490	2,343	28,210	2,136	465	25,609	96.7	67.2
I	377	6,112	6,149	536	7,062	455	387	6,220	23.3	16.2
II	387	6,419	6,435	716	7,538	513	425	6,600	24.7	17.1
III	425	6,603	6,636	576	7,741	600	430	6,811	25.4	17.6
IV	430	6,258	6,187	515	7,152	568	400	6,302	23.4	16.3
1998[1]	465	25,666	24,606	2,611	28,966	2,158	465	25,536	94.5	65.7
I	465	6,215	6,087	644	7,167	500	375	6,317	23.4	16.3
II	375	6,463	6,216	682	7,316	537	316	6,451	23.9	16.6
III	316	6,638		685		563	323			
IV	323	6,350		600		558	465			
1999[2]	298	24,275		2,790		2,340				
I	298	6,150		700		595				
II		6,050		760		610				

[1] Preliminary. [2] Forecast. *Source: Economic Research Service, U.S. Department of Agriculture (ERS-USDA)*

United States Cattle on Feed in 13 States In Thousands of Head

Year/Quarter	Number on Feed[3]	Placed on Feed	Marketings	Other Disappearance	Year/Quarter	Number on Feed[3]	Placed on Feed	Marketings	Other Disappearance
1995	9,117	22,576	21,111	732	1997[1]	10,558	24,271	22,774	930
I	9,117	5,455	4,956	197	I	10,558	5,605	5,563	239
II	9,409	4,982	5,493	199	II	10,391	4,856	6,014	275
III	8,699	5,904	5,685	152	III	8,958	7,135	5,975	155
IV	8,766	6,235	4,977	184	IV	9,963	6,675	5,222	261
1996	10,346	23,210	22,085	913	1998[2]	11,155	19,472	18,885	712
I	10,346	5,210	5,531	213	I	11,155	4,927	5,713	262
II	9,812	4,226	5,937	261	II	10,107	1,563	2,033	72
III	7,840	6,664	5,481	182	III	9,161	6,606	5,857	163
IV	8,841	7,050	5,076	257	IV	9,747	6,376	5,282	215

[1] Preliminary. [2] Estimate. [3] Beginning of Period. *Source: Economic Research Service, U.S.Department of Agriculture (ERS-USDA)*

CATTLE AND CALVES

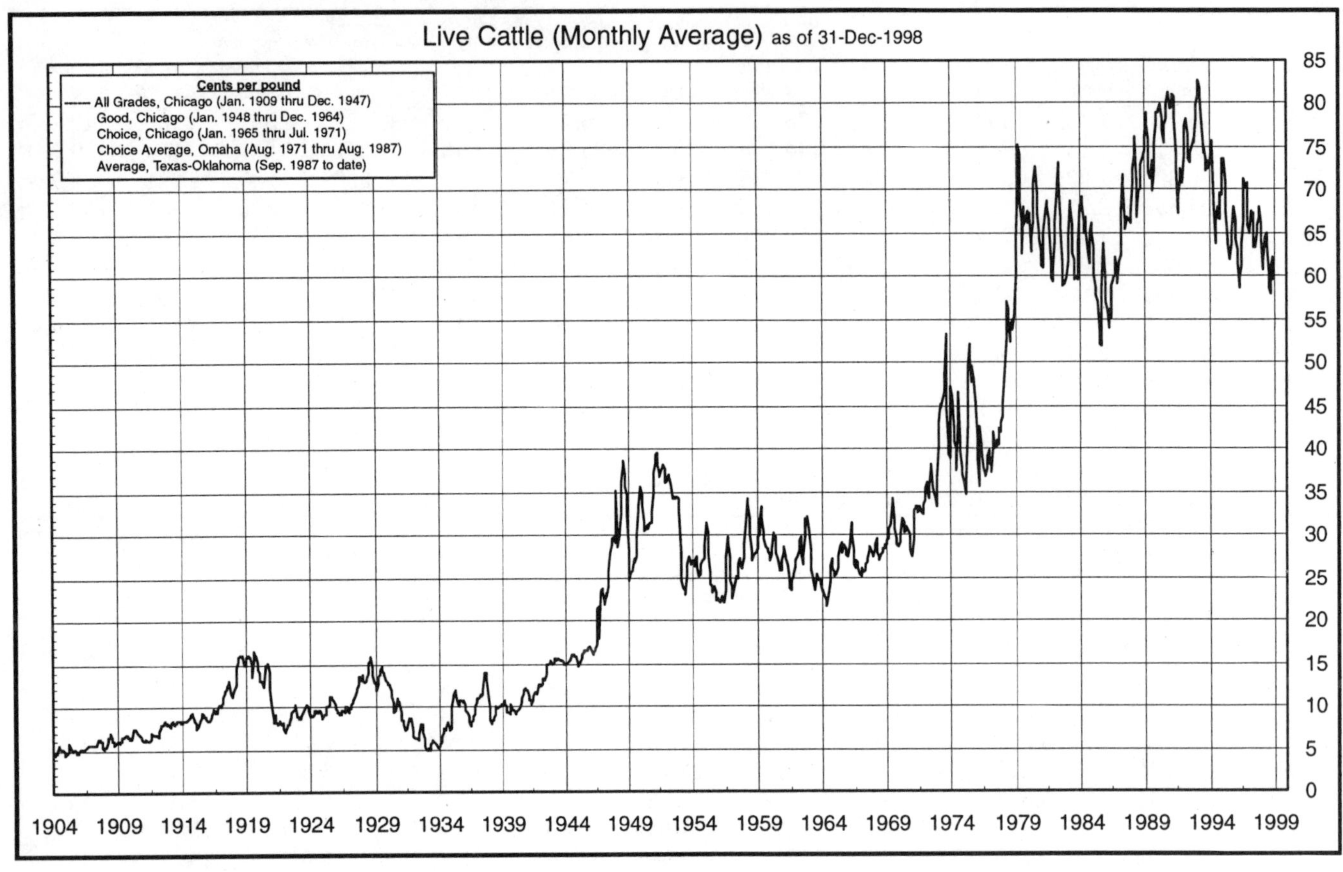

United States Cattle on Feed in 7 States, on First of Month In Thousands of Head

Year	Jan.	Feb.	Mar.	Apr.	May	June	July	Aug.	Sept.	Oct.	Nov	Dec
1989	8,045	7,970	7,931	8,252	8,087	7,795	7,235	6,763	6,631	6,958	7,911	8,331
1990	8,378	8,526	8,319	8,483	8,181	7,867	7,310	6,998	6,975	7,635	8,669	9,039
1991	8,992	8,963	8,874	8,941	8,590	8,570	7,877	7,388	7,064	7,216	8,013	8,477
1992	8,397	8,223	8,195	8,058	7,868	7,876	7,377	7,050	7,018	7,565	8,704	8,984
1993	9,163	9,140	8,851	8,781	8,409	8,393	7,973	7,703	7,794	8,224	8,219	8,418
1994	8,256	8,139	7,981	7,960	7,772	7,511	6,910	6,841	6,949	7,295	7,988	8,198
1995	8,031	8,119	8,227	8,328	8,233	8,182	7,734	7,391	7,189	7,722	8,420	8,685
1996	8,667	8,304	8,152	8,286	7,758	7,253	6,578	6,337	6,612	7,486	8,534	9,003
1997	8,943	8,813	8,769	8,904	8,484	8,231	7,679	7,536	7,850	8,558	9,390	9,718
1998[1]	9,455	9,180	8,835	8,607	8,295	8,289	7,825	7,706	7,750	8,376	9,195	9,409

[1] Preliminary. *Source: Economic Research Service, U.S. Department of Agriculture (ERS-USDA)*

United States Cattle Placed on Feedlots in 7 States In Thousands of Head

Year	Jan.	Feb.	Mar.	Apr.	May	June	July	Aug.	Sept.	Oct.	Nov.	Dec.	Total
1989	1,706	1,610	1,975	1,539	1,624	1,293	1,291	1,638	1,953	2,652	2,001	1,537	20,819
1990	1,881	1,383	1,862	1,362	1,597	1,325	1,530	1,745	2,199	2,726	1,987	1,433	21,030
1991	1,721	1,455	1,703	1,427	1,772	1,102	1,327	1,459	1,826	2,539	1,917	1,456	19,704
1992	1,565	1,502	1,516	1,425	1,724	1,319	1,432	1,641	2,189	2,688	1,813	1,694	20,508
1993	1,641	1,262	1,626	1,326	1,801	1,430	1,513	1,865	2,148	2,494	1,610	1,215	19,931
1994	1,416	1,256	1,518	1,310	1,359	1,113	1,520	1,761	1,915	2,244	1,642	1,345	18,863
1995	1,631	1,532	1,681	1,403	1,673	1,356	1,404	1,653	2,173	2,278	1,804	1,446	20,353
1996	1,312	1,441	1,666	1,150	1,242	1,068	1,483	1,965	2,267	2,536	1,953	1,423	19,506
1997	1,663	1,552	1,694	1,296	1,612	1,224	1,751	2,111	2,278	2,454	1,826	1,304	20,765
1998[1]	1,492	1,250	1,421	1,358	1,740	1,314	1,677	1,753	2,254	2,396	1,725	1,235	19,615

[1] Preliminary. *Source: Economic Research Service, U.S. Department of Agriculture (ERS-USDA)*

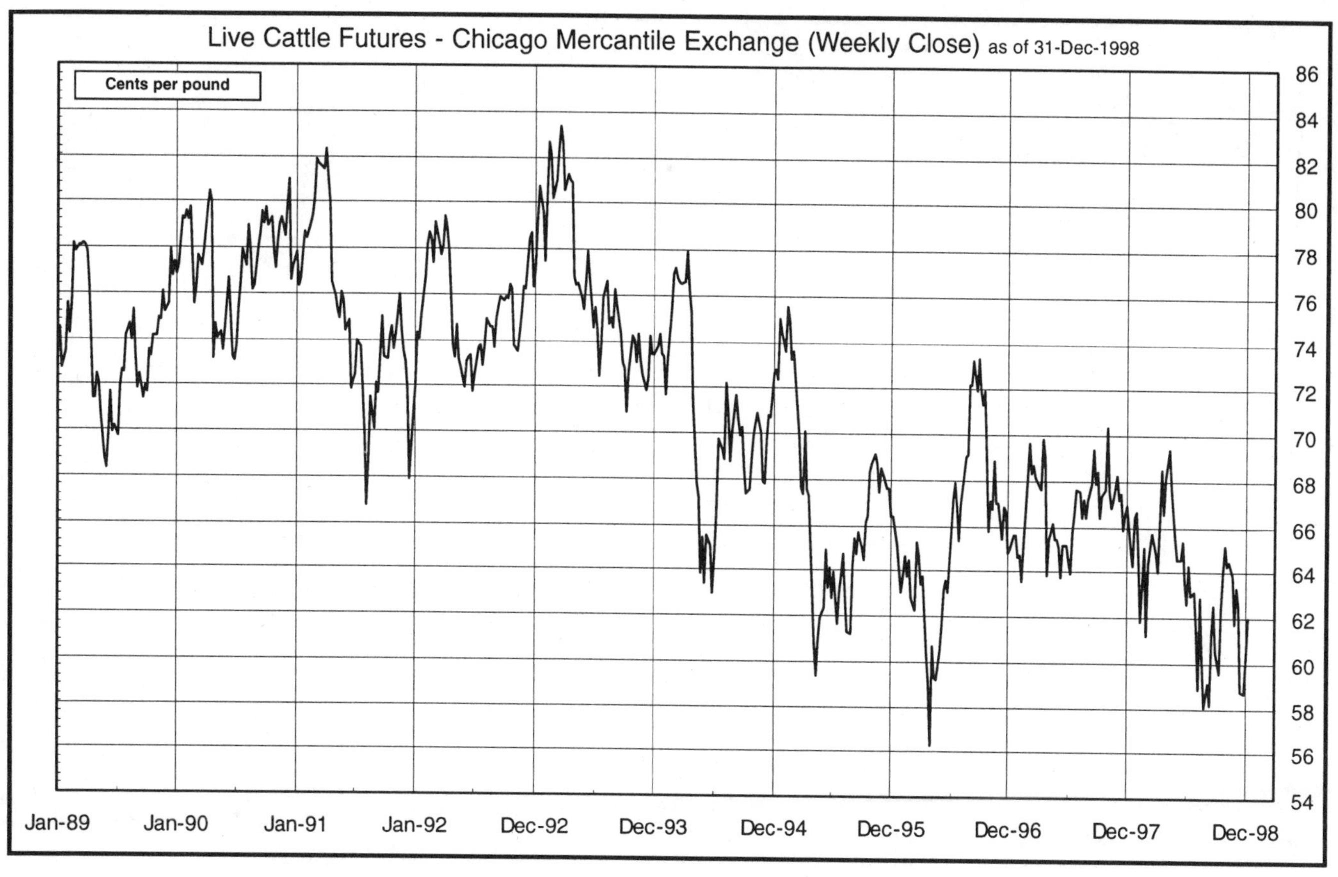

United States Cattle Marketings in 7 States In Thousands of Head

Year	Jan.	Feb.	Mar.	Apr.	May	June	July	Aug.	Sept.	Oct.	Nov.	Dec.	Total
1989	1,677	1,534	1,579	1,580	1,752	1,791	1,700	1,694	1,579	1,628	1,490	1,403	19,407
1990	1,619	1,495	1,578	1,539	1,761	1,809	1,765	1,686	1,460	1,605	1,522	1,359	19,198
1991	1,632	1,431	1,499	1,650	1,651	1,681	1,724	1,716	1,598	1,665	1,376	1,443	19,066
1992	1,640	1,410	1,536	1,490	1,594	1,702	1,674	1,592	1,581	1,473	1,442	1,414	18,548
1993	1,534	1,441	1,585	1,572	1,681	1,743	1,702	1,692	1,652	1,546	1,322	1,305	18,775
1994	1,481	1,357	1,467	1,430	1,542	1,632	1,550	1,602	1,525	1,504	1,370	1,432	18,317
1995	1,484	1,372	1,513	1,437	1,667	1,754	1,698	1,815	1,594	1,529	1,478	1,412	19,038
1996	1,626	1,541	1,476	1,613	1,747	1,696	1,678	1,653	1,342	1,431	1,418	1,415	18,636
1997	1,728	1,554	1,497	1,648	1,785	1,732	1,852	1,755	1,528	1,545	1,429	1,499	19,552
1998[1]	1,689	1,539	1,580	1,609	1,681	1,727	1,755	1,667	1,577	1,532	1,448	1,554	19,358

[1] Preliminary. *Source: Economic Research Service, U.S. Department of Agriculture (ERS-USDA)*

Quarterly Trade of Live Cattle in the United States In Head

	Imports					Exports				
Year	First Quarter	Second Quarter	Third Quarter	Fourth Quarter	Annual	First Quarter	Second Quarter	Third Quarter	Fourth Quarter	Annual
1989	515,682	287,158	132,072	524,503	1,459,415	72,822	37,867	24,117	34,334	169,140
1990	566,516	577,328	301,668	689,488	2,135,000	33,929	28,384	23,335	34,266	119,914
1991	599,398	551,390	225,710	562,556	1,939,054	49,497	62,134	103,866	95,465	310,962
1992	599,255	505,568	389,417	801,025	2,255,265	97,683	100,282	74,827	48,998	321,790
1993	672,447	635,341	469,439	721,819	2,499,046	50,733	33,286	22,049	47,348	153,416
1994	569,466	540,845	386,596	585,597	2,082,504	51,803	43,115	62,729	73,144	230,791
1995	868,694	804,686	488,515	624,350	2,786,245	26,597	18,441	19,794	29,716	94,548
1996	605,648	467,059	391,633	501,108	1,965,448	33,906	42,796	42,757	54,848	174,307
1997	494,637	500,052	423,838	627,825	2,046,352	63,217	58,153	81,095	79,879	282,344
1998[1]	538,018	503,547	373,451	678,648	2,093,664	69,824	63,459	53,145	93,365	279,793

[1] Preliminary. *Source: Economic Research Service, U.S. Department of Agriculture (ERS-USDA)*

CATTLE AND CALVES

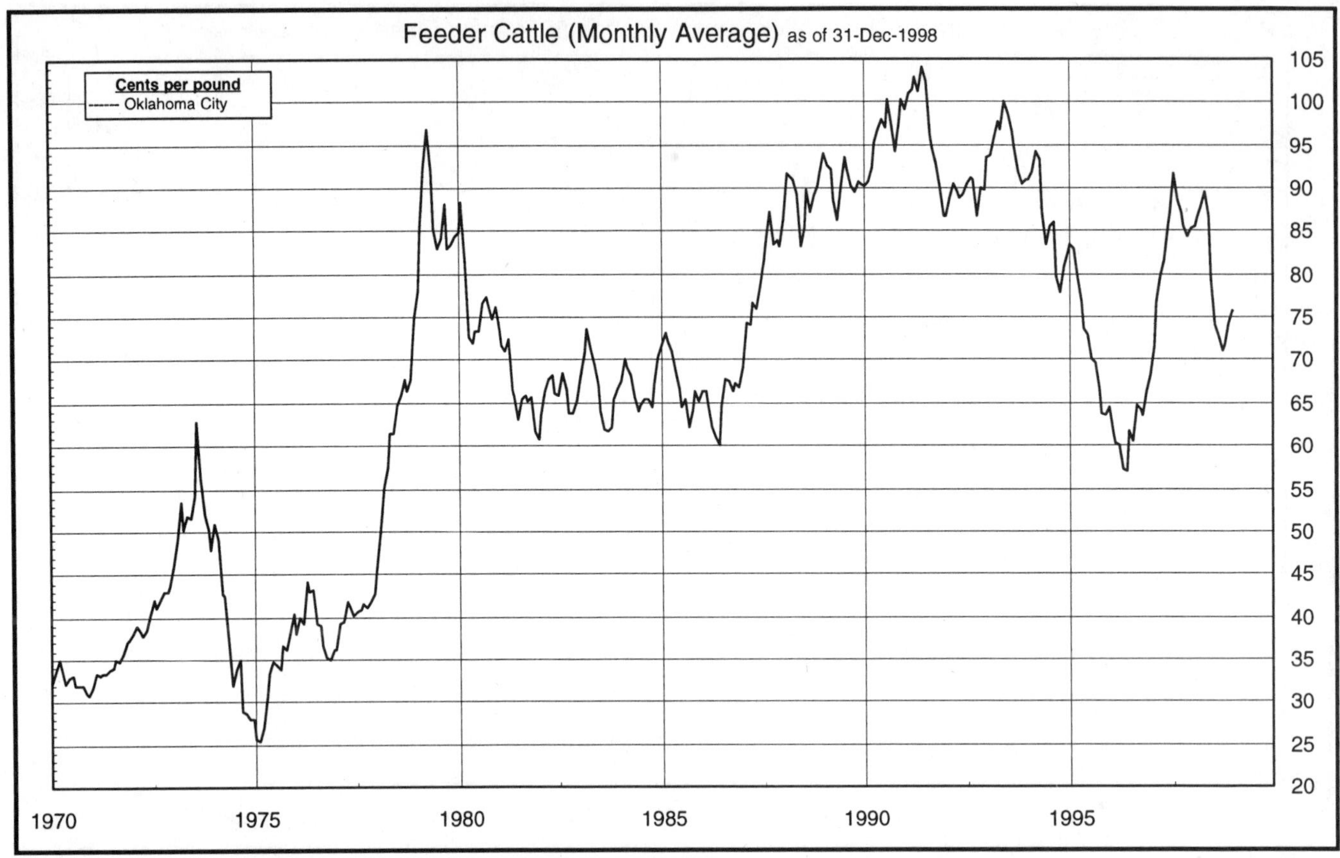

Average Wholesale Price of Slaughter Steers in Texas, Choice 2-4 (1100-1300 Lbs.) In Dollars Per 100 Lbs.

Year	Jan.	Feb.	Mar.	Apr.	May	June	July	Aug.	Sept.	Oct.	Nov.	Dec.	Average
1992	73.88	77.21	78.18	77.83	75.98	73.55	73.02	74.26	75.04	75.97	75.29	78.35	75.71
1993	80.05	80.91	82.66	81.78	80.84	77.31	74.32	75.09	73.46	72.13	73.23	72.42	77.02
1994	72.88	73.03	75.41	75.48	68.12	63.60	66.58	68.04	66.79	66.51	69.43	69.35	69.60
1995	73.60	73.79	70.64	67.54	64.27	63.08	61.81	61.95	63.80	64.89	67.94	66.14	66.62
1996	64.63	63.00	61.77	59.85	59.78	61.37	64.07	67.15	71.12	70.95	70.70	66.25	65.05
1997	65.07	65.35	67.44	67.66	67.36	63.53	63.80	65.19	66.04	66.93	67.66	65.91	66.00
1998	64.57	60.77	64.52	65.00	64.52	63.85	60.28	60.00	57.93	61.54	62.23	59.97	62.10

Source: Economic Research Service, U.S.Department of Agriculture (ERS-USDA)

Average Price of Steers (Feeder) in Oklahoma City In Dollars Per 100 Pounds

Year	Jan.	Feb.	Mar.	Apr.	May	June	July	Aug.	Sept.	Oct.	Nov.	Dec.	Average
1992	86.63	88.90	90.43	89.48	88.96	89.27	90.43	91.30	90.87	86.65	90.12	89.83	89.41
1993	93.59	93.80	95.82	97.65	96.85	100.09	98.58	96.48	94.78	91.82	90.57	91.04	95.09
1994	90.90	91.88	94.34	93.18	87.21	83.45	85.48	85.97	79.77	77.88	80.99	82.58	86.14
1995	83.41	83.05	79.50	76.62	73.69	72.89	70.09	69.62	66.71	68.60	63.45	64.44	72.67
1996	61.38	60.16	60.03	57.20	57.06	61.66	60.56	64.79	64.33	63.45	66.33	68.26	62.10
1997	71.52	76.77	79.66	81.60	85.43	87.04	91.67	88.69	87.23	85.66	84.37	85.25	83.74
1998	85.58	86.53	87.87	89.46	86.84	79.54	74.13	72.72	71.13	71.85	74.24	75.71	79.63

Source: Wall Street Journal

Federally Inspected Slaughter of Cattle in the United States In Thousands of Head

Year	Jan.	Feb.	Mar.	Apr.	May	June	July	Aug.	Sept.	Oct.	Nov.	Dec.	Total
1992	2,856	2,377	2,599	2,525	2,688	2,863	2,802	2,721	2,748	2,793	2,490	2,632	32,094
1993	2,601	2,411	2,712	2,623	2,720	2,957	2,811	2,883	2,810	2,729	2,632	2,706	32,593
1994	2,679	2,501	2,799	2,656	2,780	2,984	2,770	3,001	2,885	2,878	2,744	2,806	33,483
1995	2,802	2,524	2,890	2,591	3,064	3,187	2,878	3,160	3,019	2,982	2,897	2,741	34,735
1996	3,046	2,855	2,834	3,039	3,257	3,078	3,080	3,148	2,693	3,074	2,801	2,800	35,721
1997	3,169	2,726	2,795	2,998	3,125	3,003	3,127	3,050	2,909	3,156	2,698	2,811	35,567
1998[1]	2,977	2,691	2,838	2,872	2,906	3,050	2,987	2,987	2,938	2,991	2,717	2,834	34,787

[1] Preliminary. *Source: Agricultural Statistics Board, U.S. Department of Agriculture (ASB-USDA)*

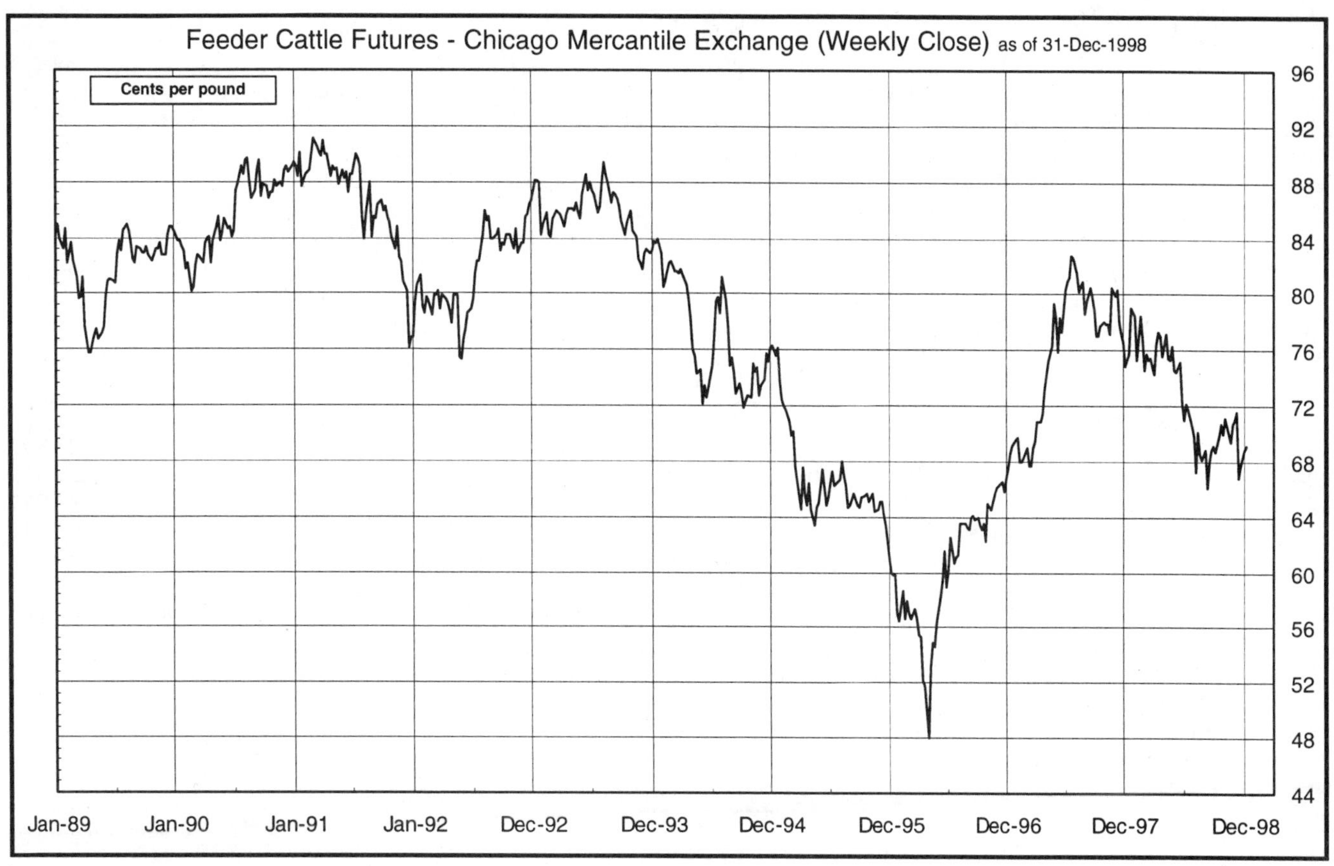

Average Open Interest of Live Cattle Futures in Chicago In Contracts

Year	Jan.	Feb.	Mar.	Apr.	May	June	July	Aug.	Sept.	Oct.	Nov.	Dec.
1989	80,464	84,909	93,240	82,267	81,588	69,981	78,045	76,582	73,530	65,807	73,962	71,508
1990	95,515	108,149	104,647	95,709	86,875	76,130	70,462	68,375	69,611	67,122	70,576	69,647
1991	74,392	79,695	84,574	83,322	78,284	70,107	67,868	68,359	74,483	70,395	75,788	74,687
1992	79,638	97,500	97,222	90,823	83,112	68,135	67,828	62,656	61,783	60,761	63,945	67,125
1993	78,481	79,256	88,113	78,144	72,183	68,287	66,617	66,560	70,275	70,559	73,571	76,042
1994	87,923	87,578	83,949	70,287	72,851	75,470	76,663	72,988	73,391	67,924	74,152	68,600
1995	80,306	78,793	76,821	64,763	61,460	56,783	58,077	55,511	58,319	62,222	69,495	69,065
1996	72,870	83,064	91,348	97,315	97,911	96,320	96,547	93,557	92,804	88,467	88,062	87,305
1997	97,014	103,437	108,157	98,354	99,640	96,279	99,042	98,590	94,137	93,579	100,368	102,741
1998	105,559	102,036	101,264	88,257	88,167	87,493	86,776	86,874	95,013	102,636	108,263	106,156

Source: Chicago Mercantile Exchange (CME)

Volume of Trading of Live Cattle Futures in Chicago In Thousands of Contracts

Year	Jan.	Feb.	Mar.	Apr.	May	June	July	Aug.	Sept.	Oct.	Nov.	Dec.	Total
1989	452.9	357.7	409.0	404.2	382.9	370.3	327.9	331.9	376.9	345.4	266.2	240.2	4,265.7
1990	400.5	350.0	354.1	327.6	372.2	263.9	298.5	327.7	273.3	320.3	268.4	240.8	3,797.4
1991	344.2	252.1	288.9	300.4	247.2	254.8	311.2	406.1	321.2	386.3	327.7	352.8	3,792.9
1992	375.6	322.5	353.8	319.1	275.9	263.9	268.9	231.0	196.0	227.9	203.8	246.7	3,319.6
1993	328.8	294.2	363.4	263.5	199.7	255.4	269.3	226.0	269.5	297.6	248.4	291.1	3,307.0
1994	280.8	291.8	262.4	264.2	372.9	363.9	318.2	317.1	270.0	308.9	275.9	254.6	3,580.9
1995	289.7	259.2	391.7	287.2	285.7	290.2	245.3	266.8	233.4	220.1	246.7	241.1	3,257.1
1996	312.0	275.4	333.2	457.5	385.9	303.1	319.8	299.5	278.1	339.4	312.6	309.7	3,926.2
1997	361.6	352.2	312.1	331.9	285.9	303.4	387.5	324.9	316.8	374.6	238.0	330.6	3,919.6
1998	355.7	400.2	327.2	400.6	296.7	321.4	334.4	369.6	370.3	373.2	318.2	349.1	4,216.5

Source: Chicago Mercantile Exchange (CME)

CATTLE AND CALVES

Beef Steer-Corn Price Ratio[1] in the United States

Year	Jan.	Feb.	Mar.	Apr.	May	June	July	Aug.	Sept.	Oct.	Nov.	Dec.	Average
1991	36.0	35.0	34.5	33.9	33.4	33.2	32.9	30.6	30.7	32.2	31.6	30.7	32.9
1992	30.3	31.0	30.7	30.8	30.2	29.8	31.7	34.7	35.0	37.3	38.2	38.7	33.2
1993	38.8	39.8	38.8	37.8	37.8	37.1	33.8	33.4	33.7	31.8	29.8	27.0	35.0
1994	27.1	26.3	27.5	28.5	26.8	24.0	28.4	31.6	30.2	32.1	34.4	31.9	29.1
1995	32.6	32.4	30.5	28.4	26.3	25.2	23.5	23.5	23.0	22.3	22.7	21.1	26.0
1996	20.3	18.1	17.2	15.1	13.9	14.2	14.0	15.0	19.1	23.6	25.8	24.9	18.4
1997	24.2	24.6	24.3	24.3	25.4	25.4	27.0	26.6	25.2	26.5	27.1	26.5	25.6
1998[2]	25.8	24.8	25.3	27.5	28.3	28.3	27.7	31.4	32.2	32.1	32.3	30.0	28.8

[1] Bushels of corn equal in value to 100 pounds of steers and heifers. [2] Preliminary. *Source: Economic Research Service, U.S. Department of Agriculture.*

Farm Value, Income and Wholesale Prices of Cattle and Calves in the United States

Year	January 1: Per Head (Dollars)	January 1: Total (Million $)	Gross Income From C. & C.[2] (Million $)	At Omaha[3]: Steers[3] Choice	At Omaha[3]: Steers[3] Select	At Omaha[3]: Heifers Select	At Omaha[3]: Heifers Choice	Feeder Heifers at Oklahoma City[5]	Cows, Boning Utility Sioux Falls[6]	Cows, Commercial Sioux Falls	Wholesale Prices, Central U.S.: Choice, 700-850 lb.	Wholesale Prices, Central U.S.: Select, 700-850 lb.	Wholesale Prices, Central U.S.: Cow[6], Canner[7]
				Dollars per 100 Pounds									
1991	655	63,090	38,697	74.03	72.46	71.44	73.86	86.04	50.66	56.08	117.24	112.73	99.42
1992	630	61,451	37,272	75.17	73.65	72.88	74.95	78.41	44.84	51.22	116.02	111.66	93.85
1993	649	64,436	39,362	76.23	74.09	73.77	76.01	82.79	47.52	56.47	117.71	113.53	95.43
1994	659	66,490	36,395	67.60	66.33	66.14	67.93	74.55	42.51	48.28	106.73	102.08	84.39
1995	615	63,157	34,310	65.64	63.94	63.69	65.46	64.43	35.58	39.03	106.09	98.45	68.67
1996	503	52,010	31,411	74.50	61.83	61.22	64.18	57.21	30.45	33.70	102.01	95.70	58.16
1997[1]	525	53,242		65.92	63.85	63.36	65.66	70.48	35.00	37.13	102.38	96.96	65.39

[1] Preliminary. [2] Excludes interfarm sales and Government payments. Cash receipts from farm marketings and value of farm consumption. [3] 1,000 to 1,100 pound weight range. [4] 1,000 to 1,200 pound weight range. [5] 700 to 750 pound weight range. Prior to 1992, 600 to 700 pound weight range. [6] All weights. [7] & cutter. NA=Not available. *Source: Economic Research Service, U.S. Department of Agriculture (ERS-USDA)*

Average Price Received by Farmers for Beef Cattle In Dollars Per 100 Pounds

Year	Jan.	Feb.	Mar.	Apr.	May	June	July	Aug.	Sept.	Oct.	Nov.	Dec.	Average
1991	76.60	77.00	78.50	78.20	75.90	73.60	71.60	68.80	68.70	70.40	67.90	67.40	72.88
1992	68.90	72.50	72.80	72.60	71.90	70.20	70.60	71.80	71.80	71.80	70.20	70.80	71.33
1993	75.10	75.80	77.20	77.30	77.10	74.50	72.50	72.70	71.40	69.10	69.30	68.50	73.38
1994	69.90	70.10	72.30	72.00	67.20	62.70	62.90	65.90	63.50	62.90	64.40	64.40	66.52
1995	67.50	68.70	66.90	63.80	60.80	60.90	59.50	59.40	59.10	58.80	60.70	60.60	62.23
1996	59.10	57.90	56.80	54.90	54.70	56.40	59.10	61.30	63.80	63.30	63.40	61.00	59.30
1997	61.40	61.90	64.80	64.80	65.10	62.30	62.80	63.90	63.60	63.30	63.30	62.90	63.34
1998[1]	62.50	60.40	61.30	63.00	63.00	61.80	58.40	57.40	56.10	58.00	58.10	62.50	60.21

[1] Preliminary. *Source: Crop Reporting Board, U.S. Department of Agriculture (CRB-USDA)*

Average Price Received by Farmers for Calves In Dollars Per 100 Pounds

Year	Jan.	Feb.	Mar.	Apr.	May	June	July	Aug.	Sept.	Oct.	Nov.	Dec.	Average
1991	98.00	104.00	106.00	109.00	107.00	106.00	103.00	98.30	96.20	93.90	90.20	87.60	99.93
1992	88.30	92.80	94.10	92.00	89.60	88.50	90.10	90.40	87.40	86.00	86.50	87.00	89.39
1993	94.70	96.00	98.60	99.60	99.20	99.10	96.90	95.10	93.50	93.90	91.60	92.80	95.92
1994	93.90	94.90	97.60	95.80	89.40	84.80	83.80	84.40	80.00	78.20	81.00	81.90	87.14
1995	85.00	86.90	84.40	81.80	77.00	76.90	72.00	70.90	68.50	66.20	64.00	63.30	74.74
1996	61.80	60.20	59.40	55.10	54.40	55.10	56.80	59.30	61.00	60.10	61.20	61.80	58.90
1997	68.10	74.90	80.00	82.20	84.30	85.40	86.90	88.00	86.90	84.30	82.90	83.30	82.27
1998[1]	86.60	88.70	89.80	90.80	88.90	81.70	76.60	76.90	74.10	75.70	77.50	86.60	82.83

[1] Preliminary. *Source: Crop Reporting Board, U.S. Department of Agriculture (CRB-USDA)*

Federally Inspected Slaughter of Calves and Vealers in the United States In Thousands of Head

Year	Jan.	Feb.	Mar.	Apr.	May	June	July	Aug.	Sept.	Oct.	Nov.	Dec.	Total
1991	150	120	119	105	102	90	108	108	115	127	125	131	1,408
1992	128	111	120	108	103	105	106	107	107	111	109	121	1,328
1993	101	97	116	96	82	91	90	95	94	94	101	103	1,159
1994	99	94	112	92	90	98	93	106	106	112	114	121	1,237
1995	121	104	118	96	114	115	111	121	119	124	125	125	1,393
1996	140	140	141	128	133	131	156	153	146	159	139	149	1,715
1997	143	122	128	126	114	115	131	123	133	137	121	142	1,534
1998[1]	125	111	125	107	99	114	131	122	132	121	109	127	1,421

[1] Preliminary. *Source: Crop Reporting Board, U.S. Department of Agriculture (CRB-USDA)*

Cement

The use of cement in the United States corresponds to areas where construction activity is the greatest. According to the U.S. Geological Survey, portland and blended cement shipments in the U.S. and Puerto Rico totaled 10.19 million metric tonnes in July 1998. This represented an increase of 6 percent from July 1997. Cumulative shipments through July 1998 were 55.52 million tonnes which was 7 percent more than in the same period of 1997. The leading portland cement producing states are California, Texas, Pennsylvania, Michigan and Missouri. Together they shipped 35 percent of the July total. The leading consuming states were California, Texas, Florida, Ohio and Michigan which took a total of 33 percent of the shipments.

Clinker cement production in July 1998 was 6.67 million tonnes, about the same as in June 1998. In the first seven months of 1998, clinker production was 42.40 million tonnes. The leading clinker producing state was California. In July 1998, California clinker production was 802,931 tonnes. The other leading producing states are Texas, Pennsylvania, Missouri and Michigan. These states shipped 44 percent of the July total.

Masonry cement shipments in July 1998 were 374,092 tonnes, a 6 percent increase from July 1997. Cumulative shipments through July 1998 were 2.24 million tonnes, an increase of 7 percent from 1997. The leading masonry cement producing state in July 1998 was Florida with 49,946 tonnes. Other major producing states include North Carolina, Georgia, Texas, Tennessee and California. For 1997, the major destination for masonry cement was Florida with 535,649 tonnes. The next major destination was North Carolina with 297,914 tonnes and Georgia at 237,250 tonnes. Texas with 231,074 tonnes was another major destination.

In June 1998, the U.S. imported 665,913 tonnes of hydraulic cement and clinker from Canada. Some 282,471 tonnes were imported from China in June while 253,582 tonnes were imported from Spain. Other large suppliers include Greece, Mexico, Turkey and Colombia. Total hydraulic cement and clinker imported into the U.S. in the first half of 1998 was 10.28 million tonnes. In the first half of 1998, imports of white cement were 302,780 tonnes. The major suppliers include Canada, Mexico and Spain.

World Production of Hydraulic Cement In Thousands of Metric Tons

Year	Brazil	China	France	Germany	India	Italy	Japan	Rep. of Korea	Russia[3]	Spain	Turkey	United States	World Total
1991	27,490	252,610	26,507	34,396	51,000	40,806	89,564	34,999	140,000	25,119	26,091	68,465	1,181,793
1992	23,903	308,220	21,165	37,529	50,000	41,347	88,253	44,444	61,700	24,615	28,607	70,883	1,239,683
1993	24,843	367,880	20,464	36,649	53,812	33,771	88,046	47,313	49,900	22,878	31,241	75,117	1,290,905
1994	25,230	421,180	21,296	40,380	57,000	32,713	91,624	50,730	37,200	25,150	29,493	79,353	1,373,013
1995	28,256	475,910	19,692	37,480	62,000	33,715	90,474	55,130	36,500	26,423	33,153	78,320	1,443,328
1996[1]	34,597	491,190	18,340	36,104	75,000	33,327	94,492	57,260	27,800	25,157	35,214	80,818	1,488,262
1997[2]	38,096	492,600	19,000	37,000	80,000	33,721	91,938	59,796	26,600	27,632	36,035	84,255	1,515,442

[1] Preliminary. [2] Estimate. [3] Formerly part of the U.S.S.R.; data not reported separately until 1992. *Source: U.S. Geological Survey (USGS)*

Salient Statistics of Cement in the United States

Year	Net Import Reliance as a % of Apparent Consumption	Production: Portland	Production: Others[3]	Production: Total	Capacity Used at (Portland Mills) %	Shipments From Mills: Total Mil. Tons	Shipments From Mills: Value[4] Mil. $	Average Value (F.O.B. Mill) $ per ton	Stocks at Mills Dec. 31	Exports[5]	Apparent Consumption	Imports for Consumption[5] by Country: Canada	Japan	Mexico	Spain	Total
		Thousand Tons							Million Tons			Thousands of Short Tons				
1991	10	64,165	3,028	67,193	72.2	68,999	3,832	55.54	6,009	633	72,413	3,127	331	1,044	699	8,701
1992	6	66,841	2,744	69,585	76.0	69,203	3,779	54.61	5,272	746	74,158	2,997	278	825	446	6,166
1993	7	70,845	2,962	73,807	79.1	72,770	4,175	55.65	4,788	625	79,198	3,629	43	783	597	7,060
1994	10	74,335	3,613	77,948	82.3	79,087	4,845	61.26	4,701	633	86,476	4,268	14	640	1,342	11,303
1995	11	73,303	3,603	76,906	81.2	78,518	5,329	67.87	5,814	759	86,003	4,886	[6]	850	1,501	13,848
1996	12	75,797	3,469	79,266	83.4	83,607	5,952	71.19	5,488	803	90,355	5,351	[6]	1,272	1,595	14,154
1997[1]	14	78,948	3,634	82,582	84.7	90,359	6,622	73.49	5,784	791	96,018	5,350	-----	995	1,845	17,596

[1] Preliminary. [2] Estimate. [3] Masonry, natural & pozzolan (slag-line). [4] Value received F.O.B. mill, excluding cost of containers. [5] Hydraulic & clinker cement. [6] Less than 1/2 unit. NA = Not available. *Source: U.S. Geological Survey (USGS)*

Shipments of Finished Portland Cement from Mills in the United States In Thousands of Metric Tons

Year	Jan.	Feb.	Mar.	Apr.	May	June	July	Aug.	Sept.	Oct.	Nov.	Dec.	Total
1993	3,370.8	3,664.1	4,882.0	5,784.1	6,617.4	7,329.2	7,199.8	7,557.4	7,237.4	7,414.5	6,269.0	5,033.3	72,359.1
1994	3,406.1	3,790.2	5,884.3	6,227.3	7,320.8	7,689.9	6,877.4	7,938.1	7,461.9	7,237.8	6,203.5	5,093.2	75,130.4
1995	3,685.2	3,959.7	5,556.6	5,668.6	6,720.6	7,336.8	6,748.1	7,660.9	7,177.0	7,736.3	6,238.3	4,667.7	73,155.6
1996	3,913.3	4,312.7	5,234.1	6,801.6	7,621.3	7,395.1	7,749.4	8,193.4	7,178.3	8,276.7	6,011.4	4,763.3	77,550.0
1997	4,111.3	4,487.1	5,739.1	7,009.5	7,489.3	7,733.7	8,132.4	7,909.2	8,186.1	8,678.9	6,108.6	5,471.9	81,073.2
1998[1]	4,559.4	4,567.0	5,878.5	7,019.7	7,430.5	8,108.6	8,309.6	7,976.5	8,101.8	8,417.7	6,670.7		84,043.6

[1] Preliminary. *Source: U.S. Geological Survey (USGS)*

Cheese

1998 world cheese production was forecast at a record 12.2 million metric tonnes vs 11.9 million in 1997; the U.S., France and Australia accounted for most of the increase. The U.S. is the world's largest producer with 3.5 million metric tonnes in 1998 vs. 3.3 million in 1997. World consumption of nearly 12 million tonnes in 1998 compares with 11.7 million in 1997 with the U.S. totals 3.6 million and 3.5 million, respectively. France and Italy combined consumed about 2.3 million tonnes in each year. Worldwide, the annual supply and demand for cheese sets new highs each year.

Most of the world's cheese is consumed where produced. Record U.S. per capita cheese consumption of 28.07 pounds in 1998 vs. 27.74 in 1997 pales relative to Europe where use tops 40 pounds in some countries, notably France.

World foreign trade of cheese is biased towards exports; almost one million metric tonnes in 1998, marginally below 1997; imports in both years hovered around 800,000 tonnes. The largest single exporter is generally New Zealand with 240,000 tonnes in 1998; collectively the E.U. exports about half the world total. U.S. exports have increased in recent years but are still small, averaging about 37,000 tonnes during 1996-98. Russia's imports totaled 220,000 tonnes in 1998 vs. 200,000 in 1997 and less than 100,000 tonnes prior to 1996. Japan is the second largest importer, generally averaging 170,000 tonnes. World stocks at yearend 1998 of 1.82 million tonnes compare with 1.91 million a year earlier; Italy accounts for about 40 percent of the total.

Cheese is a multi-billion dollar industry in the U.S. and American cheese, mostly cheddar, accounts for the largest individual variety of U.S. production and consumption. However, since the late 1980's other varieties, mostly Italian, have had a combined production that exceeds American cheese; per capita consumption of the latter has slipped in recent years to 12 pounds while other cheese use has climbed to nearly 11 pounds. Mozzarella accounts for about 80 percent of Italian cheese use.

U.S. cheese prices follow a seasonal pattern with lows in the spring and peaks in the fall, but regional differences can trigger counterseasonal price swings. Wholesale American cheese prices (40-pound blocks, Wisconsin) averaged $1.50 per pound in mid-1998, 32 cents higher than a year earlier.

Futures Markets

Cheddar Cheese futures and options are traded on both the Chicago Mercantile Exchange (CME) and the Coffee, Sugar & Cocoa Exchange, Inc. (CSCE).

World Production of Cheese In Millions of Metric Tons

Year	Argentina	Australia	Brazil	Canada	Denmark	France	Germany	Italy	Netherlands	New Zealand	United Kingdom	United States	World Total
1990	270	175	245	255	293	1,471	749	811	593	122	316	2,749	10,873
1991	290	178	290	262	285	1,500	777	885	610	125	303	2,747	10,366
1992	310	197	296	262	290	1,489	783	890	634	142	324	2,943	10,931
1993	350	211	310	271	321	1,509	821	885	637	145	331	2,961	11,172
1994	385	234	330	282	286	1,541	855	913	648	192	326	3,054	11,194
1995	370	241	360	277	311	1,579	875	942	680	197	354	3,138	11,349
1996	390	268	385	289	298	1,594	947	950	688	230	364	3,274	11,702
1997	415	285	405	336	290	1,645	988	985	693	240	374	3,324	12,051
1998[1]	420	289	421	330	286	1,670	1,001	985	690	266	368	3,375	12,210
1999[2]	435	319	434	333	290	1,675	1,021	985	688	245	365	3,440	12,367

[1] Preliminary. [2] Estimate. [3] Formerly part of the U.S.S.R.; data not reported seperately prior to 1989. *Source: Foreign Agricultural Service, U.S. Department of Agriculture (FAS-USDA)*

Supply and Distribution of All Cheese in the United States In Millions of Pounds

Year	Supply: Production: Whole Milk[2]	Supply: Production: All Cheese[3]	Supply: January 1 Commercial Stocks	Supply: Imports[4]	Supply: Total Supply	Cheese 40-Lb. Blocks Wisconsin Assembly Points ¢ per lb.	Distribution: Exports & Shipments[5]	Distribution: Gov't: Dec. 31 Stocks	Distribution: American Cheese Removed by USDA Programs	Distribution: Total Disappearance	Domestic Disapparence: American Cheese Donated	Domestic Disapparence: Total	Domestic Disapparence: Per Capita
1988	2,757	5,572	460	253	6,284	123.80	76	36.7	238.1	5,886	257	5,801	23.70
1989	2,674	5,615	361	279	6,289	138.79	74	6.6	37.4	5,959	67	5,901	23.81
1990	2,894	6,059	323	302	6,689	136.69	75	8.2	21.5	6,231	21	6,168	24.64
1991	2,769	6,055	450	301	6,810	124.41	72	23.1	76.9	6,393	60	6,337	25.01
1992	2,937	6,488	393	285	7,191	131.91	78	16.5	14.4	6,720	0	6,661	26.01
1993	2,957	6,528	454	321	7,303	131.52	87	2.2	8.3	6,853	0	6,766	26.24
1994	2,974	6,735	464	345	7,544	131.45	55	.9	6.9	7,095	0	6,994	26.82
1995	3,131	6,917	436	337	7,690	132.77	65	----	6.1	7,275	0	7,218	27.30
1996	3,281	7,218	412	335	7,964	149.14	71	----	4.6	7,473	0	7,407	27.70
1997[1]	3,285	7,329	487	311	8,127	132.40	84	----	11.3	7,635	0	7,562	28.30

[1] Preliminary. [2] Whole milk American cheddar. [3] All types of cheese except cottage, pot and baker's cheese. [4] Imports for consumption. [5]Commercial. NA = Not available. *Source: Economic Research Service, U.S. Department of Agriculture (ERS-USDA)*

Production of Cheese in the United States In Millions of Pounds

	American			Swiss,				Cream &				Total	Cottage Cheese		
Year	Whole Milk	Part Skim	Total	Including Block	Munster	Brick	Limburger	Neufchatel Cheese	Italian Varieties	Blue Mond	All Other Varieties	of All Cheese[2]	Lowfat	Curd[3]	Creamed[4]
1988	2,757	1.1	2,758	250.1	83.3	24.8	1.0	375.9	1,937.1	37.8	104.3	5,572	290.9	556.7	647.1
1989	2,674	.8	2,675	231.2	91.1	17.5	.9	401.0	2,042.9	34.6	121.2	5,615	300.9	526.9	572.3
1990	2,894	.8	2,895	261.1	100.2	17.3	.8	430.8	2,207.0	36.4	110.7	6,059	301.8	493.5	530.6
1991	2,769	.8	2,770	234.5	106.4	15.3	.7	446.7	2,328.6	34.3	118.5	6,055	321.1	490.9	497.9
1992	2,937	1.2	2,938	237.3	116.4	15.5	1.0	516.7	2,508.6	33.3	121.9	6,488	329.5	502.4	457.3
1993	2,957	3.7	2,961	231.4	117.5	12.5	.9	539.9	2,494.5	33.3	137.2	6,528	317.0	471.4	430.5
1994	2,974	24.7	2,999	221.2	113.6	12.2	.8	573.4	2,625.7	36.5	152.1	6,735	321.1	463.3	410.0
1995	3,131	24.0	3,155	221.7	109.1	10.4	.9	543.8	2,674.4	36.6	164.6	6,917	325.9	458.9	384.9
1996	3,281	NA	3,281	219.0	106.8	10.6	.7	574.7	2,812.4	38.3	106.7	7,218	329.9	448.3	360.4
1997[1]	3,285	NA	3,285	207.6	100.2	8.5	.7	614.9	2,880.4	42.8	119.8	7,329	346.7	458.5	359.5

[1] Preliminary. [2] Excludes full-skim cheddar and cottage cheese. [3] Includes cottage, pot, and baker's cheese with a butterfat content of less than 4%. [4] Includes cheese with a butterfat content of 4 to 19%. *Source: Economic Research Service, U.S. Department of Agriculture (ERS-USDA)*

Wholesale Price of Cheese, 40-lb. Blocks, Wisconsin Assembly Points In Cents Per Pound

Year	Jan.	Feb.	Mar.	Apr.	May	June	July	Aug.	Sept.	Oct.	Nov.	Dec.	Average
1989	129.1	117.6	117.9	120.4	123.9	130.8	140.6	143.3	155.8	160.3	163.6	162.2	138.8
1990	152.3	131.6	130.7	140.5	145.8	149.5	151.0	150.3	142.6	114.9	112.0	112.7	136.2
1991	111.4	111.5	111.5	111.7	115.0	121.4	128.4	136.1	139.7	140.2	135.8	130.2	124.4
1992	125.4	119.0	119.8	131.9	140.0	141.3	141.8	142.0	136.9	132.4	129.4	123.2	131.9
1993	119.3	118.6	124.3	140.8	141.8	133.7	126.3	124.8	137.4	138.9	138.7	133.7	131.5
1994	132.2	134.2	140.0	143.3	125.7	120.2	129.1	132.2	135.6	135.4	127.9	121.3	131.5
1995	124.5	130.4	131.1	122.8	122.1	126.9	126.7	132.2	141.3	145.0	145.8	144.6	132.8
1996	139.3	139.3	140.9	145.1	151.8	151.5	158.2	167.6	145.5	162.3	133.9	126.0	146.8
1997	127.9	132.3	134.0	125.6	116.5	117.9	123.3	137.6	141.4	142.4	143.8	146.1	132.4
1998[1]	144.5	144.7	138.8	129.7	123.0	151.3	162.6	166.9	171.0	183.5	188.7	192.5	158.1

[1] Preliminary. *Source: Economic Research Service, U.S. Department of Agriculture (ERS-USDA)*

Production[2] of Cheese in the United States In Millions of Pounds

Year	Jan.	Feb.	Mar.	Apr.	May	June	July	Aug.	Sept.	Oct.	Nov.	Dec.	Total
1989	456.6	419.5	488.4	472.6	494.9	485.5	464.6	460.4	448.5	464.0	453.0	489.5	5,614
1990	483.7	471.9	531.7	521.1	542.8	522.8	502.2	495.0	472.6	505.9	495.5	522.1	6,061
1991	501.7	458.0	530.1	515.4	532.3	509.0	499.5	498.2	485.0	521.0	502.3	533.7	6,061
1992	514.1	497.1	542.7	534.7	550.9	549.8	541.8	534.6	528.3	558.2	547.5	571.6	6,488
1993	517.3	492.5	563.2	561.4	576.9	563.2	537.9	525.8	531.1	560.0	540.1	558.9	6,528
1994	538.3	505.8	591.8	554.3	590.4	558.7	550.7	562.4	565.5	574.5	559.3	578.3	6,730
1995	559.3	523.3	596.0	559.6	595.3	579.2	556.5	550.8	571.3	588.6	584.7	618.4	6,883
1996	590.0	576.0	625.4	606.0	636.5	595.8	582.2	589.5	584.5	612.2	595.5	623.9	7,218
1997	598.1	577.1	638.0	598.5	642.0	623.4	613.2	596.5	604.3	615.5	594.5	627.9	7,329
1998[1]	615.7	574.2	645.2	641.3	653.1	641.1	612.5	596.0	579.9	621.2	634.8	667.6	7,483

[1] Preliminary. [2] Excludes cottage cheese *Source: National Agricultural Statistics Service, U.S. Department of Agriculture (NASS-USDA)*

Cold Storage Holdings of All Varieties of Cheese in the U.S., on First of Month In Millions of Pounds

Year	Jan.	Feb.	Mar.	Apr.	May	June	July	Aug.	Sept.	Oct.	Nov.	Dec.
1989	388.1	395.3	404.4	396.6	412.1	431.9	429.6	430.4	419.8	370.2	331.4	330.6
1990	328.0	358.4	374.9	395.8	413.4	441.6	465.0	484.6	475.7	459.9	445.4	437.3
1991	457.8	483.9	475.1	492.4	510.3	512.1	521.5	511.5	494.1	477.9	429.3	409.0
1992	415.4	440.9	445.9	449.0	449.7	455.9	465.2	496.2	487.3	449.7	441.1	462.0
1993	462.0	476.1	454.4	460.0	453.6	480.5	541.2	533.3	517.7	500.1	471.9	462.4
1994	465.2	495.2	473.6	473.3	487.9	513.4	521.4	506.3	474.7	453.0	448.3	434.2
1995	436.9	449.7	448.7	458.8	466.1	465.8	473.6	482.4	458.1	428.5	418.7	393.6
1996	412.1	441.3	466.4	490.9	525.5	541.8	542.8	536.6	506.9	495.8	494.6	480.2
1997	487.0	501.5	494.6	517.0	555.4	584.3	604.8	604.9	582.3	543.7	505.0	474.4
1998[1]	480.4	493.5	509.5	519.4	544.7	551.6	583.3	594.5	576.8	553.0	522.7	494.5

[1] Preliminary. [2] Quantities are given in "net weight." *Source: National Agricultural Statistics Service, U.S.Department of Agriculture (NASS-USDA)*

Chromium

Chromite is the ore mineral of chromium. Chromium has a wide variety of uses in metals, chemicals and refractories. Chromium enhances hardenability and resistance to corrosion and oxidation in iron, steel and nonferrous alloys. The production of stainless steel and nonferrous alloys are two of its applications. Other applications are in alloy steel, plating of metals, pigments, leather processing, surface treatments, catalysts and refractories.

World production of chromite in 1997 was 12.5 million tonnes, up almost 9 percent from 1996. The world's largest producer of chromite was South Africa with 5.78 million tonnes, up 16 percent from 1996. The next largest producer was Turkey with 1.75 million tonnes, up 37 percent from the previous year. Other significant producers include India and Kazakstan.

World ferrochromium production in 1997 was 4.42 million tonnes, up 11 percent from 1996. By far the largest producer was South Africa with 1.93 million tonnes. Other major producers included China, Kazakstan, India and Finland.

According to the U.S. Geological Survey, U.S. production of chromium ferroalloys and metal in July 1998 totaled 1,890 tonnes (chromium content). In the first seven months of 1998, production was 18,800 tonnes. For all of 1997, production was 40,900 tonnes. Net shipments in July 1998 were 3,920 tonnes. For all of 1997, net shipments were 56,300 tonnes. Stainless steel production in the second quarter of 1998 was 506,000 tonnes. For all of 1997, stainless steel production was 2.16 million tonnes.

In terms of supply, stainless steel scrap receipts in the second quarter were 159,000 tonnes. For all of 1997, stainless steel scrap receipts were 707,000 tonnes. Imports for consumption in the second quarter of 1998 of chromite ore were 71,000 tonnes, while for all of 1997 they were 303,000 tonnes. Chromium ferroalloys imported in the second quarter of 1998 were 144,000 tonnes. For 1997 they were 392,000 tonnes. Chromium metal imports in the second quarter 1998 were 2,660 tonnes. In 1997 imports were 9,800 tonnes. Stainless steel imports in April-June 1998 were 200,000 tonnes, while for all of 1997 they were 774,000 tonnes.

U.S. consumption of chromite ore in July 1998 was 23,800 tonnes. In the first seven months of 1998 it was 182,000 tonnes. For 1997, chromite ore consumption was 350,000 tonnes. Chromium ferroalloys and metal consumption in July 1998 were 24,200 tonnes. In the January-July 1998 period consumption was 200,000 tonnes. For all of 1997, consumption was 354,000 tonnes. Exports of chromite ore in the January-June 1998 period were 46,100 tonnes. For all of 1997, exports were 18,500 tonnes. Chromium ferroalloy exports in the first half of 1998 were 3,500 tonnes while for all of 1997 they were 9,180 tonnes. Stainless steel exports in first half 1998 were 112,000 tonnes, while for all of 1997 they were 199,000 tonnes.

World Mine Production of Chromium In Thousands of Metric Tons (Gross Weight)

Year	Albania	Brazil	Cuba	Finland	India	Iran	Kazakhstan[3]	Madagascar	Philippines	South Africa	Turkey	Zimbabwe	World Total
1988	1,109	410	52	700	821	60	3,700	64	129	4,245	851	561	12,896
1989	900	476	51	513	1,003	73	3,800	63	217	4,951	1,077	627	14,006
1990	950	263	50	504	1,050	77	3,800	151	183	4,620	836	573	13,200
1991	587	340	50	473	940	90	3,800	149	191	5,100	940	564	13,300
1992	322	449	50	499	1,158	130	3,500	161	81	3,363	531	522	11,000
1993	282	308	50	511	1,070	115	2,900	144	62	2,838	767	252	9,560
1994	118	360	20	573	909	354	2,020	90	76	3,599	1,270	517	10,200
1995	160	448	31	598	1,536	371	2,871	106	111	5,085	2,080	707	14,500
1996[1]	143	408	37	574	1,363	250	1,190	137	78	4,971	1,279	697	11,500
1997[2]	106	330	44	611	1,363	200	1,000	140	88	5,779	1,750	680	12,500

[1] Estimate. [2] Preliminary. [3] Formerly part of the U.S.S.R.; data not reported seperately until 1992. *Source: U.S. Geological Survey (USGS)*

Salient Statistics of Chromium in the United States In Thousands of Metric Tons (Gross Weight)

						Consumption by Primary Consumer Groups			Consumer Stocks, Dec. 31			$ per Metric Ton	
Year	% Net Import Reliance of Apparent Consumption	Production of Ferrochromium	Exports	Imports for Consumption	Reexports	Total	Metallurgical & Chemical	Refractory	Metallurgical & Chemical	Refractory	Total Stocks	South Africa[3]	Turkish[4]
1988	78	120	4	615	1	551	495	56	366	23	390	56	180
1989	78	147	40	525	2	561	517	44	368	24	392	65	185
1990	80	109	6	347	4	405	361	44	333	21	355	55	135
1991	75	68	9	310	----	375	339	36	310	11	321	50	130
1992	86	61	7	324	----	362	335	27	308	13	321	60	110
1993	81	63	10	329	2	337	314	23	259	16	275	60	110
1994	75	67	47	273	----	322	302	20	250	17	266	60	110
1995	80	73	18	416	----	W	W	W	194	11	205	80	230
1996[1]	79	37	69	362	----	W	W	W	165	8	173	80	230
1997[2]	76	61	19	350	----	W	W	W	167	8	175	75	150

[1] Preliminary. [2] Estimate. [3] Cr_2O_3, 44% (Transvaal). *Source: U.S. Geological Survey (USGS)*

Coal

U.S. coal production in the first quarter of 1998 was 279 million short tons. That was up 2 percent from the first quarter of 1996. For all of 1997, U.S. coal production was 1.09 billion tons.

Regional coal production in the first quarter 1998 was 119 million tons in Appalachia, virtually unchanged from a year earlier. Interior region coal production was 41 million tons, down 4 percent from the previous year. Western region coal production was 119 million tons or 6 percent more than in the same period of 1997. Coal production east of the Mississippi River was 145.9 million tons, down 1 percent from 1997. First quarter 1998 coal production west of the Mississippi River was 133.3 million tons, up 5 percent from a year ago.

Coal consumption in the first quarter of 1998 was 247.4 million tons, almost the same as the year before. For all of 1997, coal consumption was 1.03 billion tons. Small amounts of coal are imported. In first quarter 1998, imports of coal were 1.8 million tons or some 38 percent more than in 1997. For all of 1997, imports were 7.5 million tons.

In January-March 1998, exports of coal were 18.3 million tons, 9 percent less than in 1997. The major export destinations were Japan which took 2.5 million tons and Canada which took 2 million tons. Other large markets were Brazil, Italy and the Netherlands. U.S. steam coal exports in the first quarter were 6 million tons. The major markets were Canada and Japan. Exports of metallurgical coal were 12.3 million tons to Brazil, Japan and Italy.

World Production[3] of Coal (Monthly Average) In Thousands of Metric Tons

Year	Australia	Canada	China	Czech Rep.[4]	Germany	India	Indonesia	Kazakhstan[5]	Poland	Russia[5]	Ukraine[5]	United Kingdom	United States
1989	12,317	3,233	87,833	2,089	6,454	16,569	380	----	14,830	48,083	----	8,190	67,608
1990	13,236	3,139	90,000	1,842	6,363	16,819	611	----	12,306	39,300	----	7,442	71,137
1991	13,720	3,326	88,212	1,623	6,063	18,905	1,143	----	11,698	33,769	----	8,028	68,755
1992	14,594	2,693	91,278	1,540	6,013	19,490	1,760	10,546	10,960	16,123	----	7,273	75,413
1993	14,746	2,943	96,177	1,525	5,347	20,503	2,300	9,323	10,873	16,200	9,545	5,683	71,473
1994	14,721	3,664	100,508	1,736	4,802	20,974	2,603	8,298	11,136	14,730	7,650	3,976	78,102
1995	15,921	3,215	107,624	1,717	4,905	22,131	3,460	6,626	11,347	14,743	6,717	4,282	86,081
1996	16,154	3,359	116,117	1,653	4,428	23,782	3,945	6,086	11,425	13,875	5,852	4,109	88,574
1997[1]	20,200	NA	113,523	NA	4,267	24,663	4,352	6,268	11,496	13,800	5,813	3,861	NA
1998[2]	20,547	NA	87,928	NA	3,663	25,814	4,322	6,042	9,412	13,200	6,374	3,355	NA

[1] Preliminary. [2] Estimate. [3] All grades of anthracite and bituminous coal, but excludes recovered slurries, lignite and brown coal. [4] Formerly part of Czechoslovakia; data not reported separately until 1993. [5] Formerly part of the U.S.S.R.; data not reported separately until 1992. NA = Not available.
Source: United Nations (UN)

Production of Bituminous & Lignite Coal in the United States In Thousands of Short Tons

Year	Alabama	Colorado	Illinois	Indiana	Kentucky	Montana	Ohio	Pennsylvania	Texas	Virgina	West Virgina	Wyoming	Total U.S.
1989	27,992	17,123	59,267	33,641	167,389	37,742	33,689	67,248	53,854	43,006	153,580	171,558	980,729
1990	29,030	18,910	60,393	35,907	128,396	37,616	35,252	67,008	55,755	46,917	169,205	184,249	1,029,076
1991	27,269	17,834	60,258	31,468	158,980	38,237	30,569	61,936	53,825	41,954	167,352	193,854	995,984
1992	25,796	19,226	59,857	30,466	161,068	38,889	30,403	65,498	55,071	43,024	162,164	190,172	997,545
1993	24,768	21,886	41,098	29,295	156,299	35,917	28,816	55,394	54,567	39,317	130,525	210,129	945,424
1994	23,266	25,304	52,797	30,927	161,642	41,640	29,897	62,237	52,346	37,129	161,776	237,092	1,033,504
1995	24,640	25,710	48,180	26,007	153,739	39,451	26,118	61,576	52,684	34,099	162,997	263,822	1,032,974
1996	24,637	24,886	46,656	29,670	152,425	37,891	28,572	67,942	55,164	35,590	170,433	278,440	1,063,856
1997[1]	24,468	27,449	41,159	35,497	155,853	41,005	29,154	76,198	53,328	35,837	173,743	281,881	1,089,932
1998[2]	23,224	30,825	38,182	36,297	145,609	42,092	28,600	76,519	53,578	34,059	175,794	313,983	1,109,768

[1] Preliminary. [2] Estimate. *Source: Energy Information Administration, U.S. Department of Energy (EIA-DOE)*

Production[2] of Bituminous Coal in the United States In Thousands of Short Tons

Year	Jan.	Feb.	Mar.	Apr.	May.	June	July	Aug.	Sept.	Oct.	Nov.	Dec.	Total
1989	81,969	75,040	88,981	77,233	82,486	78,544	66,269	90,824	84,618	87,657	85,043	72,554	971,218
1990	90,304	81,796	91,357	83,350	86,615	84,720	79,585	91,558	83,107	93,418	86,772	75,676	1,028,258
1991	85,810	82,592	85,012	79,324	79,917	76,896	79,745	88,851	81,533	90,307	81,730	79,383	991,100
1992	87,979	82,102	85,835	82,364	80,197	79,968	80,768	84,401	83,555	86,265	80,240	83,021	996,695
1993	80,508	76,341	84,782	79,329	73,759	80,949	70,771	76,209	79,705	80,628	79,404	79,905	942,290
1994	76,578	81,569	95,969	87,534	82,105	86,223	77,421	93,881	88,346	85,085	86,317	87,856	1,028,884
1995	88,351	83,893	93,020	80,092	83,291	84,210	79,511	88,035	89,052	90,573	86,779	81,292	1,032,974
1996	83,013	83,671	90,392	88,158	88,562	83,824	88,331	94,664	87,388	94,195	86,400	86,493	1,059,104
1997	92,425	88,028	92,265	87,909	94,296	86,382	88,666	89,319	92,298	94,562	83,344	94,913	1,085,254
1998[1]	97,012	86,178	94,930	91,503	90,310	91,839	92,142	93,188	97,333	97,321	90,544	94,567	1,106,128

[1] Preliminary. [2] Includes small amounts of lignite. *Source: Energy Information Administration, U.S. Department of Energy (EIA-DOE)*

COAL

Production[2] of Pennsylvania Anthracite Coal   In Thousands of Short Tons

Year	Jan.	Feb.	Mar.	Apr.	May	June	July	Aug.	Sept.	Oct.	Nov.	Dec.	Total
1989	281	282	337	273	280	256	197	311	299	373	339	291	3,519
1990	237	221	259	297	329	327	225	280	323	354	310	183	3,345
1991	248	243	259	230	224	235	253	313	285	346	299	238	3,173
1992	247	257	279	296	274	287	305	337	311	322	321	306	3,542
1993	272	266	290	175	305	358	222	277	351	603	315	271	3,705
1994	318	335	415	380	375	379	346	457	412	453	452	395	4,717
1995	304	304	372	332	335	353	307	396	428	445	388	347	4,682
1996	302	349	367	371	361	335	367	418	385	557	505	434	4,751
1997	351	366	492	374	351	390	407	423	415	448	384	415	4,678
1998[1]	306	546	552	432	410	414	278	241	239	206	167	167	3,640

[1] Preliminary. [2] Represents production in Pennsylvania only.. *Source: Energy Information Administration, U.S. Department of Energy (EIA-DOE)*

Salient Statistics of Coal in the United States   In Thousands of Short Tons

Year	Production	Imports	Consumption	Exports: Brazil	Exports: Canada	Exports: Europe	Exports: Asia	Exports: Total	Total Ending Stocks[2]	Losses & Unaccounted For[3]
1989	980,729	2,851	889,699	5,681	16,777	51,604	22,734	100,815	175,087	6,811
1990	1,029,076	2,699	895,480	5,847	15,511	58,382	22,725	105,804	201,629	3,949
1991	995,984	3,390	887,621	7,052	11,178	65,520	21,788	108,969	200,682	3,731
1992	997,545	3,803	907,655	6,370	15,140	57,255	20,540	102,516	197,685	-5,826
1993	945,424	7,309	944,081	5,197	8,889	37,575	19,500	74,519	145,742	-13,924
1994	1,033,504	7,584	951,461	5,482	9,193	35,825	17,957	71,359	169,358	-5,348
1995	1,032,974	7,201	962,039	6,351	9,427	48,620	19,095	88,547	169,083	-10,136
1996	1,063,856	7,126	1,005,573	6,540	12,029	47,193	17,980	90,473	151,627	-7,608
1997	1,089,932	7,487	1,030,453	7,455	14,975	41,331	14,498	83,545	140,374	-5,326
1998[1]	1,118,101	8,472	1,024,290	36,729	15,612	36,446	13,098	77,587	150,416	

[1] Preliminary. [2] Producer & distributor and consumer stocks, excludes stocks held by retail dealers for consumption by the residential and commercial secor. [3] Equals production plus imports minus the change in producer & distributor and consumer stocks minus consumption minus exports.
Source: Energy Information Administration, U.S. Department of Energy (EIA-DOE)

Consumption and Stocks of Coal in the United States   In Thousands of Short Tons

	Consumption								Stocks, Dec. 31[3]			
	Electric Utilities				Industrial		Residential		Consumer			Producers
Year	Anthracite	Bituminous	Lignite	Total	Coke Plants	Other Industrial[2]	and Commercial	Total	Electric Utilities	Coke Plants	Other Industrials	and Distributors
1989	1,049	688,504	77,335	766,888	40,508	76,134	6,167	889,699	135,860	2,864	7,363	29,000
1990	1,031	694,317	78,201	773,549	38,877	76,330	6,724	895,480	156,166	3,329	8,716	33,418
1991	994	691,275	79,999	772,268	33,854	75,405	6,094	887,621	157,876	2,773	7,061	32,971
1992	986	698,626	80,248	779,860	32,366	74,042	6,153	892,421	154,130	2,597	6,965	33,993
1993	951	732,736	79,821	813,508	31,323	74,892	6,221	925,944	111,341	2,401	6,716	25,284
1994	1,123	737,102	79,045	817,270	31,740	75,179	6,013	930,201	126,897	2,657	6,585	33,219
1995	978	749,951	78,078	829,007	33,011	73,055	5,807	940,880	126,304	2,632	5,702	34,444
1996	1,009	795,252	78,421	874,681	31,706	70,941	6,006	983,334	114,623	2,667	5,688	28,648
1997	1,014	821,823	77,524	900,361	30,203	70,599	6,463	1,007,626	98,826	1,978	5,597	33,973
1998[1]	875	846,715	71,100	918,691	27,551	69,511	6,172	1,021,930	103,998	1,822	4,654	36,000

[1] Preliminary. [2] Including transportation. [3] Excludes stocks held at retail dealers for consumption by the residential and commercial sector.
Source: *Energy Information Administration, U.S. Department of Energy (EIA-DOE)*

Average Prices of Coal in the United States   In Dollars Per Short Ton

	End-Use Sector				Exports				End-Use Sector				Exports	
Year	Electric Utilities	Coke Plants	Other Industrial[3]	Imports[4]	Steam	Metal-lurgical	Total Average[4]	Year	Electric Utilities	Coke Plants	Other Industrial[3]	Imports[4]	Steam	Metal-lurgical	Total Average[4]
1989	30.15	47.50	33.03	34.14	37.64	45.19	42.52	1994	28.03	46.56	32.55	30.21	34.34	42.77	39.93
1990	30.45	47.73	33.59	34.45	36.81	46.51	42.63	1995	27.01	47.34	32.42	34.13	34.51	44.30	40.27
1991	30.02	48.88	33.54	33.12	36.91	46.15	42.39	1996	26.45	47.33	32.32	33.45	34.09	45.49	40.76
1992	29.36	47.92	32.78	33.46	35.73	45.41	41.34	1997	26.16	47.36	32.40	34.32	32.45	45.47	40.59
1993	28.58	47.44	32.23	29.89	36.03	44.11	41.41	1998[1]	25.88	45.85	32.33	32.71	31.19	45.37	40.25

[1] Preliminary. [2] Estimate. [3] Manufacturing plants only. [4] Based on the free alongside ship (F.A.S) value. NA = Not available.
Source: Energy Information Administration, U.S. Department of Energy (EIA-DOE)

Trends in Bituminous Coal, Lignite and Pennsylvania Anthracite in the U.S. In Thousands of Short Tons

	Bituminous Coal and Lignite							Pennsylvania Anthracite					All Mines
	Production				Labor Productivity							Labor Product.	Labor Product.
Year	Under-ground	Surface	Total	Miners[1] Employed	Under-ground	Surface	Average	Under-ground	Surface	Total	Miners[1] Employed	Short Tons Miner/Hr.	Short Tons Miner/Hr.
					Short Tons Per Miner Per Hour								
1980	336,925	486,719	823,644	224,938	1.21	3.27	1.94	583	5,473	6,056	3,631	1.11	1.93
1981	315,875	502,477	818,352	226,250	1.29	3.50	2.11	621	4,802	5,423	3,052	.92	2.10
1982	338,572	494,951	833,523	214,400	1.37	3.48	2.14	579	4,009	4,588	2,717	.59	2.11
1983	299,882	478,111	778,003	173,543	1.62	3.87	2.52	487	3,602	4,089	2,099	1.01	2.50
1984	351,474	540,285	891,759	175,746	1.72	4.10	2.65	576	3,586	4,162	2,102	1.02	2.64
1985	350,073	528,856	878,930	167,009	1.79	4.32	2.76	727	3,982	4,708	2,272	1.05	2.74
1986	359,800	526,223	886,023	152,668	2.00	4.69	3.04	638	3,654	4,292	1,977	1.03	3.01
1987	372,238	542,963	915,202	141,065	2.21	5.06	3.32	636	2,925	3,560	1,602	1.13	3.30
1988	381,546	565,164	946,710	133,913	2.38	5.41	3.58	610	2,945	3,555	1,453	1.21	3.55
1989	393,322	584,058	977,381	130,103	2.46	5.70	3.73	513	2,835	3,348	1,394	1.12	3.70
1990	424,119	601,449	1,025,570	129,619	2.54	6.07	3.86	427	3,080	3,506	1,687	1.03	3.83
1991	406,901	585,638	992,539	119,441	2.70	6.51	4.12	324	3,121	3,445	1,161	1.39	4.09
1992	406,815	587,248	994,062	108,979	2.95	6.73	4.41	424	3,058	3,483	1,217	1.33	4.36
1993	350,637	590,482	941,119	100,099	3.24	7.84	4.74	416	3,889	4,306	1,124	1.85	4.70

[1] Excludes miners employed at mines producing less than 10,000 tons. *Source: Energy Information Adminstration, U.S. Department of Energy (EIA-DOE)*

Average Mine Prices of Coal in the United States In Dollars Per Short Ton

	Average Mine Price by Method			Average Mine Prices by Rank				Bituminous & Lignite	Anthracite	All Coal CIF[3] Electric Utility
Year	Under-ground	Surface	Total	Lignite	Sub-bituminous	Bituminous	Anthracite[1]	FOB Mines[2]	FOB Mines[2]	Plants
1980	33.50	18.78	24.65	W	11.08	29.17	42.51	24.52	42.51	28.76
1981	35.78	20.60	26.40	W	12.18	31.51	44.28	26.29	44.28	32.32
1982	35.78	21.46	27.25	W	13.37	32.15	49.85	27.14	49.85	34.91
1983	34.47	20.68	25.98	W	13.03	31.11	59.29	25.85	52.29	34.99
1984	33.36	20.59	25.61	10.45	12.41	30.63	48.22	25.51	48.22	35.12
1985	32.91	20.13	25.20	10.68	12.57	30.78	45.80	25.10	45.80	34.53
1986	30.33	19.34	23.79	10.64	12.26	28.84	44.12	23.70	44.12	33.30
1987	29.63	18.58	23.07	10.85	11.32	28.19	43.65	23.00	43.65	31.83
1988	28.97	17.43	22.07	10.06	10.45	27.66	44.16	22.00	44.16	30.64
1989	28.44	17.38	21.82	9.91	10.16	27.40	42.93	21.76	42.93	30.15
1990	28.58	16.98	21.76	10.13	9.70	27.43	39.40	21.71	39.40	30.45
1991	28.56	16.60	21.49	10.89	9.68	27.49	36.34	21.45	36.34	30.02
1992	27.83	16.34	21.03	10.81	9.68	26.78	34.24	20.98	34.24	29.36
1993	26.92	15.67	19.85	11.11	9.33	26.15	32.94	20.56	37.80	28.64

[1] Produced in Pennsylvania. [2] FOB = free on board. [3] CIF = cost, insurance and freight. W = Withheld data. *Source: Energy Information Administration, U.S. Department of Energy (EIA-DOE)*

Cobalt

Cobalt is a strategic and critical metal with a variety of uses with industrial and military applications. Cobalt is found in the ores of iron and copper. The largest use of cobalt is in superalloys, which are used in making gas turbine aircraft engines. Cobalt has many other uses. It is used to make magnets; high-speed steels; cemented carbides and diamond tools; catalysts for the petroleum and chemical industries; drying agents for paints; ground coats for porcelain enamels; pigments; battery electrodes; steel-belted radial tires; and magnetic recording media.

The U.S. is the world's largest consumer of cobalt. With no mine or refinery production, the U.S. relies on imports. The U.S. Government maintains large quantities of cobalt metal in the National Defense Stockpile.

According to the U.S. Geological Survey, world cobalt mine production in 1997 was estimated at 27,000 metric tonnes (cobalt content), up less than 1 percent from 1996. The largest producer was Zambia with 6,100 tonnes, down 23 percent from 1996. The next largest producer was Canada with 5,700 tonnes, about the same as 1996. Other major producers included the Congo, Russia, Albania and Cuba.

World refinery production of cobalt in 1997 was 25,700 tonnes, almost 2 percent more than in 1996. The largest producer was Finland with 5,000 tonnes, some 20 percent more than the previous year. The next largest producer was Russia with 4,100 tonnes, down 2 percent from 1996. The other large refinery producers were Zambia, Canada, Norway and the Congo.

U.S. reported consumption of cobalt materials in July 1998 was 680 tonnes (contained cobalt). Of the total, 295 tonnes were cobalt metal, 144 tonnes were cobalt oxide and other chemical compounds, and 241 tonnes were scrap. In the January-July 1998 period, consumption was 4,840 tonnes, up 5 percent from a year ago. For all of 1997, reported consumption was 8,400 tonnes.

U.S. reported industry stocks of cobalt materials in July 1998 were 675 tonnes (contained cobalt). Of the total, cobalt metal stocks were 355 tonnes, oxide and other chemical compound stocks were 208 tonnes and scrap stocks were 113 tonnes. At the end of 1997, stocks were 738 tonnes. U.S. Government stocks of cobalt metal in July 1998 were 15,400 tonnes. At the end of 1997 they were 17,100 tonnes.

U.S. imports for consumption of cobalt in June 1998 were 559,000 kilograms, down 22 percent from the year before. The major supplier was Zambia with 121,000 kilograms. Other major suppliers were Norway, the Congo, Canada, Belgium and Finland. In the first six months of 1998, imports were 3.73 million kilograms, down 15 percent from the same period of 1997. For all of 1997, imports for consumption of cobalt were 8.43 million kilograms.

World Mine Production of Cobalt In Metric Tons (Cobalt Content)

Year	Australia	Botswana	Canada	Cuba	Finland (Refinery)	France (Refinery)	Japan (Refinery)	New Caledonia	Norway (Refinery)	Russia[3]	Zaire	Zambia	World Total
1988	1,200	291	2,398	1,783	1,132	176	109	800	1,951	2,850	26,000	7,090	43,819
1989	1,100	215	6,167	1,825	1,295	165	99	800	1,946	5,700	18,400	7,255	42,873
1990	1,200	205	5,470	1,460	1,300	150	199	800	1,830	5,500	19,000	7,000	42,300
1991	1,400	208	5,274	1,100	1,503	123	185	800	1,983	5,800	9,900	6,994	33,300
1992	1,600	208	5,102	1,150	2,100	150	105	800	2,293	4,000	5,700	6,910	27,800
1993	1,800	205	5,108	1,060	2,200	150	190	800	2,414	3,500	2,459	4,840	21,900
1994	2,300	225	4,265	972	3,000	146	161	800	2,823	3,000	826	3,600	17,800
1995	2,500	271	5,339	1,591	3,610	161	227	800	2,804	3,500	1,647	5,908	24,100
1996[1]	2,800	406	5,714	2,011	4,160	174	258	800	3,098	3,300	2,000	7,900	26,800
1997[2]	3,000	334	5,700	2,082	5,000	159	264	800	3,417	3,300	3,500	6,100	27,000

[1] Preliminary. [2] Estimate. [3] Formerly part of the U.S.S.R.; data not reported seperately until 1992. *Source: U.S. Geological Survey (USGS)*

Salient Statistics of Cobalt in the United States In Metric Tons (Cobalt Content)

					Consumption by End Uses										
Year	Net Import Reliance as a % of Apparent Consumption	Cobalt Secondary Production	Processors and Consumer Stocks Dec. 31	Imports for Consumption	Ground Coat Frit	Stainless & Heat Resisting	Catalysts	Super-Alloys	Tool Steel	Magnetic Alloys	Pigments	Drier in Paints, etc.[3]	Cutting & Wear-Resistant Material	Welding Materials	Total Apparent Uses	Price $ Per Pound[4]
1988	87	1,018	1,766	7,051	332	26	617	2,865	180	878	378	892	522	206	7,824	7.09
1989	83	1,184	1,456	5,793	366	74	819	2,860	219	870	319	718	538	136	7,172	7.64
1990	84	1,225	1,853	6,530	357	41	W	3,345	123	710	W	751	541	180	7,512	10.09
1991	80	1,578	1,622	6,920	W	51	W	3,066	W	713	W	781	525	135	7,240	16.92
1992	76	1,613	840	5,760	257	26	949	2,697	47	670	197	745	522	128	6,471	22.93
1993	79	1,566	819	5,950	W	41	935	2,530	59	569	193	732	569	171	7,310	13.79
1994	81	1,570	914	6,780	W	41	871	2,810	84	698	198	809	723	312	8,560	24.66
1995	82	1,540	818	6,440	196	38	732	2,940	146	757	172	770	748	287	8,740	29.21
1996[1]	82	2,000	770	6,710	391	38	652	3,360	95	719	191	733	722	347	9,130	25.50
1997[2]	78	2,530	738	8,430	490	38	734	4,060	112	778	201	556	789	342	11,000	23.34

[1] Preliminary. [2] Estimate. [3] Or related usage. [4] Annual spot for cathodes. W = Witheld proprietary data. *Source: U.S. Geological Survey (USGS)*

Cocoa

Cocoa is a tropical crop found mostly in a zone that extends approximately 15 degrees north and 15 degrees south of the equator. Cocoa trees attain a height of up to 35 feet and produce fruits known as pods. A mature cocoa pod is six to ten inches long and can contain 20-50 seeds or beans. In the course of a season, the cocoa tree will produce thousands of flowers but only a very small number of pods. Flowers and pods are present on the tree throughout the year but at times they are in greater numbers. After planting, cocoa trees become productive in four or five years and reach peak productivity in the tenth to eleventh year. Cocoa trees can remain productive for 50 years.

The major production area for cocoa is West Africa where about 60 percent of the world's cocoa is grown. The four major West African producers are the Ivory Coast, Ghana, Nigeria and Cameroon. The Ivory Coast is by far the largest producer with about 40 percent of world production. Ghana is the next largest producer with almost 15 percent of the market. The other major production region is Southeast Asia where Indonesia, Malaysia and Papua New Guinea are the largest producers. Indonesia has been trying to increase production while Malaysia has reduced production of cocoa so as to grow crops like palm oil. In South America, Brazil and Ecuador are the largest producers. Brazil's cocoa production has been on a gradual decline as a result of the spread of disease and poor weather. Whether Brazil can ever recover is in question as it appears the disease problem will not go away. Ecuador's crop in 1997-98 was severely damaged by El Nino. Other countries that produce cocoa include the Dominican Republic and Mexico.

The USDA estimated world cocoa production in 1998-99 at 2.69 million tonnes, about unchanged from 1997-98. The 1997-98 season was characterized as one in which El Nino related weather events took a toll on some cocoa crops while others were unscathed. In particular, Ecuador, Papua New Guinea and Indonesia saw weather related problems. The more important West African cocoa crops did not have El Nino weather related problems. As such, world cocoa production in 1997-98 was reduced by El Nino but world stocks of cocoa remain plentiful.

The USDA forecast the 1998-99 Ivory Coast crop at 1.15 million tonnes, up almost 3 percent from the previous season. The growing season in the Ivory Coast was somewhat less than optimal. There were areas that were very dry and others that received normal rainfall. The USDA noted that most of the cocoa trees in the Ivory Coast are between 8 and 25 years old which puts them at the peak of production. The USDA forecast that the Ivory Coast would export 1.05 million tonnes of cocoa which would be up 9 percent from the previous season. The Ivory Coast is by far the largest exporter of cocoa in the world. There has been a tendency for more of the cocoa producing countries to process their crops in-country. The USDA forecast the Ivory Coast would process 100,000 tonnes of its crop which would be well below the 160,000 tonnes in 1997-98.

The USDA forecast Ghana's 1998-99 cocoa crop at 360,000 tonnes, down 14 percent from 1997-98. The USDA cited unfavorable rainfall in late August and early September as the reason for the expected decline. Ghana is forecast to export 305,000 tonnes of cocoa, down 18 percent from the previous year. Ghana's in-country processing was forecast to remain unchanged at 65,000 tonnes.

The USDA forecast Indonesia's 1998-99 cocoa crop at 310,000 tonnes, just slightly higher than last season. Exports are expected to reach 230,000 tonnes or some 5 percent more than the previous season. Malaysia's cocoa output was forecast to reach 100,000 tonnes or some 6 percent less than in 1997-98. Malaysia is a net importer of cocoa. Brazil's 1998-99 cocoa output was forecast at 170,000 tonnes, an increase of almost 5 percent from 1997-98. Due to smaller crops, Brazil is becoming a net importer of cocoa.

The USDA forecast the global cocoa grind in 1998-99 at 2.9 million tonnes. That is up about 4 percent from 1997-98. It was noted that cocoa consumption would continue to grow though the rate of growth would slow due to the effect of financial instability in Russia, Eastern Europe and Asia.

Futures Markets

Cocoa futures and options are traded on the Coffee, Sugar and Cocoa Exchange (CSCE) in New York, and in London on the LIFFE. Futures are traded on the Kuala Lumpur Commodity Exchange (KLCE).

World Supply and Demand of Cocoa In Thousands of Metric Tons

Crop Year Beginning October	Stock Oct. 1	Net World Production[4]	Total Availability	Seasonal Grindings	Closing Stocks	Stock Change
1983-4	676	1,524	2,200	1,726	474	-202
1984-5	474	1,920	2,393	1,862	531	58
1985-6	531	1,942	2,474	1,877	597	65
1986-7	597	1,968	2,565	1,896	669	72
1987-8	669	2,172	2,841	2,003	838	169
1988-9	838	2,435	3,273	2,118	1,155	317
1989-90	1,155	2,401	3,556	2,212	1,343	188
1990-1	1,343	2,485	3,828	2,351	1,476	133
1991-2	1,476	2,246	3,723	2,284	1,439	-38
1992-3	1,439	2,336	3,775	2,441	1,334	-105
1993-4	1,334	2,447	3,781	2,485	1,296	-38
1994-5	1,296	2,341	3,637	2,508	1,129	-167
1995-6	1,129	2,921	4,051	2,661	1,390	261
1996-7[1]	1,390	2,663	4,053	2,752	1,301	-89
1997-8[2]	1,301	2,619	3,919	2,817	1,102	-199
1998-9[3]	1,102	2,669	3,771	2,817	954	-148

[1] Preliminary. [2] Estimate. [3] Forecast. [4] Obtained by adjusting the Gross World Crop for one percent loss in weight. *Source: E D & F Man Cocoa, Ltd.*

COCOA

World Production of Cocoa Beans In Thousands of Metric Tons

Crop Year Beginning October	Brazil	Cameroon	Colombia	Dominican Republic	Ecuador	Ghana	Indonesia	Ivory Coast	Malaysia	Mexico	Nigeria	Papua New Guinea	World Total
1989-90	356	122	58	57	102	295	135	710	240	39	155	41	2,419
1990-1	380	107	52	42	104	293	147	804	224	43	170	33	2,510
1991-2	310	108	47	48	83	243	169	748	217	51	110	41	2,269
1992-3	305	99	54	52	70	312	234	697	219	51	130	39	2,360
1993-4	280	97	49	58	79	255	251	887	204	39	142	31	2,472
1994-5	230	109	48	55	83	310	238	862	120	43	144	29	2,365
1995-6	235	117	45	55	103	404	284	1,265	116	30	163	35	2,951
1996-7[1]	170	126	45	47	101	323	327	1,132	102	35	150	28	2,690
1997-8[2]	165	127	45	60	28	404	331	1,111	57	31	167	20	2,645
1998-9[3]	145	125	45	50	60	365	350	1,100	85	35	200	35	2,696

[1] Preliminary. [2] Estimate. [3] Forecast. *Source: Foreign Agricultural Service, U.S. Department of Agriculture (FAS-USDA)*

World Consumption of Cocoa[1] In Thousands of Metric Tons

Crop Year Beginning October	Belgium	Brazil	Cote d'Ivoire	France	Germany	Italy	Malaysia	Netherlands	Singapore	United Kingdom	United States	Former USSR	World Total
1989-90	47	239	111	59	287	51	72	241	53	120	270	106	2212
1990-1	45	275	115	70	295	56	77	268	52	145	272	83	2351
1991-2	46	216	108	67	306	62	87	294	51	153	307	25	2284
1992-3	47	218	100	80	330	58	99	309	47	169	326	95	2441
1993-4	50	220	110	95	315	65	103	331	52	170	317	90	2485
1994-5	53	189	108	108	290	69	101	350	52	154	331	80	2508
1995-6	54	192	135	111	275	73	96	385	56	191	345	80	2661
1996-7[1]	55	180	150	106	265	71	103	402	55	172	394	85	2752
1997-8[2]	55	184	205	107	250	72	94	425	55	174	399	75	2817
1998-9[3]	55	200	235	115	220	73	95	430	55	172	400	50	2817

[1] Figures represent the "grindings" of cocoa beans in each country. [2] Preliminary. [3] Estimate. [4] Forecast. *Source: Foreign Agricultural Service, U.S. Department of Agriculture (FAS-USDA)*

Raw Cocoa Grindings in Selected Countries In Metric Tons

Year	Total	First Quarter	Second Quarter	Third Quarter	Fourth Quarter	Total	First Quarter	Second Quarter	Third Quarter	Fourth Quarter
	Germany[2]					Netherlands				
1989	245,997	61,960	59,211	56,994	67,832	233,529	61,071	56,392	55,129	60,937
1990	281,855	69,125	64,613	70,994	77,123	247,590	62,243	58,817	58,702	67,828
1991	290,703	73,172	72,396	70,934	73,661	274,741	64,299	71,643	63,973	74,826
1992	319,251	78,661	73,797	80,111	86,682	293,157	77,954	71,537	69,871	73,795
1993	298,681	74,119	69,805	74,010	80,747	320,060	78,338	75,548	81,183	84,991
1994	296,219	80,242	68,033	67,706	80,238	334,384	83,963	78,055	84,249	88,117
1995	258,817	69,441	56,478	61,523	71,375	355,492	91,314	85,248	85,311	93,619
1996	251,070	69,520	59,471	65,824	56,255	388,412	100,866	90,724	99,549	97,273
1997	245,244	61,379	57,402	65,233	61,230	407,340	102,338	100,132	101,817	103,053
1998[1]	219,981	62,154	47,565	55,267		408,823	104,936	108,101	108,580	
	United Kingdom					United States[3]				
1989	114,669	28,506	30,113	26,873	29,177	192,837	43,802	49,185	47,071	52,779
1990	124,791	32,116	29,322	29,419	33,934	216,740	51,559	51,683	58,278	55,220
1991	148,191	32,902	36,016	41,863	37,410	255,781	51,191	64,365	66,544	73,681
1992	159,284	39,831	37,903	37,120	44,430	313,921	70,335	74,515	84,109	84,962
1993	171,343	44,575	41,975	37,496	47,297	321,905	78,968	77,720	84,593	80,624
1994	163,170	44,131	39,063	39,591	40,385	322,629	71,398	78,805	86,247	86,179
1995	159,877	43,410	35,348	34,431	46,688	338,401	78,835	78,886	87,360	93,320
1996	189,037	50,500	44,535	48,855	45,147	351,042	79,044	82,713	93,933	95,352
1997	173,522	44,059	42,702	41,180	45,581	397,895	95,435	97,223	105,984	99,253
1998[1]	170,896	45,787	42,338	40,047		399,852	99,189	96,341	104,359	

[1] Preliminary. [2] Beginning October 1990, includes former East Germany. [3] Data incomplete January 1984-March 1991, excludes one major processor.
Source: Foreign Agricultural Service, U.S. Department of Agriculture (FAS-USDA)

Imports of Cocoa Butter in Selected Countries In Metric Tons

Year	Australia	Austria	Belgium	Canada	France	Germany	Italy	Japan	Netherlands	Sweden	Switzerland	United Kingdom	United States
1988	9,405	4,315	12,869	7,371	24,562	33,590	4,731	12,497	20,431	5,596	12,821	34,329	78,285
1989	10,291	4,599	17,748	8,224	26,597	41,765	5,932	15,280	22,924	5,735	16,276	35,045	64,353
1990	10,025	6,047	22,125	8,830	28,539	49,999	6,187	15,686	34,529	5,855	16,306	34,604	92,165
1991	11,218	5,171	24,795	8,682	28,628	54,452	7,813	15,245	29,729	6,299	16,544	26,876	90,004
1992	10,697	5,249	31,836	10,706	28,560	44,906	8,431	15,835	29,999	5,885	17,422	26,300	99,509
1993	13,129	5,417	28,989	10,225	30,611	37,269	9,851	16,422	51,559	6,390	16,711	25,941	85,400
1994	13,030	5,410	34,061	11,551	36,698	59,170	9,173	15,937	43,192	7,079	17,242	35,453	54,550
1995	12,150	7,425	26,185	11,146	40,245	69,928	12,027	12,898	38,300	7,078	17,835	30,654	57,210
1996	14,316	7,124	23,771	12,166	47,349	69,298	11,178	16,096	39,193	5,698	18,690	32,781	68,761
1997[1]	14,896	6,922	34,222	16,782	46,516	71,094	9,706	16,609	29,023	6,937	19,058	37,021	87,687

[1] Preliminary. [2] Formerly part of the U.S.S.R.; data not reported separately until 1992. NA = Not available. *Source: Food and Agricultural Organization of the United Nations (FAO-UN)*

Imports of Cocoa Liquor and Cocoa Powder in Selected Countries In Metric Tons

	Cocoa Liquior						Cocoa Powder						
Year	France	Germany	Netherlands	Japan	United Kingdom	United States	Denmark	France	Germany	Italy	Japan	Netherlands	United States
1988	31,157	793	9,014	3,445	3,022	34,454	3,138	9,750	16,455	9,498	6,470	3,432	91,337
1989	29,257	1,040	9,315	3,451	2,524	27,556	2,810	10,920	18,470	10,233	6,033	5,862	53,736
1990	35,146	1,860	9,875	3,123	1,713	25,047	3,014	12,244	21,294	11,418	6,284	6,446	58,280
1991	40,251	3,242	7,443	2,057	1,918	25,320	3,583	12,215	25,315	12,189	6,557	6,239	55,636
1992	45,056	2,540	7,130	2,246	3,611	24,255	3,291	14,896	27,745	14,469	6,067	9,412	56,089
1993	41,999	1,694	15,543	2,468	1,490	31,641	3,402	16,773	25,732	13,221	5,771	5,626	66,533
1994	42,392	2,682	14,913	2,312	4,443	26,846	3,625	19,215	28,806	12,884	6,461	10,078	67,207
1995	46,570	5,083	6,822	1,832	5,030	19,192	3,229	17,081	32,247	15,265	6,310	10,048	66,075
1996	62,938	7,437	9,926	2,133	5,069	15,357	3,711	18,398	36,211	15,006	13,069	6,678	68,658
1997[1]	61,148	10,299	8,401	1,393	5,860	17,850	4,189	19,555	35,069	15,872	8,941	4,424	71,024

[1] Preliminary. NA = Not available. *Source: E D & F Man Cococa, Ltd.*

Imports of Cocoa and Products in the United States In Thousands of Metric Tons

Year	Jan.	Feb.	Mar.	Apr.	May	June	July	Aug.	Sept.	Oct.	Nov.	Dec.	Total
1989	44	24	30	29	25	18	18	23	14	20	10	10	266
1990[2]	72	53	70	110	83	60	NA	61	41	NA	72	49	716
1991	70	53	51	74	62	66	65	59	53	NA	NA	73	761
1992	83	66	62	55	50	60	52	60	67	67	64	69	755
1993	67	57	56	61	58	61	77	58	59	71	71	98	801
1994	67	68	56	61	49	51	49	58	58	61	45	48	672
1995	68	54	44	48	47	48	48	51	53	49	54	79	643
1996	90	87	90	80	55	49	62	53	53	60	60	86	821
1997	80	47	77	71	64	54	59	47	64	61	56	88	768
1998[1]	86	105	90	71	55	65	65	62	72	63	54		860

[1] Preliminary. [2] Prior to 1990, data for cocoa bean imports only. NA = Not available. *Source: Foreign Agricultural Service, U.S. Department of Agriculture (FAS-USDA)*

Visible Stocks of Cocoa in Port of Hampton Road Warehouses[1], at End of Month In Thousands of Bags

Year	Jan.	Feb.	Mar.	Apr.	May	June	July	Aug.	Sept.	Oct.	Nov.	Dec.
1989	528.4	653.3	777.7	775.0	875.0	741.6	655.8	583.2	509.1	594.2	567.0	552.3
1990	403.6	445.9	583.2	674.3	807.4	1,064.7	917.2	67.2	1,046.5	19.0	996.5	958.2
1991	946.5	953.3	910.1	946.0	906.1	1,036.6	1,174.5	1,291.2	1,386.2	1,429.0	1,426.0	1,502.9
1992	1,588.3	1,892.1	2,233.1	2,236.2	2,236.9	2,204.8	2,150.8	2,087.4	1,982.4	2,018.6	2,043.9	2,188.5
1993	2,209.9	2,497.3	2,443.9	2,676.8	2,771.8	2,689.7	2,920.0	2,708.6	2,740.1	2,418.7	2,328.3	2,356.9
1994	2,329.6	2,441.1	2,443.9	2,522.9	2,533.1	2,460.2	2,445.4	2,335.0	2,308.4	2,360.2	2,306.9	2,253.7
1995	2,152.7	2,098.6	2,195.7	2,212.3	2,120.2	2,016.0	1,919.8	1,786.6	1,713.1	1,598.2	1,463.9	1,470.3
1996	1,439.8	1,492.8	1,458.0	1,549.6	1,561.7	1,493.9	1,412.3	1,315.4	1,239.6	1,338.9	1,108.1	1,116.2
1997	1,128.3	1,132.1	1,133.0	1,094.0	1,010.5	970.2	872.4	840.1	727.3	763.9	695.7	704.8
1998	726.5	693.4	841.9	842.5	811.6	764.7	714.3	712.3	795.4	801.9	705.9	673.0

[1] Licensed and unlicensed warehouses approved by the CSCE. *Source: Coffee, Sugar & Cocoa Exchange, Inc. (CSCE)*

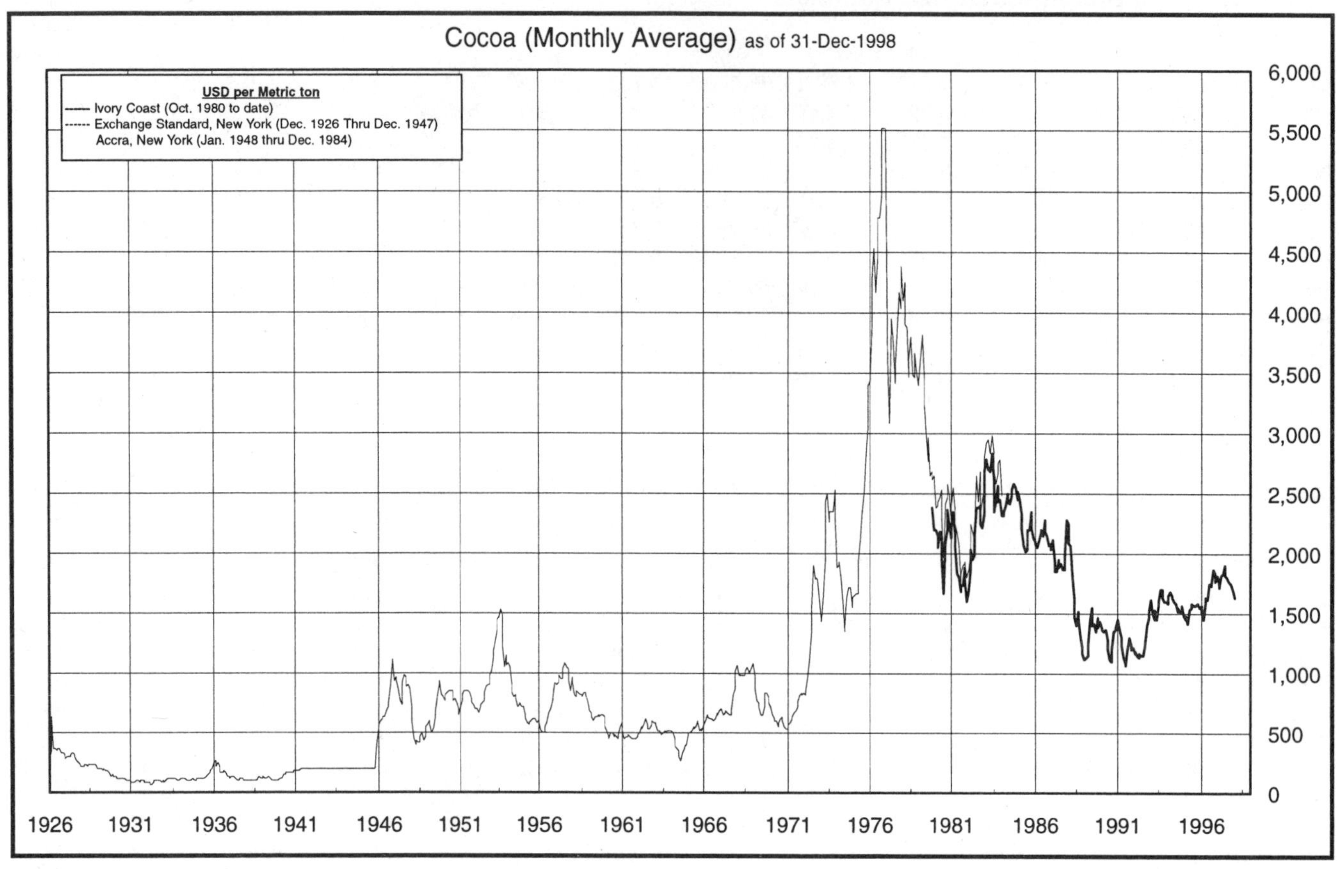

Visible Stocks of Cocoa in Philadelphia (Delaware River) Warehouses[1], at End of Month In Thousands of Bags

Year	Jan.	Feb.	Mar.	Apr.	May	June	July	Aug.	Sept.	Oct.	Nov.	Dec.
1989	86.0	67.5	88.7	96.2	114.0	112.5	100.3	100.0	54.6	46.1	51.9	53.5
1990	35.1	61.1	87.5	107.9	120.5	204.4	297.1	231.2	185.9	193.0	195.3	215.1
1991	216.2	226.9	249.3	254.9	309.2	376.8	382.8	376.8	375.5	355.1	280.5	282.7
1992	344.6	345.5	412.1	547.6	576.7	632.0	637.7	654.0	616.4	606.0	565.8	612.4
1993	562.2	589.8	603.9	606.0	653.1	678.0	665.7	648.9	600.6	611.5	685.2	781.8
1994	831.5	937.7	1,004.2	1,010.9	1,055.4	1,095.2	1,076.0	1,029.8	968.5	857.1	843.9	818.9
1995	807.5	1,034.3	1,038.9	1,020.2	963.7	924.3	860.7	759.2	852.2	727.0	666.0	735.6
1996	960.2	1,005.2	1,205.6	1,658.8	1,871.3	1,851.7	1,969.1	1,816.2	1,851.1	1,705.1	1,671.7	1,696.5
1997	1,753.0	1,634.4	1,579.6	1,641.0	1,578.7	1,625.9	1,696.2	1,637.6	1,530.9	1,491.8	1,414.2	1,394.0
1998	1,420.3	1,435.7	1,592.6	1,555.3	1,398.5	1,287.8	1,279.8	1,376.9	1,373.7	1,260.6	1,406.7	1,637.1

[1] Licensed and unlicensed warehouses approved by the CSCE. *Source: Coffee, Sugar & Cocoa Exchange, Inc. (CSCE)*

Visible Stocks of Cocoa in New York Warehouses[1], at End of Month In Thousands of Bags

Year	Jan.	Feb.	Mar.	Apr.	May	June	July	Aug.	Sept.	Oct.	Nov.	Dec.
1989	65.0	81.9	47.3	82.2	214.8	245.3	274.2	215.6	181.3	247.7	313.6	293.5
1990	288.4	267.5	311.9	335.3	294.8	359.2	431.3	409.0	442.2	406.3	413.4	397.2
1991	355.6	219.6	295.9	294.1	250.4	292.6	313.3	317.1	271.5	253.9	292.9	282.4
1992	321.2	303.7	278.7	302.6	273.4	287.8	329.7	301.5	280.5	252.3	212.7	183.3
1993	150.9	144.1	122.0	125.0	119.8	119.8	119.8	119.8	119.8	118.6	132.4	187.7
1994	271.0	275.0	280.8	296.6	358.6	394.1	447.5	447.5	467.3	427.3	407.2	556.1
1995	560.5	634.5	559.2	539.4	510.4	561.1	579.3	595.4	459.9	598.7	679.7	598.7
1996	667.6	646.1	632.7	627.2	656.1	633.5	1,191.7	1,154.2	1,121.4	973.2	950.1	919.0
1997	984.7	981.3	945.0	1,250.0	1,574.4	1,524.7	1,512.8	1,348.0	1,217.3	1,073.7	1,020.0	980.4
1998	973.9	1,342.7	1,271.3	1,675.7	1,552.3	1,516.7	1,404.6	1,293.1	1,300.1	1,126.4	989.2	1,031.6

[1] Licensed and unlicensed warehouses approved by the CSCE. *Source: Coffee, Sugar & Cocoa Exchange, Inc. (CSCE)*

Spot Cocoa Prices[1] for Selected Origins of Cocoa Beans and Products in the U.S. Dollars Per Metric Ton

Crop Year Beginning October	Cocoa Beans: Brazil	Cocoa Beans: Cote d'Ivoire	Cocoa Beans: Dominican Republic	Cocoa Beans: Ecuador	Cocoa Beans: Malaysia	Chocolate Liquor: Brazil	Chocolate Liquor: Ecuador	Cocoa Butter: African	Cocoa Butter: Other	Cocoa Cake 10-12% Fat
1988-9	1,669	1,773	1,442	1,466	1,364	2,136	1,912	3,543	3,515	945
1989-90	1,259	1,307	1,142	1,250	1,162	1,775	1,640	3,176	3,151	666
1990-1	1,222	1,289	1,091	1,168	1,131	1,704	1,646	3,232	3,199	394
1991-2	1,234	1,262	1,051	1,136	1,111	1,656	1,540	2,763	2,815	393
1992-3	1,109	1,199	969	1,123	1,020	1,571	1,513	2,517	2,572	539
1993-4	1,378	1,560	1,277	1,393	1,326	2,076	2,028	3,348	3,393	649
1994-5	1,547	1,596	1,347	1,436	1,434	2,202	2,105	3,730	3,737	560
1995-6	1,539	1,522	1,387	1,390	1,449	2,167	2,023	3,780	3,795	519
1996-7	1,641	1,631	1,498	1,511	1,539	2,305	2,163	4,022	4,021	553
1997-8[2]	1,806	1,792	1,671	1,789	1,676	2,558	2,496	4,248	4,248	636

[1] All prices are nominal and are net ex-dock or ex-warehouse, U.S. eastern seaboard north of Hatteras, for merchandise physically available in interstate commerce, in truckload and regular commercial quantities. NA = Not available. *Source: Foreign Agricultural Service, U.S. Department of Agriculture*

Average Open Interest of Cocoa Futures in New York In Contracts

Year	Jan.	Feb.	Mar.	Apr.	May	June	July	Aug.	Sept.	Oct.	Nov.	Dec.
1989	36,747	35,492	32,917	36,597	41,341	45,016	47,222	45,700	42,731	46,366	48,062	49,553
1990	52,094	52,599	55,796	51,299	51,076	50,385	49,603	49,083	47,332	50,084	44,944	41,955
1991	42,446	38,205	40,198	45,250	47,764	49,111	53,153	53,886	53,974	54,854	53,390	53,412
1992	54,464	54,797	52,110	49,904	48,076	47,690	49,924	50,532	51,706	56,101	57,426	60,521
1993	64,886	68,307	69,464	68,533	71,802	71,792	87,011	83,057	88,000	94,844	96,507	91,573
1994	89,174	87,349	91,715	82,500	82,970	72,288	72,249	69,614	73,436	74,163	72,232	75,995
1995	78,873	80,786	82,299	78,435	80,547	75,496	74,975	65,794	68,547	72,758	76,680	79,844
1996	90,478	93,533	98,049	95,390	96,346	88,232	80,873	77,134	77,942	79,572	77,139	78,592
1997	86,960	90,589	96,771	96,956	94,651	97,385	101,815	101,138	106,487	108,263	99,544	97,009
1998	90,574	82,205	78,022	73,237	79,294	74,347	74,295	73,975	71,978	74,139	74,127	73,480

Source: Coffee, Sugar & Cocoa Exchange, Inc. (CSCE)

Volume of Trading of Cocoa Futures in New York In Contracts

Year	Jan.	Feb.	Mar.	Apr.	May	June	July	Aug.	Sept.	Oct.	Nov.	Dec.	Total
1989	138,883	122,374	116,082	132,208	135,783	129,943	98,922	137,879	73,741	95,531	101,152	59,352	1,341,850
1990	121,610	128,357	166,277	191,007	194,759	181,377	126,596	143,323	75,757	120,689	116,175	69,990	1,635,917
1991	94,609	92,450	104,973	99,176	76,435	104,327	96,840	146,379	104,136	135,677	106,888	72,629	1,234,519
1992	122,576	119,375	94,131	116,804	66,185	135,373	104,660	145,815	113,589	109,888	137,815	95,024	1,397,235
1993	145,378	139,932	111,751	149,771	82,961	189,474	225,901	215,044	240,371	217,697	229,752	183,352	2,128,384
1994	178,303	190,804	205,623	188,004	267,188	251,300	193,883	241,340	142,589	183,975	210,635	164,917	2,417,006
1995	197,032	183,784	191,328	208,707	169,061	199,211	140,789	205,169	120,433	149,810	211,171	113,603	2,090,098
1996	177,720	226,701	213,189	242,988	164,749	183,544	159,070	164,719	107,634	167,227	185,226	128,809	2,121,576
1997	180,669	172,510	219,896	235,020	130,041	251,471	186,280	200,707	168,981	204,394	180,805	143,735	2,274,509
1998	175,844	145,311	171,333	192,120	143,602	183,719	131,642	156,737	115,066	125,320	155,280	114,606	1,810,580

Source: Coffee, Sugar & Cocoa Exchange, Inc. (CSCE)

Cocoa Futures - Coffee, Sugar, and Cocoa Exchange, Inc. (Weekly Close) as of 31-Dec-1998

Coconut Oil and Copra

World 1998/99 copra production is estimated at 5.38 million metric tonnes vs. 5.5 million in 1997/98. World coconut oil production at 3.3 million tonnes was 2 percent under 1997/98 while meal production of 1.8 million tonnes compares with 1.9 million, respectively. Global copra production totals only about 2 percent of world oilseed production and crop size has shown relatively little increase during the past decade. Copra, dried coconut meat, is crushed or processed to yield coconut oil and copra meal. Coconut oil, an important ingredient in cosmetics and soap is also used as a food ingredient. As an edible oil, however, foodstock use is shrinking, particularly in the U.S., as the oil has a high level of saturated fats (92 percent). U.S. coconut oil imports are mostly processed into inedible products, primarily soap, for which U.S. usage has also fallen.

Most of the world crop is processed into oil. Coconut oil accounts for less than 3 percent of the world's vegetable and marine oils. The Philippines and Indonesia produce about two-thirds of world copra output. Copra production is not only dependent on the weather, but also appears to have a biological cycle that historically has triggered sharp fluctuations in output. Foreign trade in copra products is generally small. However, amid concerns of a drought-related copra production decline in the Philippines during 1999, copra product trade thrived in 1997/98. Philippine oil exports in the October-June period of about 1 million tonnes were up 400,000 from the like year earlier period. Copra meal exports at nearly 450,000 tonnes were also ahead of the year earlier pace, but for both products export demand showed signs of slowing in mid-1998. Forecasts for 1998/99 put oil exports at 1.7 million tonnes vs. 1.8 in 1997/98; meal exports of 1.1 million tonnes compare with 1.2 million, respectively. Almost half of the coconut oil and two-thirds of the meal is imported by the E.U.-15. World carryover stocks of both coconut oil and copra are also small, for oil about 260,000 tonnes estimated at the end of 1998/99, and copra stocks at 4,000 tonnes, both about unchanged from a year earlier.

U.S. imports of edible coconut oil in 1997/98 (October/July) totaled 547,122 metric tonnes vs. 432,047 in the like year earlier period and having a value of $292 million vs. $315 million, respectively. Manufacturers are not adverse to switching to palm oil should coconut oil's premium to palm oil widen too far.

U.S. coconut oil prices for the year ending September, 1998, of $660 per metric tonne compare with a $779 average in the like 1996/97 period. World copra protein meal prices, basis Hamburg, in 1997/98 averaged $105 per tonne vs. $134 during 1996/97; the Rotterdam coconut oil price of $625 per metric tonne compares with $693, respectively, and the most recent ten year average of $541 per tonne.

World Production of Copra In Thousands of Metric Tons

Year	India	Indonesia	Ivory Coast	Malaysia	Mexico	Mozambique	New Guinea	Philippines	Sri Lanka	Thailand	Vanuatu	Vietnam	World Total
1990	450	1,392	75	76	175	72	91	1,950	61	62	28	192	4,933
1991	440	1,110	79	82	175	72	110	1,845	70	65	27	220	4,612
1992	440	1,110	65	82	200	72	117	1,845	70	65	24	220	4,624
1993	445	1,100	60	65	173	73	120	1,950	60	68	26	200	4,648
1994	455	1,270	65	60	170	74	101	1,930	60	69	27	200	4,801
1995	610	1,080	72	66	160	74	125	2,500	113	103	30	208	5,446
1996	720	1,155	75	60	204	75	178	1,725	75	61	33	210	4,880
1997[1]	680	1,300	75	60	200	76	185	2,160	100	100	48	215	5,512
1998[2]	720	1,000	75	55	190	76	150	2,100	95	90	40	210	5,108
1999[3]	700	1,050	75	52	198	73	140	1,600	90	80		208	4,595

[1] Preliminary. [2] Estimate. [3] Forecast. *Source: The Oil World*

World Supply and Distribution of Coconut Oil In Thousands of Metric Tons

	Production							Consumption						Ending Stocks		
Year	India	Indonesia	Malaysia	Philippines	Total	Exports	Imports	European Union	India	Indonesia	Philippines	United States	Total	Philippines	United States	Total
1989-90	284	782	34	1,314	3,217	1,506	1,490	535	284	576	278	386	3,061	115	128	571
1990-1	272	843	34	1,283	3,192	1,450	1,490	664	279	682	279	402	3,332	51	127	473
1991-2	267	701	33	1,110	2,852	1,343	1,321	513	278	380	257	409	2,883	115	85	420
1992-3	267	681	29	1,294	3,004	1,655	1,270	516	279	430	249	491	2,960	38	114	379
1993-4	272	746	24	1,051	2,804	1,354	1,443	547	275	379	266	483	2,950	50	74	322
1994-5	363	666	36	1,664	3,478	1,772	1,748	664	367	520	269	491	3,334	109	74	440
1995-6	422	675	35	1,173	3,049	1,373	1,404	606	423	436	292	427	3,165	90	38	354
1996-7[1]	414	756	35	1,224	3,219	1,756	1,693	691	422	213	285	504	3,132	83	68	385
1997-8[2]	426	659	35	1,520	3,415	2,010	2,020	745	426	198	278	530	3,200	50	168	611
1998-9[3]	424	626	33	958	2,798	1,358	1,384	682	430	191	273	540	3,100	45	65	335

[1] Preliminary. [2] Estimate. [3] Forecast. *Source: The Oil World*

Supply and Distribution of Coconut Oil in the United States In Millions of Pounds

Year	Rotterdam Copra Tonne $ U.S.	Rotterdam Coconut Oil, CIF $ U.S.	Imports For Consumption	Stocks Oct. 1	Total Supply	Exports	Disappearance Total Domestic	Disappearance Edible Products	Disappearance Inedible Products	Production of Coconut Oil (Refined) Total	Oct. - Dec.	Jan. - March	April - June	July - Sept.
1988-9	371	545	778	332	1,110	55	904	211	713	712.7	199.3	165.1	182.0	166.3
1989-90	251	371	1,038	152	1,190	44	866	161	705	703.1	195.4	163.8	187.3	156.6
1990-1	247	364	946	279	1,225	51	897	169	742	754.6	196.8	150.8	141.8	265.2
1991-2	397	605	838	277	1,115	22	906	164	699	733.9	145.3	158.8	159.3	270.5
1992-3	292	446	1,162	187	1,349	15	1,082	202	692	650.5	156.0	158.8	166.6	169.1
1993-4	388	564	999	251	1,250	20	1,067	234	716	536.2	155.6	129.0	131.8	119.8
1994-5	432	656	1,100	163	1,263	18	1,082	247	694	546.8	137.5	142.7	144.3	122.3
1995-6	487	746	873	163	1,036	11	941	221	453	445.0	127.5	118.4	132.8	66.4
1996-7	452	693	1,188	83	1,271	11	1,111	120	471	324.2	77.0	61.5	101.5	84.2
1997-8[1]	391	587	1,367	149	1,516	11	1,195	141	472	397.8	113.4	103.6	100.4	80.4

[1] Preliminary. NA = Not available. *Source: Bureau of the Census, U.S. Department of Commerce*

Consumption of Coconut Oil in End Products (Edible and Inedible) in the U.S. In Millions of Pounds

Year	Jan.	Feb.	Mar.	Apr.	May	June	July	Aug.	Sept.	Oct.	Nov.	Dec.	Total
1989	52.6	51.6	64.3	55.0	65.9	58.0	60.5	51.3	48.7	55.1	49.7	39.6	652.3
1990	45.4	44.9	44.3	44.6	43.2	39.4	39.8	39.5	39.2	49.7	41.0	43.9	514.9
1991		137.6			150.6			134.4			122.1		544.7
1992	72.5	70.6	76.5	70.7	78.7	74.8	65.2	70.6	77.4	75.8	76.2	66.4	875.4
1993	74.4	75.9	81.3	77.6	72.1	71.0	73.6	78.2	72.6	85.9	90.9	84.6	938.1
1994	74.4	77.4	77.5	80.4	86.6	88.8	76.0	88.4	65.1	74.6	85.1	95.0	969.3
1995	78.2	79.5	86.5	81.0	79.7	82.0	76.5	71.4	61.6	62.1	59.8	59.9	878.0
1996	47.0	54.3	60.1	60.2	68.6	54.6	55.1	47.9	44.9	49.6	50.3	47.9	640.7
1997	44.1	44.8	52.8	46.1	41.9	49.4	49.9	48.3	66.9	53.4	43.9	48.0	589.5
1998[1]	51.5	48.1	59.4	54.3	54.5	47.0	49.3	50.3	53.7	49.4	52.6		621.9

[1] Preliminary. *Source: Bureau of the Census, U.S. Department of Commerce*

Stocks of Coconut Oil (Crude and Refined) in the United States, on First of Month In Millions of Pounds

Year	Jan.	Feb.	Mar.	Apr.	May	June	July	Aug	Sept	Oct.	Nov.	Dec.
1989	275.7	278.9	247.4	205.3	167.7	134.7	189.9	177.5	149.8	150.8	218.6	238.5
1990	297.3	304.4	307.0	348.0	305.6	306.6	292.2	264.3	315.4	281.1	309.3	304.6
1991	NA	NA	359.0	NA	NA	364.3	NA	NA	279.3	NA	NA	298.0
1992	NA	266.3	274.2	239.7	211.2	173.7	178.3	141.1	187.1	187.7	225.1	278.8
1993	355.7	406.7	418.9	348.7	338.3	305.2	257.2	233.8	321.4	250.8	335.0	299.1
1994	291.7	316.5	284.5	251.5	237.6	199.9	151.4	163.7	156.0	164.1	166.2	152.9
1995	155.6	173.6	168.1	163.7	148.5	183.5	163.8	136.9	124.1	162.9	199.7	187.7
1996	164.7	229.1	200.4	217.7	173.6	175.9	171.5	116.7	113.8	84.0	78.6	65.0
1997	125.9	147.4	141.1	204.5	174.5	161.3	143.8	143.4	154.3	149.6	162.1	194.2
1998[1]	274.2	332.4	344.5	337.4	318.8	300.6	366.3	4424.6	434.4	392.6	431.8	446.7

[1] Preliminary. NA = Not avaliable. *Source: Bureau of the Census, U.S. Department of Commerce*

Average Price of Coconut Oil (Crude) Tank Cars in New York In Cents Per Pound

Year	Jan.	Feb.	Mar.	Apr.	May	June	July	Aug.	Sept.	Oct.	Nov.	Dec.	Average
1989	26.75	27.63	27.90	28.94	29.90	29.56	28.94	27.75	28.63	27.25	26.35	24.75	27.86
1990	24.31	23.69	22.10	21.63	21.15	20.31	19.16	18.58	18.26	18.18	20.45	20.13	20.66
1991	20.22	20.31	20.50	19.38	19.69	21.69	26.19	25.63	25.63	28.50	31.50	32.38	24.30
1992	39.33	36.00	34.57	34.63	33.56	32.13	29.63	27.31	27.88	26.95	27.00	25.50	31.21
1993	24.94	24.37	23.65	23.13	24.13	24.95	25.35	25.61	24.44	23.88	26.69	34.25	25.45
1994	30.30	29.69	27.31	28.19	29.45	30.25	29.56	30.35	30.63	30.60	34.19	33.69	30.35
1995	32.50	32.00	31.13	31.00	30.50	35.00	37.90	35.63	35.00	36.00	37.88	33.69	34.02
1996	35.80	36.63	36.75	38.75	39.50	42.25	41.80	42.80	47.20	48.00	49.50	50.00	42.42
1997	44.20	44.00	42.88	42.50	42.50	35.00	36.50	36.50	37.00	37.25	37.25	37.25	39.40
1998[1]	37.25	37.25	37.25	37.25	37.25	37.00	36.50	35.50	36.50	37.15	39.91	40.66	37.46

[1] Preliminary. NA = Not available. *Source: Economic Research Service, U.S. Department of Agriculture*

Coffee

Coffee prices moved lower in the second half of 1998 in response to the harvest of a large coffee crop in Brazil. Coffee prices had been moving lower in the first half of 1998 as it was anticipated that the Brazilian crop for 1998-99 would be large following a small crop in 1997-98. Coffee production tends to follow a two year cycle in which smaller crops are followed by large crops which in turn are followed by small crops. In particular, this is important with respect to Brazil which is by far the world's largest producer of coffee. The U.S.D.A. estimated the 1997-98 Brazilian crop at 23.5 million bags. That was a small crop by historical standards and on a cyclical basis it was likely it would be followed by a large crop in the 1998-99 season. Brazilian producers have planted more coffee trees so production potential is larger. In addition, while El Nino was causing problems in Colombia and Central America, Brazil experienced excellent weather. Coffee prices edged lower going into the harvest, which starts in May, as the trade expected the crop to be 40 million bags. As the crop came in, during the height of the harvest in June-August 1998, coffee prices moved to still lower ground as the crop turned out to be 35.6 million bags. That was one of the largest crops on record.

In another potentially significant development, in January 1999, Brazil's government allowed its currency to decline versus the dollar which could encourage more exports over time. Brazil produces both arabica and robusta coffee. The U.S.D.A. forecast the arabica crop at 30.6 million bags while the robusta crop was 5 million bags. The U.S.D.A. noted that the area planted to coffee in Brazil was 2.24 million hectares which was up 6 percent from the previous season. The coffee tree population is 4.27 billion trees which includes 3.33 billion bearing trees and 939 million non-bearing trees. About 580 million new seedlings were planted in the October-April 1997-98 planting season. In addition to being the largest producer of coffee, Brazil is also the largest exporter of coffee. Exports in the 1998-99 season were estimated at 19.1 million bags which would be up 29 percent from the previous year. Of the total, 17.5 million bags are coffee beans and 1.6 million bags are soluble coffee. The Brazilian government is also auctioning off its stockpile of coffee amounting to 100,000 bags a month.

With the large Brazilian crop, the U.S.D.A. forecast world coffee production at 106.8 million bags, some 9 percent more than in 1997-98. All of the gain is due to the increase in the Brazilian crop. The second largest producer of coffee is Colombia which grows only arabica coffee. Colombian coffee production has been adversely affected by dry weather related to El Nino. It had appeared that the 1998-99 Colombian crop would in fact be small because of the weather but in April 1998 the drought ended. The beneficial rains continued through September and the forecast of the new crop was increased. The U.S.D.A. increased its forecast from 11 million bags in June to 12.5 million bags in the December forecast, representing a 5 percent increase from the 1997-98 crop. Colombia has 3.1 billion bearing trees and harvested acreage of 900,000 hectares.

Outside of the large Brazilian crop, the major development in the coffee market in 1998 was hurricane Mitch which settled over Central America for days bring widespread destruction to the coffee crop as well as damaging the infrastructure in a number of countries. How much damage was done is not known as reports were still coming in 1999. The U.S.D.A. estimated Guatemala's crop at 2.83 million bags, a 29 percent decline from the 1997-98 crop. The crop was also adversely affected by the dry conditions which occurred in the January-May flowering period. The other country that was heavily damaged by the hurricane was Honduras. The 1998-99 crop was forecast to be 2.3 million bags or some 24 percent less than a year ago. Damage to the coffee crop attributable to the storm was put at 390,000 bags. For the five large Central American producers (Guatemala, Honduras, Costa Rica, El Salvador, Nicaragua) 1998-99 production was estimated at 9.83 million bags, down 21 percent from the 1997-98 season. Mexico was not directly affected by the storm but the crop will be on the small side at 4.95 million bags, the same as a year before.

Among the major robusta producers, Indonesia's 1998-99 crop was forecast to be 6.8 million bags, down 6 percent from the year before. Indonesia is the third largest coffee producer in the world. The country was severely damaged by El Nino with the dry weather resulting in a smaller crop in 1998-99. There was no firm indication as to what impact the financial turmoil in that country has had on the industry. One notable development has been the rise of Vietnam as a major producer and exporter of coffee. The 1997-98 crop was a record 6.67 million bags. After a series of successively larger crops, the 1998-99 season saw dry weather and an expected decline in production. The U.S.D.A. estimates the 1998-99 coffee crop at 6.33 million bags, down 5 percent from the year before.

In Africa, the Ivory Coast crop was forecast at 3.75 million bags, down 8 percent from the previous season. Dry weather and older trees were cited as reasons for the decline. Uganda's crop of 3.6 million bags was up 20 percent from the previous year.

The U.S.D.A. estimated world consumption of coffee in 1997-98 at 102.6 million bags with 77.1 million bags in importing countries and 25.5 million bags in exporting countries. Consumption in 1997-98 declined 3 percent from the previous season when it was 105.8 million bags. It is of interest to note that consumption of coffee in exporting countries has been increasing. For 1998-99, consumption may be lower due to very mild weather in the eastern U.S. though this could be offset by higher consumption in the exporting countries.

Futures Markets

Coffee futures are traded on the Bolsa de Mercadorias & Futuros (BM&F), the Manila International Futures Exchange Inc. (MIFE), the Singapore Commodity Exchange Ltd., the London International Financial Futures and Options Exchange (LIFFE), and the Coffee, Sugar and Cocoa Exchange Inc. (CSCE) in New York. Options are traded on the BM&F, the LIFFE and the CSCE.

World Supply and Distribution of Coffee In Thousands of 60 Kilogram Bags (132.276 Lbs. Per Bag)

Crop Year	Beginning Stocks	Production	Imports	Supply	Total Exports	Bean Exports	Rst/Grn Exports	Soluble Exports	Domestic Use	Ending Stocks
1989-90	50,193	96,958	258	147,409	83,402	80,034	129	3,239	20,995	43,012
1990-1	43,012	100,181	331	143,524	76,163	73,278	83	2,802	22,265	45,096
1991-2	45,096	104,064	291	149,451	80,887	77,844	53	2,990	22,266	46,298
1992-3	46,298	92,959	713	139,970	77,869	73,881	117	3,871	21,579	40,522
1993-4	40,522	92,319	585	133,426	76,307	71,802	108	4,397	22,927	34,192
1994-5	34,192	97,096	1,070	132,358	68,728	64,521	228	3,979	22,530	41,100
1995-6	41,100	88,749	1,081	130,930	74,106	69,165	229	4,712	24,125	32,699
1996-7[1]	32,699	103,696	1,094	137,489	84,248	79,812	192	4,244	24,366	28,875
1997-8[2]	28,875	97,675	1,232	127,782	77,264	72,729	191	4,344	25,464	25,054
1998-9[3]	25,054	106,800	1,229	133,083	79,771	75,958	190	3,623	26,310	27,002

[1] Preliminary. [2] Estimate. [3] Forecast. *Source: Foreign Agricutural Service, U.S. Department of Agriculture (FAS-USDA)*

World Production of Green Coffee In Thousands of 60 Kilogram Bags (132.276 Lbs. Per Bag)

Crop Year	Brazil	Cameroon	Colombia	Costa Rica	El Salvador	Ethiopia	Guatemala	India	Indonesia	Ivory Coast	Mexico	Uganda	World Total
1989-90	26,000	1,440	13,300	2,453	2,787	3,400	3,472	2,150	7,100	4,734	5,100	2,500	97,286
1990-1	31,000	1,450	14,500	2,565	2,603	3,500	3,282	2,970	7,480	3,300	4,550	2,700	100,417
1991-2	28,500	1,920	17,980	2,530	2,357	3,000	3,549	3,200	7,100	3,967	4,620	2,900	103,731
1992-3	24,000	837	14,950	2,620	2,894	3,500	3,584	2,700	7,350	2,500	4,180	2,800	92,894
1993-4	28,500	676	11,400	2,475	2,361	3,700	3,078	3,465	7,400	2,700	4,200	2,700	92,319
1994-5	28,000	401	13,000	2,492	2,314	3,800	3,500	3,060	6,400	3,733	4,030	3,100	97,096
1995-6	16,800	518	12,939	2,595	2,325	3,800	3,827	3,717	5,800	2,900	5,400	4,200	88,749
1996-7[1]	28,000	1,432	10,779	2,376	2,498	3,800	4,141	3,417	7,900	5,333	5,300	4,297	103,696
1997-8[2]	23,500	1,417	11,932	2,400	2,040	3,500	3,982	3,833	7,200	4,080	4,950	3,000	97,675
1998-9[3]	35,600	1,200	12,500	2,165	1,790	3,500	2,825	3,835	6,800	3,750	4,950	3,600	106,800

[1] Preliminary. [2] Estimate. [3] Forecast. *Source: Foreign Agricultural Service, U.S. Department of Agriculture (FAS-USDA)*

World Exportable[4] Production of Green Coffee In Thousands of 60 Kilogram Bags (132.276 Lbs. Per Bag)

Crop Year	Brazil	Cameroon	Colombia	Costa Rica	El Salvador	Ethiopia	Guatemala	Indonesia	Ivory Coast	Kenya	Mexico	Uganda	World Total
1989-90	17,000	1,405	11,538	2,198	2,607	2,239	3,162	5,820	4,700	1,665	3,650	2,450	75,944
1990-1	21,500	1,420	12,885	2,305	2,423	1,800	2,972	6,185	3,264	1,433	3,150	2,650	78,271
1991-2	19,500	1,895	16,580	2,270	2,173	1,400	3,239	5,550	3,929	1,483	3,170	2,845	81,729
1992-3	15,500	812	13,647	2,365	2,677	2,000	3,274	5,570	2,461	1,195	2,880	2,745	71,726
1993-4	19,100	611	9,700	2,225	2,131	2,200	2,777	5,535	2,661	1,208	2,900	2,640	69,678
1994-5	18,300	371	11,564	2,252	2,079	2,300	3,220	4,440	3,687	1,562	3,030	3,040	75,028
1995-6	6,300	453	11,439	2,360	2,055	2,300	3,527	3,750	2,852	1,788	4,340	4,140	65,248
1996-7[1]	17,000	1,332	9,279	2,118	2,268	2,300	3,856	5,820	5,282	1,115	4,450	4,217	79,826
1997-8[2]	12,000	1,317	10,372	2,150	1,805	1,900	3,682	5,110	4,025	995	3,955	2,920	72,761
1998-9[3]	23,100	1,100	10,900	1,910	1,550	1,900	2,500	5,000	3,692	894	3,950	3,520	81,150

[1] Preliminary. [2] Estimate. [3] Forecast. [4] Marketing year begins in October in some countries and April or July in others. Exportable production represents total harvested production minus estimated domestic consumption. *Source: Foreign Agricultural Service, U.S. Department of Agriculture (FAS-USDA)*

Green Coffee Imports in the United States In Thousands of 60 Kilogram Bags[2]

Year	Brazil	Colombia	Costa Rica	Domin. Republic	Ecuador	El Salvador	Ethiopia	Guatemala	Indonesia	Mexico	Peru	Venezuela	Grand Total
1988	4,213	2,235	233	366	811	829	218	609	731	1,719	436	72	15,348
1989	4,155	2,413	393	402	1,137	790	432	1,404	635	3,937	673	87	19,377
1990	3,633	2,771	403	445	876	843	234	1,871	830	3,305	473	222	19,566
1991	5,335	3,048	603	343	785	868	31	1,489	536	2,993	610	108	18,849
1992	4,253	4,852	662	254	753	1,344	23	1,812	581	3,042	526	104	21,673
1993	3,376	2,957	437	213	671	1,274	192	1,815	542	2,947	158	444	18,023
1994	2,850	2,372	325	207	969	376	215	1,403	558	2,516	249	295	14,913
1995	2,302	2,485	388	266	745	284	109	1,637	513	2,887	621	89	15,886
1996	1,852	3,011	482	255	665	401	137	1,748	1,246	3,734	441	445	17,947
1997[1]	2,331	3,179	608	150	431	500	308	1,921	1,325	2,935	652	65	18,848

[1] Preliminary. [2] 132.276 pounds per bag. *Source: Bureau of the Census, U.S. Department of Commerce*

COFFEE

Monthly Green Coffee Imports in the United States In Thousands of 60 Kilogram Bags[2]

Year	Jan.	Feb.	Mar.	Apr.	May	June	July	Aug.	Sept.	Oct.	Nov.	Dec.	Total
1988	1,175	1,683	1,427	1,179	1,141	832	1,543	1,621	1,238	1,272	1,195	1,040	15,348
1989	1,646	1,323	1,368	1,398	1,296	1,199	1,634	1,974	1,951	2,180	1,748	1,660	19,337
1990	1,950	1,989	2,358	1,783	1,658	1,548	1,451	1,261	1,229	1,611	1,140	1,591	19,566
1991	2,106	1,946	1,590	1,748	1,556	984	1,056	1,335	1,424	1,368	1,616	2,122	18,849
1992	2,262	1,944	2,125	1,698	1,534	1,795	1,806	1,692	1,644	1,615	1,508	2,050	21,673
1993	1,782	1,663	2,012	1,481	1,631	1,253	1,442	1,344	1,374	1,464	1,018	1,561	18,023
1994	1,538	1,152	1,409	1,077	1,082	1,151	1,195	1,560	1,266	1,127	1,103	1,213	14,872
1995	1,469	1,253	1,702	1,221	1,190	1,240	1,117	1,094	1,220	1,326	1,492	1,563	15,886
1996	1,824	1,657	1,753	1,395	1,444	1,236	1,329	1,341	1,364	1,279	1,485	1,828	17,936
1997[1]	1,582	1,837	1,966	1,792	1,738	1,583	1,783	1,391	1,147	1,215	1,184	1,629	18,848

[1] Preliminary. [2] 132.276 pounds per bag. *Source: Bureau of the Census, U.S. Department of Commerce*

Average Price of Brazilian[1] Coffee in New York In Cents Per Pound

Year	Jan.	Feb.	Mar.	Apr.	May	June	July	Aug.	Sept.	Oct.	Nov.	Dec.	Average
1989	145.29	128.72	128.06	131.45	128.94	115.02	78.75	67.32	67.75	60.32	65.53	67.93	98.76
1990	70.36	77.59	86.17	87.45	86.31	82.94	78.94	90.25	92.20	85.78	77.46	80.17	82.97
1991	75.59	79.39	83.83	81.58	75.56	72.44	69.24	68.15	75.08	65.91	66.03	62.14	72.91
1992	62.03	58.05	59.60	54.94	51.11	49.08	48.53	46.40	49.43	59.64	64.64	74.39	56.49
1993	67.13	66.34	62.60	54.92	57.26	55.70	65.76	73.25	75.58	71.65	74.20	74.51	66.58
1994	71.42	80.14	84.72	87.14	118.37	136.43	211.81	192.38	212.73	191.21	172.83	159.73	143.24
1995	162.81	161.07	171.48	166.54	161.72	145.22	139.68	149.54	130.26	127.23	125.33	110.46	145.95
1996	127.54	144.05	140.99	132.92	134.76	125.44	106.93	108.28	103.10	105.77	103.76	103.71	119.77
1997	127.28	160.21	179.75	183.73	209.62	184.21	158.52	158.25	167.77	152.12	149.07	171.12	166.80
1998	179.83	177.78	154.84	141.11	124.89	104.09	96.04	101.92	92.76	91.32	96.67		123.75

[1] And other Arabicas. NA = Not available. *Source: Foreign Agricultural Service, U.S. Department of Agriculture (FAS-USDA)*

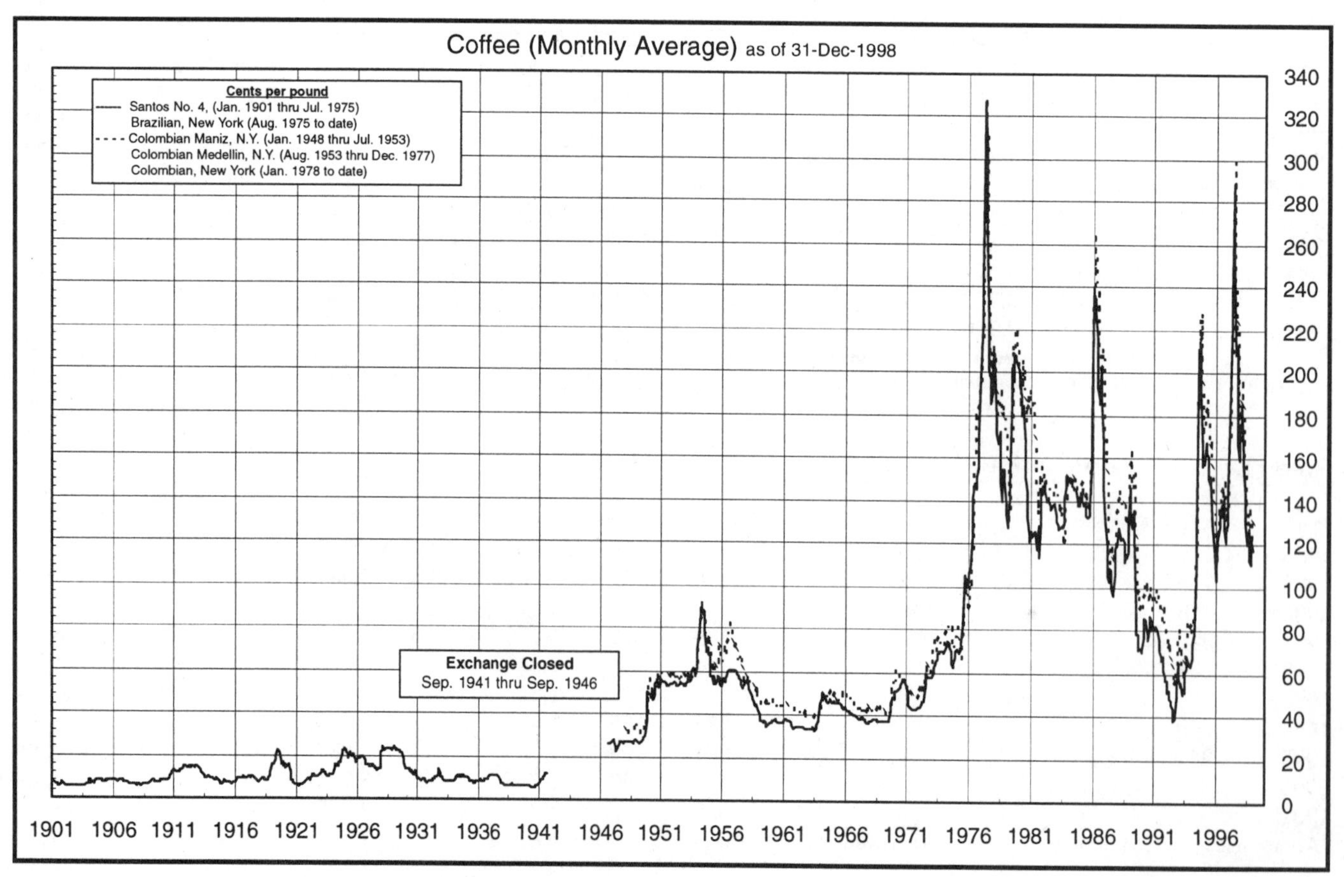

Average Monthly Retail[1] Price of Coffee in the United States In Cents Per Pound

Year	Jan.	Feb.	Mar.	Apr.	May	June	July	Aug.	Sep.	Oct.	Nov.	Dec.	Average
1991	294.5	297.1	289.4	292.4	287.9	286.6	280.5	272.4	269.2	270.6	267.3	262.5	280.9
1992	266.8	268.8	263.1	261.2	266.0	262.5	265.2	261.3	253.7	249.2	239.1	236.4	257.8
1993	235.2	245.2	246.2	247.7	251.4	253.3	254.8	250.0	249.3	241.5	243.3	248.0	247.2
1994	253.0	252.9	251.5	251.6	253.5	259.8	334.1	448.0	445.8	445.0	448.2	438.2	340.1
1995	439.8	423.4	410.8	408.4	406.7	405.9	402.7	405.1	399.6	386.5	381.4	375.2	401.8
1996	357.7	359.0	355.0	352.7	344.4	343.8	338.0	339.0	333.3	334.4	328.3	330.7	343.0
1997	330.0	331.6	351.2	389.4	410.9	442.8	462.8	466.9	461.7	439.2	430.3	416.1	411.1
1998	402.5	397.3	403.3	395.9	387.8	378.6	377.1	370.4	362.0	350.3	348.2		379.4

[1] Roasted in 13.1 to 20 ounce cans. *Source: Foreign Agricultural Service, U.S. Department of Agriculture*

Average Price of Colombian Mild Arabicas[1] in the United States In Cents Per Pound

Year	Jan.	Feb.	Mar.	Apr.	May	June	July	Aug.	Sep.	Oct.	Nov.	Dec.	Average
1991	91.55	94.23	99.36	97.27	91.51	90.18	88.02	88.09	91.95	82.88	82.43	79.70	89.76
1992	78.40	71.75	73.67	69.55	64.93	64.10	62.50	56.49	56.18	64.77	71.72	81.52	67.97
1993	71.61	72.45	67.07	59.77	67.35	68.13	76.40	84.18	86.58	83.02	85.56	87.33	75.79
1994	85.85	93.04	93.23	97.53	133.90	151.85	222.75	210.57	231.52	206.07	186.96	173.94	157.27
1995	177.23	175.07	185.75	180.30	177.18	170.87	157.22	163.21	141.49	132.08	129.09	110.47	158.33
1996	119.08	134.94	160.60	134.31	142.56	133.25	135.39	137.68	123.30	127.77	129.41	126.41	133.73
1997	146.18	188.62	212.96	199.22	318.50	227.15	190.57	193.46	196.29	169.40	161.38	183.32	198.92
1998	184.21	190.59	166.07	158.17	146.33	135.83	125.03	129.45	117.56	115.01	121.74		144.54

[1] ICO monthly and composite indicator prices on the New York Market, 1979 ICA Agreement Basis. *Source: Foreign Agricultural Service, U.S. Department of Agriculture*

Average Price of Other Mild Arabicas[1] in the United States In Cents Per Pound

Year	Jan.	Feb.	Mar.	Apr.	May	June	July	Aug.	Sep.	Oct.	Nov.	Dec.	Average
1991	86.32	89.57	93.72	91.73	87.50	85.50	82.73	81.63	87.45	79.87	78.46	75.11	84.97
1992	72.99	67.88	69.96	65.23	60.14	58.38	57.68	52.42	52.73	61.40	67.36	77.46	63.64
1993	68.66	67.46	62.77	56.88	61.48	61.61	71.46	76.56	79.87	75.05	77.07	80.00	69.91
1994	77.21	82.69	85.57	89.23	121.97	142.57	217.67	198.07	220.10	199.06	180.76	167.47	148.53
1995	171.74	168.71	178.22	172.81	168.63	151.56	143.83	151.41	131.87	125.38	123.23	103.99	149.28
1996	109.38	122.71	119.05	122.01	128.56	124.46	120.47	122.49	114.05	120.62	119.90	115.01	119.89
1997	131.83	167.20	193.82	204.43	264.50	212.55	186.52	185.17	184.38	161.45	154.15	174.25	185.02
1998	175.04	175.87	154.82	147.08	134.35	121.56	113.86	119.89	108.07	107.07	113.84		133.77

[1] ICO monthly and composite indicator prices on the New York Market, 1979 ICA Agreement Basis. *Source: Foreign Agricultural Service, U.S. Department of Agriculture*

Average Price of Robustas 1976[1] in the United States In Cents Per Pound

Year	Jan.	Feb.	Mar.	Apr.	May	June	July	Aug.	Sep.	Oct.	Nov.	Dec.	Average
1991	53.92	52.46	52.13	52.38	48.22	47.10	46.49	46.57	48.11	47.31	51.47	51.45	49.80
1992	49.44	43.22	43.08	42.32	38.79	38.07	39.60	39.92	42.39	45.50	49.08	52.09	43.63
1993	48.13	48.25	46.86	45.51	46.91	47.65	50.39	59.29	63.44	60.05	62.53	62.90	53.49
1994	60.91	62.25	66.46	72.64	96.05	113.31	164.65	162.68	182.95	170.09	154.19	130.48	119.72
1995	132.26	135.22	146.83	145.47	141.89	129.53	120.89	131.28	116.41	114.15	112.79	94.72	126.79
1996	91.99	98.99	91.99	91.45	92.10	86.46	78.14	80.16	74.83	72.97	70.51	63.08	82.72
1997	67.66	76.65	81.31	78.48	95.74	91.94	82.52	76.92	77.43	76.90	78.20	84.65	80.70
1998	86.03	85.79	84.67	90.60	92.64	84.55	78.40	79.98	80.36	80.40			84.34

[1] ICO monthly and composite indicator prices on the New York Market, 1979 ICA Agreement Basis. *Source: Foreign Agricultural Service, U.S. Department of Agriculture*

Average Price of Composite 1979[1] in the United States In Cents Per Pound

Year	Jan.	Feb.	Mar.	Apr.	May	June	July	Aug.	Sep.	Oct.	Nov.	Dec.	Average
1991	69.39	70.55	72.47	71.45	67.47	65.58	64.31	63.38	66.86	62.83	64.30	63.07	66.81
1992	61.12	55.51	56.48	53.64	49.27	48.13	48.70	45.89	47.11	52.88	57.49	64.00	53.35
1993	58.14	57.32	54.76	51.38	54.18	54.54	60.61	67.69	71.64	67.78	70.03	71.53	61.63
1994	69.17	72.37	76.11	81.19	108.42	127.91	191.44	181.53	202.39	185.64	168.12	149.14	134.45
1995	152.08	152.24	162.73	159.59	155.96	141.66	132.71	141.70	124.75	120.02	117.99	99.57	138.42
1996	100.33	110.50	105.89	107.09	110.24	105.79	99.97	102.73	96.52	98.56	97.14	90.04	102.07
1997	100.03	121.89	137.47	142.20	180.44	155.38	135.04	132.63	132.51	121.09	118.16	130.02	133.91
1998	130.61	130.78	119.93	119.66	114.23	103.84	97.32	101.25	95.82	95.01	98.26		109.70

[1] ICO monthly and composite indicator prices on the New York Market, 1979 ICA Agreement Basis. *Source: Foreign Agricultural Service, U.S. Department of Agriculture*

COFFEE

Average Open Interest of Coffee 'C' Futures in New York In Contracts

Year	Jan.	Feb.	Mar.	Apr.	May	June	July	Aug.	Sept.	Oct.	Nov.	Dec.
1989	24,544	23,684	23,246	25,870	23,663	24,716	27,184	31,410	32,404	35,019	32,687	32,096
1990	37,352	43,516	46,187	43,978	41,756	40,464	39,856	41,428	39,278	39,523	43,750	41,365
1991	42,320	41,326	39,948	39,410	41,726	43,717	42,037	40,661	42,126	43,940	41,819	40,628
1992	47,042	51,183	48,961	51,979	59,275	58,304	59,096	58,401	56,446	59,808	57,527	58,257
1993	59,193	54,249	53,618	55,578	51,797	50,918	53,871	48,541	47,649	49,809	46,901	48,812
1994	54,796	50,230	53,713	57,226	58,574	54,589	43,056	35,052	35,800	34,258	31,046	31,134
1995	34,455	35,391	36,925	34,387	34,615	34,462	30,156	27,448	27,800	28,408	24,505	26,412
1996	28,430	28,224	28,127	28,793	28,394	25,096	26,188	25,799	23,929	26,202	27,599	27,201
1997	38,516	42,888	39,092	32,644	30,324	22,552	21,497	19,818	22,788	25,109	23,636	28,577
1998	30,042	30,539	30,211	32,617	36,345	36,651	37,531	30,074	30,429	32,940	31,677	32,816

Source: Coffee, Sugar & Cocoa Exchange, Inc. (CSCE)

Volume of Trading of Coffee 'C' Futures in New York In Contracts

Year	Jan.	Feb.	Mar.	Apr.	May	June	July	Aug.	Sept.	Oct.	Nov.	Dec.	Total
1989	141,903	106,019	102,594	129,018	95,902	134,848	100,700	122,207	97,744	104,100	111,434	82,484	1,328,953
1990	130,223	174,115	211,105	144,641	128,121	147,605	127,767	172,947	119,088	113,569	175,067	119,802	1,774,050
1991	138,642	174,688	188,842	153,436	103,344	135,887	107,058	170,113	180,017	148,640	159,099	112,882	1,772,648
1992	153,332	199,420	174,662	188,232	156,944	164,586	177,493	182,741	163,214	108,707	211,678	199,374	2,152,383
1993	290,120	214,771	183,354	209,607	176,559	197,761	193,002	233,479	202,363	187,763	217,947	182,486	2,489,223
1994	188,508	219,455	208,113	284,734	380,119	304,542	210,479	196,685	159,574	177,424	184,172	142,713	2,658,073
1995	169,250	191,352	213,326	156,191	163,248	186,550	162,562	161,076	165,337	152,959	157,240	123,923	2,003,014
1996	203,369	186,526	152,797	197,442	137,454	158,929	171,800	196,991	136,054	196,696	135,305	166,213	2,039,576
1997	242,719	280,014	267,369	223,330	219,214	186,227	135,664	136,807	142,610	151,171	145,610	163,446	2,294,181
1998	155,774	194,435	186,712	194,732	157,935	189,768	165,868	189,047	156,556	172,956	197,776	133,471	2,095,030

Source: Coffee, Sugar & Cocoa Exchange, Inc. (CSCE)

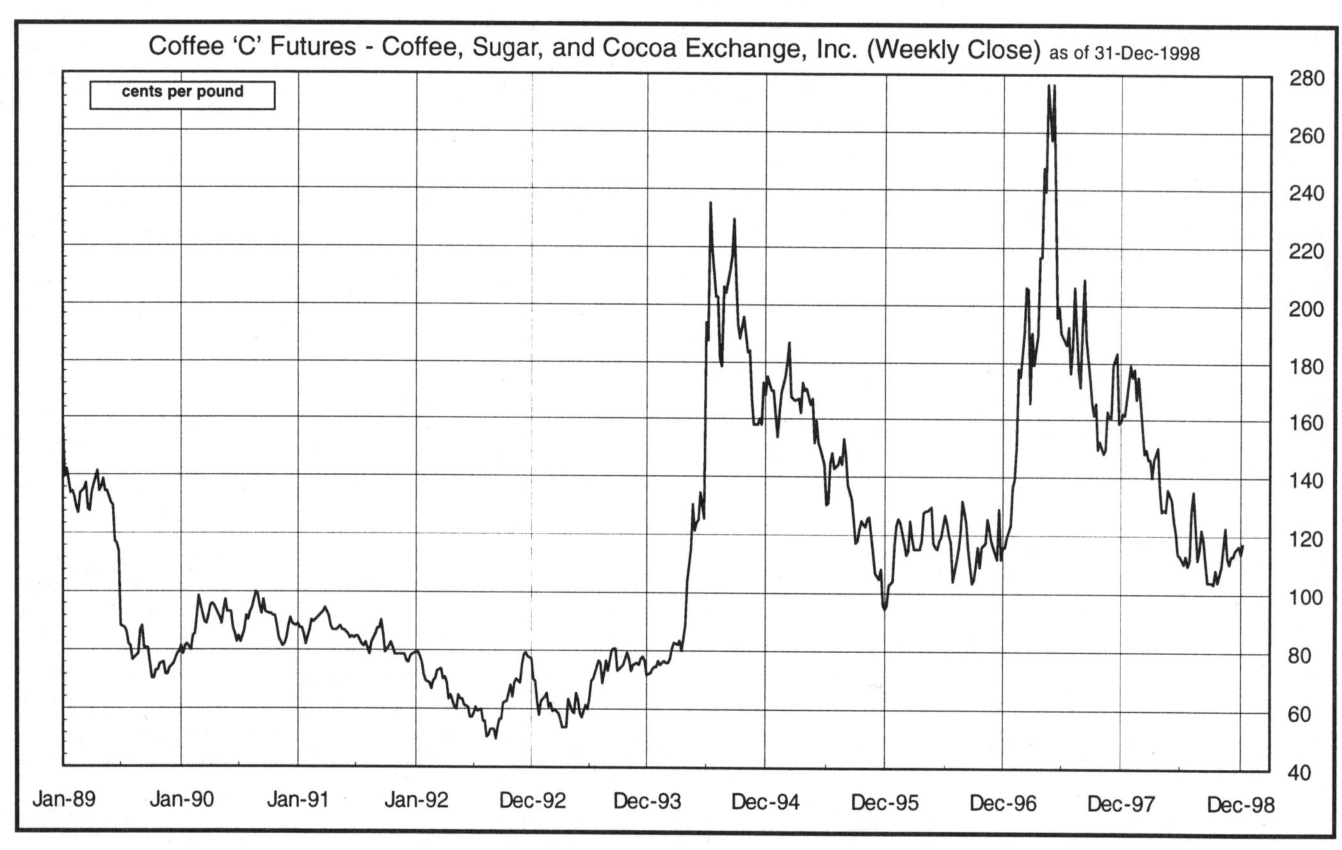

Coke

U.S. coke production in the January-March 1998 quarter was 5.22 million short tons. That was 6 percent less than in the same period of 1997. For all of 1997, coke production was 22.1 million tons. Consumption of coke in the first quarter of 1998 was 5.73 million tons, about the same as in the first quarter of 1997. For all of 1997, coke consumption was 22.8 million tons. Producer and distributor stocks of coke on March 31, 1998 were 1.11 million tons. A year earlier stocks of coke held by producers and distributors were 1.37 million tons or some 19 percent more. U.S. imports of coke in the first quarter of 1998 were 384,540 tons, an increase of 42 percent from the same period of 1997. The major supplier of coke to the U.S. was China with 198,908 tons followed by Japan with 181,505 tons. U.S. coke exports in first quarter 1998 were 79,495 tonnes, almost 26 percent more than the year before. The major export market was Mexico which took 72,139 tons followed by Europe and Canada.

Salient Statistics of Coke in the United States In Thousands of Short Tons

Year	Production at Coke Plants: Merchant Coke Plants	Furance Coke Plants	Total Coke	Breeze	Imports	Consumption[2]	Exports: Total	Canada	Mexico	Producer & Distributor Ending Stocks	Avg. Price of Coal Receipts at Coke Plants
1992	3,248	20,162	23,410	1,721	1,739	24,731	642	310	76	1,883	47.92
1993	3,209	19,973	23,182	3,424	1,534	24,303	835	417	92	1,461	47.44
1994	3,244	19,443	22,686	1,392	1,612	24,163	660	371	94	986	46.56
1995	3,239	20,509	23,749	1,463	1,816	24,500	750	579	60	1,302	47.34
1996	3,105	19,971	23,075	1,402	1,111	23,043	1,121	491	143	1,323	47.33
1997[1]	2,903	19,212	22,115	1,233	1,565	22,845	832	498	251	1,320	47.36

[1] Preliminary. [2] Equal to production plus imports minus the change in producer and distributor stocks minus exports.
Source: Energy Information Administration, U.S. Department of Energy (EIA-DOE)

Production of Petroleum Coke in the United States In Thousands of Barrels[2]

Year	Jan.	Feb.	Mar.	Apr.	May	June	July	Aug.	Sept.	Oct.	Nov.	Dec.	Total
1992	18,550	16,330	17,825	17,615	18,460	18,685	19,330	18,280	17,845	17,665	3,540	19,385	217,995
1993	18,551	17,289	19,226	18,200	18,587	18,715	20,196	19,319	18,547	18,695	18,954	19,737	226,016
1994	19,170	16,873	18,695	18,454	19,748	19,325	20,008	19,473	17,868	18,753	18,995	19,697	227,059
1995	19,079	17,117	18,556	18,519	19,774	19,949	19,527	19,722	19,184	19,292	19,349	19,887	229,955
1996	19,536	18,706	21,015	20,663	20,426	19,927	19,836	20,328	20,124	20,558	20,447	21,389	242,955
1997	19,798	17,594	20,603	21,274	22,210	21,052	21,619	22,229	21,630	21,782	20,313	21,827	251,931
1998[1]	20,929	18,968	21,998	21,834	21,790	20,856	21,790	22,469	21,526	21,234			256,073

[1] Preliminary. [2] Prior to 1993, data converted from thousands of short tons (5 barrels = 1 short ton). *Source: Energy Information Administration, U.S. Department of Energy (EIA-DOE)*

Coal Receipts and Carbonization at Coke Plants in the United States In Thousands of Short Tons

Year	Coal Receipts at Coke Plants — By State: Alabama	Indiana	Ohio	Pennsylvania	Total	By Plant Type: Merchant Coke Plants	Furance Coke Plants	Coal Carbonized at Coke Plants — By State: Alabama	Indiana	Ohio	Pennsylvania	Total	By Plant Type: Merchant Coke Plants	Furance Coke Plants
1992	3,334	6,894	3,717	9,761	32,027	4,295	27,732	3,297	7,153	3,755	9,868	32,366	4,316	28,050
1993	3,184	6,515	2,853	10,424	31,104	4,184	26,921	3,206	6,591	2,892	10,333	31,323	4,267	27,056
1994	3,242	5,023	3,064	10,776	31,719	4,205	27,514	3,253	4,841	3,092	10,849	31,740	4,218	27,522
1995	3,183	5,731	2,758	10,959	33,036	4,189	28,848	3,257	5,883	2,777	10,858	33,011	4,248	28,763
1996	3,213	5,884	1,770	10,562	31,672	4,135	27,537	3,247	5,823	1,842	10,689	31,706	4,135	27,570
1997[1]	2,966	5,676	1,823	10,272	30,138	3,800	26,338	2,956	5,715	1,848	10,334	29,443	3,826	25,618

[1] Preliminary. *Source: Energy Information Administration, U.S. Department of Energy (EIA-DOE)*

Coke Distribution and Stocks in the United States In Thousands of Short Tons

Year	Distribution — By Plant Type: Merchant Coke Plants	Furance Coke Plants	By Consumer Category: Blast Furance	Foundries	Other Industrial Plants	Total Coke	Breeze	Coke Plant Stocks, Dec. 31: Total Coke	By Plant Type: Merchant Coke Plants	Furance Coke Plants	Breeze
1992	3,253	26,718	28,075	1,290	606	29,971	2,255	1,883	267	1,616	215
1993	3,226	27,009	28,295	1,373	567	30,235	3,563	1,461	272	1,189	486
1994	3,400	25,949	27,248	1,480	621	29,349	1,735	986	122	864	105
1995	3,284	25,103	26,346	1,401	639	28,386	1,638	1,302	112	1,189	136
1996	----	----	----	----	----	----	----	1,323	160	1,163	161
1997[1]	----	----	----	----	----	----	----	1,326	79	1,247	141

[1] Preliminary. *Source: Energy Information Administration, U.S. Department of Energy (EIA-DOE)*

Copper

Copper metals and copper alloys have considerable commercial importance due to their electrical, mechanical and physical properties. Copper for commercial purposes is obtained by the reduction of copper compounds in ores and by electrolytic refining. Copper finds widespread use in alloys such as brass which is composed of copper and zinc.

The world's largest copper producer by far is Chile with almost a third of world output. The next largest producer is the U.S. followed by Canada, Peru, Australia, Poland and Zambia. In the U.S., the principal mining states are Arizona, New Mexico, Utah, Missouri and Montana.

U.S. mine production of recoverable copper in June 1998 was 151,000 metric tonnes, down 3 percent from the previous month. In the first half of 1998, mine production was 916,000 tonnes. For all of 1997 it was 1.94 million tonnes of which Arizona produced 1.25 million tonnes. Smelter production of copper in June 1998 was 104,000 tonnes, down 13 percent from June. In the January-June 1998 period, smelter production was 733,000 tonnes while for all of 1997 it was 1.44 million tonnes. In 1997, smelter copper produced from domestic and foreign ores was 1.44 million tonnes while production from scrap was 282,000 tonnes.

U.S. refinery production of copper in June 1998 was 167,000 tonnes, down 7 percent from May. In the first half of 1998, refinery production was 1.08 million tonnes and for all of 1997 it was 2.06 million tonnes. In 1997, electrolytic refinery production from domestic sources was 1.37 million tonnes. From foreign sources the total was 113,000 tonnes while production by electrowon was 579,000 tonnes.

Refinery production of secondary recoverable copper in June 1998 was 19,600 tonnes, up 10 percent from the previous month. Secondary refinery production in the first half of 1998 was 147,000 tonnes, while for all of 1997 it was 383,000 tonnes. Ingot makers secondary production in June 1998 was 10,500 tonnes, the same as the month before. For first half 1998 it was 63,200 tonnes and for all of 1997 it was 126,000 tonnes. Copper recovered by brass and wire-rod mills in first-half 1998 was 410,000 tonnes and for all of 1997 it was 804,000 tonnes.

U.S. consumption of copper in 1997 was 2.89 million tonnes. Consumption of purchased copper-base scrap was 1.73 million tonnes. U.S. stocks of refined copper at the end of June 1998 were 349,000 tonnes while at the end of 1997 they were 314,000 tonnes. Stocks of blister copper at the end of June 1998 were 104,000 tonnes and at the end of 1997 they were 180,000 tonnes.

U.S. imports of copper ores and concentrates in May 1998 were 13,100 tonnes. Imports of ores and concentrates for all of 1997 were 44,300 tonnes. Imports of refined copper in May 1998 were 57,600 tonnes while for all of 1997 they were 632,000 tonnes. U.S. exports of copper ores and concentrates in May 1998 were 2,910 tonnes and for all of 1997 were 128,000 tonnes. Exports of refined copper in May 1998 were 7,760 tonnes while for all of 1997 they were 93,300 tonnes.

Futures Markets

Copper futures and options are traded on the London Metals Exchange (LME) and the New York Mercantile Exchange, COMEX division. Copper futures are traded on the Beijing Commodity Exchange (BCE).

World Mine Production of Copper (Content of Ore) In Thousands of Metric Tons

Year	Australia	Canada[3]	Chile	China	Indonesia	Mexico	Peru	Poland	Russia[4]	South Africa	United States[3]	Zambia	World Total[2]
1988	238.3	776.5	1,451.0	282	121.5	284.9	337.5	437.0	1,000	168.5	1,420	456.6	8,727
1989	296.0	723.1	1,609.3	276	144.0	264.2	387.9	384.0	1,000	181.9	1,507	466.3	9,058
1990	330.0	793.7	1,588.4	285	164.1	293.9	339.3	330.0	950	178.7	1,588	421.0	8,950
1991	320.0	811.1	1,814.3	304	211.7	292.1	357.2	320.0	900	184.6	1,531	390.6	9,090
1992	378.0	768.6	1,932.7	334	280.8	279.0	345.6	331.9	699	176.1	1,760	429.5	9,470
1993	402.0	732.6	2,055.4	345	298.6	301.2	355.0	382.6	584	166.3	1,800	396.2	9,430
1994	415.6	616.8	2,219.9	396	322.2	294.7	346.5	378.0	573	160.1	1,850	373.2	9,520
1995	419.9	726.3	2,488.6	445	443.6	333.6	440.4	384.2	525	161.6	1,850	323.7	10,100
1996[1]	524.8	688.4	3,115.8	439	507.5	340.7	486.5	421.9	520	152.6	1,920	333.8	11,000
1997[2]	545.0	657.4	3,392.0	414	529.1	390.5	491.0	414.0	505	186.0	1,940	353.0	11,400

[1] Preliminary. [2] Estimate. [3] Recoverable. [4] Formerly part of the U.S.S.R.; data not reported separately until 1992. *Source: U.S. Geological Survey*

Commodity Exchange, Inc. Warehouse Stocks of Copper, on First of Month In Thousands of Short Tons

Year	Jan.	Feb.	Mar.	Apr.	May	June	July	Aug.	Sept.	Oct.	Nov.	Dec.
1989	13.4	14.9	17.3	29.7	21.2	25.2	23.0	20.4	15.2	11.4	10.4	9.1
1990	16.3	7.2	4.1	4.5	6.0	14.7	18.1	11.5	8.9	6.7	8.3	9.3
1991	20.2	14.7	16.4	30.2	30.9	25.0	25.1	35.9	33.6	24.4	26.8	29.3
1992	33.7	34.8	29.5	28.2	30.3	32.4	31.8	36.0	40.4	51.7	70.1	73.8
1993	105.9	124.0	114.8	107.6	110.8	108.3	105.5	113.8	100.1	94.1	96.6	80.5
1994	74.0	56.7	49.8	37.2	31.6	30.4	36.0	37.4	28.5	17.9	20.3	21.5
1995	26.7	18.7	17.7	9.0	11.5	7.0	13.1	16.7	16.5	11.2	6.0	5.0
1996	23.7	12.1	12.4	13.9	20.7	13.2	7.6	17.7	22.1	21.7	30.8	36.2
1997	29.3	18.4	24.8	43.3	48.9	42.6	44.7	30.0	46.5	61.5	68.0	82.3
1998	91.9	101.8	113.7	112.6	106.5	83.0	62.5	55.7	56.1	67.7	70.7	75.8

Source: New York Mercantile Exchange, COMEX division

Salient Statistics of Copper in the United States In Thousands of Metric Tons

Year	New Copper Produced: From Domestic Ores: Mines	Smelters	Refineries	From Foreign Ores[3]	Total New	Secondary Recovered[4]	Imports[3]: Unmanufactured	Imports[3]: Refined	Exports: Ore, Concentrate[6]	Exports: Refined[7]	Stocks, Dec. 31: COMEX	Stocks, Dec. 31: Primary Producers (Refined)	Blister & Material in Solution	Apparent Consumption: Refined Copper (Reported)	Apparent Consumption: Primary & Old Copper[8]
1988	1,417	1,043	1,282	124	1,406	518	513	332	211	58	12	97	121	2,210	2,214
1989	1,498	1,120	1,352	125	1,477	548	515	300	267	130	15	107	132	2,203	2,185
1990	1,588	1,158	1,502	75	1,577	537	512	262	258	211	18	101	119	2,150	2,168
1991	1,631	1,123	1,501	77	1,577	518	512	289	253	263	31	132	135	2,048	2,105
1992	1,765	1,180	1,615	96	1,711	555	593	289	266	177	96	205	166	2,178	2,311
1993	1,800	1,270	1,210	89	1,790	543	637	343	227	217	67	153	146	2,360	2,510
1994	1,850	1,310	1,280	64	1,840	500	763	470	261	157	24	119	171	2,680	2,690
1995	1,850	1,250	1,300	91	1,930	442	825	429	239	217	22	163	174	2,530	2,540
1996[1]	1,920	1,300	1,290	147	2,010	428	961	543	195	169	27	146	173	2,610	2,830
1997[2]	1,940	1,440	1,370	113	2,060	496	978	647	127	93	83	314	180	2,790	2,950

[1] Preliminary. [2] Estimate. [3] Also from matte, etc., refinery reports. [4] From scrap only. [5] For consumption. [6] Blister (copper content). [7] Ingots, bars, etc. [8] Old scrap only. *Source: U.S. Geological Survey (USGS)*

Consumption of Refined Copper[3] in the United States In Thousands of Metric Tons

Year	By-Products: Cathodes	Wire Bars	Ingot & Ingot Bars	Cakes & Slabs	Billets	Other[4]	By Class of Consumer: Wire Rod Mills	Brass Mills	Chemical Plants	Ingot Makers	Foundries	Miscellaneous[5]	Total Consumption
1988	1,967.4	14.0	54.2	63.0	99.0	12.7	1,667.2	493.2	1.0	2.6	14.5	31.9	2,210.4
1989	1,981.6	6.1	34.4	64.9	104.9	11.2	1,698.4	461.0	.9	1.3	14.9	26.5	2,203.1
1990	1,922.4	6.6	50.5	57.9	W	113.0	1,653.5	445.2	1.1	4.5	14.6	31.6	2,150.4
1991	1,854.9	W	24.7	33.3	W	135.4	1,591.8	458.5	.9	3.4	12.7	25.3	2,048.3
1992	1,974.9	W	20.0	43.7	W	139.6	1,675.0	458.5	.9	3.0	15.0	25.8	2,178.2
1993	2,130.0	W	37.7	55.5	W	136.0	1,819.1	503.0	.9	2.2	10.2	27.6	2,360.0
1994	2,410.0	W	37.3	73.2	W	164.0	2,060.0	568.0	1.1	4.5	11.1	30.4	2,680.0
1995	2,250.0	W	31.3	75.9	W	181.0	1,950.0	533.0	1.1	7.7	15.6	31.4	2,530.0
1996[1]	2,320.0	W	26.8	80.8	W	181.0	1,980.0	588.0	1.1	3.6	15.8	28.6	2,610.0
1997[2]	2,490.0	W	29.5	81.1	W	194.0	2,140.0	597.0	1.0	4.2	16.6	29.9	2,790.0

[1] Preliminary. [2] Estimate. [3] Primary & secondary. [4] 1991 to date include Wire Bars and Billets. [5] Includes iron and steel plants, primary smelters producing alloys other than copper, consumers of copper powder and copper shot, and other manufacturers. *Source: U.S. Geological Survey (USGS)*

London Metals Exchange Warehouse Stocks of Copper, at End of Month In Thousands of Metric Tons

Year	Jan.	Feb.	Mar.	Apr.	May	June	July	Aug.	Sept.	Oct.	Nov.	Dec.
1989	96.6	104.2	117.4	138.7	125.2	99.2	96.1	100.8	126.7	117.8	142.2	131.2
1990	121.5	106.8	71.9	67.0	92.8	67.7	126.8	161.1	227.1	221.1	199.9	220.6
1991	189.0	202.8	213.9	237.9	275.0	264.9	266.5	307.1	308.4	291.7	308.3	332.3
1992	308.6	302.7	296.4	279.7	265.4	259.1	246.8	275.2	299.7	317.8	327.0	315.8
1993	313.5	333.1	365.8	403.5	429.1	446.9	464.3	521.7	600.7	612.3	590.9	599.5
1994	597.6	554.5	504.3	446.4	379.0	350.9	338.9	367.8	359.3	333.1	318.4	301.8
1995	309.9	280.9	239.9	204.9	197.9	166.5	151.5	163.1	178.2	193.6	222.2	364.8
1996	355.1	348.4	322.3	303.9	309.7	263.0	227.6	275.5	240.7	122.1	96.1	119.6
1997	194.2	216.2	177.2	145.8	133.0	128.3	234.9	278.7	332.8	344.6	338.8	337.8
1998[1]	365.7	376.0	339.5	262.3	261.8	249.3	260.9	307.7	414.2	460.6		

[1] Preliminary. *Source: American Bureau of Metal Statistics (ABMS)*

Copper Refined from Scrap in the United States In Thousands of Metric Tons

Year	Jan.	Feb.	Mar.	Apr.	May	June	July	Aug.	Sept.	Oct.	Nov.	Dec.	Total
1989	37.4	40.8	47.0	40.1	40.8	41.1	36.6	41.4	40.6	41.3	35.9	37.1	479.9
1990	37.3	35.2	37.1	38.5	39.3	38.1	34.6	39.2	29.9	34.3	31.9	32.0	440.8
1991	35.4	32.8	40.5	39.6	38.2	35.7	32.6	33.0	28.5	37.3	32.1	32.6	417.7
1992	27.8	34.1	39.8	34.8	36.7	39.4	27.8	35.4	39.8	40.0	34.3	35.8	433.2
1993	38.1	45.9	38.9	37.8	36.4	41.1	35.0	37.6	37.4	43.0	35.4	32.2	459.8
1994	33.3	28.3	37.9	30.7	37.1	28.7	26.9	33.0	38.7	27.0	34.3	37.3	391.7
1995	30.9	30.6	36.0	32.7	33.7	28.2	18.7	25.1	25.4	25.0	26.2	24.4	319.0
1996	25.0	23.7	25.5	22.5	26.8	30.9	24.4	25.0	26.8	30.6	25.9	26.3	333.0
1997	35.9	30.0	36.4	32.6	35.4	30.8	26.4	28.4	34.3	36.5	24.6	29.3	383.0
1998[1]	25.9	28.6	23.7	31.0	17.8	21.4	24.2	23.9	23.8				293.7

[1] Preliminary. *Source: U.S. Geological Survey (USGS)*

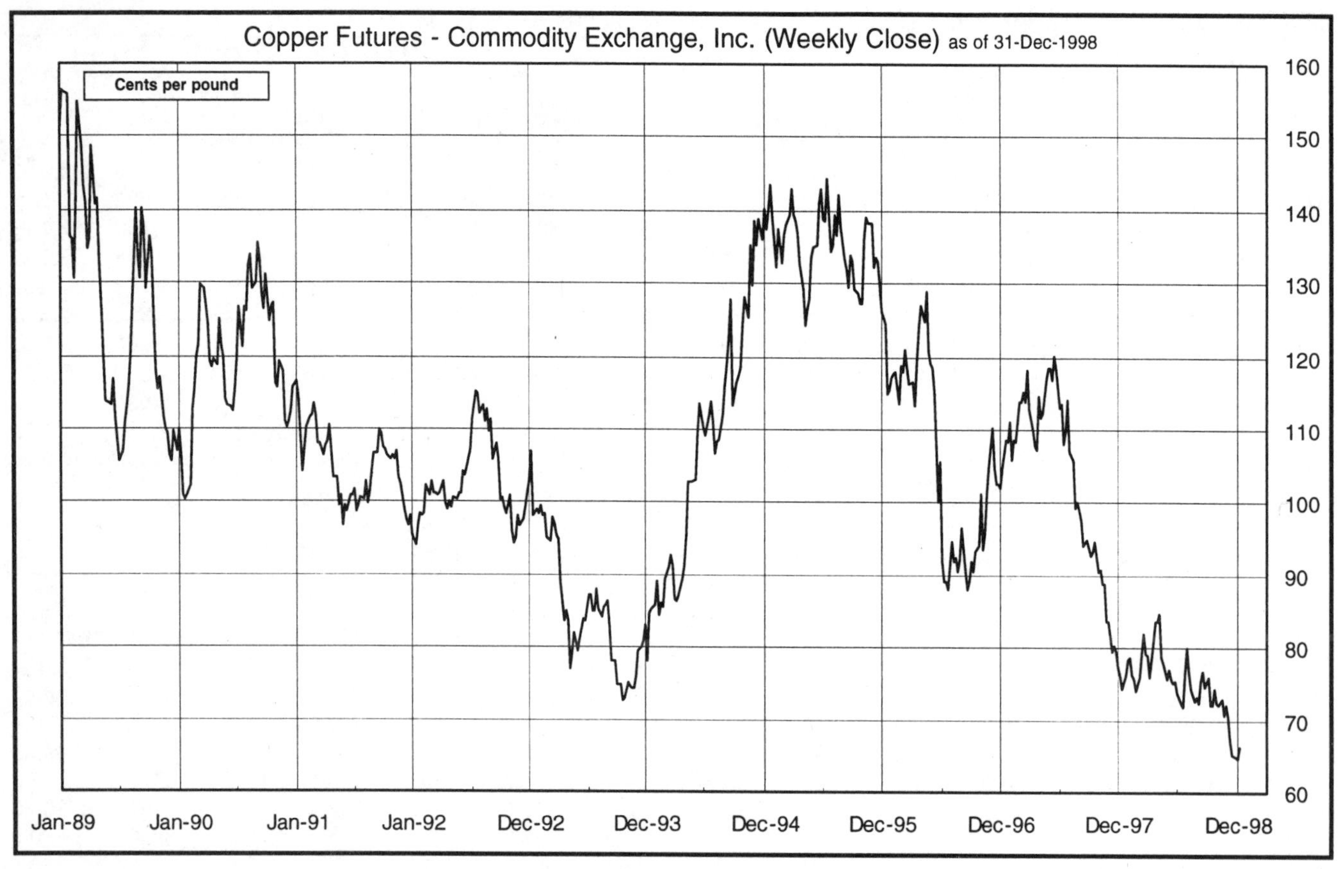

Average Open Interest of Copper Futures[1] in New York In Contracts

Year	Jan.	Feb.	Mar.	Apr.	May	June	July	Aug.	Sept.	Oct.	Nov.	Dec.
1989	33,819	34,199	35,058	36,021	30,901	28,527	26,534	28,420	28,849	27,287	31,240	32,343
1990	31,466	33,908	34,654	34,405	31,552	30,113	32,780	31,515	32,578	36,145	35,088	30,128
1991	34,927	35,978	35,026	34,096	44,153	39,879	33,100	33,333	40,347	42,028	41,618	44,283
1992	47,109	47,929	48,700	45,114	39,986	48,129	47,065	38,397	37,041	41,658	44,927	45,541
1993	47,433	48,707	48,220	51,217	52,762	56,856	54,861	54,571	54,929	57,406	63,632	69,311
1994	65,518	65,446	66,177	59,346	63,825	60,383	51,616	46,855	56,344	59,060	59,158	51,078
1995	52,632	50,770	47,267	47,793	50,089	48,200	40,968	37,744	33,709	36,476	38,475	35,996
1996	47,771	45,706	42,732	46,771	47,284	52,558	56,564	56,549	55,408	58,124	61,031	55,807
1997	54,468	56,022	58,205	50,574	56,740	56,774	47,767	44,632	49,612	54,912	67,026	67,502
1998	69,607	72,302	67,154	68,670	65,033	66,002	63,271	61,116	60,520	62,944	67,984	76,846

[1] Data for May 1988 thru December 1989 include Old copper and High Grade copper contracts. *Source: New York Mercantile Exchange, COMEX Division*

Volume of Trading of Copper Futures[1] in New York In Contracts

Year	Jan.	Feb.	Mar.	Apr.	May	June	July	Aug.	Sept.	Oct.	Nov.	Dec.	Total
1989	216,528	201,132	219,910	201,997	193,956	174,055	132,793	173,273	151,097	176,822	154,241	93,243	2,089,047
1990	152,156	148,766	179,445	181,726	164,489	163,372	141,602	154,383	156,924	161,814	133,718	114,790	1,853,185
1991	159,621	131,044	108,191	150,390	148,777	139,207	110,025	149,702	132,354	125,757	153,910	135,132	1,643,310
1992	145,245	168,015	105,003	157,473	77,722	182,091	138,225	177,581	137,423	121,392	146,062	117,931	1,674,163
1993	152,387	148,388	132,705	212,086	160,751	181,427	165,727	169,428	222,099	133,364	203,729	182,538	2,064,629
1994	197,959	233,016	231,239	207,963	247,143	297,393	188,644	242,393	219,788	208,957	290,585	178,887	2,737,967
1995	242,760	267,883	232,229	242,302	195,554	274,587	167,836	213,110	169,689	181,945	185,141	146,378	2,519,414
1996	184,431	173,689	157,553	210,836	200,469	255,172	150,445	174,351	166,537	250,420	227,800	160,216	2,311,919
1997	193,543	221,504	190,000	218,607	164,728	238,918	191,609	198,156	197,746	202,615	203,376	135,368	2,356,170
1998	172,133	223,117	197,652	264,061	175,956	217,316	202,596	213,541	196,355	195,255	250,986	174,642	2,483,610

[1] Data for May 1988 thru December 1989 include Old copper and High Grade copper contracts. *Source: New York Mercantile Exchange, COMEX Division*

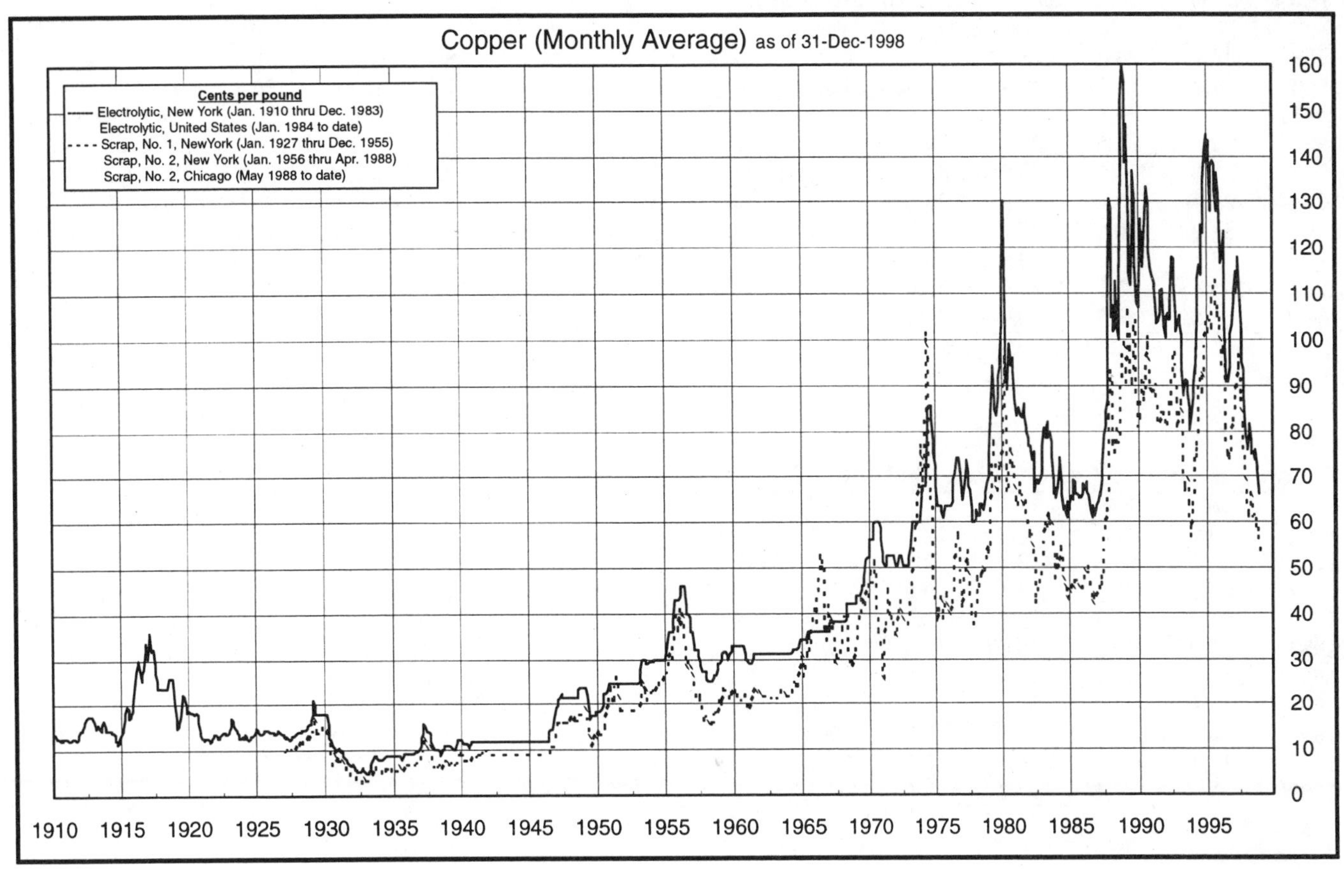

Producers' Price of Electrolytic (Wirebar) Copper, Delivered to U.S. Destinations In Cents Per Pound

Year	Jan.	Feb.	Mar.	Apr.	May	June	July	Aug.	Sept.	Oct.	Nov.	Dec.	Average
1989	164.21	146.17	154.89	150.26	132.72	121.45	119.27	133.75	143.60	137.61	123.59	115.64	136.93
1990	116.36	119.35	136.22	134.38	132.32	124.93	133.91	142.53	142.45	138.41	127.76	124.39	131.08
1991	122.59	122.73	121.24	120.35	133.11	111.72	111.90	113.48	118.92	118.90	117.26	110.33	118.54
1992	108.16	112.52	113.56	112.35	112.56	116.74	125.66	124.30	119.39	112.09	108.23	111.13	114.72
1993	112.57	110.26	107.80	99.03	92.35	94.98	93.41	97.06	92.36	81.69	86.07	91.08	96.56
1994	95.65	99.13	101.76	99.87	112.30	120.58	123.68	121.38	132.53	130.91	141.92	148.86	119.05
1995	152.02	146.00	151.14	146.03	139.80	149.51	150.00	149.77	144.14	140.00	148.48	143.78	146.72
1996	130.09	128.75	130.20	131.29	135.33	116.33	102.68	104.14	102.51	105.46	112.78	114.78	117.86
1997	120.29	122.22	126.80	121.70	127.25	129.57	121.94	114.11	107.14	105.08	99.53	95.65	115.94
1998	88.88	87.52	91.69	93.54	90.02	86.90	87.37	85.30	87.62	84.26	83.51	78.30	87.08

Source: American Metal Market (AMM)

Dealers' Buying Price of No. 2 Heavy Copper Scrap In the Chicago In Cents Per Pound

Year	Jan.	Feb.	Mar.	Apr.	May	June	July	Aug.	Sept.	Oct.	Nov.	Dec.	Average
1989	89.83	87.13	95.33	95.95	91.14	80.27	74.45	75.54	86.50	90.32	86.00	80.25	86.06
1990	78.27	71.00	78.73	88.00	88.00	84.38	84.00	85.50	91.84	89.50	86.48	83.00	84.06
1991	83.00	79.50	82.21	82.50	78.66	72.40	71.00	71.00	72.05	75.39	75.08	74.50	76.44
1992	73.21	73.37	75.23	75.16	74.00	74.27	77.18	78.38	75.38	70.27	69.00	67.18	73.55
1993	67.95	67.00	67.00	62.95	55.12	53.59	56.33	54.18	52.67	49.10	47.00	48.00	56.74
1994	50.80	56.11	59.61	62.00	64.86	72.32	76.40	74.30	75.69	76.45	78.10	82.95	69.13
1995	89.48	90.79	89.39	91.75	85.91	88.73	92.32	92.65	92.70	90.64	92.00	92.00	90.70
1996	87.17	82.90	83.24	83.29	82.95	71.48	61.43	62.00	62.00	63.00	64.84	66.00	72.53
1997	68.73	71.63	77.50	79.18	77.33	78.19	72.64	70.24	65.67	63.74	61.31	58.43	70.38
1998	53.26	52.58	53.09	54.00	52.60	49.64	48.00	47.71	46.00	44.00	40.00	40.00	48.41

Source: American Metal Market (AMM)

COPPER

Imports of Refined Copper into the United States In Thousands of Metric Tons

Year	Jan.	Feb.	Mar.	Apr.	May	June	July	Aug.	Sept.	Oct.	Nov.	Dec.	Total
1989	32.7	24.8	18.7	20.9	24.1	25.9	20.9	24.4	28.1	30.5	32.3	16.9	300.1
1990	24.7	15.8	26.5	25.3	31.3	24.0	20.6	18.0	21.4	18.4	20.8	16.7	263.6
1991	22.7	27.1	21.7	30.9	17.5	23.6	23.7	17.4	22.9	36.3	26.8	18.0	288.6
1992	22.6	24.5	31.9	25.2	25.3	26.1	24.7	25.3	24.0	19.6	20.3	20.8	289.1
1993	21.8	25.6	28.2	35.9	29.5	26.9	30.6	28.3	22.5	31.6	32.2	30.5	343.4
1994	28.7	33.6	49.8	36.8	36.1	46.8	35.6	34.4	34.7	62.4	35.9	36.2	470.0
1995	34.9	30.0	37.1	36.9	36.5	37.9	31.5	31.8	28.7	38.7	44.4	40.3	429.0
1996	43.1	41.2	48.2	49.6	56.8	44.6	53.8	64.8	62.3	46.1	61.8	47.2	543.0
1997	55.4	48.0	43.6	43.6	61.0	42.0	53.1	73.3	53.8	55.0	53.4	42.0	632.0
1998[1]	62.8	49.6	59.9	64.7	57.6	52.8	45.0	51.7					666.2

[1] Preliminary. *Source: U./S. Geological Survey (USGS)*

Exports of Refined Copper from the United States In Thousands of Metric Tons

Year	Jan.	Feb.	Mar.	Apr.	May	June	July	Aug.	Sept.	Oct.	Nov.	Dec.	Total
1989	6.2	4.8	5.9	13.5	4.3	6.6	21.4	15.8	23.4	13.7	6.3	12.1	130.2
1990	18.1	20.8	12.2	7.6	15.6	12.2	23.9	20.1	22.4	21.5	17.2	19.8	211.3
1991	33.6	21.4	37.4	16.8	31.5	23.9	20.6	20.9	17.9	13.4	15.4	17.9	270.7
1992	21.7	18.4	10.8	12.3	11.7	12.0	9.3	13.0	13.6	24.1	14.1	16.1	176.9
1993	14.0	24.9	23.6	16.3	15.4	13.1	10.7	10.1	19.5	19.5	14.9	14.5	216.7
1994	13.0	10.2	10.7	6.8	14.8	9.1	15.6	10.9	15.4	15.9	13.1	21.1	157.0
1995	11.1	24.0	25.6	18.2	23.4	38.9	16.3	16.6	12.1	9.0	12.5	9.5	217.0
1996	13.7	16.5	12.7	12.3	10.8	10.7	15.7	17.7	14.5	16.4	12.8	16.0	170.0
1997	11.1	9.8	6.5	6.5	71.9	8.2	6.9	7.5	6.3	7.4	8.2	8.5	93.3
1998[1]	6.2	12.1	12.2	7.5	7.8	6.4	7.5	6.4					99.1

[1] Preliminary. *Source: U./S. Geological Survey (USGS)*

Stocks of Refined Copper in the United States In Thousands of Short Tons (Recoverable Copper Content)

Year	Jan. 1	Feb. 1	Mar. 1	Apr. 1	May 1	June 1	July 1	Aug. 1	Sept. 1	Oct. 1	Nov. 1	Dec. 1
1989	56.3	67.5	56.3	60.6	54.3	54.4	49.1	61.8	66.1	42.3	48.1	48.2
1990	72.7	42.4	38.6	45.2	55.9	60.2	67.5	67.2	67.6	27.4	27.9	45.4
1991	72.3	72.8	53.2	68.6	63.2	52.8	52.4	71.4	64.4	48.5	48.3	63.1
1992	75.3	76.3	67.2	69.7	75.9	65.0	62.2	71.2	87.1	99.5	110.3	107.1
1993	135.4	152.7	144.3	132.3	146.0	153.6	137.1	151.0	128.4	117.2	124.6	107.1
1994	103.0	87.7	83.6	72.8	70.7	70.4	73.3	81.1	74.6	66.5	52.7	53.6
1995[2]	55.8	39.6	37.0	22.6	33.1	30.8	27.0	50.0	60.6	71.1	69.4	73.4
1996	120.0	131.4	125.5	123.1	126.3	107.9	102.8	106.2	104.7	68.0	76.0	77.5
1997	88.2	98.8	104.4	116.0	117.9	121.7	122.9	148.8	177.1	197.9	227.6	253.3
1998[1]	281.5	282.2	312.7	315.7	304.5	308.6	306.2	319.0	334.1	367.4		

[1] Preliminary. [2] New reporting method beginning January 1995. *Source: American Bureau of Metal Statistics (ABMS)*

Stocks of Refined Copper in the United States In Thousands of Short Tons (Recoverable Copper Content)

Year	Jan. 1	Feb. 1	Mar. 1	Apr. 1	May 1	June 1	July 1	Aug. 1	Sept. 1	Oct. 1	Nov. 1	Dec. 1
1989	337.5	325.7	341.0	350.3	406.5	385.7	374.2	389.8	335.8	368.7	348.1	358.3
1990	362.3	382.0	335.6	320.0	332.6	356.3	291.8	370.9	417.9	484.6	483.0	447.6
1991	439.5	464.2	447.1	501.1	559.5	595.4	593.1	605.4	664.7	653.5	644.9	676.9
1992	640.4	718.1	704.2	715.7	714.9	723.2	726.4	737.9	816.5	822.5	873.8	896.1
1993	757.1	765.9	789.6	817.2	885.1	912.2	910.4	943.8	1,040.3	1,124.3	1,133.9	1,106.1
1994	1,075.0	1,095.5	1,046.8	984.9	913.7	859.5	843.7	839.7	874.6	870.7	835.1	818.4
1995[2]	611.6	655.8	622.2	577.9	537.0	525.6	494.9	464.7	465.7	467.7	481.4	503.5
1996	560.2	566.0	552.5	517.5	498.7	563.9	507.9	476.6	544.4	499.5	391.8	362.0
1997	405.4	469.5	476.3	445.7	413.5	402.4	408.3	489.6	550.9	607.7	574.5	553.3
1998[1]	580.8	613.0	585.1	538.3	462.1	453.3	429.4	420.6	481.0	563.1		

[1] Preliminary. [2] New reporting method beginning January 1995. *Source: American Bureau of Metal Statistics (ABMS)*

Production of Refined Copper in the United States In Thousands of Short Tons (Recoverable Copper Content)

Year	Jan.	Feb.	Mar.	Apr.	May	June	July	Aug.	Sept.	Oct.	Nov.	Dec.	Total
1989	129.5	128.1	137.2	118.3	132.2	142.6	121.3	150.8	116.5	137.0	127.4	130.7	1,572
1990	136.0	122.0	150.4	140.1	147.5	136.1	125.5	132.5	130.1	141.6	141.0	125.5	1,628
1991	129.0	127.7	134.9	119.7	137.1	124.8	136.8	142.7	135.6	153.1	141.0	149.7	1,632
1992	139.9	135.6	150.6	142.8	123.0	138.5	140.3	150.1	146.9	155.3	156.8	153.7	1,734
1993	153.9	153.8	173.2	166.0	160.3	177.0	151.4	153.7	160.2	157.3	157.2	166.2	1,930
1994	160.9	150.0	167.8	157.2	165.5	160.4	148.9	165.6	162.1	157.3	153.3	159.8	1,909
1995[2]	202.7	185.5	204.8	194.6	210.0	198.3	193.8	208.8	199.0	206.5	211.3	208.1	2,423
1996	210.8	197.6	209.7	212.4	213.5	193.4	206.1	199.5	198.8	223.1	199.3	212.0	2,476
1997	220.7	200.7	216.7	216.3	205.9	196.5	222.1	213.5	226.2	241.2	229.3	230.6	2,624
1998[1]	193.3	201.4	200.7	202.7	185.5	204.8	194.6	210.0	198.3	193.8			2,382

[1] Preliminary. [2] New Reporting method beginning January 1995. *Source: American Bureau of Metal Statistics (ABMS)*

Production of Refined Copper Outside the United States In Thousands of Short Tons (Recoverable Copper Content)

Year	Jan.	Feb.	Mar.	Apr.	May	June	July	Aug.	Sept.	Oct.	Nov.	Dec.	Total
1989	387.8	372.7	411.9	404.3	430.1	388.7	409.5	413.5	421.7	436.1	434.0	402.7	4,913
1990	423.7	396.7	424.6	412.8	414.1	395.6	372.6	407.1	404.6	422.6	417.4	411.0	4,902
1991	416.5	381.1	427.7	405.5	425.3	404.5	375.1	378.7	411.4	411.8	409.2	424.5	4,871
1992	441.2	412.6	447.0	418.0	438.7	449.5	418.5	425.8	418.7	438.9	431.3	426.1	5,166
1993	429.2	405.6	475.1	426.2	440.9	447.5	421.6	449.4	448.0	425.9	447.2	436.5	5,253
1994	432.5	390.8	432.7	400.6	432.9	421.1	387.8	413.8	421.5	416.3	437.4	428.8	5,016
1995[2]	817.5	797.6	868.4	858.2	859.4	844.8	849.7	825.7	819.8	865.2	833.8	872.2	10,112
1996	903.2	869.3	929.3	922.2	916.3	918.3	908.3	931.1	938.2	972.9	935.8	992.4	11,137
1997	962.5	936.0	981.1	1,007.9	1,032.8	1,021.5	1,024.0	1,008.2	990.0	1,023.4	1,011.7	1,028.3	12,053
1998[1]	1,073.1	1,012.8	1,066.3	1,039.4	1,057.2	1,027.6	912.2	915.3	957.0	957.9			12,023

[1] Preliminary. [2] New Reporting method beginning January 1995. *Source: American Bureau of Metal Statistics (ABMS)*

Deliveries of Refined Copper to Fabricators in the United States In Thousands of Short Tons[3]

Year	Jan.	Feb.	Mar.	Apr.	May	June	July	Aug.	Sept.	Oct.	Nov.	Dec.	Total
1989	127.8	147.7	148.4	141.1	153.2	168.4	131.4	173.2	116.5	156.8	149.2	121.9	1,781
1990	167.4	132.8	163.3	156.6	153.3	144.5	129.5	132.5	130.1	140.9	130.7	108.6	1,733
1991	128.4	153.3	125.3	126.7	152.7	115.0	125.4	152.8	135.6	167.7	130.4	132.9	1,684
1992	144.9	159.0	165.9	155.5	149.4	161.4	145.8	144.1	146.9	150.4	166.2	130.0	1,813
1993	142.9	165.3	201.6	170.4	162.5	209.6	144.8	191.4	178.9	164.3	194.8	182.7	2,109
1994	193.3	168.6	204.6	178.3	187.8	171.9	154.3	194.6	188.2	188.7	167.5	175.1	2,173
1995[2]	233.8	209.2	239.1	200.9	230.0	210.5	187.1	208.8	202.9	224.7	222.4	175.5	2,545
1996	221.6	227.2	240.0	242.2	270.7	222.1	233.8	246.8	277.5	239.7	240.6	231.9	2,882
1997	246.3	234.5	240.6	247.4	254.9	228.1	241.1	258.2	252.3	259.2	256.0	236.6	2,959
1998[1]	284.5	248.4	288.1	289.2	278.7	258.0	252.4	242.1	260.7	239.1			3,169

[1] Preliminary. [2] New reporting method beginning January 1995. [3] Recoverable copper content. *Source: American Bureau of Metal Statistics (ABMS)*

Deliveries of Refined Copper to Fabricators Outside the United States In Thousands of Short Tons[3]

Year	Jan.	Feb.	Mar.	Apr.	May	June	July	Aug.	Sept.	Oct.	Nov.	Dec.	Total
1989	426.0	369.9	411.8	360.9	459.0	398.0	386.8	464.2	393.2	456.9	423.0	399.1	4,949
1990	419.9	466.3	436.7	392.9	408.3	466.7	303.7	373.5	370.8	448.9	469.1	420.7	4,972
1991	405.0	404.4	391.5	361.2	406.3	433.5	368.5	323.4	420.7	499.1	391.4	483.4	4,807
1992	453.7	408.9	441.8	416.4	413.4	432.4	410.4	364.7	432.6	403.5	406.1	461.3	5,045
1993	427.9	392.9	452.3	361.7	422.2	442.6	384.4	347.9	387.5	414.8	463.4	458.5	4,956
1994	399.8	429.5	481.2	466.5	468.9	428.1	387.9	369.2	423.5	448.9	457.1	436.0	5,197
1995[2]	758.5	810.1	892.8	882.2	853.0	867.3	863.7	814.1	803.4	835.1	796.6	726.2	9,903
1996	875.2	859.4	934.3	907.2	816.7	950.7	908.3	817.4	911.5	1,056.0	922.7	918.3	10,878
1997	862.2	889.7	977.9	1,007.1	991.1	982.7	897.8	873.9	886.2	1,009.0	980.4	966.6	11,349
1998[1]	991.2	976.5	1,059.7	1,064.8	1,001.3	1,006.5	868.2	811.0	799.3	888.0			11,360

[1] Preliminary. [2] New reporting method beginning January 1995. [3] Recoverable copper content. *Source: American Bureau of Metal Statistics (ABMS)*

Corn

U.S. corn prices, basis nearby futures, fell to a 10-year low in the second half of 1998, the lowest level since the late 1980's and reflective of near record U.S. and world corn production. The U.S. 1998/99 crop was estimated at 9.73 billion bushels (247.5 million tonnes), the second highest on record and comparing to 9.37 billion in 1997/98. The record high 10.1 billion bushel crop was realized in 1994/95. Both harvested acreage and average yield increased in 1998; acreage of 73.8 million compares with 73.7 million in 1997, while average yield of 132 bushels per acre was up from 127 bushels, respectively. In the key producing midwestern states, a record ear count per acre was realized which helped lift the overall crop outlook from initial estimates of about 247.4 million tonnes. Due to the large crop and the drop in 1998/99 exports, carryover as of August 31, 1999 was forecast at 1.71 billion bushels vs. the year earlier 1.31 billion. The stock-to-use ratio in 1998/99 was forecast at about 21 percent vs. the previous season's 15.8 percent and the very low 5 percent ratio of 1995/96. Typically, the higher the ratio, the greater the pressure that's generated on prices.

The 1998/99 overall supply/demand imbalance was manifested in futures as prices declined about $.65/bushel during the second half of calendar 1998, from near $2.75/bushel in mid-year to about $2.10 by early September, basis March '99 futures; recovering towards yearend to about $2.30. Although the price weakness was in part seasonal, the magnitude of the weakness largely reflected the anticipated buildup in carryover. In 1998/99, the average price received by farmers was forecast to range between $1.80-2.20/bushel vs. the 1997/98 average of $2.45 and the 1995/96 record high of $3.24. If a $2.00 per bushel average is realized it would be the lowest of the past decade.

Corn is by far the leading U.S. feed grain with a record large 5.9 billion bushel usage estimated for 1998/99 (October/September) vs. the previous high of 5.7 billion in 1997/98. Food, seed, and industrial use (FSI) was estimated at a record high 1.85 billion bushels vs. 1.78 billion in 1997/98. The increases in FSI use during the past few years is not surprising considering that industrial demand for corn as a sweetener--High Fructose corn syrup (HFCS)--was expected to quicken.

The U.S. is the world's largest corn exporter with Argentina a distant second. Importers are numerous, but the leaders are generally in Asia, paced by Japan, South Korea and Taiwan. U.S. exports in 1998/99 of 1.65 billion bushels (42 million tonnes) compares with 1.5 billion in 1997/98 and the record large 2.2 billion in 1995/96. The expected 1.5 billion bushel increase is attributed to larger import needs from Mexico and possibly China. Generally, Japan is the primary destination, but 1998's global financial turmoil impacted negatively on their quantity of imports. U.S. corn imports are minimal, on average about 12 million bushels.

World foreign trade in corn in 1998/99 of 61.7 million metric tonnes is lower than initially forecast and compares with 63.6 million in 1997/98, of which the U.S. accounted for about two-thirds in both years. However, this reflects a sharp drop from the mid-1990's when the U.S. supplied about 80 percent of world exports. Argentina now exports about 15 percent of the world total vs. less than 10 percent in the mid-1990's. Japan's import needs have hovered around 16 million tonnes for some time, but Mexico's needs have climbed and are forecast at 4.3 million tonnes in 1998/99. China's imports have had little pattern in the 1990's; from nothing early in the decade to 4.3 million tonnes in 1994/95 and back to 0.25 million tonnes in 1998/99. South Korea tends to be the second largest importer with 6.5 million tonnes in 1998/99 vs. 7.5 million in 1997/98.

The record large world corn production in 1998/99 of 594 million tonnes trailed initial forecasts by 4.5 million tonnes, and compares with 578 million in 1997/98 with Argentina accounting for about a third of the slippage. China, who since 1987/88 is the second largest producer, produced a near record large 124 million tonnes in 1998/99 vs. 104 million in 1997/98 and the record large 127 million in 1996/97. Together, the U.S. and China produced about 62 percent of the world's corn in 1998/99; Brazil and Mexico combined produced about 10 percent. The gains seen in China's production through the 1990's reflect increases in per capita income and meat consumption and the need for more corn as a livestock feed.

Global usage in 1998/99 of a record large 594 million tonnes compares with 578 million in 1997/98 and the previous high of 591 million in 1996/97. China's usage of 119 million tonnes compares with 118 million in 1997/98. This is the fourth consecutive year in which China's usage has topped 100 million tonnes. The U.S. is the world's largest consumer with almost a third of the total--196 million tonnes--in 1998/99. Brazil is in third place with about 36 million tonnes. World corn stocks are forecast to increase in 1998/99 by almost 4.5 million tonnes, ending the season with a nearly 90 million tonne carryover.

U.S. #2 yellow corn prices vary with the location. Typically, Gulf port prices are about 30¢ per bushel higher than prices in Central Illinois, while quotes at St. Louis run about 10¢-12¢ higher than Illinois prices. In mid-1998, #2 yellow corn in Central Illinois averaged around $2.10/bushel, down about $0.45 from a year earlier; for the Gulf ports the average was $2.48/bushel vs. $2.80, respectively.

Futures Markets

Corn futures are traded on the Beijing Commodity Exchange (BCE), the Budapest Commodity Exchange, the Tokyo Grain Exchange (TGE), the Chicago Board of Trade (CBOT), and the Mid-American Commodity Exchange (MidAm). Corn options are traded on the CBOT and the MidAm.

The CBOT also trades Iowa Corn Yield Insurance futures and options. A contract for U.S. corn yield insurance futures and options also exists although volume is very low at this time.

World Production of Corn or Maize In Thousands of Metric Tons

Crop Year	Argentina	Brazil	Canada	China	France	India	Italy	Mexico	Romania	South Africa	United States	Yugo-slavia	World Total
1989-90	5,200	22,300	6,571	78,928	13,400	9,409	6,359	9,750	6,760	8,900	191,156	9,415	460,484
1990-1	7,600	24,330	7,067	96,820	9,500	8,962	5,864	14,100	6,800	8,300	201,534	6,724	477,855
1991-2	10,600	30,800	7,413	98,770	12,930	8,060	6,240	14,689	10,500	3,125	189,868	11,500	487,307
1992-3	10,200	29,200	4,883	95,380	14,870	9,992	7,410	18,631	6,829	9,990	240,719	6,650	538,552
1993-4	10,000	32,934	6,501	102,700	14,840	9,600	8,030	19,141	8,000	13,275	160,954	5,912	475,386
1994-5	11,360	37,440	7,043	99,280	12,640	9,120	7,480	17,005	8,500	4,845	255,295	7,500	560,277
1995-6	11,100	32,480	7,271	112,000	12,390	9,440	8,450	17,780	9,923	10,200	187,970	8,375	516,903
1996-7[1]	15,500	36,160	7,380	127,470	14,430	10,612	9,550	18,922	9,610	9,012	234,518	8,100	590,395
1997-8[2]	19,360	31,000	7,180	104,300	16,750	11,088	10,140	17,000	12,680	7,550	233,864	9,700	573,979
1998-9[3]	13,500	33,500	8,900	124,000	14,800	9,500	8,600	18,000	8,000	9,000	247,943	8,200	594,735

[1] Preliminary. [2] Estimate. [3] Forecast. *Source: Foreign Agricultural Service,U.S. Department of Agriculture (FAS-USDA)*

World Supply and Demand of Course Grains In Millions of Metric Tons/Hectares

Crop Year Beginning Oct. 1	Area Harvested	Yield	Pro-duction	World Trade	Total Con-sumption	Ending Stocks	Stocks as % of Consump-tion[3]
1989-90	321.9	2.47	793.7	104.7	817.7	123.2	15.1
1990-1	316.3	2.62	828.7	89.1	817.1	134.8	16.5
1991-2	321.9	2.52	810.5	95.6	809.7	135.6	16.7
1992-3	323.9	2.69	872.2	91.9	844.1	163.6	19.4
1993-4	317.3	2.52	800.0	85.3	839.6	124.0	14.8
1994-5	323.0	2.70	871.8	98.5	858.2	137.6	16.0
1995-6	313.7	2.56	803.3	88.3	841.4	99.4	11.8
1996-7	322.6	2.81	906.6	93.4	877.9	128.1	14.6
1997-8[1]	311.6	2.83	881.3	86.6	873.0	136.4	15.6
1998-9[2]	308.0	2.86	880.5	87.5	875.2	141.7	16.2

[1] Preliminary. [2] Estimate. [3] Represents the ratio of marketing year ending stocks to total consumption. *Source: Foreign Agricultural Service, U.S. Department of Agriculture (FAS-USDA)*

Acreage and Supply of Corn in the United States In Millions of Bushels

Crop Year Beginning Sept. 1[3]	Planted	Harvested: For Grain	Harvested: For Silage	Yield Per Harvested Acre Bushels	Carry-over, Sept. 1: On Farms[3]	Carry-over, Sept. 1: Off Farms[3]	Supply: Beginning Stocks	Supply: Pro-duction	Supply: Imports	Supply: Total Supply
	In Thousands of Acres									
1989-90	72,322	64,783	6,606	116.3	967.5	962.9	1,930	7,525	2	9,458
1990-1	74,166	66,952	6,124	118.5	754.8	589.7	1,344	7,934	3	9,282
1991-2	75,957	68,822	6,101	108.6	691.2	830.0	1,521	7,475	20	9,016
1992-3	79,311	72,077	6,069	131.5	605.0	494.8	1,100	9,477	7	10,584
1993-4	73,235	62,921	6,831	100.7	1,070.7	1,042.0	2,113	6,336	21	8,470
1994-5	79,175	72,887	5,601	138.6	395.4	454.7	850	10,051	10	10,910
1995-6	71,245	64,995	5,295	113.5	740.9	816.9	1,558	7,400	16	8,974
1996-7	79,229	72,644	5,607	127.1	196.6	229.3	426	9,233	13	9,672
1997-8[1]	79,537	72,671	6,054	126.7	475.0	408.2	883	9,207	9	10,099
1998-9[2]	80,187	72,604	5,919	134.4	640.0	667.8	1,308	9,761	10	11,079

[1] Preliminary. [2] Estimate. *Source: Economic Research Service, U.S. Department of Agriculture (ERS-USDA)*

Production of Corn (for Grain) in the United States In Millions of Bushels

Year	Illinois	Indiana	Iowa	Kansas	Mich-igan	Minn-esota	Missouri	Nebraska	Ohio	South Dakota	Texas	Wis-consin	Total
1989	1,322.3	691.6	1,445.5	155.0	222.6	700.0	219.8	847.0	342.2	190.8	148.4	310.8	7,525.5
1990	1,320.8	703.1	1,562.4	188.5	238.1	762.6	205.8	934.4	417.5	234.0	130.5	354.0	7,934.0
1991	1,177.0	510.6	1,427.4	206.3	253.0	720.0	213.4	999.6	326.4	240.5	165.0	380.8	7,475.5
1992	1,646.5	877.6	1,903.7	259.5	241.5	741.0	324.0	1,066.5	507.7	277.2	202.5	306.8	9,476.7
1993	1,300.0	712.8	880.0	216.0	225.5	322.0	166.5	785.2	360.8	160.7	212.8	216.2	6,336.5
1994	1,786.2	858.2	1,930.4	304.6	260.9	915.9	273.7	1,153.7	486.5	367.2	238.7	437.1	10,102.7
1995	1,130.0	598.9	1,402.2	244.3	249.6	731.9	149.9	854.7	375.1	193.6	216.6	347.7	7,373.9
1996	1,468.8	670.4	1,711.2	357.2	211.5	868.8	340.4	1,179.8	310.8	365.0	198.2	333.0	9,232.6
1997	1,425.5	701.5	1,642.2	371.8	255.1	851.4	299.0	1,135.2	475.7	326.4	241.5	402.6	9,206.8
1998[1]	1,473.5	760.4	1,769.0	419.0	227.6	1,032.8	285.0	1,239.8	470.9	429.6	185.0	404.2	9,761.1

[1] Preliminary. *Source: National Agricultural Statistics Service, U.S. Department of Agriculture (NASS-USDA)*

CORN

Supply and Disappearance of Corn in the United States In Millions of Bushels

Crop Year Beginning Sept. 1	Supply: Beginning Stocks	Supply: Production	Supply: Imports	Supply: Total Supply	Disappearance – Domestic Use: Food, Alcohol & Industrial	Seed	Feed & Residual	Total	Exports	Total Disappearance	Ending Stocks: Gov't Owned[3]	Ending Stocks: Privately Owned[4]	Ending Stocks: Total
1994-5	850	10,051	9.6	10,962	1,686	18.2	5,523	7,227	2,178	9,405	42	1,516	1,558
Sept.-Nov.	850	10,051	2.1	10,955	409	0	2,016	2,425	449	2,875	44	8,036	8,081
Dec.-Feb.	8,081	------	3.7	8,084	409	0	1,493	1,902	590	2,493	44	5,548	5,592
Mar.-May	5,592	------	3.0	5,595	434	14.7	1,163	1,612	568	2,180	42	3,373	3,415
June-Aug.	3,415	------	.8	3,416	434	3.5	850	1,288	570	1,858	42	1,516	1,558
1995-6	1,558	7,400	16.5	8,948	1,592	20.2	4,682	6,294	2,228	8,522	30	396	426
Sept.-Nov.	1,558	7,400	3.6	8,935	413	0	1,756	2,169	660	2,830	42	6,064	6,106
Dec.-Feb.	6,106	------	5.0	6,111	401	0	1,348	1,749	562	2,311	42	3,758	3,800
Mar.-May	3,800	------	5.0	3,805	411	17.6	1,048	1,477	610	2,087	41	1,677	1,718
June-Aug.	1,718	------	2.9	1,721	367	2.6	530	899	396	1,295	30	396	426
1996-7	426	9,233	13.3	9,733	1,672	20.4	5,363	7,054	1,795	8,789	2	881	883
Sept.-Nov.	426	9,233	3.4	9,723	387	0	1,946	2,333	487	2,759	20	6,873	6,903
Dec.-Feb.	6,903	------	2.4	6,905	398	0	1,489	1,887	525	2,411	20	4,464	4,494
Mar.-May	4,494	------	3.7	4,498	443	19.9	1,108	1,571	431	2,001	10	2,486	2,497
June-Aug.	2,497	------	3.8	2,500	444	.5	819	1,264	353	1,617	2	881	883
1997-8[1]	883	9,207	9.0	10,099	1,782		5,505	7,287	1,504	8,791			1,308
Sept.-Nov.	883	9,207	2.0	10,092	429		2,036	2,465	380	2,845			7,247
Dec.-Feb.	7,247	------	1.0	7,248	418		1,510	1,928	380	2,308			4,940
Mar.-May	4,940	------	4.0	4,944	464		1,089	1,553	350	1,904			3,040
June-Aug.	3,040	------	2.0	3,042	470		870	1,340	394	1,734			1,308
1998-9[2]	1,308	9,761	10.0	11,079	1,870		5,700	7,570	1,700	9,270			1,809
Sept.-Nov.	1,308	9,761	3.0	11,072	444		2,128	2,572	450	3,022			8,050

[1] Preliminary. [2] Estimate. [3] Uncommitted inventory. [4] Includes quantity under loan and farmer-owned reserves. *Source: Economic Research Service, U.S. Department of Agriculture (ERS-USDA)*

Corn Production Estimates and Cash Prices in the United States

Crop Year	Corn for Grain Production Estimates (In Thousands of Bushels): Aug. 1	Sept. 1	Oct. 1	Nov. 1	Final	St. Louis No. 2 Yellow	Omaha No. 2 Yellow	Gulf Ports No. 2 Yellow	Kansas City No. 2 White	Chicago No. 2 Yellow	Average Farm Price[2]	Value of Production (Million Dollars)
						Dollar Per Bushel						
1990-1	7,850,164	8,118,117	8,021,697	7,934,892	7,934,028	2.49	2.28	2.67	2.98	2.41	2.28	18,192
1991-2	7,474,480	7,295,071	7,479,421	7,485,901	7,475,480	2.53	2.36	2.74	3.06	2.52	2.37	17,864
1992-3	8,762,060	7,873,436	8,592,821	9,328,850	9,476,698	2.25	2.10	2.46	2.49	2.22	2.07	19,723
1993-4	7,423,142	7,229,427	6,961,902	6,503,237	6,336,470	2.67	2.56	2.85	2.78	2.68	2.50	16,032
1994-5	9,214,420	9,257,170	9,602,340	10,010,310	10,102,735	2.51	2.33	2.78	2.91	2.43	2.26	22,992
1995-6	8,121,520	7,832,140	7,541,400	7,373,700	7,373,876	4.06	3.87	4.30	4.14	3.97	3.24	24,118
1996-7	8,694,628	8,803,928	9,012,148	9,265,288	9,293,435	2.90	2.70	3.07	3.09	2.84	2.71	25,312
1997-8[1]	9,275,870	9,267,655	9,311,705	9,359,485	9,365,574						2.45	24,394
1998-9[1]	9,592,089	9,737,949	9,743,399	9,836,069	9,836,069						1.95-2.35	

[1] Preliminary. [2] Season-average price based on monthly weighted by monthly marketings. *Source: Economic Research Service, U.S. Department of Agriculture (ERS-USDA)*

Distribution of Corn in the United States In Millions of Bushels

Year Crop Beginning Sept. 1	Food, Seed and Industrial Use: HFCS	Glucose & Dextrose	Starch	Alcohol: Fuel	Alcohol: Beverage[3]	Seed	Cereal & Other Products	Total	Livestock Feed[4]	Exports (Including Grain Equiv. of Products)	Domestic Disappearance	Total Utilization
1990-1	379	200	232	349	80	19	114	1,373	4,611	1,725	6,036	7,761
1991-2	392	210	237	398	81	20	116	1,454	4,798	1,584	6,331	7,915
1992-3	414	214	238	426	83	19	117	1,493	5,252	1,663	6,808	8,471
1993-4	444	223	223	458	106	20	118	1,571	4,684	1,328	6,293	7,621
1994-5	465	231	226	533	100	18	132	1,686	5,470	2,177	7,175	9,352
1995-6	482	237	219	396	125	20	133	1,592	4,708	2,228	6,320	8,548
1996-7	504	246	229	429	130	20	135	1,672	5,302	1,795	6,994	8,789
1997-8[1]	530	250	235	480	133	21	137	1,765	5,505	1,504	7,287	8,791
1998-9[2]	550	255	240	510	135		139	1,829	5,700	1,700	7,570	9,270

[1] Preliminary. [2] Estimate. [3] Also includes nonfuel industrial alcohol. [4] Feed and waste (residual, mostly feed). *Source: Economic Research Service, U.S. Department of Agriculture (ERS-USDA)*

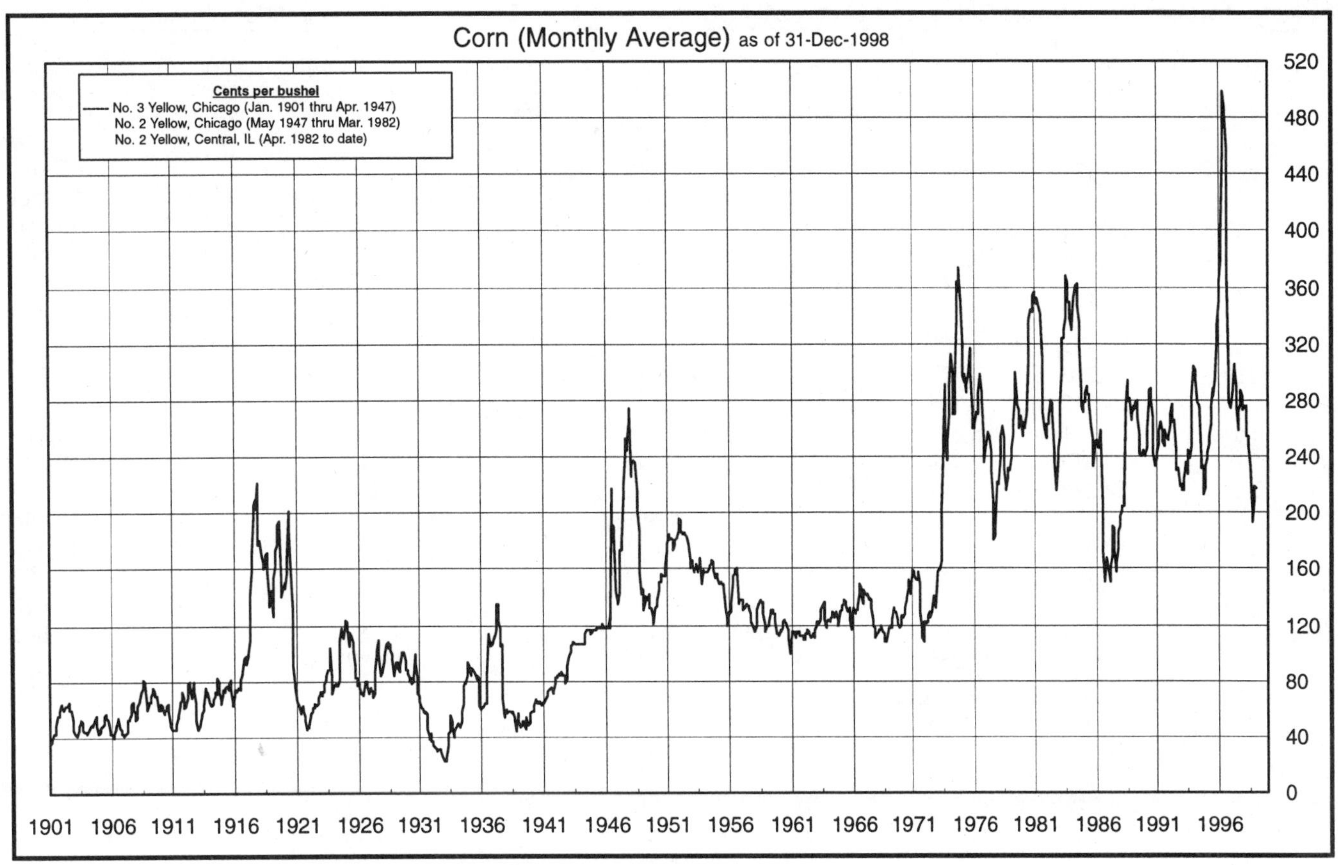

Average Cash Price of Corn, No. 2 Yellow in Central Illinois In Dollars Per Bushel

Crop Year	Sept.	Oct.	Nov.	Dec.	Jan.	Feb.	Mar.	Apr.	May	June	July	Aug.	Average
1989-90	2.35	2.25	2.29	2.29	2.29	2.34	2.44	2.64	2.73	2.70	2.68	2.54	2.46
1990-1	2.25	2.18	2.20	2.27	2.31	2.36	2.45	2.50	2.41	2.34	2.34	2.45	2.34
1991-2	2.39	2.41	2.41	2.42	2.49	2.58	2.64	2.50	2.51	2.51	2.31	2.17	2.45
1992-3	2.13	1.97	1.99	2.05	2.07	2.05	2.16	2.23	2.20	2.09	2.25	2.27	2.12
1993-4	2.22	2.27	2.63	2.81	2.89	2.83	2.76	2.61	2.58	2.61	2.19	2.13	2.54
1994-5	2.08	1.92	2.03	2.16	2.22	2.27	2.36	2.41	2.50	2.65	2.79	2.68	2.34
1995-6	2.83	3.12	3.22	3.36	3.53	3.71	3.92	4.47	4.86	4.74	4.70	4.48	3.91
1996-7	3.39	2.81	2.63	2.62	2.62	2.71	2.90	2.87	2.74	2.59	2.44	2.60	2.74
1997-8	2.61	2.66	2.70	2.60	2.60	2.58	2.59	2.41	2.37	2.29	2.16	1.86	2.45
1998-9[1]	1.78	1.94	2.09										1.94

[1] Preliminary. *Source: Economic Research Service, U.S. Department of Agriculture (ERS-USDA)*

Average Cash Price of Corn, No. 2 Yellow at Gulf Ports[2] In Dollars Per Bushel

Crop Year	Sept.	Oct.	Nov.	Dec.	Jan.	Feb.	Mar.	Apr.	May	June	July	Aug.	Average
1989-90	2.60	2.40	2.75	2.75	2.69	2.70	2.72	3.01	3.08	3.05	2.92	2.79	2.79
1990-1	2.59	2.55	2.54	2.60	2.68	2.70	2.77	2.80	2.69	2.65	2.67	2.79	2.67
1991-2	2.76	2.76	2.72	2.71	2.70	2.89	2.96	2.77	2.77	2.80	2.61	2.48	2.74
1992-3	2.50	2.40	2.42	2.39	2.39	2.40	2.48	2.55	2.50	2.36	2.59	2.55	2.46
1993-4	2.57	2.68	2.94	3.08	3.22	3.14	3.05	2.88	2.81	2.85	2.51	2.44	2.85
1994-5	2.48	2.44	2.43	2.61	2.72	2.72	2.79	2.79	2.84	3.04	3.23	3.21	2.78
1995-6	3.32	3.57	3.63	3.76	4.00	4.18	4.34	4.80	5.17	4.99	5.07	4.73	4.30
1996-7	3.69	3.27	2.97	2.97	3.02	3.08	3.25	3.17	3.01	2.86	2.69	2.86	3.07
1997-8	2.88	3.05	2.98	2.89	2.90	2.88	2.89	2.71	2.69	2.64	2.55	2.24	2.78
1998-9[1]	2.18	2.43	2.47										2.36

[1] Preliminary. [2] Barge delivered to Louisiana Gulf. *Source: Economic Research Service, U.S. Department of Agriculture (ERS-USDA)*

CORN

Weekly Outstanding Export Sales and Cumulative Exports of U.S. Corn   In Thousands of Metric Tons

1996/97			1997/98			1998/99		
Marketing Year 1996/97 Week Ending	Out-standing Sales	Cumu-lative Exports	Marketing Year 1997/98 Week Ending	Out-standing Sales	Cumu-lative Exports	Marketing Year 1998/99 Week Ending	Out-standing Sales	Cumu-lative Exports
Sept. 5, 1996	14,289	169	Sept. 4, 1997	7,730	207	Sept. 3, 1998	7,776	208
12	14,671	557	11	7,761	793	10	7,783	601
19	14,851	1,163	18	7,750	2,097	17	7,831	1,630
26	14,714	1,860	25	7,693	2,914	24	8,168	2,230
Oct. 3	14,778	2,590	Oct. 2	7,487	3,602	Oct. 1	7,907	3,097
10	15,080	3,145	9	7,279	4,445	8	7,649	3,882
17	14,555	3,890	16	7,126	5,118	15	7,796	4,840
24	14,487	4,727	23	7,121	5,593	22	8,252	5,654
31	14,298	5,776	30	7,299	6,207	29	8,202	6,536
Nov. 7	14,082	6,789	Nov. 6	7,606	6,829	Nov. 5	8,206	7,312
14	13,921	8,117	13	7,810	7,776	12	8,713	8,315
21	13,279	9,340	20	7,673	8,329	19	9,014	9,281
28	12,222	10,626	27	7,565	9,138	26	8,675	10,263
Dec. 5	11,447	11,908	Dec. 4	7,459	9,919	Dec. 3	8,699	11,108
12	10,573	13,481	11	6,921	10,830	10	8,472	12,570
19	10,708	14,340	18	6,701	11,617	17	8,515	13,690
26	10,175	15,319	25	6,634	12,031	24	8,193	14,673
Jan. 2, 1997	9,344	16,367	Jan. 1, 1998	6,481	12,764	31	7,779	15,501
9	9,371	17,249	8	6,318	13,280	Jan. 7, 1999	7,870	16,080
16	9,297	18,568	15	6,469	14,007	14	7,813	16,920
23	9,490	19,661	22	6,276	14,771	21	8,070	17,562
30	9,434	20,574	29	6,531	15,492	28	8,433	18,441
Feb. 6	9,236	21,656	Feb. 5	6,632	16,276	Feb. 4		
13	9,342	22,365	12	6,567	17,189	11		
20	8,729	23,471	19	6,634	17,755	18		
27	9,224	24,482	26	6,759	18,685	25		
Mar. 6	9,274	25,422	Mar. 5	6,771	19,374	Mar. 4		
13	9,152	26,412	12	6,821	19,970	11		
20	8,684	27,432	19	6,686	20,540	18		
27	8,145	28,252	26	6,550	21,240	25		
Apr. 3	8,054	29,273	Apr. 2	6,005	22,216	Apr. 1		
10	7,873	30,119	9	5,414	23,035	8		
17	7,706	30,777	16	5,383	23,666	15		
24	7,731	31,491	23	5,426	24,138	22		
May 1	7,320	32,495	30	5,412	24,599	29		
8	7,418	32,872	May 7	5,256	25,268	May 6		
15	7,394	33,511	14	5,520	25,837	13		
22	7,438	34,469	21	5,532	26,248	20		
29	7,379	35,118	28	5,541	27,031	27		
June 5	7,301	35,811	June 4	5,612	27,814	June 3		
12	7,151	36,477	11	5,831	28,294	10		
19	6,845	37,139	18	5,244	29,187	17		
26	6,809	37,729	25	4,825	29,928	24		
July 3	6,647	38,353	July 2	4,786	30,546	July 1		
10	6,270	38,974	9	4,497	31,299	8		
17	5,863	39,551	16	4,317	32,008	15		
24	5,077	40,325	23	4,141	32,637	22		
31	4,388	41,018	30	3,540	33,373	29		
Aug. 7	3,713	41,667	Aug. 6	3,399	34,114	Aug. 5		
14	3,074	42,287	13	3,190	35,034	12		
21	2,003	43,432	20	2,346	35,807	19		
28	6,297	0	27	1,878	36,494	26		

Source: Foreign Agricultural Service, U.S. Department of Agriculture (FAS-USDA)

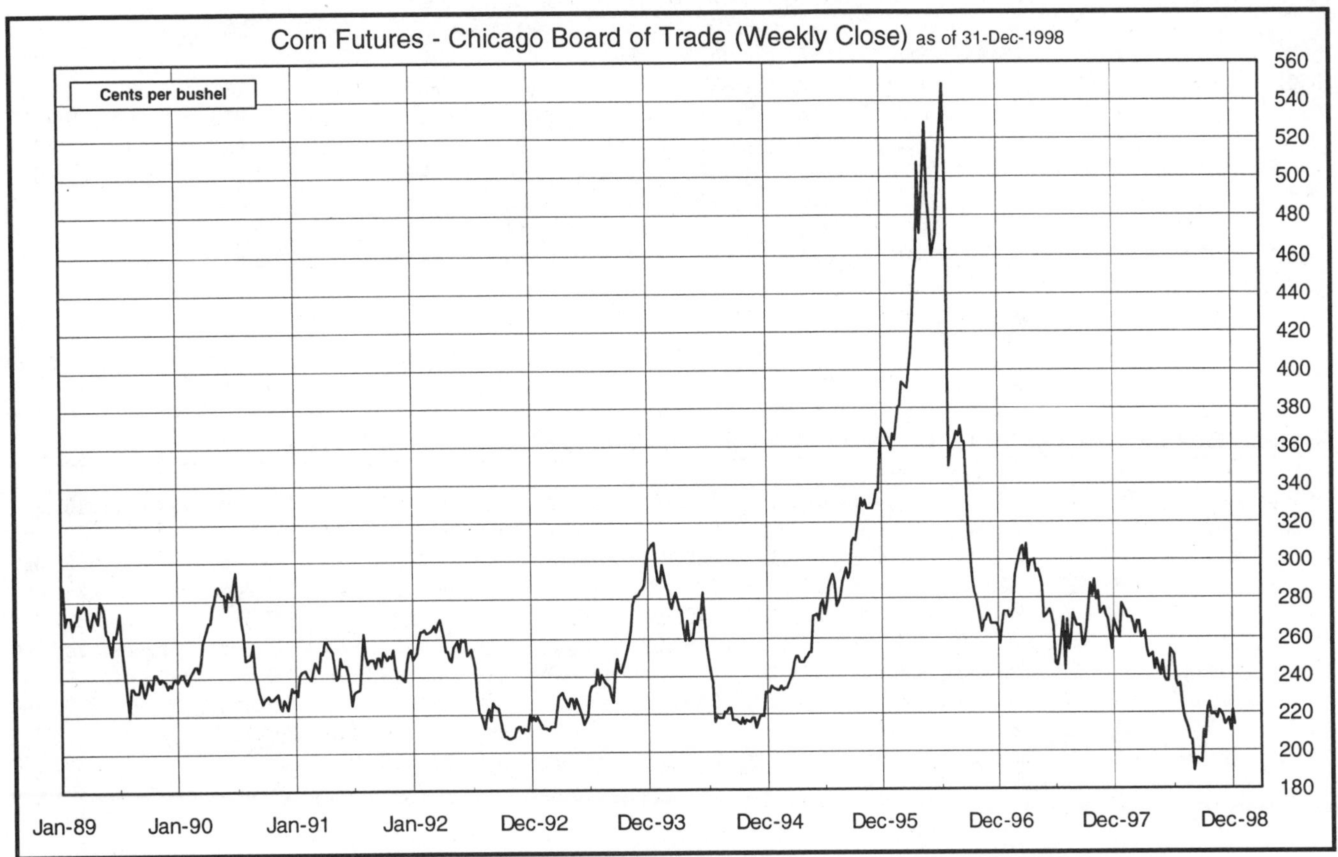

U.S. Exports[1] of Corn (Including Seed), by Country of Destination In Thousands of Metric Tons

Year Beginning Oct.	Algeria	Canada	Egypt	Israel	Japan	Mexico	Rep. of Korea	Russia[3]	Saudi Arabia	Spain	Taiwan	Vene-zuela	Total
1988-9	973	896	1,014	304	13,016	3,113	4,591	15,573	616	1,280	3,625	0	50,676
1989-90	1,146	637	1,135	250	13,885	4,585	5,680	16,371	707	1,712	5,009	593	59,854
1990-1	1,328	302	1,756	299	13,639	1,901	1,982	9,077	725	1,434	5,086	321	44,497
1991-2	827	314	1,058	369	13,481	1,041	1,508	6,533	602	1,273	4,998	552	40,693
1992-3	1,224	1,189	1,543	539	14,235	396	1,021	3,380	787	1,075	5,450	777	41,766
1993-4	1,182	640	1,437	268	12,032	1,678	631	2,337	851	1,116	4,955	751	33,057
1994-5	846	1,135	2,608	671	16,107	3,166	8,921	9	864	2,497	6,210	886	58,645
1995-6	567	751	2,106	625	14,900	6,268	7,426	58	844	1,156	5,600	479	52,681
1996-7	929	879	2,364	556	15,482	3,141	5,452	88	1,025	1,080	5,609	730	46,638
1997-8[2]	829	1,397	1,951	-----	13,994	4,373	3,364	-----	928	-----	3,488	651	37,697

[1] Excludes exports of corn by-products. [2] Preliminary. [3] Formerly part of the U.S.S.R.; data not reported separately until 1992.
Source: Economic Research Service, U.S. Department of Agriculture (ERS-USDA)

Stocks of Corn (Shelled and Ear) in the United States In Millions of Bushels

Year	On Farms Mar. 1	June 1	Sept. 1	Dec. 1	Off Farms Mar. 1	June 1	Sept. 1	Dec. 1	Total Stocks Mar. 1	June 1	Sept. 1	Dec. 1
1989	3,021.0	2,022.0	967.5	4,698.8	2,182.9	1,397.3	962.9	2,383.3	5,203.9	3,419.3	1,930.4	7,082.1
1990	2,910.5	1,623.5	754.8	4,874.0	1,901.9	1,219.7	589.7	2,066.3	4,812.4	2,843.2	1,344.5	6,940.3
1991	3,064.5	1,755.0	691.2	4,294.5	1,724.5	1,237.0	830.0	2,246.6	4,789.0	2,992.0	1,521.2	6,541.1
1992	2,610.2	1,517.5	605.5	5,736.9	1,950.8	1,221.1	494.8	2,169.5	4,561.0	2,738.6	1,100.3	7,906.4
1993	3,630.0	2,216.5	1,070.7	3,803.0	2,048.2	1,492.9	1,042.3	2,133.5	5,678.2	3,709.4	2,113.0	5,936.5
1994	2,210.0	1,203.0	395.4	5,417.5	1,785.5	1,156.9	454.7	2,663.0	3,995.7	2,359.9	850.1	8,080.5
1995	3,502.0	2,072.0	740.9	3,960.0	2,089.7	1,342.9	816.9	2,145.8	5,591.7	3,414.9	1,557.8	6,105.8
1996	2,000.2	780.1	196.6	4,800.0	1,799.3	937.8	229.3	2,103.7	3,799.5	1,717.9	425.9	6,903.7
1997	2,870.0	1,501.0	475.0	4,822.0	1,624.1	995.6	408.2	2,424.8	4,494.1	2,496.6	883.2	7,246.8
1998[1]	2,975.0	1,830.0	640.0	5,320.0	1,964.9	1,209.8	667.8	2,730.2	4,939.9	3,039.8	1,307.8	8,050.2

[1] Preliminary. *Source: National Agricultural Statistics Service, U.S. Department of Agriculture (NASS-USDA)*

Volume of Trading of Corn Futures in Chicago In Thousands of Contracts

Year	Jan.	Feb.	Mar.	Apr	May	June	July	Aug.	Sept.	Oct.	Nov.	Dec.	Total
1989	834	677	764	828	786	897	865	687	565	940	870	559	9,271
1990	650	798	925	1,148	1,429	1,353	1,102	908	606	788	1,136	580	11,423
1991	847	697	933	1,041	845	1,013	1,254	1,097	692	884	908	632	10,853
1992	901	1,003	952	869	938	1,015	866	795	689	688	996	644	10,357
1993	518	636	774	895	688	1,047	1,396	1,014	896	1,036	1,574	988	10,539
1994	1,251	1,036	1,046	1,109	1,079	1,455	748	602	615	703	1,025	861	11,530
1995	787	832	974	988	1,214	1,760	1,294	1,319	1,220	1,613	1,743	1,356	15,105
1996	1,992	1,820	1,608	2,655	2,085	1,545	1,591	1,145	1,183	1,436	1,515	1,046	19,620
1997	1,161	1,483	1,693	1,780	1,292	1,347	1,528	1,318	1,060	1,700	1,434	1,188	16,985
1998	1,250	1,277	1,433	1,620	1,149	1,771	1,415	1,231	1,126	1,319	1,217	987	15,795

Source: Chicago Board of Trade (CBT)

Average Open Interest of Corn Futures in Chicago In Contracts

Year	Jan.	Feb.	Mar.	Apr.	May	June	July	Aug.	Sept.	Oct.	Nov.	Dec.
1989	216,220	198,812	192,640	183,544	163,888	156,782	143,806	145,405	141,379	171,513	194,251	167,944
1990	178,094	202,845	229,946	252,155	250,020	242,462	212,749	207,951	206,603	211,222	230,333	203,881
1991	210,006	219,236	229,010	229,404	204,828	202,100	198,527	219,700	215,527	242,466	257,065	228,347
1992	254,195	294,957	285,429	260,527	230,359	232,189	211,221	219,796	208,613	239,888	262,345	244,803
1993	256,113	260,986	248,638	250,000	229,016	232,590	265,672	264,938	243,892	275,792	332,445	327,226
1994	346,077	336,342	327,539	305,722	262,621	246,308	215,081	208,990	212,983	243,678	262,849	250,646
1995	292,090	311,372	336,433	355,443	368,381	427,744	413,839	418,450	439,170	473,698	490,970	487,977
1996	500,837	508,496	469,697	453,707	403,118	350,066	304,265	298,894	302,170	326,373	332,809	306,256
1997	305,779	347,392	382,261	351,852	290,649	274,760	267,531	281,194	307,415	378,453	379,045	331,386
1998	328,020	341,444	358,221	366,657	337,703	327,237	297,894	318,162	321,992	332,337	342,868	322,157

Source: Chicago Board of Trade (CBT)

Corn Price Support Data in the United States

Crop Year Beginning Sept. 1	National Average Loan Rate[3]	Target Price	Placed Under Loan	% of Production	Acquired by CCC	Owned by CCC Aug. 31	CCC Inventory As of Dec. 31: CCC Owned	CCC Inventory As of Dec. 31: Under CCC Loan	Quantity Pledged	Face Amount
	$ Per Bushel	$ Per Bushel	Millions of Bushels	Millions of Bushels	Millions of Bushels	Millions of Bushels	Millions of Bushels	Millions of Bushels	Ths. Bu	Ths. $
1989-90	1.65	2.84	920	12.2	361	233	676	1,110	920,068	1,487,026
1990-1	1.57	2.75	1,071	13.5	285	371	214	1,071	1,071,040	1,616,948
1991-2	1.62	2.75	1,006	13.5	291	113	265	678	26,636	45,609
1992-3	1.72	2.75	1,646	17.4	0	56	125	1,021	15,245	28,947
1993-4	1.72	2.75	618	9.7	0	45	54	812	13,697	26,052
1994-5	1.89	2.75	2,002	19.8	0	-----	44	1,598	26,318	53,474
1995-6	1.89	2.75	970	9.2	0	-----	42	579	677,115	1,232,669
1996-7	1.89	-----	561	-----	0	-----	30	756	-----	-----
1997-8[1]	1.89	-----	1,132	-----	19	-----	2	81	-----	-----
1998-9[2]	1.89	-----	823	-----	0	-----	-----	-----	-----	-----

[1] Preliminary. [2] Estimate. [3] Finley or announced loan rate. *Source: National Agricultural Statistics Service, U.S. Department of Agriculture (NASS)*

Average Price Received by Farmers for Corn in the United States In Dollars Per Bushel

Crop Year	Sept.	Oct.	Nov.	Dec.	Jan.	Feb.	Mar.	Apr.	May	June	July	Aug.	Average
1989-90	2.29	2.22	2.24	2.27	2.31	2.32	2.37	2.51	2.62	2.63	2.62	2.51	2.36
1990-1	2.32	2.19	2.16	2.22	2.27	2.32	2.39	2.42	2.38	2.31	2.27	2.33	2.28
1991-2	2.33	2.31	2.29	2.33	2.40	2.46	2.49	2.48	2.49	2.47	2.33	2.15	2.37
1992-3	2.16	2.05	1.98	1.97	2.03	2.00	2.10	2.16	2.14	2.09	2.22	2.25	2.07
1993-4	2.21	2.28	2.45	2.67	2.70	2.79	2.74	2.65	2.60	2.61	2.29	2.16	2.50
1994-5	2.19	2.06	1.99	2.13	2.19	2.23	2.30	2.36	2.41	2.51	2.63	2.63	2.26
1995-6	2.69	2.79	2.87	3.07	3.09	3.37	3.51	3.85	4.14	4.22	4.43	4.80	3.15
1996-7	3.55	2.89	2.66	2.63	2.69	2.65	2.79	2.80	2.69	2.56	2.43	2.50	2.74
1997-8	2.52	2.54	2.51	2.52	2.56	2.55	2.54	2.41	2.34	2.28	2.20	1.90	2.41
1998-9[1]	1.83	1.91	1.93	2.01	2.01								1.94

[1] Preliminary. *Source: Economic Research Service, U.S. Department of Agriculture (ERS-USDA)*

Corn Oil

U.S. corn oil production in 1998/99 of a record 2.4 billion pounds compares with the previous record of 2.34 billion pounds in 1997/98. Seasonally, monthly production tends to peak around March and touches a low in either November or July. Seasonal consumption patterns are clouded, but on a total basis the gain in domestic usage pales against the growth in exports, especially during the past few years. Total 1998/99 disappearance of 2.4 billion pounds was a record high. Domestic usage of 1.30 billion pounds compares with 1.27 billion in 1997/98. Corn oil is cholesterol free which has enhanced its appeal among nutritional conscious consumers. Corn oil exports totaled 1.12 billion pounds in 1998/99 vs. 1.1 billion in 1997/98; in the late 1980's U.S. corn oil exports were running less than .4 billion pounds. The European Union is a major importer of U.S. corn oil, led by Italy, Spain and Greece. Saudi Arabia and Turkey are the largest individual importing nations while South Korea is Asia's largest buyer. U.S. imports are insignificant. Carryover stocks show considerable variation: from a low of 44 million pounds at the end of 1989/90 to a high of 241 million five years later and ending 1998/99 stocks of 100 million pounds vs. 105 million a year earlier.

Crude corn oil prices, basis wet/dry-milled, Central Illinois, averaged 24.95 cents a pound in calendar 1998 (vs. a marketing year average, beginning October, of 24.05 cents). Through the first nine months of calendar 1998 prices averaged 3-4 cents higher than a year earlier, and are likely to have the highest average since the mid 1980's.

Supply and Distribution of Corn Oil in the United States In Millions of Pounds

Crop Year Beginning Oct. 1	Supply				Disappearance						
	Stocks Oct. 1	Production	Imports	Total Supply	Baking and Frying Fats	Salad and Cooking Oil	Margarine	Total Edible Products	Domestic Disappearance	Exports	Total Disappearance
1992-3	196	1,878	7.0	2,081	241	547	W	945	1,220	712	1,931
1993-4	150	1,906	7.0	2,062	86	413	W	649	1,228	717	1,944
1994-5	118	2,227	10.0	2,356	100	446	W	636	1,250	865	2,115
1995-6	241	2,139	11.0	2,391	82	434	79	595	1,298	977	2,275
1996-7	116	2,230	14.0	2,361	73	386	68	527	1,244	988	2,232
1997-8[1]	129	2,335	16.0	2,492	42	339	39	446	1,271	1,118	2,390
1998-9[2]	102	2,400	15.0	2,517					1,307	1,110	2,417

[1] Preliminary. [2] Estimate. W = Withheld proprietary data. *Source: Economic Research Service, U.S. Department of Agiculture (ERS-USDA)*

Production[2] of Crude Corn Oil in the United States In Millions of Pounds

Year	Oct.	Nov.	Dec.	Jan.	Feb.	Mar.	Apr.	May	June	July	Aug.	Sept.	Total
1992-3	168.1	151.8	151.6	135.5	139.0	165.6	153.5	161.6	164.5	163.0	158.5	165.1	1,878
1993-4	160.8	153.4	162.5	140.6	138.6	166.9	155.3	164.2	171.8	164.8	162.3	165.1	1,906
1994-5	175.5	165.3	180.9	163.2	161.8	232.7	188.4	191.2	193.6	193.5	180.3	188.5	2,215
1995-6	179.5	173.8	184.5	180.6	160.4	192.9	192.1	175.9	178.4	147.1	162.2	171.2	2,099
1996-7	183.8	182.3	208.2	172.5	170.9	209.9	188.3	182.5	184.3	174.0	180.6	182.2	2,220
1997-8	199.2	207.5	202.0	171.4	162.7	201.0	203.9	201.2	201.4	192.8	202.8	188.9	2,335
1998-9[1]	209.2	199.4	189.2										2,391

[1] Preliminary. [2] Not seasonally adjusted. *Source: Bureau of the Census, U.S. Department of Commerce*

Consumption of Corn Oil, in Refining, in the United States In Millions of Pounds

Year	Oct.	Nov.	Dec.	Jan.	Feb.	Mar.	Apr.	May	June	July	Aug.	Sept.	Total
1992-3	168.1	151.8	151.6	81.2	93.6	110.5	102.4	85.8	99.9	88.0	90.9	96.4	1,320
1993-4	106.7	101.7	114.3	71.8	76.5	92.6	79.4	91.5	91.7	90.6	106.4	109.1	1,132
1994-5	103.5	107.2	116.9	100.7	92.3	109.9	97.3	95.6	108.9	97.2	78.2	95.5	1,203
1995-6	82.9	97.9	102.0	78.6	91.6	100.0	84.8	90.0	90.5	74.5	66.5	90.2	1,049
1996-7	82.0	83.0	84.7	69.7	71.0	79.5	71.4	76.1	80.4	86.9	90.8	58.5	934
1997-8	87.5	83.8	100.6	83.0	89.2	100.5	92.5	100.5	104.2	90.6	101.7	94.6	1,129
1998-9[1]	106.6	104.4											1,266

[1] Preliminary. *Source: Bureau of the Census, U.S. Department of Commerce*

Average Corn Oil Price, Wet Mill in Chicago In Cents Per Pound

Year	Oct.	Nov.	Dec.	Jan.	Feb.	Mar.	Apr.	May	June	July	Aug.	Sept.	Average
1992-3	20.43	20.60	20.75	20.75	20.87	20.79	20.80	20.75	20.60	20.67	21.50	22.23	20.90
1993-4	22.25	23.06	26.93	28.00	29.89	30.30	29.63	29.48	29.43	27.20	25.02	24.87	27.17
1994-5	24.73	24.75	24.75	28.01	27.26	28.17	27.30	26.42	26.61	27.38	26.35	25.93	26.47
1995-6	26.05	25.54	24.99	24.52	24.30	24.34	25.60	27.98	25.66	25.46	24.33	24.14	25.24
1996-7	22.67	21.96	22.27	23.39	23.97	24.38	24.60	24.66	24.82	25.34	25.36	25.15	24.05
1997-8	25.20	26.25	26.28	26.04	27.31	28.50	30.93	33.20	32.82	31.52	29.93	29.25	28.94
1998-9[1]	29.46	29.65											29.56

[1] Preliminary. *Source: Economic Research Service, U.S. Department of Agriculture (ERS-USDA)*

Cotton

U.S. cotton production in the 1998-99 (August-July) season was forecast by the USDA at 13.45 million bales. This was some 5.34 million bales less than the previous season. The 1998-99 growing season was characterized by very poor weather in some of the major production areas. California had a very cold spring which delayed plantings while Texas experienced an extreme drought characterized by excessively high temperatures. As a result of these poor conditions as well as low prices and low yields, a large amount of the cotton acreage that was planted was abandoned.

Cotton growers planted 12.87 million acres to the natural fiber, down about 930,000 acres from the previous season. Due to poor weather in a number of locations all the acreage that was planted was not harvested. In the last five seasons, an average 5.8 percent of the planted cotton acreage was abandoned or not harvested. In the previous season, 4 percent of the planted acreage was left unharvested, a total of 540,000 acres. The 1998-99 season was far different as producers left a large amount of acreage unharvested. Of the plantings of 12.87 million acres,cotton producers harvested 10.39 million acres for an abandonment rate of 19 percent. Some 2.48 million acres were unharvested. The national average cotton yield was 621 pounds per acre compared to 680 pounds a year ago. In the five previous seasons, yields were 648 pounds.

Texas was the largest producing state with 1998-99 production of 3.35 million bales. That was down 35 percent from last season. The Texas yield was 521 pounds per acre which was up 8 percent from last season. Texas harvested 3.09 million acres. California's crop was estimated at 1.50 million bales, down 43 percent from the season before. the yield was 860 pounds or some 28 percent less than the previous season. The Mississippi crop was 1.44 million bales, down 21 percent from 1997-98. The Georgia crop was 1.40 million bales or some 27 percent less than a year before. The Arkansas crop was 1.22 million bales, down 27 percent from the previous season.

At the beginning of the 1998-99 season, U.S. cotton stocks were 3.89 million bales, some 2 percent less than the previous season. U.S. imports of cotton were forecast to be 400,000 bales compared to only 10,000 bales in 1997-98. In the 1996-97 and the 1995-96 seasons, U.S. imports of cotton were about 400,000 bales each year. The high level of imports expected in 1998-99 was due to the small crop and the difficulty domestic textile mills had in finding the quality and quantity of cotton to meet their needs. With the crop of 13.45 million bales, the total supply of cotton was forecast to be 17.74 million bales, down 22 percent from the previous season.

Domestic use of cotton in the 1998-99 season was forecast to be 10.6 million bales. That represented a decline of 7 percent or 750,000 bales from the previous season. How much cotton is consumed by U.S. textile mills is dependent on a number of factors including the direction and strength of the U.S. economy as well as consumer tastes. U.S. imports of finished textiles are also an important factor. Because of the financial crises in Asia, a number of countries attempted to export their way out of difficulty and textiles are a major export item. The U.S. economy appeared to be weathering the international financial storm fairly well. Interest rates looked like they would move lower which would support the housing sector and cotton use.

More important in terms of usage is the export sector. While exports are smaller than domestic use, they tend to vary more from season to season. Since domestic use is more steady, much of the focus in the cotton market is on exports. In 1998-99, the outlook was very mixed. The USDA Step 2 cotton user marketing program was in force when the season began. The program in effect made certificate payments to exporters which in effect allowed them to sell cotton for prices that were lower than those of foreign growths. U.S. cotton prices remained stubbornly high in 1998-99 because of the small crop and the program was needed to make U.S. cotton competitive. Because of heavy use, the program ran out of funds in December 1998. There was no indication it would be refunded. U.S. cotton exports were forecast to be 4.3 million bales or some 43 percent less than the previous year. Total use of cotton in 1998-99 was projected to be 14.9 million bales or some 18 percent less than in 1997-98. Projected U.S. stocks of cotton at the end of the season in July 1999 were 2.8 million bales, down 28 percent from the prior year. The projected stocks were equivalent to 10 weeks of use.

World production of cotton was forecast to be 84.2 million bales. That was down 8 percent from the previous year. Production of cotton outside the U.S. was forecast at 70.74 million bales, down from 72.6 million bales in 1997-98. Outside of the U.S., the country that has come to dominate the cotton market is China. China produces a large amount of cotton but with a burgeoning population has become a net importer of cotton for several years. Policies in China have encouraged cotton production at the expense of other crops leading to a buildup in cotton stocks. This buildup has allowed China to assume the role of net cotton exporter. In the 1998-99 season, China was forecast to export 850,000 bales of cotton. The Chinese crop was 18.8 million bales, down from 21.1 million bales the previous year.

Among the major producers, India was forecast to produce 13 million bales, some 6 percent more than the previous year. Pakistan's crop was projected to be 7.5 million bales, up 7 percent from the 1997-98 season. In Central Asia, Uzbekistan's crop of 4.6 million bales was down 13 percent. Australia's cotton crop of 3.3 million bales was up 6 percent.

Futures Markets

Cotton futures and options are traded on the New York Cotton Exchange (NYCE). Cotton futures are traded on the Bolsa de Mercadorias & Futuros (BM&F). Cotton Yarn futures are traded on the Nagoya Textile Exchange, the Osaka Textile Exchange, and the Tokyo Commodity Exchange (TOCOM).

Supply and Distribution of All Cotton in the United States In Thousands of 480-Pound Bales

Crop Year Beginning Aug. 1	Area Planted (1,000 acres)	Area Harvested (1,000 acres)	Yield Lbs./acre	Supply Beginning Stocks[3]	Supply Production[4]	Supply Imports	Supply Total	Disappearance Mill Use	Disappearance Exports	Disappearance Total	Unaccounted	Ending Stocks	Farm Price[5] (Cents Per Lb.)	"A" Index Price[6] (Cents Per Lb.)	of Production Million $
1989-90	10,587	9,538	614	7,092	12,196	2	19,290	8,759	7,694	16,453	163	3,000	66.2	82.34	3,877.9
1990-1	12,348	11,732	634	3,000	15,505	4	18,509	8,657	7,793	16,450	285	2,344	67.1	82.87	5,075.8
1991-2	14,052	12,960	652	2,344	17,614	13	19,971	9,613	6,646	16,259	-8	3,704	58.1	62.90	4,913.2
1992-3	13,240	11,143	699	3,704	16,219	1	19,923	10,250	5,201	15,451	190	4,662	54.9	56.87	4,273.9
1993-4	13,438	12,783	606	4,662	16,134	6	20,802	10,418	6,862	17,280	8	3,530	58.4	70.75	4,520.9
1994-5	13,720	13,322	708	3,530	19,662	20	23,212	11,198	9,402	20,600	38	2,650	72.0	92.66	6,796.7
1995-6	16,931	16,007	537	2,650	17,900	408	20,958	10,604	7,675	18,322	-27	2,609	76.5	85.61	6,574.6
1996-7	14,634	12,868	707	2,609	18,942	403	21,954	11,126	6,865	17,991	8	3,971	70.5	78.66	6,408.1
1997-8[1]	13,808	13,270	680	3,971	18,793	13	22,777	11,349	7,500	18,849	-44	3,887	66.3	72.11	6,142.3
1998-9[2]	12,866	10,375	612	3,887	13,231	300	17,418	10,600	4,500	15,100	-18	2,300			

[1] Preliminary. [2] Estimate. [3] Excludes preseason ginnings (adjusted to 480-lb. bale net weight basis). [4] Includes preseason ginnings. [5] Marketing year average price. [6] Average of 5 cheapest types of SLM 1 3/32" staple length cotton offered on the European market. *Source: Economic Research Service, U.S. Department of Agriculture (ERS-USDA)*

World Production of All Cotton In Thousands of 480-Lb. Bales

Crop Year Beginning Aug. 1	Argentina	Brazil	China	Egypt	India	Iran	Mexico	Pakistan	Sudan	Turkey	United States	Uzbekistan[3]	World Total
1989-90	1,272	3,030	17,400	1,324	10,599	524	769	6,687	584	2,835	12,196	7,605	79,780
1990-1	1,355	3,215	20,700	1,378	9,135	553	813	7,522	380	3,007	15,505	7,317	86,980
1991-2	1,148	3,445	26,100	1,338	9,291	543	831	10,000	386	2,578	17,614	6,628	95,992
1992-3	666	2,113	20,700	1,620	10,775	465	138	7,073	276	2,635	16,218	5,851	82,709
1993-4	1,075	1,860	17,200	1,882	9,487	310	110	6,282	250	2,666	16,134	6,067	76,049
1994-5	1,608	2,526	19,900	1,225	10,814	762	458	6,250	400	2,886	19,662	5,778	85,610
1995-6	1,930	1,791	21,900	1,088	12,649	800	860	8,200	490	3,911	17.900	5,740	92,174
1996-7	1,493	1,300	19,300	1,568	13,781	825	1,077	7,300	460	3,600	18,942	4,750	89,179
1997-8[1]	1,350	1,750	21,100	1,550	12,000	----	960	7,000	400	3,800	18,793	5,300	91,167
1998-9[2]	1,500	1,800	18,800	1,200	12,500	----	1,000	7,500	300	3,700	13,231	4,600	83,685

[1] Preliminary. [2] Estimate. [3] Formerly part of the U.S.S.R.; data not reported separately until 1989. *Source: Foreign Agricultural Service, U.S. Department of Agriculture (FAS-USDA)*

World Supply and Demand of Cotton In Thousands of 480-Lb. Bales

Crop Year Beginning Aug. 1	Beginning Stocks United States	Beginning Stocks Uzbekistan[3]	Beginning Stocks China	Beginning Stocks World Total	Production United States	Production Uzbekistan[3]	Production China	Production World Total	Consumption United States	Consumption Russia[3]	Consumption China	Consumption World Total	Exports United States	Exports Uzbekistan[3]	Exports China	Exports World Total
1989-90	7,092	473	5,971	31,423	12,196	7,605	17,400	79,741	8,759	5,831	20,000	86,579	7,694	6,810	865	31,275
1990-1	3,000	460	4,379	25,771	15,505	7,317	20,700	86,968	8,657	5,469	20,000	85,677	7,793	5,393	928	29,656
1991-2	2,344	1,555	5,956	27,073	17,614	6,628	26,100	95,659	9,613	4,539	20,500	86,045	6,646	5,200	602	28,196
1992-3	3,704	2,295	12,284	37,403	16,218	5,851	20,700	82,445	10,250	2,200	21,500	85,765	5,201	5,500	684	25,583
1993-4	4,662	1,845	10,442	35,121	16,134	6,067	17,200	76,697	10,418	2,200	21,300	85,353	6,862	5,800	749	26,731
1994-5	3,530	737	6,101	26,507	19,662	5,778	19,900	85,534	11,198	1,263	20,200	84,688	9,402	5,006	183	28,476
1995-6	2,650	956	9,678	28,977	17,900	5,740	21,900	92,174	10,647	1,150	19,500	85,444	7,675	4,500	21	27,359
1996-7	2,609	1,304	13,202	33,813	18,942	4,750	19,300	89,179	11,126	1,100	21,000	88,626	6,865	4,550	10	26,494
1997-8[1]	3,971	822	14,755	36,678	18,793	5,300	21,100	91,167	11,349	1,200	20,800	88,235	7,500	4,400	34	26,310
1998-9[2]	3,887	977	16,855	40,124	13,231	4,600	18,800	83,685	10,600	950	19,800	86,446	4,500	3,800	1,800	24,961

[1] Preliminary. [2] Estimate. [3] Formerly part of the U.S.S.R.; data not reported separately until 1989. *Source: Foreign Agricultural Service, U.S. Department of Agriculture (FAS-USDA)*

World Consumption of All Cotton in Specified Countries In Thousands of 480-Lb. Bales

Crop Year Beginning Aug. 1	Brazil	China	Egypt	France	Germany	India	Italy	Japan	Mexico	Pakistan	United States	Uzbekistan[3]	World Total
1989-90	3,445	20,000	1,352	600	1,435	8,667	1,450	3,229	725	4,801	8,759	9,200	86,579
1990-1	3,215	20,000	1,457	530	955	9,018	1,470	3,027	712	5,648	8,657	8,700	85,677
1991-2	3,215	19,000	1,465	484	830	8,674	1,447	2,783	772	6,482	9,613	860	86,136
1992-3	3,445	21,500	1,640	470	680	9,761	1,400	2,301	740	6,634	10,250	950	85,770
1993-4	3,675	20,900	1,530	500	750	9,950	1,375	2,060	825	6,500	10,418	925	85,325
1994-5	4,000	20,200	1,350	500	660	10,334	1,525	1,800	800	6,750	11,198	750	84,574
1995-6	3,904	19,500	1,010	450	610	12,282	1,470	1,529	1,000	7,000	10,647	875	85,444
1996-7	3,900	21,000	900	440	600	13,000	1,560	1,400	1,550	7,000	11,126	800	88,626
1997-8[1]	3,400	20,800	950	550	650	12,600	1,600	1,300	2,050	7,100	11,349	750	88,235
1998-9[2]	3,250	19,800	1,000	530	660	12,500	1,600	1,300	2,200	7,300	10,600	800	86,446

[1] Preliminary. [2] Estimate. [3] Formerly part of the U.S.S.R.; data not reported separately until 1991. *Source: Foreign Agricultural Service, U.S. Department of Agriculture (FAS-USDA)*

COTTON

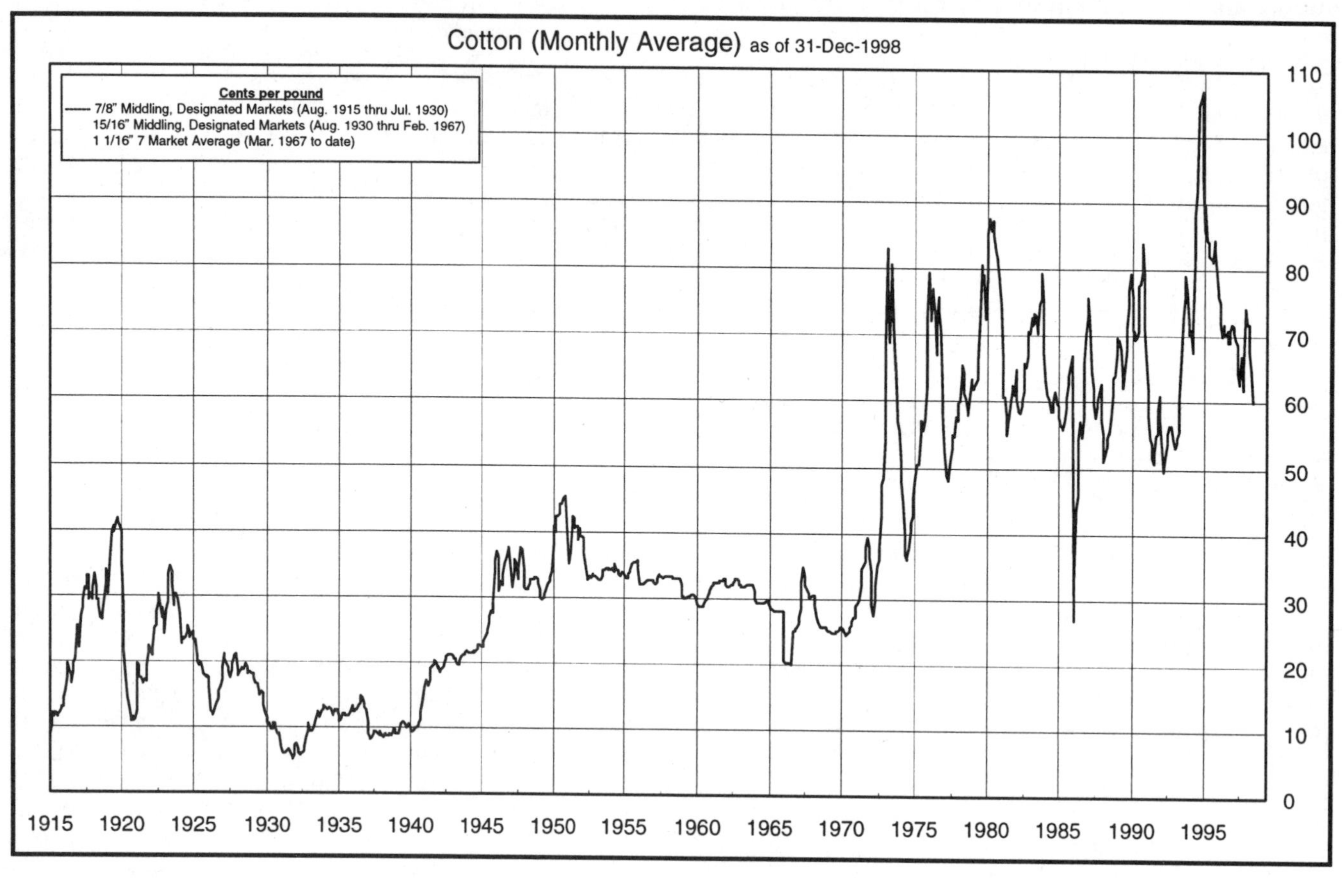

Average Spot Cotton Prices[2], C.I.F. Northern Europe In U.S. Cents Per Pound

Crop Year Beginning Aug. 1	Argentina "C"[3] 1 1/16"	Australia M 1 3/32"	Cotlook Index A	Cotlook Index B	Egypt Giza[4] 81	Greece M 1 3/32"	Mexico[5] M 1 3/32"	Pakistan Sind/ Punjab[6]	Tanzania AR"[7] Type 3	Turkey Izmir[8] 1 3/32"	U.S. Calif. ACALA SJV[9]	U.S. Memphis Terr.[10] M 1 3/32"	U.S. Orleans/ Texas[11] M 1 1/32"
1980-1	82.06	------	94.20	84.20	137.66	100.41	95.48	85.11	103.78	97.43	101.85	99.99	89.14
1981-2	63.55	------	73.80	64.40	115.73	81.06	75.36	65.56	87.92	77.65	79.79	75.87	66.76
1982-3	62.63	------	76.65	66.60	110.07	85.25	76.37	65.58	87.19	83.28	84.94	77.95	68.11
1983-4	83.32	90.83	87.65	80.40	134.07	94.42	87.54	75.51	95.23	92.64	94.90	87.23	78.41
1984-5	60.95	60.33	69.15	59.55	134.01	76.14	70.10	56.20	77.29	75.92	76.20	73.88	65.95
1985-6	49.42	50.05	49.00	40.95	111.40	50.98	53.16	37.92	55.81	57.06	59.43	65.01	52.26
1986-7	68.97	66.59	62.05	55.05	112.59	63.53	64.64	55.11	67.41	64.63	74.27	61.96	56.38
1987-8	64.13	76.14	72.30	67.50	145.11	83.85	73.75	65.88	87.96	86.43	81.17	74.24	72.07
1988-9	64.11	72.14	66.35	61.30	176.85	63.07	61.54	56.98	69.09	68.98	77.13	69.00	63.92
1989-90	77.05	84.16	82.40	77.40	189.54	83.76	82.50	76.75	86.68	90.49	88.59	83.90	78.93
1990-1	77.06	85.58	82.90	77.80	177.43	84.24	84.46	77.19	89.62	81.32	92.84	88.13	80.35
1991-2	55.08	65.97	63.05	58.50	128.10	65.90	68.19	58.14	68.90	74.66	74.47	66.35	63.41
1992-3	64.31	64.01	57.70	53.70	99.24	56.92	------	52.66	62.24	------	68.37	63.08	58.89
1993-4	80.20	72.81	70.60	67.30	88.35	58.81	------	54.42	69.83	59.80	77.55	72.80	69.78
1994-5	101.88	81.05	92.75	92.40	93.70	88.64	82.65	73.75	------	------	106.40	98.67	95.70
1995-6	82.98	93.75	85.61	81.06	------	84.95	94.94	81.86	96.20	90.38	103.49	94.71	90.37
1996-7	79.71	83.24	78.59	74.80	------	75.85	79.60	73.37	79.22	------	89.55	82.81	79.77
1997-8[1]	69.96	77.49	72.19	70.69	------	72.03	81.70	72.93	84.04	------	85.11	78.12	74.74

[1] Preliminary. [2] Generally for prompt shipment. [3] 1 1/32" prior to January 20, 1984; 1 1/16" since. [4] Giza 67 until December 1983; Giza 69/75/81 until November 1990; Giza 81 since. [5] S. Brazil Type 5, 1 1/16" until 1987/88; Brazilian Type 5/6, 1 1/16" since. [6] Sind SG until June 1984; Sind/Punjab SG until January 1985; Afzal 1" until January 1986; Afzal 1 1/32" since. [7] No. 1/2 until February 1986; AR' Mwanza No. 3 until January 1992; AR' Type 3 since. [8] Izmir ST 1 White 1 1/16" RG prior to 1981/82; 1 1/32" from 1981/82 until January 1987; Izmir/Antalya ST 1 White 1 3/32" RG since. [9] SM 1 1/8". [10] SM 1 1/16" prior to 1981-82; Middling 1 3/32 inches since. [11] Middling 1" prior to 1988/89; Middling 1 1/32" since. NA = Not available. *Source: International Cotton Advisory Committee (ICAC)*

Average Price of Strict Low Middling 1-1/16", Cotton[2] at Designated U.S. Markets ¢ Per Pound (Net Weight)

Year	Aug.	Sept.	Oct.	Nov.	Dec.	Jan.	Feb.	Mar.	Apr.	May	June	July	Average
1989-90	69.88	68.46	69.40	68.33	63.56	62.21	64.95	68.06	71.31	74.61	77.06	79.53	69.78
1990-1	76.27	71.01	70.54	69.48	69.92	70.50	77.69	77.92	79.94	83.94	79.05	71.33	74.80
1991-2	66.44	62.39	58.28	54.70	53.89	51.54	50.76	52.01	54.97	55.45	58.82	60.93	56.68
1992-3	57.56	53.49	49.47	49.98	51.85	53.72	55.38	56.45	56.17	56.37	54.38	54.35	54.10
1993-4	53.04	54.01	54.58	55.61	60.29	66.53	72.69	72.74	76.12	79.30	76.85	71.71	66.12
1994-5	70.32	71.10	67.58	72.00	81.92	88.11	91.89	104.20	104.94	105.38	106.96	93.26	88.14
1995-6	85.90	90.00	84.65	84.16	82.18	81.81	81.56	81.13	84.69	83.22	80.23	76.84	83.03
1996-7	76.15	75.24	72.21	70.12	71.98	70.53	70.53	71.12	69.09	69.30	71.03	71.83	71.59
1997-8	71.61	70.75	69.46	68.90	64.57	62.75	63.66	67.04	61.88	65.21	73.50	74.18	67.79
1998-9[1]	71.87	71.75	67.61	64.95	59.88	56.20							65.38

[1] Preliminary. [2] Color 41, leaf 4, staple 34, mike 35-36 and 43-49, strength 23.5-26.4. *Source: Agricultural Marketing Service, U.S Department of Agriculture (AMS-USDA)*

Average Spot Cotton, 1-3/32", Price (SLM) at Designated U.S. Markets In Cents Per Pound (Net Weight)

Year	Aug.	Sept.	Oct.	Nov.	Dec.	Jan.	Feb.	Mar.	Apr.	May	June	July	Average
1989-90	72.45	71.24	71.55	70.23	65.61	63.83	66.39	69.55	72.85	76.32	78.73	81.34	71.67
1990-1	78.06	72.87	72.19	70.97	71.61	72.14	79.38	79.86	81.99	85.94	81.02	73.28	76.61
1991-2	68.24	64.18	59.74	55.57	54.62	52.39	51.84	53.11	56.30	56.90	60.26	62.35	57.96
1992-3	59.08	54.99	50.96	51.41	53.37	55.24	56.86	58.30	58.03	58.23	56.24	56.22	55.74
1993-4	54.89	55.90	56.46	57.34	61.76	67.97	73.99	74.15	77.55	80.42	78.01	72.97	67.62
1994-5	71.46	72.42	68.82	73.38	83.41	89.92	94.25	106.66	107.50	107.93	109.52	96.31	90.13
1995-6	88.31	92.71	87.06	86.43	84.25	84.32	84.04	83.65	87.25	85.90	82.71	78.86	85.46
1996-7	77.97	76.92	73.90	71.74	75.75	72.53	72.86	73.60	71.23	71.38	73.25	74.04	73.76
1997-8	73.69	72.64	71.13	70.35	66.30	64.55	65.78	69.25	64.31	67.66	76.02	76.63	69.86
1998-9[2]	73.93	73.75	69.90	67.18	62.18								69.39

[1] Preliminary. *Source: Economic Research Service, U.S. Department of Agriculture (ERS-USDA)*

Average Spot Prices of U.S. Cotton,[1] Base Quality--(SLM) at Designated Markets In Cents Per Pound

Crop Year Beginning Aug. 1	Dallas (East Tex.-Okl.)	Fresno (San Joaquin Valley)	Greenville (South-east)	Green-wood (South Delta)	Lubbock (West Texas)	Memphis (North Delta)	Phoenix Desert (South-west)	Average
1989-90	67.11	73.47	70.64	69.50	67.06	69.51	71.19	69.78
1990-1	71.40	78.30	75.90	75.53	71.09	75.49	75.90	74.80
1991-2	55.63	57.50	57.70	56.21	55.79	56.18	57.77	56.68
1992-3	53.78	52.84	56.73	55.03	53.53	55.03	51.61	54.10
1993-4[2]	66.22	65.04	67.46	67.04	65.92	67.04	64.16	66.12
1994-5	86.96	93.73	87.17	87.25	86.66	87.25	87.96	88.14
1995-6	80.89	87.40	83.86	83.76	80.64	83.76	80.90	83.03
1996-7	70.29	74.47	72.06	71.84	69.98	72.11	69.88	71.59
1997-8	65.93	71.79	68.60	68.36	65.88	68.36	66.79	67.79
1998-9[3]	64.04	72.15	66.75	66.89	64.31	66.89	62.55	66.22

[1] Prices are for mixed lots, net weight, uncompressed in warehouse. [2] 1993/94 prices are for mixed lots, net weight, compressed, F.O.B. car/truck. *Source: Agricultural Marketing Service, U.S. Department of Agriculture (AMS-USDA)*

Average Price[1] Received by Farmers for Upland Cotton in the United States In Cents Per Pound

Year	Aug.	Sept.	Oct.	Nov.	Dec.	Jan.	Feb.	Mar	Apr.	May	June	July	Average
1989-90	60.4	63.8	65.8	65.6	61.9	60.2	61.0	63.9	65.8	66.2	64.0	63.9	63.6
1990-1	64.6	65.1	67.7	68.4	67.1	64.9	67.9	68.9	69.5	70.1	67.5	66.3	67.1
1991-2	66.3	64.9	62.9	61.2	55.7	51.7	49.8	50.3	53.1	53.2	58.0	56.3	56.8
1992-3	52.7	52.8	53.9	52.7	54.3	53.0	53.8	56.3	55.1	54.4	53.6	53.7	53.7
1993-4	52.4	51.4	52.4	53.3	56.5	62.7	65.7	66.6	67.5	69.0	63.3	58.7	58.1
1994-5	66.8	65.9	66.2	68.5	73.3	78.7	80.2	82.6	77.6	76.2	86.5	80.1	72.0
1995-6	72.2	74.8	74.2	75.0	75.7	76.4	75.7	76.8	78.9	76.7	76.9	73.6	75.4
1996-7	71.9	71.6	71.5	69.7	69.3	67.9	68.1	69.3	67.6	68.3	67.1	67.5	69.3
1997-8	67.0	69.6	69.4	67.9	63.8	61.1	62.5	63.9	63.6	63.5	69.7	68.0	65.2
1998-9[2]	66.2	67.1	66.4	65.1	60.7	59.1							64.1

[1] Weighted average by sales. [2] Preliminary. *Source: Agricultural Marketing Service, U.S. Department of Agriculture (AMS-USDA)*

COTTON

Purchases Reported by Exchanges in Designated U.S. Spot Markets[1] In Running Bales

Year Beginning Aug. 1	Aug.	Sept.	Oct.	Nov.	Dec.	Jan.	Feb.	Mar.	Apr.	May	June	July	Market Total
1987-8	152,935	252,669	650,349	718,829	1,065,457	622,727	571,851	463,739	266,545	572,702	336,191	117,645	5,791,639
1988-9	288,187	166,692	230,724	163,642	323,025	383,699	811,630	388,169	307,937	282,564	261,958	282,288	3,890,515
1989-90	119,516	49,237	89,853	214,910	258,849	388,519	333,417	206,528	157,187	86,966	42,299	46,312	1,993,593
1990-1	36,735	53,948	154,499	376,790	600,752	516,421	180,949	66,869	138,503	101,180	45,731	40,551	2,312,928
1991-2	50,469	55,637	179,671	347,393	776,233	1,043,190	1,063,959	699,026	302,102	110,764	134,500	105,795	4,868,739
1992-3	81,778	233,424	325,600	853,846	1,049,780	1,321,861	317,451	330,381	224,874	208,962	189,401	231,390	5,368,748
1993-4	143,237	173,896	321,119	1,071,518	1,213,655	500,246	602,766	318,008	234,331	318,244	83,083	40,699	5,020,802
1994-5	92,401	98,251	426,371	1,075,829	1,491,429	608,701	233,159	149,762	49,192	44,228	43,821	13,244	4,326,388
1995-6	60,442	38,855	73,857	209,279	381,943	765,502	153,758	241,197	225,797	73,459	59,042	31,324	2,314,455
1996-7	62,884	73,925	148,337	477,331	613,430	696,494	412,095	242,606	72,234	130,163	201,557	93,205	3,224,261
1997-8	48,504	106,503	323,400	367,010	617,470	655,432	482,625	396,946	92,072	210,906	105,139	39,647	3,445,654
1998-9	25,868	50,890	113,688	226,833	492,092	411,971							2,642,684

[1] Commencing September 1, 1988, spot transactions are for seven markets. *Source: Agricultural Marketing Service, U.S. Department of Agriculture (AMS-USDA)*

Production of Cotton (Upland and American-Pima) in the United States In Thousands of 480-Pound Bales

	Upland												Total
Year	Alabama	Arizona	Arkansas	California	Georgia	Louisiana	Mississippi	Missouri	North Carolina	South Carolina	Tennessee	Texas	American-Pima
1982	460	1,095	534	3,073	235	870	1,760	204	102	155	339	2,700	98.7
1983	183	725	323	1,971	112	532	900	73	43	53	151	2,380	94.7
1984	447	1,097	612	2,913	281	1,056	1,650	187	120	170	337	3,680	130.4
1985	545	928	703	3,114	370	742	1,655	204	117	180	419	3,910	155.1
1986	330	675	602	2,245	185	673	1,190	196	109	87	396	2,535	205.9
1987	397	849	901	2,989	338	977	1,745	330	98	106	634	4,635	284.6
1988	380	865	1,044	2,824	370	948	1,825	306	133	140	584	5,215	334.2
1989	383	649	851	2,661	342	868	1,555	269	141	154	476	2,870	691.7
1990	375	811	1,081	2,734	405	1,177	1,850	314	263	145	495	4,965	358.5
1991	553	898	1,576	2,548	722	1,414	2,275	429	640	344	701	4,710	398.4
1992	621	725	1,681	2,817	744	1,299	2,131	541	468	226	834	3,265	508.3
1993	469	790	1,094	2,918	733	1,105	1,550	376	429	204	545	5,095	369.3
1994	726	862	1,772	2,902	1,537	1,512	2,132	615	829	393	885	4,968	337.7
1995	492	793	1,468	2,312	1,941	1,375	1,841	513	798	376	724	4,460	367.6
1996	789	778	1,636	2,390	2,079	1,286	1,876	591	1,002	455	675	4,345	528.5
1997[1]	550	847	1,683	2,191	1,919	986	1,821	565	930	410	662	5,140	548.0
1998[2]	570	580	1,220	1,150	1,550	645	1,450	350	1,005	350	545	3,500	430.0

[1] Preliminary. *Source: Agricultural Statistics Board, U.S. Department of Agriculture (ASB-USDA)*

Cotton Production and Yield Estimates

	Forecast of Production (1,000 Bales of 480 Lbs.[1])						Actual	Forecasts of Yields (Lbs. Per Harvested Acre)						Actual
Year	Aug.1	Sept.1	Oct. 1	Nov. 1	Dec. 1	Jan. 1	Crop	Aug.1	Sept.1	Oct. 1	Nov. 1	Dec. 1	Jan. 1	Yield
1983	7,810	7,776	7,550	7,497	7,725	------	7,771	503	501	487	504	506	------	508
1984	12,569	13,276	13,272	13,271	13,292	------	12,982	583	615	620	613	610	------	600
1985	13,780	13,655	13,638	13,875	13,810	13,534	13,432	638	632	633	644	644	630	630
1986	10,676	10,506	10,006	9,875	9,792	9,785	9,731	573	565	539	546	539	553	552
1987	12,907	12,846	13,336	13,936	14,281	14,724	14,760	615	616	640	671	695	703	706
1988	14,934	14,709	14,714	14,837	15,197	15,446	15,411	616	605	605	612	627	623	619
1989	11,834	12,279	11,991	12,102	12,083	12,233	12,196	618	603	607	608	619	619	614
1990	14,864	14,722	14,540	14,905	15,399	15,617	15,499	622	616	609	622	640	640	634
1991	17,648	17,868	17,614	13,429	14,052	17,542	17,614	630	638	620	635	630	656	652
1992	16,533	16,943	15,885	16,204	16,259	16,260	16,219	696	685	694	698	696	700	699
1993	18,545	17,867	17,014	16,297	16,284	16,176	16,134	668	645	614	594	597	607	606
1994	19,195	19,025	19,303	19,453	19,573	19,728	19,662	690	690	690	695	699	710	708
1995	21,811	20,266	18,771	18,838	18,236	17,971	17,900	663	615	574	567	551	540	537
1996	18,577	17,900	18,189	18,594	18,738	18,951	18,942	686	661	673	698	704	709	705
1997	17,783	18,418	18,410	18,848	18,819	18,977	18,793	637	658	665	673	672	686	673
1998	14,263	13,563	13,288	13,231	13,452	------	13,796	640	614	616	612	621	------	618

[1] Net weight bales. *Source: Agricultural Statistics Board, U.S. Department of Agriculture (ASB-USDA)*

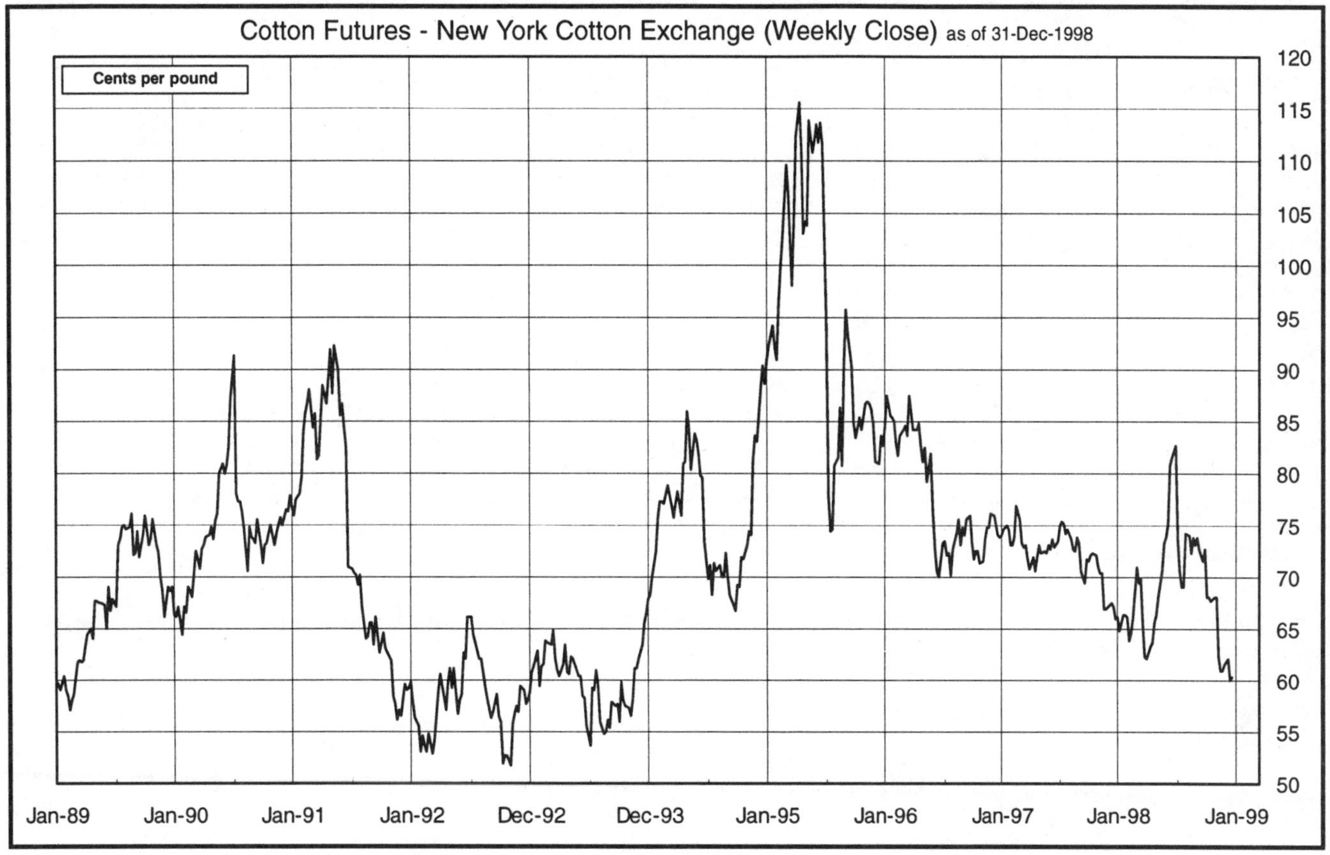

Average Open Interest of No. 2 Cotton Futures in New York In Contracts

Year	Jan.	Feb.	Mar.	Apr.	May	June	July	Aug.	Sept.	Oct.	Nov.	Dec.
1989	31,415	30,978	36,725	36,657	40,761	38,693	40,059	45,894	49,629	49,072	48,136	42,349
1990	40,237	36,291	36,073	37,829	37,908	38,556	36,083	34,042	35,250	40,431	43,997	40,241
1991	43,003	46,793	44,001	43,957	50,086	46,637	40,924	39,616	38,252	39,772	39,295	36,066
1992	38,097	40,095	38,592	36,228	37,839	36,861	35,891	42,241	46,168	46,577	40,425	38,487
1993	41,946	38,657	38,576	33,641	33,012	34,057	32,118	33,872	37,393	36,479	38,567	45,975
1994	54,424	55,558	53,724	54,670	52,830	51,001	52,357	50,597	50,955	51,561	53,563	59,065
1995	71,353	75,100	79,090	71,488	71,714	68,159	65,656	69,653	69,528	65,768	38,475	35,996
1996	58,001	60,231	57,542	61,795	64,555	62,342	61,921	60,182	58,168	58,415	57,397	47,652
1997	59,909	65,392	72,130	76,779	73,464	70,296	73,893	79,309	87,134	92,430	89,150	87,120
1998	89,358	86,739	81,236	85,505	84,562	90,178	81,652	78,571	85,378	88,970	88,917	77,873

Source: New York Cotton Exchange (NYCE)

Volume of Trading of No. 2 Cotton Futures in New York In Contracts

Year	Jan.	Feb.	Mar.	Apr.	May	June	July	Aug.	Sept.	Oct.	Nov.	Dec.	Total
1989	124,764	135,963	113,028	118,573	135,044	167,442	91,381	151,034	165,255	143,713	178,889	124,034	1,649,120
1990	135,260	116,806	126,820	121,203	139,489	135,040	132,329	129,081	103,936	142,670	150,958	98,895	1,534,611
1991	133,415	179,656	148,918	156,978	174,690	122,242	116,458	115,175	107,742	125,558	150,545	82,867	1,614,244
1992	134,531	134,184	149,711	167,778	173,128	153,194	105,534	142,323	144,844	129,680	161,194	105,157	1,701,258
1993	171,180	135,400	136,965	135,300	105,920	128,985	130,886	122,280	110,989	107,571	178,350	139,344	1,603,027
1994	210,011	207,421	210,363	252,614	179,591	208,945	161,688	128,879	140,574	179,604	205,936	203,021	2,289,998
1995	223,073	290,600	286,098	219,187	214,052	185,276	183,171	199,050	191,534	196,676	195,601	141,116	2,525,434
1996	215,882	196,225	147,393	251,786	236,684	264,047	131,183	177,430	166,629	229,305	229,281	128,010	2,373,855
1997	201,610	253,475	302,609	258,851	175,227	314,406	234,718	202,008	212,966	216,771	266,800	197,839	2,837,280
1998	221,308	289,222	310,075	362,688	218,595	407,922	226,138	230,752	195,690	303,849	272,775	161,816	3,200,830

Source: New York Cotton Exchange (NYCE)

COTTON

Supply and Distribution of Upland Cotton in the United States In Thousands of 480-Pound Bales

Crop Year Beginning Aug. 1	Area: Planted (1,000 Acres)	Area: Harvested (1,000 Acres)	Area: Yield Lbs./Acre	Supply: Beginning Stocks[3]	Supply: Production[4]	Supply: Imports	Supply: Total	Disappearance: Mill Use	Disappearance: Exports	Disappearance: Total	Ending Stocks	Farm Price[5] Cents/Lb.
1985-6	10,601	10,145	628	4,024	13,277	33	17,334	6,352	1,855	8,207	9,289	56.8
1986-7	9,933	8,357	547	9,289	9,525	3	18,817	7,385	6,570	13,955	4,942	51.5
1987-8	10,259	9,894	702	4,942	14,475	2	19,419	7,565	6,345	13,910	5,718	63.7
1988-9	12,325	11,759	615	5,718	15,077	5	20,800	7,711	5,883	13,594	7,026	55.6
1989-90	10,210	9,166	602	7,026	11,504	2	18,532	8,686	7,242	15,928	2,798	63.6
1990-1	12,117	11,505	632	2,798	15,147	4	17,949	8,592	7,378	15,970	2,262	67.1
1991-2	13,802	12,716	650	2,262	17,216	13	19,491	9,548	6,348	15,896	3,583	56.8
1992-3	12,977	10,863	694	3,583	15,710	1	19,294	10,190	4,869	15,059	4,456	53.7
1993-4	13,248	12,594	601	4,456	15,764	6	20,226	10,346	6,555	16,901	3,303	58.1
1994-5	13,552	13,156	705	3,303	19,324	18	22,645	11,109	8,978	20,087	2,588	72.0
1995-6	16,717	15,796	533	2,588	17,532	400	20,520	10,538	7,375	17,913	2,543	75.4
1996-7	14,376	12,612	701	2,543	18,413	403	21,359	11,020	6,399	17,419	3,920	69.3
1997-8[1]	13,558	13,021	673	3,920	18,245	13	22,178	11,234	7,060	18,294	3,822	65.2
1998-9[2]	12,552	10,128	606	3,822	12,785	300	16,907	10,500	4,160	14,660	2,224	

[1] Preliminary. [2] Estimate. [3] Excludes preseason ginnings (adjusted to 480-lb. bale net weight basis). [4] Includes preseason ginnings. [5] Marketing year average price. [6] Average of 5 cheapest types of SLM 1 3/32" staple length cotton offered on the European market. *Source: Economic Research Service, U.S. Department of Agriculture (ERS-USDA)*

Daily Rate of Upland Cotton Mill Consumption[2] on Cotton-System Spinning Spindles in the United States
In Thousands of Running Bales

Crop Year Beginning Aug. 1	Aug.	Sept.	Oct.	Nov.	Dec.	Jan.	Feb.	Mar.	Apr.	May.	June	July	Average
1985-6	22.9	22.5	24.6	23.9	19.5	23.8	24.9	24.6	24.8	25.2	24.4	20.9	23.4
1986-7	26.7	26.2	27.3	26.5	23.1	27.3	28.1	29.4	28.7	29.3	28.3	27.0	27.3
1987-8	30.3	30.1	31.0	30.3	24.4	28.4	29.5	29.5	27.8	27.6	26.5	21.7	28.1
1988-9	28.8	27.7	27.6	26.1	22.9	28.3	29.2	30.0	31.2	32.2	31.9	27.9	28.6
1989-90	32.9	32.8	33.0	30.6	25.9	29.9	31.4	31.5	30.9	31.8	32.8	27.8	30.9
1990-1	33.8	41.4	33.2	30.2	29.7	----	32.3	----	----	34.0	----	----	33.5
1991-2	33.6	----	----	33.1	----	34.6	36.3	35.7	35.6	37.3	35.2	33.9	35.0
1992-3	38.5	37.8	39.7	37.6	31.5	39.1	39.5	38.8	38.7	39.4	37.8	34.5	37.8
1993-4	39.8	38.4	39.4	36.4	31.4	36.9	37.9	39.0	39.3	39.5	40.4	40.3	38.2
1994-5	41.0	41.4	41.1	41.8	41.7	42.6	42.1	42.4	41.1	40.2	39.2	37.2	41.0
1995-6	38.8	39.4	37.6	38.1	37.9	37.5	38.1	39.5	39.4	39.6	40.6	39.8	38.9
1996-7	40.5	40.7	40.5	41.5	41.1	41.2	40.4	39.4	41.0	41.0	40.9	42.5	40.9
1997-8	40.7	42.4	42.0	42.4	43.9	41.9	41.7	41.1	40.5	40.8	40.0	41.5	41.6
1998-9[1]	39.3	38.7	39.9	37.3	37.4								38.5

[1] Preliminary. [2] Not seasonally adjusted. *Source: Bureau of the Census, U.S. Department of Commerce*

Consumption of American and Foreign Cotton in the United States In Thousands of Running Bales

Year	Aug.	Sept.	Oct.	Nov.	Dec.	Jan.	Feb.	Mar.	Apr.	May	June	July	Total
1985-6	458	562	493	477	486	595	499	492	620	503	489	522	6,198
1986-7	534	523	683	529	576	546	562	734	573	586	708	540	7,096
1987-8	606	753	621	606	610	568	590	738	556	551	662	433	7,294
1988-9	577	693	552	523	572	568	584	751	623	645	798	559	7,444
1989-90	689	860	690	642	685	630	658	826	650	667	826	559	8,383
1990-1	680	835	671	610	601	----	2,068	----	----	2,212	----	----	8,367
1991-2	2,215	----	----	2,199	----	870	730	898	718	752	885	682	9,949
1992-3	776	950	799	756	792	788	796	976	778	792	951	694	9,846
1993-4	801	965	792	731	790	743	785	999	806	830	1,032	744	10,019
1994-5	870	1,070	873	838	897	858	878	1,097	847	842	999	681	10,750
1995-6	829	1,020	798	761	801	744	787	1,029	810	824	1,040	731	10,174
1996-7	847	1,028	829	816	858	810	819	1,014	834	840	1,044	781	10,519
1997-8	868	1,100	872	855	951	848	861	1,068	839	854	1,017	770	10,902
1998-9[1]	835	1,013	834	758	796								10,167

[1] Preliminary. *Source: Bureau of the Census, U.S. Department of Commerce*

Exports of All Cotton[2] from the United States In Thousands of Running Bales

Year	Aug.	Sept.	Oct.	Nov.	Dec.	Jan.	Feb.	Mar.	Apr.	May	June	July	Total
1985-6	166	218	180	198	236	189	202	206	125	69	68	19	1,876
1986-7[2]	374	496	489	525	664	591	518	750	500	465	554	439	6,365
1987-8	355	304	316	612	536	698	879	649	565	537	486	359	6,296
1988-9	248	173	292	352	524	756	514	597	575	795	515	649	5,990
1989-90	431	384	507	469	516	909	840	882	818	495	510	550	7,311
1990-1	480	355	433	591	639	1,112	950	804	960	488	404	273	7,489
1991-2	219	126	239	396	674	961	725	791	787	535	430	466	6,349
1992-3	252	263	277	342	528	501	502	533	639	401	317	395	4,950
1993-4	287	248	345	405	571	738	512	743	761	854	770	626	6,860
1994-5	531	333	341	710	1,098	1,115	1,383	1,392	1,104	684	410	300	9,402
1995-6	315	245	452	733	1,230	1,262	1,295	777	576	343	263	183	7,675
1996-7	257	171	277	573	899	666	728	848	711	631	604	501	6,866
1997-8	458	299	400	581	774	734	777	888	669	477	574	571	7,202
1998-9[1]	402	280	265										3,788

[1] Preliminary. [2] Data prior to 1986-7 are for American Cotton only. *Source: Foreign Agricultural Service, U.S. Department of Agriculture (FAS-USDA)*

U.S. Exports of American Cotton to Countries of Destination In Thousands of 480-Pound Bales

Crop Year Beginning Aug. 1	Canada	China	Hong Kong	Indo-nesia	Italy	Japan	Rep. of Korea	Mexico	Philip-pines	Taiwan	Thai-land	United Kingdom	Total
1985-6	98	------	1	105	91	520	513	------	8	46	17	35	1,958
1986-7	70	------	52	324	263	1,723	1,330	------	153	907	239	56	6,685
1987-8	153	------	88	287	406	1,569	1,450	------	135	424	248	69	6,582
1988-9	148	793	108	307	239	1,381	1,302	------	50	254	172	37	6,147
1989-90	197	670	244	499	431	1,594	1,365	117	134	320	375	74	7,694
1990-1	191	1,233	306	561	425	1,437	1,168	202	132	358	317	36	7,793
1991-2	181	792	335	739	240	1,107	1,024	213	181	380	368	60	6,646
1992-3	154	1	100	429	144	839	1,031	557	117	279	150	65	5,201
1993-4	165	1,183	314	653	96	790	976	653	168	356	277	65	6,862
1994-5	253	2,257	347	925	83	1,061	951	558	173	352	441	89	9,402
1995-6	294	1,847	223	794	115	940	769	618	144	255	331	85	7,675
1996-7[1]	253	1,756	129	594	46	630	568	733	84	255	197	66	6,865
1997-8[2]	311	745	151	485	86	682	760	1,605	55	384	226	13	7,604

[1] Preliminary. [2] Estimate. *Source: Foreign Agricultural Service, U.S. Department of Agriculture (FAS-USDA)*

Cotton[1] Government Loan Program in the United States

Crop Year Beginning Aug. 1	Support Price	Target Price	Put Under Support	% of Pro-duction	Acquired	Owned July 31	Crop Year Beginning Aug. 1	Support Price	Target Price	Put Under Support	% of Pro-duction	Acquired	Owned July 31
	--- ¢ per Pound ---		Ths Bales		----- Ths. Bales -----			--- ¢ per Pound ---		Ths Bales		---- Ths. Bales ----	
1986-7	55.00	81.0	6,170	64.8	12	24	1992-3	52.35	72.9	8,302	52.9	10	[8]
1987-8	52.25	79.4	5,362	37.0	131	3	1993-4	52.35	72.9	7,721	49.0	3	14
1988-9	51.80	75.9	11,231	74.5	66	35	1994-5	50.00	72.9	4,716	24.4	[3]	[3]
1989-90	50.00	73.4	3,732	32.4	2	27	1995-6	51.92	72.9	3,478	19.8	0	0
1990-1	50.27	72.9	3,205	21.1	1	4	1996-7	51.92	-----	3,340	18.1	0	0
1991-2	50.77	72.9	6,312	36.6	8	[3]	1997-8[2]	51.92	-----	-----	-----	-----	-----

[1] Upland. [2] Preliminary. [3] Less than 500 bales. NA = Not available. *Source: Economic Research Service, U.S. Department of Agriculture (ERS)*

Production Cotton Cloth[1] in the United States In Millions of Square Yards

Year	First Quarter	Second Quarter	Third Quarter	Fourth Quarter	Total Year	Year	First Quarter	Second Quarter	Third Quarter	Fourth Quarter	Total Year
1987	1,158	1,217	1,219	1,178	4,772	1993	1,150	1,144	1,071	1,039	4,403
1988	1,252	1,255	1,072	1,052	5,632	1994	1,073	1,125	1,131	1,143	4,473
1989	1,157	1,192	1,134	1,106	4,589	1995	1,169	1,137	1,090	1,093	4,488
1990	1,202	1,127	1,087	1,048	4,463	1996	1,182	1,230	1,198	1,187	4,796
1991	1,081	1,148	1,082	1,093	4,404	1997	1,211	1,276	1,283	1,309	5,078
1992	1,154	1,172	1,130	1,144	4,600	1998[2]	1,315	1,198	1,311		5,099

[1] Cotton broadwoven goods over 12 inches in width. [2] Preliminary. *Source: Bureau of the Census, U.S. Department of Commerce*

Cotton Ginnings[1] in the United States To: In Thousands of Running Bales

Crop Year	Aug. 1	Sept. 1	Sept. 15	Oct. 1	Oct. 15	Nov. 1	Nov. 15	Dec. 1	Dec. 15	Jan. 1	Jan. 15	Feb. 1	Total Crop
1989-90	90	382	523	981	2,772	5,948	8,388	10,353	11,246	11,548	11,681	11,771	11,913
1990-1	120	583	1,090	2,616	4,739	7,955	10,207	12,428	13,863	14,516	14,809	14,963	15,082
1991-2	NA	699	983	2,467	4,955	8,351	10,752	13,260	15,067	15,888	16,402	16,765	17,146
1992-3	14	446	740	1,664	4,046	7,584	10,296	12,597	14,083	14,944	15,311	15,527	15,786
1993-4	9	435	748	1,846	4,471	7,975	10,952	13,244	14,695	15,321	15,517	15,590	15,675
1994-5	113	680	943	2,324	5,002	8,878	12,479	15,587	17,465	18,438	18,842	19,028	19,127
1995-6	17	433	898	2,455	4,795	8,430	11,262	14,199	16,101	17,011	17,292	17,416	17,469
1996-7	48	342	637	2,146	4,780	8,876	11,906	14,623	16,528	17,681	18,101	18,308	18,439
1997-8	2	359	683	1,210	3,752	7,930	11,601	14,735	16,662	17,613	18,013	18,170	18,301
1998-9[2]	146	524	739	2,055	4,324	7,362	9,310	11,272	12,558	13,067	13,366	13,464	

[1] Excluding linters. [2] Preliminary. NA = Not available. *Source: National Agricultural Statistics Service, U.S. Department of Agriculture (NASS-USDA)*

Fiber Prices in the United States In Cents Per Pound

	Cotton[1]		Rayon[2]		Polyester[3]		Price Ratios[4] in Percent	
Year	Actual	Raw[5] Equivalent	Actual	Raw[5] Equivalent	Actual	Raw[5] Equivalent	Cotton/ Rayon	Cotton/ Polyester
1988	64.89	72.10	90.67	94.44	73.83	76.91	.77	.94
1989	71.99	79.99	109.75	114.32	85.67	89.24	.70	.90
1990	79.29	88.10	119.92	124.91	82.58	86.02	.71	1.03
1991	79.05	87.83	122.00	127.08	73.50	76.56	.69	1.15
1992	61.92	68.80	114.08	118.84	73.50	76.56	.58	.90
1993	62.43	69.37	111.42	116.06	72.50	75.52	.60	.92
1994	78.69	87.43	103.00	107.29	74.92	78.04	.82	1.12
1995	100.76	111.95	118.67	123.61	88.83	92.53	.91	
1996	86.24	95.83	118.00	122.92	81.10	84.48	.78	1.14
1997	76.29	84.77	115.00	119.79	69.50	72.40	.71	1.17
Nov.	74.97	83.30	115.00	119.79	71.00	73.96	.70	1.13
Dec.	71.57	79.52	115.00	119.79	71.00	73.96	.66	1.08
1998[6]	75.18	83.54	112.10	116.77	64.40	67.09	.72	1.26
Jan.	69.45	77.17	115.00	119.79	71.00	73.96	.64	1.04
Feb.	69.48	77.20	115.00	119.79	71.00	73.96	.64	1.04
Mar.	72.95	81.06	115.00	119.79	71.00	73.96	.68	1.10
Apr.	69.50	77.22	115.00	119.79	71.00	73.96	.65	1.04
May	71.78	79.76	115.00	119.79	65.00	67.71	.67	1.18
June	80.87	89.86	115.00	119.79	64.00	66.67	.75	1.35
July	83.62	92.91	115.00	119.79	62.00	64.58	.78	1.44
Aug.	79.80	88.67	110.00	114.58	58.00	60.42	.77	1.47
Sept.	79.02	87.80	105.00	109.38	58.00	60.42	.80	1.45
Oct.	75.35	83.72	101.00	105.21	53.00	55.21	.80	1.52

[1] SLM-1 1/16" at group B Mill points, net weight. [2] 1.5 and 3.0 denier, regular rayon staples. [3] Reported average market price for 1.5 denier polyester staple for cotton blending. [4] Raw fiber equivalent. [5] Actual prices converted to estimated raw fiber equivalent as follows: cotton, divided by 0.90, rayon and polyester, divided by 0.96. *Source: Economic Research Service, U.S. Department of Agriculture (ERS-USDA)*

Average Producer Price Index of Gray Cotton Broadwovens Index 1982=100

Year	Jan.	Feb.	Mar.	Apr.	May	June	July	Aug.	Sept.	Oct.	Nov.	Dec.	Average
1989	112.4	111.3	110.9	110.9	110.5	110.1	109.4	109.8	109.8	110.8	110.9	113.5	110.9
1990	113.7	113.8	113.8	114.0	114.1	109.9	115.1	115.1	112.3	112.5	116.1	116.4	113.8
1991	113.3	113.6	114.1	114.5	114.9	115.2	115.3	115.3	115.3	115.4	115.7	115.6	114.9
1992	116.9	116.8	116.7	116.7	116.8	117.5	117.3	117.3	117.2	116.9	117.1	117.2	117.0
1993	117.0	116.8	115.9	116.3	115.7	115.7	115.2	115.2	112.5	114.1	114.1	114.9	115.3
1994	109.9	110.8	115.4	115.7	114.9	114.9	115.0	117.5	117.6	118.9	117.2	118.0	115.5
1995	117.8	120.2	120.7	121.6	123.4	123.6	124.1	125.4	125.3	123.7	123.7	123.8	122.8
1996	123.6	123.7	122.0	122.0	121.1	120.7	120.7	119.9	119.7	120.4	120.0	120.4	121.2
1997	120.3	120.8	120.7	120.8	121.2	120.6	121.4	121.6	121.4	120.8	121.6	121.2	121.0
1998[1]	122.8	122.0	122.1	121.5	121.8	120.8	120.0	119.1	119.1	118.1	117.1	118.0	120.2

[1] Preliminary. *Source: Bureau of Labor Statistics (0337-01), U.S. Department of Commerce (BLS)*

Cottonseed and Products

Cottonseed production is directly related to the amount of cotton produced. For the U.S., the 1998-99 season was an unusual one. The growing season weather was less than optimal leading to very large abandonment of planted cotton acreage. Texas suffered through a severe drought leading producers to leave fields unharvested. California had a cold spring that delayed plantings. Not only does poor weather lead to less acreage harvested but low yields and low prices can also cause producers to abandon acreage. The 1998-99 season had aspects of all of these. Weather in some of the most important growing areas was poor, yields were low and prices were low.

U.S. cotton planted acreage was 12.87 million acres, down 7 percent from the 1997-98 level of 13.81 million. Harvested acreage was only 10.39 million acres in 1998-99, down 22 percent from the previous year. The abandonment rate was 19 percent, much above the 1997-98 rate of 4 percent. On average, between 4 percent and 8 percent of cotton acreage is not harvested. The USDA reported that U.S. cottonseed production in 1998-99 was 4.58 million metric tonnes, down 27 percent from 1997-98.

World cottonseed production in the 1998-99 season was forecast at 32.50 million tonnes, down 6 percent from 1997-98. The decline in the U.S. accounted for all of the world decline in cottonseed production. China is the other major producer of cotton and therefore cottonseed. Chinese production of cottonseed in 1998-98 was forecast to be 7.40 million tonnes, down 11 percent from the previous years total of 8.28 million tonnes. India had a larger cotton crop with cottonseed production estimated at 5.50 million tonnes, some 8 percent more than the previous year. Pakistan's cottonseed production was estimated at 3.30 million tonnes, some 10 percent above the previous year. Uzbekistan produced 2 million tonnes, down 13 percent from 1997-98.

World Production of Cottonseed In Thousands of Metric Tons

Crop Year	Argentina	Australia	Brazil	China	Egypt	Greece	India	Mexico	Pakistan	Turkey	United States	Former U.S.S.R.	World Total
1990-1	538	686	1,352	8,340	504	365	3,980	294	3,275	977	5,415	4,550	33,919
1991-2	435	724	1,313	10,499	491	355	4,090	307	4,352	878	6,283	4,283	37,691
1992-3	275	528	800	8,340	571	410	4,740	52	3,080	905	5,652	3,557	32,196
1993-4	390	466	920	6,655	655	460	4,120	31	2,740	892	5,754	3,600	29,688
1994-5	631	474	980	7,727	411	574	4,709	187	2,959	930	6,898	3,360	33,105
1995-6	760	595	690	8,487	384	725	5,339	344	3,604	1,263	6,213	3,150	35,254
1996-7	564	859	560	7,481	560	540	5,890	421	3,230	1,259	6,480	2,580	34,498
1997-8[1]	542	941	580	8,188	563	590	4,830	329	3,180	1,260	6,291	2,780	34,252
1998-9[2]	590	1,017	620	7,125	475	570	5,450	346	3,330	1,280	4,521	2,880	32,481

[1] Preliminary. [2] Estimate. *Source: Oil World*

Salient Statistics of Cottonseed in the United States

Crop Year Beginning Aug. 1	Supply: Stocks	Supply: Production	Total Supply	Disappearance: Crush	Disappearance: Exports	Disappearance: Other	Total Disappearance	Farm Price $/Ton	Value of Production Mil. $	Products Produced: Oil Millions Lbs.	Products Produced: Meal Thousand Sh. Tons
	In Thousands of Short Tons										
1990-1	366	5,969	6,337	3,369	53	2,264	5,686	121	722.3	1,154	1,691
1991-2	651	6,926	7,579	3,981	161	2,977	7,119	71	492.3	1,279	1,765
1992-3	460	6,230	6,690	3,629	192	2,504	6,325	98	608.4	1,137	1,533
1993-4	365	6,343	6,708	3,470	157	2,649	6,276	113	714.4	1,119	1,563
1994-5	432	7,604	8,036	3,947	232	3,306	7,485	101	771.3	1,312	1,830
1995-6	551	6,849	7,399	3,882	114	2,886	6,882	106	730.4	1,229	1,748
1996-7	517	7,144	7,681	3,860	116	3,182	7,158	126	914.6	1,310	1,807
1997-8[1]	523	6,935	7,553	3,885	149	2,957	6,990	121	839.1	1,289	1,793
1998-9[2]	563	5,182	5,945	2,650	75	3,020	5,745	-----	-----	995	1,283

[1] Preliminary. [2] Estimate. *Source: Economic Research Service, U.S. Department of Agriculture (ERS-USDA)*

Average Wholesale Price of Cottonseed Meal (41% Solvent) at Memphis In Dollars Per Short Ton

Year	Jan.	Feb.	Mar.	Apr.	May	June	July	Aug.	Sept.	Oct.	Nov.	Dec.	Average
1990	160.00	150.00	146.25	150.00	155.00	147.50	161.50	169.50	178.75	163.00	147.50	141.25	155.85
1991	125.00	118.10	125.00	122.50	118.10	117.20	127.50	130.90	133.10	131.00	144.40	162.00	129.57
1992	156.25	140.10	124.25	121.25	127.50	132.50	133.75	146.90	163.00	154.40	157.50	174.50	144.33
1993	164.40	149.40	153.50	149.00	143.10	153.00	170.30	178.50	193.75	173.10	181.00	180.00	165.75
1994	170.30	173.10	174.00	166.25	157.75	154.10	152.50	144.50	145.00	134.40	120.50	114.20	150.55
1995	106.75	97.50	100.30	98.10	92.75	108.75	116.90	116.50	137.60	153.25	165.00	185.80	123.27
1996	208.80	202.80	195.60	220.00	191.25	192.20	201.56	193.10	193.10	183.25	196.60	224.50	200.23
1997	207.20	183.75	189.10	189.10	193.75	190.30	170.75	176.25	192.00	189.10	189.10	190.50	188.41
1998[1]	153.10	139.10	128.70	116.25	105.00	129.40	146.65	130.30	115.60	106.50	107.90	117.90	124.70

[1] Preliminary. *Source: Economic Research Service, U.S. Department of Agriculture (ERS-USDA)*

COTTONSEED AND PRODUCTS

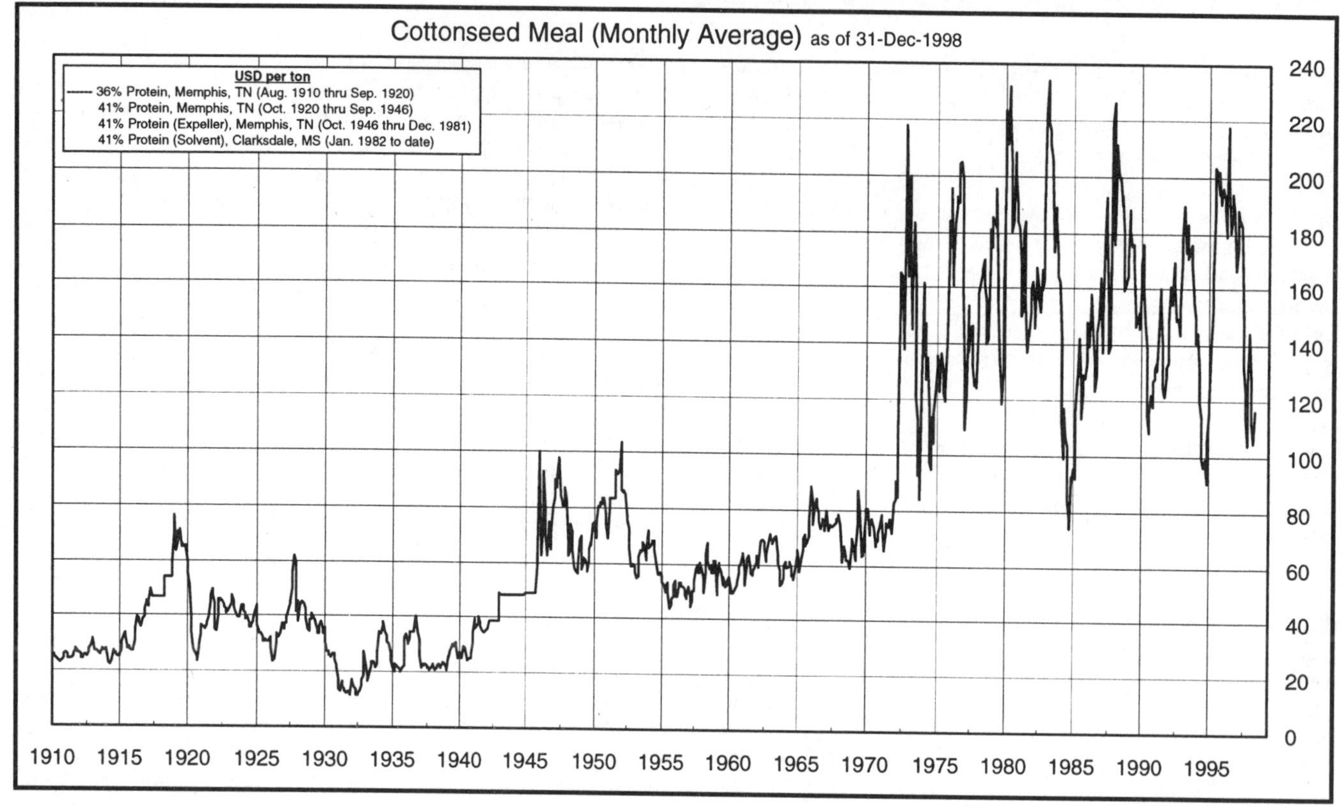

Supply & Distribution of Cottonseed Oil in the United States In Millions of Pounds

Crop Year Beginning Oct. 1	Supply: Stocks	Supply: Production	Supply: Imports	Supply: Total Supply	Disappearance: Domestic	Disappearance: Exports	Disappearance: Total	Per Capita Consump. of Salad & Ck. Oils -- In Lbs.--	Utilization Food Uses: Shortening	Utilization Food Uses: Salad & Cooking Oils	Utilization Food Uses: Total	Prices: U.S.[3] (Crude) $/Tonne	Prices: Rott[4] (Cif) $/Tonne
1992-3	78	1,137	37.7	1,253	995	177	1,172	26	238	353	640	551	688
1993-4	81	1,119	26.0	1,226	873	248	1,121	25	217	289	558	684	750
1994-5	106	1,312	0	1,417	1,006	329	1,335	26	217	262	532	683	671
1995-6	82	1,229	.3	1,311	996	221	1,217	27	218	235	497	575	613
1996-7	94	1,216	.3	1,310	1,012	232	1,244	26	271	265	556	564	590
1997-8[1]	66	1,223	.1	1,289	1,003	208	1,211	29	187	171	379	663	693
1998-9[2]	79	850	66.4	995	850	100	950					758	769

[1] Preliminary. [2] Estimate. [3] F.O.B.; Greenwood, MS. (Tank Cars). [4] Rotterdam;U.S. PBSY *Source: Economic Research Service, U.S. Department of Agriculture (ERS-USDA)*

United States Consumption of Crude Cottonseed Oil in Refining In Millions of Pounds

Year	Oct.	Nov.	Dec.	Jan.	Feb	Mar.	Apr.	May	June	July	Aug.	Sept.	Total
1992-3	75.7	93.3	95.5	107.3	85.1	77.5	92.8	79.3	74.7	65.1	68.6	57.6	972.5
1993-4	82.7	113.0	103.8	110.8	96.7	111.5	69.6	74.8	73.2	74.6	88.4	64.2	1,063.3
1994-5	81.9	97.2	109.8	107.7	87.1	96.2	87.2	72.8	73.4	76.0	83.3	71.6	1,044.4
1995-6	76.1	91.8	89.7	94.5	87.2	92.2	83.4	77.3	55.5	56.2	64.3	54.4	922.5
1996-7	67.2	85.1	85.1	88.7	83.3	80.8	77.4	79.2	58.4	55.3	59.0	39.2	858.7
1997-8	73.1	73.1	77.2	85.0	75.7	70.2	72.1	57.1	51.9	54.9	57.5	30.1	778.1
1998-9[1]	52.9	49.6	50.2										610.8

[1] Preliminary. *Source: Bureau of the Census, U.S. Department of Commerce*

United States Exports of Cottonseed Oil (Crude and Refined) In Thousands of Pounds

Year	Jan.	Feb.	Mar.	Apr.	May	June	July	Aug.	Sept.	Oct.	Nov.	Dec	Total
1992	68,977	69,631	19,704	19,753	13,071	13,443	16,027	7,947	13,090	8,101	4,625	17,308	271,677
1993	23,904	14,238	6,294	27,370	25,849	17,685	5,066	7,065	19,246	7,079	15,103	14,075	182,974
1994	32,011	11,093	21,156	26,595	34,921	11,583	24,303	24,644	25,265	17,487	33,385	36,613	299,056
1995	18,808	43,454	48,471	34,500	28,775	22,692	18,490	11,973	NA	9,896	30,268	13,223	280,550
1996	26,407	8,103	38,597	24,628	16,052	14,135	7,827	21,197	10,903	12,526	10,345	20,918	211,638
1997	25,722	26,835	22,647	22,230	30,319	9,535	25,207	24,717	8,919	15,351	24,217	8,164	243,863
1998[1]	24,003	15,077	16,150	22,874	20,791	22,994	15,348	14,392	8,818	11,023	6,614		194,273

[1] Preliminary. NA = Not available. *Source: Economic Research Service, U.S. Department of Agriculture (ERS-USDA)*

Cottonseed Crushed (Consumption) in the United States In Thousands of Short Tons

Year	Aug.	Sept.	Oct.	Nov.	Dec.	Jan.	Feb.	Mar.	Apr.	May	June	July	Total
1990-1	157.3	176.1	274.9	339.4	320.8	------------	973.0	------------	------------	864.5	------------	------	3,106
1991-2	813.6	------------	------------	1,145.2	------------	420.6	378.3	381.3	297.8	245.4	292.1	270.2	4,245
1992-3	245.7	162.9	323.2	353.3	372.1	413.3	334.6	324.1	323.8	296.4	242.7	237.2	3,629
1993-4	182.9	162.6	300.4	391.4	375.0	391.0	335.2	358.6	265.7	257.7	239.4	210.2	3,470
1994-5	192.1	195.5	343.9	386.2	397.5	404.6	360.5	391.0	345.4	304.0	316.5	310.0	3,947
1995-6	264.4	245.5	337.1	386.7	362.4	402.3	373.5	381.4	349.6	325.2	223.7	209.2	3,861
1996-7	229.2	225.0	331.7	355.1	352.6	381.0	362.8	362.2	334.4	351.3	280.8	294.0	3,860
1997-8	244.4	178.6	329.7	374.5	371.3	428.4	352.3	370.8	359.1	309.1	278.8	277.6	3,875
1998-9[1]	246.0	174.9	272.7	254.3	262.8								2,906

[1] Preliminary. *Source: Economic Research Service, U.S. Department of Agriculture (ERS-USDA)*

Production of Cottonseed Cake and Meal in the United States In Thousands of Short Tons

Year	Aug.	Sept.	Oct.	Nov.	Dec.	Jan.	Feb.	Mar.	Apr.	May	June	July	Total
1990-1	68.7	77.4	128.2	160.1	148.8	------------	456.2	------------	------------	409.1	------------	-------	1,449
1991-2	388.6	------------	------------	533.9	------------	192.6	170.5	173.5	138.2	111.7	129.9	127.8	1,967
1992-3	111.2	76.0	143.7	150.2	160.5	176.2	146.6	136.4	140.9	126.1	103.0	101.0	1,572
1993-4	76.7	71.5	130.1	172.2	166.6	161.8	151.8	164.0	119.6	116.1	106.9	93.4	1,531
1994-5	90.6	89.4	154.2	171.5	176.9	184.1	162.2	174.3	154.2	137.4	143.9	137.2	1,776
1995-6	120.1	113.6	159.9	178.2	161.0	183.8	169.8	168.3	158.7	147.1	102.4	102.7	1,766
1996-7	100.9	99.1	146.1	161.5	158.2	174.5	164.6	162.1	152.2	160.7	128.6	123.2	1,732
1997-8	128.2	92.1	147.8	168.7	178.2	194.4	158.5	170.4	162.3	141.8	128.8	124.0	1,795
1998-9[1]	114.7	77.1	118.7	115.9	122.5								1,317

[1] Preliminary. *Source: Bureau of the Census, U.S. Department of Commerce*

U.S. Production of Crude Cottonseed Oil[2] In Millions of Pounds

Year	Aug.	Sept.	Oct.	Nov.	Dec.	Jan.	Feb.	Mar.	Apr.	May	June	July	Total
1990-1	58.7	57.6	86.2	104.0	102.3	------------	309.9	------------	------------	283.0	------------	------	1,002
1991-2	263.7	-----------	------------	398.9	------------	137.4	127.2	121.5	97.5	79.3	91.8	91.3	1,409
1992-3	77.8	56.8	99.5	110.2	117.6	134.7	107.2	104.9	101.7	96.1	77.7	76.5	1,161
1993-4	59.1	51.7	93.5	122.2	117.5	124.7	99.9	119.6	85.3	85.2	78.4	69.8	1,107
1994-5	61.7	61.0	109.8	122.6	125.6	133.4	115.6	125.2	110.4	97.7	102.4	96.6	1,262
1995-6	87.8	84.3	105.2	121.6	111.6	130.9	121.4	125.6	110.4	101.9	73.3	76.7	1,251
1996-7	70.3	69.4	98.9	114.8	115.9	123.9	114.8	114.7	103.7	109.8	86.9	85.9	1,209
1997-8	80.6	66.0	97.8	120.3	119.6	136.4	111.1	115.5	112.7	96.1	87.3	88.8	1,232
1998-9[1]	77.8	59.6	78.3	80.0	80.6								903

[1] Preliminary. [2] Not seasonally adjusted. *Source: Bureau of the Census, U.S. Department of Commerce*

United States Production of Refined Cottonseed Oil In Millions of Pounds

Year	Aug.	Sept.	Oct.	Nov.	Dec.	Jan.	Feb.	Mar.	Apr.	May	June	July	Total
1990-1	57.8	53.7	75.4	96.0	90.0	------------	253.9	------------	------------	256.3	------------	-------	883
1991-2	209.3	------------	------------	205.0	------------	103.2	105.6	97.9	85.6	73.4	82.1	81.1	1,043
1992-3	69.3	46.3	72.6	90.2	91.9	103.1	82.0	74.5	88.8	75.6	70.8	62.4	928
1993-4	65.1	54.6	79.4	109.1	100.6	107.2	93.4	107.8	66.9	71.6	70.0	72.2	998
1994-5	86.3	62.9	80.0	94.4	106.2	104.2	94.4	92.6	84.2	70.1	70.7	72.6	1,019
1995-6	80.5	69.0	74.0	89.5	86.9	91.7	84.6	89.8	81.7	75.0	53.8	54.5	931
1996-7	62.4	53.0	64.9	82.8	82.2	85.9	80.7	78.1	75.2	76.9	56.4	53.6	852
1997-8	57.4	38.1	48.3	71.0	74.8	82.2	73.1	68.2	69.8	55.2	50.3	53.0	741
1998-9[1]	55.8	29.1	51.1	47.9	48.5								558

[1] Preliminary. *Source: Bureau of the Census, U.S. Department of Commerce*

U.S. Stocks of Cottonseed Oil (Crude & Refined) at End of Month In Millions of Pounds

Year	Aug.	Sept.	Oct.	Nov.	Dec.	Jan.	Feb.	Mar.	Apr.	May	June	July
1990-1	75.9	80.4	83.0	93.5	102.7	------------	145.8	------------	------------	124.3	------------	-------
1991-2	136.3	------------	------------	163.3	------------	193.1	183.6	180.3	171.5	154.0	139.9	119.8
1992-3	94.3	81.0	93.1	101.7	123.2	148.4	152.6	167.1	157.0	159.2	144.8	143.8
1993-4	85.8	54.6	79.4	109.1	100.6	107.2	93.4	107.8	66.9	71.6	70.0	72.1
1994-5	112.4	105.6	103.5	117.0	114.7	122.2	150.5	129.9	120.8	95.7	96.9	92.2
1995-6	87.8	82.1	82.6	89.3	94.8	118.2	147.2	151.2	155.6	143.3	128.1	125.4
1996-7	101.2	94.1	97.5	102.5	106.0	120.9	133.7	137.5	131.7	116.1	103.4	85.9
1997-8	78.0	66.4	68.6	86.4	105.3	133.8	141.2	140.7	159.8	150.4	130.9	118.8
1998-9[1]	97.3	78.6	89.1	110.0	85.5							

[1] Preliminary. *Source: Bureau of the Census, U.S. Department of Commerce*

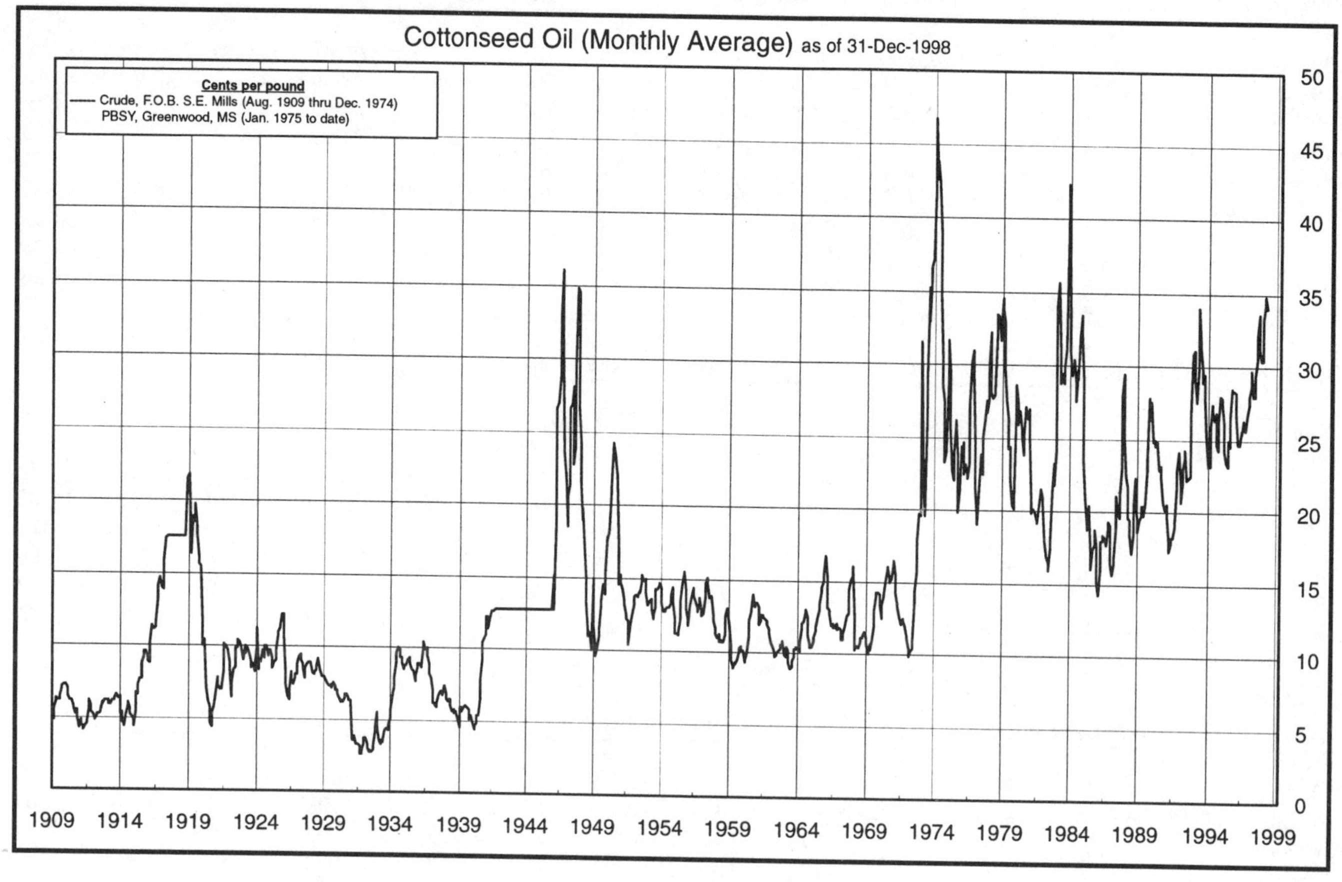

Average Price of Crude Cottonseed Oil, PBSY, Greenwood, MS[1] (Tank Cars) In Cents Per Pound

Year	Jan.	Feb.	Mar.	Apr.	May	June	July	Aug.	Sept.	Oct.	Nov.	Dec.	Average
1989	19.19	17.56	20.25	21.06	21.80	20.25	19.63	18.60	19.75	19.95	20.81	20.50	19.95
1990	19.95	20.19	22.88	22.83	26.90	26.94	26.00	24.60	24.88	24.80	24.19	24.75	24.08
1991	23.75	22.88	23.00	22.13	20.67	20.31	20.50	21.00	19.88	17.98	17.41	18.07	20.63
1992	18.50	18.13	19.25	19.38	21.38	22.58	24.45	21.86	21.04	22.17	22.96	23.91	21.30
1993	24.09	22.03	22.24	22.55	22.70	26.76	30.74	30.45	28.98	24.79	26.69	30.39	26.03
1994	33.16	29.96	29.60	29.06	29.66	27.55	24.20	23.71	24.51	23.64	24.85	25.50	27.12
1995	28.70	29.95	27.14	27.61	27.51	30.04	30.63	30.26	28.61	27.61	26.27	26.10	26.36
1996	24.45	24.35	24.25	26.77	28.46	27.94	28.25	27.81	26.13	24.55	24.28	24.29	25.96
1997	25.21	25.44	26.18	25.10	25.19	25.01	26.53	27.11	28.03	28.47	29.11	26.78	26.51
1998	27.69	29.37	30.46	32.47	33.13	30.22	29.40	30.11	33.26	33.99	34.16	33.57	31.49

[1] Data prior to 1995 are F.O.B. Valley Points, Southeastern mills. *Source: Economic Research Service, U.S Department of Agriculture (ERS-USDA)*

United States Exports of Cottonseed Oil to Important Countries In Thousands of Metric Tons

Year	Canada	Dominican Republic	Egypt	Guat-emala	Japan	Mexico	Nether-lands	Salvador	South Korea	Turkey	Venez-uela	Total
1988	4.8	3.1	29.6	.5	21.5	8.2	2.7	26.3	7.7	13.5	46.2	167.8
1989	6.6	5.1	39.4	6.0	34.3	3.2	3.4	30.5	21.0	2.0	53.7	209.4
1990	6.8	6.0	14.7	.4	36.7	1.4	2.9	21.0	36.0	-----	9.2	136.3
1991	7.8	2.1	14.7	-----	24.1	4.8	3.4	13.0	13.0	5.5	4.2	97.0
1992	11.3	1.0	8.2	3.2	15.3	8.5	17.4	26.5	10.9	7.0	3.7	123.3
1993	10.9	-----	-----	.5	17.6	5.8	.2	30.8	6.6	.5	1.5	83.1
1994	10.8	-----	7.5	12.3	29.8	10.3	1.9	26.1	16.9	-----	4.5	135.7
1995	12.0	-----	10.3	1.9	17.9	5.7	1.5	37.8	19.2	-----	2.8	133.7
1996	23.2	-----	-----	1.7	15.8	3.3	-----	20.6	8.1	2.0	-----	100.0
1997[1]	28.1	-----	-----	.4	11.3	2.5	4.2	25.3	1.9	2.5	-----	110.6

[1] Prelminary. *Source: The Oil World*

Bridge/CRB Futures Index

The Bridge Commodity Research Bureau Futures Price Index was first calculated by Commodity Research Bureau, Inc. in 1957 and made its innaugural appearance in the 1958 CRB Commodity Year Book.

The Index was originally comprised of two cash markets and 26 futures markets which were traded on exchanges in the U.S. and Canada. It included barley and flaxseed from the Winnipeg exchange; cocoa, coffee "B", copper, cotton, cottonseed oil, grease wool, hides, lead, potatoes, rubber, sugar #4, sugar #6, wool tops and zinc from New York exchanges; and corn, oats, wheat, rye, soybeans, soybean oil, soybean meal, lard, onions, and eggs from Chicago exchanges. In addition to those 26, the Index also included the spot New Orleans cotton and Minneapolis wheat markets.

Like the Bureau of Labor Statistics spot index, the Bridge CRB Futures Price Index is calculated to produce an unweighted geometric mean of the individual commodity price relatives. In other words, a ratio of the current price to the base year average price. Currently, 1967 is the base year the Index is calculated against (1967 = 100).

The formula considers all future delivery contracts which expire on or before the end of the sixth calendar month from the current date, up to a maximum of five delivery months per commodity. However, a minimum of two delivery months must be used to calculate the current price, even if the second contract is outside of the six month window. Contracts are excluded from the calculation when in their delivery period.

The 1998 closing value of 191.22 was 16.55 percent lower than 1997's close of 229.14, the third consecutive lower close, and the lowest yearly close since 1975. Only one of the 17 component commodities, frozen concentrated orange juice, finished 1998 with a gain.

Futures Markets

Futures and options on the CRB Futures Index are traded on the New York Futures Exchange (NYFE).

CRB Futures Price Index Component Commodities by Group

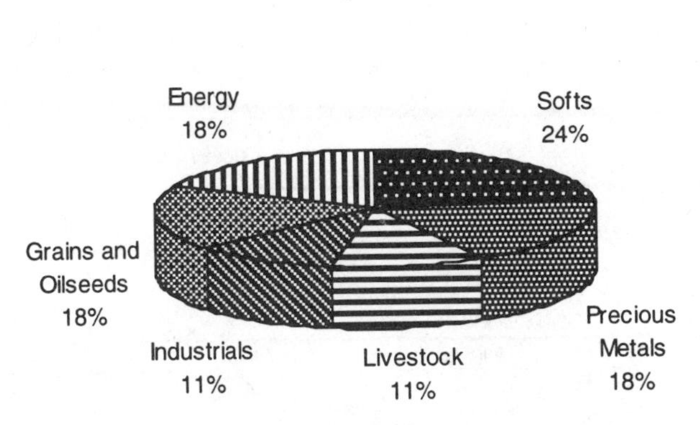

Groups:	*Components:*
Energy -	Crude Oil, Heating Oil, Natural Gas
Grains and Oilseeds-	Corn, Soybeans, Wheat
Industrials -	Copper, Cotton
Livestock -	Live Cattle, Live Hogs
Precious Metals -	Gold, Platinum. Silver
Softs -	Cocoa, Coffee, Orange Juice, Sugar

The CRB Futures Price Index is computed using a three-step process:

1) Each of the Index's 17 component commodities is arithmetically averaged using the prices for all of the designated contract months which expire on or before the end of the sixth calendar month from the current date, except that: a) no contract shall be included in the calculation while in delivery; b) there shall be a minimum of two contract months for each component commodity (adding contracts beyond the six month window, if necessary); c) there shall be a maximum of five contract months for each commodity (dropping the most deferred contracts to remain at five, if necessary). The result is that the Index extends six to seven months into the future depending on where one is in the current month. For example, live cattle's average price on October 30, 1995 would be computed as follows:

$$\text{Cattle Average} = \frac{\text{Dec. '96} + \text{Feb. '97}}{2}$$

2) These 17 component averages are then geometrically averaged by multiplying all of the numbers together and taking the 17th root.

$$\text{Geometric Average} = \sqrt[17]{\text{Crude Avg. x Heating Avg. x ...Sugar Avg.}}$$

3) The resulting average is divided by 30.7766, the 1967 base-year average for these 17 commodities. That result is then multiplied by an adjustment factor of .8486. This adjustment factor is necessitated by the nine revisions to the Index since its inception in 1957. Finally, that result is multiplied by 100 in order to convert the Index into percentage terms:

$$\text{CRB Futures Index} = \frac{\text{Current Geometric Average}}{\text{1967 Geometric Avg. (30.7766)}} \text{ x .8486 x 100}$$

BRIDGE/CRB FUTURES INDEX

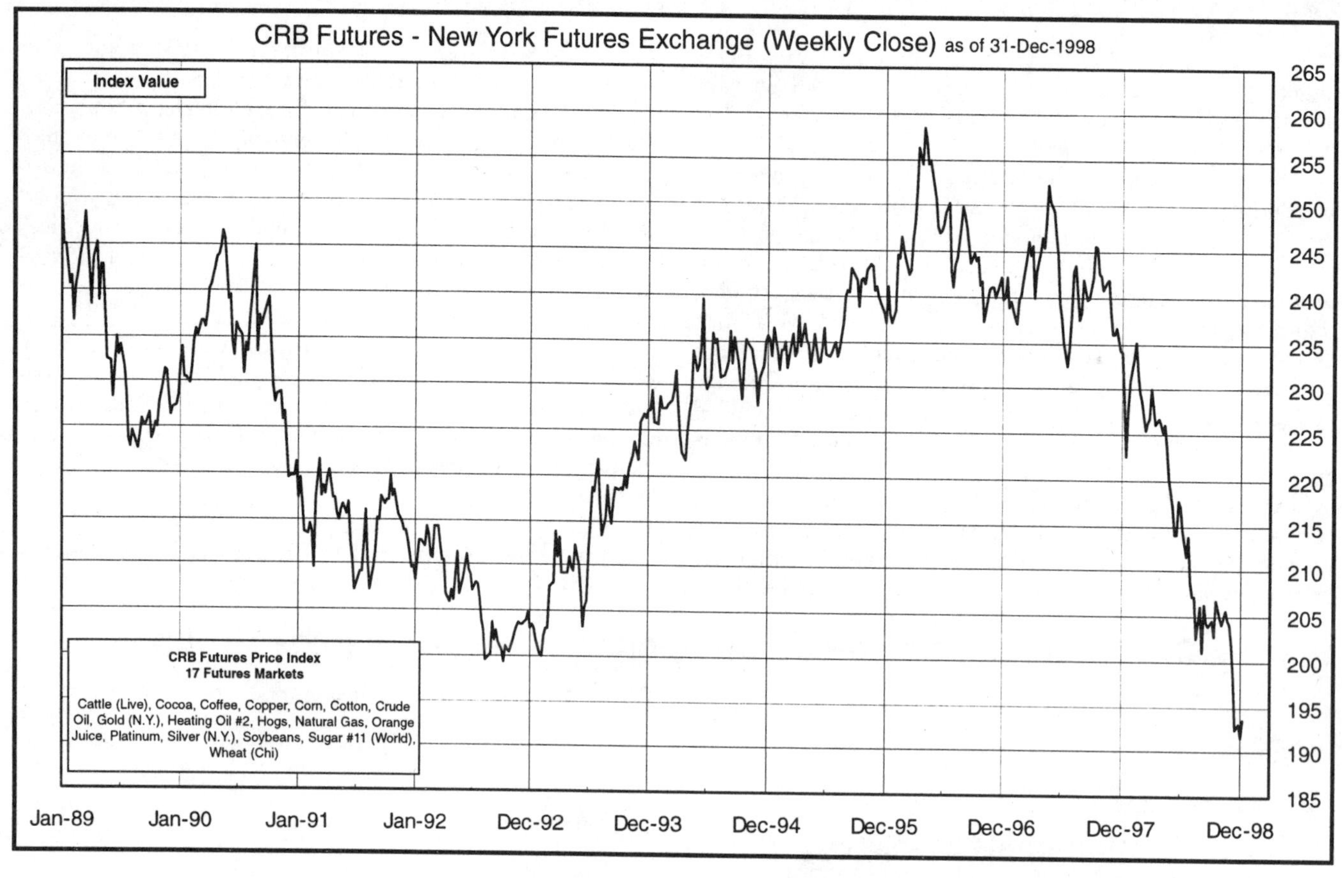

Average Open Interest of CRB Futures Index in New York In Contracts

Year	Jan.	Feb.	Mar.	Apr.	May	June	July	Aug.	Sept.	Oct.	Nov.	Dec.
1989	2,679	3,008	2,491	2,274	2,117	2,104	1,891	1,992	1,861	1,907	2,215	2,209
1990	1,889	1,229	1,476	1,858	1,499	1,459	1,289	1,286	1,181	1,247	1,505	1,530
1991	1,443	1,593	1,524	1,620	1,511	1,524	1,168	1,071	1,045	1,172	1,357	1,383
1992	1,435	1,472	1,185	1,347	1,311	1,087	951	1,179	1,075	1,226	1,283	1,406
1993	1,969	1,984	1,842	2,201	2,564	2,947	2,616	2,409	2,128	2,383	2,432	2,351
1994	2,607	3,146	2,680	2,691	2,339	2,698	3,838	5,146	4,562	4,942	4,535	2,800
1995	2,144	2,164	2,147	2,370	2,016	2,144	2,053	2,070	2,062	1,942	2,003	1,640
1996	1,934	1,826	1,753	2,355	1,881	1,890	1,562	1,345	1,596	1,853	1,861	1,866
1997	1,944	2,128	2,090	2,245	2,192	1,817	1,957	1,741	1,656	1,843	1,789	1,752
1998	1,679	1,557	1,626	1,509	1,641	1,895	1,832	1,719	1,839	2,162	2,639	2,787

Source: New York Futures Exchange (NYFE)

Volume of Trading of CRB Futures Index in New York In Contracts

Year	Jan.	Feb.	Mar.	Apr.	May	June	July	Aug.	Sept.	Oct.	Nov.	Dec.	Total
1989	8,805	10,045	12,035	11,437	13,145	13,824	11,917	9,846	7,918	7,412	9,613	8,551	124,548
1990	6,505	5,829	7,042	6,670	7,191	6,687	6,477	6,415	4,096	4,744	4,409	3,842	69,907
1991	5,835	5,391	6,715	6,432	3,671	5,557	4,853	5,876	4,414	3,766	4,132	4,543	61,185
1992	4,895	6,031	4,136	5,697	5,496	4,487	4,162	4,617	3,874	3,183	5,277	4,400	56,255
1993	3,620	5,720	8,050	7,340	8,680	10,722	12,418	8,590	6,192	4,350	8,535	6,954	91,908
1994	6,956	7,473	10,085	10,274	11,298	14,652	10,560	8,967	7,445	6,575	10,186	5,515	109,986
1995	6,151	5,545	5,763	7,955	7,877	7,573	6,875	10,094	7,376	5,030	5,865	5,309	81,413
1996	7,490	6,041	6,428	10,784	9,526	5,543	7,476	5,816	6,311	6,527	5,990	3,181	81,113
1997	6,645	4,942	5,245	8,600	8,156	7,776	6,248	7,685	4,537	4,588	3,468	3,592	71,482
1998	7,659	4,623	3,953	3,890	2,933	5,634	3,394	4,578	5,101	4,013	8,814	4,401	58,993

Source: New York Futures Exchange (NYFE)

Currencies

Trading in the world's currencies expanded rapidly during the 1990's and by the decade's end is projected to approach $2 trillion per day. Most of the trading is via electronic transfers for central banks and commercial banks, but a growing portion of the trading is on organized exchanges where intraday price swings often have speculative based roots that can exaggerate short term price swings. However, the U.S. dollar is the fulcrum from which the longer term market value of many currencies is determined. During the first half of 1998, the world's major currencies showed mixed results against the U.S. dollar; but on balance the dollar retained its strength reflecting a combination of cyclical and secular factors. The U.S. economy was undoubtedly the world's strongest and U.S. interest rates were high enough to attract foreign capital at a record level. Moreover, the economic crisis that took hold in 1997, notably in Asia, persisted into 1998 and the so called "safe haven buying" maintained a strong private sector enthusiasm for the U.S. dollar.

The second half of 1998 proved more volatile and the U.S. dollar weakened against a number of currencies. The reason was largely a reaction to three interest rate cuts by the Federal Reserve that dampened the enthusiasm for the dollar, notwithstanding foreign interest rate cuts. Moreover, the Asian and Latin American economic problems, while far from being resolved, at least lost some of their intensity in both real and psychological terms. Whether they flare up again in 1999 is basically anybody's guess, the uncertainty of which is apt to prevent the dollar from lapsing into any sustained slippage.

In mid-1998 the J-yen was trading around 140 yen to the U.S. dollar, ranging between 145 and 135 into early October; by yearend the parity was close to 115, almost unchanged from a year earlier. Japan's economic problems ran deep (with unemployment in late 1998 at a record high 4.4%) while fresh monetary and fiscal policies enacted in 1998 were seen as too little and too late. Ironically, Japan's central bank, which had voiced its determination to hold the J-yen's value via intervention if needed, proved hollow in the closing months of 1998.

The Canadian dollar and Russian ruble also plunged against the U.S. dollar in 1998, but the C-dollar finally stabilized in the fourth quarter while the ruble continued to fall. The latter tumbled to a 20 to 1 parity in December from 6 to 1 in mid-summer in a direct market response to Russia's default on debt obligations. The C-dollar at yearend 1998 was near $0.65 vs. $0.70 a year earlier. However, most the C-dollar's break came in the first eight months of 1998, the action ultimately forcing the Bank of Canada to abandon a policy adopted in early 1995 to intervene in the FOREX market whenever the U.S. dollar moved 70 basis points, in either direction, against the C-dollar.

The major European currencies firmed against the U.S. dollar in the closing months of 1998 as the FOREX market awaited the formal introduction, on January 1, 1999, of a single monetary policy and foreign exchange rate policy conducted in the euro. The European Monetary Union (EMU) commenced in May, 1998, and was the long awaited result of the Maastricht Treaty signed in early 1992. Two key questions focused on the euro as it neared its implementation: will it be strong or weak against the U.S. dollar and will it last? Advocates feel it will ultimately rival the U.S. dollar as the world's reserve currency; skeptics feel it will fail due to Europe's seperative political history.

The FINEX dollar moved in a narrow range into late summer, pivoting about 100. Following the early autumn Federal Reserve easing of monetary policy the index fell to about 91, and towards yearend was pivoting about 94. The dollar's outlook for 1999 looks promising. The U.S. economy's strong growth rate is apt to slow, but still prove much better than growth in most of the world's key economies. U.S. monetary policy could ease again, but not as much as seen in 1998, and with the new European union it's likely that any easing is apt to be on a global basis.

Futures Markets

The Chicago Mercantile Exchange International Monetary Market (IMM) trades futures and options on the Deutsche mark, Japanese yen, Mexican peso, Australian dollar, British pound, Canadian dollar, French franc, Swiss franc, Brazilian real, South African rand, Russian Ruble, the Euro, and the New Zealand dollar. Chicago's MidAmerica Commodity Exchange (MidAm) trades smaller futures contracts on many of the IMM currencies. The FINEX division of the New York Cotton Exchange (NYCE) trades futures and options on a composite Dollar Index and also offers crossrate futures contracts: D-mark/J-yen, D-mark/French franc and D-mark/B-pound. Currency futures and options are also traded on the Philadelphia Board of Trade (PBOT). 1999 is likely to see many new currency contracts added by various exchanges.

CRB Currency Index 1977 = 100

Year	Jan.	Feb.	Mar.	Apr.	May	June	July	Aug.	Sep.	Oct.	Nov.	Dec.	Average
1989	130.38	129.50	127.85	126.75	121.86	119.28	123.21	121.77	120.01	122.28	122.64	125.11	124.22
1990	126.68	127.50	124.71	125.11	127.77	127.85	131.67	136.42	137.52	141.69	143.64	140.48	132.59
1991	140.91	142.85	134.41	130.85	130.02	126.44	126.33	128.27	130.86	131.57	134.66	136.78	132.83
1992	136.15	133.37	129.33	129.78	132.13	135.42	139.83	142.26	140.65	136.30	129.70	129.91	134.57
1993	127.91	126.74	127.99	132.20	132.73	131.17	129.44	130.64	132.87	131.38	129.31	129.14	130.13
1994	128.54	129.57	130.89	130.57	132.23	134.18	137.60	137.51	139.78	141.94	140.29	137.85	135.08
1995	139.31	140.54	147.85	152.52	150.20	150.85	150.58	145.41	143.89	146.33	145.21	143.83	146.38
1996	141.69	141.01	141.12	139.61	138.11	138.37	139.53	140.52	139.51	138.74	139.92	137.47	139.63
1997	134.61	130.36	129.56	128.71	130.83	131.75	130.14	126.84	128.02	129.07	129.58	126.93	129.70
1998	125.06	126.10	125.65	124.96	124.33	122.86	121.89	120.65	126.18	130.98	128.86	130.69	125.68

Closing value. *Source: Bridge/CRB*

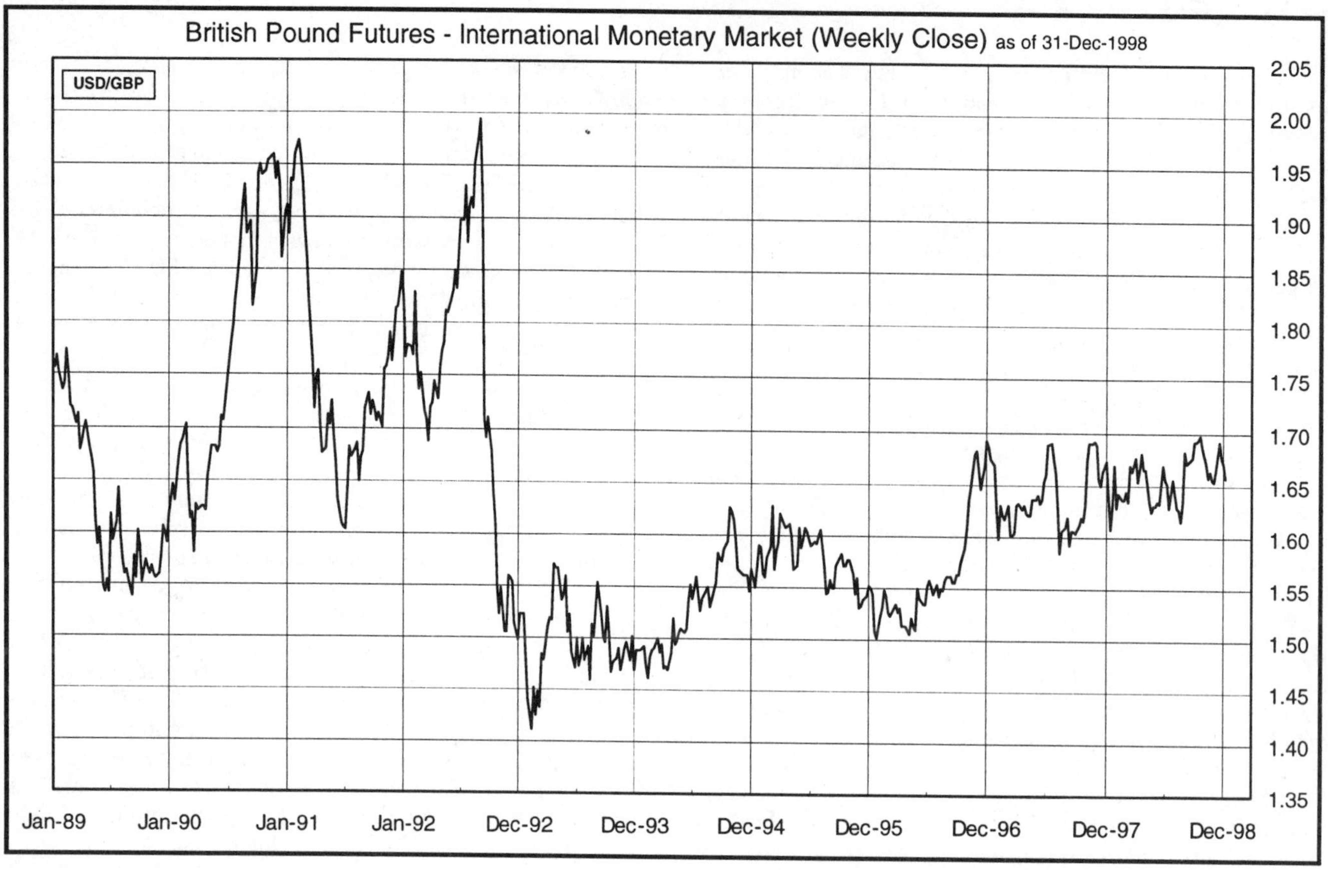

British Pound Futures - International Monetary Market (Weekly Close) as of 31-Dec-1998

USD/GBP

2.05
2.00
1.95
1.90
1.85
1.80
1.75
1.70
1.65
1.60
1.55
1.50
1.45
1.40
1.35

Jan-89 Jan-90 Jan-91 Jan-92 Dec-92 Dec-93 Dec-94 Dec-95 Dec-96 Dec-97 Dec-98

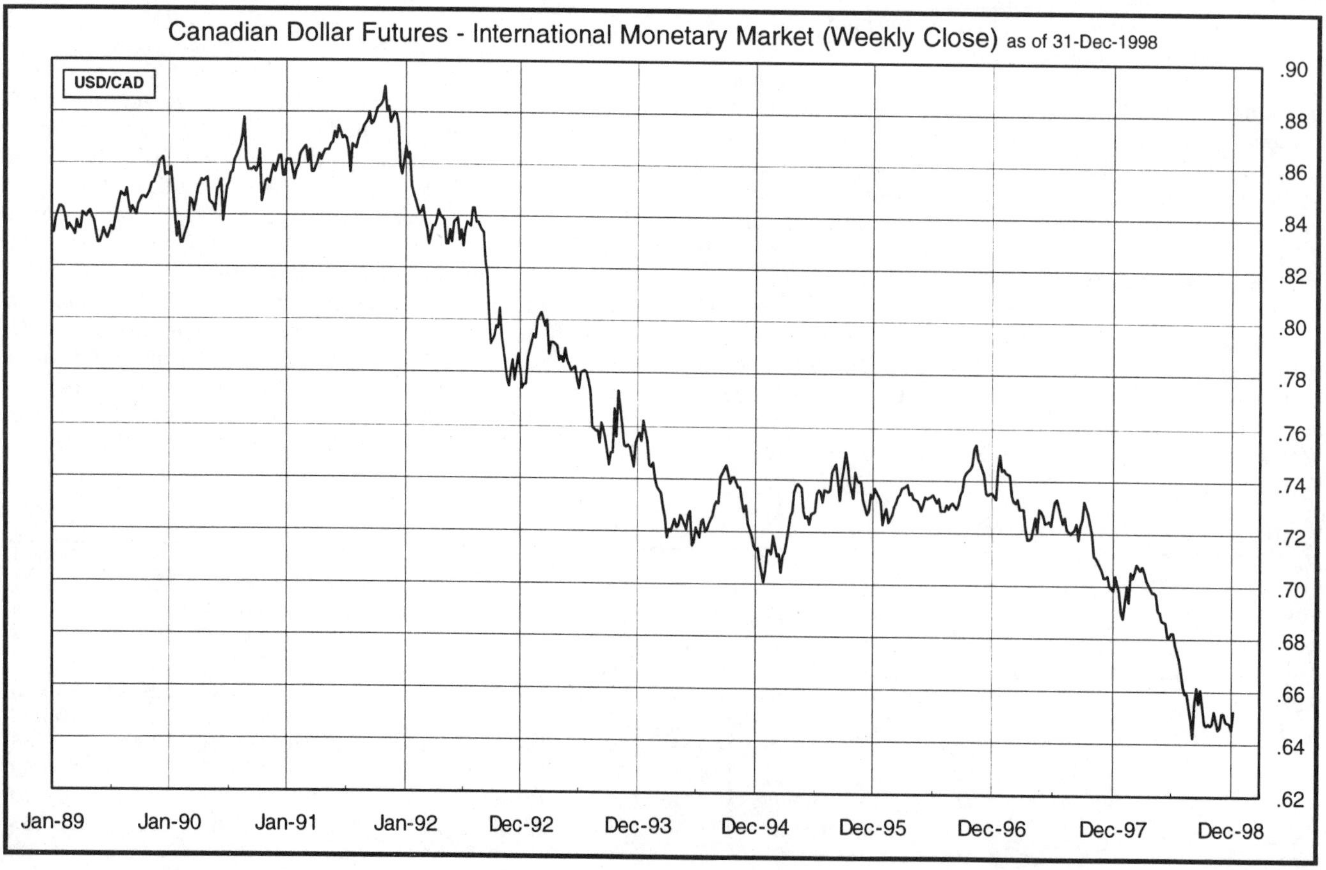

Canadian Dollar Futures - International Monetary Market (Weekly Close) as of 31-Dec-1998

USD/CAD

.90
.88
.86
.84
.82
.80
.78
.76
.74
.72
.70
.68
.66
.64
.62

Jan-89 Jan-90 Jan-91 Jan-92 Dec-92 Dec-93 Dec-94 Dec-95 Dec-96 Dec-97 Dec-98

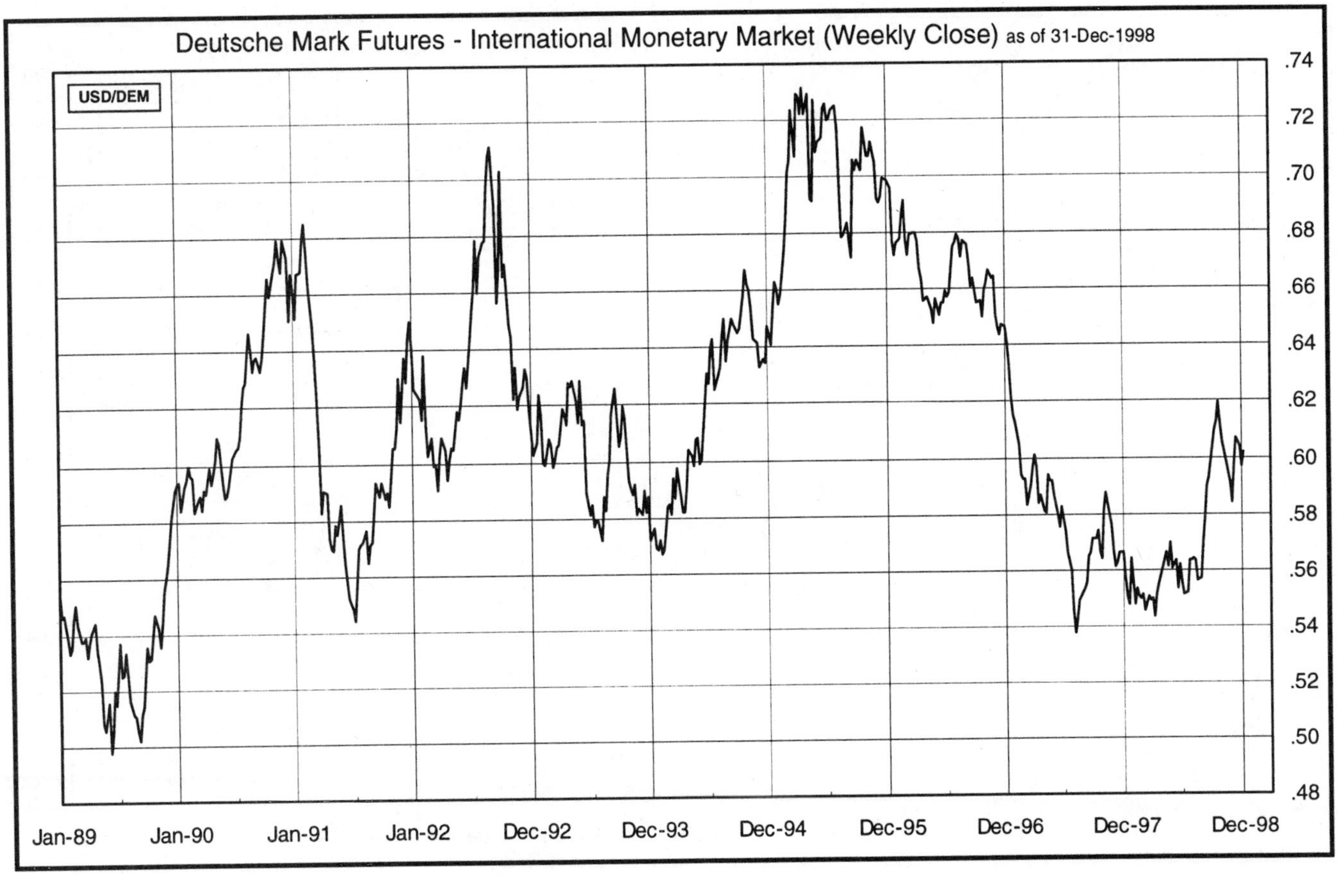

Deutsche Mark Futures - International Monetary Market (Weekly Close) as of 31-Dec-1998

USD/DEM

.74 .72 .70 .68 .66 .64 .62 .60 .58 .56 .54 .52 .50 .48

Jan-89 Jan-90 Jan-91 Jan-92 Dec-92 Dec-93 Dec-94 Dec-95 Dec-96 Dec-97 Dec-98

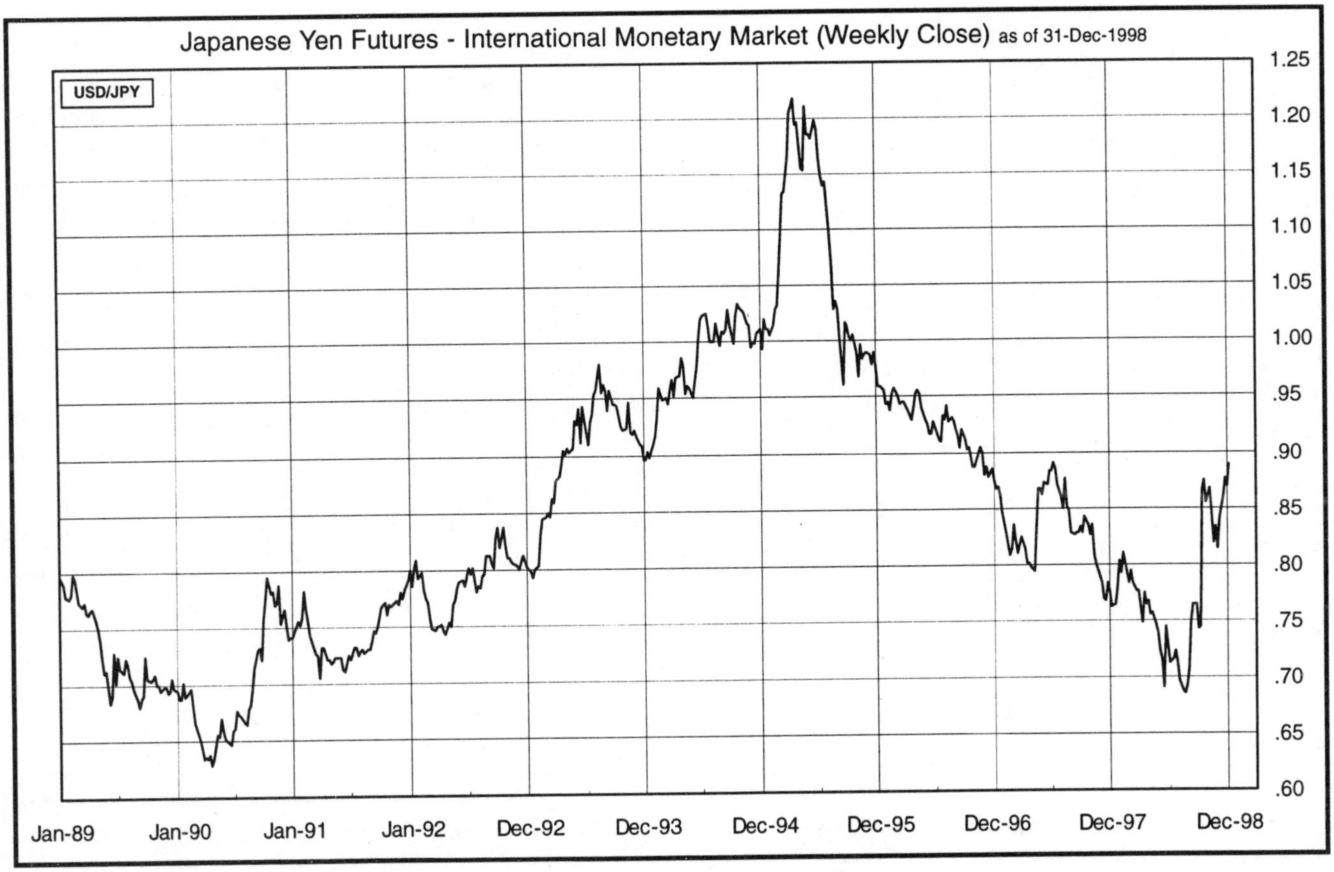

Japanese Yen Futures - International Monetary Market (Weekly Close) as of 31-Dec-1998

USD/JPY

1.25 1.20 1.15 1.10 1.05 1.00 .95 .90 .85 .80 .75 .70 .65 .60

Jan-89 Jan-90 Jan-91 Jan-92 Dec-92 Dec-93 Dec-94 Dec-95 Dec-96 Dec-97 Dec-98

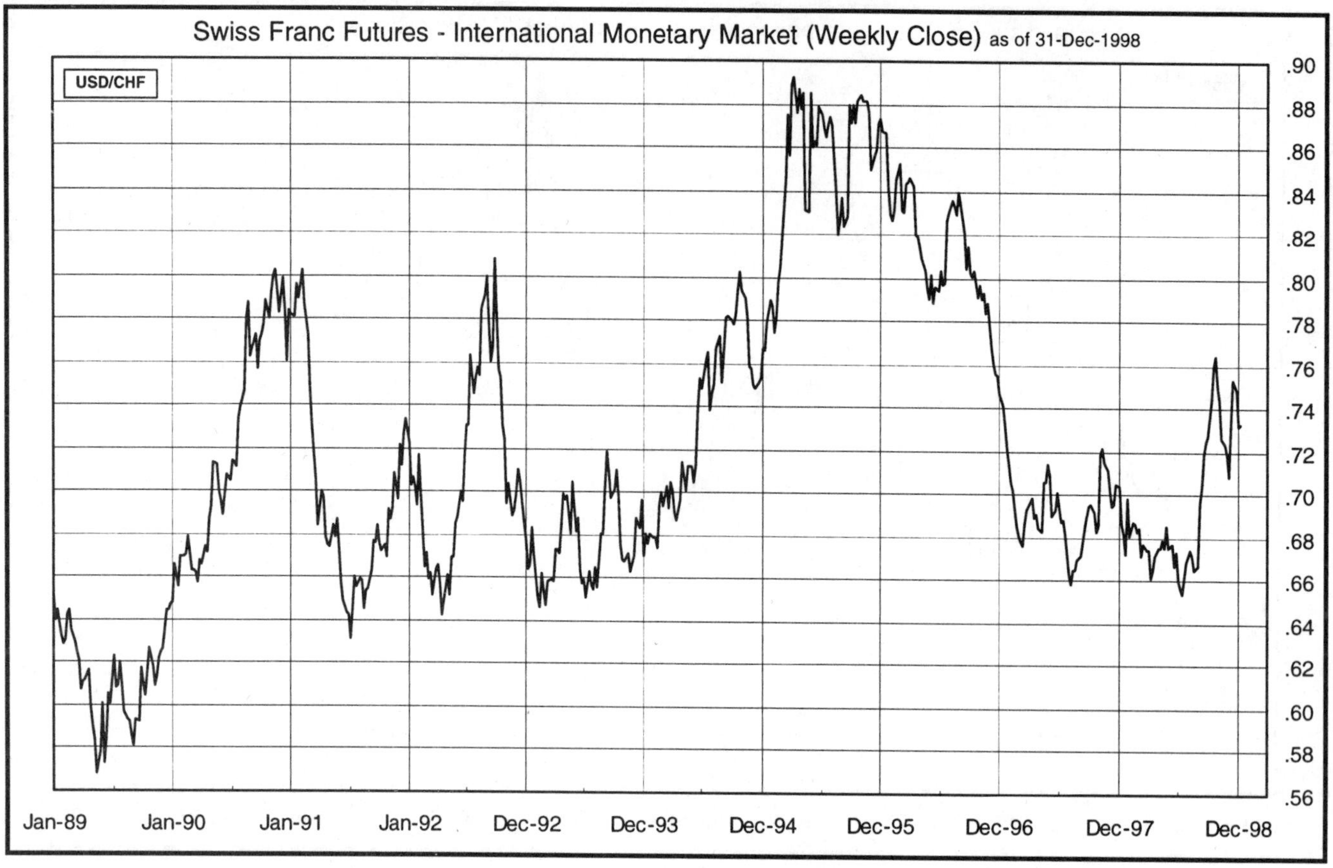

Swiss Franc Futures - International Monetary Market (Weekly Close) as of 31-Dec-1998
USD/CHF
.90
.88
.86
.84
.82
.80
.78
.76
.74
.72
.70
.68
.66
.64
.62
.60
.58
.56
Jan-89
Jan-90
Jan-91
Jan-92
Dec-92
Dec-93
Dec-94
Dec-95
Dec-96
Dec-97
Dec-98

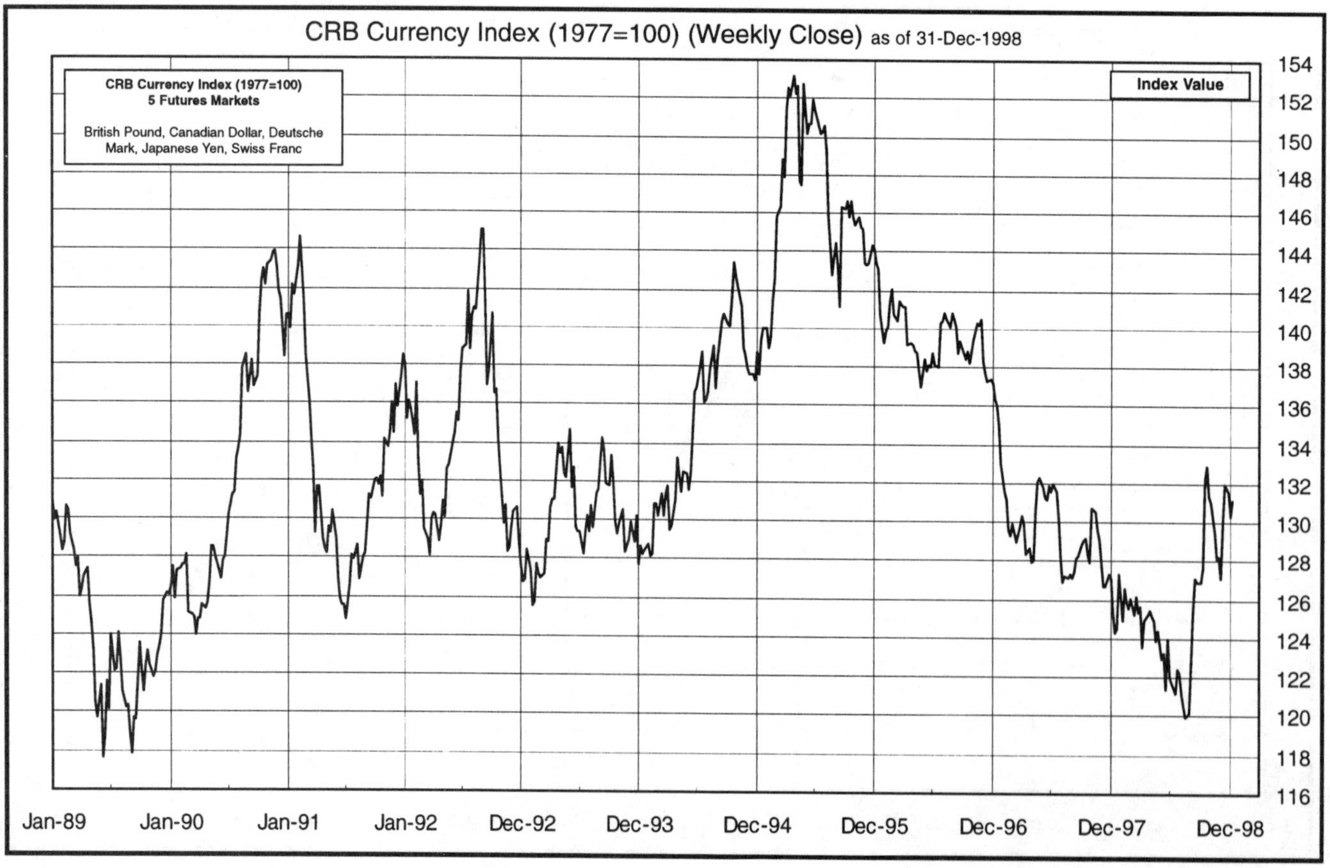

CRB Currency Index (1977=100) (Weekly Close) as of 31-Dec-1998
CRB Currency Index (1977=100)
5 Futures Markets
British Pound, Canadian Dollar, Deutsche Mark, Japanese Yen, Swiss Franc
Index Value
154
152
150
148
146
144
142
140
138
136
134
132
130
128
126
124
122
120
118
116
Jan-89
Jan-90
Jan-91
Jan-92
Dec-92
Dec-93
Dec-94
Dec-95
Dec-96
Dec-97
Dec-98

Canadian Dollars per U.S. Dollar

Year	January	February	March	April	May	June	July	August	September	October	November	December	Average
1990	1.1718	1.1967	1.1800	1.1640	1.1749	1.1728	1.1571	1.1453	1.1578	1.1600	1.1637	1.1604	1.1670
1991	1.1563	1.1545	1.1572	1.1535	1.1497	1.1438	1.1493	1.1451	1.1372	1.1281	1.1310	1.1474	1.1461
1992	1.1569	1.1827	1.1923	1.1871	1.1990	1.1955	1.1916	1.1906	1.2208	1.2440	1.2683	1.2711	1.2083
1993	1.2774	1.2595	1.2467	1.2616	1.2686	1.2788	1.2817	1.3078	1.3210	1.3253	1.3166	1.3307	1.2896
1994	1.3175	1.3419	1.3645	1.3821	1.3805	1.3831	1.3818	1.3777	1.3536	1.3495	1.3649	1.3896	1.3656
1995	1.4120	1.3995	1.4065	1.3749	1.3607	1.3772	1.3609	1.3550	1.3495	1.3449	1.3525	1.3685	1.3718
1996	1.3664	1.3753	1.3651	1.3591	1.3690	1.3649	1.3687	1.3717	1.3691	1.3501	1.3382	1.3621	1.3633
1997	1.3484	1.3555	1.3727	1.3947	1.3793	1.3844	1.3769	1.3894	1.3865	1.3863	1.4127	1.4272	1.3845
1998	1.4407	1.4335	1.4159	1.4294	1.4449	1.4647	1.4865	1.5344	1.5212	1.5430	1.5400	1.5429	1.4831

Average. *Source: Bridge Information Systems, Inc.*

German (Deutsche) Marks per U.S. Dollar

Year	January	February	March	April	May	June	July	August	September	October	November	December	Average
1990	1.6936	1.6764	1.7056	1.6857	1.6646	1.6828	1.6373	1.5711	1.5703	1.5235	1.4850	1.4969	1.6161
1991	1.5092	1.4812	1.6132	1.7013	1.7178	1.7833	1.7886	1.7440	1.6951	1.6913	1.6222	1.5597	1.6589
1992	1.5802	1.6193	1.6594	1.6486	1.6209	1.5713	1.4892	1.4459	1.4486	1.4860	1.5866	1.5826	1.5616
1993	1.6144	1.6427	1.6459	1.5939	1.6050	1.6541	1.7137	1.6927	1.6198	1.6396	1.6997	1.7106	1.6527
1994	1.7422	1.7340	1.6907	1.6969	1.6557	1.6269	1.5705	1.5637	1.5488	1.5188	1.5410	1.5705	1.6216
1995	1.5312	1.4996	1.4044	1.3792	1.4085	1.3988	1.3874	1.4457	1.4599	1.4133	1.4178	1.4397	1.4321
1996	1.4627	1.4644	1.4763	1.5053	1.5329	1.5274	1.5026	1.4819	1.5068	1.5277	1.5124	1.5517	1.5043
1997	1.6056	1.6749	1.6940	1.7120	1.7029	1.7269	1.7932	1.8398	1.7867	1.7556	1.7317	1.7787	1.7335
1998	1.8182	1.8115	1.8269	1.8127	1.7745	1.7928	1.7968	1.7858	1.7003	1.6400	1.6827	1.6699	1.7593

Average. *Source: Bridge Information Systems, Inc.*

Japanese Yen per U.S. Dollar

Year	January	February	March	April	May	June	July	August	September	October	November	December	Average
1990	145.13	145.70	153.35	158.52	153.77	153.74	149.00	147.47	138.76	129.56	129.18	133.88	144.84
1991	133.67	130.58	137.48	137.05	138.12	139.66	137.97	136.87	134.41	130.78	129.74	127.93	134.52
1992	125.24	127.65	132.79	133.51	130.61	126.72	125.69	126.10	222.58	121.23	123.80	123.94	134.99
1993	124.94	120.77	116.99	112.22	110.10	107.29	107.57	103.74	105.41	107.00	107.78	109.89	111.14
1994	111.33	106.22	105.00	103.36	103.76	102.37	98.65	99.88	98.78	98.36	98.08	100.08	102.16
1995	99.67	98.14	90.40	83.59	84.96	84.55	87.22	94.72	100.49	100.76	101.93	101.84	94.02
1996	105.66	105.57	105.90	107.23	106.42	108.91	109.21	107.84	109.87	112.40	112.35	114.01	108.78
1997	117.93	122.90	122.72	125.66	118.93	114.25	115.30	117.90	120.85	121.06	125.35	129.62	121.04
1998	129.39	125.71	129.04	131.79	135.01	140.40	140.75	144.51	134.45	120.49	120.41	117.01	130.75

Average. *Source: Bridge Information Systems, Inc.*

Swiss Francs per U.S. Dollar

Year	January	February	March	April	May	June	July	August	September	October	November	December	Average
1990	1.5179	1.4885	1.5128	1.4851	1.4202	1.4253	1.3909	1.3086	1.3061	1.2814	1.2563	1.2802	1.3894
1991	1.2712	1.2690	1.3891	1.4382	1.4557	1.5304	1.5507	1.5204	1.4819	1.4797	1.4357	1.3825	1.4337
1992	1.4045	1.4567	1.5072	1.5179	1.4895	1.4234	1.3322	1.2948	1.2763	1.3193	1.4276	1.4231	1.4060
1993	1.4775	1.5197	1.5199	1.4572	1.4471	1.4767	1.5138	1.4947	1.4158	1.4421	1.4966	1.4629	1.4770
1994	1.4707	1.4558	1.4295	1.4363	1.4120	1.3723	1.3256	1.3176	1.2895	1.2636	1.2974	1.3275	1.3665
1995	1.2865	1.2694	1.1691	1.1362	1.1678	1.1564	1.1542	1.1958	1.1868	1.1444	1.1440	1.1624	1.1811
1996	1.1810	1.1942	1.1945	1.2194	1.2546	1.2574	1.2324	1.2022	1.2333	1.2583	1.2757	1.3296	1.2361
1997	1.3925	1.4543	1.4622	1.4614	1.4298	1.4419	1.4810	1.5123	1.4702	1.4507	1.4057	1.4393	1.4501
1998	1.4756	1.4616	1.4896	1.5050	1.4782	1.4951	1.5126	1.4927	1.4002	1.3376	1.3856	1.3600	1.4495

Average. *Source: Bridge Information Systems, Inc.*

U.S. Dollars per British Pound

Year	January	February	March	April	May	June	July	August	September	October	November	December	Average
1990	1.6513	1.6960	1.6246	1.6376	1.6775	1.7112	1.8101	1.9008	1.8803	1.9481	1.9635	1.9208	1.7852
1991	1.9347	1.9641	1.8214	1.7514	1.7259	1.6491	1.6482	1.6839	1.7253	1.7214	1.7780	1.8311	1.7695
1992	1.8083	1.7776	1.7251	1.7562	1.8101	1.8555	1.9193	1.9445	1.8510	1.6547	1.5269	1.5497	1.7649
1993	1.5330	1.4383	1.4621	1.5465	1.5492	1.5090	1.4973	1.4928	1.5251	1.5027	1.4808	1.4904	1.5023
1994	1.4933	1.4787	1.4921	1.4832	1.5038	1.5261	1.5446	1.5421	1.5647	1.6073	1.5864	1.5582	1.5317
1995	1.5742	1.5727	1.6004	1.6087	1.5886	1.5960	1.5955	1.5668	1.5595	1.5782	1.5612	1.5411	1.5786
1996	1.5289	1.5376	1.5278	1.5159	1.5154	1.5417	1.5538	1.5501	1.5595	1.5863	1.6629	1.6660	1.5622
1997	1.6590	1.6258	1.6095	1.6285	1.6325	1.6457	1.6717	1.6044	1.6020	1.6331	1.6887	1.6606	1.6385
1998	1.6347	1.6402	1.6615	1.6720	1.6370	1.6509	1.6429	1.6355	1.6814	1.6933	1.6613	1.6713	1.6568

Average. *Source: Bridge Information Systems, Inc.*

CURRENCIES

Average Open Interest of Canadian Dollar Futures in Chicago In Contracts

Year	January	February	March	April	May	June	July	August	September	October	November	December
1990	26,426	29,204	23,848	24,048	33,823	30,809	39,843	42,092	34,998	29,434	31,250	25,272
1991	29,072	28,214	25,550	24,894	29,310	33,136	25,113	25,310	30,909	28,805	27,453	22,311
1992	19,724	24,020	24,118	21,354	24,020	22,860	24,773	27,665	28,221	27,827	28,025	24,923
1993	20,410	24,376	25,877	23,639	27,438	29,784	29,385	45,397	40,639	43,476	32,469	28,879
1994	28,277	38,157	48,411	42,730	44,363	42,845	35,370	39,582	49,312	40,706	42,353	59,763
1995	55,863	44,677	33,706	45,394	47,832	36,677	44,930	42,629	49,526	43,032	40,047	40,592
1996	31,028	37,674	38,551	41,411	46,470	37,141	37,522	42,063	44,014	68,674	82,817	72,586
1997	55,949	56,600	72,803	82,732	73,747	57,243	43,937	59,112	56,387	59,265	75,027	74,221
1998	63,300	67,862	61,528	58,938	64,859	74,027	71,313	75,193	60,863	51,967	61,318	50,271

Source: International Monetary Market (IMM), division of the Chicago Mercantile Exchange (CME)

Average Open Interest of Deutsche Mark Futures in Chicago In Contracts

Year	January	February	March	April	May	June	July	August	September	October	November	December
1990	63,745	73,216	72,357	63,058	70,475	65,113	64,765	72,684	58,241	61,839	76,650	67,322
1991	51,211	73,463	72,824	71,737	79,162	80,318	68,046	73,860	70,525	59,236	85,248	77,632
1992	60,390	69,246	76,614	74,945	85,123	74,761	79,297	93,027	82,287	87,679	126,380	132,676
1993	134,432	140,184	126,046	118,747	131,816	159,334	165,356	147,140	108,958	103,720	135,960	145,414
1994	146,742	144,594	118,301	99,177	125,321	108,586	94,767	106,647	108,742	88,784	101,376	101,548
1995	79,425	92,975	79,700	61,954	71,050	60,698	46,832	63,789	63,820	53,300	59,123	70,267
1996	74,553	79,549	70,804	75,370	86,672	71,984	65,130	73,623	74,561	71,361	70,936	72,887
1997	79,970	97,156	94,187	81,216	83,567	84,285	116,221	115,947	88,075	68,767	76,424	84,700
1998	100,408	80,368	94,147	101,005	136,541	111,089	98,008	102,060	155,231	137,632	105,209	82,045

Source: International Monetary Market (IMM), division of the Chicago Mercantile Exchange (CME)

Average Open Interest of Japanese Yen Futures in Chicago In Contracts

Year	January	February	March	April	May	June	July	August	September	October	November	December
1990	60,012	67,723	82,783	71,709	79,850	62,252	62,760	65,050	77,686	74,890	77,115	65,365
1991	43,552	64,694	57,115	49,060	52,964	55,727	53,045	56,496	66,174	74,353	74,585	64,219
1992	63,856	67,714	71,702	63,938	63,079	64,596	56,465	58,353	53,462	44,488	45,941	46,887
1993	50,066	70,195	81,979	76,696	82,028	81,103	72,186	80,780	73,002	83,097	84,812	95,817
1994	101,792	94,470	73,286	57,281	65,835	70,759	73,734	72,798	63,419	63,091	80,053	92,834
1995	86,569	86,852	77,649	63,379	67,644	56,285	48,680	63,463	73,830	67,336	73,335	70,268
1996	80,645	78,915	71,643	76,655	73,832	85,398	77,941	73,535	86,723	76,620	72,130	67,301
1997	73,391	82,542	78,466	81,117	85,984	73,322	62,488	82,369	96,468	90,080	130,606	121,001
1998	95,338	101,448	97,183	97,389	106,139	132,732	113,084	145,241	108,808	88,991	89,108	79,262

Source: International Monetary Market (IMM), division of the Chicago Mercantile Exchange (CME)

Average Open Interest of Swiss Franc Futures in Chicago In Contracts

Year	January	February	March	April	May	June	July	August	September	October	November	December
1990	36,339	42,435	34,953	32,853	45,464	42,862	39,769	48,544	40,269	37,216	44,166	37,220
1991	31,489	36,483	49,061	40,026	38,601	43,476	36,031	35,881	29,833	24,949	32,342	32,439
1992	24,653	33,640	42,825	36,230	38,269	36,668	30,159	33,707	33,167	34,767	45,428	44,901
1993	52,713	49,472	48,002	43,514	47,832	42,343	40,703	44,329	60,446	49,320	58,406	49,670
1994	41,914	46,280	44,134	37,450	42,071	49,162	45,223	43,746	44,495	39,587	51,539	55,424
1995	39,726	44,364	39,358	30,270	30,586	26,766	23,121	30,267	34,228	34,889	38,033	44,741
1996	42,280	42,902	36,924	39,233	46,810	44,848	38,300	40,298	43,695	47,613	53,581	59,405
1997	51,652	54,114	51,121	45,725	48,651	42,530	55,279	58,098	49,296	43,585	51,822	48,560
1998	57,740	46,160	67,722	67,303	63,477	77,564	85,984	70,569	81,465	57,413	44,810	43,436

Source: International Monetary Market (IMM), division of the Chicago Mercantile Exchange (CME)

Average Open Interest of British Pound Futures in Chicago In Contracts

Year	January	February	March	April	May	June	July	August	September	October	November	December
1990	23,272	30,729	26,219	23,909	33,355	35,528	37,898	41,820	33,458	32,213	39,623	32,790
1991	23,686	34,680	33,558	29,900	30,697	33,792	26,443	21,578	28,215	22,882	31,792	26,443
1992	21,578	28,215	22,882	31,595	36,426	35,529	27,160	28,041	30,137	30,330	33,121	27,935
1993	26,614	41,752	40,238	38,544	39,654	34,953	26,056	32,446	33,560	29,733	37,246	33,606
1994	39,223	43,878	35,554	44,725	46,577	41,801	37,633	34,988	40,751	42,648	49,684	65,834
1995	47,740	44,935	36,805	23,161	26,571	28,402	22,662	34,932	38,900	34,485	43,634	49,804
1996	40,315	50,106	52,349	54,954	52,573	61,461	55,080	50,862	53,868	51,934	62,128	47,652
1997	40,479	38,370	43,742	37,701	40,956	48,890	60,592	50,829	41,801	35,752	56,825	44,667
1998	33,616	31,282	38,712	41,256	47,303	55,511	39,156	49,645	63,756	53,458	54,004	53,578

Source: International Monetary Market (IMM), division of the Chicago Mercantile Exchange (CME)

United States Merchandise Trade Balance[1] In Millions of Dollars

Year	January	February	March	April	May	June	July	August	September	October	November	December	Total
1989	-8,639	-8,622	-6,954	-7,191	-9,463	-8,724	-10,582	-11,034	-8,971	-11,780	-10,754	-6,687	-115,245
1990	-9,640	-6,150	-6,369	-6,527	-7,308	-6,476	-10,759	-10,509	-9,157	-12,805	-10,529	-6,211	-109,030
1991	-7,079	-4,201	-1,889	-3,411	-4,158	-3,948	-7,894	-7,450	-7,111	-8,735	-4,942	-5,908	-74,068
1992	-5,470	-2,178	-3,527	-5,772	-5,409	-6,718	-9,893	-10,218	-9,693	-9,706	-8,644	-7,276	-96,106
1993	-6,113	-5,905	-8,886	-8,428	-6,542	-11,749	-12,609	-11,949	-12,516	-12,638	-11,521	-9,115	-132,575
1994	-11,999	-13,573	-11,477	-13,405	-14,079	-14,009	-15,831	-14,232	-14,566	-14,926	-15,292	-13,272	-166,192
1995	-15,746	-14,221	-14,487	-16,051	-16,010	-15,862	-15,887	-13,415	-13,243	-13,108	-12,324	-12,600	-173,729
1996	-15,623	-12,911	-14,574	-15,897	-16,826	-14,839	-17,757	-16,759	-17,976	-15,320	-15,176	-17,695	-191,337
1997	-18,167	-16,780	-14,896	-16,505	-16,982	-15,610	-15,864	-16,909	-16,524	-16,270	-16,605	-16,962	-197,955
1998[2]	-17,076	-18,120	-20,504	-21,335	-22,578	-20,530	-21,029	-22,735	-20,802	-20,629			-246,406

[1] Not seasonally adjusted. [2] Preliminary. *Source: Bureau of Economic Analysis, U.S. Department of Commerce (BEA)*

Index of Real Trade-Weighted Dollar Exchange Rates for Total Agricultural[2] 1985 = 100

Year		Jan.	Feb.	Mar.	Apr.	May	June	July	Aug.	Sept.	Oct.	Nov.	Dec.
1991	U.S. Markets	75.8	75.0	78.4	79.4	79.7	80.8	80.5	79.8	78.4	78.3	77.1	76.3
	U.S. Competitors	75.3	75.1	76.4	77.0	77.3	77.8	77.8	76.9	75.8	77.0	76.4	76.2
1992	U.S. Markets	75.5	76.4	80.9	78.2	76.5	76.0	74.7	74.2	74.2	75.2	77.6	77.3
	U.S. Competitors	76.2	76.8	81.1	76.6	77.4	76.6	75.6	75.1	77.2	75.7	77.7	77.4
1993	U.S. Markets	78.2	78.4	78.3	77.0	77.3	76.0	77.1	76.8	76.0	76.6	77.4	77.9
	U.S. Competitors	78.3	78.6	79.1	78.4	78.9	77.7	78.5	78.7	78.0	78.3	78.6	78.1
1994	U.S. Markets	77.0	77.0	97.1	97.4	97.0	96.9	95.3	95.2	94.3	93.8	94.2	96.7
	U.S. Competitors	78.3	78.3	107.3	107.6	105.7	104.5	101.5	101.2	100.1	98.4	99.1	100.5
1995	U.S. Markets	99.2	98.6	96.7	92.5	92.0	92.0	92.2	94.8	96.6	96.7	98.3	98.0
	U.S. Competitors	98.9	98.0	95.3	93.9	94.5	93.8	92.7	94.5	95.6	94.4	94.4	94.8
1996	U.S. Markets	99.4	99.2	99.4	99.4	99.4	100.1	100.4	99.4	100.1	101.1	100.8	101.5
	U.S. Competitors	96.0	96.0	96.3	97.0	97.9	97.5	96.7	96.2	96.8	97.4	96.5	97.8
1997	U.S. Markets	103.0	105.3	107.0	110.2	104.3	107.8	107.6	109.3	106.9	106.9	112.8	117.1
	U.S. Competitors	99.8	102.8	105.9	107.3	103.9	106.8	110.5	113.3	110.6	110.6	110.7	114.0
1998[1]	U.S. Markets	119.0	117.6	117.1	115.2	117.7	117.6	120.0	118.7	114.6			
	U.S. Competitors	118.2	116.6	116.5	114.2	116.2	116.3	116.3	112.1	108.8			

[1] Preliminary. [2] Real indexes adjust nominal exchange rates for differences in rates of inflation to avoid the distortion caused by high-inflation countries. A higher value means the dollar has appreciated. Federal Reserve Board Index of trade-weighted value of the U.S. Dollar against ten major currencies. Weights are based on relative importance in world financial markets. *Source: Economic Research Service, U.S. Department of Agriculture (ERS-USDA)*

United States Balance on Current Account[1] In Millions of Dollars

Year	1st Quarter	2nd Quarter	3rd Quarter	4th Quarter	Annual
1989	-21,747	-25,379	-30,740	-26,274	-104,139
1990	-17,319	-19,241	-30,591	-24,473	-91,624
1991	15,599	3,597	-15,834	-7,744	-4,383
1992	115	-10,986	-19,878	-20,625	-51,374
1993	-8,010	-19,884	-28,772	-29,467	-86,133
1994	-17,470	-28,892	-39,749	-37,714	-123,825
1995	-23,334	-32,545	-36,282	-23,093	-115,254
1996	-19,973	-31,732	-49,194	-34,016	-134,915
1997	-28,128	-33,393	-48,222	-45,472	-155,215
1998[2]	-37,218	-54,423	-72,128		-218,359

[1] Not seasonally adjusted. [2] Preliminary. *Source: Bureau of Economic Analysis, U.S. Department of Commerce (BEA)*

Merchandise Trade and Account Balances In Billions of Dollars

	Merchandise Trade Balance					Current Account Balance				
Year	Canada	Germany	Japan	Switzerland	U.K.	Canada	Germany	Japan	Switzerland	U.K.
1990	9.5	69.2	69.4	-7.2	-33.4	-19.8	48.9	44.7	8.6	-33.3
1991	6.1	19.0	96.1	-5.9	-18.1	-22.4	-17.8	68.2	10.6	-14.0
1992	7.5	27.9	124.5	-1.0	-23.0	-21.0	-19.1	112.4	15.1	-17.8
1993	10.1	41.2	139.3	1.7	-20.2	-21.8	-14.0	131.9	19.5	-15.5
1994	14.9	50.8	144.1	1.6	-17.0	-13.0	-20.3	130.5	17.5	-2.5
1995	25.4	65.0	131.2	.9	-18.3	-4.7	-22.6	110.4	21.4	-5.8
1996	30.7	71.3	83.6	.9	-19.8	3.3	-13.8	65.8	21.3	-3.6
1997	17.5	71.7	101.7	-.4	-20.6	-9.2	-4.7	94.5	20.9	7.9
1998[1]	10.4	88.3	126.0	1.5	-29.2	-12.6	8.1	121.1	22.2	-8.1
1999[2]	9.8	101.5	150.0	1.5	-31.7	-12.2	17.3	138.7	24.7	-17.9

[1] Estimate. [2] Projection. *Source: Organization for Economic Cooperation and Development (OECD)*

CURRENCIES

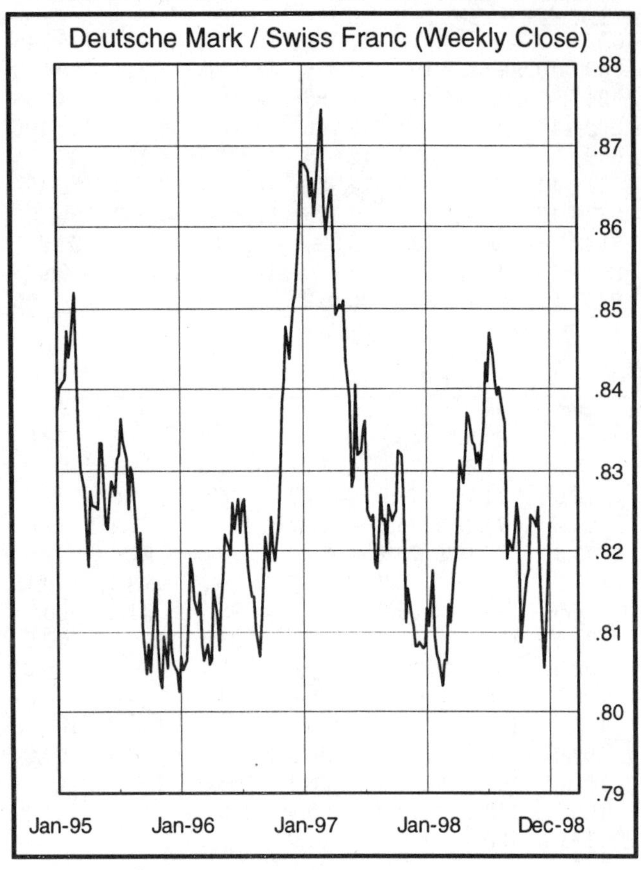

Deutsche Mark / Swiss Franc (Weekly Close)
.88
.87
.86
.85
.84
.83
.82
.81
.80
.79
Jan-95
Jan-96
Jan-97
Jan-98
Dec-98

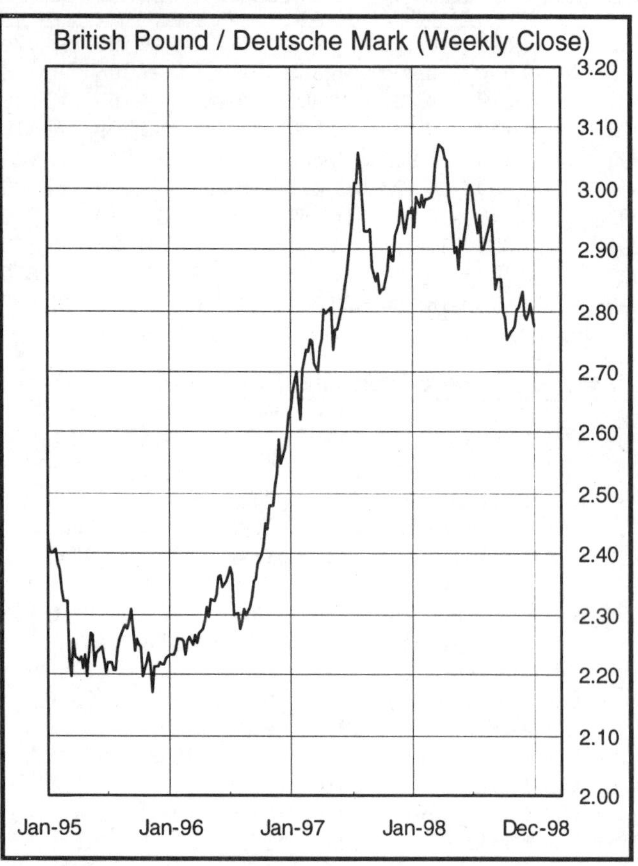

British Pound / Deutsche Mark (Weekly Close)
3.20
3.10
3.00
2.90
2.80
2.70
2.60
2.50
2.40
2.30
2.20
2.10
2.00
Jan-95
Jan-96
Jan-97
Jan-98
Dec-98

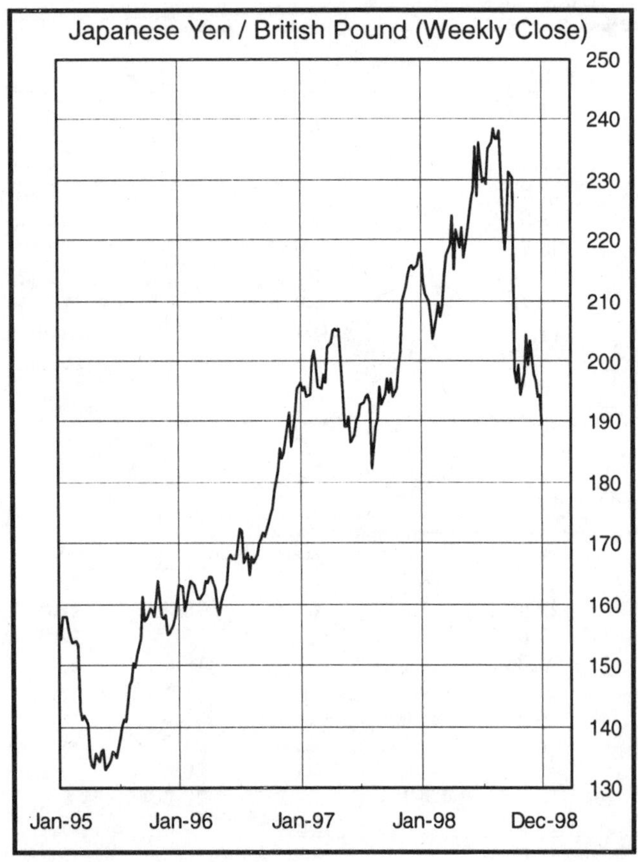

Japanese Yen / British Pound (Weekly Close)
250
240
230
220
210
200
190
180
170
160
150
140
130
Jan-95
Jan-96
Jan-97
Jan-98
Dec-98

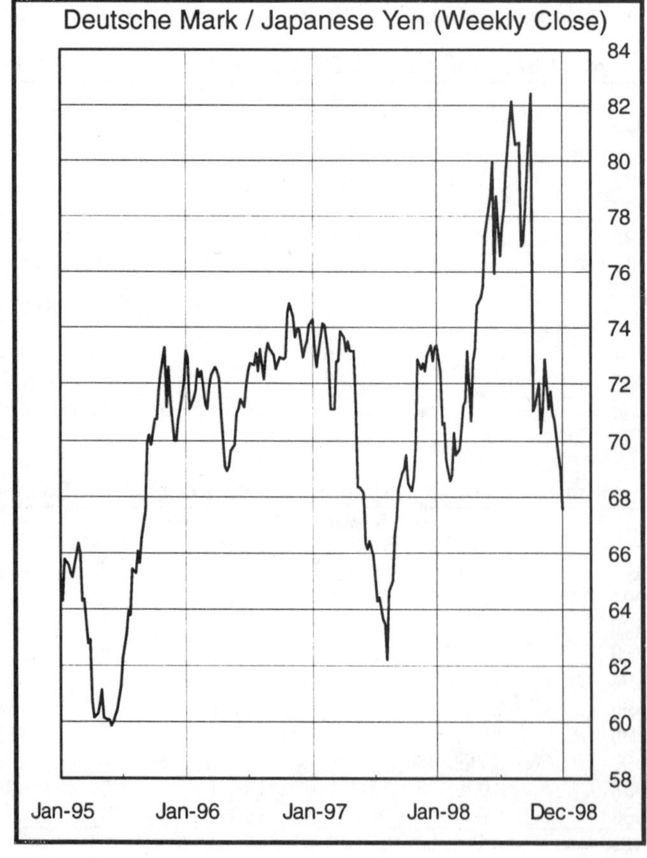

Deutsche Mark / Japanese Yen (Weekly Close)
84
82
80
78
76
74
72
70
68
66
64
62
60
58
Jan-95
Jan-96
Jan-97
Jan-98
Dec-98

Diamonds

Diamonds have unique properties that give them value in industrial and research applications. Diamonds are the hardest substance known and as such find use in cutting, drilling, grinding and polishing. Industrial-grade diamonds are used primarily as abrasives.

World production of natural diamonds (gemstones and industrial) in 1997 was estimated at 110 million carats. This was some 6 percent less than in 1996. World production of gemstone diamonds in 1997 was 52.2 million carats, 4 percent less than in 1996. The leading producer of gemstones in 1997 was Australia with 18.1 million carats. Botswana was the next largest producer with 13 million carats followed by Russia, South Africa and the Congo.

World production of industrial diamonds in 1997 was 57.7 million carats, down 8 percent from 1996. The largest producer was Australia with 22.1 million carats, down 4 percent from 1996. The next largest producers was the Congo with 12.5 million carats. Other large producers include Russia with 1997 production of 9.6 million carats, followed by South Africa with 5.8 million carats. Botswana produced 5 million carats of industrial diamonds in 1997.

World Production of Natural Gem Diamonds In Thousands of Carats

Year	Angola	Australia	Botswana	Brazil	Central African Republic	China	Ghana	Namibia	Russia[3]	Sierra Leone	South Africa	Zaire	World Total
1992	1,100	18,078	11,160	653	307	200	570	1,520	9,000	180	4,600	8,934	57,300
1993	130	18,844	10,310	1,000	370	230	106	1,120	8,000	90	4,600	2,006	47,600
1994	270	19,500	10,550	300	401	230	118	1,312	8,500	155	5,050	4,000	51,400
1995	2,600	18,300	11,500	676	400	230	126	1,382	9,000	113	5,070	4,000	54,200
1996[1]	2,250	18,897	12,700	200	350	230	142	1,420	9,250	162	4,280	3,600	54,400
1997[2]	1,110	18,100	13,000	300	400	230	140	1,500	9,550	110	4,380	2,500	52,200

[1] Preliminary. [2] Estimate. [3] Formerly part of the U.S.S.R.; data not reported separately until 1992. *Source: U.S. Geological Survey (USGS)*

World Production of Natural Industrial Diamonds In Thousands of Carats

Year	Angola	Australia	Botswana	Brazil	Central African Republic	China	Ghana	Russia[3]	Sierra Leone	South Africa	Venezuela	Zaire	World Total
1992	80	22,095	4,790	665	107	800	140	9,000	116	5,600	176	4,567	48,500
1993	15	23,032	4,420	600	125	850	484	8,000	68	5,700	155	13,620	57,400
1994	30	23,800	5,000	600	131	850	473	8,500	100	5,800	203	13,000	58,800
1995	300	22,400	5,300	600	130	900	505	9,000	101	5,880	66	13,000	58,600
1996[1]	250	23,096	5,000	600	120	900	573	9,250	108	5,670	55	17,000	63,000
1997[2]	124	22,100	5,000	600	100	900	560	9,550	90	5,790	50	12,500	57,700

[1] Preliminary. [2] Estimate. [3] Formerly part of the U.S.S.R.; data not reported separately until 1992. *Source: U.S. Geological Survey (USGS)*

World Production of Synthetic Diamonds In Thousands of Carats

Year	Belarus[3]	China	Czech Republic[4]	France	Greece	Ireland	Japan	Russia[3]	South Africa	Sweden	Ukraine[3]	United States	World Total
1992	30,000	15,000	10,000	3,500	750	60,000	30,000	80,000	60,000	25,000	10,000	90,000	422,000
1993	30,000	15,500	5,000	3,500	1,000	65,000	32,000	80,000	60,000	25,000	10,000	103,000	440,000
1994	25,000	15,500	5,000	3,500	1,000	65,000	32,000	80,000	60,000	25,000	8,000	104,000	434,000
1995	25,000	15,500	5,000	3,000	1,000	60,000	32,000	80,000	60,000	25,000	8,000	115,000	440,000
1996[1]	25,000	15,500	5,000	3,000	750	60,000	32,000	80,000	60,000	25,000	8,000	114,000	439,000
1997[2]	25,000	16,000	5,000	3,500	750	60,000	32,000	80,000	60,000	25,000	8,000	125,000	451,000

[1] Preliminary. [2] Estimate. [3] Formerly part of the U.S.S.R.; data not reported separately until 1992. [4] Formerly part of Czechoslovakia; data not reported separately until 1993. W = Withheld proprietary data. *Source: U.S. Geological Survey (USGS)*

Salient Statistics of Industrial Diamonds in the United States In Millions of Carats

	Bort, Grit & Powder & Dust — Natural and Synthetic								Stones (Natural)							
	Production															
Year	Manufactured Diamond	Secondary	Imports for Consumption	Exports & Reexports	In Manufactured Products	Gov't Sales	Apparent Consumption	Price Value of Imports $ Per Carat	Secondary Production	Imports for Consumption	Exports & Reexports	Gov't Sales	Apparent Consumption	Price Value of Imports $ Per Carat	Net Import Reliance % of Consumption
1993	105.0	15.9	133.0	107.0	.6	-----	146.0	.61	.1	5.2	3.4	1.3	1.9	6.85	95
1994	104.0	16.0	174.0	150.0	.4	2.0	146.0	.51	.1	2.8	.5	3.1	5.5	9.41	98
1995	115.0	26.1	188.0	98.0	-----	.2	231.0	.43	.3	4.1	.5	.3	4.2	6.62	86
1996	114.0	20.0	218.0	105.0	-----	1.0	248.0	.46	.4	2.9	.5	.5	3.3	7.54	88
1997[1]	125.0	10.0	254.0	126.0	-----	.7	264.0	.43	.5	2.8	.6	1.2	3.9	7.69	87
1998[2]	130.0	10.0	250.0	102.0	-----	-----	288.0	.42	.5	3.8	.9	.4	3.8	5.32	87

[1] Preliminary. [2] Estimate. NA = Not avaliable. W = Withheld proprietary data. *Source: U.S. Geological Survey (USGS)*

Eggs

Global production and consumption of eggs and egg products in 1998 extended the steady uptrend of recent years reflecting egg's strong position as a low-priced protein source. The U.S. accounts for about 12 percent of the world's total production (almost 80 billion eggs in 1988), most of which is consumed domestically. However, the U.S. is the largest exporter with 2.8 billion eggs in 1998 vs. 2.7 billion in 1997, about half of which were shell eggs. Forecasts for 1999 place exports at a near record large 3 billion eggs. Japan and Canada generally account for nearly half the total value of U.S. egg and product exports. Hong Kong, once a strong buyer of U.S. eggs, has seen its trade shift more to China. The European Union, paced by the Netherlands, imports U.S. eggs, but the demand within the union has relatively large variance and, as in Asia, demand is also subject to currency fluctuations. As of late 1998, it was uncertain what effect the adoption of a single European currency might have on egg imports from the U.S.

China is the world's largest producer and consumer of eggs, followed by the U.S. China's production has more than doubled since the early 1990's, with a record 360 billion produced in 1998 vs. 336 billion in 1997: total world production of 735 billion compares with 707 billion, respectively. However, a major difference persists between the two nations in respect to usage. Much of China's production is directly consumed as fresh brown eggs, whereas in the U.S. about a third of production is processed and white eggs are favored for table use. U.S. per capita table egg and product usage in 1998 was estimated at 245 vs. 242 in 1997, of which about 70 percent were table eggs. U.S. consumer preference, however, is showing signs of favoring egg products relative to tablestock. Total per capita egg usage is much higher abroad, notably Asia, than in the U.S. Japan's usage in the 1990's has hovered near 345 pieces. China's usage was a record high 288 in 1998 vs. 250 in 1995; Taiwan's usage in 1998 of 331 compares with an annual average of less than 300 in the first half of the 1990's.

Foreign trade in eggs is expanding; estimated at 7.3 billion in 1998 vs. 6.9 billion in 1997. After the U.S., the E.U. is the largest exporter with 1.6 billion in 1998, about unchanged from 1997. China's exports have nearly doubled in recent years, totaling 1.1 billion in 1998. Asia takes about 60 percent of the imports, paced by Japan and Hong Kong. Japan's import breakdown includes hatched, table, dried and preserved eggs as well as egg albumen and yolks.

There are definitive seasonal swings in U.S. egg production and table consumption. The table egg flocks typically reach a low in mid-summer and then increase throughout the year with monthly production peaking in the winter. Table egg consumption tends to be highest in the summer. Wholesale prices lack a clear seasonality, but on balance are highest during the winter months.

The New York wholesale market egg price in 1998 averaged $0.73-78 cents per dozen, the 1997 average was $0.81. Prices are forecast to fall again in 1999, to a range of $0.70-$.75 per dozen.

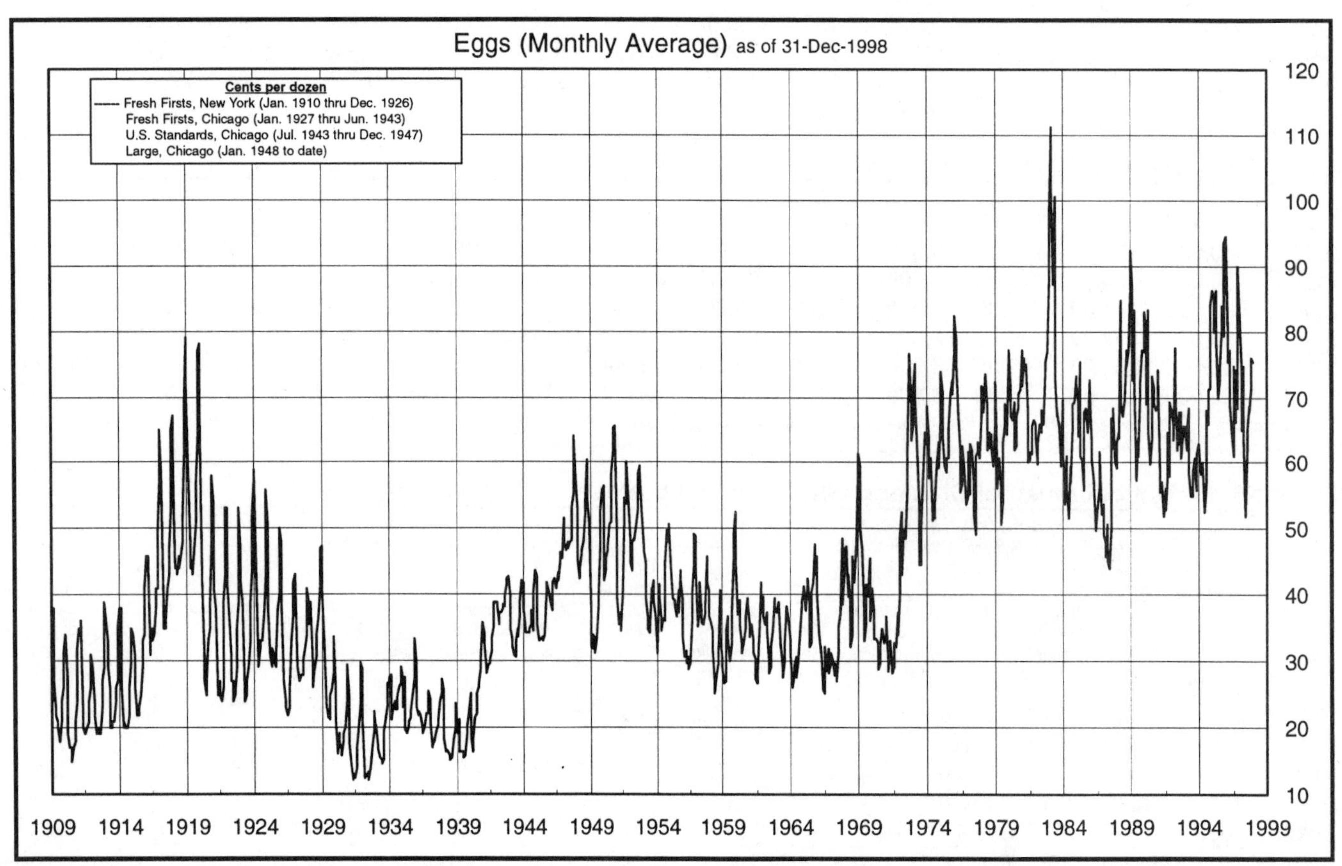

World Production of Eggs In Millions of Eggs

Year	Brazil	China	France	Germany	Italy	Japan	Mexico	Russia[4]	Spain	Ukraine[4]	United Kingdom	United States	World Total[4]
1990	13,454	158,920	14,629	16,800	11,454	40,318	18,040	47,470	10,659	16,287	10,658	67,987	526,296
1991	13,655	184,400	15,300	15,525	11,568	41,638	19,840	46,900	10,184	15,188	12,485	69,612	529,075
1992	14,190	230,980	15,375	15,165	11,454	42,911	19,650	42,900	8,675	13,445	10,699	70,860	541,859
1993	12,700	235,960	15,355	13,678	11,502	43,252	21,471	40,300	8,454	11,766	10,645	72,072	593,734
1994	13,460	281,010	16,370	13,960	11,599	43,047	25,896	37,400	9,670	10,145	10,620	74,136	644,545
1995	16,065	301,860	16,911	13,838	12,017	42,167	25,760	33,720	9,983	9,500	10,644	74,592	668,567
1996	15,932	312,640	16,500	13,922	11,923	42,786	26,045	31,500	8,952	8,633	10,668	76,452	681,964
1997	12,596	336,000	16,084	14,025	12,298	42,588	27,170	31,900	9,450	8,246	10,752	77,515	709,629
1998[1]	13,600	345,000	16,250	14,075	12,290	42,400	29,000	35,000	9,250	8,400	10,480	79,764	728,471
1999[2]	13,872	360,000	16,400	14,090	12,250	42,000	30,000	36,000	9,350	8,500	10,250	81,480	749,481

[1] Preliminary. [2] Estimate. [3] Forecast. [4] Formerly part of the U.S.S.R.; data not reported separately until 1987. [4] Selected countries.
Source: Foreign Agricultural Service, U.S. Department of Agriculture (FAS-USDA)

Salient Statistics of Eggs in the United States

Year	Hens & Pullets: On Farm Dec. 1[3] (Thousands)	Hens & Pullets: Average Number During Year (Thousands)	Rate of Lay Per Layer During Year[4] (Number)	Eggs: Total Produced (Millions)	Eggs: Price in ¢ Per Dozen	Value of Production[5] Million $	Total Egg Production (Million Dozen)	Imports[6] (Million Dozen)	Exports[6] (Million Dozen)	Used for Hatching (Million Dozen)	Consumption: Total (Million Dozen)	Consumption: Per Capita Eggs[6] (Number)
1989	271,064	270,415	250	67,503	68.9	3,877	5,598	25.2	91.6	641.8	4,917	238.6
1990	271,963	270,946	251	68,134	70.8	4,021	5,666	9.1	100.8	678.5	4,916	236.0
1991	279,325	275,451	252	69,465	67.6	3,915	5,779	2.3	154.5	708.6	4,938	234.6
1992	282,034	278,824	254	70,749	57.6	3,397	5,885	4.3	157.0	732.0	5,020	235.9
1993	290,626	284,770	253	71,936	63.4	3,800	5,960	4.7	158.9	769.6	5,082	236.2
1994	298,509	291,018	254	73,911	61.4	3,780	6,177	3.7	187.6	803.0	5,186	238.7
1995	298,753	293,854	253	74,591	62.4	3,880	6,216	4.1	208.9	847.2	5,167	235.7
1996	303,754	297,958	256	76,281	74.9	4,762	6,371	5.4	253.1	863.8	5,262	237.8
1997[1]	312,137	303,604	255	77,532	70.2	4,531	6,460	6.9	227.8	894.8	5,345	239.3
1998[2]	320,694	312,058	256	79,717			6,632	4.5	236.0	926.9	5,471	242.9

[1] Preliminary. [2] Estimate. [3] All layers of laying age. [4] Number of eggs produced during the year divided by the average number of all layers of laying age on hand during the year. [5] Value of sales plus value of eggs consumed in households of producers. [6] Shell-egg equivalent of eggs and egg products.
Source: National Agricultural Statistics Service, U.S. Department of Agriculture (NASS-USDA)

Average Wholesale Price of Shell Eggs (Large) Delivered, Chicago In Cents Per Dozen

Year	Jan.	Feb.	Mar.	Apr.	May	June	July	Aug.	Sept.	Oct.	Nov.	Dec.	Average
1989	64.57	63.79	84.68	69.10	67.27	69.55	69.30	77.09	74.70	76.90	86.48	92.25	74.64
1990	86.50	72.63	83.14	72.35	57.41	63.90	61.19	70.91	72.37	77.09	77.00	83.00	73.12
1991	80.19	69.00	83.10	64.59	59.93	63.35	73.07	71.30	68.80	67.96	68.50	74.12	70.33
1992	59.16	55.68	55.73	57.17	52.00	56.05	52.82	57.86	64.83	58.14	69.30	68.05	58.90
1993	65.65	63.61	77.50	71.07	61.90	67.64	62.79	67.59	60.64	64.21	65.55	65.55	66.14
1994	62.07	64.89	68.28	58.34	55.12	55.05	58.75	60.63	59.21	55.93	61.50	62.88	60.22
1995	58.55	58.24	60.22	59.87	52.50	56.84	68.10	65.93	71.10	71.34	83.93	86.35	66.08
1996	85.25	80.00	86.12	78.88	69.77	73.00	74.73	80.59	83.80	79.13	93.68	94.60	81.63
1997	79.77	75.18	77.25	68.55	64.40	61.02	74.66	66.07	74.26	68.39	89.87	82.68	73.51
1998	75.20	64.92	74.68	63.64	51.91	61.86	65.00	68.76	67.76	71.45	75.85	75.27	68.03

[1] Preliminary. *Source: National Agricultural Statistics Service, U.S. Department of Agriculture (NASS-USDA)*

Total Egg Production in the United States In Cents Per Dozen

Year	Jan.	Feb.	Mar.	Apr.	May	June	July	Aug.	Sept.	Oct.	Nov.	Dec.	Total
1989	5,758	5,182	5,782	5,569	5,696	5,498	5,648	5,613	5,450	5,658	5,543	5,781	67,178
1990	5,708	5,172	5,838	5,655	5,769	5,533	5,703	5,718	5,533	5,783	5,696	5,879	67,987
1991	5,865	5,316	5,935	5,666	5,796	5,643	5,840	5,855	5,675	5,915	5,811	6,035	69,352
1992	5,951	5,558	6,042	5,832	5,918	5,693	5,908	5,919	5,753	6,019	5,913	6,112	70,618
1993	6,030	5,432	6,067	5,861	6,009	5,816	5,992	6,015	5,876	6,144	6,085	6,296	71,623
1994	6,186	5,598	6,320	6,073	6,189	5,992	6,205	6,272	6,125	6,377	6,265	6,516	74,121
1995	6,369	5,714	6,448	6,177	6,251	6,010	6,145	6,146	5,990	6,260	6,232	6,523	74,265
1996	6,398	5,954	6,495	6,243	6,340	6,169	6,440	6,447	6,235	6,495	6,409	6,696	76,321
1997[1]	6,577	5,909	6,625	6,355	6,519	6,292	6,457	6,500	6,366	6,664	6,572	6,841	77,677
1998[2]	6,766	6,109	6,869	6,603	6,665	6,456	6,720	6,694	6,480	6,791	6,723	7,008	79,884

[1] Preliminary. [2] Estimate. *Source: National Agricultural Statistics Service, U.S. Department of Agriculture (NASS-USDA)*

EGGS

Per Capita Disappearance of Eggs[4] in the United States In Number of Eggs

Year	First Quarter	Second Quarter	Third Quarter	Fourth Quarter	Total	Total Consumption (Million Dozen)	Year	First Quarter	Second Quarter	Third Quarter	Fourth Quarter	Total	Total Consumption (Million Dozen)
1988	53.2	49.3	49.4	50.7	202.6	4,138	1994	45.0	43.0	43.9	46.0	177.9	3,864
1989	49.2	47.2	47.5	49.0	192.2	3,978	1995	44.0	43.1	42.7	45.0	174.9	3,834
1990	47.0	46.3	46.0	47.7	186.8	3,891	1996	44.5	42.1	43.4	45.0	175.0	3,886
1991	46.7	43.8	45.1	47.0	182.6	3,844	1997[1]	59.0	59.2	59.5	61.8	239.5	3,881
1992	45.1	44.1	44.4	46.7	180.3	3,838	1998[2]	60.1	60.1	60.9	63.0	244.1	3,908
1993	46.1	44.0	43.8	46.0	179.7	3,825	1999[3]	60.3	60.4	61.3	63.5	245.5	3,904

[1] Preliminary. [2] Estimate. [3] Forecast. [4] Data through 1996 are for Shell eggs. *Source: Economic Research Service, U.S. Department of Agriculture (ERS-USDA)*

Egg-Feed Ratio[1] in the United States

Year	Jan.	Feb.	Mar.	Apr.	May	June	July	Aug.	Sept.	Oct.	Nov.	Dec.	Average
1989	8.3	8.2	11.1	9.0	8.4	8.8	9.2	11.6	11.8	12.1	13.6	14.3	10.5
1990	14.3	11.5	13.0	11.0	8.5	9.0	7.9	9.9	10.9	12.1	12.4	12.3	11.1
1991	13.2	11.1	12.6	10.0	8.6	8.8	10.4	9.8	9.4	9.7	9.9	11.2	10.4
1992	8.4	7.8	7.4	7.6	6.7	7.0	7.3	8.1	9.6	9.3	11.2	11.1	8.5
1993	10.5	10.3	11.7	10.6	9.2	9.8	8.2	8.9	8.1	8.8	8.8	8.3	9.4
1994	7.9	8.0	8.6	7.9	7.2	7.1	7.9	9.0	9.2	9.0	10.3	10.2	8.5
1995	9.7	9.6	9.2	9.2	7.8	7.8	8.0	8.7	9.2	8.9	10.4	10.6	9.1
1996	10.1	8.9	9.3	8.1	6.6	6.7	6.3	6.9	8.1	9.3	11.3	12.5	8.7
1997	10.0	9.9	8.6	7.4	7.1	6.6	8.2	7.8	9.3	8.7	11.4	11.0	8.8
1998[2]	10.1	8.3	9.4	8.5	6.8	8.0	7.9	10.7	10.7	11.3	12.6	12.8	9.8

[1] Pounds of laying feed equivalent in value to one dozen eggs. [2] Preliminary. *Source: Economic Research Service, U.S. Department of Agriculture (ERS)*

Total Eggs -- Supply and Distribution in the United States In Millions of Dozen

	Supply				Utilization			Consumption	
Year & Quarters	Beginning Stocks	Production	Imports[4]	Total Supply	Exports[4]	Eggs Used for Hatching	Ending Stocks	Total	Per Capita (Number)
1993 I	13.5	1,461	.9	1,475	37.1	187.3	11.9	1,237	57.7
II	11.9	1,474	1.5	1,487	34.5	196.6	11.7	1,244	57.9
III	11.7	1,490	1.4	1,503	42.0	192.4	11.4	1,258	58.4
IV	11.4	1,535	.9	1,548	45.3	191.4	10.7	1,300	60.2
1994 I	10.7	1,509	1.0	1,520	40.2	195.3	12.1	1,273	58.8
II	12.1	1,521	1.1	1,535	45.5	205.3	11.9	1,272	58.6
III	11.9	1,550	1.0	1,563	49.3	202.8	13.8	1,297	59.6
IV	13.8	1,597	.6	1,611	52.6	199.6	14.9	1,344	61.6
1995 I	14.9	1,549	1.1	1,565	45.5	207.1	14.9	1,297	59.4
II	14.9	1,545	1.2	1,561	50.1	214.1	17.9	1,279	58.4
III	17.9	1,533	1.0	1,552	47.0	213.0	13.0	1,279	58.3
IV	13.0	1,589	.8	1,602	66.4	212.9	11.2	1,312	59.6
1996 I	11.2	1,571	1.5	1,583	59.3	217.4	9.8	1,297	58.8
II	9.8	1,563	1.6	1,574	65.6	217.2	9.6	1,282	58.0
III	9.6	1,594	1.2	1,604	66.0	215.8	11.9	1,311	59.1
IV	11.9	1,632	1.0	1,645	62.2	214.3	8.5	1,360	61.2
1997[1] I	8.5	1,592	1.9	1,602	61.7	221.2	6.5	1,313	58.9
II	6.5	1,595	1.5	1,603	50.3	227.3	6.3	1,319	59.1
III	6.3	1,606	1.6	1,614	51.6	225.1	8.2	1,329	59.5
IV	8.2	1,667	1.9	1,678	64.2	221.2	7.4	1,385	61.8
1998[2] I	7.4	1,637	1.5	1,646	60.0	226.9	7.9	1,351	60.2
II	7.9	1,640	1.0	1,649	57.0	235.0	10.0	1,347	59.9
III	10.0	1,665	1.0	1,676	57.0	235.0	10.0	1,374	60.9
IV	10.0	1,690	1.0	1,701	62.0	230.0	10.0	1,399	61.9
1999[3] I	10.0	1,665	1.0	1,676	60.0	240.0	10.0	1,366	60.3
II									
III									

[1] Preliminary. [2] Estimate. [3] Forecast. [4] Shell-egg equivalent of eggs and egg products. *Source: Economic Research Service, U.S. Department of Agriculture (ERS-USDA)*

Hens and Pullets of Laying Age (Layers) in the United States, on First of Month In Thousands

Year	Jan.	Feb.	Mar.	Apr.	May	June	July	Aug.	Sept.	Oct.	Nov.	Dec.
1989	272,243	272,780	271,590	269,278	267,269	267,239	267,088	266,253	267,656	267,919	270,006	271,064
1990	271,164	272,826	271,921	272,813	270,664	269,040	265,647	266,767	267,004	268,835	270,274	271,963
1991	273,917	275,533	274,446	272,541	272,150	272,944	272,779	272,998	274,277	276,187	278,433	279,325
1992	280,697	279,274	279,117	279,009	276,757	275,645	275,179	275,091	274,010	279,233	280,183	282,034
1993	281,639	282,933	282,005	282,480	281,468	280,795	280,517	282,201	282,341	284,771	285,298	290,626
1994	290,413	289,625	290,416	290,979	289,125	288,398	287,454	288,484	292,116	294,576	295,719	298,509
1995	300,331	298,202	297,689	296,290	294,697	290,806	289,018	286,519	289,595	290,889	294,486	298,293
1996	299,261	298,320	298,348	298,029	295,123	293,740	294,044	296,612	296,911	298,433	299,910	303,754
1997	305,011	303,449	304,276	303,997	302,766	300,692	299,007	298,844	300,138	305,664	307,146	312,137
1998[1]	310,296	310,946	313,068	312,557	308,709	307,994	307,809	307,833	308,769	311,835	316,234	320,694

[1] Preliminary. *Source: National Agricultural Statistics Service, U.S. Department of Agriculture (NASS-USDA)*

Eggs Laid Per Hundred Layers in the United States In Number of Eggs

Year	Jan.	Feb.	Mar.	Apr.	May	June	July	Aug.	Sept.	Oct.	Nov.	Dec.	Average
1989	2,154	1,937	2,178	2,111	2,165	2,089	2,148	2,135	2,071	2,142	2,098	2,181	2,117
1990	2,149	1,940	2,185	2,120	2,171	2,105	2,179	2,181	2,104	2,189	2,140	2,208	2,139
1991	2,186	1,977	2,217	2,124	2,168	2,108	2,186	2,190	2,106	2,175	2,124	2,208	2,147
1992	2,176	2,036	2,216	2,148	2,186	2,110	2,196	2,204	2,125	2,200	2,140	2,226	2,164
1993	2,192	1,970	2,209	2,132	2,182	2,112	2,175	2,183	2,124	2,209	2,167	2,237	2,158
1994	2,199	1,987	2,246	2,160	2,204	2,142	2,222	2,230	2,152	2,227	2,180	2,176	2,177
1995	2,130	1,919	2,173	2,092	2,137	2,075	2,137	2,135	2,065	2,140	2,108	2,183	2,108
1996	2,141	1,996	2,178	2,105	2,153	2,099	2,180	2,172	2,094	2,171	2,124	2,199	2,134
1997	2,161	1,943	2,176	2,093	2,156	2,093	2,155	2,165	2,096	2,172	2,122	2,193	2,127
1998[1]	2,170	1,946	2,183	2,115	2,150	2,086	2,172	2,165	2,081	2,157	2,109		2,121

[1] Preliminary. *Source: National Agricultural Statistics Service, U.S. Department of Agriculture (NASS-USDA)*

Egg-Type Chicks Hatched by Commercial Hatcheries in the United States In Thousands

Year	Jan.	Feb.	Mar.	Apr.	May	June	July	Aug.	Sept.	Oct.	Nov.	Dec.	Total
1989	26,602	27,271	32,597	36,135	38,376	34,708	29,828	32,217	32,862	33,456	29,666	29,284	383,002
1990	32,004	32,107	36,509	36,915	37,895	34,471	31,582	32,949	31,219	32,926	29,809	31,046	398,432
1991	34,487	34,837	37,041	39,775	38,404	36,227	33,696	33,656	34,007	34,307	30,400	32,717	419,554
1992	32,496	31,950	36,490	35,755	38,513	34,568	32,265	28,349	28,760	32,843	27,718	31,612	391,319
1993	34,885	34,009	38,264	37,163	36,742	35,587	33,980	31,455	31,775	31,634	30,074	30,448	405,986
1994	33,236	31,086	33,489	35,657	35,322	31,985	29,613	31,295	31,587	32,066	26,075	30,166	381,577
1995	32,374	32,743	36,019	35,078	37,540	34,996	29,572	31,442	33,586	33,383	29,129	30,639	396,501
1996	31,523	34,627	37,474	35,628	38,607	34,076	33,331	32,393	32,070	33,065	31,437	33,017	407,248
1997	33,815	35,762	37,410	38,873	39,078	36,861	33,838	33,125	37,181	35,328	27,846	35,890	425,007
1998[1]	37,234	34,573	39,986	39,926	39,602	39,206	36,567	33,514	38,611	35,039	30,810	35,430	440,498

[1] Preliminary. *Source: National Agricultural Statistics Service, U.S. Department of Agriculture (NASS-USDA)*

Cold Storage Holdings of Frozen Eggs in the United States, on First of Month In Millions of Pounds[1]

Year	Jan.	Feb.	Mar.	Apr.	May	June	July	Aug.	Sept.	Oct.	Nov.	Dec.
1989	19.6	19.7	19.0	14.8	15.3	16.2	15.1	16.5	15.0	14.4	14.9	13.4
1990	13.6	14.2	15.2	16.8	19.7	16.8	18.1	17.1	17.1	16.6	16.8	17.2
1991	14.7	14.8	14.0	14.1	13.0	13.5	14.2	18.1	16.3	16.5	17.0	15.1
1992	16.0	20.0	19.2	19.7	18.8	18.9	21.1	19.5	20.2	20.0	21.7	18.7
1993	17.2	16.7	16.9	15.1	14.3	15.5	15.1	17.6	18.1	14.4	14.0	13.5
1994	13.7	14.8	15.8	15.6	16.3	15.2	15.4	19.0	19.7	17.8	20.0	19.1
1995	19.5	19.5	18.3	18.5	17.3	18.1	22.9	20.6	18.0	16.2	14.4	12.5
1996	13.8	15.6	16.2	12.4	11.5	11.4	11.7	13.5	15.0	14.9	12.6	10.4
1997	10.2	11.0	11.5	8.5	8.5	8.3	8.6	8.9	11.1	10.8	10.9	10.3
1998[2]	9.7	12.0	12.3	10.4	9.2	12.9	10.2	11.8	9.0	8.3	9.0	9.3

[1] Converted on basis 39.5 pounds frozen eggs equal 1 case [2] Preliminary. *Source: National Agricultural Statistics Service, U.S. Department of Agriculture*

Electric Power

U. S. net generation of electric power in the January-July 1998 period was 1.86 trillion kilowatthours. That was 4 percent higher than in 1997 when it was 1.8 trillion kilowatthours. For all of 1997, U.S. electric power generation was 3.12 trillion kilowatthours. For 1998, coal powered utilities provided 56 percent of the electricity generated. Nuclear powered plants provided 20 percent of the electricity while hydroelectric power accounted for 11 percent.

In July 1998, U.S. generation of electric power was 318 billion kilowatthours. That was an increase of 9 percent from the previous month and 4 percent higher than a year ago. Electric power generation tends to be highest in the months of July and August. Of the July 1998 total electric power output, some 173 billion kilowatthours were provided by coal-powered electric utilities. Another 13.6 billion kilowatthours came from petroleum-powered electric utilities. Gas-powered electric utilities generated 42.1 billion kilowatthours. Nuclear-powered electric utilities provided 61.5 billion kilowatthours. Hydroelectric-based utilities generated 26.7 billion kilowatthours in July 1998. Geothermal-powered utilities provided 448 million kilowatthours while other alternatively powered utilities such as biomass, wind, photoelectric and solar thermal generated 173 million kilowatthours.

Electric utility consumption of coal in July 1998 was 87.5 million short tons. That was up 10 percent from the previous month and up 3 percent from a year ago. For the January-July 1998 period, coal consumption was 526.7 million tons, an increase of 3 percent from the year before. Petroleum consumption by electric utilities in July 1998 was 22.8 million barrels, an increase of 14 percent from the previous month and 51 percent more than a year ago. For the January-July 1998 period, petroleum consumption was 102.2 million barrels, up 52 percent from the same period of 1997. Electric utility consumption of gas in July 1998 was 448.9 million cubic feet, an increase of 18 percent from the previous month and some 5 percent more than a year ago. For the first seven months of 1998, gas consumption by electric utilities was 1.81 billion cubic feet, up 12 percent from the same period of 1997.

Electric utility stocks of coal at the end of July 1998 were 109.8 million short tons, down 7 percent from June 1998 and just about the same as a year before. Stocks of petroleum at the end of July 1998 were 46.7 million barrels, up 5 percent from the previous month and 2 percent more than a year ago.

Retail sales of electricity to residential customers in July 1998 were 121.3 billion kilowatthours, up 23 percent from the previous month and 11 percent more than a year ago. For the January-July 1998 period, sales to residential customers were 647.8 billion kilowatthours, up 6 percent from the same period of 1997.

World Electricity Production (Monthly Average) In Millions of Kilowatt Hours

Year	Australia	Canada	China	Germany	India	Italy	Japan	Rep. of Korea	Russia[3]	South Africa	Ukraine[3]	United Kingdom	United States
1988	11,592	42,164	49,460	35,228	18,427	16,931	62,811	7,122	142,090	13,062	------	25,761	239,875
1989	12,316	41,628	49,549	36,716	20,428	17,570	66,563	7,873	143,500	13,527	------	25,153	246,659
1990	12,923	40,169	51,500	37,433	22,025	18,074	71,439	8,972	139,455	13,782	------	26,581	250,979
1991	13,071	42,326	55,918	44,949	23,893	18,503	74,007	9,885	136,156	14,026	------	26,900	254,818
1992	13,313	41,803	61,562	44,761	25,081	18,854	74,611	10,914	84,038	14,008	21,044	27,240	256,209
1993	13,646	42,591	67,723	37,722	26,961	18,566	75,559	12,036	79,716	14,572	19,159	26,834	262,158
1994	13,929	44,502	75,312	37,786	29,250	19,292	80,361	13,754	72,993	15,650	17,425	27,637	272,354
1995	14,450	44,868	81,979	38,207	31,675	20,093	82,490	15,388	71,669	15,752	16,167	27,870	278,776
1996	14,777	45,747	88,275	45,586	32,808	21,227	84,345	17,124	70,600	16,679	15,086	28,989	288,256
1997[1]	14,404	44,956	91,277	45,133	35,105	22,329	75,439	18,704	68,722	17,525	17,100	27,470	285,455
1998[2]	14,587		92,532		37,287		75,540	17,702	67,450	17,325	16,726	30,327	

[1] Preliminary. [2] Estimate. [3] Formerly part of the U.S.S.R.; data not reported separately until 1992. *Source: United Nations*

Installed Capacity, Capability & Peak Load of the U.S. Electric Utility Industry In Millions of Kilowatt Hours

	Installed Generating Capacity at Dec. 31													Capacity	Total	
		Type of Prime Mover				Type of Ownership						Capability	Non-Co incident	Margin Non-Co incident	Electric Utility	Annual Peak
Year	Total Electric Utility Industry	Hydro	Gas Turbine & Steam	Nuclear Power	Internal Combustion	Investor Owned	Cooperative	Sub-total Gov't.	Municipal Utilities	Federal	Power Districts, State Projects	at Winter Peak Load	Winter Peak Load	Peak Load (%)	Industry Generation	Load Factor (%)
1988	723.9	86.9	526.6	103.4	7.0	557.8	26.4	139.7	40.4	64.8	34.5	676.9	466.5	20.0	2,704.3	59.5
1989	730.9	87.5	529.1	106.7	7.5	562.1	26.4	142.4	40.7	67.2	34.5	685.2	496.4	22.3	2,784.3	62.2
1990	735.1	87.2	531.1	108.0	8.7	568.8	26.3	139.9	40.1	65.4	34.4	696.8	484.0	20.4	2,808.2	60.4
1991	740.0	88.7	534.1	108.4	8.8	573.0	26.5	140.5	40.4	65.6	34.5	703.2	485.4	20.2	2,825.0	60.9
1992	741.7	89.7	534.5	107.9	9.6	572.9	26.0	142.7	41.6	66.1	35.0	707.8	493.0	21.1	2,797.2	61.1
1993	744.7	90.2	536.9	107.8	9.8	575.2	26.1	143.4	41.8	66.1	35.5	712.0	521.7	17.1	2,882.5	61.0
1994	746.0	90.3	537.9	107.9	9.9	574.8	26.4	144.7	42.0	66.3	36.4	715.1	518.3	16.7	2,910.7	61.2
1995	750.5	91.1	541.6	107.9	9.9	578.7	27.1	144.8	42.2	65.9	36.6	727.7	544.7	13.2	2,994.5	59.8
1996[1]	754.9	90.9	544.8	109.2	10.0	581.1	26.9	146.9	42.7	67.2	36.9	740.5	545.1	14.9	3,073.1	61.0
1997[2]	756.8	90.9	546.6	109.2	10.0	582.5	26.9	147.4	43.2	67.2	37.0				3,119.1	

[1] Preliminary. *Source: Edison Electric Institute (EEI)*

Available Electricity and Energy Sales in the United States — In Billions of Kilowatt Hours

	Net Generation								Sales to Ultimate Customers								
	Electric Utility Industry																
Year	Total[2]	Hydro	Natural Gas	Coal	Fuel Oil	Nuclear	Other Sources[3]	Total	Total Million $	Total	Residential	Inter-Departmental	Commercial	Industrial	Street & Highway Lighting	Other Public Auth.	Railways & Railroads
1984	2,416	321.2	297.4	1,342	119.8	327.6	8.6	2,488	143,093	2,281	782	5.8	578.1	835	14.2	59.9	4.5
1985	2,470	281.1	291.9	1,402	100.2	383.7	10.7	2,568	149,162	2,306	792	5.3	605.9	820	14.6	62.2	4.7
1986	2,487	290.8	248.5	1,386	136.6	414.0	11.5	2,599	152,467	2,355	820	5.2	629.0	819	15.0	61.9	4.7
1987	2,572	249.7	272.6	1,464	118.5	455.3	12.3	2,719	155,700	2,435	846	4.5	658.4	843	14.4	63.0	4.9
1988	2,704	222.9	252.8	1,541	148.9	527.0	12.0	2,879	162,388	2,554	886	4.2	697.8	881	14.6	64.6	5.1
1989	2,784	265.1	266.6	1,554	158.3	529.4	11.3	2,985	169,627	2,621	898	4.3	715.9	912	14.6	69.3	5.3
1990	2,808	279.9	264.1	1,560	117.0	576.9	10.7	3,041	176,468	2,684	915	4.2	738.9	931	15.2	72.8	5.3
1991	1,825	275.5	264.2	1,551	111.5	612.6	10.1	3,100	185,118	2,764	948	2.6	753.3	934	15.6	76.1	5.3
1992	2,797	239.6	263.9	1,576	88.9	618.8	10.2	3,107	187,283	2,735	929	2.6	755.7	949	15.8	77.2	5.2
1993	2,883	265.1	258.9	1,639	99.5	610.3	9.6	3,210	197,992	2,860	994	2.7	803.1	957	18.1	69.7	5.4
1994	2,911	243.7	291.1	1,635	91.0	640.4	8.9	3,283	202,597	2,936	1,008	3.0	833.5	990	18.5	70.6	5.8
1995	2,995	293.7	307.3	1,653	60.8	673.4	6.4	3,395	207,652	3,017	1,042	2.1	863.5	1,006	17.9	69.9	5.5
1996	3,073	324.5	262.3	1,737	67.0	674.7	7.2	3,473	212,390	3,103	1,082	2.5	887.1	1,028	18.0	70.3	5.3
1997[1]	3,171	318.6	296.9	1,812	94.1	642.3	7.3	3,119	215,183	3,157	1,093	2.3	924.1	1,042	19.0	71.3	5.2

[1] Preliminary. [2] Includes internal combustion. [3] Includes electricity produced from geothermal, wood, waste, wind, solar, etc.
Source: Edison Electric Insititute (EEI)

Electric Power Production by Electric Utilities in the United States — In Millions of Kilowatt Hours

Year	Jan.	Feb.	Mar.	Apr.	May	June	July	Aug.	Sept.	Oct.	Nov.	Dec.	Total
1984	216,632	189,564	200,107	181,084	192,217	209,648	221,245	229,296	195,198	190,936	190,380	199,996	2,416,304
1985	227,856	198,242	194,970	184,877	196,790	205,363	226,722	226,050	202,499	194,789	192,427	219,255	2,469,841
1986	217,470	192,336	196,834	186,074	197,315	215,015	242,672	225,166	206,692	197,754	196,432	213,551	2,487,310
1987	222,749	194,034	201,849	189,496	206,074	225,589	247,915	247,645	213,008	203,009	200,258	220,500	2,572,127
1988	237,897	216,937	214,013	196,000	208,371	232,747	257,461	267,693	220,179	210,608	209,593	232,752	2,704,250
1989	232,747	219,826	226,742	208,042	220,124	235,689	257,050	258,687	227,150	219,910	219,300	259,038	2,784,304
1990	237,289	212,880	226,034	211,070	222,908	249,175	266,375	268,527	237,017	224,694	213,748	237,434	2,808,151
1991	248,455	210,821	221,400	209,004	234,373	248,427	271,976	268,115	233,885	223,430	221,377	233,760	2,825,023
1992	243,970	217,761	224,665	210,837	220,355	236,842	266,148	255,203	234,760	221,289	221,263	244,126	2,797,219
1993	245,782	224,617	234,801	211,374	222,396	249,633	282,292	279,132	236,603	223,629	225,855	246,412	2,882,525
1994	261,697	225,011	231,544	214,817	227,703	263,859	278,149	274,645	237,663	227,972	224,745	242,906	2,910,712
1995	253,077	228,127	233,675	217,381	236,381	256,083	292,827	304,709	245,574	234,409	234,117	258,170	2,994,529
1996	268,713	245,388	247,989	226,423	251,570	268,644	289,329	290,458	250,672	240,674	241,077	258,138	3,079,074
1997	274,119	234,251	244,551	231,053	243,175	266,672	304,426	294,328	266,498	253,218	245,004	267,609	3,124,904
1998[1]	265,384	235,266	256,351	232,807	264,952	291,198	317,684	312,868	279,486	251,589	239,281		3,214,763

[1] Preliminary. *Source: Energy Information Administration, U.S. Department of Energy*

Use of Fuels for Electric Generation in the United States

	Consumption of Fuel									
Year	Coal (Thousand Short Tons)	Fuel Oil (Thousand Barrels)[2]	Gas (Million Cubic Feet)	Total Fuel in Coal Equivalent[3] (Thousand Short Tons)	Net Generation by Fuels[4] (Million Kw. Hr.)	Pounds of Coal Per Kw. Hr. (Pounds)	Cost of Fossil-Fuel at Elec. Util. ¢ Mil. BTU	Average Cost of Fuel Per Kw. Hr. (¢)	Heat Rate BTU Per Kw. Hr.	Cost Per Million BTU Consumed (¢)
1984	664,399	204,479	3,111,342	909,156	1,758,882	.990	219.1	2.41	10,385	232.0
1985	693,841	173,414	3,044,083	926,793	1,794,276	.990	209.4	2.27	10,429	217.7
1986	685,056	230,482	2,602,370	907,720	1,770,925	.989	175.0	1.92	10,423	184.5
1987	717,894	199,378	2,844,051	944,420	1,854,895	.981	170.6	1.84	10,354	177.7
1988	758,372	248,096	2,635,613	984,969	1,942,353	.984	164.3	1.76	10,328	170.7
1989	766,888	267,451	2,787,012	1,004,964	1,978,577	.987	167.5	1.79	10,312	174.0
1990	773,549	196,054	2,787,332	988,300	1,940,712	.997	168.9	1.80	10,366	174.1
1991	772,268	184,886	2,789,014	987,469	1,926,801	.996	160.3	1.75	10,322	169.6
1992	779,860	147,335	2,765,608	983,484	1,928,683	.990	159.0	1.72	10,340	166.6
1993	813,508	162,454	2,682,440	1,017,086	1,997,605	.993	159.5	1.72	10,351	166.6
1994	817,270	151,004	2,987,146	1,033,575	2,017,646	.999	152.6	1.59	10,425	152.6
1995	829,007	102,150	3,196,507	1,039,174	2,021,064	1.003	145.3	1.48	10,173	145.2
1996	874,681	113,274	2,732,107	1,063,755	2,066,666	1.007	151.9	1.55	10,176	151.9
1997[1]	900,361	125,146	2,968,453				152.2			

[1] Preliminary. [2] 42-gallon barrels. [3] Coal equivalents are calculated on the basis of Btu instead of generation data. [4] Excludes wood & waste fuels.
Source: Edison Electric Institute (EEI)

Fertilizer

The three primary fertilizer chemicals used in the United States are nitrogen, phosphorus and potassium. They provide the basic nutrients to plants. The basic nitrogen fertilizer is ammonia, which is comprised of nitrogen and natural gas. Ammonia can be supplied in liquid form below the surface of the soil or converted into solid nitrogenous fertilizers. Nitrogen is a requirement for proper nutrition and maturation of the crop plant. Phosphorus is an essential element for plant and animal nutrition. Phosphorus is produced from phosphate rock minerals. Potash denoted a variety of mined and manufactured salts, all containing the element potassium in water soluble form. As a fertilizer, potassium in water-soluble form activates plant enzymes, aids photosynthesis in the leaves and increases disease resistance.

Nitrogen is an essential element of life and a part of all plant and animal proteins. Some crops such as alfalfa, soybeans and peanuts can convert atmospheric nitrogen into a usable form through the process of fixation. All commercial fertilizers contain their nitrogen in the ammonium and/or nitrate form. Commercial production of anhydrous ammonia is based on reacting nitrogen with hydrogen under high temperatures and pressures.

The U.S. Geological Survey reported that in 1997, U.S. production of ammonia was 14.3 million tonnes, an increase of 8 percent from 1996. 1997 U.S. exports of ammonia in 1997 were 395,000 tonnes, a decline of 9 percent from the previous year. Imports for consumption of ammonia in 1997 were 3.53 million tonnes, up 4 percent from 1996. U.S. consumption of ammonia in 1997 was 16.8 million tonnes, 3 percent more then in 1996. Producer stocks of ammonia on December 31, 1997 were 1.53 million tonnes, 74 percent above 1996. Stocks of nitrogen solutions at the end of 1997 were 385,000 tonnes, up 55 percent from the previous year.

1997 world production of ammonia was estimated at 102 million tonnes, unchanged from the previous year. The U.S. was the largest producer. The next largest producer was the Ukraine with 3.4 million tonnes, up 3 percent from 1996.

Phosphorus is an essential element for plant nutrition. Phosphate rock minerals are the only significant global resource of phosphorus. U.S. marketable production of phosphate rock in 1997 was 43.3 million tonnes. In the first seven months of 1998, production was 25.7 million tonnes. Small amounts of phosphate rock are imported into the U.S. and in the first five months of 1998, imports were 478,000 tonnes. The U.S. is the leading producer and consumer of phosphate rock which is used to manufacture phosphate fertilizers. Approximately 90 percent of the phosphate rock mined is used to manufacture chemical fertilizers. Production in 1997 declined 5 percent due to temporary mine closures. Most of the marketable rock mined in the U.S. is mined in Florida and North Carolina. Phosphate rock is also mined in Idaho and Utah where it is used to produce high-analysis phosphate fertilizers and elemental phosphorus.

U.S. production of potash in 1997 was 2.8 million tonnes, slightly above 1996. Imports for consumption in 1997 were 9.03 million tonnes, some 11 percent more than in 1996. Potash exports in 1997 were 1.07 million tonnes or some 3 percent less than in 1996. U.S. apparent consumption of potash in 1997 was 11 million tonnes, up 10 percent from 1996.

World Production of Ammonia In Thousands of Metric Tons of Contained Nitrogen

Year	Canada	China	France	Germany	India	Indonesia	Japan	Mexico	Netherlands	Poland	Russia[3]	United States	Total
1990	3,054	17,500	1,586	2,690	7,010	2,789	1,531	2,164	3,188	1,962	18,200	12,680	97,160
1991	3,016	18,000	1,604	2,123	7,132	2,706	1,553	2,221	3,033	1,531	17,100	12,803	93,800
1992	3,104	18,000	1,848	2,113	7,452	2,688	1,602	2,203	2,588	1,490	8,786	13,400	93,600
1993	3,410	19,000	1,871	2,100	7,176	2,888	1,471	1,758	2,472	1,163	8,138	12,600	91,700
1994	3,470	20,100	1,480	2,170	7,503	3,012	1,483	2,030	2,479	1,230	7,300	13,300	93,700
1995	3,773	22,600	1,470	2,518	8,287	3,336	1,584	1,992	2,580	1,415	7,900	13,000	99,800
1996[1]	3,840	23,000	1,500	2,485	8,549	3,647	1,567	2,054	2,652	1,405	7,900	13,200	102,000
1997[2]	3,980	24,000	1,500	2,470	8,600	3,770	1,570	1,450	2,500	1,500	7,150	14,300	102,000

[1] Preliminary. [2] Estimate. [3] Formerly part of the U.S.S.R.; data not reported separately until 1992. *Source: U.S. Geological Survey (USGS)*

Salient Statistics of Nitrogen[3] (Ammonia) in the United States In Thousands of Metric Tons

Year	Net Import Reliance as a % of Apparent Consumption	Production[3] (Fixed): Fertilizer	Production[3] (Fixed): Non-fertilizer	Production[3] (Fixed): Total	Imports[4] (Fixed)	Exports	Nitrogen[5] Compounds: Produced	Nitrogen[5] Compounds: Consumption	Stocks, Dec. 31: Ammonia	Stocks, Dec. 31: Fixed Nitrogen Compounds	Ammonia Consumption (Apparent)	Average Price ($ Per Tonne): Urea F.O.B. Gulf[6] Coast	Urea F.O.B. Corn Belt	Ammonium Nitrate: F.O.B. Corn Belt	Ammonia F.O.B. Gulf Coast
1990	15	11,573	1,107	12,680	2,673	482	9,851	9,902	797	1,451	14,923	155-156	155-165	120-125	106
1991	14	11,559	1,244	12,803	2,742	580	9,770	9,815	936	1,607	14,826	142-143	146-160	108-130	117
1992	14	12,000	1,349	13,400	2,690	354	10,404	10,448	1,059	1,789	15,600	142-146	149-160	138-149	106
1993	17	11,300	1,320	12,620	2,657	378	10,000	10,100	852	1,600	15,100	139-141	141-165	138-149	121
1994	19	11,600	1,750	13,350	3,450	215	10,000	11,700	956	1,650	16,500	219-226	204-215	165-176	211
1995	16	11,600	1,410	13,010	2,630	319	10,400	10,700	959	1,580	15,300	217-222	220-235	162-170	191
1996[1]	13	11,500	1,720	13,220	3,390	435	11,502	11,100	881	1,390	16,300	188-190	197-210	160-170	225
1997[2]	14	12,300	1,980	14,280	3,530	395	11,000	11,400	1,530	2,240	16,800	102-103	125-135	122-125	130

[1] Preliminary. [2] Estimate. [3] Anhydrous ammonia, synthetic. [4] For consumption. [5] Major downstream nitrogen compounds. [6] Granular.
Source: U.S. Geological Survey (USGS)

World Production of Phosphate Rock, Basic Slag & Guano   In Thousands of Metric Tons (Gross Weight)

Year	Brazil	China	Egypt	Israel	Jordan	Morocco	Russia[3]	Senegal	Syria	Togo	Tunisia	United States	World Total
1988	4,672	17,000	1,154	3,479	6,611	25,015	37,000	2,326	2,186	3,464	6,103	45,389	166,436
1989	3,655	20,000	1,355	3,922	6,900	18,067	37,500	2,273	2,256	3,355	6,610	49,817	167,342
1990	2,968	21,550	1,151	3,516	6,082	21,396	36,800	2,147	1,633	2,314	6,258	46,343	162,783
1991	3,280	22,000	1,652	3,370	4,433	17,900	28,400	1,741	1,359	2,965	6,352	48,096	150,731
1992	2,850	21,400	2,000	3,595	4,296	19,145	11,500	2,284	1,266	2,083	6,400	46,965	139,000
1993	3,419	21,200	1,585	3,680	4,129	18,193	9,400	1,667	931	1,794	5,500	35,494	119,000
1994	3,937	24,100	632	3,961	4,217	19,764	8,000	1,587	1,203	2,149	5,699	41,100	127,000
1995	3,888	19,300	765	4,063	4,984	20,200	8,800	1,502	1,551	2,570	7,241	43,500	130,000
1996[1]	3,823	21,000	808	3,839	5,355	20,855	8,500	1,427	2,189	2,731	7,167	45,400	135,000
1997[2]	3,850	20,000	800	4,047	5,896	23,367	7,500	1,535	2,392	2,631	7,068	43,300	135,000

[1] Preliminary. [2] Estimate. [3] Formerly part of the U.S.S.R.; data not reported separately until 1992. *Source: U.S. Geological Survey (USGS)*

Salient Statistics of Phosphate Rock in the United States   In Thousands of Metric Tons

Year	Mine Production	Marketable Production	Value Million $	Imports for Consumption	Exports	Apparent Consumption	Stocks, Dec. 31 (Producer)	Price - $ Avg. Per Metric Ton (F.O.B. Mine)	Avg. Price of Florida & North Carolina - $ Tonne - F.O.B. Mine (-60% to +74%) - Domestic	Export	Average
1988	162,299	45,389	888	676	8,092	41,025	9,323	19.56	18.29	25.24	19.56
1989	170,268	49,817	1,084	705	7,842	42,143	11,027	21.76	20.65	28.67	21.76
1990	151,277	46,343	1,075	451	6,238	43,967	8,912	23.20	22.44	30.43	23.55
1991	154,485	48,096	1,109	552	5,082	40,177	10,168	23.06	22.67	31.69	23.69
1992	154,936	46,965	1,058	1,530	3,723	42,920	12,612	22.53	22.47	31.69	23.32
1993	107,000	35,500	759	534	3,200	38,300	9,220	21.38	21.26	28.51	21.89
1994	157,000	41,100	869	1,800	2,800	42,900	5,980	21.14	21.79	25.60	22.08
1995	165,000	43,500	947	1,800	2,760	42,700	5,710	21.75	21.29	28.35	21.75
1996[1]	179,000	45,400	1,060	1,800	1,570	43,700	6,390	23.40	22.90	35.82	23.40
1997[2]	162,000	43,300	1,060	1,830	335	43,300	7,390	24.60	20.32	35.25	24.60

[1] Preliminary. [2] Estimate. *Source: U.S. Geological Survey (USGS)*

World Production of Marketable Potash   In Thousands of Metric Tons (K_2O Equivalent)

Year	Belarus[3]	Brazil	Canada	China	France	Germany	Israel	Jordan	Russia[3]	Spain	United Kingdom	United States	World Total
1988	------	54	8,154	22	1,502	5,800	1,244	785	11,301	855	460	1,521	31,820
1989	------	97	7,333	42	1,195	5,388	1,273	792	10,200	741	462	1,595	29,276
1990	------	66	6,989	29	1,292	4,960	1,311	841	9,000	686	488	1,713	27,493
1991	------	101	7,406	32	1,129	3,855	1,320	818	8,560	585	495	1,749	26,136
1992	3,311	85	7,270	21	1,141	3,460	1,300	794	3,470	594	529	1,705	23,900
1993	1,947	173	3,836	25	890	2,861	1,309	822	2,628	661	555	1,510	20,400
1994	3,021	234	8,037	74	870	3,286	1,259	930	2,498	684	580	1,400	23,100
1995	3,211	215	8,855	80	799	3,278	1,330	1,112	2,800	760	582	1,480	24,700
1996[1]	2,720	243	8,120	110	751	3,332	1,500	1,060	2,620	680	618	1,390	23,400
1997[2]	3,250	243	9,301	115	665	3,423	1,488	849	3,400	640	565	1,400	25,700

[1] Preliminary. [2] Estimate. [3] Formerly part of the U.S.S.R.; data not reported separately until 1992. *Source: U.S. Geological Survey (USGS)*

Salient Statistics of Potash in the United States   In Thousands of Metric Tons (K_2O Equivalent)

									--------- $ Per Ton ---------		
Year	Net Import as % of Consumption	Production	Sales by Producers	Value Million $	Imports for Consumption	Exports	Apparent Consumption	Producer Stocks, Dec. 31	Avg. Value Per Ton of Product - $	Avg. Value of K2O Equiv.	Avg. Price[3] $ Per Tonne
1988	73	1,521	1,427	240.3	4,217	380	5,264	248	85.75	168.37	132.00
1989	66	1,595	1,536	271.5	3,410	446	4,500	307	90.28	176.74	137.00
1990	68	1,713	1,716	303.3	4,164	470	5,410	303	89.46	176.80	130.00
1991	67	1,749	1,709	304.5	4,158	624	5,243	343	91.52	178.20	131.00
1992	67	1,705	1,766	334.4	4,248	663	5,351	283	96.45	189.36	134.00
1993	72	1,510	1,480	286.0	4,360	415	5,430	305	94.36	192.72	130.74
1994	76	1,400	1,470	284.0	4,800	464	5,810	234	95.93	193.50	125.34
1995	75	1,480	1,400	284.0	4,820	409	5,820	312	98.58	202.43	137.99
1996[1]	77	1,390	1,430	299.0	4,940	481	5,890	265	101.08	208.57	134.07
1997[2]	76	1,400	1,400	320.0	5,490	466	6,500	W	108.00	227.00	138.00

[1] Preliminary. [2] Estimate. [3] Unit of K_2O, standard 60% muriate F.O.B. mine. *Source: U.S. Geological Survey (USGS)*

Fish

The U.S. Department of Agriculture reported that U.S. aquacultural production continues to increase. The increase is being led by catfish. Still, U.S. aquaculture faces competition from foreign aquaculture, wild harvest seafood and meat products.

The USDA reported that catfish sales to processors in 1998 are expected to be about 560 million pounds, about 7 percent higher than in 1997. Through August 1998, catfish sales were some 8 percent higher than the year before. Sales in the fourth quarter were expected to be lower. Catfish producers have been helped by lower costs for feeds like corn and soybeans. In the latest survey of the industry, catfish producers indicated that their inventories of broodfish, foodsize fish and fingerlings were higher than in the previous year. This implies that catfish production in 1999 will likely increase. Catfish producers reported that pond acreage in 1998 was 164,600 acres, up slightly from a year ago.

In the first half of 1998, U.S. shrimp imports were 305 million pounds, some 21 percent higher than in the first half of 1997. With the strong economy, shrimp imports are expected to reach record levels both in terms of quantity and value. Higher imports of shrimp into the U.S. will be in part related to the strength of the dollar and partly to the efforts of Asian exporters to increase export earnings. There had been concerns that the economic crises in Asia would in fact affect production but that has not been the case. The major suppliers of shrimp to the U.S. are Ecuador, Thailand, Mexico and Indonesia. Other large suppliers are India and Bangladesh.

U.S. imports of Atlantic salmon in the first half of 1998 totaled 104 million pounds which represented a 38 percent increase from the first half of 1997. All of the Atlantic salmon import categories; fresh whole fish, frozen whole fish and fresh and frozen fillets, showed increases. Much of the growth came from the import of fresh or frozen fillets from Chile. Imports of filleted products have increased substantially. A strong economy boosts restaurant sales which is the major outlet for salmon products. The major suppliers of salmon to the U.S. are Canada and Chile.

U.S. imports of crawfish in the first half of 1988 totaled 865,000 pounds, an increase of 47 percent from the same period of 1997. China is a dominant supplier of crawfish to the U.S. though exports are expected to decline somewhat due to a tariff on frozen crawfish meat. U.S. exports of crawfish in the first half of 1998 were 1.7 million pounds.

Fishery Products -- Supply in the United States In Millions of Pounds[2]

					Domestic Catch					Imports				
Year	Grand Total	For Human Food - Finfish	For Human Food - Shellfish[3]	For Industrial Use[4]	Total	% of Grand Total	For Human Food - Finfish	For Human Food - Shellfish[3]	For Industrial Use[4]	Total	% of Grand Total	For Human Food - Finfish	For Human Food - Shellfish[3]	For Industrial Use[4]
1987	15,744	7,919	2,642	5,183	6,896	43.8	2,769	1,177	2,950	8,848	56.2	5,150	1,465	2,233
1988	14,628	7,786	2,719	4,123	7,192	49.2	3,306	1,282	2,604	7,436	50.8	4,480	1,437	1,519
1989	15,485	9,735	2,533	3,217	8,463	54.7	4,897	1,307	2,259	7,022	45.3	4,838	1,226	958
1990	16,349	10,120	2,542	3,687	9,404	57.5	5,747	1,294	2,363	6,945	42.5	4,373	1,248	1,324
1991	16,364	10,186	2,834	3,344	9,484	58.0	5,564	1,467	2,453	6,879	42.0	4,622	1,367	890
1992	16,106	10,297	2,945	2,864	9,637	59.8	6,182	1,436	2,019	6,469	40.2	4,115	1,509	845
1993	20,334	10,796	3,025	6,513	10,467	51.5	6,770	1,444	2,253	9,867	48.5	4,026	1,581	4,260
1994	19,309	10,719	2,995	5,595	10,461	54.2	6,612	1,324	2,525	8,848	45.8	4,107	1,671	3,070
1995	16,484	10,692	2,891	2,900	9,788	59.4	6,414	1,252	2,121	6,696	40.6	4,278	1,639	779
1996[1]	16,474	10,699	2,927	2,848	9,565	58.1	6,205	1,271	2,089	6,909	41.9	4,494	1,656	759

[1] Preliminary. [2] Live weight, except percent. [3] For univalue and bivalues mollusks (conchs, clams, oysters, scallops, etc.) the weight of meats, excluding the shell is reported. [4] Fish meal and sea herring. *Source: Fisheries Statistics Division, U.S. Department of Commerce*

Fisheries -- Landings of Principal Species in the United States In Millions of Pounds

	Fish									Shellfish					
Year	Cod, Atlantic	Flounder	Halibut	Herring, Sea	Menhaden	Pollock	Salmon, Pacific	Tuna	Whiting	Clams (Meats)	Crabs	Lobsters (American)	Oysters (Meats)	Scallops (Meats)	Shrimp
1987	59	200	76	207	2,712	598	562	100	35	134	386	46	40	41	363
1988	76	229	82	222	2,086	1,290	606	111	36	132	456	49	32	43	331
1989	78	202	75	209	1,989	2,385	786	89	39	138	458	53	30	41	352
1990	96	255	70	221	1,962	3,129	733	62	44	139	499	61	29	42	346
1991	93	405	66	230	1,977	2,873	783	36	37	134	650	63	32	40	320
1992	62	646	67	282	1,644	2,952	716	57	36	142	624	56	36	34	338
1993	51	599	63	216	1,983	3,258	888	55	36	148	604	57	34	19	293
1994	39	427	58	214	2,324	3,133	901	72	36	131	447	66	38	25	283
1995	30	423	45	265	1,847	2,853	1,137	14	34	134	364	66	40	20	307
1996[1]	31	460	49	318	1,755	2,630	877	85	35	123	392	71	38	18	317

[1] Preliminary. NA = Not available. *Source: Fisheries Statistics Division, U.S. Department of Commerce*

U.S. Fisheries: Quantity & Value of Domestic Catch & Consumption & World Fish Oil Production

	Disposition					For	For			Fish	World[2]
	Fresh & Frozen	Canned	Cured	For Meal, Oil, Etc.	Total	Human Food	Industrial Products	Ex-vessel Value[3]	Average Price	Per Capita Consumption	Fish Oil Production
Year	Millions Pounds							Million $	¢ Lb.	Lbs.	1,000 Tonnes
1990	6,501	751	126	2,026	9,404	7,041	2,363	3,522	37.4	15.0	1,386
1991	6,541	674	119	2,150	9,484	7,031	2,453	3,308	34.9	14.8	1,105
1992	7,288	543	110	1,696	9,637	7,618	2,019	3,678	38.2	14.7	1,187
1993	7,744	649	115	1,959	10,467	8,214	2,253	3,471	33.2	14.9	1,184
1994	7,475	622	95	2,269	10,461	7,936	2,525	3,807	36.8	NA	1,470
1995	7,099	769	90	1,830	9,788	7,667	2,121	3,770	38.5	NA	1,302
1996[1]	7,054	678	93	1,740	9,565	7,475	2,090	3,487	36.5	NA	1,337

[1] Preliminary. [2] Crop year on a marketing year basis. [3] At the Dock Prices. *Source: Fisheries Statistics Division, U.S. Department of Commerce*

Imports of Seafood Products into the United States In Thousands of Pounds

	Fresh			Frozen								
Year	Atlantic Salmon	Pacific Salmon	Shrimp	Trout	Atlantic Salmon	Pacific Salmon	Shrimp	Oysters[2]	Mussels[3]	Clams[4]	Canned Salmon	Prepared Shrimp[5]
1992	48,843	40,075	8,347	6,197	5,302	10,199	558,580	16,800	7,657	6,192	2,671	36,782
1993	62,860	33,920	11,649	4,741	7,714	11,659	556,213	17,293	9,658	5,818	2,053	44,765
1994	68,254	31,952	NA	3,878	7,851	11,210	580,010	15,415	11,032	8,265	3,190	47,912
1995	95,739	33,371	NA	4,076	9,982	8,849	539,630	14,866	15,483	5,930	3,582	57,577
1996	116,606	43,962	NA	4,552	10,752	8,514	507,823	14,222	21,241	6,596	4,182	74,648
1997[1]	150,135	38,999	NA	5,403	14,956	25,662	572,111	14,531	26,903	5,703	3,675	76,213

[1] Preliminary. [2] Oysters fresh or prepared. [3] Mussels fresh or prepared. [4] Clams, fresh or prepared. [5] Shrimp, canned, breaded or prepare.
NA = Not available. *Source: Bureau of the Census, U.S. Department of Commerce*

Exports of Seafood Products into the United States In Thousands of Pounds

	Fresh			Frozen								
Year	Atlantic Salmon	Pacific Salmon	Shrimp	Trout	Atlantic Salmon	Pacific Salmon	Shrimp	Oysters[2]	Mussels[3]	Clams[4]	Canned Salmon	Prepared Shrimp[5]
1992	1,396	20,655	3,558	1,201	406	240,072	18,082	1,105	2,317	4,999	85,369	11,134
1993	4,018	24,275	2,776	955	373	257,751	16,524	1,454	2,291	4,217	84,520	11,539
1994	1,184	22,483	NA	1,958	384	260,469	13,622	2,634	1,935	3,785	90,393	15,778
1995	6,823	26,142	NA	1,545	231	266,706	14,795	2,531	1,896	3,968	95,611	14,837
1996	7,280	42,999	NA	1,867	322	223,346	11,180	2,097	1,603	5,126	94,842	17,665
1997	7,504	25,529	NA	1,709	322	152,516	11,967	2,890	1,157	4,916	81,407	14,826

[1] Preliminary. [2] Oysters fresh or prepared. [3] Mussels fresh or prepared. [4] Clams, fresh or prepared. [5] Shrimp, canned, breaded or prepare.
NA = Not available. *Source: Bureau of theCensus, U.S. Department of Commerce*

World Production of Fish Meal In Thousands of Metric Tons

Year	Chile	Spain	Denmark	EU-12	FSU-12	Iceland	Japan	Norway	Peru	South Africa	Thailand	United States	World Total
1990-1	1,144.2	123.9	302.6	556.2	643.9	87.6	841.8	220.8	1,308.5	87.9	292.8	310.4	6,303.6
1991-2	1,322.1	122.1	351.7	602.5	465.1	158.9	509.6	239.9	1,095.6	150.3	313.4	312.2	5,948.5
1992-3	1,091.2	101.6	300.1	531.2	355.0	197.7	395.0	250.8	1,767.3	128.3	349.3	352.5	6,202.4
1993-4	1,526.1	91.0	352.7	569.5	295.0	190.5	343.0	216.8	2,254.4	75.4	372.8	447.8	7,085.7
1994-5	1,549.7	70.1	363.4	573.1	280.0	173.8	239.0	225.0	2,052.6	91.2	383.9	338.3	6,906.2
1995-6[1]	1,387.6	76.4	322.9	532.1	260.0	271.0	197.0	233.8	1,702.7	62.0	380.0	329.1	6,385.8
1996-7[2]	1,209.9	75.0	334.5	539.4	260.0	272.0	184.0	257.0	2,150.5	61.0	385.0	345.0	6,661.8
1997-8[3]	1,050.0	77.0	355.0	565.2	250.0	250.0	179.0	243.0	840.0	70.0	380.0	341.0	5,155.0

[1] Preliminary. [2] Estimate. [3] Forecast. *Source: The Oil World*

World Production of Fish Oil In Thousands of Metric Tons

Year	Canada	Chile	China	Denmark	Iceland	Japan	Norway	Peru	South Africa	FSU-12	United States	World Total	Fish Oil CIF[4]
1990-1	10.7	201.0	12.4	107.2	39.4	331.7	97.6	215.1	12.1	132.0	127.8	1,383.0	307
1991-2	11.0	155.9	8.7	114.5	63.0	186.1	92.9	102.1	16.1	104.2	84.4	1,042.1	361
1992-3	11.8	165.3	9.4	90.3	86.0	102.0	112.3	250.9	17.0	71.6	119.0	1,140.6	375
1993-4	9.9	280.0	11.0	112.0	96.5	90.9	122.7	426.5	8.5	52.7	141.2	1,457.5	332
1994-5	10.1	323.1	9.9	118.3	85.0	57.7	94.1	388.1	3.8	48.5	109.6	1,367.9	405
1995-6[1]	10.6	280.2	12.0	120.0	120.5	45.8	93.7	410.0	8.0	43.0	110.4	1,367.7	461
1996-7[2]	10.5	166.5	12.0	120.0	134.6	51.2	86.4	407.1	7.0	41.0	110.0	1,259.7	502
1997-8[3]	10.5	147.0	12.6	119.5	120.0	55.0	83.0	115.0	7.5	39.5	115.0	940.1	691

[1] Preliminary. [2] Estimate. [3] Forecast. [4] Any origin, N.W. Europe, $ per tonne. *Source: The Oil World*

Monthly Production of Catfish--Round Weight Processed--in the U.S. In Thousands of Pounds (Live Weight)

Year	Jan.	Feb.	Mar.	Apr.	May	June	July	Aug.	Sept.	Oct.	Nov.	Dec.	Total
1989	26,948	28,559	29,458	27,310	28,892	27,598	27,827	28,371	30,366	31,670	29,096	25,805	341,900
1990	33,066	31,884	33,120	30,980	31,542	28,967	29,540	31,108	27,566	29,211	27,913	25,538	360,435
1991	32,206	33,036	35,951	31,205	31,322	31,588	32,720	32,912	33,244	35,400	31,114	30,172	390,870
1992	36,200	39,228	45,048	41,177	39,111	36,813	36,128	37,958	37,857	39,212	35,073	33,562	457,367
1993	40,327	40,277	43,521	39,920	37,030	35,496	37,086	37,706	37,072	39,472	36,557	34,549	459,013
1994	36,714	35,035	40,446	34,494	34,163	34,595	35,901	39,813	38,716	39,072	36,054	34,266	439,269
1995	38,807	38,515	42,200	36,588	37,030	36,047	35,800	38,827	37,634	39,456	34,119	31,863	446,886
1996	38,475	38,004	46,376	38,557	39,583	36,810	39,025	40,463	38,807	42,070	37,210	36,874	472,254
1997	42,409	45,067	48,431	45,721	43,409	42,282	43,376	44,154	43,472	46,275	40,137	40,216	524,949
1998[1]	46,723	47,606	53,761	49,393	45,218	46,244	46,383	47,739	46,579	47,904	43,224	43,581	564,355

[1] Preliminary. *Source: Economic Research Service, U.S. Department of Agriculture (ERS-USDA)*

Average Price Paid to Producers for Farm-Raised Catfish in the U.S. In Cents Per Pound (Live Weight)

Year	Jan.	Feb.	Mar.	Apr.	May	June	July	Aug.	Sept.	Oct.	Nov.	Dec.	Average
1989	78	78	77	76	76	75	71	68	65	64	64	68	71.7
1990	72	74	78	78	78	78	76	76	76	76	75	72	75.8
1991	69	69	69	69	66	65	63	60	59	58	57	53	63.1
1992	53	56	60	63	63	61	59	58	59	61	62	63	59.8
1993	63	67	70	71	72	72	72	73	73	73	73	73	71.0
1994	74	77	79	80	80	80	80	80	80	77	77	77	78.4
1995	78	79	79	79	79	79	79	79	78	78	78	78	78.6
1996	77	78	78	78	79	79	79	78	77	76	75	73	77.3
1997	73	73	73	73	73	72	71	70	69	69	69	69	71.0
1998[1]	69	73	78	79	79	78	76	74	73	71	70	70	74.2

[1] Preliminary. *Source: Economic Research Service, U.S. Department of Agriculture (ERS-USDA)*

Sales and Prices of Fresh Catfish in the United States

Year	Jan.	Feb.	Mar.	Apr.	May	June	July	Aug.	Sept.	Oct.	Nov.	Dec.	Total/Avg.
						In Thousands of Pounds							
SALES--Whole													
1995	3,221	3,373	3,856	3,086	2,997	2,903	2,951	3,184	3,108	3,166	2,962	2,847	37,654
1996	3,673	3,593	4,168	3,508	3,230	2,868	3,001	3,107	3,215	3,324	2,763	2,925	39,375
1997	3,402	3,632	4,133	3,770	3,456	3,447	3,481	3,284	3,370	3,598	3,002	3,051	41,626
1998[1]	3,700	4,049	4,308	3,856	3,421	3,340	3,342	3,270					43,929
Fillets[2]													
1995	3,054	3,281	3,646	3,369	3,350	3,246	3,115	3,348	3,162	3,295	2,897	2,845	38,608
1996	3,439	3,866	4,366	3,883	3,824	3,374	3,556	3,615	3,645	3,758	3,254	3,222	43,802
1997	3,627	4,272	4,531	4,084	4,126	3,894	4,033	4,135	4,009	4,464	3,623	3,543	48,341
1998[1]	4,292	4,784	5,130	4,634	4,371	4,220	4,542	4,622					54,893
Other[3]													
1995	998	1,115	1,437	1,328	1,234	1,172	934	1,035	1,067	1,166	1,049	938	13,473
1996	1,097	1,263	1,438	1,154	1,124	937	1,045	1,128	1,081	1,228	1,063	982	13,540
1997	1,287	1,497	1,562	1,530	1,430	1,307	1,385	1,332	1,358	1,498	1,212	1,147	16,545
1998[1]	1,499	1,712	1,721	1,509	1,395	1,453	1,246	1,369					17,856
						In Dollars Per Pound							
PRICE--Whole													
1995	1.69	1.69	1.68	1.69	1.69	1.71	1.70	1.69	1.68	1.67	1.63	1.65	1.68
1996	1.63	1.64	1.68	1.68	1.73	1.77	1.73	1.71	1.67	1.65	1.64	1.60	1.68
1997	1.59	1.60	1.58	1.56	1.56	1.52	1.51	1.53	1.54	1.52	1.54	1.50	1.55
1998[1]	1.52	1.57	1.63	1.61	1.65	1.60	1.60	1.63					1.60
Fillets[2]													
1995	2.89	2.90	2.92	2.93	2.90	2.90	2.91	2.90	2.91	2.92	2.90	2.89	2.91
1996	2.88	2.85	2.86	2.87	2.88	2.92	2.91	2.88	2.85	2.83	2.84	2.81	2.87
1997	2.80	2.79	2.80	2.78	2.78	2.77	2.75	2.74	2.73	2.69	2.67	2.71	2.75
1998[1]	2.71	2.75	2.85	2.86	2.86	2.85	2.84	2.82					2.82
Other[3]													
1995	1.82	1.80	1.93	1.99	1.99	1.97	1.81	1.86	1.84	1.84	1.87	1.81	1.88
1996	1.77	1.75	1.77	1.84	1.87	1.90	1.86	1.81	1.77	1.74	1.75	1.73	1.80
1997	1.72	1.67	1.68	1.64	1.68	1.68	1.70	1.69	1.65	1.60	1.66	1.64	1.67
1998[1]	1.61	1.65	1.72	1.78	1.78	1.76	1.79	1.71					1.73

[1] Preliminary. [2] Includes regular, shank and strip fillets; excludes breaded products. [3] Includes steaks, nuggets and all other products not reported.
Source: Economic Research Service, U.S. Department of Agriculture (ERS-USDA)

Flaxseed and Linseed Oil

U.S. flaxseed acreage trended lower from early in the 1980's into the mid-1990's with a record low 96,000 acres planted in 1996; acreage has since rebounded to 146,000 acres in 1997, and 335,000 in 1998, with an accompanying large jump in crop production. Flaxseed (from which linseed oil is derived), is considered a minor U.S. oilseed with average production of 3.5 million bushels in the first half of the 1990's. World production of flaxseed is also small, averaging about 2.3 million metric tonnes in the 1990's.

1998/99 (June/May) U.S. production of 5.3 million bushels compares with 2.1 million in 1997/98 and is the highest since 1991/92's crop of 6.2 million bushels as recent higher prices encouraged larger acreage. Still, since the mid-1970's, U.S. flaxseed production has dropped 80 percent. Imports of flaxseed, primarily from Canada--the world's largest producer with a third of production--were forecast at 6.7 million bushels in 1998/99 vs. a record large 9.3 million in 1997/98. The U.S. has been a net importer of flaxseed since 1978 with imports averaging almost 7 million bushels in the 1990's, twice the 1980's yearly rate. Total 1998/99 supplies of 13.2 million bushels, the highest since 1987/88, includes a carryover of 1.2 million bushels; supplies in 1997/98 totaled 12.3 million bushels. Disappearance in 1998/99 was forecast at 11.4 million bushels vs. 11.1 million in 1998/99 which, if realized, would boost ending carryover to almost 3 million bushels, the highest in ten years. Most of the crop is crushed, estimated at 10.8 million bushels in 1998/99 vs. 10.5 million in 1997/98.

1998/99 U.S. domestic demand for linseed oil was 155 million pounds, with exports put at 50 million pounds vs. a record 66 million in 1996/97. Production in 1998/99 of 215 million pounds compares to 210 million in 1997/98. Linseed oil is used as a drying agent in paint, but its domestic use has fallen in line with the acceptance of water based latex paints. Annual usage in the 1990's has averaged about 190 million pounds, at least 15 million under the like 1980 period. Carryover stocks as of May 31, 1999 are estimated at 45 million pounds, marginally higher than a year earlier. Linseed meal production in 1998/99 of 199,000 short tons compares with 194,000 in 1997/98. Total meal disappearance of 200,000 tons compares with 195,000, respectively. 40 percent of the production was exported in both years.

The average price received by U.S. farmers for flaxseed in 1998/99 was expected to average between $5.00-$5.70 per bushel vs. the 1997/98 average of $5.75. Linseed oil prices in 1998/99 were forecast between $0.37-.40 per pound vs. $0.363 in 1997/98, basis Minneapolis. 1998/99 linseed meal prices, basis 34 percent protein Minneapolis, were forecast between $70-84 per ton vs $110 in 1997/98 and $169.74 in 1996/97.

Futures Markets

Flaxseed futures are traded on the Winnipeg Commodity Exchange (WCE). Prices are quoted in Canadian dollars per metric ton.

World Production of Flaxseed In Thousands of Metric Tons

Crop Year	Argentina	Australia	Bangladesh	Canada	China	Egypt	France	Hungary	India	Romania	United States	Former USSR	World Total
1988-9	446	3	43	328	490	28	32	11	361	38	41	220	2,215
1989-90	526	2	47	498	400	21	31	11	326	49	31	227	2,352
1990-1	458	4	48	889	535	28	34	10	339	53	97	197	2,923
1991-2	341	5	55	635	410	24	26	13	292	23	158	140	2,458
1992-3	177	5	49	334	430	21	29	10	268	18	84	130	1,969
1993-4	112	8	49	627	410	22	27	11	330	28	88	120	2,177
1994-5	152	6	48	960	511	18	44	4	325	7	74	110	2,474
1995-6[1]	149	15	49	1,105	420	16	27	4	308	5	56	113	2,518
1996-7[2]	72	7	46	851	480	17	15	4	319	6	41	100	2,240
1997-8[3]	74	6	48	967	420	18	20	4	320	6	55	85	2,337

[1] Preliminary. [2] Estimate. [3] Forecast. *Source: The Oil World*

Supply and Distribution of Flaxseed in the United States In Thousands of Bushels

Crop Year Beginning June	Planted (1,000 Acres)	Harvested (1,000 Acres)	Yield Per Acre Bushels	Supply: Beginning Stocks	Supply: Production	Supply: Imports	Supply: Total Supply	Distribution: Seed	Distribution: Crush	Distribution: Exports	Distribution: Residual	Total Distribution
1989-90	195	163	7.5	1,307	1,215	7,260	9,782	211	8,250	1,054	23	9,538
1990-1	260	253	15.1	244	3,812	6,715	10,771	288	8,800	549	163	9,800
1991-2	356	342	18.1	971	6,200	4,371	11,542	139	9,050	541	256	9,986
1992-3	171	165	19.9	1,556	3,288	6,035	10,879	167	8,600	230	337	9,334
1993-4	206	191	18.2	1,545	3,480	5,118	10,143	144	8,650	126	69	8,989
1994-5	178	171	17.1	1,155	2,922	6,005	10,082	134	8,550	72	156	8,912
1995-6	165	147	15.0	1,170	2,211	7,248	10,681	91	9,000	119	202	9,399
1996-7[1]	96	92	17.4	1,230	1,602	8,390	11,222	123	10,000	144	502	10,769
1997-8[2]	146	135	16.1	453	2,171	9,636	12,260	271	10,500	174	134	11,079
1998-9[3]	335	322	16.5	1,181	5,315	6,731	13,227	284	10,750	175	268	11,302

[1] Preliminary. [2] Estimate. [3] Forecast. *Source: Economic Research Service, U.S. Department of Agriculture (ERS-USDA)*

FLAXSEED AND LINSEED OIL

Production of Flaxseed in the United States, by States In Thousands of Bushels

Crop Year	Minnesota	North Dakota	South Dakota	Other States	Total	Crop Year	Minnesota	North Dakota	South Dakota	Other States	Total
1989	95	980	140	------	1,215	1994	126	2,450	304	42	2,922
1990	238	3,118	456	------	3,812	1995	171	1,725	260	55	2,211
1991	640	4,860	578	122	6,200	1996	60	1,386	126	30	1,602
1992	220	2,730	322	16	3,288	1997	96	1,997	252	75	2,420
1993	170	2,886	323	101	3,480	1998[1]	432	5,817	294	165	6,708

[1] Preliminary. *Source: National Agricultural Statistics Service, U.S. Department of Agriculture (NASS-USDA)*

Factory Shipments of Paints, Varnish and Lacquer in the United States In Millions of Dollars

Year	First Quarter	Second Quarter	Third Quarter	Fourth Quarter	Total	Year	First Quarter	Second Quarter	Third Quarter	Fourth Quarter	Total
1989	2,614.4	3,149.9	3,100.0	2,665.7	11,239	1994	3,039.8	3,783.0	3,736.2	3,240.8	13,800
1990	2,754.7	3,188.6	3,080.1	2,632.6	11,762	1995	3,330.3	3,838.0	3,814.5	3,423.4	14,406
1991	2,498.4	3,158.7	3,123.0	2,611.2	11,707	1996	3,438.6	4,161.9	3,954.9	3,428.9	14,984
1992	2,852.3	3,464.1	3,308.7	2,816.4	12,441	1997	3,515.2	4,023.4	3,924.1	3,323.0	14,786
1993	2,894.1	3,600.5	3,448.9	2,993.7	12,937	1998[1]	3,519.7	4,152.8	3,993.8		15,555

[1] Preliminary. *Source: The Oil World*

Consumption of Linseed Oil in Inedible Products in the United States In Millions of Pounds

Year	July	Aug.	Sept.	Oct.	Nov.	Dec.	Jan.	Feb.	Mar.	Apr.	May	June	Total
1991-2		----------- 29.0 -----------			----------- 23.2 -----------		15.5	15.5	13.0	15.0	15.3	11.4	133.4
1992-3	16.3	14.8	11.5	11.2	6.9	8.0	8.3	8.5	11.8	10.5	12.6	13.0	133.4
1993-4	14.9	8.1	11.2	9.0	7.2	10.7	10.2	7.5	9.9	8.5	11.5	11.7	120.4
1994-5	10.7	10.8	12.3	12.2	9.0	10.0	12.6	8.2	11.4	8.1	10.0	9.7	124.9
1995-6	8.8	10.0	9.4	10.6	7.4	6.9	8.8	8.5	7.2	8.1	10.1	9.5	105.3
1996-7	9.0	10.8	7.8	6.0	6.7	6.1	6.7	7.1	6.3	8.3	8.9	8.5	92.3
1997-8	8.9	7.7	8.6	6.7	7.5	6.4	8.0	6.0	6.2	5.9	6.8	5.7	84.3
1998-9[1]	7.2	6.8	6.4	5.6	4.6	6.5							74.3

[1] Preliminary. *Source: Bureau of the Census, U.S. Department of Commerce*

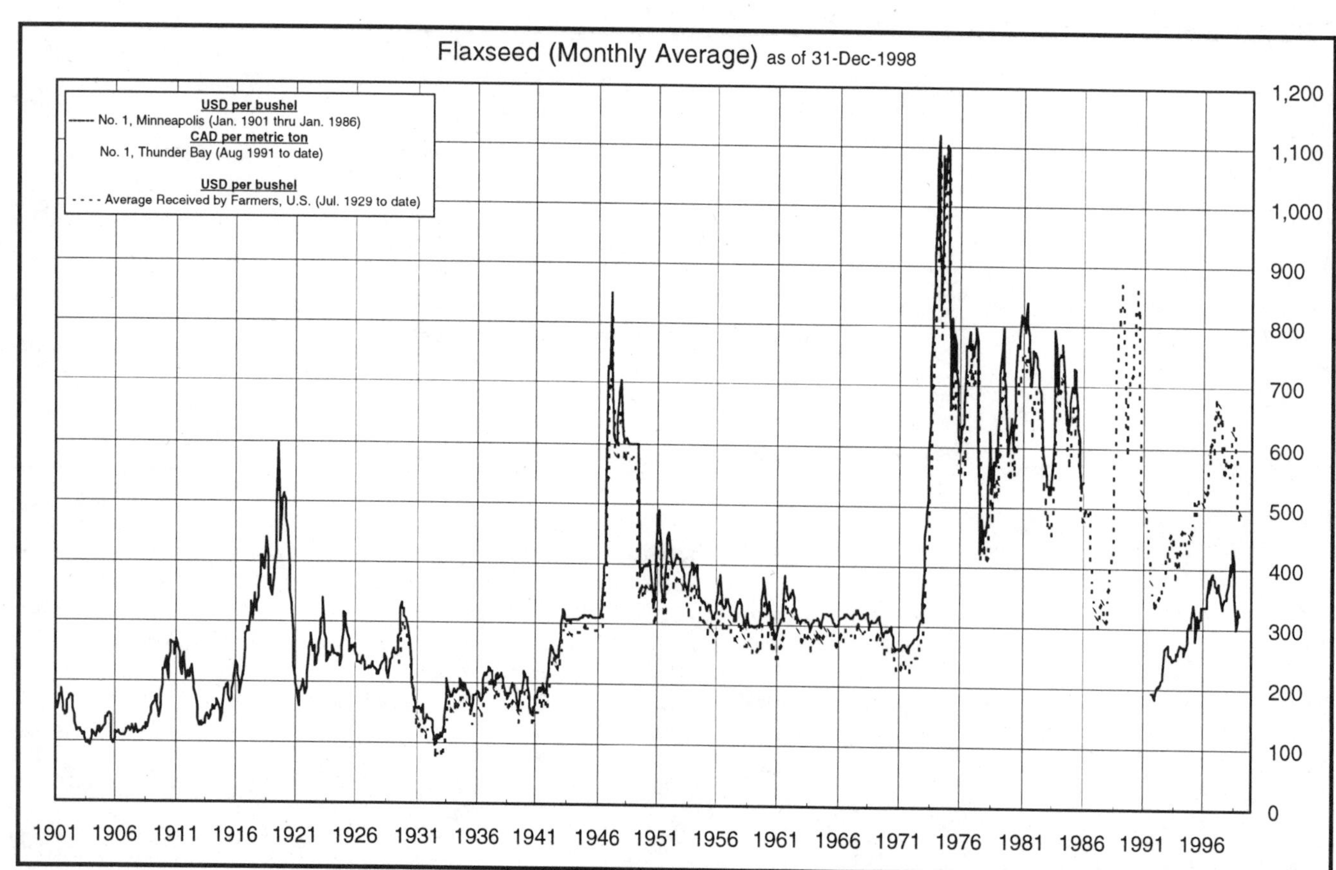

Supply and Distribution of Linseed Oil in the United States In Millions of Pounds

Crop Year Beginning June	Supply: Stocks June 1	Supply: Pro-duction	Supply: Total	Disappearance: Exports	Disappearance: Domestic	Disappearance: Total Disappearance	Average Price at Minneapolis Cents/Lb.
1989-90	48	165	213	12	164	176	40.2
1990-1	37	176	213	6	167	173	38.0
1991-2	40	182	222	12	170	182	32.0
1992-3	40	172	212	8	150	158	31.5
1993-4	54	174	228	7	162	165	31.8
1994-5	63	171	237	24	168	192	33.7
1995-6	45	180	228	23	155	178	36.5
1996-7	50	200	256	66	155	221	36.0
1997-8[1]	35	210	250	58	155	208	37.8
1998-9[2]	42	215	262	62	155	217	36.5-38.5

[1] Preliminary. [2] Forecast. *Source: Economic Research Service, U.S. Department of Agriculture (ERS-USDA)*

World Production and Price of Linseed Oil In Thousands of Metric Tons

Year	Argentina	Bang-ladesh	Belgium	China	Egypt	Germany	India	Japan	United Kingdom	United States	Former U.S.S.R.	World Total	Rotterdam Ex-Tank $ Tonne
1989-90	158.8	11.6	12.9	104.1	11.7	44.9	92.9	31.4	11.4	76.1	11.5	646.6	756
1990-1	141.5	12.0	12.2	126.9	12.3	57.5	94.2	34.7	16.8	84.0	10.1	685.8	502
1991-2	114.0	13.5	14.7	111.0	11.3	56.1	83.8	31.9	27.0	87.9	9.1	638.4	377
1992-3	62.3	12.6	25.5	114.0	8.1	56.8	78.0	28.4	27.2	80.0	9.6	571.5	450
1993-4	32.2	12.7	28.8	121.8	8.7	77.2	90.7	30.7	35.2	78.7	9.9	617.9	476
1994-5	46.8	13.0	35.2	127.8	9.3	104.0	91.4	29.2	41.4	81.7	10.2	700.3	657
1995-6	47.8	13.0	44.3	117.3	8.0	72.0	88.1	30.0	28.9	80.0	12.1	659.0	579
1996-7	16.9	12.5	52.1	114.0	9.6	52.2	88.8	31.0	34.1	99.3	11.2	644.0	560
1997-8[1]	29.0	12.9	57.6	120.0	9.8	59.4	85.1	31.0	36.1	97.1	11.0	670.0	633

[1] Preliminary. [2] Forecast. *Source: The Oil World*

Average Price Received by Farmers for Flaxseed in the United States In Dollars Per Bushel

Year	July	Aug.	Sept.	Oct.	Nov.	Dec.	Jan.	Feb.	Mar.	Apr.	May	June	Average
1989-90	5.90	6.49	7.07	7.09	7.15	7.14	7.24	7.69	8.03	8.60	8.23	8.31	7.41
1990-1	7.56	5.86	5.36	5.15	5.16	5.15	5.12	4.82	4.90	4.66	4.33	3.98	5.17
1991-2	3.92	3.69	3.55	3.39	3.31	3.46	3.39	3.43	3.51	3.53	3.61	3.66	3.54
1992-3	3.70	3.68	4.12	4.09	4.08	4.24	4.11	4.46	4.52	4.40	4.42	4.45	4.19
1993-4	4.29	3.79	4.24	4.09	4.05	4.18	4.38	4.61	4.64	4.60	4.43	4.25	4.30
1994-5	4.28	4.52	4.54	4.49	4.51	4.71	4.76	4.94	5.13	5.10	4.91	5.03	4.74
1995-6	5.11	5.21	5.11	5.11	5.17	5.03	5.26	5.21	5.28	5.31	6.13	5.90	5.32
1996-7	6.19	6.15	5.89	6.49	6.38	6.77	6.43	6.74	6.66	6.43	6.45	5.99	6.38
1997-8	6.07	5.53	5.72	5.81	5.71	5.72	5.82	6.27	6.24	6.22	6.34	6.18	5.97
1998-9[1]	6.17	5.45	5.09	4.86	4.97	5.01	5.03						5.23

[1] Preliminary. *Source: National Agricultural Statistics Service, U.S. Department of Agriculture (NASS-USDA)*

Stocks of Linseed Oil (Crude & Refined) at Factories & Warehouses in the U.S. In Millions of Pounds

Year	July 1	Aug. 1	Sept. 1	Oct. 1	Nov. 1	Dec. 1	Jan. 1	Feb. 1	Mar. 1	Apr. 1	May 1	June 1
1989-90	48.4	43.8	23.2	21.5	23.9	30.3	29.9	39.5	36.7	39.1	38.3	36.8
1990-1	28.2	21.9	17.2	41.8	41.4	47.5	---	61.7	---	---	75.4	---
1991-2	---	60.6	---	---	64.2	---	73.1	51.2	62.3	45.6	45.7	41.4
1992-3	34.6	35.5	29.7	41.3	49.1	47.7	39.9	44.2	45.1	49.1	42.8	43.1
1993-4	45.2	39.0	42.1	47.0	27.9	19.3	22.5	38.0	42.0	49.4	52.0	62.6
1994-5	60.3	56.5	49.4	60.6	48.1	39.3	38.6	38.9	31.0	35.7	37.9	44.8
1995-6	39.5	44.6	37.4	46.0	48.0	44.5	45.3	58.9	64.0	62.0	60.6	47.2
1996-7	51.3	50.9	59.0	46.1	38.8	41.8	49.2	48.1	53.9	50.5	44.5	45.6
1997-8	39.9	35.2	40.3	33.3	38.6	40.3	46.9	60.8	55.8	63.1	54.6	49.4
1998-9[1]	49.6	45.3	38.5	55.4	35.7	44.5	51.0					

[1] Preliminary. *Source: Bureau of the Census, U.S. Department of Commerce*

FLAXSEED AND LINSEED OIL

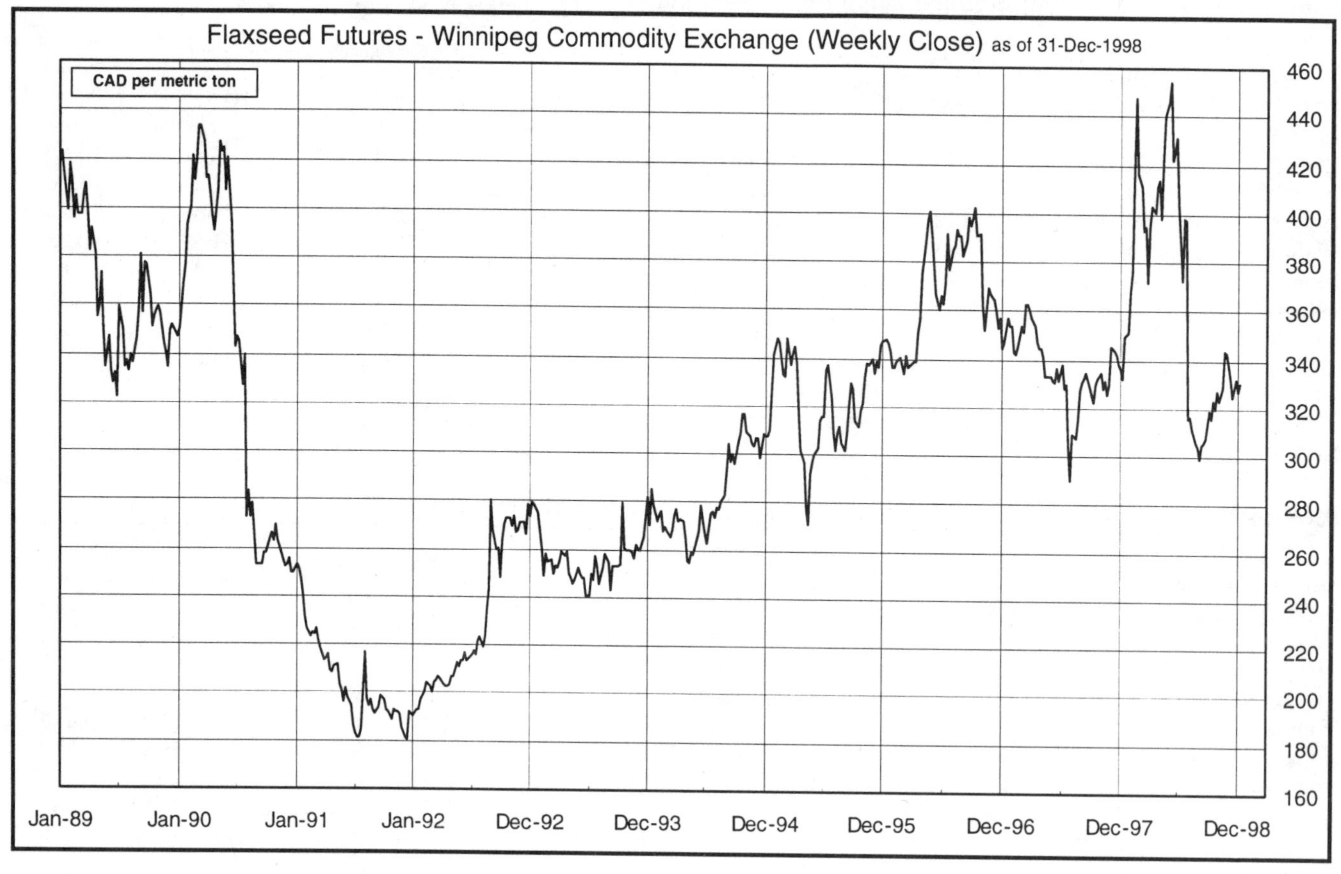

Wholesale Price of Raw Linseed Oil at Minneapolis in Tank Cars In Cents Per Pound

Year	July	Aug.	Sept.	Oct.	Nov.	Dec.	Jan.	Feb.	Mar.	Apr.	May	June	Average
1989-90	39.00	39.00	39.50	40.00	40.00	40.00	40.00	40.00	41.60	42.00	42.00	43.00	40.51
1990-1	44.00	40.40	39.75	36.80	36.00	36.00	36.00	36.00	36.00	36.00	36.50	36.00	37.45
1991-2	36.00	36.00	36.00	30.00	30.00	30.00	30.00	30.00	30.00	30.00	30.00	30.00	31.50
1992-3	30.00	30.00	32.00	32.00	32.00	32.00	32.00	32.00	32.00	32.00	32.00	28.50	31.38
1993-4	32.00	32.00	32.00	32.00	32.00	32.00	32.00	32.00	32.00	32.00	32.00	32.00	32.00
1994-5	30.31	32.00	32.00	33.50	35.00	35.00	35.00	35.00	35.00	35.00	35.00	35.00	33.98
1995-6	35.00	35.50	37.00	37.00	37.00	37.00	37.00	37.00	37.00	37.00	37.00	37.00	36.71
1996-7	37.00	37.20	37.50	37.00	33.75	32.12	36.00	36.00	36.00	36.00	36.00	36.00	35.88
1997-8	36.00	36.00	36.00	37.00	37.00	37.00	36.00	36.00	36.00	36.00	37.00	37.00	36.42
1998-9[1]	37.00	37.00	37.00										37.00

[1] Preliminary. *Source: Economic Research Service, U.S. Department of Agriculture (ERS-USDA)*

Average Open Interest of Flaxseed Futures in Winnipeg In Contracts

Year	Jan.	Feb.	Mar.	Apr.	May	June	July	Aug.	Sept.	Oct.	Nov.	Dec.
1989	7,864	7,875	5,422	6,038	6,479	8,297	8,609	9,234	8,191	5,120	4,613	3,349
1990	3,812	5,165	5,701	5,790	4,839	4,985	4,950	4,908	4,651	4,477	5,079	4,502
1991	4,033	4,140	4,175	4,861	4,137	4,642	5,317	6,106	6,173	5,733	5,669	5,333
1992	5,620	6,772	7,864	7,984	7,786	7,321	6,299	6,553	5,623	4,860	6,734	5,979
1993	7,810	8,052	6,203	5,672	5,505	5,321	4,246	5,777	5,923	3,568	3,763	3,922
1994	6,118	6,201	5,946	5,519	4,683	3,945	4,301	4,654	4,997	3,077	4,888	5,251
1995	6,242	8,731	7,505	7,121	8,107	7,212	6,436	5,557	6,230	5,245	5,937	4,414
1996	6,059	6,056	4,402	5,192	6,970	4,435	3,102	2,989	3,257	3,438	4,326	5,119
1997	5,420	5,356	5,591	5,151	4,923	4,075	3,891	4,031	7,131	8,284	7,255	7,955
1998	10,059	10,190	9,707	8,540	6,480	6,874	6,030	6,767	7,421	7,221	7,564	5,828

Source: Winnipeg Commodity Exchange (WCE)

Fruits

The U.S. Department of Agriculture indicated that in the second half of 1998, the grower price for fruit and nuts would likely average slightly higher than in the same period of 1997. Grower prices for noncitrus fruit were expected to be higher. Partly to blame for the higher prices were weather-related problems in California which resulted in smaller fruit crops. California is the major fruit producer. Lower production of stone fruit and pears in the fall of 1998 would work to increase retail fruit prices while a larger apple crop would act to lower prices.

The U.S.D.A. forecast 1998 apple production at 11.3 billion pounds, an increase of 9 percent from 1997. The largest apple producing state is Washington which was forecast to have a crop of 6.1 billion pounds, an increase of 22 percent from 1997. California's apple crop was estimated at 915 million pounds or some 5 percent less than the year before. The Michigan crop was forecast at a billion pounds, down 5 percent from the year before. New York's apple harvest was projected at 1.04 billion pounds, some 7 percent less than in 1997.

The U.S.D.A. forecast U.S. pear production in 1998 at 1.84 billion pounds, a 12 percent decline from 1997. California Bartlett pear production in 1998 was forecast at 540 million pounds, a decline of 4 percent from the previous season. The smaller crop was due to unfavorable weather on the Pacific Coast. Washington state production of Bartlett and other pears was estimated at 760 million pounds, down 16 percent from the previous season. Oregon production of Bartlett and other pears was forecast at 420 million pounds, a decline of 18 percent from 1997.

U.S. production of peaches in 1998 was forecast by the U.S.D.A. at 2.42 billion pounds, down 9 percent from 1997 when output was 2.65 billion pounds. California is by far the largest producer of peaches. California Clingstone peach production is estimated at 1.05 billion pounds, down 9 percent from 1997. California Freestone peach production was estimated at 650 million pounds, a 12 percent decline from 1997. South Carolina peach production was estimated at 140 million pounds in 1998, down 12 percent from the season before. Georgia production was 70 million pounds, a decline of 56 percent from the previous year.

U.S. sweet cherry production in 1998 was estimated at nearly 386 million pounds, a decline of 13 percent from 1997. The Washington state sweet cherry crop was forecast at 182 million pounds, about 1 percent less than the previous year. Oregon sweet cherry production was estimated at 100 million pounds, unchanged from the year before. Michigan sweet cherry production rose 11 percent to 60 million pounds in 1998 while California's crop fell 70 percent in 1998 to 30 million pounds.

Commercial Production for Selected Fruits in the United States — In Thousands of Short Tons

Year	Apples	Cherries[2]	Cranberries	Grapes	Grapefruit	Lemons	Nectarines	Oranges	Peaches	Pears	Pineapples	Prunes & Plums	Strawberries	Tangelos	Tangerines	Total All Fruits
1992	5,284	373	208	6,052	2,224	766	236	8,909	1,336	923	550	829	668	117	260	29,482
1993	5,342	339	196	6,023	2,791	942	205	10,992	1,330	948	370	588	724	137	247	31,750
1994	5,750	359	234	5,874	2,661	984	242	10,329	1,257	1,046	365	879	825	150	318	31,872
1995	5,293	363	210	5,922	2,912	897	176	11,432	1,151	948	345	744	804	142	287	32,150
1996	5,196	290	234	5,554	2,718	992	247	11,427	1,058	821	347	952	814	110	349	31,618
1997[1]	5,193	368	275	7,282	2,888	958	264	12,677	1,326	1,044	324	899	817	178	418	35,487

[1] Preliminary. [2] Sweet and tart. *Source: Economic Research Service, U.S. Department of Agriculture (ERS-USDA)*

Utilized Production of Selected Fruits in the United States — In Thousands of Short Tons

Year	Utilized Production: Citrus[1]	Utilized Production: Noncitrus[2]	Utilized Production: Total	Value of Production: Citrus[1]	Value of Production: Noncitrus[2]	Value of Production: Total
	In Thousands of Short Tons			In Thousands of Dollars		
1992	12,452	17,124	29,576	2,401,351	6,036,615	8,437,966
1993	15,274	16,563	31,837	2,151,173	6,135,411	8,286,584
1994	14,561	17,341	31,903	2,268,330	6,269,879	8,542,929
1995	15,799	16,358	32,178	2,328,915	6,818,439	9,147,354
1996	15,712	16,114	31,826	2,515,774	7,261,536	9,777,310
1997[3]	17,247	18,390	35,637	2,574,167	8,080,056	10,654,223

[1] Year harvest was completed. [2] Includes bushberries (beginning 1992), cranberries and strawberries. [3] Preliminary. *Source: Economic Research Service, U.S. Department of Agriculture (ERS-USDA)*

Average Retail Prices for Selected Fruits in the United States — In Dollars Per Pound

Year	Red Delicious Apples	Bananas	Anjou Pears	Thompson Seedless Grapes	Lemons	Grapefruit	Oranges: Navel	Oranges: Valencias
1993	.834	.439	.846	1.465	1.084	.529	.557	.654
1994	.803	.462	.802	1.642	1.090	.513	.545	.587
1995	.835	.490	.774	1.551	1.136	.548	.625	.648
1996	.930	.490	.916	1.685	1.114	.574	.707	.703
1997	.907	.487	.985	1.712	1.154	.520	.592	.682
1998[1]	.964	.481	.897	1.769	1.001	.490	.516	.559

[1] Estimate. *Source: Economic Research Service, U.S. Department of Agriculture (ERS-USDA)*

FRUITS

Utilization of Fruit Production, and Value in the U.S. In Thousands of Short Tons (Fresh Equivalent)

Year	Utilized Production	Fresh	Processed: Canned	Dried	Juice	Frozen	Wine	Other	Value of Utilized Production $1,000
1988	15,911	5,909	2,374	2,546	1,415	459	2,983	224	5,102,962
1989	16,345	6,104	2,266	2,857	1,580	479	2,869	190	5,279,382
1990	15,640	6,093	2,244	2,440	1,448	506	2,717	192	5,525,279
1991	15,740	6,215	2,119	2,417	1,583	501	2,739	167	6,021,210
1992	17,124	6,522	2,386	2,369	1,743	584	3,256	264	6,036,615
1993	16,563	6,400	2,042	2,339	1,743	627	3,029	181	6,135,411
1994	17,341	6,711	2,092	2,816	1,881	669	2,711	227	6,269,879
1995	16,358	6,294	1,754	2,400	1,853	652	2,992	205	6,818,439
1996	16,114	6,322	1,873	2,275	1,577	610	3,043	180	7,261,536
1997[1]	18,390	6,663	2,138	2,645	1,700	699	4,036	236	8,080,056

[1] Preliminary. *Source: Economic Research Service, U.S. Department of Agriculture (ERS-USDA)*

Average Price Indexes for Fruits in the United States

Year	Index of all Fruit and Nut Prices Received by Growers (1990-92 = 100)	Producer Price Index (1982 = 100): Fresh Fruit	Dried Fruit	Canned Fruits and Juices	Frozen Fruits and Juices	Consumer Price Index (1982-84 = 100): Fresh Fruit	Processed Fruit
1988	96	112.8	98.9	120.3	130.0	143.0	121.9
1989	99	110.4	103.1	122.6	124.5	152.4	125.9
1990	97	116.1	107.0	126.9	138.9	170.9	136.6
1991	112	129.4	111.5	128.6	115.1	193.9	131.8
1992	99	83.2	114.3	134.6	125.7	184.2	137.7
1993	91	84.3	117.6	126.1	110.9	188.8	132.3
1994	89	82.2	120.9	126.0	111.9	201.2	133.1
1995	99	85.8	121.0	129.4	115.8	219.0	137.2
1996	118	100.8	124.2	137.5	123.9	234.4	145.2
1997[1]	108	101.3	124.9	137.5	117.3	236.3	148.8

[1] Estimate. *Source: Economic Research Service, U.S. Department of Agriculture (ERS-USDA)*

Fresh Fruit: Per Capita Consumption[1] in the United States In Pounds

Year	Citrus Fruit: Oranges	Tangerines & Tangelos	Lemons	Grapefruit	Total	Noncitrus Fruit: Apples	Apricots	Avocados	Bananas	Cherries	Cranberries
1988	13.90	1.77	2.47	6.69	25.39	19.84	.15	1.58	24.29	.53	.11
1989	12.17	1.71	2.39	6.60	23.56	21.22	.10	1.54	24.71	.62	.07
1990	12.38	1.31	2.60	4.43	21.37	19.60	.16	1.07	24.36	.39	.05
1991	8.46	1.38	2.60	5.87	19.07	18.18	.13	1.41	25.12	.40	.07
1992	12.91	1.94	2.54	5.95	24.36	19.25	.15	1.43	27.26	.53	.08
1993	14.24	1.87	2.65	6.23	25.97	19.17	.13	2.17	26.80	.43	.07
1994	13.06	2.11	2.68	6.12	24.96	19.58	.15	1.34	28.06	.53	.08
1995	11.97	2.01	2.87	6.07	24.12	18.95	.10	1.37	27.42	.29	.08
1996	12.77	2.19	2.90	5.93	24.95	19.01	.09	1.60	28.02	.41	.08
1997[2]	14.31	2.52	2.79	6.26	26.81	18.46	.14	1.42	27.65	.55	.08

[1] All data on calendar-year basis except for citrus fruits; apples, August; grapes and pears, July; grapefruit, September; lemons, August of prior year; all other citrus, November. [2] Preliminary. *Source: Economic Research Service, U.S. Department of Agriculture (ERS-USDA)*

Fresh Fruit: Per Capita Consumption[1] in the United States In Pounds

Year	Noncitrus - Continued: Grapes	Kiwifruit	Mangos	Nectarines & Peaches	Pears	Pineapples	Papaya	Plums & Prunes	Strawberries	Total Noncitrus	Total Fruit
1989	7.94	.33	.51	5.86	3.20	2.04	.14	1.41	3.25	73.07	96.63
1990	7.92	.49	.54	5.54	3.22	2.05	.18	1.55	3.24	70.55	91.92
1991	7.26	.44	.85	6.43	3.15	1.92	.17	1.42	3.58	70.73	89.80
1992	7.19	.33	.68	6.02	3.14	2.00	.24	1.78	3.61	73.84	98.20
1993	7.04	.53	.90	5.95	3.38	2.05	.28	1.28	3.64	73.92	99.87
1994	7.32	.57	.98	5.49	3.48	2.04	.30	1.62	4.09	75.62	100.57
1995	7.52	.56	1.13	5.44	3.40	1.93	.37	.94	4.16	73.65	97.77
1996	6.94	.55	1.36	4.49	3.10	1.92	.55	1.45	4.39	73.96	98.91
1997[2]	8.05	.48	1.46	5.66	3.48	2.38	.48	1.53	4.19	76.01	102.82

[1] All data on calendar-year basis except for citrus fruits; apples, August; grapes and pears, July; grapefruit, September; lemons, August of prior year; all other citrus, November. [2] Preliminary. *Source: Economic Research Service, U.S. Department of Agriculture (ERS-USDA)*

Gas

The U.S. Energy Information Agency reported that gross withdrawals of natural gas in July 1998 were 2.04 trillion cubic feet, up 3 percent from the previous month and marginally higher than a year ago. For all of 1997, gross withdrawals of natural gas were 24.3 trillion cubic feet. Natural gas repressuring in July 1998 was 283 billion cubic feet, slightly higher than the previous month and 4 percent lower than a year ago. For all of 1997, natural gas repressuring was 3.68 trillion cubic feet.

Nonhydrocarbon gases removed in July 1998 were 44 billion cubic feet, some 5 percent above a year ago. For all of 1997, nonhydrocarbon gases removed totaled 503 billion cubic feet. Vented and flared natural gas in July 1998 amounted to 21 billion cubic feet, up 5 percent from the previous month and down 5 percent from a year ago. For all of 1997, vented and flared natural gas was 258 billion cubic feet.

Market production (wet) of natural gas in September 1998 was 1.64 trillion cubic feet, down 3 percent from the previous month but 1 percent more than a year ago. For the January-September 1998 period, market production (wet) of natural gas was 15 trillion cubic feet, up almost 1 percent from the same period in 1997. For all of 1997, marketed wet production was 19.9 trillion cubic feet.

Extraction loss in September 1998 was 80 billion cubic feet, down 2 percent from the previous month but 1 percent higher than a year ago. In the January-September 1998 period, extraction loss totaled 725 billion cubic feet, up almost 1 percent from the same period in 1997. For all of 1997, natural gas extraction loss was 965 billion cubic feet. Extraction loss annually amounts to between four and five percent of marketed production.

Natural dry gas production in September 1998 in the U.S. was 1.56 trillion cubic feet. That was 3 percent less than in August 1998 but 1 percent more than a year ago. In the January-September 1998 period, dry gas production was 14.2 trillion cubic feet, up 1 percent from the comparable period in 1997. For all of 1997, dry gas production was 18.9 trillion cubic feet.

Dry natural gas consumption in September 1998 was 1.45 trillion cubic feet, down 7 percent from the previous month and 1 percent more than a year ago. For the January-September 1998 period, dry natural gas consumption was 15.93 trillion cubic feet, down 2 percent from the year before. For all of 1997, dry natural gas consumption was 21.98 trillion cubic feet. Net imports of dry natural gas in September 1998 were 231 billion cubic feet. In January-September 1998, net imports were 2.14 trillion cubic feet while for all of 1997 they were 2.84 trillion cubic feet.

Futures Markets

Natural gas futures and options are traded on the New York Mercantile Exchange (NYMEX) and the Kansas City Board of Trade (KCBT). Futures are traded on the International Petroleum Exchange (IPE).

World Production of Natural Gas (Monthly Average Marketed Production[3]) In Terajoule[4]

Year	Australia	Canada	China	Germany	Indonesia	India	Italy	Mexico	Netherlands	Romania	Russia[5]	United Kingdom	United States
1989	51,406	331,923	48,816	44,734	128,193	33,715	49,618	75,131	210,184	92,312	2,245,667	143,708	1,569,198
1990	66,445	342,826	49,380	44,162	195,448	36,795	54,389	79,594	211,717	79,931	2,311,092	158,628	1,614,310
1991	62,194	362,029	49,955	52,460	158,214	43,284	53,037	79,009	239,349	68,977	2,286,626	176,344	1,609,083
1992	67,696	397,229	50,052	51,911	165,761	43,297	57,117	95,688	240,043	67,900	1,743,167	176,661	1,614,941
1993	72,848	437,922	52,297	47,904	171,828	44,475	60,792	93,646	244,205	68,891	1,708,083	196,792	1,667,401
1994	87,356	438,335	55,230	50,535	190,775	47,219	64,142	97,285	207,317	65,057	1,525,232	203,875	1,700,081
1995	78,460	607,608	55,872	55,451	203,633	53,422	64,467	100,488	209,229	60,258	1,891,583	213,987	1,683,692
1996	90,912	625,469	63,792	60,310	248,574	59,452	63,864	112,850	236,803	58,843	1,846,065	360,395	1,727,420
1997[1]	93,006	622,414	78,195	59,984	291,502	61,246	62,852	170,284	201,193	51,364	1,903,589	270,136	NA
1998[2]	90,891		69,404	56,421	270,619	64,067		181,766	260,080	45,369	1,887,641	334,060	

[1] Preliminary. [2] Estimate. [3] Compares all gas collected & utilized as fuel or as a chemical industry raw material, including gas used in oilfields as a fuel by producers. [4] Terajoule = 10 to the 12th power Joule = approximately 10 to the 9th power BTU. [5] Formerly part of the U.S.S.R., data not reported separately until 1992. NA = not avaliable. *Source: United Nations*

Marketed Production of Natural Gas in the United States, by States In Million of Cubic Feet

Year	Alaska	California	Colorado	Kansas	Louisiana	Michigan	Mississippi	New Mexico	Oklahoma	Texas	Wyoming	Total
1988	378,638	399,663	191,544	592,845	5,180,267	146,145	124,053	791,819	2,167,050	6,286,029	509,058	17,918,465
1989	393,729	362,860	216,737	601,196	5,078,125	155,988	102,645	854,615	2,237,037	6,241,425	665,699	18,095,147
1990	402,907	362,748	242,997	573,603	5,241,989	172,151	94,616	965,104	2,258,471	6,343,146	735,728	18,593,792
1991	437,822	378,384	285,961	628,459	5,034,361	195,749	108,031	1,038,284	2,153,852	6,280,654	776,528	18,532,439
1992	443,597	365,632	323,041	658,007	4,914,300	194,815	91,697	1,268,863	2,017,356	6,145,862	842,576	18,711,808
1993	430,350	315,851	400,985	686,347	4,991,138	204,635	80,695	1,409,429	2,049,942	6,249,624	634,957	18,981,915
1994	555,402	309,427	453,207	712,730	5,169,705	222,657	63,448	1,557,689	1,934,864	6,353,844	696,018	19,709,525
1995	469,550	279,555	523,084	721,436	5,108,366	238,203	95,533	1,625,837	1,811,734	6,330,048	673,775	19,506,474
1996	480,828	286,494	572,071	712,796	5,240,747	245,740	103,263	1,554,087	1,734,887	6,449,022	666,036	19,750,793
1997[1]	474,612	291,098	583,198	689,349	5,475,266	310,591	107,137	1,497,069	1,713,127	6,431,484	719,932	19,846,087

[1] Preliminary. *Source: Energy Information Administration, U.S. Department of Energy (EIA-DOE)*

World Production of Natural Gas Plant Liquids   Thousand Barrels Per Day

Year		Algeria	Canada	Mexico	Saudi Arabia	Former USSR	United States	Persian Gulf[2]	OAPEC[3]	OPEC[4]	World
1990	Average	130	426	428	620	425	1,559	930	1,107	1,281	4,632
1991	Average	140	431	457	680	420	1,659	931	1,113	1,299	4,827
1992	Average	140	460	454	713	390	1,697	1,003	1,185	1,364	4,973
1993	Average	145	506	459	704	380	1,736	1,040	1,238	1,435	5,169
1994	Average	140	539	461	698	340	1,727	1,081	1,272	1,475	5,297
1995	Average	145	581	447	701	180	1,762	1,106	1,301	1,506	5,474
1996	Average	145	599	423	697	185	1,830	1,082	1,295	1,501	5,582
1997	Average	145	631	386	723	200	1,817	1,108	1,310	1,488	5,571
1998[1]	Average	145	641	420	714	230	1,753	1,164	1,388	1,554	5,706

[1] Preliminary. [2] Bahrain, Iran, Iraq, Kuwait, Qatar, Saudi Arabia and the United Arab Emirates. [3] Organization of Arab Petroleum Exporting Countries. [4] Organization of Petroleum Exporting Countries. *Source: Energy Information Administration, U.S. Department of Energy (EIA-DOE)*

Recoverable Reserves and Deliveries of Natural Gas in the United States   In Billions of Cubic Feet

Year	Gross Withdrawals Natural Gas	Recoverable Reserves of Natural Gas Dec. 31[2]	Deliveries: Residential	Commercial	Electric Utility Plants[3]	Industrial	Total Deliveries	Consumption: Lease & Plant Fuel	Used as Pipline Fuel	Heating Value BTU per Cubic Foot
1989	21,074	167,116	4,781	2,718	2,787	6,816	17,102	1,070	629	1,031
1990	21,523	169,346	4,391	2,623	2,786	7,018	16,819	1,236	660	1,031
1991	21,750	167,062	4,556	2,729	2,789	7,231	17,305	1,129	601	1,030
1992	22,132	165,015	4,690	2,803	2,766	7,527	17,786	1,171	588	1,030
1993	22,726	162,415	4,956	2,863	2,682	7,981	18,483	1,172	624	1,027
1994	23,581	163,837	4,848	2,895	2,987	8,167	18,899	1,124	685	1,028
1995	23,744	165,146	4,850	3,034	3,197	8,580	19,660	1,220	700	1,027
1996	24,052	166,474	5,241	3,161	2,732	8,870	20,006	1,250	711	1,027
1997[1]	24,213	167,223	5,014	3,286	2,969	8,753	20,022	1,202	752	1,026

[1] Preliminary. [2] Estimated proved recoverable reserves of dry natural gas. [3] Figures include gas other than natural (impossible to segregate); therefore, shown separately from other consumption. *Source: Energy Information Administration, U.S. Department of Energy (EIA-DOE)*

Gas Utility Sales in the United States by Types and Class of Service   In Trillions of BTU's

Year	Total Utility Sales	Number of Customers (Millions)	Class by Service: Residential	Commercial	Industrial	Electric Generation	Other	Revenue -- Million $ From Sales to Customers: Total	Residential	Commercial	Industrial	Electric Generation	Other
1989	10,551	53.4	4,798	2,322	1,963	1,280	188	47,493	26,172	11,074	9,217	449	582
1990	9,842	54.3	4,468	2,192	1,890	1,120	171	45,153	25,000	10,604	6,034	2,962	553
1991	9,601	55.2	4,546	2,198	1,743	888	226	44,647	25,729	10,669	5,326	2,250	674
1992	9,907	56.1	4,694	2,209	1,959	813	231	46,178	26,702	10,865	5,837	2,077	698
1993	10,151	57.0	5,054	2,397	2,009	524	168	50,137	29,787	12,076	6,162	1,480	632
1994	9,248	57.9	4,845	2,253	1,690	420	159	49,852	30,552	12,276	5,529	1,170	597
1995	9,221	58.7	4,803	2,281	1,591	328	218	46,436	28,742	11,573	4,816	836	549
1996[1]	9,532	59.8	5,198	2,395	1,519	271	148	51,115	32,021	12,726	4,257	783	545
1997[2]	8,913	59.8	5,021	2,244	1,279	245	124	51,517	33,068	12,666	4,518	766	498

[1] Preliminary. [2] Estimate. NA = Not available. *Source: American Gas Association (AGA)*

Salient Statistics of Gas in the United States

Year	Supply: Marketed Production	Extraction Loss	Dry Production	Storage Withdrawals	Imports (Consumed)	Total Supply	Disposition: Consumption	Exports	Added to Storage	Total Disposition	Average Price Delivered to Consumers: Wellhead Price	Imports	Exports	Residential	Commercial	Industrial	Electric Utilities
	In Billions of Cubic Feet										$ Per Thousand Cubic Feet						
1988	17,918	816	17,103	2,270	1,294	20,315	18,030	74	2,211	20,315	1.69	1.84	2.74	5.47	4.63	2.95	2.33
1989	18,095	785	17,311	2,854	1,382	21,435	18,801	107	2,528	21,435	1.69	1.82	2.51	5.64	4.74	2.96	2.43
1990	18,594	784	17,810	1,986	1,532	21,302	18,716	86	2,499	21,300	1.71	1.94	3.10	5.80	4.83	2.93	2.38
1991	18,532	835	17,698	2,752	1,773	21,836	19,035	129	2,672	21,836	1.64	1.82	2.59	5.82	4.81	2.69	2.18
1992	18,712	872	17,840	2,772	2,138	22,360	19,544	216	2,599	22,360	1.74	1.85	2.25	5.89	4.88	2.84	2.36
1993	18,982	886	18,095	2,799	2,350	23,254	20,279	140	2,835	23,254	2.04	2.03	2.59	6.16	5.22	3.07	2.61
1994	19,710	889	18,821	2,508	2,624	24,207	20,708	162	2,796	24,207	1.85	1.87	2.50	6.41	5.44	3.05	2.28
1995	19,506	908	18,599	2,974	2,841	24,837	21,581	154	2,566	24,837	1.55	1.49	2.39	6.06	5.05	2.71	2.02
1996[1]	19,751	958	18,793	2,911	2,937	25,635	21,967	153	2,906	25,635	2.17	1.97	2.97	6.34	5.40	3.42	2.69
1997[2]	19,865	964	18,901	2,824	2,994	25,517	21,973	157	2,800	25,517	2.32	2.17	3.02	6.94	5.79	3.59	2.74

[1] Preliminary. [2] Estimate. *Source: Energy Information Administration, U.S. Department of Energy (EIA-DOE)*

Average Open Interest of Natural Gas Futures in New York In Contracts

Year	Jan.	Feb.	Mar.	Apr.	May	June	July	Aug.	Sept.	Oct.	Nov.	Dec.
1990	-----	-----	-----	1,320	2,699	4,268	6,130	8,760	11,077	12,998	13,813	10,814
1991	10,523	13,825	13,125	13,225	16,782	18,502	19,235	21,460	23,853	24,003	21,692	19,065
1992	24,718	28,661	29,851	33,626	41,456	49,642	49,829	57,346	68,306	77,034	80,349	74,569
1993	69,499	77,053	91,132	116,366	136,074	132,667	124,038	126,443	129,940	130,619	124,627	129,963
1994	127,254	128,336	118,480	119,908	120,894	120,956	111,044	135,652	156,238	145,766	139,471	139,054
1995	148,448	151,882	157,097	150,101	148,797	144,402	143,942	140,297	135,226	133,969	140,301	166,227
1996	155,024	150,521	149,809	159,132	147,616	156,959	151,913	135,191	138,657	144,944	147,854	151,498
1997	156,231	162,567	171,467	181,745	206,685	197,637	199,296	213,640	235,509	242,184	231,556	210,259
1998	192,652	198,853	203,402	251,344	255,837	264,517	255,878	273,350	275,868	252,827	236,292	240,832

Source: New York Mercantile Exchange (NYMEX)

Volume of Trading of Natural Gas Futures in New York In Thousands of Contracts

Year	Jan.	Feb.	Mar.	Apr.	May	June	July	Aug.	Sept.	Oct.	Nov.	Dec.	Total
1990	-----	-----	-----	4.1	6.4	10.5	14.3	17.3	15.2	25.3	15.9	22.3	131.4
1991	29.2	14.9	22.8	20.3	28.7	51.2	37.0	33.1	42.3	46.6	49.0	50.2	425.3
1992	89.0	45.4	77.9	98.9	137.5	116.4	156.0	192.2	268.7	300.0	213.5	227.6	1,923.2
1993	194.3	274.4	318.8	443.0	471.5	365.9	335.6	353.3	459.6	417.1	449.7	613.9	4,697.1
1994	667.6	470.9	373.5	344.7	411.1	465.8	438.8	724.2	578.7	594.2	621.9	721.8	6,413.2
1995	733.0	557.8	676.1	524.5	621.3	622.5	641.8	745.6	548.3	664.4	763.0	988.5	8,086.7
1996	887.2	655.7	694.6	620.0	590.7	681.3	829.0	628.8	679.1	924.4	802.8	820.4	8,813.9
1997	922.8	693.6	664.7	836.3	945.4	803.7	812.9	1,313.8	1,377.1	1,394.0	1,104.8	1,054.6	11,923.6
1998	1,005.6	1,089.1	1,193.5	1,625.9	1,245.2	1,568.8	1,310.4	1,237.0	1,656.3	1,339.5	1,243.1	1,464.0	15,978.3

Source: New York Mercantile Exchange (NYMEX)

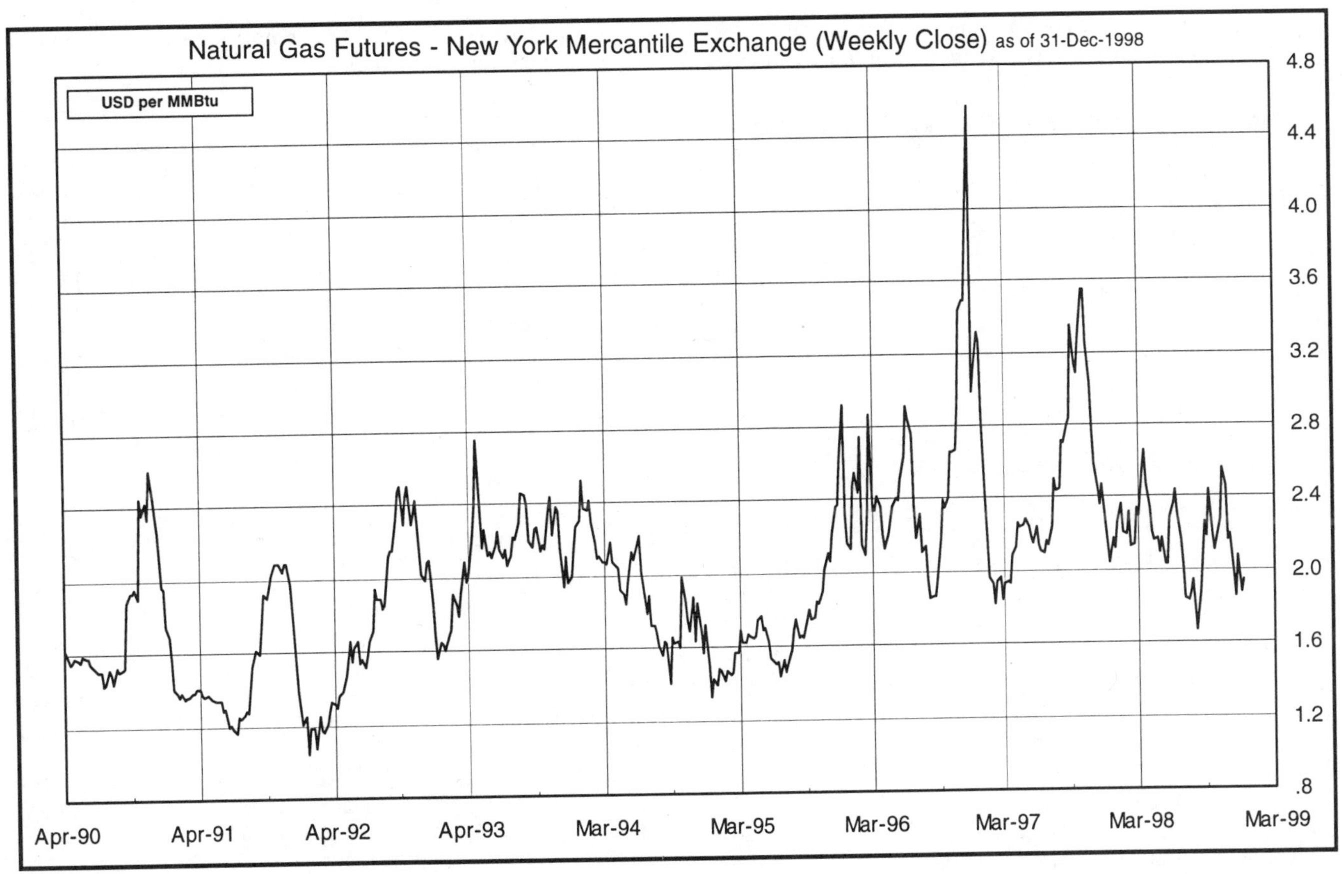

Gasoline

Gasoline prices fell in 1998, a reflection of burdensome supplies of product. With large supplies of petroleum, production of finished motor gasoline increased and with it prices at the pump fell to some of the lowest inflation adjusted levels in history. On a seasonal basis, gasoline production by refineries increases in the summer months and declines in the winter months. The peak driving season between June and September is considered the heaviest and refineries increase output of product to build inventories heading into the season. At the end of the summer driving season, refineries switch to the production of heating oil for the winter heating season. Late 1998 saw extremely mild weather in the eastern U.S. which likely led to increased travel though that was not enough to raise prices. To some extent, technology and the application of new technology to discover and develop crude oil reserves has led to the glut of petroleum which in turn has increased the supply of gasoline.

U.S. production of finished motor gasoline in August 1998 was 8.2 million barrels per day. That represented a decline of 1 percent from July 1998. Production in June reached a season high 8.37 million barrels per day. Production in August 1997 was 1 percent higher than in August 1997 and 5 percent above August 1996. Over the January-August 1998 period, production of finished motor gasoline averaged 7.98 million barrels per day. That was nearly 3 percent above the same period of 1997 and some 5 percent higher than in the like period of 1996. For all of 1997, gasoline production averaged 7.87 million barrels per day.

U.S. imports of finished gasoline in August 1998 averaged 351,000 barrels per day, an increase of 9 percent from the previous month. Imports in August 1998 were 20 percent higher than in August 1997 and were 1 percent more than in August 1996. In the January-August 1998 period, imports averaged 303,000 barrels per day. That represented an 8 percent decline from the same period in 1997 and some 17 percent less than the same period of 1996. For all of 1997, imports of finished motor gasoline averaged 309,000 barrels per day.

U.S. exports of motor gasoline in August 1998 averaged 127,000 barrels per day, an increase of almost 9 percent from the previous month. Exports were 27 percent less than in August 1997 but were 55 percent higher than in August 1996. In the January-August 1998 period, imports averaged 120,000 barrels per day. That was down 1 percent from the comparable period in 1997 but some 17 percent more than in 1996. For all of 1997, exports averaged 137,000 barrels per day.

Finished gasoline supplied in August 1998 averaged 8.58 million barrels per day. In January-August 1998 they averaged 8.15 million barrels per day, up 2 percent from 1997. Total gasoline ending stocks at the end of August 1998 were 208 million barrels. That was down 3 percent from the previous month. Stocks at the end of 1997 were 210 million barrels. Stocks of finished gasoline at the end of August 1998 were 164 million barrels, down 5 percent from the previous month. At the end of 1997, stocks were 166 million barrels.

Futures Market

Unleaded gasoline futures and options are traded on the New York Mercantile Exchange (NYMEX).

Average Price of Unleaded Gasoline in New York In Cents Per Gallon

Year	Jan.	Feb.	Mar.	Apr.	May	June	July	Aug.	Sept.	Oct.	Nov.	Dec.	Average
1989	50.24	48.47	54.91	69.98	67.97	63.75	56.34	52.81	59.29	55.76	50.80	53.94	57.02
1990	64.20	59.59	56.15	61.86	64.24	64.55	65.25	89.61	99.85	95.68	88.10	68.07	73.10
1991	68.88	65.82	74.25	72.07	70.28	63.59	65.23	69.90	62.17	64.41	65.10	55.55	66.44
1992	53.04	55.14	54.10	59.75	63.48	64.51	59.94	62.06	61.63	60.81	58.22	53.24	58.83
1993	52.96	52.54	54.33	59.35	59.37	54.78	51.80	53.13	48.61	50.22	44.30	37.68	51.59
1994	42.40	43.75	44.04	48.98	50.62	52.84	54.52	55.61	46.53	51.14	52.32	46.87	49.14
1995	50.99	51.43	50.74	61.01	64.76	59.47	51.45	53.45	56.10	48.89	51.15	53.44	54.41
1996	50.70	53.26	58.56	69.17	65.10	58.03	61.65	61.17	62.43	65.52	69.23	68.58	61.95
1997	67.64	62.49	61.28	58.59	62.08	55.17	58.58	70.42	62.17	58.35	55.60	51.75	60.34
1998	47.85	45.14	44.13	46.98	48.26	43.95	42.29	40.14	42.70	43.71	36.78	30.92	42.74

Source: New York Mercantile Exchange (NYMEX)

Average Open Interest of Unleaded Regular Gasoline Futures in New York In Contracts

Year	Jan.	Feb.	Mar.	Apr.	May	June	July	Aug.	Sept.	Oct.	Nov.	Dec.
1989	55,838	57,011	59,012	69,547	68,478	61,519	56,913	52,158	51,910	55,312	65,392	71,464
1990	77,580	80,425	75,368	71,132	62,121	72,105	68,826	59,528	60,558	61,253	56,332	56,569
1991	54,807	75,337	81,393	74,801	71,900	73,633	74,503	87,073	90,680	100,606	111,745	125,578
1992	124,896	117,155	108,388	89,775	79,680	80,394	81,110	76,741	71,264	68,059	71,110	77,508
1993	80,610	93,630	100,657	96,607	88,311	94,926	104,260	103,371	100,921	107,339	126,649	150,359
1994	135,366	120,204	118,977	122,092	96,525	89,854	86,401	76,213	67,881	70,258	71,245	63,679
1995	61,015	67,631	65,201	76,323	76,269	69,676	64,379	58,426	62,089	58,782	57,902	70,098
1996	64,561	64,990	70,100	71,895	66,172	52,882	55,394	55,618	57,119	59,993	58,416	62,760
1997	68,188	84,693	92,520	97,619	90,407	78,492	83,082	103,538	103,250	94,602	92,852	103,497
1998	106,353	102,656	108,667	117,521	107,235	100,792	89,846	86,902	85,188	81,991	87,306	103,079

Source: New York Mercantile Exchange (NYMEX)

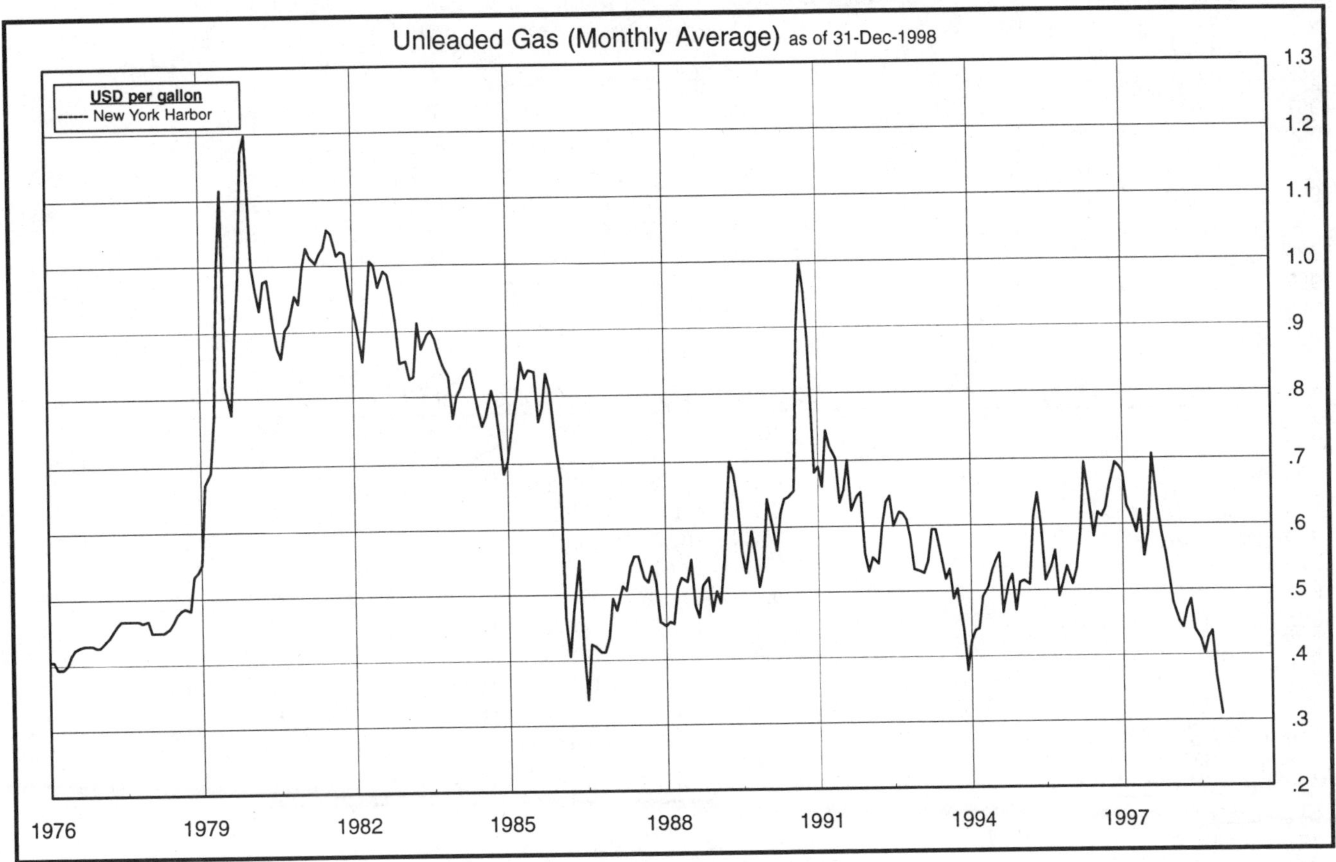

Volume of Trading of Unleaded Regular Gasoline Futures in New York In Contracts

Year	Jan.	Feb.	Mar.	Apr.	May	June	July	Aug.	Sept.	Oct.	Nov.	Dec.	Total
1989	354,167	258,669	373,936	510,964	407,445	443,205	356,939	310,546	412,753	375,489	328,277	352,168	4,484,558
1990	540,633	349,439	461,438	481,665	527,637	472,377	456,342	549,702	373,102	386,472	314,051	248,137	5,160,995
1991	366,772	351,188	525,432	541,073	482,943	446,350	396,429	562,085	386,421	477,111	537,834	529,940	5,603,578
1992	565,922	558,476	604,678	668,490	580,088	620,114	600,897	545,520	469,844	563,856	435,847	461,025	6,674,757
1993	531,780	558,770	584,899	539,785	571,860	611,951	594,740	721,852	642,959	629,733	674,814	729,717	7,392,860
1994	634,027	526,505	615,594	677,891	636,990	673,034	601,980	748,415	569,384	684,670	582,359	519,987	7,470,836
1995	592,329	506,640	736,704	663,743	780,568	680,792	565,655	556,589	573,551	473,014	480,507	461,695	7,071,787
1996	543,818	449,537	570,341	676,193	623,347	467,953	533,793	463,830	469,036	527,553	487,624	499,314	6,312,339
1997	590,066	563,180	605,121	623,169	618,312	555,543	721,386	795,404	664,906	613,557	509,893	614,608	7,475,145
1998	613,643	612,266	766,430	789,293	681,052	753,120	680,551	591,985	654,247	670,159	577,799	601,724	7,992,269

Source: New York Mercantile Exchange (NYMEX)

Production of Finished Motor Gasoline in the United States Thousand Barrels Per Day

Year	Jan.	Feb.	Mar.	Apr.	May	June	July	Aug.	Sept.	Oct.	Nov.	Dec.	Average
1989	6,937	6,650	6,612	6,811	6,894	7,275	7,360	7,155	7,069	6,845	7,046	6,884	6,963
1990	6,879	6,989	6,613	6,775	6,610	7,101	7,238	7,326	7,274	6,880	6,940	6,887	6,959
1991	6,629	6,573	6,643	6,742	7,063	7,351	7,274	7,247	7,030	6,749	7,018	7,354	6,975
1992	7,013	6,726	6,683	6,954	7,092	7,198	7,195	6,817	7,071	7,198	7,323	7,411	7,058
1993	7,228	7,144	6,904	7,126	7,446	7,442	7,337	7,335	7,573	7,394	7,652	7,725	7,360
1994	7,097	6,790	6,760	7,195	7,348	7,455	7,380	7,432	7,385	7,151	7,849	7,867	7,312
1995	7,303	7,243	7,168	7,529	7,678	7,843	7,747	7,642	7,785	7,544	7,739	7,821	7,588
1996	7,333	7,303	7,242	7,475	7,724	7,820	7,811	7,696	7,585	7,496	7,835	7,784	7,593
1997	7,308	7,315	7,322	7,822	8,056	8,180	7,947	8,048	8,147	8,039	7,984	8,143	7,862
1998[1]	7,749	7,485	7,591	8,029	8,057	8,372	8,287	8,200	8,029	7,995	8,263	8,327	8,035

[1] Preliminary. *Source: Energy Information Adminstration, U.S. Department of Energy (EIA-DOE)*

GASOLINE

Disposition of Finished Motor Gasoline, Total Product Supplied in the U.S. Thousand Barrels Per Day

Year	Jan.	Feb.	Mar.	Apr.	May	June	July	Aug.	Sept.	Oct.	Nov.	Dec.	Average
1989	6,745	7,119	7,421	7,157	7,381	7,780	7,296	7,717	7,240	7,302	7,353	7,410	7,328
1990	6,643	7,179	7,338	7,121	7,358	7,519	7,496	7,796	6,914	7,226	7,241	6,978	7,235
1991	6,645	6,838	7,017	7,137	7,437	7,456	7,561	7,528	7,083	7,281	7,008	7,224	7,188
1992	6,869	6,963	7,137	7,238	7,328	7,460	7,639	7,380	7,344	7,338	7,102	7,396	7,268
1993	6,639	7,112	7,389	7,435	7,585	7,700	7,785	7,864	7,607	7,382	7,533	7,661	7,476
1994	6,980	7,275	7,395	7,564	7,644	7,922	7,884	7,975	7,615	7,548	7,464	7,924	7,601
1995	7,163	7,481	7,788	7,651	7,894	8,220	7,888	8,187	7,786	7,781	7,866	7,742	7,789
1996	7,254	7,552	7,729	7,869	7,998	8,089	8,135	8,216	7,641	8,038	7,875	7,775	7,849
1997	7,312	7,651	7,808	8,067	8,128	8,260	8,471	8,195	8,004	8,166	7,955	8,093	8,007
1998[1]	7,590	7,755	7,956	8,137	8,070	8,437	8,659	8,500	8,308	8,405	8,136	8,371	8,197

[1] Preliminary. *Source: Energy Information Adminstration, U.S. Department of Energy (EIA-DOE)*

Stocks of Finished Gasoline[2] on Hand in the United States In Millions of Barrrels

Year	Jan.	Feb.	Mar.	Apr.	May	June	July	Aug.	Sept.	Oct.	Nov.	Dec.
1989	207.8	205.7	191.1	190.6	185.8	180.1	192.1	183.8	187.5	184.8	187.1	179.1
1990	197.6	203.3	187.9	186.3	180.3	177.7	182.0	175.4	190.5	181.9	178.7	182.4
1991	189.1	182.7	174.4	171.9	173.7	178.5	173.5	172.8	179.1	168.3	173.3	183.3
1992	192.8	191.4	182.9	185.0	187.4	189.5	182.0	168.2	170.0	168.7	178.2	179.1
1993	197.8	201.9	189.0	184.0	186.8	184.2	176.8	166.7	171.2	175.6	182.6	187.1
1994	194.1	186.2	175.6	176.4	179.0	176.9	172.9	167.6	169.2	161.7	176.6	175.9
1995	182.7	180.0	167.8	167.1	167.1	163.5	166.0	154.6	158.9	155.6	155.6	161.3
1996	168.7	168.4	158.3	159.8	161.8	163.8	163.7	154.9	161.3	149.1	150.7	157.0
1997	164.9	161.3	153.8	152.0	157.8	163.9	150.6	149.6	158.1	158.0	161.1	166.1
1998[1]	175.3	172.8	166.4	168.3	174.9	177.7	172.5	168.8	164.7	160.0		

[1] Preliminary. [2] Includes oxygenated and other finished. *Source: Energy Information Administration, U.S. Department of Energy (EIA-DOE)*

Average Refiner Price of Finished Motor Gasoline to End Users[1] In Cents Per Gallon

Year	Jan.	Feb.	Mar.	Apr.	May	June	July	Aug.	Sept.	Oct.	Nov.	Dec.	Average
1989	65.6	66.1	68.4	81.7	85.5	84.5	82.0	76.6	74.9	74.7	72.7	72.1	75.6
1990	78.8	76.5	75.1	77.9	80.2	81.5	80.8	92.4	101.2	108.7	107.2	98.4	88.3
1991	88.8	79.5	74.0	77.0	82.0	81.9	78.9	81.1	80.2	77.9	79.1	76.0	79.7
1992	71.2	70.2	71.0	74.6	80.3	84.0	83.5	82.3	82.3	81.3	81.4	78.5	78.4
1993	76.9	76.1	75.7	77.8	80.1	79.8	77.6	76.2	74.9	75.3	72.5	68.0	75.9
1994	66.8	67.6	67.3	69.5	71.1	74.1	77.0	81.5	79.6	76.9	77.5	75.1	73.8
1995	74.5	73.3	73.1	77.3	83.4	83.9	80.0	76.9	75.8	73.6	71.8	73.0	76.5
1996	74.6	74.8	79.8	88.1	92.7	90.3	87.5	84.9	84.4	84.4	86.7	85.9	84.7
1997	86.6	86.1	84.3	83.9	84.5	83.3	81.5	86.8	87.2	84.3	81.6	77.8	83.9
1998[2]	73.3	69.0	65.6	67.4	71.0	70.4	69.4	66.7	65.4	66.4			68.5

[1] Excludes aviation and taxes. [2] Preliminary.. *Source: Energy Information Administration, U.S. Department of Energy (EIA-DOE)*

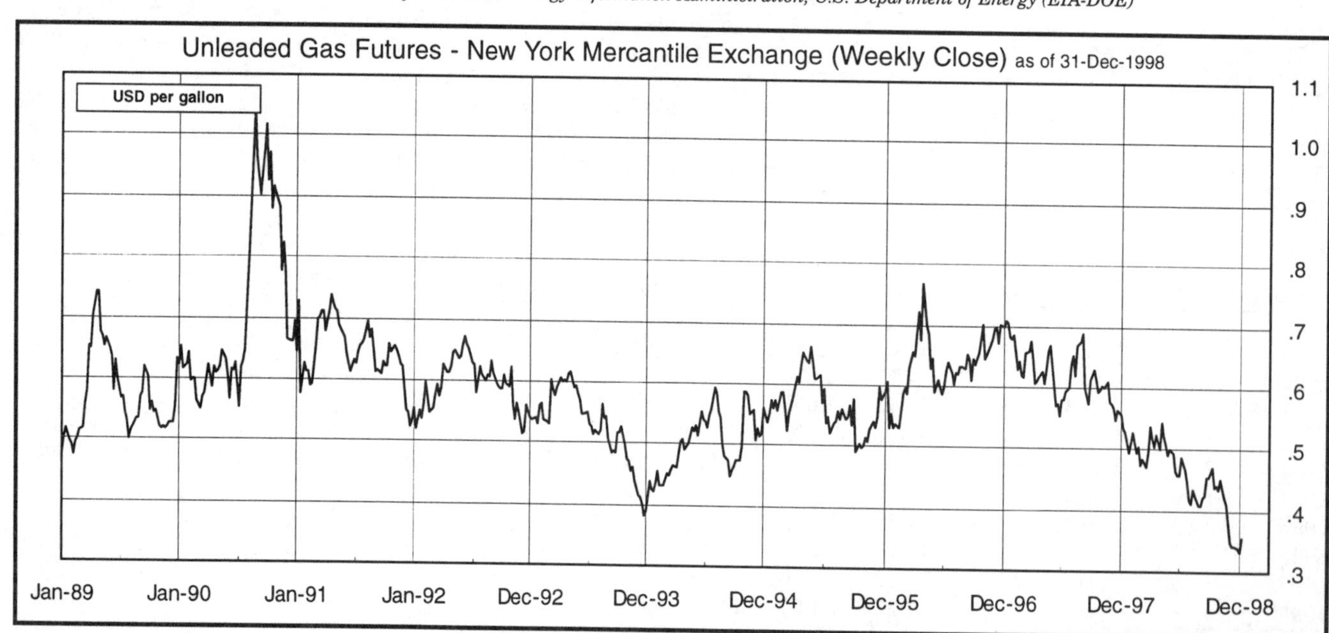

Average Retail Price of Unleaded Premium Motor Gasoline[2] in the United States In Cents Per Gallon

Year	Jan.	Feb.	Mar.	Apr.	May	June	July	Aug.	Sept.	Oct.	Nov.	Dec.	Average
1989	109.1	110.0	111.5	122.1	127.8	127.8	126.4	123.3	121.3	120.9	118.7	117.0	119.7
1990	123.0	122.7	121.8	123.3	124.8	127.1	127.2	136.9	146.7	155.4	155.9	153.7	134.9
1991	143.1	132.1	126.4	128.1	133.1	133.8	131.3	131.8	132.4	130.7	131.8	130.9	132.1
1992	126.7	124.8	125.0	126.8	131.7	135.9	136.3	134.8	134.6	134.5	135.1	133.0	131.6
1993	131.3	130.1	129.4	130.4	131.9	132.1	130.5	129.4	128.2	132.3	130.5	126.8	130.2
1994	124.0	124.5	124.3	126.0	127.4	130.0	132.7	136.7	136.4	134.5	135.4	133.7	130.5
1995	132.4	131.6	130.6	132.5	138.3	141.1	138.4	135.2	133.2	131.5	129.2	129.0	133.6
1996	131.7	131.1	134.8	143.1	150.7	148.1	145.3	142.1	141.7	140.8	142.8	143.8	141.3
1997	144.1	143.4	141.5	141.3	140.9	141.1	138.8	143.3	145.8	142.6	139.7	136.3	141.6
1998[1]	131.9	127.1	122.9	123.7	127.5	127.9	126.8	124.4	123.0	123.6	122.5		125.6

[1] Preliminary. [2] Including taxes. *Source: Energy Information Administration, U.S. Department of Energy (EIA-DOE)*

Average Retail Price of Unleaded Regular Motor Gasoline[2] in the United States In Cents Per Gallon

Year	Jan.	Feb.	Mar.	Apr.	May	June	July	Aug.	Sept.	Oct.	Nov.	Dec.	Average
1989	91.8	92.6	94.0	106.5	111.9	111.4	109.2	105.7	102.9	102.7	99.9	98.0	102.1
1990	104.2	103.7	102.3	104.4	106.1	108.8	108.4	119.0	129.4	137.8	137.7	135.4	116.4
1991	124.7	114.3	108.2	110.4	115.6	116.0	112.7	114.0	114.3	112.2	113.4	112.3	114.0
1992	107.3	105.4	105.8	107.9	113.6	117.9	117.5	115.8	115.8	115.4	115.9	113.6	112.7
1993	111.7	110.8	109.8	111.2	112.9	113.0	110.9	109.7	108.5	112.7	111.3	107.0	110.8
1994	104.3	105.1	104.5	106.4	108.0	110.6	113.6	118.2	117.7	115.2	116.3	114.3	111.2
1995	112.9	112.0	111.5	114.0	120.0	122.6	119.5	116.4	114.8	112.7	110.1	110.1	114.7
1996	112.9	112.4	116.2	125.1	132.3	129.9	127.2	124.0	123.4	122.7	125.0	126.0	123.1
1997	126.1	125.5	123.5	123.1	122.6	122.9	120.5	125.3	127.7	124.2	121.3	117.7	123.4
1998[1]	113.1	108.2	104.1	105.2	109.2	109.4	107.9	105.2	103.3	104.2	102.8		106.6

[1] Preliminary. [2] Including taxes. *Source: Energy Information Administration, U.S. Department of Energy (EIA-DOE)*

Average Retail Price of All-Types[2] Motor Gasoline[3] in the United States In Cents Per Gallon

Year	Jan.	Feb.	Mar.	Apr.	May	June	July	Aug.	Sept.	Oct.	Nov.	Dec.	Average
1989	94.4	95.5	97.4	109.8	115.2	115.0	113.2	109.6	107.3	107.1	104.6	103.0	106.0
1990	109.0	108.6	107.6	109.6	111.4	114.0	113.9	124.6	134.7	143.1	143.2	141.0	121.7
1991	130.4	119.8	113.8	115.9	120.9	121.4	118.5	119.6	119.9	118.0	119.3	118.2	119.6
1992	113.5	111.7	112.2	114.3	119.7	123.9	123.8	122.1	122.2	121.9	122.3	120.1	119.0
1993	118.2	117.2	116.3	117.5	119.3	119.4	117.4	116.3	115.1	119.3	117.8	113.6	117.3
1994	110.9	111.4	110.9	112.8	114.3	116.7	119.9	124.3	123.7	121.2	122.2	120.3	117.4
1995	119.0	118.1	117.3	119.7	125.6	128.1	125.2	122.2	120.6	118.5	116.1	116.0	120.5
1996	118.6	118.1	121.9	130.5	137.8	135.4	132.8	129.8	129.3	128.7	130.8	131.8	128.8
1997	131.8	131.2	129.3	128.8	128.4	128.6	126.3	131.0	133.4	130.0	127.1	123.6	129.1
1998[1]	118.6	113.7	109.7	110.6	114.6	114.8	113.4	110.8	109.1	109.9	108.6		112.2

[1] Preliminary. [2] Includes types of motor oil not shown seperately. [3] Including taxes. *Source: Energy Information Administration, U.S. Department of Energy (EIA-DOE)*

Refiner Sales Prices of Finished Aviation Gasoline to End Users[2] in the United States In Cents Per Gallon

Year	Jan.	Feb.	Mar.	Apr.	May	June	July	Aug.	Sept.	Oct.	Nov.	Dec.	Average
1989	89.2	89.7	90.6	99.1	107.0	107.1	105.5	101.9	100.7	100.4	98.6	97.3	99.5
1990	102.0	102.4	100.9	101.4	103.6	104.2	103.9	112.8	125.6	134.4	131.7	122.5	112.0
1991	112.1	106.4	101.3	101.2	105.3	105.2	103.6	105.8	105.7	104.6	104.3	102.0	104.7
1992	98.5	98.5	98.0	99.1	102.4	106.4	106.8	105.7	104.9	104.3	103.4	101.3	102.7
1993	100.3	99.9	99.4	100.7	102.2	102.5	99.7	98.8	98.2	98.0	95.7	91.2	99.0
1994	88.6	88.4	89.0	91.3	92.3	95.6	95.9	101.7	101.1	100.0	100.0	99.2	95.6
1995	99.6	99.8	99.0	101.3	105.8	106.4	101.8	99.2	101.3	96.8	95.4	96.0	100.5
1996	97.6	100.6	105.0	111.2	114.4	113.5	113.7	114.4	114.3	115.0	115.1	115.3	111.6
1997	113.7	114.9	113.8	114.7	115.7	114.6	112.5	114.6	115.6	113.9	113.0	107.7	113.8
1998[1]	104.3	101.1	98.2	98.6	99.9	99.0	98.4	95.9	94.1	95.1			98.5

[1] Preliminary. [2] Excluding taxes. *Source: Energy Information Administration, U.S. Department of Energy (EIA-DOE)*

Gold

The speculative based enthusiasm for gold continued to wane during 1998, as has been the case for some time. Gold began 1998 around $300.00 per ounce and at yearend was near $290.00, basis N.Y. nearest futures. During the year there were some temporary spikes in both directions, an upward push in the spring that carried to about $320.00 an ounce and a mid-summer slide that ran to about $275.00. Neither move had much speculative play if one uses daily trading volume and changes in futures open interest as a clue. On balance, the price bias was negative.

The rational for gold's weakness since mid-1997 has been that central banks were selling, or threatening to sell, their gold inventories. That fear was not as strong in 1998 as it was in 1997 when gold's price fell by $50.00/oz. However, the loss of faith in gold has been persistent as the "ultimate store of value" attitudes have given way to traders access to the world's currency and interest rate markets as possible inflation hedges. Inflationary pressures were and are dormant in most of the industrialized nations with deflation seen as a greater threat. Much of the former speculative interest towards gold has gone into the burgeoning world equity markets. Even in the second half of 1998, when the world's equity markets dropped in the wake of fresh fears of economic meltdowns in some countries, gold's price showed only a tepid upward reaction that briefly carried through $300.00 an ounce.

What price may prove to be gold's bottom and/or what it might take for fresh speculative buying enthusiasm to resurface is not discernible. Moreover, the metal's fundamentals are not encouraging. Should prices carry to about $260.00 an ounce, the effect will likely close a number of marginal producing mines, conversely, a run to the mid-$300's is likely to encourage increased production. World production costs average in the mid $200 an ounce range.

A major uncertainty overhanging the gold market in 1999 is the position of the new European Central Bank (ECB) towards the metal. In mid-1998, it was believed within the banking community that gold would represent 10-15 percent of total ECB reserves, but the speculative based consensus focused on 10-30 percent. In either case, a sizable tonnage of gold, perhaps as much as 12,000 tons, may lie outside the ECB reserves and be subject to sale, more likely in the year 2000 than in 1999. This overhanging inventory is strictly European and does not include the 8,000 plus tons in the U.S., the world's largest holder.

Annual world gold production (mined) in the 1990's has held around 2,250,000 kilograms. South Africa, the world's largest producer, has seen production drop since the mid-1990's. The U.S., the second largest producer since 1991, produced 338,000 kg. in 1997, the highest total to date of the 1990's. 173,000 kg. were produced in the first half of 1998, suggesting that the full year's output will top 1997.

World demand in 1998 could be a record high; total demand in the second quarter of 634,000 kg. was 9 percent below a year earlier, but 50 percent higher than in the first quarter of 1998 with jewelry demand the cornerstone of the recovery. Jewelry fabrication demand had shown virtually no growth in the industrial nations since 1990, but has apparently quickened in Europe and the U.S. Identified world gold resources are estimated at 75,000 tons with South Africa having about one-half of the resources and the U.S. 12 percent. Of the estimated 125,000 tons of gold mined from historical times through 1997, about 15 percent is believed to have been lost or unaccounted for. Of the remaining 100,000 plus tons, about two-thirds is privately held in the form of coin, jewelry and bullion.

The U.S. is a net gold exporter, mostly refined bullion shipped to Europe. Exports in 1997 totaled 476,000 kg. vs. 200,000 kg. in the first half of 1998. U.S. gold imports in 1997 of 209,000 kg. compare to 150,000 through mid-1998, the largest percentage coming from Australia and Canada.

Futures Markets

Gold futures are traded on the Bolsa de Mercadorias & Futuros (BM&F), The Hong Kong Futures Exchange Ltd. (HKFE), the Tokyo Commodity Exchange (TOCOM), the Singapore International Monetary Exchange Ltd. (SIMEX), the Chicago Board of Trade (CBOT), the Mid America Commodity Exchange, (MidAm), and the New York Mercantile Exchange, COMEX division (COMEX). Gold options are traded on the the Vancouver Stock Exchange (VSE), the European Options Exchange (EOE-Optiebeurs), the MidAm, and the COMEX. Futures and options on Krugerrands are traded on the South Africa Futures Exchange (SAFEX).

World Mine Production of Gold In Kilograms (1 Kilogram = 32.1507 Troy Ounces)

Year	Australia	Brazil	Canada	Chile	China	Ghana	Indonesia	Papua N.Guinea	Russia[3]	South Africa	United States	Uzbekistan[3]	World Total
1988	156,950	112,159	134,813	20,614	78,000	11,601	4,738	38,129	277,600	621,000	200,914	------	1,873,803
1989	203,563	52,527	159,527	22,559	90,000	13,358	6,155	27,538	304,000	607,460	265,731	------	2,013,913
1990	244,137	101,913	169,412	27,503	100,000	16,840	11,158	31,938	302,000	605,100	294,189	------	2,180,000
1991	234,218	89,578	176,552	28,879	120,000	26,311	16,879	60,780	260,000	601,110	294,062	------	2,190,000
1992	243,400	85,862	161,402	33,774	125,000	31,032	37,983	71,190	146,000	614,071	330,212	70,000	2,290,000
1993	247,196	69,894	152,929	33,638	130,000	38,911	42,097	61,671	149,500	619,201	331,000	70,000	2,280,000
1994	256,188	70,535	146,428	38,786	132,000	43,478	42,600	59,286	146,600	580,201	327,000	70,000	2,270,000
1995	253,504	64,424	152,032	44,585	140,000	53,087	62,909	53,405	132,170	523,809	317,000	70,000	2,250,000
1996[1]	289,530	60,011	166,378	53,174	145,000	49,211	65,000	51,119	123,000	497,583	326,000	72,000	2,310,000
1997[2]	311,360	59,000	169,050	49,500	175,000	52,000	68,000	47,500	115,000	483,443	360,000	75,000	2,420,000

[1] Preliminary. [2] Estimate. [3] Formerly part of the U.S.S.R.; data not reported separately until 1992. *Source: U.S. Geological Survey (USGS)*

Salient Statistics of Gold in the United States In Kilograms (1 Kilogram = 32.1507 Troy Ounces)

			Refinery Production				Stocks, Dec. 31				Consumption			
Year	Mine Production	Value Million $	Domestic & Foreign Ores	Secondary (Old Scrap)	Exports (Excluding Coinage)	Imports for Consumption	Treasury Department[3]	Futures Exch.	Industry	Official World Reserves[4]	Dental	Industrial[5]	Jewelry & Arts	Total
1988	200,914	2,831.3	137,829	61,391	328,237	92,457	8,145,696	44,634	38,360	35,829	7,576	37,226	67,027	111,836
1989	265,731	3,268.6	183,685	51,943	211,091	152,504	8,147,169	69,727	30,462	35,603	7,927	37,621	69,524	115,078
1990	294,189	3,640.8	225,183	43,980	296,397	97,519	8,146,432	50,881	37,065	35,572	8,700	30,996	78,514	118,216
1991	294,062	3,434.7	224,675	48,088	284,127	178,749	8,145,696	49,893	39,411	35,501	8,485	21,793	84,096	114,375
1992	330,212	3,662.4	283,951	53,396	368,851	174,341	8,145,000	46,453	36,713	35,199	6,543	20,360	83,508	110,410
1993	331,013	3,840.0	243,000	152,000	792,680	169,305	8,143,000	78,514	34,400	34,900	6,173	19,663	65,600	91,400
1994	327,000	4,050.0	241,000	148,000	471,000	114,000	8,142,000	49,100	32,700	34,800	5,430	17,013	53,700	76,100
1995	317,000	3,950.0	NA	NA	347,000	126,000	8,140,000	45,400	NA	34,600	NA	NA	NA	NA
1996[1]	326,000	4,090.0	NA	NA	471,000	159,000	8,140,000	20,700	NA	34,400	NA	NA	NA	NA
1997[2]	360,000	3,850.0	270,000	100,000	476,000	209,000	8,140,000	15,200	NA	34,000	NA	NA	NA	NA

[1] Preliminary. [2] Estimate. [3] Includes gold in Exchange Stabilization Fund. [4] Held by market economy country central banks and governments and international monetary organizations. [5] Including space and defense. *Source: U.S. Geological Survey (USGS)*

Monthly Average Gold Price (Handy & Harman) in New York Dollars Per Troy Ounce

Year	Jan.	Feb.	Mar.	Apr.	May	June	July	Aug.	Sept.	Oct.	Nov.	Dec.	Average
1989	404.01	387.78	390.14	384.40	371.32	367.60	394.71	364.92	361.89	366.88	392.32	408.12	382.92
1990	410.10	416.80	393.10	374.30	369.20	352.30	362.50	395.00	389.50	380.70	381.70	378.20	383.61
1991	383.60	363.80	363.40	358.40	356.80	366.70	367.50	356.20	348.80	358.70	359.50	361.10	362.18
1992	354.50	353.90	344.30	338.50	337.20	340.80	353.00	343.00	345.40	344.40	335.10	334.70	343.74
1993	329.00	329.40	330.10	341.90	366.70	371.90	392.40	378.50	354.90	364.20	373.50	383.70	359.67
1994	387.02	382.01	384.13	378.20	381.21	385.64	385.44	380.43	391.80	389.77	349.43	379.60	384.14
1995	378.55	376.51	382.12	391.11	385.46	387.56	386.40	383.63	382.22	383.14	385.53	387.42	384.22
1996	399.59	404.73	396.21	392.96	391.98	385.58	383.69	387.43	382.97	381.07	378.46	369.02	387.81
1997	355.10	346.71	351.67	344.47	343.75	340.75	324.08	324.03	322.74	324.87	307.10	288.65	331.16
1998[1]	289.18	297.49	295.90	308.40	299.39	292.31	292.79	283.76	289.01	295.92	293.89	291.29	294.11

[1] Preliminary. *Sources: U.S. Geological Survey (USGS)*

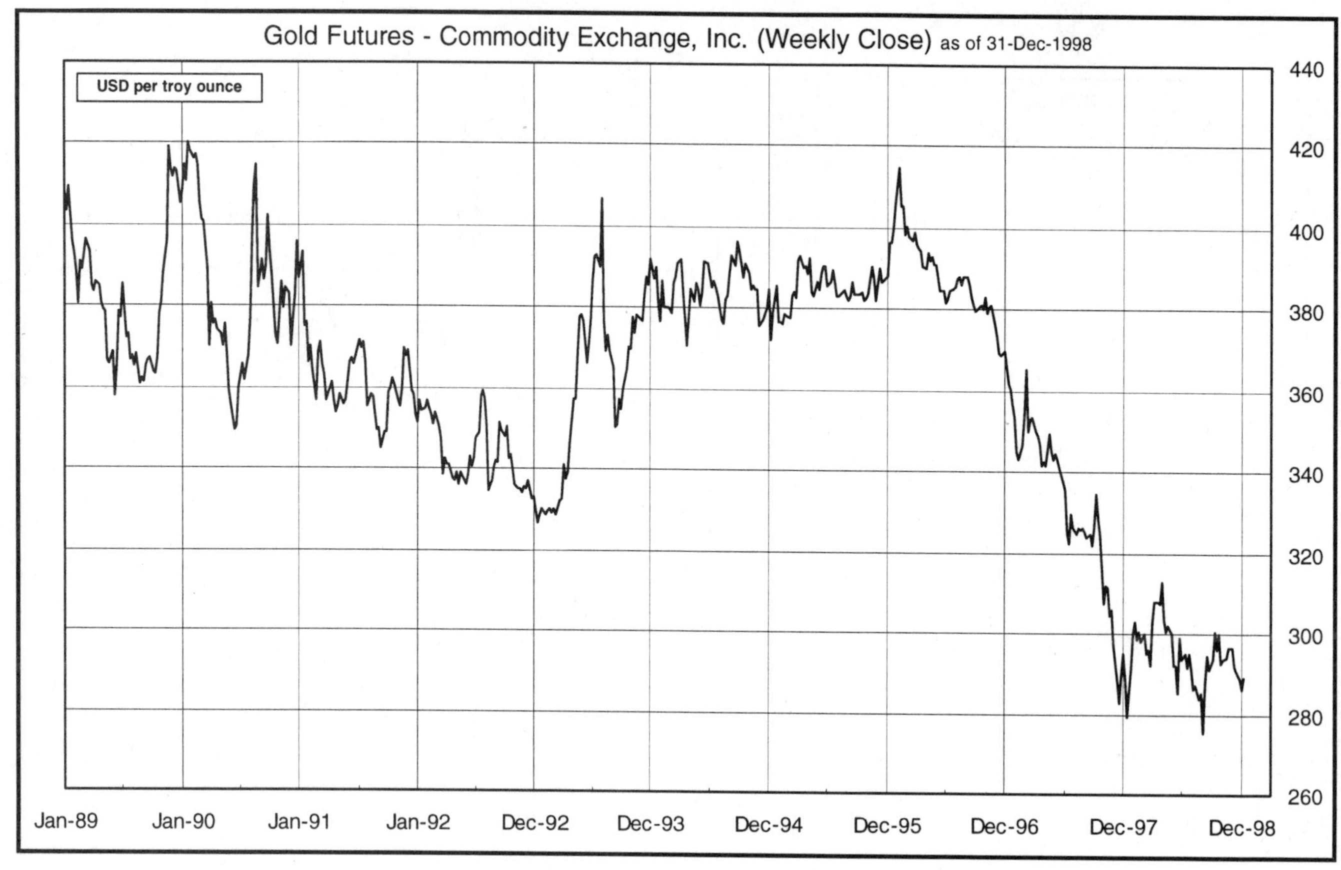

Average Open Interest of Gold Futures in New York (COMEX) In Thousands of Contracts

Year	Jan.	Feb.	Mar.	Apr.	May	June	July	Aug.	Sept.	Oct.	Nov.	Dec.
1989	162,226	166,455	167,419	160,215	180,709	164,196	154,517	150,414	151,836	146,262	154,927	151,788
1990	147,884	132,400	126,890	118,750	117,707	113,958	105,496	120,579	116,331	113,873	111,638	110,343
1991	104,666	98,000	98,429	101,266	100,341	88,961	94,467	99,790	105,053	96,302	109,030	109,004
1992	106,110	103,319	109,796	106,485	109,947	98,127	111,039	102,239	102,376	102,232	109,965	100,328
1993	112,420	109,093	115,505	142,208	172,491	170,829	200,168	180,509	166,201	152,531	152,853	154,730
1994	156,045	139,354	146,269	144,386	147,738	146,255	148,915	155,641	167,981	166,041	166,536	178,998
1995	184,549	170,972	168,651	191,667	173,805	174,075	175,727	176,135	185,128	185,854	170,674	141,751
1996	210,695	226,160	203,968	201,826	203,056	192,423	185,374	159,435	185,907	192,606	187,145	185,994
1997	199,710	190,524	167,595	157,176	160,512	170,640	207,352	198,099	201,267	188,365	212,757	188,558
1998	180,994	171,507	183,358	180,267	158,157	172,250	169,180	192,623	183,351	186,680	164,304	153,063

Source: New York Mercantile Exchange, COMEX Division

Volume of Trading of Gold Futures in New York (COMEX) In Thousands of Contracts

Year	Jan.	Feb.	Mar.	Apr.	May	June	July	Aug.	Sept.	Oct.	Nov.	Dec.	Total
1989	900.4	800.0	993.8	682.4	932.0	936.6	756.1	591.1	630.0	681.2	1,228.4	876.4	10,008.4
1990	1,327.1	885.1	975.6	472.4	745.2	541.0	747.4	1,191.5	729.4	879.9	705.3	530.1	9,730.0
1991	957.3	497.8	617.7	446.1	584.4	520.0	551.4	457.2	429.1	551.0	677.3	510.6	6,799.9
1992	729.8	388.4	607.3	425.4	485.4	427.2	734.6	500.2	465.3	414.1	504.1	320.1	6,001.9
1993	506.0	446.2	661.4	640.4	1,140.7	809.6	1,171.7	808.8	728.9	565.2	892.3	533.2	8,904.4
1994	981.8	584.0	889.5	589.2	922.6	740.2	723.8	626.0	645.6	651.2	687.8	461.5	8,503.2
1995	881.9	420.0	1,087.5	613.0	777.0	588.1	669.9	500.5	495.5	387.7	982.5	378.1	7,781.6
1996	1,384.7	987.5	943.6	647.1	858.5	582.1	749.8	541.9	541.9	528.5	795.2	458.8	8,694.5
1997	1,102.8	830.2	899.4	508.5	762.1	522.7	1,147.5	667.8	715.8	988.0	808.8	588.1	9,541.9
1998	1,078.2	534.2	877.2	698.1	845.2	718.7	712.4	680.0	851.7	769.6	705.6	519.0	8,990.1

Source: New York Mercantile Exchange, COMEX Division

Commodity Exchange, Inc. (COMEX) Depository Warehouse Stocks of Gold In Thousands of Troy Ounces

Year	Jan. 1	Feb. 1	Mar. 1	Apr. 1	May 1	June 1	July 1	Aug. 1	Sept. 1	Oct. 1	Nov. 1	Dec. 1
1989	1,434	1,408	1,454	1,532	1,606	1,634	1,602	1,602	1,433	1,483	1,731	2,263
1990	2,241	2,225	2,245	2,220	2,048	1,809	1,582	1,530	1,539	1,564	1,585	1,347
1991	1,636	1,686	1,540	1,298	1,458	1,711	1,772	1,875	1,220	1,342	1,302	1,479
1992	1,605	1,362	1,435	1,411	1,591	1,618	1,605	1,733	1,688	1,947	1,766	1,524
1993	1,507	1,340	1,365	1,426	1,383	2,231	2,247	2,448	2,437	2,425	2,349	2,552
1994	2,524	2,955	2,958	2,862	2,802	2,434	2,665	2,574	2,030	1,904	1,843	1,867
1995	1,577	1,498	1,386	1,360	1,391	1,488	1,505	1,608	1,448	1,745	1,395	1,315
1996	1,460	1,869	1,412	1,429	1,335	1,711	1,263	1,273	1,402	1,283	1,060	1,104
1997	666	837	583	1,000	946	878	850	914	733	894	615	761
1998	488	446	481	720	658	1,077	1,055	1,092	911	958	827	819

Source: New York Mercantile Exchange, COMEX division

Central Gold Bank Reserves In Millions of Troy Ounces

	Industrial Countries															
Year	Belgium	Canada	France	Germany	Italy	Japan	Nether-lands	Switzer-land	United Kingdom	United States	Industrial Total	Deve-loping Oil	Deve-loping Non-Oil	IMF[2]	Bank for Int'l Settle-ments	World Total
1988	33.7	17.1	81.9	95.2	66.7	24.2	43.9	83.3	19.0	261.9	895.2	42.0	103.3	103.4	6.6	1,150.5
1989	30.2	16.1	81.9	95.2	66.7	24.2	43.9	83.3	19.0	261.9	891.5	42.1	101.2	103.4	6.6	1,144.8
1990	30.2	14.8	81.9	95.2	66.7	24.2	43.9	83.3	18.9	261.9	889.4	41.5	101.7	103.4	7.8	1,143.8
1991	30.2	13.0	81.9	95.2	66.7	24.2	43.9	83.3	18.9	261.9	887.3	42.0	102.4	103.4	6.6	1,141.6
1992	25.0	9.9	81.9	95.2	66.7	24.2	43.9	83.3	18.6	261.8	877.4	42.0	100.3	103.4	6.8	1,129.9
1993	25.0	6.1	81.9	95.2	66.7	24.2	35.1	83.3	18.5	261.8	860.4	42.4	108.1	103.4	8.6	1,123.0
1994	25.0	3.9	81.9	95.2	66.7	24.2	34.8	83.3	18.4	261.7	856.9	42.4	106.6	103.4	7.0	1,116.2
1995	20.5	3.4	81.9	95.2	66.7	24.2	34.8	83.3	18.4	261.7	848.7	41.9	111.9	103.4	7.3	1,113.2
1996	15.3	3.1	81.9	95.2	66.7	24.2	34.8	83.3	18.4	261.7	840.1	42.5	115.5	103.4	6.6	1,108.2
1997[1]	15.3	3.1	81.9	95.2	66.7	24.2	27.1	83.3	18.4	261.7	822.0	42.3	115.1	103.4	6.2	1,089.0

[1] Preliminary. [2] International Monetary Fund. *Source: American Metal Market (AMM)*

Mine Production of Recoverable Gold in the United States, by States In Kilograms

Year	Arizona	California	Idaho	Montana	Nevada	Alaska	Colorado	South Dakota	New Mexico	Utah	Other States	Total
1989	2,768	29,804	3,057	12,434	153,995	5,756	3,448	16,123	1,076	W	37,270	265,731
1990	5,000	29,607	W	13,012	179,078	3,232	2,357	17,870	888	W	43,145	294,189
1991	6,195	30,404	3,348	13,715	178,488	3,200	3,181	16,371	W	W	39,161	295,957
1992	6,656	33,335	4,037	13,994	203,393	5,003	3,763	18,681	W	W	41,350	329,124
1993	2,710	35,800	4,324	14,300	211,000	2,780	W	19,200	995	W	37,300	331,000
1994	2,540	28,880	3,610	13,300	203,000	5,740	4,420	W	W	W	50,100	306,000
1995	1,920	25,600	8,850	12,400	210,000	4,410	W	W	W	W	53,700	317,000
1996	1,740	23,800	7,410	9,110	213,000	5,020	W	W	W	W	57,500	318,000
1997	2,140	24,400	W	5,290	243,000	W	W	W	W	W	67,900	338,000
1998[1]	1,800	20,900	W	W	243,000	W	W	W	W	W	65,400	331,000

[1] Preliminary. [2] January through October. W = Withheld proprietary data, included in "Other States." *Source: U.S. Geological Survey (USGS)*

Consumption of Gold, by End-Use in the United States In Kilograms

	Jewelry and the Arts					Industrial				
Year	Gold-filled & Other	Electro-plating	Karat Gold	Total	Dental	Gold-filled & Other	Electro-plating	Karat Gold	Total	Grand Total
1987	9,256	3,133	58,635	71,024	6,944	21,010	12,343	1,892	35,245	113,319
1988	7,598	1,469	57,959	67,027	7,576	21,034	15,088	1,104	37,226	111,836
1989	7,364	1,283	60,877	69,524	7,927	15,723	20,684	1,215	37,621	115,078
1990	8,132	429	69,952	78,514	8,700	12,725	17,251	1,020	30,996	118,216
1991	3,848	373	79,875	84,096	8,485	8,102	12,624	1,068	21,793	114,375
1992	3,546	581	79,381	83,508	6,543	8,802	10,476	1,082	20,360	110,410
1993	3,532	373	61,700	65,600	6,173	9,474	9,094	1,095	19,663	91,400
1994	3,650	369	49,700	53,700	5,430	7,450	9,470	96	17,000	76,100
1995	NA	NA	NA	NA	NA	NA	NA	NA	NA	NA
1996[1]	NA	NA	NA	NA	NA	NA	NA	NA	NA	NA

[1] Preliminary. *Source: U.S. Geological Survey (USGS)*

GOLD

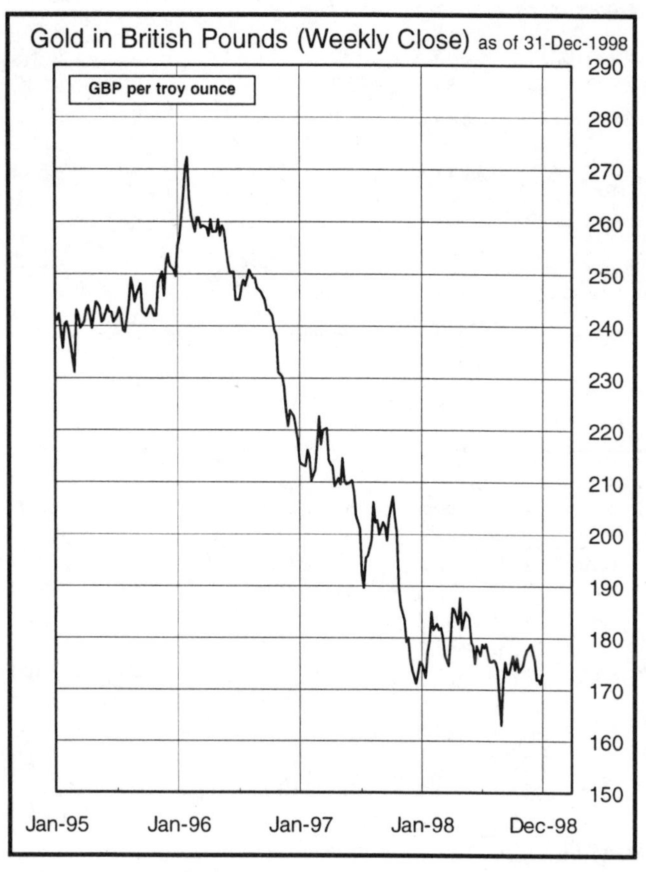

Gold in British Pounds (Weekly Close) as of 31-Dec-1998
GBP per troy ounce
290
280
270
260
250
240
230
220
210
200
190
180
170
160
150
Jan-95
Jan-96
Jan-97
Jan-98
Dec-98

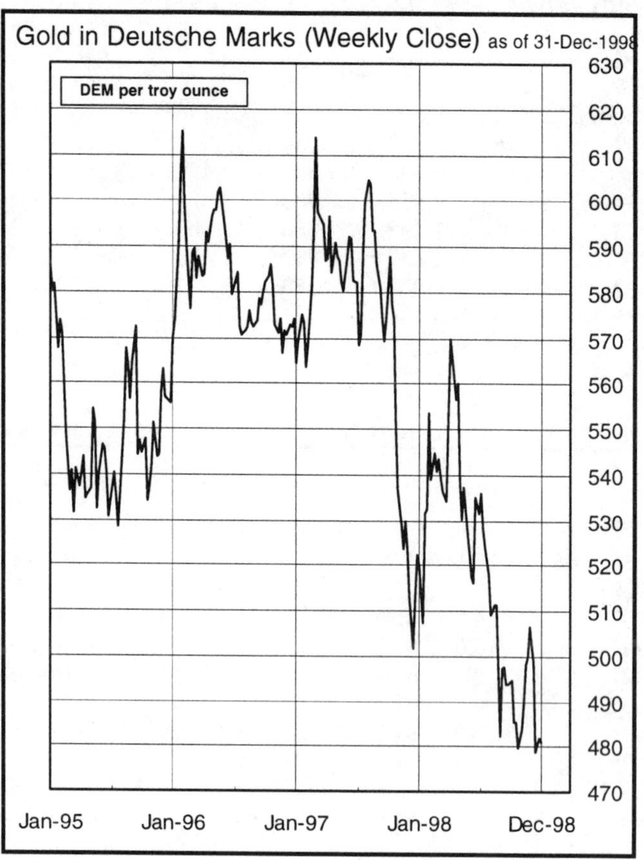

Gold in Deutsche Marks (Weekly Close) as of 31-Dec-1998
DEM per troy ounce
630
620
610
600
590
580
570
560
550
540
530
520
510
500
490
480
470
Jan-95
Jan-96
Jan-97
Jan-98
Dec-98

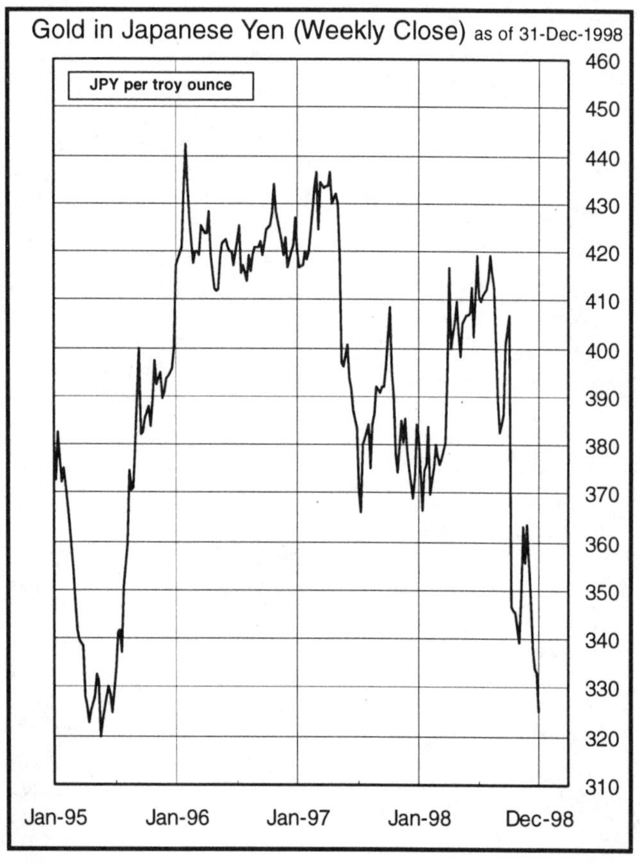

Gold in Japanese Yen (Weekly Close) as of 31-Dec-1998
JPY per troy ounce
460
450
440
430
420
410
400
390
380
370
360
350
340
330
320
310
Jan-95
Jan-96
Jan-97
Jan-98
Dec-98

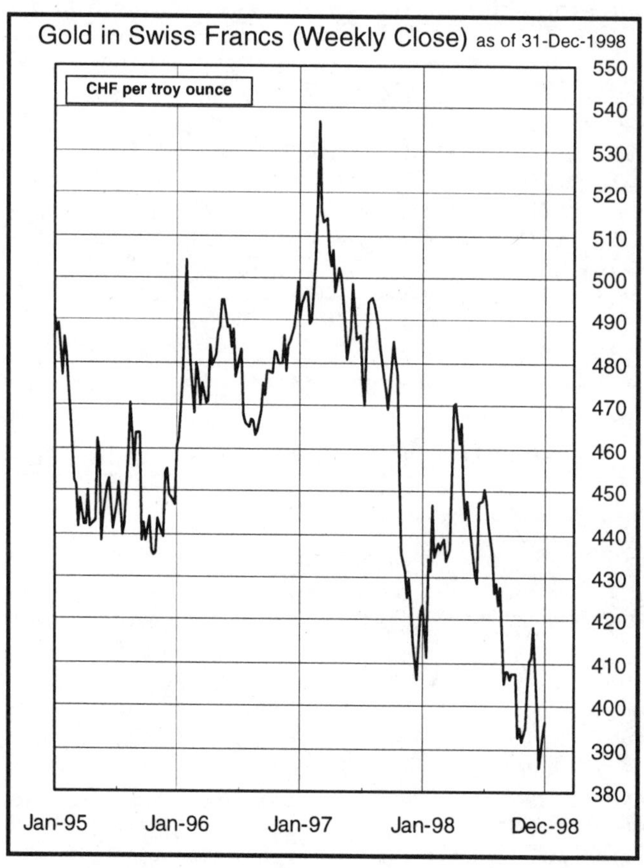

Gold in Swiss Francs (Weekly Close) as of 31-Dec-1998
CHF per troy ounce
550
540
530
520
510
500
490
480
470
460
450
440
430
420
410
400
390
380
Jan-95
Jan-96
Jan-97
Jan-98
Dec-98

Grain Sorghum

The U.S. remains the world's largest producer of grain sorghum (milo) despite a steady decline in production, and for the 1998 crop, the lowest harvested acreage since 1953. World production in 1998/99 of 59.7 million metric tonnes compares with 60.6 million in 1997/98, with the U.S. producing nearly a quarter of the crop with a near record low 13.2 million tonnes vs. 13.5 million in 1997/98. However, unlike most of the world's sorghum producing nations who consume their production domestically, the U.S. generally consumes at most two-thirds and exports the balance.

India's 1998/99 crop, the second largest producer, of 10 million tonnes was unchanged from 1997/98. Significantly, India sorghum acreage generally accounts for nearly a third of the world's acreage, but India's average yield tends to be the world's lowest. In contrast, China's average yield tends to be one of the highest, but sorghum acreage is contracting. China's lower than expected 1998/99 crop of 4.5 million tonnes compares with the most recent five year average of nearly 5 million tonnes.

World 1998/99 usage of 60 million tonnes compares with 61 million in 1997/98 with India and Mexico the largest users. World sorghum trade is small; averaging in recent years around 6.4 million tonnes vs. an early 1990's average of about 9 million tonnes. The U.S., with average exports near 5 million tonnes, is by far the largest exporter, mostly to Mexico and Japan, the two largest importers. Argentine exports are increasing, totaling 1.2 million tonnes each in 1998/99 and 1997/98, nearly double the mid-1990's average. The world carryover totaled nearly 10 million tonnes at yearend 1992/93, falling to 2.6 million by 1995/96 and forecast at 4.0 at the end of 1998/99, almost a third of which will be in the U.S.

The U.S. sorghum crop year begins September 1. Kansas and Texas are the largest producing states with Nebraska a distant third. Production in 1998/99 of 521 million bushels compares with 653 in 1997/98 and 803 million in 1996/97. Total U.S. supplies in 1998/99 of only 570 million bushels compares with 701 million in 1997/98. No sorghum is imported into the U.S.. Disappearance in 1998/99 of 515 million bushels compares with 652 million in 1997/98, of which 275 million will be used as a feed and 195 million exported vs. 387 million and 210 million, respectively. The projected ending 1998/99 carryover of 55 million bushels compares with a carryin of 49 million.

Sorghum prices received by farmers during 1998/99 were forecast to have a range of $1.65-$2.05 per bushel vs. the year earlier $2.20 and a 1990's high of $3.19 in 1995/96 when prices were buoyed by low production. In late calendar 1998, #2 sorghum's cash price of around $4.20 per cwt. compared with $4.95 a year earlier, basis Gulf port.

World Supply and Demand of Grain Sorghum   In Thousands of Metric Tons

	Exports				Imports				Total	Utilization				Ending Stocks		
Crop Year	Argentina	Non-U.S.	U.S.	Total	Japan	Mexico	Unaccounted	Total	Production	China	Mexico	U.S.	Total	Non-U.S.	U.S.	Total
1993-4	426	1,750	5,318	7,068	2,852	3,089	543	7,068	55,899	5,416	6,307	11,687	61,216	2,873	1,208	4,081
1994-5	192	756	5,653	6,409	2,334	2,544	118	6,409	57,964	6,355	5,644	10,223	57,932	2,294	1,819	4,113
1995-6	811	1,691	4,757	6,448	2,298	1,764	484	6,448	55,249	4,927	6,900	8,021	56,702	2,193	467	2,660
1996-7[1]	615	920	5,207	6,127	2,637	2,091	261	6,127	69,311	5,377	8,500	14,441	67,428	3,337	1,206	4,543
1997-8[2]	1,300	1,605	5,150	6,755	2,774	3,250	76	6,755	59,589	3,650	9,050	11,167	59,620	3,270	1,242	4,512
1998-9[3]	1,200	1,725	4,800	6,525	2,700	2,700	330	6,525	59,728	4,350	9,250	8,129	59,691	3,155	1,394	4,549

[1] Preliminary. [2] Estimate. [3] Forecast. *Source: Foreign Agricultural Service, U.S. Department of Agriculture (FAS-USDA)*

Salient Statistics of Grain Sorghum in the United States

	Acreage	For Grain					For Silage			Sorghum Grain Stocks			
	Planted[4] for All Purposes	Acreage Harvested	Production 1,000	Yield Per Harvested Acre	Price in Cents Per	Value of Production	Acreage Harvested 1,000	Production 1,000	Yield Per Harvested Acre	Dec. 1 On Farms	Dec. 1 Off Farms	June 1 On Farms	June 1 Off Farms
Year	1,000 Acres	1,000 Acres	Bushels	Bushels	Bushel	Million $	Acres	Tons	Tons	1,000 Bushels	1,000 Bushels	1,000 Bushels	1,000 Bushels
1993-4	9,882	8,916	534,172	59.9	231	1,234.5	351	3,914	11.2	105,950	340,198	32,075	96,035
1994-5	9,827	8,917	649,206	72.8	213	1,323.8	329	3,932	12.0	126,650	295,809	44,570	114,212
1995-6	9,454	8,278	460,373	55.6	319	1,395.4	368	3,652	9.9	79,090	222,186	13,955	56,433
1996-7[1]	13,097	11,811	795,274	67.3	234	1,986.3	423	4,976	11.8	144,590	322,767	38,815	80,329
1997-8[2]	10,052	9,158	633,545	69.2	221	1,408.9	412	5,385	13.1	96,625	274,244	27,200	68,907
1998-9[3]	9,626	7,723	519,933	67.3	155-185	952.5	305	3,487	11.4	95,900	237,831		

[1] Preliminary. [2] Estimate. [3] Forecast. NA = Not available. *Source: Economic Research Service, U.S. Department of Agriculture (ERS-USDA)*

Production of All Sorghum for Grain in the United States, by States   In Thousands of Bushels

Year	Arkansas	Colorado	Illinois	Kansas	Louisiana	Mississippi	Missouri	Nebraska	New Mexico	Oklahoma	South Dakota	Texas	Total
1993	12,470	7,140	17,430	176,400	7,200	4,225	39,420	73,750	7,425	14,500	10,500	156,750	534,172
1994	18,375	7,140	17,820	231,000	8,364	5,250	49,500	117,600	7,410	14,000	11,375	153,400	649,206
1995	13,135	4,620	11,730	173,600	5,880	2,665	35,770	56,840	3,380	12,800	4,800	129,600	460,373
1996	16,280	13,260	12,600	354,200	11,628	5,040	50,960	97,850	7,425	28,910	7,975	182,400	795,274
1997	11,100	6,000	10,465	265,200	6,600	2,475	36,800	60,750	9,988	22,500	11,360	185,850	633,545
1998[1]	6,890	10,545	7,918	264,000	7,500	2,340	26,560	56,400	2,925	15,300	9,940	105,800	519,933

[1] Preliminary. *Source: National Agricultural Statistics Service, U.S Department of Agriculture (NASS-USDA)*

GRAIN SORGHUM

Grain Sorghum Quarterly Supply and Disappearance in the United States In Millions of Bushels

Crop Year Beginning Sept. 1	Supply				Disappearance: Domestic Use						Ending Stocks		
	Beginning Stocks	Pro-duction	Imports	Total Supply	Food, Alcohol & Industrial	Seed	Feed & Residual	Total	Export	Total	Gov't. Owned[3]	Privately Owned[4]	Total Stocks
1995-6	71.6	460.4	0	532.0	9.5	1.6	304.7	315.8	197.8	513.6	0	18.4	18.4
Sept.-Nov.	71.6	460.4	0	532.0	1.0	0	176.0	177.0	53.7	230.7	.7	300.6	301.3
Dec.-Feb.	301.3	-----	0	301.3	1.2	0	70.7	71.9	66.8	138.7	.7	161.9	162.6
Mar.-May	162.6	-----	0	162.6	4.1	.9	51.0	56.0	36.2	92.2	.7	69.7	70.4
June-Aug.	70.4	-----	0	70.4	3.2	.7	6.9	10.8	41.2	52.0	0	18.4	18.4
1996-7	18.4	795.0	0	821.4	38.7	1.3	528.5	568.5	205.4	773.9	0	47.5	47.5
Sept.-Nov.	18.4	795.0	0	821.3	11.0	0	286.8	297.8	56.2	354.0	0	467.4	467.4
Dec.-Feb.	467.4	-----	0	467.4	10.6	0	123.5	134.1	59.0	193.1	0	274.3	274.3
Mar.-May	274.3	-----	0	274.3	11.0	.7	82.4	94.1	61.0	155.2	0	119.1	119.1
June-Aug.	119.1	-----	0	119.1	6.1	.6	35.7	42.4	29.2	71.7	0	47.5	47.5
1997-8[1]	47.0	634.0	0	681.0	55.0	1.4	365.0	632.0	212.0	844.0	0	49.0	49.0
Sept.-Nov.	47.0	634.0	0	681.0	18.0	0	239.0	307.0	49.0	356.0	0	374.0	374.0
Dec.-Feb.	374.0	-----	0	374.0	18.0		38.0	139.0	83.0	222.0	0	235.0	235.0
Mar.-May	235.0	-----	0	235.0	12.0		71.0	139.0	55.0	194.0	0	96.0	96.0
June-Aug.	96.0	-----	0	96.0	6.0		17.0	47.0	24.0	71.0	0	49.0	49.0
1998-9[2]	49.0	520.0	0	569.0	45.0		275.0	505.0	185.0	690.0	0	64.0	64.0
Sept.-Nov.	49.0	520.0	0	569.0	15.0		180.0	235.0	41.0	276.0	0	334.0	334.0

[1] Preliminary. [2] Forecast. [3] Uncommitted inventory. [4] Includes quantity under loan & farmer-owned reserve. *Source: Economic Research Service, U.S. Department of Agriculture (ERS-USDA)*

Average Price of Sorghum Grain, No. 2, Yellow at Kansas City In Dollars Per Hundred Pounds (Cwt.)

Year	Sept.	Oct.	Nov.	Dec.	Jan.	Feb.	Mar.	Apr.	May	June	July	Aug.	Average
1991-2	4.24	4.30	4.27	4.35	4.44	4.62	4.78	4.41	4.54	4.51	4.05	3.77	4.36
1992-3	3.76	3.60	3.61	3.70	3.70	3.66	3.70	3.72	3.82	3.58	3.99	4.01	3.74
1993-4	3.89	4.03	4.60	4.91	4.93	4.81	4.64	4.33	4.38	4.43	3.79	3.73	4.37
1994-5	3.72	3.55	3.60	3.81	3.92	3.90	4.01	4.08	4.27	4.50	4.93	4.85	4.10
1995-6	5.08	5.45	5.68	6.19	6.39	6.58	6.81	7.79	8.17	7.79	7.24	6.74	6.66
1996-7	5.29	4.64	4.31	4.22	4.24	4.46	4.88	4.83	4.63	4.48	4.18	4.28	4.54
1997-8	4.13	4.36	4.30	4.26	4.33	4.36	4.40	4.10	4.09	4.03	3.74	3.27	4.11
1998-9[1]	2.98	3.17											3.08

[1] Preliminary. *Source: Economic Research Service, U.S. Department of Agriculture (ERS-USDA)*

Exports of Grain Sorghum, by Country of Destination from the United States In Metric Tons

Year Beginning October	Canada	Ecuador	Ethiopia	Israel	Japan	Jordon	Mexico	South Africa	Spain	Sudan	Turkey	World Total
1991-2	1,613	36,000	42,150	104,952	1,738,075	120,001	4,956,607	19,031	174,758	122,183	99,394	7,454,616
1992-3	1,795	9,501	0	217,110	1,933,012	0	3,970,069	56,186	188,893	4,287	132,182	6,651,528
1992-3	1,795	9,501	0	217,110	1,933,012	0	3,970,069	56,186	188,893	4,287	132,182	6,651,528
1993-4	1,699	0	86,697	66,264	1,681,976	0	3,118,139	0	169,454	48,042	0	5,245,524
1994-5	3,713	0	0	214,073	1,987,738	0	2,543,696	0	398,339	12,304	0	5,652,585
1995-6[1]	5,734	0	25,700	356,868	1,616,384	0	1,665,541	332	431,578	0	0	4,757,055
1996-7[2]	3,347	0	10,020	456,271	2,203,669	0	2,189,598	0	125,827	8,000	138,590	5,206,964

[1] Preliminary. [2] Estimate. *Source: Economic Research Service, U.S. Department of Agriculture (ERS-USDA)*

Grain Sorghum Price Support Program and Market Prices in the United States

Year	Price Support Operations: Put Under Price Support									No. 2 Yellow ($ Per Cwt.)			
	Quantity	% of Pro-duction	Aquired by CCC	Owned by CCC at Year End	Basic Loan Rate	Target Price	Findley Loan Rate	Effective Base[3]	Partici-pation Rate[4]	Kansas City	Texas High Plains	Los Angeles	Gulf Ports
	Million Cwt.				$ Per Bushel			Mil. Acres	% of Base				
1991-2	9.5	2.9	5.4	4.5	1.80	2.61	1.54	13.5	77.1	4.36	4.78	5.69	4.86
1992-3	27.2	5.5	0	2.2	1.91	2.61	1.63	13.6	78.6	3.74	4.06	5.11	4.27
1993-4	8.2	2.6	0	1.4	1.89	2.61	1.63	13.5	81.6	4.37	4.95	----	4.90
1994-5	25.2	6.9	0	.4	1.89	2.61	1.80	13.5	81.1	4.10	4.75	----	4.62
1995-6	4.0	1.6	0	0	1.84	2.61	1.80	13.3	76.9	6.66	7.30	----	7.19
1996-7[1]	11.4	2.5	0	0	----	[5]	1.81	13.2	98.8	4.54	5.02	----	5.03
1997-8[2]	----	----	----	----	----	[5]	1.76	----	----	----	----	----	----

[1] Preliminary. [2] Estimate. [3] National effective crop acreage base as determined by ASCS. [4] Percentage of effective base acres enrolled in acreage reduction programs. [5] Beginning 1996-7, target prices are no longer applicable. *Source: Economic Research Service, U.S. Department of Agriculture (ERS-USDA)*

Hay

U.S. total hay production in the 1990's held fairly constant at about 150 million tons (marketing year, May 1 to April 30); the 1997/98 crop of 152 million tons compares with 149 million in 1996/97. Harvested acreage of 61 million acres was about unchanged from a year earlier, but the average yield of 2.50 tons per acre was up slightly from 1996/97. California is generally the largest producing state, but in 1997/98 Texas produced 10.8 million tons vs 7.8 million in 1996/97, while California's crop of 8.6 million tons compares with 8 million, respectively. Alfalfa and alfalfa mixtures account for more than half of total hay production, totaling about 79 million tons in both 1996/97 and 1997/98, with California the largest producer. Alfalfa yields are nearly twice as high as other hays.

Roughage consuming animal units (RCAU) in 1998/99 were expected to be down 1% from 1997/98, the lowest since 1990/91. The supply of hay per RCAU in 1998/99 was forecast at 2.31 tons vs 2.28 tons a year earlier. The key to hay prices generally rests on the number of dairy cows and producer intentions to plant acreage to hay for forage. The season average prices for all hay in 1997/98 were $100 per ton, up from $95.80 in 1996/97 and a record. Prices received by farmers for all hay during calendar 1998 (May through September) averaged about $12 per ton below a year earlier. Alfalfa farm prices during the indicated 1998 period of $95.30 per ton compare with the year earlier average of $111.46. Farm prices for hay other than alfalfa averaged $75.68 vs $76.56 a year earlier.

Salient Statistics of All Hay in the United States

Year Crop Beginning May	Acres Harvested 1,000 Acres	Yield Per Acre Tons	Production	Carryover May 1	Disappearance	Supply Per Animal Unit	Disappearance	Animal Units Fed[3] Millions	Farm Price $ Per Ton	Farm Production Value Million $	Retail Price Paid by Farmers for Seed, April 15: Alfalfa (Certified)	Timothy	Red Clover	Sudan-Grass
			Millions of Tons			In Tons					Dollars Per Cwt.			
1993-4	59,679	2.46	146.8	21.0	145.7	2.20	1.91	76.3	84.7	10,957	269.00	80.60	148.00	45.20
1994-5	58,735	2.55	150.1	22.1	151.4	2.21	1.94	77.9	86.7	11,114	266.00	76.00	148.00	47.90
1995-6	59,629	2.59	154.2	20.8	154.2	2.25	1.98	78.3	82.2	11,042	274.00	71.00	134.00	51.80
1996-7	61,169	2.45	149.8	20.7	152.8	2.24	2.01	76.9	95.8	12,727	277.00	76.00	172.00	51.90
1997-8[1]	61,084	2.50	152.5	17.4	NA	2.33	NA	NA	102.5	13,250	282.00	73.00	153.00	51.40
1998-9[2]	60,016	2.52	151.3							11,720				

[1] Preliminary. [2] Estimate. [3] Roughage-consuming animal units fed annually. *Source: Economic Research Service, U.S. Department of Agriculture (ERS)*

Production of All Hay in the United States, by States In Thousands of Tons

Year	California	Idaho	Iowa	Minnesota	Missouri	New York	North Dakota	Ohio	Oklahoma	South Dakota	Texas	Wisconsin	Total
1993	7,590	4,844	4,803	5,970	7,335	7,323	5,043	3,475	4,248	8,190	7,506	6,260	146,799
1994	8,210	4,438	5,775	7,530	6,770	7,415	4,510	4,384	4,198	7,330	8,455	6,550	150,060
1995	8,341	5,080	5,665	6,943	6,818	6,975	5,095	4,035	4,174	9,050	8,136	6,820	154,166
1996	8,008	4,760	5,310	5,998	7,270	7,455	4,825	3,400	4,940	8,200	7,815	6,050	149,779
1997	8,408	4,730	5,190	6,398	7,340	6,790	4,375	3,850	5,108	7,810	10,955	6,353	152,536
1998[1]	8,115	5,549	5,332	7,110	7,703	7,680	4,190	3,875	3,380	8,160	6,870	6,370	151,338

[1] Preliminary. *Source: Agricultural Statistics Board, U.S. Department of Agriculture (ASB-USDA)*

Hay Production and Farm Stocks in the United States In Thousands of Short Tons

Year	Production: Alfalfa & Mixtures	All Others	All Hay	Corn for Silage[1]	Sorghum Silage[1]	Farm Stocks: May 1	Dec. 1
1993	80,305	66,494	146,799	81,829	3,914	21,010	100,953
1994	81,336	68,724	150,060	88,588	3,932	22,096	105,296
1995	84,515	69,651	154,166	77,867	3,652	20,775	109,438
1996	79,139	70,640	149,779	86,581	4,976	20,739	105,179
1997	78,535	74,001	152,536	97,192	5,385	17,424	103,044
1998[2]	82,010	69,328	151,338	94,525	3,487	21,827	111,839

[1] Not included in all tame hay. [2] Preliminary. *Source: Agricultural Statistics Board, U.S. Department of Agriculture (ASB-USDA)*

Mid-Month Price Received by Farmers of All Hay (Baled) in the United States In Dollars Per Ton

Year	May	June	July	Aug.	Sept.	Oct.	Nov.	Dec.	Jan.	Feb.	Mar.	Apr.	Average[2]
1993-4	86.60	79.60	76.90	77.50	78.80	82.30	84.20	83.50	85.70	86.90	90.80	98.20	84.70
1994-5	100.00	88.70	82.50	83.10	82.40	86.80	86.60	85.50	84.80	85.00	86.70	90.30	86.00
1995-6	90.40	83.90	80.60	81.10	80.30	83.00	81.00	80.30	81.70	81.20	83.40	90.30	82.10
1996-7	97.10	92.30	89.60	92.90	90.10	93.00	92.00	90.80	97.90	105.00	108.00	117.00	97.14
1997-8	118.00	108.00	98.40	99.00	103.00	103.00	101.00	97.70	98.10	97.20	97.50	101.00	101.83
1998-9[1]	103.00	91.80	88.60	88.50	86.50	85.20	81.40	78.40	78.80				86.91

[1] Preliminary. [2] Marketing year average. *Source: Economic Research Service, U.S. Department of Agriculture (ERS-USDA)*

Heating Oil

Heating oil prices moved to very low levels in late 1998 on a combination of large supplies of petroleum and very mild weather in the northeast United States. Advances in the technology of the petroleum industry have allowed larger amounts of petroleum to be found and older reserves to be more fully developed. The result is that there is more petroleum coming to the market and that has resulted in greater production of products like distillate fuel oil and motor gasoline putting downward pressure on prices. Until the end of 1998, weather in the northeast U.S., where most heating oil is consumed, was much warmer than normal. This led to less need to heat and heating oil usage was lower. Weather over the last four years has been warmer than normal leading some to question whether this is the start of a new trend toward gradually rising temperatures.

U.S. distillate fuel oil production in September 1998 was 3.48 million barrels per day, about unchanged from the previous month and about the same as the year before. Over the January-September 1998 period, production averaged 3.45 million barrels per day, some 3 percent more than the same period of 1997 and 7 percent more than the comparable period of 1996. For all of 1997, distillate fuel oil production averaged 3.39 million barrels per day.

U.S. imports of distillate fuel oil in September 1998 averaged 191,000 barrels per day. That was 10 percent more than the previous month and 9 percent less than a year ago. Over the January-September 1998 period, imports averaged 192,000 barrels per day. That represented a decline of 18 percent from the comparable period in 1997 and 6 percent less than the same period in 1996.

U.S. exports of distillate fuel oil in September 1998 were 177,000 barrels per day, up 18 percent from the previous month and 11 percent more than a year ago. In the January-September 1998 period, exports averaged 143,000 barrels per day, down 5 percent from the comparable period of 1997 and 20 percent less than the like period of 1996. For all of 1997, exports averaged 152,000 barrels per day.

Product supplied in September 1998 was 3.23 million barrels per day, down 7 percent from the previous month and 2 percent less than a year ago. In the January-September 1998 period, product supplied averaged 3.43 million barrels, up 1 percent from the same period in 1997 and 3 percent higher than in 1996. For all of 1997, product supplied averaged 3.44 million barrels per day.

U.S. ending stocks of distillate fuel oil at the end of September 1998 were 152 million barrels. This was 9 percent above the level of stocks in September 1997 and 32 percent higher than in September 1996. Stocks were the highest level since December 1984 when they were 161 million barrels.

U.S. production of residual fuel oil in September 1998 averaged 737,000 barrels per day, down 5 percent from August 1998 and 7 percent more than a year ago. Over the January-September 1998 period, residual fuel oil production averaged 768,000 barrels per day, up 12 percent from the like period of 1997 and 6 percent more than in 1996. For all of 1997, production averaged 708,000 barrels per day.

In September 1998, imports averaged 223,000 barrels per day, down 3 percent from the previous month. Imports in January-September 1998 were 209,000 barrels per day, up 5 percent from the same period in 1997 and 12 percent less than in the like period of 1996. For all of 1997, imports averaged 194,000 barrels per day.

Exports of residual fuel oil in September 1998 averaged 119,000 barrels per day, up 13 percent from August 1998 and 31 percent above the rate of a year ago. In the first nine months of 1998, exports averaged 142,000 barrels per day, 20 per cent higher than in the same period of 1997 and 41 percent more than in the like period of 1996. For all of 1997, exports averaged 120,000 barrels per day.

U.S. ending stocks of residual fuel oil in September 1998 were 39 million barrels, down 7 percent from the month before. September stocks were 11 percent more than a year ago and 3 percent higher than in 1996. At the end of 1997, stocks were 40 million barrels.

Futures Markets

Heating oil futures and options are traded on the New York Mercantile Exchange (NYMEX). In London, gasoil futures and options are listed on the International Petroleum Exchange (IPE).

Average Price of No. 2 Heating Oil in New York In Cents Per Gallon

Year	Jan.	Feb.	Mar.	Apr.	May	June	July	Aug.	Sept.	Oct.	Nov.	Dec.	Average
1989	54.35	51.47	56.86	53.98	50.76	48.51	49.35	49.75	55.78	58.80	59.20	80.91	55.81
1990	73.26	57.48	57.93	58.51	53.99	48.22	53.14	75.23	88.82	93.95	87.51	79.73	68.98
1991	74.96	70.80	61.92	56.36	55.04	53.67	57.74	60.48	61.54	66.58	64.33	53.35	61.31
1992	51.72	53.39	52.49	56.22	57.38	61.26	60.24	58.29	61.90	62.72	56.52	54.98	57.25
1993	53.14	56.02	58.13	55.49	54.53	52.62	49.74	50.70	51.96	54.00	50.30	43.47	52.51
1994	49.93	55.81	49.18	48.01	47.98	49.37	49.93	49.51	47.90	48.23	49.62	48.41	49.49
1995	47.98	47.64	45.95	49.40	50.31	47.75	46.65	49.14	50.21	48.89	51.89	57.76	49.46
1996	55.64	61.24	65.19	67.90	57.59	51.56	55.58	60.42	67.61	72.34	70.13	72.13	63.11
1997	69.90	61.15	54.83	57.74	56.31	52.32	53.11	54.02	53.19	57.24	56.23	51.09	56.43
1998	46.59	44.26	42.12	42.97	41.07	37.88	36.24	34.48	40.15	38.29	35.59	31.38	39.25

Source: New York Mercantile Exchange (NYMEX)

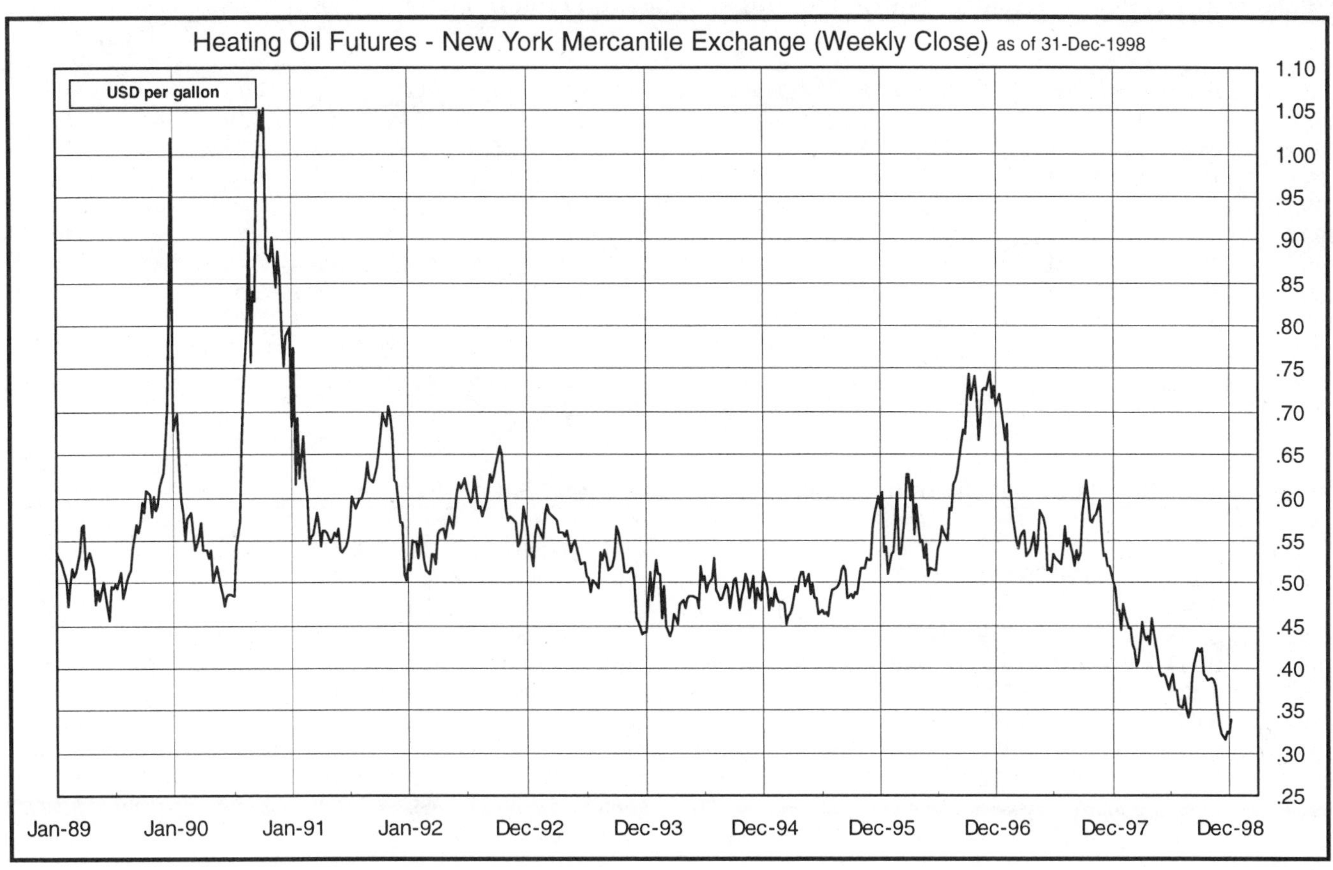

Average Open Interest of No. 2 Heating Oil Futures in New York In Contracts

Year	Jan.	Feb.	Mar.	Apr.	May	June	July	Aug.	Sept.	Oct.	Nov.	Dec.
1989	75,038	63,791	60,455	57,533	49,174	49,527	59,799	69,578	88,642	97,064	99,293	105,240
1990	83,020	68,065	67,389	76,954	85,349	112,506	116,108	103,280	97,589	93,631	92,399	81,864
1991	74,216	81,742	81,103	82,419	89,482	102,887	115,896	125,463	135,804	144,026	128,330	117,182
1992	108,337	96,543	91,508	90,816	87,459	101,185	98,623	109,787	119,595	129,951	140,952	135,380
1993	130,536	125,603	130,438	107,363	102,708	113,898	131,816	142,054	166,253	172,940	175,781	199,299
1994	196,390	185,607	186,539	164,417	140,658	129,005	124,764	149,571	172,071	165,475	152,570	148,298
1995	128,664	112,508	118,700	121,974	115,501	122,163	136,722	140,214	149,934	152,244	139,232	138,596
1996	114,324	95,745	90,080	94,161	98,038	97,699	109,524	119,366	138,513	141,217	127,512	108,558
1997	100,333	105,223	122,149	139,981	135,523	141,864	151,403	149,243	151,407	141,008	126,528	145,153
1998	171,177	163,114	177,158	174,587	176,663	196,903	205,071	198,527	188,096	188,019	192,835	184,100

Source: New York Mercantile Exchange (NYMEX)

Volume of Trading of No. 2 Heating Oil Futures In New York In Thousands of Contracts

Year	Jan.	Feb.	Mar.	Apr.	May	June	July	Aug.	Sept.	Oct.	Nov.	Dec.	Total
1989	534.0	422.7	430.4	372.6	335.0	445.8	372.4	402.4	475.4	554.7	574.7	820.7	5,741.0
1990	754.9	415.4	462.5	451.7	517.0	463.3	519.0	723.2	505.8	612.3	522.0	429.8	6,376.9
1991	603.7	523.9	392.5	387.2	399.9	425.1	507.8	595.9	538.2	689.1	781.3	835.6	6,680.2
1992	815.2	574.0	550.1	592.1	586.7	601.1	645.0	663.7	625.7	709.5	808.2	807.1	8,005.5
1993	829.0	660.5	747.3	537.5	482.0	543.4	632.2	721.9	833.8	761.8	886.6	988.9	8,625.1
1994	1,085.7	875.7	766.8	631.7	629.3	723.7	612.3	783.2	706.8	721.4	652.3	798.1	8,986.8
1995	779.8	608.7	716.0	622.8	729.8	618.8	612.7	563.6	714.2	650.8	659.5	990.1	8,266.8
1996	977.2	768.1	666.2	586.5	530.9	402.0	530.2	624.4	766.5	1,014.2	725.0	750.7	8,341.9
1997	794.4	719.0	588.6	710.1	592.0	679.4	679.6	694.7	828.3	742.7	619.3	722.9	8,371.0
1998	793.6	641.8	776.4	578.4	688.5	904.9	720.2	683.0	748.2	768.2	766.5	793.9	8,863.8

Source: New York Mercantile Exchange (NYMEX)

HEATING OIL

Stocks of Distillate and Residual Fuel in the United States, on First of Month In Millions of Barrels

Year	Jan.	Feb.	Mar.	Apr.	May	June	July	Aug.	Sept.	Oct.	Nov.	Dec.	Residual Fuel Oil Stocks Jan. 1	Residual Fuel Oil Stocks July 1
1989	123.5	120.3	107.5	96.6	98.4	99.3	99.6	115.0	116.3	123.2	121.7	119.8	44.6	44.1
1990	105.7	118.0	112.2	99.7	99.5	102.8	109.4	125.2	136.0	136.3	132.4	132.2	43.8	46.8
1991	112.1	111.7	101.6	98.2	102.9	106.9	113.7	124.7	131.4	140.1	138.3	144.5	47.6	43.7
1992	143.5	126.7	108.8	97.7	92.1	96.4	104.5	114.6	122.8	127.8	136.8	146.3	49.9	40.9
1993	140.6	130.7	110.4	97.3	99.5	102.8	110.0	120.7	128.2	131.3	145.3	149.2	42.6	45.7
1994	140.9	117.5	102.9	99.4	102.6	112.4	119.5	134.2	138.6	144.7	146.0	147.3	44.2	39.4
1995	140.2	122.1	115.4	114.6	118.3	114.7	125.0	130.9	131.7	131.4	135.4	130.2	41.9	36.0
1996	130.2	113.8	97.3	89.7	90.1	95.7	101.6	106.8	110.3	115.0	114.7	121.8	36.8	34.8
1997	126.7	111.3	105.9	101.8	97.5	108.4	118.2	123.0	132.9	138.9	136.2	140.5	45.9	39.2
1998[1]	139.0	133.1	127.9	124.4	125.7	136.8	139.1	148.8	150.5	152.5	147.5	154.6	40.4	39.8

[1] Preliminary. *Source: Energy Information Administration, U.S. Department of Energy (EIA-DOE)*

Production of Distillate Fuel Oil in the United States Thousand Barrels Per Day

Year	Jan.	Feb.	Mar.	Apr.	May	June	July	Aug.	Sept.	Oct.	Nov.	Dec.	Average
1989	2,974	2,797	2,713	2,789	2,750	2,809	2,848	2,907	2,952	2,906	3,063	3,266	2,899
1990	3,130	2,753	2,657	2,803	2,874	2,996	3,008	3,131	2,968	2,928	2,915	2,917	2,925
1991	2,845	2,870	2,865	2,819	2,929	2,941	2,998	2,961	3,055	3,040	3,103	3,107	2,962
1992	2,818	2,661	2,749	2,930	2,933	2,995	3,067	2,865	2,983	3,251	3,240	3,179	2,974
1993	2,914	2,815	2,919	3,047	2,994	3,093	3,186	3,100	3,205	3,432	3,474	3,382	3,132
1994	3,114	3,018	3,096	3,249	3,317	3,285	3,191	3,187	3,285	3,203	3,270	3,232	3,205
1995	3,054	2,954	3,157	3,126	3,111	3,109	3,056	3,145	3,287	3,169	3,341	3,344	3,155
1996	3,110	3,145	3,110	3,305	3,258	3,291	3,139	3,295	3,403	3,626	3,665	3,558	3,325
1997	3,119	3,089	3,258	3,291	3,525	3,517	3,362	3,427	3,452	3,488	3,543	3,578	3,389
1998[1]	3,321	3,297	3,385	3,447	3,521	3,526	3,583	3,472	3,399	3,223	3,439	3,502	3,427

[1] Preliminary. *Source: Energy Information Administration, U.S. Department of Energy (EIA-DOE)*

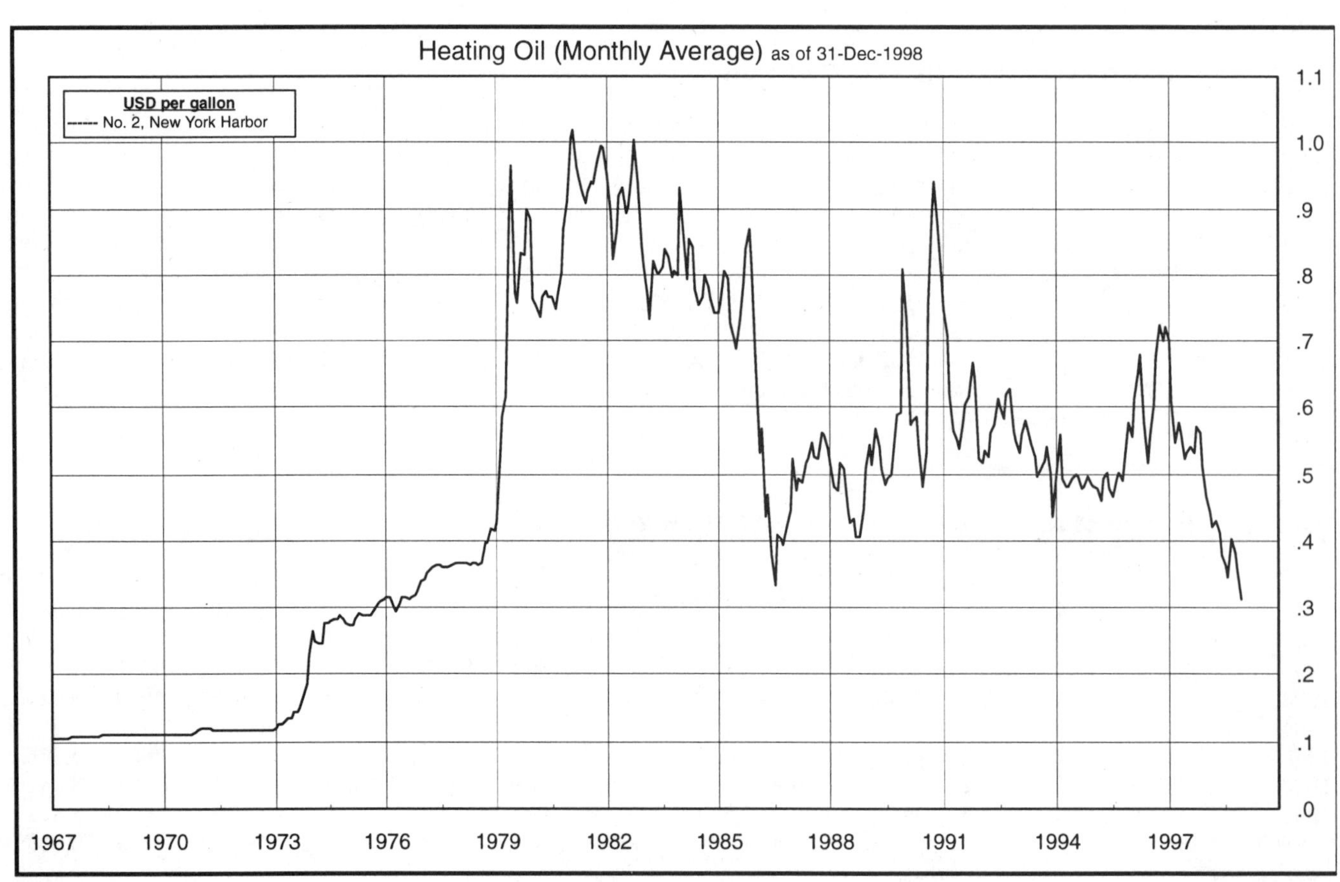

Imports of Distillate Fuel Oil in the United States Thousand Barrels Per Day

Year	Jan.	Feb.	Mar.	Apr.	May	June	July	Aug.	Sept.	Oct.	Nov.	Dec.	Average
1989	346	331	439	301	290	233	334	254	249	261	307	324	306
1990	505	357	281	308	209	257	236	293	226	190	238	239	278
1991	192	139	206	258	186	209	155	168	237	207	249	252	205
1992	232	217	238	202	179	157	172	229	237	263	236	229	216
1993	182	224	235	209	153	168	130	159	137	242	214	160	184
1994	161	276	318	226	202	182	164	211	193	159	166	187	203
1995	313	289	188	125	109	176	157	171	142	162	262	235	193
1996	243	271	253	258	215	185	194	195	187	246	192	253	224
1997	293	246	245	256	220	219	223	202	210	213	161	232	227
1998[1]	187	183	220	189	178	193	212	173	194	226	152	234	195

[1] Preliminary. *Source: Energy Information Administration, U.S. Department of Energy (EIA-DOE)*

Disposition of Distillate Fuel Oil, Total Product Supplied in the United States Thousand Barrels Per Day

Year	Jan.	Feb.	Mar.	Apr.	May	June	July	Aug.	Sept.	Oct.	Nov.	Dec.	Average
1989	3,303	3,427	3,428	2,975	2,954	3,002	2,596	2,966	2,889	3,127	3,311	3,914	3,157
1990	3,185	3,260	3,277	3,043	2,900	2,923	2,726	3,218	2,864	2,960	3,094	2,816	3,021
1991	3,367	2,976	2,984	2,839	2,765	2,775	2,648	2,770	2,865	3,047	2,921	3,087	2,921
1992	3,231	3,219	3,207	3,039	2,753	2,679	2,710	2,705	2,908	3,056	2,929	3,316	2,979
1993	3,128	3,465	3,420	2,943	2,685	2,863	2,674	2,820	2,973	2,983	3,218	3,357	3,041
1994	3,698	3,581	3,307	3,116	2,912	3,062	2,663	3,063	3,133	3,066	3,180	3,203	3,162
1995	3,389	3,675	3,344	3,106	2,899	3,267	2,732	3,044	3,285	3,104	3,233	3,449	3,207
1996	3,681	3,722	3,453	3,385	3,118	3,194	3,046	3,184	3,178	3,575	3,460	3,434	3,368
1997	3,780	3,422	3,515	3,523	3,240	3,235	3,279	3,124	3,302	3,659	3,411	3,665	3,430
1998[1]	3,566	3,585	3,589	3,408	3,219	3,492	3,322	3,442	3,417	3,537	3,300	3,395	3,439

[1] Preliminary. *Source: Energy Information Administration, U.S. Department of Energy (EIA-DOE)*

Production of Residual Fuel Oil in the United States Thousand Barrels Per Day

Year	Jan.	Feb.	Mar.	Apr.	May	June	July	Aug.	Sept.	Oct.	Nov.	Dec.	Average
1989	949	930	937	904	934	953	862	903	856	1,001	1,075	1,140	954
1990	1,163	1,060	976	882	884	926	987	944	909	799	846	1,021	950
1991	1,001	1,050	995	916	929	933	871	925	838	814	896	1,051	934
1992	965	957	990	900	964	894	838	815	810	818	895	862	892
1993	820	840	818	896	908	795	762	752	822	841	899	869	835
1994	809	852	859	846	860	779	807	838	800	755	835	871	826
1995	903	776	778	789	748	746	797	801	811	724	705	874	788
1996	774	776	701	671	732	731	646	732	713	693	712	753	719
1997	800	789	639	617	618	727	645	643	688	711	786	810	705
1998[1]	766	673	789	852	773	749	782	778	749	668	741	817	762

[1] Preliminary. *Source: Energy Information Adminstration, U.S. Department of Energy (EIA-DOE)*

Supply and Disposition of Residual Fuel Oil in the United States

	Supply		Disposition				
Year	Total Production	Imports	Stock Change	Exports	Product Supplied	Ending Stocks	Average Sales to End Users[3]
	Thousand Barrels per Day					Mil. Barrels	¢ per Gallon
1989	885	565	[2]	186	1,264	47	38.5
1990	950	504	13	211	1,229	49	44.4
1991	934	453	4	226	1,158	50	34.0
1992	892	375	-20	193	1,094	43	33.6
1993	835	373	4	123	1,080	44	33.7
1994	826	314	-6	125	1,021	42	35.2
1995	788	187	-13	136	852	37	39.2
1996	726	248	24	102	848	46	45.5
1997	708	194	-15	120	797	40	42.3
1998[1]	762	211	13	141	819	44	30.9

[1] Preliminary. [2] Less than +500 barrels per day and greater than -500 barrels per day. [3] Refiner price excluding taxes.
Source: Energy Information Administration, U.S. Department of Energy (EIA-DOE)

Hides and Leather

The major producers of bovine hides and skins are the U.S., Argentina, Brazil and Russia. The U.S. is the largest producer with about 40 percent of the world market in terms of production. The U.S. Department of Agriculture forecast world production of bovine hides and skins in 1998 at 3.82 million tonnes, down slightly from the year before. After the U.S., Brazil is the next largest producer of bovine hides and skins followed by Argentina.

The U.S. cattle and calf population in 1998 was forecast to be 99.5 million head, a decline of 2 percent from the previous season. Brazil's cattle inventory in 1998 was projected to be 144.5 million head which would be 1 percent less than the previous season. Argentina's cattle inventory was forecast to be 50.3 million head, or some 3 percent less than a year ago. Among the world's major cattle producing countries, the 1998 total inventory was estimated at 1.03 billion head, virtually the same as the inventory in 1997.

U.S. exports of cattlehides in 1997 were 19.2 million pieces. This represented a decline of 6 percent from the prior year. For 1997, the major market for U.S. cattle hides was the Republic of Korea which took 7.5 million pieces or 39 percent of all U.S. exports. The next largest market was Taiwan which took 2.9 million pieces or some 15 percent of the U.S. export total. Mexico imported 2.5 million pieces in 1997. Japan took 1.8 million pieces in 1997 which represented a decline of 24 percent from the previous year. A country that is becoming a larger market for U.S. cattle hides is China. In 1997, China took almost 1.6 million hides, down 6 percent from 1996. Still, as recently as 1993, China imported only 207,000 cattle hides from the U.S. In 1997, Canada imported 1.32 million pieces from the U.S., an increase of almost 15 percent from the previous year.

Most U.S. leather is used in the shoe industry. U.S. production of nonrubber footwear and slippers in the first quarter of 1998 was 32.8 million pair. That represented an increase of 4 percent from the first quarter of 1997. Of the total, production of women's shows was 33 percent with men's shoes making up 28 percent. Production of slippers made up 32 percent of the total.

In the second quarter of 1998, U.S. nonrubber footwear and slipper production was 31.8 million pair or some 4 percent less than in the second quarter of 1997. In the second quarter of 1998, production of women's shoes was 9.8 million pair while production of men's shoes was 8.7 million pair. Slipper production in second quarter 1998 was 11.5 million pair. For the first half of 1998, U.S. nonrubber footwear and slipper production was 64.6 million pair. For all of 1997, nonrubber footwear and slipper production was 123.7 million pair. This was down very slightly from the 1996 total production of 128 million pair. In 1995, U.S. nonrubber footwear and slipper production was substantially higher at almost 147 million pair.

World Production of Bovine Hides and Skins   In Thousands of Metric Tons

Year	Argentina	Australia	Brazil	Canada	Colombia	France	Germany	Italy	Mexico	Russia[3]	United Kingdom	United States	World Total
1990	307	149	447	78	105	175	247	92	181	503	92	1,057	4,077
1991	308	153	448	75	104	182	251	95	155	502	93	1,061	4,076
1992	298	162	442	77	88	180	205	98	160	466	88	1,073	3,983
1993	303	154	565	73	79	160	175	95	161	460	77	1,078	3,969
1994	305	152	573	74	77	151	158	93	166	350	81	1,106	3,850
1995	301	145	608	75	84	154	156	93	170	310	85	973	4,190
1996	306	145	615	81	88	158	164	92	160	280	90	992	4,192
1997	295	166	590	85	92	158	164	92	161	270	84	976	4,211
1998[1]	255	157	596	86	94	148	154	92	162	235	83	984	4,161
1999[2]	260	152	605	84	96	143	150	92	159	215	76	910	NA

[1] Preliminary. [2] Forecast. [3] Formerly part of the U.S.S.R.; data not reported separately until 1990. *Source: Foreign Agricultural Service, U.S. Department of Agriculture (FAS-USDA)*

Salient Statistics of Hides and Leather in the United States

	New Supply of Cattle Hides				Wholesale Prices - ¢ Lb.		Production			Wholesale Leather Indexes		Footwear	
	Domestic Slaughter									Upper			
Year	Federally Inspected	Uninspected[4]	Total Production	Net Exports	Heavy Native Cows[2]	Heavy Native[3] Steers	All U.S. Tanning	Cattle-Hide	Value of Leather Exports $1,000	Men	Women	Production[5]	Export
	Thousands of Equivalent Hides						In 1,000 Equiv. Hides			1982 = 100		Mil. Pairs	
1988	34,048	1,031	35,079	24,527	86.50	87.3	13,300	11,475	506,483	121.3	112.5	234,852	18,394
1989	33,010	907	33,917	22,500	83.16	89.4	12,932	11,242	624,925	127.5	116.2	221,790	14,358
1990	32,391	851	33,242	20,920	92.58	92.0	14,820	13,018	750,836	135.8	120.9	184,568	15,174
1991	31,887	803	32,690	18,636	76.92	78.9	14,800	13,021	680,348	141.0	124.0	167,386	18,109
1992	32,094	780	32,874	17,810	81.71	75.9	15,900	14,474	705,038	145.0	126.4	168,451	21,401
1993	32,593	731	33,324	17,117	82.16	78.9	18,057	16,931	764,120	145.3	129.3	171,733	20,700
1994	33,483	713	34,196	16,259	94.99	87.3	18,842	18,117	811,951	144.7	127.2	163,000	22,505
1995	34,879	760	35,639	18,336	93.89	87.6	18,092	17,480	870,247	150.1	129.0	147,550	20,571
1996	36,583	177	36,760	18,626	92.15	86.4	18,769	18,135	950,510	152.4	132.1	127,315	23,726
1997[1]	35,567	925	36,492	17,562	90.99	86.1	19,592	18,930	1,145,664	156.4	132.2	136,832	28,300

[1] Preliminary. [2] Central U.S., heifers. [3] FOB, Chicago. [4] Includes farm slaughter; diseased and condemned animals and hides taken off fallen animals. [5] Other than rubber. *Sources: Leather Industries of America; Bureau of the Census, U.S. Department of Commerce*

Production of All Footwear (Shoes, Sandals, Slippers, Athletic, Etc.) in the U.S. In Millions of Pairs

Year	First Quarter	Second Quarter	Third Quarter	Fourth Quarter	Total	Year	First Quarter	Second Quarter	Third Quarter	Fourth Quarter	Total
1989	56.2	52.8	50.8	50.8	221.9	1994	42.5	40.8	40.1	39.5	163.0
1990	53.5	52.3	49.6	46.2	184.6	1995	37.2	38.3	34.8	36.7	147.0
1991	48.1	37.8	41.8	41.2	169.0	1996	33.2	31.8	29.7	33.2	128.0
1992	41.1	40.8	43.6	39.3	164.8	1997	31.4	33.1	28.6	30.6	123.7
1993	43.3	44.6	42.8	41.0	171.7	1998[1]	32.8	31.8	29.3		125.2

[1] Preliminary. *Source: Bureau of the Census, U.S. Department of Commerce*

Average Factory Price[2] of Footwear in the United States In Dollars Per Pair

Year	First Quarter	Second Quarter	Third Quarter	Fourth Quarter	Total	Year	First Quarter	Second Quarter	Third Quarter	Fourth Quarter	Total
1989	15.43	16.37	16.97	17.87	16.98	1994	25.77	23.60	21.49	22.44	23.22
1990	18.04	18.65	19.91	20.72	19.37	1995	19.61	21.46	25.37	21.26	21.79
1991	22.14	20.40	19.74	18.52	20.14	1996	23.65	22.78	22.14	20.38	22.07
1992	20.19	22.21	21.15	20.46	20.96	1997	21.99	21.15	21.79	21.82	21.69
1993	21.62	21.67	21.37	21.79	21.61	1998[1]	24.00	23.82	19.94		22.59

[1] Preliminary. [2] Average value of factory shipments per pair. *Source: Bureau of the Census, U.S. Department of Commerce*

Imports and Exports of All Cattle Hides in the United States In Thousands of Hides

	Imports		U.S. Exports -- By Country of Destination										
Year	Total	From Canada	Total	Canada	Italy	Japan	Rep. of Korea	Mexico	Portugal	Romania	Spain	Taiwan	Thailand
1988	642	481	24,687	759	319	7,140	9,986	1,865	44	624	142	2,493	35
1989	901	1,043	23,401	614	343	6,268	10,322	1,284	46	1,154	64	1,886	70
1990	661	678	21,582	674	136	6,802	9,839	1,438	29	253	175	1,476	91
1991	1,549	1,088	20,185	561	138	4,662	9,300	2,702	7	0	39	2,058	123
1992	1,536	1,457	19,347	684	107	4,647	8,589	2,729	100	4	30	1,823	160
1993	1,660	1,597	18,777	965	354	4,167	7,919	2,217	79	1	60	1,950	386
1994	1,731	-----	17,990	995	309	3,133	7,472	1,553	168	72	141	2,491	332
1995	1,759	-----	20,095	952	332	3,246	8,283	899	111	63	215	3,017	781
1996	1,702	-----	20,328	1,149	522	2,372	7,956	2,123	64	171	189	2,871	455
1997[1]	1,633	-----	19,195	1,320	469	1,802	7,470	2,501	55	-----	148	2,866	323

[1] Preliminary. *Source: Leather Industries of America (LIA)*

Imports of Bovine Hides and Skins by Selected Countries In Metric Tons

Year	Brazil	Canada	Hong Kong	Italy	Japan	Mexico	Portugal	Rep. of Korea	Spain	Taiwan	Turkey	United States	World Total
1991	8	18	67	156	206	70	30	392	39	100	15	67	1,249
1992	11	17	80	131	188	71	32	385	26	91	28	65	1,266
1993	21	26	81	141	188	71	39	372	35	94	37	57	1,352
1994	16	28	95	243	139	60	56	356	29	112	17	56	1,417
1995	33	35	100	250	152	30	43	342	42	112	43	53	1,617
1996	20	34	79	263	123	71	42	341	33	124	50	57	1,586
1997	13	39	64	254	114	96	37	323	44	140	60	52	1,537
1998[1]	13	37	67	250	85	120	35	250	48	145	65	61	1,536
1999[2]	13	38	66	250	85	125	39	230	46	145	70	65	NA

[1] Preliminary. [2] Forecast. *Source: Foreign Agricultural Service, U.S. Department of Agriculture (FAS-USDA)*

Exports of Bovine Hides and Skins by Selected Countries In Metric Tons

Year	Australia	Brazil	Canada	Germany	Hong Kong	Italy	Nether-lands	New Zealand	Poland	Russia	United Kingdom	United States	World Total
1991	149	60	90	63	69	8	70	33	13	22	18	637	1,288
1992	144	71	74	38	75	9	66	31	17	28	19	610	1,261
1993	142	76	87	40	76	7	35	21	5	150	25	581	1,290
1994	96	84	79	24	93	10	37	22	2	216	22	602	1,343
1995	85	148	90	34	100	10	47	22	2	195	22	510	1,352
1996	93	174	97	33	72	20	47	28	3	212	24	506	1,426
1997	115	216	96	35	60	16	48	27	3	210	25	473	1,476
1998[1]	124	220	98	22	63	15	45	25	4	202	25	470	1,454
1999[2]	110	230	100	22	63	14	49	30	4	190	23	417	NA

[1] Preliminary. [2] Forecast. *Source: Foreign Agricultural Service, U.S. Department of Agriculture (FAS-USDA)*

HIDES AND LEATHER

Utilization of Bovine Hides and Skins by Selected Countries In Metric Tons

Year	Argentina	Brazil	Colombia	Germany	Italy	Japan	Mexico	Rep. of Korea	Spain	Taiwan	Turkey	United States	World Total
1990	307	395	100	176	425	261	233	380	129	74	74	388	3,960
1991	308	396	98	143	435	253	225	400	119	101	78	491	4,009
1992	298	382	97	129	435	229	231	400	98	91	90	528	3,977
1993	302	510	94	100	435	226	232	385	98	94	95	554	3,905
1994	304	505	96	83	550	200	226	374	94	112	85	560	3,865
1995	300	493	89	79	570	191	200	355	98	112	100	516	4,416
1996	308	461	91	80	615	165	230	353	95	124	110	543	4,350
1997	294	387	92	101	570	150	252	347	106	140	120	555	4,272
1998[1]	254	389	93	99	550	131	277	282	110	145	123	575	4,246
1999[2]	259	388	94	96	550	130	279	252	107	145	126	558	

[1] Preliminary. [2] Forecast. *Source: Foreign Agricultural Service, U.S. Department of Agriculture (FAS-USDA)*

Wholesale Price of Hides (Packer Native Steer) F.O.B. Chicago In Cents Per Pound

Year	Jan.	Feb.	Mar.	Apr.	May	June	July	Aug.	Sept.	Oct.	Nov.	Dec.	Average
1989	83.95	87.42	94.61	87.50	85.18	85.03	90.35	92.39	95.90	94.68	92.91	90.85	90.06
1990	92.68	92.76	95.50	99.95	99.57	97.90	96.69	91.74	87.51	84.70	82.90	84.40	82.19
1991	81.64	75.84	76.50	86.32	88.77	86.60	84.05	77.18	74.05	75.30	75.30	71.29	79.40
1992	70.55	67.84	69.68	75.95	80.05	76.77	76.50	72.76	77.62	81.18	80.05	81.00	75.83
1993	79.82	81.05	81.48	81.44	80.35	76.95	76.62	79.27	80.52	81.76	80.81	79.83	79.99
1994	75.07	75.08	79.00	84.75	87.33	88.77	90.38	89.76	93.90	93.67	93.19	91.13	86.84
1995	90.10	91.42	97.99	102.32	99.64	92.45	85.74	82.46	82.45	82.16	78.02	73.02	88.15
1996	73.67	75.11	77.96	84.58	87.56	82.51	89.45	96.06	98.91	101.51	94.60	90.65	87.71
1997	89.77	93.47	99.44	99.40	89.44	81.45	80.20	83.92	84.86	86.35	89.20	82.61	88.34
1998	66.88	77.33	82.61	83.72	85.05	83.13	81.17	81.11	75.23	67.95	67.53	68.26	76.66

Source: The Wall Street Journal

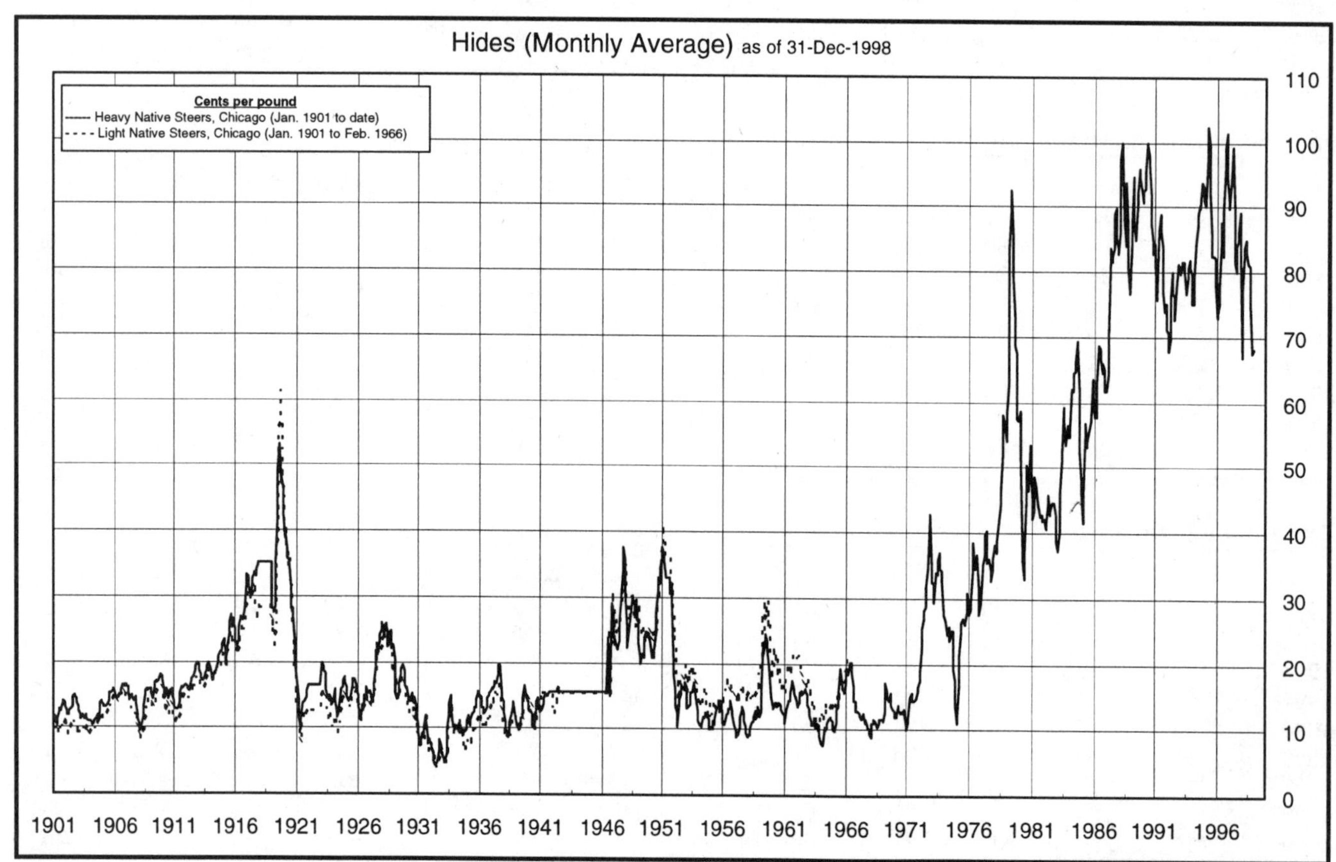

Hogs

The U.S. hog industry in 1998 was dismal for the small, independent producer as live hog prices fell to an inflation adjusted 50 year low. This suggests a continuing trend of industry concentration into corporate based finishing and marketing operations.

The world's hog inventory in early 1998 of a record high 807 million head compares with 792 million in 1997. Head expansion in China and the U.S. accounted for much of the gain. World pork consumption also hit a new high in 1998 at 82.9 million metric tonnes vs. 80.2 million in 1997, but on a per capita basis the 1998 estimate of 18.7 kilograms per person trails the 1995 record of 19.6 kg.

China is the world's largest hog producer with more than half the total while the U.S. is a distant second. China's 1998 inventory of a record large 475 million head compares with 457 million in 1997 and an annual average in the first half of the 1990's of less than 400 million. In the U.S., the 1998 total of 59.9 million head compares with 56.1 million in 1997. Germany's inventory, the largest in the European Union, of nearly 25 million head compares with 24.3 million in 1997. The protracted slide in Russia's and the Ukraine's inventory persisted into 1998, the combined total of 26.5 million head compares with 30.7 million in 1997 and over 50 million as recently as 1992.

The September 1, 1998 U.S. inventory of 62.9 million head compares with 61.2 million a year earlier. About 7 million head were kept for breeding in late 1998, marginally higher from a year earlier with the balance to be marketed. The increase in the 1998 inventory was expected given the higher mid-1997 hog prices and prospects for lower feed costs in 1998. Farrowing intentions during the closing months of 1998 and into the first quarter of 1999 were about 3 percent above the year earlier periods. Although the U.S. hog inventory is only about 8 percent of the world total, slaughter runs about 10-12 percent and pork production somewhat higher. U.S. per capita pork use in 1998 of 51.9 pounds compares with 48.7 pounds in 1997 and a forecast of 53.6 pounds in 1999.

More than half the inventory share of U.S. hog marketing's now come from contract hog operations. In a contractual agreement, the contractor provides the hogs, feed, medication and supplies while the contractee provides the housing, utilities and labor. Most hog production still occurs in Corn Belt states, with Iowa the leader. Southern states, led by North Carolina, have seen a dramatic growth in contractual operations in recent years. Still, most U.S. producers continue to raise hogs in farrow-to-finish operations. As of September 1, 1998, the total number of hogs under contract, owned by operations with over 5,000 head total inventory, but raised by contractees, accounted for 29 percent of the total U.S. inventory vs. 26 percent a year earlier.

Commercial U.S. hog slaughter in the Jan-July 1998 period of 64.8 million head compares with 51.5 million in the like 1997 period, with an average dressed weight of 188 pounds in both years. Pork production for the year 1998 was estimated at 18.8 billion pounds vs. 17.2 billion in 1997. Based upon fall 1998 inventory and breeding intentions, pork production in 1999 is forecast at a record high 19.6 billion pounds, but could prove higher if the late 1998 pressure on prices persists and marginal producers opt to liquidate herds rather than maintain operations.

The U.S. is among the world's largest pork exporters-449,000 metric tonnes in 1998 vs. 474,000 in 1997; the world total of 2.4 million tonnes compares with 2.5 million, respectively, with Denmark the largest exporter in 1998 with 485,000 tonnes. Japan, Russia, Canada and Mexico are the largest importers of U.S. pork. However, continued depreciation of the J-yen against the U.S. dollar and Japan's sluggish economy tempered exports to Japan in 1998 and likely into 1999. Import demand from Mexico and Russia is apt to be higher, but much of the increase will be for lower-valued pork cuts. The U.S. imports pork products, mostly from Canada and Denmark--261,000 tonnes in 1998 vs. 287,000 in 1997; while live hogs are imported from Canada.

Wholesale barrow and gilt hog prices during 1998 averaged about $34-$36 per cwt., basis Iowa/Minnesota vs. $51.36 in 1997 and are forecast at $34-$37 in 1999.

Futures Markets

Lean hog futures and options are traded on the Chicago Mercantile Exchange (CME); futures settle to the CME lean hog Index (TM) which tracks the value of lean pork at select U.S. packing plants. Live hog futures are traded on the Mid-America Commodity Exchange (MidAm)and the Budapest Commodity Exchange.

Salient Statistics of Pigs and Hogs in the United States

	Pig Crop						Value of Hogs on Farms, Dec. 1		Hog Marketings	Quantity Produced (Live Wt.)	Value of Production	Hogs Slaughtered in Thousand Heads				
	Spring[3]			Fall[4]								Commercial				
	Sows Farrowed	Pig Crop	Pigs Per Liter	Sows Farrowed	Pig Crop	Pigs Per Liter	$ Per	Total	Thousand			Federally				
Year	- 1,000s of Head -		Liter	- 1,000s of Head -		Liter	Head	Million $	Head	Mil. Lbs.	Mil. $	Inspected	Other	Total	Farm	Total
1989	6,028	47,141	7.82	5,767	44,779	7.76	79.1	4,253	92,432	21,907	9,281	86,328	2,364	88,692	315	89,007
1990	5,732	45,223	7.89	5,709	44,877	7.86	85.4	4,648	89,240	21,287	11,346	82,901	2,235	85,136	296	85,431
1991	5,988	47,413	7.92	6,071	47,902	7.89	68.8	3,966	92,220	22,727	11,067	85,952	2,217	88,169	276	88,445
1992	6,260	50,466	8.06	6,012	48,676	8.10	71.2	4,147	98,589	23,947	9,854	92,611	2,278	94,889	268	95,157
1993	6,028	49,006	8.13	5,954	48,044	8.07	74.9	4,338	98,351	23,693	10,628	90,933	2,135	93,068	229	93,296
1994	6,257	51,217	8.18	6,139	50,262	8.19	53.2	3,192	100,747	24,437	9,692	93,435	2,261	95,696	208	95,905
1995	6,046	50,077	8.28	5,843	48,739	8.35	70.7	4,120	102,684	24,426	9,829	94,203	2,123	96,325	210	96,535
1996	5,648	47,887	8.46	5,449	46,571	8.55	94.0	5,284	101,852	23,267	12,013	90,534	1,860	92,394	183	92,577
1997[1]	5,595	48,393	8.65	5,885	51,190	8.70	81.0	4,880	104,554	24,094	12,634	90,228	1,733	91,960	176	92,136
1998[2]	6,015	52,469	8.73	6,044	52,512	8.69						99,285	1,744	101,028		

[1] Preliminary. [2] Estimate. [3] December-May. [4] June-November. *Source: Economic Research Service, U.S. Department of Agriculture (ERS-USDA)*

HOGS

World Hog Numbers in Specified Countries as of January 1 In Thousands of Head

Year	Brazil	Canada	China	Denmark	France	Germany	Philip-pines	Poland	Russia	Spain	Ukraine	United States	World Total
1990	32,120	10,650	352,810	9,120	12,275	34,178	8,124	18,685	40,000	16,910	19,947	53,788	795,188
1991	32,550	10,468	362,408	9,282	12,013	30,818	8,007	19,739	38,500	16,001	19,427	54,416	760,788
1992	33,050	10,498	369,646	9,767	12,067	26,063	8,022	20,725	35,384	17,209	17,839	57,469	728,789
1993	31,050	10,577	384,210	10,345	13,015	26,514	7,954	21,059	31,520	18,260	16,175	58,202	740,758
1994	31,200	10,851	393,000	10,870	14,791	26,075	8,227	17,422	28,600	18,234	15,298	57,904	744,211
1995	31,338	11,673	414,619	10,864	14,593	24,698	8,941	19,138	24,859	18,295	13,946	59,990	761,835
1996	32,068	11,588	441,692	10,709	14,523	23,737	9,023	20,343	22,630	18,600	13,070	58,264	784,866
1997	31,369	11,483	457,130	11,081	14,976	24,283	9,750	17,697	19,500	18,651	11,175	56,141	791,747
1998[1]	31,427	11,842	475,000	11,392	15,430	24,795	10,210	18,498	16,579	19,269	10,000	60,915	808,853
1999[2]	31,682	12,200	NA	11,985	15,810	25,665	10,912	19,500	16,513	19,300	9,900	62,200	NA

[1] Preliminary. [2] Forecast. *Source: Foreign Agricultural Service, U.S. Department of Agricultures (FAS-USDA)*

Hogs and Pigs on Farms in the United States on December 1 In Thousands of Head

Year	Georgia	Illinois	Indiana	Iowa	Kansas	Minne-sota	Missouri	Nebraska	North Carolina	Ohio	South Dakota	Wis-consin	Total
1989	1,200	5,700	4,350	13,500	1,450	4,450	2,700	4,200	2,570	2,080	1,720	1,150	53,821
1990	1,100	5,700	4,400	13,800	1,500	4,500	2,800	4,300	2,800	2,000	1,770	1,200	54,477
1991	1,130	5,900	4,600	15,000	1,430	4,900	2,700	4,500	3,650	1,925	1,950	1,180	57,684
1992	1,100	5,900	4,600	16,400	1,440	4,700	2,850	4,650	4,500	1,800	1,830	1,210	59,815
1993	1,000	5,450	4,300	15,000	1,350	4,750	3,000	4,300	5,400	1,630	1,750	1,170	57,904
1994	1,020	5,350	4,500	14,500	1,310	4,850	3,500	4,350	7,000	1,800	1,740	1,040	59,990
1995	900	4,800	4,000	13,400	1,230	4,950	1,100	4,050	8,200	1,800	1,450	900	58,264
1996	800	4,400	3,750	12,200	1,450	4,850	3,450	3,600	9,300	1,500	1,200	800	56,171
1997	520	4,700	3,950	14,600	1,530	5,700	3,550	3,500	9,600	1,700	1,400	740	61,158
1998[1]	430	4,850	4,050	15,300	1,590	5,700	3,300	3,400	9,700	1,700	1,400	690	62,156

[1] Preliminary. *Source: National Agricultural Statistics Service, U.S. Department of Agriculture (NASS-USDA)*

Hog-Corn Price Ratio[1] in the United States

Year	Jan.	Feb.	Mar.	Apr.	May	June	July	Aug.	Sept.	Oct.	Nov.	Dec.	Average
1989	20.5	20.8	21.6	21.4	23.4	22.9	23.2	23.3	19.0	21.0	20.1	21.2	22.1
1990	22.0	22.5	21.5	21.0	22.7	23.7	23.9	22.0	22.3	23.3	25.9	21.5	22.4
1991	22.0	22.5	21.5	21.0	22.7	23.7	23.9	22.0	19.9	18.9	16.6	16.6	20.9
1992	15.3	16.3	15.7	16.5	18.1	18.9	19.1	20.5	19.5	20.5	20.8	21.2	18.5
1993	20.3	22.0	22.1	21.0	21.9	23.0	20.6	21.0	21.6	20.6	17.3	15.2	20.6
1994	16.1	17.2	16.2	16.1	16.4	16.3	18.6	19.4	16.2	15.4	14.1	14.5	16.4
1995	16.8	17.5	16.4	15.1	15.4	16.8	17.6	18.5	18.0	16.4	13.9	14.2	16.4
1996	13.7	13.8	13.9	12.9	13.7	13.4	13.2	13.9	15.4	19.2	20.5	21.1	15.4
1997	20.0	19.9	17.7	19.2	21.6	22.6	24.3	22.1	20.0	18.6	18.0	16.5	20.0
1998[2]	14.1	14.0	13.7	14.5	18.0	18.5	16.7	18.5	16.1	14.3	9.7	7.3	14.6

[1] Bushels of corn equal in value to 100 pounds of hog, live weight [2] Preliminary. *Source: Economic Research Service, U.S. Department of Agriculture*

Cold Storage Holdings of Frozen Pork[1] in the United States, on First of Month In Millions of Pounds

Year	Jan.	Feb.	Mar.	Apr.	May	June	July	Aug.	Sept.	Oct.	Nov.	Dec.
1989	357.9	377.6	393.5	392.8	432.6	428.1	380.1	342.6	277.9	278.0	275.8	279.2
1990	255.8	272.5	303.9	294.6	320.3	320.3	292.6	256.4	224.7	225.8	231.9	221.5
1991	233.6	247.0	281.2	289.0	340.0	333.3	312.3	277.9	282.4	280.5	299.7	308.0
1992	311.1	341.2	364.0	372.2	362.6	344.9	319.0	307.0	266.7	297.3	306.8	316.7
1993	314.5	329.5	344.4	330.4	378.5	371.6	351.3	342.5	308.9	311.2	324.8	313.0
1994	299.2	348.8	356.9	393.1	429.7	437.6	410.8	393.7	364.0	352.7	385.4	383.2
1995	365.3	389.6	395.1	416.8	422.3	434.9	431.1	408.3	354.0	332.6	321.6	347.1
1996	334.8	382.2	385.5	352.9	385.5	381.3	351.8	322.7	322.9	340.3	333.3	316.4
1997	313.8	342.2	383.9	404.7	440.2	413.4	406.2	388.7	371.8	346.6	354.2	334.1
1998[2]	346.4	446.1	464.5	458.8	487.0	477.4	426.8	414.6	392.6	388.7	411.9	443.4

[1] Excludes lard. [2] Preliminary. *Source: Economic Research Service, U.S. Department of Agriculture (ERS-USDA)*

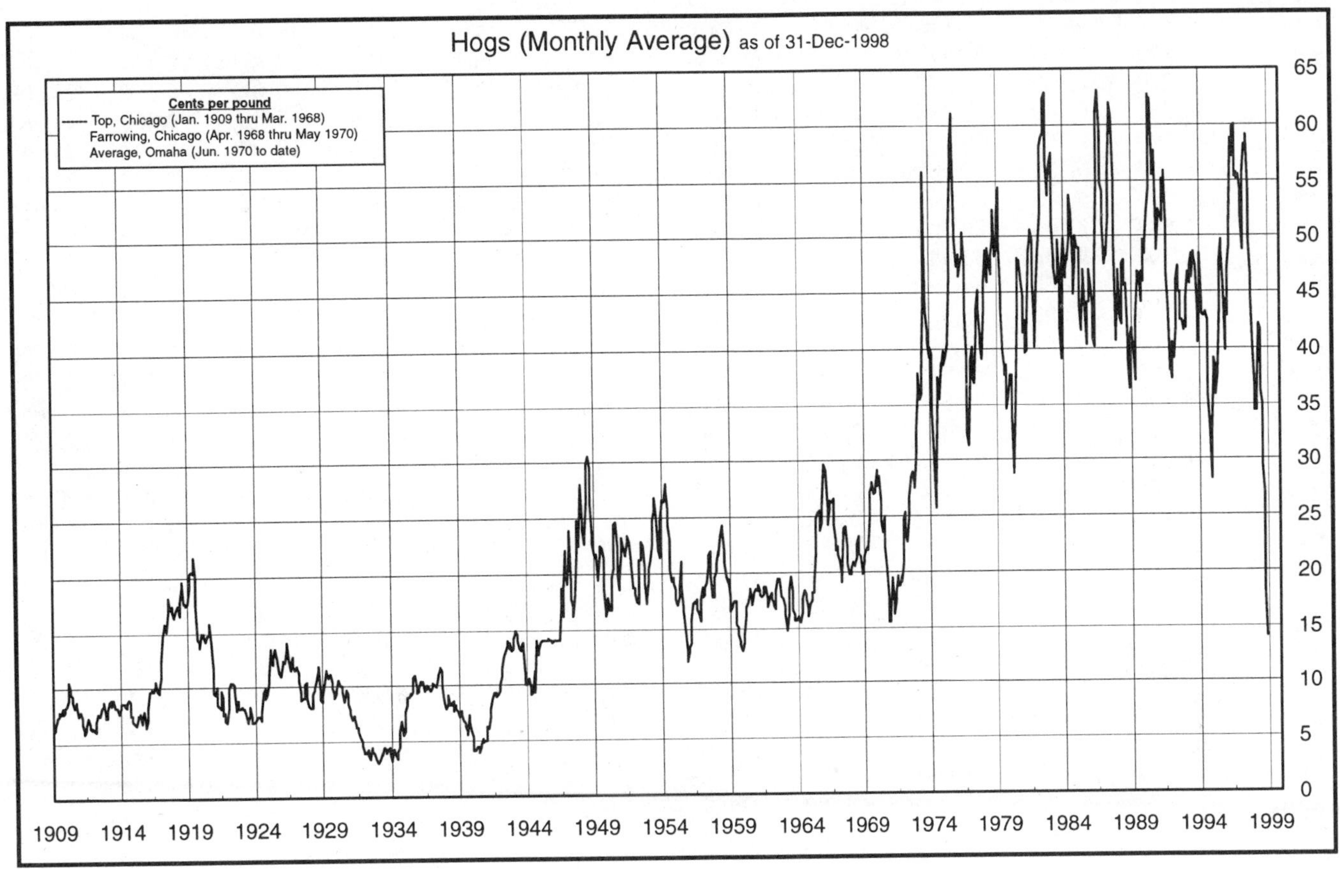

Average Wholesale Price of Hogs, Average (All Weights) in Sioux City In Dollars Per Hundred Pounds (Hwt.)

Year	Jan.	Feb.	Mar.	Apr.	May	June	July	Aug.	Sept.	Oct.	Nov.	Dec.	Average
1988	44.59	47.45	43.19	42.28	47.75	48.26	45.60	45.98	41.28	38.92	36.52	40.58	43.53
1989	41.64	41.11	39.88	37.22	42.40	46.24	47.26	47.04	44.58	47.49	47.21	49.65	44.31
1990	48.41	49.48	52.56	54.63	62.80	61.34	62.54	56.37	55.64	58.02	50.17	48.96	55.08
1991	51.32	52.31	51.92	51.42	54.83	54.79	55.74	51.11	46.76	43.51	38.29	38.93	49.24
1992	37.15	40.45	39.09	42.01	45.90	47.59	44.98	44.88	42.50	42.57	41.98	42.12	42.60
1993	41.66	44.57	46.76	45.46	47.10	48.52	46.38	48.67	48.40	47.27	42.76	40.38	45.66
1994	43.99	48.12	44.30	42.72	42.27	42.76	42.62	42.37	35.49	32.56	28.25	31.59	39.75
1995	37.82	39.09	37.94	35.88	37.35	43.03	47.18	49.46	48.67	45.42	40.02	43.80	42.14
1996	42.39	46.93	49.06	50.88	58.29	56.45	59.47	60.49	54.60	55.41	54.42	55.47	53.66
1997[1]	52.96	51.36	48.52	54.41	57.84	57.43	58.89	54.17	49.45	46.12	44.86	40.33	51.36

[1] Preliminary. *Source: Economic Research Service, U.S. Department of Agriculture (ERS-USDA)*

Average Price Received by Farmers for Hogs in the United States In Cents Per Pound

Year	Jan.	Feb.	Mar.	Apr.	May	June	July	Aug.	Sept.	Oct.	Nov.	Dec.	Average
1989	40.90	40.40	39.30	36.90	41.60	45.10	45.90	45.60	43.40	46.60	45.00	48.20	43.24
1990	47.30	48.20	51.30	53.80	61.20	60.30	60.80	55.90	54.30	56.80	50.20	47.80	53.99
1991	50.00	52.20	51.50	50.90	54.10	54.70	54.20	51.20	46.40	43.60	38.00	38.60	48.78
1992	36.80	40.20	39.10	41.00	45.10	46.70	44.60	44.10	42.10	42.00	41.10	41.70	42.04
1993	41.20	44.00	46.50	45.40	46.90	48.10	45.70	47.30	47.80	46.90	42.50	40.40	45.23
1994	43.50	47.90	44.40	42.70	42.70	42.70	42.20	41.80	35.40	31.80	28.00	30.80	39.49
1995	36.90	39.10	37.80	35.70	37.20	42.30	46.30	48.60	48.40	45.70	39.90	43.50	41.78
1996	42.30	46.50	48.70	49.70	56.80	56.40	58.60	59.70	54.70	55.60	54.40	55.60	53.25
1997	53.80	52.80	49.40	53.80	58.20	57.80	58.90	55.30	50.40	47.30	45.10	41.60	52.03
1998[1]	36.00	35.70	34.80	35.60	42.20	42.20	36.70	35.10	29.50	27.40	18.70	14.70	32.38

[1] Preliminary. *Source: Economic Research Service, U.S. Department of Agriculture (ERS-USDA)*

Quarterly 10 -- U.S. State Hogs & Pigs Report   In Thousands of Head

Year[2]	Inventory[3]	Breeding[3]	Market[3]	Farrowings	Pig Crop	Year[2]	Inventory[3]	Breeding[3]	Market[3]	Farrowings	Pig Crop
1989	43,210	5,335	37,875	9,203	71,807	1994	57,904	7,130	50,739	12,376	101,400
I	43,210	5,335	37,875	2,109	16,439	I	57,904	7,130	50,739	2,885	23,368
II	41,655	5,440	36,215	2,580	20,309	II	57,350	7,210	50,140	3,390	27,984
III	44,020	5,565	38,455	2,324	18,167	III	60,715	7,565	53,150	3,107	25,547
IV	45,200	5,335	39,865	2,190	16,890	IV	62,320	7,415	54,905	2,997	24,517
1990	42,200	5,275	36,925	8,960	70,589	1995	59,990	7,060	52,930	11,847	98,516
I	42,200	5,275	36,925	2,013	15,748	I	59,990	7,060	52,930	2,886	23,851
II	40,190	5,245	34,945	2,458	19,576	II	58,465	6,998	51,467	3,170	26,373
III	42,630	5,405	37,225	2,236	17,684	III	59,560	7,180	52,380	2,976	24,813
IV	44,120	5,300	38,820	2,238	17,459	IV	60,540	6,898	53,642	2,815	23,479
1991	42,900	5,257	37,643	9,516	75,330	1996	58,264	6,839	51,425	11,114	94,458
I	42,900	5,257	37,643	2,129	16,700	I	58,264	6,839	51,425	2,735	23,054
II	41,990	5,450	36,540	2,577	20,555	II	55,741	6,701	49,040	2,930	24,833
III	44,520	5,700	38,820	2,413	19,260	III	56,038	6,682	49,356	2,718	23,244
IV	46,950	5,685	41,265	2,433	18,551	IV	56,961	6,577	50,384	2,731	23,327
1992	45,735	5,610	40,125	10,202	82,497	1997	56,124	6,578	49,546	11,480	99,583
I	45,735	5,610	40,125	2,296	18,532	I	56,141	6,667	49,474	2,684	23,164
II	44,800	5,555	39,245	2,663	21,570	II	55,049	6,637	48,412	2,911	25,229
III	47,255	5,845	41,410	2,501	20,395	III	57,366	6,789	50,577	2,946	25,696
IV	49,175	5,840	43,335	2,398	19,351	IV	60,456	6,858	53,598	2,939	25,494
1993	58,202	7,109	51,093	11,982	97,050	1998[1]	61,158	6,957	54,200	12,059	104,981
I	58,202	7,109	51,093	3,665	29,739	I	61,158	6,957	54,200	2,929	25,480
II	47,145	5,735	41,410	2,363	19,267	II	60,163	6,942	53,220	3,086	26,989
III	58,395	7,320	51,075	2,972	24,041	III	62,213	6,958	55,254	3,054	26,634
IV	59,030	7,130	51,900	2,982	24,003	IV	63,488	6,875	56,612	2,990	25,878

[1] Preliminary. [2] Quarters are December preceding year-February (I), March-May (II), June-August (III) and September-November (IV). [3] Beginning of period. *Source: National Agricultural Statistics Service, U.S.Department of Agriculture (NASS-USDA)*

Federally Inspected Hog Slaughter in the United States   In Thousands of Head

Year	Jan.	Feb.	Mar.	Apr.	May	June	July	Aug.	Sept.	Oct.	Nov.	Dec.	Total
1989	7,116	6,619	7,569	7,199	7,277	6,881	6,131	7,392	7,493	7,823	7,815	7,012	86,328
1990	7,407	6,643	7,279	6,785	6,799	6,152	5,938	7,110	6,716	7,546	7,334	7,140	82,901
1991	7,461	6,469	7,044	7,320	6,948	6,296	6,557	7,098	7,177	8,292	7,744	7,708	85,951
1992	8,144	7,153	7,934	7,610	6,897	7,166	7,461	7,494	8,217	8,599	7,796	8,142	92,613
1993	7,649	6,921	7,958	7,840	6,988	7,338	7,010	7,473	7,763	7,857	7,952	8,184	90,993
1994	7,285	6,783	8,148	7,609	7,383	7,452	6,941	7,997	8,192	8,585	8,516	8,547	93,435
1995	7,882	7,157	8,628	7,379	8,012	7,731	6,918	8,083	7,752	8,358	8,424	7,881	94,203
1996	8,129	7,506	7,549	7,886	7,485	6,395	7,187	7,509	7,541	8,423	7,469	7,455	90,534
1997	7,610	6,836	7,437	7,590	6,971	6,859	7,169	7,197	7,872	8,625	7,601	8,461	90,228
1998[1]	8,454	7,590	8,335	8,198	7,443	7,596	8,130	8,024	8,443	9,192	8,650	9,231	99,285

[1] Preliminary. *Source: National Agricultural Statistics Service, U.S. Department of Agriculture (NASS-USDA)*

Average Live Weight of All Hogs Slaughtered Under Federal Inspection   In Pounds Per Head

Year	Jan.	Feb.	Mar.	Apr.	May	June	July	Aug.	Sept.	Oct.	Nov.	Dec.	Average
1989	249	247	247	251	251	251	247	247	246	248	251	250	249
1990	249	248	248	250	251	252	249	249	248	250	253	252	250
1991	251	250	250	252	254	253	251	250	251	253	256	255	252
1992	255	253	252	253	254	254	251	250	252	252	255	255	253
1993	254	253	253	254	254	256	254	252	252	254	257	258	254
1994	254	254	254	256	255	256	252	252	255	259	261	260	256
1995	258	256	257	258	258	258	256	253	252	255	259	258	257
1996	257	254	255	255	255	256	251	250	250	255	258	257	254
1997	257	256	256	256	256	257	253	252	255	257	261	260	256
1998[1]	259	258	257	257	256	255	252	252	253	257	262	261	257

[1] Preliminary. *Source: Economic Research Service, U.S. Department of Agriculture (ERS-USDA)*

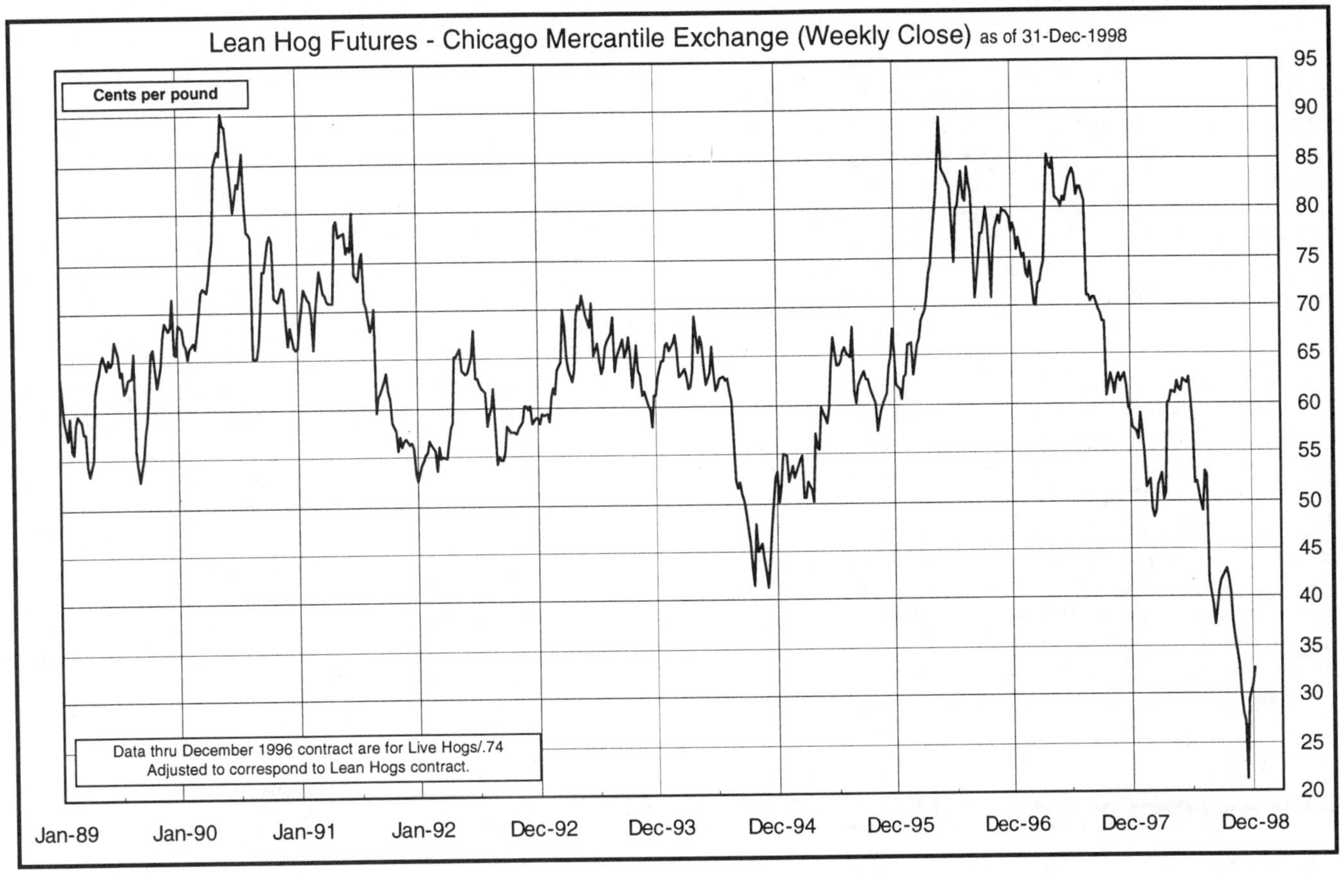

Average Open Interest of Lean[1] Hogs Futures in Chicago In Contracts

Year	Jan.	Feb.	Mar.	Apr.	May	June	July	Aug.	Sept.	Oct.	Nov.	Dec.
1989	31,923	30,853	29,014	30,414	29,646	27,353	25,375	25,345	28,308	33,936	35,913	29,693
1990	30,335	31,018	37,789	39,257	47,291	43,631	32,942	29,964	26,982	25,691	27,648	25,757
1991	22,742	24,798	24,449	22,400	25,871	21,275	18,154	16,771	17,281	18,462	21,572	19,167
1992	23,854	31,545	32,441	32,430	30,947	26,362	24,935	24,535	27,535	32,555	32,738	30,468
1993	27,210	25,620	28,264	24,139	22,581	19,840	19,026	20,761	20,544	20,051	21,167	24,096
1994	31,899	32,123	31,012	31,713	30,889	27,327	26,414	25,335	28,957	32,077	36,304	33,516
1995	36,705	30,958	30,736	28,035	28,294	28,729	29,959	31,599	34,183	31,312	31,519	35,127
1996	35,253	34,823	38,730	42,900	41,916	36,620	35,616	32,541	32,591	34,329	33,148	32,163
1997	33,105	33,953	31,289	34,071	41,978	37,398	36,141	33,712	31,483	36,928	39,363	39,394
1998	45,908	42,241	38,965	33,610	34,257	32,456	32,085	31,199	34,165	34,051	42,224	45,241

[1] Data prior to November 1995 are for Live Hogs, November 1995 thru December 1996 are Live Hogs and Lean Hogs, January 1997 to date are Lean Hogs.
Source: Chicago Mercantile Exchange (CME)

Volume of Trading of Lean[1] Hogs Futures in Chicago In Thousands of Contracts

Year	Jan.	Feb.	Mar.	Apr.	May	June	July	Aug.	Sept.	Oct.	Nov.	Dec.	Total
1989	188.2	135.0	152.8	130.7	175.2	147.5	141.9	131.8	149.6	181.5	205.9	151.6	1,891.9
1990	181.0	119.9	189.7	188.8	278.3	277.0	212.5	170.4	147.0	160.3	186.1	130.4	2,241.3
1991	177.9	150.3	148.0	157.0	155.7	120.8	131.1	120.9	102.9	118.4	104.5	94.8	1,695.8
1992	135.2	137.0	140.4	138.2	116.7	131.2	148.8	102.2	116.6	149.5	117.0	123.3	1,556.1
1993	131.5	101.9	160.0	131.0	120.2	121.1	112.5	91.5	109.4	102.7	116.1	103.0	1,401.8
1994	144.7	97.6	146.9	93.1	127.4	144.4	116.2	122.1	110.7	129.0	150.7	172.1	1,554.0
1995	155.8	115.8	181.9	116.8	145.4	155.3	139.0	144.6	135.3	132.1	142.5	136.2	1,700.7
1996	177.3	138.0	150.1	216.5	208.7	177.4	185.9	157.5	158.1	203.8	170.6	152.1	2,095.9
1997	180.2	159.6	200.1	212.8	222.8	188.6	181.6	146.3	150.0	175.1	152.9	130.9	2,100.9
1998	180.2	182.7	174.8	133.0	155.7	167.8	185.4	158.0	165.0	173.2	219.0	241.8	2,136.4

[1] Data prior to November 1995 are for Live Hogs, November 1995 thru December 1996 are Live Hogs and Lean Hogs, January 1997 to date are Lean Hogs.
Source: Chicago Mercantile Exchange (CME)

Honey

China is the world's largest producer of honey, followed by the U.S. and Argentina. World production has fallen 50 percent since the mid-1980's with lower output in most countries; Argentina is the notable exception with recent annual output averaging about 65,000 tonnes vs. 40,000 in the 1980's. Several factors influence a country's annual honey production with weather being foremost. However, the long term downtrend in production also reflects a contraction in the number of beekeepers and producing bee colonies in some countries, the U.S. being one. A lingering problem results from the more aggressive Africanized bees who have virtually wiped out or greatly curtailed production in some countries, notably Brazil and Mexico.

China's honey production of about 150,000 tonnes in 1997 compares with an annual average during the first half of the 1990's of 175,000 tonnes; the decline largely reflecting fewer beekeepers. The demand side has also been contained due to quality control problems that have plagued China's domestic consumption in recent years. In China honey is considered a healthy food, but demand for pharmaceutical purposes has fallen. China is the world's largest honey exporter for which more stringent quality control standards are set, but shipments have tapered off during the past few years. China's major export markets are generally Japan, Germany, the U.S. and the U.K.

U.S. honey production in 1997 of 192.4 million pounds compares with 198.2 million in 1996, and is the lowest to date for the 1990's. Six states account for more than half of U.S. production paced by California (30 million pounds in 1997), followed by the Dakotas (40 million pounds combined), Minnesota, Montana and Florida. However, U.S. imports reached a record 167.4 million pounds in 1997 vs. 150.6 million in 1996, and only 88 million in 1995. The U.S. also exports a small quantity of honey, about 9 million pounds per year. The U.S. is the world's largest market for industrial honey (used in cereals, bakery and health food products) which accounts for half of total domestic usage. The food service industry takes about 15 percent. The U.S. average honey yield per colony in 1997 of 74.6 pounds compares with 77.3 pounds in 1996; and bee colonies of 2.58 million compare with 2.56 million, respectively. At the turn of the decade U.S. colonies averaged more than 3 million.

U.S. prices for the 1997 honey crop averaged 75.2 cents per pound vs. a record high 88.8 cents in 1996. The average price is based on retail sales by producers and sales to private processors and co-ops.

World Production of Honey In Metric Tons

Year	Argentina	Australia	Brazil	Canada	China	Germany	Japan	Mexico	Russia[2]	United States	Total[3]
1989	40,000	26,198	32,000	27,815	189,000	29,000	5,343	48,530	225,000	80,266	703,152
1990	47,000	27,561	30,000	32,115	193,000	23,000	4,854	51,000	236,219	89,717	732,466
1991	54,000	20,604	32,300	31,606	206,000	25,000	4,202	58,770	240,000	99,414	714,790
1992	61,000	18,948	18,841	30,339	178,000	24,677	3,800	48,852	47,000	100,055	531,512
1993	59,000	22,556	19,000	30,760	176,000	26,357	3,500	48,000	49,600	104,620	539,393
1994	64,000	24,000	19,000	32,920	177,000	22,233	3,500	41,500	43,900	98,500	526,553
1995	70,000	24,000	19,200	30,575	178,000	36,685	3,500	49,228	44,000	95,490	550,678
1996	57,000	-----	-----	24,895	184,000	14,674	-----	47,997	-----	89,850	418,416
1997	70,000	-----	-----	30,021	188,000	15,069	-----	53,681	-----	87,270	444,041
1998[1]	60,000	-----	-----	33,000	140,000	15,000	-----	56,500	-----	89,000	393,500

[1] Preliminary. [2] Formerly part of the U.S.S.R.; data not reported separately until 1992. [3] Only for countries listed. *Source: Foreign Agricultural Service, U.S. Department of Agriculture (FAS-USDA)*

Salient Statistics of Honey in the United States In Millions of Pounds

									------- Program Activity -------					Per
Year	Number of Colonies (1,000)	Yield Per Colony Pounds	Stocks Jan. 1	Total U.S. Production	Imports for Consumption	Domestic Disappearance	Exports	Total Supply	Placed Under Loan	CCC Take Over	Net Gov't. Expenditure[3] Mil. $	Domestic Avg. Price All Honey (¢ Lb.)	National Avg. Price Support (¢ Lb.)	Capita Consumption Lbs.
1989	3,443	51.4	192.4	177.0	77.3	292.0	10.0	446.7	161.7	2.8	41.7	49.8	56.4	1.0
1990	3,210	61.6	144.7	197.8	77.0	303.4	12.4	419.5	183.5	1.1	46.7	53.7	53.8	1.0
1991	3,181	68.9	103.7	219.2	92.2	303.4	9.6	415.1	112.9	3.2	18.6	55.6	53.8	1.0
1992	3,030	72.8	109.3	220.6	114.6	330.5	10.4	444.5	122.7	4.1	16.6	55.0	53.8	1.0
1993	2,876	80.2	103.5	230.6	133.6	342.0	8.5	467.8	136.8	16.4	22.1	53.9	53.8	1.0
1994	2,770	78.4	117.3	217.2	123.2	355.2	8.3	457.7	73.4	0	-.2	52.8	50.0	1.0
1995	2,648	79.6	94.1	210.5	88.6	341.6	9.3	393.2	64.4	0	-9.3	68.5	50.0	1.0
1996	2,566	77.4	42.2	198.1	150.6	334.1	9.9	390.9	-----	-----	-----	-----	-----	-----
1997[1]	2,579	74.5	47.0	192.4	167.4	328.8	8.9	406.8	-----	-----	-----	-----	-----	-----
1998[2]	2,550	76.9	69.1	196.2	132.3	332.9	9.9	397.5	-----	-----	-----	-----	-----	-----

[1] Preliminary. [2] Forecast. [3] Fiscal year. *Source: Economic Research Service, U.S. Department of Agriculture (ERS-USDA)*

Interest Rates, U.S.

Federal Reserve policy eased during 1998; the action was not unexpected, but the implementation was surprising in that one downward move came between the Fed's periodic open market committee meetings and not, as usual, immediately after the FOMC meets. The Fed eased monetary policy three times during the second half of 1998; the first half could be described as a wait and see approach even though the market(s) across the interest rate spectrum were suggesting lower rates were coming. The market's emphasis, however, was on long-term rates which fell below 5 percent in October, a record low. At yearend 1998, the 30-year T-bond yield of 5.09 percent compared with 5.92 percent a year earlier; 3 month T-bills were at 4.45 percent vs. 5.19 percent; fed funds were at 5.00 percent vs. 5.84 percent, the prime rate at 7.75 percent vs. 8.50 percent, and the discount rate at 4.50 percent vs. 5.00 percent, respectively.

Late summer and early fall of 1998 was a tumultuous time for the U.S. equity markets and it was obvious that some Fed action was necessary to restore confidence, in the U.S. and abroad. The Fed's first easing was seen as too little and too late. The timing of the second easing caught the marketplace by surprise and it revitalized the equities market with a 300 point plus rally within 24 hours, basis the Dow-Jones 30 industrial index. The third rate reduction--25 basis points-- followed the FOMC's November 17th meeting, lowering the fed funds target rate around 4.75 percent and the discount rate to 4.50 percent, respectively. In effect the Fed's three pronged action solidified the market's positive psychology by suggesting the Federal Reserve had opted to make the world safe for investments.

Notwithstanding the equity market concerns, the Fed had supporting economic evidence during 1998 that an easier monetary policy could be implemented with little, if any, risk to the economy. Ironically, this outlook would seem to be at odds with traditional fed policy. The U.S. gross national product proved stronger than expected with employment at a record high and unemployment at its lowest level since the 1970's. And consumers were spending, perhaps at too fast a clip at times, but confidence remained high throughout the year. It was a scenario that from a historical stance would be expected to trigger inflation, containment of which has always been the Fed's priority. Instead, inflation proved almost non-existent despite the economy's record long cyclical expansion. If the Fed had any fears, it was not focused on inflation, but deflation; reflecting declining world oil prices, metals prices and a host of other basic commodities. Moreover, the strong economy with its higher tax revenues proved a windfall for the federal government and for the first time in years a budget surplus was realized.

Initial forecasts for 1999 suggest a slowing economy. In late 1998 there were signs that the tight labor market was easing, partly in response to another round of corporate downsizing. Assuming domestic growth slows to around 2 1/2 percent, which the Fed has long considered acceptable, a case can be made for still lower interest rates in 1999. Supporting this view is the likely effort by the Fed to a coordinated easier monetary policy by the world's central banks.

Futures Markets

A futures (and options) contract exists for almost every maturity on the yield curve, as well as for municipal and commercial credit risks. Major U.S. contracts include T-bills and Eurodollars on Chicago's International Monetary Market (IMM), and T-bonds and 10-year T-notes on the Chicago Board of Trade (CBOT). Futures are also traded in Chicago on 2 and 5-Year T-notes, municipal bonds, 30 day fed funds, and one month LIBOR. Smaller size contracts on some interest rate instruments are listed at the MidAmerica Commodity Exchange (MidAm).

U.S. Producer Price Index[2] (Wholesale, All Commodities) 1982 = 100

Year	Jan.	Feb.	Mar.	Apr.	May	June	July	Aug.	Sept.	Oct.	Nov.	Dec.	Average
1990	114.9	114.4	114.2	114.1	114.6	114.3	114.5	116.5	118.3	120.8	120.1	118.7	116.3
1991	119.0	117.2	116.2	116.0	116.5	116.4	116.1	116.2	116.1	116.4	116.4	115.9	116.5
1992	115.6	116.0	116.1	116.3	117.2	118.0	117.9	117.7	118.0	118.1	117.8	117.6	117.2
1993	118.0	118.4	118.7	119.3	119.7	119.5	119.2	118.7	118.7	119.1	119.0	118.6	118.9
1994	119.1	119.3	119.7	119.7	119.9	120.5	120.7	121.2	120.9	120.9	121.5	121.9	120.4
1995	122.9	123.5	123.9	124.6	124.9	125.3	125.3	125.1	125.2	125.3	125.4	125.7	124.8
1996	126.3	126.2	126.4	127.4	128.1	128.0	128.0	128.3	128.2	128.0	128.2	129.1	127.7
1997	129.7	128.5	127.3	127.0	127.4	127.2	126.9	127.2	127.5	127.8	127.9	126.8	127.6
1998[1]	125.4	125.0	124.7	124.9	125.1	124.8	124.9	124.2	123.9	124.0	123.5	122.7	124.4

[1] Preliminary. [2] Not seasonally adjusted. *Source: Bureau of Labor Statistics, U.S. Department of Commerce (BLS)*

U.S. Consumer Price Index[2] (Retail Price Index for All Items: Urban Consumers) 1982-1984 = 100

Year	Jan.	Feb.	Mar.	Apr.	May	June	July	Aug.	Sept.	Oct.	Nov.	Dec.	Average
1990	127.4	128.0	128.7	128.9	129.2	129.9	130.4	131.6	132.7	133.5	133.8	133.8	130.7
1991	134.6	134.8	135.0	135.2	135.6	136.0	136.2	136.6	137.2	137.4	137.8	137.9	136.2
1992	138.1	138.6	139.3	139.5	139.7	140.2	140.5	140.9	141.3	141.8	142.0	141.9	140.3
1993	142.6	143.1	143.6	144.0	144.2	144.4	144.4	144.8	145.1	145.7	145.8	145.8	144.5
1994	146.2	146.7	147.2	147.4	147.5	148.0	148.4	149.0	149.4	149.5	149.7	149.7	148.2
1995	150.3	150.9	151.4	151.9	152.2	152.5	152.5	152.9	153.2	153.7	153.6	153.5	152.4
1996	154.4	154.9	155.7	156.3	156.6	156.7	157.0	157.3	157.8	158.3	158.6	158.6	156.9
1997	159.1	159.6	159.8	160.0	160.1	160.4	160.6	160.9	161.3	161.6	161.8	161.9	160.6
1998[1]	161.9	162.0	162.0	162.4	162.9	163.0	163.3	163.6	163.6	164.0	164.3	164.5	163.1

[1] Preliminary. [2] Not seasonally adjusted. *Source: Bureau of Labor Statistics, U.S. Department of Commerce (BLS)*

Average Open Interest of 3-Month[1] Treasury Bill Futures in Chicago In Thousands of Contracts

Year	Jan.	Feb.	Mar.	Apr.	May	June	July	Aug.	Sept.	Oct.	Nov.	Dec.
1989	29,023	26,612	25,672	20,433	21,864	19,934	20,950	22,687	25,216	29,118	34,224	33,469
1990	39,168	38,358	27,668	31,274	25,128	21,171	26,524	37,903	35,723	46,974	53,284	50,146
1991	55,371	53,484	38,259	43,538	53,941	51,178	55,514	55,999	47,509	50,865	57,680	51,750
1992	51,312	45,902	35,539	44,757	47,734	41,091	38,399	35,638	29,781	32,556	35,379	29,566
1993	32,544	35,756	32,556	39,115	40,724	34,614	30,895	34,177	28,983	30,121	33,800	30,996
1994	36,456	41,150	43,243	51,485	41,164	34,580	32,572	29,559	24,522	32,325	30,077	22,322
1995	21,065	26,289	33,420	35,873	34,608	25,930	20,534	19,195	18,929	16,781	16,384	11,279
1996	14,769	16,906	14,161	14,460	15,709	10,285	8,973	9,770	6,536	6,906	7,516	7,002
1997	8,114	9,793	9,968	10,390	10,048	8,949	8,425	9,760	7,899	9,497	11,223	10,679
1998	10,295	11,647	7,903	4,993	3,818	4,123	4,330	4,407	2,840	1,929	2,123	2,264

[1] 90-day U.S. Treasury Bill. *Source: International Monetary Market (IMM), division of the Chicago Mercantile Exchange (CME)*

Volume of Trading of 3-Month[1] Treasury Bill Futures in Chicago In Thousands of Contracts

Year	Jan.	Feb.	Mar.	Apr.	May	June	July	Aug.	Sept.	Oct.	Nov.	Dec.	Total
1989	109.6	146.5	143.2	119.2	126.3	101.4	89.3	126.9	135.9	149.1	130.1	124.9	1,502.4
1990	169.3	153.6	118.5	120.3	102.4	96.7	138.1	206.6	168.9	178.5	223.7	193.1	1,869.6
1991	252.9	197.9	166.8	164.0	188.2	173.3	141.7	223.2	111.0	110.8	140.8	141.6	1,912.2
1992	143.8	137.9	145.0	115.9	106.5	106.1	85.8	76.2	103.0	127.0	106.5	83.4	1,337.1
1993	86.1	100.4	97.0	65.6	103.2	106.0	71.7	75.7	89.3	69.1	87.4	66.0	1,071.3
1994	59.8	137.0	115.9	104.4	99.4	89.4	53.7	60.9	77.6	57.4	81.2	83.8	1,020.5
1995	72.2	80.0	90.3	37.4	58.7	49.9	28.1	41.5	44.4	36.9	46.6	34.2	620.2
1996	32.0	36.0	36.5	17.9	16.6	25.2	12.0	19.4	19.8	10.8	10.4	14.3	250.9
1997	10.6	19.4	20.6	11.6	16.6	14.9	11.5	15.4	19.0	20.4	16.8	22.1	199.1
1998	18.5	14.3	14.4	9.5	9.4	7.6	3.4	7.6	5.2	4.8	3.9	5.7	104.2

[1] 90-day U.S. Treasury Bill. *Source: International Monetary Market (IMM), division of the Chicago Mercantile Exchange (CME)*

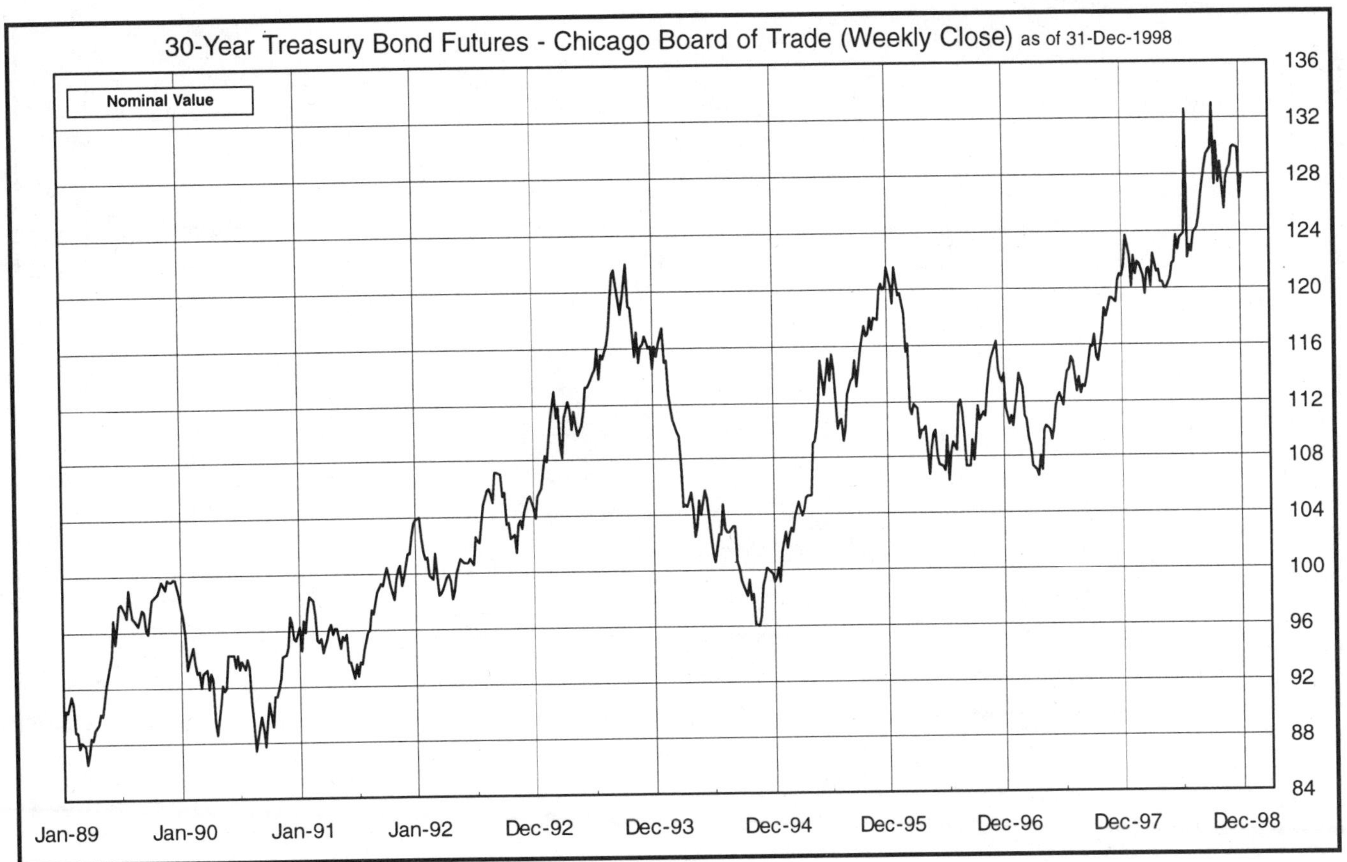

Average Open Interest of 30-Year U.S. Treasury Bond Futures in Chicago In Thousands of Contracts

Year	Jan.	Feb.	Mar.	Apr.	May	June	July	Aug.	Sept.	Oct.	Nov.	Dec.
1989	395,874	366,704	303,891	308,850	330,016	312,318	325,851	321,493	283,133	301,719	355,555	314,252
1990	315,671	324,954	294,968	280,745	303,544	278,889	285,934	317,197	297,075	286,291	288,581	254,775
1991	257,229	279,378	250,028	283,473	279,443	254,983	273,774	325,303	310,110	304,198	317,445	301,604
1992	343,156	353,782	318,737	313,742	346,542	347,293	370,850	427,723	385,645	364,250	362,231	321,706
1993	336,327	375,435	361,675	362,404	370,485	349,285	361,393	396,411	388,188	360,859	359,739	337,575
1994	380,057	422,902	454,539	500,790	497,296	421,286	441,884	451,462	447,924	436,684	449,642	397,554
1995	384,356	389,908	369,989	367,964	399,500	421,234	438,267	381,237	361,394	395,346	447,409	426,384
1996	382,001	403,403	395,338	381,926	413,944	443,644	464,145	471,203	420,622	409,950	463,731	479,086
1997	497,539	545,775	509,573	493,511	554,418	480,669	530,011	608,474	624,231	723,321	719,186	737,703
1998	744,894	764,309	766,233	806,559	888,215	1,040,659	1,084,889	1,061,223	837,986	769,932	782,677	662,025

Source: Chicago Board of Trade (CBT)

Volume of Trading of 30-Year U.S. Treasury Bond Futures in Chicago In Thousands of Contracts

Year	Jan.	Feb.	Mar.	Apr.	May	June	July	Aug.	Sept.	Oct.	Nov.	Dec.	Total
1989	5,806.0	6,300.0	5,605.0	4,858.0	6,673.0	7,995.0	5,231.0	7,640.0	4,792.0	6,329.0	5,828.0	3,244.0	70,303.0
1990	7,215.0	7,438.0	7,175.0	5,653.0	6,189.0	5,279.0	4,895.0	8,855.0	4,939.0	6,659.0	6,570.0	4,691.0	75,559.0
1991	5,804.0	5,717.0	5,658.0	5,957.0	6,186.0	5,582.0	4,293.0	6,592.0	4,765.0	6,450.0	6,239.0	4,643.0	67,886.0
1992	7,523.4	6,270.1	6,793.4	4,810.1	5,417.7	4,828.8	6,081.0	6,085.5	5,953.3	6,870.7	5,287.8	4,083.0	70,004.8
1993	5,577.4	6,482.7	7,902.9	6,156.1	6,799.8	5,817.2	6,218.4	6,914.5	7,443.9	6,537.4	8,193.5	5,384.5	79,428.5
1994	7,287.8	8,430.2	10,836.7	9,557.4	9,999.0	9,804.0	6,987.0	7,910.0	7,913.0	7,004.0	8,533.0	5,699.0	99,960.0
1995	7,058.0	7,714.0	9,623.8	5,835.4	8,721.5	8,446.7	5,790.2	7,083.7	7,317.1	6,927.2	6,626.3	5,232.1	86,375.9
1996	7,528.6	8,781.4	7,199.3	6,010.6	7,932.3	6,520.6	6,422.1	6,625.8	6,926.1	6,772.4	7,297.7	6,708.4	84,725.1
1997	8,104.7	7,522.8	7,493.3	7,519.9	8,339.1	7,400.2	7,679.8	10,228.1	8,356.2	12,467.6	7,735.5	6,980.4	99,827.7
1998	9,595.3	9,368.1	9,763.9	8,516.7	9,054.1	10,208.6	8,070.9	12,024.8	11,159.2	10,698.1	8,155.0	5,609.2	112,224.1

Source: Chicago Board of Trade (CBT)

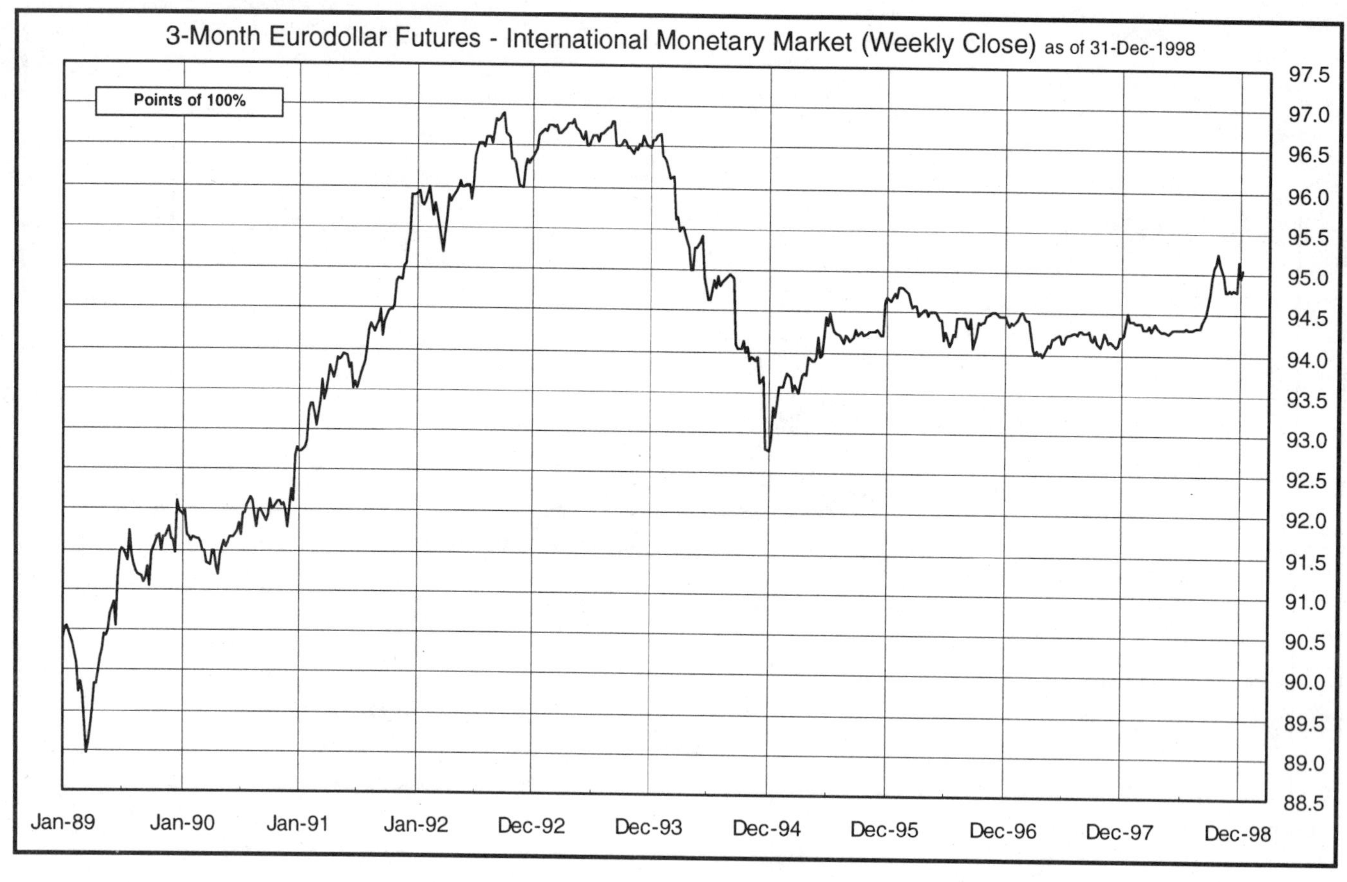

Average Open Interest of 3-Month Eurodollar Futures in Chicago In Thousands of Contracts

Year	Jan.	Feb.	Mar.	Apr.	May	June	July	Aug.	Sept.	Oct.	Nov.	Dec.
1989	574.8	672.3	731.3	749.7	756.9	720.4	690.2	714.0	637.9	591.5	663.6	661.9
1990	638.5	662.9	653.2	616.9	662.8	676.3	690.6	740.0	697.8	678.2	728.4	664.1
1991	630.9	722.7	741.1	767.6	857.4	835.2	797.9	883.1	916.7	949.5	1,054.7	1,067.2
1992	1,129.8	1,213.7	1,244.6	1,269.1	1,377.2	1,382.7	1,434.1	1,549.9	1,537.0	1,537.6	1,547.0	1,418.7
1993	1,429.4	1,586.7	1,643.3	1,653.4	1,782.8	1,739.1	1,777.7	1,918.4	1,940.7	2,026.5	2,149.0	2,150.2
1994	2,300.5	2,529.5	2,568.1	2,627.3	2,734.3	2,565.2	2,599.1	2,703.8	2,699.6	2,561.2	2,660.3	2,606.3
1995	2,443.6	2,535.4	2,463.9	2,447.4	2,503.3	2,390.8	2,279.5	2,374.6	2,347.2	2,290.3	2,405.5	2,480.5
1996	2,519.4	2,638.6	2,511.4	2,483.5	2,571.8	2,590.1	2,504.4	2,485.5	2,392.4	2,349.7	2,378.2	2,225.7
1997	2,190.8	2,333.2	2,423.1	2,523.1	2,671.3	2,706.5	2,699.2	2,788.0	2,769.3	2,815.1	2,799.5	2,661.6
1998	2,713.4	2,821.5	2,797.9	2,892.6	3,089.0	3,093.9	3,027.7	3,223.0	3,359.9	3,303.4	3,297.4	3,000.1

Source: International Monetary Market (IMM), division of the Chicago Mercantile Exchange (CME)

Volume of Trading of 3-Month Eurodollar Futures in Chicago In Thousands of Contracts

Year	Jan.	Feb.	Mar.	Apr.	May	June	July	Aug.	Sept.	Oct.	Nov.	Dec.	Total
1989	2,257.0	3,107.0	3,848.0	4,471.0	3,941.0	4,116.0	3,193.0	3,980.0	2,977.0	3,971.0	2,914.0	2,043.0	40,818.0
1990	3,244.0	2,459.0	2,727.0	2,566.0	3,132.0	2,473.0	2,947.0	3,857.0	2,730.0	2,898.0	2,982.0	2,680.0	34,696.0
1991	2,859.0	2,635.0	3,445.0	3,208.0	2,458.0	2,972.0	2,629.0	4,035.0	3,000.0	3,505.0	3,301.0	3,196.0	37,243.0
1992	5,365.7	4,418.5	5,582.8	4,942.2	4,819.0	4,602.6	5,357.8	4,016.3	4,705.2	6,691.6	5,461.3	4,568.1	60,531.1
1993	5,556.8	5,003.8	6,013.8	4,059.4	5,977.8	5,672.9	5,656.7	4,494.2	6,340.6	4,888.4	6,269.8	4,477.3	64,411.4
1994	6,074.8	8,745.3	9,468.9	9,639.2	11,494.0	9,348.0	7,810.0	7,128.0	7,641.0	7,992.0	9,715.0	9,766.0	104,823.0
1995	10,341.1	10,429.3	9,549.0	6,069.2	9,897.1	10,104.7	6,669.9	7,013.5	7,171.1	6,477.9	6,055.2	5,952.1	95,730.0
1996	7,485.7	9,267.2	9,526.3	6,872.4	7,413.7	7,415.0	8,323.2	6,967.5	8,232.5	7,014.5	5,056.9	5,308.1	88,883.1
1997	7,903.4	6,918.0	8,936.4	9,351.7	8,447.4	8,049.7	7,291.6	9,295.4	7,634.7	12,569.7	6,314.1	7,058.2	99,770.2
1998	10,908.0	7,861.4	8,842.1	9,488.4	7,202.4	8,349.5	5,452.3	9,811.3	13,593.9	11,756.9	9,627.8	6,578.5	109,472.5

Source: International Monetary Market (IMM), division of the Chicago Mercantile Exchange (CME)

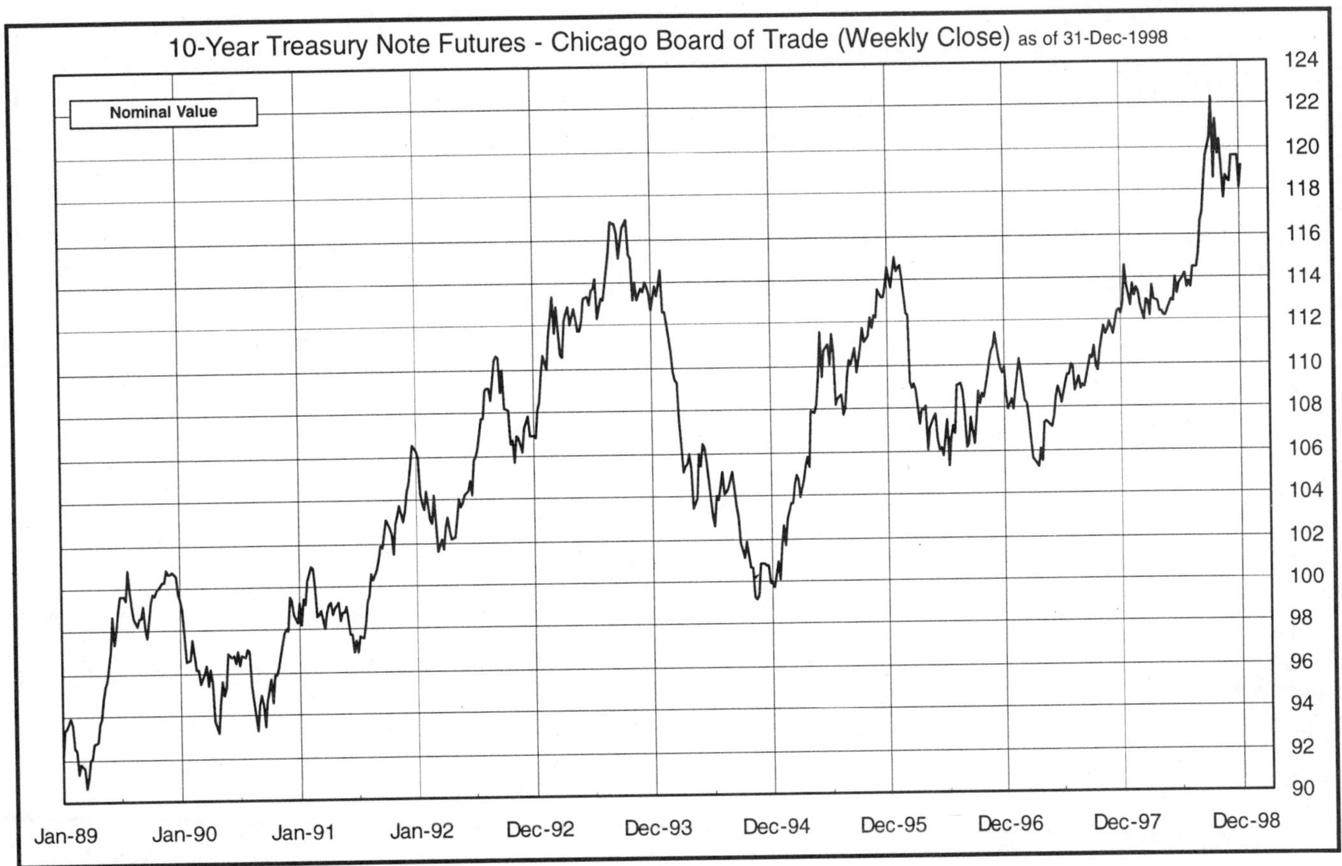

Average Open Interest of 10-Year U.S. Treasury Note Futures in Chicago In Contracts

Year	Jan.	Feb.	Mar.	Apr.	May	June	July	Aug.	Sept.	Oct.	Nov.	Dec.
1989	76,964	84,605	78,966	86,661	88,511	76,364	77,211	76,538	71,138	82,844	82,149	72,238
1990	73,155	82,211	76,939	76,030	82,174	78,498	71,413	75,644	72,900	67,309	73,744	76,697
1991	72,621	79,355	79,413	71,451	84,203	81,884	85,527	94,379	96,836	93,187	95,450	87,063
1992	119,739	114,521	106,497	102,862	112,666	126,228	143,924	158,831	179,045	191,725	199,990	195,705
1993	190,018	206,852	198,653	209,221	229,378	217,521	233,458	238,189	237,243	237,877	273,336	262,831
1994	264,848	258,643	300,080	328,821	294,091	254,612	232,373	253,233	273,564	277,313	301,000	271,992
1995	282,978	285,187	265,747	263,816	273,945	289,052	306,046	323,078	277,011	278,832	270,527	249,073
1996	260,374	297,850	285,501	319,234	331,032	293,416	302,330	326,391	291,208	284,581	313,298	303,702
1997	332,285	343,661	323,982	348,683	350,814	336,927	363,744	407,147	387,284	398,645	404,980	374,448
1998	430,335	507,986	474,916	494,417	533,214	513,369	512,173	604,862	555,268	482,928	508,299	503,533

Source: Chicago Board of Trade (CBT)

Volume of Trading of 10-Year U.S. Treasury Note Futures in Chicago In Thousands of Contracts

Year	Jan.	Feb.	Mar.	Apr.	May	June	July	Aug.	Sept.	Oct.	Nov.	Dec.	Total
1989	450.5	547.9	468.3	431.6	625.6	637.3	453.0	629.6	465.8	555.8	516.7	327.4	6,109.5
1990	491.3	650.5	480.9	381.1	638.7	427.4	415.0	703.0	399.3	449.6	574.3	442.6	6,053.7
1991	507.7	519.6	508.3	466.5	566.9	456.6	318.9	705.9	467.2	573.2	661.3	591.4	6,342.0
1992	929.6	866.4	824.9	531.2	758.9	683.3	859.4	1,047.7	1,138.5	1,300.2	1,225.8	1,052.1	11,218.0
1993	1,134.6	1,286.3	1,763.1	1,089.5	1,341.4	1,390.6	1,147.0	1,390.7	1,523.7	1,279.5	1,926.6	1,328.2	16,601.2
1994	1,484.3	1,935.7	2,572.4	2,213.5	2,399.4	2,250.2	1,621.8	2,028.7	1,932.9	1,635.1	2,253.6	1,750.2	24,078.0
1995	1,752.6	1,978.8	2,458.7	1,368.2	2,236.5	2,495.8	1,588.9	2,028.7	1,859.0	1,459.7	1,730.8	1,487.6	22,445.4
1996	1,649.1	2,313.1	2,075.8	1,632.1	2,211.3	1,715.6	1,556.3	1,865.7	1,810.4	1,494.7	1,904.5	1,711.2	21,939.7
1997	1,780.5	1,939.9	2,051.8	1,703.2	2,025.6	1,942.3	1,509.6	2,535.9	2,062.5	2,593.7	1,825.6	1,991.2	23,961.8
1998	2,393.5	2,748.7	2,817.5	2,342.1	2,695.9	2,681.9	1,704.1	3,632.2	3,560.3	2,882.7	2,912.2	2,111.5	32,482.6

Source: Chicago Board of Trade (CBT)

Average Open Interest of 5-Year Treasury Note Futures in Chicago In Contracts

Year	Jan.	Feb.	Mar.	Apr.	May	June	July	Aug.	Sept.	Oct.	Nov.	Dec.
1989	34,728	40,203	45,320	46,371	48,195	42,496	44,985	34,675	37,474	42,669	57,901	73,798
1990	81,705	74,568	74,999	60,841	59,417	56,485	54,004	64,100	75,955	78,370	82,981	93,549
1991	80,059	82,666	83,109	74,612	75,799	65,543	72,197	86,981	85,794	91,096	102,890	99,291
1992	116,322	121,667	125,155	130,826	135,111	144,386	143,928	143,203	127,418	122,113	129,548	127,690
1993	139,207	150,443	152,711	158,607	169,234	152,262	152,403	160,258	159,754	154,501	181,492	206,914
1994	200,812	213,037	200,626	185,083	192,659	186,026	189,828	182,027	181,518	181,578	176,322	205,150
1995	206,539	210,192	199,357	200,087	213,531	189,332	176,329	173,897	163,419	162,121	177,915	171,023
1996	163,026	184,523	200,253	191,690	179,951	177,370	174,484	179,599	154,764	138,246	155,820	154,764
1997	176,691	208,928	219,540	235,543	227,882	225,691	226,306	225,792	234,309	233,480	248,377	257,886
1998	257,094	270,048	282,327	277,540	274,145	257,193	264,756	389,118	382,855	383,809	353,399	326,860

Source: Chicago Board of Trade (CBT)

Volume of Trading of 5-Year Treasury Note Futures in Chicago In Thousands of Contracts

Year	Jan.	Feb.	Mar.	Apr.	May	June	July	Aug.	Sept.	Oct.	Nov.	Dec.	Total
1989	91.1	156.8	128.1	89.2	167.3	162.0	142.3	205.2	121.2	148.3	253.4	116.9	518.6
1990	184.5	277.5	164.9	107.6	266.6	140.8	131.6	320.4	189.0	197.9	305.7	40.8	544.4
1991	220.5	318.5	252.3	181.4	307.6	232.4	179.7	385.4	243.9	291.5	419.9	353.1	1,064.5
1992	498.6	543.8	560.0	322.2	590.1	551.5	484.2	565.7	582.1	539.0	640.8	563.2	1,743.0
1993	539.5	673.1	886.0	447.6	755.9	753.8	506.4	711.3	753.8	472.6	908.0	715.8	2,096.4
1994	695.9	1,235.1	1,295.4	917.1	1,202.0	1,154.9	834.8	944.9	1,107.3	840.6	1,156.7	1,078.0	12,463.0
1995	988.5	1,296.2	1,386.9	783.4	1,291.1	1,402.9	828.6	1,100.5	1,008.7	769.6	996.0	784.7	12,637.1
1996	837.3	1,312.0	1,084.6	815.7	1,135.5	878.3	881.7	1,061.8	979.0	689.5	831.1	957.1	11,463.4
1997	927.5	1,156.7	1,271.1	984.4	1,190.6	1,143.8	761.4	1,244.6	1,243.7	1,314.1	1,068.1	1,182.8	13,488.7
1998	1,451.9	1,482.0	1,390.7	1,154.7	1,281.1	1,376.9	944.0	2,480.5	1,913.5	1,583.1	1,722.7	1,279.1	18,060.0

Source: Chicago Board of Trade (CBT)

United States Federal Funds Rate In Percent

Year	Jan.	Feb.	Mar.	Apr.	May	June	July	Aug.	Sept.	Oct.	Nov.	Dec.	Annual
1989	9.12	9.36	9.85	9.84	9.81	9.53	9.24	8.99	9.02	8.84	8.55	8.45	9.22
1990	8.23	8.24	8.28	8.26	8.18	8.29	8.15	8.13	8.20	8.11	7.81	7.31	8.10
1991	6.91	6.25	6.12	5.91	5.78	5.90	5.82	5.66	5.45	5.21	4.81	4.43	5.69
1992	4.03	4.06	3.98	3.73	3.82	3.76	3.25	3.30	3.22	3.10	3.09	2.92	3.52
1993	3.02	3.03	3.07	2.96	3.00	3.04	3.06	3.03	3.09	2.99	3.02	2.96	3.02
1994	3.05	3.25	3.34	3.56	4.01	4.25	4.26	4.47	4.73	4.76	5.29	5.45	4.20
1995	5.53	5.92	5.98	6.05	6.01	6.00	5.85	5.74	5.80	5.76	5.80	5.60	5.84
1996	5.56	5.22	5.31	5.22	5.56	5.27	5.40	5.22	5.30	5.24	5.31	5.29	5.30
1997	5.25	5.19	5.39	5.51	5.50	5.56	5.52	5.54	5.54	5.50	5.52	5.50	5.46
1998	5.56	5.51	5.49	5.45	5.49	5.56	5.54	5.55	5.51	5.07	4.83		5.41

Source: Bureau of Economic Analysis (BEA), U.S. Department of Commerce

United States Municipal Bond Yield[1] In Percent

Year	Jan.	Feb.	Mar.	Apr.	May	June	July	Aug.	Sept.	Oct.	Nov.	Dec.	Annual
1989	7.35	7.44	7.59	7.49	7.25	7.02	6.96	7.06	7.26	7.22	7.14	6.98	7.23
1990	7.10	7.22	7.29	7.39	7.35	7.24	7.19	7.32	7.53	7.49	7.18	7.09	7.28
1991	7.08	6.91	7.10	7.02	6.95	7.13	7.05	6.90	6.80	6.68	6.73	6.69	6.92
1992	6.54	6.74	6.76	6.67	6.57	6.49	6.13	6.16	6.25	6.41	6.36	6.22	6.44
1993	6.16	5.86	5.85	5.76	5.73	5.63	5.57	5.45	5.29	5.25	5.47	5.35	5.61
1994	5.31	5.40	5.91	6.23	6.19	6.11	6.23	6.21	6.28	6.52	6.97	6.80	6.18
1995	6.53	6.22	6.10	6.02	5.95	5.84	5.92	6.06	5.91	5.80	5.64	5.45	5.95
1996	5.43	5.43	5.79	5.94	5.98	6.02	5.92	5.76	5.87	5.72	5.59	5.64	5.76
1997	5.72	5.63	5.76	5.88	5.70	5.53	5.35	5.41	5.39	5.38	5.33	5.19	5.52
1998	5.06	5.10	5.21	5.23	5.20	5.12	5.14	5.10	4.99	4.93	5.03		5.10

[1] 20-bond average. *Source: Bureau of Economic Analysis (BEA), U.S. Department of Commerce*

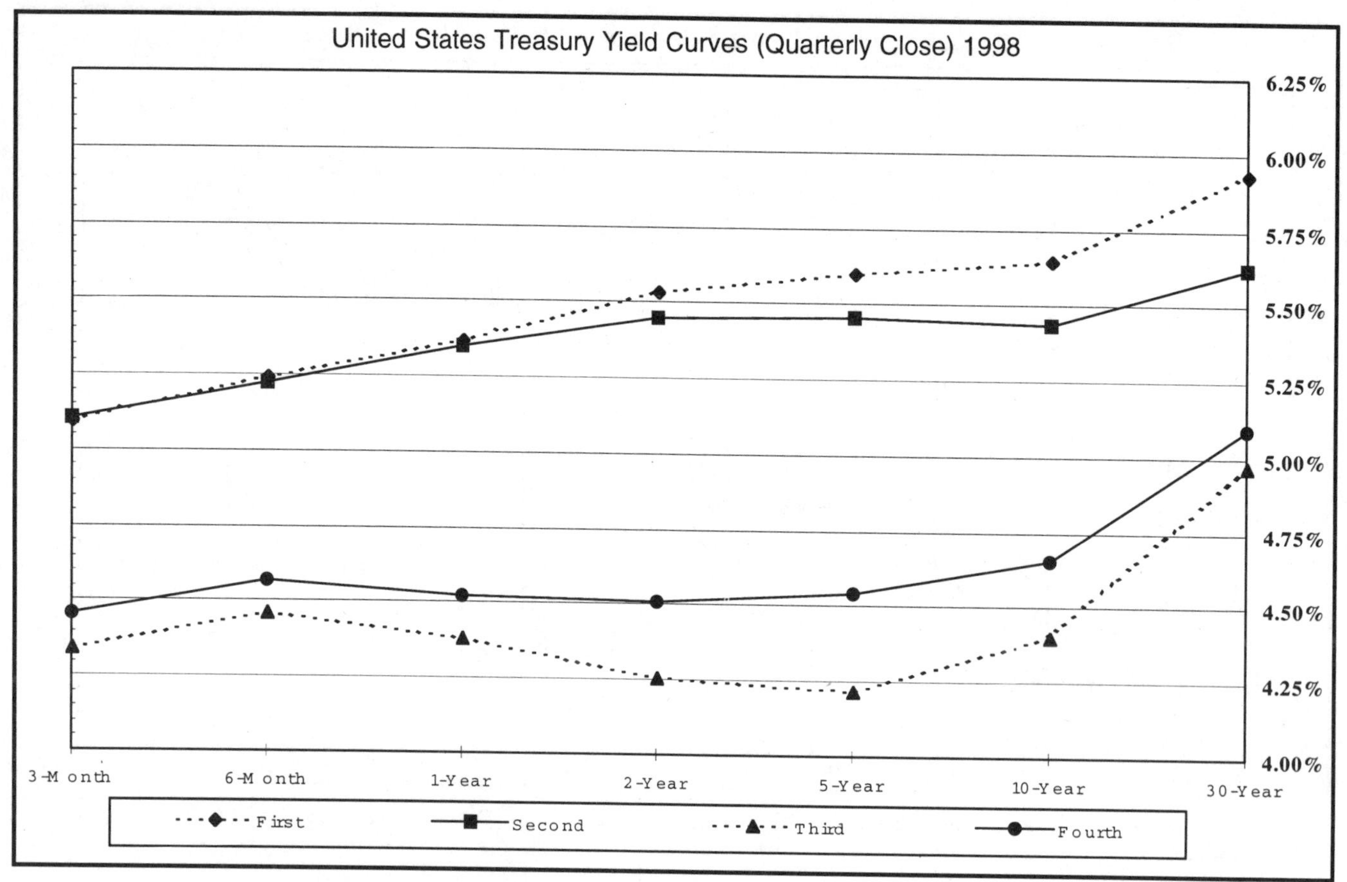

United States Industrial Production Index[1] (Seasonally Adjusted) 1992 = 100

Year	Jan.	Feb.	Mar.	Apr.	May	June	July	Aug.	Sept.	Oct.	Nov.	Dec.	Average
1989	99.7	98.9	99.8	100.1	99.5	99.3	98.3	98.7	98.5	98.1	98.5	98.9	99.0
1990	98.5	99.0	99.4	98.9	99.3	99.3	99.2	99.4	99.5	99.0	97.7	97.1	98.9
1991	96.7	95.9	95.0	95.3	96.0	97.2	97.2	97.4	98.3	98.2	98.1	97.4	96.9
1992	97.5	98.1	98.9	99.6	100.0	99.7	100.4	100.1	100.5	101.3	101.9	101.9	100.0
1993	102.3	102.8	102.8	103.2	102.6	102.8	103.1	102.8	103.9	104.1	104.6	105.4	103.4
1994	105.7	106.2	107.0	107.4	108.1	108.6	109.1	109.2	109.3	109.9	110.6	111.6	108.6
1995	111.9	111.6	111.7	111.4	111.5	111.7	111.7	112.6	113.0	112.5	112.7	112.8	114.5
1996	112.4	113.8	113.2	114.3	114.8	115.5	115.5	115.8	116.0	116.2	120.6	120.9	118.5
1997	121.3	122.1	122.5	123.1	123.3	123.5	124.5	125.2	125.6	129.3	129.9	130.3	126.7
1998[2]	130.3	130.2	130.7	131.3	131.9	130.6	130.5	132.4	131.9	132.2	131.8		131.2

[1] Total Index of the Federal Reserve Index of Quantity Output. [2] Preliminary. *Source: Bureau of Economic Analysis, U.S. Department of Commerce*

U.S. Gross National Product, National Income, and Personal Income In Billions of Current Dollars[1]

Year	Gross Domestic Product I	II	III	IV	Annual Average	National Income I	II	III	IV	Annual Average	Personal Income I	II	III	IV	Annual Average
1989	6,009	6,053	6,086	6,093	6,060	4,203	4,231	4,245	4,301	4,245	4,409	4,472	4,502	4,574	4,489
1990	6,154	6,174	6,145	6,081	6,139	4,396	4,461	4,475	4,507	4,460	4,689	4,772	4,838	4,868	4,792
1991	6,048	6,074	6,089	6,104	6,079	4,493	4,529	4,555	4,599	4,720	4,885	4,951	4,979	5,059	4,969
1992	6,175	6,214	6,261	6,327	6,244	4,889	4,941	4,912	5,103	4,990	5,161	5,236	5,233	5,429	5,277
1993	6,326	6,357	6,393	6,469	6,386	5,160	5,237	5,282	5,389	5,267	5,369	5,504	5,544	5,659	5,519
1994	6,509	6,588	6,645	7,096	6,947	5,423	5,556	5,636	5,747	5,591	5,616	5,767	5,838	5,911	5,758
1995	7,171	7,211	7,305	7,392	7,270	5,816	5,873	5,965	6,040	5,924	5,980	6,030	6,094	6,185	6,072
1996	7,495	7,629	7,703	7,818	7,662	6,120	6,227	6,304	6,374	6,256	6,284	6,390	6,477	6,550	6,425
1997	7,955	8,063	8,171	8,255	8,111	6,509	6,605	6,705	6,768	6,647	6,667	6,744	6,821	6,905	6,784
1998[2]	8,384	8,441	8,538		8,454	6,875	6,946	7,032		6,951	7,004	7,082	7,161		7,082

[1] Seasonally adjusted at annual rates. [2] Preliminary *Source: Bureau of Economic Analysis, U.S. Department of Commerce (BEA)*

United States Money Supply M1[2] In Billions of Dollars

Year	Jan.	Feb.	Mar.	Apr.	May	June	July	Aug.	Sept.	Oct.	Nov.	Dec.	Average
1989	786.0	784.2	782.9	780.1	774.9	773.4	778.7	779.3	781.6	787.0	788.1	794.2	782.5
1990	795.3	798.2	801.7	806.3	804.6	810.3	810.4	816.0	821.6	819.8	822.0	825.8	811.0
1991	826.7	832.8	839.8	842.5	849.1	858.6	861.3	867.2	870.6	877.5	888.6	897.3	859.3
1992	910.0	926.2	936.8	944.3	952.4	954.2	963.2	975.4	988.2	1,003.9	1,016.7	1,025.0	966.4
1993	1,032.0	1,034.0	1,038.4	1,047.8	1,067.5	1,075.4	1,084.7	1,094.5	1,104.2	1,114.3	1,123.6	1,129.8	1,078.9
1994	1,132.8	1,137.3	1,140.1	1,142.4	1,143.5	1,144.7	1,150.9	1,149.7	1,150.8	1,150.4	1,150.4	1,150.7	1,145.3
1995	1,150.3	1,148.4	1,147.1	1,150.4	1,145.1	1,142.7	1,145.0	1,144.0	1,141.6	1,135.7	1,133.1	1,129.0	1,142.7
1996	1,122.2	1,119.8	1,126.2	1,123.5	1,117.1	1,115.5	1,108.8	1,099.8	1,093.3	1,080.3	1,080.1	1,081.1	1,106.3
1997	1,080.8	1,078.8	1,075.0	1,068.3	1,064.3	1,065.4	1,065.6	1,071.1	1,063.5	1,061.9	1,069.2	1,076.0	1,070.0
1998[1]	1,073.7	1,076.5	1,081.1	1,080.7	1,077.7	1,074.5	1,071.8	1,069.0	1,072.1	1,078.5	1,087.3		1,076.6

[1] Preliminary. [2] M1--This measure is currency, travelers checks, plus demand deposits at commercial banks and interest-earning checkable deposits at all depository institutions. *Source: Bureau of Economic Analysis,U.S. Department of Commerce (BEA)*

United States Money Supply M2[2] In Billions of Dollars

Year	Jan.	Feb.	Mar.	Apr.	May	June	July	Aug.	Sept.	Oct.	Nov.	Dec.	Average
1989	2,999.8	3,000.4	3,007.2	3,014.3	3,019.1	3,034.8	3,060.2	3,081.5	3,100.8	3,122.5	3,141.1	3,160.9	3,061.9
1990	3,173.1	3,185.3	3,196.9	3,209.3	3,207.0	3,221.0	3,230.2	3,248.4	3,262.3	3,265.3	3,269.6	3,279.5	3,229.0
1991	3,293.4	3,311.1	3,329.4	3,337.9	3,348.0	3,359.1	3,361.0	3,360.5	3,360.0	3,363.9	3,372.5	3,379.6	3,348.0
1992	3,387.7	3,407.1	3,410.5	3,408.8	3,407.4	3,401.3	3,402.2	3,408.9	3,418.2	3,432.0	3,435.3	3,434.0	3,412.8
1993	3,431.3	3,424.0	3,420.4	3,423.6	3,447.6	3,452.9	3,452.7	3,456.8	3,463.6	3,469.7	3,480.2	3,486.6	3,450.8
1994	3,490.8	3,491.7	3,494.3	3,503.0	3,504.0	3,493.7	3,502.1	3,498.2	3,498.4	3,499.4	3,500.9	3,502.1	3,498.2
1995	3,506.3	3,506.1	3,506.7	3,519.1	3,534.9	3,562.9	3,583.1	3,604.4	3,620.1	3,629.8	3,639.3	3,655.0	3,572.3
1996	3,669.9	3,685.0	3,713.9	3,724.5	3,725.6	3,741.9	3,750.0	3,762.7	3,775.3	3,788.1	3,798.3	3,821.8	3,746.6
1997	3,840.7	3,853.3	3,868.9	3,890.0	3,892.5	3,908.0	3,922.5	3,954.8	3,979.3	3,999.3	4,023.6	4,046.4	3,932.6
1998[1]	4,071.6	4,104.5	4,133.2	4,166.1	4,175.9	4,194.0	4,210.8	4,240.8	4,292.9	4,338.5	4,377.4		4,209.6

[1] Preliminary. [2] M2--This measure adds to M1 overnight repurchase agreements (RPs) issued by commercial banks and certain overnight Eurodollars (those issued by Caribbean branches of member banks) held by U.S. nonbank residents, general purpose and broker/dealer money market mutual shares (MMMF), and savings and small-denomination time deposits. *Source: Bureau of Economic Analysis, U.S. Department of Commerce (BEA)*

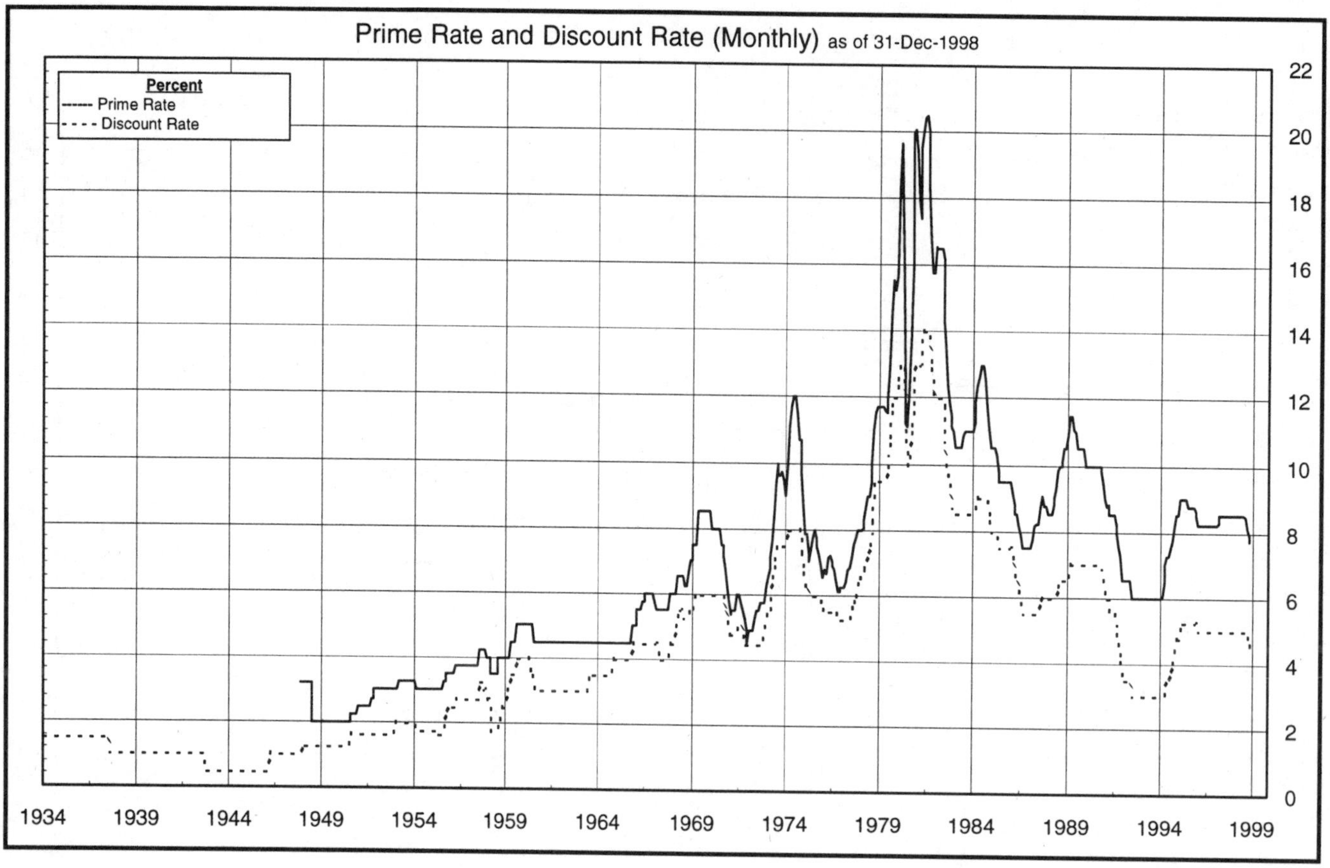

Prime Rate and Discount Rate (Monthly) as of 31-Dec-1998

Percent
Prime Rate
Discount Rate

22 20 18 16 14 12 10 8 6 4 2 0

1934 1939 1944 1949 1954 1959 1964 1969 1974 1979 1984 1989 1994 1999

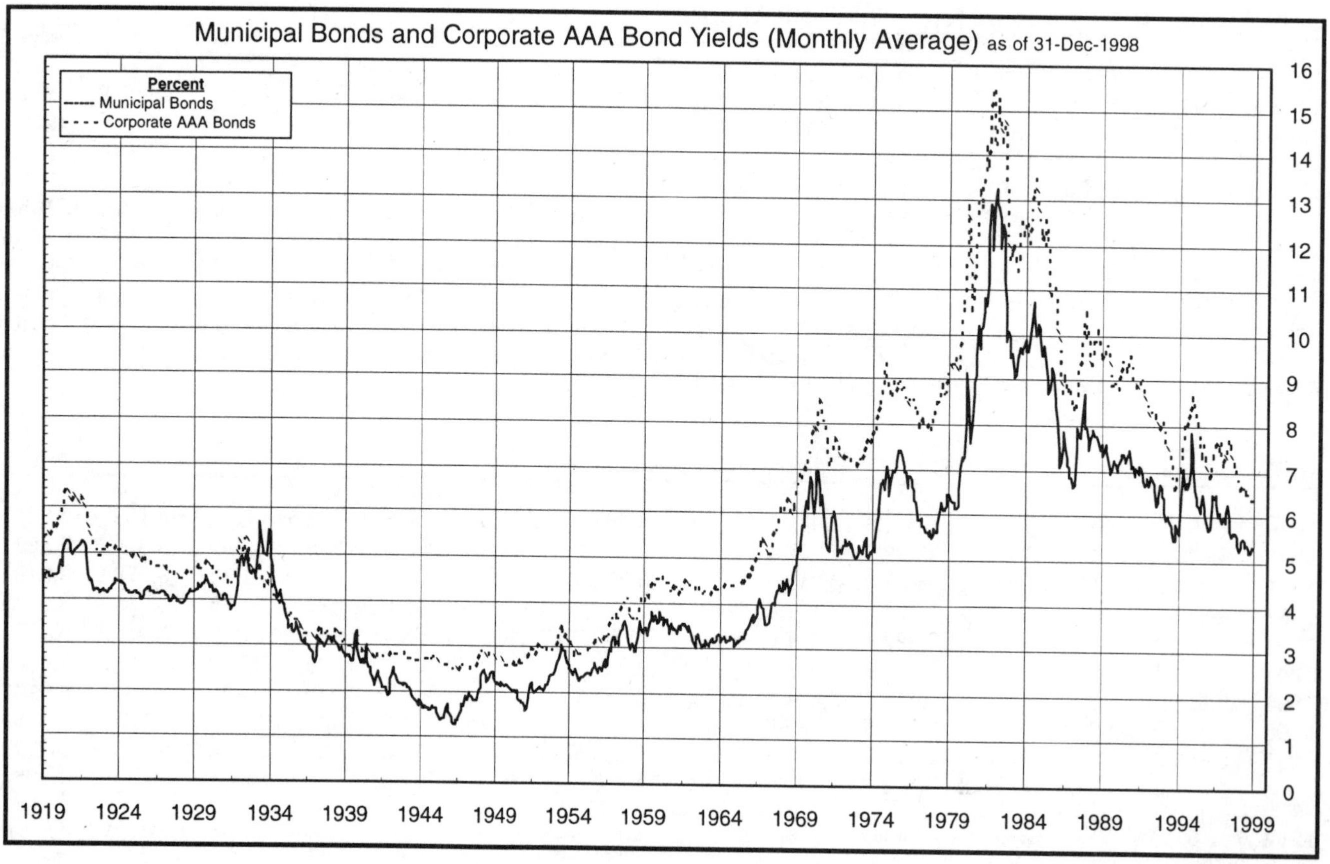

Municipal Bonds and Corporate AAA Bond Yields (Monthly Average) as of 31-Dec-1998

Percent
Municipal Bonds
Corporate AAA Bonds

16 15 14 13 12 11 10 9 8 7 6 5 4 3 2 1 0

1919 1924 1929 1934 1939 1944 1949 1954 1959 1964 1969 1974 1979 1984 1989 1994 1999

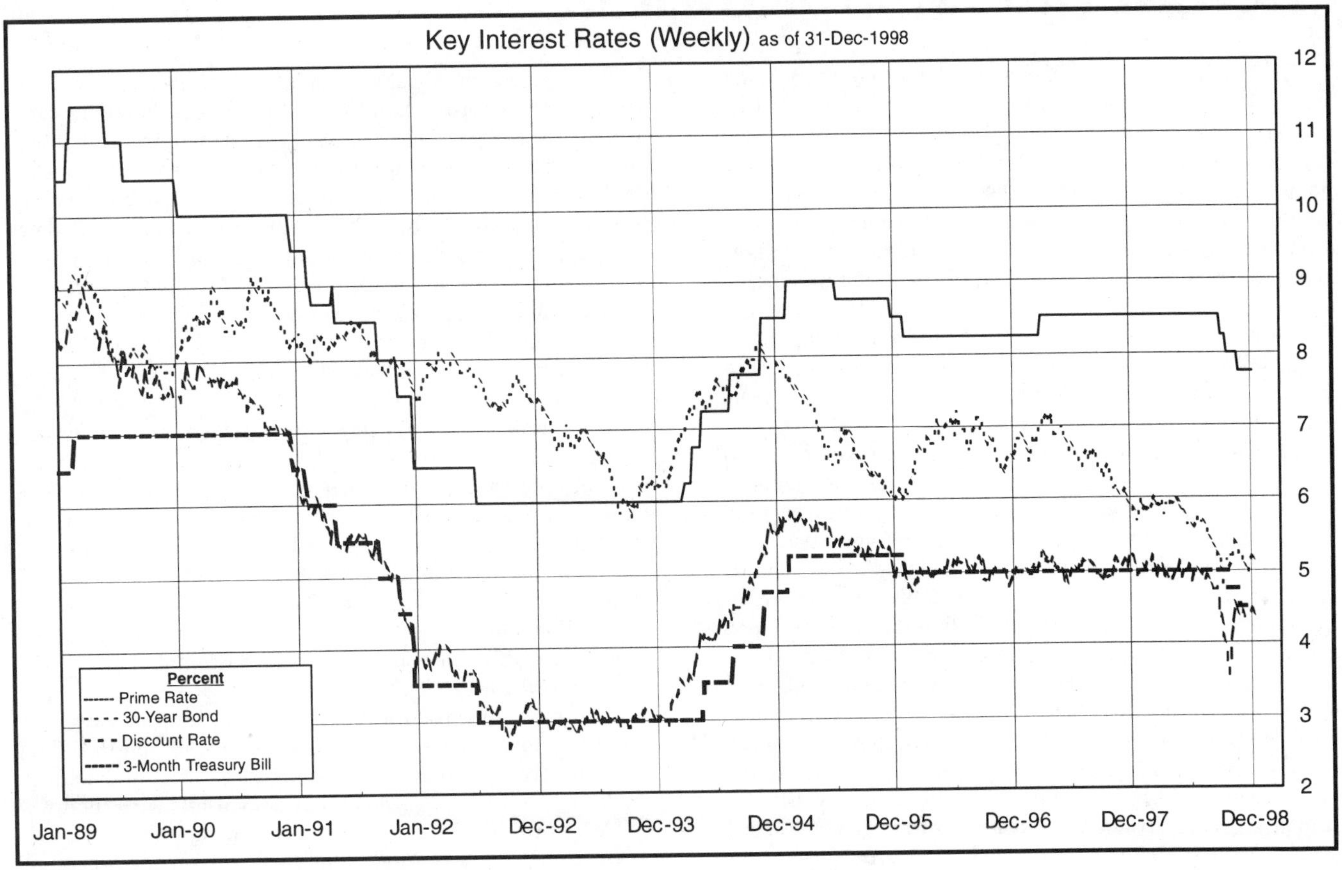

Key Interest Rates (Weekly) as of 31-Dec-1998

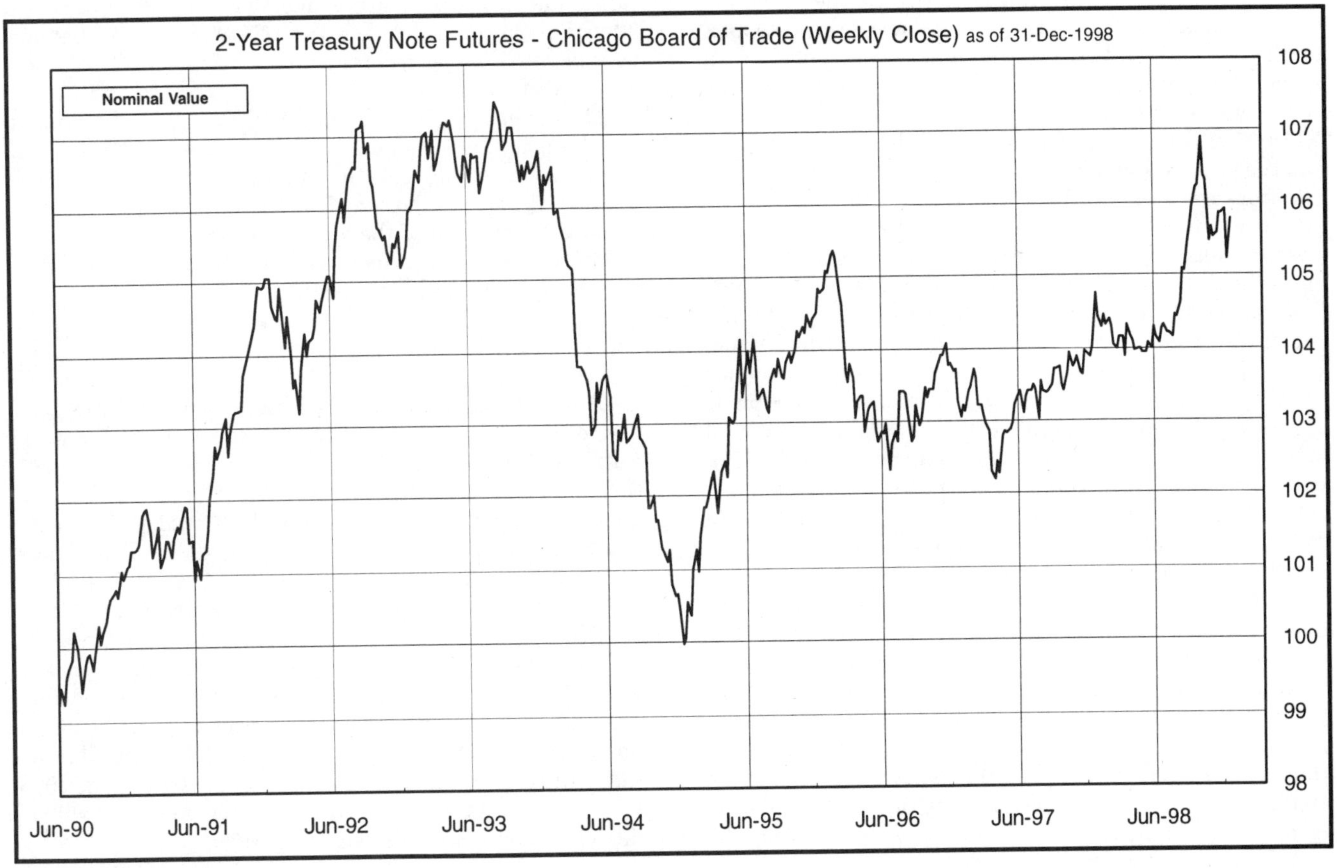

2-Year Treasury Note Futures - Chicago Board of Trade (Weekly Close) as of 31-Dec-1998

Interest Rates, Worldwide

Three major factors influenced global monetary policy during 1998: (1) The European Monetary Union (EMU) commenced in May with the approval of the newly formed European Central Bank (ECB). Eleven EMU participating member nations joined together in preparation for the January 1, 1999 launch of the ECB initiating a single monetary and foreign exchange rate policy conducted in a single currency, the euro; (2) a coordinated interest rate cut to a benchmark 3 percent by ten of the EMU nations in early December and followed later in the month by Italy; and (3) the U.S. Federal Reserve officially lowered short-term rates three times in the closing months of 1998, despite a strong economy and tight labor market.

The Fed's action sent a strong message to the global markets that in effect said that the U.S. is committed to defending the global economy. The latter, of course, is not a blanket panacea as economic and/or political turmoil in Russia, Brazil and Asia lie beyond the Fed's far reaching scope. Still, a very strong positive variable prevailed in the world economies in 1998 that allowed easier monetary policies, specifically the absence of inflationary pressures due to lower basic commodity prices, such as crude oil. Indeed, if there was a common concern it focused on deflation and the need to stimulate demand with a combination of monetary and fiscal incentives. This concern was also evident in 1997, but seemed to have hardened in 1998. Ironically, the continued strength in equity markets around the world was seen as masking global apprehension towards slowing economic growth in many countries and underlying fears of a global recession in 1999. The U.S. may prove the exception, but the fear of a global slide seems to have deep roots and, justified or not, is likely to keep central bank policy in an easier mode throughout 1999 although not with the same intensity as seen in 1998.

In 1998, hundreds of billions of dollars were pumped into the global economy in an effort to mitigate the dramatic loss of wealth in Asia, Latin America and Russia. To some extent the efforts were successful. However, since the crisis was not caused by high interest rates, it's possible that low interest rates may not be the cure. Many of the world's 1998 financial problems were the result of excess capacity and ebbing demand. a scenario that largely defied traditional central bank strategy. The major question for 1999 is how the major western economies can continue to prosper while the rest of the world is in the doldrums. The International Monetary Fund, in late 1998, lowered its projection for 1999 world economic growth to 2.2 percent vs. a forecast of 2.5 percent made in late summer, citing eroding conditions in Japan, Russia and Latin America. World growth was placed at 2.2 percent in 1998 vs. 4.2 percent in 1997.

In Europe, sensing that the global slowdown had begun to chill Europe, Germany's Bundesbank in early December started the ball rolling for a coordinated EMU rate cut to enhance the credibility of the euro and the fledgling ECB in world markets. Germany's 50 basis point cut in the repo rate at yearend was the Bundesbank first change in more than a year and officially set the benchmark basic bank lending rate of all eleven members of the EMU. The odds favor further unified rate reductions in 1999. However, The ECB has also formally stated its intention to assure flexibility in interest rates; the key central bank refinancing rate would stay at 3 percent at least in the early months of 1999, but selected rates around it could be changed, such as the deposit rate. Still, the EMU countries will no longer be able to use interest rates to influence the performance of their national economies or implement any major independent fiscal policy changes, assuming the EMU holds together with a viable and globally accepted central bank.

In the U.K., not yet a participating member of the EMU, key lending rates were also cut three times in late 1998. Twice the cut was a larger than expected 1/2 percent, the central bank citing slowing economic conditions across Europe. Still, at yearend, the U.K.'s repurchase rate of 6.25 percent, the rate at which the central bank lends to commercial banks, was still more than twice the rest of Europe.

In Canada, however, the central bank in mid-summer raised its overnight lending rate by 1 percent to 6 percent in an effort to halt the slide of the Canadian dollar against the U.S. dollar, but the action was generally seen as counterproductive when viewed against a backdrop of slowing economic growth into 1999.

In Japan, interest rates fell to record lows in 1998 and actually offered negative returns for a time in mid-fall. This never before seen slide reflected broad distrust of Japanese banks and a run into Government obligations with the safety factor offsetting the lack of return on capital.

In the U.S., at yearend, long term rates near 5 percent were still seen as too high relative to an annualized inflation rate under 2 percent, suggesting that the U.S. Treasury's 30-year bond could slide another 1/2 percent in 1999, if one assumes that a real net return of 3 percent over inflation still holds true.

On balance, global deflation and rising unemployment are the primary economic fears as the year 2000 nears. If deflation does take root, the implications may favor more downward pressure on longer term rates, as seen in 1998, while the front end of the yield curve is buoyed somewhat by uncertainties as to how central banks may attempt to deal with deflationary pressures.

Futures Markets

A number of actively traded interest rate futures markets exist worldwide. The London International Financial Futures Exchange (LIFFE) trades contracts on 3-month Sterling prices and British government bonds, called long gilts. LIFFE also offers futures on Euromarks, Euroswiss, Italian government bonds and German government bonds, called bunds. The latter is also traded in Frankfurt. Canadian Bankers Acceptances are traded on the Montreal Exchange. Notional bond and PIBOR futures are traded on the Paris MATIF. Euroyen futures and Japanese yen government bonds are traded in Tokyo. Libor and eurodollars are traded on Chicago's Mercantile Exchange, with the latter also on the Mid-America Exchange. Additional interest rate futures contracts are likely to begin trading in 1998. New interest rate futures denominated in euros will be introduced on several exchanges in 1999.

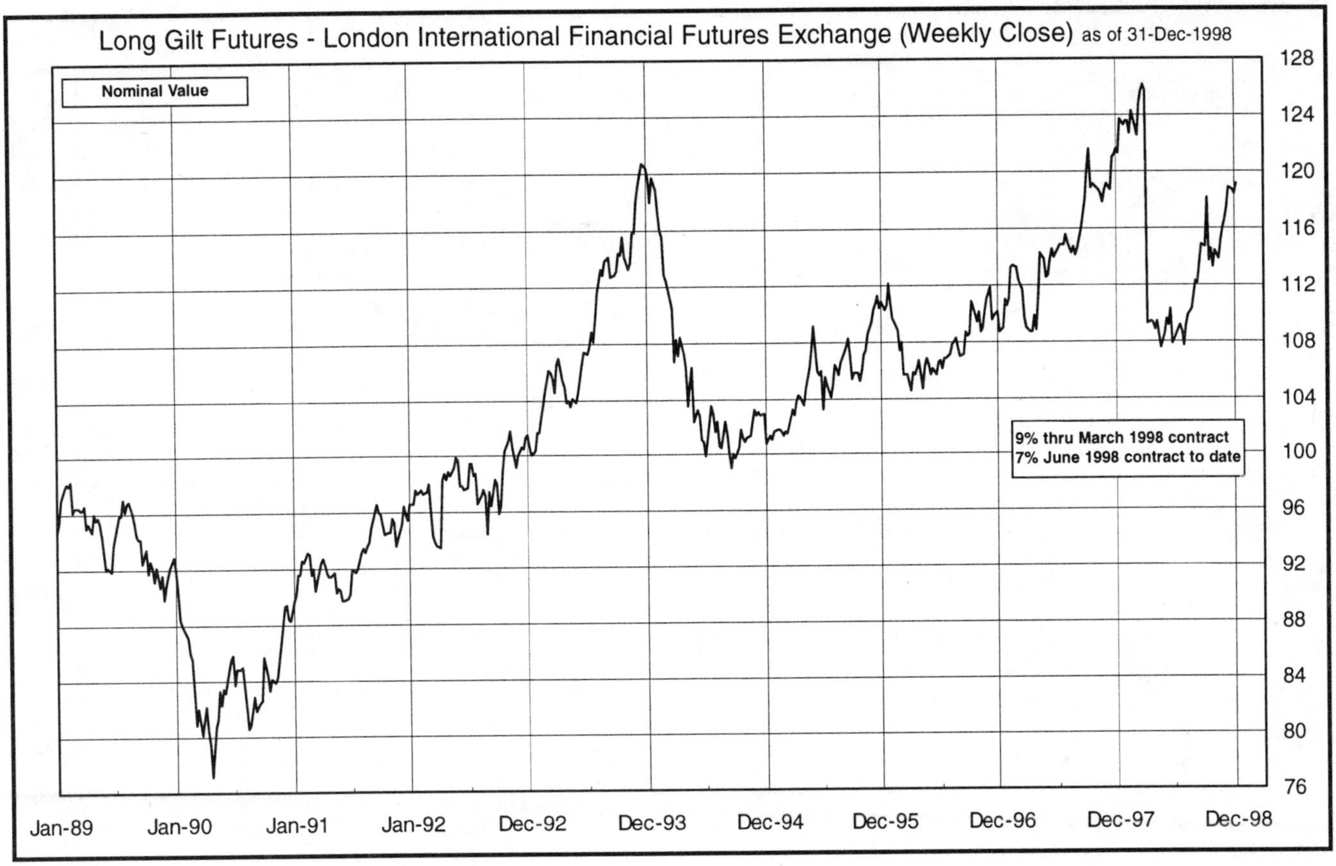

Long Gilt Futures - London International Financial Futures Exchange (Weekly Close) as of 31-Dec-1998

Nominal Value

9% thru March 1998 contract
7% June 1998 contract to date

128
124
120
116
112
108
104
100
96
92
88
84
80
76

Jan-89 Jan-90 Jan-91 Jan-92 Dec-92 Dec-93 Dec-94 Dec-95 Dec-96 Dec-97 Dec-98

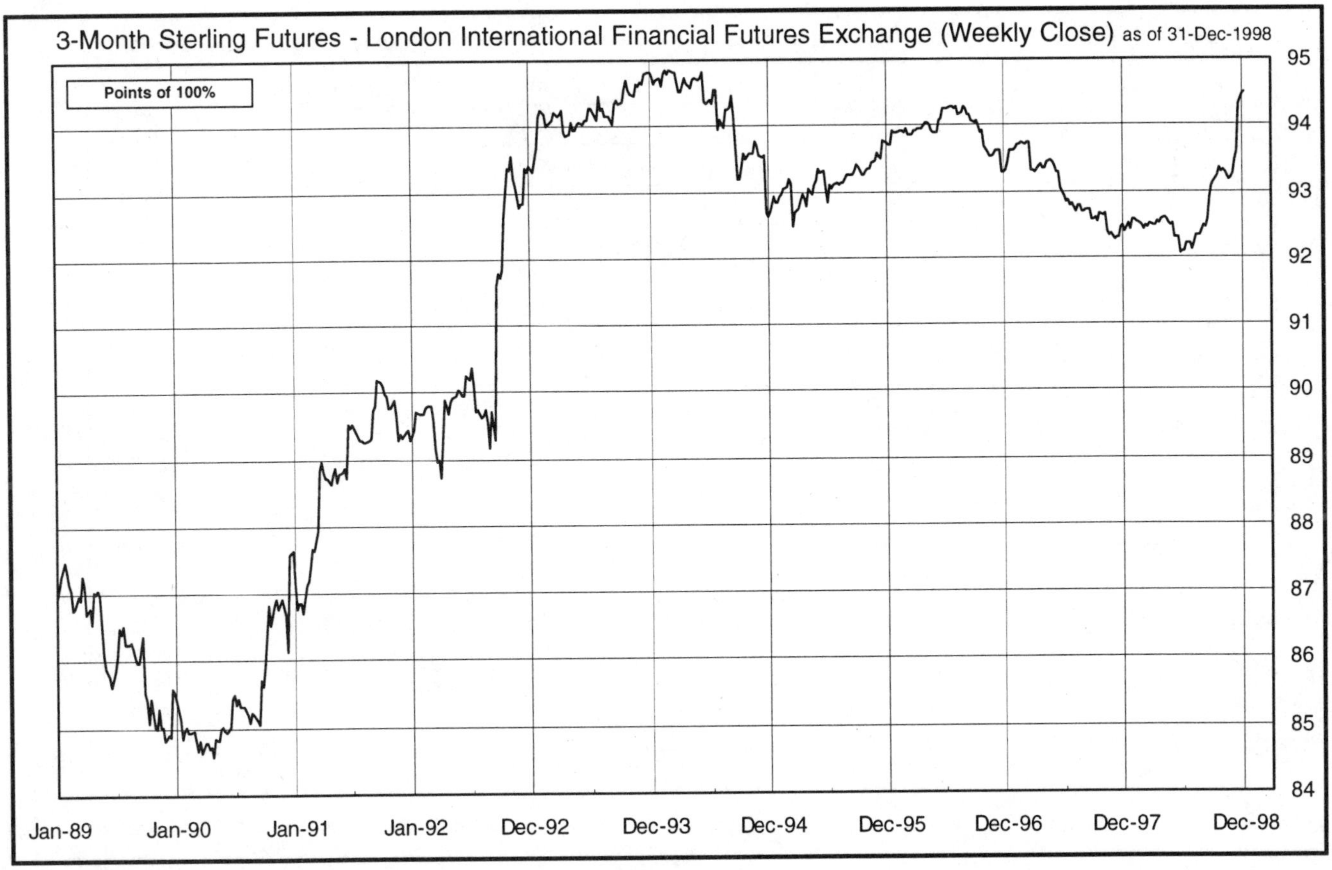

3-Month Sterling Futures - London International Financial Futures Exchange (Weekly Close) as of 31-Dec-1998

Points of 100%

95
94
93
92
91
90
89
88
87
86
85
84

Jan-89 Jan-90 Jan-91 Jan-92 Dec-92 Dec-93 Dec-94 Dec-95 Dec-96 Dec-97 Dec-98

INTEREST RATES, WORLDWIDE

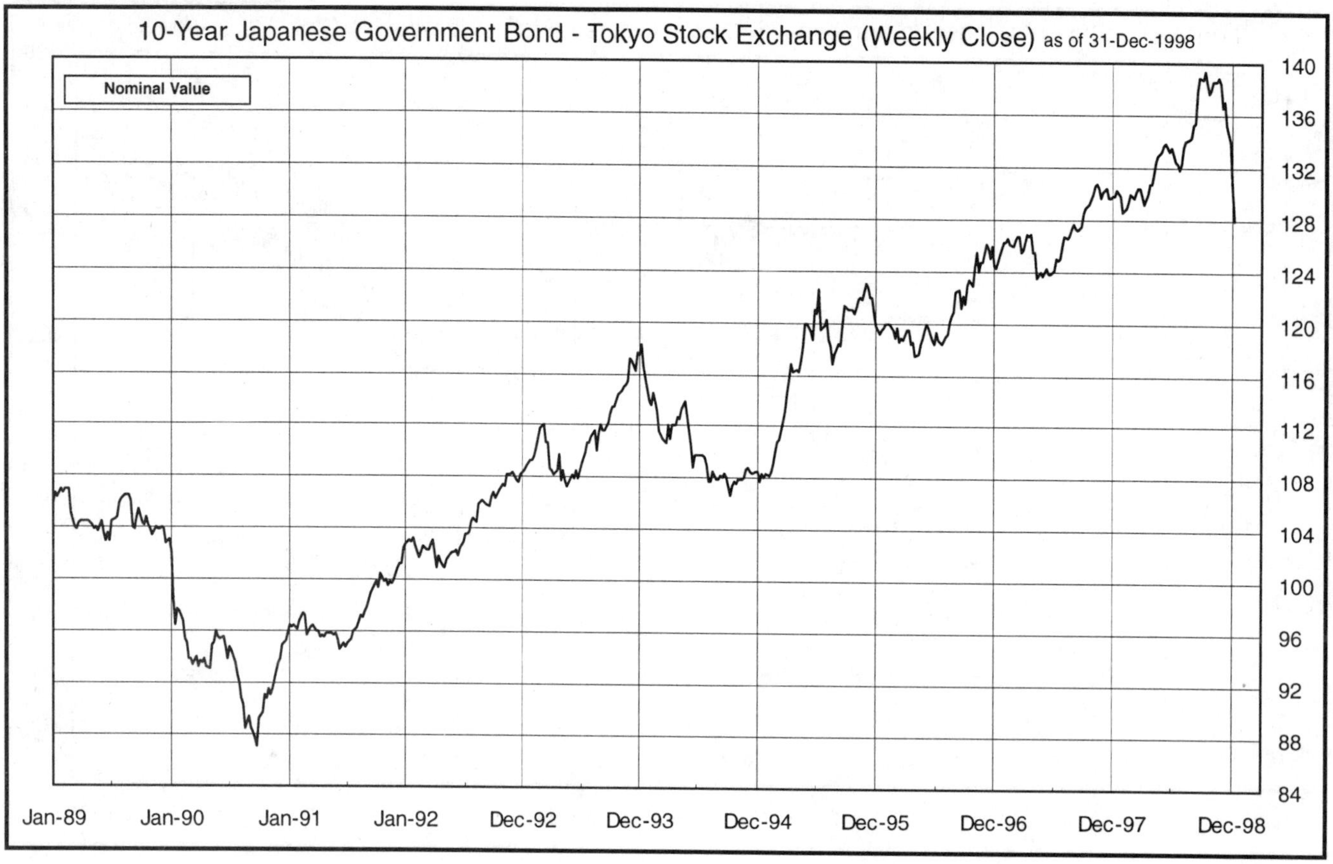

10-Year Japanese Government Bond - Tokyo Stock Exchange (Weekly Close) as of 31-Dec-1998

3-Month Euroyen - Tokyo International Financial Futures Exchange (Weekly Close) as of 31-Dec-1998

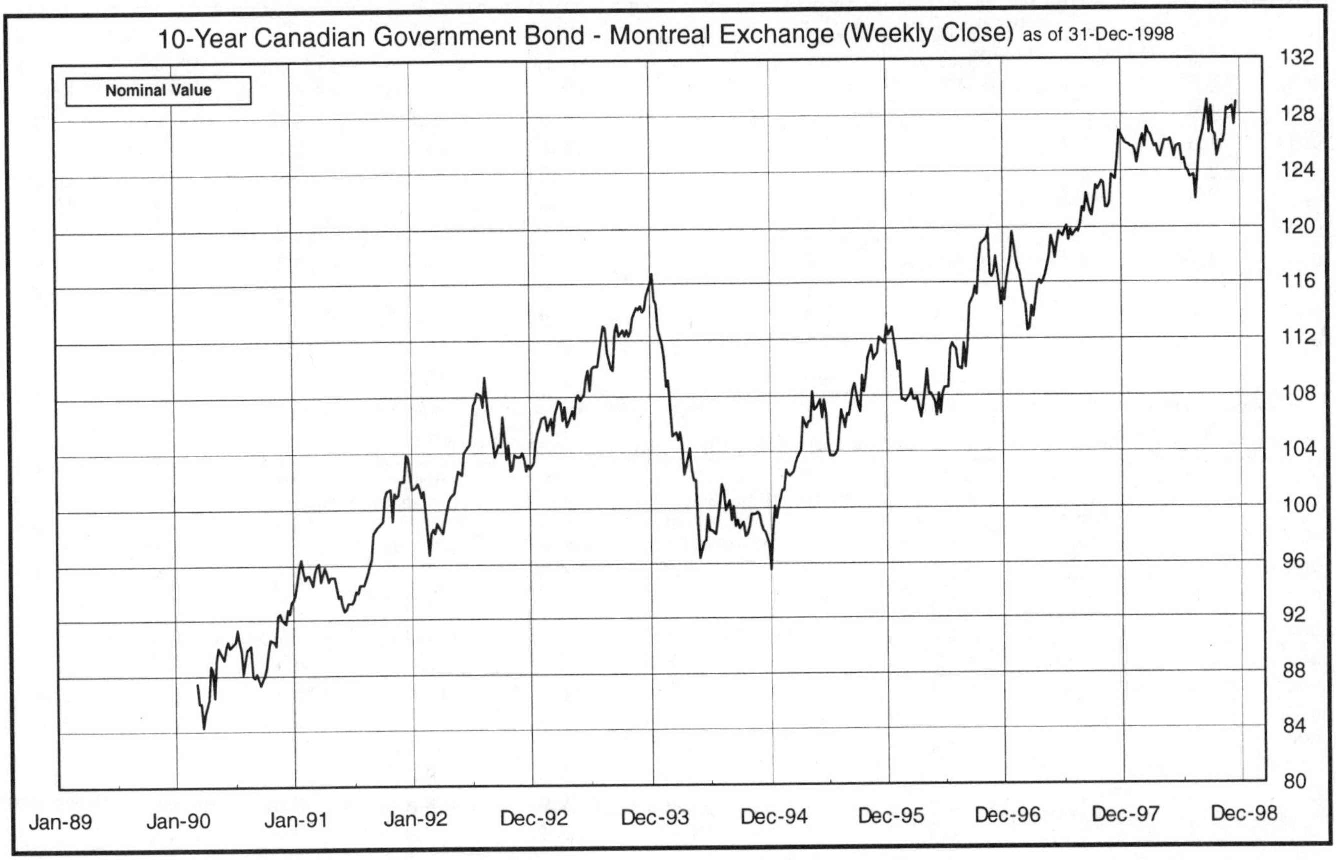

10-Year Canadian Government Bond - Montreal Exchange (Weekly Close) as of 31-Dec-1998

Nominal Value

132
128
124
120
116
112
108
104
100
96
92
88
84
80

Jan-89 Jan-90 Jan-91 Jan-92 Dec-92 Dec-93 Dec-94 Dec-95 Dec-96 Dec-97 Dec-98

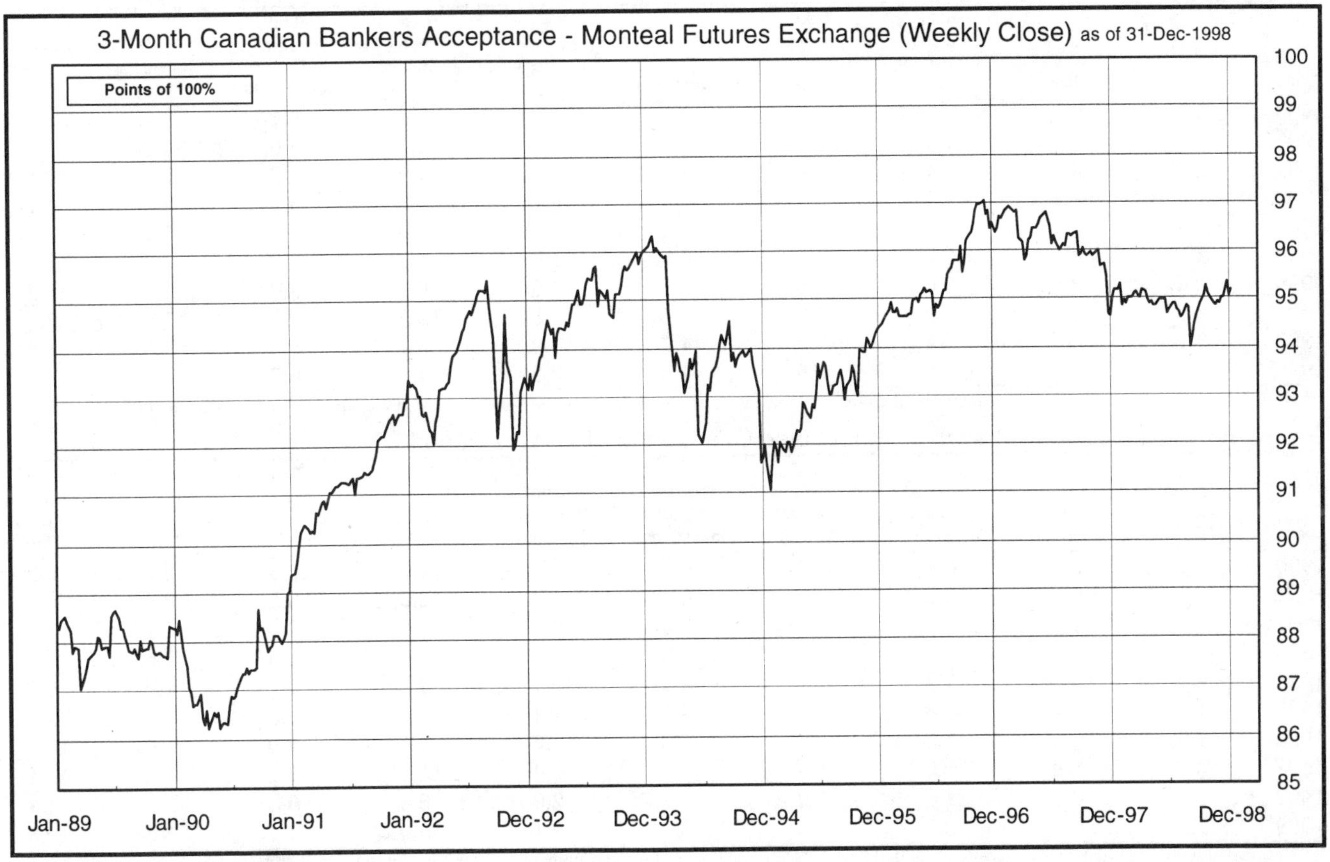

3-Month Canadian Bankers Acceptance - Monteal Futures Exchange (Weekly Close) as of 31-Dec-1998

Points of 100%

100
99
98
97
96
95
94
93
92
91
90
89
88
87
86
85

Jan-89 Jan-90 Jan-91 Jan-92 Dec-92 Dec-93 Dec-94 Dec-95 Dec-96 Dec-97 Dec-98

Australia -- Economic Statistics   Percentage Change from Previous Period

Year	Real GDP	Nominal GDP	Real Private Consump-tion	Real Public Consump-tion	Grossed Fixed Investment	Real Total Domestic Demand	Real Exports of Goods & Services	Real Imports of Goods & Services	Consumer Prices[1]	Unem-ployment Rate
1990	1.2	5.8	2.6	4.2	-8.2	-.9	8.5	-4.0	7.3	7.0
1991	-1.3	1.0	.8	2.7	-9.3	-2.5	13.3	-2.3	3.2	9.5
1992	2.7	4.1	3.6	1.7	2.3	3.5	5.2	7.9	1.0	10.7
1993	4.0	5.4	2.6	-.1	3.7	3.3	7.5	5.3	1.8	10.9
1994	5.3	6.5	4.6	5.2	11.6	5.9	9.0	15.4	1.9	9.7
1995	4.1	6.7	4.9	2.4	3.9	4.7	4.8	10.1	4.6	8.6
1996	3.7	5.9	3.1	3.1	6.2	3.6	11.1	9.8	2.6	8.5
1997	2.8	4.8	3.4	2.3	11.1	3.2	11.4	14.0	.3	8.6
1998	3.6	5.6	4.1	2.5	3.8	5.5	-.9	7.5	NA	8.2
1999[2]	2.4	4.9	3.0	4.6	2.5	2.7	5.5	5.5	NA	8.1

[1] National accounts implicit private consumption deflator. [2] Forecast. *Source: Organization for Economic Co-operation and Development (OECD)*

Canada -- Economic Statistics   Percentage Change from Previous Period

Year	Real GDP	Nominal GDP	Real Private Consump-tion	Real Public Consump-tion	Grossed Fixed Investment	Real Total Domestic Demand	Real Exports of Goods & Services	Real Imports of Goods & Services	Consumer Prices[1]	Unem-ployment Rate
1990	.3	3.3	1.3	3.7	-3.6	2.9	4.7	2.3	4.8	8.2
1991	-1.9	.8	-1.4	2.8	-3.5	-1.4	2.3	3.2	5.6	10.4
1992	.9	2.2	1.8	1.0	-1.3	.9	7.9	6.2	1.5	11.3
1993	2.5	3.8	1.9	-.2	-2.9	1.5	12.0	8.1	1.9	11.2
1994	3.9	5.1	3.1	-1.8	7.1	3.0	11.8	9.1	.2	10.4
1995	2.2	4.8	1.7	-.4	-2.8	1.0	9.3	6.7	2.2	9.5
1996	1.2	2.7	2.4	-1.3	4.8	1.1	5.7	5.2	1.6	9.7
1997	3.7	4.2	4.1	-.1	11.4	5.3	8.0	13.3	1.6	9.2
1998	3.0	3.0	2.9	.5	4.9	2.9	6.8	7.0	NA	8.4
1999[2]	2.4	4.1	2.4	1.0	5.3	2.4	6.2	6.2	NA	8.1

[1] National accounts implicit private consumption deflator. [2] Forecast. *Source: Organization for Economic Co-operation and Development (OECD)*

France -- Economic Statistics   Percentage Change from Previous Period

Year	Real GDP	Nominal GDP	Real Private Consump-tion	Real Public Consump-tion	Grossed Fixed Investment	Real Total Domestic Demand	Real Exports of Goods & Services	Real Imports of Goods & Services	Consumer Prices[1]	Unem-ployment Rate
1990	2.5	5.7	2.7	2.1	2.8	2.8	5.4	6.1	3.4	8.9
1991	.8	4.1	1.4	2.8	2.8	.6	4.1	3.0	3.2	9.4
1992	1.2	3.3	1.4	3.4	-2.8	.2	4.9	1.2	2.4	10.4
1993	-1.3	1.1	.2	3.4	-6.7	-2.2	-.4	-3.5	2.1	11.7
1994	2.8	4.4	1.4	1.1	1.3	3.0	6.0	6.7	1.7	12.2
1995	2.1	3.7	1.7	1.1	2.5	1.8	6.3	5.1	1.7	11.5
1996	1.6	2.7	2.0	2.6	-.5	.9	5.2	3.0	2.0	12.3
1997	2.3	3.3	.9	1.2	-.5	.8	12.5	7.7	1.2	12.4
1998	3.1	3.9	3.4	1.5	4.6	3.9	5.7	8.2	NA	11.8
1999[2]	2.4	3.5	2.6	2.0	4.6	3.0	4.0	5.7	NA	11.2

[1] National accounts implicit private consumption deflator. [2] Forecast. *Source: Organization for Economic Co-operation and Development (OECD)*

Germany[2] -- Economic Statistics   Percentage Change from Previous Period

Year	Real GDP	Nominal GDP	Real Private Consump-tion	Real Public Consump-tion	Grossed Fixed Investment	Real Total Domestic Demand	Real Exports of Goods & Services	Real Imports of Goods & Services	Consumer Prices[1]	Unem-ployment Rate
1990	5.7	9.1	5.4	2.2	8.5	5.2	11.0	10.3	2.7	6.2
1991	5.0	9.1	5.6	.4	6.0	4.7	12.6	13.1	3.6	6.7
1992	2.2	7.9	2.8	4.1	3.5	2.8	-.3	2.0	5.1	7.7
1993	-1.2	2.8	.1	-.5	-5.6	-1.4	-5.0	-5.9	4.5	8.8
1994	2.7	5.2	1.2	2.1	3.5	2.7	7.9	7.7	2.7	9.6
1995	1.2	3.4	1.8	2.0	3.5	1.4	6.6	7.3	1.8	9.4
1996	1.3	2.3	1.6	2.7	-1.2	.7	5.1	2.9	1.5	10.3
1997	2.2	2.9	.5	-.7	.1	1.4	11.1	8.1	1.8	11.4
1998	2.7	3.9	1.6	1.0	2.8	2.6	6.8	6.5	NA	11.2
1999[3]	2.2	3.5	2.1	1.2	3.2	2.1	5.0	4.9	NA	10.8

[1] National accounts implicit private consumption deflator. [2] Data are for Western Germany only, except for foreign trade statistics. [3] Forecast.
Source: Organization for Economic Co-operation and Development (OECD)

Italy -- Economic Statistics   Percentage Change from Previous Period

Year	Real GDP	Nominal GDP	Real Private Consumption	Real Public Consumption	Grossed Fixed Investment	Real Total Domestic Demand	Real Exports of Goods & Services	Real Imports of Goods & Services	Consumer Prices[1]	Unemployment Rate
1990	2.2	10.0	2.4	1.3	3.6	2.5	6.8	8.9	6.1	9.1
1991	1.1	8.9	2.7	1.7	.8	1.8	-.8	2.7	6.5	8.6
1992	.6	5.2	1.0	1.1	-1.8	.5	5.9	5.4	5.3	8.8
1993	-1.2	3.2	-2.4	.5	-12.8	-4.5	9.1	-8.1	4.2	10.2
1994	2.2	5.7	1.4	-.6	.5	1.5	10.7	8.4	3.9	11.3
1995	2.9	8.2	1.9	-1.0	7.1	2.3	11.6	9.6	5.4	12.0
1996	.7	5.7	.8	.2	.4	.3	-.2	-2.0	3.8	12.1
1997	1.5	4.2	2.4	-.7	.6	2.5	6.3	11.8	1.8	12.3
1998	1.5	4.2	1.3	.9	3.3	2.1	5.2	8.5	NA	12.2
1999[2]	2.1	4.1	2.4	.4	4.0	2.3	3.5	4.1	NA	12.1

[1] National accounts implicit private consumption deflator. [2] Forecast. *Source: Organization for Economic Co-operation and Development (OECD)*

Japan -- Economic Statistics   Percentage Change from Previous Period

Year	Real GDP	Nominal GDP	Real Private Consumption	Real Public Consumption	Grossed Fixed Investment	Real Total Domestic Demand	Real Exports of Goods & Services	Real Imports of Goods & Services	Consumer Prices[1]	Unemployment Rate
1990	5.1	7.5	4.4	1.5	8.5	5.2	6.9	7.9	3.1	2.1
1991	3.8	6.6	2.5	2.0	3.3	2.9	5.2	-3.1	3.3	2.1
1992	1.0	2.8	2.1	2.0	-1.5	.4	4.9	-.7	1.7	2.2
1993	.3	.9	1.2	2.4	-2.0	.1	1.3	-.3	1.2	2.5
1994	.6	.8	1.9	2.4	-.8	1.0	4.6	8.9	.7	2.9
1995	1.5	.8	2.1	3.3	1.7	2.3	5.4	14.2	-.1	3.1
1996	3.9	3.4	2.9	1.5	9.5	4.8	3.5	11.5	.1	3.4
1997	.8	1.4	1.1	-.1	-3.5	-.5	10.8	-.2	1.7	3.4
1998	-2.6	-1.9	-1.8	.5	-7.2	-3.3	-2.1	-7.9	NA	4.2
1999[2]	.2	-.2	.2	.5	-.3	-.1	3.3	2.1	NA	4.6

[1] National accounts implicit private consumption deflator. [2] Forecast. *Source: Organization for Economic Co-operation and Development (OECD)*

Switzerland -- Economic Statistics   Percentage Change from Previous Period

Year	Real GDP	Nominal GDP	Real Private Consumption	Real Public Consumption	Grossed Fixed Investment	Real Total Domestic Demand	Real Exports of Goods & Services	Real Imports of Goods & Services	Consumer Prices[1]	Unemployment Rate
1990	3.7	8.2	1.2	5.4	3.8	3.9	2.1	2.6	5.4	.5
1991	-.8	5.2	1.6	3.5	-2.9	-.6	-2.1	-1.6	5.9	1.1
1992	-.1	2.6	.1	.7	-6.6	-2.7	3.0	-4.2	4.0	2.5
1993	-.5	2.2	-.9	-.1	-2.7	-1.0	1.5	.1	3.3	4.5
1994	.5	2.2	1.0	2.0	6.5	2.7	1.8	7.9	.9	4.7
1995	.6	1.7	.5	-.1	1.8	1.8	1.6	5.1	1.8	4.2
1996	2.1	.4	.4	1.4	-2.7	1.8	2.5	2.7	.8	4.7
1997	1.7	1.6	1.2	-.1	1.5	1.0	9.0	7.2	.5	5.2
1998	1.7	2.5	1.7	.3	3.6	2.2	5.5	6.8	NA	4.0
1999[2]	1.6	3.0	1.6	.4	3.6	2.0	4.5	5.5	NA	3.4

[1] National accounts implicit private consumption deflator. [2] Forecast. *Source: Organization for Economic Co-operation and Development (OECD)*

United Kingdom -- Economic Statistics   Percentage Change from Previous Period

Year	Real GDP	Nominal GDP	Real Private Consumption	Real Public Consumption	Grossed Fixed Investment	Real Total Domestic Demand	Real Exports of Goods & Services	Real Imports of Goods & Services	Consumer Prices[1]	Unemployment Rate
1990	.6	8.3	.7	2.5	-2.3	-.3	4.9	.5	9.5	5.9
1991	-1.5	5.1	-1.7	2.9	-8.7	-2.7	-.2	-5.0	5.9	8.2
1992	.1	4.1	.4	.5	-.7	.8	4.1	6.8	3.7	10.2
1993	2.3	5.1	2.9	-.8	.8	2.2	3.9	3.2	1.6	10.3
1994	4.4	6.0	2.9	1.4	3.6	3.5	9.2	5.4	2.5	9.4
1995	2.8	5.4	1.7	1.6	2.9	1.8	9.5	5.5	3.4	8.6
1996	2.6	5.9	3.6	1.7	4.9	3.0	7.5	9.1	2.4	8.0
1997	3.5	6.3	4.2	1.8	6.1	3.9	8.4	9.5	3.1	6.9
1998	2.7	5.0	3.0	2.1	7.0	3.9	2.7	6.7	NA	6.5
1999[2]	.8	3.9	1.3	1.5	2.0	1.2	2.9	4.1	NA	7.4

[1] National accounts implicit private consumption deflator. [2] Forecast. *Source: Organization for Economic Co-operation and Development (OECD)*

Iron and Steel

Iron and steel scrap are the basic raw materials for the production of new steel and cast iron products. Scrap is readily available from manufacturing operations and from the recovery of products that have reached the end of their useful lives. As such, the steel and foundry industries in the U.S. have been structured to recycle scrap. Slags are the nonmetallic by-products of many metallurgical operations. They consist mostly of calcium, magnesium and aluminum silicates in various combinations. Slags are also co-products in steelmaking processes. Steel slag is a hard, dense material somewhat similar to air-cooled iron slag. Its high density and hardness make it suitable for use in road construction. Iron and steel slags are also used in cement manufacturing, concrete aggregates, fill, glass manufacture and as a mineral supplement in soil.

According to the U.S. Geological Survey, U.S. production or iron ore in the Lake Superior region in July 1998 was 5.43 million metric tonnes, down 4 percent from the June 1998 total. In the January-June 1998 period, iron ore production was 35.71 million tonnes, up 2 percent from the year before. For all of 1997, Lake Superior iron ore production was 62.48 million tonnes. Virtually all U.S. iron ore is produced in the Lake Superior district. Shipments of iron ore for the Lake Superior district in July 1998 was 6.39 million tonnes, up 1 percent from the previous month. Cumulative shipments in the first seven months of 1998 were 32.38 million tonnes, up 5 percent from the same period of 1997. For all of 1997, shipments from the Lake Superior district were 62.47 million tonnes.

U.S. exports of iron ore and agglomerates in June 1998 were 400,000 tonnes, down from 726,000 tonnes in May. In the first half of 1998, exports totaled 2.70 million tonnes virtually all of which was shipped to Canada.

U.S. imports for consumption of iron ore and agglomerates in June 1998 were 1.30 million tonnes. In the January-June 1998 period, imports were 7.63 million tonnes which was down 2 percent from a year ago. In the first half of 1998, the major suppliers of iron ore and agglomerates to the U.S. were Canada, with 3.45 million tonnes, followed by Brazil with 2.99 million tonnes. Other suppliers included Venezuela, Australia and Sweden.

U.S. iron and steel scrap receipts from dealers and other sources in June 1998 were 3.4 million tonnes. For the first half of 1998, total scrap receipts from dealers were 21 million tonnes. Production of recirculating scrap in first half 1998 was 7 million tonnes.

U.S. consumption of iron and steel scrap in June 1998 was 4.5 million tonnes while for the first half of 1998 it was 28 million tonnes. Most scrap was consumed in electric furnaces which took 20 million tonnes in first half 1998. Pig iron consumption in January-June 1998 was 26 million tonnes with most used in basic oxygen process furnaces.

World Production of Raw Steel (Ingots and Castings) In Thousands of Metric Tons

Year	Brazil	Canada	China	France	Germany	Italy	Japan	Rep. of Korea	Russia[3]	Ukraine[3]	United Kindom	United States	World Total
1988	24,657	14,866	59,430	19,121	41,021	23,760	105,681	19,118	163,037	-----	18,950	90,650	780,122
1989	25,055	15,458	61,587	19,340	41,073	25,213	107,908	21,873	160,096	-----	18,740	88,852	785,973
1990	20,567	12,281	66,349	19,016	38,434	25,467	110,339	23,125	154,414	-----	17,841	89,726	770,458
1991	22,617	12,987	71,000	18,434	42,169	25,112	109,649	26,001	77,093	45,002	16,474	79,737	733,591
1992	23,934	13,933	80,935	17,972	39,711	24,835	98,132	28,055	67,029	41,759	16,212	84,322	719,679
1993	25,207	14,387	89,539	17,106	37,625	25,720	99,623	33,026	58,346	32,609	16,625	88,792	727,546
1994	25,747	13,897	92,613	18,031	40,837	26,151	98,295	33,745	48,812	24,081	17,286	91,243	725,338
1995	25,076	14,415	95,360	18,100	42,051	27,767	101,640	36,772	51,589	22,309	17,604	95,190	752,350
1996[1]	25,237	14,735	101,236	17,633	39,793	24,285	98, 801	38,903	49,253	22,332	17,992	94,670	749,377
1997[2]	26,153	15,554	107,567	19,767	45,007	25,770	104,545	42,554	46,355	24,740	18,489	97,512	792,855

[1] Preliminary. [2] Estimate. [3] Formerly part of the U.S.S.R.; data not reported separately until 1992. *Source: U.S. Geological Survey (USGS)*

Average Wholesale Prices of Iron and Steel in the United States

Year	No. 1 Heavy Melting Steel Scrap: Pittsburgh	No. 1 Heavy Melting Steel Scrap: Chicago	Pittsburgh Prices: Hot Rolled Sheet[2]	Sheet Bars: Hot Rolled	Sheet Bars: Cold Finished	Hot Rolled Strip	Carbon Steel Plates	Cold Rolled Strip	Galvanized Sheets	Rail Road Steel Scrap[3]	Used Steel Cans[4]
	-- $ Per Gross Ton --		Cents Per Pound							-- $ Per Gross Ton --	
1988	113.78	113.47	21.50	17.25	21.23	22.10	21.64	37.24	31.05	150.25	NA
1989	106.80	108.33	22.21	19.60	25.21	22.10	23.50	37.24	32.48	145.23	60.18
1990	106.61	108.62	22.25	20.43	25.37	22.10	23.75	37.24	33.55	131.59	77.16
1991	95.18	95.19	22.88	20.60	25.75	23.15	24.50	38.86	35.35	129.69	89.00
1992	88.72	88.52	19.13	17.48	24.03	23.50	24.50	39.40	30.88	117.40	88.73
1993	116.30	115.26	20.99	18.44	23.83	23.50	25.12	39.40	30.90	142.18	91.79
1994	136.76	131.91	22.93	NA	25.70	23.50	27.61	39.40	32.24	169.00	102.33
1995	142.34	143.17	25.32	NA	25.70	24.88	29.98	39.40	34.47	NA	126.32
1996	137.28	136.07	23.94	NA	25.81	25.00	31.16	NA	35.90	NA	122.29
1997[1]	133.38	139.40	18.12	NA	25.67	NA	32.00	NA	28.60	NA	108.20

[1] Preliminary. [2] 10 gauge. [3] Specialties scrap. [4] Consumer buying prices. NA = Not available. *Source: American Metal Market (AMM)*

Salient Statistics of Steel in the United States In Thousands of Net Tons

		Producer Price Index for Steel Mill Products	Raw Steel Production							Net Shipments	Total Steel Products	
			By Type of Furnace									
Year	Pig Iron Production	(1982=100)	Basic Oxygen	Open Hearth	Electric[2]	Stainless	Carbon	Alloy	Total	Steel Mill Products	Exports	Imports
1989	55,873	114.5	58,348	4,442	35,154	1,926	86,230	9,786	97,943	84,100	5,098	19,699
1990	54,750	112.1	58,471	3,496	36,939	2,037	86,590	10,279	98,606	84,981	5,001	19,401
1991	48,637	109.5	52,714	1,408	33,774	1,878	77,879	8,139	87,896	78,846	7,112	17,743
1992	52,224	106.4	57,642	-----	35,308	1,993	82,458	8,498	92,949	82,241	5,016	19,033
1993	53,082	108.2	59,353	-----	38,524	1,956	86,865	9,056	97,877	89,022	4,727	21,796
1994	54,426	113.4	61,028	-----	39,551	2,022	89,535	9,022	100,579	95,084	4,852	32,705
1995	56,097	120.1	62,523	-----	42,407	2,265	92,656	10,009	104,930	96,859	7,080	24,409
1996	54,485	115.7	60,433	-----	44,876	1,911	93,019	5,948	100,878	100,531	5,031	29,164
1997	54,679	116.4	61,053	-----	47,508	2,067	97,509	6,282	105,858	105,538	6,036	31,157
1998[1]	53,174	113.9	59,686	-----	47,958	2,050	94,325	5,769	102,143	102,143	5,520	41,520

[1] Preliminary. [2] Includes crucible sheets. NA = Not available. *Sources: American Iron & Steel Institute (AISI); U.S. Geological Survey (USGS)*

Production of Steel Ingots, Rate of Capability Utilization[1] in the United States In Percents

Year	Jan.	Feb.	Mar.	Apr.	May	June	July	Aug.	Sept.	Oct.	Nov.	Dec.	Average
1989	88.2	89.8	90.9	92.2	88.1	86.2	80.8	79.2	80.0	83.0	77.4	73.3	84.5
1990	83.1	85.1	85.7	85.2	85.7	84.5	82.0	85.5	84.6	85.1	83.8	75.0	84.0
1991	74.6	73.1	71.7	72.5	70.0	71.7	74.8	75.2	78.5	78.0	78.0	74.4	74.2
1992	80.5	82.4	83.5	85.3	83.5	82.1	78.9	78.7	78.3	80.9	80.4	77.7	82.2
1993	84.8	89.0	87.0	87.4	88.3	87.5	86.9	86.2	87.7	90.2	86.3	85.9	89.1
1994	87.7	92.2	91.3	91.4	91.2	88.7	87.1	87.7	90.0	92.0	92.6	94.3	93.0
1995	93.8	95.6	96.0	92.9	91.6	90.1	86.8	88.3	93.6	90.3	92.1	90.2	91.7
1996	92.2	92.6	93.8	90.5	89.7	91.3	86.6	87.1	87.7	88.0	87.0	87.9	89.5
1997	85.3	89.3	89.6	89.2	87.9	87.0	85.1	86.4	91.2	86.9	89.6	86.3	87.8
1998[2]	90.0	95.2	93.1	92.5	89.1	86.1	83.0	86.4	83.0	81.0	74.4	74.8	85.7

[1] Based on tonnage capability to produce raw steel for a full order book. [2] Preliminary. *Sources: American Iron and Steel Institute; U.S. Geological Survey*

Production of Steel Ingots in the United States In Thousands of Short Tons

Year	Jan.	Feb.	Mar.	Apr.	May	June	July	Aug.	Sept.	Oct.	Nov.	Dec.	Total
1989	8,729	8,022	8,997	8,738	8,633	8,171	7,955	7,790	7,617	8,175	7,386	7,222	97,943
1990	8,241	7,624	8,505	8,209	8,529	8,142	8,101	8,452	8,094	8,424	8,021	7,422	98,906
1991	7,577	6,608	7,283	7,089	7,076	7,017	7,338	7,386	7,457	7,711	7,461	7,348	87,896
1992	7,754	7,432	8,043	7,875	7,968	7,584	7,542	7,526	7,249	7,742	7,449	7,438	92,949
1993	7,942	7,528	8,148	7,926	8,278	7,937	8,066	8,001	7,878	8,409	7,786	8,008	97,877
1994	8,003	7,598	8,323	8,180	8,437	7,941	7,996	8,053	7,993	8,477	8,256	8,684	100,579
1995	8,918	8,211	9,131	8,548	8,696	8,286	8,308	8,455	8,668	8,685	8,574	8,678	103,142
1996	8,981	8,438	9,136	8,588	8,798	8,661	8,585	8,627	8,407	8,702	8,276	8,689	104,356
1997	8,735	8,266	9,175	8,882	9,048	8,662	8,692	8,818	9,006	9,128	9,116	9,071	107,488
1998[1]	9,510	9,087	9,839	9,524	9,483	8,863	8,832	9,194	8,548	8,681	7,710	8,013	107,643

[1] Preliminary. *Source: American Iron and Steel Institute (AISI)*

Shipments of Steel Products[1] by Market Classifications in the United States In Thousands of Net Tons

Year	Appliances Utensils & Cutlery	Auto-motive	Con-tainers, Packaging & Shipping Materials	Cons-truction Including Maint.	Con-tactors Products	Electrical Equip-ment	Export	Machinery, Industrial Equipment & Tools	Oil and Gas	Rail Trans-portation	Steel for Converting & Pro-cessing[2]	Steel Service Center & Dis-tributors	All Other[3]	Total Ship-ments
1989	1,721	11,763	4,459	8,318	3,182	2,449	3,183	2,409	1,203	1,229	8,235	20,769	15,180	84,100
1990	1,540	11,100	4,474	9,245	2,870	2,453	2,487	2,388	1,892	1,080	9,441	21,111	14,900	84,981
1991	1,388	10,015	4,278	9,161	2,306	2,102	4,476	1,982	1,425	999	8,265	19,464	12,985	78,846
1992	1,503	11,092	3,974	9,536	2,694	2,136	2,650	1,951	1,454	1,052	9,226	21,328	13,645	82,241
1993	1,592	12,719	4,355	10,516	2,913	2,213	2,110	2,191	1,526	1,223	9,451	23,714	14,499	89,022
1994	1,736	14,753	4,495	10,935	3,348	2,299	1,710	2,427	1,703	1,248	10,502	24,153	15,775	95,084
1995	1,538	13,512	3,877	11,761	3,337	2,320	3,767	2,024	2,736	1,136	8,444	20,573	21,832	96,859
1996	1,648	14,400	3,998	12,981	-----	2,329	2,211	2,329	2,987	1,134	8,070	22,156	26,286	100,531
1997	1,633	14,342	4,140	14,295	-----	2,390	2,511	1,684	3,154	1,117	9,085	21,670	29,518	105,538
1998[4]	1,663	14,059	3,742	14,438	-----	2,309	2,435	1,627	2,093	1,287	7,258	20,724	30,509	102,143

[1] All grades including carbon, alloy and stainless steel. [2] Net total after deducting shipments to reporting companies for conversion or resale. [3] Includes agricultural; bolts, nuts, rivets and screws; forgings (other than automotive); shipbuilding and marine equipment; aircraft; mining, quarrying and lumbering; other domestic and commercial equipment machinery; ordinance and other direct military; seven shipments of non-reporting companies. [4] Preliminary.
Source: American Iron and Steel Institute (AISI)

IRON AND STEEL

Net Shipments of Steel Products[1] in the United States — In Thousands of Net Tons

Year	Cold Finished Bars	Rails & Accessories	Wire Drawn	Tin Mill Products	Plates (Cut & Coils)	Sheet & Strip Galv. (Hot Dipped)	Hot Rolled Bars	Pipe & Tubing	Structural Shapes & Steel Piling	Reinforcing Bars	Hot Rolled Sheets	Cold Rolled Sheets	Carbon	Alloy	Stainless
1989	1,472	562	1,002	4,126	7,384	8,543	6,301	4,011	4,987	5,015	13,281	13,854	78,485	4,143	1,472
1990	1,486	519	918	4,031	7,945	7,878	6,655	4,652	5,670	5,305	13,388	13,199	78,818	4,647	1,516
1991	1,341	486	865	4,041	6,942	6,910	5,431	4,488	5,245	4,859	13,161	11,532	73,480	3,917	1,449
1992	1,458	562	900	3,927	7,102	8,199	5,806	4,198	5,081	4,781	13,361	12,692	76,625	4,101	1,514
1993	1,580	679	802	4,123	7,538	9,712	6,339	4,445	4,973	5,033	14,873	12,758	83,106	4,381	1,534
1994	1,786	631	788	4,137	8,556	10,943	7,088	4,965	5,506	4,929	15,654	13,016	88,505	4,859	1,720
1995	1,758	609	703	3,942	9,044	11,345	7,004	5,436	6,611	4,714	16,402	12,677	90,485	5,115	1,894
1996	1,685	721	652	4,108	8,673	11,456	6,999	5,895	6,140	5,762	17,466	14,089	93,019	5,948	1,911
1997	1,796	825	619	4,058	8,855	12,369	8,045	6,548	6,011	6,142	18,136	13,317	97,509	6,282	2,067
1998[2]	1,768	881	655	3,714	8,865	13,481	7,835	5,410	5,452	6,286	15,728	13,193	94,325	5,769	2,050

[1] All grades, including carbon, alloy and stainless steel. [2] Preliminary. *Source: American Iron and Steel Institute (AISI)*

World Production of Pig Iron (Excludes Ferro-Alloys) — In Thousands of Metric Tons

Year	Belgium	Brazil	China	France	Germany	India	Italy	Japan	Russia[4]	Ukraine[4]	United Kindom	United States	World Total
1988	9,147	23,649	57,040	14,786	34,676	11,925	11,349	79,295	116,158	------	13,056	50,861	553,395
1989	8,868	24,621	58,200	15,071	35,197	12,420	11,795	80,197	116,628	------	12,638	50,977	561,762
1990	9,416	21,360	62,380	14,415	32,058	13,395	11,883	80,229	111,763	------	12,277	50,058	549,000
1991	9,354	22,926	67,650	13,408	30,608	14,176	10,856	79,985	90,900	------	11,883	44,510	528,000
1992	8,533	23,152	75,890	12,730	28,547	15,126	10,462	73,144	45,824	34,663	11,542	47,890	523,000
1993	8,178	23,982	87,390	12,679	26,970	15,674	11,066	73,738	40,871	26,999	11,534	48,200	531,000
1994	8,974	25,177	97,409	13,293	29,923	17,808	11,157	73,776	36,116	21,200	11,943	49,400	543,000
1995	9,199	25,090	105,293	12,860	29,828	18,626	11,684	74,905	39,762	20,000	12,238	50,900	564,000
1996[1]	8,628	24,121	107,225	12,108	30,012	20,000	10,347	74,597	36,061	18,143	12,830	49,400	561,000
1997[2]	8,077	25,000	115,440	13,424	30,939	20,000	11,348	78,519	37,327	20,561	13,057	49,600	585,000

[1] Preliminary. [2] Estimate. [4] Formerly part of the U.S.S.R.; data not reported separately until 1992. *Source: U.S. Geological Survey (USGS)*

Production of Pig Iron (Excludes Ferro-Alloys) in the United States — In Thousands of Short Tons

Year	Jan.	Feb.	Mar.	Apr.	May	June	July	Aug.	Sept.	Oct.	Nov.	Dec.	Total
1989	4,964	4,654	5,112	4,990	4,917	4,707	4,604	4,172	4,403	4,692	4,322	4,202	55,873
1990	4,638	4,221	4,681	4,549	4,746	4,530	4,656	4,788	4,629	4,673	4,523	4,264	54,925
1991	4,077	3,470	4,047	3,830	3,885	3,830	4,179	4,121	4,175	4,251	4,300	4,338	48,503
1992	4,390	4,175	4,524	4,400	4,444	4,232	4,347	4,299	4,065	5,329	4,268	4,306	52,224
1993	4,503	4,503	4,454	4,328	4,555	4,351	4,522	4,504	4,367	4,652	4,218	4,514	53,103
1994	3,970	3,858	3,957	4,099	4,394	4,519	4,518	4,446	4,320	4,564	4,619	4,928	54,426
1995	4,820	4,453	4,916	4,568	4,674	4,499	4,576	4,688	4,727	4,687	4,738	4,762	56,115
1996	4,811	4,476	4,813	4,430	4,556	4,578	4,524	4,498	4,404	4,443	4,307	4,523	54,485
1997	4,489	4,243	4,713	4,440	4,690	4,452	4,420	4,443	4,605	4,662	4,717	4,861	54,680
1998[1]	4,955	4,433	4,881	4,600	4,731	4,299	4,418	4,502	4,170	4,212	3,837	4,119	53,174

[1] Preliminary. *Source: American Iron and Steel Institute (AISI)*

Salient Statistics of Ferrous Scrap and Pig Iron in the United States — In Thousands of Metric Tons

	Consumption: Ferrous Scrap & Pig Iron Charged To												Stocks--Dec. 31 Ferrous Scrap & Pig Iron at Consumers		
	Mfg. of Pig Iron & Steel Ingots & Castings			Iron Foundries & Misc. Users			Mfg. of Steel Castings	All Uses							
Year	Scrap	Pig Iron	Total	Scrap	Pig Iron	Total	(Scrap)	Ferrous Scrap	Pig Iron	Grand Total	Imports of Scrap[2]	Exports of Scrap[3]	Scrap	Pig Iron	Total Stocks
1988	51,054	52,163	103,217	16,513	1,393	17,906	2,126	69,692	53,567	123,259	942	9,161	4,131	188	4,319
1989	52,733	50,210	102,943	13,270	892	14,162	1,894	67,897	51,122	119,019	1,016	11,149	4,293	246	4,539
1990	54,361	49,337	103,698	13,085	835	13,920	1,850	69,296	50,193	119,489	1,324	11,580	4,292	147	4,439
1991	48,778	44,095	92,873	11,126	656	11,782	1,609	61,513	44,765	106,278	1,073	9,502	4,072	190	4,262
1992	50,144	47,263	97,407	11,444	619	12,063	1,640	63,228	47,894	111,122	1,316	9,262	3,752	181	3,933
1993	53,084	48,092	101,176	12,658	676	13,334	1,900	68,000	48,777	116,777	1,390	9,805	3,725	220	3,945
1994	53,801	50,257	104,057	14,000	1,000	15,000	2,000	70,000	51,000	121,000	1,740	8,813	4,100	400	4,500
1995	56,000	51,000	107,000	13,000	1,100	14,100	2,000	72,000	52,000	124,000	2,090	10,400	4,200	620	4,820
1996	56,000	50,000	106,000	13,000	1,100	14,100	2,700	72,000	52,000	124,000	2,600	8,440	5,200	600	5,800
1997[1]	58,000	51,000	109,000	13,000	1,200	14,200	1,800	73,000	52,000	125,000	2,870	8,930	5,500	510	6,010

[1] Preliminary. [2] Includes tinplate and terneplate. [3] Excludes used rails for rerolling and other uses and ships, boats, and other vessels for scrapping.
Source: U.S. Geological Survey (USGS)

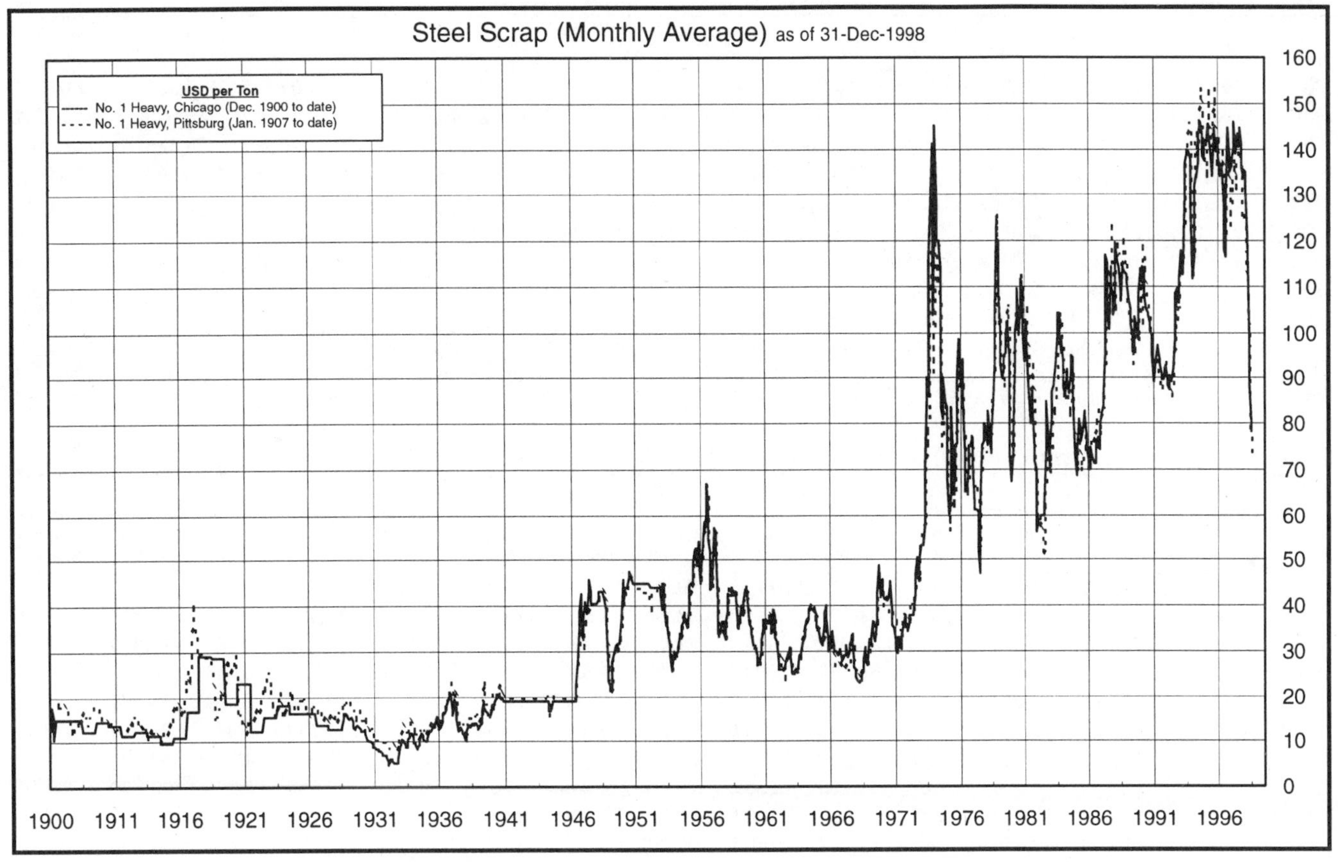

Consumption of Pig Iron in the U.S., by Type of Furnace or Equipment In Thousands of Metric Tons

Year	Open Hearth	Electric	Cupola	Basic Oxygen Process	Air & Other Furnace	Direct Casting	Total
1989	1,582	1,051	389	49,380	30	536	52,968
1990	2,072	982	332	47,307	19	387	51,099
1991	997	574	265	42,955	13	106	44,910
1992	-----	429	215	47,194	7	49	47,894
1993	-----	519	292	47,848	34	84	48,777
1994	-----	1,700	520	49,138	4	39	51,401
1995	-----	1,700	500	50,000	W	72	52,272
1996	-----	2,900	-----	45,000	-----	W	47,900
1997[1]	-----	2,400	400	50,000	W	W	52,800
1998[2]	-----	2,900	-----	42,000	W	W	44,900

[1] Preliminary. [2] Estimate. W = withheld. *Source: U.S. Geological Survey (USGS)*

Wholesale Price of No. 1 Heavy Melting Steel Scrap in Chicago In Dollars Per Gross Ton

Year	Jan.	Feb.	Mar.	Apr.	May	June	July	Aug.	Sept.	Oct.	Nov.	Dec.	Average
1989	114.10	118.32	113.00	113.00	113.00	113.00	108.00	108.00	108.00	101.09	96.00	94.50	108.33
1990	104.00	102.29	98.00	109.43	114.55	111.67	108.50	116.00	113.76	112.50	107.73	105.00	108.62
1991	104.76	100.74	98.00	97.80	93.18	87.50	87.74	94.14	98.50	97.50	91.97	90.50	95.19
1992	90.50	90.50	90.50	90.50	89.70	87.68	87.50	87.55	88.50	85.50	85.50	88.36	88.52
1993	98.34	109.50	109.50	106.50	106.50	111.27	118.50	114.18	113.50	125.88	131.50	138.00	115.26
1994	138.00	138.00	138.00	138.00	123.64	110.50	117.20	133.63	134.50	132.50	137.50	141.50	131.91
1995	152.05	147.50	140.20	141.50	144.50	141.64	141.50	149.76	144.90	141.50	136.50	136.50	143.17
1996	143.41	144.50	139.50	139.50	142.50	139.50	134.50	136.95	140.35	130.89	120.76	120.50	136.07
1997	131.14	143.50	139.70	132.59	136.50	136.50	143.50	146.50	139.60	139.63	142.50	142.50	139.51
1998	144.29	140.39	135.50	133.50	135.30	135.50	131.50	120.88	107.79	85.64	78.71	76.68	118.81

Source: American Metal Market (AMM)

IRON AND STEEL

World Production of Iron Ore[3] In Thousands of Metric Tons (Gross Weight)

Year	Australia	Brazil	Canada	China	India	Maur-itania	Russia[4]	South Africa	Sweden	Ukraine[4]	United States	Vene-zula	World Total
1988	99,450	146,008	39,934	154,380	49,961	10,004	249,754	25,248	20,440	------	57,515	18,932	967,218
1989	105,810	157,900	40,509	171,850	53,418	12,110	241,348	29,958	21,763	------	59,032	18,053	1,013,383
1990	110,508	152,300	34,855	168,300	53,700	11,590	236,000	30,291	19,877	------	56,408	20,119	983,000
1991	117,134	151,500	39,307	176,070	56,880	10,246	199,000	29,075	19,328	------	56,761	21,296	955,618
1992	112,101	146,447	33,167	197,600	54,870	8,202	82,100	28,226	19,277	75,700	55,593	18,070	924,887
1993	120,534	150,000	31,830	234,660	57,375	9,360	76,100	29,385	18,728	65,500	55,676	16,871	953,316
1994	128,493	168,245	37,703	240,200	60,473	11,440	73,300	30,489	19,663	51,300	58,454	18,318	981,979
1995	142,936	174,643	36,628	249,350	65,173	11,330	75,900	31,946	19,058	50,400	62,501	18,954	1,019,582
1996[1]	147,100	183,600	36,030	249,550	66,657	11,400	69,600	30,830	20,273	47,600	62,083	18,412	1,024,136
1997[2]	157,766	183,000	37,284	243,000	67,000	11,700	70,800	33,125	21,893	53,000	62,971	18,359	1,035,942

[1] Preliminary. [2] Estimate. [3] Iron ore, iron ore concentrates and iron ore agglomerates. [4] Formerly part of the U.S.S.R.; data not reported separately until 1992. *Source: U.S. Geological Survey (USGS)*

Salient Statistics of Iron Ore[3] in the United States In Thousands of Metric Tons

Year	Net Import Reliance % of Apparent Consumption	Production Total	Production Lake Superior	Production Other Regions	Ship-ments	Value Million $ (at Mine)	Average Value $ at Mine Per Ton	Stocks--Dec. 31 Mines	Stocks--Dec. 31 Con-suming Plants	Stocks--Dec. 31 Lake Erie Docks	Imports	Exports	Con-sumption	Value Million $ Imports
1988	18	57,515	56,038	1,477	57,113	1,716.7	30.06	2,957	18,005	2,537	20,183	5,285	83,694	484.5
1989	22	59,032	56,981	2,052	58,299	1,939.9	33.27	4,575	15,730	2,171	19,596	5,365	80,447	522.3
1990	21	56,408	54,628	1,780	57,010	1,570.0	27.52	4,795	15,911	2,273	18,054	3,199	76,855	559.5
1991	14	56,761	55,636	1,124	56,775	1,900.0	33.40	4,850	17,612	2,981	13,335	4,045	66,366	436.8
1992	10	55,593	55,018	575	55,569	1,730.0	31.10	3,780	16,093	2,981	12,504	5,055	75,067	395.8
1993	14	55,661	54,814	848	56,300	1,380.0	24.50	2,500	16,500	2,290	14,100	5,060	76,800	419.0
1994	18	58,382	57,848	367	57,610	1,410.0	24.50	2,790	16,300	2,230	17,500	4,980	80,200	499.0
1995	14	62,489	62,026	427	61,100	1,730.0	28.40	4,240	17,100	2,140	17,600	5,270	83,100	491.0
1996[1]	14	62,073	61,748	383	62,200	1,770.0	28.50	4,650	18,800	2,250	18,400	6,260	79,600	556.0
1997[2]	15	62,480	62,480	W	62,737	1,890.0	30.10	4,860	20,200	2,880	18,600	6,350	79,500	552.0

[1] Preliminary. [2] Estimate. [3] Usable iron ore exclusive of ore containing 5% or more manganese and includes byproduct ore.
Source: U.S. Geological Survey (USGS)

U.S. Imports (for Consumption) of Iron Ore[2] In Thousands of Metric Tons

Year	Australia	Brazil	Canada	Chile	Maur-itania	Peru	Sweden	Vene-zuela	Total
1989	394	5,169	8,538	61	594	186	57	4,232	19,596
1990	14	4,276	9,344	138	666	59	54	3,503	18,054
1991	NA	2,481	7,299	103	459	157	51	2,763	13,335
1992	163	2,442	6,834	107	280	70	64	2,540	12,504
1993	254	2,872	7,442	68	206	1	60	3,170	14,097
1994	675	3,610	10,073	134	124	2	45	2,778	17,466
1995	570	4,810	9,050	57	317	54	47	2,500	17,600
1996	511	5,173	9,800	164	275	43	48	2,140	18,392
1997	742	5,080	9,970	228	-----	252	57	2,090	18,600
1998[1]	558	5,312	7,531	48	-----	126	276	971	15,015

[1] Preliminary. [2] Including agglomerates. *Source: U.S. Geological Survey (USGS)*

Total[1] Iron Ore Stocks in the United States, at End of Month In Thousands of Metric Tons

Year	Jan.	Feb.	Mar.	Apr.	May	June	July	Aug.	Sept.	Oct.	Nov.	Dec.
1988	20,997	20,925	20,041	20,119	19,789	19,341	19,835	20,801	22,210	22,140	22,485	22,755
1989	23,189	23,252	22,685	21,145	21,670	21,544	22,286	22,275	22,588	21,429	21,448	22,476
1990	22,088	21,986	20,958	20,609	20,501	21,019	21,863	22,110	22,268	22,027	22,042	22,978
1991	22,572	22,218	21,316	20,757	21,756	23,174	23,319	24,329	25,148	25,117	25,358	25,445
1992	24,527	23,162	20,922	20,550	21,501	22,492	23,046	21,721	22,735	23,190	23,433	22,856
1993	21,296	20,806	19,235	18,996	19,180	22,036	22,905	21,575	22,629	21,355	21,615	21,341
1994	19,013	17,816	15,953	14,883	15,251	16,592	17,864	18,931	20,554	20,760	21,552	21,339
1996	22,277	20,744	19,779	20,104	23,426	21,822	22,445	23,663	24,116	24,866	25,465	25,701
1997	25,913	25,262	24,745	24,812	25,001	25,620	26,076	26,971	27,562	28,029	28,053	27,912
1998[2]	27,977	26,317	24,039	25,251	25,576	26,197	27,606	29,037	30,301	30,095		

[1] All stocks at mines, furnance yards and at U.S. docks. [2] Preliminary. *Source: U.S. Geological Survey (USGS)*

Lard

Production of lard is directly related to commercial pork production. As such, the largest producers of hogs are the largest producers of lard. China is by far the largest producer of lard followed by the United States. China produces about 40 percent of the world's lard while the U.S. produces about 7 percent. Other large producers include the former Soviet Union, Germany and Brazil.

The U.S. Department of Agriculture reported that U.S. beginning stocks of lard for the 1998-99 season were 45 million pounds. The season begins in October. Stocks were substantially higher than in the previous season. At the start of the 1997-98 season, lard stocks were 19.9 million pounds.

U.S. production of lard in the 1998-99 season was forecast at 1.1 billion pounds, an increase of nearly 4 percent from the previous season. Small amounts of lard are imported. In the 1998-99 season, U.S. lard imports are estimated at 2 million pounds, the same as in 1997-98. The total supply of lard in 1998-99 was projected to be 1.15 billion pounds, some 6 percent more than in 1997-98.

In terms of usage, domestic use of lard was projected to be 990 million pounds, an increase of nearly 8 percent from the previous year. Exports of lard in the 1998-99 season were forecast at 110 million pounds, down 8 percent from the previous year. Total use of lard was projected to be 1.1 billion pounds, an increase of nearly 6 percent from 1997-98. Use of lard has been fairly steady for several years. Projected ending stocks of lard were 47 million pounds, an increase of 4 percent from the 45 million pounds at the end of the 1997-98 season.

World Production of Lard In Thousands of Metric Tons

Year Beginning Oct. 1	Brazil	Canada	China	France	Germany	Italy	Japan	Poland	Romania	Spain	United States	Former U.S.S.R.	World Total
1989-90	151.0	75.6	1,519.5	129.2	534.4	178.5	91.0	136.8	130.1	156.1	412.3	844.4	5,441.8
1990-1	158.6	75.6	1,605.6	137.3	476.3	187.6	87.0	288.3	129.0	169.7	415.0	762.8	5,586.2
1991-2	165.7	76.9	1,698.4	135.5	411.3	188.0	85.0	303.3	117.7	170.6	447.7	653.6	5,497.5
1992-3	175.5	77.0	1,767.6	142.9	418.2	192.1	85.8	292.9	113.7	185.8	445.0	573.8	5,523.6
1993-4	186.2	76.0	1,984.8	151.3	409.5	189.5	82.4	243.3	115.9	192.8	451.0	465.0	5,605.9
1994-5	202.9	78.3	2,178.6	153.2	404.8	191.3	83.8	275.1	105.2	196.7	471.2	414.1	5,822.7
1995-6[1]	217.2	79.8	2,346.5	154.6	405.6	198.5	76.3	290.6	102.6	206.5	449.3	371.6	5,984.5
1996-7[2]	227.0	80.3	2,528.7	157.3	396.1	197.6	74.1	277.9	100.0	211.8	437.0	344.7	6,117.5
1997-8[3]	237.8	82.0	2,706.0	159.1	402.1	193.9	73.0	285.1	99.0	215.2	482.8	343.2	6,368.6

[1] Preliminary. [2] Estimate. [3] Forecast. *Source: The Oil World*

Supply and Distribution of Lard in the United States In Millions of Pounds

	Supply			Disappearance						
Year	Production	Stocks Oct. 1	Total Supply	Domestic	Baking or Frying Fats	Margarine[2]	Exports	Total Disappearance	Direct Use	Per Capita (Lbs.)
1990-1	933.6	22.9	959.9	825.4	264.0	35.0	110.0	935.8	439.2	3.3
1991-2	1,016.3	24.1	1,042.9	884.8	274.0	43.0	131.0	1,015.7	423.7	3.3
1992-3	1,011.2	27.2	1,041.5	886.1	310.0	37.0	129.2	1,015.3	438.6	3.5
1993-4	1,014.7	26.2	1,043.6	890.4	296.0	31.0	118.8	1,009.2	573.0	3.4
1994-5	1,052.4	34.4	1,089.0	924.4	306.0	43.0	140.4	1,064.7	584.4	3.4
1995-6	1,012.6	24.3	1,038.8	921.8	266.0	33.0	94.3	1,016.1	600.5	3.5
1996-7	979.0	22.7	1,002.9	879.6	254.7	15.0	103.3	982.9	602.4	3.5
1997-8[1]	1,064.7	19.9	1,086.8	924.6	250.6	15.0	121.8	1,046.4	-----	3.4
1998-9[2]	1,120.0	40.4	1,162.4	992.4	-----	-----	130.0	1,122.4	-----	-----

[1] Preliminary. [2] Includes edible tallow. [3] Forecast. *Source: Economic Research Service, U.S. Department of Agriculture (ERS)*

Consumption of Lard (Edible and Inedible) in the United States In Millions of Pounds

Year	Jan.	Feb.	Mar.	Apr.	May	June	July	Aug.	Sept.	Oct.	Nov.	Dec.	Total
1990	27.0	27.3	30.9	26.3	32.1	29.2	22.8	32.0	31.3	34.6	33.8	30.6	357.9
1991	----------	97.3	----------	----------	94.7	----------	----------	95.2	----------	----------	105.9	----------	393.1
1992	33.9	31.6	39.9	40.0	38.7	39.6	42.9	41.1	47.6	46.4	41.0	37.2	479.9
1993	40.1	34.4	45.9	36.8	38.2	38.8	32.6	38.4	41.8	44.0	43.0	40.3	474.3
1994	33.5	33.9	36.2	34.6	35.9	34.4	32.4	37.5	43.4	43.8	44.7	41.7	452.0
1995	37.5	34.7	41.2	36.2	42.2	44.4	34.9	35.9	35.9	40.1	38.9	36.8	458.7
1996	30.5	35.4	36.7	46.9	36.8	31.4	32.6	33.9	30.9	34.5	34.7	33.6	417.9
1997	26.5	30.5	31.0	36.5	39.9	36.2	36.1	35.0	37.4	39.0	41.5	40.4	429.8
1998[1]	34.1	29.9	31.1	29.6	28.5	35.9	33.0	33.0	37.1	37.7	38.9	33.9	402.7

[1] Preliminary. *Source: Bureau of the Census, U.S. Department of Commerce*

LARD

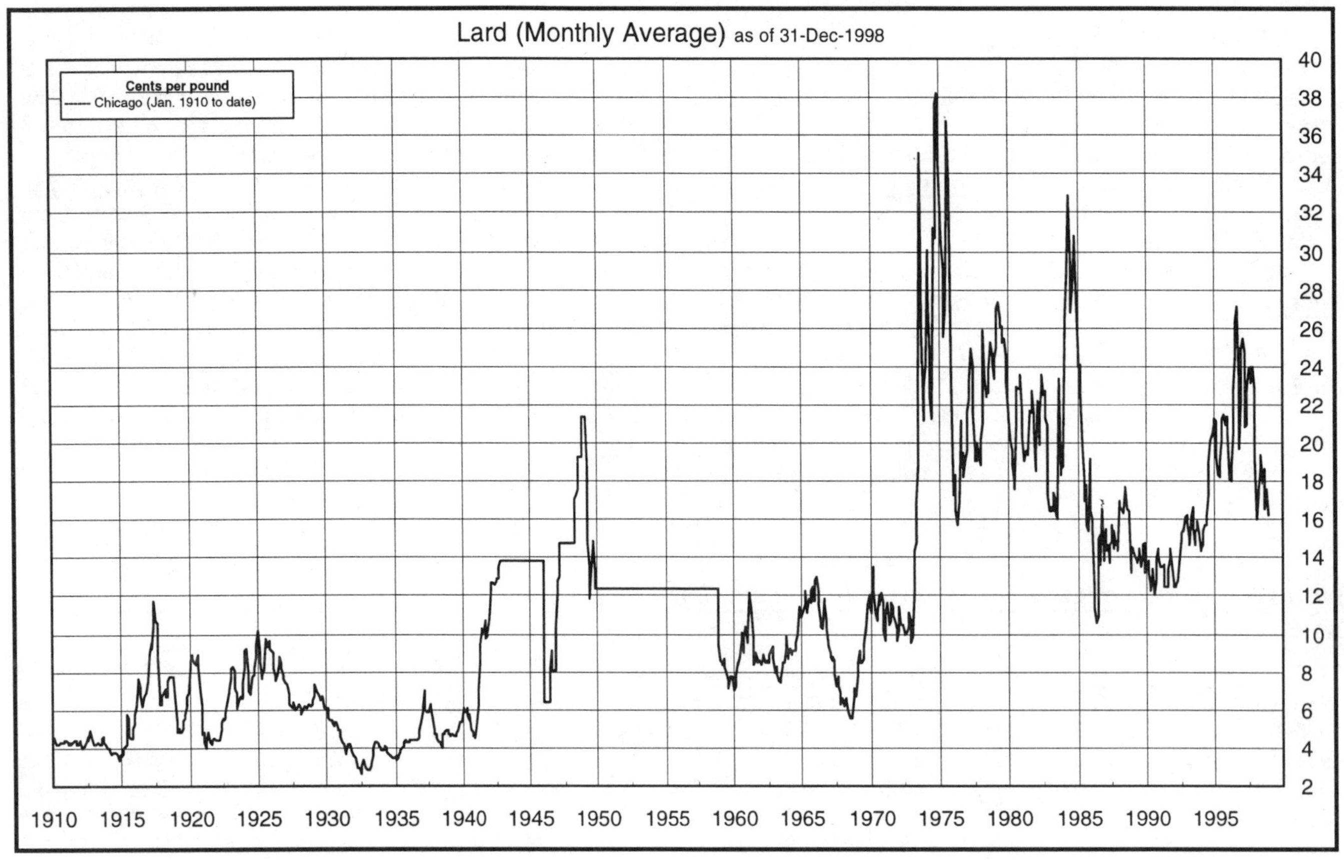

Average Wholesale Price of Lard--Loose, Tank Cars, in Chicago In Cents Per Pound

Year	Jan.	Feb.	Mar.	Apr.	May	June	July	Aug.	Sept.	Oct.	Nov.	Dec.	Average
1989	14.50	14.40	14.10	13.80	13.70	14.10	14.40	13.50	14.20	14.60	14.80	13.20	14.11
1990	13.50	13.80	13.20	12.50	12.30	13.20	13.40	12.10	12.70	14.00	14.50	14.10	13.28
1991	13.50	13.50	13.50	13.70	12.50	12.50	12.40	13.40	14.00	14.40	13.60	12.20	13.27
1992	12.50	12.50	12.60	12.60	13.90	15.00	15.00	15.30	15.50	15.40	16.10	16.30	14.39
1993	15.80	15.00	14.70	16.20	16.70	15.50	14.60	15.40	15.50	15.90	15.30	14.30	15.41
1994	14.50	14.60	15.40	15.70	15.80	16.30	17.20	18.90	20.10	20.40	20.40	20.90	17.52
1995	21.21	21.13	19.25	18.34	18.25	19.02	20.25	21.30	21.48	20.90	21.38	21.35	20.32
1996	20.52	18.17	18.01	18.67	20.47	22.61	24.55	26.30	27.09	23.11	19.70	22.17	21.78
1997	24.93	25.47	24.69	20.82	20.94	22.68	23.83	23.95	23.14	23.41	23.97	22.85	23.39
1998	19.09	16.03	17.36	17.64	18.66	19.38	17.93	18.65	16.58	17.39	17.60	16.27	17.72

Source: The Wall Street Journal

Cold Storage Holdings of All Lard[1] in the United States, on First of Month In Millions of Pounds

Year	Jan.	Feb.	Mar.	Apr.	May	June	July	Aug.	Sept.	Oct.	Nov.	Dec.
1989	37.4	38.2	37.1	27.3	34.2	37.6	41.3	32.4	28.9	41.6	29.0	36.6
1990	32.0	33.7	37.6	28.5	31.6	27.4	25.2	25.9	22.8	22.9	22.2	30.3
1991	----------	24.4	----------	----------	28.3	----------	----------	24.0	----------	----------	24.1	----------
1992	37.4	27.2	28.9	28.3	26.7	23.2	24.8	29.2	26.9	27.2	22.2	24.8
1993	22.7	25.9	27.2	24.0	22.8	25.8	31.1	27.4	23.6	26.2	24.6	30.1
1994	37.7	38.0	31.8	28.8	25.1	27.4	27.0	25.5	29.7	34.4	34.0	35.8
1995	40.6	50.3	46.4	43.0	36.8	27.1	25.8	22.1	30.2	24.3	19.9	21.6
1996	38.4	38.6	25.8	28.8	21.5	23.2	23.7	30.5	20.7	22.7	20.1	18.8
1997	18.9	16.3	18.5	19.2	18.9	18.7	23.0	23.2	21.5	19.9	21.3	19.7
1998[2]	22.2	30.1	38.3	42.5	41.6	47.6	43.7	44.8	38.8	40.4	34.8	26.3

[1] Stocks in factories and warehouses (except that in hands of retailers). [2] Preliminary. *Source: Bureau of the Census, U.S. Department of Commerce*

Lead

Lead is used in the production of batteries, fuel tanks, ammunition, electrical equipment, cans and containers, and as solder for pipes and plumbing. Lead finds use as a covering for power and communication cables but by far the dominant use of lead is in lead-acid batteries. Lead and the compounds that contain lead are very toxic and there has been a concerted effort to reduce the use of lead. Some of the substitutes for lead include plastic, tin, iron, aluminum and bismuth.

The U.S. Geological Survey reported that lead was mined in 44 countries in 1997 with the top five producers accounting for 69 percent of production. In 1997, world mine production of lead was 3.01 million metric tonnes, down 3 percent from 1996. China was the largest producer of mined lead with 1997 output of 650,000 tonnes, up 1 percent from 1996. Australia was the next largest producer of mined lead with 1997 output of 531,000 tonnes, almost 2 percent more than in 1996. U.S. mine production in 1997 was 459,000 tonnes, up 5 percent from the previous year. U.S. production of lead has been increasing for a number of years. Alaska and Missouri were the dominant producers with over 90 percent of U.S. lead output. Other producing states included Colorado, Idaho and Montana. Lead was produced at 16 mines while primary lead was processed at two smelters. Other major producers of lead include Peru and Canada.

World lead refinery production in 1997 was estimated at 5.76 million tonnes, up 1 percent from 1996. Of the total, primary refinery production was 2.9 million tonnes while secondary refinery production was 2.86 million tonnes. U.S. refinery production of lead in 1997 was 1.45 million tonnes, up almost 4 percent from 1996. Secondary lead, derived principally from scrapped lead-acid batteries, accounted for 76 percent of refined lead production in the United States. China produced 646,000 tonnes of refined lead in 1997, down 8 percent from 1996.

U.S. mine production of lead in July 1998 was 34,600 tonnes compared to 34,700 tonnes in the previous month. In the January-July 1998 period mine production (recoverable lead) was 252,000 tonnes, down 2 percent from the year before. U.S. refinery production of lead in July 1998 was 28,900 tonnes, up 42 percent from the previous month. In the first seven months of 1998, refinery production was 193,000 tonnes, down 6 percent from the same period in 1997.

U.S. lead imports for consumption of ore and concentrates (lead content) were 5,690 tonnes in June 1998. In the January-June 1998 period imports were 11,600 tonnes, an increase of 49 percent from 1997. For all of 1997, imports of lead ore and concentrates were 17,800 tonnes. Imports of refined lead metal in June 1998 were 21,700 tonnes and in the first half of 1998 they were 129,000 tonnes. That was down 12 percent from the year before. For all of 1997, refined lead metal imports were 265,000 tonnes.

U.S.-reported consumption of lead in July 1998 was 124,000 tonnes, down 2 percent from the previous month. In the January-July 1998 period, reported consumption of lead was 875,000 tonnes, up 20 percent from a year ago. For all of 1997, reported lead consumption was 1.6 million tonnes. Stocks of lead at primary refineries at the end of July 1998 were 13,700 tonnes while stocks at secondary smelters and consumers were 64,700 tonnes.

World Smelter (Primary and Secondary) Production of Lead In Thousands of Metric Tons

Year	Australia[3]	Belgium[4]	Canada[3]	China[2]	France	Germany	Italy	Japan	Mexico[3]	Spain	United Kingdom[3]	United States	World Total
1990	229.0	105.8	183.6	296.0	432.7	411.0	166.8	327.4	232.2	110.0	329.4	1,330	5,950
1991	239.4	110.7	212.4	330.0	438.0	362.5	208.2	332.4	161.8	169.0	311.0	1,230	5,770
1992	231.8	116.3	252.9	365.0	444.6	354.3	186.3	330.2	177.0	120.0	346.8	1,220	5,420
1993	243.0	131.1	217.0	412.0	258.7	334.2	182.8	309.5	188.0	123.0	364.0	1,230	5,250
1994	237.0	123.5	251.6	468.0	260.0	331.7	205.9	292.2	171.0	140.0	352.5	1,280	5,390
1995	241.0	121.7	281.4	608.0	290.1	311.2	180.4	287.6	176.0	80.0	320.7	1,390	5,600
1996[1]	228.0	125.4	309.4	706.0	293.9	237.1	209.8	287.4	160.0	86.0	345.6	1,400	5,690
1997[2]	238.0	111.0	275.0	646.0	282.8	240.0	210.0	296.8	178.0	88.0	391.0	1,450	5,760

[1] Preliminary. [2] Estimate. [3] Refined & bullion. [4] Includes scrap. NA - not avaliable. *Source: U.S. Geaological Survey (USGS)*

Consumption of Lead in the United States, by Products In Metric Tons

Year	Ammunition	Bearing Metals	Pipes, Traps & Bends[2]	Cable Covering	Calking Lead	Casting Metals	Other Metal Products[3]	Total Other Oxides[4]	Sheet Lead	Solder	Storage Battery: Grids, Post, etc.	Storage Battery: Oxides	Brass and Bronze	Total Consumption
1990	58,210	5,212	9,281	18,253	1,688	14,843	3,812	56,484	21,013	16,490	571,187	448,450	9,943	1,275,226
1991	58,458	3,669	8,975	17,472	1,074	14,141	3,254	59,617	22,334	14,750	591,884	415,233	8,997	1,246,337
1992	64,845	4,785	11,652	15,992	1,045	17,111	3,024	63,225	21,006	13,518	629,147	373,185	9,175	1,236,571
1993	65,100	4,830	5,740	17,165	961	18,500	5,360	63,600	21,200	14,400	677,000	374,000	5,750	1,290,000
1994	62,400	5,560	3,370	16,000	764	18,900	5,330	62,700	21,500	12,200	797,000	425,000	6,320	1,450,000
1995	70,900	6,490	2,210	5,640	935	18,100	5,220	61,700	27,900	16,200	711,000	618,000	5,260	1,560,000
1996	52,100	4,350	1,810	W	767	18,900	5,220	62,100	19,400	9,020	635,000	706,000	5,460	1,540,000
1997[1]	55,300	2,490	1,860	4,930	1,390	18,300	7,570	67,000	19,100	9,580	634,000	761,000	4,410	1,600,000

[1] Preliminary. [2] Including building. [3] Including terne metal, type metal, and lead consumed in foil, collapsible tubes, annealing, plating, galvanizing and fishing weights. [4] Includes paints, glass and ceramic products, and other pigments and chemicals. NA = not avaliable. W = Withheld proprietary data.
Source: U.S. Geological Survey (USGS)

LEAD

Salient Statistics of Lead in the United States   In Thousands of Metric Tons

Year	Net Import Reliance as a % of Apparent Consumption	--- of Refined Lead From --- Domestic Ores[3]	Foreign Ores3	Total Primary	Total Value of Refined Mil. USD	------ Secondary Lead Recovered ------ As Soft Lead	In Antimonial Lead	In Other Alloys	Total	Total Value of Secondary Mil. USD	-- Stocks, Dec. 31 -- Primary	Consumer[4]	Average Price --- ¢ Per Pound --- New York	London[5]
1988	13	371.3	20.7	392.1	321.0	367.1	331.3	38.0	736.4	603.0	15.4	89.9	37.14	29.73
1989	8	379.0	17.4	396.5	343.9	438.0	418.6	34.7	891.3	773.3	15.6	82.4	39.35	30.63
1990	3	385.6	18.0	403.7	409.5	461.4	425.4	35.6	922.2	935.6	25.5	86.3	46.02	37.05
1991	6	323.9	21.9	345.7	255.2	421.9	426.9	35.8	884.6	652.9	9.1	71.7	33.48	25.30
1992	10	284.0	20.8	304.8	235.9	452.9	424.5	23.1	916.3	709.1	20.5	82.3	35.10	24.50
1993	15	310.7	24.9	335.6	234.4	444.0	417.0	17.0	893.0	625.0	14.3	80.5	31.74	18.42
1994	19	328.0	23.4	351.4	288.0	527.0	371.0	16.1	931.0	763.0	9.3	68.8	37.17	24.83
1995	17	374.0	W	374.0	348.0	584.0	400.0	19.2	1,020.0	951.0	14.2	79.4	42.28	28.08
1996[1]	16	326.0	W	326.0	351.0	625.0	420.0	9.2	1,070.0	1,150.0	8.1	72.1	48.83	31.22
1997[2]	14	343.0	W	343.0	352.0	663.0	411.0	14.2	1,110.0	1,130.0	11.9	88.7	46.54	28.29

[1] Preliminary. [2] Estimate. [3] And base bullion. [4] Also at secondary smelters. [5] LME data in USD per metric ton beginning July 1993.
W = Withheld proprietary data. E = Net exporter.. *Source: U.S. Geological Survey (USGS)*

United States Foreign Trade of Lead   In Thousands of Metric Tons

Year	---- Exports ---- Ore Concentrate	Unwrought Lead[3]	Wrought Lead[4]	Scrap	Ash & Residues[5]	---- Imports for Consumption ---- Ores, Flue Dust or Fume & Mattes	Base Bullion	Pigs & Bars	Reclaimed Scrap, Etc.	Value Mil. USD	---- General Imports From: ---- Ore, Flue ------ Dust & Matte ------ Australia	Canada	Peru	--------- Pigs & Bars --------- Canada	Mexico	Peru
1988	20.9	7.5	6.0	81.9	15.5	20.6	4.00	148.6	7.30	124.8	1.4	221.8	11.4	104.8	30.9	-----
1989	57.0	28.5	5.4	59.9	10.0	5.1	5.80	115.7	.70	95.7	1.9	189.9	12.9	90.5	19.2	2.3
1990	56.6	57.2	6.8	75.0	13.0	10.7	2.70	90.6	.30	91.2	1.2	124.3	7.1	70.7	25.0	1.0
1991	88.0	94.4	7.6	72.0	11.0	12.4	.40	116.5	.10	82.6	1.0	226.7	3.9	83.6	11.9	.5
1992	72.3	64.3	5.3	63.2	2.1	5.3	.20	190.7	.20	120.6	-----	239.9	21.2	124.7	56.1	9.8
1993	41.8	51.4	7.1	54.1	1.7	.5	-----	195.6	.08	99.4	-----	55.7	13.6	130.8	40.3	18.3
1994	38.7	48.2	5.3	88.1	20.6	.5	.58	230.8	.14	146.6	.5	.2	-----	159.0	31.9	25.6
1995	65.5	48.2	9.0	105.0	8.0	2.6	.03	264.0	.08	191.7	1.5	-----	.1	182.0	54.3	22.1
1996[1]	59.7	44.0	16.7	85.3	19.4	6.6	.01	268.0	.19	217.0	-----	4.4	-----	192.0	56.9	17.1
1997[2]	42.2	37.4	15.9	88.4	16.8	17.8	.03	265.0	.07	186.0	-----	96.5	10.2	187.0	70.4	6.4

[1] Preliminary. [2] Estimate. [3] And lead alloys. [4] Blocks, pigs, etc. [5] Formerly drosses and flue dust. *Source: U.S. Geological Survey (USGS)*

Annual Mine Production of Recoverable Lead in the United States   In Metric Tons

Year	Total	Idaho	Missouri	Montana	Other States	Missouri's % of Total
1988	384,983	W	353,194	8,266	23,523	92%
1989	410,915	W	366,931	W	43,984	89%
1990	483,704	W	380,781	W	102,923	79%
1991	465,931	W	351,995	W	113,936	76%
1992	397,923	W	300,589	W	97,334	76%
1993	353,607	W	276,569	W	77,800	78%
1994	363,443	W	290,738	9,940	63,100	80%
1995	386,000	W	359,000	8,350	18,200	93%
1996[1]	426,000	W	397,000	7,970	21,200	93%
1997[2]	448,000	W	412,000	9,230	26,600	92%

[1] Preliminary. [2] Estimate. W = Withheld. NA = Not available. *Source: U.S. Geological Survey (USGS)*

Mine Production of Recoverable Lead in the United States   In Thousands of Metric Tons

Year	Jan.	Feb.	Mar.	Apr.	May	June	July	Aug.	Sept.	Oct.	Nov.	Dec.	Total
1989	33.3	31.0	34.4	33.2	33.8	36.1	33.2	38.6	34.3	35.1	32.9	30.1	410.9
1990	42.4	39.0	39.9	37.4	40.8	38.8	42.3	47.2	37.9	43.0	38.5	36.6	483.7
1991	41.5	41.1	41.6	37.8	43.5	36.4	47.5	41.1	36.1	38.9	28.0	26.1	465.9
1992	36.0	34.0	34.0	31.2	31.5	32.4	33.8	32.5	32.5	33.3	30.8	31.7	392.7
1993	33.3	30.5	34.2	30.6	28.5	29.5	25.8	27.5	28.4	27.3	29.5	28.5	355.2
1994	27.6	28.8	33.0	31.3	32.4	29.1	29.4	30.4	31.2	28.0	31.7	29.9	363.4
1995	29.6	30.3	35.2	28.9	32.7	34.8	32.5	33.5	29.9	34.1	31.6	32.1	385.0
1996	36.9	36.4	35.6	35.9	37.5	33.8	35.6	34.1	26.9	35.2	33.6	35.7	426.0
1997	36.7	36.7	37.2	38.6	38.6	35.1	33.4	33.7	34.4	35.4	31.7	32.8	415.0
1998[1]	36.4	35.4	37.8	37.3	35.7	34.7	34.3	35.6	36.1	40.3	37.8		437.9

[1] Preliminary. *Source: U.S. Geological Survey (USGS)*

Average Price of Pig Lead, U.S. Primary Producers (Common Corroding)[1] In Cents Per Pound

Year	Jan.	Feb.	Mar.	Apr.	May	June	July	Aug.	Sept.	Oct.	Nov.	Dec.	Average
1989	40.22	37.00	35.00	35.03	36.14	38.82	39.97	41.30	43.00	43.00	40.55	38.55	39.05
1990	39.73	41.74	54.45	48.10	45.00	45.14	50.62	51.00	49.08	44.52	41.33	37.03	45.65
1991	34.18	33.00	33.00	33.00	32.00	31.80	33.00	33.00	33.70	35.00	35.00	35.00	33.47
1992	35.00	35.00	35.00	35.00	35.00	35.00	36.91	40.00	40.00	36.64	32.63	32.00	35.68
1993	32.00	32.00	32.00	32.00	32.00	32.00	32.00	32.00	32.00	32.00	32.00	33.00	32.08
1994	34.00	34.00	34.00	34.00	34.00	35.73	37.70	38.00	40.00	42.00	43.70	44.00	37.59
1995	44.00	44.00	42.00	42.00	42.00	42.00	42.00	43.65	44.00	44.00	46.10	48.00	43.65
1996	48.00	49.50	50.96	52.00	52.00	52.00	50.29	49.18	50.00	50.00	50.00	50.00	50.33
1997	50.00	50.00	48.70	48.00	48.00	48.00	48.00	48.00	48.00	48.00	48.00	48.00	48.39
1998	48.00	48.00	48.00	48.00	48.00	48.00	48.00	48.00	48.00	48.00	45.47	45.00	47.54

[1] New York Delivery. *Source: American Metal Market (AMM)*

Refiners Production[1] of Lead in the United States In Metric Tons

Year	Jan.	Feb.	Mar.	Apr.	May	June	July	Aug.	Sept.	Oct.	Nov.	Dec.	Total
1989	37,195	32,659	35,381	30,845	32,841	32,206	32,387	34,474	35,653	31,480	32,024	29,303	396,455
1990	34,927	34,383	33,476	35,018	33,022	30,210	30,845	34,474	33,929	38,375	33,476	31,571	403,657
1991	30,763	30,863	33,771	30,248	27,031	22,371	27,973	28,204	29,411	29,846	26,428	28,813	345,714
1992	29,121	27,691	33,366	27,456	26,742	22,441	24,993	21,587	19,365	22,945	23,674	25,414	304,791
1993	29,627	26,693	30,197	27,578	29,814	28,253	16,734	22,817	32,725	31,220	27,953	31,312	335,014
1994	29,908	30,685	31,420	29,059	31,588	31,707	30,661	27,335	31,185	32,874	29,301	30,447	366,170
1995	32,100	29,100	32,600	32,300	32,600	28,300	31,000	29,300	30,600	34,200	30,100	31,500	374,000
1996	34,700	30,400	30,900	28,600	27,500	21,700	25,500	24,700	25,400	25,300	26,100	25,500	326,000
1997	28,800	28,500	31,900	30,400	30,800	28,700	25,900	28,000	21,600	30,500	29,000	28,700	343,000
1998[2]	29,200	25,900	30,000	29,700	29,500	20,300	28,900	NA	NA	NA	NA		331,714

[1] Represents refined lead produced from domestic ores by primary smelters plus small amounts of secondary material passing through these smelters. Includes GSA metal purchased for remelt. [2] Preliminary. *Source: U.S. Geological Survey (USGS)*

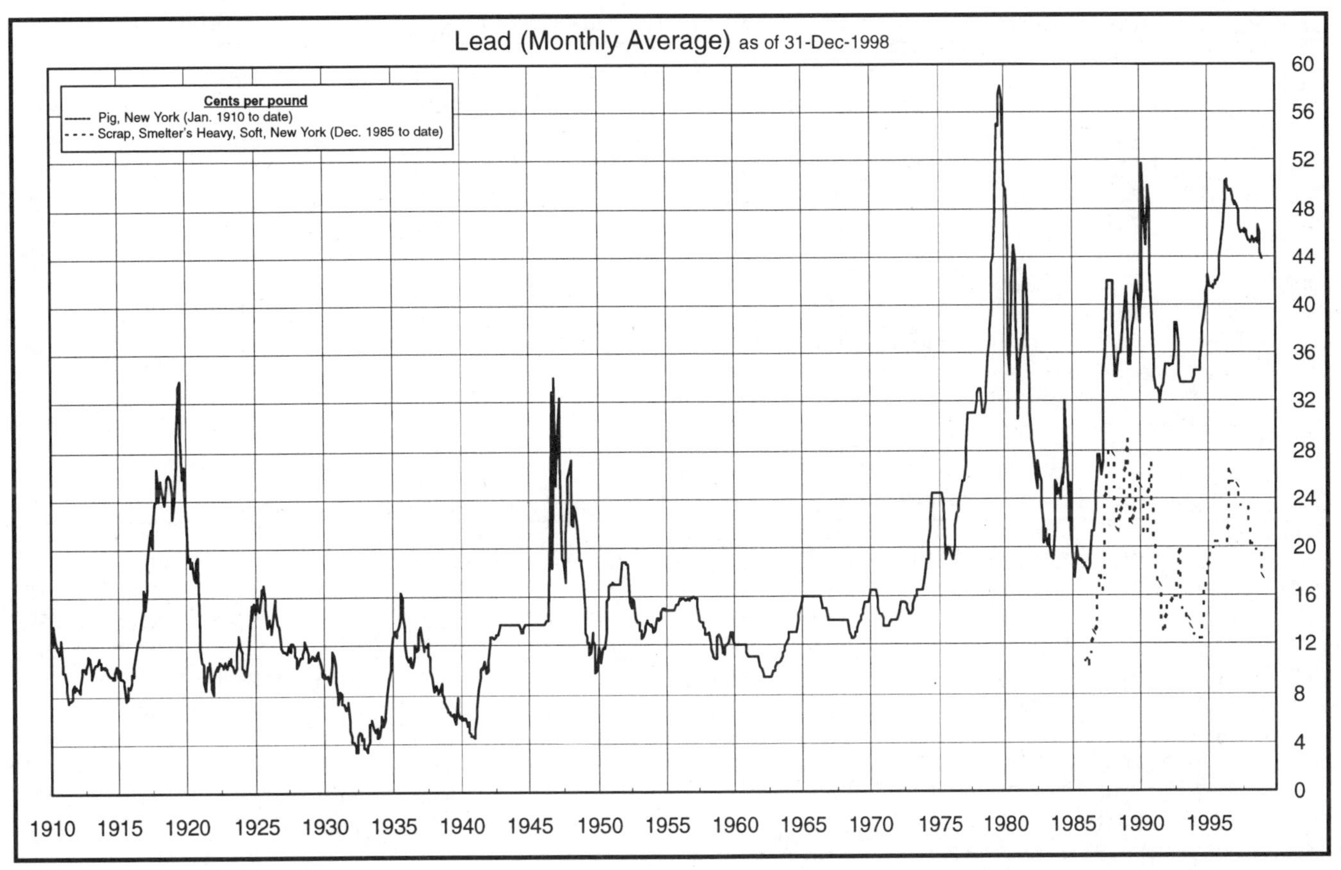

LEAD

Total Stocks of Lead[1] in the United States at Refiners, at End of Month In Metric Tons

Year	Jan.	Feb.	Mar.	Apr.	May	June	July	Aug.	Sept.	Oct.	Nov.	Dec.
1989	26,037	32,931	39,191	37,558	29,665	28,940	31,389	27,942	27,488	18,779	14,606	15,604
1990	14,697	18,325	16,420	21,138	19,323	19,596	20,775	19,958	20,593	23,769	22,771	25,492
1991	24,177	24,333	26,990	21,261	17,474	16,195	15,362	9,072	6,608	4,091	4,491	9,089
1992	9,774	15,785	21,682	25,220	28,940	26,490	26,634	22,347	17,736	14,971	14,796	20,543
1993	28,069	33,338	34,058	34,306	35,775	32,162	22,753	14,797	15,086	14,408	13,456	14,289
1994	11,964	12,633	12,048	11,445	11,598	10,251	12,368	9,256	8,897	10,659	9,060	9,271
1995	8,200	9,750	11,500	14,500	16,700	16,200	21,300	14,000	12,800	9,820	9,830	14,200
1996	15,000	15,000	15,000	15,000	15,000	19,600	19,900	14,200	12,200	7,060	7,830	8,160
1997	8,460	11,800	21,400	19,900	15,000	10,900	6,530	7,790	5,370	7,310	8,710	11,900
1998[2]	13,000	15,900	18,700	20,900	11,400	11,400	13,700	NA	NA	NA	NA	

[1] Primary refineries. [2] Preliminary. *Source: U.S. Geological Survey (USGS)*

Total[1] Lead Consumption in the United States In Thousands of Metric Tons

Year	Jan.	Feb.	Mar.	Apr.	May	June	July	Aug.	Sept.	Oct.	Nov.	Dec.	Total
1989	104.7	98.3	101.2	99.2	101.3	101.6	95.2	102.7	105.9	114.0	106.2	97.3	1,283
1990	104.1	106.7	111.9	101.1	106.2	103.2	97.7	112.4	104.6	109.0	104.3	97.3	1,275
1991	101.3	105.3	101.2	101.3	98.4	92.4	90.8	101.9	102.7	106.9	102.4	92.7	1,246
1992	102.5	99.3	108.3	98.5	96.0	103.5	94.8	104.8	106.6	105.4	98.2	92.9	1,215
1993	108.9	107.5	112.3	104.6	109.2	113.8	106.8	112.6	117.1	113.2	109.3	102.2	1,357
1994	107.0	115.2	112.8	111.6	113.5	115.2	114.3	115.5	115.9	121.2	118.7	113.0	1,384
1995	119.0	119.0	119.0	109.0	110.0	113.0	115.0	105.0	115.0	116.0	118.0	116.0	1,370
1996	107.0	100.0	106.0	111.0	113.0	106.0	104.0	146.0	140.0	147.0	163.0	143.0	1,530
1997	139.0	138.0	138.0	140.0	137.0	141.0	116.0	119.0	122.0	123.0	117.0	117.0	1,600
1998[2]	116.0	115.0	119.0	128.0	127.0	129.0	128.0	128.0	129.0	129.0	127.0		1,500

[1] Represents total consumption of primary and secondary lead as metal, in chemicals, or in alloys. [2] Preliminary. *Source: U.S. Bureau of Mines (USGS)*

Lead Recovered from Scrap in the United States In Thousands of Metric Tons (Lead Content)

Year	Jan.	Feb.	Mar.	Apr.	May	June	July	Aug.	Sept.	Oct.	Nov.	Dec.	Total
1989	62.1	58.6	67.5	64.1	65.3	66.3	61.6	65.9	64.4	73.5	67.1	66.9	808.6
1990	68.7	69.6	73.0	69.4	66.9	67.9	67.0	71.8	71.0	77.5	72.3	77.3	923.0
1991	79.0	74.4	71.0	72.0	72.0	70.7	69.8	70.0	72.3	74.6	70.7	75.9	883.7
1992	76.1	71.5	66.5	71.0	73.3	72.3	71.1	77.7	77.5	79.6	76.9	74.3	888.5
1993	71.1	76.8	71.7	80.2	78.9	72.5	70.3	76.6	76.3	77.0	77.9	79.3	903.6
1994	74.0	76.0	84.2	81.7	81.1	79.0	78.9	79.8	78.4	76.4	81.0	80.4	949.0
1995	82.5	80.8	84.4	72.8	73.7	72.5	79.9	71.5	82.3	80.0	82.3	82.1	945.0
1996	75.7	76.2	84.2	83.7	84.7	80.7	81.2	89.0	92.1	98.8	97.3	93.2	1,100.0
1997	88.0	89.8	91.7	86.0	88.2	85.7	86.7	94.7	97.3	96.2	95.2	91.7	1,110.0
1998[1]	95.0	92.0	92.6	94.1	92.5	89.7	89.3	95.7	94.4	95.0	93.0		1,116.3

[1] Preliminary. *Source: U.S. Geological Survey (USGS)*

Domestic Shipments[1] of Lead in the United States, by Refiners In Thousands of Short Tons

Year	Jan.	Feb.	Mar.	Apr.	May	June	July	Aug.	Sept.	Oct.	Nov.	Dec.	Total
1988	33.5	29.5	39.2	33.0	41.4	44.7	32.0	34.7	33.7	43.0	38.5	35.5	438.7
1989	29.3	28.5	32.2	35.7	45.1	36.4	32.8	41.5	40.0	44.2	40.2	31.1	437.1
1990	39.3	33.9	39.1	33.5	38.4	32.9	32.6	38.9	36.6	38.9	37.9	31.7	433.7
1991	35.4	33.8	34.3	39.8	33.9	26.0	31.8	37.9	35.1	35.7	28.7	26.7	399.2
1992	31.3	23.9	30.4	26.3	25.6	27.2	27.3	28.7	26.3	28.5	26.3	21.7	323.5
1993	24.6	23.6	32.5	30.0	31.3	35.1	28.9	34.0	35.5	35.5	31.7	33.5	376.2
1994	35.9	32.8	35.2	32.7	34.7	36.7	31.6	33.4	34.8	34.3	34.0	33.3	409.3
1995	36.5	30.3	35.1	31.1	33.7	31.9	28.6	40.3	34.9	40.9	33.2	29.8	406.4
1996	37.2	32.4	29.5	30.2	29.4	26.7	27.7	33.5	30.1	33.5	28.1	27.6	366.0
1997[2]	31.5	27.8	24.7	35.2	39.2	36.1	33.4	29.4	26.4	31.5	30.4	28.1	377.8

[1] Includes GSA metal. *Source: American Metal Market (AMM)*

Lumber & Plywood

A strong U.S. economy and lower interest rates have resulted in an increase in housing starts which in turn has increased softwood lumber consumption. Through the first seven months of 1998, consumption of softwood lumber in the U.S. increased 1.4 percent from the same period of 1997. Total softwood lumber consumption in the period was 30.4 billion board feet compared to 30 billion board feet in 1997. It would appear that unless there is a severe downturn in the economy, softwood lumber consumption will set a new modern day record. What is interesting is that actual U.S. production of softwood lumber in the first seven months of 1998 was lower which implies that imports were higher. While U.S. lumber production was lower, structural panel production was higher. Shipments of particle board were also higher. As U.S. imports of lumber increased, exports of lumber and wood products declined rather substantially led by a steep decline in shipments to the Pacific Rim.

U.S. softwood lumber production in July 1998 was 3.05 billion board feet, about the same level as the month before but some 2 percent less than a year ago. In the Southern Pine region, production in July 1998 was 1.4 billion board feet, down 6 percent from the level in June 1998. Softwood lumber production in July 1998 in the West Coast region was 706 million board feet, some 6 percent more than in the previous month. Production in the Inland region in July was 622 million board feet, virtually unchanged from the previous month. Production in the California Redwood region in July was 159 million board feet, some 23 percent more than the month before. Other softwood production was 166 million board feet, unchanged from the previous month. Total shipments of softwood lumber in July 1998 were 3.1 billion board feet, down 2 percent from the previous month. Shipments from the Southern Pine region in July 1998 were 1.41 billion board feet, down 5 percent from the month before. West Coast region softwood lumber shipments were 726 million board feet in July, an increase of almost 2 percent from the previous month. Inland region shipments were 618 million board feet, down 5 percent from June 1998. California Redwood region shipments were 176 million board feet, some 23 percent above the June 1998 total. Other softwood lumber shipments were 169 million board feet.

Orders received for softwood lumber in July 1998 were 3.12 billion board feet, down 4 percent from June 1998. Orders received from the Southern Pine region were 1.39 billion board feet, down 5 percent from June 1998. Orders received from the West Coast region were 735 million board feet, down 5 percent while orders received from the Inland region were 645 million board feet. Orders received from the California Redwood region were 176 million board feet while other softwood orders received were 170 million board feet.

At the end of July 1998, unfilled orders for softwood lumber from the West Coast region were 458 million board feet. Unfilled orders from the California Redwood region were 88 million board feet while unfilled orders from the Inland region were 325 million board feet. Gross stocks of softwood lumber at the end of July 1998 in the West Coast region were 681 million board feet. Gross stocks in the Inland region were 976 million board feet while stocks in the California Redwood region were 209 million board feet.

In the January-July 1998 period, total U.S. softwood lumber production was 20.3 billion board feet. That was down 1.7 percent from the same period in 1997. Softwood lumber production in the Southern Pine region in the first seven months of 1998 was 9.39 billion board feet. That was down 2.3 percent from the same period in 1997. Production in the West Coast region was 4.63 billion board feet which was down .1 percent from the year before. Inland region softwood lumber production was 4.28 billion board feet or some 2.1 percent less than in 1997. California Redwood region lumber production in the 1998 period was 921 million board feet, 2.6 percent less than in 1997. Other softwood production in the first seven months of 1998 was 1.11 billion board feet.

Maple flooring production in January-July 1998 was 14.04 million square feet, while structural panel production was 16.90 billion square feet.

Futures Markets

Lumber futures and options are traded on the Chicago Mercantile Exchange (CME). The CME also began trading an Oriented Strand Board contract late in 1996.

United States Housing Starts: Seasonally Adjusted Annual Rate In Thousands

Year	Jan.	Feb.	Mar.	Apr.	May	June	July	Aug.	Sept.	Oct.	Nov.	Dec.	Average
1989	1,621	1,425	1,422	1,339	1,331	1,397	1,427	1,332	1,279	1,410	1,351	1,251	1,382
1990	1,551	1,437	1,289	1,248	1,212	1,177	1,171	1,115	1,110	1,014	1,145	969	1,203
1991	798	965	921	1,001	996	1,036	1,063	1,049	1,015	1,079	1,103	1,079	1,009
1992	1,176	1,250	1,297	1,099	1,214	1,145	1,139	1,226	1,186	1,244	1,214	1,227	1,201
1993	1,210	1,210	1,083	1,258	1,260	1,280	1,254	1,300	1,343	1,392	1,376	1,533	1,292
1994	1,272	1,337	1,564	1,465	1,526	1,409	1,439	1,450	1,474	1,450	1,511	1,455	1,446
1995	1,383	1,325	1,246	1,278	1,309	1,294	1,464	1,404	1,378	1,382	1,451	1,404	1,360
1996	1,444	1,520	1,429	1,522	1,476	1,488	1,492	1,515	1,470	1,407	1,486	1,353	1,470
1997	1,394	1,547	1,477	1,480	1,404	1,502	1,461	1,383	1,501	1,529	1,523	1,540	1,478
1998[1]	1,545	1,616	1,585	1,546	1,538	1,620	1,704	1,621	1,579	1,694	1,662	1,720	1,619

[1] Preliminary. Total privately owned. *Source: Bureau of the Census, U.S. Department of Commerce*

LUMBER

World Production of Industrial Roundwood by Selected Countries In Thousands of Cubic Meters

Year	Austria	Canada	Czech[3] Republic	Finland	France	Germany	Japan	Poland	Russia[4]	Spain	Sweden	Turkey	United States
1989	13,575	170,625	16,856	42,670	34,276	41,806	31,202	18,980	305,300	15,691	51,430	5,728	416,900
1990	14,160	173,897	16,398	40,196	34,913	40,934	29,300	15,549	305,300	13,790	49,071	5,960	430,200
1991	12,535	159,039	13,770	31,616	33,754	29,823	27,938	14,334	275,300	12,988	47,600	5,502	388,310
1992	9,255	165,436	8,820	35,279	32,596	29,159	26,934	15,720	164,000	11,624	49,720	8,458	403,100
1993	9,107	173,133	9,706	37,758	29,563	29,357	25,570	15,940	136,030	11,419	50,200	9,408	401,520
1994	11,101	181,054	11,172	44,319	32,442	36,018	25,696	16,711	83,650	12,990	52,100	9,211	410,781
1995[1]	10,746	181,054	11,716	45,799	33,561	35,210	25,696	17,677	83,050	12,997	59,800	10,745	408,948
1996[2]			12,317	42,178				17,696	67,000		52,600	10,229	406,625

[1] Preliminary. [2] Estimate. [3] Formerly part of Czechoslovakia; data not reported separately until 1992. [4] Formerly part of the U.S.S.R.; data not reported separately until 1992. NA = Not available. *Source: Food and Agricultural Organization of the United Nations (FAO-UN)*

Lumber Production and Consumption in the United States In Millions of Board Feet

	Production						Domestic Consumption							
	Softwood						Softwood							
Year	California Redwood	Inland Region	Southern Pine	West Coast	Total	Total Hardwood	Inland Region	Southern Pine	West Coast	Softwood Imports	Total	U.S. Hardwood	Hardwood Imports	Total Lumber
1990	2,214	11,395	12,676	10,029	38,130	12,170	11,180	12,108	8,096	13,806	48,513	10,636	390	59,539
1991	2,053	11,348	12,544	9,811	37,545	12,415	11,134	12,125	7,950	13,638	47,966	11,970	375	60,311
1992	1,972	10,452	12,911	8,751	35,791	12,660	10,390	12,388	7,184	12,148	45,003	11,070	255	56,328
1993	1,657	9,510	12,507	7,908	33,161	11,633	9,302	12,147	6,454	11,742	42,225	10,278	226	52,730
1994	1,474	8,097	15,010	7,902	34,107	12,311	7,856	14,618	6,833	16,380	48,104	11,127	394	59,625
1995	1,305	7,015	14,708	7,452	32,233	12,434	6,956	14,384	6,530	17,396	47,749	11,372	380	59,501
1996	1,371	7,079	15,262	7,745	33,266	NA	7,073	15,112	6,821	18,214	49,883	11,235	511	62,304
1997[1]	1,511	7,383	16,113	7,772	34,667	NA	7,180	15,993	7,012	18,002	50,863	NA	NA	NA
I	383	1,825	3,874	1,914	8,456	NA	1,804	3,765	1,603	4,051	11,827	NA	NA	NA
II	425	1,915	4,239	2,041	9,117	NA	1,873	4,300	1,889	4,823	13,590	NA	NA	NA
III	399	1,911	4,154	1,978	8,928	NA	1,830	4,134	1,796	4,680	13,178	NA	NA	NA
IV	304	1,732	3,846	1,839	8,166	NA	1,673	3,794	1,724	4,448	12,268	NA	NA	NA
1998[1] I	381	1,833	3,851	1,947	8,473	NA	1,772	3,674	1,811	4,368	12,304	NA	NA	NA
II	381	1,829	4,143	1,976	8,807	NA	1,835	3,960	1,969	4,785	13,332	NA	NA	NA
III	453	1,853	4,017	2,080	8,886	NA	1,849	4,083	1,958	4,851	13,589	NA	NA	NA

[1] Preliminary. NA = not avaliable. *Source: American Forest & Paper Association (AF&PA)*

Stocks (Gross) of Softwood Lumber in the United States, on First of Month In Millions of Board Feet

Year	Jan.	Feb.	Mar.	Apr.	May	June	July	Aug.	Sept.	Oct.	Nov.	Dec.
1989	4,999	4,896	4,818	4,837	4,810	4,740	4,746	4,748	4,797	4,762	4,908	4,934
1990	4,898	5,022	5,022	5,020	4,961	5,043	4,831	4,783	4,752	4,810	4,834	4,809
1991	4,734	4,925	4,949	4,946	4,849	4,600	4,699	4,684	4,793	4,786	4,741	4,710
1992	4,616	4,603	4,567	4,608	4,730	4,731	4,678	4,606	4,418	4,419	4,365	4,263
1993	4,669	4,217	4,166	4,239	4,490	4,618	4,599	4,526	4,418	4,445	4,282	4,298
1994	4,207	4,512	4,656	4,816	4,883	4,649	4,738	4,432	4,349	4,539	4,235	4,294
1995	4,403	4,336	4,344	4,653	4,352	4,663	4,508	4,323	4,342	4,359	4,361	4,335
1996	4,293	4,435	4,459	4,357	4,251	4,153	4,156	4,038	3,918	3,965	3,939	3,906
1997	3,973	4,019	4,113	4,067	3,963	4,017	3,915	3,871	3,875	3,927	3,925	3,865
1998[1]	3,884	3,970	4,048	4,062	4,158	4,084	NA	NA	NA	NA	NA	

[1] Preliminary. *Source: American Forest & Paper Association (AF&PA)*

Lumber (Softwood)[2] Production in the United States In Millions of Board Feet

Year	Jan.	Feb.	Mar.	Apr.	May	June	July	Aug.	Sept.	Oct.	Nov.	Dec.	Total
1989	3,849	3,311	3,758	3,773	4,025	4,273	3,683	4,023	3,787	4,172	3,811	3,615	46,080
1990	4,160	3,862	4,300	4,121	4,084	3,944	3,976	4,060	3,602	4,015	3,412	2,914	46,450
1991	3,534	3,410	3,661	3,958	3,837	3,762	3,664	3,808	3,682	3,933	3,473	3,254	43,976
1992	3,836	3,628	4,121	3,862	3,632	3,911	3,882	3,746	3,736	4,048	3,617	3,425	45,444
1993	3,545	3,596	3,954	3,809	3,555	3,787	3,685	3,930	3,824	4,103	3,883	3,576	45,247
1994	3,839	3,662	4,097	3,735	3,972	4,113	3,785	4,124	4,135	4,145	3,636	3,851	47,094
1995	4,084	3,577	3,931	3,675	3,805	3,897	3,641	3,866	3,757	4,105	3,549	3,297	45,184
1996	2,600	2,606	2,757	2,903	2,833	2,819	2,942	3,077	2,858	3,179	2,758	2,424	33,756
1997	3,012	2,791	2,866	3,149	2,890	3,027	3,097	2,889	2,905	3,094	2,536	2,487	34,743
1998[1]	2,767	2,760	2,928	3,084	2,647	3,051	3,079	2,930	2,953	3,167	2,647		34,923

[1] Preliminary. [2] Data prior to 1996 are for Softwood and Hardwood. *Source: American Forest & Paper Association (AF&PA)*

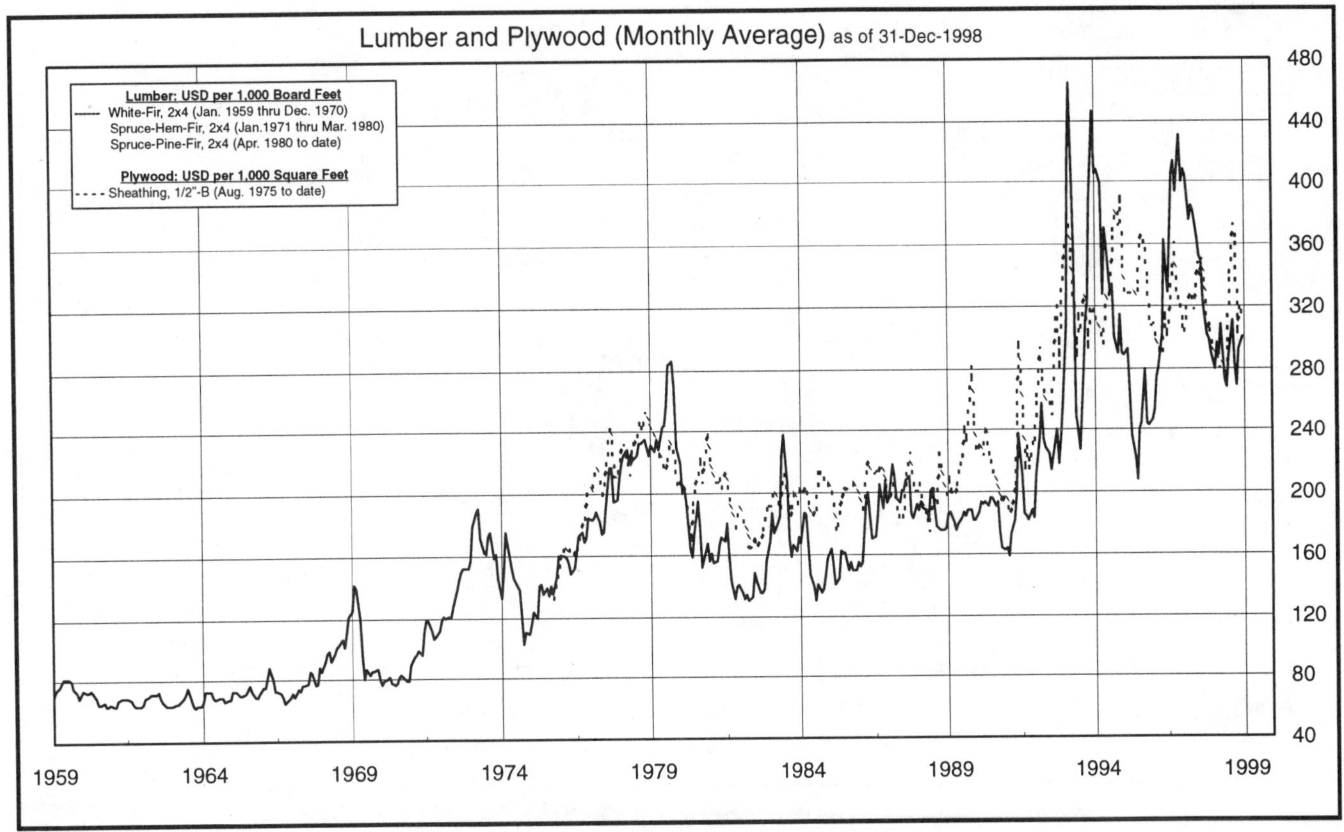

Lumber (Softwood)[2] Shipments in the United States In Millions of Board Feet

Year	Jan.	Feb.	Mar.	Apr.	May	June	July	Aug.	Sept.	Oct.	Nov.	Dec.	Total
1989	3,914	3,417	3,877	3,846	4,163	4,420	3,760	3,977	3,823	4,081	3,854	3,626	50,476
1990	4,035	3,870	4,317	4,173	3,952	4,176	3,912	3,987	3,453	3,890	3,357	2,873	47,773
1991	3,240	3,301	3,617	4,037	4,028	3,764	3,412	3,926	3,676	4,012	3,477	3,370	44,559
1992	3,912	3,693	4,078	3,682	3,565	3,936	3,884	3,878	3,692	4,147	3,745	3,491	45,703
1993	3,575	3,649	3,852	3,563	3,402	3,759	3,721	3,997	3,724	4,211	3,798	3,617	44,868
1994	3,576	3,663	3,912	3,761	4,192	4,091	4,039	4,163	3,914	4,321	3,603	3,696	46,931
1995	3,971	3,584	3,855	3,831	3,765	4,026	3,826	3,870	3,760	4,055	3,478	3,367	45,388
1996	2,460	2,581	2,863	3,002	2,934	2,813	3,058	3,196	2,813	3,206	2,792	2,353	34,071
1997	2,966	2,697	2,890	3,253	2,834	3,126	3,139	2,885	2,852	3,096	2,598	2,461	34,797
1998[1]	2,685	2,685	2,863	3,019	2,684	3,175	3,132	2,963	2,948	3,205	2,682		34,954

[1] Preliminary. [2] Data prior to 1996 are for Softwood and Hardwood. *Source: American Forest & Paper Association (AF&PA)*

Imports and Exports of Lumber in the United States, by Type In Millions of Board Feet

	Imports[2]								Exports[2]						
	Softwood								Softwood						
Year	Cedar	Douglas Fir	Hemlock	Pine	Spruce	Total	Total Hardwood	Total Lumber	Douglas Fir	Hemlock	Ponderosa/White Pine	Southern Pine	Total	Total Hardwood	Total Lumber
1989	786.0	603.4	469.5	335.8	7,387.4	13,638.4	375.1	14,022.5	1,018.2	670.9	197.0	442.3	3,319.1	856.0	4,213.1
1990	652.8	375.4	362.4	87.6	3,535.7	12,148.2	255.4	12,429.4	818.5	549.4	215.2	374.7	2,970.4	877.7	3,900.0
1991	700.6	354.1	287.8	55.7	2,248.3	11,741.5	226.2	11,998.2	798.1	497.7	222.9	396.0	2,863.2	934.3	3,858.9
1992	666.4	355.3	300.0	91.4	2,410.5	13,380.5	276.4	13,681.9	735.0	396.7	308.7	440.5	2,650.7	977.2	3,687.1
1993	615.3	327.6	354.9	84.6	3,104.1	15,259.9	335.0	15,625.4	664.9	340.4	273.3	339.6	2,376.4	1,008.9	3,468.9
1994	702.6	336.2	399.2	97.2	2,948.5	16,380.3	394.4	16,787.1	591.9	283.2	157.2	356.7	2,186.6	1,040.9	3,333.4
1995	768.0	395.4	258.1	97.1	2,827.7	17,395.3	379.7	17,786.9	637.9	227.0	106.7	334.6	1,987.5	1,100.5	3,189.5
1996	726.6	264.4	257.1	133.4	1,988.8	18,213.5	396.8	18,640.6	685.4	194.9	96.6	314.5	1,935.3	1,141.0	3,173.4
1997	586.1	263.9	249.8	314.2	1,040.4	18,014.3	464.5	18,505.9	435.8	104.6	122.1	299.3	1,820.0	1,281.4	3,189.0
1998[1] I	149.8	63.7	72.8	83.6	214.2	4,367.7	133.5	4,506.4	63.3	12.0	30.7	70.6	334.5	284.9	674.9
II	133.7	104.0	75.2	95.3	220.8	4,785.1	137.9	4,933.4	60.3	9.2	32.5	69.1	302.5	286.1	639.7
III	121.3	154.6	63.2	95.3	210.2	4,850.8	155.3	5,016.0	64.9	7.9	25.0	61.0	295.5	264.2	617.3

[1] Preliminary. [2] Includes sawed timber, board planks and scantings, flooring, box shook and railroad ties. *Source: American Forest & Paper Association*

Average Open Interest of Random Lumber[1] Futures in Chicago In Contracts

Year	Jan.	Feb.	Mar.	Apr.	May	June	July	Aug.	Sept.	Oct.	Nov.	Dec.
1989	7,982	7,484	7,436	8,244	7,363	7,921	8,248	8,055	7,065	7,192	6,600	6,167
1990	6,078	6,061	4,991	4,957	4,538	4,359	3,570	3,028	2,881	3,105	2,632	2,001
1991	1,922	2,003	2,023	2,354	2,076	2,601	2,571	2,181	2,276	2,480	2,206	1,606
1992	1,969	2,651	2,743	2,467	1,900	1,774	1,338	1,369	1,507	1,441	1,745	2,155
1993	2,194	2,432	2,163	2,055	2,302	2,658	2,254	2,141	2,011	2,080	2,140	2,721
1994	2,571	2,814	2,638	2,563	1,936	1,838	1,705	1,854	2,102	2,169	1,702	1,967
1995	1,757	1,923	2,142	2,509	2,742	3,252	2,896	2,918	2,809	3,039	2,626	2,940
1996	3,378	4,040	3,752	4,395	5,666	4,972	3,280	5,243	4,743	4,797	4,341	3,691
1997	3,745	3,211	3,048	3,337	2,895	3,137	2,767	3,119	3,267	4,006	3,606	4,068
1998	4,249	3,332	3,394	4,102	4,353	4,773	4,048	4,081	3,466	4,295	3,434	3,893

[1] Data July 1995 thru March 1996, Lumber and Random Lumber. *Source: Chicago Mercantile Exchange (CME)*

Volume of Trading of Random Lumber[1] Futures in Chicago In Contracts

Year	Jan.	Feb.	Mar.	Apr.	May	June	July	Aug.	Sept.	Oct.	Nov.	Dec.	Total
1989	29,963	25,857	23,947	31,427	26,789	26,712	20,258	19,514	18,790	18,965	17,286	14,395	273,903
1990	27,416	21,914	20,948	18,362	19,053	16,084	16,465	13,446	8,914	11,839	15,794	11,749	201,984
1991	10,535	13,460	10,326	11,309	15,135	19,029	19,350	14,912	12,214	14,054	10,295	9,902	160,521
1992	17,073	16,778	17,557	13,713	14,059	13,807	12,177	13,043	12,127	11,261	11,514	17,425	170,534
1993	14,915	15,080	14,808	14,661	14,241	15,308	13,287	13,358	12,400	13,248	18,150	18,728	178,184
1994	16,837	15,204	17,323	17,380	14,996	14,348	11,542	13,327	14,856	13,032	10,997	13,121	172,963
1995	12,150	12,909	15,088	12,139	14,536	20,126	13,766	16,919	15,718	18,981	15,551	14,803	182,686
1996	22,954	19,960	20,956	27,094	28,271	26,100	19,302	27,792	31,982	32,042	25,236	22,525	304,214
1997	28,561	20,946	21,071	24,624	18,248	24,797	20,308	18,503	21,736	24,416	15,131	21,977	260,318
1998	19,556	20,339	20,881	24,673	20,519	24,112	21,763	20,453	19,412	19,578	22,002	16,559	249,847

[1] Data July 1995 thru March 1996, Lumber and Random Lumber. *Source: Chicago Mercantile Exchange (CME)*

Production of Plywood by Selected Countries In Thousands of Cubic Meters

Year	Austria	Canada	Finland	France	Germany	Italy	Japan	Poland	Romania	Russia[3]	Spain	Sweden	United States
1992	150	1,838	462	484	429	427	5,954	132	100	1,268	120	55	17,109
1993	150	1,824	621	460	416	415	5,263	133	100	1,042	200	73	17,093
1994	150	1,834	700	594	397	427	4,865	124	97	890	210	85	17,380
1995	150	1,831	778	559	498	418	4,865	115	83	939	210	108	17,140
1996	150	1,814	869	470	507	418	NA	112	83	930	125	117	18,640
1997[1]	150	1,830	960	510	500	400	NA	115	90	930	125	116	17,709
1998[2]	150	1,825	980	530	520	400	NA	120	90	950	125	116	17,190

[1] Preliminary. [2] Estimate. [3] Formerly part of the U.S.S.R.; data not reported separately until 1992. NA = Not available.
Source: Food and Agricultural Organization of the United Nations (FAO-UN)

Imports of Plywood by Selected Countries In Thousands of Cubic Meters

Year	Austria	Belgium	Canada	Denmark	France	Germany	Italy	Japan	Netherlands	Sweden	Switzerland	United Kingdom	United States
1992	79	300	242	198	423	879	216	3,003	583	106	110	1,397	1,649
1993	77	436	288	152	263	865	241	4,105	612	98	118	1,157	1,630
1994	104	267	288	171	234	1,003	257	4,074	560	126	144	1,202	1,547
1995	116	146	353	188	260	1,177	323	4,074	552	112	136	1,127	1,769
1996	130	275	167	193	262	1,549	300	NA	524	135	129	1,743	1,570
1997[1]	130	250	200	195	277	1,000	300	NA	524	137	130	1,750	1,751
1998[2]	130	250	200	200	277	1,100	300	NA	524	137	130	1,750	1,746

[1] Preliminary. [2] Estimate. NA = Not available. *Source: Food and Agricultural Organization of the United Nations (FAO-UN)*

Exports of Plywood by Selected Countries In Thousands of Cubic Meters

Year	Austria	Baltic States[3]	Belgium	Canada	Finland	France	Germany	Italy	Netherlands	Poland	Russia[3]	Spain	United States
1992	119	25	132	412	348	228	122	90	72	56	226	32	1,618
1993	129	90	87	416	542	194	110	104	99	41	464	60	1,562
1994	158	143	134	511	627	193	131	108	102	66	568	67	1,346
1995	130	138	88	818	668	183	149	96	72	60	670	48	1,395
1996	120	151	100	646	772	216	133	90	58	60	612	40	1,605
1997[1]	120	NA	90	625	850	246	110	100	58	55	630	40	1,805
1998[2]	120	NA	90	635	860	246	110	100	58	50	650	40	2,027

[1] Preliminary. [2] Estimate. [3] Formerly part of the U.S.S.R.; data not reported separately until 1992. NA = Not available. *Source: Food and Agricultural Organization of the United Nations (FAO-UN)*

Selected World Prices of Plywood

Year	Jan.	Feb.	Mar.	Apr.	May	June	July	Aug.	Sept.	Oct.	Nov.	Dec.	Average
Southeast Asia, Lauan, Wholesale Price, Spot Tokyo In U.S. Cents Per Sheet[1]													
1994	564.97	600.26	617.10	647.05	637.21	629.58	649.70	630.99	566.50	567.91	562.70	539.99	601.16
1995	551.01	599.11	656.48	665.11	635.41	627.00	562.66	560.56	527.43	526.55	539.65	540.20	582.60
1996	529.12	548.59	529.22	521.11	535.48	523.62	521.39	538.27	528.50	525.09	526.22	518.62	528.77
1997	500.31	479.63	489.39	485.57	511.91	524.85	512.10	500.68	480.05	454.68	438.61	424.25	483.50
1998	409.19	413.35	387.32	371.74	363.05	356.51							383.53
Canada, Export Unit Value, F.O.B. In Canadian Dollar Per Cubic Meter													
1992	426.14	409.62	373.22	396.94	387.59	395.95	354.61	373.58	385.20	395.29	410.59	353.95	388.56
1993	392.59	396.65	393.73	424.19	515.51	448.76	408.39	435.72	505.58	517.58	494.52	476.08	450.78
1994	442.04	574.74	553.92	553.81	542.95	458.48	472.29	510.01	526.42	454.20	462.90	499.71	504.29
1995	473.77	480.78											477.28
Finland, Export Unit Value, F.O.B. In Markka Per Cubic Meter													
1994	3,758	3,518	3,829	3,822	3,800	4,029	3,963	3,916	4,041	3,680	3,631	3,569	3,796
1995	3,681	3,809	3,751	3,897	3,752	3,769	3,771	3,543	3,430	3,370	3,268	2,923	3,579
1996	3,084	2,548	3,129	3,296	3,075	3,225	3,070	3,003	3,245	3,036	3,264	2,900	3,060
1997	3,021	2,943	3,032	3,157	3,174	3,336	3,220	3,222	3,321	3,408	3,465	3,563	3,235
United Kingdom, Import Unit Value, C.I.F. In Pound Sterling Per Cubic Meter													
1994	256.36	252.50	263.47	299.61	291.19	209.08	275.85	272.06	294.44	276.46	213.94	247.54	262.71
1995	232.68	239.77	257.68	264.72	229.18	268.11	256.09	241.61	263.31	285.36	275.38	282.68	258.05
1996	238.86	249.65	224.40	273.23	256.16	275.38	269.36	247.83	253.37	261.66	260.77	293.42	258.67
1997	235.57	234.39	340.66	378.17	274.27	256.75	248.45	276.09	268.64	277.69	270.27	294.06	262.92

[1] Sheet measurement = 1.2cm X 90.0cm X 1.8cm. *Source: Food and Agricultural Organization of the United Nations (FAO-UN)*

Magnesium

Magnesium has a density that is two-thirds that of aluminum. Because of that property, magnesium finds widespread use in aircraft and automobile parts, photo optical instruments, engines, luggage, water heaters and dry-cell batteries. Among the magnesium compounds, magnesium sulfate is used in explosives, fertilizers and paper production. Magnesium oxide is used in water treatment, household cleaners and pharmaceuticals.

Magnesium is an extremely abundant element in the Earth's crust. It is the third most plentiful element dissolved in seawater. Magnesium metal can be recovered from seawater as well as lake brines. World primary production of magnesium in 1997 was 392,000 tonnes, up 7 percent from 1996. The U.S. is the largest producer of magnesium with primary production in 1997 at 125,000 tonnes, down 6 percent from 1996. The next largest producer was China with 92,000 tonnes of output in 1997, an increase of 26 percent from a year ago. Russian production was 39,500 tonnes or some 13 percent more than in 1996. Other large producers include France, the Ukraine and Brazil. Global secondary production of magnesium in 1997 was 106,000 tonnes, up 6 percent from 1996. The U.S. is the largest secondary magnesium producer in the world with 1997 production of 80,200 tonnes. That represented a 14 percent increase from 1996. The next largest producer was Japan with 22,797 tonnes in 1997, up 7 percent from 1996.

U.S. imports of magnesium metal in May 1998 were 942 tonnes. That was down substantially from the April import total of 2,410 tonnes. In the January-May 1998 period, imports of magnesium metal were 12,100 tonnes. For all of 1997, imports of metal were 19,700 tonnes. Imports of magnesium waste and scrap in May 1998 were 531 tonnes, down 16 percent from the previous month. In the January-May period, imports of waste and scrap were 2,830 tonnes. For all of 1997, imports were 3,990 tonnes. Imports of alloys (magnesium content) in May 1998 were 3,060 tonnes, down 25 percent from April. In the January-May 1998 period, magnesium alloy imports were 18,100 tonnes. For all of 1997, alloy imports were 41,000 tonnes. Total U.S. magnesium imports in the first five months of 1998 were 33,300 tonnes. For all of 1997 they were 65,100 tonnes.

U.S. exports of magnesium metal in May 1998 were 1,510 tonnes, down 26 percent from the previous month. In the January-May 1998 period, metal exports were 6,550 tonnes while for all of 1997 they were 17,100 tonnes. Magnesium waste and scrap exports in January-May 1998 were 5,230 tonnes and for 1997 were 11,200 tonnes. Alloy exports in the January-May 1998 period were 5,820 tonnes while in 1997 they were 9,180 tonnes. Total exports in the first five months of 1998 were 18,100 tonnes while for all of 1997, U.S. magnesium exports were 40,500 tonnes.

World Production of Magnesium (Primary and Secondary) In Metric Tons

	Primary Production								Secondary Production				
Year	Brazil	Canada	China	France	Norway	Russia[4]	United States	World Total	Japan	United Kingdom	United States	Former USSR	World Total
1988	5,865	7,600	3,200	13,776	50,317	91,000	141,983	334,348	15,099	1,000	50,207	8,000	75,825
1989	6,200	7,000	3,500	14,600	49,827	91,000	152,066	344,447	20,270	1,000	51,200	8,000	81,970
1990	8,700	25,300	5,900	14,000	48,222	88,000	139,333	354,000	23,308	900	54,808	7,500	88,100
1991	7,800	35,512	8,600	14,050	44,322	80,000	131,288	342,000	17,158	800	50,543	7,000	77,100
1992	7,300	25,800	10,600	13,660	30,404	40,000	137,000	295,000	12,978	800	57,000	6,500	78,900
1993	9,700	23,000	11,800	10,982	27,300	30,000	132,000	269,000	13,215	1,000	58,900	6,000	80,700
1994	9,700	28,900	24,000	12,280	27,635	35,400	128,000	282,000	19,009	1,000	62,100	5,000	88,700
1995	9,700	48,100	93,600	14,450	28,000	37,500	142,000	395,000	11,767	1,000	65,100	6,000	85,500
1996[1]	9,000	54,000	73,100	14,000	28,000	35,000	133,000	368,000	21,243	1,000	70,200	6,000	100,000
1997[2]	9,000	5,770	92,000	12,000	28,000	39,500	125,000	392,000	22,797	1,000	80,200	NA	106,000

[1] Preliminary. [2] Estimate. [4] Formerly part of the U.S.S.R.; data not reported separately until 1992. *Source: U.S. Geological Survey (USGS)*

Salient Statistics of Magnesium in the United States In Metric Tons

	Production								Domestic Consumption of Primary Magnesium					
		Secondary							Structural Products					
Year	Primary (Ingot)	New Scrap	Old Scrap	Total	Exports[3]	Imports for Consumption	Stocks Dec. 31[4]	$ Price per Pound[5]	Castings	Wrought	Total	Aluminum Alloys	Other Uses[6]	Total
1988	141,983	22,567	27,640	50,207	49,802	14,407	25,000	1.58-1.63	7,069	10,138	17,207	53,671	29,915	100,793
1989	152,066	23,229	27,971	51,200	56,631	12,289	26,000	1.63	7,455	9,653	17,108	53,821	34,297	88,118
1990	139,333	23,424	31,384	54,808	51,834	26,755	26,000	1.43-1.63	9,078	10,944	20,022	45,060	31,026	76,086
1991	131,288	23,059	27,484	50,543	55,160	31,863	27,000	1.43	8,857	8,802	17,659	45,809	28,404	74,213
1992	136,947	26,191	30,854	57,045	51,951	11,844	13,000	1.46-1.53	10,223	8,843	19,066	41,003	33,758	74,761
1993	132,144	28,313	30,577	58,890	38,815	37,248	26,000	1.43-1.46	12,543	9,870	22,413	46,498	32,202	78,700
1994	128,000	32,500	29,600	62,100	45,200	29,100	20,030	1.63	15,676	7,690	23,366	61,100	27,900	89,000
1995	142,000	35,400	29,800	65,100	38,300	34,800	21,193	1.93-2.25	15,231	8,510	23,741	60,200	25,100	85,300
1996[1]	133,000	41,100	30,100	71,200	40,500	46,600	25,000	1.70-1.80	16,400	8,080	24,480	52,300	25,500	77,800
1997[2]	125,000	49,700	30,500	80,200	40,500	65,100	23,000	1.60-1.70	20,679	6,840	27,519	50,000	23,000	73,000

[1] Preliminary. [2] Estimate. [3] Metal & alloys in crude form & scrap. [4] Estimate of Industry Stocks, metal. [5] Magnesium (99.8%), F.O.B. Valasco, Texas. [6] Distributive or sacrificial purposes. *Source: U.S. Geological Survey (USGS)*

Manganese

Manganese is primarily used in the steel industry as an alloy. Manganese increases the metal's hardness so virtually all steel contains some manganese. Manganese is essential in iron and steel production because of its sulfur-fixing, deoxidizing and alloying properties. Steelmaking accounts for most of the demand for manganese though it finds use in aluminum alloys and is used in oxide form in dry cell batteries. Manganese also finds use in plant fertilizers and animal feeds. Manganese ore, when converted to a metallic alloy with iron, forms the compound ferromanganese.

1997 manganese ore world production was estimated at 7.68 million metric tonnes (metal content). That represents a 5 percent decline from 1996. For 1997, the world's largest producer of manganese ore was China with 1.4 million tonnes, down 8 percent from the previous year. South Africa produced 1.32 million tonnes followed by the Ukraine with 1.03 million tonnes and Australia with 1.02 million tonnes.

U.S. imports for consumption of manganese in June 1998 were 60,800 tonnes, manganese content. Of the total, 16,400 tonnes were in the form of manganese ore and manganese dioxide; another 44,400 tonnes were in the form of manganese ferroalloy and manganese metal. In June 1997, manganese imports were 41,400 tonnes. In the Jan-June 1998 period, U.S. imports of manganese were 354,000 tonnes. Of the total, 82,100 tonnes were manganese ore and manganese dioxide, and 271,000 tonnes were ferroalloy and manganese metal. In the first half of 1997 U.S. imports were 263,000 tonnes.

U.S. imports of silicomanganese in June 1998 were 27,500 tonnes, gross weight, with 18,300 tonnes manganese content. In the first half of 1998, silicomanganese imports were 193,000 tonnes, gross weight, with 128,000 tonnes manganese content. The major suppliers of silicomanganese to the U.S. in the first half of 1998 were South Africa, Australia, India and Mexico. Together they supply about 70 percent of the U.S. requirements.

U.S. imports for consumption of ferromanganese in June 1998 were 31,600 tonnes, gross weight, with 24,600 tonnes manganese content. Of the total, low carbon manganese was 904 tonnes, gross weight, 811 tonnes manganese content. Medium carbon manganese imports in June 1998 were 5,680 tonnes, gross weight, with 4,560 tonnes manganese content. High carbon ferromanganese imports in June 1998 were 25,000 tonnes, gross weight, 193,00 tonnes manganese content. In the Jan-June 1998 period, U.S. imports or ferromanganese were 174,000 tonnes, gross weight, 136,000 tonnes manganese content. The major suppliers of low carbon ferromanganese were Italy and Japan, of medium carbon Mexico and Japan, and of high carbon South Africa, France and Australia.

World Production of Manganese Ore — In Thousands of Metric Tons (Gross Weight)

Year	Australia[2] 37-53[4]	Brazil 30-50	China 30	Gabon 50-53	Georgia[5] 29-30	Ghana 30-50	Hungary[3] 30-33	India 10-54	Mexico 27-50	Morocco 50-53	South Africa 30-48 +	Ukraine[5] 29-30	World Total
1988	1,985	1,991	3,212	2,254	-----	260	81	1,333	444	30	4,023	9,108	25,013
1989	2,124	1,904	3,200	2,592	-----	297	84	1,334	394	32	4,884	9,141	26,260
1990	1,920	2,300	4,080	2,423	-----	247	60	1,385	451	49	4,402	8,500	26,108
1991	1,412	2,000	5,150	1,620	-----	320	30	1,401	254	59	3,146	7,240	22,900
1992	1,251	1,703	5,300	1,556	500	276	18	1,810	407	44	2,464	5,819	21,800
1993	2,092	1,837	5,860	1,290	300	295	59	1,655	363	43	2,507	3,800	20,800
1994	1,920	2,199	3,570	1,436	150	270	55	1,632	307	31	2,851	2,979	18,000
1995	2,177	2,398	6,900	1,930	100	217	-----	1,764	472	-----	3,199	3,200	23,300
1996	2,109	2,506	7,600	1,980	97	266	-----	1,797	485	-----	3,240	3,070	24,100
1997[1]	2,136	2,000	7,000	1,900	-----	300	-----	1,800	534	-----	3,112	3,040	22,700

[1] Preliminary. [2] Metallurgical Ore. [3] Concentrate. [4] Range of percentage of manganese. [5] Formerly part of the U.S.S.R.; data not reported separately until 1992. *Source: U.S. Geological Survey (USGS)*

Salient Statistics of Manganese in the United States — In Thousands of Metric Tons (Gross Weight)

Year	Net Import Reliance as a % of Apparent Consumption	Manganese Ore (35% or More Manganese): Imports for Consumption	Exports	Consumption	Stocks, Dec. 31[3]	Ferromanganese: Imports for Consumption	Exports	Consumption	Avg. Price Mn. Metallurgical Ore $ Lg. Ton Unit[4]	Silicomanganese: Exports	Imports
1988	100	464	62	503	415	482	3	425	1.75	8.3	256.0
1989	100	580	52	559	470	432	8	399	2.76	6.5	281.5
1990	100	307	70	497	379	380	7	413	3.78	1.8	224.5
1991	100	234	66	473	275	320	15	346	3.72	2.9	258.3
1992	100	247	13	438	276	304	13	339	3.25	9.2	257.2
1993	100	232	16	389	302	347	18	341	2.60	9.4	316.0
1994	100	331	15	449	269	336	11	347	2.40	6.8	273.0
1995	100	394	15	486	309	310	11	348	2.40	7.8	305.0
1996[1]	100	478	32	478	319	374	10	326	2.55	5.3	323.0
1997[2]	100	357	84	510	275	304	12	337	2.44	5.4	306.0

[1] Preliminary. [2] Estimate. [3] Including bonded warehouses; excludes Government stocks; also excludes small tonnages of dealers' stocks. [4] 46-48% Mn, C.I.F., U.S. Ports. *Source: U.S. Geological Survey (USGS)*

MANGANESE

Imports[3] of Manganese Ore (20% or More Mn) in the United States In Metric Tons (Mn Content)

Year	Australia	Brazil	Gabon	Mexico	Morocco	South Africa	Total	Customs Value Thous. $
1988[4]	35,675	24,498	133,045	32,197	85	-----	225,499	29,074
1989	54,828	84,626	99,463	8,916	18	19,612	270,786	43,794
1990	32,544	20,662	67,828	2,732	18	9,958	148,944	40,054
1991	16,485	2,583	79,997	4,673	44	-----	117,255	40,332
1992	25,519	15,541	75,354	3,930	56	-----	120,400	29,967
1993	30,171	5,573	66,659	7,317	43	6,006	115,770	24,927
1994	23,200	4,530	112,000	13,700	56	7,780	161,000	29,800
1995	31,600	7,080	104,000	23,600	37	13,100	187,000	33,300
1996[1]	48,900	5,640	140,000	16,100	9	20,800	231,000	42,400
1997[2]	17,200	9,100	99,500	30,100	37	-----	156,000	30,900

[1] Preliminary. [2] Estimate. [3] Imports for consumption. [4] Manganese content of 35% or more prior to 1989. *Source: U.S. Geological Survey (USGS)*

Average Price of Ferromanganese[1] (High Carbon - F.O.B. Plant) In Dollars Per Gross Ton -- Carloads

Year	Jan.	Feb.	Mar.	Apr.	May	June	July	Aug.	Sept.	Oct.	Nov.	Dec.	Average
1988	382.50	382.50	414.50	422.50	435.63	440.00	457.50	475.00	530.00	550.00	550.00	550.00	465.84
1989	550.00	550.50	573.75	597.50	640.00	640.00	640.00	634.00	610.00	610.00	610.00	610.00	605.48
1990	610.00	610.00	610.00	610.00	610.00	610.00	610.00	610.00	610.00	610.00	610.00	610.00	610.00
1991	610.00	610.00	610.00	610.00	610.00	610.00	610.00	610.00	610.00	610.00	610.00	610.00	610.00
1992	610.00	610.00	610.00	610.00	610.00	610.00	610.00	610.00	610.00	610.00	610.00	610.00	610.00
1993	610.00	610.00	610.00	610.00	610.00	610.00	610.00	610.00	610.00	610.00	610.00	610.00	610.00
1994	610.00	610.00	610.00	610.00	610.00	527.50	500.00	500.00	500.00	500.00	500.00	500.00	548.13
1995	500.00	500.00	500.00	500.00	500.00	500.00	500.00	518.75	525.00	525.00	542.50	560.00	514.27
1996	560.00	552.50	550.00	550.00	541.00	535.00	533.13	527.50	527.50	527.50	501.25	477.50	531.91
1997	477.50	467.50	470.00	482.50	490.00	490.00	490.00	492.50	475.00	475.00	475.00	475.00	480.00

[1] Domestic standard. *Source: American Metal Market (AMM)*

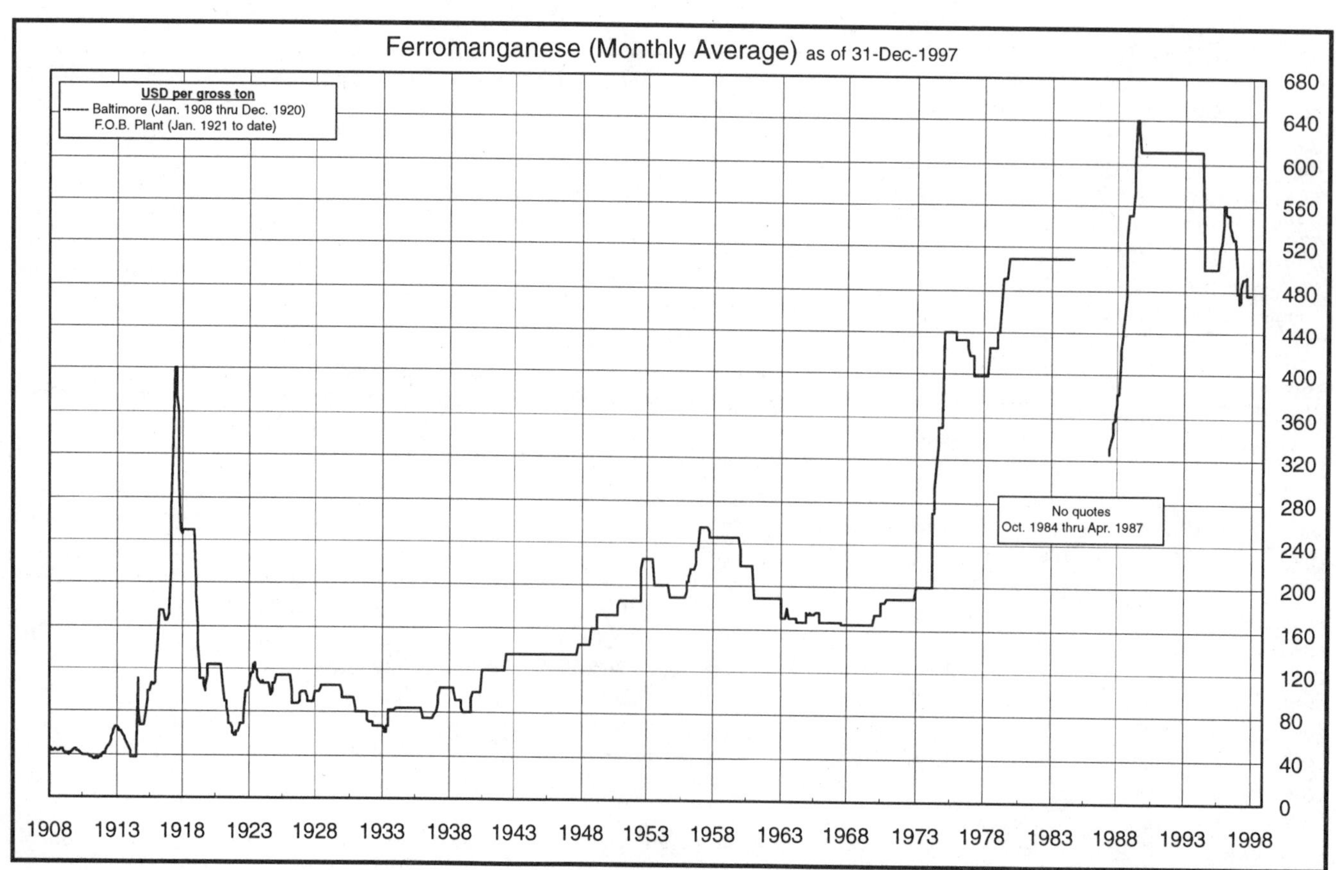

Meats

U.S. commercial red meat production--the combined total of beef, veal, lamb and pork output--jumped nearly 20 percent in the first half of 1998, to 29.7 billion pounds from 24.8 billion a year earlier, easily suggesting a record high output for the year. Red meat accounts for nearly 60 percent of total U.S. meat production with the balance from poultry. The combined red meat and poultry half year total of 52 billion pounds in 1998 compares with 44.1 billion in 1997 with beef production in that time frame of 17.2 billion pounds comparing with 14.8 billion in 1997 and pork production of 12.2 billion pounds vs. 9.6 billion, respectively. Initial estimates for 1998 placed beef output at 24.8 billion pounds and pork at 18.5 billion; beef is apt to be much higher and pork about on target. U.S. veal and lamb production are insignificant.

Worldwide, China is the largest red meat producer at 50 million metric tonnes, most of it pork; in 1998, Chinese production accounted for almost one-third of the world total with the U.S. second with less than one-half of China's output. The slide in red meat production from the former U.S.S.R. still shows little sign of abating, estimated at only 5.5 million tonnes in 1998 vs. almost 6 million in 1997.

U.S. per capita beef consumption (retail weight) in 1998 of 68.5 pounds compares with 66.9 in 1997 and a forecast of 63.2 pounds in 1999. Pork use of 52 pounds compares with 48.7 in 1997 and 53.6 pounds forecast for 1999. The gain in pork use partially reflects the aggressive advertising campaign by the pork industry associating pork as a white meat instead of a red meat. The beef industry's advertising campaign focuses on the ease (timewise) of preparing beef for dinner. For both meats, however, consumer preferences have shifted to foods containing less fat which has benefited poultry at red meat's expense; per capita retail broiler and turkey consumption totaled 90.1 pounds in 1998 and are forecast at 92.9 pounds in 1999.

Choice steers (basis Nebraska) averaged $61-65/cwt. in 1998 vs. $66.32 in 1997; forecasts for 1999 are from $71 to $76. Midwest barrow prices of $34-36/cwt. in 1998 compare with $51.36 in 1997 and estimates for 1999 of $34-37/cwt., which if realized is another reason for the anticipated increase in per capita pork use, relative to beef.

U.S. red meat imports in 1998 of 3.2 billion pounds compares with 3 billion in 1997 and forecasts of 3.3 billion in 1999 with beef imports accounting for about 80 percent of the totals. U.S. red meat exports, again mostly beef, totaled 3.4 billion pounds in 1998 vs. 3.2 billion in 1997 and a 1999 forecast of 3.5 billion pounds. Japan is the major importer of U.S. red meat. The U.S. imports live cattle from Canada and Mexico and beef and veal from Australia and New Zealand.

World Total Meat Production[3] In Thousands of Metric Tons

Year	Argentina	Australia	Brazil	Canada	China[4]	France	Germany	Italy	Mexico	Russia[5]	United Kingdom	United States	World Total
1990	2,738	2,683	4,650	2,022	25,132	3,816	6,111	2,583	2,658	8,204	2,331	17,597	120,078
1991	2,735	2,704	5,513	2,022	27,238	3,963	5,552	2,608	2,535	7,526	2,389	17,956	121,244
1992	2,602	2,810	5,620	2,107	29,406	3,997	4,994	2,648	2,626	6,748	2,297	18,589	116,309
1993	2,630	2,780	5,795	2,052	32,254	3,901	4,796	2,642	2,718	6,260	2,236	18,488	115,852
1994	2,682	2,807	5,850	2,137	36,968	3,868	5,092	2,618	2,852	5,659	2,323	19,361	123,388
1995	2,668	2,644	7,530	2,204	42,653	3,941	5,053	2,602	2,942	4,860	2,359	19,812	130,280
1996	2,636	2,650	7,750	2,226	47,721	3,973	5,161	2,668	2,832	4,597	2,088	19,634	135,364
1997	2,622	2,912	7,590	2,331	50,500	4,046	5,053	2,631	2,891	4,020	2,189	19,667	137,720
1998[1]	2,285	2,894	7,743	2,415	52,700	4,055	5,137	2,652	2,906	3,611	2,254	20,410	141,022
1999[2]	2,353	2,863	7,880	2,475	52,700	4,034	5,231	2,632	2,910	3,449	2,195	19,942	141,022

[1] Preliminary. [2] Forecast. [3] Includes beef, veal, pork, sheep and goat meat. [4] Predominately pork production. [5] Formerly part of the U.S.S.R.; data not reported separately until 1990. *Source: Foreign Agricultural Service, U.S. Department of Agriculture (FAS-USDA)*

Production and Consumption of Red Meats in the United States (Carcass Weight)

	Beef			Veal			Lamb & Mutton			Pork (Excluding Lard)			All Meats		
	Commercial Production	Consumption Total	Consumption Per Capita	Commercial Production	Consumption Total	Consumption Per Capita	Commercial Production	Consumption Total	Consumption Per Capita	Commercial Production	Consumption Total	Consumption Per Capita	Commercial Production	Consumption Total	Consumption Per Capita
Year	-- Million Pounds --		Lb.[4]	- Million Pounds -		Lb.[4]	- Million Pounds -		Lb.[4]	-- Million Pounds --		Lb.[4]	-- Million Pounds --		Lb.[4]
1990	22,634	24,114	96.2	327	316	1.3	358	397	1.6	15,300	16,030	64.1	38,608	40,782	163.2
1991	22,800	24,261	95.4	306	296	1.2	358	397	1.6	15,948	16,399	64.9	39,402	41,214	163.1
1992	22,968	24,261	95.0	310	299	1.2	343	388	1.5	17,185	17,475	68.4	40,795	42,437	166.1
1993	22,942	24,006	93.0	267	286	1.1	329	381	1.5	17,030	17,419	67.5	40,568	42,092	163.1
1994	24,278	25,124	96.4	283	290	1.2	304	345	1.3	17,658	17,829	68.4	42,523	43,588	167.3
1995	25,115	25,534	97.0	308	319	1.2	264	338	1.1	17,085	16,826	63.3	42,772	43,017	162.6
1996	25,419	25,863	97.4	367	378	1.4	264	334	1.1	17,085	16,814	63.3	43,135	43,389	163.2
1997[1]	25,384	25,706	95.9	324	323	1.2	257	324	1.1	17,244	16,460	61.4	43,209	42,813	159.6
1998[2]	25,666	25,231	93.3	250	272	1.0	247	306	1.0	18,992	17,667	65.3	45,155	43,476	160.6
1999[3]	24,275									18,875			43,150		

[1] Preliminary. [2] Estimate. [3] Forecast. [4] Carcass Weight. *Source: Economic Research Service, U.S. Department of Agriculture (ERS-USDA)*

MEATS

Total Red Meat Imports (Carcass Weight Equivalent) of Principal Countries In Thousands of Metric Tons

Year	Canada	France	Germany	Hong Kong	Italy	Japan	Rep. of Korea	Nether-lands	Russia[3]	Singa-pore	United Kingdom	United States	World Total
1991	232	1,035	1,240	306	1,106	1,206	201	181	740	140	896	1,463	6,509
1992	237	1,027	1,338	265	1,231	1,388	187	208	292	147	885	1,424	5,733
1993	292	1,010	1,319	280	1,139	1,480	134	207	227	150	889	1,449	6,118
1994	313	1,044	1,447	298	1,103	1,628	191	238	865	28	785	1,434	6,844
1995	283	40	149	223	37	1,840	247	25	1,084	28	285	1,284	7,024
1996	276	45	143	202	62	1,904	240	31	939	41	276	1,253	6,482
1997	310	47	133	238	65	1,721	276	56	1,079	34	283	1,388	6,836
1998[1]	290	43	122	300	70	1,763	175	50	875	37	266	1,493	6,719
1999[2]	290	44	138	340	70	1,824	185	50	704	28	264	1,609	6,719

[1] Preliminary. [2] Forecast. [3] Formerly part of the U.S.S.R.; data not reported separately until 1992. *Source: Foreign Agricultural Service, U.S. Department of Agriculture (FAS-USDA)*

Total Red Meat Exports (Carcass Weight Equivalent) of Principal Countries In Thousands of Metric Tons

Year	Argentina	Australia	Brazil	Canada	China	Denmark	France	India	Ireland	Nether-lands	New Zealand	United States	World Total
1991	402	1,391	290	375	494	1,097	757	151	529	1,438	845	669	8,040
1992	301	1,510	470	453	195	1,657	864	110	643	1,491	884	789	7,484
1993	283	1,469	425	494	315	1,272	917	120	672	1,470	858	779	7,290
1994	378	1,473	383	518	295	1,394	1,054	110	613	1,499	896	976	7,675
1995	463	1,329	315	520	310	1,313	999	129	372	1,425	923	1,211	7,954
1996	472	1,291	330	658	279	445	291	162	305	195	985	1,294	8,541
1997	438	1,465	354	780	218	536	282	171	271	202	964	1,445	8,884
1998[1]	281	1,501	419	765	148	499	225	170	238	181	972	1,525	8,429
1999[2]	286	1,490	425	825	148	510	155	180	202	164	868	1,539	8,429

Preliminary. [2] Estimate. [3] Formerly part of the U.S.S.R.; data not reported separately until 1992. *Source: Foreign Agricultural Service, U.S. Department of Agriculture (FAS-USDA)*

United States Meat Imports by Type of Product In Metric Tons

	Beaf and Veal				Pork							
Year	Fresh, Chilled & Frozen	Canned, including Sausage	Other Pre-pared or Preserved	Lamb Mutton and Goat, Except Canned	Fresh and Frozen	Canned[2]	Other Pre-pared or Preserved	Sausage, all Types	Mixed Sausage	Other Meats[3]	Variety Meats, Fresh or Frozen	Total
1988	703,415	67,109	10,124	19,239	281,965	143,356	10,214	2,906	2,732	17,449	8,905	1,253,995
1989	638,999	56,302	13,842	20,917	226,172	118,598	10,328	2,656	2,620	23,581	11,102	1,105,045
1990	694,163	57,636	10,939	19,056	233,536	31,539	13,375	3,421	1,874	18,560	11,423	1,100,710
1991	709,997	60,511	12,929	19,100	215,935	82,339	16,948	2,144	1,533	22,979	18,266	1,162,681
1992	728,922	64,303	10,641	23,853	185,671	61,005	16,553	2,453	1,674	19,225	20,059	1,134,359
1993	720,079	59,786	14,560	24,468	207,653	75,440	17,689	2,695	1,368	18,679	25,298	1,167,714
1994	714,450	61,575	13,335	23,277	209,026	75,443	17,577	2,237	1,900	18,724	27,407	1,164,951
1995	641,918	52,012	13,528	29,919	194,387	61,904	15,571	2,553	1,935	19,550	25,972	1,059,249
1996[1]	640,678	53,388	13,618	33,097	183,555	55,247	15,281	2,418	1,639	21,934	32,472	1,053,327

[1] Preliminary. [2] Includes canned hams, shoulders and bacon. [3] Mostly mixed lucheon meats. *Source: Foreign Agricultural Service, U.S. Department of Agriculture (FAS-USDA)*

United States Meat Exports by Type of Product In Metric Tons

	Beef and Veal			Pork			Other Pork Prepared or Preserved					
Year	Fresh, Chilled & Frozen	Prepared and Preserved	Lamb and Mutton, Fresh or Frozen	Fresh, Chilled & Frozen	Hams & Shoul-ders, Cured	Bacon	Not Canned	Canned	Sausage, Bologna & Frank-furters	Variety Meats, Fresh, Chilled & Frozen	Other Meats[2]	Total
1988	214,530	14,083	619	54,598	2,138	1,045	4,924	268	8,439	302,087	75,084	677,815
1989	373,110	8,810	2,076	79,318	6,101	3,788	2,204	1,395	11,968	245,235	78,550	812,555
1990	339,925	7,783	2,490	66,756	5,567	4,518	4,310	1,036	14,208	226,623	70,558	743,774
1991	395,697	10,251	3,790	76,193	4,702	5,443	6,133	1,278	24,025	280,721	61,440	869,673
1992	436,455	12,064	3,278	116,496	8,181	7,396	5,812	2,352	22,796	303,295	57,154	975,279
1993	411,003	14,464	3,605	129,240	5,208	7,092	4,579	2,350	34,198	338,689	45,905	996,333
1994	517,507	13,545	3,766	149,318	8,477	12,076	4,470	2,973	46,925	373,662	34,734	1,167,453
1995	581,731	13,653	2,509	228,164	12,074	13,830	6,263	3,564	56,829	449,599	34,118	1,402,334
1996[1]	596,891	14,565	2,475	267,419	9,733	15,838	7,541	5,343	92,476	469,320	26,239	1,507,840

[1] Preliminary. [2] Includes sausage ingredients, cured (excluding canned); meat and meat products canned; and baby food, canned. *Source: Foreign Agricultural Service, U.S. Department of Agriculture (FAS-USDA)*

Exports and Imports of Meats in the United States (Carcass Weight Equivalent)[3]

Year	Exports: Beef and Veal	Exports: Lamb and Mutton	Exports: Pork[4]	Exports: All Meat	Imports: Beef and Veal	Imports: Lamb and Mutton	Imports: Pork[4]	Imports: All Meat
	In Millions of Pounds							
1990	1,006	6	238	1,250	2,356	41	898	3,295
1991	1,188	10	283	1,481	1,406	41	775	3,223
1992	1,324	8	407	1,739	2,440	50	645	3,135
1993	1,275	8	435	1,718	2,401	53	740	3,194
1994	1,611	9	532	2,152	2,369	49	743	3,161
1995	1,821	6	771	2,598	2,103	64	664	2,831
1996	1,878	4	970	2,852	2,072	72	619	2,764
1997[1]	2,136	5	1,037	3,174	2,343	83	632	3,058
1998[2]	2,165	4	1,244	3,130	2,642	109	693	3,157

[1] Preliminary. [2] Estimate. [3] Includes meat content of minor meats and of mixed products. *Source: Economic Research Service, U.S. Department of Agriculture (ERS-USDA)*

Average Wholesale Prices of Meats in the United States In Cents Per Pound

Year	Composite Retail Price of Beef, Choice, Grade 3	Composite Retail Price of Pork[3]	Wholesale Value[4] Beef	Wholesale Value[4] Pork	Net Farm Value of Pork[5]	Cow Beef Canner & Cutter, Central US	Boxed Beef Cut-out, Choice 1-3, Central US, 550-700 lbs.	Pork Carcass Cut-out, U.S., No. 2	Lamb Carcass, Choice-Prime, East Coast, 55-65 lbs.	Pork Loins, Central US, 14-18 lbs.	Skinned Ham, Central US, 20-26 lbs.[6]	Pork Bellies, Central US, 12-14 lbs.
1990	281.00	212.60	189.60	118.30	87.20	102.41	123.21	74.00	121.47	117.52	84.87	53.80
1991	288.30	211.90	182.50	108.90	78.40	99.42	118.31	67.02	117.33	108.39	75.68	47.79
1992	284.60	198.00	179.60	98.90	67.80	93.85	116.73	58.37	131.66	101.41	67.42	30.39
1993	293.40	197.60	182.50	102.90	72.50	95.43	118.74	62.19	143.97	107.47	67.85	41.62
1994	282.90	198.10	166.70	98.90	62.90	84.39	108.47	57.29	147.62	101.50	58.12	40.00
1995	284.30	194.80	163.90	98.80	66.70	68.22	106.68	59.98	163.45	107.74	58.56	43.04
1996	280.20	220.90	158.10	117.20	84.60	58.18	103.09	72.39	177.58	118.49	72.41	69.97
1997[1]	279.53	231.54				64.30	103.26	70.87	178.99	108.06	62.75	71.41
1998[2]	277.81	228.41				61.33	99.72	52.80	156.75	99.75	44.75	51.94

[1] Preliminary. [2] Estimate. [3] Sold as retail cuts (ham, bacon, loin, etc.). [4] Quantity equivalent to 1 pound of retail cuts. [5] Portion of gross farm value minus farm by-product allowance. [6] Prior to 1995, 17-20 pounds. *Source: Economic Research Service, U.S. Department of Agriculture (ERS-USDA)*

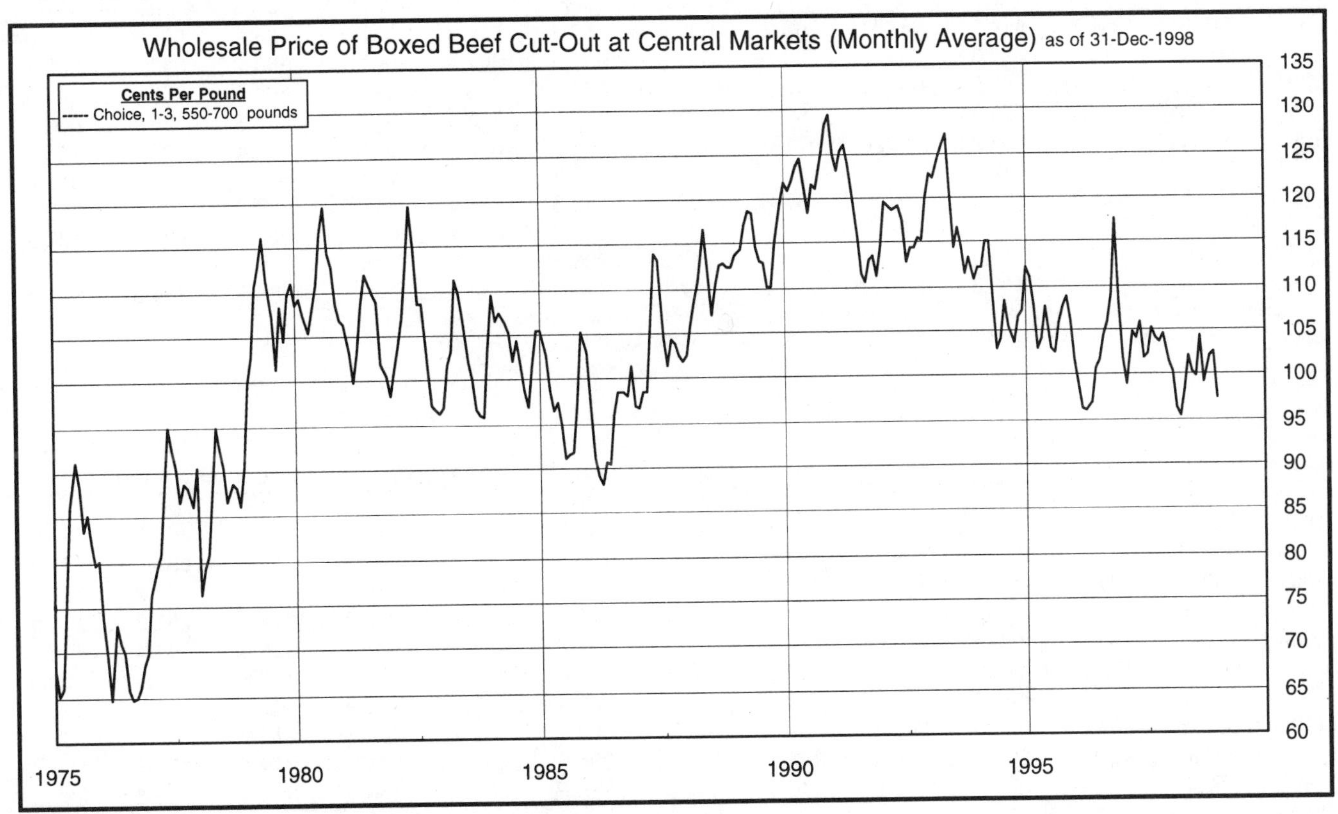

Average Wholesale Price of Boxed Beef Cut-Out[1], Choice, at Central Markets In Cents Per Pound

Year	Jan.	Feb.	Mar.	Apr.	May	June	July	Aug.	Sept.	Oct.	Nov.	Dec.	Average
1989	113.62	114.30	117.09	118.58	118.53	114.53	113.17	112.83	110.08	110.04	115.06	119.52	114.78
1990	121.75	120.97	122.10	123.62	124.56	121.53	118.54	121.52	121.18	124.96	128.32	129.48	123.21
1991	125.04	123.24	125.45	125.96	123.76	120.61	115.82	111.54	110.61	113.04	113.43	111.18	118.31
1992	114.38	119.65	119.14	118.66	119.18	117.53	112.79	114.36	114.40	115.51	115.26	119.95	116.73
1993	122.69	122.13	124.80	126.12	127.19	120.52	114.48	116.73	114.65	111.52	113.26	110.83	118.74
1994	112.11	112.23	115.03	114.98	108.85	102.92	104.19	108.38	105.49	103.63	106.66	107.22	108.47
1995	112.17	111.12	107.87	103.03	104.21	107.65	103.03	102.55	105.82	107.77	108.88	106.08	106.68
1996	101.71	98.86	96.36	96.01	96.90	100.70	101.53	104.43	105.93	109.10	117.53	108.03	103.09
1997	101.90	98.98	104.87	104.17	105.97	101.83	102.38	105.14	104.06	103.72	104.63	101.50	103.26
1998[2]	100.26	96.27	95.34	98.32	102.09	100.38	99.96	104.28	99.28	102.08	102.61	97.49	99.86

[1] Choice 1-3, 550-700 pounds. [2] Preliminary. *Source: Economic Research Service, U.S. Department of Agriculture (ERS-USDA)*

Production (Commercial) of All Red Meats in the United States In Millions of Pounds (Carcass Weight)

Year	Jan.	Feb.	Mar.	Apr.	May	June	July	Aug.	Sept.	Oct.	Nov.	Dec.	Total
1989	3,265	3,004	3,325	3,131	3,397	3,343	3,048	3,483	3,317	3,523	3,411	3,171	39,418
1990	3,354	2,972	3,259	3,049	3,320	3,175	3,100	3,431	3,096	3,499	3,273	3,080	38,608
1991	3,430	2,954	3,081	3,285	3,291	3,059	3,253	3,425	3,308	3,708	3,324	3,284	39,402
1992	3,623	3,090	3,376	3,259	3,237	3,423	3,441	3,406	3,560	3,656	3,289	3,434	40,794
1993	3,304	3,012	3,396	3,299	3,212	3,481	3,342	3,504	3,516	3,499	3,449	3,554	40,568
1994	3,366	3,126	3,591	3,382	3,431	3,615	3,361	3,756	3,720	3,795	3,666	3,714	42,523
1995	3,560	3,210	3,751	3,304	3,758	3,798	3,424	3,860	3,697	3,795	3,748	3,553	43,458
1996	3,823	3,519	3,512	3,690	3,767	3,439	3,585	3,707	3,396	3,827	3,435	3,432	43,132
1997	3,735	3,278	3,444	3,592	3,571	3,492	3,657	3,619	3,665	4,005	3,453	3,715	43,226
1998[1]	3,836	3,476	3,726	3,701	3,582	3,732	3,781	3,770	3,827	4,033	3,725	3,945	45,134

[1] Preliminary. *Source: Economic Research Service, U.S. Department of Agriculture (ERS-USDA)*

Cold Storage Holdings of All[1] Meat in the United States, at End of Month In Millions of Pounds

Year	Jan.	Feb.	Mar.	Apr.	May	June	July	Aug.	Sept.	Oct.	Nov.	Dec.
1989	745.0	758.7	474.5	747.5	763.7	683.5	652.0	576.3	557.0	538.2	554.2	536.0
1990	564.7	609.6	637.5	653.0	632.8	591.6	565.9	507.4	507.5	536.7	536.7	536.4
1991	566.2	588.6	606.2	597.7	640.1	614.1	589.7	593.2	592.8	594.7	650.2	644.9
1992	707.9	690.5	725.4	706.8	692.2	665.3	646.0	595.6	613.4	637.8	626.6	615.1
1993	649.4	654.6	652.9	692.0	671.0	660.8	664.2	650.7	671.7	702.4	720.3	726.7
1994	807.7	800.5	842.5	858.0	837.5	822.6	816.2	771.9	788.5	822.7	827.5	802.0
1995	838.7	833.8	834.0	852.7	831.2	820.8	803.6	733.4	711.3	732.3	757.0	749.7
1996	779.5	781.6	729.3	748.6	716.2	687.9	642.7	657.4	678.4	655.5	627.1	621.3
1997	655.9	669.9	719.5	752.5	719.7	742.9	726.3	731.5	728.2	739.1	741.0	722.4
1998[2]	802.8	821.8	816.3	849.3	814.4	771.0	747.2	728.2	738.7	794.9	794.3	821.0

[1] Includes beef and veal, mutton and lamb, pork and products, rendered pork fat, and miscellaneous meats. Excludes lard. [2] Preliminary.
Source: Economic Research Service, U.S. Department of Agriculture (ERS-USDA)

Cold Storage Holdings of Frozen Beef in the United States, on First of Month In Millions of Pounds

Year	Jan.	Feb.	Mar.	Apr.	May	June	July	Aug.	Sept.	Oct.	Nov.	Dec.
1989	317.5	315.1	313.4	298.9	275.4	244.1	241.8	249.2	242.4	231.8	220.7	237.6
1990	251.7	259.8	267.6	304.3	293.3	270.4	256.5	265.4	240.5	243.0	267.4	277.2
1991	300.4	298.9	271.3	276.9	265.6	234.7	247.1	273.2	259.4	276.7	298.2	306.3
1992	315.9	329.1	298.9	313.7	302.1	303.5	299.4	294.1	288.9	275.2	291.2	275.9
1993	272.8	286.4	279.9	293.9	276.7	262.1	271.7	285.3	307.5	326.8	344.4	376.3
1994	401.0	430.2	414.4	423.2	399.5	367.9	379.4	388.9	377.2	406.8	410.6	419.5
1995	411.2	420.3	407.7	385.4	392.2	359.1	352.3	359.3	344.9	347.7	381.6	381.4
1996	389.6	367.9	362.6	347.3	335.6	307.4	306.7	291.1	305.2	312.2	295.9	288.1
1997	284.9	290.3	260.8	290.4	285.4	278.7	305.6	302.8	324.6	349.1	351.6	378.2
1998[1]	350.2	331.1	331.0	330.0	335.5	310.2	316.5	303.0	306.7	323.1	358.2	328.3

[1] Preliminary. *Source: Economic Research Service, U.S. Department of Agriculture (ERS-USDA)*

Mercury

Beginning in late 1990 nearly all domestic mercury production was of secondary origin, derived from recycled mercury-containing devices. No domestic mine produced mercury as its primary product. Several companies, however, were engaged in mercury refining, the three largest being in the eastern and central United States. Strict U.S. and foreign environmental policies and the advancement of new technology are affecting both primary and secondary mercury production, working almost in tandem to reduce the demand for mercury in commercial products. However, even as the content in products declines, regulations on mercury disposal will result in more recycling to recover contained mercury. The trend for the past several years has been to substitute other materials for mercury rather than develop large-scale recycling programs. The largest domestic use of mercury in 1997 continued to be in the electrolytic production of chlorine and caustic soda.

Mercury is the only common metal that is liquid at room temperature. It is also highly toxic. The last producing U.S. mercury mine (in Nevada) closed in 1990. Since then the only prime virgin mercury produced in the U.S. has been recovered as a by-product of gold mining operations.

World production of mercury is largely limited to four countries with another six marginal producers (annual production less than 100 metric tonnes). World production in 1997 of 2,730 metric tonnes compares with 2,580 tonnes in 1996. Spain, the world's largest producer, reportedly has an annual production capacity of 3,500 tonnes, but this decade's highest output of 1,497 tonnes in 1995 compares with 1,000 tonnes in 1997. (One tonne equals 29 flasks of 76 pounds each.) In Kyrgyzstan, the government privatized a 650-ton capacity mining complex by opening ownership to foreign investors; production at which totaled 611 tonnes in 1997 vs. 584 in 1996. Algeria and China produced 370 and 500 tonnes respectively in 1997, vs. 368 and 510 in 1996.

U.S. secondary production totaled 52 tonnes in 1997 vs. 446 in 1996. EPA restrictions banning landfill disposal and/or transport of mercury-containing wastes has encouraged more efficient recovery methods, especially from fluorescent lamps. The U.S. government has a National Defense primary mercury stockpile, but tight restrictions are in place as to how much can be sold each year. Reportedly, the goal is to reduce the government's inventory to zero, but the last disposal of 86 tonnes occurred in 1994.

U.S. industrial consumption of refined mercury totaled 346 tonnes in 1997 vs. 372 tonnes in 1996. In the mid-1980's battery production alone consumed almost 30,000 tonnes; battery use is now near zero as manufacturers produce alkaline and zinc-carbon batteries. Chlorine and caustic soda manufacture accounted for 160 tonnes in 1997 vs. 136 tonnes in 1996. Substitutes for mercury include lithium and composite ceramic materials.

U.S. foreign trade in mercury is small. Imports totaled 164 tonnes in 1997 vs. 340 tonnes in 1996; exports, however, rose to 134 tonnes from 45 tonnes, respectively, with Hong Kong taking 97 tonnes.

Mercury is sold in 34.5 kilogram flasks. The U.S. average dealer price in 1996 was $262/flask (N.Y.) vs. the 1980's average near $300/fl. In 1997, the free market price averaged $160/flask while the U.S. dealer price was not officially available. Historically mercury's world price is considered more reflective of true market values.

World Mine Production of Mercury In Metric Tons (1 tonne = 29.008216 flasks)

Year	Algeria	China	Finland	Kyrgyzstan[3]	Mexico	Spain	Tajikistan[3]	Turkey	Ukraine[3]	United States	World Total
1989	587	1,200	159	------	651	1,224	------	197	850	414	5,464
1990	637	1,000	141	------	735	425	------	60	800	562	4,100
1991	431	760	74	------	340	100	------	25	750	58	2,540
1992	476	580	85	300	21	36	100	5	100	64	1,920
1993	459	520	101	350	12	64	80	------	80	W	1,800
1994	414	470	83	379	12	393	55	------	50	W	1,960
1995	292	780	90	380	15	1,497	50	------	40	W	3,250
1996[1]	368	510	88	584	15	862	45	------	30	W	2,580
1997[2]	370	500	90	611	15	1,000	40	------	25	W	2,730

[1] Preliminary. [2] Estimate. [3] Formerly part of the U.S.S.R.; data not reported separately until 1992. *Source: U.S. Geological Survey*

Salient Statistics of Mercury in the United States In Metric Tons

Year	Producing Mines	Secondary Production: Industrial	Secondary Production: Government[3]	N.D.S.[4] Shipments	Consumer & Dealer Stocks, Dec. 31	Industrial Demand	Exports	Imports
1989	10	137	180	170	217	121	221	131
1990	9	108	193	52	197	720	311	15
1991	8	165	215	103	313	554	786	56
1992	9	176	103	267	436	621	977	92
1993	9	350	-----	543	384	558	389	40
1994	7	466	-----	86	469	483	316	129
1995	8	534	-----	-----	321	436	179	377
1996[1]	6	446	-----	-----	446	372	45	340
1997[2]	5	52	-----	-----	203	346	134	164

[1] Preliminary. [2] Estimate. [3] Secondary mercury shipped from the Department of Energy. [4] National Defense Stockpile.
Source: U.S. Geological Survey (USGS)

MERCURY

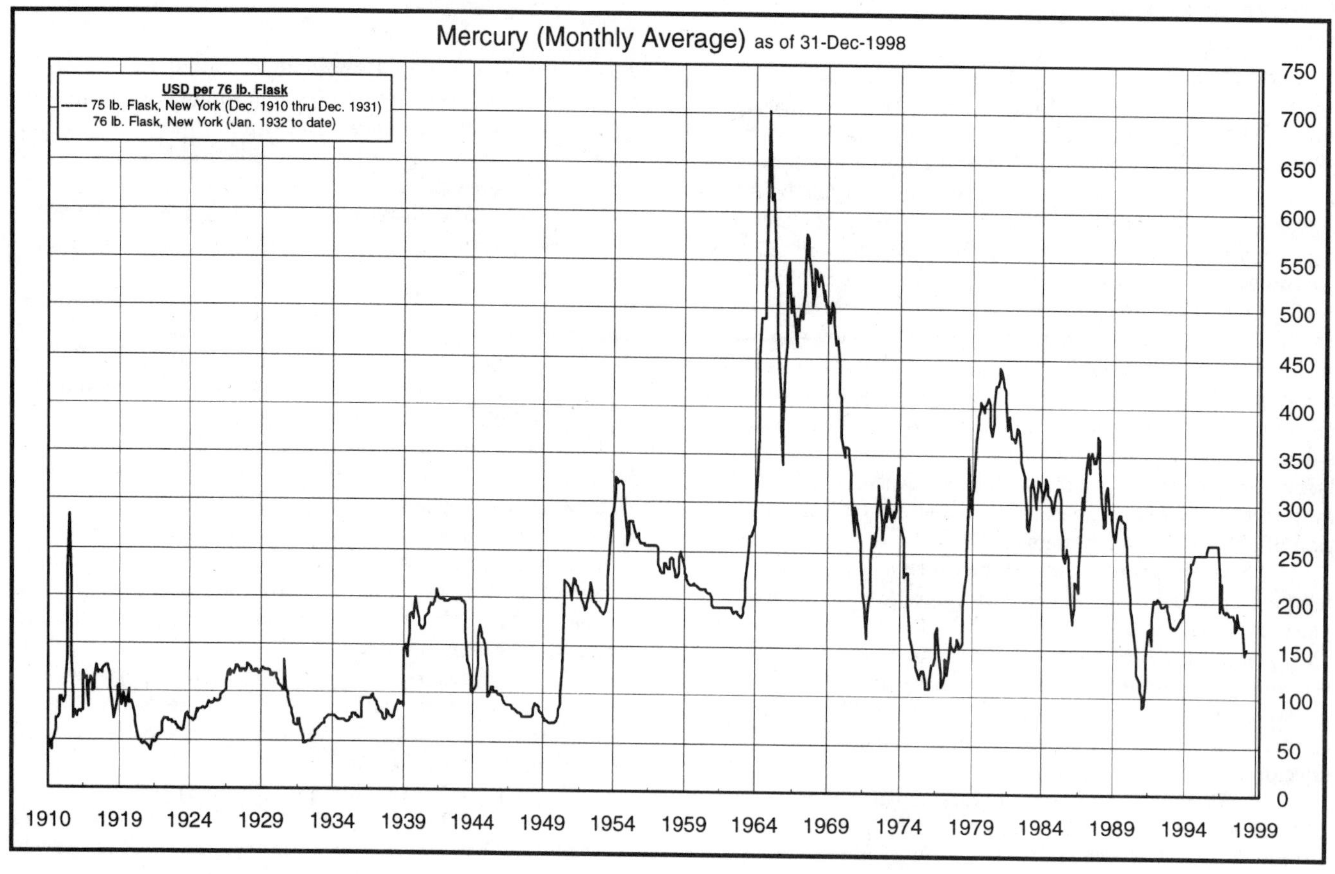

Average Price of Mercury in New York In Dollars Per Flask of 76 Pounds (34.5 Kilograms)

Year	Jan.	Feb.	Mar.	Apr.	May	June	July	Aug.	Sept.	Oct.	Nov.	Dec.	Average
1989	292.50	318.42	330.00	327.50	315.68	308.86	293.03	273.80	265.13	267.61	282.50	292.50	297.29
1990	292.50	292.50	287.84	285.00	285.00	285.00	281.45	262.50	259.34	235.54	198.75	182.50	262.33
1991	181.55	169.08	150.36	140.68	129.77	119.75	110.36	102.50	98.00	94.02	127.50	150.12	131.14
1992	162.86	177.24	180.00	180.00	190.63	202.50	202.50	203.45	207.50	207.50	207.50	207.50	194.10
1993	207.50	207.50	207.50	207.50	207.50	201.30	191.00	191.00	185.00	185.00	181.00	175.00	195.57
1994	175.00	175.00	179.78	180.00	180.95	186.64	196.50	200.00	203.10	205.00	217.50	230.71	194.18
1995	235.00	240.00	241.30	250.00	250.00	250.00	250.00	250.00	250.00	250.00	250.00	250.00	247.19
1996	250.00	250.00	261.67	268.33	265.00	265.00	265.00	265.00	265.00	265.00	262.63	235.48	259.84
1997	233.98	232.76	228.88	228.64	220.00	199.05	200.00	198.10	190.83	198.83	191.47	187.00	209.13
1998	187.00	187.00	187.00	187.00	187.00	181.55	175.00	175.00	175.00	175.00	175.00	175.00	180.55

Source: American Metal Market (AMM)

Mercury Consumed in the United States In Metric Tons

Year	Batteries	Chlorine & Caustic Soda	Catalysts, Misc.	Dental Equip.	Electrical Lighting	General Lab Use	Measuring Control Instrument	Paints	Wiring Devices & Switches	Other Uses	Grand Total
1988	448	354	86	53	31	26	77	197	176	55	1,503
1989	250	379	40	39	31	18	87	192	141	32	1,212
1990	106	247	29	44	33	32	108	14	70	38	720
1991	18	184	26	41	39	30	90	6	71	49	554
1992	13	209	20	42	55	28	80	-----	82	92	621
1993	10	180	18	35	38	26	65	-----	83	103	558
1994	6	135	25	24	27	24	53	-----	79	110	483
1995	-----	154	-----	32	30	-----	43	-----	84	93	436
1996[1]	-----	136	-----	31	29	-----	41	-----	49	86	372
1997[2]	-----	160	-----	40	29	-----	24	-----	57	36	346

[1] Preliminary. [2] Estimate. NA = Not available. *Source: U.S. Geological Survey (USGS)*

Milk

U.S. milk production in 1998 at an estimated 71.7 million metric tonnes compares with 71 million in 1997. The U.S. milk cow inventory continues to shrink, but the effect is offset by increases in milk per cow production. In late 1998, higher milk prices and lower prices for concentrate feeds were expected to provide producers incentives to expand production in 1999, however, uncertainty about supplies of dairy-quality forage may temper producer intentions. The number of dairy cows in 1998 of about 9.2 million head compares with 9.3 million in 1997, and the 1993-97 average of almost 9.5 million. As of mid-1998, U.S. farm milk prices were up with the June Basic Formula Prices (BFP) 22 percent over a year earlier ($13.10 per cwt. vs. $10.74). For 1997, BFP prices averaged $12.05 per cwt. vs. $13.39 in 1996. The BFP average through January-July 1998 was $12.87, but strengthening towards mid-year. Milk's average manufacturing grade price in 1997 of $12.18 per cwt. compares with $13.38 in 1996, and for 1998 is forecast to average over $13.00. Retail prices generally show more variance than wholesale values, due largely to differences in transportation and marketing costs. Retail fluid milk and cream prices in 1997 averaged almost 45 percent over the 1982-1994 average.

The milk industry continues to aggressively advertise milk as a beverage in an effort to reverse the tide of fluid milk's 30-year consumption decline and defend itself from competing iced teas and bottled water. The strategy, employing well known sports and T.V. celebrities, may work more with children than adults. It is believed that more than half of U.S. adults over 35 have eliminated milk from their diet. U.S. consumer milk usage patterns have changed: plain whole milk sales during the past ten years have dropped sharply, but plain low fat milk sales have increased at least 10 percent while skim milk sales have tripled. About 87 percent of U.S. milk output is produced in 22 states. California and Wisconsin are the leading milk producing states. Seasonally, milk production is highest during the April-June quarter, during which a nationwide 40.9 billion pounds were produced in 1998 vs. 40.7 billion a year earlier; of which California's production was 7.1 billion pounds in both years and Wisconsin at about 5.8 billion.

The U.S. is the world's largest fluid milk producer with average annual production during 1996-98 of 70.9 million metric tonnes. 1998 world production of a near record 384 million tonnes compares with 382 million in 1997. Russia and the Ukraine combined produced an estimated 46 million tonnes in 1998, continuing the steady decline seen in the 1990's; production in 1993 totaled 65 million tonnes. Other major producers include India and Germany, each in excess of 25 million tonnes during 1998. Percentagewise, Brazil shows the highest growth rate, producing almost 22 million tonnes in 1998 vs. 16.5 million in 1993-1994.

India is the world's largest consumer of fluid milk with a record 33 million tonnes in 1998 vs. the U.S. total of 26.8 million tonnes. On a per capita basis, the U.S. total of 100 kilograms is well under most European nations. Pricewise, U.S. fluid milk prices are lower than abroad, especially relative to Japan, but dried milk prices tend to be higher due largely to a government support program.

Futures Markets

Nonfat dry milk and raw milk futures and options are traded on the Coffee, Sugar, & Cocoa Exchange Inc. (CSCE). Fluid milk futures and options are traded on the Chicago Mercantile Exchange (CME).

World Fluid Milk Production (Cow's Milk) In Thousands of Metric Tons

Year	Brazil	France	Germany	India	Italy	Netherlands	New Zealand	Poland	Russia[3]	Ukraine[3]	United Kingdom	United States	World Total
1992	15,538	25,315	28,106	29,400	11,300	10,901	8,603	13,060	46,776	19,114	14,428	68,440	379,917
1993	16,250	25,049	28,080	30,600	10,400	10,953	8,735	12,650	46,300	18,377	14,645	68,303	377,633
1994	16,700	25,322	27,866	31,000	10,365	10,964	9,719	11,822	42,800	18,138	14,920	69,701	378,408
1995	18,375	25,413	28,621	32,500	10,500	11,294	9,684	11,420	39,300	17,181	14,700	70,500	380,789
1996	19,480	25,083	28,776	33,500	10,800	11,013	10,405	11,690	35,800	16,000	14,640	69,971	379,893
1997	20,600	24,957	28,700	34,500	10,818	10,922	11,500	11,980	34,100	13,650	14,830	71,035	381,518
1998[1]	21,630	24,700	28,500	35,500	10,800	11,200	11,640	12,100	34,000	13,700	14,600	71,375	384,892
1999[2]	22,495	24,500	28,500	36,000	10,800	11,100	11,460	12,550	33,000	13,600	14,550	72,650	387,471

[1] Preliminary. [2] Estimate. [3] Formerly part of the U.S.S.R.; data not reported separately until 1989. *Source: Foreign Agricultural Service, U.S. Department of Agriculture (FAS-USDA)*

Milk-Feed Price Ratio[1] in the United States In Pounds

Year	Jan.	Feb.	Mar.	Apr.	May	June	July	Aug.	Sept.	Oct.	Nov.	Dec.	Average
1991	2.57	2.52	2.42	2.34	2.41	2.54	2.73	2.82	2.94	3.14	3.25	3.19	2.74
1992	3.04	2.86	2.77	2.79	2.68	2.81	3.06	3.20	3.22	3.23	3.23	3.13	3.00
1993	2.96	2.87	2.77	2.79	2.81	2.91	2.78	2.70	2.80	2.79	2.77	2.65	2.80
1994	2.62	2.51	2.51	2.50	2.36	2.44	2.61	2.74	2.81	2.92	2.96	2.81	2.65
1995	2.73	2.75	2.73	2.60	2.53	2.46	2.39	2.50	2.55	2.60	2.69	2.55	2.59
1996	2.57	2.44	2.30	2.16	2.07	2.18	2.21	2.30	2.65	2.94	2.85	2.70	2.45
1997	2.42	2.36	2.26	2.16	2.16	2.11	2.25	2.35	2.44	2.63	2.73	2.80	2.39
1998[2]	2.77	2.74	2.72	2.70	2.55	2.87	2.98	3.57	3.96	4.15	4.24	4.27	3.29

[1] Pounds of 16% protein mixed dairy feed equal in value to one pound of whole milk. [2] Preliminary. *Source: Economic Research Service, U.S. Department of Agriculture (ERS-USDA)*

Salient Statistics of Milk in the United States In Millions of Pounds

Year	Number of Milk Cows on Farms[3] (Thousands)	Supply: Production: Per Cow[4] (Pounds)	Supply: Production: Total[4]	Supply: Beginning Stocks[5]	Supply: Imports	Supply: Total Supply	Utilization: Exports[5]	Utilization: Domestic: Fed to Calves	Utilization: Domestic: Humans	Utilization: Total Use	Average Farm Price Received Per Cwt.: All Milk, Whole-sale	Average Farm Price Received Per Cwt.: Milk Eligible for Fluid Market	Average Farm Price Received Per Cwt.: Milk, Manu-facturing Grade	Per Capita Consumption[6] (Fluid Milk in Lbs.)
1991	9,826	15,031	147,697	13,359	2,625	163,681	2,845	1,480	142,897	147,841	12.24	12.33	11.12	233
1992	9,688	15,570	150,847	15,840	2,520	169,246	7,569	1,436	144,519	155,032	13.09	13.16	11.87	231
1993	9,589	15,704	150,582	14,214	2,806	167,602	7,894	1,408	148,178	158,032	12.84	12.88	11.80	226
1994	9,500	16,175	153,664	9,570	2,880	166,072	5,555	1,305	152,791	160,312	13.01	13.02	11.85	226
1995	9,458	16,433	155,425	5,760	2,936	164,121		1,230			12.74	12.78	11.78	226
1996[1]	9,351	16,498	154,268	4,168	2,911	161,347		1,189			14.88	14.95	13.38	224
1997[2]	9,250	16,960	156,850	4,714	2,697	164,261					13.34	13.38	12.18	222

[1] Preliminary. [2] Estimate. [3] Average number on farms during year including dry cows, excluding heifers not yet fresh. [4] Excludes milk sucked by calves. [5] Government and commercial. [6] Product pounds of commercial sales and on farm consumption. *Source: Economic Research Service, U.S. Department of Agriculture (ERS-USDA)*

Utilization of Milk in the United States In Millions of Pounds (Milk Equivalent)

Year	Butter from Whey Cream	Creamery Butter[2]	Cheese[3]	Cottage Cheese (Creamed)	Canned Milk[4]	Bulk Condensed Whole Milk: Unsweet-ened	Bulk Condensed Whole Milk: Sweet-ened	Dry Whole Milk Products	Ice Cream[5]	Other Frozen Dairy Products	Other Manu-factured Pro-ducts[6]	Used on Farms: Farm-Churned Butter	Used on Farms: Total
1991	4,296	30,039	46,769	644	1,194	364	236	785	2,092	12,726	356	494	1,974
1992	4,150	30,478	49,458	592	1,872	417	301	1,227	2,367	11,825	188	455	1,892
1993	4,500	29,493	49,871	557	1,178	244	324	1,130	1,995	12,063	199	428	1,836
1994	4,592	29,127	51,143	524	1,184	205	277	1,227	2,083	13,182	216	394	1,700
1995	4,735	28,388	52,589	494	1,049	203	254	1,262	2,053	13,041	252	346	1,576
1996[1]	4,911	26,187	53,937	461	1,013	242	266	983	2,058	13,190	217	301	1,489

[1] Preliminary. [2] Excludes whey butter. [3] American and other. [4] Includes evaporated and sweetened condensed. [5] Milk equivalent of butter and condensed milk used in ice cream. [6] Whole milk equivalent of dry cream, malted milk powder, part-skim milk, dry or concentrated ice cream mix, dehydrated butterfat and other miscellaneous products using milkfat. *Source: National Agricultural Statistics Service, U.S. Department of Agriculture (NASS-USDA)*

Milk Production[1] in the United States In Millions of Pounds

Year	Jan.	Feb.	Mar.	Apr.	May	June	July	Aug.	Sept.	Oct.	Nov.	Dec.	Total
1992	12,671	12,132	13,155	12,838	13,346	12,893	12,844	12,577	12,094	12,476	12,064	12,626	150,847
1993	10,728	9,908	11,060	10,927	11,410	12,957	12,894	12,492	11,978	12,272	11,872	12,427	150,582
1994	12,721	11,662	13,209	13,118	13,719	13,079	13,020	12,837	12,360	12,732	12,330	12,871	153,664
1995	13,147	12,142	13,640	13,343	13,875	13,302	13,152	12,793	12,381	12,716	12,297	12,844	155,425
1996	13,085	12,431	13,537	13,230	13,576	12,832	12,809	12,624	12,241	12,714	12,324	12,928	154,331
1997	13,126	12,141	13,694	13,406	13,902	13,375	13,319	13,059	12,427	12,814	12,362	12,977	156,602
1998[2]	13,282	12,188	13,694	13,510	14,015	13,296	13,162	12,942	12,415	12,956	12,611	13,370	157,441

[1] Excludes milk sucked by calves. [2] Preliminary. *Source: Economic Research Service, U.S. Department of Agriculture (ERS-USDA)*

Average Price Received by U.S. Farmers for All Milk (Sold to Plants) In Dollars Per Hundred Pounds (Cwt.)

Year	Jan.	Feb.	Mar.	Apr.	May	June	July	Aug.	Sept.	Oct.	Nov.	Dec.	Average
1992	13.40	12.90	12.50	12.60	12.80	13.20	13.40	13.50	13.50	13.40	13.10	12.80	13.09
1993	12.50	12.20	12.20	12.60	12.90	13.00	12.80	12.40	12.80	13.10	13.60	13.50	12.80
1994	13.60	13.40	13.50	13.40	12.80	12.60	12.20	12.40	12.80	13.00	13.10	12.80	12.97
1995	12.60	12.60	12.70	12.30	12.30	12.10	12.00	12.40	12.80	13.40	14.00	13.90	12.76
1996	14.00	13.80	13.70	13.90	14.30	14.80	15.40	15.90	16.50	16.40	15.20	14.30	14.85
1997	13.40	13.50	13.50	13.20	12.70	12.20	12.10	12.70	13.10	14.10	14.70	14.80	13.33
1998[1]	14.70	14.70	14.40	14.00	13.20	14.00	14.10	15.40	16.60	17.60	17.90	18.00	15.38

[1] Preliminary. *Source: Economic Research Service, U.S. Department of Agriculture (ERS-USDA)*

Average Farm Price of Milk Eligible for Fluid Market In Dollars Per Hundred Pounds (Cwt.)

Year	Jan.	Feb.	Mar.	Apr.	May	June	July	Aug.	Sept.	Oct.	Nov.	Dec.	Average
1992	13.50	13.00	12.50	12.60	12.90	13.30	13.40	13.50	13.60	13.50	13.20	12.90	13.16
1993	12.60	12.30	12.20	12.70	13.00	13.10	12.80	12.50	12.80	13.10	13.60	13.60	12.86
1994	13.60	13.50	13.50	13.50	12.90	12.70	12.20	12.50	12.80	13.10	13.10	12.90	13.03
1995	12.70	12.60	12.60	12.30	12.30	12.20	12.10	12.50	12.80	13.40	14.00	14.00	12.79
1996	14.00	13.90	13.70	13.90	14.30	14.90	15.50	16.00	16.60	16.40	15.30	14.40	14.91
1997	13.40	13.50	13.60	13.20	12.80	12.30	12.20	12.80	13.10	14.10	14.70	14.80	13.38
1998[1]	14.70	14.80	14.50	14.00	13.30	14.00	14.10	15.50	16.70	17.60	17.90	18.00	15.43

[1] Preliminary. *Source: Economic Research Service, U.S. Department of Agriculture (ERS-USDA)*

Molasses

Molasses is a heavy, viscous fluid produced as a by-product of raw sugar refining. About 50 gallons of molasses are produced for each ton of raw sugar refined. Molasses contains 33 percent sucrose. U.S. supplies of molasses are about three million metric tonnes per year. Of this total, a third comes from mainland sugar mills, a quarter from beet sugar refiners and smaller amounts from Hawaiian cane and cane refiners. Beet molasses is used primarily as a livestock food and a yeast by the pharmaceutical industry.

To a large extent, production of molasses is related to refinement of sugar. Some countries produce and export raw sugar while others produce and refine sugar leading to the production of molasses. To that extent, the price of molasses and the price of sugar are related. A larger-than-expected sugar cane or beet crop can put some countries in the position of being net exporters of molasses. Countries with smaller-than-expected crops could then be out in the position of being net importers.

The world sugar market in 1998-99 is characterized by a surplus of sugar. Production has exceeded consumption which has led to a buildup in world stocks of sugar. This has increased availability of molasses. Large supplies of sugar lead to large supplies of molasses and that implies that prices will be weak. Other sources of reduced demand came from Asia where financial problems have reduced usage. All of this is reflected in prices which remain well below year ago levels.

As of mid-January 1999, cane blackstrap molasses in New Orleans was priced at $37.50 per short ton compared to $57.50 per ton a year earlier. That is a decline of 33 percent. Cane blackstrap molasses in Savannah, Georgia was priced at $60.00 per ton, some 22 percent less than a year ago. In Stockton, California, in January 1999, cane blackstrap molasses was priced at $60.00 per ton, 25 percent less than a year earlier. In the January 1999 U.S.D.A. supply/demand report, U.S. sugar production was estimated at 8.26 million short tons, up 3 percent from the year before.

The U.S. imports molasses from countries like Australia, Mexico, Colombia and the Dominican Republic.

World Production of Sugarcane, by Selected Countries — In Thousands of Metric Tons

Crop Year	Australia	Brazil	China	Cuba	India	Indonesia	Mexico	Pakistan	Phillip-pines	South Africa	Thailand	United States	World Total
1990-1	25,140	75,000	57,620	67,500	135,494	28,074	36,000	22,604	18,600	18,083	40,563	24,018	707,497
1991-2	21,306	87,000	67,898	62,000	148,814	28,100	35,300	24,796	22,816	20,078	47,505	26,272	753,303
1992-3	29,400	90,000	73,011	47,150	123,985	32,000	39,700	27,276	23,850	12,955	34,711	26,264	719,671
1993-4	31,951	91,000	63,549	46,000	116,638	33,000	34,100	34,182	22,753	11,244	37,569	26,680	706,433
1994-5	34,860	110,000	60,300	39,000	159,593	30,545	40,134	34,193	18,415	15,683	50,459	25,485	783,373
1995-6	37,378	93,000	65,417	45,500	184,708	30,000	42,300	28,151	22,774	16,750	57,693	25,835	842,937
1996-7[1]	39,878	101,000	68,500	45,000	147,858	28,600	42,000	25,580	23,500	22,512	59,000	24,055	845,645
1997-8[2]	40,878	105,000	69,400	45,500	137,184	29,000		31,600			60,000		

[1] Preliminary. [2] Estimate. *Source: Economic Reseach Service, U.S. Department of Agriculture (ERS-USDA)*

World Production of Sugarbeets, by Selected Countries — In Thousands of Metric Tons

Crop Year	Belgium-Luxembrg	China	France	Germany	Italy	Poland	Russia[3]	Spain	Turkey	Ukraine[3]	United Kingdom	United States	World Total
1990-1	6,857	14,525	25,520	30,366	11,600	16,721	31,091	7,358	13,986	44,265	8,000	24,959	303,149
1991-2	6,043	16,289	24,403	25,926	11,400	11,412	24,280	6,679	15,474	36,168	7,672	25,485	277,368
1992-3	6,174	15,069	26,491	27,177	14,762	11,052	25,548	7,234	15,563	28,783	9,180	26,438	274,751
1993-4	6,120	11,938	25,514	28,606	10,510	15,621	25,468	8,622	15,463	33,717	8,988	23,813	272,746
1994-5	5,729	12,406	23,943	24,211	11,905	11,630	13,945	8,100	12,757	28,138	8,360	29,024	247,798
1995-6	6,291	13,984	25,121	26,049	12,932	13,309	19,110	7,450	10,989	28,000	8,360	25,460	257,984
1996-7[1]	6,100	13,900	24,400	27,000	11,150	17,460	16,500	7,700	14,383	25,500	8,432	24,104	254,335
1997-8[2]	6,000	14,000	24,500	26,500	12,500	14,000	17,000	6,800	15,100	25,400	8,400	26,134	256,393

[1] Preliminary. [2] Estimate. [3] Formerly part of U.S.S.R. *Source: Economic Reseach Service, U.S. Department of Agriculture (ERS-USDA)*

U.S. Annual Average Prices of Molasses, by Types (F.O.B. Tank Car or Truck) — In Dollars Per Short Ton[2]

	Blackstrap							Beet Molasses	
Year	New Orleans	South Florida	Baltimore	Upper Mississippi	Savannah	California Ports[3]	Houston	Montana/ Wyoming & Nebraska	Red River Valley[4]
1991	67.02	74.58	89.15	94.78	82.52	80.00	69.52	71.92	66.16
1992	61.27	68.36	80.41	92.95	76.70	78.43	63.75	67.81	57.50
1993	55.48	62.36	76.03	89.26	70.00	74.24	57.12	72.63	64.44
1994	65.53	72.23	85.94	91.97	79.23	83.31	69.86	NA	NA
1995	72.00	79.92	86.30	99.11	87.48	90.30	76.37	NA	NA
1996	74.88	83.07	91.27	104.71	92.55	97.11	79.41	NA	NA
1997	58.14	68.00	76.84	90.69	77.51	83.38	62.13	NA	NA
1998[1]	48.26	61.43	65.16	79.99	70.61	71.26	50.76	NA	NA

[1] Preliminary. [2] To convert dollars per short ton to cents per gallon divide by 171. [3] Los Angeles and Stockton. [4] North Dakota and Minnesota.
NA = Not available. *Source: Agricultural Marketing Service, U.S. Department of Agriculture (AMS-USDA)*

MOLASSES

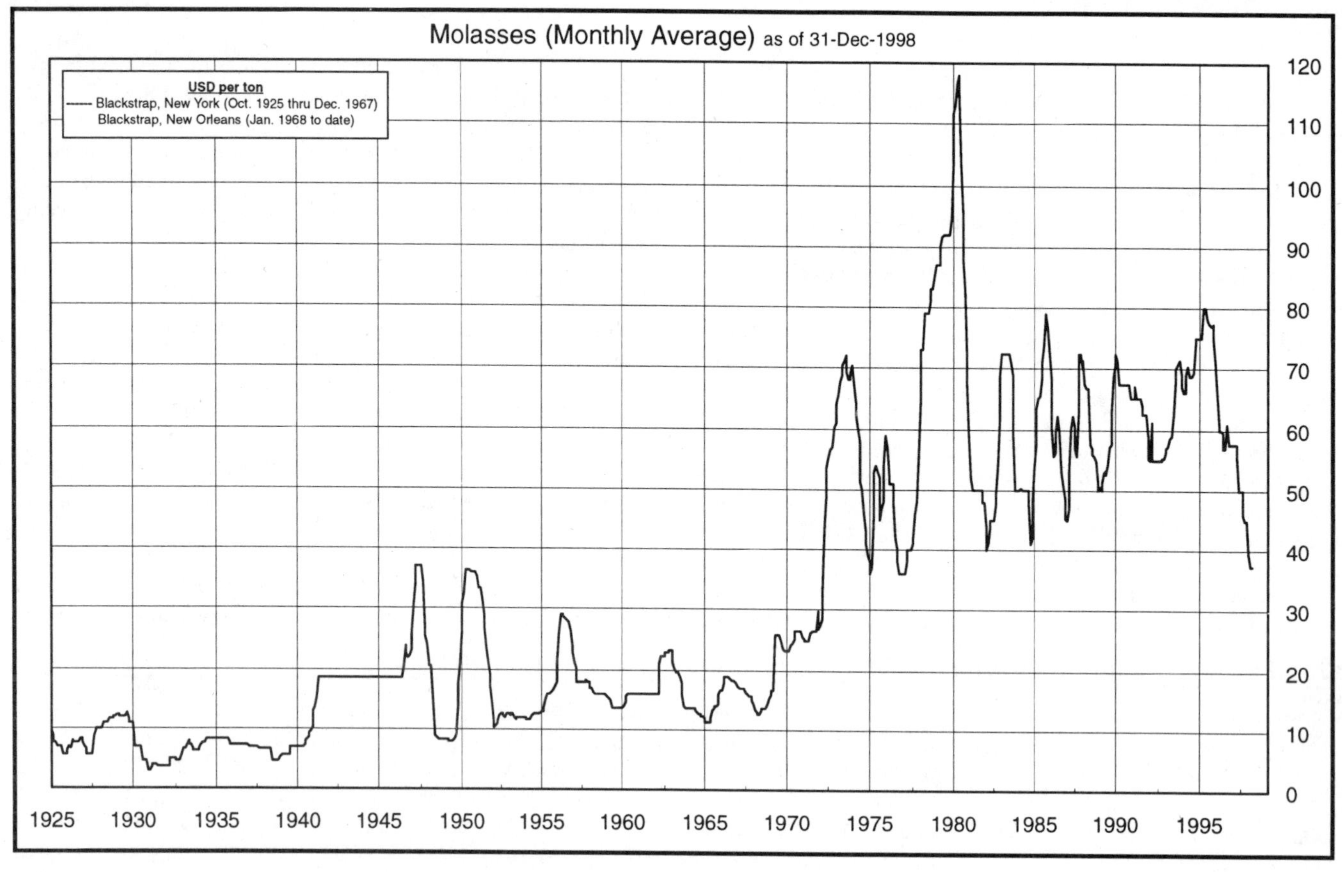

Salient Statistics of Molasses[3] in the United States In Metric Tons

Year	Production: Hawaii	Production: Mainland: Mainland Mills[4]	Production: Mainland: Refiners Black-strap	Production: Mainland: Beet	Production: Puerto Rico	In Shipments From Hawaii	Inedible Imports From: Total Imports	Inedible Imports From: Brazil	Inedible Imports From: Dominican Republic	Inedible Imports From: Mexico	Mainland Exports[5]	Total U.S. Supply	Production of Edible Molasses (1,000 Gallons)
1987	260,930	726,854	110,784	1,137,014	35,385	152,087	962,151	95,004	123,619	183,525	366,957	2,721,954	1,630
1988	252,516	775,936	101,257	1,006,353	40,694	178,476	969,870	142,897	102,792	93,605	299,217	2,749,692	1,925
1989	218,009	808,355	122,786	974,179	34,864	169,270	926,870	107,109	147,235	75,634	293,535	2,707,925	1,990
1990	228,968	741,749	105,124	948,820	24,959	214,045	1,078,924	70,986	145,543	88,401	212,263	2,876,399	1,405
1991	188,252	807,652	126,000	1,165,962	27,882	184,337	1,258,637	10,342	137,271	235,244	242,635	3,299,953	1,825
1992	182,849	782,566	123,000	950,312	25,097	183,657	1,115,863	-----	127,500	117,722	282,098	2,873,300	1,460
1993	187,915	831,661	113,000	692,465	22,802	190,371	1,040,858	-----	163,180	47,596	255,907	2,612,448	1,480
1994[1]	180,884	824,453	114,000	1,200,000	18,531	151,172	1,556,640	-----	121,320	197,753	277,098	3,459,167	1,500
1995[2]	146,000	886,826	114,000	1,040,000	16,156	146,000	1,048,726	-----	132,983	172,177	274,868	2,960,684	

[1] Preliminary. [2] Estimate. [3] Feed and industrial molasses. [4] Includes high-test molasses from frozen cane. [5] Excluding exports from Hawaii and Puerto Rico. NA = Not available. *Source: Agricultural Marketing Service, U.S. Department of Agriculture (AMS-USDA)*

Wholesale Price of Blackstrap Molasses (Cane) at New Orleans In Dollars Per Short Ton

Year	Jan.	Feb.	Mar.	Apr.	May	June	July	Aug.	Sept.	Oct.	Nov.	Dec.	Average
1989	66.90	66.25	57.50	56.90	55.75	55.60	55.00	51.25	50.00	50.50	50.00	51.25	55.58
1990	52.75	53.13	52.50	54.25	57.19	57.50	62.75	68.75	70.63	72.25	71.25	67.50	61.70
1991	67.50	67.50	67.50	67.50	67.50	67.50	67.50	67.50	65.25	65.00	65.00	65.00	66.69
1992	65.00	65.00	65.00	65.00	63.75	62.50	62.50	62.50	58.75	55.31	55.00	55.00	61.28
1993	55.00	55.00	55.00	55.00	55.00	55.00	55.00	55.25	55.31	56.25	56.75	57.19	55.48
1994	57.75	57.50	59.38	62.50	68.00	70.00	70.63	71.25	69.38	67.50	66.25	66.25	65.53
1995	69.00	70.31	68.75	68.75	68.75	69.38	74.25	75.00	75.00	75.00	75.00	75.00	72.02
1996	80.00	80.00	80.00	78.00	77.50	77.50	77.50	77.50	75.00	70.00	65.63	60.75	74.95
1997	60.00	60.00	59.00	56.56	56.88	60.31	57.50	57.50	57.50	57.50	57.50	57.50	58.15
1998[1]	57.50	55.63	51.00	50.00	50.00	46.00	45.00	45.00	45.00	37.50	37.50	37.50	46.47

[1] Preliminary. *Source: Agricultural Marketing Service, U.S. Department of Agriculture (AMS-USDA)*

Molybdenum

Molybdenum is a silver-gray metal that is used principally as an alloying agent in cast irons, steels and superalloys. It is used to enhance strength, toughness and wear resistance. In the form of molybdic acid or ferromolybdenum it is combined with or added to chromium, manganese, nickel, tungsten and other alloy metals. Molybdenum finds significant usage as a refractory metal in chemical applications. Since there are so many uses for molybdenum-contained materials and few acceptable substitutes, demand for molybdenum is expected to increase in the future.

World mine output of molybdenum was estimated to be 140,000 metric tonnes (molybdenum contained in concentrate) in 1997. That was some 5 percent more than in 1996. Molybdenum production and reserves are concentrated in a few countries. The major producers are the U.S., China, Chile, Russia and Canada. These countries provide about 90 percent of the world's molybdenum. These countries also possess about 90 percent of the estimated world reserves. U.S. mine production of molybdenum in 1997 was 60,900 tonnes (contained molybdenum), an increase of 11 percent from 1996. U.S. shipments of molybdenum in 1997 were 59,100 tonnes, an increase of 2 percent from 1996. On December 31, 1997, stocks of molybdenum concentrate at mines and plants were 3,660 tonnes. This was some 48 percent higher than the stocks a year earlier.

The U.S. Geological Survey reported that production of molybdenum concentrate in July 1998 was 4,060 tonnes (contained molybdenum). That was down 6 percent from the production level in June. In the first seven months of 1998, U.S. production of molybdenum concentrate was 31,600 tonnes. For all of 1997 it was 60,100 tonnes. Domestic shipments of molybdenum concentrate in July 1998 were 3,280 tonnes compared to 3,350 tonnes in June. In the January-July 1998 period, domestic shipments were 19,800 tonnes while for all of 1997 they were 12,100 tonnes. Exports in July 1998 were 926 tonnes compared to 1,040 tonnes in June. In the first seven months of 1998, exports of concentrate were 12,400 tonnes while for all of 1997 they were 20,000 tonnes.

U.S. exports of molybdenum ores and concentrates in June 1998 were 3.94 million kilograms. That was down from the 4.09 million kilograms exported in May 1998. In the first half of 1998, exports totaled 25.5 million kilograms. For all of 1997, exports were 57.2 million kilograms. In 1998, the major markets were the Netherlands, Chile, the United Kingdom, Japan and Belgium. U.S. exports of ferromolybdenum in June 1998 were 172,000 kilograms. For the first half of 1998, exports were 491,000 kilograms while for all of 1997 they were 678,000 kilograms. The major destination was Canada.

World Mine Production of Molybdenum   In Metric Tons (Contained Molybdenum)

Year	Bulgaria	Canada[3]	Chile	China	Iran	Kazak hstan[4]	Mexico	Mongolia	Peru	Russia[4]	United States	Uzbek- isten[4]	World Total
1988	200	13,535	15,515	14,400	700	------	4,456	1,400	2,444	17,000	43,051	------	112,860
1989	190	14,073	16,550	15,700	785	------	4,189	1,580	3,177	17,000	63,105	------	136,494
1990	150	11,994	13,830	15,700	542	------	2,000	1,578	2,510	17,000	61,611	------	127,028
1991	120	11,329	14,434	13,200	395	------	1,716	1,716	3,031	16,000	53,364	------	115,000
1992	120	9,405	14,840	19,200	1,320	700	1,458	1,610	3,220	5,000	49,725	700	108,000
1993	120	9,700	14,899	18,300	1,000	600	1,705	2,050	2,980	10,300	36,800	700	99,500
1994	100	10,250	16,028	21,400	670	534	2,610	2,100	2,765	7,700	46,800	700	112,000
1995	400	9,113	17,889	33,000	560	400	3,883	1,830	3,411	8,800	60,900	500	142,000
1996[1]	400	8,789	17,415	29,600	560	400	4,211	2,200	3,711	8,500	54,900	500	133,000
1997[2]	------	7,540	17,900	32,000	600	400	4,300	1,992	3,835	8,500	60,900	500	140,000

[1] Preliminary. [2] Estimate. [3] Shipments. [4] Formerly part of the U.S.S.R.; data not reported separately until 1992. *Source: U.S. Geological Survey*

Salient Statistics of Molybdenum in the United States   In Metric Tons (Contained Molybdenum)

	Concentrate							Primary Products[4]							
		Shipments						Net Production				Shipments			
Year	Production	Total (Includes Exports)	Value Mil. $	For Exports	Consumption	Imports for Consumption	Stocks, Dec. 31[3]	Grand Total	Molybdic Oxide[5]	Molybdenum Metal Powder	Price Avg. Value $ Kl.[6]	To Domestic Destinations	Oxide for Exports (Gross Weight)	Consumption	Producer Stocks, Dec. 31
1988	43,051	45,240	266.9	23,500	35,690	514	4,777	29,782	25,404	4,378	7.61	20,535	W	17,422	7,116
1989	63,105	61,733	421.4	51,232	41,877	238	6,969	16,545	16,545	W	8.05	18,277	1,391	17,204	6,675
1990	61,611	61,580	346.3	41,380	35,455	478	7,672	15,727	15,727	W	7.39	17,983	787	18,060	5,919
1991	53,364	53,607	249.9	22,424	32,998	161	5,291	20,782	18,739	2,043	5.27	19,105	1,571	16,901	9,422
1992	49,725	45,098	189.9	33,439	15,243	831	11,905	13,880	11,916	1,964	4.85	17,305	557	17,200	7,480
1993	36,800	39,200	165.1	28,280	13,800	3,400	11,200	11,989	10,697	1,292	5.13	16,000	1,042	17,700	6,150
1994	46,800	40,000	284.0	14,568	17,200	2,280	5,510	16,000	14,900	1,070	4.60	21,400	2,240	19,100	3,940
1995	60,900	61,700	651.0	18,600	25,500	5,570	5,390	22,900	20,900	1,970	17.47	24,000	2,840	19,900	4,820
1996[1]	54,900	57,900	456.0	19,700	24,500	5,480	2,470	24,100	20,400	1,970	7.30	24,100	1,790	20,900	5,780
1997[2]	60,900	59,100	406.0	20,000	24,300	6,330	3,660	25,900	22,700	2,000	8.50	25,900	1,240	20,000	6,500

[1] Preliminary. [2] Estimate. [3] At mines and at plants making molybdenum products. [4] Comprises ferromolybdenum, molybdic oxide, and molybdenum salts and metal. [5] Includes molybdic oxide briquets, molybdic acid, molybdenum trioxide, and all others. [6] U.S. producer price per kilogram of molybdenum contained in technical-grade molybdic oxide. W = Withheld proprietary data. *Source: U.S. Geological Survey (USGS)*

Nickel

Nickel is used in the production of stainless steel and other corrosion-resistant alloys. About a fifth of the nickel produced in the U.S. is used in plating to provide hard, tarnish-resistant, polishable surfaces. Nickel is used in coins to replace silver, in rechargeable batteries and in electronic circuitry. Nickel-based alloys are used in wire, bars, sheets and in tubular forms. Elemental nickel is used to make nickel-base corrosion resistant alloys. Nickel plating techniques, like electroless coating or single-slurry coating, are employed in such applications as turbine blades, helicopter rotors, extrusion dies and rolled steel strip.

U.S. reported consumption of nickel (exclusive of scrap) in the January-June 1998 period was 52,600 tonnes vs. 52,700 tonnes in the same period of 1997. Consumption of nickel cathodes, pellets, briquets and powder in the first half of 1998 was 43,300 tonnes, 5 percent higher than in the same period of 1997. Consumption of ferronickel in first half 1998 was 7,090 tonnes or some 23 percent less than the year before. Consumption of nickel oxide-sinter, salts and other forms in first half 1998 was 2,250 tonnes, down 5 percent from 1997. In the first half of 1998, some 38 percent of nickel consumption was in making stainless and heat resisting steel; 17 percent was used in superalloys; 16 percent was used in other nickel steel products and nickel alloys while 14 percent was used in electroplating.

U.S. ending stocks of nickel (exclusive of scrap) held by consumers in June 1998 were 4,680 tonnes (nickel content). Stocks of cathodes, pellets, briquets and powder were 3,310 tonnes or some 17 percent less than a year earlier. Stocks of ferronickel in June 1998 were 1,140 tonnes, much above the 389 tonnes of stocks held a year earlier. Stocks of oxide-sinter, salts and other forms were 231 tonnes, down 25 percent from June 1997.

U.S. consumption of purchased secondary nickel or scrap in January-June 1998 was 31,400 tonnes (nickel content). That was some 1 percent less than in the same period of 1997. Consumption of ferrous scrap in first half 1998 was 26,300 tonnes, down 1 percent from the year before. Consumption of nonferrous scrap was 5,050 tonnes, about unchanged from 1997. For all of 1997, nickel scrap consumption was 62,300 tonnes. U.S. stocks of nickel scrap in June 1998 were 4,460 tonnes or some 11 percent less than the year before. Stocks of ferrous scrap were 4,280 tonnes while stocks of nonferrous scrap were 174 tonnes.

U.S. imports for consumption of nickel in January-May 1998 were 74,000 tonnes, some 4 percent higher than in 1997. The major supplier was Canada with 29,000 tonnes followed by Russia with 14,600 tonnes. Other large suppliers are Norway, Australia and the Dominican Republic.

Futures Markets

Nickel is traded on the London Metals Exchange (LME).

World Mine Production of Nickel In Metric Tons (Contained Nickel)

Year	Australia[3]	Botswana	Brazil	Canada	China	Dominican Republic	Greece	Indonesia	New Caledonia	Philippines	Russia[4]	South Africa	World Total
1988	62,358	26,000	18,677	216,589	32,700	29,345	13,131	57,982	71,200	10,349	280,000	30,000	952,215
1989	67,041	23,700	18,826	200,899	34,250	31,264	16,097	62,987	96,200	15,380	280,000	28,900	984,078
1990	67,000	23,200	24,100	196,225	33,000	28,700	18,500	68,308	85,100	15,818	280,000	29,000	974,000
1991	69,000	23,500	26,400	192,259	31,000	29,062	19,300	71,681	114,492	13,658	245,000	27,700	991,000
1992	57,683	23,000	29,372	186,384	32,800	42,641	17,000	77,600	113,000	13,022	280,000	28,400	1,010,000
1993	64,717	23,000	32,154	188,080	30,700	37,423	12,940	65,757	97,092	7,663	244,000	29,868	926,000
1994	78,962	19,041	32,663	149,886	36,900	45,588	18,821	81,175	97,323	9,895	240,000	30,751	929,000
1995	98,467	18,672	25,469	180,984	41,800	44,051	19,947	88,183	121,457	15,075	251,000	29,803	1,030,000
1996[1]	113,134	24,200	25,600	183,059	43,000	45,000	20,000	90,000	142,200	14,700	230,000	33,613	1,080,000
1997[2]	120,000	22,600	27,200	182,000	41,000	47,000	18,000	76,000	157,000	15,000	230,000	31,800	1,080,000

[1] Preliminary. [2] Estimate. [3] Content of nickel and sulfate and concentrates. *Source: U.S. Geological Survey (USGS)*

Salient Statistics of Nickel in the United States In Metric Tons (Contained Nickel)

Year	Net Import Reliance as a % of Apparent Consumption	Production: Plant[4]	Production: Secondary[5]	Nickel Consumed[1], By Uses: Alloy Steels	Cast Irons	Copper Base Alloys	Electroplating Anodes	Nickel Alloys	Stainless & Heat Resisting Steels	Super Alloys	Chemicals	Apparent Consumption	Stocks, Dec. 31: At Consumers' Plants	Stocks, Dec. 31: At Producer Plants	Primary & Secondary Nickel: Exports	Primary & Secondary Nickel: Imports	Avg. Price LME[6] $ Lb.
1988	74	-----	49,371	7,330	2,359	6,890	19,520	19,046	80,107	13,537	1,816	159,156	15,081	6,967	27,916	127,680	6.25
1989	71	347	52,131	6,094	2,318	9,928	21,604	18,757	68,866	10,956	1,164	157,103	16,562	6,326	31,460	137,017	6.04
1990	64	3,701	57,367	7,007	2,646	7,594	15,550	16,315	96,120	15,713	1,500	170,042	13,971	8,065	37,057	145,600	4.02
1991	61	7,065	53,521	5,536	1,185	6,938	15,474	16,882	84,292	13,787	1,363	156,663	15,940	11,794	36,902	138,210	3.70
1992	59	8,960	55,871	4,988	1,202	6,313	16,538	15,946	83,460	10,872	51	159,373	17,480	10,140	33,860	128,510	3.18
1993	63	4,880	54,702	4,940	805	6,078	16,611	17,004	87,300	10,783	1,170	158,000	14,430	15,700	33,180	132,710	2.40
1994	64	-----	58,590	5,930	499	7,940	15,500	20,500	88,700	11,700	2,670	164,000	11,000	10,200	41,920	133,070	2.88
1995	60	8,290	64,600	9,570	491	8,510	15,600	21,800	103,000	14,100	5,210	181,000	12,300	12,700	51,550	156,930	3.73
1996[2]	59	15,100	59,200	6,240	563	7,300	16,200	19,700	94,000	12,600	5,310	183,000	12,900	11,200	46,700	150,060	3.40
1997[3]	54	16,100		7,500	W	W	14,100	W	42,400	11,700	W		14,200	11,500	56,500	158,000	3.14

[1] Exclusive of scrap. [2] Preliminary. [3] Estimate. [4] Smelter & refinery. [5] From purchased scrap (ferrous & nonferrous). [6] London Metal Exchange

W = Withheld proprietary data. *Source: U.S. Geological Survey (USGS)*

Oats

Within the U.S. and worldwide feed grain complex, oat production is the smallest crop. The U.S. 1998/99 crop (June to May) of 170 million bushels compares with 176 million in 1997/98 and the record low 155 million in 1996/97. The U.S. harvested oat acreage in 1998/99 of 2.8 million is the second smallest acreage on record; by comparison, in the 1980's plantings averaged about 12 million acres. Average yield, however, has increased, averaging 60.5 bushels/acre for the 1998 crop, unchanged from 1997, vs. an average of about 55 bushels in 1993-96. The Dakota's are the largest producing states, followed by Wisconsin.

Imports, mostly from Canada, help complement U.S. supplies. They are forecast to be only 90 million bushels in 1998/99 vs. 98 million in crop-year 1997/98, and would seem to underscore the well entrenched contraction in U.S. oat demand.

Oat 1998/99 carryin stocks as of June 1, 1998, of a near record low 74 million bushels compare with 67 million a year earlier. The total supply for 1998/99 of 334 million bushels compares with 341 million in 1997/98. Disappearance was estimated at 262 million vs. 267 million, respectively. Feed and residual use was forecast at 165 million bushels in 1998/99 vs. 170 million in 1997/98. Feed, seed and industrial use was placed at 95 million, unchanged from 1997/98. U.S. oat exports of about 2 million bushels are insignificant. Carryover stocks on May 31, 1999, are forecast at 72 million bushels.

The declining supply/demand data has failed to bolster prices which during calendar 1997 and into 1998 slipped steadily lower, briefly going under a $1.00/bushel in September 1998, basis nearby futures, vs. a high for the year near $1.50/bushel.The average farm price for 1998/99 was forecast at $1.10-1.30/bus. vs. $1.60 in 1997/98, and $1.96 in 1996/97, the highest farm price of the 1990's.

World oat production in the mid 1980's totaled about 50 million metric tonnes, for 1998/99 the total was less than 26.5 million as less acreage continues to be allocated to oats. In 1998/99 world acreage of 16.5 million hectare compares with 17 million in 1997/98 with an average yield 1.61 tonnes per hectare vs. 1.82, respectively. Russia remains the world's largest producer, but their 1998/99 crop of 5.5 million tonnes compares with 9.4 million in 1997/98 and is about half the country's production in the mid-1980's. Among the few major producers only Canada has shown any real growth in production during the 1990's with a record high 4.4 million tonnes produced in 1996/97 and 4 million in 1998/99.

Most of the world's oat production is consumed domestically and world trade is small. In 1998/99 exports were put at 1.9 million tonnes vs. 2.2 million in 1997/98, with Canada accounting for 1.5 million and 1.25 million, respectively. Importing nations are more numerous, but the U.S. is the consistent leader although with a lower than expected 1.5 million tonnes forecast for 1998/99 vs. 1.8 million in 1997/98.

Futures Markets

Oat futures and options are traded on the Chicago Board of Trade (CBOT) and the Winnipeg Commodity Exchange (WCE). Oat futures are traded on the Mid-America Commodity Exchange (MidAm).

World Production of Oats In Thousands of Metric Tons

Crop Year	Argentina	Australia	Canada	China	France	Germany	Italy	Poland	Sweden	Turkey	United States	Former U.S.S.R.	World Total
1989-90	620	1,640	3,546	622	970	2,010	296	2,186	1,455	270	5,423	14,972	39,554
1990-1	434	1,530	2,692	685	830	2,104	298	2,119	1,584	270	5,189	15,081	39,042
1991-2	400	1,690	1,794	650	740	1,867	359	1,873	1,426	280	3,534	12,342	32,785
1992-3	450	1,937	2,823	640	700	1,314	333	1,229	807	280	4,298	13,974	33,587
1993-4	440	1,652	3,550	640	710	1,730	370	1,500	1,295	280	2,994	14,422	35,162
1994-5	350	920	3,640	600	680	1,660	360	1,240	990	300	3,320	13,850	33,160
1995-6	350	1,880	2,860	640	620	1,420	300	1,500	950	280	2,350	10,690	28,830
1996-7[1]	310	1,700	4,360	600	620	1,610	350	1,580	1,200	250	2,250	10,030	30,590
1997-8[2]	510	1,300	3,490	400	560	1,600	280	1,630	1,280	250	2,560	11,480	30,870
1998-9[3]	350	1,200	3,970	650	640	1,300	340	1,500	1,000	250	2,470	7,510	26,680

[1] Preliminary. [2] Estimate. [3] Forecast. *Source: Foreign Agricultural Service, U.S. Department of Agriculture (FAS-USDA)*

Official Oats Crop Production Reports in the United States In Thousands of Bushels

Year	July 1	Aug. 1	Sept. 1	Oct. 1	Dec.	Final	Year	July 1	Aug. 1	Sept. 1	Oct. 1	Dec.	Final
1987	------	392,843	------	------	------	373,713	1993	262,860	249,830	249,830	208,138	------	206,770
1988	------	206,330	206,330	210,766	------	217,375	1994	248,151	247,753	247,753	229,717	------	229,008
1989	387,593	380,690	380,690	370,693	------	373,587	1995	181,508	186,167	186,167	------	------	162,027
1990	374,457	365,337	365,337	358,288	------	357,654	1996	154,968	157,663	------	------	------	153,245
1991	280,016	259,666	259,666	242,526	------	243,851	1997	182,672	187,127	------	------	------	167,246
1992	256,381	276,381	------	------	------	294,229	1998	183,201	177,211	------	------	------	167,122

Source: National Agricultural Statistics Service, U.S. Department of Agriculture (NASS-USDA)

OATS

Oat Stocks in the United States In Thousands of Bushels

Year	On Farms Mar. 1	On Farms June 1	On Farms Sept. 1	On Farms Dec. 1	Off Farms Mar. 1	Off Farms June 1	Off Farms Sept. 1	Off Farms Dec. 1	Total Stocks Mar. 1	Total Stocks June 1	Total Stocks Sept. 1	Total Stocks Dec. 1
1989	------	59,930	------	------	------	38,404	------	------	------	98,334	------	------
1990	140,000	82,850	234,700	194,700	74,749	74,062	117,009	99,398	214,749	156,912	351,709	294,098
1991	138,600	92,400	173,600	148,100	90,659	78,831	110,487	96,508	229,259	171,231	284,087	244,608
1992	98,150	61,000	199,900	161,200	76,735	66,721	94,717	81,292	174,885	127,721	294,617	242,492
1993	110,250	66,130	161,000	124,200	64,875	47,063	58,004	69,517	175,125	113,193	219,004	193,717
1994	85,050	53,940	144,300	113,400	61,502	51,583	75,551	78,664	146,552	105,523	219,851	192,064
1995	78,400	46,750	107,200	87,200	70,575	53,848	72,967	65,804	148,975	100,598	180,167	153,004
1996	57,350	32,600	93,400	80,650	55,268	33,708	38,716	45,218	112,618	66,308	132,116	125,868
1997	56,200	33,100	107,950	83,200	39,362	33,576	48,972	61,051	95,562	66,676	156,922	144,251
1998[1]	58,800	34,500	110,300	81,500	52,653	39,501	51,525	61,841	111,453	74,001	161,825	143,341

[1] Preliminary. *Source: National Agriucultural Statistics Service, U.S. Department of Agriculture (NASS-USDA)*

Oats Supply and Utilization in the United States

Crop Year Beginning June 1	Acreage Planted (1,000 Acres)	Acreage Harvested (1,000 Acres)	Yield Per Acre (Bushels)	Production	Imports	Total Supply	Feed & Residual	Food, Alcohol & Industrial	Seed	Exports	Total Use	Ending Stocks	Farm Price	Findley Loan Rate	Target Price
				In Millions of Bushels									Dollars Per Bushel		
1989-90	12,085	6,882	54.3	373.6	66.4	538.3	265.6	91.6	23.4	.8	381.4	156.9	1.49	.85	1.50
1990-1	10,423	5,945	60.1	357.5	63.4	578.0	286.1	100.9	19.1	.6	406.7	171.2	1.14	.81	1.45
1991-2	8,654	4,806	50.6	243.5	74.8	489.4	235.2	107.2	17.8	1.9	362.1	127.7	1.21	.83	1.45
1992-3	7,961	4,492	65.4	294.8	55.0	476.9	233.0	107.2	17.8	5.7	363.7	113.2	1.32	.88	1.45
1993-4	7,937	3,803	54.4	206.8	106.8	426.8	193.3	110.0	15.0	3.0	321.3	105.5	1.36	.88	1.45
1994-5	6,639	4,010	57.1	229.0	93.2	427.7	201.1	79.2	12.8	1.0	327.1	100.6	1.22	.97	1.45
1995-6	6,336	2,962	54.7	162.0	80.5	343.2	182.7	80.0	12.1	2.1	276.9	66.3	1.68	.97	1.45
1996-7	4,661	2,685	57.8	155.3	97.5	319.1	154.9	81.4	13.6	2.5	252.0	67.0	1.96	1.03	-----
1997-8[1]	5,169	2,911	60.5	176.1	98.0	341.0	170.0	81.4	13.6	2.1	267.0	74.0	1.59	1.11	-----
1998-9[2]	4,992	2,936	60.4	170.0	90.0	334.0	165.0			2.0	262.0	72.0	1.10-1.30	2.11	-----

[1] Preliminary. [2] Forecast. *Source: Economic Research Service, U.S. Department of Agriculture (ERS-USDA)*

Production of Oats in the United States, by States In Thousands of Bushels

Year	Illinois	Iowa	Michigan	Minnesota	Nebraska	New York	North Dakota	Ohio	Penn-slyvania	South Dakota	Texas	Wisconsin	Total
1989	16,000	54,000	20,100	46,750	8,640	9,145	20,150	15,750	13,770	44,000	6,600	46,860	373,587
1990	11,560	40,800	13,050	48,180	13,440	8,235	16,100	2,280	15,840	53,200	9,225	47,570	357,654
1991	6,600	21,250	5,400	22,800	11,880	5,000	10,200	1,292	8,400	38,500	7,200	26,500	243,851
1992	7,930	25,125	8,400	35,000	15,400	7,700	37,400	12,070	13,735	42,900	5,720	34,410	294,229
1993	4,590	9,000	7,150	23,750	6,880	6,510	37,100	9,000	10,000	26,520	7,420	24,150	206,770
1994	5,490	26,660	6,270	24,750	7,500	7,040	33,550	6,720	8,480	31,360	5,200	25,380	229,008
1995	5,360	14,625	5,130	18,000	4,500	5,310	21,600	6,900	9,440	11,500	5,040	18,700	162,027
1996	4,620	12,920	3,600	15,120	7,455	3,850	19,000	5,130	7,560	21,600	3,400	17,400	153,245
1997	5,550	16,790	4,880	17,400	5,850	5,850	18,700	6,660	8,990	14,850	6,760	20,160	167,246
1998[1]	3,920	10,915	4,830	19,530	5,320	6,510	26,040	6,500	8,480	20,100	6,890	18,300	167,122

[1] Preliminary. *Source: National Agricultural Statistics Service, U.S. Department of Agriculture (NASS-USDA)*

Average Cash Price of No. 2 Heavy White Oats in Toledo In Dollars Per Bushel

Year	June	July	Aug.	Sept.	Oct.	Nov.	Dec.	Jan.	Feb.	Mar.	Apr.	May	Average
1988-9	2.71	2.79	2.66	2.55	2.41	2.04	2.08	2.25	2.10	1.96	1.83	1.79	2.26
1989-90	1.53	1.39	1.30	1.30	1.34	1.37	1.46	1.40	1.37	1.41	1.46	1.47	1.40
1990-1	1.33	1.19	1.14	1.09	1.11	1.10	1.15	1.12	1.12	1.22	1.22	1.26	1.17
1991-2	1.14	1.24	1.29	1.28	1.31	1.30	1.34	1.41	1.58	1.61	1.48	1.50	1.37
1992-3	1.46	1.47	1.46	1.58	1.54	1.58	1.55	1.54	1.49	1.43	1.53	1.50	1.51
1993-4	1.42	1.50	1.49	1.43	1.41	1.38	1.37	1.43	1.40	1.37	1.37	1.25	1.40
1994-5	1.35	1.26	1.26	1.32	1.35	1.28	1.27	1.34	1.45	1.43	1.48	1.59	1.37
1995-6	1.65	1.76	1.83	1.90	1.76	1.91	2.21	2.14	2.06	2.17	2.32	2.05	1.98
1996-7	NQ	2.45	2.34	2.19	2.02	1.96	1.96	1.99	2.16	2.26	2.12	2.08	2.14
1997-8[1]	2.12	1.79	1.84	1.80	1.77								1.86

[1] Preliminary. NQ = No Quote. *Source: Economic Research Service, U.S. Department of Agriculture (ERS-USDA)*

Volume of Trading in Oat Futures in Chicago In Contracts

Year	Jan	Feb	Mar	Apr	May	June	July	Aug	Sept	Oct	Nov	Dec	Total
1989	33,700	27,320	30,140	37,740	27,740	39,040	29,740	34,980	20,840	17,340	38,380	12,900	349,860
1990	24,660	31,740	33,880	45,140	54,000	46,360	32,040	49,600	25,200	27,800	47,380	15,560	433,360
1991	20,040	30,280	30,320	42,720	20,580	44,940	37,100	41,060	17,860	20,300	34,560	15,200	354,960
1992	31,020	84,020	42,260	47,060	42,020	54,540	22,200	40,160	25,100	16,580	35,220	19,400	459,580
1993	20,480	26,500	26,060	63,140	33,420	43,120	33,300	32,080	26,880	40,780	72,320	37,260	455,340
1994	47,980	57,060	39,800	53,820	34,300	69,760	20,760	39,340	28,840	24,900	56,940	19,680	493,180
1995	13,512	37,014	29,490	45,536	34,116	107,082	29,862	45,677	31,676	38,641	52,321	47,005	511,932
1996	61,451	52,079	34,608	77,395	47,161	34,498	38,960	33,316	30,801	37,579	37,856	16,154	501,858
1997	34,238	51,608	39,607	41,988	27,028	29,632	25,473	26,486	21,241	42,630	38,187	19,214	397,332
1998	21,150	51,247	25,551	65,381	23,490	55,376	29,870	42,156	27,131	31,426	51,172	18,924	442,874

Source: Chicago Board of Trade (CBT)

Average Open Interest of Oat Futures in Chicago In Contracts

Year	Jan.	Feb.	Mar.	Apr.	May	June	July	Aug.	Sept.	Oct.	Nov.	Dec.
1989	10,068	10,245	10,152	10,057	9,521	9,766	9,793	9,454	9,765	11,167	11,862	11,248
1990	11,227	11,809	11,355	12,243	12,513	10,891	10,743	12,112	12,965	14,804	15,115	11,758
1991	11,890	12,832	13,895	15,620	14,223	13,091	11,117	10,894	10,368	11,560	11,257	9,355
1992	9,555	15,499	15,359	15,052	15,329	14,773	12,759	11,100	9,869	9,178	8,781	7,287
1993	7,398	7,739	7,655	11,579	13,357	12,020	10,894	11,381	11,171	14,116	20,057	20,547
1994	21,193	20,137	20,194	19,882	18,312	14,575	11,710	13,923	14,743	16,266	15,354	13,376
1995	13,133	13,231	13,000	15,426	16,054	13,611	11,019	11,348	11,012	11,970	12,542	13,003
1996	13,253	14,095	14,231	14,497	13,897	11,697	11,336	11,803	11,457	11,918	11,150	8,550
1997	8,088	9,650	12,649	11,024	9,830	9,395	8,131	8,606	8,618	10,953	11,816	10,964
1998	12,782	15,368	16,553	17,748	17,441	16,437	14,255	15,052	14,771	16,263	18,466	17,048

Source: Chicago Board of Trade (CBT)

OATS

Average Cash Price of No. 2 Heavy White Oats in Minneapolis In Dollars Per Bushel

Year	June	July	Aug	Sept	Oct	Nov	Dec	Jan	Feb	Mar	Apr	May	Average
1989-90	1.97	1.72	1.59	1.58	1.61	1.68	1.70	1.56	1.48	1.57	1.63	1.68	1.65
1990-1	1.52	1.37	1.25	1.23	1.29	1.30	1.24	1.22	1.18	1.27	1.32	1.36	1.30
1991-2	1.25	1.33	1.38	1.35	1.41	1.42	1.49	1.50	1.68	1.66	1.57	1.59	1.47
1992-3	1.55	1.49	1.45	1.58	1.52	1.59	1.63	1.66	1.63	1.63	1.66	1.57	1.58
1993-4	1.54	1.63	1.63	1.66	1.56	1.51	1.56	1.57	1.52	1.55	1.46	1.37	1.55
1994-5	1.47	1.36	1.44	1.44	1.44	1.41	NQ	1.46	1.42	1.54	1.62	1.76	1.36
1995-6	1.73	1.92	1.96	2.04	2.11	2.63	2.50	2.40	2.31	2.47	2.56	2.68	2.28
1996-7	2.11	2.48	2.36	2.08	2.06	1.87	1.86	1.89	1.94	1.99	1.88	1.81	2.03
1997-8	1.89	1.76	1.80	1.78	1.75	1.65	1.71	1.68	1.59	1.65	1.54	1.58	1.70
1998-9[1]	1.52	1.42	1.21	1.30	1.29	1.32	1.31						1.34

[1] Preliminary. NQ = No Quote. *Source: Economic Research Service, U.S. Department of Agriculture (ERS-USDA)*

Average Price Received by Farmers for Oats in the United States In Dollars Per Bushel

Year	June	July	Aug	Sept	Oct	Nov	Dec	Jan	Feb	Mar	Apr	May	Average
1989-90	1.82	1.53	1.47	1.38	1.47	1.48	1.53	1.47	1.43	1.39	1.44	1.45	1.49
1990-1	1.33	1.15	1.06	1.09	1.14	1.16	1.17	1.13	1.13	1.16	1.16	1.16	1.14
1991-2	1.08	1.08	1.09	1.12	1.21	1.25	1.25	1.31	1.44	1.44	1.46	1.43	1.21
1992-3	1.38	1.32	1.23	1.28	1.31	1.35	1.36	1.42	1.42	1.43	1.45	1.51	1.32
1993-4	1.43	1.36	1.32	1.31	1.33	1.39	1.42	1.42	1.42	1.39	1.32	1.49	1.36
1994-5	1.31	1.20	1.16	1.18	1.21	1.18	1.18	1.22	1.22	1.33	1.36	1.41	1.22
1995-6	1.38	1.52	1.48	1.43	1.50	1.72	1.91	1.93	1.96	2.04	2.13	2.48	1.46
1996-7	2.17	2.13	2.00	1.83	1.84	1.85	1.72	1.83	1.81	1.91	1.87	1.86	1.96
1997-8	1.81	1.68	1.57	1.47	1.62	1.66	1.57	1.60	1.62	1.63	1.61	1.53	1.61
1998-9[1]	1.39	1.19	1.02	1.06	1.10	1.10	1.17	1.14					1.15

[1] Preliminary. *Source: National Agricultural Statistics Service, U.S. Department of Agriculture (ERS-USDA)*

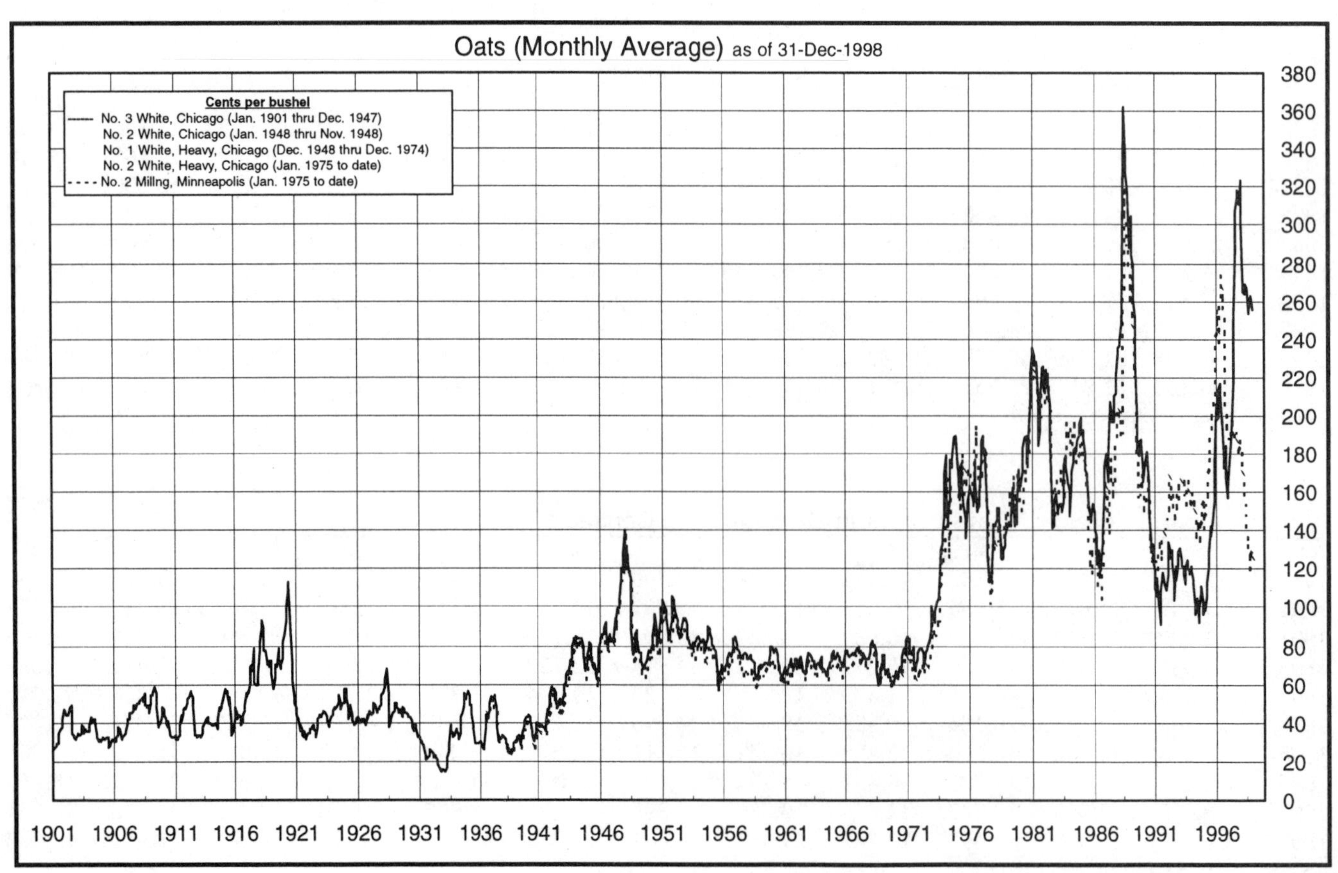

Olive Oil

The U.S.D.A. forecast world olive oil production in 1998-99 at 2.4 million metric tonnes. That represented an increase of 2 percent from the 1997-98 marketing year. Olive oil production tends to be somewhat cyclical in that large crops follow small ones in a two year cycle. That is a common pattern among tree crops. In 1994-95, world olive oil production was 1.8 million tonnes which was followed by the 1995-96 crop of 1.4 million tonnes, a 19 percent decline. That crop was in turn followed by the 1996-97 crop of 2.3 million tonnes or some 64 percent larger. The major producers of olive oil are Spain, Italy, Greece, Tunisia, Turkey, Syria and Morocco.

The European Union is the leader in world production accounting for about three-fourths of world output. European Union olive oil production in 1998-99 was forecast by the U.S.D.A. to be 1.9 million tonnes, a decline of 5 percent from 1997-98. Production of olive oil by Tunisia was forecast to be 200,000 tonnes, up substantially from the 100,000 tonne output of 1997-98; that represented a cyclical decline from the 1996-97 output of 210,000 tonnes. Olive oil production by Turkey was estimated to be 110,000 tonnes in 1998-99, another large increase from the 1997-98 crop of 60,000 tonnes. That crop was also down on a cyclical basis from the 1996-97 output of 200,000 tonnes.

European Union imports of olive oil in 1998-99 were forecast to be 628,000 tonnes, virtually unchanged from the previous year. Exports of olive oil in 1998-99 were forecast to be 865,000 tonnes, the same level as in 1997-98.

World consumption of olive oil has been trending higher. Global consumption in 1998-99 was forecast to be 2.3 million tonnes, an increase of 1 percent from the previous year. Consumption in the European Union was forecast to be 1.6 million tonnes, down 4 percent from 1996-97. U.S. olive oil consumption is forecast to be 181,000 tonnes in 1998-99, an increase of 16 percent from the previous year. In the October-July period, U.S. imports of olive oil were 304,784 tonnes, a 19 percent decline from the comparable period of 1996-97. Small amounts of olive oil are exported with 1997-98 U.S. exports projected to be 10,000 tonnes.

World Production of Olive Oil (Pressed Oil) In Thousands of Metric Tons

Crop Year	Algeria	Argentina	Greece	Italy	Jordan	Libya	Morocco	Portugal	Spain	Syria	Tunisia	Turkey	World Total
1989-90	16.0	10.5	316.3	624.2	7.5	8.0	70.0	44.3	594.9	33.0	137.0	39.0	1,938.6
1990-1	6.0	11.0	187.0	176.4	9.0	7.0	40.0	22.0	690.6	92.0	189.0	92.0	1,579.1
1991-2	37.0	9.5	423.5	727.9	5.5	10.0	55.5	72.7	640.5	47.0	264.0	70.0	2,393.5
1992-3	26.5	10.5	339.0	469.8	15.5	6.0	43.0	26.9	673.9	95.0	133.0	65.0	1,974.0
1993-4	21.0	8.5	275.0	451.5	9.5	8.0	45.5	36.1	593.2	71.0	251.0	55.0	1,875.2
1994-5	14.0	10.0	389.8	464.4	15.0	6.5	50.0	36.2	547.0	101.5	106.5	181.5	1,963.6
1995-6	23.0	11.5	362.0	540.0	15.5	4.0	40.0	48.6	320.0	84.0	64.5	45.5	1,598.4
1996-7[1]	46.0	12.0	470.0	400.0	26.0	10.0	121.0	49.0	1,028.0	138.0	289.0	222.0	2,854.0
1997-8[2]	7.0	13.0	410.0	704.0	16.0	6.0	75.0	43.0	1,175.0	78.0	99.0	45.0	2,705.0
1998-9[3]	23.0	16.0	430.0	540.0	21.0	8.0	70.0	43.0	797.0	131.0	161.0	221.0	2,498.0

[1] Preliminary. [2] Estimate. [3] Forecast. *Source: The Oil World*

Average Unit Value of Olive Oil Imports in the United States In Dollars Per Metric Ton

Year	Jan.	Feb.	Mar.	Apr.	May	June	July	Aug.	Sept.	Oct.	Nov.	Dec.	Average
1989	1,642	1,642	1,890	1,930	2,005	1,981	1,919	1,919	1,862	1,917	1,910	2,017	1,886
1990	1,892	1,940	1,931	2,034	2,047	2,047	2,044	2,169	2,142	2,029	2,245	2,170	2,058
1991	2,195	2,213	2,355	2,188	2,283	2,274	2,281	2,282	2,401	2,250	2,417	2,523	2,305
1992	2,448	2,365	2,317	2,271	2,270	2,267	2,299	2,302	2,206	2,204	2,189	2,295	2,286
1993	2,132	2,071	1,853	1,823	1,779	1,820	1,805	1,815	1,836	1,788	1,885	1,852	1,872
1994	1,838	1,752	1,891	1,850	1,872	1,889	1,943	2,001	2,032	2,141	2,215	2,126	1,963
1995	2,245	2,316	2,470	2,629	2,795	2,857	3,032	3,112	3,110	3,253	3,256	3,322	2,866
1996	3,704	4,056	4,267	4,411	4,361	4,233	4,300	4,149	4,131	4,129	4,114	3,932	4,149
1997	3,580	3,138	2,962	2,781	2,732	2,496	2,482	2,431	2,401	2,393	2,429	2,391	2,685
1998[1]	2,329	2,242	2,264	2,177	2,135	2,165	1,958	1,984	2,051	2,393	2,429		2,145

[1] Preliminary. *Source: Foreign Agricultural Service, U.S. Department of Agriculture (FAS-USDA)*

World Supply and Distribution of Olive Oil In Thousands of Metric Tons

Crop Year	Production	Exports	Imports	Consumption	Ending Stocks	Crop Year	Production	Exports	Imports	Consumption	Ending Stocks
1987-8	2,095	509	519	1,929	1,936	1993-4	1,875	397	406	2,042	576
1988-9	1,552	558	575	1,870	634	1994-5	1,964	451	459	2,004	544
1989-90	1,939	579	573	1,861	706	1995-6	1,598	307	312	1,839	308
1990-1	1,579	316	333	1,879	419	1996-7[1]	2,854	466	462	2,300	860
1991-2	2,394	346	349	1,931	836	1997-8[2]	2,705	460	463	2,430	1,138
1992-3	1,974	377	365	2,068	734	1998-9[3]	2,498	490	490	2,510	1,126

[1] Preliminary. [2] Estimate. [3] Forecast. *Source: The Oil World*

Onions

The U.S.D.A. forecast fresh onion production in 1998 at 5.7 billion pounds, an increase of nearly 2 percent from 1997. Over the last five seasons, U.S. production of fresh onions has averaged nearly 5.5 billion pounds. Imports of fresh onions in 1998 were forecast at 550 million pounds, a 5 percent decline from 1997. Over the last five seasons, imports have averaged just over 550 million pounds per year. Season beginning stocks of onions were almost 973 million pounds, some 3 percent more than a year ago. The total supply of onions in 1998 was forecast to be 7.22 billion pounds, some 1 percent more than in 1997.

In terms of utilization, U.S. exports of onions in 1998 were forecast at 625 million pounds, 4 percent more than in 1997. Exports set a high in 1994 at 802 million pounds. Over the last five seasons, exports have averaged 655 million pounds. Shrink and loss accounted for 740 million pounds, about the same as the previous year. Domestic use of fresh onions in 1998 was 4.88 billion pounds, a 1 percent increase from 1997. Projected ending stocks of onions were 975 million pounds, just slightly above a year ago.

Per capita use of fresh onions has been trending higher. Per capita use in 1998 was projected at 18 pounds, up from 17.9 pounds in 1997. In 1988, per capita use was 14.5 pounds while in 1978 it was 11.1 pounds. Since 1973, per capita use of fresh onions has increased over 75 percent.

Salient Statistics of Onions in the United States

Crop Year	Harvested Acres	Yield Per Acre	Production 1,000 Cwt.	Price Per Cwt.	Farm Value $1,000	Jan. 1 Stocks Frozen	Annual Pack Frozen	Imports Canned	Exports (Fresh)	Imports (Fresh)	Per Capita[3] Utilization --Lbs., Farm Weight-- All	Fresh
						Millions of Pounds						
1993	152,580	380	57,956	16.80	831,986	34.2	213.7	4.7	437.9	510.2	18.5	16.5
1994	160,350	396	63,531	9.87	626,778	36.1	241.3	4.2	802.1	544.7	17.5	16.5
1995	164,000	391	64,182	11.10	633,692	51.2	246.8	4.0	662.1	483.7	18.9	17.6
1996	166,210	386	64,106	10.50	604,789	48.8	259.5	3.6	586.3	625.2	18.8	17.9
1997[1]	165,910	414	68,769	11.90	728,772	40.8	230.1	3.8	600.0	576.0	18.8	17.9
1998[2]	164,140	397	65,131	14.30	830,976	42.2			625.0	550.0	19.0	18.0

[1] Preliminary. [2] Forecast. [3] Includes fresh and processing. *Source: Economic Research Service, U.S. Department of Agriculture (ERS-USDA)*

Production of Onions in the United States In Thousands of Hundred Pounds (Cwt.)

	Spring				Summer										
Year	Arizona	California	Texas	Total (All)	California	Colorado	Idaho	Michigan	Minnesota	New Mexico	New York	Oregon (Malheur)	Texas	Total (All)	Grand Total
1993	631	3,300	2,768	8,193	13,035	5,735	4,698	2,201	22	4,074	3,720	5,940	936	49,763	57,956
1994	688	2,948	4,704	10,297	12,710	6,125	5,547	2,178	312	3,318	3,844	7,378	837	53,324	63,531
1995	672	3,300	3,763	10,110	12,658	6,141	5,481	1,856	125	4,095	4,032	7,134	870	54,072	64,182
1996	760	2,736	4,030	9,290	13,330	5,200	5,590	1,798	114	3,266	2,736	7,080	924	52,079	61,369
1997	746	3,204	1,661	9,087	12,760	5,355	5,658	1,952	165	-----	3,660	7,440	-----	56,221	65,308
1998[1]	1,175	2,992	2,907	9,298	11,480	5,940	4,960	1,215	143	-----	3,306	6,840	-----	52,971	62,269

[1] Preliminary. *Source: Agricultural Statistics Board, U.S. Department of Agriculture (ASB-USDA)*

Cold Storage Stocks of Fresh Onions in the United States In Thousands of Pounds

Year	Jan.	Feb.	Mar.	Apr.	May	June	July	Aug.	Sept.	Oct.	Nov.	Dec.
1993	25,634	25,246	24,648	21,336	19,061	16,384	17,571	24,457	26,828	26,219	26,145	29,205
1994	27,349	25,740	21,630	20,530	20,156	21,067	21,877	30,794	35,832	38,571	42,691	41,044
1995	37,472	36,240	35,402	33,906	30,071	30,790	31,309	32,175	32,081	33,594	36,360	34,877
1996	35,354	35,819	31,784	32,782	27,670	29,200	27,511	27,536	27,659	30,288	27,889	32,261
1997	30,481	29,255	32,227	31,811	29,693	28,061	29,314	28,520	27,336	26,908	29,831	30,513
1998[1]	31,187	28,724	27,710	24,428	23,443	22,787	22,179	21,468	18,731	24,553	27,070	25,965

[1] Preliminary. *Source: National Agricultural Statistics Service, U.S. Department of Agriculture (NASS-USDA)*

F.O.B. Price Received by Growers for Onions in the United States In Dollars Per Hundred Pounds (Cwt.)

Year	Jan.	Feb.	Mar.	Apr.	May	June	July	Aug.	Sept.	Oct.	Nov.	Dec.	Season Average
1993	16.60	14.00	17.30	31.00	23.60	10.40	12.70	14.80	13.30	12.10	18.70	24.50	16.80
1994	31.40	33.90	18.80	10.80	8.64	8.49	12.30	9.54	9.32	10.60	12.20	12.70	9.87
1995	13.50	17.50	17.90	20.00	14.60	10.50	13.70	9.67	10.00	9.89	9.52	10.00	9.87
1996	10.70	10.10	8.11	8.86	9.54	11.10	12.10	12.60	12.70	11.50	10.40	10.20	10.60
1997	9.75	7.87	8.09	14.90	13.30	16.50	14.20	13.50	10.30	9.20	10.10	11.00	12.60
1998[1]	13.20	16.00	21.20	21.70	18.50	15.90	21.30	15.10	12.90	12.70			

[1] Preliminary. *Source: Economic Research Service, U.S. Department of Agriculture (ERS-USDA)*

Oranges and Orange Juice

U.S. production of frozen concentrated orange juice (FCOJ) continued to trend higher in 1997-98. The 1996-97 crop was large at 226.2 million boxes and the initial outlook for the 1997-98 crop was that it would be even larger. Several factors appear to be contributing to the continued increase in Florida production. One factor, and maybe the most important, is that there are a large number of trees coming into production bearing more fruit. The amount of acreage planted in Florida has increased significantly and the number of trees planted on that acreage has increased. As a result, there are more trees on more acreage. Additionally, following the freezes of the 1980's, many of the groves have been moved to the south of the state making them far less vulnerable to damage from freezes. On top of that, recent winters have been milder leading to still larger crops.

The 1997-98 Florida orange crop turned out to be a record 244 million boxes. The early midseason and Navel crop was 140 million boxes while the Valencia crop was 104 million boxes. U.S. orange production in 1997-98 was 320.5 million boxes. California orange production in 1997-98 increased to 74 million boxes. The 1998-99 season was extreme in Florida. A wet winter was followed by a very dry spring. There were many questions going into the 1998-99 season as to what sort of crop would be produced given the extremes in growing conditions. In the October crop production report, the U.S.D.A. surprised the market with a Florida crop forecast of 190 million boxes. That was well below trade expectations. The December crop report also showed the crop to be 190 million boxes with a projected yield of 1.57 gallons per box. The U.S. orange crop was 254.4 million boxes. The Florida early midseason and Navel crop was 112 million boxes while the Valencia crop was 78 million boxes. The California crop was hit by very cold weather in late December 1998 resulting in losses.

Going into the 1998-99 season, there was a large inventory of juice remaining from the harvest of the record 1997-98 crop. The Florida Citrus Processors Association reported that for the last week of the 1997-98 season, cumulative movement of juice was 260.4 million gallons, down 2 percent from the previous season. Cumulative imports of FCOJ for the season were 38.94 million gallons or some 10 percent less than the year before. The net cumulative pack from the record crop was 253.7 million gallons, up 5 percent from the 1996-97 season. The inventory of FCOJ at the end of the 1997-98 season was 104.6 million gallons, up over 50 percent from the inventory at the end of the 1996-97 season.

Brazil continued to produce a lot of FCOJ. In mid-December 1998, the Brazilian Citrus Exporters Association reported production of 1.12 million tonnes, down 8 percent from 1997-98 but larger than had been expected.

Futures Market

Frozen concentrated orange juice futures and options are traded on the Citrus Associates of the New York Cotton Exchange (NYCE).

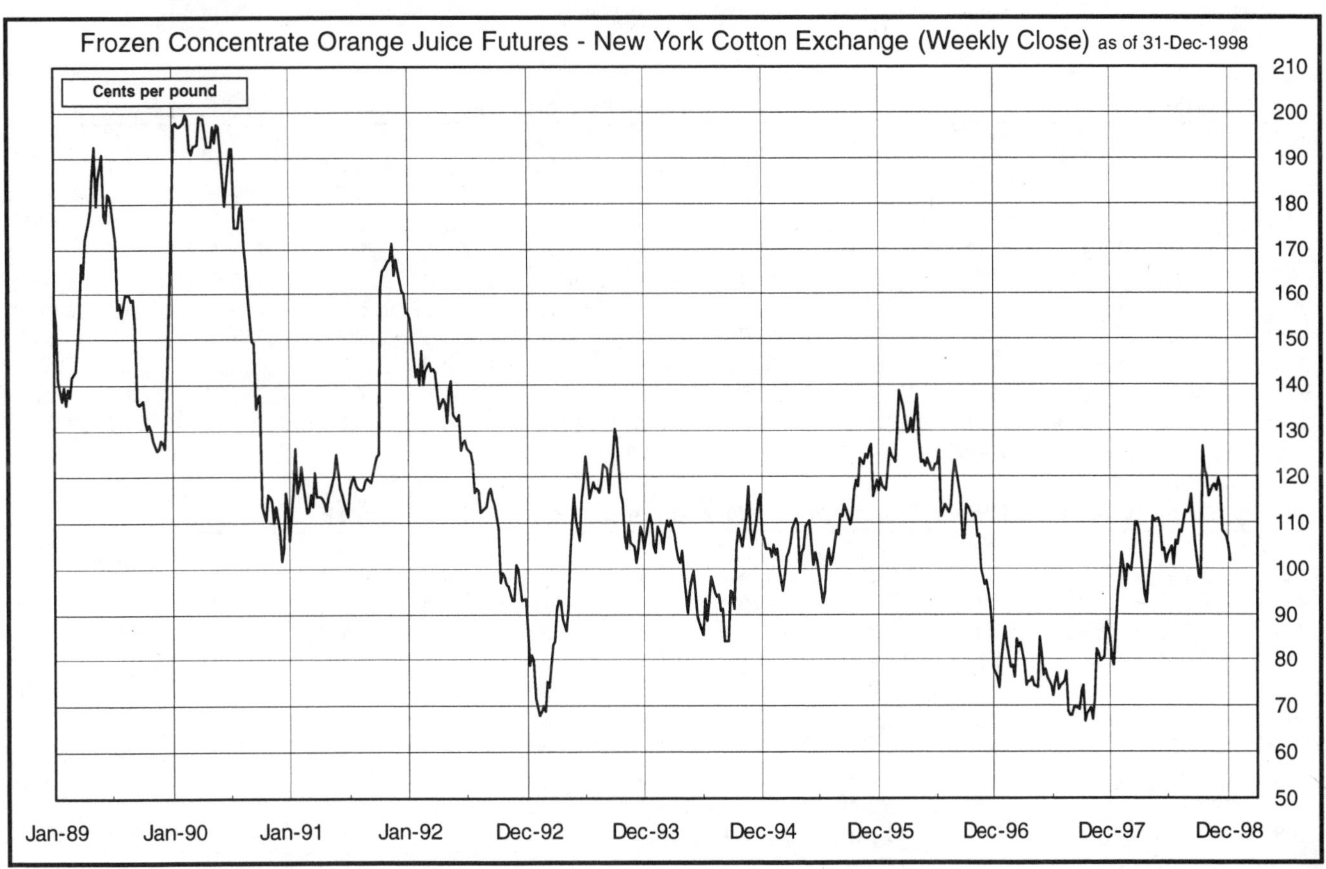

ORANGES AND ORANGE JUICE

World Production of Oranges In Thousands of Metric Tons

Season	Argentina	Australia	Brazil	Egypt	Greece	Italy	Mexico	Morocco	South Africa	Spain	Turkey	United States	World Total
1987-8	650	394	10,400	1,387	462	1,343	1,942	891	681	2,442	700	7,903	30,990
1988-9	620	544	14,150	1,199	770	2,170	2,000	994	629	2,216	740	8,272	35,835
1989-90	750	458	12,036	1,397	932	2,067	1,900	775	697	2,400	740	7,083	33,361
1990-1	600	485	12,362	1,574	819	1,760	2,300	1,103	648	2,590	735	7,222	33,938
1991-2	640	595	14,974	1,694	820	1,842	2,100	780	680	2,651	830	8,175	38,193
1992-3	660	578	14,484	1,771	1,042	2,111	2,913	874	712	2,926	820	10,074	41,582
1993-4	746	651	13,710	1,324	854	2,100	3,174	916	739	2,509	840	9,462	39,595
1994-5[1]	712	416	16,520	1,513	865	1,710	3,500	657	770	2,644	920	10,641	43,539
1995-6[2]	640	543	16,450	1,360	850	1,770	2,600	870	850	2,440	880	10,747	42,932
1996-7[3]	700	544	19,054	1,613	880	2,100	3,500	770	970	2,145	800	11,734	47,644

[1] Preliminary. [2] Estimate. [3] Forecast. NA = Not available. *Source: Foreign Agricultural Service, U.S. Department of Agriculture (FAS-USDA)*

Salient Statistics of Oranges & Orange Juice in the United States

Season	Production[4] California	Production[4] Florida	Production[4] Total U.S.	Farm Price $ Per Box	Farm Value Million $	Florida Crop Processed: Frozen Concentrates	Florida Crop Processed: Chilled Products	Florida Crop Processed: Total Processed	Florida Crop Processed: Yield Per Box Gallons[5]	Frozen Concentrated Orange Juice-Florida: Carry-in	Frozen Concentrated Orange Juice-Florida: Pack	Frozen Concentrated Orange Juice-Florida: Total Supply	Frozen Concentrated Orange Juice-Florida: Total Season Movement	Brazilian U.S. Imports of Frozen Concentrated OJ: Pack	Brazilian U.S. Imports of Frozen Concentrated OJ: Exports Total	Brazilian U.S. Imports of Frozen Concentrated OJ: Exports To U.S.
	Million Boxes					Million Boxes				In Million Gallons (42° Brix)						
1988-9	58.9	146.6	207.2	8.90	1,848.5	107.4	29.5	146.6	1.5	42.1	239.1	281.2	235.0	245.8	243.8	123.1
1989-90	71.4	110.2	184.5	7.96	1,465.1	70.1	33.5	110.2	1.2	46.3	184.7	231.0	191.1	362.0	330.7	132.4
1990-1	25.6	151.6	179.0	8.70	1,584.7	100.4	38.2	151.6	1.5	40.0	221.2	261.2	229.2	294.8	284.5	87.7
1991-2	67.4	139.8	209.6	7.43	1,545.2	90.6	37.0	139.8	1.6	31.8	211.7	243.5	212.6	274.1	279.3	107.8
1992-3	66.8	186.6	255.8	5.77	1,489.9	128.3	47.2	186.6	1.6	31.0	292.0	322.9	269.4	394.8	418.2	103.1
1993-4	63.6	174.4	240.5	6.37	1,541.3	111.7	51.0	174.4	1.6	53.5	261.7	315.2	256.6	388.2	387.5	102.0
1994-5	56.0	205.5	263.6	6.08	1,624.1	144.7	54.8	199.8	1.5	58.6	274.2	332.8	290.4	356.9	370.7	96.5
1995-6[1]	58.0	203.3	263.9	6.85	1,821.6	132.9	64.5	197.7	1.5	42.4	284.5	326.9	285.7	-----	360.8	65.9
1996-7[2]	64.0	226.2	292.6	6.16	1,834.1	153.8	68.9	222.9	1.6	41.2	301.7	342.9	273.9	-----	398.3	67.5
1997-8[3]	74.0	244.0	320.5	6.13	2,000.1	160.9	77.3	238.2	1.6							

[1] Preliminary. [2] Estimate. [3] Forecast. [4] Fruit ripened on trees, but destroyed prior to picking in not included. [5] 42° Brix equivalent.
Sources: Economic Research Service, U.S. Department of Agriculture (ERS-USDA); Florida Department of Citrus

Cold Storage Stocks of Orange Juice Concentrate in the U.S., on First of Month In Millions of Pounds

Year	Jan.	Feb.	Mar.	Apr.	May	June	July	Aug.	Sept.	Oct.	Nov.	Dec.
1989	721.6	980.9	1,155.9	1,087.0	1,144.8	1,296.1	1,324.8	1,167.5	932.6	808.4	725.7	669.7
1990	749.6	926.6	1,046.5	1,119.2	980.9	1,148.2	1,074.8	1,008.1	901.4	797.1	802.0	871.3
1991	1,031.6	1,195.8	1,199.5	1,236.9	1,363.2	1,304.7	1,110.6	1,007.5	876.9	765.2	617.3	655.4
1992	828.4	1,130.7	1,150.0	1,102.9	1,269.3	1,294.8	1,143.8	978.0	874.9	741.9	665.5	638.0
1993	892.9	1,135.9	1,282.8	1,297.5	1,440.9	1,462.3	1,351.8	1,147.0	1,029.6	875.7	813.3	890.9
1994	955.5	1,248.9	1,429.0	1,273.8	1,499.6	1,615.2	1,521.8	1,449.1	1,257.5	1,119.6	1,026.1	1,055.9
1995	1,353.1	1,704.0	1,685.1	1,773.3	1,864.6	1,833.8	1,631.6	1,424.1	1,233.7	1,038.3	830.3	897.7
1996	1,050.6	1,295.4	1,353.0	1,322.3	1,443.9	1,596.9	1,535.0	1,423.6	1,238.6	965.6	732.7	691.0
1997	1,069.4	1,522.6	1,677.6	1,752.9	1,993.4	2,176.0	1,977.7	1,761.8	1,571.8	1,287.8	1,140.9	1,214.4
1998[1]	1,503.4	1,945.9	2,029.7	2,025.0	2,473.7	2,612.8	2,447.9	2,240.2	2,025.1	1,796.3	1,534.2	1,540.2

[1] Preliminary. *Source: Agricultural Statistics Board, U.S. Department of Agriculture (ASB-USDA)*

Average Open Interest of Frozen Concentrated Orange Juice Futures in New York In Contracts

Year	Jan.	Feb.	Mar.	Apr.	May	June	July	Aug.	Sept.	Oct.	Nov.	Dec.
1989	7,169	6,959	7,009	7,821	8,374	9,767	8,340	7,531	6,857	7,218	7,029	9,887
1990	9,667	11,067	11,877	11,952	10,528	10,229	9,413	7,485	6,867	5,939	5,802	6,983
1991	6,773	6,457	5,739	6,255	5,762	6,338	5,653	6,556	9,854	11,924	9,877	9,101
1992	9,095	10,033	9,872	11,309	10,791	9,776	10,109	12,132	11,910	14,224	16,669	17,455
1993	17,733	18,199	19,030	20,210	18,525	19,267	20,000	18,899	18,287	18,825	18,422	20,367
1994	17,544	18,137	19,073	21,607	21,450	23,530	24,829	21,874	22,739	23,385	26,859	26,413
1995	27,439	25,885	26,407	30,172	27,057	26,844	23,537	17,881	20,918	22,460	26,303	24,202
1996	22,943	21,670	25,232	23,788	21,724	20,934	20,159	19,834	18,029	18,000	22,513	26,405
1997	29,171	26,929	26,331	28,955	29,868	33,639	31,799	34,339	36,057	40,365	41,811	46,169
1998	38,885	37,893	36,843	33,146	35,749	32,608	25,503	26,394	28,017	26,506	21,984	24,562

Source: Citrus Association of the New York Cotton Exchange (NYCE)

Volume of Trading of Frozen Concentrated Orange Juice Futures in New York In Contracts

Year	Jan.	Feb.	Mar.	Apr.	May	June	July	Aug.	Sept.	Oct.	Nov.	Dec.	Total
1989	26,156	26,419	28,501	26,855	30,272	32,051	23,403	19,698	17,119	18,069	15,893	39,668	304,104
1990	53,133	32,035	31,676	28,025	23,656	45,028	21,302	24,029	13,131	21,793	16,473	30,739	342,574
1991	35,037	28,221	17,298	17,116	17,991	20,956	14,905	20,187	26,412	42,016	23,228	24,171	287,076
1992	30,508	28,177	21,371	31,725	21,253	22,473	21,877	27,208	26,912	29,604	33,133	44,979	339,230
1993	43,634	46,067	58,298	52,554	53,566	60,330	49,415	52,381	56,838	63,808	44,167	58,073	640,131
1994	46,166	51,123	43,075	55,955	48,236	60,110	37,069	55,711	52,209	73,155	54,978	76,037	653,824
1995	50,875	66,370	51,292	78,288	32,607	80,165	41,357	67,528	38,781	64,904	45,688	71,077	688,932
1996	59,666	82,057	46,272	65,752	62,247	44,827	40,884	58,346	44,239	40,680	39,291	70,676	654,937
1997	84,982	89,875	66,340	82,772	62,890	78,690	47,242	118,286	55,081	108,413	100,941	134,349	1,029,861
1998	96,020	81,554	66,235	101,651	70,909	79,319	48,844	85,544	81,187	98,639	29,541	75,171	914,614

Source: Citrus Association of the New York Cotton Exchange (NYCE)

Retail and Nonretail Sales of Orange Juice in the United States In Millions of SSE Gallons

Crop Year	Retail Sales	% Change[2]	Nonretail Sales	% Change[2]	Apparent Con- sumption	% Change[2]	Per Capita Con- sumption	% Change[2]
1987-8	667	-4.9%	432	12.2%	1,229	-1.1%	5.0	-2.0%
1988-9	690	3.4%	401	-7.2%	1,238	.7%	5.0	0
1989-90	628	-9.0%	317	-20.9%	1,079	-12.8%	4.3	-14.0%
1990-1	701	11.6%	296	-6.6%	1,146	6.2%	4.5	4.7%
1991-2	689	-1.7%	268	-9.5%	1,112	-3.0%	4.3	-4.4%
1992-3	748	8.6%	371	38.4%	1,328	19.4%	5.1	18.6%
1993-4	740	-1.1%			1,368	3.0%	5.2	2.0%
1994-5	740	0			1,355	-1.0%	5.1	-1.9%
1995-6[1]	718	-2.9%			1,363	.6%	4.9	-3.9%
1996-7[1]	700	-2.5%			1,320	-3.1%	NA	NA

[1] Estimate. [2] Percentage change from previous period. *Source: Florida Department of Citrus*

Producer Price Index of Frozen Orange Juice Concentrate 1982 = 100

Year	Jan.	Feb.	Mar.	Apr.	May	June	July	Aug.	Sept.	Oct.	Nov.	Dec.	Average
1989	136.4	127.7	126.5	126.5	131.7	139.2	140.6	140.3	134.0	131.6	123.1	121.7	131.6
1990	137.6	162.4	162.8	159.9	159.7	160.0	160.4	160.8	150.9	147.2	120.9	117.8	150.0
1991	114.4	114.4	111.7	111.7	111.0	111.0	111.0	107.2	107.4	116.0	127.3	131.5	114.6
1992	135.1	134.7	134.7	134.3	126.2	118.5	115.5	114.5	112.5	106.5	104.2	98.8	119.6
1993	91.6	88.8	88.2	89.0	89.3	97.5	104.5	104.5	104.7	104.7	107.9	107.9	98.2
1994	107.9	104.8	104.2	104.2	102.7	101.2	100.2	100.1	99.9	99.8	100.7	100.5	102.2
1995	107.4	105.4	107.6	107.6	109.1	109.1	109.1	105.3	101.0	101.6	106.1	107.3	106.4
1996	109.4	112.5	117.2	119.5	119.5	119.5	115.3	113.6	113.6	112.8	112.8	108.8	114.5
1997	106.9	106.9	106.0	107.6	107.7	107.3	105.3	105.8	102.7	101.4	95.0	94.2	103.9
1998[1]	94.9	101.2	104.1	103.2	108.8	109.1	109.5	109.6	109.9	110.7	119.8	122.0	108.6

[1] Preliminary. *Source: Bureau of Labor Statistics, U.S. Department of Commerce (BLS)*

Average Price of Oranges (Equivalent On-Tree) Received by Growers in the U.S. In Dollar Per Box

Year	Jan.	Feb.	Mar.	Apr.	May	June	July	Aug.	Sept.	Oct.	Nov.	Dec.	Average
1989	6.51	6.45	6.26	7.28	8.39	8.51	7.27	6.52	6.54	6.29	7.34	6.34	6.98
1990	5.92	5.82	6.00	6.47	6.97	6.61	5.74	4.38	4.48	5.04	5.78	5.76	5.75
1991	5.64	6.28	6.94	7.09	7.95	19.43	17.40	18.45	21.39	9.87	6.27	5.79	11.04
1992	5.90	6.02	5.81	6.14	6.16	4.26	1.85	1.02	1.05	2.43	4.10	3.67	4.03
1993	3.37	3.21	3.41	4.00	4.03	4.09	5.02	7.25	11.85	11.44	5.95	3.81	5.62
1994	3.76	3.90	4.66	4.83	5.04	4.94	4.08	4.24	3.44	2.92	3.44	3.43	4.06
1995	3.43	3.59	4.22	4.61	4.90	5.63	7.44	7.30	7.26	7.90	3.57	3.55	5.28
1996	3.97	4.39	5.20	6.11	6.63	6.72	6.97	8.15	13.70	10.94	4.30	3.91	6.75
1997	3.97	3.98	4.46	4.94	5.15	5.11	6.64	7.03	7.15	3.90	2.41	2.81	4.80
1998[1]	3.15	3.53	4.75	5.82	5.68	6.41	5.85	5.37	4.97	5.42	5.87	4.74	5.13

[1] Preliminary. *Source: Economic Research Service, U.S. Department of Agriculture (ERS-USDA)*

Palm Oil

Palm oil is a tropical edible oil but competes directly with other cooking oils such as soybean and sunflower oils that are grown in more temperate climates. Palm oil is the world's second largest vegetable oil crop (after soybeans), but first in foreign trade. Almost all the world's production comes from Malaysia and Indonesia.

1998/99 world palm oil production was forecast at 17.7 million metric tonnes (October/September), 4 percent above 1997/98's 17 million tonnes. Still, world 1998/99 production was a record high as is consumption at 17.7 million tonnes vs. 17.4 million in 1997/98. Annual usage was less than 12 million tonnes earlier in the 1990's. World carryover stocks remain low, estimated at 1.49 million tonnes at the end of 1998/99 vs. 1.58 million a year earlier. Indonesia's 1998/99 crop of 5.5 million tonnes compares with 5 million in 1997/98. Malaysia's crop of 8.8 million compares with 8.6 million in 1997/98.

Two-thirds of world production is exported to meet global consumption; 12.1 million tonnes in 1998/99 vs. 11.9 million in 1997/98. Malaysia accounted for about 7.4 million tonnes in both years. Palm oil exports go mostly to Europe, the world's largest importer of crude vegetable oils. China and Pakistan also import at least one million tonnes each.

U.S. palm oil imports during the first ten months of the 1997/98 crop year (through July) totaled 101,463 metric tonnes vs. 125,756 in the like 1996/97 period with a value of $45.6 million vs $55.5 million, respectively. The U.S. does not re-export any palm oil.

World palm oil prices traversed a wide range during 1986/87-1996/97 averaging $414 per metric ton. For 1997/98 the average was $601, basis Malaysia FOB vs. $526 in 1995/96. Helping to support prices are the low world stocks in importing countries and continued strong usage in Europe, China and India. The U.S. average 1997/98 price of $684 per metric tonne compares with $608 in the like 1996/97 period.

Futures Markets

Crude Palm Oil and Crude Palm Kernal Oil are traded on the Kuala Lumpur Commodity Exchange (KLCE).

World Palm Oil Statistics In Thousands of Metric Tons

Crop Year	Production: Colombia	Production: Indonesia	Production: Ivory Coast	Production: Malaysia	Production: Nigeria	Production: Thailand	Production: World Total	Imports: China	Imports: Pakistan	Imports: World Total	Exports: Indonesia	Exports: Malaysia	Exports: World Total
1992-3	303	3,453	302	7,122	640	289	13,486	1,107	1,102	9,319	1,733	6,212	9,377
1993-4	348	3,630	305	7,103	640	311	13,782	1,653	1,080	10,354	1,965	6,737	10,372
1994-5	391	4,144	282	7,771	638	346	15,064	1,786	1,215	10,685	1,904	6,728	10,572
1995-6	393	4,587	277	8,264	607	369	16,112	1,178	1,166	10,537	2,082	6,896	10,589
1996-7[1]	440	4,724	250	9,000	615	386	17,087	1,851	1,020	11,730	2,419	7,794	11,895
1997-8[2]	437	5,158	251	8,509	571	375	16,920	1,478	1,229	11,682	2,521	7,800	11,720
1998-9[3]	424	5,350	265	8,532	570	366	17,165	1,700	1,060	11,743	2,800	7,500	11,713

[1] Preliminary. [2] Estimate. [3] Forecast. *Source: The Oil World*

Supply and Distribution of Palm Oil in the United States In Thousands of Metric Tons

Year Beginning Oct.	Stocks Oct. 1	Imports	Total Supply	Consumption: Edible Products	Consumption: Inedible Products	Consumption: Total End Products	Total Disappearance	Exports	Prices: U.S. Import Value[4]	Prices: Malaysia, F.O.B., RBD	Prices: Palm Kernel Oil, Malaysia, C.I.F. Rotterdam
				In Millions of Pounds					U.S. $ Per Metric Ton		
1993-4	14.9	167.0	181.9	86.2	118.2	204.4	162.0	3.6	370	451	566
1994-5	16.4	98.7	115.1	38.1	113.6	151.7	101.8	5.9	538	647	680
1995-6	7.4	106.9	114.3	6.7	103.9	110.6	91.0	9.2	511	545	729
1996-7[1]	14.0	146.4	160.4		91.8	91.8	135.0	4.2	432	544	680
1997-8[2]	21.4	130.0	151.4		93.8	93.8	144.0	9.7	464	640	606
1998-9[3]	15.0				78.4	78.4				685	

[1] Preliminary. [2] Estimate. [3] Forecast. [4] Market value in the foreign country, excluding import duties, ocean freight and marine insurance.
Sources: The Oil World; Economic Research Service, U.S. Department of Agriculture (ERS-USDA)

Average Wholesale Palm Oil Prices, CIF, Bulk, U.S. Ports In Cents Per Pound

Year	Jan.	Feb.	Mar.	Apr.	May	June	July	Aug.	Sept.	Oct.	Nov.	Dec.	Average
1992	21.91	21.05	21.92	22.05	21.51	21.77	21.19	21.00	21.50	21.86	22.18	22.24	21.68
1993	23.18	23.09	22.99	22.26	21.95	21.01	20.31	19.84	19.43	18.83	19.74	21.90	21.21
1994	21.91	21.67	21.72	23.08	26.27	28.94	27.44	30.18	32.15	31.93	34.95	36.83	28.09
1995	34.26	33.82	36.18	35.56	32.80	33.06	33.68	32.59	30.86	31.45	31.96	30.00	33.02
1996	27.08	26.52	26.33	27.52	28.57	25.43	24.78	24.46	27.24	26.13	26.95	27.45	26.54
1997	28.68	29.25	28.00	28.18	28.93	27.25	26.17	25.55	25.37	27.33	27.28	25.05	27.25
1998[1]	29.30	29.59	30.53	32.10	35.20	31.11	31.42	32.33	33.14				31.64

[1] Preliminary. *Source: Economic Research Service, U.S. Department of Agriculture (ERS-USDA)*

Paper

The world's largest producer of paper and paperboard is the United States. Between 1991 and 1996, U.S. paper and paperboard production averaged 79.5 million metric tonnes. The next largest producer is Canada. Between 1991 and 1996, Canada's production of paper and paperboard averaged 17.7 million tonnes. Other large producers of paper and paperboard include Finland, Sweden, Japan, Germany, France, Italy and the United Kingdom.

The world's largest producer of newsprint is Canada. In 1997, production was estimated at 793.5 thousand tonnes per month. That was almost 6 percent above the level of 1996. Between 1992 and 1997, Canadian production of newsprint averaged 763.5 thousand tonnes. Production has been increasing at the rate of almost 2 percent per year over the last five years. The U.S. is the second largest producer of newsprint. U.S. production in 1997 was 534.5 thousand tonnes per month, an increase of 2 percent from 1996. Between 1992 and 1996, U.S. production of newsprint averaged 531.2 thousand tonnes per month. U.S. production of newsprint has been holding steady. Japan is the third largest producer of newsprint with production in 1997 averaging 265.8 thousand tonnes per month. That is up almost 2 percent from 1996. Other large producers of newsprint include Sweden, Germany, Finland and South Korea. U.S. production of newsprint in 1997 was estimated at 6.41 million tonnes, down 8 percent from 1996. Canada's production in 1997 was 9.52 million tonnes, up 2 percent from 1996. Canada exports close to 90 percent of its production.

Production of Paper and Paperboard by Selected Countries — In Thousands of Metric Tons

Year	Austria	Canada	Finland	France	Germany	Italy	Japan	Netherlands	Russia[2]	Spain	Sweden	United Kingdom	United States
1991	3,090	16,559	8,776	7,190	12,904	5,795	29,056	2,862	9,590	3,579	8,349	4,951	72,724
1992	3,252	16,585	9,147	7,690	13,214	6,040	28,324	2,835	5,765	3,449	8,378	5,151	75,161
1993	3,300	17,528	9,990	7,975	13,034	6,019	27,764	2,855	4,459	3,348	8,781	5,406	77,167
1994	3,603	18,349	10,909	8,701	14,457	6,705	28,527	3,011	3,412	3,503	9,284	5,829	80,948
1995	3,599	18,713	10,942	8,619	14,827	6,810	28,527	2,967	4,073	3,684	9,159	6,093	85,526
1996[1]		18,414	10,441			6,358		2,987	3,212		9,038	6,188	85,173

[1] Preliminary. [2] Formerly part of the U.S.S.R.; data not reported separately until 1992. *Source: Food and Agricultural Organization of the United Nations (FAO-UN)*

Production of Newsprint by Selected Countries (Monthly Average) — In Thousands of Metric Tons

Year	Australia	Brazil	Canada	China	Finland	France	Germany	India	Japan	Rep. of Korea	Russia[3]	Sweden	United States
1992	33.6	18.9	729.0	40.8	104.8	55.8	94.2	24.7	271.1	50.2	78.6	147.5	535.3
1993	33.1	22.2	761.0	48.3	118.7	66.7	105.8	23.5	243.1	61.9	70.4	193.8	534.3
1994	33.5	22.1	776.8	52.6	119.4	70.3	156.3	22.3	247.7	72.3	86.5	201.3	528.3
1995	37.4	24.6	768.8	65.2	112.5	56.4	146.0	26.3	258.2	79.7	121.5	196.1	529.3
1996	36.5	23.1	798.3	75.1	133.6	65.6	142.4	24.8	261.7	99.2	103.8	181.9	525.3
1997[1]	34.0	22.1	793.5	60.6	123.3	76.5	150.7	23.3	266.0	117.5	-----	200.9	534.5
1998[2]	33.7	22.4	-----	64.4	124.7	75.7	148.0	27.1	270.3	128.1	-----	206.1	-----

[1] Preliminary. [2] Estimate. [3] Formerly part of the U.S.S.R.; data not reported separately until 1992. *Source: Statistical Division, United Nations (UN)*

Index Price of Paperboard — 1982 = 100

Year	Jan.	Feb.	Mar.	Apr.	May	June	July	Aug.	Sept.	Oct.	Nov.	Dec.	Average
1992	133.4	133.6	133.4	134.3	134.3	134.3	134.2	134.6	135.9	135.7	133.9	133.6	134.3
1993	133.0	131.6	131.3	130.6	129.9	128.9	128.6	128.0	128.0	129.7	130.2	130.5	130.0
1994	130.2	130.1	131.1	133.4	133.1	133.5	137.8	143.5	146.9	153.6	156.0	156.7	140.5
1995	165.3	171.2	172.3	183.8	188.2	188.4	189.9	190.6	190.3	188.8	185.7	182.2	183.1
1996	175.7	172.6	166.6	161.8	154.0	150.6	148.0	145.5	145.6	146.6	146.9	147.6	155.1
1997	147.1	144.2	139.7	137.2	136.8	137.5	137.8	143.8	148.4	150.1	154.4	156.1	144.4
1998[1]	155.9	156.1	156.0	155.2	154.2	153.7	152.2	150.9	149.0	147.0	145.9	144.3	151.7

[1] Preliminary. *Source: Bureau of Labor Statistics, U.S. Department of Commerce (BLS - 0914)*

Index Price of Wood Pulp, Bleached Suphate Softwood — 1982 = 100

Year	Jan.	Feb.	Mar.	Apr.	May	June	July	Aug.	Sept.	Oct.	Nov.	Dec.	Average
1992	121.6	123.7	125.2	131.8	132.1	131.4	134.2	136.1	135.1	133.7	132.0	132.8	130.8
1993	121.6	118.1	112.7	112.3	112.7	112.7	110.7	108.9	108.6	107.1	105.5	104.0	111.2
1994	106.7	106.9	109.6	113.5	113.4	118.0	119.4	124.3	130.3	137.1	141.4	142.2	121.9
1995	150.9	153.0	187.5	193.0	202.4	215.2	217.8	223.3	218.8	223.3	217.0	212.7	201.2
1996	195.0	175.4	155.5	123.5	111.1	120.1	126.9	129.0	129.4	130.3	129.3	131.5	138.1
1997	129.6	125.9	123.9	119.0	121.8	123.9	130.9	134.4	135.7	135.7	136.8	136.2	129.5
1998[1]	132.0	131.3	127.8	118.7	118.0	122.8	125.7	122.8	117.2	117.9	110.1	109.9	121.2

[1] Preliminary. *Source: Bureau of Labor Statistics, U.S. Department of Commerce (BLS - 0911-0211)*

Index Price of Shipping Sack Paper[2] 1982 = 100

Year	Jan.	Feb.	Mar.	Apr.	May	June	July	Aug.	Sept.	Oct.	Nov.	Dec.	Average
1992	148.9	148.9	154.0	154.0	154.0	148.9	148.9	148.9	155.7	155.7	155.7	155.7	152.4
1993	155.7	155.7	155.7	155.7	151.8	151.8	151.8	151.8	151.8	151.8	152.5	152.5	153.2
1994	151.3	150.9	154.3	154.5	159.3	163.9	169.9	170.3	176.6	178.2	184.9	185.5	166.6
1995	190.4	204.5	209.5	212.0	221.5	224.2	224.2	224.2	224.0	223.4	212.8	207.3	214.8
1996	205.2	202.2	201.5	194.7	194.3	193.1	189.9	185.7	183.0	183.0	185.8	185.8	192.0
1997	185.8	186.4	186.7	186.5	184.3	184.1	183.9	188.1	182.0	188.5	196.9	197.6	187.6
1998[1]	197.1	197.2	197.2	197.2	196.3	196.3	194.4	194.4	194.4	194.4	194.4	194.4	195.6

[1] Preliminary. [2] Unbleached kraft. *Source: Bureau of Labor Statistics, U.S. Department of Commerce (BLS - 0913-0307)*

Producer Price Index of Standard Newsprint 1982 = 100

Year	Jan.	Feb.	Mar.	Apr.	May	June	July	Aug.	Sept.	Oct.	Nov.	Dec.	Average
1992	115.3	114.8	112.3	108.8	108.3	106.6	106.6	106.7	109.5	109.2	110.6	109.6	109.9
1993	110.4	111.2	114.1	113.9	113.0	113.1	112.7	112.6	111.3	111.2	111.0	111.0	112.1
1994	109.9	109.5	110.7	110.6	112.2	113.8	116.9	116.9	121.7	123.8	126.8	127.3	116.7
1995	135.8	134.6	140.1	147.4	152.3	164.8	166.1	166.1	174.5	186.2	186.2	186.2	161.8
1996	186.2	186.2	185.2	182.7	173.5	164.4	157.4	148.7	145.7	133.1	127.3	123.1	159.5
1997	121.1	120.9	123.1	128.6	135.9	137.2	138.6	139.4	139.4	139.4	141.3	141.8	133.9
1998[1]	142.2	142.5	141.8	142.3	140.0	140.3	143.4	143.1	145.6	146.8	147.5	143.4	143.2

[1] Preliminary. *Source: Bureau of Labor Statistics, U.S. Department of Commerce (BLS - 0913-02)*

Index Price of Coated Printing Paper, No. 3 1982 = 100

Year	Jan.	Feb.	Mar.	Apr.	May	June	July	Aug.	Sept.	Oct.	Nov.	Dec.	Average
1992	126.8	123.6	123.7	123.7	122.3	121.7	122.1	121.7	121.7	124.2	123.4	123.3	123.2
1993	123.4	123.3	123.3	123.4	123.4	123.3	123.0	123.0	123.2	122.9	122.9	122.9	123.2
1994	122.0	122.1	121.8	122.2	121.6	121.6	121.6	125.2	130.7	131.7	132.9	136.3	125.8
1995	139.5	145.8	150.2	153.1	147.7	152.0	159.3	159.3	160.4	160.3	160.3	160.3	154.0
1996	160.2	159.7	159.4	159.2	155.6	153.5	153.0	152.5	152.2	151.8	151.9	152.9	155.2
1997	152.7	153.1	152.9	153.2	153.2	154.6	154.5	154.5	153.2	153.3	153.2	153.3	153.5
1998[1]	153.8	154.7	154.2	154.2	154.1	154.0	154.0	153.8	153.7	153.4	153.4	151.9	153.8

[1] Preliminary. *Source: Bureau of Labor Statistics, U.S. Department of Commerce (BLS - 0913-0113)*

International Paper Prices--Export Unit Value

Year	Jan.	Feb.	Mar.	Apr.	May	June	July	Aug.	Sept.	Oct.	Nov.	Dec.	Average
NEWSPRINT - Finland	In Markka Per Metric Ton												
1994	2,339	2,273	2,320	2,366	2,349	2,364	2,318	2,360	2,295	2,262	2,236	2,275	2,313
1995	2,563	2,589	2,577	2,614	2,598	2,667	3,037	3,122	3,172	3,187	3,214	3,191	2,885
1996	3,320	3,412	3,438	3,463	3,442	3,362	3,265	3,110	3,010	3,709	2,899	2,841	3,207
1997	2,741	2,662	2,669	2,667	2,701	2,602	2,642	2,709	2,736	2,697	2,706	2,755	2,694
PRINTING AND WRITING - Finland		In Markka Per Metric Ton											
1994	3,471	3,290	3,370	3,375	3,484	3,507	3,524	3,490	3,498	3,472	3,501	3,666	3,471
1995	3,816	3,897	3,905	4,066	4,165	4,284	4,473	4,416	4,439	4,555	4,569	4,400	4,235
1996	4,556	4,555	4,503	4,374	4,265	4,069	3,871	3,743	3,644	3,644	3,667	3,654	4,027
1997	3,620	3,579	3,648	3,651	3,698	3,656	3,620	3,649	3,725	3,738	3,799	3,803	3,687

Source: Food and Agricultural Organization of the United Nations (FAO-UN)

International Paper Prices--Import Unit Value

Year	Jan.	Feb.	Mar.	Apr.	May	June	July	Aug.	Sept.	Oct.	Nov.	Dec.	Average
NEWSPRINT - United Kingdom		In Pounds Per Metric Ton											
1994	304	317	308	317	305	317	295	319	288	310	308	319	309
1995	344	353	348	363	376	384	428	465	470	473	469	241	393
1996	498	534	529	514	518	513	504	476	461	412	435	427	485
1997	439	400	394	380	372	380	200	385	374	368	373	377	370
PRINTING AND WRITING - United Kingdom			In Pounds Per Metric Ton										
1994	441	457	454	459	474	487	525	489	526	534	546	559	496
1995	613	571	611	617	643	619	670	698	718	713	675	684	653
1996	709	776	683	639	661	635	607	919	664	631	629	684	686
1997	606	561	580	561	554	530	555	549	594	559	602	565	568

Source: Food and Agricultural Organization of the United Nations (FAO-UN)

Peanuts and Peanut Oil

World raw peanut (groundnut) production of a near record large 28 million metric tonnes in 1998/99 compares with 27.1 million in 1997/98 and the record 28.4 million in 1996/97. On a shelled basis the totals would be about 25 percent lower. Peanuts are the world's fourth largest oilseed crop, generally just ahead of sunflowerseed. However, among the major oilseeds for which world acreage has generally increased, the area devoted to peanuts in the 1990's would show little change were it not for China.

China (10.2 million tonnes in 1998/99) and India (8.30 million) produce more than half of the world's crop with the U.S. a distant third (1.64 million). Foreign trade in peanuts is small as most of the crop is consumed locally. World imports during 1998/99 of 1.6 million tonnes were marginally lower than in 1997/98; exports of 1.66 million tonnes compare with 1.64 million, respectively. The world's peanut crush is among the smallest of the major oilseeds; 14.5 million tonnes in 1998/99, about a tenth of the soybean crush. More of the world's peanut crop is allocated to meal production than oil, production of which totaled 5.8 million tonnes in 1998/99 vs. 5.5 million in 1997/98, and about equal to consumption in both years. Peanut oil production in 1998/99 of 4.4 million tonnes compares with 4.2 million in 1997/98. Foreign trade in meal and oil is small.

The average world peanut oilseed price in 1997/98 (October/September) of $1055 per metric tonne, basis Rotterdam, compares with $926 in 1996/97, and a 1986/87-1996/97 average of $982 per ton, during which time the yearly average saw a high of $1539 and a low of $818. Rotterdam meal prices in 1997/98 averaged $134 per metric ton vs. $235 in 1996/97, and the ten year average of $201; oil prices of $965 per ton compare with $959 and $806, respectively. In the U.S., the average price for peanut meal, basis southeast mills FOB, during 1997/98 of $176 per ton compares with $229 in 1996/97; peanut oil prices averaged $1065 and $985, respectively.

In the U.S., the 1998/99 crop (October/September) of 3.5 billion pounds was slightly under 1997/98 and compares with 3.6 billion in 1996/97. U.S. peanut production is largely concentrated in the southeast. Peanuts are also grown in the southern plains states where irrigation may be needed and production costs run higher, but not necessarily realized yield per acre. The average yield for the 1998 crop was put at 2,448 pounds per acre vs. 2,459 a year earlier. The acreage harvested of 1.47 million acres compares with 1.41 million, respectively. Georgia is the largest producing state with at least a third of total production (1.3 billion pounds in 1998) followed by Texas (with the largest gains in production in recent years), North Carolina and Alabama. Total supplies in 1998/99 of 4.4 billion pounds compare with 4.5 billion for 1997/98 and include an estimated October 1, 1998 carryin of 765 million pounds vs. 795 million a year earlier. U.S. peanut imports are generally small, 152 million pounds in 1998/99. Imports, however, have seen wide swings at times, from 401 million pounds in 1980 to 2 million in the early 1990's.

Total U.S. peanut disappearance in 1998/99 of 3.7 billion pounds is unchanged from 1997/98. The crush was forecast at 612 million pounds vs. 546 million, and exports at 640 million vs. 700 million, respectively. As a direct food, 2.1 billion pounds were forecast for 1998/99, marginally higher than in 1997/98. Peanut use as a direct foodstuff has slipped during the past decade. Per capita U.S. peanut use has fallen from a high of 7 pounds (kernel basis) in 1989 to under 6 pounds by the mid-1990's.

Contributing to the decline is reduced demand for peanut butter, a drop in snack peanut consumption and no growth in peanut based candies. Exports of peanuts and products in 1997/98 (October/July) of 4.9 million tonnes compares with 5.1 million in the like 1996/97 period; with Canada the primary importer followed by the Netherlands and the U.K..

Futures Markets

Peanut futures are traded on the Beijing Commodity Exchange (BCE).

World Production of Peanuts (in the Shell) In Thousands of Metric Tons

Crop Year	Argen-tina	Burma	China	India	Indo-nesia	Nigeria	Senegal	South Africa	Sudan	Thailand	United States	Zaire	World Total
1989-90	336	459	5,365	8,088	875	350	113	350	400	161	1,810	380	22,059
1990-1	574	440	6,368	7,514	860	250	703	112	325	162	1,634	380	22,206
1991-2	400	440	6,300	7,065	890	220	724	114	400	160	2,235	380	22,138
1992-3	225	425	5,953	8,850	890	250	580	172	390	162	1,943	380	23,050
1993-4	210	390	8,420	7,760	870	250	620	190	390	170	1,540	380	23,990
1994-5	280	445	9,682	8,255	880	250	720	105	390	165	1,927	380	26,278
1995-6	460	500	10,200	7,400	1,060	1,580	830	190	370	150	1,570	580	28,400
1996-7	300	570	10,140	9,020	990	330	650	140	370	150	1,660	560	28,440
1997-8[1]	650	590	9,650	8,000	1,000	350	550	100	370	150	1,600	560	27,140
1998-9[2]	600	580	10,200	8,300	1,000	380	550	100	370	150	1,680	580	28,090

[1] Preliminary. [2] Estimate. *Source: Foreign Agricultural Service, U.S. Department of Agriculture (FAS-USDA)*

Salient Statistics of Peanuts in the United States

Crop Year	Acreage Planted (1,000 Acres)	Acreage Harvested for Nuts (1,000 Acres)	Average Yield Per Acre In Lbs.	Production 1,000 Lbs.	Season Farm Price ¢ Lb.	Farm Value Million Dollars	Thousand Pounds (Year Beg. August) Exports: Unshelled	Exports: Shelled	Imports: Unshelled	Imports: Shelled
1985-6	1,490.4	1,467.4	2,810	4,122,787	24.3	1,003.4	83,747	721,690	1,493	1,942
1986-7	1,564.7	1,535.2	2,408	3,700,745	29.2	1,073.3	75,687	441,954	328	1,598
1987-8	1,567.4	1,547.4	2,337	3,619,440	28.0	1,021.9	76,345	407,557	880	1,949
1988-9	1,657.4	1,628.4	2,445	3,980,917	27.9	1,115.2	105,746	437,867	650	2,094
1989-90	1,665.2	1,644.7	2,426	3,989,995	28.0	1,116.5	126,682	577,807	55	1,477
1990-1	1,840.0	1,809.5	1,991	3,602,770	34.7	1,257.2	250,851	401,149	6,429	20,571
1991-2	2,039.2	2,015.7	2,444	4,926,570	28.3	1,392.0	997,000	630,000	5,000	27,000
1992-3	1,686.6	1,669.1	2,567	4,284,416	30.0	1,285.4	951,000	611,250	2,000	2,000
1993-4	1,733.5	1,689.8	2,008	3,392,415	30.4	1,030.9	555,000	352,500	2,000	1,420
1994-5	1,641.0	1,618.5	2,624	4,247,455	28.9	1,229.0	878,000	659,905	74,000	55,385
1995-6	1,537.5	1,517.0	2,282	3,461,475	29.3	1,013.3	824,000	564,021	153,000	108,303
1996-7	1,401.5	1,380.0	2,653	3,661,205	28.1	1,029.8	666,000	440,438	127,000	95,057
1997-8[1]	1,434.0	1,413.8	2,503	3,539,380	26.1	1,002.7	681,000	------	141,000	------
1998-9[2]	1,511.0	1,465.5	2,683	3,931,275	28.3	1,008.5	685,000	------	152,000	------

[1] Preliminary. [2] Estimate. *Source: Economic Research Service, U.S. Department of Agriculture (ERS-USDA)*

Supply and Disposition of Peanuts (Farmer's Stock Basis) & Support Program in the United States

Crop Year Beginning Aug. 1	Supply: Production	Supply: Imports	Supply: Stocks Aug. 1	Supply: Total	Disposition: Exports	Disposition: Crushed for Oil	Disposition: Seed, Loss & Residual	Disposition: Food	Total Disappearance	Government Support Program: Support Price (¢ per Lb.)	Additional (¢ per Lb.)	Amount Put Under Support: Quantity Mil. Lbs.	Amount Put Under Support: % of Prod.
	Million Pounds												
1985-6	4,123	2	1,424	5,549	1,043	812	826	2,023	4,704	27.95	7.4	1,359	33.0
1986-7	3,697	2	845	4,544	663	514	291	2,073	3,541	30.37	7.5	290	7.8
1987-8	3,616	2	1,003	4,621	618	560	539	2,071	3,788	30.41	7.5	700	19.3
1988-9	3,981	2	833	4,816	688	814	217	2,254	3,974	30.76	7.5	540	13.6
1989-90	3,990	2	843	4,835	989	624	211	2,312	4,136	30.79	7.5	401	10.0
1990-1	3,603	27	701	4,331	652	689	288	2,020	3,649	31.57	7.5	576	16.0
1991-2	4,927	5	683	5,615	997	1,103	254	2,207	4,561	32.14	7.5	1,070	21.7
1992-3	4,284	2	1,055	5,341	951	891	227	2,122	3,991	33.75	6.6	436	10.2
1993-4	3,392	2	1,350	4,744	553	670	372	2,088	3,683	33.75	6.6	324	9.6
1994-5	4,247	74	1,061	5,382	878	982	316	2,009	4,184	33.92	6.6	820	19.3
1995-6	3,461	153	1,198	4,812	824	999	238	1,993	4,054	33.92	6.6	818	24.0
1996-7	3,661	127	758	4,545	666	692	363	2,029	3,751	30.50	6.6	320	8.7
1997-8[1]	3,537	141	795	4,473	681	544	300	2,099	3,624	30.50	6.6	-----	-----
1998-9[2]	3,611	152	848	4,612	685	675	307	2,135	3,802	30.50	8.8	-----	-----

[1] Preliminary. [2] Estimate. *Source: Economic Research Service, U.S. Department of Agriculture (ERS-USDA)*

Production of Peanuts (Harvested for Nuts) in the United States, by States In Thousands of Pounds

Crop Year	Alabama	Florida	Georgia	New Mexico	North Carolina	Oklahoma	South Carolina	Texas	Virgina	Total
1985	590,000	216,000	1,921,320	31,992	451,990	170,980	34,200	422,625	283,680	4,122,787
1986	494,940	233,160	1,632,575	28,700	440,440	184,500	25,530	385,000	275,900	3,700,745
1987	465,300	215,800	1,575,000	29,760	392,200	222,750	31,200	441,000	243,000	3,616,010
1988	561,680	228,600	1,801,550	30,552	419,985	225,040	32,110	417,500	263,900	3,980,917
1989	537,750	214,890	1,849,500	43,680	370,120	210,700	32,500	484,700	246,155	3,989,995
1990	386,560	233,120	1,347,500	50,000	475,600	235,320	30,105	534,650	309,915	3,602,770
1991	638,485	279,660	2,228,550	51,075	461,700	243,800	33,600	682,500	307,200	4,926,570
1992	591,180	202,510	1,820,465	58,236	406,980	236,180	32,500	680,150	256,215	4,284,416
1993	473,220	194,880	1,383,545	56,680	299,585	233,580	24,500	550,175	176,250	3,392,415
1994	446,220	207,480	1,862,630	51,660	485,465	261,000	36,250	605,570	291,180	4,247,455
1995	483,360	193,590	1,414,880	43,000	347,040	201,880	30,800	540,000	206,925	3,461,475
1996	449,805	236,160	1,433,770	37,950	367,500	195,210	32,550	689,000	219,260	3,661,205
1997	372,490	228,060	1,333,830	46,710	329,640	184,800	30,450	822,150	191,250	3,539,380
1998[1]	411,600	220,000	1,537,000	55,000	400,000	172,500	24,725	900,450	210,000	3,931,275

[1] Preliminary. *Source: Agricultural Statistics Board, U.S. Department of Agriculture (ASB-USDA)*

PEANUTS AND PEANUT OIL

Supply and Reported Uses of Shelled Peanuts and Products in the United States — In Thousands of Pounds

Crop Year Beginning Aug. 1	Shelled Peanuts -- Stocks Aug.1 --- Edible	Oil Stock[2]	Shelled Peanuts ------ Production ----- Edible	Oil Stock[2]	Reported Used (Shelled Peanuts--Raw Basis) — Edible Grades Used in: Candy[3]	Snacks[4]	Sandwich Spread	Butter[5]	Other Products	Total	Shelled Peanuts Crushed[6]	Crude Oil Production	Cake & Meal Production
1989-90	513,679	44,397	2,319,780	374,859	330,158	392,811	------	897,318	36,682	1,656,969	469,351	193,000	261,465
1990-1	455,586	15,194	1,836,052	330,102	305,324	355,258	------	742,384	37,888	1,440,854	517,712	213,112	299,820
1991-2	386,155	65,950	2,538,398	616,170	327,617	346,255	------	886,367	34,173	1,594,412	828,986	356,276	459,457
1992-3	871,207	57,829	2,376,782	533,641	328,324	352,775	------	797,910	24,981	1,503,990	669,942	285,904	377,301
1993-4	679,639	42,054	1,748,734	425,710	362,418	348,867	------	727,006	36,301	1,474,592	503,674	212,216	292,093
1994-5	732,272	57,188	1,741,824	511,635	349,630	301,548	------	709,823	36,854	1,397,855	738,221	314,189	415,394
1995-6	752,814	58,188	1,253,451	491,818	350,663	277,089	------	728,076	32,015	1,387,843	751,281	320,909	420,919
1996-7	498,954	41,000	1,692,581	305,674	360,846	290,102	------	727,531	33,825	1,412,304	520,413	220,877	294,590
1997-8[1]	509,476	14,091	1,694,016	290,882	360,840	310,458	------	735,829	35,823	1,442,950	409,249	178,853	228,276

[1] Preliminary. [2] Includes straight run oil stock peanuts. [3] Includes peanut butter made by manufacturers for own use in candy. [4] Formerly titled "Salted Peanuts." [5] Includes peanut butter made by manufacturers for own use in cookies and sandwiches, but excludes peanut butter used in candy. [6] All crushings regardless of grade. *Source: National Agricultural Statistics Service, U.S. Department of Agriculture (NASS-USDA)*

Shelled Peanuts (Raw Basis) Used in Primary Products, by Type — In Thousands of Pounds

Crop Year Beginning Aug. 1	Virginia: Candy[2]	Snack Peanuts	Peanut Butter[3]	Total	Runner: Candy[2]	Snack Peanuts	Peanut Butter[3]	Total	Spanish: Candy[2]	Snack Peanuts	Peanut Butter[3]	Total
1989-90	28,701	130,000	90,622	263,014	278,062	234,661	773,985	1,306,810	23,395	28,150	32,711	87,145
1990-1	26,043	142,113	101,069	286,242	259,995	189,254	580,691	1,049,423	19,286	23,841	60,624	105,189
1991-2	51,312	142,514	89,045	297,570	244,815	180,609	759,747	1,203,233	31,490	23,132	37,575	93,609
1992-3	49,223	124,875	92,355	275,895	259,498	203,732	674,962	1,152,775	19,603	24,168	30,593	75,320
1993-4	44,889	99,381	63,270	222,641	298,325	227,286	365,047	1,179,396	19,204	22,200	28,689	72,555
1994-5	26,857	97,389	51,354	190,916	302,697	185,377	644,711	1,152,110	20,076	18,782	13,758	54,829
1995-6	25,176	93,041	71,310	203,183	304,285	169,142	634,350	1,123,719	21,202	14,906	22,416	60,941
1996-7	24,158	91,882	64,274	193,166	318,924	176,851	634,387	1,149,347	17,764	21,369	28,870	69,791
1997-8[1]	26,776	81,949	59,228	183,648	314,702	208,075	652,438	1,194,038	19,362	20,434	24,163	65,264

[1] Preliminary. [2] Includes peanut butter made by manufacturers for own use in candy. [3] Includes peanut butter made by manufacturers for own use in cookies and sandwiches, but excludes peanut butter used in candy. *Source: National Agricultural Statistics Service, U.S. Department of Agriculture (NASS-USDA)*

Production, Consumption, Stocks and Foreign Trade of Peanut Oil in the U.S. — In Millions of Pounds

Crop Year Beginning Aug. 1	Production: Crude	Refined	Consumption: In Refining	In End Products	Stocks Dec. 31: Crude	Refined	Imports for Consumption	Exports
1990-1	213.1	131.7	229.1	169.0	19.3	5.8	10.0	25.0
1991-2	261.5	125.6	132.3	141.0	27.5	3.1	1.0	151.0
1992-3	285.9	181.1	188.4	182.1	46.2	5.3	0	59.0
1993-4	212.2	155.2	163.7	149.1	6.5	3.9	11.0	61.0
1994-5	319.9	120.0	126.1	118.9	5.0	2.8	5.0	21.5
1995-6	329.0	125.7	129.9	126.0	19.9	2.8	3.2	47.8
1996-7	233.9	133.5	138.9	138.4	85.6	2.8	5.0	13.0
1997-8[1]	144.3	104.0	111.6	121.6	42.6	3.0	5.0	35.0
1998-9[2]	111.7	114.9	123.7	170.2	47.2	3.8		

[1] Preliminary. [2] Forecast. NA = Not available. *Source: Bureau of the Census, U.S. Department of Commerce*

Production of Crude Peanut Oil in the United States — In Millions of Pounds

Year	Jan.	Feb.	Mar.	Apr.	May	June	July	Aug.	Sept.	Oct.	Nov.	Dec.	Total
1989	10.5	20.8	27.8	24.3	19.0	33.4	26.6	22.4	NA	7.4	11.6	9.8	213.6
1990	11.1	15.8	14.2	22.2	24.9	24.1	14.0	8.5	2.1	14.4	12.5	15.9	179.7
1991		70.8			71.1			59.5			60.1		261.5
1992	28.0	26.8	42.5	40.9	39.8	40.6	37.3	31.3	35.1	24.2	19.2	15.6	381.3
1993	16.9	17.0	24.1	28.8	23.3	29.0	25.6	22.5	3.6	8.6	16.4	14.6	230.4
1994	18.1	18.3	21.2	18.7	25.6	15.4	21.7	16.8	17.2	11.9	18.4	24.2	227.5
1995	27.9	28.6	42.7	36.9	39.2	29.2	26.9	26.3	17.4	13.2	19.5	24.3	332.0
1996	29.2	31.9	36.8	36.8	36.7	33.3	31.4	31.5	27.1	21.1	20.6	21.8	358.2
1997	19.9	16.1	18.8	17.9	13.3	15.9	9.9	12.1	6.1	12.2	11.6	14.0	167.7
1998[1]	16.4	14.5	14.3	13.0	10.8	10.0	9.5	6.3	5.8	6.9	13.6	13.9	134.9

[1] Preliminary. NA = Not available. *Source: Bureau of the Census, U.S. Department of Commerce*

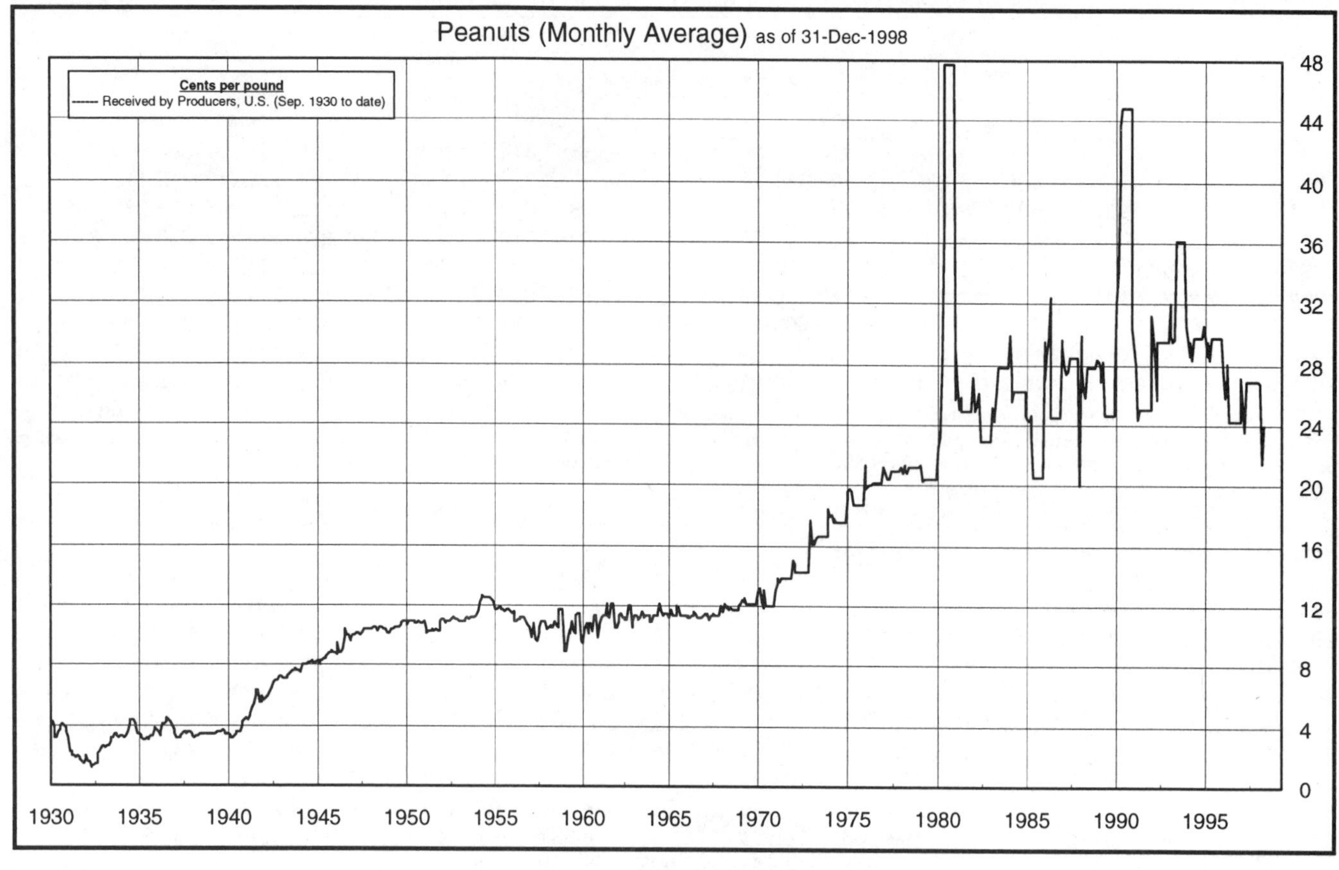

Average Price Received by Producers in United States for Peanuts in the Shell — In Cents Per Pound

Crop Year	Aug.	Sept.	Oct.	Nov.	Dec.	Jan.	Feb.	Mar.	Apr.	May.	June	July	Average[1]
1989-90	28.4	28.2	27.7	26.9	28.2	24.6	NQ	NQ	NQ	NQ	NQ	NQ	27.3
1990-1	26.5	32.2	34.0	40.1	43.6	44.8	NQ	NQ	NQ	NQ	NQ	NQ	34.7
1991-2	30.4	29.3	28.1	24.4	25.1	NQ	NQ	NQ	NQ	NQ	NQ	NQ	28.3
1992-3	NQ	31.3	29.9	28.2	25.7	29.5	NQ	NQ	NQ	NQ	NQ	NQ	30.0
1993-4	NQ	32.0	30.0	29.5	29.7	36.1	NQ	NQ	NQ	NQ	NQ	NQ	30.4
1994-5	NQ	30.6	28.6	25.9	25.8	25.7	NQ	NQ	NQ	NQ	NQ	NQ	27.9
1995-6	30.6	29.7	28.6	29.5	28.3	29.8	NQ	NQ	NQ	NQ	NQ	NQ	29.4
1996-7	NQ	27.6	25.8	27.1	28.1	24.3	NQ	NQ	NQ	NQ	NQ	NQ	26.6
1997-8	23.3	27.1	25.4	25.0	30.7	24.7	NQ	NQ	NQ	NQ	NQ	NQ	26.0
1998-9[2]	NQ	26.8	26.3	21.5	24.0	27.9							25.3

[1] Weighted average by sale. [2] Preliminary. NQ = No quote. *Source: National Agricultural Statistics Service, U.S. Department of Agriculture (NASS)*

Average Price of Domestic Crude Peanut Oil (in Tanks) F.O.B. Southeast Mills — In Cents Per Pound

Year	Oct.	Nov.	Dec.	Jan.	Feb.	Mar.	Apr.	May	June	July	Aug.	Sept.	Average
1989-90	39.06	41.50	41.60	43.25	46.00	43.40	41.25	45.25	46.90	46.88	49.05	51.13	44.64
1990-1	48.13	44.20	43.00	41.00	42.83	47.60	46.75	43.33	42.25	41.50	35.33	30.66	42.22
1991-2	34.33	27.67	23.50	23.50	23.63	23.17	25.00	27.88	25.60	26.19	23.88	22.00	25.53
1992-3	23.63	25.58	30.30	30.88	27.17	26.00	27.50	30.00	30.20	33.00	39.50	35.93	29.97
1993-4	40.20	43.33	43.17	46.10	46.12	44.50	43.40	44.25	43.75	44.00	45.00	43.10	43.91
1994-5	46.00	50.88	53.80	50.25	41.83	41.00	41.25	40.25	39.00	39.13	41.50	41.30	43.85
1995-6	42.50	41.63	39.20	37.25	36.00	36.60	39.25	42.80	43.00	43.00	42.60	40.80	40.39
1996-7	41.50	39.20	40.75	43.50	43.88	44.75	45.00	46.20	47.88	48.06	48.00	47.25	44.66
1997-8	49.63	51.00	51.25	51.60	51.00	51.00	50.00	47.20	45.50	44.00	43.75	43.88	48.32
1998-9[1]	45.40	45.00	44.25	44.00									44.66

[1] Preliminary. *Source: Agricultural Marketing Service, U.S. Department of Agriculture (AMS-USDA)*

Pepper

Pepper prices increased in the January-October 1998 period due to a decline in world production in 1997. The price of black pepper (Malabar-Lampong-Brazilian) in January 1998 was $1.99 per pound. By May 1998, the price had increased to $2.63 per pound and in October 1998 it was $2.43 per pound. The price of black pepper in January 1998 was some 44 percent more than a year earlier though the October price was some 8 percent less than the prior year. Between January 1998 and October 1998, the price of black pepper increased 22 percent.

The price of white pepper (Muntok) did not increase over the same period. In January 1998, the New York spot price was $3.48 per pound, an increase of 36 percent from the previous year. By May 1998, white pepper prices were $3.93 per pound, but by October 1998 they had fallen back to $3.40 per pound. That was 6 percent less than the previous year. In the first 10 months of 1998, white pepper prices declined 2 percent.

One reason for the higher pepper prices was a decline in world pepper production in 1997. The International Pepper Community (IPC) reported that 1997 world production of pepper was 174,794 metric tonnes. That represented a decline of 9 percent from 1996.

India is the world's largest producer of pepper. In 1997, the I.P.C. reported that production was 60,000 tonnes, down 8 percent from 1996. India produces about a third of the world pepper crop. India is also the largest exporter of pepper with 1997 shipments estimated at 42,500 tonnes, an increase of almost 8 percent from 1996. India plants about 200,000 hectares to black pepper and exports about 70 percent of its production. The next largest producer of pepper is Indonesia with 1997 output estimated at 35,000 tonnes, a decline of 11 percent from the previous year. Indonesia was adversely affected by weather events related to El Nino. Indonesia's pepper exports in 1997 were estimated at 32,835 tonnes, down 9 percent from 1996.

After Indonesia, the next largest pepper producer is Vietnam. Production in 1997 was estimated at 20,000 tonnes, unchanged from 1996. Vietnam was not adversely affected by El Nino in 1997 though there has been dry weather in 1998. Malaysia's pepper production in 1997 was estimated at 18,000 tonnes, an increase of almost 13 percent from 1996. Malaysian exports of pepper in 1997 were 21,000 tonnes, an increase of 9 percent from 1996. Brazil's pepper production in 1997 fell sharply to 15,000 tonnes, a decline of 42 percent from the large 1996 crop of 25,700 tonnes. Brazilian exports of pepper in 1997 were 12,000 tonnes, down 48 percent from 1996. China's pepper production in 1997 was 12,000 tonnes, an increase of 2 percent from 1996. Exports in 1997 increased substantially to 2,235 tonnes, from 519 tonnes in 1996. Pepper production by Thailand was 7,074 tonnes, down 8 percent from 1996. Thailand's exports of pepper were 325 tonnes, down 4 percent from 1996.

World Exports of Pepper (Black and White) and Prices in the United States

	Exports (In Metric Tons)								New York Spot Prices (¢ Per Pound)				
									Indonesian			Indian	
Year	Brazil	India	Indonesia	Madagascar	Malaysia	Mexico	Sri Lanka	Vietnam	Lampong Black	Muntok White	Brazilian Black	Malabar Black	Tellicherry[2]
1988	24,393	47,258	41,568	2,497	19,190	2,602	2,714	2,612	173.9	243.4	170.3	170.3	220.6
1989	27,717	25,120	42,138	1,417	26,260	2,388	1,576	7,551	138.2	146.2	136.2	135.9	174.8
1990	28,014	34,429	47,675	1,222	27,706	2,663	2,609	1,288	99.1	90.3	97.1	97.1	139.1
1991	47,553	18,735	49,667	1,844	25,458	1,861	2,058	16,252	71.1	70.1	67.1	67.1	117.8
1992	26,277	22,684	62,136	1,948	22,919	3,636	2,143	22,347	56.1	70.8	54.7	54.7	86.1
1993	26,254	47,677	27,684	2,001	16,737	2,430	5,032	20,138	62.5	114.6	62.3	62.3	84.0
1994	22,231	36,536	36,036	2,066	23,275	2,615	1,850	19,500	95.3	151.9	95.0	95.0	110.7
1995	22,158	25,270	57,781	1,274	14,869	3,085	2,082	17,900	116.8	182.3	116.8	116.8	150.9
1996[1]	24,178	------	36,849	1,570	28,124	4,200	2,612	25,000	114.8	178.9	114.8	114.8	140.0
1997[1]									206.7	304.6	206.7	206.7	225.8

[1] Preliminary. [2] Extra bold. *Sources: Foreign Agricultural Service, U.S. Department of Agriculture; Food and Agricultural Organization of the United Nations*

United States Imports of Unground Pepper from Specified Countries In Metric Tons

	Black Pepper							White Pepper					
Year	Brazil	India	Indonesia	Malaysia	Singapore	Sri Lanka	Total	Brazil	China	Indonesia	Malaysia	Singapore	Total
1988	6,033	7,481	11,131	1,400	104	344	26,939	20	2	4,169	12	26	4,326
1989	11,038	1,272	11,016	6,732	324	375	31,819	37	38	5,272	63	90	5,549
1990	8,778	6,679	8,444	6,768	457	644	32,980	17	15	5,506	24	86	5,721
1991	15,069	2,308	11,330	8,154	391	396	38,860	2	7	4,938	37	96	5,174
1992	6,601	9,892	20,768	2,073	52	310	40,590	51	2	5,089	29	261	5,544
1993	4,580	21,985	7,666	209	-----	539	35,969	322	114	4,304	137	363	5,481
1994	8,215	21,097	11,877	829	90	386	43,011	312	756	3,974	228	302	6,102
1995	3,165	10,836	19,630	268	30	327	34,465	414	280	4,037	164	211	5,266
1996	4,267	18,350	17,213	1,084	101	411	41,602	519	54	4,370	150	391	5,765
1997[1]	4,328	23,404	13,610	2,203	678	585	45,319	75	522	3,755	199	750	5,751

[1] Preliminary. *Source: Foreign Agricultural Service, U.S. Department of Agriculture (FAS-USDA)*

PEPPER

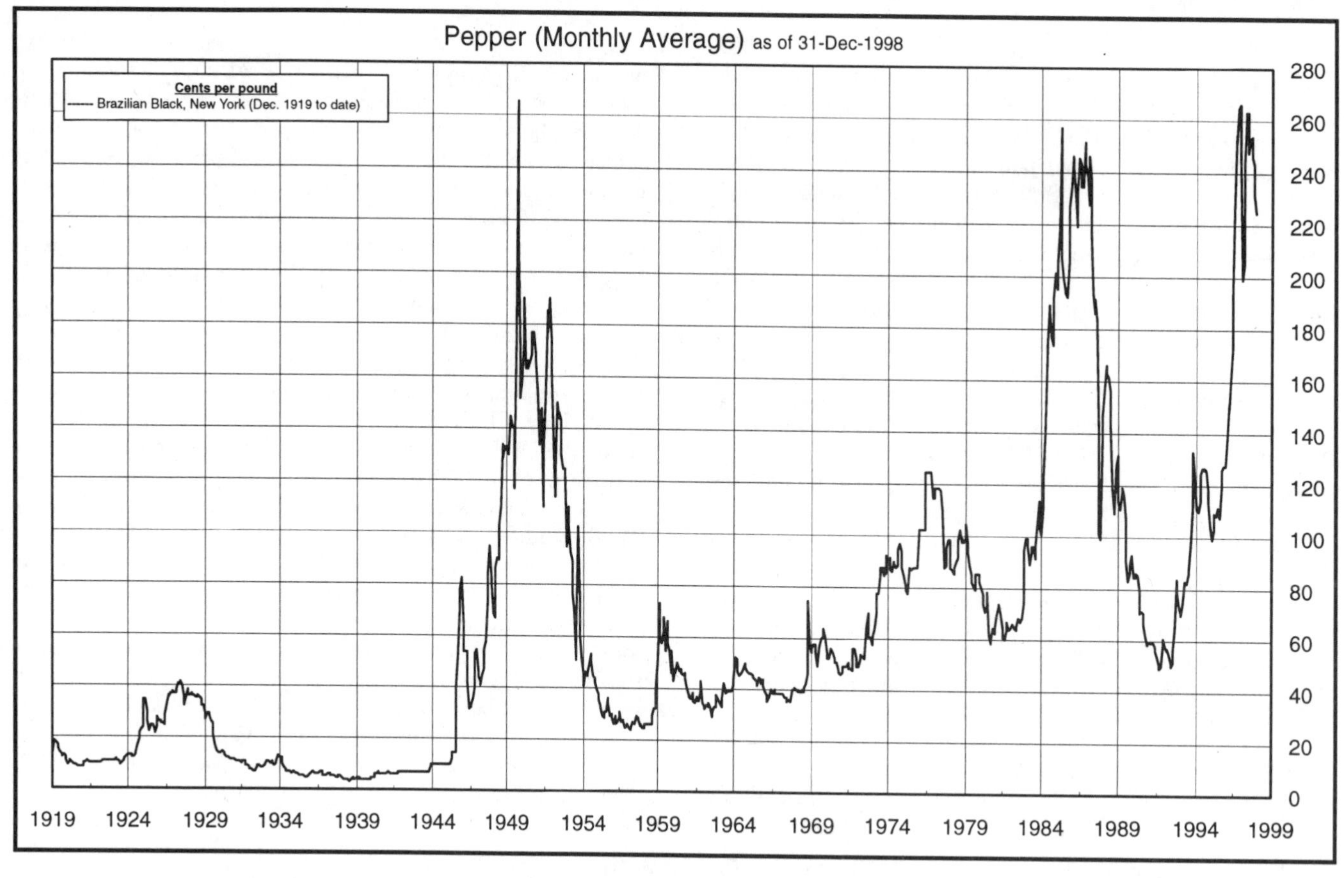

Average Black Pepper Prices in New York (Brazilian) In Cents Per Pound

Year	Jan.	Feb.	Mar.	Apr.	May	June	July	Aug.	Sept.	Oct.	Nov.	Dec.	Average
1989	156.8	161.8	159.0	160.0	154.5	141.8	115.5	108.0	108.2	124.7	131.3	112.4	136.2
1990	107.0	110.8	115.4	115.0	106.0	91.0	82.3	85.8	88.5	92.3	89.6	81.8	97.1
1991	79.0	78.5	78.6	74.5	66.8	70.0	68.8	61.6	59.5	56.8	55.8	55.0	67.1
1992	55.6	54.5	56.0	55.3	54.0	54.0	50.8	49.0	50.0	57.8	61.0	58.0	54.7
1993	56.0	56.5	54.3	51.2	50.0	51.5	55.8	64.8	84.0	79.0	74.2	70.8	62.3
1994	69.3	74.3	82.0	82.8	82.0	86.5	87.8	97.8	112.2	131.5	123.5	110.4	95.0
1995	111.0	110.0	114.2	124.8	127.3	126.0	127.0	126.3	118.2	113.5	104.8	99.0	116.8
1996	99.3	103.3	109.2	108.3	111.2	109.5	108.0	119.8	126.5	127.5	127.6	128.0	114.8
1997	138.6	151.8	149.0	161.8	173.4	193.8	229.5	255.0	251.3	264.8	266.3	245.0	206.7
1998	199.4	205.5	243.8	262.8	262.8	247.5	253.0	253.8	246.3	243.3			241.8

Source: Foreign Agricultural Service, U.S. Department of Agriculture (FAS-USDA)

Average White Pepper Prices in New York (Indonesian)[1] In Cents Per Pound

Year	Jan.	Feb.	Mar.	Apr.	May	June	July	Aug.	Sept.	Oct.	Nov.	Dec.	Average
1989	176.3	178.8	179.8	169.2	156.3	147.6	141.5	135.0	125.6	121.2	116.0	107.6	146.2
1990	102.3	100.5	99.2	95.5	93.8	82.8	80.0	88.2	91.5	88.0	83.2	78.0	90.3
1991	77.0	72.5	71.4	70.0	67.4	66.0	66.3	63.2	67.0	70.8	78.6	71.5	70.1
1992	70.0	70.0	70.0	70.0	68.0	65.0	64.2	65.0	72.7	79.2	78.5	77.4	70.8
1993	79.0	89.0	85.3	84.0	81.3	87.3	97.0	121.5	181.3	172.6	154.7	142.4	114.6
1994	144.5	139.5	141.3	140.8	137.0	143.3	143.4	156.3	159.2	167.5	176.5	173.0	151.9
1995	179.5	175.8	168.0	181.3	195.0	184.2	187.5	190.8	191.0	182.0	178.5	174.2	182.3
1996	174.5	177.5	181.6	179.5	172.6	164.8	154.0	169.6	181.5	193.5	191.8	205.8	178.9
1997	256.0	264.5	255.0	250.0	241.0	248.8	280.3	324.0	332.5	362.0	433.8	407.5	304.6
1998	348.0	346.3	362.5	390.0	393.0	358.8	354.0	356.3	348.8	340.0			359.8

[1] Muntok white. *Source: Foreign Agricultural Service, U.S. Department of Agriculture (FAS-USDA)*

Petroleum

U.S. domestic field production of petroleum in September 1998 was 8.44 million barrels per day. This was up less than 1 percent from August 1998 and 3 percent less than a year ago. Petroleum includes crude oil, natural gas plant liquids and other liquids. In the January-September 1998 period, field production of petroleum averaged 8.53 million barrels per day. That was down 1 percent from the comparable period of 1997 and 1 percent less than in 1996. For all of 1997, field production of petroleum was 8.61 million barrels per day. U.S. field production of petroleum has been trending lower for many years. In 1973, production averaged almost 11 million barrels per day. Advances in petroleum engineering technology have allowed more petroleum products to be found and old fields to be more fully exploited.

U.S. production of natural gas plant liquids in September 1998 was 1.7 million barrels per day. That was 1 percent less than the previous month and 8 percent less than a year ago. In the January-September 1998 period, production averaged 1.77 million barrels per day. That was down 3 percent from the like period of 1997 and 2 percent less than 1996. For all of 1997, natural gas plant liquids production averaged 1.82 million barrels per day.

U.S. imports of petroleum products (not including crude oil) in September 1998 were 1.84 million barrels per day, up 9 percent from August 1998 and 8 percent higher than a year ago. In the January-September 1998 period, imports of petroleum products averaged 1.82 million barrels, down 10 percent from the comparable period of 1997 and 7 percent less than in 1996. For all of 1997, petroleum product imports averaged 1.94 million barrels per day. U.S. exports of petroleum products in September 1998 averaged 883,000 barrels per day, up 21 percent from the previous month and 1 percent higher than a year earlier. In the January-September 1998 period, exports averaged 846,000 barrels per day, down 3 percent from 1997 and 2 percent less than in 1996. For all of 1997, exports averaged 896,000 barrels per day.

U.S. domestic field production of crude oil in September 1998 averaged 6.3 million barrels per day, about unchanged from the previous month. In the first nine months of 1998, U.S. domestic crude oil production averaged 6.39 million barrels per day, down 1 percent from the same period of 1997 and 1 percent less than in 1996. For all of 1997, domestic crude oil production averaged 6.45 million barrels per day. In 1973, crude oil production was 9.21 million barrels per day.

Alaskan crude oil production in September 1998 averaged 1.09 million barrels per day, down 4 percent from the previous month. In the first nine months of 1998, production averaged 1.18 million barrels per day, down 10 percent from 1997 and 16 percent less than in 1996. In 1973 Alaskan crude oil production was 198,000 barrels per day and it peaked in 1988 at 2.02 million barrels per day.

U.S. imports of crude oil in September 1998 averaged 8.38 million barrels per day, down 8 percent from August. In the January-September 1998 period, imports averaged 8.56 million barrels per day, up 4 percent from 1997 and 14 percent more than in the same period of 1996. For all of 1997, imports averaged 8.23 million barrels per day. U.S. imports of crude oil have been on a steady increase for many years. In 1973, imports averaged 3.24 million barrels per day.

Refinery inputs of crude oil in September 1998 averaged 14.97 million barrels per day, down 4 percent from the previous month. In the first nine months of 1998, refinery inputs averaged 14.95 million barrels per day, up 2 percent from the same period of 1997 and 5 percent more than in 1996. For all of 1997, refinery inputs averaged 14.66 million barrels per day.

U.S. stocks of crude oil at the end of September 1998 were 885 million barrels, unchanged from August. Stocks were 2 percent higher than a year earlier. Stocks in the Strategic Petroleum Reserve in September 1998 were 563 million barrels. Reserves have been at that level since December 1996.

Futures Markets

Futures and options contracts on light sweet crude oil, heating oil and unleaded gasoline are traded on the New York Mercantile Exchange (NYMEX). Propane and natural gas futures also are traded there. London's International Petroleum Exchange (IPE) trades Brent crude oil futures and options on those futures. The IPE also trades heating oil futures and options (termed gas oil) and unleaded gasoline futures. High-sulfur fuel oil futures are traded on the SIMEX in Singapore.

World Production of Crude Petroleum In Thousands of Barrels Per Day

Year	Canada	China	Indonesia	Iran	Kuwait	Mexico	Nigeria	Russia[3]	Saudi Arabia	United Kingdom	United States	Venezuela	Total World
1989	1,560	2,757	1,409	2,810	1,783	2,520	1,716	11,715	5,064	1,802	7,613	1,907	59,863
1990	1,553	2,774	1,462	3,088	1,175	2,553	1,810	10,975	6,410	1,820	7,355	2,137	60,566
1991	1,548	2,835	1,592	3,312	190	2,680	1,892	9,992	8,115	1,797	7,417	2,375	60,207
1992	1,605	2,845	1,504	3,429	1,058	2,669	1,943	7,632	8,332	1,825	7,171	2,371	60,216
1993	1,679	2,890	1,511	3,540	1,852	2,673	1,960	6,730	8,198	1,915	6,847	2,450	60,246
1994	1,746	2,939	1,510	3,618	2,025	2,685	1,931	6,135	8,120	2,375	6,662	2,588	61,003
1995	1,805	2,990	1,503	3,643	2,057	2,618	1,993	5,995	8,231	2,489	6,560	2,750	62,331
1996	1,837	3,131	1,547	3,686	2,062	2,855	2,188	5,850	8,218	2,568	6,465	3,053	64,054
1997[1]	1,893	3,200	1,546	3,664	2,083	3,023	2,317	5,884	8,562	2,517	6,452	3,315	66,317
1998[2]	1,990	3,197	1,516	3,638	2,092	3,067	2,157	5,931	8,415	2,596	6,357	3,179	66,991

Includes lease condensate. [1] Preliminary. [2] Estimate. [3] Formerly part of the U.S.S.R.; data not reported separately until 1992.

Source: Energy Information Administration, U.S. Department of Energy (EIA-DOE)

Refiner Sales Prices of Petroleum Products for Resale (Excluding Taxes) In Cents Per Gallon

Year	Jan.	Feb.	Mar.	Apr.	May	June	July	Aug.	Sept.	Oct.	Nov.	Dec.	Average
						Residual Fuel Oil (Sulfur 1% or less)							
1992	30.3	32.7	30.8	31.6	33.1	35.9	38.0	37.7	37.9	41.4	39.2	35.9	35.1
1993	36.8	35.5	39.1	38.4	34.8	33.7	32.7	31.6	31.9	32.1	30.7	27.5	33.7
1994	33.8	39.3	30.0	29.4	31.7	35.8	37.8	37.1	32.6	32.6	35.7	36.9	34.5
1995	39.1	37.1	38.3	36.8	40.4	39.9	36.8	35.5	36.4	35.3	36.6	44.7	38.3
1996	49.9	42.8	47.1	48.3	45.0	40.4	41.4	42.0	42.8	47.9	49.1	51.4	45.7
1997	46.2	43.7	39.6	37.6	36.6	39.4	38.5	39.4	40.1	44.6	46.5	38.7	41.5
1998[1]	35.2	30.7	29.4	32.9	31.9	29.3	30.7	26.9	29.9	31.0			30.8
						No. 2 Fuel Oil							
1992	51.9	54.0	53.7	56.5	58.8	61.7	61.3	60.1	62.7	64.6	58.8	55.7	57.9
1993	54.4	56.9	59.0	57.5	56.9	55.0	51.0	51.0	54.8	58.1	53.1	45.1	54.4
1994	50.7	54.2	49.7	48.9	49.0	49.8	50.9	51.4	50.1	50.8	51.0	49.5	50.6
1995	49.4	49.1	48.1	50.4	52.4	49.3	48.1	51.0	52.0	50.5	53.4	57.3	51.1
1996	56.8	58.9	62.8	67.5	61.1	53.7	57.1	62.1	68.7	72.7	71.4	71.2	63.9
1997	69.8	64.5	57.7	58.6	58.8	54.5	53.8	55.3	54.3	59.0	58.4	53.4	58.9
1998[1]	48.9	47.7	44.9	44.9	43.4	39.9	38.8	36.9	41.8	41.2			42.8
						No. 2 Diesel Fuel							
1992	51.4	54.1	54.0	57.0	60.1	62.7	61.8	60.4	63.3	65.5	60.4	56.4	59.1
1993	54.9	57.4	60.0	59.8	59.6	57.2	53.2	53.2	58.9	65.8	58.9	46.8	57.0
1994	49.1	52.8	52.9	52.3	51.7	52.2	53.7	54.1	54.2	55.2	55.1	50.8	52.9
1995	50.1	50.6	51.2	54.8	55.9	52.6	51.4	54.2	55.7	54.6	56.3	57.6	53.8
1996	56.2	57.9	61.9	70.1	67.0	59.1	60.0	64.9	71.7	75.4	73.2	71.0	65.9
1997	69.9	67.8	62.5	61.7	60.7	56.5	55.8	58.9	57.8	61.7	61.5	55.0	60.6
1998[1]	49.6	48.3	45.8	48.2	47.0	43.6	42.6	41.4	45.6	45.6			45.8
						Kerosine-Type Jet Fuel							
1992	53.9	55.2	54.6	56.9	60.8	63.3	64.8	63.9	64.3	66.0	61.5	58.9	60.5
1993	57.7	60.4	60.3	59.8	60.1	58.5	55.1	55.1	56.6	60.5	58.7	51.0	57.7
1994	52.6	56.0	52.4	50.8	50.6	51.5	53.8	54.4	54.0	54.4	56.3	53.1	53.4
1995	52.3	52.1	50.1	52.6	54.7	53.1	51.3	53.1	55.2	54.1	56.3	58.6	53.9
1996	60.3	57.2	59.6	65.3	62.2	57.5	59.6	64.5	71.6	73.6	72.2	73.0	64.6
1997	73.5	71.4	61.8	60.5	59.4	58.1	56.8	59.4	58.8	61.3	61.3	55.6	61.2
1998[1]	53.4	50.2	45.7	46.6	46.9	43.5	43.8	42.9	44.6	45.9			46.4
						Propane (Consumer Grade)							
1992	30.9	30.2	29.5	29.0	29.4	31.6	31.5	32.9	35.4	36.6	36.2	36.3	32.8
1993	40.2	36.7	38.2	36.2	34.0	33.8	33.3	33.3	34.1	34.7	33.6	30.9	35.1
1994	32.3	34.0	31.8	30.5	30.4	29.9	29.8	31.0	31.7	33.5	35.0	35.8	32.5
1995	35.6	34.5	34.3	33.0	33.2	32.6	32.1	33.2	33.8	34.4	34.7	37.9	34.4
1996	41.6	44.1	41.1	37.8	36.2	36.2	36.9	38.9	45.3	51.1	58.0	67.7	46.1
1997	59.9	44.7	41.3	37.7	36.9	36.4	35.9	37.5	39.5	41.1	39.6	37.5	41.6
1998[1]	35.4	33.1	31.2	30.3	29.3	26.6	25.7	25.7	26.3	27.6			29

[1] Preliminary. *Source: Energy Information Administration, U.S. Department of Energy (EIA-DOE)*

Supply and Disposition of Crude Oil in the United States

	Supply								Disposition		Ending Stocks		
	Field Production		Imports			Unaccounted for Crude Oil	Stock Withdrawal[3]						
Yearly Average	Total Domestic	Alaskan	Total	SPR[2]	Other		SPR[2]	Other	Refinery Inputs	Exports	Total	SPR[2]	Other Primary
	Thousands of Barrels Per Day										Million of Barrels		
1989	7,613	1,874	5,843	56	5,787	200	56	30	13,401	142	921	580	341
1990	7,355	1,773	5,894	27	5,867	258	16	-51	13,409	109	908	586	323
1991	7,417	1,798	5,782	0	5,782	195	-47	5	13,301	116	893	569	325
1992	7,171	1,714	6,083	10	6,073	258	17	-18	13,411	89	893	575	318
1993	6,847	1,582	6,787	15	6,772	168	34	47	13,613	98	922	587	335
1994	6,662	1,559	7,063	12	7,051	266	13	5	13,866	99	929	592	337
1995	6,560	1,484	7,230	0	7,230	193	0	-93	13,973	95	895	592	303
1996	6,465	1,393	7,508	0	7,508	215	-71	-53	14,195	110	850	566	284
1997	6,452	1,296	8,225	0	8,225	145	-7	57	14,662	108	868	563	305
1998[1]	6,343	1,177	8,586	0	8,586	111	26	53	14,850	111	890	569	322

[1] Preliminary. [2] Strategic Petroleum Reserve. [3] A negative number indicates a decrease in stocks and a positive number indicates an increase. Note: Crude oil includes lease condensate. Stocks of Alaskan crude oil in transit were included beginning in January 1981. *Source: Energy Information Administration, U.S. Department of Energy (EIA-DOE)*

Crude Petroleum Refinery Operations Ratio[1] in the United States In Percent of Capacity

Year	Jan.	Feb.	Mar.	Apr.	May	June	July	Aug.	Sept.	Oct.	Nov.	Dec.	Average
1989	86.0	83.0	84.0	84.0	86.0	90.0	89.0	89.0	88.0	86.0	86.0	84.0	86.3
1990	88.0	88.0	84.0	85.0	87.0	89.0	93.0	91.0	91.0	84.0	84.0	83.0	87.3
1991	83.0	84.0	83.0	85.0	87.0	90.0	89.0	89.0	88.0	83.0	84.0	87.0	86.0
1992	83.0	81.0	85.0	86.0	89.0	92.0	92.0	89.0	91.0	89.0	90.0	88.0	87.9
1993	87.0	87.0	89.0	91.0	93.0	95.0	95.0	93.0	93.0	92.0	92.0	91.0	91.5
1994	89.8	88.7	87.6	92.4	95.4	95.8	95.5	96.4	94.4	89.8	92.7	92.6	92.6
1995	89.6	87.9	86.7	90.5	94.0	95.6	94.0	94.0	95.6	90.5	92.1	93.3	92.0
1996	90.6	89.1	90.6	93.7	94.4	95.4	93.9	95.0	95.5	94.6	94.7	94.3	93.5
1997	89.3	87.3	90.7	92.6	97.3	97.7	97.1	98.6	99.7	96.7	95.6	97.2	95.0
1998[2]	93.3	91.3	94.4	96.4	97.1	98.9	99.2	99.8	95.0	89.7	94.7		95.4

[1] Based on the ration of the daily average crude runs to stills to the rated capacity of refineries per day. [2] Preliminary.
Source: Energy Information Administration, U.S. Department of Energy (EIA-DOE)

Crude Oil Refinery Inputs in the United States In Thousands of Barrels Per Day

Year	Jan.	Feb.	Mar.	Apr.	May	June	July	Aug.	Sept.	Oct.	Nov.	Dec.	Average
1989	13,330	12,765	12,963	12,956	13,405	13,905	13,848	13,861	13,791	13,360	13,420	13,165	13,401
1990	13,491	13,487	12,876	13,051	13,386	13,689	14,212	14,142	14,104	12,825	12,953	12,708	13,409
1991	12,735	13,046	12,839	13,042	13,539	13,918	13,703	13,800	13,694	12,896	12,929	13,465	13,301
1992	12,923	12,486	13,083	13,260	13,679	14,059	13,953	13,426	13,714	13,584	13,547	13,194	13,411
1993	12,938	12,865	13,200	13,538	13,829	14,129	14,136	13,844	13,841	13,729	13,686	13,571	13,613
1994	13,286	13,130	12,985	13,809	14,272	14,351	14,344	14,491	14,234	13,529	13,968	13,951	13,866
1995	13,604	13,365	13,480	13,817	14,303	14,553	14,403	14,276	14,402	13,598	13,833	14,011	13,973
1996	13,708	13,529	13,755	14,263	14,401	14,535	14,319	14,423	14,483	14,276	14,276	14,194	14,181
1997	13,632	13,425	14,047	14,283	15,083	15,139	14,958	15,217	15,297	14,790	14,654	14,898	14,626
1998[1]	14,313	14,034	14,590	14,961	15,104	15,368	15,496	15,660	14,854	14,001	14,769	14,990	14,850

[1] Preliminary. *Source: Energy Information Administration, U.S. Department of Energy (EIA-DOE)*

Production of Major Refined Petroleum Products in the Continental United States In Millions of Barrels

Year	Asphalt	Aviation Gasoline	Fuel Oil: Distillate	Fuel Oil: Residual	Gasoline	Jet Fuel	Kerosene	Natural Gas Plant Liquids	Lubricants	Liquefied Gases: Total	Liquefied Gases: at L.P.G.[2]	Liquefied Gases: at L.P.G.[3]
1988	162.1	9.3	1,046.3	338.7	2,555	501.3	28.8	614.2	62.3	665.2	482.6	182.6
1989	154.9	9.2	1,152.2	500.1	2,684	543.6	30.8	586.1	58.1	653.5	451.3	202.2
1990	164.0	8.5	1,067.5	346.6	2,650	555.6	15.5	598.3	59.7	638.4	456.2	182.2
1991	156.8	8.0	1,081.0	341.1	2,554	525.0	14.0	639.2	57.0	683.1	487.5	195.6
1992	153.0	7.9	1,088.4	326.1	2,591	512.0	14.8	668.0	57.5	721.9	499.7	222.2
1993	165.6	7.9	1,139.7	303.9	2,644	518.8	17.5	631.2	58.4	849.4	633.5	215.9
1994	164.8	7.9	1,169.7	301.4	2,621	528.4	21.1	630.2	62.1	734.2	511.1	223.2
1995	170.4	7.8	1,151.7	287.6	2,722	516.8	19.2	643.2	63.7	759.9	521.1	238.8
1996	167.8	7.3	1,213.6	265.5	2,769	554.5	22.8	669.8	63.3	789.1	546.7	242.5
1997[1]	177.0	7.2	1,238.0	258.3	2,826	567.3	23.9	663.3	65.9	799.4	547.3	252.2

[1] Preliminary. *Source: Energy Information Administration, U.S. Department of Energy (EIA-DOE)*

Stocks of Petroleum and Products in the United States on January 1 In Millions of Barrels

Year	Crude Petroleum	Strategic Reserve	Refined Products: Total	Asphalt	Aviation Gasoline	Fuel Oil: Distillate	Fuel Oil: Residual	Finished Gasoline	Jet Fuel	Kerosene	Liquefied Gases[2]	Lubricants	Motor Gasoline: Total	Motor Gasoline: Finished[3]
1989	889.9	559.5	561.6	20.8	2.1	123.5	44.6	192.0	43.8	7.3	97.3	13.3	228	190
1990	921.1	579.9	508.3	20.6	2.1	105.7	43.8	179.1	40.9	5.1	80.2	13.8	213	177
1991	908.4	585.7	566.8	18.7	1.7	132.2	48.6	182.4	52.1	5.6	97.9	12.4	220	181
1992	893.1	568.5	576.7	22.3	1.6	143.5	49.9	183.3	48.8	5.8	92.3	12.3	219	182
1993	892.9	574.7	549.1	17.7	1.6	140.6	42.6	179.1	43.1	5.7	88.7	13.3	216	178
1994	922.5	587.1	465.8	19.1	1.8	140.9	44.2	185.7	40.4	4.1	106.6	11.8	226	187
1995	928.9	591.7	468.0	18.6	2.3	145.2	41.9	175.9	46.8	8.0	108.0	11.5	215	176
1996	895.0	591.6	401.2	26.3	2.2	106.3	34.8	162.8	38.4	4.0	99.2	11.7	206	161
1997	868.1	565.8	452.6	22.3	1.7	139.0	40.4	166.1	43.9	7.3	89.5	13.2	203	157
1998[1]	868.1	563.4	451.6	22.1	1.7	138.4	40.5	166.4	44.0	7.3	95.2	12.9	166	166

[1] Preliminary. [2] Includes ethane and ethylene at plants and refineries. [3] Includes oxygenated. *Source: Energy Information Administration, U.S. Department of Energy (EIA-DOE)*

Stocks of Crude Petroleum in the United States, on First of Month In Millions of Barrels

Year	Jan.	Feb.	Mar.	Apr.	May	June	July	Aug.	Sept.	Oct.	Nov.	Dec.
1989	889.9	894.8	896.6	892.5	907.4	915.7	903.0	907.6	916.3	912.0	914.3	930.5
1990	921.1	932.9	924.0	955.9	953.1	968.7	970.9	966.2	959.2	932.7	935.7	924.7
1991	908.4	905.3	912.8	905.3	907.2	924.3	915.3	910.6	913.8	909.1	910.7	912.0
1992	893.1	909.7	914.8	907.1	916.5	912.0	894.6	902.2	898.3	893.5	906.2	899.4
1993	892.9	902.0	908.1	914.7	930.4	935.0	935.1	935.2	919.6	906.4	916.5	924.1
1994	922.5	925.3	922.6	932.6	930.6	922.7	919.6	924.2	920.2	927.0	934.9	938.0
1995	922.2	920.8	931.0	929.4	924.1	919.6	907.3	899.5	897.5	902.8	910.6	894.9
1996	894.9	894.7	892.9	888.8	889.7	889.7	898.9	891.3	890.8	875.8	881.5	869.1
1997	849.7	865.9	862.1	877.6	883.9	890.5	885.3	873.0	864.2	866.6	879.3	886.9
1998[1]	868.1	884.3	885.7	899.8	914.6	916.1	896.4	902.6	893.5	873.0	897.4	906.2

[1] Preliminary. *Source: Energy Information Administration, U.S. Department of Agriculture (EIA-DOE)*

Production of Crude Petroleum in the United States In Thousands of Barrels Per Day

Year	Jan.	Feb.	Mar.	Apr.	May	June	July	Aug.	Sept.	Oct.	Nov.	Dec.	Average
1989	7,937	7,788	7,575	7,772	7,816	7,624	7,444	7,544	7,548	7,453	7,536	7,337	7,613
1990	7,546	7,497	7,433	7,407	7,328	7,106	7,173	7,287	7,224	7,542	7,387	7,338	7,355
1991	7,500	7,637	7,546	7,509	7,409	7,320	7,347	7,316	7,368	7,437	7,328	7,299	7,417
1992	7,361	7,389	7,348	7,293	7,169	7,167	7,131	6,922	7,030	7,126	7,024	7,103	7,171
1993	6,961	6,943	6,974	6,881	6,847	6,795	6,688	6,758	6,712	6,839	6,912	6,858	6,847
1994	6,817	6,770	6,746	6,612	6,688	6,611	6,501	6,544	6,609	6,658	6,628	6,760	6,662
1995	6,682	6,794	6,600	6,604	6,629	6,579	6,449	6,447	6,416	6,421	6,585	6,530	6,560
1996	6,495	6,577	6,571	6,444	6,394	6,458	6,338	6,360	6,482	6,481	6,476	6,506	6,465
1997	6,387	6,514	6,470	6,483	6,401	6,341	6,316	6,282	6,388	6,435	6,450	6,475	6,411
1998[1]	6,438	6,538	6,465	6,484	6,384	6,290	6,322	6,276	6,069	6,270	6,189	6,403	6,343

[1] Preliminary. *Source: Energy Information Administration, U.S. Department of Energy (EIA-DOE)*

U.S. Foreign Trade of Petroleum and Products In Thousands of Barrels Per Day

	Exports		Imports						Exports		Imports				
Year	Total[2]	Petroleum Products	Crude	Petroleum Products	Distillate Fuel Oil	Residual Fuel Oil	Net Imports[3]	Year	Total[2]	Petroleum Products	Crude	Petroleum Products	Distillate Fuel Oil	Residual Fuel Oil	Net Imports[3]
1979	471	236	6,519	1,937	193	1,151	7,985	1989	859	717	5,843	2,217	306	629	7,202
1980	544	258	5,263	1,646	142	939	6,365	1990	857	748	5,894	2,123	278	504	7,161
1981	595	367	4,396	1,599	173	800	5,401	1991	1,001	885	5,782	1,844	205	453	6,626
1982	815	579	3,488	1,325	93	776	4,298	1992	950	861	6,083	1,805	216	375	6,938
1983	739	575	3,329	1,722	174	699	4,312	1993	1,003	904	6,787	1,833	184	373	7,618
1984	722	541	3,426	2,011	272	681	4,715	1994	942	843	7,063	1,933	203	314	8,054
1985	781	577	3,201	1,866	200	510	4,286	1995	949	855	7,230	1,605	193	187	7,886
1986	785	631	4,178	2,045	247	669	5,439	1996	981	871	7,508	1,971	230	248	8,498
1987	764	613	4,674	2,004	255	565	5,914	1997	1,003	896	8,225	1,936	228	194	9,158
1988	815	661	5,107	2,295	302	644	6,587	1998[1]	942	831	8,586	1,846	195	211	9,490

[1] Preliminary. [2] Includes crude oil. [3] Equals imports minus exports. *Source: Energy Information Administration, U.S. Department of Energy (EIA)*

Domestic First Purchase Price of Crude Petroleum at Wells[1] In Dollars Per Barrel

Year	Jan.	Feb.	Mar.	Apr.	May	June	July	Aug.	Sept.	Oct.	Nov.	Dec.	Average
1989	13.80	14.24	15.65	17.04	16.76	16.42	16.32	15.01	15.58	16.25	16.30	17.01	15.86
1990	18.49	18.16	16.57	14.52	13.82	12.79	14.03	21.87	28.46	30.86	27.53	22.63	20.03
1991	19.60	16.28	15.13	16.16	16.44	15.58	16.36	16.60	16.71	17.72	17.12	14.68	16.54
1992	13.99	14.04	14.12	15.36	16.38	17.96	17.80	17.07	17.20	17.16	16.00	14.94	15.99
1993	14.70	15.53	15.94	16.15	16.03	15.06	13.83	13.75	13.39	13.72	12.45	10.38	14.25
1994	10.49	10.71	10.94	12.31	14.02	14.93	15.34	14.50	13.62	13.84	14.14	13.43	13.19
1995	14.00	14.69	14.68	15.84	15.85	15.02	14.01	14.13	14.49	13.68	14.03	15.02	14.62
1996	15.43	15.54	17.63	19.58	17.94	16.94	17.63	18.29	19.93	21.09	20.20	21.34	18.46
1997	21.76	19.38	17.85	16.64	17.24	15.90	15.91	16.21	16.44	17.68	16.84	15.06	17.24
1998[2]	13.48	12.16	11.53	11.64	11.49	10.00	10.46	10.18	11.28	11.36			11.36

[1] Buyers posted prices. [2] Preliminary. *Source: Energy Information Adiministration, U.S. Department of Energy (EIA-DOE)*

Volume of Trading of Crude Oil Futures in New York In Thousands of Contracts

Year	Jan.	Feb.	Mar.	Apr.	May	June	July	Aug.	Sept.	Oct.	Nov.	Dec.	Total
1989	1,919.0	1,524.0	2,053.0	2,070.0	1,911.0	2,082.0	1,663.0	1,343.0	1,541.0	1,521.0	1,425.0	1,483.0	20,535.0
1990	2,164.0	1,790.0	1,794.0	1,813.0	1,945.0	1,839.0	2,046.0	2,716.0	2,073.0	2,437.0	1,769.0	1,302.0	23,687.0
1991	1,997.0	1,478.0	1,605.0	1,885.0	1,741.0	1,411.0	1,675.0	1,598.0	1,543.0	2,064.0	2,051.0	1,960.0	21,008.0
1992	2,097.0	1,630.0	1,620.0	1,889.0	1,885.0	2,006.0	1,796.0	1,531.0	1,541.0	1,797.0	1,542.0	1,778.0	21,110.0
1993	2,139.0	1,886.0	1,895.0	1,459.0	1,641.0	2,018.0	2,616.0	2,200.0	2,679.0	1,945.0	2,378.0	2,122.0	24,869.0
1994	2,296.0	1,933.0	2,228.0	2,382.0	2,602.0	2,576.0	2,186.0	2,544.0	1,897.0	2,195.0	2,195.9	1,778.2	16,812.0
1995	2,133.5	1,657.3	2,289.8	2,220.1	2,408.9	2,172.4	1,749.3	1,793.8	1,968.0	1,834.6	1,739.1	1,647.2	23,614.0
1996	2,260.1	1,928.3	2,399.3	2,489.9	2,161.3	1,601.7	1,732.1	1,657.0	1,912.6	2,098.0	1,643.1	1,604.3	23,487.8
1997	1,949.9	1,973.7	2,086.6	2,033.7	2,134.9	2,098.6	2,221.4	2,053.7	2,027.5	2,574.0	1,770.2	1,847.2	24,771.4
1998	2,468.3	2,208.3	2,902.8	2,451.1	2,603.6	3,079.5	2,375.0	2,066.7	2,617.8	2,592.4	2,552.9	2,577.3	30,495.6

Source: New York Mercantile Exchange (NYMEX)

Average Open Interest of Crude Oil Futures in New York In Contracts

Year	Jan.	Feb.	Mar.	Apr.	May	June	July	Aug.	Sept.	Oct.	Nov.	Dec.
1989	204,066	210,299	224,322	248,032	231,390	222,748	221,389	209,702	230,990	235,716	242,677	257,974
1990	273,193	300,069	287,013	287,538	278,600	285,384	275,771	262,746	266,313	269,167	242,500	232,405
1991	249,759	272,396	285,417	303,942	286,159	277,587	278,704	267,186	264,223	298,434	292,889	284,453
1992	310,763	331,050	316,544	340,315	335,545	364,155	331,972	316,066	314,446	301,381	308,467	330,134
1993	352,316	369,180	385,768	381,954	384,309	396,832	423,041	428,418	404,172	397,121	404,046	427,756
1994	427,705	438,929	424,462	410,974	427,071	414,257	409,251	396,657	395,194	413,206	388,932	391,151
1995	373,798	379,329	353,805	364,929	350,826	346,051	357,718	343,636	342,360	334,170	329,786	348,954
1996	389,935	400,236	427,306	460,841	424,994	376,164	367,405	364,458	395,358	410,387	385,415	368,331
1997	365,522	384,737	408,751	409,719	401,663	397,245	411,292	424,529	405,389	419,821	404,597	424,333
1998	424,810	445,167	468,438	463,961	450,611	467,998	476,516	486,499	486,047	481,657	487,175	502,565

Source: New York Mercantile Exchange (NYMEX)

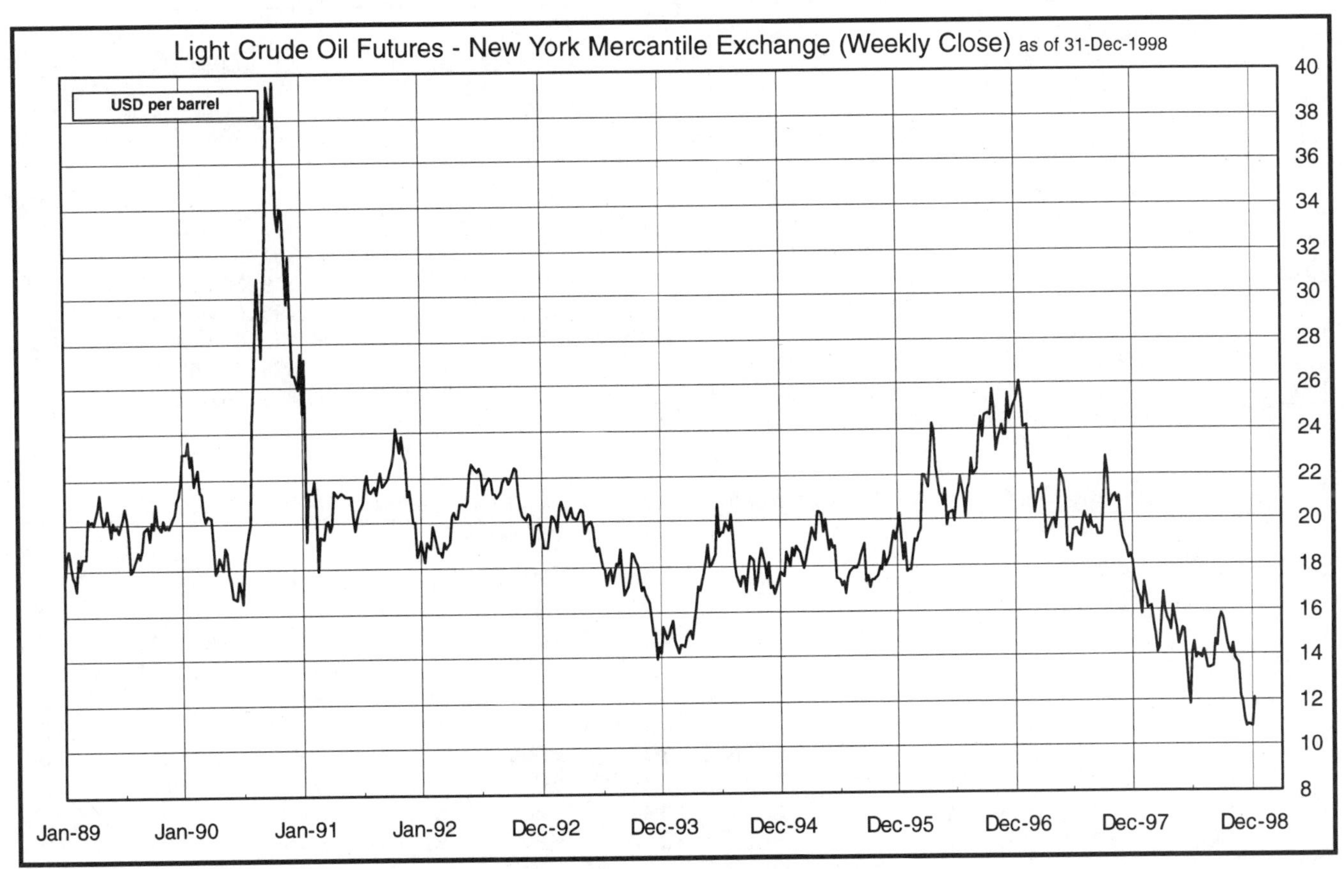

Plastics

On a volume basis, plastics are one of the most used materials in the U.S. for industrial and commercial purposes. The most important developments in the industry have occurred since 1910. The period of 1930-40 saw the initial commercial development of today's major thermoplastics: polyvinyl chloride, low density polyethylene, polystyrene and polymethyl methacrylate. In 1939, World War Two brought plastics into great demand mostly as substitutes for material that was in short supply, such as natural rubber. In the U.S., the production of synthetic rubbers led to the development of more plastic materials.

U.S. plastic resin sales in 1997 were 82.7 billion pounds, dry weight basis, up 5 percent from 1996. Sales of plastic resin continue to increase. Of the total, plastic resin sales for the packaging industry in 1997 were 21.8 billion pounds, an increase of 2 percent from 1996. The packaging industry consumed 26 percent of plastic resins in 1996. The building and construction industry took 17.1 billion pounds, an increase of almost 6 percent from 1996. Some 21 percent of plastic resins go to the building and construction market. Consumer and institutional markets took 10.6 billion pounds, an increase of 8 percent from 1996. Other major markets for plastic resins included transportation, electrical/electronic, furniture and furnishings, adhesives, ink/coatings and industrial/machinery.

Of the plastic resin sales in 1997, 74 billion pounds were thermoplastics. In terms of the major markets, packaging took 29.3 percent, building and construction 15.4 percent, consumer and institutional products took 14 percent, transportation took 4.6 percent, furniture and furnishings 4.2 percent, electrical/electronic took 3.9 percent, adhesives/inks/coatings 2.3 percent and industrial/machinery 1 percent. Exports of thermoplastics took an additional 12.7 percent.

The remaining 8.7 billion pounds of plastic resins are in the form of thermosets. Of this total, the major markets were building and construction, 65.5 percent; transportation, 7.9 percent; furniture and furnishings 7.2 percent; adhesives/inks/coatings, 3.5 percent; consumer and institutional products, 3.4 percent; electrical/electronic, 3.2 percent; packaging, .6 percent; exports, 3.5 percent.

An important thermoset resin is unsaturated polyester. The domestic reinforced plastic total use in 1997 was 1.12 billion pounds. Of that total, marine and marine accessories took 262 million pounds, transportation took 156 million pounds, construction took 553 million pounds, electrical/electronic took 59 million pounds, consumer goods took 62 million pounds and other reinforced plastics took 24 million pounds.

Domestic non-reinforced plastics total use in 1997 was 430 million pounds. Construction took 250 million pounds with consumer goods taking 40 million pounds. Gel coats/surface resins/protective coatings took 83 million pounds.

Plastics Production by Resin in the United States In Millions of Pounds

	Thermosets				Thermoplastics										
Year	Polyester Unsaturated	Phenolic	Epoxy	Total Thermosets	Thermoplastic Polyester	Polyvinyl Chloride	Polystyrene	Polypropylene	Nylon	Low Density Polyethylene[1]	High Density Polyethylene	Total Thermoplastics	Total Selected Plastics	Other Plastics	Total Plastics
1988	1,404	3,066	486	6,588	1,652	8,350	5,187	7,274	566	10,397	8,400	43,251	49,839	9,923	59,762
1989	1,319	2,879	510	6,407	1,630	8,478	5,104	7,238	569	9,695	8,102	42,189	48,596	9,933	58,529
1990	1,221	2,946	499	6,364	1,879	9,096	5,021	8,310	558	11,148	8,337	45,646	52,010	9,950	61,960
1991	1,075	2,658	497	5,909	2,115	9,164	4,954	8,330	576	11,582	9,213	47,146	53,055	9,731	62,786
1992	1,175	2,923	457	6,335	2,413	9,989	5,096	8,421	668	11,917	9,808	49,751	56,086	10,285	66,371
1993	1,264	3,078	512	6,868	2,549	10,257	5,382	8,628	768	12,067	9,941	51,159	58,027	10,777	68,854
1994	1,468	3,229	601	7,513	3,196	11,712	5,848	9,539	943	12,600	11,117	56,794	64,307	11,664	75,971
1995	1,577	3,204	632	7,519	3,785	12,295	5,656	10,890	1,020	12,886	11,211	59,331	66,850	11,834	78,684
1996	1,557	3,476	662	8,129	4,031	13,220	6,065	11,991	1,103	14,145	12,373	64,526	72,655	11,640	84,295
1997	1,621	3,734	654	8,647	4,260	14,084	6,380	13,320	1,222	14,579	12,557	67,872	76,519	12,287	88,806

[1] Includes LDPE and LLDPE. *Source: The Society of the Plastics Industry, Inc. (SPI)*

Total Resin Sales and Captive Use by Important Markets In Millions of Pounds (Dry Weight Basis)

Year	Adhesive, Inks & Coatings	Building & Construction	Consumer & Industrial	Electrical & Electronics	Exports	Furniture & Furnishings	Industrial & Machinery	Packaging	Transportation	Other	Total
1989	1,211	11,096	6,217	3,145	[1]	2,285	475	14,711	2,547	10,911	52,598
1990	1,373	11,803	5,861	3,165	[1]	2,190	636	16,568	2,504	11,811	55,910
1991	1,391	10,650	5,689	2,896	7,418	2,255	587	16,723	2,328	6,616	56,553
1992	1,723	11,876	6,093	2,766	6,950	2,559	617	18,284	2,817	6,877	60,562
1993	1,572	12,885	6,015	2,981	6,632	2,759	768	19,569	3,221	7,234	63,636
1994	1,789	14,715	9,266	3,325	6,889	3,118	836	19,551	3,795	7,515	70,799
1995	1,795	14,321	9,054	2,966	7,742	3,198	818	19,334	3,916	8,050	71,194
1996	1,833	16,199	9,804	3,137	8,722	3,477	980	21,271	3,964	9,361	78,748
1997	2,019	17,117	10,649	3,150	9,667	3,721	950	21,767	4,102	9,573	82,715

[1] Included in other. *Source: The Society of the Plastics Industry, Inc. (SPI)*

Average Producer Price Index of Plastic Materials in the United States 1982 = 100

Year	Jan.	Feb.	Mar.	Apr.	May	June	July	Aug.	Sept.	Oct.	Nov.	Dec.	Average
Plastic Resins and Materials (066)													
1990	122.2	121.6	122.2	123.0	123.5	123.0	122.1	122.3	123.6	125.1	128.6	131.2	124.0
1991	131.1	128.7	125.4	122.9	120.6	117.0	115.0	114.9	114.9	116.4	116.7	116.0	120.0
1992	115.4	115.6	114.2	114.2	114.7	115.2	115.9	117.7	117.5	118.2	118.1	118.1	116.2
1993	118.3	118.0	117.6	117.1	116.3	116.9	116.9	117.6	117.4	116.9	116.2	116.2	117.1
1994	115.0	114.7	114.5	116.5	117.7	119.1	119.6	121.5	126.3	131.9	134.1	138.1	122.4
1995	142.5	144.1	145.9	148.5	149.0	148.9	147.0	144.8	142.7	139.2	135.8	132.2	143.4
1996	129.9	128.4	128.4	127.7	130.6	132.1	133.2	135.2	137.9	138.0	138.0	137.7	133.1
1997	137.0	137.5	138.7	138.9	139.1	139.6	139.3	137.4	136.0	135.9	134.6	133.9	137.3
1998[1]	134.0	132.2	131.0	130.7	128.8	126.8	125.0	123.7	123.1	119.0	117.1	115.9	125.6
Thermoplastic Resins (0662)													
1990	122.9	121.9	122.5	123.5	124.1	123.4	122.4	122.5	124.1	125.8	130.5	134.0	124.8
1991	132.1	129.4	125.5	122.9	120.2	116.2	113.8	113.7	114.6	115.5	116.0	115.3	119.6
1992	114.7	114.7	113.0	112.9	113.4	114.1	114.8	117.1	116.8	117.6	117.6	117.5	115.4
1993	117.5	117.1	116.3	115.8	114.8	115.4	115.5	116.4	116.4	116.4	115.5	114.6	116.0
1994	113.0	112.7	112.5	115.0	116.2	117.9	118.4	120.1	125.4	131.6	133.9	138.4	121.3
1995	143.1	145.0	147.1	150.3	151.0	151.2	148.7	146.2	143.7	139.6	135.5	131.1	144.4
1996	128.4	126.7	126.8	125.9	129.4	131.1	132.5	134.8	137.8	137.9	137.9	137.6	132.2
1997	136.7	137.3	138.6	138.8	139.0	139.7	139.3	137.0	135.5	135.3	133.8	133.0	137.0
1998[1]	133.0	130.7	129.5	129.2	127.0	124.7	122.5	121.0	120.5	115.9	113.7	112.4	123.3
PE Resin, Low, Film & Sheeting (0662-0301)													
1990	151.9	145.3	146.1	145.9	152.5	151.7	144.9	141.9	152.3	145.6	149.8	157.4	148.8
1991	158.1	150.7	142.6	135.8	130.1	121.9	117.8	114.8	113.9	123.2	131.3	124.6	130.4
1992	126.5	130.9	126.7	121.3	123.5	122.4	132.9	138.9	145.2	149.3	148.6	150.6	134.7
1993	NA	151.4	145.6	141.8	135.5	137.1	132.2	136.6	129.2	128.4	127.6	127.4	135.7
1994	121.6	119.4	119.3	120.8	127.6	134.5	136.3	140.8	146.6	155.4	172.8	182.2	139.8
1995	188.5	196.0	202.0	210.6	215.4	211.1	205.7	194.4	185.0	173.4	167.5	157.4	192.3
1996	146.4	139.9	137.6	139.5	147.6	158.8	166.0	165.3	190.1	195.2	195.9	196.6	164.9
1997	191.8	189.0	189.7	193.8	196.8	199.4	197.9	201.0	190.2	185.1	182.5	177.2	191.2
1998[1]	181.3	181.0	168.7	NA	159.1	162.9	158.0	152.8	NA	NA	NA	NA	166.3
Styrene Plastics Materials (0662-06)													
1990	113.1	114.7	117.2	116.8	116.8	115.2	113.7	113.7	116.8	123.4	127.8	124.2	117.8
1991	123.3	122.7	115.4	115.5	112.4	121.9	109.2	107.7	108.3	113.0	113.0	111.5	114.5
1992	109.5	109.6	109.1	109.1	110.3	109.4	110.4	112.6	111.2	112.5	111.7	111.5	110.6
1993	110.7	110.5	110.0	110.4	111.0	111.3	111.2	111.1	110.6	109.1	106.5	106.4	109.9
1994	105.8	104.1	104.1	108.1	108.3	109.2	110.4	110.6	116.0	123.3	125.3	126.2	112.6
1995	129.0	127.0	132.5	134.7	135.9	137.5	135.1	133.2	132.1	130.1	127.9	126.1	131.8
1996	125.7	123.5	125.0	118.3	120.1	122.7	123.4	123.3	123.6	122.8	122.0	120.9	122.6
1997	120.6	123.1	123.0	121.6	121.6	121.6	122.7	117.7	118.0	116.5	113.5	113.7	119.5
1998[1]	113.3	113.9	115.5	114.9	114.1	112.8	111.3	111.2	110.1	107.3	106.6	106.0	111.4
Thermosetting Resins (0663)													
1990	122.8	124.0	124.1	124.4	124.3	124.7	124.7	124.8	125.0	125.6	124.0	126.6	124.6
1991	130.1	129.1	128.9	127.1	126.3	125.2	124.9	124.9	123.9	124.5	123.8	123.1	126.0
1992	123.1	124.1	123.9	124.3	124.4	124.4	124.7	125.0	125.0	125.3	125.1	125.2	124.5
1993	126.1	126.5	127.4	127.5	127.8	128.0	127.7	127.7	127.9	127.8	127.8	128.3	127.5
1994	128.2	128.1	128.1	127.8	128.7	129.1	129.7	132.1	134.9	137.7	140.1	141.5	132.2
1995	144.3	145.1	145.4	145.2	144.7	143.5	144.0	143.5	142.9	142.3	142.4	142.1	143.8
1996	141.8	141.9	141.2	141.3	141.4	141.2	140.6	141.5	141.7	142.0	142.0	142.2	141.6
1997	142.1	142.3	142.7	143.1	143.2	143.0	142.8	142.9	143.0	143.1	142.9	142.9	142.8
1998[1]	143.6	144.0	143.2	142.9	142.6	142.7	142.5	142.2	141.4	140.6	140.1	139.6	142.1
Phenolic & Tar Acid Resins (0663-02)													
1990	148.2	149.4	149.1	148.7	148.5	147.3	143.9	142.5	141.5	139.0	138.2	143.7	145.0
1991	146.4	147.3	142.4	140.7	138.3	132.8	131.6	131.5	128.3	129.7	126.5	125.5	135.1
1992	125.4	126.4	125.1	124.7	125.6	125.6	127.7	127.6	127.9	129.7	128.8	128.5	126.9
1993	128.5	130.3	130.5	131.4	133.7	134.1	133.9	132.8	133.1	132.1	132.0	132.9	132.1
1994	133.0	130.9	129.7	131.3	134.1	135.9	139.2	143.7	147.2	154.7	161.0	161.5	141.9
1995	164.6	166.4	165.1	162.5	158.6	153.5	152.0	148.5	147.7	146.2	143.2	142.6	154.2
1996	142.7	142.6	141.9	142.2	143.1	143.4	143.2	147.2	148.7	149.1	149.8	150.5	145.4
1997	150.5	151.2	150.9	152.7	152.9	152.6	151.9	152.7	153.1	152.5	151.9	151.8	152.0
1998[1]	153.1	154.9	153.0	151.0	148.7	148.8	148.5	149.0	143.4	139.8	140.5	138.6	147.4

[1] Preliminary. NA = Not available. *Source: Bureau of Labor Statistics, U.S. Department of Commerce (BLS)*

Platinum-Group Metals

Within the platinum metals group (PGM), only platinum is viewed as a precious metal due to its use in jewelry, but towards mid-1998 palladium could have easily been classified as a precious metal as its price soared to a record high, besting gold's price at the time by about $100 an ounce. The reason for the price strength had nothing to do with inflation fears and the traditional need for some viable hedge as gold tends to be seen; for palladium it was simply a case of the marketplace reacting to a perceived logistical supply shortage.

Given the strong world demand for a cleaner environment: focusing largely on the use of catalytic converters to control emissions from gasoline-powered vehicles, the year-to-year demand for platinum group metals is expected to increase. Both platinum and palladium are used in converters. Platinum is expected to remain the dominant metal, primarily due to the need to use up to three times as much palladium to obtain the same desired emissions reduction. However, there is an inherent supply problem in that the metals are found in only a few countries, some of which lack political and economic stability, notably Russia. In 1997, platinum's average merchant price (N.Y.) of $394.93 per ounce compared with palladium's $181.98, a spread of $213. Comparable 1996 values were $397.23 and $130.40, respectively, and a $267 spread, platinum over. During 1998, platinum futures, basis nearest contract, started the year near $350 an ounce, climbed to $440 in mid-spring, and at yearend were back to about $360. Palladium, however, in 1998 went from about $200/oz. to almost $420 in mid-spring, and in the fourth quarter pivoted about the $275/oz. area until late in the period when prices shot up again to about $330, narrowing the spread between the two metals to about $30 near yearend. Clearly, during the past few years the bias has favored palladium, apparently reflecting the view that the metal's annual demand exceeds supply, perhaps by as much as 20 percent.

Platinum still tends to be viewed as a precious metal and its price, justified or not, mirrors gold and silver's price action. Palladium used to follow, taking its cue from platinum. In 1998, speculative interest in the precious metals, including platinum, dropped due partly to the buoyancy in the equity markets that siphoned capital away from the metals and partly from the absence of inflation fears. Moreover, there were no major problems in South Africa, the world's largest platinum producer, that may have hindered mine production and/or shipments of the metals. Generally the short term variables on PGM's prices are supply sensitive. However, Russia, the world's largest palladium producer, was a totally different story as uncertainty mounted regarding Russian exports. Although the fears eased in mid-year, Russia opted to resume palladium exports as ingots rather than in the more usable sponge form which then required buyers, notably autocatalyst manufacturers, to pay added refiner costs, effectively keeping the metal's base price high. In late 1998, Russia's palladium export policy was still mired in uncertainty.

Six metals make up the platinum group (PGM); statistical data is limited to platinum and palladium; for iridium, osmium, rhodium (formerly the most expensive) and ruthenium (the least expensive) the data is spotty at best. Mineable deposits of the PGM's are rare, production occurs as a byproduct of some other metal, usually nickel or copper. World production in 1997 of 288,000 kilograms compares with 283,000 in 1996. However, early in the 1990's, a shift developed in the production breakdown with more palladium produced than platinum, generally by about 10,000 kg. In 1997 about 154,000 kg. of platinum were produced and 119,000 kg. of palladium. Other 1997 PGM metals production of 15,700 kg. compares with 15,600 kg. in 1996. The global PGM reserve base at yearend 1997 was estimated between 65-70 million kg. and reserves around 55 56 million, almost all in South Africa with the balance in Russia.

South Africa is the largest producer with 125,000 kg. of platinum in 1997 vs. 123,000 in 1996; palladium production at a record high 55,900 kg. compares with 54,800 in 1996. Russia is believed to have produced 17,000 kg. of platinum in 1997, unchanged from 1996, and 47,000 kg. of palladium, also unchanged. U.S. production is relatively minor, 2,610 kg. of platinum in 1997 and 8,400 kg. of palladium, vs 1,840 kg. and 6,100 kg. in 1996, respectively. There is only one operational platinum mine in the western hemisphere: the Stillwater Mine in Montana which smelts the ore locally but then ships the resulting PGM-bearing matte to Belgium for refining. Reportedly there are large deposits of PGM in the Montana region, but high extracting costs and potential environmental restrictions are restraining factors.

In the U.S., the automotive industry is the largest consumer of PGM. The metal(s) have no competitive substitutes when used as an emission control catalyst, but the percentage of each metal used in the catalysts can be varied. Western world demand for "platinum" in 1997 was estimated at 56,900 kg. vs. 58,000 kg. in 1996. The decline was due to a fall in the use of platinum-rich catalyst systems on gasoline vehicles in Europe. Most North American made vehicles continued to be equipped with platinum based converters, as are Japanese cars exported to North America.

The U.S. imports half of the world's PGM production. U.S. imports of platinum in 1997 totaled 76,000 kg. with South Africa supplying about 46,000 kg.; the U.S. imported about 148,000 kg. of palladium with Russia supplying about 65,000 kg. and South Africa almost 20,000 kg. The U.S. exports PGM's, most of which is refined palladium, 23,000 kg. of platinum in 1997 and 43,800 kg. of palladium. Belgium and Switzerland took more than a third of the platinum exports while Mexico, Belgium and Taiwan took about half of the palladium.

Producers maintain an artificial price for the platinum group metals, but dealer or market prices are generally much lower. Generally platinum has a premium to gold; in late 1998 the metal was about $75 an ounce over gold vs. a year earlier differential near $80 an ounce.

Futures Markets

Platinum and palladium futures and options are traded on the New York Mercantile Exchange (NYMEX). In Japan, platinum and palladium futures are listed on the Tokyo Commodity Exchange (TOCOM).

World Mine Production of Platinum In Kilograms

Year	Australia	Canada	Colombia[3]	Finland	Japan	Russia[4]	Serbia/ Montenegro[5]	South Africa	United States	Zimbabwe	World Total
1989	100	4,467	973	60	1,031	32,000	23	82,884	1,430	25	122,994
1990	100	5,040	1,320	60	1,430	31,000	21	87,800	1,810	21	129,000
1991	100	4,680	1,600	60	988	30,000	22	88,900	1,500	19	128,000
1992	100	4,800	1,956	60	629	28,000	19	94,900	1,650	9	132,000
1993	100	5,000	1,722	60	661	20,000	10	109,000	2,050	4	139,000
1994	100	6,000	1,084	60	691	15,000	10	114,000	1,960	7	139,000
1995	100	9,320	973	60	730	18,000	10	118,000	1,590	10	149,000
1996[1]	100	8,080	669	60	816	17,000	10	123,000	1,840	100	151,000
1997[2]	100	7,550	500	60	680	17,000	10	125,000	2,610	100	154,000

[1] Preliminary. [2] Estimate. [3] Placer platinum. [4] Formerly part of the U.S.S.R.; data not reported separately until 1992 [5] Formerly part of Yugoslavia.; data not reported separately until 1992 *Source: U.S. Geological Survey (USGS)*

World Mine Production of Palladium and Other Group Metals In Kilograms

	Palladium										Other Group Metals		
Year	Australia	Canada	Finland	Japan	Russia[3]	Serbia[4] Montenegro	South Africa	United States	Zimbabwe	World Total	Russia[3]	South Africa	World Total
1989	400	4,676	100	821	85,000	199	35,800	4,850	43	131,889	10,500	15,000	26,746
1990	400	5,270	100	1,050	84,000	130	38,300	5,930	31	135,000	10,000	15,800	27,200
1991	400	6,440	100	1,050	82,000	155	38,000	5,200	30	133,000	9,500	16,000	26,100
1992	400	5,800	100	986	70,000	130	41,000	5,440	19	124,000	6,000	17,000	24,300
1993	400	6,000	100	1,183	50,000	72	48,000	6,780	11	113,000	4,000	19,000	24,400
1994	400	7,000	100	1,277	40,000	50	47,800	6,440	17	103,000	3,000	22,100	27,100
1995	400	5,950	100	2,174	48,000	50	49,400	5,260	20	111,000	3,600	22,800	27,200
1996[1]	400	5,160	100	2,180	47,000	50	54,800	6,100	120	116,000	3,500	11,400	15,600
1997[2]	400	4,810	100	1,900	47,000	50	55,900	8,400	120	119,000	3,500	11,500	15,700

[1] Preliminary. [2] Estimate. [3] Formerly part of the U.S.S.R.; data not reported separately until 1992 [4] Formerly part of Yugoslavia.; data not reported separately until 1992 *Source: U.S. Geological Survey (USGS)*

Platinum–Group Metals Sold to Consuming Industries in the United States In Kilograms

	Automotive		Chemical		Electrical		Dental & Medical		Jewelry & Decorative		Petroleum		All Platinum–Group Metals			
Year	Platinum	Other[3]	Platinum	Other[3]	Platinum	Other[3]	Platinum	Other[3]	Platinum	Other[3]	Platinum	Other[3]	Platinum	Palladium	Other[3]	Total
1989	18,774	6,869	2,424	2,233	3,894	19,514	632	8,601	418	396	2,859	2,570	33,698	39,273	5,512	78,483
1990	20,967	5,990	2,080	2,574	3,907	19,791	687	6,287	431	387	3,274	1,488	36,055	35,116	6,316	77,487
1991	18,643	5,338	861	1,749	3,910	14,428	598	4,918	626	500	3,163	181	31,112	25,747	5,738	62,597
1992	20,503	5,860	1,716	2,297	2,922	15,738	640	5,386	881	1,417	1,036	790	31,095	28,935	6,816	66,846
1993	19,446	10,124	2,364	3,121	2,125	12,699	687	5,562	1,024	1,422	1,204	709	29,879	26,840	8,544	65,063
1994	21,756	11,413	3,104	1,889	2,790	7,961	902	5,092	1,345	824	1,581	422	34,044	21,509	7,387	62,940
1995	27,990	12,440	2,022	2,395	4,510	18,225	778	6,158	1,337	1,431	3,421	871	43,524	45,188	-----	88,712
1996[1]	28,550	12,627	2,115	2,457	4,541	17,665	778	6,285	1,493	1,493	3,514	902	44,489	45,157	-----	89,646
1997[2]	28,923	15,146	2,239	2,426	4,945	19,997	840	6,376	2,115	1,617	3,390	871	46,184	50,227	-----	96,411

[1] Preliminary. [2] Estimate. [3] Includes palladium, iridium, osmium, rhodium, and ruthenium. *Sources: U.S. Geological Survey (USGS); American Metal Market (AMM)*

Salient Statistics of Platinum and Allied Metals[3] in the United States In Kilograms

		Mine Production				Refiner, Importer & Dealer Stocks as of Dec. 31				Imports for Consumption		Exports		
Year	Net Import Reliance as a % of Apparent Consumption	Platinum	Palladium	Refinery Production (Secondary)	Total Refined	Platinum	Palladium	Other[4]	Total	Refined	Total	Refined	Total	Apparent Consumption
1989	90	1,430	4,850	50,186	50,525	14,791	15,182	2,570	32,543	111,107	113,278	23,082	38,301	101,209
1990	88	1,810	5,930	71,248	71,312	13,421	14,425	2,478	30,324	120,631	125,354	20,148	55,044	117,043
1991	90	1,730	6,050	72,349	72,564	10,349	12,263	1,701	24,313	121,741	125,661	27,401	39,624	111,798
1992	87	1,840	6,470	64,309	64,309	14,187	10,641	2,118	26,946	129,419	132,006	31,060	57,830	109,469
1993	89	2,050	6,780	65,792	65,792	10,263	8,324	176	18,763	148,790	153,165	43,798	78,486	123,273
1994	91	1,960	6,440	63,000	63,000	10,304	9,345	123	19,772	167,681	170,907	46,259	88,561	127,000
1995	---	1,590	5,260	------	------	------	------	------	------	214,143	220,613	41,825	50,575	-----
1996[1]	84	1,840	6,100	------	------	------	------	------	------	248,860	255,880	39,709	48,836	-----
1997[2]	---	2,610	8,400	------	------	------	------	------	------	253,114	258,424	67,656	81,249	-----

[1] Preliminary. [2] Estimate. [3] Includes platinum, palladium, iridium, osmium, rhodium, and ruthenium. [4] Includes iridium, osmium, rhodium, and ruthenium. NA = Not available. *Source: U.S. Geological Survey (USGS)*

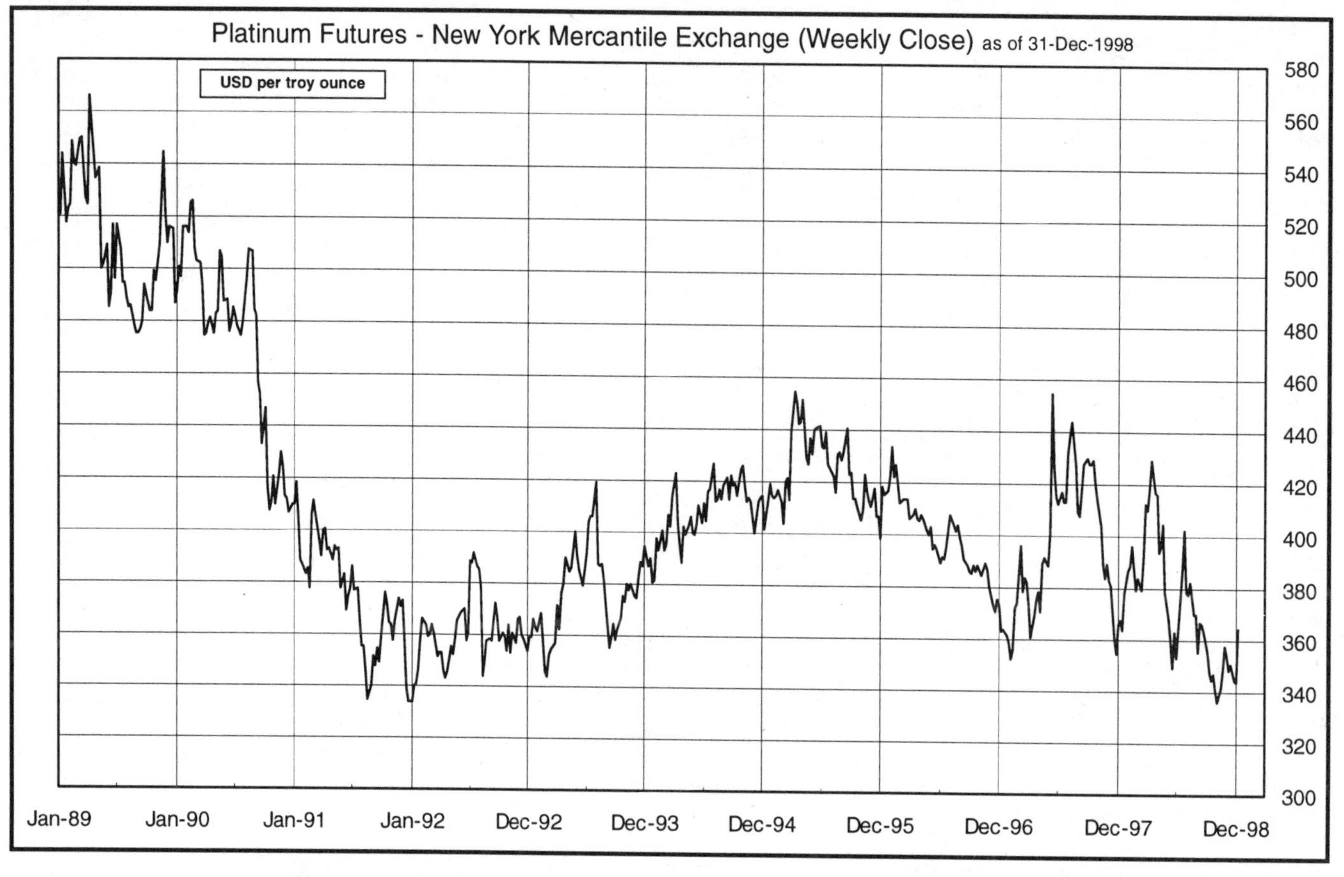

Average Open Interest of Platinum Futures in New York In Contracts

Year	Jan.	Feb.	Mar.	Apr.	May	June	July	Aug.	Sept.	Oct.	Nov.	Dec.
1989	19,334	18,648	19,736	19,895	19,661	20,597	17,310	19,121	19,165	16,981	19,934	20,392
1990	19,510	17,970	15,888	15,915	16,688	15,652	15,496	17,254	18,494	17,472	16,313	16,994
1991	15,497	16,043	16,083	14,334	15,779	18,273	17,503	19,214	18,611	15,933	13,579	14,533
1992	15,464	14,231	14,272	14,130	15,353	19,070	20,402	18,444	17,574	14,079	13,532	14,282
1993	11,889	14,315	12,990	15,490	19,641	17,919	20,931	18,892	16,883	15,690	16,658	19,633
1994	18,779	19,655	21,673	22,834	21,880	22,835	24,804	25,049	24,245	24,159	26,287	26,661
1995	23,285	23,058	23,470	23,657	20,984	21,533	20,801	25,288	23,489	24,498	22,137	21,534
1996	23,130	21,535	23,156	25,081	26,343	27,720	25,861	25,455	28,511	28,305	27,423	29,143
1997	25,890	26,092	22,364	16,568	18,933	18,440	13,280	14,180	13,639	13,466	12,396	13,501
1998	10,791	10,932	13,220	13,559	12,048	11,471	10,607	9,733	11,950	14,601	15,709	13,289

Source: New York Mercantile Exchange (NYMEX)

Volume of Trading of Platinum Futures in New York In Thousands of Contracts

Year	Jan.	Feb.	Mar.	Apr.	May	June	July	Aug.	Sept.	Oct.	Nov.	Dec.	Total
1989	113.6	96.6	148.5	107.3	111.6	126.9	69.8	86.8	85.1	56.4	99.8	88.1	1,190.5
1990	85.6	80.9	81.3	55.3	65.2	70.1	52.7	73.8	77.2	68.0	50.1	56.8	817.1
1991	50.8	42.3	72.7	43.0	51.1	55.7	40.6	45.7	55.8	42.9	41.9	60.3	598.6
1992	47.9	38.3	54.1	29.3	37.7	82.0	61.0	50.6	51.8	28.5	42.3	53.8	577.3
1993	29.4	55.6	61.4	50.6	65.8	72.5	59.8	56.4	58.6	37.0	44.0	60.3	651.2
1994	48.3	65.3	94.4	62.6	65.1	88.3	84.2	75.4	92.4	60.9	77.3	81.6	895.8
1995	61.4	38.6	131.3	69.9	60.4	75.4	53.4	62.5	98.8	55.9	56.3	82.8	846.7
1996	80.5	70.3	86.3	54.2	47.9	88.8	53.3	53.7	90.1	47.1	42.0	88.3	802.5
1997	60.5	83.3	86.2	57.7	67.0	72.5	38.7	36.4	62.5	46.2	28.9	58.6	698.6
1998	38.2	35.5	65.9	36.2	36.2	47.5	35.2	27.5	58.3	44.4	42.7	60.8	528.3

Source: New York Mercantile Exchange (NYMEX)

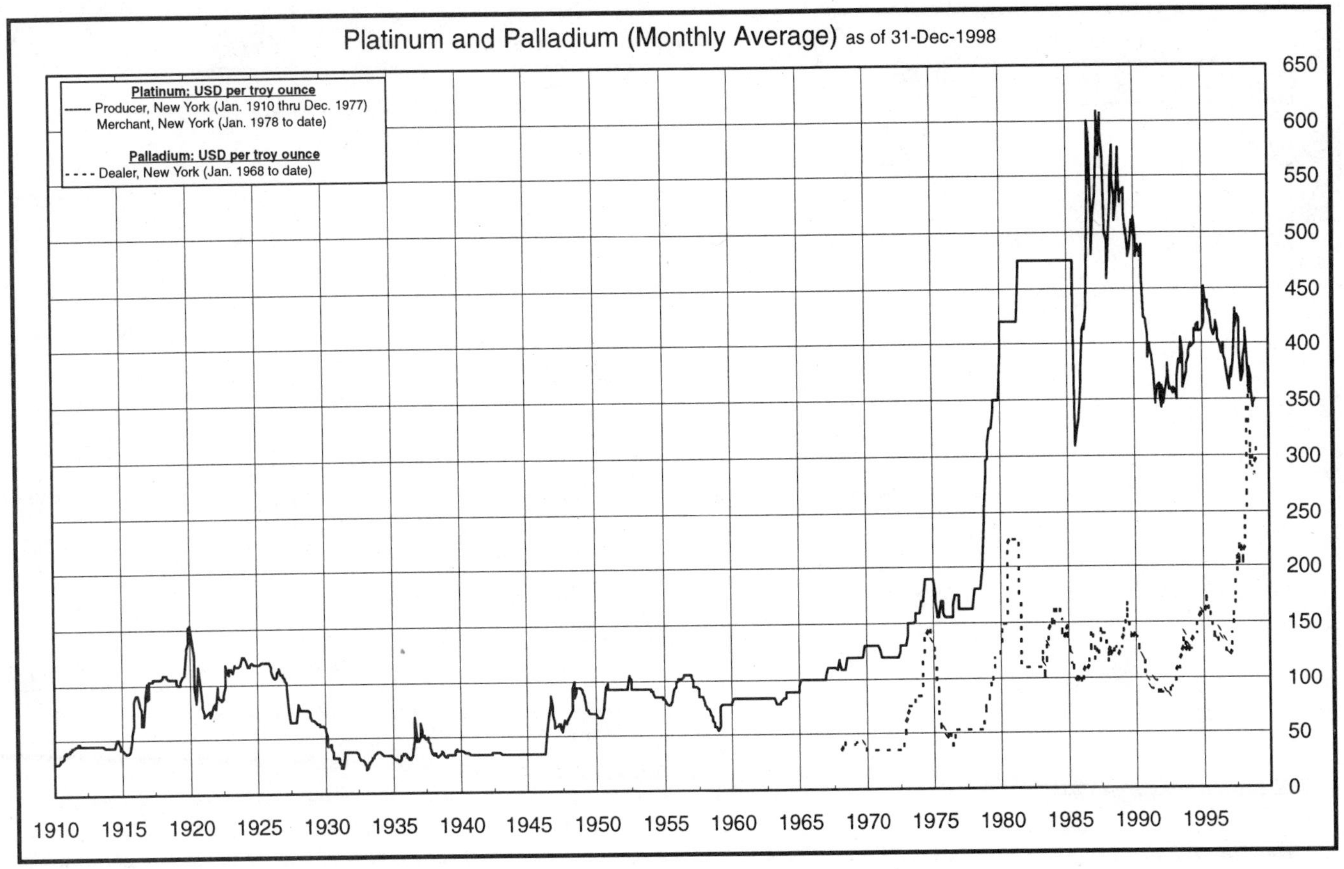

Average Merchant's Price of Platinum in the United States In Dollars Per Troy Ounce

Year	Jan	Feb	Mar	Apr	May	Jun	Jul	Aug	Sep	Oct	Nov	Dec	Average
1989	528.69	532.66	538.26	539.96	517.20	498.81	503.16	485.20	479.29	485.48	508.73	507.24	510.39
1990	949.93	517.34	500.32	478.33	485.89	486.60	476.93	492.02	463.87	423.78	424.12	446.94	474.26
1991	408.92	385.53	403.12	398.16	373.06	374.25	375.38	351.68	348.01	362.52	364.01	356.65	375.11
1992	341.88	362.97	356.84	347.73	354.75	368.17	378.89	360.20	361.60	359.75	355.81	361.98	359.21
1993	359.99	361.53	349.31	365.98	385.50	384.54	401.10	394.69	365.29	369.19	376.98	383.85	374.75
1994	390.30	393.95	398.29	400.38	395.41	401.42	408.25	411.91	415.93	421.11	415.73	408.83	405.13
1995	414.27	415.22	415.37	446.24	439.02	436.58	435.21	425.61	430.31	414.49	413.55	410.17	424.67
1996	416.13	420.02	411.19	404.28	401.60	392.64	393.86	400.03	389.86	384.24	382.36	370.60	397.23
1997	359.66	364.99	379.18	370.39	387.14	430.79	415.23	424.55	425.48	423.20	392.83	365.76	394.93
1998[1]	374.07	386.63	398.99	413.45	389.40	355.20	379.18	370.42	359.33	342.31	347.04	349.82	372.15

[1] Preliminary. *Source: American Metal Market (AMM)*

Average Dealer[1] Price of Palladium in the United States In Dollars Per Troy Ounce

Year	Jan.	Feb.	Mar.	Apr.	May	June	July	Aug.	Sept.	Oct.	Nov.	Dec.	Average
1989	135.74	141.79	152.84	165.46	155.17	152.92	151.36	135.97	137.85	137.84	139.35	139.75	145.50
1990	135.80	136.63	131.25	128.18	120.08	117.40	116.60	116.17	106.62	96.12	94.84	90.93	115.89
1991	86.61	85.11	86.44	95.25	96.61	97.39	95.57	84.55	82.49	81.87	85.96	82.72	88.38
1992	82.96	86.04	84.50	83.71	82.90	80.98	86.49	86.04	90.67	95.07	95.01	104.88	88.27
1993	110.39	112.57	106.22	113.79	119.94	125.36	139.74	137.37	121.95	130.04	123.62	125.60	122.22
1994	124.40	130.92	132.43	133.22	135.76	137.03	145.28	151.83	152.99	154.90	158.10	153.80	142.56
1995	156.67	157.53	161.18	170.91	160.87	158.59	156.27	138.81	143.76	137.36	135.57	132.37	150.83
1996	131.59	142.10	140.67	138.05	134.36	132.95	134.55	128.82	123.10	119.39	119.30	119.90	130.40
1997	124.73	141.26	139.55	143.73	173.38	209.47	195.73	221.57	200.38	214.21	217.05	202.64	181.98
1998[2]	229.70	239.68	265.73	326.67	360.55	291.50	310.82	290.62	288.81	283.45	284.00	306.05	289.80

[1] Based on wholesale quantities, prompt delivery. [2] Preliminary. *Sources: American Metal Market (AMM); U.S. Geological Survey (USGS)*

Volume of Trading of Palladium Futures in New York In Contracts

Year	Jan.	Feb.	Mar.	Apr.	May	June	July	Aug.	Sept.	Oct.	Nov.	Dec.	Total
1989	12,852	16,296	12,978	48,699	28,266	13,062	15,477	15,351	11,235	8,862	17,745	10,836	211,659
1990	4,893	19,026	6,930	5,355	13,104	5,670	4,452	11,130	5,407	7,150	9,592	3,178	95,887
1991	5,017	10,542	5,380	7,245	10,521	4,447	5,230	10,114	2,914	5,668	8,150	2,971	78,199
1992	7,217	7,323	3,429	2,833	8,011	2,881	4,965	6,752	5,066	5,359	6,461	7,912	68,209
1993	7,708	14,461	8,057	10,034	12,190	7,368	7,043	13,356	6,977	9,220	12,477	4,790	113,681
1994	8,250	14,953	6,067	6,676	15,481	6,514	9,024	21,741	15,690	9,603	21,384	8,390	143,773
1995	10,684	17,092	21,001	12,775	17,413	9,615	11,816	18,948	9,754	9,320	16,662	11,633	166,713
1996	13,725	33,519	11,931	16,416	27,467	8,989	9,896	23,740	10,721	8,149	28,870	12,187	205,610
1997	13,908	43,160	22,796	21,604	36,422	17,647	18,097	18,751	8,331	13,094	13,143	11,763	238,716
1998	11,506	17,786	18,678	14,042	17,942	7,370	4,241	8,737	6,214	4,962	12,839	6,933	131,250

Source: New York Mercantile Exchange (NYMEX)

Average Open Interest of Palladium Futures in New York In Contracts

Year	Jan.	Feb.	Mar.	Apr.	May	June	July	Aug.	Sept.	Oct.	Nov.	Dec.
1989	6,460	6,758	6,636	9,082	9,173	9,116	8,307	7,616	7,105	6,847	7,123	6,660
1990	6,296	6,350	5,276	5,359	5,476	5,361	5,493	5,717	5,165	5,100	5,316	4,565
1991	4,658	4,559	4,319	4,686	4,559	4,302	4,454	4,429	4,429	4,384	4,337	4,042
1992	3,984	4,071	4,101	4,206	4,137	3,852	3,762	3,362	3,041	2,982	2,901	3,246
1993	3,718	4,213	4,365	4,897	5,312	4,513	4,655	5,080	4,360	4,495	4,472	4,484
1994	4,626	4,995	4,672	4,303	5,116	4,530	5,807	6,851	6,625	6,511	7,726	6,917
1995	7,484	7,579	7,102	7,231	6,519	6,413	6,739	6,852	5,950	6,120	6,486	6,090
1996	6,365	7,539	6,682	7,099	8,713	8,143	7,977	8,805	8,129	7,971	8,227	7,727
1997	8,291	10,946	10,528	9,759	9,947	7,072	5,538	4,973	3,822	4,282	4,291	4,030
1998	4,062	4,873	5,220	5,369	4,371	4,219	4,166	3,488	2,959	3,048	2,938	2,700

Source: New York Mercantile Exchange (NYMEX)

Pork Bellies

Wholesale pork belly prices, basis Chicago futures, turned sharply lower in late 1997 and the weakness persisted into the first quarter of 1998, carrying prices to $0.40/lb., the lowest level since mid-1995. A 10 percent jump in hog production and like gain in belly output was the primary bearish factor. Although prices recovered mid-year, the gains were marginal due to a 9 percent increase in 1998 pork production and expected like gain in 1999. Although the futures market has lost much of its speculative following, it's still a viable forward pricing media for producers and users.

Pork bellies, or bacon, are obtained from the underside of a hog. A hog has two bellies, generally weighing 8-18 pounds, depending on the commercial slaughter weight. Slaughter weights now average 255 pounds per hog, resulting in a dressed weight of about 190 pounds. Bellies account for about 12 percent of a hog's live weight, but represent a somewhat larger percentage of the total cutout value of the realized pork products. Bellies deliverable against futures generally weigh 12-14 pounds.

Historically, there are definitive seasonal trends for pork bellies, but a change may be taking hold. Bellies are a storable commodity with the movement into cold storage building early in the calendar year and peaking mid-year. Net withdrawals from storage then carry stocks to a low around October. The cycle then begins anew. However, this storage pattern of peaks and valleys could be flattening if the 1998 trends offer a clue: fewer fresh bellies went into storage in early 1998, perhaps reflecting a shift in usage as more bacon is now used in fast-food outlets. In the past retail bacon demand followed a time tested pattern; peaking in the summer and tapering off to a low during the winter months, suggesting the highest prices in the summer and the lowest in the winter. The opposite was not unusual with contra-seasonal price moves partially attributed to supply logistics; notably, the availability of storage stocks deliverable against futures at exchange approved warehouses. The fact that no futures contract months are traded between August and the following February often added to price distortions. The price trends in 1999 may support ideas that supply/demand logistics have changed.

Belly prices (cash and futures) have been sensitive to the inventory in cold storage during the year and to the weekly net movement in and out of storage. Storage movements can afford a clue to demand although a better measure is the weekly quantity of bellies being sliced into bacon. Bacon is not a consumer necessity, but demand can be buoyed and/or slowed by consumer disposable income levels. Consumer dietary standards have changed in recent years, but the earlier negative effects on bacon consumption may have run their course. Retail bacon prices in mid-1998 averaged $2.52 a pound, down 20 cents from a year earlier; wholesale prices of $0.79 compare with $.086, respectively.

U.S. foreign trade in bacon, as a processed product, is small. Imports are largely from Denmark and exports go to Eastern Europe.

Futures Markets

Frozen pork belly futures and options are traded on the Chicago Mercantile Exchange (CME). In 1998 the CME introduced futures on fresh pork bellies.

Average Retail Price of Bacon, Sliced In Dollars Per Pound

Year	Jan.	Feb.	Mar.	Apr.	May	June	July	Aug.	Sept.	Oct.	Nov.	Dec.	Average
1989	1.80	1.80	1.79	1.75	1.68	1.69	1.71	1.72	1.72	1.77	1.82	1.96	1.77
1990	1.97	2.01	1.99	1.98	2.04	2.15	2.21	2.24	2.18	2.21	2.24	2.28	2.13
1991	2.26	2.30	2.32	2.27	2.31	2.31	2.31	2.22	2.16	2.12	2.07	1.99	2.22
1992	1.96	1.95	1.92	1.92	1.90	1.93	1.95	1.94	1.93	1.89	1.85	1.86	1.92
1993	1.87	1.84	1.80	1.89	1.91	1.95	2.00	1.95	1.98	1.99	2.01	2.02	1.93
1994	2.04	2.02	2.02	2.06	1.99	1.99	2.00	1.99	1.97	1.97	1.92	1.89	1.99
1995	1.93	1.93	1.91	1.89	1.92	1.90	1.91	1.97	2.04	2.12	2.16	2.17	1.99
1996	2.14	2.20	2.20	2.24	2.35	2.49	2.54	2.68	2.81	2.72	2.66	2.64	2.47
1997	2.66	2.65	2.66	2.66	2.63	2.69	2.72	2.76	2.75	2.73	2.67	2.61	2.68
1998[1]	2.64	2.62	2.54	2.44	2.44	2.46	2.52	2.51	2.58	2.57	2.62	2.58	2.54

[1] Preliminary. *Source: Economic Research Service, U.S. Department of Agriculture (ERS-USDA)*

Frozen Pork Belly Storage Stocks in the United States, on First of Month In Thousands of Pounds

Year	Jan.	Feb.	Mar.	Apr.	May	June	July	Aug.	Sept.	Oct.	Nov.	Dec.
1989	113,137	116,191	121,556	127,617	143,751	142,340	126,676	94,107	49,083	32,031	39,358	67,489
1990	85,026	77,255	85,789	96,945	102,899	105,482	87,983	55,859	23,352	4,785	5,506	24,044
1991	46,998	48,750	54,529	68,094	80,382	79,936	72,032	45,915	29,832	15,944	25,558	48,311
1992	71,318	76,894	75,925	85,095	96,653	92,677	78,646	54,544	26,854	21,973	26,044	49,970
1993	70,576	65,280	65,919	66,064	79,430	77,903	70,251	46,630	20,811	10,964	14,345	33,563
1994	53,168	55,999	54,921	63,099	72,230	79,018	73,583	57,747	30,636	18,260	22,656	40,725
1995	61,073	62,776	64,228	78,975	78,539	77,919	67,607	47,055	17,435	6,255	13,478	37,092
1996	47,587	46,498	46,381	47,655	57,174	63,522	56,767	28,533	18,996	12,702	16,206	30,943
1997	37,930	38,030	44,277	54,767	54,015	55,274	52,274	33,657	18,346	11,148	14,408	25,365
1998[1]	44,763	55,249	55,368	54,441	58,600	59,462	52,010	31,433	14,786	9,452	16,440	41,711

[1] Preliminary. *Source: National Agricultural Statistics Service, U.S. Department of Agriculture (NASS-USDA)*

Weekly Pork Belly Storage Movement

1997	Stocks[1] in Thousands of Pounds				1998	Stocks[1] in Thousands of Pounds			
Week Ending	In	Out	On Hand	Net Movement	Week Ending	In	Out	On Hand	Net Movement
Jan. 4	2,868	6	30,680	2,862	Jan. 3	4,946	119	25,190	4,827
11	1,094	165	31,609	929	10	3,255	83	28,362	3,172
18	429	270	31,768	159	17	2,154	245	30,271	1,909
25	402	685	31,485	-283	24	1,541	230	31,582	1,311
Feb. 1	837	813	31,345	24	31	66	854	30,794	-788
8	880	720	31,659	160	Feb. 7	282	1,021	30,055	-739
15	2,035	380	33,314	1,655	14	706	663	30,098	43
22	1,459	586	34,187	873	21	613	612	30,099	1
Mar. 1	1,220	489	34,918	731	28	734	404	30,429	330
8	1,902	57	36,763	1,845	Mar. 7	1,048	534	30,943	514
15	2,536	9	39,290	2,527	14	748	701	30,806	47
22	968	6	40,252	962	21	719	369	31,156	350
29	277	41	40,488	236	28	286	1,101	30,341	-815
Apr. 5	798	541	40,745	257	Apr. 4	98	1,250	29,189	-1,152
12	1,030	677	41,098	353	11	897	989	27,488	-92
19	161	570	40,715	-383	18	1,757	2,132	28,476	-375
26	189	1,394	39,510	-1,205	25	3,197	1,108	30,565	2,089
May 3	415	1,369	38,556	-954	May 2	1,193	169	31,589	1,024
10	1,530	337	39,749	1,193	9	1,232	291	32,530	941
17	1,415	469	40,695	946	16	301	239	32,592	62
24	531	813	40,413	-282	23	965	286	33,271	679
31	213	350	40,276	-137	30	274	874	32,671	-600
June 7	262	368	40,170	-106	June 6	10	1,315	31,366	-1,305
14	1,545	392	41,323	1,153	13	49	2,061	29,354	-2,012
21	457	252	41,258	205	20	725	1,352	28,727	-627
28	16	1,195	40,349	-1,179	27	92	1,658	27,161	-1,566
July 5	92	1,633	38,808	-1,541	July 4	181	2,580	24,762	-2,399
12	75	2,284	36,599	-2,209	11	15	3,632	21,145	-3,617
19	239	3,164	33,674	-2,925	18	0	2,604	18,541	-2,604
26	97	3,687	30,084	-3,590	25	50	2,836	15,755	-2,786
Aug. 2	79	3,503	26,660	-3,424	Aug. 1	0	2,630	13,125	-2,630
9	6	3,603	23,063	-3,597	8	40	2,299	10,866	-2,259
16	41	2,600	20,504	-2,559	15	43	2,693	8,216	-2,650
23	66	2,779	17,791	-2,713	22	48	2,546	5,718	-2,498
30	49	2,083	15,757	-2,034	29	230	936	5,012	-706
Sept. 6	38	1,722	14,073	-1,684	Sept. 5	841	816	5,037	25
13	44	2,259	11,858	-2,215	12	417	1,313	4,141	-896
20	57	2,945	8,970	-2,888	19	0	788	3,352	-788
27	9	1,378	7,601	-1,369	26	368	648	3,072	-280
Oct. 4	222	1,143	6,680	-921	Oct. 3	452	472	3,052	-20
11	181	1,382	5,479	-1,201	10	379	226	3,205	153
18	876	774	5,581	102	17	805	124	3,886	681
25	1,065	994	5,652	71	24	627	209	4,304	418
Nov. 1	232	1,042	4,842	-810	31	1,846	195	5,955	1,651
8	NA	NA	NA	NA	Nov. 7	2,392	203	8,144	2,189
15	1,836	42	8,062	1,794	14	3,613	163	11,594	3,450
22	622	0	8,684	622	21	2,901	126	14,369	2,775
29	2,058	90	10,652	1,968	28	4,992	92	19,269	4,900
Dec. 6	2,241	66	12,827	2,175	Dec. 5	1,946	22	21,193	1,924
13	1,693	85	14,435	1,608	12	1,981	17	23,157	1,964
20	1,505	96	15,844	1,409	19	5,005	0	35,079	5,005
27	4,735	216	20,363	4,519	26	0	0	35,079	0

[1] 57 Chicago and Outside Combined Chicago Mercantile Exchange approved warehouses. *Source: Chicago Mercantile Exchange (CME)*

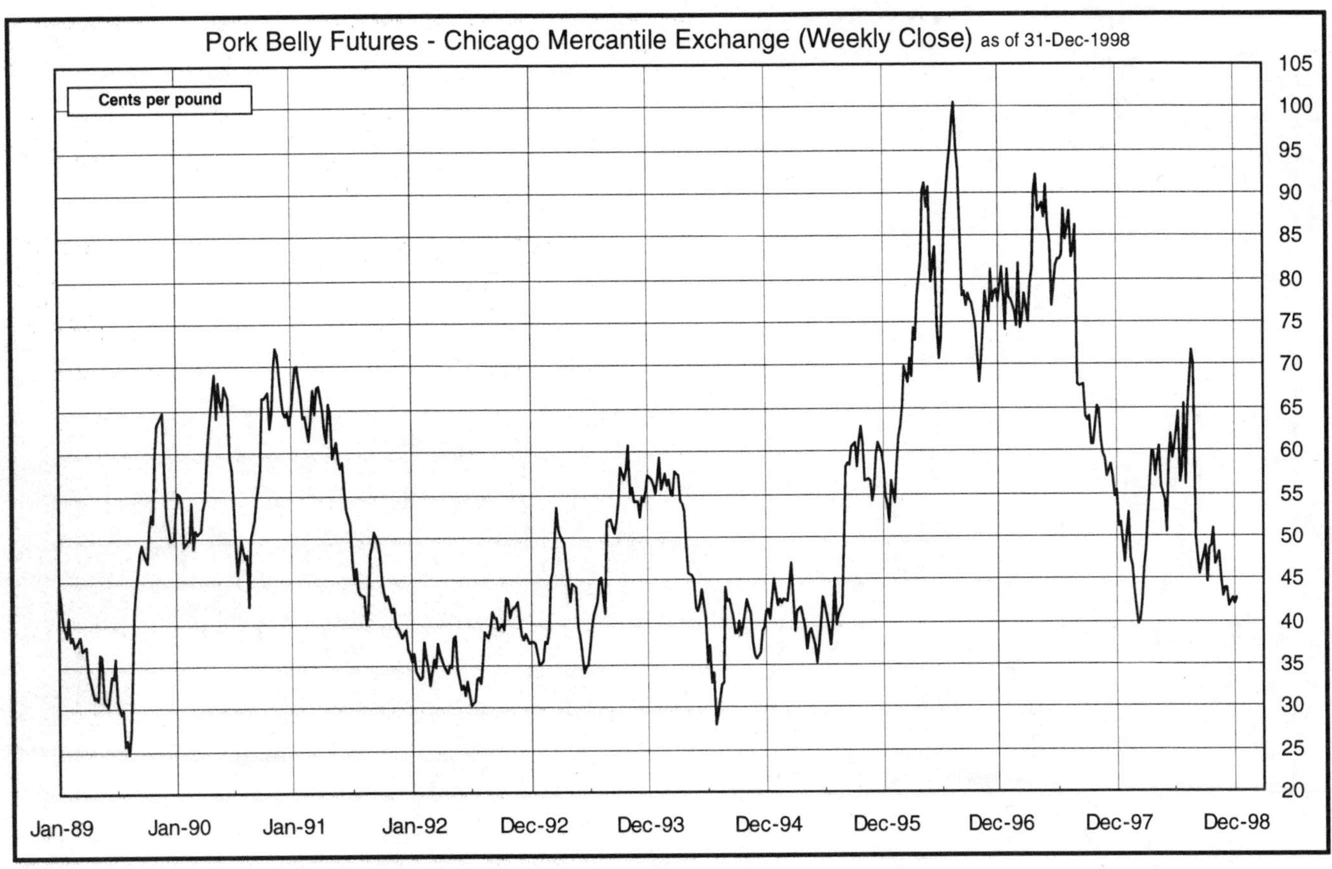

Average Open Interest of Frozen Pork Belly Futures in Chicago In Contracts

Year	Jan.	Feb.	Mar.	Apr.	May	June	July	Aug.	Sept.	Oct.	Nov.	Dec.
1989	20,453	20,444	21,897	22,117	24,931	25,898	20,053	12,724	11,916	12,501	14,802	13,844
1990	12,885	12,114	13,017	15,338	14,513	13,038	11,146	6,104	6,059	7,851	11,419	12,589
1991	11,777	10,187	9,776	11,509	10,436	10,111	7,356	6,176	7,532	10,813	13,173	12,844
1992	12,521	12,195	11,901	12,345	12,497	13,598	12,623	7,149	6,540	7,033	9,251	10,953
1993	10,623	9,244	8,283	8,626	10,096	11,092	9,031	5,427	4,644	7,241	8,701	9,121
1994	11,053	10,426	9,375	9,894	8,092	8,248	7,836	7,841	8,398	10,072	10,141	10,216
1995	10,294	9,080	7,809	7,367	8,017	7,036	5,666	4,271	6,246	7,007	7,103	7,282
1996	7,094	8,028	10,521	10,753	10,018	8,136	6,432	6,296	6,056	6,395	6,050	6,480
1997	7,504	7,930	7,260	7,165	8,950	7,203	5,905	4,791	5,242	7,520	8,302	9,009
1998	9,187	9,145	9,082	7,825	6,786	5,406	4,185	3,493	2,933	3,841	4,987	7,085

Source: Chicago Mercantile Exchange (CME)

Volume of Trading of Frozen Pork Belly Futures in Chicago In Contracts

Year	Jan.	Feb.	Mar.	Apr.	May	June	July	Aug.	Sept.	Oct.	Nov.	Dec.	Total
1989	107,577	89,922	84,768	90,353	145,975	152,207	119,733	91,200	75,155	106,389	141,983	105,714	1,310,976
1990	109,036	100,813	129,476	133,946	165,880	143,663	122,187	74,653	53,428	76,549	112,752	80,746	1,303,129
1991	106,078	89,975	88,056	111,195	119,773	96,273	74,255	59,176	65,604	80,707	63,331	50,773	1,005,196
1992	80,697	79,700	67,470	57,565	73,137	73,081	78,588	54,663	39,839	64,248	60,724	54,440	784,152
1993	77,380	62,871	63,988	62,403	62,400	70,124	65,496	42,613	37,992	47,780	60,163	49,099	698,799
1994	60,316	67,250	58,183	53,839	56,575	58,424	50,450	47,626	38,375	45,525	49,280	47,803	633,646
1995	62,994	54,330	59,324	43,501	49,453	53,571	45,869	36,623	31,112	35,444	47,061	42,631	561,913
1996	48,563	56,623	61,669	61,703	61,868	55,337	55,121	45,399	39,182	48,973	42,709	35,502	612,649
1997	60,761	53,604	56,750	76,072	62,190	54,043	55,043	36,153	31,154	44,277	31,663	33,609	595,319
1998	41,894	50,105	47,249	61,910	36,058	48,913	41,133	33,832	24,006	30,538	30,093	35,521	481,252

Source: Chicago Mercantile Exchange (CME)

PORK BELLIES

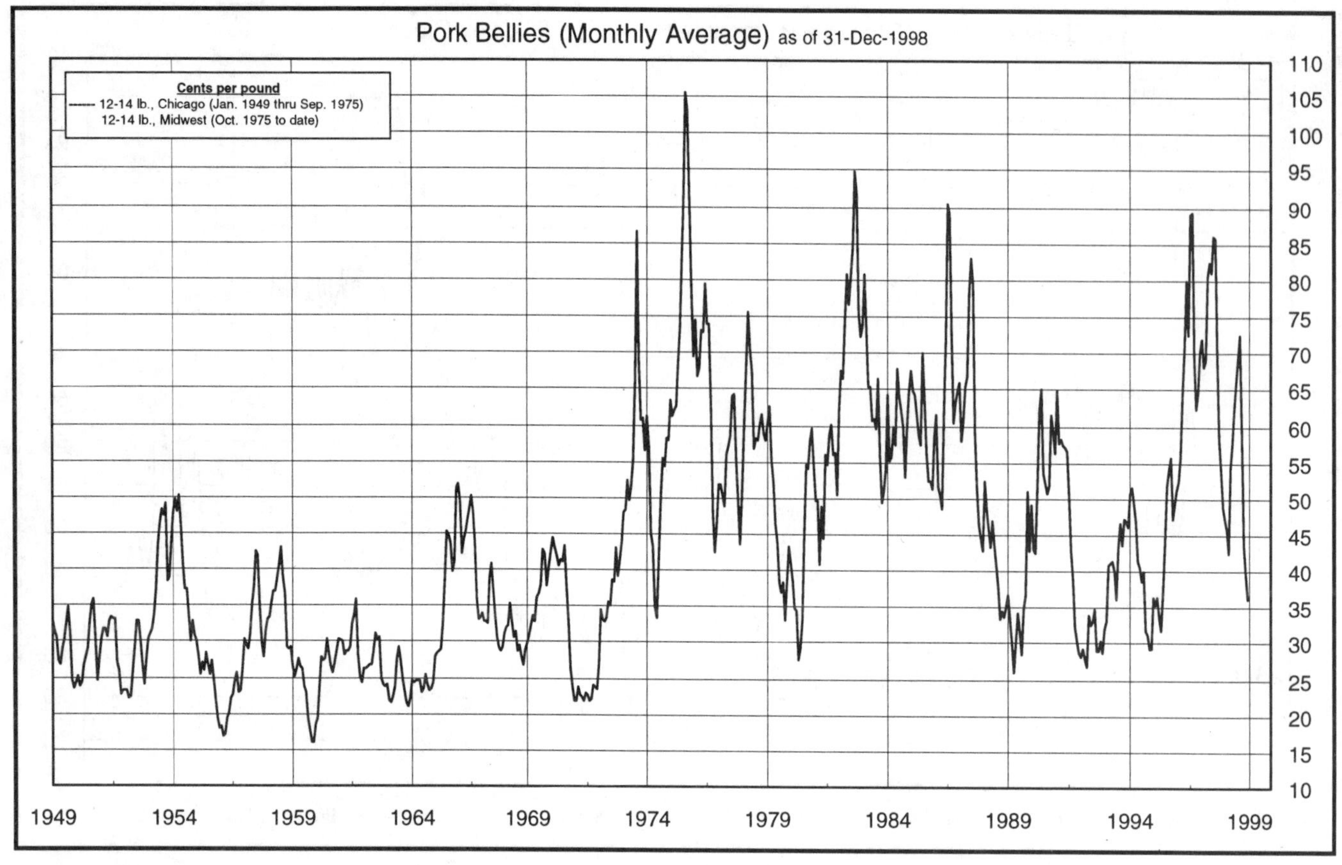

Average Price of Pork Bellies (12-14 lbs.) Midwest In Cents Per Pound

Year	Jan.	Feb.	Mar.	Apr.	May	June	July	Aug.	Sept.	Oct.	Nov.	Dec.	Average
1989	36.91	31.41	30.19	25.49	29.11	32.90	31.52	28.82	34.23	36.88	49.96	42.23	34.14
1990	48.65	42.53	42.60	52.60	61.48	65.15	53.18	51.08	51.31	59.83	60.57	56.58	53.80
1991	64.11	57.20	58.52	57.25	57.50	56.48	50.40	42.01	38.97	32.26	30.04	28.79	47.79
1992	28.05	29.44	28.01	26.93	34.09	32.78	32.77	35.13	29.09	29.13	30.48	28.80	30.39
1993	31.97	33.22	41.28	41.19	39.86	36.24	44.51	46.68	43.82	47.25	47.21	46.21	41.62
1994	50.63	51.66	49.68	46.84	41.40	40.39	38.64	39.60	31.50	31.33	29.09	29.29	40.00
1995	36.03	35.80	36.30	33.83	31.70	37.94	43.10	52.42	54.43	56.20	47.28	51.45	43.04
1996	52.33	56.33	64.50	69.86	79.50	72.64	89.49	88.40	68.12	63.07	65.27	70.07	69.97
1997	72.04	68.42	59.05	80.54	82.58	80.68	86.70	85.43	72.25	57.97	53.77	47.52	70.58
1998[1]	43.00	45.89	42.28	54.65	57.87	63.10	68.46	72.99	57.49	42.05	39.13	36.31	51.94

[1] Preliminary. *Source: Economic Research Service, U.S. Department of Agriculture (ERS-USDA)*

Average Price of Pork Loins (14-18 lbs.) Central, U.S. In Cents Per Pound

Year	Jan.	Feb.	Mar.	Apr.	May	June	July	Aug.	Sept.	Oct.	Nov.	Dec.	Average
1989	89.35	90.97	91.77	91.59	99.95	108.28	115.10	110.03	105.25	111.98	91.75	107.28	101.11
1990	101.36	107.75	117.26	120.68	136.06	125.62	144.14	119.56	121.64	113.71	98.94	103.50	117.52
1991	107.67	109.13	110.33	104.81	120.48	123.49	121.73	117.54	105.85	100.87	88.63	90.19	108.39
1992	96.89	99.13	94.10	98.65	108.94	113.94	108.22	111.18	102.98	96.98	89.64	96.22	101.41
1993	98.22	100.05	100.61	107.61	111.16	122.28	113.40	116.73	116.74	111.85	98.68	92.33	107.47
1994	103.90	110.75	100.45	101.89	103.99	103.84	109.79	112.86	105.34	95.65	80.00	89.50	101.50
1995	96.94	102.20	95.30	93.33	103.50	118.81	124.65	127.98	117.63	108.23	93.94	110.39	107.74
1996	110.00	116.43	120.49	119.70	131.61	115.73	126.16	118.18	112.28	115.40	115.39	120.45	118.49
1997	112.50	109.50	106.58	117.16	125.68	116.28	122.53	119.28	112.07	99.68	85.99	79.44	108.89
1998[1]	76.50	103.03	104.56	102.51	130.64	113.13	106.51	105.90	97.23	99.63	79.90	72.49	99.34

[1] Preliminary. *Source: Economic Research Service, U.S. Department of Agriculture (ERS-USDA)*

Potatoes

Potatoes, the nation's largest vegetable crop in quantity, have seen annual production in the 1990's average about 450 million cwt., almost 100 million more than the average of the 1980's. Total production in 1997 of 466 million cwt. trailed the 1996 record high of 499 million cwt. due to a reduction in acreage--from 1.5 million acres to 1.4 million, and a dip in average yield to 346 cwt./acre from 1996's record high 350 cwt. U.S. potato production is seeing a slow change in that producers are making more use of biogenetic seed with built in pesticides; a major uncertainty, however, focuses on consumer acceptance of "engineered" fresh potatoes on the retail level.

More than half of the U.S. crop is processed and about a fifth is consumed as tablestock. Total consumption (sales) in 1997 of 428 million cwt. compares with a record high 451 million in 1996 with the decline largely in the production of french fries, down from a record high 145 million cwt. in 1996 to 132 million in 1997. The jury is still out as to whether the U.S. consumer's affinity for deep fried processed potatoes has peaked; the odds suggest otherwise as fast food retailers are making concerted marketing efforts to enhance demand. Tablestock use (fresh potatoes) in 1997 of 130.5 million cwt. compares with 130.9 million in 1996. Non-sale use, i.e. seed and shrinkage, totaled almost 38 million cwt. in 1997 vs. 47.6 million in 1996.

Potatoes are grown in all fifty states but the crop is divided into four seasonal groups based on harvest time. The fall crop, consisting of about two dozen states, accounts for 85-90 percent of total production and is usually harvested from September through November. The winter crop is the smallest and harvested only in Florida and California from January into March. Spring and summer crop production tend to be similar in size. The seasonal disparities reflect major differences in planted acreage and realized yield which is consistently higher in the fall producing states. The marketing season follows the harvest, but the movement of the fall crop can extend into the following July with supplies drawn from storage. The inventoried fall crop can serve as a supply buffer in the event the spring and summer crops are short. Large fall stocks can be a depressant on prices should earlier crops prove large. Generally about a third of farm marketings occur in September/October.

Idaho is the nation's largest producer with a 1997 fall crop of 140 million cwt. vs. 143 million in 1996. Washington's crop, at a distant second, of 88 million cwt. compares with 95 million in 1996. As usual, Washington's average yield was the nation's highest, 580 cwt./acre in 1997 vs. Idaho's 353 cwt./acre. Maine, once the largest fall producing state, realized a crop of only 19 million cwt. vs. 21 million in 1996; the steady decline in Maine's ranking--to about seventh in recent years--largely reflects the wide variety of tubers grown, whereas in Idaho production is focused on one type of potato, the Russet Burbank, enhancing marketing consistency and consumer preference. The value of the 1997 crop was estimated at $2.6 billion, up 7 percent from 1996, but 13 percent below 1995's record high. The average price received by farmers in 1997 of $5.62 per cwt. compares with $4.92 in 1996 and $6.77 in 1995. On the retail level, processed potato prices are usually about three times higher than tablestock.

Frozen french fries account for most of all frozen use. Chips and shoestrings account for about 20 percent of total processing use; in 1997 there were 119 chip producing plants in the U.S. vs. 122 in 1996, most of which are located in the Eastern half of the U.S. Foreign trade in U.S. potatoes is small: Japan imports processed potatoes, mostly french fries; Canada exports fresh potatoes which are used mostly for seed.

Futures Markets

Potato futures and options are traded on the New York Cotton Exchange (NYCE) and the London Commodity Exchange (LCE). Potato futures are traded on the Marche a Terme International de France (MATIF).

Salient Statistics of Potatoes in the United States

Crop Year	Acreage Planted (1,000 Acres)	Acreage Harvested (1,000 Acres)	Yield Per Harvested Acre (Cwt.)	Total Production (In Thousands of Cwt.)	Farm Disposition — Used Where Grown: Seed & Feed (In Thousands of Cwt.)	Farm Disposition — Used Where Grown: Shrinkage & Loss (In Thousands of Cwt.)	Farm Disposition — Sold[2] (In Thousands of Cwt.)	Farm Price ($ Cwt.)	Value of Production[3] (Million $)	Value of Sales (Million $)	Stocks on Jan. 1 (1,000 Cwt)	Foreign Trade[5] (Fresh) Domestic Exports (Millions of Lbs.)	Foreign Trade[5] Imports (Millions of Lbs.)	Consumption[5] Per Capita Fresh (in Pounds)	Consumption[5] Per Capita Total (in Pounds)
1989	1,305	1,282	289	370,444	5,722	24,974	339,748	7.36	2,717	2,501	173,550	467,836	509,347	50.0	127.0
1990	1,400	1,371	293	402,110	5,949	28,329	367,832	6.08	2,409	2,240	194,460	327,333	482,903	46.8	124.1
1991	1,408	1,374	304	417,622	5,995	32,429	379,198	4.96	2,043	1,880	211,005	341,682	437,349	50.4	135.5
1992	1,339	1,315	323	425,367	5,925	33,807	385,637	5.52	2,336	2,129	215,990	537,939	273,515	48.6	130.7
1993	1,385	1,317	326	428,693	5,931	30,152	392,610	6.17	2,637	2,424	217,300	539,345	541,382	49.3	134.9
1994	1,416	1,380	339	467,054	5,878	37,166	424,010	5.58	2,590	2,367	238,560	655,026	405,899	50.3	140.2
1995	1,398	1,372	323	443,606	5,745	29,530	408,331	6.77	2,992	2,762	223,550	583,938	458,926	49.5	138.4
1996	1,455	1,426	350	499,254	6,221	41,222	451,190	4.91	2,425	2,220	261,320	564,010	690,768	50.0	145.4
1997[1]	1,384	1,354	345	467,091	5,464	32,186	427,887	5.64	2,622	2,403	246,550	670,270	512,321	48.9	143.2
1998[1]	1,423	1,394	343	477,754				5.24	2,493		246,220			48.7	143.9

[1] Preliminary. [2] For all purposes, including food, seed processing & livestock feed. [3] Farm weight basis, excluding canned and frozen potatoes.

Source: Economic Research Service, U.S. Department of Agriculture (ERS-USDA)

POTATOES

Cold Storage Stocks of All Frozen Potatoes in the United States, on First of Month   In Millions of Pounds

Year	Jan.	Feb.	Mar.	Apr.	May	June	July	Aug.	Sept.	Oct.	Nov.	Dec.
1989	988.7	927.4	944.3	947.3	968.7	986.7	961.5	739.9	611.3	734.2	878.7	938.0
1990	917.3	932.7	995.6	1,041.2	1,059.0	1,061.3	977.6	769.3	688.1	852.5	995.6	999.5
1991	975.8	993.3	988.9	1,041.5	1,052.3	1,167.2	1,216.5	935.5	880.1	985.5	1,148.0	1,037.2
1992	980.8	996.5	1,036.3	1,082.7	1,077.6	1,137.3	1,131.4	966.4	948.7	949.1	1,067.1	1,038.7
1993	963.2	971.2	1,028.2	1,046.6	912.7	979.5	989.8	932.8	902.8	1,019.5	1,184.7	1,130.7
1994	1,006.4	1,019.9	1,057.1	1,054.4	1,050.5	1,118.9	1,099.9	979.8	1,028.2	1,108.7	1,189.0	1,163.5
1995	1,096.6	1,156.0	1,179.9	1,169.0	1,138.0	1,125.4	1,116.5	992.4	992.6	1,145.3	1,225.6	1,174.5
1996	1,123.7	1,147.2	1,172.5	1,164.6	1,112.1	1,076.4	1,059.7	907.1	957.8	1,124.9	1,225.2	1,146.3
1997	1,098.4	1,111.5	1,180.1	1,177.1	1,195.8	1,213.3	1,271.4	1,214.3	1,130.8	1,270.0	1,354.7	1,313.5
1998[1]	1,163.5	1,147.2	1,235.7	1,278.3	1,225.1	1,282.8	1,316.5	1,234.7	1,204.5	1,266.9	1,341.0	1,290.9

[1] Preliminary. *Source: Agricultural Statistics Board, U.S. Department of Agriculture (ASB-USDA)*

Potato Crop Production Estimates, Stocks and Disappearance in the United States   In Millions of Cwt.

	Crop Production Estimates					Total Storage Stocks[2]						Fall Crop				
	Total Crop			Fall Crop			Following Year					1,000 Cwt.				
Year	Oct. 1	Nov. 1	Dec. 1	Oct. 1	Nov. 1	Dec. 1	Jan. 1	Feb. 1	Mar. 1	Apr. 1	May 1	Production	Disappearance (Sold)	Dec. 1 Stocks	Average Price $/Cwt.	Value of Sales $1,000
1989	------	367.3	------	------	342.5	202.1	173.6	144.3	116.6	84.3	50.7	316,097	295,605	202,050	6.76	1,999,104
1990	------	393.2	------	------	371.7	225.5	194.5	162.9	134.5	101.2	63.0	344,200	320,033	225,500	5.42	1,734,476
1991	------	417.6	------	------	379.5	242.1	211.0	178.5	145.8	108.9	69.1	363,541	334,893	242,070	4.16	1,393,749
1992	------	425.4	------	------	372.4	246.8	216.0	184.6	152.8	115.8	75.0	368,516	341,209	246,820	5.17	1,762,984
1993	------	428.7	------	------	372.4	249.4	217.3	185.5	153.4	115.2	72.9	376,954	353,052	249,710	5.65	1,981,017
1994	------	467.9	------	------	412.4	273.3	238.6	202.5	169.6	129.8	87.6	410,839	380,818	272,290	5.06	1,914,311
1995	------	444.8	------	------	402.4	256.7	223.6	189.4	156.0	115.9	75.9	394,785	370,679	256,710	6.43	2,372,983
1996	------	491.5	------	------	447.9	295.1	261.3	226.1	189.2	147.6	103.2	443,704	408,247	295,100	4.35	1,772,037
1997	------	459.4	------	------	417.5	278.8	246.6	212.6	175.9	134.2	92.8	413,513	387,089	278,830	5.20	2,010,344
1998[1]	------	471.0	------	------	429.0	282.3	246.2	211.1				424,897		282,300		

[1] Preliminary. [2] Held by growers and local dealers in the fall producing areas. *Source: Agricultural Statistics Board, U.S. Department of Agriculture*

Production of Potatoes by Seasonal Groups in the United States   In Thousands of Cwt.

		Spring			Summer			Fall								
Year	Winter	California	Florida	Total	New Mexico	Virgina	Total	Colorado	Idaho	Maine	Minnesota	North Dakota	Oregon	Washington	Wisconsin	Total
1989	2,764	7,875	6,860	20,852	4,025	1,440	22,155	20,603	102,475	22,000	13,860	15,070	23,308	64,310	23,120	324,673
1990	2,343	8,438	8,714	24,163	3,400	1,980	23,097	22,750	119,070	20,520	14,280	16,675	23,450	67,980	23,075	352,507
1991	2,609	8,284	6,600	20,636	3,450	1,485	22,647	23,800	122,175	18,170	17,160	30,030	22,170	75,435	23,275	371,730
1992	2,998	7,238	7,750	21,535	952	1,980	21,309	22,110	127,050	24,300	16,080	27,690	21,075	69,300	25,160	379,525
1993	2,552	7,508	6,068	19,654	1,290	1,760	14,922	25,270	126,192	19,890	14,780	21,090	23,103	88,500	22,588	391,565
1994	2,372	7,790	8,588	22,646	1,088	1,425	17,381	25,795	138,801	18,375	20,035	28,200	27,514	88,920	25,740	424,655
1995	2,473	6,230	7,830	20,193	1,344	2,040	17,931	23,808	132,657	17,160	20,790	25,410	24,788	80,850	26,000	403,009
1996	3,273	7,538	7,765	22,417	1,404	1,463	19,176	29,175	142,800	21,175	24,600	28,820	30,124	94,990	33,150	454,388
1997	3,431	8,073	7,150	22,299	1,248	1,268	18,171	24,993	140,314	19,080	20,440	22,000	27,319	88,160	30,175	423,190
1998[1]	2,980	6,198	7,358	21,137	962	1,380	19,269	25,360	139,650	18,060	21,170	28,670	26,229	93,225	30,895	434,368

[1] Preliminary. *Source: Agricultural Statistics Board, U.S. Department of Agriculture (ASB-USDA)*

Utilization of Potatoes in the United States   In Thousands of Cwt.

	Sales											Non-sales			
		For Processing							Other Sales						
Crop Year	Table Stock	Chips, Shoestrings	For Dehydration	Frozen French Fries	Other Frozen Products	Canned Potatoes	Other Canned Products[2]	Starch & Flour	Livestock Feed	Seed	Total Sale	Used on Farms Where Grown	Shrinkage & Loss	Total Non-sales	Total
1988	108,348	44,539	28,786	95,466	17,558	2,941	2,031	1,416	3,330	21,146	325,561	4,827	25,067	30,877	356,438
1989	113,932	43,071	32,187	100,459	19,115	3,138	1,858	898	2,800	22,290	339,748	4,735	24,974	30,696	370,444
1990	119,545	44,489	38,838	108,455	23,915	2,526	2,075	1,699	3,264	23,026	367,832	5,035	28,329	34,278	402,110
1991	126,953	45,850	40,395	111,128	23,097	2,465	1,886	1,739	3,652	22,033	379,198	4,988	32,429	38,424	417,622
1992	127,215	48,455	38,078	112,496	23,016	2,710	2,557	1,610	3,928	23,529	385,637	4,746	33,807	39,730	425,367
1993	123,802	48,987	40,795	121,087	25,190	1,879	2,458	1,691	2,498	24,223	392,610	4,808	30,152	36,083	428,693
1994	133,989	49,299	41,381	136,531	26,362	2,503	3,006	2,176	4,147	24,616	424,010	4,732	37,166	43,044	467,054
1995	124,482	47,284	45,065	129,029	27,073	3,342	2,385	1,668	3,224	25,779	408,331	4,783	29,530	35,275	443,606
1996	130,907	48,305	54,261	145,489	28,972	2,785	2,167	1,956	12,073	24,140	451,190	4,937	41,222	47,579	498,633
1997[1]	130,508	48,130	48,389	131,628	33,397	2,822	2,675	1,311	3,603	25,424	427,887	4,138	32,186	37,650	465,537

[1] Preliminary. [2] Hash, stews and soups. *Source: Agricultural Statistics Board, U.S. Department of Agriculture (ASB-USDA)*

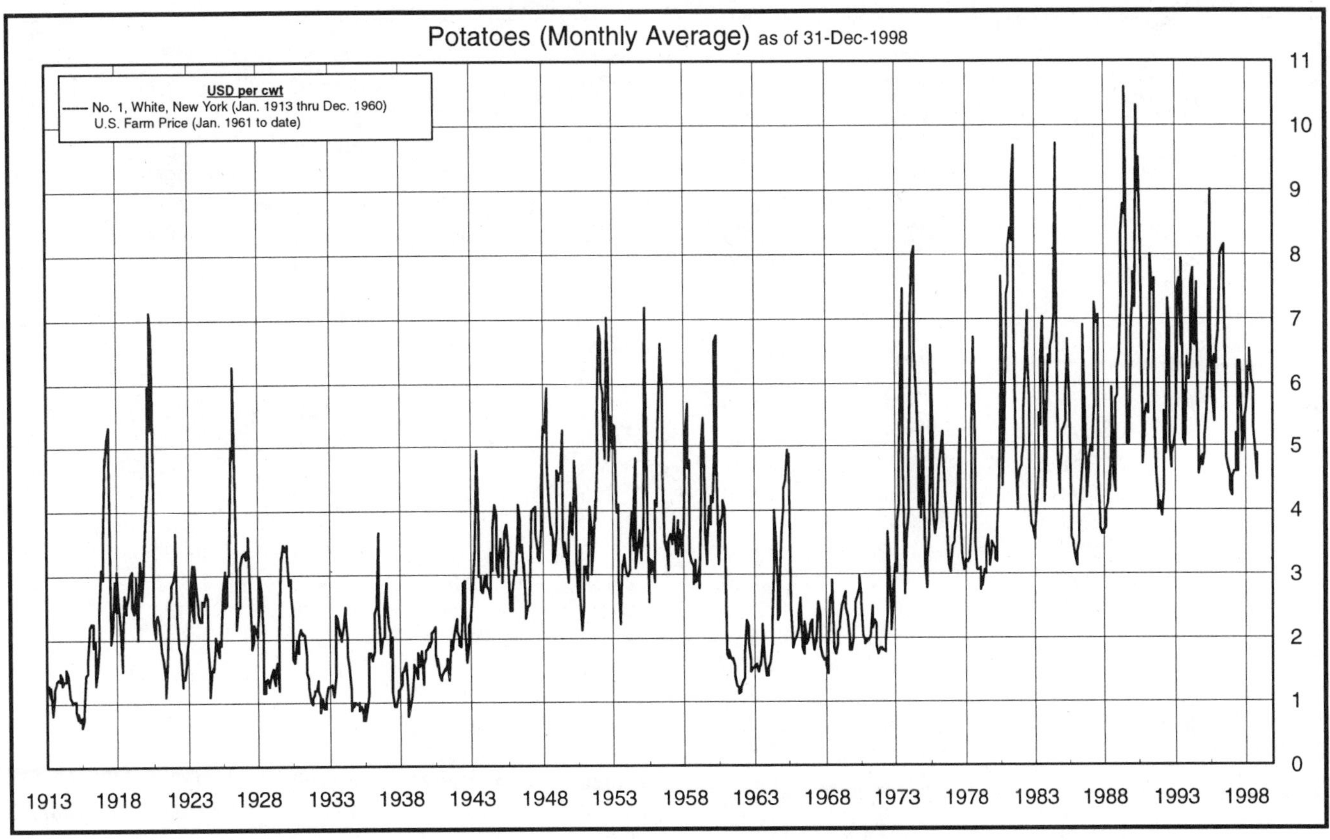

Per Capita Utilization of Potatoes in the United States in Pounds (Farm Weight)

Year	Total	Fresh	Processing: Freezing	Chips & Shoe-string	Dehy-drating	Canning	Total
1990	127.7	45.8	50.2	17.0	12.8	1.9	81.9
1991	130.4	46.4	51.3	17.3	13.7	1.7	84.0
1992	132.4	48.9	51.0	17.5	13.2	1.8	83.5
1993	136.9	49.7	54.5	17.6	13.4	1.7	87.2
1994	140.2	48.6	59.3	17.1	13.5	1.7	91.6
1995	137.9	50.7	55.3	16.9	13.0	2.0	87.2
1996	145.4	50.0	60.4	16.5	16.7	1.8	95.4
1997	142.2	48.9	60.2	16.1	16.2	1.8	94.3
1998[1]	143.9	48.7	60.6	16.3	16.4	1.9	95.2
1999[2]	143.5	48.2	60.4	16.2	16.9	1.8	95.3

[1] Preliminary. [2] Forecast. *Source: Agricultural Statistics Board, U.S. Department of Agriculture (ASB-USDA)*

Average Price Received by Farmers for Potatoes in the United States In Dollars Per Cwt.

Year	Jan.	Feb.	Mar.	Apr.	May	June	July	Aug.	Sept.	Oct.	Nov.	Dec.	Season Average
1989	6.24	6.43	7.34	8.33	8.78	8.61	10.60	7.58	5.06	5.03	6.32	6.81	7.36
1990	7.36	7.71	9.17	10.30	9.32	8.96	9.50	8.09	5.36	4.73	5.24	5.46	6.08
1991	5.66	5.53	6.15	7.03	7.98	7.51	7.95	5.39	4.51	4.06	3.99	4.29	4.96
1992	4.07	4.08	4.64	5.16	4.43	4.71	7.00	6.64	4.89	4.55	4.90	5.06	5.52
1993	5.15	5.29	6.06	7.19	7.18	6.45	7.61	6.05	5.12	4.96	6.40	6.12	6.17
1994	6.02	6.43	7.67	6.69	6.59	6.67	7.49	6.99	5.03	4.57	4.80	4.86	5.58
1995	4.88	4.90	5.39	5.54	5.77	6.98	8.60	6.81	5.76	5.38	6.42	6.29	6.77
1996	6.65	6.92	7.51	7.83	8.09	8.14	8.09	5.79	4.83	4.76	4.43	4.32	5.11
1997	4.23	4.50	4.60	4.61	5.26	4.62	5.60	6.34	5.09	4.93	5.13	5.29	5.68
1998[1]	5.55	5.86	6.25	6.17	6.52	6.04	5.93	5.30	4.92	4.47	4.81	5.20	

[1] Preliminary. *Source: Agricultural Statistics Board, U.S. Department of Agriculture (ASB-USDA)*

POTATOES

Potatoes Processed[1] in the United States, Eight States In Thousands of Cwt.

States	Storage Season	to Dec. 1	to Jan. 1	to Feb. 1	to Mar. 1	to Apr. 1	to May 1	Entire Season
Idaho and	1989-90	22,200	28,140	34,240	40,270	46,330	51,810	66,010
Oregon-	1990-1	24,780	31,100	37,550	44,220	51,030	58,660	78,500
Malheur Co	1991-2	22,980	28,910	35,700	42,840	50,260	57,290	78,690
	1992-3	22,180	29,080	35,710	42,800	50,090	57,090	80,570
	1993-4	24,090	30,540	37,150	44,720	53,070	61,440	85,780
	1994-5	26,620	34,230	42,330	49,890	57,990	66,680	90,300
	1995-6	27,310	35,040	43,260	51,530	59,060	66,690	89,250
	1996-7	31,060	38,210	45,420	54,640	62,570	70,720	96,970
	1997-8	26,880	33,950	41,050	49,470	57,620	65,750	91,450
	1998-9	27,510	34,700	42,670				
Maine[2]	1989-90	2,055	2,660	3,510	4,000	4,620	5,210	6,900
	1990-1	2,105	2,690	3,420	3,900	4,460	5,120	6,750
	1991-2	2,015	2,450	3,050	3,350	3,900	4,445	5,210
	1992-3	1,195	1,630	2,205	2,720	3,390	4,020	5,055
	1993-4	1,350	1,720	2,210	2,505	2,890	3,275	4,555
	1994-5	1,505	1,840	2,265	2,540	2,985	3,330	4,770
	1995-6	1,455	1,850	2,430	2,850	3,435	3,965	5,725
	1996-7	1,790	2,115	2,820	3,280	3,820	4,420	6,495
	1997-8	1,245	1,655	2,285	2,725	3,335	3,900	5,870
	1998-9	1,180	1,710	2,260				
Washington and	1989-90	23,635	28,015	33,170	38,610	44,510	49,595	57,695
Oregon-Other	1990-1	24,780	29,830	35,170	39,950	45,600	50,780	61,450
	1991-2	26,345	30,570	35,320	41,320	47,120	52,605	65,210
	1992-3	26,840	31,550	35,950	41,670	46,530	51,630	63,510
	1993-4	28,260	33,350	39,010	45,020	51,290	57,180	70,690
	1994-5	28,670	33,480	39,120	46,070	52,940	59,540	76,780
	1995-6	30,000	35,170	39,460	45,280	51,730	57,360	70,250
	1996-7	31,670	36,660	41,700	48,740	55,570	62,320	80,970
	1997-8	28,580	33,990	38,690	46,400	53,720	59,780	76,930
	1998-9	33,460	38,895	45,650				
Other States[3]	1989-90	6,340	8,010	9,860	11,535	13,240	15,100	20,610
	1990-1	6,585	8,605	10,405	12,425	14,635	17,010	24,005
	1991-2	7,515	9,350	11,580	13,585	15,685	17,935	24,990
	1992-3	7,140	9,220	11,265	13,305	15,550	17,555	25,070
	1993-4	7,605	9,515	11,605	13,720	16,080	18,705	25,690
	1994-5	9,725	13,110	15,630	18,260	21,115	24,060	32,260
	1995-6	12,650	15,630	18,815	21,985	25,510	28,610	33,580
	1996-7	13,720	17,000	20,645	24,085	27,650	30,830	43,100
	1997-8	11,645	13,960	17,115	19,905	23,515	26,365	37,842
	1998-9	11,020	13,785	17,510				
Total	1989-90	54,230	66,825	80,780	94,415	108,700	121,715	151,215
	1990-1	58,250	72,225	86,545	100,495	115,725	131,570	170,705
	1991-2	58,855	71,280	85,650	101,095	116,965	132,275	174,100
	1992-3	57,355	71,480	85,130	100,495	115,560	130,295	174,205
	1993-4	61,305	75,125	89,975	105,965	123,330	140,600	186,715
	1994-5	66,520	82,660	99,345	116,760	135,030	153,610	204,110
	1995-6	71,415	87,690	103,965	121,645	139,735	156,625	198,805
	1996-7	78,240	93,985	110,585	130,745	149,610	168,290	227,535
	1997-8	68,355	83,620	99,120	118,510	138,210	155,795	212,092
	1998-9	73,170	89,090	108,090				

[1] Total quantity received and used for processing regardless of the state in which the potatoes were produced. Excluding quantities used for potato chips in Maine, Michigan, Minnesota, North Dakota or Wisconsin. [2] Includes Maine grown potatoes only. [3] Michigan, Minnesota, North Dakota and Wisconsin.
Source: National Agricultural Statistics Service, U.S. Department of Agriculture (NASS-USDA)

Rayon and Other Synthetic Fibers

World Cellulosic Fiber Production In Thousands of Metric Tons

Year	Austria	Brazil	China	Czech Republic	Finland	Germany	India	Japan	Taiwan	United Kingdom	United States	Former U.S.S.R.	Total
1989	136.0	55.0	204.0	56.9	64.8	278.4	198.7	272.9	147.6	55.0	263.3	584.0	2,943
1990	135.0	54.5	214.3	55.0	63.8	199.1	216.7	275.8	147.9	71.0	229.2	544.0	2,757
1991	120.0	53.0	242.0	33.5	47.4	118.0	215.4	266.4	149.1	63.0	220.7	401.7	2,433
1992	128.3	54.2	249.0	39.3	56.0	139.9	219.9	254.4	139.3	65.0	224.5	292.3	2,327
1993	131.2	56.7	276.2	41.0	56.5	127.1	238.9	244.4	130.8	67.2	228.9	258.3	2,286
1994	134.3	62.8	336.1	41.7	58.5	136.2	239.7	218.9	149.3	67.4	226.0	176.0	2,340
1995	139.4	53.1	435.0	35.0	57.5	143.5	262.1	212.7	139.6	67.1	226.0	188.4	2,439
1996	145.0	34.4	432.0	31.4	49.8	143.6	251.9	198.2	144.7	62.3	215.3	127.3	2,274
1997[1]	145.0	37.9	450.0	27.3	62.0	155.0	242.4	184.1	148.4	70.0	208.3	401.2	2,309
1998[2]	-----	51.4	558.0	51.2	-----	-----	371.4	265.6	163.9	-----	233.2	-----	3,228

[1] Preliminary. [2] Producing capacity. *Source: Fiber Economics Bureau, Inc. (FEB)*

World Noncellulosic Fiber Production (Except Olefin) In Thousands of Metric Tons

Year	Brazil	China	Germany	India	Italy/ Malta	Japan	Rep. of Korea	Mexico	Spain	Taiwan	United States	Former U.S.S.R.	Total
1989	245.8	1,223.2	952.3	366.7	547.7	1,380.9	1,189.9	352.8	252.3	1,523.1	3,119.4	874.0	14,747
1990	207.8	1,342.8	777.0	436.6	578.3	1,425.0	1,269.7	366.8	255.0	1,621.5	2,886.0	893.5	14,894
1991	219.1	1,488.9	797.0	439.6	564.6	1,429.8	1,365.2	395.3	241.1	1,841.4	2,902.9	804.8	15,273
1992	218.2	1,586.7	817.3	538.0	589.9	1,448.8	1,451.4	426.6	257.0	2,042.6	2,980.6	656.8	15,911
1993	233.3	1,871.9	758.8	608.9	551.6	1,365.1	1,581.3	406.5	240.3	2,122.8	3,016.1	669.8	16,653
1994	239.1	2,299.2	807.6	681.0	599.9	1,374.0	1,673.5	418.4	273.6	2,295.9	3,193.3	658.1	17,908
1995	227.4	2,283.7	771.3	738.0	551.3	1,400.0	1,858.2	516.6	252.3	2,410.5	3,238.9	636.1	18,384
1996	229.4	2,711.5	-----	916.4	-----	1,399.0	2,025.2	554.3	-----	2,561.0	3,280.3	1,359.8	19,697
1997[1]	246.1	2,948.1	-----	1,267.5	-----	1,433.6	2,402.2	583.4	-----	2,932.4	3,403.7	-----	21,683
1998[2]	320.7	3,873.0	-----	1,747.0	-----	1,785.3	2,808.8	715.0	-----	3,629.0	3,859.9	-----	27,514

[1] Preliminary. [2] Producing capacity. *Source: Fiber Economics Bureau, Inc. (FEB)*

World Production of Synthetic Fibers In Thousands of Metric Tons

	Noncellulosic Fiber Production (Except Olefin)							Glass Fiber Production							
	By Fibers				World Total										
Year	Acrylic & Mod-acrylic	Nylon & Aramid	Polyester	Other Fibers[3]	Yarn & Monofil-aments	Staple & Tow & Fiberfill	Total	Europe	Japan	Other Americas	United States	Total	China	Former U.S.S.R.	Cigarette Tow Pro-duction
1989	2,341	3,795	8,459	152	6,847	7,900	14,747	470	345	65	735	1,680	70	133	443
1990	2,320	3,738	8,678	158	7,035	7,859	14,894	445	371	60	675	1,631	75	120	464
1991	2,385	3,605	9,116	167	7,241	8,032	15,273	441	293	75	650	1,561	65	133	480
1992	2,363	3,662	9,729	157	7,673	8,238	15,911	442	307	83	700	1,652	75	130	475
1993	2,297	3,707	10,512	136	8,478	8,174	16,652	508	312	86	794	1,865	77	69	482
1994	2,472	3,770	11,500	162	9,107	8,797	17,904	545	313	87	959	2,076	78	64	536
1995	2,446	3,740	11,953	247	9,686	8,698	18,384	567	318	96	981	2,438	85	55	550
1996	2,589	3,857	12,995	256	10,323	9,374	19,697	585	316	94	996	2,492	98	54	584
1997[1]	2,709	4,015	14,687	273	11,530	10,154	21,683	610	328	100	1,032	2,560	75	55	584
1998[2]	3,206	5,258	18,666	384	14,713	12,802	27,514	770	363	110	1,225	2,953	65	50	-----

[1] Preliminary. [2] Producing capacity. [3] Alginate, azion, spandex, saran, etc. *Source: Fiber Economics Bureau, Inc. (FEB)*

Artificial (Cellulosic) Fiber Distribution in the United States In Millions of Pounds

	Yarn & Monofilament					Staple & Tow					
	Producers' Shipments					Producers' Shipments					
Year	Domestic	Exports	Total	Imports	Domestic Con-sumption	Domestic	Exports	Total	Imports	Domestic Con-sumption	Glass Fiber Ship-ments
1989	187.3	31.7	219.0	26.3	213.6	338.2	16.2	354.4	54.0	392.2	1,530.1
1990	172.7	34.0	206.7	24.2	196.9	291.7	12.5	304.2	111.6	403.3	1,519.1
1991	179.9	32.3	212.2	30.8	210.7	255.5	8.1	263.6	92.0	347.5	1,488.5
1992	182.9	35.1	218.0	32.1	215.0	260.7	6.9	267.6	85.6	346.3	1,629.7
1993	196.5	31.5	228.0	40.4	236.9	273.6	10.3	283.9	89.5	363.1	1,780.6
1994	190.3	32.9	223.2	32.9	223.2	252.3	30.7	283.0	65.7	318.0	2,016.0
1995	169.3	41.5	210.8	34.0	203.3	259.8	28.7	288.5	40.8	300.6	2,163.0
1996	169.0	49.6	218.6	39.3	208.3	225.3	20.0	245.3	35.3	260.6	2,196.0
1997[1]	145.9	41.2	187.1	42.9	188.8	205.3	60.1	265.4	51.6	256.9	2,275.0

[1] Preliminary. *Source: Fiber Economics Bureau, Inc. (FEB)*

RAYON AND OTHER SYNTHETIC FIBERS

Man-Made Fiber Production in the United States In Millions of Pounds

	-Artificial (Cellulosic) Fibers- - Rayon & Acetate -			Synthetic (Noncellulosic) Fibers											
				Yarn & Monofilament				Staple & Tow							
Year	Filament Yarn & Monofilament	Staple & Tow	Total Cellulostic	Nylon	Polyester	Olefin	Total Yarn	Nylon	Polyester	Acrylic & Modacrylic	Olefin	Total Staple	Total Noncellulosic	Total Manufactured Fibers	Total Glass Fiber
1989	217	363	580	1,759	1,209	1,257	4,225	981	2,385	543	382	4,291	8,516	9,096	1,620
1990	206	299	505	1,671	1,107	1,417	4,194	990	2,090	505	406	3,991	8,185	8,690	1,488
1991	213	273	486	1,667	1,208	1,408	4,282	869	2,202	454	459	3,984	8,266	8,752	1,433
1992	220	275	495	1,651	1,270	1,528	4,449	904	2,308	439	474	4,125	8,573	9,068	1,543
1993	227	278	505	1,700	1,284	1,659	4,643	959	2,274	433	483	4,149	8,791	9,296	1,751
1994	225	273	498	1,805	1,492	1,870	5,167	935	2,366	442	549	4,292	9,459	9,957	2,114
1995	208	290	498	1,829	1,597	1,907	5,333	874	2,290	432	521	4,117	9,450	9,948	2,282
1996	219	245	464	1,920	1,560	1,957	5,437	875	2,259	478	465	4,078	9,515	9,979	2,326
1997[1]	187	266	453	2,005	1,642	2,058	5,704	793	2,454	440	629	4,317	10,012	10,465	2,408
1998[2]	144	216	360	2,050	1,536	2,155	5,740	804	2,331	355	638	4,129	9,868	10,228	

[1] Preliminary. [2] Estimate. *Source: Fiber Economics Bureau, Inc. (FEB)*

Domestic Distribution of Synthetic (Noncellulosic) Fibers in the United States In Millions of Pounds

	Yarn & Monofilament								Staple & Tow								
	Producers' Shipments								Producers' Shipments								
	Domestic								Domestic								
Year	Nylon	Polyester	Olefin	Total	Exports	Total	Imports	Domestic Consumption	Nylon	Polyester	Acrylic & Modacrylic	Olefin	Total	Exports	Total	Imports	Domestic Consumption
1989	1,575.3	1,110.7	1,226.0	3,912.0	237.9	4,149.9	182.2	4,094.2	955.3	2,261.3	414.8	363.4	3,994.8	253.3	4,248.1	192.4	4,187.2
1990	1,537.5	1,046.2	1,404.9	3,988.6	265.1	4,253.7	154.7	4,143.3	950.2	2,015.4	352.2	387.9	3,705.7	278.9	3,984.6	209.8	3,915.5
1991	1,493.9	1,114.0	1,380.6	3,988.5	246.9	4,235.4	174.8	4,163.3	835.0	2,127.9	319.2	437.5	3,719.6	277.8	3,997.4	263.1	3,982.7
1992	1,570.1	1,229.6	1,496.1	4,295.8	194.8	4,490.6	209.3	4,505.1	891.7	2,202.1	322.3	441.0	3,857.1	267.2	4,124.3	397.7	4,255.0
1993	1,612.7	1,228.4	1,631.5	4,472.6	174.6	4,647.2	295.8	4,768.4	907.9	2,157.8	333.0	468.2	3,866.9	297.1	4,164.0	509.0	4,375.9
1994	1,700.0	1,402.8	1,838.2	4,941.0	204.9	5,145.9	377.7	5,318.7	911.7	2,221.3	319.6	489.0	3,941.6	390.9	4,332.5	622.9	4,564.5
1995	1,741.4	1,439.8	1,870.3	5,051.5	259.0	5,310.5	393.6	5,445.1	828.5	2,100.4	266.1	458.0	3,653.0	398.7	4,051.7	624.9	4,277.9
1996	1,801.2	1,428.7	1,953.2	5,183.1	275.2	5,458.3	482.0	5,665.1	843.8	2,015.6	287.9	439.2	3,586.5	465.3	4,051.8	607.7	4,194.2
1997[1]	1,877.1	1,530.3	2,013.2	5,420.6	274.4	5,695.0	589.0	6,009.6	757.2	2,219.7	288.6	405.0	3,670.5	455.1	4,125.6	672.8	4,343.3

[1] Preliminary. *Source: Fiber Economics Bureau, Inc. (FEB)*

Mill Consumption of Fiber & Products and Per Capita Consumption in the U.S. In Millions of Pounds

	Cellulosic Fibers				Noncellulosic Fibers								Per Capita[4] Mill Consumption (Pounds)				
Year	Yarn & Monofilament	Staple & Tow	Net Waste	Total Cellulostic	Noncellulostic	Net Waste	Total Noncellulostic	Total Manufactured Fibers[2]	Cotton	Wool	Other Fibers[3]	Grand Total	Man-made Fibers[2]	Cotton	Wool	Other Fibers[3]	Total All Fibers
1989	213.6	392.2	-5.0	600.8	8,281.4	127.4	8,408.8	9,009.6	3,985.9	139.6	77.9	13,213.0	40.6	23.4	1.1	2.0	67.1
1990	196.9	403.3	-1.3	598.9	8,058.8	179.3	8,238.1	8,837.0	4,036.5	135.4	75.7	13,084.6	39.3	23.2	1.1	2.2	65.8
1991	210.7	347.5	-1.7	556.5	8,135.9	168.8	8,304.7	8,861.2	4,347.5	159.0	78.6	13,446.3	39.1	24.6	1.2	2.0	66.9
1992	215.0	346.3	-3.6	557.7	8,760.1	181.1	8,941.2	9,498.9	4,714.7	159.1	76.3	14,449.0	41.5	27.6	1.2	1.9	72.2
1993	236.9	363.1	-5.6	594.4	9,144.3	189.8	9,334.1	9,928.5	4,921.9	166.6	73.8	15,090.8	43.2	29.2	1.3	1.8	75.5
1994	223.2	318.0	-21.4	519.8	9,883.2	102.4	9,985.6	10,505.4	5,191.6	168.1	54.8	15,919.9	45.4	30.2	1.4	2.7	79.7
1995	203.3	300.6	-22.7	481.2	9,722.5	76.3	9,798.8	10,280.0	5,199.9	161.8	65.6	15,642.7	43.7	30.2	1.4	2.5	77.8
1996	208.2	260.7	-12.8	456.1	9,909.5	99.8	10,009.3	10,465.4	5,191.9	142.9	46.0	15,801.3	44.2	29.6	1.3	1.8	76.9
1997[1]	188.8	256.9	-18.4	427.3	10,492.1	102.7	10,594.8	11,022.1	5,419.5	139.9	45.8	16,582.4	46.0	31.2	1.3	2.1	80.6

[1] Preliminary. [2] Excludes Glass Fiber. [3] Includes silk, linen, jute and sisel & others. [4] Mill consumption plus imports less exports of semimanufactured and unmanufactured products. *Source: Fiber Economics Bureau, Inc. (FEB)*

Producer Price Index of Grey Synthetic Broadwovens 1982 = 100

Year	Jan.	Feb.	Mar.	Apr.	May	June	July	Aug.	Sept.	Oct.	Nov.	Dec.	Average
1989	114.3	112.0	112.2	112.2	112.1	113.1	114.7	115.0	115.0	115.8	115.9	115.3	114.0
1990	115.6	115.7	115.6	115.7	115.5	115.6	115.7	115.2	115.3	115.6	115.8	116.1	115.7
1991	115.7	114.7	114.4	114.1	114.3	113.9	114.8	116.4	116.5	116.5	116.8	118.2	115.5
1992	119.0	119.9	120.3	120.9	121.8	122.0	122.6	122.0	121.7	120.8	119.4	119.9	120.9
1993	119.6	119.1	119.1	119.2	117.1	118.4	118.0	118.0	116.9	117.3	115.2	114.5	117.7
1994	113.5	112.8	112.9	113.2	113.2	113.3	113.1	113.3	114.1	111.8	112.9	113.8	113.2
1995	114.8	116.8	116.7	116.3	116.6	117.1	115.4	114.8	116.9	116.4	114.7	116.2	116.1
1996	114.3	114.1	116.9	117.9	116.8	115.7	116.1	117.1	116.9	117.2	116.6	117.0	116.4
1997	117.9	118.3	118.3	117.9	118.4	119.0	118.8	118.5	119.4	118.7	117.6	119.6	118.5
1998[1]	120.1	120.4	119.7	120.2	119.8	119.7	118.0	118.1	116.8	114.2	115.6	115.1	118.1

[1] Preliminary. *Source: Bureau of Labor Statistics, U.S. Department of Commerce (BLS)*

Rice

1998 global rice trade reached a record 24.9 million metric tonnes, 6 million tonnes over 1997. The surge in trade was demand driven reflecting crop shortfalls in some producing nations that increased their import needs. Record crops in Thailand, China and India, however, allowed exporters to increase shipments to meet the huge demand.

Asia accounts for most of the world's exports. Thailand is the major exporter--6.2 million tonnes in 1998 vs. 5.3 million in 1997; Vietnam is now in second place--3.6 million tonnes in 1998 vs. 3.3 million in 1997. Previously India was second, but that country's exports have shown sharp variance in recent years: from 4.2 million in 1995 to 2 million in 1997 and 3.5 million in 1998. The U.S. is among the top exporters with 3.0 million tonnes in 1998 vs. 2.3 million in 1997. The Western hemisphere is the primary destination for U.S. rice and is generally higher priced than Asian rice.

Importing nations are more numerous, but only a few import at least one million tonnes: Indonesia required an exceptionally large 5.7 million tonnes in 1998 vs. only .8 million in 1997. China's imported 2 million tonnes as recently as 1995 but now averages 0.5 million tonnes. On a regional basis, the Middle East tends to be the largest importer. Low quality rice constitutes a major portion of total world rice imports; an extremely price sensitive sector, dominated by Asian sellers.

World carryover 1997/98 stocks of 52.2 million are forecast to slide to 43.4 million at the end of 1998/99; China generally holds about half the total followed by India. World rough rice production in 1998/99 of 558 million tonnes compares with the record 570 million in 1997/98. World milled rice consumption of a record 385.1 million tonnes in 1998/99 compares with the previous year's record 384.4 million tonnes. China is the world's largest producer and consumer with about a third of each, with India second.

U.S. rough rice production in 1998/99 (August/July) of 177.7 million cwt. compares with 178.9 million in 1997/98. 1998/99 U.S. rice acreage was 3.2 million acres. The long grain yield for the 1998/99 crop of 5,576 pounds/acre compares with 6,121 pounds in 1996/97. Domestic rice usage of a record 108.9 million cwt. in 1998/99 compares with 106.9 million in 1997/98. Since the late 1980's domestic per capita rice consumption has increased from 16 pounds to 25 pounds with the increase partly attributed to Hispanic and Asian immigration and increased emphasis on grains in the diet. Moreover, exotic rice varieties have whetted consumer appetites, much of which is grown in California. U.S. ending 1998/99 stocks of 23.8 million cwt. (rough) compare with 25 million a year earlier and carryover that averaged close to 30 million cwt. earlier in the 1990's.

The U.S. average farm price in 1998/99 was forecast to range between $9.25 to $10.25 per cwt. vs $9.65 in 1997/98.

Futures Market

Rough rice futures and options are traded on the Chicago Board of Trade (CBOT).

World Rice Supply and Distribution[4] In Thousands of Metric Tons

	Exports			Imports					Utilization			Ending Stocks		
Year	U.S.	Non-U.S.	Total	Brazil	Iran	Saudi Arabia	Unaccounted	Total	China	India	Total	China	India	Total
1994-5	3,073	17,920	20,993	987	1,633	615	778	20,993	129,000	77,307	366,877	21,515	14,083	50,120
1995-6	2,624	16,881	19,505	786	1,294	786	1,394	19,505	130,000	79,203	371,225	21,732	11,000	50,131
1996-7[1]	2,292	16,748	19,040	845	875	659	1,762	19,040	132,134	80,707	379,113	25,556	9,500	51,187
1997-8[2]	3,000	22,480	25,480	1,200	500	700	1,474	25,480	135,900	80,700	384,385	28,146	8,800	51,772
1998-9[3]	2,750	18,270	21,020	1,000	650	700	1,400	21,020	137,000	80,700	384,981	21,396	7,600	43,425

[1] Preliminary. [2] Estimate. [3] Forecast. [4] Production is on a rough basis; all other data are reported on a milled basis. *Source: Foreign Agricultural Service, U.S. Department of Agriculture (FAS-USDA)*

World Production of Rough Rice In Thousands of Metric Tons

Year	Bangladesh	Brazil	Burma	China	India	Indonesia	Japan	Rep. of Korea	Pakistan	Philippines	Thailand	Vietnam	World Total
1994-5	25,252	11,235	16,000	175,930	121,752	49,743	14,977	6,882	5,171	10,475	21,400	24,615	540,542
1995-6	26,533	10,038	17,000	185,214	119,442	51,100	13,435	6,386	5,905	11,174	21,800	26,792	551,009
1996-7[1]	28,326	9,504	15,517	195,100	121,980	49,360	12,930	7,189	6,461	11,177	20,700	27,273	563,488
1997-8[2]	27,948	8,529	15,345	200,700	125,263	46,500	12,532	7,365	6,547	9,923	22,803	27,533	569,438
1998-9[3]	27,003	10,000	16,034	188,571	122,262	50,769	10,852	6,351	6,901	10,615	22,652	27,273	558,103

[1] Preliminary. [2] Estimate. [3] Forecast. *Source: Foreign Agricultural Service, U.S. Department of Agriculture (FAS-USDA)*

World Exports of Rice (Milled Basis) In Thousands of Metric Tons

Year	Argentina	Australia	Burma	China	European Union	Guyana	India	Pakistan	Thailand	Uruguay	Vietnam	United States	World Total
1994	215	570	619	1,519	185	183	600	1,399	4,738	396	2,222	2,794	16,425
1995	342	519	645	32	323	203	4,201	1,592	5,931	470	2,308	3,073	20,993
1996	367	475	265	265	301	233	3,556	1,677	5,281	596	3,040	2,624	19,505
1997[1]	500	700	15	938	367	285	1,959	1,982	5,272	640	3,268	2,292	19,040
1998[2]	400	700	80	3,300	350	250	3,500	2,000	6,100	525	3,600	3,000	25,480
1999[3]	550	650	100	1,250	350	300	2,000	2,000	5,800	625	3,500	2,750	21,020

[1] Preliminary. [2] Estimate. [3] Forecast. *Source: Foreign Agricultural Service, U.S. Department of Agriculture (FAS-USDA)*

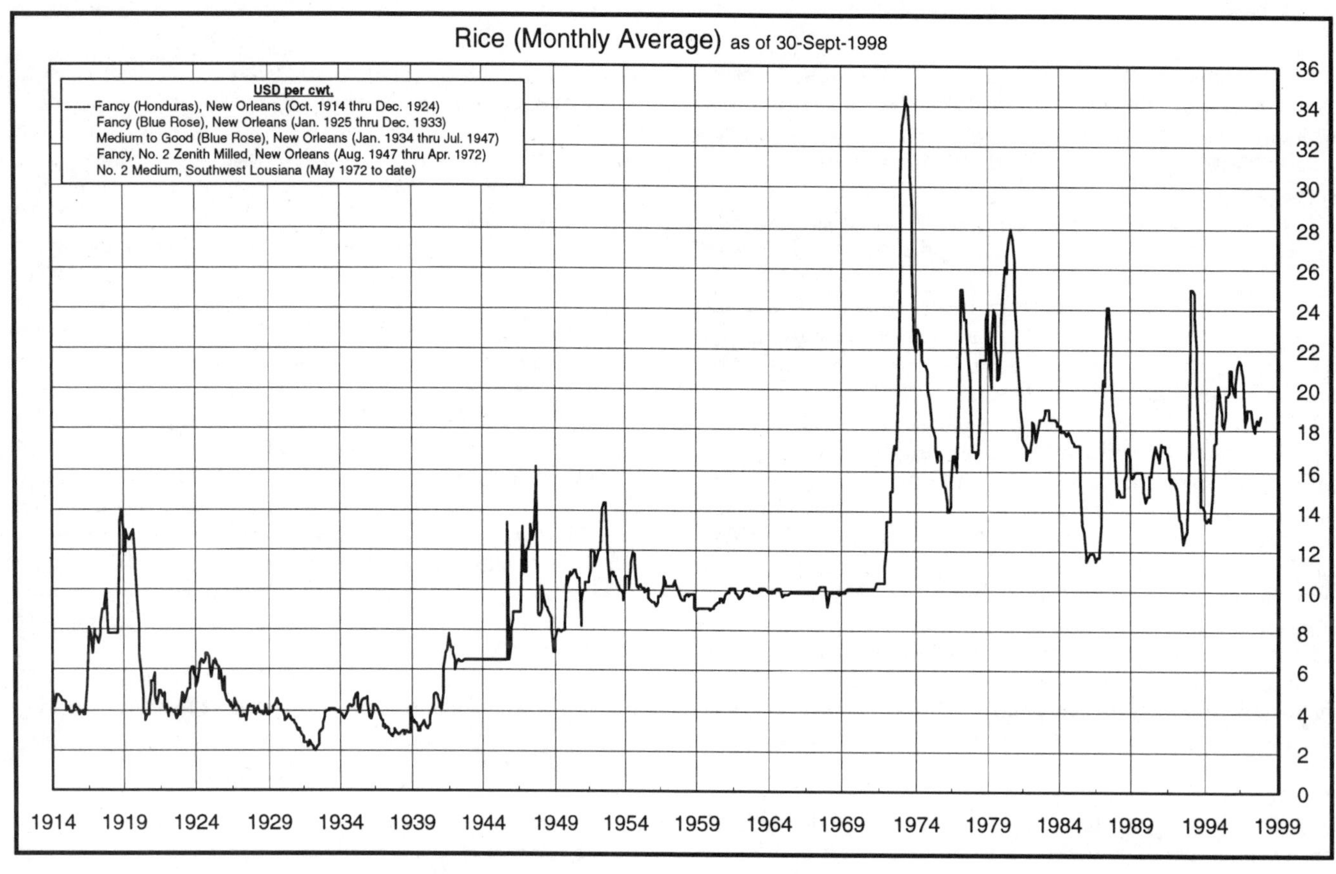

Average Wholesale Price of Rice No. 2 (Medium)[1] Southwest Louisiana In Dollars Per Cwt. Bagged

Year	Aug.	Sept.	Oct.	Nov.	Dec.	Jan.	Feb.	Mar.	Apr.	May	June	July	Average
1988-9	16.40	16.20	14.50	14.50	14.00	13.90	13.75	13.50	13.50	14.60	14.65	15.75	14.60
1989-90	15.55	15.30	14.80	14.30	14.04	14.80	15.13	15.13	15.50	15.75	15.65	15.30	15.10
1990-1	14.75	13.90	13.50	13.50	13.50	14.90	14.90	15.05	16.05	16.15	16.50	16.35	14.90
1991-2	15.85	16.00	16.00	16.00	16.00	16.00	15.90	15.50	15.50	15.15	14.50	14.50	15.60
1992-3	14.50	14.00	14.50	14.15	13.40	13.40	13.00	12.80	12.40	11.94	12.00	12.00	13.15
1993-4	12.25	12.45	15.65	21.95	24.00	24.00	23.88	23.80	24.00	23.70	22.00	20.00	20.65
1994-5	18.30	15.88	15.00	15.00	14.00	13.80	14.16	14.38	14.38	14.70	14.75	14.55	14.91
1995-6	15.44	17.50	20.25	20.13	20.00	20.00	19.88	19.25	19.13	19.38	19.40	19.50	19.15
1996-7	19.50	19.50	19.25	19.25	19.00	18.81	19.19	19.25	19.25	19.25	18.40	19.00	19.14
1997-8[2]	18.25	18.35	18.63	19.00	19.00	19.00	19.00	18.20	18.00	18.13	18.50	18.50	18.55

[1] U.S. No. 2--broken not to exceed 4%. [2] Preliminary. *Source: Economic Research Service, U.S. Department of Agriculture (ERS-USDA)*

Average Price Received by Farmers for Rice (Rough) in the U.S. In Dollars Per Hundred Pounds (Cwt.)

Year	Aug.	Sept.	Oct.	Nov.	Dec.	Jan.	Feb.	Mar.	Apr.	May	June	July	Average[2]
1989-90	7.41	7.59	7.41	7.03	7.05	7.44	7.57	7.55	7.41	7.28	7.18	7.05	7.35
1990-1	6.66	6.21	6.02	6.29	6.13	6.39	6.75	7.07	7.43	7.44	7.43	7.21	6.68
1991-2	7.16	7.67	7.65	7.84	7.98	7.84	7.97	7.78	7.46	7.18	6.97	6.99	7.58
1992-3	6.60	6.41	6.40	6.42	6.39	6.36	6.06	5.64	5.52	5.24	5.02	4.92	5.89
1993-4	5.19	5.21	6.10	8.06	8.91	8.98	10.10	10.20	9.93	10.00	8.88	7.80	7.98
1994-5	6.87	6.89	6.47	6.53	6.56	6.78	6.71	6.64	6.70	6.75	7.03	7.17	6.78
1995-6	7.64	7.95	8.77	9.12	9.36	9.33	9.10	9.31	9.34	9.69	9.74	9.68	9.15
1996-7	10.10	10.00	9.66	9.41	9.82	9.95	10.10	10.20	10.30	10.20	9.90	10.00	9.96
1997-8	9.94	9.85	10.00	9.71	9.67	9.52	9.66	9.55	9.30	9.41	9.51	9.57	9.64
1998-9[1]	8.95	9.35	9.25	8.98	9.06	9.12							9.19

[1] Preliminary. [2] Weighted average by sales. *Source: Economic Research Service, U.S. Department of Agriculture*

Salient Statistics of Rice, Rough & Milled (Rough Equivalent) in the United States In Millions of Cwt.

Crop Year Beginning August	Supply: Stocks August 1	Supply: Production	Supply: Imports	Supply: Total Supply	Disappearance: Domestic: Food	Domestic: Brewers	Domestic: Seed	Domestic: Total	Residual	Exports	Total Disappearance	CCC Stocks July 31	Government Support Program: Put Under Price Support	Loan Rate ($ Per Cwt.): Rough[3]: Long	Rough[3]: Medium	Rough[3]: All Classes	Milled Long
1993-4	39.4	156.1	6.9	202.5	71.2	14.3	4.3	89.8	11.6	75.3	176.7	0	30.9	6.67	6.11	6.50	10.75
1994-5	25.8	197.8	7.0	230.9	74.0	14.5	4.1	92.5	8.2	98.9	199.6	.1	131.2	6.64	6.13	6.50	10.72
1995-6	31.3	173.9	7.4	212.6	77.0	15.6	3.7	96.3	8.3	83.0	187.6	0	100.9	6.68	6.12	6.50	10.69
1996-7	25.0	171.3	10.0	206.3	80.0	15.4	4.0	99.4	1.3	78.4	179.1	0	68.9	6.68	6.17	6.50	10.77
1997-8[1]	27.2	178.9	9.2	215.3	82.0	15.4	4.0	101.4	1.0	85.2	187.6	0	67.6	6.67	6.14	6.50	10.69
1998-9[2]	27.7	180.4	10.0	218.0	83.5	15.4	4.0	102.9	5.5	85.0	193.4	0	64.3	6.68	6.14	6.50	10.71

[1] Preliminary. [2] Estimate. [3] Loan rate for each class of rice is the sum of the whole kernels' loan rate weighted by its milling yield (average 56%) and the broken kernels' loan rate weighted by its milling yield (average 12%). *Source: Economic Research Service, U.S. Department of Agriculture (ERS-USDA)*

Acreage, Yield, Production and Prices of Rice in the United States

Crop Year	Acreage Harvested (1,000 Acres): Southern States	Acreage Harvested: California	Acreage Harvested: United States	Yield Per Harvested Acre (In Lbs.): California	Yield: United States	Production (1,000 Cwt.): Southern States	Production: California	Production: United States	Value of Production $1,000	Wholesale Prices ($ Per Cwt.): Arkansas[2]	Wholesale Prices: Houston[3]	Milled Rice, Average C.I.F. at Rotterdam ($ Per Metric Ton): U.S. No. 2[4]	Thai "A"[5]	Thai "B"[5]
1993-4	2,396	437	2,833	8,300	5,510	119,839	36,271	156,110	1,246,875	21.15	20.75	413	413	335
1994-5	2,831	485	3,316	8,500	5,964	156,555	41,224	197,779	1,336,570	14.47	14.70	325	412	331
1995-6	2,628	465	3,093	7,600	5,621	138,519	35,352	173,871	1,587,236	19.10	19.15	404	-----	407
1996-7	2,304	500	2,804	7,490	6,120	134,140	37,459	171,599	1,690,270	19.02	20.95	428	-----	380
1997-8	2,587	516	3,103	8,250	5,897	140,446	42,546	182,992	1,756,136	18.14	19.61	417	-----	345
1998-9[1]	2,839	478	3,317	6,840	5,669	155,353	32,698	188,051	1,617,954	-----	-----	397	-----	385

[1] Preliminary. [2] F.O.B. mills, Arkansas, medium. [3] Houston, Texas (long grain). [4] Milled, 4%, container, FAS. 5 SWR, 100%, bulk. NA = Not available. *Source: Economic Research Service, U.S. Department of Agriculture (ERS-USDA)*

U.S. Exports of Milled Rice, by Country of Destination In Thousands of Metric Tons

Year Beginning October	Canada	Haiti	Iran	Ivory Coast	Jamaica	Mexico	Netherlands	Peru	Saudi Arabia	South Africa	Switzerland	United Kingdom	Total
1991-2	143.7	116.9	11.6	73.4	46.3	157.0	67.7	43.6	179.6	136.6	94.2	59.8	2,279
1992-3	146.0	152.9	184.3	107.3	39.4	241.5	120.9	61.6	223.5	122.1	71.2	72.2	2,710
1993-4	141.3	57.2	60.4	34.2	53.8	234.0	92.8	47.0	180.5	110.9	64.8	82.4	2,433
1994-5	160.0	210.2	240.6	92.0	88.5	309.6	170.3	81.8	176.1	106.1	91.2	58.7	3,763
1995-6	172.1	149.6	24.5	61.3	63.1	359.1	113.9	97.8	141.5	169.9	80.3	85.4	2,826
1996-7[1]	162.9	178.7	-----	35.6	27.4	381.3	54.0	35.1	150.9	108.5	64.2	101.0	2,560

[1] Preliminary. [2] Formerly part of the U.S.S.R.; data not reported separately until 1992. *Source: Economic Research Service, U.S. Department of Agriculture*

U.S. Exports of Rice, by Export Program In Thousands of Metric Tons

Fiscal Year	PL 480	Section 416	CCC Credit Programs[2]	CCC African Relief Exports	EEP[3]	Export Programs[4]	Exports Outside Specified Export Programs	Total U.S. Rice Exports	% Export Programs as a Share of Total Exports
1993	199	0	235	0	278	850	1,860	2,710	31
1994	222	0	155	0	46	433	2,001	2,434	18
1995	196	0	321	0	113	644	3,123	3,767	17
1996	182	0	215	0	23	420	2,411	2,831	15
1997	116	0	89	0	0	205	2,359	2,564	8
1998[1]	183	0	80	0	0	263	2,837	3,100	9

[1] Preliminary. [2] May not completely reflect exports made under these programs. [3] Sales not shipments. [4] Adjusted for estimated overlap between CCC export credit and EEP shipments. *Source: Economic Research Service, U.S. Department of Agriculture*

Production of Rice (Rough) in the United States, by Type and Variety In Thousands of Cwt.

Year	Long Grain	Medium Grain	Short Grain	Total	Year	Long Grain	Medium Grain	Short Grain	Total
1989	109,161	41,441	3,885	154,487	1994	133,445	63,390	944	197,779
1990	107,806	47,328	954	156,088	1995	121,730	51,241	900	173,871
1991	109,137	47,567	753	157,457	1996	113,629	56,901	1,069	171,599
1992	128,015	50,633	1,010	179,658	1997	124,485	57,091	1,416	182,992
1993	103,064	51,873	1,173	156,110	1998[1]	141,624	44,453	1,974	188,051

[1] Preliminary. *Source: National Agricultural Statistics Service, U.S. Department of Agriculture (NASS-USDA)*

Rubber

According to the International Rubber Study Group, world production of natural rubber in 1997 was 6.41 million metric tonnes. That represented an increase of 1 percent from 1996. Estates production of natural rubber in 1997 was 1.68 million tonnes, the same level as in 1996. Smallholdings production of rubber was 4.73 million tonnes, almost 2 percent more than in 1996. In the January-May 1998 period, world production of natural rubber was 2.56 million tonnes. Estates production of rubber in the same period was 690,000 tonnes. Smallholdings production was 1.87 million tonnes.

World consumption of natural rubber in 1997 was 6.57 million tonnes, an increase of 7 percent from 1996. In the January-May 1998 period, consumption of natural rubber was 2.79 million tonnes. Producer stocks of natural rubber at the end of May 1998 were 460,000 tonnes, some 2 percent less than a year before. Consumer's reported stocks of rubber at the end of May 1998 were 388,000 tonnes, up 14 percent from the year before. Consumer's total stocks of rubber in May 1998 were 660,000 tonnes, down 8 percent from a year earlier. Stocks afloat in May 1998 were 340,000 tonnes compared to 480,000 tonnes a year before. World stocks of natural rubber in May 1998 were 1.46 million tonnes, 13 percent less than the stocks in May 1997.

World production of synthetic rubber in 1997 was 10.06 million tonnes. That was almost 3 percent above 1996. Production of synthetic rubber in the January-May 1998 period was 4.29 million tonnes. Global consumption of synthetic rubber in 1997 was 10.05 million tonnes, up almost 5 percent from 1996. In the first five months of 1998, world consumption of synthetic rubber was 4.25 million tonnes.

Reported world stocks of synthetic rubber at the end of May 1997 were 1.13 million tonnes. At the end of May 1997 they were 1.09 million tonnes. Russian Federation stocks of synthetic rubber in May 1998 were 100,000 tonnes. That represented a substantial decline from a year earlier when stocks were 210,000 tonnes. China's stocks of synthetic rubber at the end of May 1998 were 80,000 tonnes. That was down from the May 1997 stock level of 110,000 tonnes. Stocks elsewhere were 830,000 tonnes or some 19 percent more than the year before. Stocks afloat were 260,000 tonnes at the end of May 1998. World stocks of synthetic rubber in May 1998 were 2.40 million tonnes, up 2 percent from the year before.

U.S. consumption of natural rubber and synthetic rubber in 1997 was 3.38 million tonnes, an increase of 6 percent from 1996. In the first half of 1998, U.S. consumption of synthetic and natural rubber was 1.76 million tonnes. China's consumption of natural and synthetic rubber in 1997 was 1.94 million tonnes, up 15 percent from the year before. Japan's consumption in 1997 was 1.88 million tonnes, an increase of 2 percent from 1996. Russian Federation consumption of rubber in 1997 was 534,000 tonnes, up 18 percent from the year before. Other large users of rubber were Germany, France and Brazil.

U.S. reported stocks of natural rubber held by consumers in May 1998 were 58.4 million pounds, up almost 6 percent from the year before. The U.S. stockpile of natural rubber from the Defense Logistics Agency in June 1998 was 70.3 million pounds. U.S. reported stocks of synthetic rubber in June 1998 were 405.8 million pounds, about the same as a year before.

The major producers of natural rubber are Thailand, Indonesia and Malaysia. Thailand's production of natural rubber in 1997 was 2.03 million tonnes, an increase of 3 percent from 1996. Production of natural rubber by Indonesia in 1997 was 1.58 million tonnes, an increase of 3 percent from 1997. Malaysia production in 1997 was 971,100 tonnes or 10 percent less than in 1996. Other producers of natural rubber include Sri Lanka, Vietnam, China, India and the Ivory Coast.

The major exporters of natural rubber are also the largest producers. Thailand's net exports of natural rubber in 1997 were 1.84 million tonnes. Malaysia exported 586,800 tonnes while Indonesia exported 1.40 million tonnes. Other large exporters are Vietnam, Sri Lanka and Liberia.

Futures Markets

Rubber futures are traded on the Kobe Rubber Exchange (KRE), the Tokyo Commodity Exchange, (TOCOM), the Kuala Lumpur Commodity Exchange (KLCE), and the Singapore Commodity Exchange Ltd.

U.S. Imports of Natural Rubber (Includes Latex & Guayule) In Thousands of Metric Tons

Year	Jan.	Feb.	Mar.	Apr.	May	June	July	Aug.	Sept.	Oct.	Nov.	Dec.	Total
1989	99.3	52.2	99.1	74.6	87.5	63.8	77.9	65.6	69.1	69.5	78.9	69.1	880.9
1990	72.3	58.6	81.9	63.1	89.5	77.7	60.4	61.0	83.0	55.7	81.7	75.7	820.1
1991	59.9	54.1	69.5	90.9	59.6	56.7	53.4	52.4	65.5	74.4	71.3	68.9	776.2
1992	77.5	75.2	84.7	64.7	79.0	73.8	80.5	77.2	73.9	81.3	68.1	77.5	913.4
1993	95.3	79.9	93.9	86.3	74.1	81.2	83.6	77.8	69.2	73.4	86.0	86.9	987.6
1994	87.5	74.7	102.6	78.9	88.3	77.8	66.7	85.0	78.8	89.3	70.0	76.0	975.6
1995	81.7	86.9	102.3	90.2	94.1	93.4	78.0	81.0	81.5	89.2	79.1	68.7	1,026.1
1996	105.4	86.1	82.2	90.6	65.1	70.4	79.0	81.0	82.1	113.6	73.5	85.0	1,014.0
1997	94.2	92.0	93.9	88.2	93.0	65.1	76.8	90.1	87.5	86.8	87.6	89.0	1,044.2
1998[1]	104.4	76.6	102.8	81.0	98.0	92.9	96.4	100.8					1,129.4

[1] Preliminary. *Source: International Rubber Study Group (IRSG)*

World Production[1] of Rubber In Thousands of Metric Tons

Year	Natural: China	India	Indo-nesia	Malaysia	Sri Lanka	Thailand	Vietnam	World Total	Synthetic: Ger-many	Japan	United States	Russia[3]	World Total
1988	239.8	254.8	1,235.0	1,661.6	122.4	978.9	60.0	5,020	499.6	1,298.8	2,334.7	2,435	10,160
1989	242.8	288.6	1,256.0	1,415.6	110.7	1,178.9	85.0	5,150	507.6	1,352.7	2,261.4	2,358	10,150
1990	264.2	323.5	1,262.0	1,291.0	113.1	1,275.3	103.0	5,120	524.5	1,425.8	2,114.5	2,277	9,910
1991	296.4	360.2	1,284.0	1,255.7	103.9	1,341.2	87.0	5,170	504.4	1,377.3	2,050.0	2,105	9,270
1992	309.3	383.0	1,387.0	1,173.2	106.1	1,531.0	114.0	5,440	544.7	1,389.9	2,300.0	1,611	9,300
1993	326.1	428.1	1,301.3	1,074.3	104.2	1,553.4	97.0	5,290	569.7	1,309.8	2,180.0	1,103	8,600
1994	374.0	464.0	1,360.8	1,100.6	105.3	1,717.9	121.0	5,710	621.6	1,349.0	2,390.0	632	8,880
1995	424.0	499.6	1,466.8	1,089.3	105.7	1,804.8	123.0	6,040	480.0	1,497.6	2,530.0	837	9,510
1996	430.0	540.1	1,543.0	1,082.5	112.5	1,970.0	123.0	6,330	548.1	1,519.9	2,486.0	775	9,780
1997[2]	444.0	563.6	1,551.8	971.1	105.8	2,029.6	124.0	6,370	555.1	1,591.5	2,620.0	730	10,110

[1] Including rubber in the form of latex. [2] Preliminary. *Source: International Rubber Study Group (IRSG)*

World Consumption of Natural and Synthetic Rubber In Thousands of Metric Tons

Year	Natural: Brazil	France	Ger-many	Japan	United Kingdom	United States	World Total	Synthetic: France	Ger-many	Japan	United Kingdom	United States	World Total
1988	125.3	181.0	203.6	623.0	140.0	858.3	5,100	315.0	471.0	1,042.0	226.5	2,016.8	9,940
1989	124.3	184.0	221.1	657.0	132.5	866.9	5,190	358.0	476.0	1,103.0	240.0	2,051.0	10,070
1990	121.3	179.0	208.7	677.0	136.0	807.5	5,200	351.0	511.0	1,133.0	223.0	1,820.8	9,710
1991	125.0	183.0	210.7	689.5	119.0	755.8	5,100	342.0	502.0	1,118.5	201.0	1,768.1	9,310
1992	123.4	179.0	212.8	685.4	124.5	910.2	5,320	365.4	506.0	1,080.6	231.0	1,959.6	9,380
1993	131.7	168.5	174.9	631.0	119.0	966.7	5,440	314.7	488.0	1,022.0	212.0	2,001.0	8,640
1994	144.7	179.8	186.4	639.8	135.0	1,001.7	5,680	400.1	512.2	1,026.2	217.0	2,117.6	8,820
1995	155.2	176.0	211.7	692.0	118.0	1,003.9	6,000	430.2	426.4	1,085.0	226.0	2,172.0	9,290
1996	145.0	182.2	193.0	714.5	112.0	1,001.7	6,130	436.1	478.0	1,124.5	230.0	2,186.6	9,590
1997[1]	150.0	192.3	212.0	713.0	120.0	1,066.8	6,580	416.2	504.0	1,163.0	234.0	2,316.1	10,150

[1] Preliminary. *Source: International Rubber Study Group (IRSG)*

World Stocks of Natural & Synthetic Rubber (by Countries) on January 1 In Thousands of Metric Tons

Year	Total Synthetic	In Producing Countries: Africa	Indo-nesia	Malaysia	Sri Lanka	Thailand	Vietnam	Total Natural	In Consuming Countries (Reported Stocks): Brazil	India	Japan	United States	Total
1989	1,800	23.2	100	286.5	23.2	53.0	6.0	540	20.5	80.9	97.2	61.7	260
1990	988	26.9	110	248.3	27.0	53.7	8.0	510	16.0	78.4	105.6	92.0	292
1991	1,011	21.7	114	190.3	29.8	83.7	11.0	490	12.0	92.9	91.6	94.3	291
1992	973	24.4	68	196.1	17.3	89.3	9.0	460	9.0	106.0	92.7	109.4	317
1993	982	19.6	110	187.2	16.0	89.0	12.0	540	17.0	90.9	82.9	108.0	442
1994	924	21.6	80	159.2	17.2	115.4	9.0	520	25.0	96.4	85.4	71.3	410
1995	888	16.9	80	187.0	16.5	96.1	11.0	430	17.0	94.1	72.9	45.2	363
1996	1,002	21.2	90	175.6	17.0	112.2	12.0	460	13.0	127.4	77.1	67.1	414
1997	1,065	21.5	60	190.3	17.6	145.5	12.0	470	7.0	123.4	86.8	79.3	419
1998[1]	1,092	25.1	60	231.8	17.9	158.0	12.0	530	6.0	138.0	87.2	57.2	359

[1] Preliminary. *Source: International Rubber Study Group (IRSG)*

Net Exports of Natural Rubber from Producing Areas In Thousands of Metric Tons

Year	Cambodia	Guat-emala	Indonesia	Liberia	Malaysia	Nigeria	Sri Lanka	Thailand	Vietnam	Other Africa[2]	Other Asia[3]	World Total
1988	21.0	9.8	1,132.0	105.6	1,563.6	65.8	99.3	906.4	37.9	107.0	36.8	4,070
1989	32.0	11.0	1,151.8	106.0	1,364.8	101.3	86.0	1,100.6	57.7	115.0	38.2	4,170
1990	28.0	13.4	1,077.3	19.0	1,185.6	121.0	86.7	1,150.8	75.9	118.0	37.6	3,990
1991	21.0	14.3	1,220.0	32.0	1,041.2	63.0	76.4	1,231.9	62.9	126.0	44.0	3,950
1992	20.0	15.7	1,268.1	30.0	939.1	70.4	78.6	1,412.9	80.9	135.0	44.6	4,060
1993	21.0	16.9	1,214.3	45.0	769.8	79.7	69.6	1,396.8	65.0	134.0	52.8	3,840
1994	32.0	22.3	1,244.8	31.0	782.1	49.6	69.1	1,605.0	80.0	143.0	63.9	4,200
1995	30.0	23.2	1,323.8	13.0	777.5	99.2	68.2	1,635.5	82.0	142.0	60.5	4,260
1996	31.0	29.2	1,434.3	13.5	709.8	69.0	72.1	1,763.0	83.0	175.0	70.2	4,450
1997[1]	32.0	30.0	1,403.8	49.2	586.8	68.0	61.4	1,837.1	81.0	184.0	74.8	4,410

[1] Preliminary. [2] Includes Cameroon, Cote d'Ivoire, Gabon, Ghana and Zaire. [3] Includes Myanmar, Papua New Guinea and the Philippines.
Source: International Rubber Study Group (IRSG)

RUBBER

Average Spot Crude Rubber Prices (Smoked Sheets[1]) in New York In Cents Per Pound

Year	Jan.	Feb.	Mar.	Apr.	May	June	July	Aug.	Sept.	Oct.	Nov.	Dec.	Average
1989	55.95	59.34	56.69	55.23	52.07	49.50	49.20	47.21	46.13	46.09	45.63	44.84	50.66
1990	44.72	45.75	45.92	45.64	45.80	46.00	45.80	47.46	48.43	46.50	46.23	47.03	46.27
1991	47.47	48.92	48.09	45.92	45.17	45.26	44.59	44.45	44.25	44.52	44.75	44.16	45.63
1992	43.11	43.95	44.50	45.86	46.41	46.57	46.78	47.05	46.86	47.83	48.00	48.03	46.25
1993	48.51	48.30	46.41	44.15	43.78	43.78	43.30	43.85	44.54	44.23	44.90	44.70	45.04
1994	44.92	46.11	49.62	50.83	51.43	55.13	62.49	66.35	67.15	73.51	71.76	77.35	59.72
1995	85.68	92.61	94.15	93.43	89.50	80.57	72.13	68.54	70.70	73.59	83.19	83.39	82.29
1996	80.25	79.90	79.76	75.08	76.99	75.10	71.03	69.13	68.75	66.32	66.32	66.14	72.90
1997	65.06	64.76	63.53	59.97	57.71	57.30	51.96	52.45	51.89	51.36	47.99	40.53	55.38
1998	40.21	43.96	41.70	41.23	42.65	41.28	40.03	38.58	38.62	40.26	39.96	38.20	40.56

[1] No. 1 ribbed, plantation rubber. *Source: Wall Street Journal*

Natural Rubber Prices in London In British Pounds Per Metric Ton

Year	Jan.	Feb.	Mar.	Apr.	May	June	July	Aug.	Sept.	Oct.	Nov.	Dec.	Average
Buyers' Price RSS 1 (CIF)													
1995	1,141.9	1,170.8	1,209.6	1,189.2	1,174.9	1,004.9	894.9	886.0	921.4	946.7	1,082.6	1,099.7	1,060.2
1996	1,063.1	1,066.1	1,057.3	990.8	1,025.1	999.6	912.0	881.2	880.5	829.8	803.3	800.3	942.4
1997	777.6	783.6	800.9	731.3	715.1	699.6	605.9	604.1	592.5	573.9	525.9	461.4	654.3
1998	464.6	516.9	470.7	473.3	487.0	461.5	473.8	456.6	469.3	490.2			476.4
Buyers' Prices RSS 3 (CIF)													
1995	1,122.9	1,157.0	1,188.2	1,174.2	1,161.0	988.2	882.7	859.2	911.3	941.4	1,074.2	1,093.6	1,046.2
1996	1,057.3	1,058.6	1,049.9	981.4	1,015.5	984.6	895.2	863.0	862.0	814.7	790.7	782.1	929.6
1997	762.2	769.4	788.7	721.3	708.9	696.9	588.7	592.1	575.8	553.0	490.1	411.4	636.5
1998	416.0	500.3	445.5	465.6	480.7	451.0	466.3	439.1	454.3	478.0			459.7
Sellers' Prices SMR 20 (CIF)													
1995	1,227.5	1,228.8	1,151.5	1,116.9	1,053.0	926.3	796.9	839.1	871.2	887.5	1,066.5	1,065.0	1,019.2
1996	1,059.5	1,019.4	1,006.3	915.0	894.0	838.1	821.0	830.6	844.4	814.5	778.8	777.5	883.3
1997	767.5	769.4	765.0	697.5	663.1	653.8	597.0	600.0	580.6	567.5	530.0	468.3	640.7
1998	477.5	539.4	485.0	487.0	495.0	438.8	417.0	396.3	403.0	416.9			455.6

Source: International Rubber Study Group (IRSG)

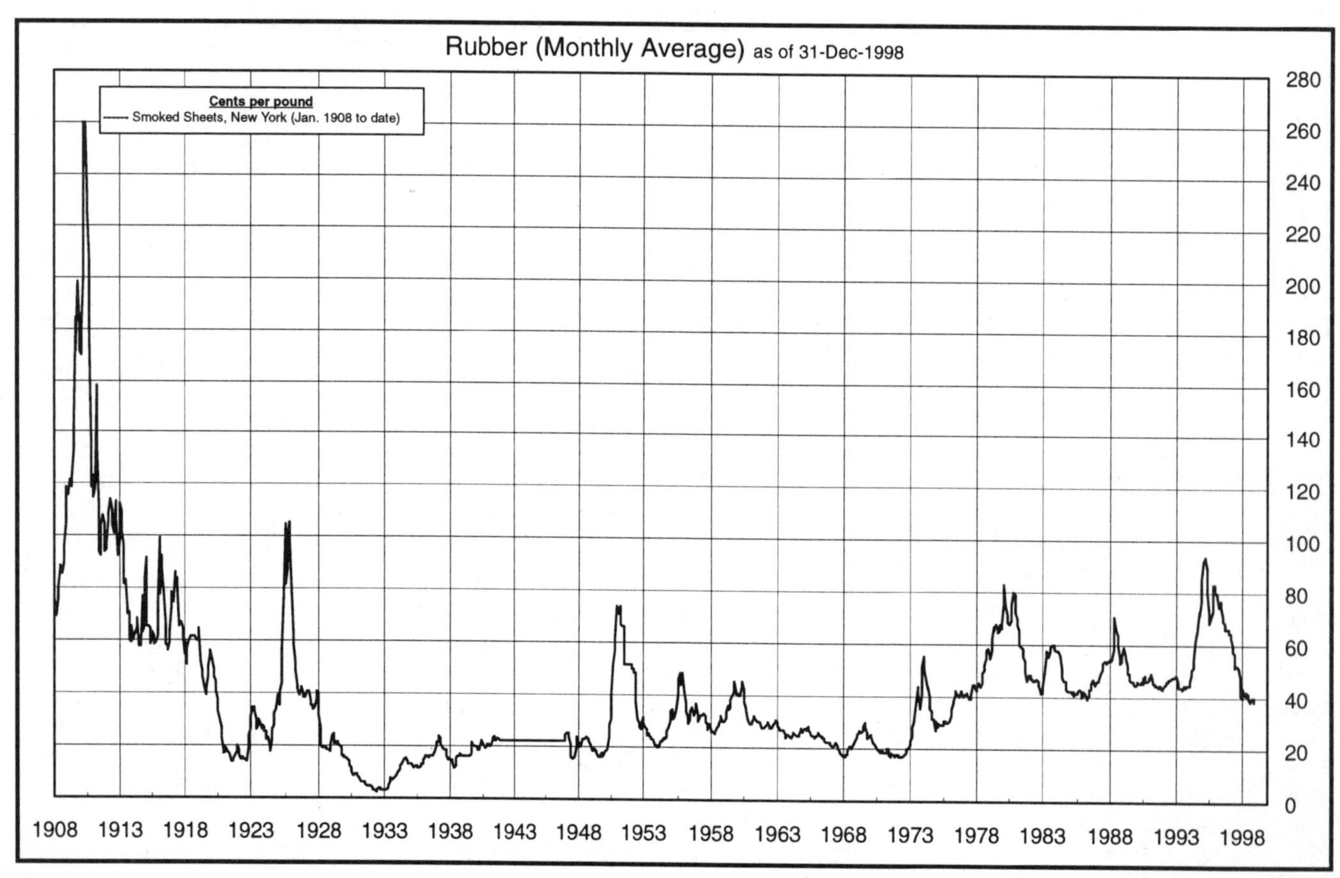

Consumption of Natural Rubber in the United States In Thousands of Metric Tons

Year	Jan.	Feb.	Mar.	Apr.	May	June	July	Aug.	Sept.	Oct.	Nov.	Dec.	Total
1989	89.9	51.1	96.6	68.4	87.9	65.1	82.7	70.8	72.0	62.1	84.6	50.9	866.9
1990	62.6	57.3	79.0	65.2	87.4	73.9	57.4	74.1	78.8	59.8	75.6	69.8	807.5
1991	60.0	60.0	65.0	65.0	65.0	60.0	55.0	55.0	65.0	70.0	65.0	66.0	755.8
1992	83.4	63.3	85.9	66.9	80.6	78.6	82.6	79.5	70.2	84.6	64.4	70.2	910.2
1993	96.3	76.0	93.4	93.4	67.9	76.8	77.3	84.9	72.0	73.6	82.9	72.2	966.7
1994	92.8	84.9	93.1	82.7	89.6	84.6	76.2	87.8	74.8	90.1	66.4	78.7	1,001.7
1995	70.5	75.8	98.4	90.3	92.2	93.3	85.0	82.7	83.1	89.9	81.4	61.3	1,003.9
1996	102.5	85.8	81.2	87.9	65.6	76.7	81.9	88.1	83.3	108.4	72.1	68.2	1,001.7
1997	94.2	92.0	93.9	88.2	93.0	65.1	76.8	90.1	87.5	86.8	87.5	89.0	1,044.1
1998[1]	104.5	76.6	102.7	81.0	98.0	92.9	96.4	100.7					1,129.2

[1] Preliminary. *Source: International Rubber Study Group (IRSG)*

Stocks of Natural Rubber in the United States, on First of Month In Thousands of Metric Tons

Year	Jan.	Feb.	Mar.	Apr.	May	June	July	Aug.	Sept.	Oct.	Nov.	Dec.
1989	61.7	71.1	67.5	77.4	82.2	86.7	86.2	86.2	88.1	83.3	87.7	83.9
1990	92.0	100.2	100.2	101.6	97.1	97.3	99.8	101.6	87.2	90.3	84.7	89.6
1991	94.3	94.0	88.0	93.0	119.0	113.0	110.0	108.0	106.0	106.0	110.0	117.0
1992	109.4	103.6	112.7	110.4	107.5	105.9	101.1	99.0	96.7	100.3	97.0	100.7
1993	108.0	49.4	53.3	53.7	46.7	52.9	57.3	63.6	56.5	53.7	53.4	56.5
1994	71.3	65.9	55.7	65.2	61.4	60.0	53.2	43.8	41.0	45.0	44.2	47.8
1995	45.2	56.4	67.5	71.4	71.2	72.6	73.0	66.0	64.4	62.8	62.1	59.8
1996	67.1	70.0	70.3	71.2	73.9	73.4	67.1	64.2	57.2	56.0	61.1	62.4
1997	79.3	74.2	74.2	76.9	77.5	62.2	55.2	53.6	52.1	51.2	52.4	55.2
1998[1]	57.2	61.2	65.5	63.5	60.9	66.7	53.6	57.9	54.7			

[1] Preliminary. *Source: International Rubber Study Group (IRSG)*

Stocks of Synthetic Rubber in the United States, on First of Month In Thousands of Metric Tons

Year	Jan.	Feb.	Mar.	Apr.	May	June	July	Aug.	Sept.	Oct.	Nov.	Dec.
1989	276.3	288.9	287.7	294.4	289.6	300.4	303.7	308.7	314.1	323.4	329.6	414.8
1990	404.0	393.5	392.5	385.8	406.8	397.5	395.0	414.9	420.8	419.6	405.0	393.9
1991	403.7	406.0	403.0	404.0	402.0	388.0	394.0	385.0	356.0	334.0	330.0	325.0
1992	403.7	386.0	381.2	383.9	393.2	389.2	372.8	382.7	382.1	375.1	378.6	401.1
1993	406.9	345.9	345.7	346.0	340.5	351.8	342.1	341.6	333.6	326.4	319.9	321.4
1994	331.1	313.3	313.3	307.9	306.0	314.2	302.5	323.2	318.5	304.6	299.4	299.5
1995	305.4	307.4	302.8	293.5	319.4	315.6	325.9	349.2	355.7	354.6	347.0	351.5
1996	366.2	355.3	342.0	354.8	365.4	360.0	367.0	377.3	366.0	362.8	354.1	370.6
1997	400.0	402.5	402.6	410.7	415.0	412.0	406.1	397.1	382.6	386.8	374.9	377.8
1998[1]	392.3	402.5	389.7	392.8	400.0	414.8	405.8	417.3	403.7			

[1] Preliminary. *Source: International Rubber Study Group (IRSG)*

Production of Synthetic Rubber in the United States In Thousands of Metric Tons

Year	Jan.	Feb.	Mar.	Apr.	May	June	July	Aug.	Sept.	Oct.	Nov.	Dec.	Total
1989	206.3	177.5	193.6	174.1	179.7	175.0	186.2	164.2	176.0	191.0	182.9	194.8	2,261
1990	173.5	180.1	182.5	187.8	174.6	172.0	171.9	180.9	180.4	190.3	167.4	153.1	2,115
1991	168.0	163.0	184.0	174.0	173.0	159.0	154.0	133.0	159.0	159.0	173.0	164.0	2,050
1992	180.0	190.0	200.0	210.0	200.0	190.0	190.0	200.0	210.0	200.0	195.0	175.0	2,300
1993	120.0	160.0	220.0	190.0	200.0	180.0	190.0	180.0	180.0	180.0	190.0	180.0	2,180
1994	180.0	180.0	210.0	200.0	210.0	200.0	200.0	210.0	190.0	210.0	200.0	200.0	2,390
1995	220.0	200.0	210.0	210.0	240.0	220.0	210.0	230.0	210.0	200.0	200.0	190.0	2,540
1996	200.0	190.0	220.0	210.0	200.0	210.0	200.0	210.0	200.0	210.0	220.0	216.0	2,486
1997	220.0	200.0	220.0	230.0	220.0	200.0	220.0	220.0	230.0	210.0	210.0	203.0	2,589
1998[1]	230.0	200.0	230.0	220.0	240.0	210.0	220.0	210.0					2,640

[1] Preliminary. *Source: International Rubber Study Group (IRSG)*

RUBBER

Consumption of Synthetic Rubber in the United States In Thousands of Metric Tons

Year	Jan.	Feb.	Mar.	Apr.	May	June	July	Aug.	Sept.	Oct.	Nov.	Dec.	Total
1989	158.5	166.8	186.8	163.1	172.1	166.3	160.9	171.1	162.5	170.6	180.5	150.5	2,051
1990	159.6	158.7	161.6	144.1	161.5	151.6	137.1	149.5	155.6	175.3	147.1	119.1	1,821
1991	145.0	140.0	160.0	150.0	160.0	135.0	140.0	140.0	160.0	140.0	150.0	149.0	1,768
1992	167.8	159.5	174.7	158.9	162.6	184.2	154.5	177.7	180.2	171.5	155.1	148.2	1,960
1993	161.3	154.4	189.4	172.8	164.5	173.6	166.0	173.9	162.0	169.4	162.3	151.4	2,001
1994	177.7	160.8	191.8	173.0	173.5	187.5	164.9	187.1	176.0	178.8	175.7	170.8	2,118
1995	188.6	182.2	194.3	179.1	212.7	188.7	160.0	190.7	182.4	178.1	169.7	145.5	2,172
1996	188.0	173.7	186.9	176.8	184.9	178.5	177.0	197.3	182.9	201.0	177.8	165.5	2,187
1997	191.6	181.2	189.9	187.9	195.2	185.1	203.9	206.2	201.6	200.9	179.7	186.9	2,310
1998[1]	196.7	192.8	215.5	195.2	200.3	202.1	192.8	205.6					2,402

[1] Preliminary. *Source: International Rubber Study Group (IRSG)*

Exports of Synthetic Rubber in the United States In Thousands of Metric Tons

Year	Jan.	Feb.	Mar.	Apr.	May	June	July	Aug.	Sept.	Oct.	Nov.	Dec.	Total
1989	42.4	45.7	55.0	41.3	54.4	51.3	43.7	48.2	54.5	54.6	43.6	44.4	450.6
1990	45.6	39.0	50.2	42.6	42.7	41.0	37.4	43.1	42.0	50.8	50.3	39.0	523.7
1991	43.8	46.1	44.0	45.2	47.9	40.4	42.8	43.2	43.1	46.3	47.3	42.2	532.3
1992	52.3	55.1	51.3	59.1	58.2	51.6	46.5	52.8	58.0	51.4	48.1	39.7	624.1
1993	47.1	34.1	57.7	47.4	52.4	46.9	46.9	43.8	48.8	46.6	49.0	41.9	562.6
1994	48.8	46.4	55.4	57.0	52.4	49.6	50.2	62.8	60.7	59.9	56.9	55.0	655.1
1995	54.9	51.6	62.7	55.6	58.6	58.6	50.0	54.9	53.0	60.4	53.9	52.6	666.8
1996	61.1	57.7	64.0	68.0	48.2	66.8	62.3	57.1	63.9	65.2	58.6	58.6	731.5
1997	63.1	58.2	57.5	74.2	66.9	61.6	64.1	70.0	65.6	65.6	63.0	58.7	768.5
1998[1]	61.1	60.8	62.8	59.8	66.9	61.8	60.1	64.4					746.6

[1] Preliminary. *Source: International Rubber Study Group (IRSG)*

Production of Tyres (Car and Truck) in the United States In Thousands of Units

Year	First Quarter	Second Quarter	Third Quarter	Fourth Quarter	Total	Year	First Quarter	Second Quarter	Third Quarter	Fourth Quarter	Total
1980	45,329	35,764	36,174	41,997	159,263	1989	56,716	56,626	50,086	49,444	212,870
1981	47,853	46,042	45,658	42,209	181,762	1990	55,915	53,856	51,163	49,729	210,663
1982	47,304	45,602	42,656	42,938	178,500	1991	51,296	52,796	49,183	51,115	202,391
1983	45,859	47,451	45,370	47,353	186,923	1992	57,890	57,319	57,554	57,487	230,250
1984	53,369	53,588	50,957	51,463	209,375	1993	61,809	60,752	57,702	57,184	237,447
1985	54,460	49,385	46,468	46,610	196,923	1994	63,586	63,331	57,018	59,442	243,696
1986	49,240	45,687	46,855	48,507	190,289	1995	63,800	63,800	63,800	63,754	255,521
1987	51,205	50,210	49,723	51,839	202,978	1996	64,000	64,000	64,000	63,700	255,723
1988	54,677	52,986	51,195	52,493	211,351	1997[1]					264,020

[1] Preliminary. [2] Estimate. *Source: International Rubber Study Group (IRSG)*

Foreign Trade of Tyres (Car and Truck) in the United States In Thousands of Units

	Imports					Exports				
Year	First Quarter	Second Quarter	Third Quarter	Fourth Quarter	Total	First Quarter	Second Quarter	Third Quarter	Fourth Quarter	Total
1988	11,383	12,059	12,383	12,783	48,608	4,203	4,120	3,712	4,034	16,069
1989	12,802	14,518	12,609	12,749	52,678	4,104	4,254	5,267	4,704	18,329
1990	13,713	13,564	11,951	11,633	50,861	5,453	5,532	6,031	6,730	23,746
1991	12,011	13,008	11,320	10,158	46,497	6,407	6,388	6,623	6,342	25,760
1992	10,760	12,496	11,850	12,285	47,391	6,243	6,475	7,125	6,646	26,489
1993	11,519	13,045	12,688	13,036	50,288	7,266	6,930	7,163	7,133	28,492
1995	14,883	14,977	13,762	12,718	56,340	8,438	8,502	8,478	9,174	34,592
1996	13,163	13,864	12,543	13,186	52,756	8,244	10,013	8,672	9,401	36,330
1997[1]	13,359	14,487	15,314	16,064	59,224	9,466	11,386	10,456	11,085	42,393
1998[2]	17,046	17,728				12,840	10,678			

[1] Preliminary. [2] Estimate. *Source: International Rubber Study Group (IRSG)*

Rye

The world's rye production is insignificant relative to other grains, with U.S. production in recent years accounting for about 1 percent of the world's output. However, the annual slippage in world and U.S. rye production into the first half of the 1990's has since shown some signs of stabilizing, although it's unlikely that any viable recovery in output is taking root. In the U.S., rye is a minor crop within the small grain complex (includes oats, barley and wheat) and likely to remain so, but the U.S. is apt to stay a net importer of rye.

The major producing states are Georgia, the Dakotas and Oklahoma, the four accounting for about half of 1998/99's (June/May) total production of 12.8 million bushels vs. a record low 8.9 million in 1997/98. Although production increased about 4 million bushels (100,000 tonnes) for the 1998/99 crop due to a moderate rise in both acreage and average yield, the crop's 44 percent year to year statistical increase does not hide the fact that U.S. production is still well under the annual average of the 1980's. Moreover, production is erratic: Georgia's 1998 crop of 1 million bushels compares with 1.8 million in 1996, while Oklahoma's crop of 1.9 million in 1998 is twice that of 1996. In the U.S. rye is used as an animal feed and as an ingredient in bread and some whiskeys, with about a third of the total supply used as a feedstuff, a third as a foodstuff, and the balance as seed and for whisky. U.S. rye exports are minimal as are carryover stocks. The contraction in U.S. supply/demand statistics reflects the lack of interest towards the grain by producers and users alike; only about 1.5 million acres are now allocated to rye vs. 5 million acres to oats and 70 million to wheat.

Production on a world basis, as of the mid-1990's, appears to have stabilized in the 20 to 25 million metric tonne range, but still pales against the mid-1980's average of more than 30 million tonnes. World production in 1998/99 of 22.2 million metric tonnes compares with the previous two crop years of 24.4 and 22.3 million tonnes, respectively, reflecting relatively steady acreage and average yield during the past few years. Eastern Europe is the major producing area with more than half the world's crop: 14.4 million tonnes in 1998/99 with Poland accounting for 5.9 million tonnes vs. 5.3 million in 1997/98. Russia, once the world's largest producer, saw its crop fall to 4.5 million tonnes in 1998/99 vs. 7.5 million in 1997/98, the decline reflecting an average yield of only 1.13 metric tonnes per hectare vs. 1.88 in 1997/98. Within the European Union, Germany's production of 4.7 million tonnes in 1998/99 compares with 4.6 million in 1997/98. Canada, whose output is not much larger than the U.S., exports most of its crop to the U.S.

World trade in 1998/99 (October/September) of 1.9 million metric tonnes compares with less than a million tonnes in 1997/98 and 1.4 million in 1996/97. Canada is now the largest exporter, 200,000 tonnes in 1998/99. Importing nations are more numerous, but focused on Japan, China and Korea. U.S. imports are fairly consistent at about 100,000 tonnes.

World Production of Rye In Thousands of Metric Tons

Crop Year	Austria	Canada	Czech Republic[5]	Denmark	France	Germany	Poland	Russia[4]	Spain	Turkey	Ukraine[4]	United States	World Total
1989-90	381	873	708	487	270	3,867	6,216	-----	336	320	18,288	347	33,412
1990-1	396	599	736	545	240	3,988	6,044	-----	267	240	21,193	258	36,861
1991-2	350	339	484	395	210	3,324	5,899	-----	242	240	14,061	248	27,359
1992-3	278	265	255	308	205	2,422	3,981	13,890	230	240	1,160	304	28,656
1993-4	290	320	300	323	190	2,984	5,000	9,150	300	230	1,180	263	26,090
1994-5	320	400	280	380	180	3,450	5,300	6,000	220	250	940	290	21,890
1995-6	310	310	260	500	200	4,520	6,290	4,100	170	260	1,210	260	21,890
1996-7[1]	150	310	200	340	230	4,210	5,650	5,900	300	250	1,100	230	22,230
1997-8[2]	210	320	260	450	210	4,580	5,300	7,500	230	250	1,350	230	24,440
1998-9[3]	200	390	260	500	210	4,740	5,900	4,500	230	250	1,400	330	21,970

[1] Preliminary. [2] Estimate. [3] Forecast. [4] Formerly part of the U.S.S.R.; data not reported separately until 1992. [5] Formerly part of Czechoslovakia; data not reported separately until 1992. *Source: Foreign Agricultural Service, U.S. Department of Agriculture (FAS-USDA)*

Production of Rye in the United States, by States In Thousands of Bushels

Year	Georgia	Kansas	Michigan	Minnesota	Nebraska	North Dakota	Oklahoma	Penns-ylvania	South Carolina	South Dakota	Texas	Wisconsin	Total
1989	1,610	80	825	1,088	600	1,064	532	576	644	3,240	126	360	13,647
1990	1,320	130	580	868	750	780	420	496	594	1,870	140	465	10,176
1991	1,300	115	360	648	1,000	992	665	297	630	1,152	228	435	9,761
1992	1,560	130	496	720	1,040	1,496	798	720	675	1,666	280	330	11,952
1993	1,380	693	420	667	500	1,050	660	340	380	1,600	363	260	10,340
1994	1,890	325	442	810	546	700	945	320	600	1,485	435	875	11,341
1995	1,155	400	544	609	480	726	810	330	440	1,650	380	480	10,064
1996	1,820	150	351	480	323	528	975	216	520	1,476	190	384	8,936
1997	1,430	300	450	400	240	513	1,080	400	250	728	330	432	8,132
1998[1]	1,050	375	420	837	288	2,196	1,540	495	400	1,400	400	360	11,795

[1] Preliminary. *Source: Agricultural Statistics Board, U.S. Department of Agriculture (ASB-USDA)*

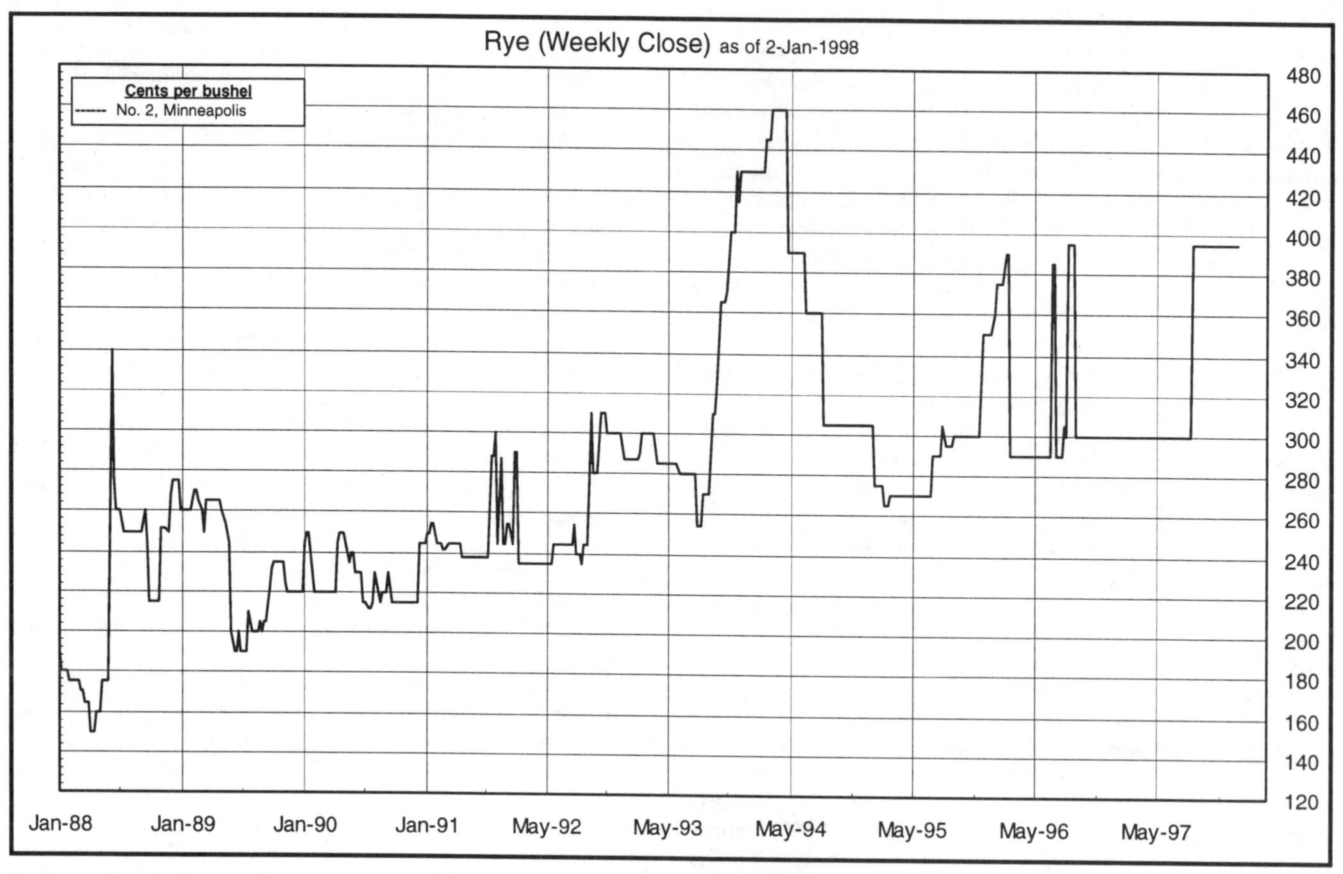

Salient Statistics of Rye in the United States In Thousands of Bushels

Crop Year Beginning June 1	Supply: Stocks June 1	Supply: Production	Supply: Imports	Supply: Total Supply	Disappearance – Domestic Use: Food	Industry	Seed	Feed & Residual	Total	Exports	Total Disappearance	Acreage: Planted (1,000 Acres)	Harvested for Grain (1,000 Acres)	Yield Per Harvested Acre Bushels
1989-90	10,300	13,647	30	23,977	3,500	2,000	3,000	9,035	17,535	800	18,335	2,014	484	28.2
1990-1	5,642	10,176	3,895	19,713	3,500	2,000	3,000	7,670	16,173	213	16,383	1,625	375	27.1
1991-2	3,327	9,761	4,542	17,630	3,500	2,000	3,000	7,528	16,028	53	16,081	1,671	396	24.6
1992-3	1,523	11,952	3,099	16,100	3,500	2,000	3,000	5,984	14,484	14	14,498	1,582	406	29.4
1993-4	1,555	10,340	4,607	16,502	3,600	2,000	3,000	6,915	15,515	16	15,531	1,493	381	27.1
1994-5	971	11,341	4,386	16,698	3,300	2,000	3,000	6,912	15,212	35	15,247	1,613	407	27.9
1995-6	1,451	10,064	3,760	15,275	3,300	2,000	3,000	6,001	14,301	41	14,342	1,602	385	26.1
1996-7[1]	933	8,936	4,327	14,196	3,400	2,000	3,000	5,057	13,490	32	13,522	1,457	345	25.9
1997-8[2]	800	8,132	4,500	13,432	3,500	3,000	2,000	4,900	13,400	100	13,400	1,400	316	25.7
1998-9[3]		11,795										1,571	418	28.2

[1] Preliminary. [2] Estimate. [3] Forecast. *Source: Economic Research Service, U.S. Department of Agriculture (ERS-USDA)*

United States Rye Crop Production Reports and CCC Operations In Thousands of Bushels

Crop Year Beginning June 1	Official Crop Reports: July 1	Aug. 1	Dec. 1	Final	National Average Support Rate: $ Per Bushel	% of Parity	Placed Under Loan Total	Percentage of Production	Acquired by CCC
1990-1	------	10,098	------	10,176	1.33	31	200	2.0	0
1991-2	------	9,761	------	9,761	1.38	32	100	1.0	0
1992-3	------	11,952	------	11,952	1.46	34	200	1.7	0
1993-4	------	10,340	------	10,340	1.46	35	100	1.0	0
1994-5	------	11,138	------	11,341	1.61	38	100	0.9	0
1995-6	------	9,928	------	10,064	1.61	42	100	1.0	0
1996-7[1]	------	------	------	8,936	[4]	------	------	------	------
1997-8[2]	------	------	------	8,132	[4]	------	------	------	------
1998-9[3]	------	------	------	11,795	[4]	------	------	------	------

[1] Preliminary. [2] Estimate. [3] Forecast. [4] The Federal Agriculture Improvement and Reform Act of 1996 did not extend authority for price support for rye beyond the 1995-6 marketing year. *Source: National Agricultural Statistics Service, U.S. Department of Agriculture (NASS-USDA)*

Average Price of Cash Rye No. 2 in Minneapolis In Cents Per Bushel

Year	July	Aug.	Sept.	Oct.	Nov.	Dec.	Jan.	Feb.	Mar.	Apr.	May	June	Average
1989-90	206	203	214	235	229	225	245	220	222	241	242	232	226
1990-1	215	222	220	220	190	245	252	243	242	242	245	245	232
1991-2	216	238	195	288	288	279	251	263	235	235	235	245	247
1992-3	245	241	267	295	303	298	288	290	300	289	285	282	282
1993-4	280	270	280	354	387	427	430	430	452	460	400	383	372
1994-5	360	336	305	305	305	305	285	267	270	270	270	270	296
1995-6	287	298	299	300	300	350	368	346	290	290	290	304	310
1996-7	325	364	314	300	300	300	300	300	300	300	300	300	309
1997-8	300	327	395	395	395	395	NQ	NQ	NQ	NQ	NQ	NQ	382
1998-9[1]	NQ	NQ	NQ	NQ	NQ	NQ	NQ	NQ					

[1] Preliminary NQ = No qoute. *Source: Agricultural Marketing Service, U.S. Department of Agriculture (AMS-USDA)*

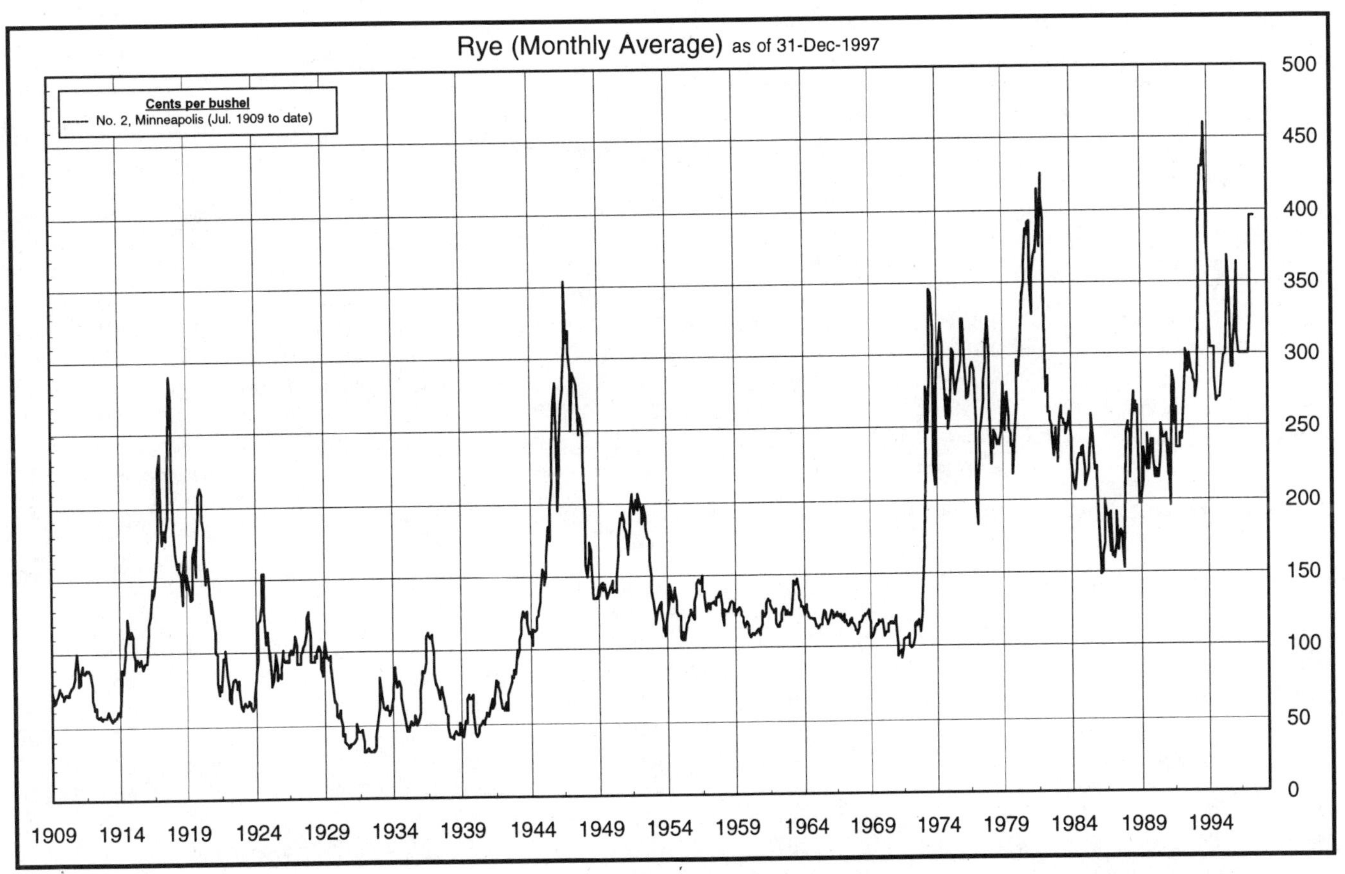

Salt

Salt, or sodium chloride, is a basic commodity with many uses. Salt is added to food to enhance flavor and to remove ice in winter. Salt is used in the manufacture of caustic soda and as a feedstock for chlorine. Salt is produced by a number of companies in the U.S. which employ a number of methods. Salt can be produced by solar evaporation, by vacuum pan, mined as rock salt, or taken from the ocean as brine. There are no economic substitutes for salt. Calcium chloride and calcium magnesium acetate, hydrochloric acid, and potassium chloride can be used for deicing, some chemical processes, and to flavor food but at increased cost.

The U.S. Geological Survey reported that U.S. production of salt in 1997 was 41.7 million metric tonnes, down 1 percent from 1996. Twenty-seven companies operated 67 plants in 14 states. Salt sold by type was: brine, 51 percent; rock salt, 32 percent; vacuum pan, 9 percent; and solar salt, 8 percent. Salt sold or used by producers in 1997 was 41,400 tonnes, down 3 percent from 1996. U.S. salt imports for consumption in 1997 were 8 million tonnes, down 25 percent from 1996. The major suppliers of salt to the U.S. were Canada, Mexico, Chile and the Bahamas. U.S. exports of salt in 1997 were 675,000 tonnes, down 22 percent from 1996. Apparent consumption of salt in 1997 was 48.7 million tonnes, down 7 percent from the previous year. U.S. producer stocks of salt at the end of 1997 were estimated at roughly 300,000 tonnes. The chemical industry consumed 42 percent of total salt sales. Salt was used mostly in the chlorine and caustic soda manufacturing sector. Salt for highway deicing accounted for 34 percent of demand.

World production of salt in 1997 was estimated at 192 million tonnes, unchanged from 1996. The U.S. was the largest producer followed by China with production of 30 million tonnes. The next largest producer was Canada with 12.1 million tonnes followed by Germany with 11 million tonnes.

World Production of All Salt   In Thousands of Metric Tons

Year	Australia	Canada	China	France	Germany	India	Italy	Mexico	Poland	Spain	United Kingdom	United States	World Total
1990	7,227	11,261	20,000	6,605	15,719	9,503	4,432	7,135	4,055	3,377	6,434	36,918	183,000
1991	7,791	11,993	24,100	6,500	14,870	9,503	3,954	7,533	3,840	4,070	6,828	36,400	191,000
1992	7,693	11,171	28,100	6,116	12,708	9,503	3,821	7,395	3,887	3,610	6,101	36,100	184,000
1993	7,737	10,900	29,500	6,980	12,688	9,503	3,730	7,490	3,817	3,410	6,790	39,300	187,000
1994	7,685	11,700	29,700	7,536	10,273	9,503	3,953	7,458	4,074	4,932	7,000	39,800	191,000
1995	8,148	10,957	29,800	7,539	15,224	9,503	3,552	7,670	4,214	4,776	6,650	42,200	199,000
1996[1]	7,905	12,248	29,000	7,860	15,907	9,503	3,600	8,508	4,163	4,000	6,610	42,300	201,000
1997[2]	8,722	13,264	29,300	7,160	15,700	9,500	3,600	7,933	3,968	4,000	6,600	41,500	201,000

[1] Preliminary. [2] Estimate. *Source: U.S. Geological Survey (USGS)*

Salient Statistics of the Salt Industry in the United States   In Thousands of Metric Tons

Year	Net Import Reliance as a % of Apparent Consumption	Average Value FOB Mine Vacuum & Open Pan $ Ton	Production: Total	Production: Open & Vacuum Pan	Production: Solar	Production: Rock	Production: Brine	Sold or Used by Producers: Open & Vacuum Pan	Sold or Used by Producers: Rock Salt	Sold or Used by Producers: Brine	Sold or Used by Producers: Total Salt	Value[3] Million $	Imports for Consumption	Exports: Total	Exports: To Canada	Apparent Consumption
1990	9	110.58	36,794	3,662	2,985	12,772	17,374	3,655	13,056	17,724	36,916	826.7	5,969	2,266	2,087	40,619
1991	11	114.75	36,316	3,654	2,813	11,188	18,660	3,623	11,064	18,640	35,902	801.5	6,188	1,777	1,288	40,313
1992	11	113.20	36,016	3,811	3,221	11,411	17,574	3,763	10,910	34,784	34,784	802.6	5,394	992	718	39,186
1993	12	111.97	39,200	3,864	2,960	14,253	18,100	3,850	13,401	18,100	38,200	904.0	5,868	688	499	43,400
1994	18	115.35	40,100	3,960	3,020	15,100	18,000	3,930	14,900	18,000	39,700	990.0	9,630	742	573	48,600
1995	14	118.63	42,100	3,950	3,540	14,000	20,600	3,920	13,000	20,500	40,800	1,000.0	7,090	670	558	47,200
1996[1]	19	120.54	42,200	3,920	3,270	13,500	21,500	3,900	14,500	21,500	42,900	1,060.0	10,600	869	710	52,600
1997[2]	14	119.61	41,400	3,980	3,170	12,900	21,400	3,990	12,200	21,400	40,600	993.0	9,160	748	624	49,000

[1] Preliminary. [2] Estimate. [3] Values are fob mine or refinery and do not include cost of cooperage or containers. *Source: U.S. Geological Survey (USGS)*

Salt Sold or Used by Producers in the U.S. by Classes & Consumers or Uses   In Thousands of Metric Tons

Year	Chemical[2]	Tanning Leather	Textile & Dyeing	Meat Packers	Canning	Baking	Agricultural Distribution	Feed Dealers	Feed Manufacturers	Rubber	Oil	Paper & Pulp	Metal Processing	Water Treatment	Grocery Stores	Water Conditioning Distrib.	Ice Control and/or Stabilization
1990	19,258	99	206	543	288	155	562	999	495	41	719	257	314	449	811	1,019	10,253
1991	20,014	76	232	370	255	142	546	1,097	335	138	554	237	293	432	897	889	9,360
1992	18,538	67	271	389	252	161	553	1,020	392	34	1,208	230	217	435	849	899	7,814
1993	19,273	67	313	418	322	152	808	1,120	476	37	1,220	110	216	419	823	527	13,600
1994	18,400	82	304	410	342	157	842	1,070	478	33	1,290	150	239	440	934	505	16,400
1995	21,100	74	290	410	332	155	726	1,040	407	67	2,420	152	236	413	847	563	12,900
1996	22,400	83	288	407	336	169	661	1,150	403	71	2,430	122	199	534	855	719	17,700
1997[1]	22,400	78	273	416	334	167	307	1,110	683	68	2,440	107	177	471	800	624	15,000

[1] Preliminary. [2] Chloralkali producers and other chemical. *Source: U.S. Geological Survey (USGS)*

Sheep & Lambs

The mid-1998 total of all sheep and lambs of 9.4 million head compares with 9.9 million a year earlier. Of the total, the breeding inventory was 5.6 million head vs. 5.82 million in mid-1997. The 1998 lamb crop of 4.87 million head was 7 percent under the 1997 crop of 5.24 million. The USDA evaluates the U.S. sheep inventory on the basis of five regional districts, the largest (#3) comprises Colorado, S. Dakota, Montana, Utah and Wyoming.

Commercial lamb production in the first half of 1998 of 164 million pounds compares with 152 million in the like 1997 period, reflecting a slaughter of 2.5 million head vs. 2.3 million a year earlier. The U.S. is a net importer of lamb, mostly from New Zealand and Australia, totaling 38.1 million pounds (carcass weight) through the first half of 1998 vs. 25.9 million in the second half of 1997. The U.S. also imported mutton at a monthly average of 3.5 million pounds during the first half of 1998.

Choice slaughter lamb prices in mid-1998 were lower than a year ago; the August average of $81.25 per cwt. compared with $90.25 a year earlier, basis San Angelo, Texas.

Although the demand for sheep meat is low in the U.S., abroad it's notably higher, especially in countries with large sheep herds utilized for wool production. Thus, the price of wool is a key factor is determining the availability of sheep meat. World sheep numbers declined steadily during the first half of the 1990's, but have since recovered due to increases in China and India, which have more than offset declines in Australia and New Zealand.

World Sheep and Goat Numbers in Specified Countries on January 1 In Thousands of Head

Year	Argentina	Australia	China	India	Kazakhstan[3]	New Zealand	Romania	Russia[3]	South Africa	Spain	Turkey	United Kingdom	World Total
1991	27,552	173,982	210,021	160,207	35,700	57,852	14,062	58,200	37,585	24,037	45,000	30,147	962,853
1992	25,706	161,073	206,210	161,084	34,556	55,162	13,879	55,255	36,076	24,625	44,700	28,932	931,903
1993	24,500	140,542	207,329	162,155	34,420	52,568	12,079	51,368	35,770	24,615	44,600	29,493	900,400
1994	23,500	132,569	217,314	163,156	34,208	50,298	12,276	43,700	33,800	23,872	44,000	29,333	886,483
1995	21,626	123,210	240,528	164,242	25,132	50,135	12,119	34,500	33,385	23,058	43,000	29,484	876,169
1996	17,956	121,200	276,857	173,519	19,600	48,816	11,086	28,336	35,145	21,322	42,400	28,797	900,998
1997	17,295	120,200	304,150	175,976	13,742	47,394	10,317	23,519	35,830	23,981	41,100	28,256	915,782
1998[1]	16,432	119,600	335,000	178,462	10,896	46,970	9,747	20,697	36,821	24,512	39,500	30,118	942,098
1999[2]	17,252	119,300	------	180,130	8,800	46,150	9,300	18,213	37,966	24,520	37,400	29,361	------

[1] Preliminary. [2] Forecast. [3] Formerly part of the U.S.S.R.; data not reported separately until 1986. *Source: Foreign Agricultural Service, U.S. Department of Agriculture (FAS-USDA)*

Salient Statistics of Sheep & Lambs in the United States In Thousands of Head

	--Inventory, Jan. 1 --				--- Marketings[3]---		---------- Slaughter ----------					Production (Live Weight)	Farm Value, ------ Jan. 1 ------	
Year	Without New Crop Lambs	With New Crop Lambs	Lamb Crop	Total Supply	Sheep	Lambs	Farm	Commercial	Total[4]	Net Exports	Total Disappearance	Mil. Lbs.	All Million $	$ Per Head
1990	11,358	12,132	7,685	19,817	1,628	6,823	96	5,654	5,750	448	12,290	780.8	901.1	79.3
1991	11,174	11,930	7,651	19,581	1,719	7,187	91	5,722	5,813	787	11,763	796.1	732.6	65.6
1992	10,797	11,507	7,225	18,732	1,923	7,007	88	5,497	5,585	770	11,173	746.0	660.7	61.2
1993	10,201	10,906	6,379	17,285	1,952	6,752	84	5,184	5,268	750	10,159	688.6	714.2	70.6
1994	9,079	9,714	5,897	15,611	1,527	6,358	69	4,939	5,008	760	8,899	625.9	681.4	69.9
1995	8,886	8,886	5,606	14,492	990	6,228	69	4,560	4,628	680	5,807	599.4	663.4	74.7
1996	8,461	8,461	5,282	13,743	1,019	5,923	65	4,184	4,249	264	5,488	560.2	732.2	86.5
1997[1]	8,024	8,024	5,356	13,380	-----	-----	-----	3,907	3,907	-----	5,946	-----	761.7	96.0
1998[2]	7,825	7,825	5,013	12,838	-----	-----	-----	3,801	3,801	-----	-----	-----	776.3	102.0

[1] Preliminary. [2] Estimate. [3] Excludes interfarm sales. [4] Includes all commercial and farm. *Source: Economic Research Service, U.S. Department of Agriculture (ERS-USDA)*

Sheep and Lambs[3] on Farms in the United States on January 1 In Thousands of Head

Year	California	Colorado	Idaho	Iowa	Minnesota	Montana	New Mexico	Ohio	South Dakota	Texas	Utah	Wyoming	Total
1991	1,015	710	272	465	300	683	462	305	640	2,000	508	830	11,200
1992	995	710	273	345	293	658	445	215	602	2,140	488	870	10,749
1993	995	685	250	320	245	554	405	190	591	2,000	490	885	10,500
1994	1,120	647	266	267	231	534	340	198	550	1,895	442	813	9,742
1995	1,060	545	270	294	190	490	315	162	530	1,700	445	790	8,886
1996	1,000	535	273	345	185	465	265	153	500	1,650	395	680	8,461
1997	960	575	285	285	180	432	235	130	450	1,400	375	720	7,937
1998[1]	800	575	285	265	165	415	290	135	420	1,530	420	710	7,825
1999[2]	810	440	265	260	175	380	275	125	420	1,350	400	660	7,238

[1] Preliminary. [2] Estimate. [3] Includes sheep & lambs on feed for market and stock sheep & lambs. *Source: Economic Research Service, U.S. Department of Agriculture (ERS-USDA)*

SHEEP AND LAMBS

Average Wholesale Price of Slaughter Lambs (Choice) at San Angelo, Texas — In Dollars Per 100 Pounds

Year	Jan.	Feb.	Mar.	Apr.	May	June	July	Aug.	Sept.	Oct.	Nov.	Dec.	Average
1990	54.80	60.38	63.69	63.13	62.25	53.56	53.25	51.20	51.75	52.50	50.42	48.08	55.42
1991	47.63	45.81	54.88	55.50	57.70	55.75	55.50	54.31	53.25	51.20	52.08	54.92	53.21
1992	58.56	57.69	66.55	74.63	68.88	64.50	58.17	52.38	53.61	52.81	56.93	67.25	61.00
1993	69.88	73.38	75.50	71.25	62.50	57.75	57.00	58.97	66.08	63.75	65.69	68.44	65.85
1994	56.67	62.31	61.19	51.25	60.94	66.92	75.33	79.50	76.08	69.96	73.60	67.50	66.77
1995	65.38	75.08	73.75	68.58	77.20	81.63	83.70	87.00	80.00	75.50	72.00	70.50	75.86
1996	74.44	85.63	84.07	83.10	86.17	97.50	92.67	83.75	84.40	82.58	80.00	88.88	85.27
1997	94.63	100.81	97.50	95.50	83.17	83.25	78.94	90.25	85.45	82.75	80.33	83.52	88.01
1998[1]	74.38	74.31	71.50	63.00	73.00	91.21	82.21	81.25	69.50	67.20	63.33	71.44	73.53

[1] Preliminary. *Source: Economic Research Service, U.S. Department of Agriculture (ERS-USDA)*

Federally Inspected Slaughter of Sheep & Lambs in the United States — In Thousands of Head

Year	Jan.	Feb.	Mar.	Apr.	May.	June	July	Aug.	Sept.	Oct.	Nov.	Dec.	Total
1990	479	431	481	466	465	426	430	463	422	490	465	449	5,467
1991	495	449	546	436	442	388	431	438	456	501	449	471	5,502
1992	468	422	481	503	374	419	427	400	470	452	413	460	5,289
1993	380	384	476	461	396	462	394	413	410	391	403	430	5,000
1994	383	409	515	402	418	377	302	382	384	381	393	411	4,756
1995	373	363	456	420	355	347	296	355	344	356	364	358	4,388
1996	352	353	403	374	313	271	313	315	313	365	324	336	4,032
1997	294	317	386	321	308	293	295	288	310	324	299	337	3,771
1998[1]	301	300	377	367	270	283	269	263	295	312	290	344	3,671

[1] Preliminary. *Source: Economic Research Service, U.S. Department of Agriculture (ERS-USDA)*

Cold Storage Holdings of Lamb and Mutton in the U.S., on First of Month — In Thousands of Pounds

Year	Jan.	Feb.	Mar.	Apr.	May	June	July	Aug.	Sept.	Oct.	Nov.	Dec.
1990	7,625	7,844	8,468	7,905	8,390	8,052	9,685	10,107	9,144	8,929	8,458	8,099
1991	8,414	9,438	9,829	8,070	7,277	8,436	8,002	6,917	6,130	5,287	5,739	6,659
1992	6,296	7,255	6,670	8,455	8,580	9,870	10,968	11,711	9,314	8,751	8,520	8,406
1993	7,864	6,343	6,620	6,661	11,064	11,181	13,152	13,495	12,241	12,615	11,843	10,161
1994	8,372	9,198	9,507	11,194	11,505	11,368	12,124	12,026	11,016	9,261	8,946	8,796
1995	10,913	11,621	10,825	12,679	14,934	13,992	12,306	10,679	10,240	7,412	7,503	7,846
1996	7,606	9,794	13,017	12,247	13,649	12,187	13,726	13,164	14,645	11,249	10,494	9,788
1997	8,899	9,473	9,862	11,163	13,027	15,220	16,594	18,535	19,383	16,119	16,894	16,534
1998[1]	13,741	13,920	15,284	16,226	16,306	16,655	16,040	16,188	14,530	12,253	12,558	11,914

[1] Preliminary. *Source: Economic Research Service, U.S. Department of Agriculture (ERS-USDA)*

Average Price Received by Farmers for Sheep in the U.S. — In Dollars Per Hundred Pounds (Cwt.)

Year	Jan.	Feb.	Mar.	Apr.	May	June	July	Aug.	Sept.	Oct.	Nov.	Dec.	Average
1990	32.20	30.90	30.00	23.50	19.70	19.60	24.70	24.30	18.90	19.20	20.40	22.40	23.82
1991	23.50	19.90	21.50	21.30	18.30	21.00	20.30	19.20	18.90	18.20	19.80	22.60	20.38
1992	28.10	29.80	31.60	28.30	23.10	22.60	24.00	25.80	25.00	25.30	25.50	33.20	26.86
1993	33.10	35.20	36.10	27.30	29.10	28.90	29.00	28.50	25.80	24.60	25.70	30.30	29.47
1994	35.10	37.00	34.30	29.60	29.30	33.60	30.10	29.40	27.90	27.30	30.50	34.70	31.57
1995	32.80	37.50	31.90	29.50	27.90	28.30	28.60	27.00	26.00	24.50	23.80	26.00	28.65
1996	34.40	33.80	34.00	27.30	25.30	26.60	30.50	29.10	30.20	28.80	29.80	34.20	30.33
1997	41.80	41.30	42.50	37.50	34.00	36.60	39.40	38.40	33.90	35.80	38.90	37.70	38.15
1998[1]	42.00	39.60	42.20	35.40	30.70	30.70	30.00	28.90	27.70	26.60	26.80	30.30	32.58

[1] Preliminary. *Source: Economic Research Service, U.S. Department of Agriculture (ERS-USDA)*

Average Price Received by Farmers for Lambs in the U.S. — In Dollars Per Hundred Pounds (Cwt.)

Year	Jan.	Feb.	Mar.	Apr.	May	June	July	Aug.	Sept.	Oct.	Nov.	Dec.	Average
1990	56.40	59.80	66.00	62.90	59.80	55.40	54.40	54.00	52.80	51.90	50.10	48.60	56.01
1991	48.00	45.80	51.10	54.80	57.60	55.30	57.70	53.40	51.80	51.70	50.70	52.00	52.49
1992	53.50	55.20	63.40	69.30	68.80	65.60	62.20	55.90	56.70	55.40	58.20	65.20	60.78
1993	67.30	72.70	76.00	68.10	61.50	55.70	53.90	59.20	64.50	64.50	65.80	66.00	64.60
1994	60.60	59.40	58.60	54.50	54.50	63.00	72.80	75.50	71.20	68.00	70.60	69.10	64.82
1995	67.50	70.40	74.80	74.60	80.40	85.70	85.70	85.60	82.70	77.60	77.10	76.50	78.22
1996	76.10	84.30	86.60	85.90	90.30	100.70	98.30	89.10	88.50	87.00	84.60	88.20	88.30
1997	94.60	99.80	99.70	96.40	90.80	86.50	81.10	92.70	90.20	87.20	83.10	83.90	90.50
1998[1]	78.40	75.00	70.00	66.10	63.30	88.70	81.00	79.90	71.40	67.30	62.20	64.50	72.32

[1] Preliminary. *Source: Economic Research Service, U.S. Department of Agriculture (ERS-USDA)*

Silk

Silk is the cloth and thread made from silkworms. The fiber used in commercial silk production is produced primarily by the mulberry silkworm. Silk is produced in a number of countries depending mostly on a favorable climate and adequate labor. A primary requirement of silk production is an ample supply of mulberry trees. The mulberry leaf-feeding silkworm thrives on mulberry leaves. The silkworm spins a cocoon made of silk fiber which is then collected for a process called reeling. Reeling is the bringing together of two or more cocoons to form them into one continuous strand of raw silk.

The Food and Agricultural Organization of the United Nations estimates that world production of raw silk in 1997 was 83,000 metric tonnes. That represented a decline of 1 percent from the previous year. In the 1993-1997 period, world production of silk averaged 101,000 tonnes per year. The world's largest producer of silk in 1997 was China with 51,000 tonnes, unchanged from the previous year. The next largest producer of raw silk is India with 16,000 tonnes in 1997, unchanged from 1996. India's production has been trending higher for several years. The next largest producer is North Korea with 1997 output of 5,000 tonnes, unchanged from the previous year. Uzbekistan's production was estimated at 2,000 tonnes, unchanged from 1996. Two countries that have seen a substantial increase in silk production are Iran and Vietnam. Iran's 1997 production was 1,000 tonnes. In 1993 it was 480 tonnes. Vietnam's 1997 production was 1,000 tonnes while in 1993 it was 550 tonnes.

Among the major importers, Japan in 1996 took 6,098 tonnes. That represented an increase of 41 percent from the previous year. Imports by India in 1996 were 4,773 tonnes, an increase of 12 percent from the previous year. Italy imported 4,400 tonnes of silk in 1996 while Hong Kong imported 3,978 tonnes.

China is the largest exporter of silk. Exports in 1996 were 15,791 tonnes, down 6 percent from the previous year. Exports by Hong Kong were 4,165 tonnes, down 20 percent from the previous year. Japan's exports were 946 tonnes while Brazil exported 1,071 tonnes.

Futures Markets

Raw silk is traded in Japan on the Kobe Raw Silk Exchange (KSE). Dry Cocoons are traded on the Manila International Futures Exchange Inc., (MIFE).

World Production of Raw Silk In Metric Tons

Year	Brazil	China	India	Iran	Japan	North Korea	South Korea	Kyrgyzstan[3]	Thailand	Turkmenistan[3]	Uzbekistan[3]	Viet Nam	World Total
1986	1,200	39,098	9,300	280	8,336	3,600	1,342	-----	1,400	-----	3,710	350	69,178
1987	1,800	40,940	9,498	900	7,864	3,700	1,413	-----	1,200	-----	4,200	360	72,597
1988	1,900	42,041	10,255	900	6,862	3,800	1,355	-----	1,250	-----	4,300	420	73,866
1989	1,697	50,244	10,500	537	6,078	4,000	1,400	-----	1,250	-----	3,900	400	80,745
1990	1,693	55,003	11,000	537	6,000	4,200	971	-----	1,250	-----	4,094	500	85,987
1991	2,077	60,002	14,000	537	5,527	4,400	837	-----	1,300	-----	4,100	500	93,880
1992	2,296	70,302	15,000	537	5,085	4,500	870	1,200	1,300	600	2,200	500	105,220
1993	2,450	76,801	14,168	480	4,254	4,600	683	1,000	1,500	500	2,000	550	109,790
1994	2,450	84,001	14,500	600	2,400	4,700	700	1,000	1,600	500	2,000	600	115,796
1995	2,450	80,001	15,000	600	2,400	4,700	700	1,000	1,600	500	2,000	650	112,350
1996[1]	2,000	51,000	16,000	1,000	3,000	5,000	-----	1,000	1,000	1,000	2,000	1,000	84,000
1997[2]	2,000	51,000	16,000	1,000	3,000	5,000	-----	1,000	1,000	1,000	2,000	1,000	83,000

[1] Preliminary. [2] Estimate. [3] Formerly part of the U.S.S.R.; data not reported separately until 1992. *Source: Food and Agricultural Organization of the United Nations (FAO-UN)*

World Trade of Silk by Selected Countries In Metric Tons

	Imports							Exports					
Year	France	Hong Kong	India	Italy	Japan	South Korea	World Total	Brazil	China	Hong Kong	Japan	North Korea	World Total
1986	572	3,179	2,100	7,133	8,943	3,747	29,835	692	16,349	4,115	586	1,060	27,931
1987	770	6,652	2,100	7,339	8,342	5,582	35,864	648	18,368	7,778	794	1,200	34,886
1988	771	7,489	1,411	8,094	10,259	4,851	39,216	670	20,168	8,553	442	1,200	37,276
1989	1,012	6,362	1,400	7,740	8,512	3,763	35,968	534	19,314	6,748	417	1,100	39,064
1990	796	3,928	1,647	4,775	7,111	3,204	27,322	1,064	13,066	4,102	380	1,200	27,977
1991	579	4,347	2,100	5,297	6,933	3,519	29,623	2,052	15,178	4,186	405	900	29,188
1992	693	4,400	2,843	4,337	5,137	3,627	28,239	1,552	13,474	4,358	701	800	26,433
1993	1,001	5,475	4,977	5,634	5,982	4,494	36,086	1,495	15,652	7,204	904	1,200	35,634
1994	1,047	6,165	5,750	9,235	5,772	4,128	44,136	1,739	21,004	6,149	1,265	1,400	41,998
1995	663	4,775	4,276	5,612	4,331	3,513	37,135	966	16,788	5,176	925	1,000	35,671
1996[1]	675	3,978	4,773	4,400	6,098	3,737	NA	1,071	15,791	4,165	946	1,000	NA

[1] Preliminary. *Source: Food and Agricultural Organization of the United Nations (FAO-UN)*

Silver

Silver prices began to firm in late 1997 from a base of about $5.00 an ounce, climaxing with an explosive rally in mid-February 1998 that carried nearby futures values to almost $7.50 an ounce, a near ten-year high. The catalyst for the strength was that a noted U.S. financier had accumulated nearly 130 ounces of physical silver which triggered a speculative run into futures; it also proved short lived. The higher prices choked off demand for physical silver and there was talk that the financier had either stopped buying or liquidated his holdings. As 1998 progressed, futures drifted lower in lethargic trading and at yearend were again in the $5.00/oz. range. Contributing to the curtailed 1998 trading interest were (1) the strong equity markets which siphoned risk capital away from silver and (2) the persistent assurance from the Federal Reserve and world credit markets of little inflationary pressure.

Many variables impact on silver's price but which are more important at any given time are not easily discernible. The fundamental approach focuses on tangible supply/demand data which is often rationalized to support price swings in either direction. These moves then can be exaggerated, as likely occurred in early 1998, by chart and computer generated buy or sell signals. Further clouding the market's outlook is that silver's price is quoted in different markets and perhaps at the same time, different prices. The primary price references are: (l) the London spot which is fixed daily at 12:15 P.M., (2) the COMEX spot settlement and (3) the Handy & Harmon price which is the cash quotation accepted by most commercial users.

Inflation fears, real or perceived, retain a fading belief of a direct tandem price correlation between gold and silver. Still, silver is likely to retain its nickname as the poor man's gold. During the early 1998 silver rally gold prices hardly budged. Even the protracted drawdown on futures based (notably COMEX) approved vault silver stocks failed to reawaken fundamentalist buying interest. At yearend 1997, futures exchange stocks of 3,430 metric tonnes compares with 4,550 tonnes a year earlier and over 10,000 tonnes in early 1995. However, declining COMEX silver inventories do not necessarily mean increased consumption, but perhaps a reallocation of inventory placement, either in U.S. vaults and/or exported for inventory placement abroad. Still, there were signs of improving world demand for silver in late 1998 with some U.S. fabricators expressing concern about the availability of high quality physical silver.

World mine production of silver in 1997 of 16,400 metric tonnes compares with 15,200 tonnes in 1996 and a 1993-97 annual average of almost 15,000 tonnes. Less than 20 percent of the world's silver comes from primary mines, most is obtained as a by-product of copper, lead, zinc and gold mining. Accordingly, the annual gains or contractions in silver production are apt to be a reaction to the price strength or weakness of the host metals associated with silver.

Mexico is the world's largest producer with an estimated 2,679 tonnes in 1997 vs. 2,578 in 1996; Peru and the U.S. vie for second place: 2,150 tonnes for the U.S. in 1997 and Peru at 2,077 vs. 1996 production of 1,570 tonnes and 1,970 tonnes, respectively. Nevada is the largest producing state followed by Idaho. Silver is also obtained from secondary supplies such as scrap and old coinage. U.S. recycling of silver scrap in 1997 totaled 1,360 tonnes.

Global silver demand in 1997 grew 6 percent to an estimated 24,999 tonnes, the highest so far of the 1990's. The increase was largely due to a 3 percent jump, to 7,230 tonnes, from the photographic industry due to increased demand for color film, primarily from India and China. U.S. industrial demand in 1997, notably from the electronics sector, was estimated at 5,000 tonnes, up 6 percent. Industrial demand includes (1) industrial and decorative; (2) photographic; (3) jewelry/silverware; and (4) coinage.

U.S. imports of silver (ore, concentrates and refined) in 1997 totaled 2.5 million kilograms vs. 3 million in 1996; with Mexico and Canada supplying 79 percent of the 1997 total. Exports of 3.1 million kg. in 1997 compare with 2.95 million with the U.K. taking almost 2 million kg. in 1997. For the first time since 1980, the U.S. was a net exporter of silver during 1997.

Futures Markets

Silver futures are traded on the Tokyo Commodity Exchange (TOCOM), the Chicago Board of Trade (CBOT), the Mid America Commodity Exchange (MidAm), and the New York Mercantile Exchange, COMEX division (COMEX). Options are traded on the European Options Exchange (EOE-Optiebeurs), the CBOT, and the COMEX.

World Mine Production of Silver In Thousands of Kilograms (Metric Tons)

Year	Australia	Bolivia	Canada[3]	Chile	China	Kazakhstan[4]	Rep. of Korea	Mexico	Peru	Poland	Sweden	United States	World Total[2]
1988	1,118	232	1,443	507	110	2,500	227	2,359	1,552	1,063	208	1,661	15,484
1989	1,075	267	1,371	545	125	2,500	239	2,400	1,840	1,003	228	2,008	16,425
1990	1,173	311	1,501	655	130	2,500	238	2,425	1,930	832	243	2,121	16,600
1991	1,180	376	1,339	678	150	2,200	265	2,295	1,927	899	239	1,860	15,600
1992	1,218	282	1,220	1,029	170	900	333	2,098	1,614	798	210	1,800	14,600
1993	1,092	333	896	970	840	500	215	2,420	1,631	767	255	1,640	14,400
1994	1,045	352	768	983	810	506	257	2,215	1,768	1,064	276	1,490	14,200
1995	939	425	1,285	1,041	910	489	299	2,324	1,929	1,001	268	1,560	14,900
1996[1]	1,013	384	1,309	1,047	1,140	480	254	2,528	1,970	935	272	1,570	15,200
1997[2]	1,106	390	1,222	1,091	1,300	500	268	2,679	2,077	1,000	280	2,150	16,400

[1] Preliminary. [2] Estimate. [3] Shipments. [4] Formerly part of the U.S.S.R.; data not reported separately until 1992

Source: U.S. Geological Survey (USGS)

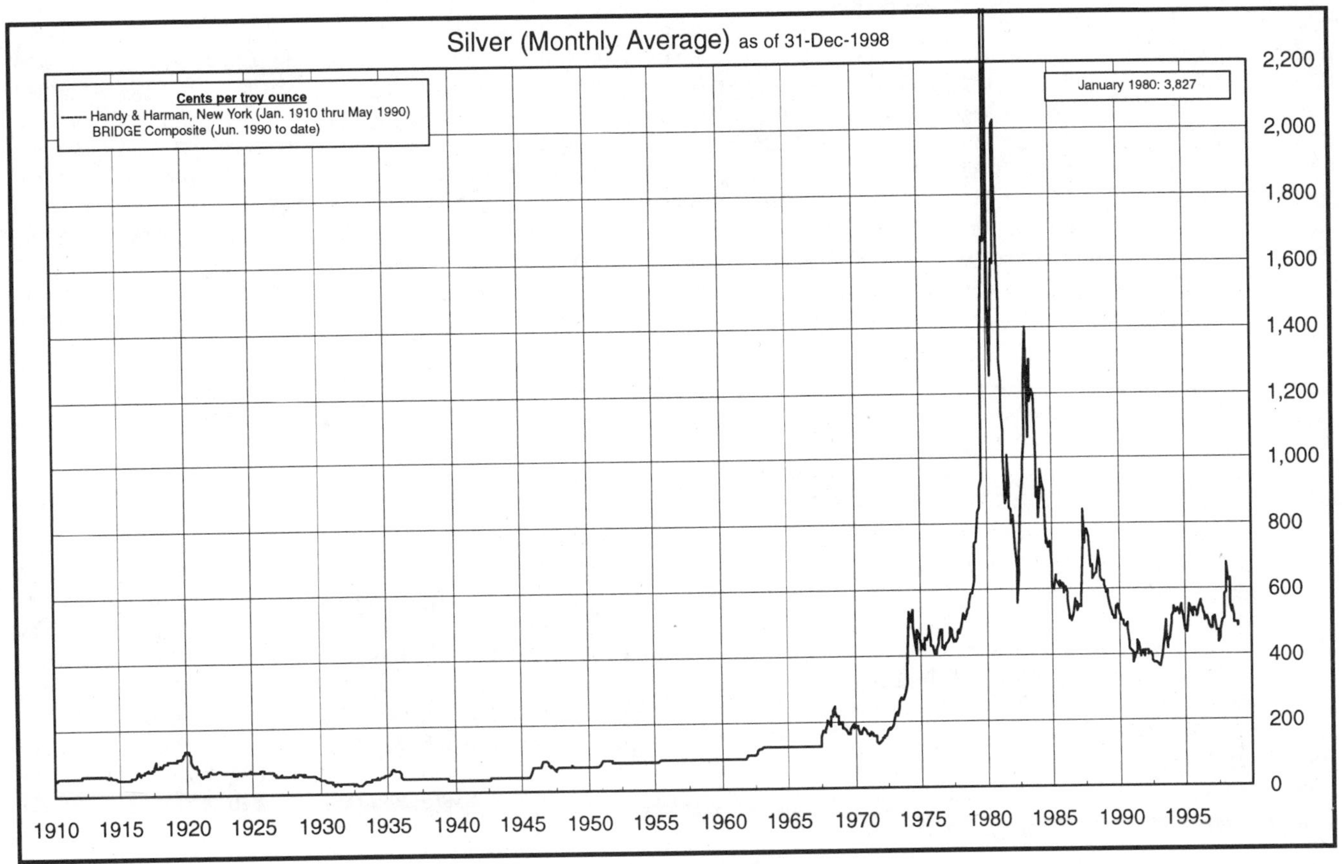

Average Price of Silver in New York (Handy & Harman) In Cents Per Troy Ounce (.999 Fine)

Year	Jan.	Feb.	Mar.	Apr.	May	June	July	Aug.	Sept.	Oct.	Nov.	Dec.	Average
1989	597.17	589.08	592.98	579.08	544.70	528.02	523.65	517.93	513.30	513.30	546.53	554.28	550.00
1990	524.30	527.84	505.82	504.58	507.39	490.60	485.90	498.15	479.03	436.59	416.90	406.84	482.00
1991	402.82	372.34	396.90	397.07	404.07	438.85	430.38	393.80	403.60	410.22	406.05	390.90	403.92
1992	412.08	413.71	410.36	403.00	406.83	405.64	394.89	379.67	376.33	373.66	376.32	370.98	393.62
1993	367.93	364.39	364.80	396.36	445.02	437.50	503.74	480.61	417.19	433.45	450.25	496.83	429.84
1994	513.14	527.24	545.11	530.87	543.64	539.34	528.65	519.54	552.88	544.10	519.60	476.88	528.42
1995	476.36	469.53	464.83	552.42	555.25	535.27	517.58	539.59	540.78	534.48	529.30	514.75	519.18
1996	547.03	562.75	551.38	540.14	536.02	513.58	502.95	500.98	510.50	492.76	482.76	479.23	518.34
1997	476.39	508.76	519.88	476.41	475.80	474.60	435.96	451.36	472.69	501.15	506.00	571.53	489.21
1998	584.58	672.61	617.18	628.86	558.65	526.05	546.82	516.45	502.67	500.18	498.39	488.71	553.43

Source: American Metal Market (AMM)

Average Price of Silver London (Spot Fix) In Pence Per Troy Ounce (.999 Fine)

Year	Jan.	Feb.	Mar.	Apr.	May	June	July	Aug.	Sept.	Oct.	Nov.	Dec.	Average
1988	373.09	361.12	350.19	343.97	349.76	393.77	416.27	392.67	378.37	361.99	348.15	334.87	367.02
1989	337.32	335.09	346.81	341.28	333.69	340.21	322.29	324.61	326.77	323.99	348.64	348.92	335.80
1990	317.67	311.77	312.45	309.08	302.29	287.85	269.56	263.50	255.45	225.76	212.45	210.97	273.23
1991	209.50	190.10	216.00	227.61	234.43	266.86	263.97	235.06	234.22	238.90	229.09	228.03	231.15
1992	227.68	233.21	238.36	230.72	225.02	219.32	206.74	197.03	203.89	226.06	246.94	240.01	224.58
1993	240.39	254.41	249.55	256.16	287.61	289.42	335.27	324.64	276.85	285.48	306.07	332.78	286.55
1994	344.48	354.77	364.74	358.95	360.86	353.28	341.86	336.67	353.15	339.73	326.64	306.49	345.14
1995	302.80	300.36	290.35	341.95	248.74	336.31	323.80	343.72	348.99	340.29	339.90	336.05	329.44
1996	359.20	367.64	362.03	392.85	354.25	334.68	325.81	330.93	322.98	310.78	290.51	289.77	336.79
1997	287.63	311.95	323.99	293.08	291.43	289.16	272.73	280.36	295.67	308.69	300.76	348.90	300.36

Source: American Metal Market (AMM)

SILVER

Average Open Interest of Silver Futures in New York In Contracts

Year	Jan.	Feb.	Mar.	Apr.	May	June	July	Aug.	Sept.	Oct.	Nov.	Dec.
1989	93,582	95,876	93,953	99,598	90,996	86,804	83,466	88,886	85,248	88,406	91,459	93,606
1990	94,397	93,713	96,182	96,701	95,784	103,575	99,098	99,668	92,436	91,093	84,181	80,364
1991	91,685	101,352	99,564	99,791	94,921	105,646	97,554	95,536	87,079	90,791	89,765	91,390
1992	97,179	93,352	88,445	96,427	87,355	84,002	80,879	81,695	74,265	72,090	77,633	72,296
1993	80,155	86,241	87,127	100,985	105,931	102,539	107,537	109,427	93,891	93,316	101,576	110,029
1994	112,584	116,652	112,745	119,314	121,296	126,255	122,138	118,081	113,261	117,224	126,666	134,099
1995	132,158	139,806	132,317	129,063	112,723	108,941	101,842	111,251	95,433	101,763	105,453	95,551
1996	99,316	107,667	92,186	101,011	99,529	110,247	105,627	103,618	93,448	95,809	93,238	83,879
1997	91,385	94,539	90,531	97,434	87,510	90,145	96,777	89,250	79,344	100,464	96,695	93,761
1998	95,717	108,284	91,730	83,045	79,451	91,563	78,353	82,530	74,848	74,451	76,440	78,716

Source: New York Mercantile Exchange, COMEX Division

Volume of Trading of Silver Futures in New York In Thousands of Contracts

Year	Jan.	Feb.	Mar.	Apr.	May	June	July	Aug.	Sept.	Oct.	Nov.	Dec.	Total
1989	317,152	408,485	447,323	354,235	278,496	484,711	272,254	360,381	244,926	261,102	622,123	345,423	4,376,611
1990	343,175	413,287	210,193	364,055	328,804	433,848	242,288	524,815	201,273	308,449	323,664	219,758	3,913,609
1991	309,841	420,092	446,491	395,957	255,548	547,495	344,683	320,639	268,660	252,983	349,698	242,617	4,154,704
1992	408,179	320,226	229,010	322,364	184,825	295,358	197,946	266,347	173,165	125,537	355,728	127,654	3,016,339
1993	167,201	315,916	242,974	476,554	433,460	523,961	503,935	531,772	428,366	338,189	520,591	373,005	4,855,924
1994	489,055	555,136	484,134	585,058	516,396	729,414	339,298	535,722	377,540	455,049	589,220	348,323	5,994,345
1995	390,453	501,454	541,807	592,620	500,522	476,481	280,651	655,854	344,182	272,362	447,095	179,755	5,183,236
1996	415,801	583,767	368,175	547,629	334,973	549,631	296,905	460,686	316,366	321,781	415,441	259,653	4,870,808
1997	401,995	530,514	360,871	493,999	280,536	472,306	340,245	425,471	335,400	430,397	488,024	333,762	4,893,520
1998	352,688	550,800	368,127	360,130	310,130	393,971	278,774	367,257	283,475	280,066	319,216	229,982	4,094,616

Source: New York Mercantile Exchange, COMEX Division

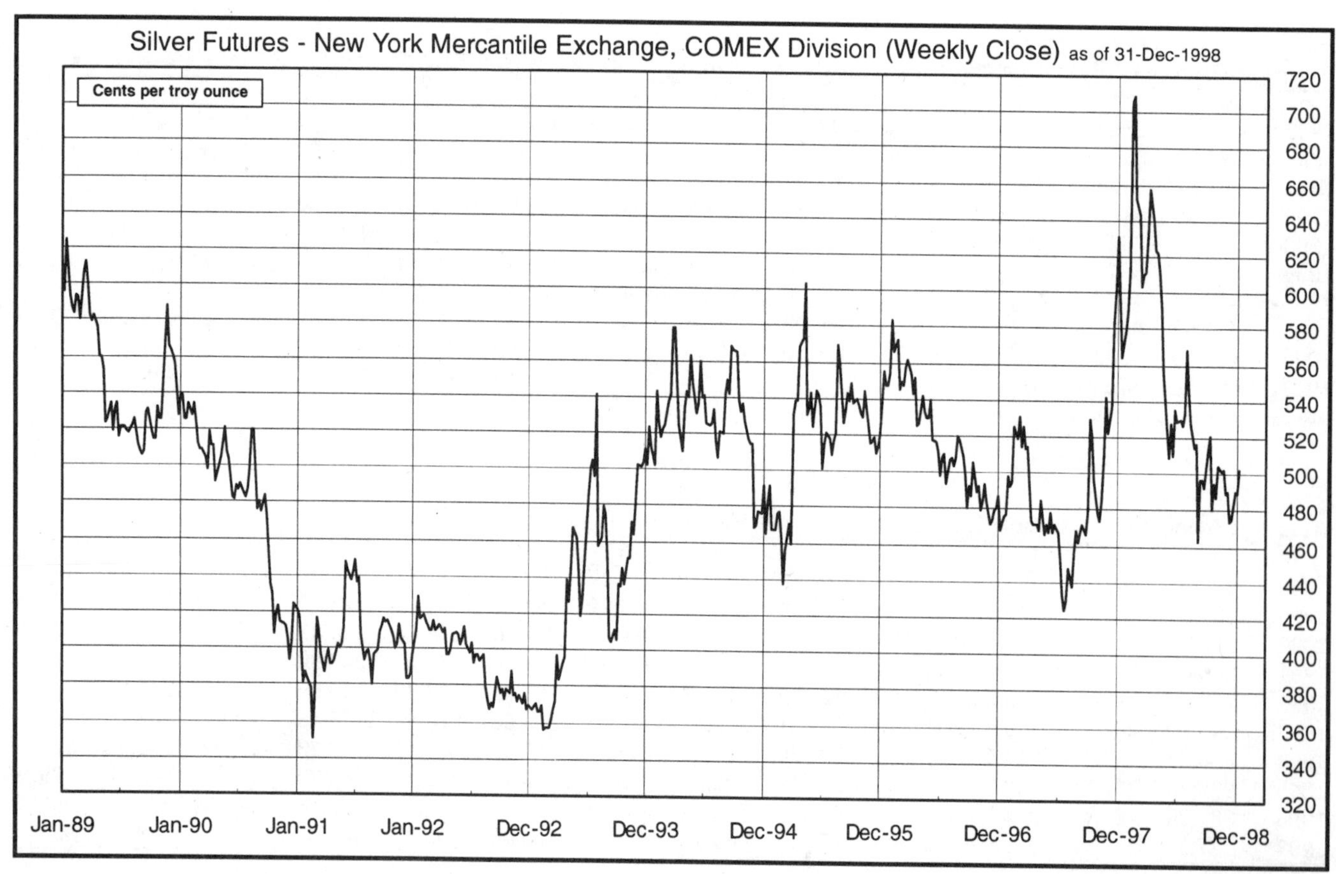

Mine Production of Recoverable Silver in the United States, by State In Metric Tons

Year	Arizona	Idaho	Montana	Nevada	Total	Year	Arizona	Idaho	Montana	Nevada	Total
1986	140	349	148	199	1,074	1992	153	255	195	586	1,740
1987	114	NA	185	379	1,241	1993	157	190	125	713	1,610
1988	152	340	192	608	1,661	1994	183	158	71	602	1,390
1989	171	439	194	625	2,007	1995	220	182	76	766	1,640
1990	173	442	220	646	2,125	1996	189	234	11	594	1,570
1991	148	337	222	578	1,848	1997[1]	190	341	W	866	2,150

[1] Preliminary. [2] Estimate. NA = Not available. *Source: U.S. Geological Survey (USGS)*

Consumption of Silver in the United States, by End Use In Millions of Troy Ounces

Year	Brazing Alloys & Solders	Catalysts	Batteries[2]	Mirrors	Electrical Contacts - Conductors	Photo-graphic Materials	Silver-plate	Jewelry[4]	Sterling Ware	Total Net Industrial Con-sumption	Coinage	Total Con-sumption
1988	NA	2.6	2.5	1.1	23.0	62.5	2.6	2.9	3.5	117.5	7.9	125.4
1989	NA	2.8	2.8	1.1	23.5	65.2	2.7	2.4	3.4	126.0	6.8	132.8
1990	2.8	3.0	3.0	1.2	23.3	67.0	2.8	2.0	3.5	118.2	9.4	131.0
1991	5.6	3.3	3.1	1.1	21.2	65.0	2.8	2.0	3.5	112.3	10.8	128.2
1992	6.5	3.8	3.1	1.2	23.1	63.5	2.9	3.0	3.9	114.5	8.4	128.6
1993	7.2	4.0	3.3	1.3	28.6	64.0	3.0	3.3	4.0	117.4	8.2	135.6
1994	7.7	----------	16.9	----------	31.6	67.8	----------	12.0	----------	136.3	8.7	145.0
1995	8.0	----------	17.9	----------	36.0	70.3	----------	12.5	----------	144.9	8.1	152.9
1996	8.2	----------	18.2	----------	36.3	74.4	----------	12.4	----------	150.2	6.1	156.3
1997[1]	8.4		------------		41.9	79.0	----------	12.5	----------	161.5	5.5	167.0

[1] Preliminary. [2] Beginning 1994; includes batteries, catalysts, and mirrors. [3] Beginning 1994; includes silverplate, jewelry, and sterlingware.
Source: The Silver Institute

Commodity Exchange, Inc. (COMEX) Warehouse of Stocks of Silver In Thousands of Troy Ounces

Year	Jan. 1	Feb. 1	Mar. 1	Apr. 1	May 1	June 1	July 1	Aug. 1	Sept. 1	Oct. 1	Nov. 1	Dec. 1
1989	182,657	190,243	194,802	200,995	203,207	206,049	210,385	207,286	212,283	226,570	237,946	238,773
1990	240,796	243,421	252,104	253,773	255,421	251,626	253,326	255,814	260,184	258,614	257,685	265,339
1991	266,206	263,832	257,851	263,563	263,686	266,087	276,961	270,804	269,661	265,874	262,835	270,734
1992	271,692	278,990	270,449	262,239	267,003	267,818	271,259	273,743	278,575	278,526	280,712	275,156
1993	272,824	273,629	271,856	265,580	270,800	273,947	277,228	278,745	276,819	275,370	277,666	263,138
1994	251,685	250,730	239,374	240,187	233,950	236,459	246,291	249,417	255,198	259,634	265,710	258,618
1995	260,708	264,045	235,114	211,028	189,668	184,570	181,269	175,764	156,544	156,529	156,110	156,932
1996	159,695	143,426	151,336	139,059	141,789	150,141	168,079	155,441	151,283	141,673	129,911	148,451
1997	204,051	195,450	193,381	191,676	189,498	201,682	184,691	169,079	164,296	138,775	133,470	128,252
1998	110,437	103,778	89,458	86,926	89,715	89,628	85,911	79,136	78,681	73,142	74,260	76,818

Source: New York Mercantile Exchange, COMEX Division

Production[1] of Refined Silver in the United States, from All Sources In Metric Tons

Year	Jan.	Feb.	Mar.	Apr.	May	June	July	Aug.	Sept.	Oct.	Nov.	Dec.	Total
1989	312	295	307	300	373	279	240	290	248	246	314	280	3,485
1990	278	244	221	271	267	274	256	241	237	249	303	252	3,093
1991	273	209	229	228	285	236	220	254	263	259	250	268	2,973
1992	414	388	396	375	408	295	366	350	323	393	331	364	4,403
1993	359	406	374	357	315	266	293	275	292	293	261	303	3,794
1994	278	327	319	307	209	371	239	288	273	254	297	281	3,443
1995	279	273	340	281	381	355	331	404	364	340	384	351	4,083
1996	373	299	332	321	327	316	354	314	333	344	304	403	4,020
1997	343	262	296	331	250	326	292	344	331	281	340	382	3,780
1998[1]	338	486	426	372	377	363	382	311	450	433			3,938

[1] Preliminary. [2] Through 1991; output of commercial bars .999 fine, including U.S. Mint purchases of crude. Production is from both foreign and domestic silver.Beginning 1992; U.S. mine production of recoverable silver plus imports of refined silver. [2] Preliminary. *Source: U.S. Geological Survey (USGS)*

U.S. Exports of Refined Silver to Selected Countries In Thousands of Troy Ounces

Year	Canada	France	Germany	Hong Kong	Japan	Singapore	South Korea	Switzer-land	United Arab Emirates	United Kingdom	Uruguay	Other Countries	Total
1988	1,073	157	480	[2]	6,030	[2]	166	70	[2]	4,894	[2]	82	14,270
1989	2,597	61	519	[2]	5,997	[2]	588	88	[2]	3,722	[2]	55	13,828
1990	2,586	64	749	[2]	16,568	1,005	298	74	[2]	2,060	152	93	23,664
1991	736	22	350	755	6,519	1,593	2,823	8	3,462	8,628	259	73	25,318
1992	2,177	44	140	497	4,554	2,126	[2]	70	6,922	10,856	671	47	29,274
1993	4,910	[2]	34	1,002	3,414	2,500	1,492	38	4,403	3,673	530	44	22,673
1994	4,289	[2]	8	456	9,275	16	3,084	[2]	3,627	4,896	1,353	193	27,902
1995	1,667	431	[3]	[2]	2,737	2,209	2,929	1,170	10,285	63,882	937	41	86,644
1996	[2]	[2]	[3]	265	18,100	[2]	[2]	[2]	52,800	67	[2]	[2]	71,232
1997[1]	1,125	[2]	[2]	19,290	12,217	[2]	[2]	[2]	2	172,649	[2]	[2]	71,232

[1] Preliminary. [2] Included in "other countries", if any. *Source: American Bureau of Metal Statistics (ABMS)*

U.S. Imports of Silver from Selected Countries In Thousands of Troy Ounces

	Ores and Concentrates				Refined Bullion						
Year	Canada	Mexico	Other Countries	Total	Canada	Chile	Mexico	Peru	Uruguay	Other Countries	Total
1988	288	1,511	31	6,151	31,361	211	37,471	11	[2]	139	72,663
1989	56	129	28	225	37,203	724	53,262	2,761	1,958	0	98,429
1990	12	189	2	203	33,518	1,671	40,204	8,141	2,265	165	86,741
1991	42	277	29	348	25,389	6,640	34,448	13,748	[2]	17	81,198
1992	646	126	11	814	24,937	2,002	40,230	16,841	400	2	85,572
1993	299	836	12	1,147	28,622	1,058	27,241	12,709	[2]	28	70,189
1994	369	3,805	97	4,271	28,678	1,923	22,135	12,663	[2]	32	66,141
1995	312	6,269	-----	6,825	27,640	4,694	29,200	13,732	[2]	78	84,446
1996	189	3,890	-----	4,079	30,640	2,424	[2]	9,002	[2]	28	89,034
1997[1]	177	8,938	-----	9,253	35,687	1,511	31,958	8,970	[2]	180	78,126

[1] Preliminary. [2] Included in "other countries", if any. *Source: American Bureau of Metal Statistics (ABMS)*

World Silver Consumption[1] In Millions of Troy Ounces

	Industrial Uses										Coinage							
Year	Canada	France	Ger-many	India	Italy	Japan	Mexico	United Kingdom	United States	World Total	Austria	Canada	France	Ger-many	Mexico	United States	World Total	World Total
1988	11.0	21.3	44.0	22.4	37.9	100.4	7.1	22.8	112.0	568.6	.6	1.1	2.2	3.2	2.0	7.9	25.3	593.9
1989	12.0	22.1	46.7	25.6	43.1	100.8	7.2	24.6	120.0	599.2	.4	3.3	2.2	3.2	1.7	6.8	26.3	625.5
1990	4.0	22.4	51.7	42.3	45.7	106.9	14.1	24.7	118.9	651.8	.5	1.9	2.2	2.4	1.2	9.1	31.6	683.4
1991	3.8	26.9	52.2	44.9	57.4	109.3	14.3	24.7	112.3	672.3	.6	.9	2.0	5.5	1.6	10.5	28.4	700.7
1992	1.6	29.7	49.3	58.1	61.1	105.4	15.6	26.3	114.5	687.7	.5	.8	2.1	5.4	8.7	8.1	32.8	720.5
1993	1.6	27.6	45.6	109.9	57.5	105.5	15.6	27.9	123.5	736.1	.5	1.2	2.1	2.6	17.1	8.2	40.5	776.6
1994	1.6	26.5	45.8	91.8	53.2	108.4	15.3	31.4	132.6	716.9	.5	1.5	1.0	7.0	13.0	8.7	42.9	759.9
1995	2.0	29.7	43.6	98.7	51.0	112.7	16.9	31.6	144.8	750.4	.6	.7	1.1	2.4	.6	8.1	23.8	774.2
1996	2.0	26.6	41.0	128.4	53.1	112.1	20.3	33.8	150.2	791.7	.4	.7	.3	4.6	.5	6.1	22.3	814.0
1997[2]	2.1	28.0	42.3	131.0	57.9	120.0	23.3	34.9	161.5	836.0	.3	.7	.3	3.7	.4	5.5	27.4	863.4

[1] Non-communist areas only. [2] Preliminary. NA = Not available. *Source: The Silver Institute*

Soybean Meal

The world supply/demand statistics for soybean meal showed persistent growth through the 1990's and the pace could quicken in the year ahead due to the expansion in global poultry numbers. Soybean meal, a high protein feed used in formulating livestock and poultry rations, is obtained from the processing (crush) of soybeans and is the world's top protein meal with about 60 percent of total production. Cottonseed and rapeseed meal account for a combined total of about 20 percent. The U.S. is the largest producer followed by Brazil.

World soybean meal production in the mid-1990's averaged about 88 million metric tonnes. In crop year 1998/99 a record large 102 million tonnes were produced, of which the U.S. produced a near record large 34.4 million tonnes. Brazil's production reached a record 32 million tonnes. Argentina is the world's third largest producer with 15.8 million tonnes in 1998/99, virtually unchanged from the past few years.

Part of the growth in meal production has been indirectly derived from the strong worldwide demand for vegetable oils, but the primary reason is that more countries have increasing livestock numbers and a burgeoning need for high protein feed; a fact that is underscored by the sharp expansion in the world's soybean meal trade. Significantly, many of the recent gains in foreign trade have come from developing nations in Latin America and Asia.

World meal consumption in 1998/99 of a record large 102 million tonnes compares with 99 million in 1997/98. The U.S. is the largest single consumer with about 27 million tonnes, but the European Union and Asia run a close second with about 25 million tonnes each in 1998/99. Asia's usage has nearly doubled during the past decade reflecting the strong growth in that region's poultry production. China's 1998/99 consumption of 12.5 million tonnes compares with an annual average of less than 10 million prior to 1996/97. China's 1998/99 meal imports of a record large 4.4 million tonnes, the most of any other country, compares with 1.5 million tonnes three years ago. Earlier in the 1990's, China was a net exporter of soybean meal. France, the second largest importer, took 3.9 million tonnes vs. 3.3 million in the mid-1990's.

World carryover at the end of the 1998/99 season is forecast at 3.7 million tonnes, marginally lower than a year earlier. As usual, Argentina and Brazil account for at least a third of the carryover.

U.S. soymeal production (October-September) in 1998/99 of 38.3 million (short) tons compares with 37.7 million in 1997/98. Total 1998/99 supplies of 38.6 million tons compares with 38 million in 1997/98, including an October 1st carryin of about 0.2 million tons at the start of each crop year. Total supplies in the early 1990's averaged 30 million tons. Domestic usage has climbed steadily in recent years and is expected to total a record high 38.4 million tons in 1998/99 vs. 37.7 million in 1997/98. The gain, as in other countries, is largely due to increases in poultry production. It now appears that poultry demand controls the U.S. soybean crush, not soybean oil demand. Cattle accounts for minor soybean meal use, hogs a little more.

U.S. soybean meal exports in 1998/99 were forecast at a near record large 8.2 million metric tonnes vs. the record 8.4 million in 1997/98; the decline reflecting some easing in demand from China, increased competition from Brazil and Argentina, and larger oilseed production in Western Europe.

U.S. soybean meal prices, basis 48 percent protein, Decatur, Illinois, were expected to average between $130-$150 per short ton in 1998/99 vs. $185.54 in 1997/98, which if realized, would be the lowest crop year average since $136.40 in 1984/85. There is a moderate seasonality to prices with the crop year's high generally reached in September and October, before the weight of the new soybean harvest (and crush) enters the supply pipelines.

Futures Markets

Soybean meal futures and options are traded on the Chicago Board of Trade. A smaller futures contract is traded on the Mid-America Commodity Exchange.

World Supply and Demand of Soybean Meal In Thousands of Metric Tons

Year Beginnin Oct. 1	Production					Exports			Imports		Consumption			Ending Stocks		
	Brazil	China	EC-12	United States	Total	Brazil	United States	Total	France	Total	EC-12	United States	Total	Brazil	United States	Total
1989-90	12,350	3,020	10,580	25,150	70,089	9,430	4,830	26,010	3,480	25,730	19,900	20,220	68,950	1,114	290	4,070
1990-1	11,160	3,280	9,950	25,700	69,500	8,200	4,960	26,890	3,430	27,200	20,190	20,810	70,130	860	260	3,660
1991-2	11,740	2,750	10,530	27,060	73,200	8,780	6,300	28,620	3,550	28,250	21,170	20,870	73,360	520	210	3,140
1992-3	12,170	3,630	10,980	27,550	76,380	8,170	5,650	27,550	3,500	27,870	22,240	22,000	76,050	600	190	3,800
1993-4	14,500	6,160	9,850	27,680	81,200	10,310	4,860	29,950	3,800	29,260	22,680	22,940	80,600	610	140	3,710
1994-5	15,870	6,550	11,490	30,180	87,170	10,450	6,090	30,920	3,790	31,270	24,420	24,080	87,100	980	200	4,370
1995-6	17,040	6,050	10,910	29,510	89,100	11,940	5,450	33,780	3,340	32,860	22,650	24,140	88,310	970	190	4,310
1996-7	15,720	6,950	11,620	31,040	91,810	10,660	6,350	33,960	3,270	34,350	22,070	24,780	92,730	840	190	3,780
1997-8[1]	15,730	8,280	12,010	34,630	100,050	10,300	8,480	36,900	3,800	36,390	23,870	26,190	99,570	810	200	3,760
1998-9[2]	15,810	8,100	12,070	34,680	102,060	10,150	7,850	38,220	3,950	38,050	24,670	26,850	101,890	820	230	3,760

[1] Preliminary. [2] Forecast. *Source: Foreign Agricultural Service, U.S. Department of Agriculture (FAS-USDA)*

SOYBEAN MEAL

Average Open Interest of Soybean Futures in Chicago In Contracts

Year	Jan.	Feb.	Mar.	Apr.	May	June	July	Aug.	Sept.	Oct.	Nov.	Dec.
1989	71,792	71,599	67,542	58,923	58,794	64,212	59,547	60,925	59,271	60,038	63,552	57,219
1990	60,010	71,773	74,762	76,897	77,307	69,658	63,824	62,033	58,915	68,888	76,899	70,901
1991	62,172	60,017	56,179	59,107	49,973	57,068	55,629	54,342	67,765	68,627	68,263	71,900
1992	67,575	56,453	55,370	59,528	57,204	60,519	66,315	66,861	66,648	72,403	73,255	72,881
1993	63,178	70,384	64,550	66,121	78,386	74,191	91,435	73,770	75,267	77,065	83,802	85,039
1994	87,612	91,142	82,193	89,453	85,553	81,721	84,461	82,691	85,508	94,483	101,030	98,717
1995	97,661	101,253	101,846	99,898	90,237	86,090	83,712	74,233	79,450	85,290	103,824	110,193
1996	95,903	90,010	87,468	101,204	91,453	88,641	77,961	80,727	93,373	88,969	90,007	84,399
1997	86,204	97,618	107,763	111,413	113,848	110,780	114,372	108,923	111,447	118,409	125,201	116,760
1998	114,243	122,979	131,390	137,251	136,212	136,216	126,108	139,239	140,904	141,426	134,095	122,788

Source: Chicago Board of Trade (CBT)

Volume of Trading of Soybean Meal Futures in Chicago In Thousands of Contracts

Year	Jan.	Feb.	Mar.	Apr.	May	June	July	Aug.	Sept.	Oct.	Nov.	Dec.	Total
1989	408.1	320.7	382.4	388.8	406.7	403.8	410.7	393.1	382.8	364.8	330.1	294.8	4,487
1990	308.6	276.4	400.2	428.4	421.0	398.3	460.2	435.3	401.6	476.3	448.7	448.5	4,904
1991	323.4	281.8	310.3	429.3	296.8	412.5	484.3	463.6	394.7	410.8	351.6	339.6	4,499
1992	368.7	290.5	312.6	312.2	388.1	381.0	426.0	333.6	327.6	320.2	327.9	357.1	4,146
1993	295.5	288.1	346.6	307.9	356.7	518.2	575.5	460.5	402.4	315.6	469.3	380.6	4,717
1994	405.6	339.8	330.7	380.7	467.2	456.3	384.5	354.4	366.3	317.4	370.4	420.5	4,594
1995	283.6	307.5	404.4	410.9	532.7	479.6	610.8	491.8	481.9	449.0	523.4	625.6	5,601
1996	496.4	442.9	435.8	656.0	439.2	442.4	507.2	490.3	425.9	581.1	491.9	452.1	5,861
1997	479.0	481.8	509.5	576.6	581.9	569.8	579.7	452.2	531.3	589.5	561.1	512.5	6,425
1998	458.5	454.3	449.8	592.6	499.5	749.8	675.1	536.7	504.1	553.2	521.2	559.1	6,554

Source: Chicago Board of Trade (CBT)

Supply and Distribution of Soybean Meal in the United States — In Thousands of Short Tons

Year Beginning Oct. 1	Supply: For Stocks Oct. 1	Supply: Production	Supply: Total Supply	Distribution: Domestic	Distribution: Exports	Distribution: Total	$ Ton Decatur 48% Protein Solvent	$ Tonne: Decatur 44% Solvent	$ Tonne: Brazil FOB 45-46% Protein	$ Tonne: Rotterdam CIF
1989-90	173	27,719	27,928	22,291	5,319	27,610	186.48	192	181	204
1990-1	318	28,325	28,688	22,934	5,469	28,403	181.40	187	178	198
1991-2	285	29,831	30,183	23,008	6,945	29,953	189.20	194	184	203
1992-3	230	30,364	30,687	24,251	6,232	30,483	193.75	201	185	207
1993-4	204	30,514	30,788	25,282	5,356	30,638	192.86	199	182	202
1994-5	150	33,269	33,483	26,542	6,717	33,260	162.55	167	172	184
1995-6	223	32,527	32,826	26,611	6,002	32,613	236.00	248	256	256
1996-7[1]	212	34,211	34,525	27,321	6,994	34,316	270.90	286	289	278
1997-8[2]	210	38,171	38,437	28,889	9,330	38,219	185.54	193	201	197
1998-9[3]	218	37,757	38,025	29,850	7,900	37,750	130-145	151	158	159

[1] Preliminary. [2] Estimate. [3] Forecast. *Source: Economic Research Service, U.S. Department of Agriculture (ERS-USDA)*

U.S. Exports of Soybean Cake & Meal, by Country of Destination — In Thousands of Metric Tons

Year	Algeria	Australia	Canada	Dominican Republic	Italy	Japan	Mexico	Netherlands	Philippines	Russia[2]	Spain	Venezuela	Total
1988	411.4	35.5	718.1	92.7	543.6	33.0	332.3	553.9	110.6	1,122.0	71.2	851.3	6,348
1989	389.1	7.7	569.2	66.2	188.6	10.8	269.5	269.0	59.1	1,417.9	44.2	283.8	4,712
1990	373.5	28.2	555.5	130.5	146.4	20.8	253.0	229.7	200.7	1,568.4	19.6	332.2	4,826
1991	323.5	99.4	651.2	142.6	33.5	24.1	303.6	339.8	150.4	2,271.0	5.5	405.9	5,536
1992	237.8	75.9	582.5	146.7	93.4	167.2	454.4	420.0	434.8	765.1	92.3	473.8	6,236
1993	266.1	90.6	646.7	200.8	91.5	208.7	187.8	580.8	295.7	697.1	203.8	425.0	5,536
1994	248.3	247.0	706.3	209.2	27.1	76.9	367.5	465.6	257.9	159.5	92.6	258.9	4,825
1995	216.7	190.2	798.7	219.2	70.2	246.7	340.0	751.6	593.4	11.1	127.7	181.4	5,890
1996	203.4	157.2	687.3	260.7	85.9	225.5	292.2	452.6	423.2	5.1	51.8	274.9	5,860
1997[1]	250.8	136.1	651.6	261.1	284.1	263.3	142.1	449.0	483.1	8.3	329.1	336.7	6,994

[1] Preliminary. [2] Formerly part of the U.S.S.R.; data not reported separately until 1992. *Source: The Oil World*

Production of Soybean Cake & Meal[2] in the United States — In Thousands of Short Tons

Crop Year	Oct.	Nov.	Dec.	Jan.	Feb.	Mar.	Apr.	May	June	July	Aug.	Sept.	Total	Yield of Meal from Soybeans in lbs.
1989-90	2,246.2	2,492.5	2,519.6	2,548.6	2,187.2	2,432.3	2,263.7	2,224.2	2,183.4	2,196.6	2,237.1	2,187.3	27,718	47.63
1990-1	2,508.8	2,513.2	2,431.5	----------	7,082.0	----------	----------	6,640.8	----------	----------	7,148.9	----------	28,325	47.47
1991-2	----------	7,920.4	----------	2,665.5	2,393.8	2,544.4	2,411.3	2,262.5	2,372.4	2,434.2	2,429.0	2,397.3	29,831	47.51
1992-3	2,698.1	2,697.3	2,763.4	2,781.2	2,430.4	2,691.3	2,519.1	2,536.3	2,373.0	2,324.1	2,188.3	2,361.8	30,364	47.54
1993-4	2,707.1	2,714.8	2,696.7	2,632.3	2,458.1	2,696.3	2,510.0	2,446.4	2,330.7	2,398.0	2,406.6	2,517.1	30,514	47.62
1994-5	2,812.5	2,903.5	3,027.8	3,007.5	2,755.0	3,048.5	2,829.8	2,697.9	2,492.1	2,565.4	2,589.8	2,535.8	33,269	47.33
1995-6	2,893.2	2,948.9	2,972.3	2,945.2	2,652.1	2,757.5	2,683.1	2,534.6	2,566.2	2,656.3	2,513.4	2,404.1	32,527	47.69
1996-7	2,992.8	3,151.8	3,263.8	3,251.7	2,966.8	3,089.1	2,709.1	2,618.1	2,573.2	2,517.4	2,465.2	2,611.0	34,211	47.36
1997-8	3,344.0	3,390.6	3,624.2	3,596.0	3,278.9	3,478.1	3,172.1	2,956.2	2,794.7	2,941.0	2,665.0	2,930.0	38,171	47.40
1998-9[1]	3,426.1	3,367.4	3,425.1										40,874	

[1] Preliminary. [2] At oil mills; including millfeed and lecithin. *Source: Economic Research Service, U.S. Department of Agriculture (ERS-USDA)*

Stocks (at Oil Mills)[2] of Soybean Cake & Meal in the U.S., on First of Month — In Thousands of Short Tons

Year	Oct.	Nov.	Dec.	Jan.	Feb.	Mar.	Apr.	May	June	July	Aug.	Sept.
1989-90	172.9	220.5	194.3	328.2	254.0	262.0	311.8	307.9	252.6	262.5	267.7	232.0
1990-1	318.3	290.9	313.6	----------	455.8	----------	----------	527.8	----------	----------	425.0	----------
1991-2	----------	285.0	----------	281.0	258.3	291.3	315.6	310.4	310.2	274.7	260.5	209.9
1992-3	230.0	307.9	411.3	360.8	440.0	420.5	336.9	268.5	328.4	257.3	386.1	353.8
1993-4	204.4	375.1	282.3	290.1	230.0	283.1	277.3	333.0	325.2	254.3	267.5	144.9
1994-5	149.6	240.9	231.6	241.1	197.7	227.1	173.1	382.7	337.6	222.6	252.0	203.8
1995-6	223.4	196.9	241.3	394.8	302.2	229.9	369.3	382.1	306.8	406.2	298.8	218.3
1996-7	212.4	200.2	291.8	254.4	263.0	198.5	322.6	280.1	256.5	317.3	303.2	257.4
1997-8	206.6	218.2	412.2	262.0	269.3	280.7	238.0	210.4	290.2	193.1	205.3	187.2
1998-9[1]	218.1	271.9	352.3	313.9								

[1] Preliminary. [2] Including millfeed and lecithin. *Source: Economic Research Service, U.S. Department of Agriculture (ERS-USDA)*

SOYBEAN MEAL

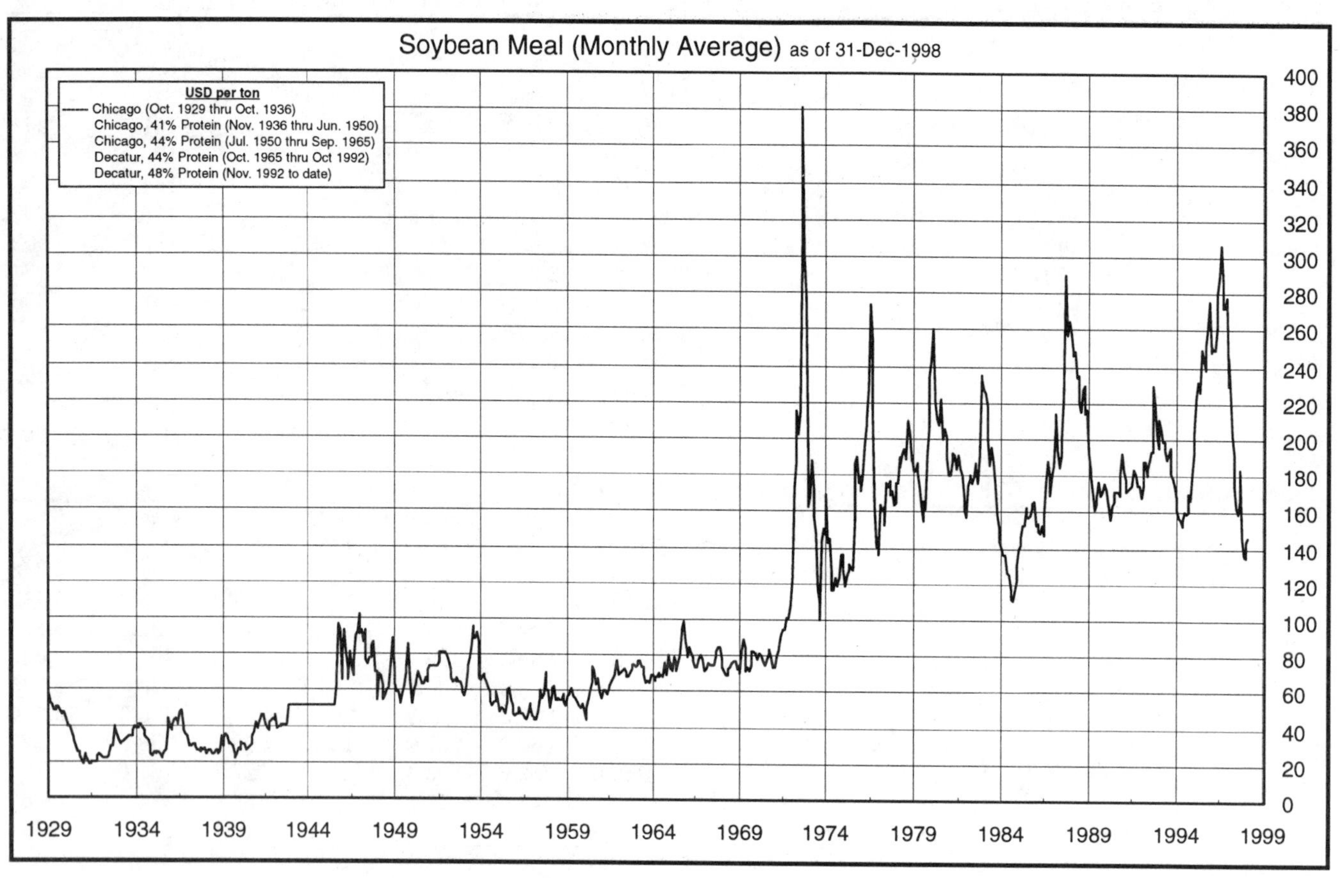

Average Price of Soybean Meal (44% Solvent) at Decatur In Dollars Per Short Ton--Bulk

Year	Oct.	Nov.	Dec.	Jan.	Feb.	Mar.	Apr.	May	June	July	Aug.	Sept.	Average
1988-9	259.75	248.20	246.00	249.30	234.10	237.10	220.75	214.70	227.50	231.50	215.50	227.50	234.33
1989-90	191.60	183.40	179.40	172.30	161.90	165.10	165.40	176.20	169.10	171.30	172.40	176.90	173.75
1990-1	172.50	163.80	164.80	153.70	163.50	165.75	171.50	171.00	171.10	169.70	177.60	191.90	169.74
1991-2	183.00	178.00	170.70	172.70	174.30	174.20	174.80	182.75	181.70	173.90	174.40	175.10	176.30
1992-3	168.60	170.90	176.40	175.60	167.50	172.40	175.60	181.70	181.30	217.60	206.90	186.50	181.75
1993-4	180.60	195.70	192.50	185.90	184.40	182.00	176.40	191.10	183.00	168.10	165.60	162.50	180.65
1994-5	156.40	150.90	145.40	145.10	149.40	145.70	151.00	148.10	149.10	160.10	157.50	171.75	152.54
1995-6	183.40	194.10	213.60	220.50	216.70	215.70	237.90	232.30	227.90	242.30	251.10	265.50	225.08
1996-7	238.00	242.70	240.90	240.70	253.60	270.40	277.70	296.00	275.90	261.49	261.60	265.70	260.39
1997-8	216.00	231.60	214.90	193.10	182.10	165.30	152.75	150.30	157.80	173.30	135.70	126.90	174.98

Source: Economic Research Service, U.S. Department of Agriculture (ERS-USDA)

Average Price of Soybean Meal (48% Solvent) at Decatur In Dollars Per Short Ton--Bulk

Year	Oct.	Nov.	Dec.	Jan.	Feb.	Mar.	Apr.	May	June	July	Aug.	Sept.	Average
1989-90	208.10	194.90	191.60	183.80	172.90	176.40	178.00	189.40	182.00	183.92	186.75	190.00	186.48
1990-1	185.40	174.25	175.90	167.00	174.50	177.60	182.50	182.10	183.25	181.00	188.75	204.25	181.40
1991-2	196.30	190.25	183.10	184.00	185.40	185.90	187.20	195.25	203.90	186.25	186.00	187.00	189.20
1992-3	180.60	181.90	187.60	188.75	179.90	183.60	187.40	193.25	193.10	229.90	219.10	199.90	193.75
1993-4	194.50	209.40	206.00	198.30	198.40	195.40	188.90	193.75	195.50	181.10	178.60	174.50	192.86
1994-5	168.50	161.00	156.90	156.40	151.30	156.90	161.90	159.10	160.40	170.45	166.70	180.99	162.55
1995-6	193.90	204.10	223.60	232.00	228.30	226.57	249.30	244.30	238.80	252.50	261.20	276.40	235.90
1996-7	248.50	251.50	250.60	249.20	262.40	280.50	288.60	306.40	287.90	273.60	273.30	278.30	270.90
1997-8	229.30	245.30	222.50	202.85	192.75	174.20	162.50	160.00	168.55	183.40	146.25	135.80	185.28
1998-9	135.70	144.45	146.40	138.80									141.34

Source: Economic Research Service, U.S. Department of Agriculture (ERS-USDA)

Soybean Oil

World soybean oil supply/demand has shown a continuous progression of new record highs. World production in 1998/99 of a record 23.1 million metric tonnes compares with the previous year's high of 22.8 million. The U.S., the world's largest soybean oil producer, generally accounts for about a third of total production, producing twice that of Brazil, the second largest producer.

World usage of soybean oil in 1998/99 of a record large 23.2 million tonnes compares with 23.1 million in 1997/98. The U.S. is the largest consumer with China a distant second.

World carryover stocks at the end of 1998/99 were estimated at 2.3 million tonnes, a shade under 1997/98 with nearly a third of the total in the U.S.

Global soybean oil exports in 1998/99 were estimated at a near record 6.75 million tonnes, about unchanged from 1997/98. Argentina is the largest exporter while Brazil and the U.S. vie for second place. U.S. exports in 1998/99 of 1.2 million tonnes compare with 1.3 million in 1997/98. Importing nations are numerous: China is now the largest single importer, 2.0 million tonnes in 1998/99, unchanged from 1997/98.

The U.S. soybean oil crop year begins October 1st. Production in 1998/99 of a near record high 18.1 billion pounds was a shade under the 1997/98 record. During the first half of the 1990's production averaged about 14 billion pounds. The oil content of U.S. soybeans correlates directly with temperatures and sunshine during the pod-filling stages. Carryin stocks on October 1, 1998 totaled about 1.3 billion pounds vs. 1.5 billion a year earlier. The U.S. supply for 1998/99 of a near record high 19.5 billion pounds compares with 19.7 billion in 1997/98. Disappearance in 1998/99 of 18.0 billion pounds compares with 18.4 billion in 1997/98. Bean oil stocks were forecast to build during 1998/99, lifting the yearend carryover to about 1.45 billion pounds.

Domestic soybean oil use in 1998/99 could reach a record high 15.4 billion pounds vs. 15.1 billion in 1997/98 as domestic prices should prove competitive to other fats and oils. A comparative price advantage, relative to Brazilian bean oil and Malaysian palm oil, helped boost exports to a record pace in the first half of the crop year but the pace slowed in the spring as competition from South American soybean oil expanded.

Crude soybean oil prices (basis Decatur) in 1998/99 were expected to range from 25.50¢ to 28.50¢ per pound vs. a 25.80¢ per pound average in 1997/98. The record high 30.6 cents was realized during 1983/84.

Futures Markets

Soybean oil futures and options are traded on the Chicago Board of Trade (CBT).

World Supply and Demand of Soybean Oil In Thousands of Metric Tons

Year Beginning Oct. 1	Production: Brazil	Production: EC-12	Production: United States	Production: Total	Exports: Brazil	Exports: United States	Exports: Total	Imports: India	Imports: Total	Consumption: Brazil	Consumption: EC-12	Consumption: India	Consumption: United States	Consumption: Total	Stocks[3]: United States	Stocks[3]: Total
1989-90	2,980	2,350	5,900	16,000	870	610	3,940	30	3,970	2,000	1,610	340	5,480	15,950	590	1,740
1990-1	2,679	2,243	6,082	15,909	686	356	3,635	20	3,587	2,136	1,661	370	5,515	15,886	810	1,988
1991-2	2,815	2,337	6,507	16,851	658	748	3,558	100	3,487	2,167	1,703	442	5,554	16,366	1,016	2,470
1992-3	2,910	2,540	6,250	17,200	690	640	4,210	40	3,900	2,280	2,000	560	5,920	17,220	710	2,050
1993-4	3,470	2,240	6,330	18,250	1,350	690	4,850	40	4,730	2,320	1,850	710	5,870	18,410	500	1,770
1994-5	3,800	2,580	7,080	19,710	1,550	1,220	6,080	60	6,100	2,470	1,920	560	5,860	19,440	520	2,050
1995-6	4,030	2,470	6,910	20,180	1,600	450	5,280	60	5,300	2,530	1,950	770	6,110	19,780	910	2,640
1996-7	3,720	2,630	7,150	20,680	1,290	920	5,920	50	5,890	2,600	1,800	710	6,470	20,730	690	2,550
1997-8[1]	3,740	2,770	8,230	22,810	1,180	1,440	6,700	240	6,740	2,730	1,830	1,100	6,880	22,770	630	2,640
1998-9[2]	3,740	2,780	8,280	23,280	1,200	1,230	6,780	150	6,710	2,780	1,860	1,080	6,990	23,410	720	2,450

[1] Preliminary. [2] Forecast. [3] End of season. *Source: Foreign Agricultural Service, U.S. Department of Agriculture (FAS-USDA)*

Supply and Distribution of Soybean Oil in the United States In Millions of Pounds

Year Beginning Oct. 1	Production	Imports	Stocks Oct. 1	Exports	Domestic Disappearance: Food: Total Domestic	Food: Shortening	Food: Margarine	Food: Cooking & Salad Oils	Food: Other Edible	Food: Total Food	Non-Food: Paint & Varnish	Non-Food: Resins & Plastics	Non-Food: Total Non-Food	Total Disappearance
1989-90	13,004	22	1,715	1,353	12,083	3,934	1,754	4,726	124	10,537	38	112	272	13,436
1990-1	13,408	17	1,305	780	12,164	4,090	1,811	4,693	130	10,722	49	106	295	12,944
1991-2	14,345	1	1,786	1,648	12,245	4,091	1,911	4,961	148	11,112	46	98	301	13,893
1992-3	13,778	10	2,239	1,419	14,473	4,465	1,970	4,717	254	11,505	38	95	296	14,473
1993-4	13,951	68	1,555	1,529	14,471	4,773	1,840	4,999	221	11,832	46	115	304	14,471
1994-5	15,613	17	1,103	2,680	15,597	4,714	1,693	5,546	222	12,175	49	124	287	15,597
1995-6	15,240	95	1,137	992	13,465	4,702	1,699	5,317	159	11,877	48	119	297	14,457
1996-7	15,752	53	2,015	2,037	14,264	4,578	1,667	6,119	68	12,432	51	132	333	16,300
1997-8[1]	18,143	60	1,520	3,077	15,264	4,688	1,623	6,188	72	12,570	49	128	490	18,341
1998-9[2]	18,070	63	1,382	2,550	15,600						31	118	580	18,150

[1] Preliminary. [2] Forecast. *Source: Economic Research Service, U.S. Department of Agriculture (ERS-USDA)*

SOYBEAN OIL

Stocks of Soybean Oil (Crude & Refined) in the United States, at End of Month In Millions of Pounds

Crop Year Beginning Oct.		Oct.	Nov.	Dec.	Jan.	Feb.	Mar.	Apr.	May	June	July	Aug.	Sept.
1992-3	Crude	1,856.1	1,885.0	2,041.5	2,177.8	2,110.4	2,029.0	2,068.9	2,006.4	1,967.0	1,848.8	1,518.6	1,352.9
	Refined	220.2	220.2	238.6	232.3	226.4	217.1	229.0	234.3	207.0	211.8	201.2	201.9
1993-4	Crude	1,239.6	1,209.9	1,189.3	1,184.2	1,184.0	1,192.3	1,329.8	1,346.2	1,330.0	1,352.6	1,124.0	904.7
	Refined	213.1	189.7	217.5	230.4	216.9	209.8	223.5	220.6	223.8	218.2	215.4	198.4
1994-5	Crude	850.8	811.4	826.6	880.6	876.7	838.3	860.5	893.9	885.9	906.3	895.3	905.7
	Refined	204.7	215.5	231.7	236.2	252.1	221.3	229.1	236.5	225.8	235.7	204.7	231.0
1995-6	Crude	990.4	908.9	1,154.3	1,237.4	1,264.2	1,366.6	1,490.1	1,531.7	1,672.4	1,951.4	1,874.3	1,799.3
	Refined	990.4	908.9	1,154.3	1,237.4	1,264.2	1,366.6	1,490.1	1,531.7	1,672.4	1,951.4	1,874.3	1,799.3
1996-7	Crude	1,796.5	1,711.6	1,805.1	1,928.5	1,982.6	1,938.2	1,929.9	1,919.4	1,917.8	1,760.3	1,492.8	1,321.1
	Refined	196.4	186.8	222.0	243.8	220.6	233.1	233.9	223.9	220.1	217.8	207.1	199.0
1997-8	Crude	1,307.0	1,303.6	1,439.8	1,518.8	1,459.1	1,498.6	1,533.3	1,577.6	1,451.7	1,535.9	1,240.1	1,167.4
	Refined	218.6	221.9	239.8	269.1	252.1	264.0	324.3	279.4	260.9	243.2	213.0	215.0
1998-9[1]	Crude	1,195.0	1,142.0	1,041.1									
	Refined	221.7	264.4	246.5									

[1] Preliminary. *Source: Bureau of the Census, U.S. Department of Commerce*

U.S. Exports of Soybean Oil[1], by Country of Destination In Metric Tons

Year Beginning Oct. 1	Canada	Ecuador	Ethiopia	Haiti	India	Mexico	Morocco	Pakistan	Panama	Peru	Turkey	Vene-zuela	Grand Total
1987-8	7,344	19,050	17,605	3,411	151,600	11,537	35,821	396,737	3,736	1,144	17,098	4,866	850,015
1988-9	5,364	30,930	8,960	2,846	28,127	17,730	80,023	453,067	6,695	5,778	0	29,055	753,576
1989-90	5,443	26,314	22,858	1,688	16,391	4,435	77,985	309,502	3,174	5,206	0	8,198	613,902
1990-1	3,790	20,832	14,948	4,946	13,544	11,087	73,255	66,209	8,123	6,566	16,460	0	353,959
1991-2	11,153	528	19,619	4,737	67,577	23,383	127,602	250	11,143	32,696	81,976	13	747,465
1992-3	28,585	17	8,272	6,753	49,452	44,194	57,995	0	641	36,340	58,436	0	643,796
1993-4	4,401	0	24,509	1,747	46,846	18,499	31,563	72,204	248	24,081	34,920	26	693,697
1994-5	24,886	12,698	8,391	49,793	28,949	58,623	29,053	25,500	13,342	8,692	5,750	2,016	1,215,804
1995-6	43,912	1,155	4,546	15,041	20,841	46,643	------	------	9,512	35,999	1,960	1,877	449,876
1996-7[2]	60,318	6,587	19,492	36,436	26,675	81,901	46,682	------	3,623	37,726	6,952	517	923,871

[1] Crude & refined oil combined as such. [2] Preliminary. *Source: Foreign Agricultural Service, U.S. Department of Agriculture (FAS-USDA)*

Production of Crude Soybean Oil[2] in the United States In Millions of Pounds

Year	Oct.	Nov.	Dec.	Jan.	Feb.	Mar.	Apr.	May	June	July	Aug.	Sept.	Total
1989-90	1,057	1,146	1,161	1,187	1,022	1,142	1,067	1,050	1,036	1,038	1,059	1,038	13,004
1990-1	1,188	1,168	1,138	------------	3,331	------------	------------	3,171	------------	------------	3,412	------------	13,408
1991-2	------------	3,772	------------	1,270	1,147	1,228	1,167	1,096	1,152	1,177	1,179	1,158	14,345
1992-3	1,238	1,200	1,239	1,247	1,102	1,216	1,148	1,152	1,083	1,070	1,006	1,078	13,778
1993-4	1,241	1,228	1,218	1,192	1,122	1,231	1,155	1,123	1,070	1,099	1,104	1,168	13,951
1994-5	1,328	1,342	1,403	1,400	1,289	1,419	1,333	1,275	1,183	1,205	1,228	1,208	15,613
1995-6	1,354	1,360	1,382	1,360	1,236	1,292	1,259	1,197	1,221	1,263	1,171	1,139	15,234
1996-7	1,401	1,430	1,473	1,474	1,348	1,413	1,254	1,216	1,196	1,176	1,141	1,231	15,752
1997-8	1,591	1,580	1,689	1,685	1,558	1,655	1,526	1,418	1,337	1,409	1,285	1,410	18,143
1998-9[1]	1,628	1,598	1,610										19,345

[1] Preliminary. [2] Not seasonally adjusted. *Source: Economic Research Service, U.S. Department of Agriculture (ERS-USDA)*

Production of Refined Soybean Oil in the United States In Millions of Pounds

Year	Oct.	Nov.	Dec.	Jan.	Feb.	Mar.	Apr.	May	June	July	Aug.	Sept.	Total
1989-90	936.8	912.0	873.9	887.8	800.6	800.6	812.7	952.8	915.1	903.7	931.1	935.7	10,745
1990-1	1,028.0	980.6	934.7	------------	2,717.1	------------	------------	2,865.5	------------	------------	2,952.8	------------	11,479
1991-2	------------	2,918.1	------------	933.8	876.7	1,041.3	973.1	993.3	977.9	979.2	997.6	1,040.7	11,732
1992-3	1,095.6	999.4	951.0	960.1	935.4	1,054.9	1,039.7	950.6	1,042.8	978.2	1,066.7	1,109.7	12,184
1993-4	1,094.3	1,053.5	1,030.8	960.1	945.5	1,056.6	1,018.5	1,012.0	1,017.3	968.0	1,107.2	1,044.6	12,308
1994-5	1,123.0	1,079.2	1,060.6	1,002.5	968.2	1,063.6	1,010.4	1,077.0	993.5	940.9	1,076.8	1,039.8	12,435
1995-6	1,119.2	1,088.8	1,018.5	979.9	934.3	1,042.6	997.3	1,009.3	962.8	971.9	1,115.8	1,058.7	12,299
1996-7	1,111.7	1,064.1	1,025.7	969.8	931.5	1,057.1	1,023.7	1,026.2	984.8	1,019.1	1,094.3	1,072.5	12,381
1997-8	1,173.9	1,156.3	1,110.1	1,092.6	1,047.4	1,148.2	1,094.8	1,140.7	1,053.1	1,083.9	1,173.4	1,114.5	13,389
1998-9[1]	1,200.6	1,108.8	1,041.2										13,402

[1] Preliminary. *Source: Bureau of the Census, U.S. Department of Commerce*

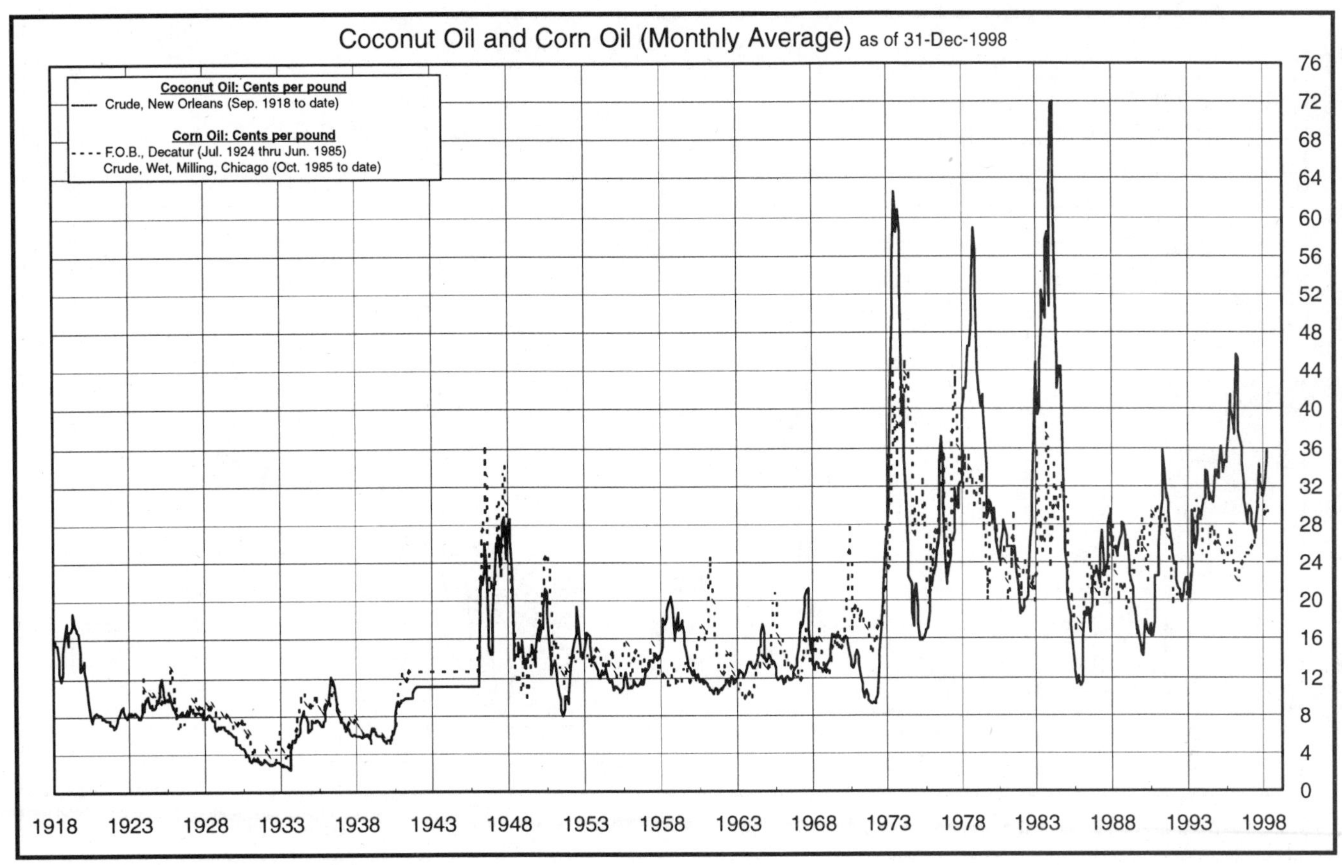

Consumption of Soybean Oil in End Products in the United States In Millions of Pounds

Year	Jan.	Feb.	Mar.	Apr.	May	June	July	Aug.	Sept.	Oct.	Nov.	Dec.	Total
1989	780.8	729.5	834.7	800.8	851.9	854.2	774.7	876.9	876.2	923.2	889.7	887.0	10,080
1990	901.3	815.7	952.0	893.6	950.9	927.8	866.0	905.4	895.7	984.1	912.9	878.0	10,883
1991	--------	2,690.3	------------	--------	2,831.8	------------	--------	2,837.7	------------	--------	2,907.8	------------	11,268
1992	880.4	867.0	1,010.1	947.9	956.7	962.1	935.5	932.4	1,019.8	1,061.7	951.8	946.1	11,472
1993	934.5	942.2	1,092.6	1,044.6	981.2	1,036.0	1,019.3	1,097.3	1,103.3	1,123.6	1,092.1	1,029.2	12,496
1994	924.5	939.1	1,084.7	1,040.6	1,001.4	1,023.8	974.9	1,119.2	1,075.4	1,123.3	1,103.4	1,063.8	12,474
1995	991.1	950.0	1,093.8	1,006.2	1,077.3	1,020.8	948.7	1,046.1	1,042.3	1,092.0	1,067.7	1,002.6	12,339
1996	964.9	927.4	1,026.4	999.8	1,020.6	946.2	959.9	1,123.3	1,042.8	1,137.1	1,080.9	1,093.1	12,322
1997	1,086.0	979.7	1,104.9	1,060.4	1,034.1	995.2	991.4	1,126.1	1,067.8	1,128.5	1,100.0	1,087.8	12,762
1998[1]	1,045.8	1,020.2	1,129.7	1,066.5	1,101.6	1,070.1	1,062.2	1,123.4	1,122.0	1,231.5	1,150.2	1,040.4	13,164

[1] Preliminary. *Source: Bureau of the Censue, U.S. Department of Commerce*

U.S. Exports of Soybean Oil (Crude and Refined) In Millions of Pounds

Year	Jan.	Feb.	Mar.	Apr.	May	June	July	Aug.	Sept.	Oct.	Nov.	Dec.	Total
1989	104.5	65.8	112.4	105.5	161.4	72.1	159.3	181.1	265.6	116.2	82.5	113.4	1,540
1990	95.4	136.2	164.4	33.0	112.0	161.9	122.6	82.8	132.9	85.4	43.9	12.1	1,183
1991	--------	71.8	------------	--------	132.3	------------	--------	434.8	------------	--------	336.1	------------	975
1992	140.0	171.9	134.6	155.4	69.1	129.1	163.7	205.2	142.5	169.5	113.2	91.6	1,686
1993	146.8	188.0	143.3	61.1	154.8	75.4	59.9	116.0	99.7	190.4	88.6	200.2	1,524
1994	120.4	144.6	94.4	46.1	111.6	36.1	57.7	184.6	254.0	154.8	303.2	305.9	1,813
1995	217.4	367.6	564.2	236.2	90.8	160.4	91.0	109.4	79.4	69.3	205.4	95.9	2,287
1996	189.1	97.0	68.0	75.3	63.9	16.1	27.1	28.0	56.7	121.0	303.8	213.3	1,259
1997	190.7	239.2	301.1	84.9	28.9	44.9	144.1	212.9	152.1	217.2	424.0	199.7	2,240
1998[1]	449.4	387.6	268.6	191.1	148.1	204.7	161.8	316.0	108.9	189.6	343.5		3,021

[1] Preliminary. *Source: Economic Research Service, U.S. Department of Agriculture (ERS-USDA)*

SOYBEAN OIL

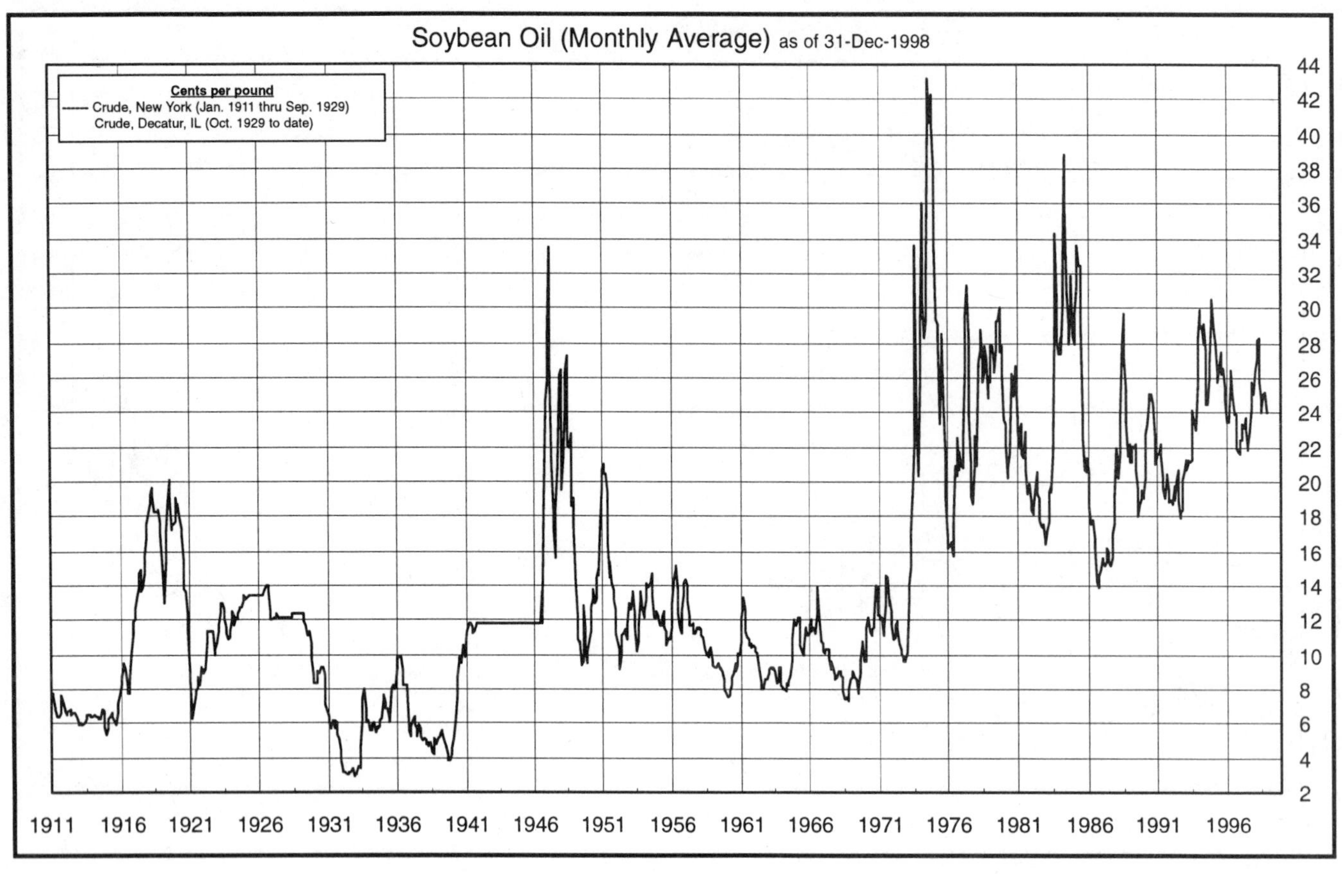

Stocks of Soybean Oil (Crude and Refined) at Factories and Warehouses in the U.S. In Millions of Pounds

Year	Oct. 1	Nov. 1	Dec. 1	Jan. 1	Feb. 1	Mar. 1	Apr. 1	May 1	June 1	July 1	Aug. 1	Sept. 1
1989-90	1,715	1,515	1,532	1,605	1,718	1,703	1,695	1,716	1,551	1,422	1,433	1,380
1990-1	1,305	1,216	1,320	--------	1,464	------------	--------	1,875	------------	--------	1,853	------------
1991-2	--------	1,786	------------	2,217	2,159	2,402	2,400	2,423	2,433	2,427	2,421	2,363
1992-3	2,239	2,076	2,111	2,280	2,410	2,337	2,246	2,298	2,241	2,174	2,061	1,720
1993-4	1,555	1,453	1,400	1,407	1,415	1,401	1,402	1,553	1,567	1,554	1,571	1,339
1994-5	1,103	1,056	1,027	1,055	1,117	1,129	1,060	1,090	1,130	1,112	1,142	1,100
1995-6	1,137	1,196	1,132	1,409	1,513	1,521	1,654	1,747	1,759	1,888	2,156	2,091
1996-7	2,015	1,993	1,898	2,027	2,172	2,203	2,171	2,164	2,143	2,138	1,978	1,700
1997-8	1,520	1,526	1,526	1,680	1,788	1,711	1,763	1,858	1,857	1,713	1,779	1,453
1998-9[1]	1,382	1,417	1,406	1,288								

[1] Preliminary. *Source: Economic Research Service, U.S. Department of Agriculture (ERS-USDA)*

Average Price of Crude Domestic Soybean Oil (in Tank Cars) F.O.B. Decatur In Cents Per Pound

Year	Oct.	Nov.	Dec.	Jan.	Feb.	Mar.	Apr.	May	June	July	Aug.	Sept.	Average
1989-90	19.02	19.57	19.11	19.28	20.27	22.80	23.35	24.72	25.03	24.69	25.05	24.45	22.28
1990-1	22.59	21.05	21.55	21.56	21.66	22.21	21.50	20.23	19.65	19.05	20.23	20.46	21.00
1991-2	19.57	18.78	18.99	18.77	18.88	19.74	19.00	20.15	20.71	18.82	17.87	18.28	19.10
1992-3	18.36	20.10	20.52	21.23	20.72	21.00	21.24	21.15	21.30	24.13	23.47	23.61	21.40
1993-4	22.98	25.37	28.09	29.91	28.84	29.03	27.94	29.10	27.60	24.53	24.51	26.11	27.00
1994-5	27.06	29.84	30.61	29.01	28.15	28.33	27.16	26.00	26.78	27.60	26.56	26.26	27.71
1995-6	26.56	25.41	24.76	23.69	23.65	23.60	25.82	26.50	24.95	24.10	23.99	23.92	24.70
1996-7	21.95	21.80	21.60	22.45	22.41	23.29	23.17	23.68	22.97	21.89	22.06	22.88	22.50
1997-8	24.31	25.73	25.08	25.09	26.51	27.09	28.10	28.28	25.83	24.88	23.99	25.13	25.84
1998-9[1]	25.21	25.20	23.99	22.88									24.32

[1] Preliminary. *Source: Economic Research Service, U.S. Department of Agriculture (ERS-USDA)*

Average Open Interest of Soybean Oil Futures in Chicago In Contracts

Year	Jan.	Feb.	Mar.	Apr.	May	June	July	Aug.	Sept.	Oct.	Nov.	Dec.
1989	77,741	81,676	78,235	77,249	73,623	76,572	70,644	68,652	63,751	63,911	69,248	68,166
1990	73,368	80,842	87,615	92,845	103,116	103,747	88,763	81,310	73,841	78,548	86,786	75,995
1991	72,987	71,607	76,800	70,361	70,954	73,870	73,864	70,058	66,128	61,227	69,657	63,901
1992	68,619	73,919	75,508	68,749	65,084	71,507	64,450	72,569	70,228	65,243	76,168	76,908
1993	73,683	68,887	66,803	68,598	65,814	73,892	83,730	72,746	64,927	62,348	80,136	94,990
1994	97,198	99,640	100,334	98,659	97,595	83,165	93,994	88,196	81,735	86,901	108,327	114,928
1995	101,171	103,856	97,715	87,300	76,175	75,171	81,650	77,064	70,410	71,652	85,241	84,138
1996	87,214	85,611	87,859	95,954	95,422	86,366	81,440	80,090	83,211	98,514	97,496	86,119
1997	89,112	89,348	102,388	101,191	101,544	104,433	105,346	95,282	94,521	107,471	119,877	106,406
1998	105,798	121,657	142,100	160,004	159,248	139,934	117,487	112,177	115,879	115,260	110,386	104,738

Source: Chicago Board of Trade (CBT)

Volume of Trading of Soybean Oil Futures in Chicago In Thousands of Contracts

Year	Jan.	Feb.	Mar.	Apr.	May	June	July	Aug.	Sept.	Oct.	Nov.	Dec.	Total
1989	317.8	347.7	368.1	384.7	426.4	386.3	414.5	348.8	320.8	341.0	344.2	298.6	4,298.9
1990	294.1	397.1	413.9	447.7	488.8	441.5	462.3	405.6	319.2	344.1	370.2	266.3	4,650.8
1991	330.2	259.4	355.0	342.1	364.6	322.9	433.8	399.8	303.2	340.6	297.9	369.3	4,118.8
1992	344.2	293.1	400.0	255.8	381.8	352.3	413.1	298.0	425.9	346.8	365.8	405.5	4,282.3
1993	341.4	281.1	378.4	291.5	261.6	434.7	513.3	444.6	449.3	302.1	465.2	448.6	4,611.8
1994	442.0	401.6	366.0	391.2	442.4	378.2	397.5	357.9	415.4	476.9	516.7	477.4	5,063.2
1995	424.4	363.7	464.4	355.9	457.7	418.2	377.4	330.5	303.9	317.2	431.7	366.4	4,611.3
1996	354.6	355.2	375.2	443.4	376.7	423.1	512.6	449.0	425.9	414.0	396.2	454.3	4,980.3
1997	473.3	381.9	504.0	445.8	389.7	439.6	442.8	375.1	418.0	413.7	489.5	511.4	5,285.0
1998	443.6	557.0	497.9	673.1	624.5	648.1	629.6	491.2	558.0	383.8	450.1	540.4	6,497.3

Source: Chicago Board of Trade (CBT)

Soybeans

U.S. soybean prices fell nearly $2.00 per bushel during calendar year 1998, extending a decline that took hold in early 1997; the added weakness carried to almost $5.00/bu. towards yearend 1998, basis nearby futures, the lowest level in years. Although futures recovered somewhat by yearend, the entrenched weakness reflected both near record 1998/99 world supplies and ending carryover stocks.

The 1998/99 world production of 153.6 million metric tonnes trailed initial forecasts by almost 3 million tonnes and compared to the 1997/98 record large 156 million tonnes; still, production proved well above the growth trend into the mid-1990's when production averaged less than 120 million tonnes. Although the 1998/99 U.S. crop proved lower than expected, a record large 2.77 billion bushels (75.4 million tonnes) were still realized. The U.S. produces nearly half of the world's soybeans and Brazil, the second largest producer, about a third. Soybean production is expanding is a number of countries, but the U.S. ranking is well entrenched as is Brazil's runner-up slot. A key question area is China, who during the past few years has vied with Argentina to be the third largest producer; in 1998/99 China produced 13.5 million tonnes and Argentina 16.5 million; both totals below their record large 1997/98 crops. The odds would seem to favor stronger growth in China in line with their expanding poultry flocks and the derived need for high protein soybean meal. However, as China's economy becomes more market sensitive, growers may switch to higher priced crops as happened in the mid-1990's as soybean acreage was moved into corn and cotton production. It is possible that China's soybean acreage has temporarily peaked at around 8 million hectares, suggesting that further production gains will be dependent on realizing higher average yields, estimated at 1.69 tonnes per hectare in 1998/99. Brazil's soybean crop is sown about the same time the U.S. crop is harvested and was forecast at 29 million tonnes in 1998/99 vs. 31 million in 1997/98. Percentagewise, Argentina's bean production shows the fastest year-to-year gain in the 1990's, however, unlike Brazil, Argentine soybean farmers have significantly lower production costs and a better transportation structure. Brazil soybean acreage is nearly double Argentina's, 12.8 million hectares vs. 7.1 million in 1998/99, respectively, but yield per acre is lower, 2.27 tonnes/hectare in Brazil vs. 2.32 tonnes in Argentina. Brazil's crop year encompasses February to January; Argentina's is April to March.

World soybean trade in 1998/99 of a near record large 38.1 million tonnes compares with the 1997/98 record of 40 million. The U.S. now accounts for about 60 percent of world exports, a somewhat lower percentage than earlier in the 1990's; 22.6 million tonnes in 1998/99 vs. 23.9 million in 1997/98. Brazil's exports, however, have since doubled, totaling 8.3 million tonnes in 1998/99 vs. 9.1 million in 1997/98, and about 3.5 million in the mid-1990's. Importing nations are more numerous, the biggest are generally the European Union and Japan. The ending 1998/99 world bean carryover of 23.2 million tonnes compares with the year earlier 19.2 million; generally the U.S., Brazil and Argentina account for about 80 percent of total world stocks.

U.S. farmers harvested an estimated record large 71.6 million acres of soybeans in 1998 vs. 69.6 million in 1997. An average yield of 40.6 bushels per acre was realized vs. 38.8 bushels in 1997, and the record high 41.4 bushels in 1994. Iowa is the largest producing state with Illinois a close second followed by Minnesota and Indiana.

U.S. soybean crop year begins September 1st. Carryover stocks on August 31, 1998, of 200 million bushels brought total 1998/99 supplies to 2.8 billion bushels vs. 2.7 billion in 1997/98. Total disappearance in 1998/99 was put at 2.6 billion bushels, of which at least 1.6 billion will be crushed, 0.8 billion exported and about 150 million allocated to seed and residual. Carryover as of August 31, 1999 is forecast at a record large 395 million bushels. Projected carryover as a percentage of usage in 1998/99 was forecast near 15 percent, twice that of 1997/98.

The 1998/99 season could yet prove to have a more or less intense demand than initially expected, much will depend on the crush and export demand during December-February which tends to be the seasonal high. Early in the season the export outlook was eclipsed by the more dominant domestic crush market. Major foreign buyers for U.S. beans in 1997/98 included Brazil, China and the European Union; Brazil's 1998/99 needs are expected to fall and a slowing Chinese economy could dampen imports relative to recent years. Still, should a more positive soybean usage outlook shows signs of materializing it is apt to show in early calendar year prices. Demand bull years in soybeans generally show counterseasonal strength in January and February, however, if total usage holds neutral and/or weakens then prices, manifested chiefly in futures, tend to witness what is referred to as the "February break." If the latter develops it is not unusual for prices to penetrate the harvest lows of the previous October-December quarter.

The U.S.D.A.'s average price received by farmers in 1998/99 was forecast at $5.00 to $5.70 per bushel vs. $6.45 in 1997/98. The highest farm price during the past decade was $7.42 in 1988/89, and the low was $5.56 in 1992/93.

Futures Markets

Soybean futures are traded on the Bolsa de Mercadorias & Futuros (BM&F), the Kansai Agricultural Commodities Exchange (KANEX), the Tokyo Grain Exchange (TGE), the Manila International Futures Exchange Inc. (MIFE), the Chicago Board of Trade (CBOT), and the Mid America Commodity Exchange (MidAm). Options are traded on the TGE, the CBOT, and the MidAm.

World Production of Soybeans   In Thousands of Metric Tons

Crop Year[4]	Argentina	Bolivia	Brazil	Canada	China	India	Indonesia	Mexico	Paraguay	Thailand	United States	Former USSR	World Total
1989-90	10,750	173	20,340	1,219	10,227	1,806	1,315	984	1,575	672	52,354	956	107,367
1990-1	11,500	352	15,750	1,262	11,000	2,602	1,400	575	1,300	530	52,416	880	104,155
1991-2	11,315	384	19,456	1,460	9,713	2,492	1,555	725	1,315	436	54,065	830	108,050
1992-3	11,240	278	22,710	1,455	10,304	3,106	1,870	573	1,794	435	59,546	620	117,508
1993-4	12,200	491	24,963	1,851	14,600	3,700	1,709	497	1,890	480	50,919	660	117,058
1994-5	12,500	710	25,900	2,251	16,000	3,150	1,565	523	2,200	528	68,490	465	137,730
1995-6	12,430	887	24,150	2,293	13,500	4,350	1,689	190	2,400	386	59,240	321	124,980
1996-7[1]	11,200	862	26,800	2,170	13,220	4,000	1,517	56	2,770	359	64,840	304	131,730
1997-8[2]	18,700	1,023	31,000	2,737	14,730	4,900	1,357	170	2,800	373	73,550	290	156,190
1998-9[3]	16,500		29,000		13,500				3,100		75,190		153,660

[1] Preliminary. [2] Estimate. [3] Forecast. [4] Split year includes Northern Hemisphere crops harvested in the late months of the first year shown combined with Southern Hemisphere crops harvested in the early months of the following year. *Source: Foreign Agricultural Service, U.S. Department of Agriculture*

Supply and Distribution of Soybeans in the United States   In Millions of Bushels

Crop Year Beginning Sept. 1	Supply: Stocks, Sept. 1: Farms	Supply: Stocks, Sept. 1: Mills, Elevators[3]	Supply: Stocks, Sept. 1: Total	Supply: Production	Supply: Total Supply	Distribution: Crushings	Distribution: Exports	Distribution: Seed, Feed & Residual	Distribution: Total Distribution
1989-90	87.3	94.7	182.0	1,923.7	2,108.2	1,146.4	622.9	99.7	1,869.1
1990-1	86.0	153.1	239.1	1,925.9	2,168.6	1,187.3	557.3	94.9	1,839.5
1991-2	118.4	210.6	329.0	1,986.5	2,319.0	1,253.5	683.9	103.1	2,040.6
1992-3	105.0	173.4	278.4	2,190.4	2,470.8	1,279.0	769.6	130.0	2,178.6
1993-4	125.0	167.3	292.3	1,871.0	2,169.7	1,275.6	589.1	95.8	1,960.5
1994-5	59.1	150.0	209.1	2,516.7	2,731.3	1,405.2	838.1	153.2	2,396.5
1995-6	105.1	229.7	334.8	2,176.8	2,516.1	1,369.5	851.2	111.9	2,332.6
1996-7	59.5	123.9	183.5	2,382.0	2,574.7	1,435.9	881.8	125.6	2,441.0
1997-8[1]	43.6	87.8	131.4	2,703.0	2,839.0	1,597.0	870.0	158.0	2,626.0
1998-9[2]	84.3	115.5	199.8	2,757.0	2,963.0	1,590.0	810.0	153.0	2,553.0

[1] Preliminary. [2] Estimate. [3] Also warehouses. *Source: Economic Research Service, U.S. Department of Agriculture (ERS-USDA)*

U.S. Soybean Price Support Program & Official Crop Production Reports   In Millions of Bushels

Crop Year Beginning Sept.	Quantity Put Under Support	% of Production	Stocks Sept. 1	National Average Support: % of Parity	National Average Support: $ Per Bu.	Crop Production Reports (In Thousands of Bushels): Aug. 1	Sept. 1	Oct. 1	Nov. 1	Dec. 1	Final
1989-90	208.9	10.9	182.0	37	4.53	1,905,300	1,889,265	1,926,385	1,936,545	----------	1,926,806
1990-1	241.4	12.5	239.1	36	4.50	1,836,017	1,834,602	1,823,462	1,903,832	----------	1,925,947
1991-2	158.8	8.0	329.0	40	5.02	1,868,825	1,816,825	1,933,570	1,961,840	----------	1,986,539
1992-3	182.1	8.3	278.4	41	5.02	2,079,487	NA	NA	NA	----------	2,190,354
1993-4	87.1	4.8	292.3	40	5.02	1,902,023	1,909,188	1,890,808	1,833,788	----------	1,870,958
1994-5	375.0	14.9	209.1	40	4.92	2,282,367	2,316,077	2,458,087	2,522,527	----------	2,516,694
1995-6	181.8	8.4	334.8	39	4.92	2,245,901	2,284,551	2,190,661	2,182,991	----------	2,176,814
1996-7	195.9	12.2	183.5	-----	4.97	2,299,675	2,269,505	2,346,220	2,402,610	----------	2,380,274
1997-8	265.5	10.1	131.4	-----	5.26	2,744,451	2,745,891	2,721,843	2,736,115	----------	2,688,750
1998-9[1]	306.1	9.0	199.8	-----	5.26	2,824,744	2,908,604	2,768,919	2,762,609	----------	2,756,794

[1] Preliminary. NA = Not available. *Source: National Agricultural Statistics Service, U.S. Department of Agriculture (NASS-USDA)*

Soybean Stocks in the United States   In Thousands of Bushels

Year	On Farms: Mar. 1	On Farms: Jun. 1	On Farms: Sept. 1	On Farms: Dec. 1	Off Farms[1]: Mar. 1	Off Farms[1]: Jun. 1	Off Farms[1]: Sept. 1	Off Farms[1]: Dec. 1	Total Stocks: Mar. 1	Total Stocks: Jun. 1	Total Stocks: Sept. 1	Total Stocks: Dec. 1
1989	415,000	229,200	87,320	793,400	475,246	235,311	94,709	816,583	890,246	464,511	182,029	1,609,983
1990	535,800	255,300	86,000	754,000	519,705	340,614	153,139	929,963	1,055,505	595,914	239,139	1,683,963
1991	555,500	336,500	118,400	810,000	634,619	387,022	210,642	968,957	1,190,119	723,522	329,042	1,778,957
1992	505,000	279,000	105,000	876,100	672,343	416,671	173,437	959,885	1,177,343	695,671	278,437	1,835,985
1993	576,900	319,800	124,970	697,400	638,667	363,613	167,314	876,220	1,215,567	683,413	292,284	1,573,620
1994	425,700	195,000	59,080	985,800	595,917	360,260	150,037	1,116,156	1,021,617	555,260	209,117	2,101,956
1995	635,300	348,800	105,130	861,500	734,898	443,072	229,684	971,929	1,370,198	791,872	334,814	1,833,429
1996	512,000	234,100	59,523	935,100	678,356	388,701	123,935	889,984	1,190,356	622,801	183,458	1,825,084
1997	514,000	216,000	43,600	1,048,000	541,912	283,890	88,233	951,417	1,055,912	499,890	131,833	1,999,417
1998	637,000	318,000	84,300	1,187,000	565,922	275,654	115,499	999,756	1,202,922	593,654	199,799	2,186,756

[1] Includes stocks at mills, elevators, warehouses, terminals and processors. NA = Not available. *Source: National Agricultural Statistics Service, U.S. Department of Agriculture (NASS-USDA)*

SOYBEANS

Commercial Stocks of Soybeans in the United States, on First of Month In Millions of Bushels

Year	Jan.	Feb.	Mar.	Apr.	May	June	July	Aug.	Sept.	Oct.	Nov.	Dec.
1989	81.3	75.6	63.8	53.4	35.8	31.2	21.1	18.6	14.1	11.4	62.1	71.3
1990	65.8	62.1	57.8	53.2	56.2	54.4	48.1	41.4	26.1	24.1	89.7	90.7
1991	90.2	78.1	70.5	56.2	43.5	35.5	33.3	25.5	25.3	29.7	80.6	84.0
1992	76.0	75.9	67.1	67.8	58.5	57.2	51.7	32.1	18.6	59.0	75.1	79.9
1993	71.5	63.5	54.5	48.5	44.0	32.1	26.6	24.4	15.8	9.6	52.3	60.2
1994	62.6	65.3	54.4	46.3	40.7	34.7	29.9	24.3	19.8	11.5	68.1	83.4
1996	57.2	57.2	59.2	54.7	56.2	44.9	36.9	32.7	12.0	5.3	55.2	50.6
1997	32.6	28.8	22.9	26.0	29.2	24.7	14.3	12.8	6.3	4.5	50.2	49.4
1998	35.3	31.2	22.9	18.4	14.5	14.2	10.2	9.7	8.7	18.6	43.5	40.6
1999	39.1	31.5										

Source: Livestock Division, U.S. Department of Agriculture (LD-USDA)

Salient Statistics of Soybeans in the United States

Crop Year	Planted	Acreage Harvested	Yield Per Acre (Bu.)	Farm Price ($ Bu.)	Farm Value (Million Dollars)	Pounds Per Bushel Crushed: Yield of Oil	Yield of Meal	-U.S. Exports of Soybeans Crop Year (Oct-Sept) in Thous of Metric Tons-: Grand Total	Germany	Japan	Netherlands	Spain	Taiwan	former USSR
	--- 1,000 Acres ---													
1989-90	60,820	59,538	32.3	5.69	10,916	11.17	47.63	16,933	818	3,480	2,721	1,565	2,016	342
1990-1	57,795	56,512	34.1	5.74	11,042	11.23	47.47	15,161	760	3,584	2,085	1,027	1,087	354
1991-2	59,180	58,011	34.2	5.58	11,092	11.42	47.51	19,277	814	3,891	3,167	1,459	2,034	543
1992-3	59,180	58,233	37.6	5.56	12,168	10.84	47.54	20,400	893	3,984	3,362	1,424	2,369	46
1993-4	60,135	57,347	32.6	6.40	11,950	10.87	47.62	16,364	807	3,527	2,661	921	1,700	0
1994-5	61,670	60,859	41.4	5.48	13,756	11.08	47.33	23,584	1,228	4,061	4,130	1,714	2,586	0
1995-6	62,575	61,624	35.3	6.72	14,737	11.15	47.69	22,372	1,286	3,730	3,706	1,218	2,631	16,578
1996-7	64,205	63,409	37.6	7.35	17,440	10.91	47.36	24,027	1,299	3,663	3,352	1,517	1,902	------
1997-8[1]	70,850	69,884	39.0	6.47	17,373	11.25	47.40							
1998-9[2]	72,690	71,570	40.6	5.35	14,660	11.23	47.26							

[1] Preliminary. [2] Forecast. NA = Not available. *Source: Economic Research Service, U.S. Department of Agriculture (ERS-USDA)*

Production of Soybeans for Beans in the United States, by State In Millions of Bushels

Year	Arkansas	Illinois	Indiana	Iowa	Kentucky	Michigan	Minnesota	Mississippi	Missouri	Nebraska	Ohio	Tennessee	Total
1989	75.2	354.0	166.1	322.9	36.9	38.9	185.0	40.0	121.8	81.9	125.4	29.8	1,923.7
1990	90.5	354.9	171.4	327.9	39.0	43.3	179.4	39.9	124.5	81.4	135.7	33.8	1,925.9
1991	89.6	341.3	171.6	349.5	36.7	52.8	195.3	46.8	135.1	82.4	135.7	31.5	1,986.5
1992	104.3	405.5	194.4	359.5	42.2	47.5	172.8	59.5	161.5	103.3	147.2	33.3	2,190.4
1993	92.3	387.0	223.1	257.3	38.0	54.7	115.0	42.9	118.8	90.0	156.2	32.2	1,871.0
1994	115.6	429.1	215.3	442.9	42.4	57.0	224.0	57.0	173.3	134.4	173.6	38.3	2,516.7
1995	88.4	378.3	196.7	407.4	41.4	59.6	234.9	37.8	132.8	101.0	153.1	34.6	2,176.8
1996	112.0	398.9	203.7	415.8	44.8	46.7	224.2	54.3	149.9	135.5	157.2	38.5	2,380.3
1997	109.8	427.9	230.6	478.4	42.1	71.6	255.5	64.2	174.6	143.8	191.0	40.8	2,688.8
1998[1]	85.0	468.6	235.2	501.6	36.0	73.7	285.6	48.0	170.0	165.0	193.2	35.1	2,756.8

[1] Preliminary. *Source: Agricultural Statistics Board, U.S. Department of Agriculture (ASB-USDA)*

Stocks of Soybeans at Mills in the United States, on First of Month In Millions of Bushels

Crop Year	Sept.	Oct.	Nov.	Dec.	Jan.	Feb.	Mar.	Apr.	May	June	July	Aug.
1989-90	23.8	24.5	96.3	108.5	89.7	93.6	91.4	83.5	73.0	67.5	58.8	46.9
1990-1	45.2	34.5	130.1	130.7	------	106.5	------------	------	78.5	------------	------	61.2
1991-2	------	------	67.0	------------	126.9	121.4	109.6	94.7	79.8	73.5	65.7	56.2
1992-3	43.8	46.3	132.3	137.4	119.1	111.2	97.2	90.1	83.6	67.7	67.1	55.3
1993-4	42.0	28.0	108.6	114.9	120.9	126.1	118.5	119.7	98.7	97.8	90.0	63.5
1994-5	47.9	46.8	114.1	124.3	108.0	114.7	114.3	112.6	94.1	81.2	69.1	55.1
1995-6	52.8	54.2	125.6	129.1	120.0	123.3	121.9	110.6	104.2	92.5	70.4	57.4
1996-7	40.7	23.4	101.1	117.4	106.0	112.6	122.2	104.9	89.2	78.2	64.0	43.6
1997-8	28.3	37.0	126.4	124.3	110.3	98.7	93.4	72.0	56.9	41.0	42.5	44.1
1998-9[1]	32.8	66.5	175.0	154.3								

[1] Preliminary. *Source: Economic Research Service, U.S. Department of Agriculture (ERS-USDA)*

U.S. Exports of Soybeans In Millions of Bushels

Year	Sept.	Oct.	Nov.	Dec.	Jan.	Feb.	Mar.	Apr.	May	June	July	Aug.	Total
1989-90	17.9	74.0	76.6	65.7	76.3	74.9	87.3	43.6	22.8	35.2	20.8	28.3	623.4
1990-1	27.9	29.8	62.8	55.8	------	190.1	-----------	------	117.7	-----------	------	73.9	557.9
1991-2	26.8	------	235.6	-----------	73.8	90.6	63.3	56.6	28.3	27.3	42.6	39.2	683.9
1992-3	50.1	98.0	84.2	73.6	89.1	104.7	79.7	48.7	34.6	39.4	42.7	24.6	769.5
1993-4	30.1	73.6	72.4	73.9	71.0	67.8	53.6	34.8	27.5	26.7	17.1	40.7	589.1
1994-5	42.3	99.9	78.5	104.2	89.3	91.4	83.1	80.7	45.2	35.5	41.2	46.7	838.1
1995-6	70.7	77.4	65.5	89.6	106.2	82.9	93.5	52.9	42.1	51.8	46.0	52.6	851.2
1996-7	41.6	95.7	152.4	121.7	106.0	105.4	66.9	58.2	40.8	32.3	23.2	37.5	881.8
1997-8	42.6	170.3	152.4	120.5	91.1	94.8	55.9	36.3	27.7	23.2	29.0	26.6	870.4
1998-9[1]	27.9	135.4	105.2										1,074.2

[1] Preliminary. *Source: Economic Research Service, U.S. Department of Agriculture (ERS-USDA)*

Spread Between Value of Products and Soybean Price in the United States In Cents Per Bushel

Year	Sept.	Oct.	Nov.	Dec.	Jan.	Feb.	Mar.	Apr.	May	June	July	Aug.	Average
1989-90	171	141	113	87	78	58	70	85	109	103	97	99	101
1990-1	99	77	58	64	63	73	79	75	72	74	91	99	77
1991-2	118	120	94	82	74	74	75	78	87	104	80	83	89
1992-3	98	93	87	93	94	77	77	79	82	84	120	97	90
1993-4	95	108	105	92	93	99	88	85	89	88	94	118	96
1994-5	146	167	143	137	130	109	114	109	86	102	87	90	118
1995-6	88	107	82	88	82	77	79	94	73	76	77	71	82
1996-7	109	117	126	115	94	95	86	80	107	96	123	151	108
1997-8	207	127	140	112	80	76	55	56	56	55	77	68	92
1998-9	74	68	50	56									62

Source: Economic Research Service, U.S. Department of Agriculture (ERS-USDA)

Soybean Crushed (Factory Consumption) in the U.S. In Millions of Bushels--One Bushel=60 Pounds

Year	Sept.	Oct.	Nov.	Dec.	Jan.	Feb.	Mar.	Apr.	May	June	July	Aug.	Total
1989-90	74.1	94.8	104.1	105.4	107.2	91.8	102.1	95.1	93.4	92.0	92.2	94.2	1,146
1990-1	92.1	106.1	106.0	102.7	--------	297.9	------------	--------	280.1	------------	--------	202.5	1,187
1991-2	98.9	--------	333.3	------------	112.0	100.8	107.2	101.6	95.2	100.0	102.3	102.3	1,254
1992-3	101.2	113.9	113.1	116.2	116.8	102.2	113.0	105.9	106.5	99.9	98.0	92.2	1,279
1993-4	98.4	113.7	114.4	114.1	110.7	103.3	113.3	105.6	103.0	97.2	101.0	101.0	1,276
1994-5	105.9	119.3	122.5	128.5	127.3	116.5	128.1	119.4	114.2	105.6	108.4	109.5	1,405
1995-6	107.4	120.6	123.4	125.1	122.8	111.2	115.5	112.1	106.3	107.5	111.9	105.7	1,370
1996-7	100.9	127.0	133.1	138.1	137.3	125.1	130.1	114.8	110.7	108.9	106.1	103.8	1,436
1997-8	110.8	142.2	142.8	153.1	151.9	138.2	147.0	133.9	123.9	117.5	123.8	111.9	1,597
1998-9[1]	123.9	145.0	143.0	144.6									1,669

[1] Preliminary. *Source: Economic Research Service, U.S. Department of Agriculture (ERS-USDA)*

SOYBEANS

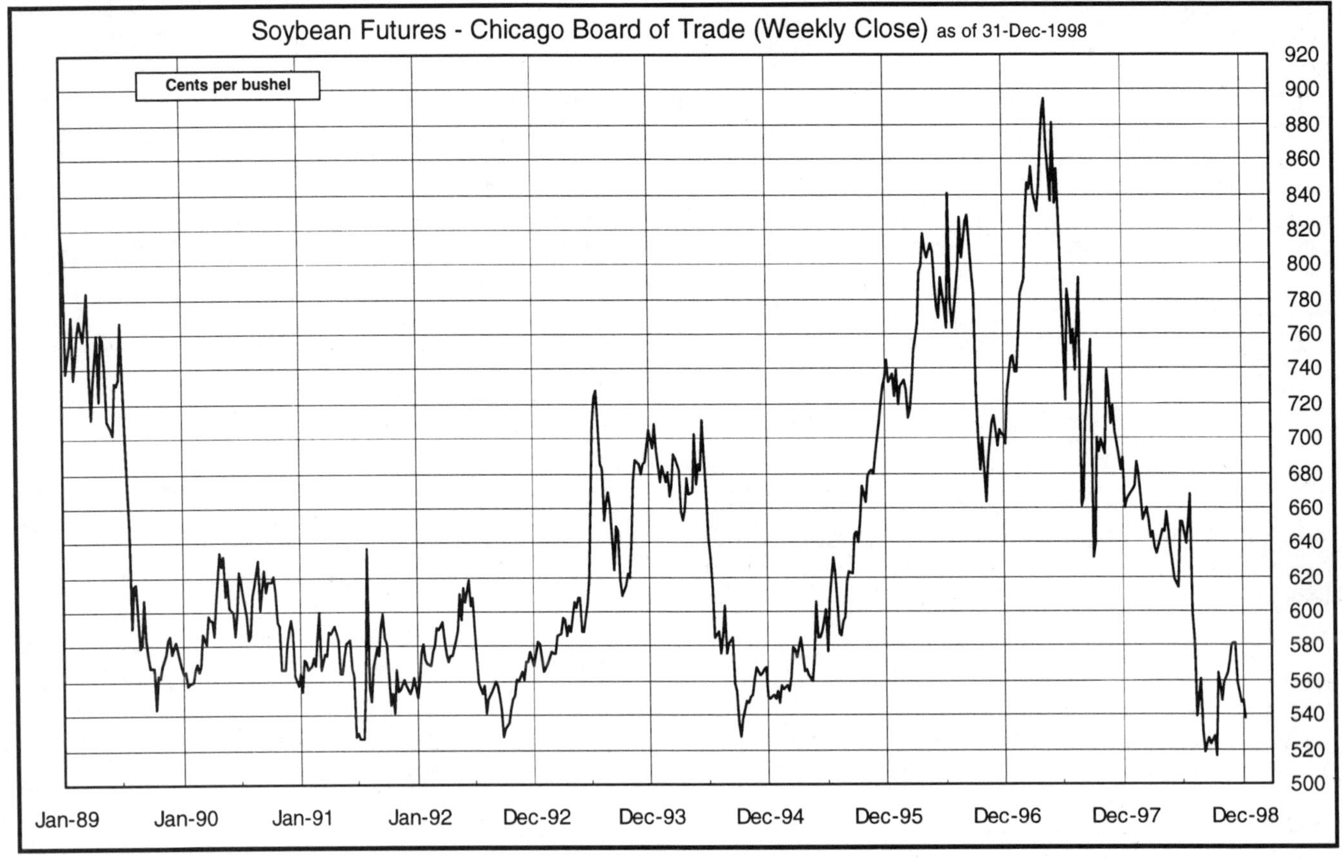

Average Open Interest of Soybean Futures in Chicago In Millions of Bushels

Year	Jan.	Feb.	Mar.	Apr.	May	June	July	Aug.	Sept.	Oct.	Nov.	Dec.
1989	119,700	114,468	115,992	102,736	96,802	94,453	83,407	75,926	80,966	100,793	96,432	98,672
1990	95,718	99,367	111,395	123,005	131,173	118,009	96,789	91,706	97,929	119,841	125,136	123,552
1991	109,311	110,421	110,318	106,995	102,369	103,362	91,449	86,132	98,050	114,206	112,407	112,782
1992	114,871	118,317	132,639	121,171	121,398	137,896	116,208	106,830	104,115	125,734	118,877	114,261
1993	121,726	126,682	126,681	138,155	137,821	142,721	199,681	183,422	163,647	159,641	161,170	168,694
1994	177,648	167,217	156,059	147,569	145,798	150,203	132,010	121,126	126,947	147,198	137,187	136,351
1995	138,345	138,794	137,843	138,624	133,533	143,119	143,671	135,584	144,409	167,200	174,775	194,021
1996	198,731	199,150	192,927	207,284	191,989	179,548	180,817	182,324	196,361	178,872	155,937	152,966
1997	157,728	176,242	189,352	188,617	186,792	159,720	141,658	133,732	150,606	172,098	148,760	150,201
1998	135,340	142,778	147,900	152,732	143,994	149,563	133,532	140,236	158,627	163,759	143,814	146,463

Source: Chicago Board of Trade (CBT)

Volume of Trading of Soybean Futures in Chicago In Thousands of Contracts

Year	Jan.	Feb.	Mar.	Apr.	May	June	July	Aug.	Sept.	Oct.	Nov.	Dec.	Total
1989	1,044.4	853.0	952.0	944.0	917.4	893.2	795.4	634.4	570.8	802.2	649.4	578.6	9,635
1990	655.6	534.6	826.6	884.4	1,126.0	1,041.8	1,037.6	905.6	642.8	1,132.0	859.8	655.0	13,577
1991	745.0	620.8	715.4	808.0	684.4	776.2	992.4	943.2	662.4	876.2	571.2	619.0	8,974
1992	804.4	738.4	688.0	558.8	873.8	1,054.6	933.2	630.8	572.2	867.4	613.2	665.4	9,000
1993	683.4	624.6	675.8	761.2	778.0	1,287.0	1,643.2	1,180.0	925.0	962.2	1,188.0	941.4	11,649
1994	1,134.6	898.5	922.0	919.3	1,158.4	1,197.0	892.4	688.4	622.6	857.0	825.8	633.2	10,749
1995	614.0	572.0	799.6	698.3	949.4	1,050.8	1,196.7	817.0	800.2	1,127.8	840.4	1,145.4	10,612
1996	1,302.6	1,122.9	1,009.4	1,683.2	1,149.3	989.5	1,295.9	989.8	1,050.2	1,002.7	1,695.6	940.1	14,231
1997	1,119.8	1,254.2	1,405.9	1,585.5	1,391.1	1,355.6	1,217.4	835.0	852.3	1,505.8	1,010.7	1,006.6	14,540
1998	875.7	971.2	935.9	1,116.2	973.6	1,378.8	1,286.3	884.5	864.4	1,264.6	867.0	1,012.9	12,431

Source: Chicago Board of Trade (CBT)

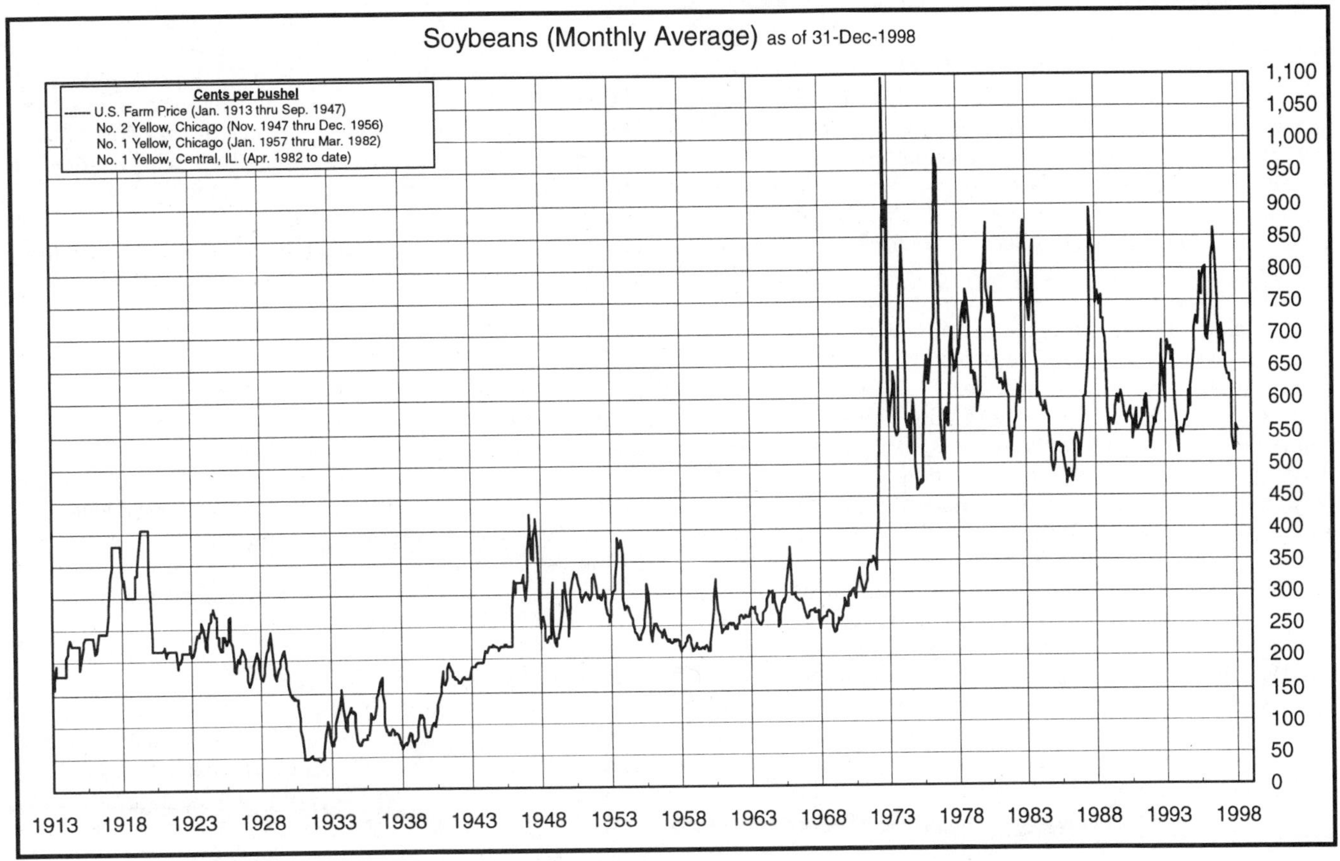

Average Cash Price of No. 1 Yellow Soybeans at Illinois Processor In Cents Per Bushel

Year	Sept.	Oct.	Nov.	Dec.	Jan.	Feb.	Mar.	Apr.	May	June	July	Aug.	Average
1989-90	600	564	570	582	572	585	600	600	620	609	619	626	596
1990-1	628	614	587	591	576	585	592	601	589	583	554	578	590
1991-2	598	568	571	568	577	581	593	585	609	619	580	564	584
1992-3	554	535	560	572	582	575	587	597	607	606	689	679	595
1993-4	643	606	664	694	701	686	692	670	689	685	603	576	659
1994-5	557	531	566	567	558	560	574	578	580	577	623	602	573
1995-6	632	656	686	717	737	730	726	791	808	778	795	816	739
1996-7	820	711	704	708	737	769	833	854	878	837	769	741	780
1997-8	703	684	727	699	679	680	662	649	649	640	642	556	664
1998-9[1]	533	536	572	558									550

[1] Preliminary. *Source: Economic Research Service, U.S. Department of Agriculture (ERS-USDA)*

Average Price Received by Farmers for Soybeans in the United States In Cents Per Bushel

Year	Sept.	Oct.	Nov.	Dec.	Jan.	Feb.	Mar.	Apr.	May	June	July	Aug.	Average
1989-90	570	555	566	564	565	556	565	582	597	588	597	600	569
1990-1	599	588	578	572	571	565	576	577	567	556	536	566	574
1991-2	564	548	548	545	554	559	567	566	587	594	559	540	558
1992-3	536	526	536	546	558	556	565	573	581	590	656	656	556
1993-4	621	601	632	664	672	671	673	657	677	672	592	558	640
1994-5	547	530	536	541	547	540	551	555	556	568	590	583	548
1995-6	598	615	640	676	677	701	700	743	769	741	762	782	672
1996-7	779	694	690	691	713	738	797	823	840	816	752	725	735
1997-8	672	650	685	671	669	657	640	626	626	616	614	543	639
1998-9[1]	525	518	540	537	522								528

[1] Preliminary. *Source: Economic Research Service, U.S. Department of Agriculture (ERS-USDA)*

Stock Index Futures, U.S.

1998 proved to be a record year for U.S. equity markets despite an autumn correction caused by economic difficulties in Russia and Brazil. All the major stock indices showed strong returns, adding about $2.6 trillion of value to the market, but the real emphasis focused on the high tech internet related companies traded on the NASDAQ. The latter index outperformed all others, up 39.63 percent, its second best year ever, closing 1998 at a record 2192.69. The bellwether Dow Jones Industrial Average gained 16.10 percent; closing 1998 at 9,181.43, marginally below its record high of 9,380.20 reached in November. The S & P 500 index gained 26.67 percent to a near record high 1229.23. The Wilshire 5000 rose 21.72 percent. The Value Line Index gained 5.5 percent while the broad based Russell 2000 lost 3.5 percent. Trading volume again soared to record highs with the New York Stock Exchange trading 170 billion shares vs. 134 billion in 1997. The NASDAQ volume topped 198 billion shares vs. 164 billion in 1997.

Market volatility was the rule rather than the exception, partially reflecting burgeoning computer driven day trading in outlandishly valued Internet stocks. Beginning July 20, the Dow Jones Industrials fell from a record high 9400 to 7400 on September 1. By late November, the Dow was again at a new high, triggering widespread talk of the Dow at 10,000 by yearend or early 1999. The catalyst for the fourth quarter rally was a series of interest rate cuts by the Federal Reserve, one of which sparked a 350 point jump in the Dow in a single day. However, by mid-December the Dow was again under 9000 with the once positive outlook clouded by uncertainties over President Clinton's impeachment, fresh troubles in Iraq and 1999 economic weakness.

The U.S. economy grew robustly in 1998, with the gross domestic product up more than 3 percent, unemployment at a 24 year low, and inflation at its lowest level in years, up an annualized rate of only 1.5 percent. Moreover, the Federal Government realized a budget surplus of over $70 billion, tempering the Treasury's borrowing needs. This resulted in lower interest rates and enhanced the demand for U.S. equities. Indeed, mainstream America saw stocks as the best investment vehicle and poured billions into the market during 1998 as consumer confidence remained strong throughout the entire year.

At yearend there was concern that equities could not repeat the strength of the past few years during 1999. Forecasts of eroding corporate profits and real gross domestic product dipping below 3 percent were pervasive. But if the economy slows, inflation is apt to remain benign, suggesting at worst a steady monetary policy. The latter would likely maintain the opportunity cost's attractiveness of equities vs. capital inflows into bank deposits. On balance, the bullish momentum seemed to be deep rooted at yearend 1998 and capable of supporting new record highs for the major stock indices in 1999.

Futures Markets

The Chicago Mercantile Exchange's (CME) IOM division trades futures and options on the S&P 500, the S&P MidCap 400, and the NASDAQ 100. The Chicago Board of Trade (CBOT) lists futures and options on the Dow Jones Industrial Average. The New York Futures Exchange (NYFE) trades futures and options on the New York Stock Exchange Composite Index. The Kansas City Board of Trade (KCBT) lists futures and options on the Value Line Index. Additional futures and options on stock indices are likely to be added in 1999.

Dow Jones Industrial Average (30 Stocks)

Year	Jan.	Feb.	Mar.	Apr.	May	June	July	Aug.	Sept.	Oct.	Nov.	Dec.	Average
1989	2,234.7	2,304.3	2,283.1	2,348.9	2,439.5	2,494.9	2,554.0	2,691.1	2,693.4	2,692.0	2,642.5	2,728.5	2,508.9
1990	2,679.2	2,614.2	2,700.1	2,708.4	2,793.8	2,894.8	2,934.2	2,681.9	2,550.7	2,460.5	2,518.6	2,610.9	2,679.0
1991	2,587.6	2,863.0	2,920.1	2,925.5	2,928.4	2,968.1	2,978.2	3,006.1	3,010.4	3,019.7	2,986.1	2,958.6	2,929.3
1992	3,227.1	3,257.3	3,247.4	3,294.1	3,376.8	3,337.8	3,329.4	3,307.4	3,293.9	3,198.7	3,238.5	3,303.1	3,284.3
1993	3,277.7	3,367.3	3,440.7	3,423.6	3,478.2	3,513.8	3,529.4	3,597.0	3,592.3	3,625.8	3,674.7	3,744.1	3,522.1
1994	3,868.4	3,905.6	3,817.0	3,661.5	3,708.0	3,737.6	3,718.3	3,797.5	3,880.6	3,868.1	3,792.5	3,770.3	3,793.8
1995	3,872.5	3,953.7	4,062.8	4,230.7	4,391.6	4,510.8	4,684.8	4,639.3	4,746.8	4,760.5	4,935.8	5,136.1	4,493.8
1996	5,179.4	5,518.7	5,612.2	5,579.9	5,616.7	5,671.5	5,496.3	5,685.5	5,804.0	5,995.1	6,318.4	6,435.9	5,742.8
1997	6,707.0	6,917.5	6,901.1	6,657.5	7,242.4	7,599.6	7,990.7	7,948.4	7,866.6	7,875.8	7,677.4	7,909.8	7,441.1
1998	7,808.4	8,323.6	8,709.5	9,037.4	9,080.1	8,873.0	9,097.1	8,478.5	7,909.8	8,164.3	9,005.8	9,018.7	8,625.5

Monthly average. *Source: The Wall Street Journal*

Dow Jones Transportation Average (20 Stocks)

Year	Jan.	Feb.	Mar.	Apr.	May	June	July	Aug.	Sept.	Oct.	Nov.	Dec.	Average
1989	1,009.3	1,073.0	1,046.3	1,098.0	1,139.8	1,159.3	1,223.1	1,407.1	1,462.7	1,342.0	1,188.1	1,183.0	1,194.3
1990	1,139.8	1,083.4	1,160.3	1,164.8	1,163.1	1,181.9	1,150.0	951.1	881.3	850.8	848.1	908.5	1,040.3
1991	962.2	1,110.4	1,113.5	1,138.8	1,167.6	1,205.2	1,204.7	1,204.7	1,182.3	1,241.5	1,237.1	1,233.3	1,166.8
1992	1,378.7	1,412.2	1,409.0	1,356.9	1,380.4	1,333.3	1,303.1	1,254.6	1,275.2	1,286.1	1,375.9	1,430.2	1,349.6
1993	1,488.1	1,533.2	1,541.6	1,619.7	1,583.4	1,533.9	1,553.7	1,631.6	1,623.9	1,660.5	1,732.6	1,763.2	1,605.5
1994	1,812.1	1,810.4	1,719.9	1,614.7	1,602.2	1,619.2	1,596.2	1,602.8	1,553.7	1,485.8	1,473.7	1,415.3	1,608.8
1995	1,515.8	1,547.2	1,584.6	1,648.9	1,646.2	1,699.3	1,852.1	1,883.9	1,961.4	1,922.9	2,008.3	2,029.5	1,775.0
1996	1,932.7	2,030.0	2,136.0	2,180.0	2,229.1	2,213.4	2,053.1	2,060.4	2,050.8	2,100.1	2,224.3	2,273.9	2,123.7
1997	2,295.0	2,341.4	2,427.8	2,464.0	2,635.1	2,711.4	2,858.0	2,925.8	3,086.0	3,239.9	3,155.7	3,233.5	2,781.1
1998	3,275.8	3,456.8	3,521.5	3,586.5	3,401.9	3,373.2	3,459.3	3,021.1	2,763.0	2,647.8	2,953.4	3,027.6	3,207.3

Monthly average. *Source: The Wall Street Journal*

Dow Jones Public Utilities (15 Stocks)

Year	Jan.	Feb.	Mar.	Apr.	May	June	July	Aug.	Sept.	Oct.	Nov.	Dec.	Average
1989	188.9	186.6	182.8	188.0	196.3	206.7	215.5	218.1	216.0	215.7	221.0	232.1	205.6
1990	223.2	221.2	217.0	210.7	212.4	211.2	205.0	201.2	199.8	207.2	210.3	210.6	210.8
1991	205.3	213.7	213.2	214.4	211.2	204.6	199.6	204.4	208.0	213.6	216.7	219.3	210.3
1992	215.7	206.8	204.4	206.1	213.2	212.5	219.1	220.2	220.0	217.2	217.7	220.2	214.4
1993	222.0	234.2	240.0	242.1	237.8	241.5	246.5	252.0	253.0	243.1	227.1	227.1	238.9
1994	222.3	215.6	207.0	196.5	185.5	182.9	181.8	188.9	179.6	179.9	177.7	181.0	191.6
1995	186.9	194.0	187.9	192.7	197.6	204.5	202.5	202.8	207.2	216.4	215.3	221.4	202.4
1996	228.4	228.6	216.3	209.5	211.2	210.0	212.8	214.8	217.2	222.3	234.0	232.1	219.8
1997	235.8	230.5	223.7	213.8	222.1	223.5	232.0	231.9	238.9	242.9	249.2	263.9	234.0
1998	265.6	267.9	279.0	285.4	281.2	291.1	289.3	279.4	289.1	307.0	308.1	309.0	287.7

Source: The Wall Street Journal

Standard & Poor's 500 Composite Price Index

Year	Jan.	Feb.	Mar.	Apr.	May	June	July	Aug.	Sept.	Oct.	Nov.	Dec.	Average
1989	285.4	294.0	292.7	302.3	313.9	323.7	331.9	346.6	347.3	347.4	340.2	348.6	322.8
1990	340.0	330.5	338.5	338.2	350.3	360.4	360.0	330.8	315.4	307.1	315.3	328.8	334.6
1991	325.5	362.3	372.3	379.7	378.0	378.3	380.2	389.4	387.2	386.9	385.9	388.5	376.2
1992	416.1	412.6	407.4	407.4	414.8	408.3	415.1	417.9	418.5	412.5	422.8	435.6	415.7
1993	435.2	441.7	450.2	443.1	445.3	448.1	447.3	454.1	459.2	463.9	462.9	466.0	451.4
1994	473.0	471.6	463.8	447.2	451.0	454.8	451.4	464.2	467.0	463.8	461.0	455.2	460.3
1995	465.3	481.9	493.2	507.9	523.8	539.4	557.4	559.1	578.8	582.9	595.5	614.6	541.6
1996	614.4	649.5	647.1	547.2	661.2	668.5	644.1	662.7	674.9	701.5	735.7	743.3	662.5
1997	766.1	798.4	792.2	763.9	833.1	876.3	925.3	927.7	937.0	951.2	938.9	962.4	872.7
1998	963.4	1,023.7	1,076.8	1,112.2	1,108.4	1,108.4	1,156.6	1,074.6	1,020.7	1,032.5	1,144.5	1,190.0	1,084.3

Source: The Wall Street Journal

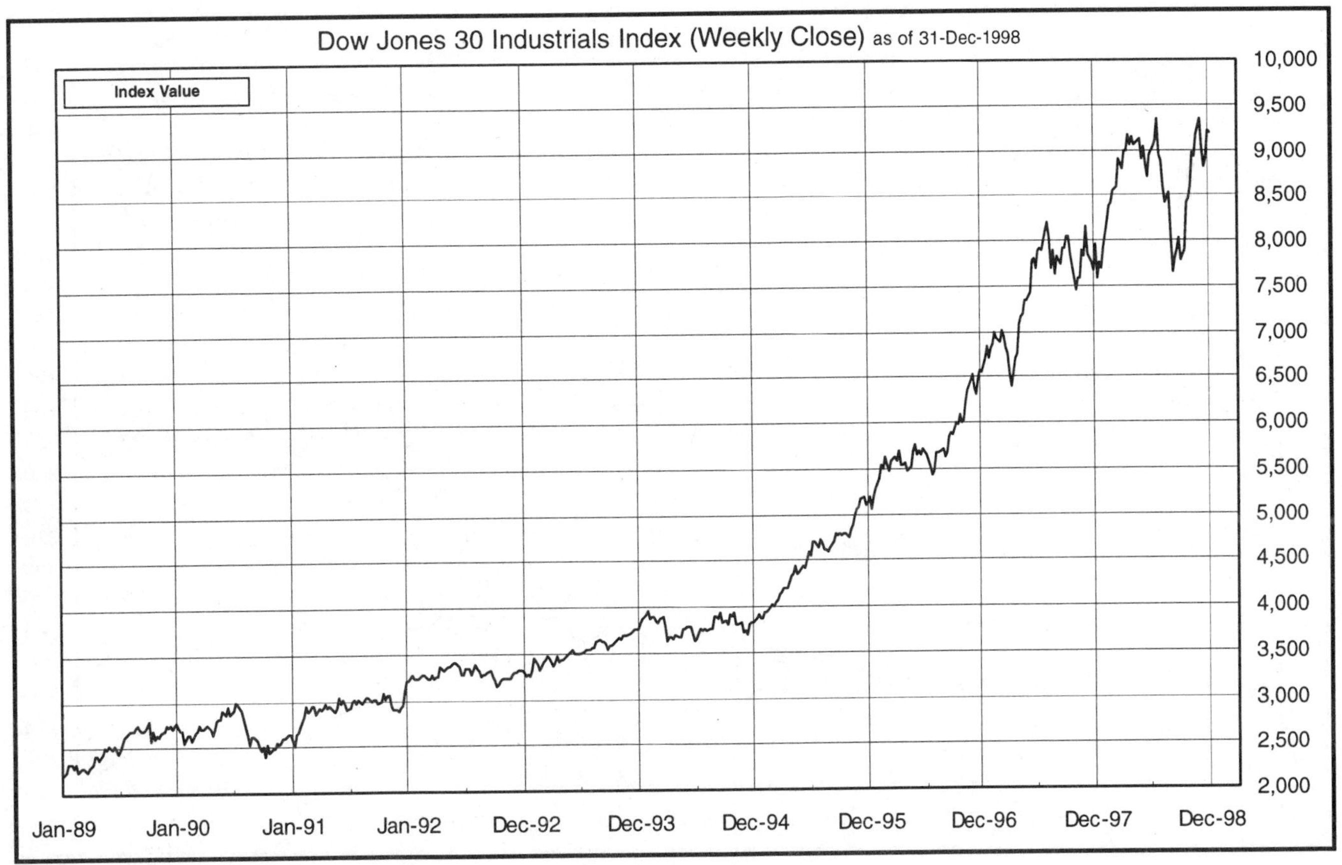

Major Market Index (MMI) (Weekly Close) as of 31-Dec-1998

NYSE Composite Index (Weekly Close) as of 31-Dec-1998

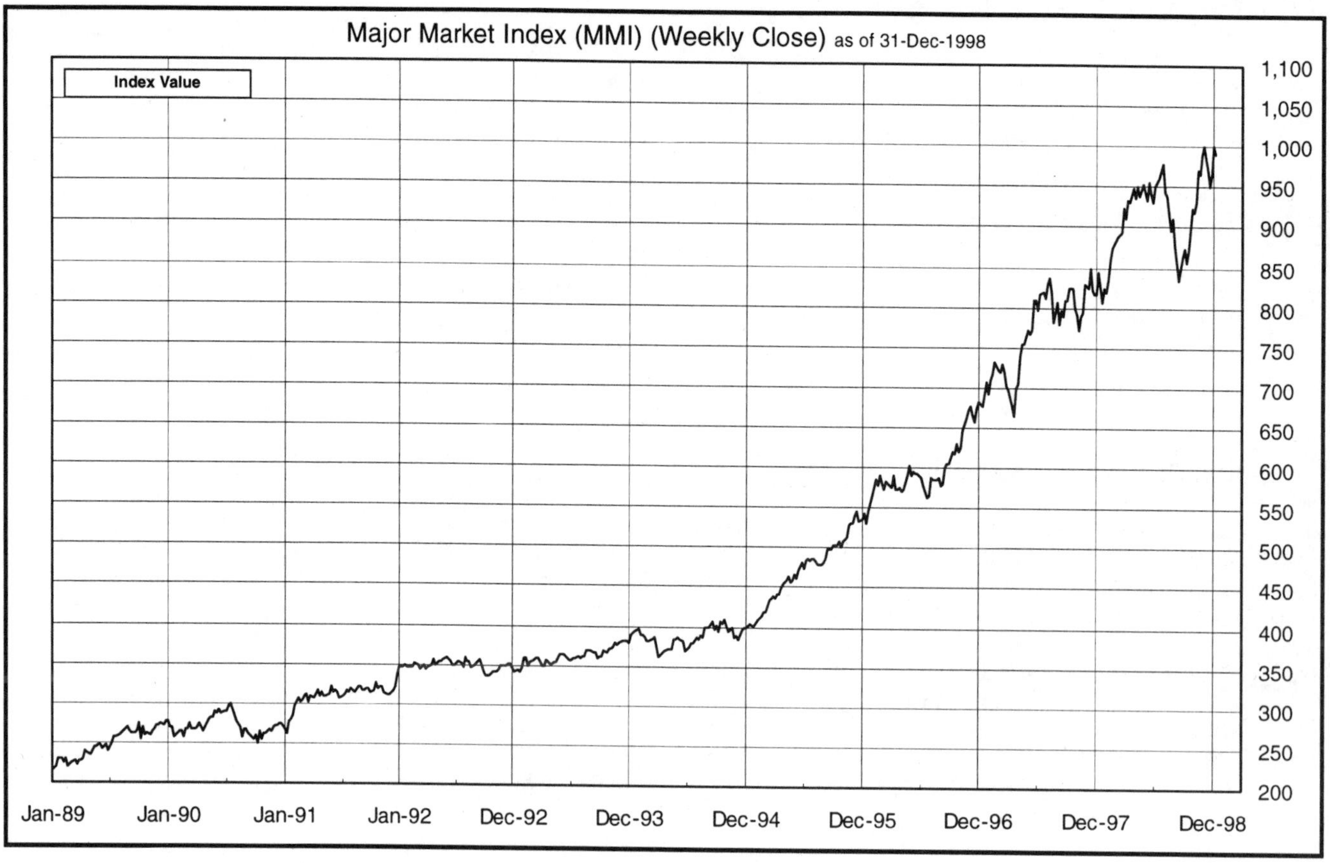

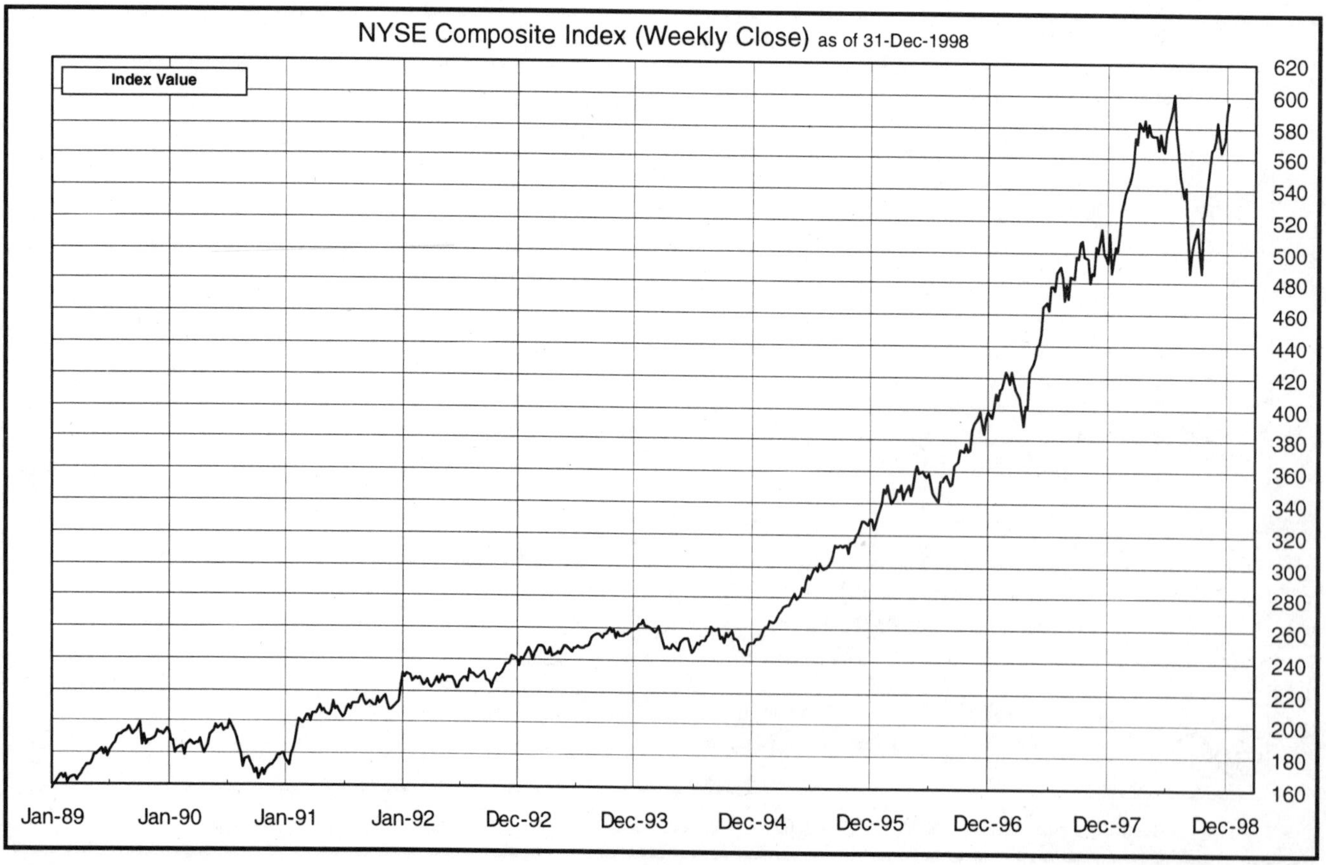

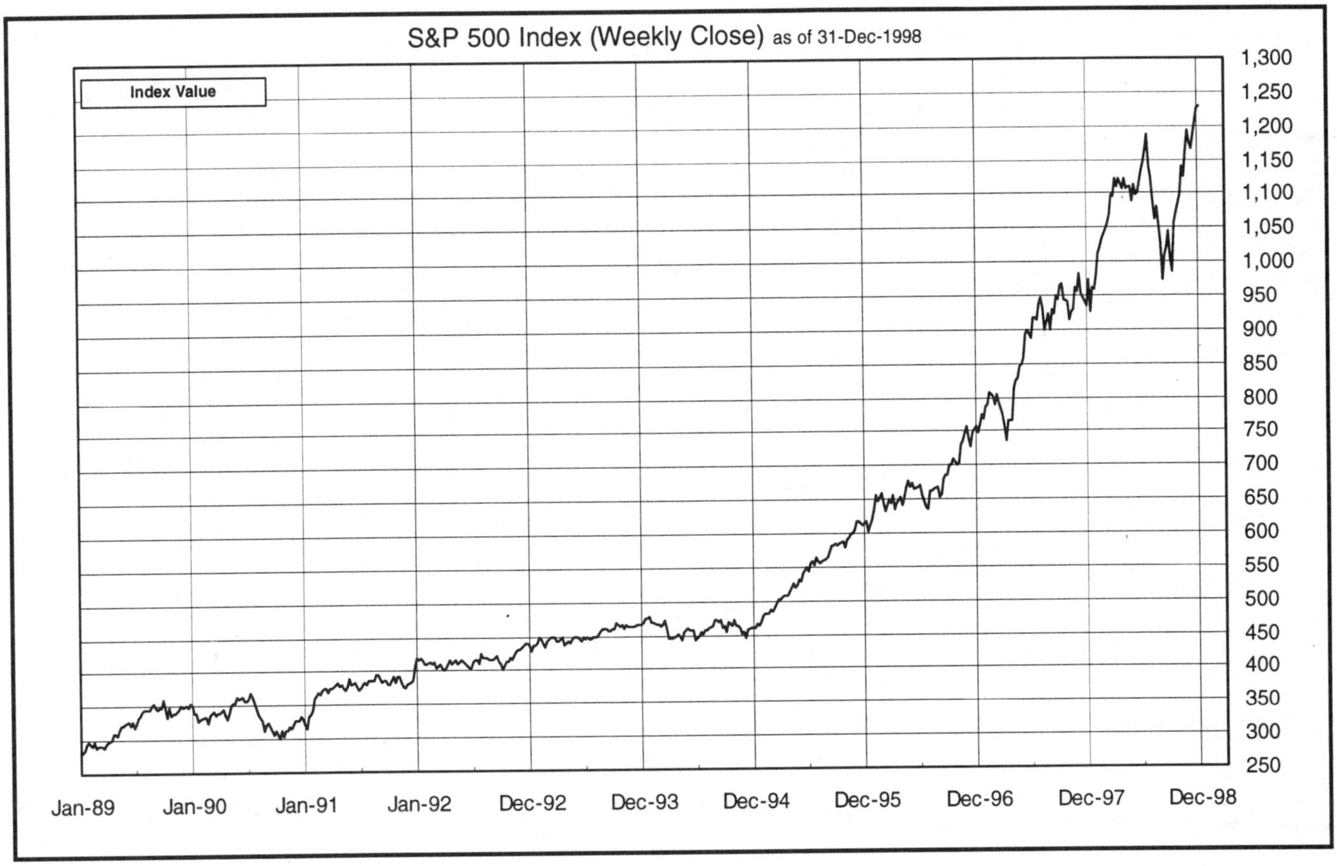
S&P 500 Index (Weekly Close) as of 31-Dec-1998
Index Value
1,300
1,250
1,200
1,150
1,100
1,050
1,000
950
900
850
800
750
700
650
600
550
500
450
400
350
300
250
Jan-89
Jan-90
Jan-91
Jan-92
Dec-92
Dec-93
Dec-94
Dec-95
Dec-96
Dec-97
Dec-98

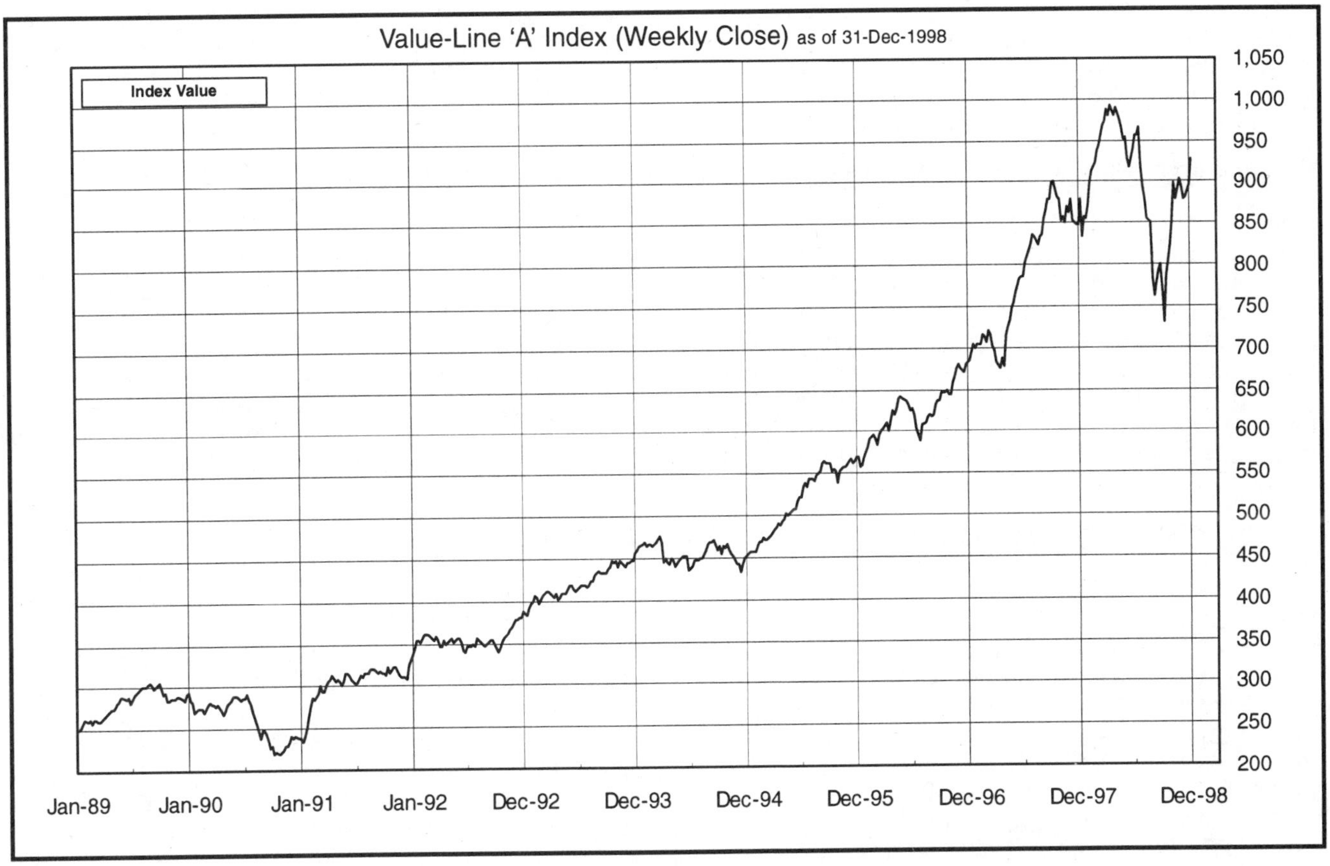
Value-Line 'A' Index (Weekly Close) as of 31-Dec-1998
Index Value
1,050
1,000
950
900
850
800
750
700
650
600
550
500
450
400
350
300
250
200
Jan-89
Jan-90
Jan-91
Jan-92
Dec-92
Dec-93
Dec-94
Dec-95
Dec-96
Dec-97
Dec-98

Composite Index of Leading Indicators 1987 = 100

Year	Jan.	Feb.	Mar.	Apr.	May	June	July	Aug.	Sept.	Oct.	Nov.	Dec.	Average
1990	100.0	99.6	99.9	99.7	99.7	99.7	99.6	99.1	98.8	98.2	97.9	98.0	99.2
1991	97.8	98.1	98.5	98.8	99.1	99.3	99.8	99.5	99.5	99.5	99.4	99.1	99.0
1992	99.4	99.7	99.9	99.9	100.0	99.9	99.9	99.9	99.9	100.1	100.4	101.0	100.0
1993	100.7	100.7	100.1	100.4	100.2	100.3	100.1	100.3	100.4	100.5	100.8	101.2	100.5
1994	101.2	101.0	101.5	101.4	101.4	101.4	101.2	101.5	101.4	101.5	101.6	101.6	101.4
1995	101.5	101.1	100.7	100.6	100.4	100.5	100.7	101.0	101.1	100.9	100.9	101.2	100.9
1996	100.5	101.4	101.6	101.8	102.1	102.3	102.3	102.4	102.5	102.5	102.5	102.6	102.0
1997	102.8	103.3	103.4	103.3	103.6	103.6	103.9	104.0	104.3	104.4	104.7	104.6	103.8
1998[1]	104.8	105.2	105.4	105.4	105.4	105.2	105.6	105.7	105.6	105.7	106.2	106.5	105.6

[1] Preliminary. *Source: Bureau of Economic Analysis, U.S. Department of Commerce (BEA)*

Civilian Unemployment Rate in the United States

Year	Jan.	Feb.	Mar.	Apr.	May	June	July	Aug.	Sept.	Oct.	Nov.	Dec.	Average
1990	5.4	5.3	5.2	5.4	5.4	5.2	5.5	5.7	5.9	5.9	6.2	6.3	5.6
1991	6.4	6.6	6.8	6.7	6.9	6.9	6.8	6.9	6.9	7.0	7.0	7.3	6.9
1992	7.3	7.4	7.4	7.4	7.6	7.8	7.7	7.6	7.6	7.3	7.4	7.4	7.5
1993	7.3	7.1	7.0	7.1	7.1	7.0	6.9	6.8	6.7	6.8	6.6	6.5	6.9
1994	6.7	6.6	6.5	6.4	6.0	6.1	6.1	6.1	5.9	5.8	5.6	5.4	6.1
1995	5.6	5.5	5.4	5.7	5.6	5.6	5.7	5.7	5.7	5.5	5.6	5.6	5.6
1996	5.7	5.5	5.5	5.5	5.5	5.3	5.4	5.2	5.2	5.2	5.3	5.3	5.4
1997	5.4	5.3	5.2	4.9	4.8	5.0	4.9	4.9	4.9	4.8	4.6	4.7	5.0
1998[1]	4.6	4.6	4.7	4.3	4.4	4.5	4.5	4.5	4.5	4.5	4.4	4.3	4.5

[1] Preliminary. *Source: Bureau of Economic Analysis, U.S. Department of Commerce (BEA)*

Capacity Utilization Rates (Total Industry) Percent

Year	Jan.	Feb.	Mar.	Apr.	May	June	July	Aug.	Sept.	Oct.	Nov.	Dec.	Average
1990	82.6	82.9	83.2	82.6	82.8	82.7	82.5	82.5	82.5	81.9	80.7	80.1	82.3
1991	79.6	78.9	78.1	78.2	78.7	79.5	79.5	79.5	80.1	79.9	79.7	79.1	79.2
1992	79.0	79.4	79.9	80.4	80.6	80.2	80.6	80.2	80.5	81.0	81.3	81.2	80.4
1993	81.4	81.7	81.6	81.7	81.2	81.2	81.3	81.0	81.7	81.8	82.1	82.5	81.6
1994	82.6	82.8	83.2	83.3	83.7	83.9	84.1	83.9	83.8	84.1	84.4	84.9	83.9
1995	84.9	84.5	84.3	83.9	83.7	83.6	83.4	83.8	83.9	83.3	83.2	83.0	83.4
1996	82.4	83.2	82.6	83.1	83.2	83.5	83.2	83.2	83.1	83.0	82.5	82.5	82.4
1997	82.4	82.6	82.5	82.6	82.4	82.3	82.6	82.8	82.7	83.4	83.4	83.4	82.9
1998[1]	83.0	82.6	82.6	82.6	82.6	81.5	81.1	82.0	81.3	81.4	81.0	80.9	81.9

[1] Preliminary. *Source: Bureau of Economic Analysis, U.S. Department of Commerce (BEA)*

Manufacturers New Orders, Durable Goods In Billions of Constant Dollars

Year	Jan.	Feb.	Mar.	Apr.	May	June	July	Aug.	Sept.	Oct.	Nov.	Dec.	Average
1990	124.02	127.57	135.14	127.83	131.90	129.10	131.58	127.67	128.36	130.67	117.87	123.12	127.90
1991	119.26	120.00	112.54	117.55	120.64	116.85	132.82	125.62	122.36	123.66	124.96	116.97	121.10
1992	122.15	122.14	124.63	127.60	125.65	128.77	125.51	123.79	125.86	128.69	125.49	135.19	126.29
1993	129.56	133.47	128.50	130.20	126.93	131.29	128.27	128.99	130.31	133.01	135.60	136.82	131.08
1994	142.23	138.88	140.91	141.21	142.61	146.15	142.60	145.92	146.93	145.72	149.89	152.88	144.66
1995	153.42	151.82	151.72	146.32	149.74	148.21	147.45	152.12	156.78	154.37	154.09	158.89	154.10
1996	158.86	155.10	157.67	156.01	162.59	162.67	168.25	162.76	170.45	170.59	169.34	166.02	163.79
1997	171.73	174.80	170.02	173.13	177.05	176.93	175.82	181.08	181.15	181.33	189.71	181.44	177.03
1998[1]	184.33	183.87	184.17	187.35	181.58	182.22	186.22	190.39	193.18	189.31	190.05	194.24	187.24

[1] Preliminary. *Source: Bureau of Economic Analysis, U.S. Department of Commerce (BEA)*

Change in Manufacturing and Trade Inventories In Billions of Dollars

Year	Jan.	Feb.	Mar.	Apr.	May	June	July	Aug.	Sept.	Oct.	Nov.	Dec.	Average
1990	19.9	7.6	22.2	39.8	64.5	-15.2	64.0	55.9	41.3	24.2	25.3	-50.3	24.9
1991	60.8	-24.8	-99.2	-25.7	-50.0	-32.7	-10.5	-1.1	37.2	16.2	8.8	47.3	-6.1
1992	-60.6	-0.3	13.8	28.3	-22.3	53.6	28.4	21.4	-8.4	4.6	11.8	23.9	7.9
1993	34.9	31.8	66.7	43.7	12.9	25.6	7.3	39.0	34.8	27.2	63.2	1.6	32.4
1994	15.3	45.1	-8.1	42.1	114.2	56.3	60.8	98.6	60.3	71.8	65.3	64.5	57.2
1995	127.4	78.5	100.6	97.6	54.4	48.1	42.9	50.6	51.4	61.8	24.1	-39.7	58.5
1996	66.2	14.2	-27.7	61.5	-8.4	80.3	123.6	-272.1	90.6	143.4	86.1	72.0	18.0
1997	107.0	103.4	76.3	56.2	25.2	76.8	20.9	19.1	91.5	55.2	43.1	28.2	43.4
1998[1]	23.5	89.1	75.5	21.6	-6.4	5.9	4.3	47.9	72.0	30.0	58.2	-17.7	38.3

[1] Preliminary. *Source: Bureau of Economic Analysis, U.S. Department of Commerce (BEA)*

Comparison of International Stock Price Indexes 1990 = 100

Year	Jan.	Feb.	Mar.	Apr.	May	June	July	Aug.	Sept.	Oct.	Nov.	Dec.	Average
United States													
1993	131.9	133.3	135.8	132.3	135.3	135.4	134.7	139.3	137.9	140.6	138.8	140.2	136.3
1994	144.8	140.4	134.0	135.5	137.2	133.5	137.7	142.9	139.1	142.0	136.4	138.1	138.5
1995	141.4	146.5	150.5	154.7	160.3	163.7	168.9	168.9	175.7	174.8	182.0	185.1	164.4
1996	191.2	192.5	194.0	196.6	201.1	201.6	192.4	196.0	206.6	212.0	227.6	222.7	202.9
1997	236.3	237.7	227.6	240.9	255.0	266.1	286.8	270.4	284.7	274.9	287.2	291.7	263.3
1998[1]	294.7	315.4	331.2	334.2	327.9	340.8	336.9	287.7	305.7	330.2	349.8	369.5	327.0
Canada													
1993	96.6	100.9	105.3	110.8	113.5	115.9	116.0	120.9	116.6	124.4	122.2	126.3	114.1
1994	133.1	129.3	126.6	124.7	126.5	117.7	122.2	127.1	127.3	125.4	119.7	123.2	125.2
1995	117.4	120.6	126.1	125.1	130.0	132.3	134.9	132.0	132.4	130.3	136.2	137.8	129.6
1996	145.2	144.2	145.3	150.4	153.4	147.4	144.1	150.3	154.7	163.7	175.9	173.2	154.0
1997	178.6	180.0	171.0	174.7	186.6	188.2	201.0	193.3	205.8	200.0	190.4	195.8	188.8
1998[1]	195.8	207.3	220.9	224.0	221.9	215.3	202.6	161.7	164.0	181.5	185.4	189.6	197.5
France													
1993	97.5	109.1	111.8	106.7	103.9	108.5	114.8	122.0	116.4	120.1	116.1	124.8	112.6
1994	128.4	123.1	114.6	119.2	111.7	104.1	114.2	113.8	103.4	104.9	108.7	103.5	112.5
1995	98.9	97.8	102.3	105.6	107.2	102.3	105.6	103.6	98.4	99.8	100.6	103.0	102.1
1996	111.2	109.5	112.5	118.1	116.1	116.9	109.8	108.4	117.4	117.8	127.4	127.4	116.0
1997	138.5	143.5	146.2	145.2	142.2	157.3	169.2	152.4	165.5	150.7	157.3	165.0	152.8
1998[1]	174.5	188.3	213.3	213.5	222.4	231.3	229.8	200.9	176.0	193.8	211.5	216.9	206.0
Germany[2]													
1993	84.3	90.2	91.2	88.1	88.0	90.6	96.6	102.8	101.4	110.0	109.3	117.5	97.5
1994	115.1	110.7	112.3	117.8	109.7	106.4	111.5	114.5	105.2	107.7	105.9	108.3	110.4
1995	103.8	108.2	98.6	103.5	106.6	106.6	112.8	113.7	111.4	109.3	111.9	114.0	108.4
1996	123.7	123.2	123.3	123.0	124.4	126.3	122.1	125.6	130.4	130.6	139.0	139.7	127.6
1997	147.0	157.8	167.8	167.1	172.2	183.8	209.6	184.1	195.3	177.8	186.0	196.3	178.7
1998[1]	204.9	217.5	234.9	237.1	251.6	262.2	266.6	221.8	205.6	209.2	229.6	225.3	230.5
Italy													
1993	75.8	79.9	73.9	81.9	83.9	83.5	87.7	98.4	92.8	90.8	85.4	96.4	85.9
1994	103.1	102.5	112.6	124.5	113.8	107.4	110.5	107.5	105.8	98.9	97.4	98.5	106.9
1995	102.8	97.5	93.3	99.8	98.8	94.9	98.8	99.0	96.1	90.5	86.1	91.8	95.8
1996	96.5	94.5	90.4	102.4	104.1	102.4	93.4	93.2	99.0	94.0	102.4	103.7	98.0
1997	119.8	115.4	115.3	119.5	117.9	130.0	144.5	136.6	155.0	144.6	149.4	164.0	134.3
1998[1]	184.0	194.3	239.3	220.9	236.1	222.1	240.5	208.1	184.6	194.1	223.7	231.5	214.9
Japan													
1993	59.1	58.8	64.5	72.6	71.3	68.0	70.7	72.9	69.7	68.4	56.9	60.4	66.1
1994	70.2	69.4	66.3	68.4	72.8	71.6	70.9	71.6	67.9	69.3	66.2	68.4	69.4
1995	64.7	59.2	56.0	58.3	53.6	50.4	57.9	62.9	62.1	61.2	65.0	68.9	60.0
1996	72.2	69.8	74.3	76.5	76.2	78.2	71.8	70.0	74.8	71.0	72.9	67.2	72.9
1997	63.6	64.4	62.5	66.4	69.6	71.5	70.5	63.2	62.1	57.1	57.7	52.9	63.5
1998[1]	57.7	58.4	57.3	54.3	54.4	54.9	56.8	48.9	46.5	47.1	51.6	48.0	53.0
United Kingdom													
1993	126.0	129.0	130.1	128.3	129.6	132.3	133.8	142.0	139.2	144.6	143.8	155.4	136.2
1994	161.3	154.8	144.3	146.0	138.7	135.2	142.8	150.3	139.6	141.9	141.2	140.5	144.7
1995	136.8	137.4	142.1	145.8	150.8	150.0	157.3	158.8	160.2	160.2	165.2	166.6	152.6
1996	170.2	170.0	170.3	176.9	174.2	171.5	169.6	177.0	179.7	180.8	183.4	186.0	175.8
1997	192.8	194.7	194.0	197.3	203.3	201.8	212.0	210.3	226.8	211.9	211.4	222.7	206.6
1998[1]	234.3	247.9	257.0	257.6	258.9	253.4	252.6	225.5	216.6	231.4	242.7	247.0	243.7

[1] Preliminary. [2] Federal Republic of Germany. Not seasonally adjusted. *Source: Economic and Statistics Administration, U.S. Department of Census*

Corporate Profits After Tax--Quarterly In Billions of Dollars

Year	I	II	III	IV	Average	Year	I	II	III	IV	Average
1987	144.4	167.3	173.8	180.6	166.5	1993	282.5	296.1	298.4	324.0	300.3
1988	201.0	217.1	220.3	231.0	217.4	1994	312.1	342.5	361.6	377.7	348.5
1989	219.3	206.7	196.9	204.4	206.8	1995	401.0	405.9	411.8	418.8	409.4
1990	221.7	232.2	233.9	237.1	231.2	1996	438.7	450.0	447.5	454.0	454.1
1991	240.7	236.4	238.6	247.6	240.8	1997	467.2	475.3	504.7	487.1	488.3
1992	267.2	275.2	240.4	270.6	263.4	1998[1]	479.2	481.8	473.2		478.1

[1] Preliminary. *Source: Bureau of Economic Analysis, U.S. Department of Commerce (BEA)*

STOCK INDEX FUTURES, U.S.

Productivity: Index of Output Per Hour, All Persons, Nonfarm Business--Quarterly 1992 = 100

Year	I	II	III	IV	Average	Year	I	II	III	IV	Average
1987	94.1	94.7	94.5	95.2	94.6	1993	100.1	99.7	100.1	100.8	100.2
1988	94.9	95.0	95.4	95.9	95.3	1994	100.2	100.5	101.0	101.2	100.7
1989	95.5	95.7	96.0	96.1	95.8	1995	100.5	100.9	101.3	101.1	100.7
1990	96.4	96.7	96.4	95.5	96.3	1996	101.5	101.7	102.0	102.4	103.7
1991	96.1	96.8	97.4	97.6	97.0	1997	103.4	104.0	105.6	105.9	105.1
1992	99.3	99.9	99.7	101.1	100.0	1998[1]	106.8	106.8	107.4		107.0

[1] Preliminary. *Source: Bureau of Economic Analysis, U.S. Department of Commerce (BEA)*

Consumer Confidence, The Conference Board 1985 = 100

Year	Jan.	Feb.	Mar.	Apr.	May	June	July	Aug.	Sept.	Oct.	Nov.	Dec.	Average
1990	106.5	106.7	110.6	107.3	107.3	102.4	101.7	84.7	85.6	62.6	61.7	61.3	91.5
1991	55.1	59.4	81.1	79.4	76.4	78.0	77.7	76.1	72.9	60.1	52.7	52.5	68.5
1992	50.2	47.3	56.5	65.1	71.9	72.6	61.2	59.0	57.3	54.6	65.6	78.1	61.6
1993	76.7	68.5	63.2	67.6	61.9	58.6	59.2	59.3	63.8	60.5	71.9	79.8	65.9
1994	82.6	79.9	86.7	92.1	88.9	92.5	91.3	90.4	89.5	89.1	100.4	103.4	90.6
1995	101.4	99.4	100.2	104.6	102.0	94.6	101.4	102.4	97.3	96.3	101.6	99.2	100.0
1996	88.4	98.0	98.4	104.8	103.5	100.1	107.0	112.0	111.8	107.3	109.5	114.2	104.6
1997	118.7	118.9	118.5	118.5	127.9	129.9	126.3	127.6	130.2	123.4	128.1	136.2	125.4
1998[1]	128.3	137.4	133.8	137.2	136.3	138.2	137.2	133.1	126.4	119.3	126.4	126.7	131.7

[1] Preliminary. *Source: The Conference Board (Copyrighted)*

Average Open Interest of NYSE Composite Stock Index Futures in New York In Contracts

Year	Jan.	Feb.	Mar.	Apr.	May	June	July	Aug.	Sept.	Oct.	Nov.	Dec.
1990	6,350	6,098	5,443	4,925	5,129	5,160	4,732	6,079	6,003	5,272	4,983	4,554
1991	4,736	5,720	5,264	5,488	6,190	6,010	5,056	5,997	5,869	5,512	6,438	6,195
1992	5,216	5,290	5,469	4,575	4,867	5,858	6,491	7,049	6,647	6,034	6,430	5,890
1993	5,033	5,083	4,113	3,613	4,222	4,340	3,714	4,178	3,997	4,315	4,721	4,539
1994	4,653	4,471	4,823	3,720	3,839	3,969	3,903	3,982	4,142	4,494	4,244	4,617
1995	3,695	4,159	4,113	3,476	3,396	3,254	3,205	3,029	2,966	2,683	3,125	3,403
1996	3,644	4,139	3,245	2,822	2,839	2,547	2,492	2,526	2,759	2,798	2,649	3,050
1997	3,126	3,232	3,194	2,801	3,154	2,744	2,316	2,823	2,780	2,384	3,005	4,354
1998	4,803	5,216	5,252	4,754	4,888	5,990	10,154	12,249	10,574	8,554	7,977	9,806

Source: New York Futures Exchange (NYFE)

Average Open Interest of Value Line Stock Index Futures in Kansas City In Contracts

Year	Jan.	Feb.	Mar.	Apr.	May	June	July	Aug.	Sept.	Oct.	Nov.	Dec.
1990	1,245	1,355	1,463	1,514	1,544	1,404	1,311	1,297	1,250	1,210	1,325	1,381
1991	1,534	2,211	2,107	2,326	2,384	2,138	1,860	1,884	1,764	1,509	1,857	2,100
1992	2,127	2,208	1,657	1,169	1,117	1,049	833	867	1,029	962	1,101	1,632
1993	1,999	1,822	1,356	934	1,188	1,118	1,100	1,181	1,039	1,057	1,302	1,461
1994	1,921	1,649	1,289	768	839	823	812	850	898	915	1,011	1,478
1995	1,600	1,365	1,077	802	759	648	580	565	568	489	627	1,025
1996	1,163	783	571	530	418	435	347	411	403	318	370	503
1997	548	447	352	218	321	361	324	342	313	255	202	211
1998	140	151	136	102	109	253	166	184	177	112	96	76

Source: Kansas City Board of Trade (KCBT)

Average Open Interest of S&P 500 Index Futures in Chicago In Contracts

Year	Jan.	Feb.	Mar.	Apr.	May	June	July	Aug.	Sept.	Oct.	Nov.	Dec.
1990	224,392	248,558	248,920	236,700	255,436	237,730	226,100	265,136	319,214	303,980	314,880	320,520
1991	296,224	337,606	317,988	296,212	314,206	309,696	285,330	304,134	303,218	288,558	307,796	290,648
1992	294,868	286,026	283,884	273,982	283,514	299,924	306,070	327,226	336,526	340,130	356,684	359,884
1993	329,228	347,382	357,878	348,554	365,792	380,106	364,378	382,622	416,780	390,218	402,748	392,350
1994	376,450	391,648	420,130	401,636	438,218	599,134	434,056	455,742	475,868	461,188	487,162	502,740
1995	427,004	442,628	445,584	420,104	443,296	453,364	420,024	422,608	417,812	402,794	441,780	447,528
1996	406,400	428,058	419,688	368,620	399,070	407,914	369,248	382,266	413,944	374,726	416,102	448,382
1997	393,086	396,528	417,542	377,100	392,034	417,006	372,274	392,812	423,449	391,922	402,044	417,717
1998	394,410	408,851	417,721	365,746	371,732	412,739	370,410	385,820	434,838	405,395	421,928	435,907

Source: Index and Option Market (IOM), division of the Chicago Mercantile Exchange (CME)

Average Open Interest of S & P 400 Midcap Index Futures in Chicago   In Contracts

Year	Jan.	Feb.	Mar.	Apr.	May	June	July	Aug.	Sept.	Oct.	Nov.	Dec.
1992		2,776	3,060	3,017	3,712	4,476	4,073	4,350	4,762	4,355	5,778	6,883
1993	7,197	9,048	9,095	8,759	8,640	9,336	8,731	10,183	10,728	12,955	13,343	13,261
1994	13,183	11,999	12,748	10,801	10,829	11,902	11,970	12,369	15,002	13,702	13,896	14,494
1995	13,787	13,355	11,130	9,275	9,329	9,929	11,198	11,708	13,107	11,702	12,341	12,863
1996	11,088	10,474	11,375	8,700	9,254	10,403	9,763	10,867	11,168	9,641	10,596	11,107
1997	11,215	11,825	11,258	9,721	10,807	10,877	11,292	12,346	13,505	11,595	11,874	13,329
1998	12,688	13,319	14,363	14,130	13,352	13,940	12,964	13,589	14,893	16,645	16,768	17,569

Source: International Monetary Market (IMM); division of the Chicago Mercantile Exchange (CME)

Average Open Interest of NASDAQ 100 Index Futures in Chicago   In Contracts

Year	Jan.	Feb.	Mar.	Apr.	May	June	July	Aug.	Sept.	Oct.	Nov.	Dec.
1996	-----	-----	-----	1,364	3,336	6,182	5,977	4,737	7,957	10,999	10,465	8,897
1997	6,610	7,064	8,073	7,627	7,587	8,270	6,346	8,255	8,444	6,235	8,831	8,210
1998	6,918	8,184	9,314	7,652	8,833	11,128	9,991	9,507	9,233	8,187	9,176	10,838

Source: International Monetary Market (IMM); division of the Chicago Mercantile Exchange (CME)

Average Open Interest of Dow Jones Industrials Index Futures in Chicago   In Contracts

Year	Jan.	Feb.	Mar.	Apr.	May	June	July	Aug.	Sept.	Oct.	Nov.	Dec.
1997	-----	-----	-----	-----	-----	-----	-----	-----	-----	5,249	11,542	15,952
1998	14,853	15,558	14,421	13,846	14,464	16,226	15,707	17,586	18,569	17,416	17,795	17,597

Source: Chicago Board of Trade (CBT)

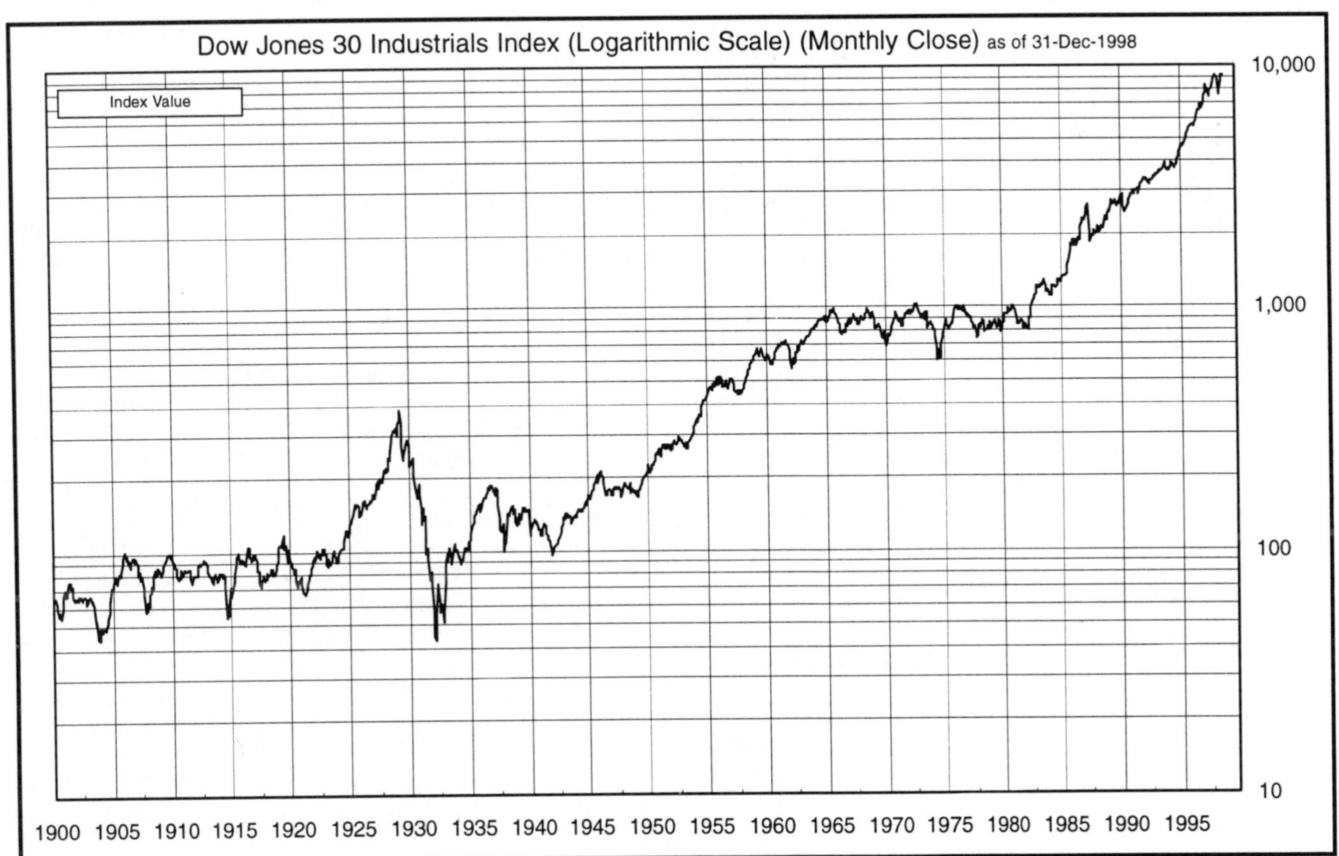

Stock Index Futures, Worldwide

The world's equity markets moved higher in 1998, gaining about 15 percent. However, there were noticeable weak spots that persisted throughout the year and for a time in mid-summer almost all the world's markets witnessed a major shakeout. Despite the seesaw year, corporate merger and acquisition activity was at a record high. An estimated $2.49 trillion in mergers occurred worldwide vs. $1.62 trillion in 1997. Oil mergers set the pace as low prices spurned an industry consolidation to reduce operating costs.

The world economic setting was sharply divided with Japan, Russia, Brazil and emerging nations facing sharply curtailed growth while domestic demand in the U.S. and Western Europe remained strong. The latter helped push world economic growth in 1998 to +2.2 percent vs. 1997 growth of +4.2 percent. However, revised estimates for 1999 place world growth at 2.2 percent vs. initial forecasts of 2.5 percent with the slippage worldwide. The bright spot is the continued absence of inflationary pressures due to low basic commodity prices suggesting that the major central banks will have the leeway to ease interest rates or that government fiscal policies will be more stimulative. However, there are lingering problems that seem to defy solution: (1) unemployment remains high in a number of countries (in Japan an unheard of 4.4 percent); (2) the 1997 Asian crisis has deep roots that carried into 1998 and are likely to persist into 1999; and (3) the economic and political turmoil in Russia has no predictable end.

Russia's equity market, which statistically led the world's markets with a near 200 percent gain in 1997, collapsed in 1998. From May to August alone the Russian Trading System index lost two-thirds of its value while interest rates soared in the wake of Russia's default and the ruble's value against all major currencies crumbled. For the year the Russian stock market fell 87.5 percent. The Russian crisis impacted on the global markets; in mid-August virtually every equity market went into a tailspin with the greatest percentile losses seen in South America: Brazil's market was off 45 percent from its mid-April peak; Argentina's market witnessed a 49 percent break from its late March high, and Mexico's market was down nearly 40 percent. In contrast, the U.S. markets lost only 14 percent and most Western European markets were off between 15 to 20 percent.

The overall picture brightened in the fourth quarter which virtually erased the mid-summer losses. In Western Europe a general rebound developed that carried the European-wide index up 18 percent and nearly 25 percent for the year. Eastern European nations did not fare nearly as well as their markets were down 66 percent primarily due to Russia. The best performer in Europe in 1998 was Finland whose equity market doubled due largely to two telephone equipment companies, but at the opposite end was Norway where only a minor gain was recorded for the year as low crude oil prices depressed oil company stocks.

For the year, the U.K. gained 10 percent; France gained 24 percent; Germany +15 percent; Switzerland +14 percent and Italy up almost 40 percent.

The 1999 outlook for European markets, as in the U.S., is mixed as all countries are faced with the same uncertainties--corporate profits and economic growth. And, as of January 1, 1999, the new European Monetary Union.

In the U.S., the bellwether Dow Jones Industrial Average advanced 16.10 percent in 1998, closing the year about 2 percent below its mid-November record high. The S&P 500 composite gained 27 percent; the high-tech weighted NASDAQ composite 39.66 percent, and the Wilshire 5000, which measures almost all U.S. stocks, gained 22 percent. Canada's market, however, fell 5 percent for the year while Australia's market gained 8 percent.

In almost all markets price volatility was the rule rather than the exception, reflecting burgeoning public participation with the buying, especially in the U.S., prompted by a strong non-inflationary economy and optimistic consumer confidence towards the future. Price corrections, while steep at times, were seen as buying opportunities.

In some countries, including Indonesia and Japan, much of the fourth quarter rebound came from a slide in the value of the U.S. dollar. In Japan, the weaker dollar accounted for about four-fifths of the quarter's 26.9 percent gain, lifting the Nikkei's 225 index up 5.5 percent for the year; in yen the Japanese market was down 8.5 percent. In Indonesia, the stock market gained 120 percent in dollar terms in the fourth quarter, but was down nearly 30 percent for the year. South Korea was a notable exception, its stock market gained 123 percent in the fourth quarter and was up 119 percent for the year. Hong Kong's Hang Seng index closed 1998 fairly close to its year earlier level. In Latin America, nearly all markets were held in check or depressed by doubts about Brazil's ability to reform its financial problems. For the year, Brazil's, Columbia's and Mexico's equity markets all dropped about 40 percent.

Cyclically, the U.S economy's expansionary phase has persisted for an unprecedented 90 plus months and appears likely to carry into 1999 although at a somewhat slower growth rate. The flow of capital into equities, estimated at $2 billion per week on average, much of it emanating from pension programs, shows little sign of slowing. While the U.S. equity markets would seem ripe for the long awaited correction, the public's bias was still solidly positive at yearend 1998, abetted in part by a strong consensus that the federal reserve would maintain an easy monetary policy, as would other key central banks, the implication of which is that most of the world's equity markets in 1999 should do fairly well, notwithstanding any latent fears that may exist as the year 2000 nears.

Futures Markets

During the 1990's, futures and options on stock indices have taken their place alongside debt instrument futures and options as the most successful exchange traded contracts. Because of this, nearly every global futures exchange lists a variety of stock index contracts, primarily on those indices based on their domestic stock markets. The list of stock indices traded worldwide has grown too large for this space, but a listing is available in the worldwide futures exchange volume tables in the front section of this Yearbook.

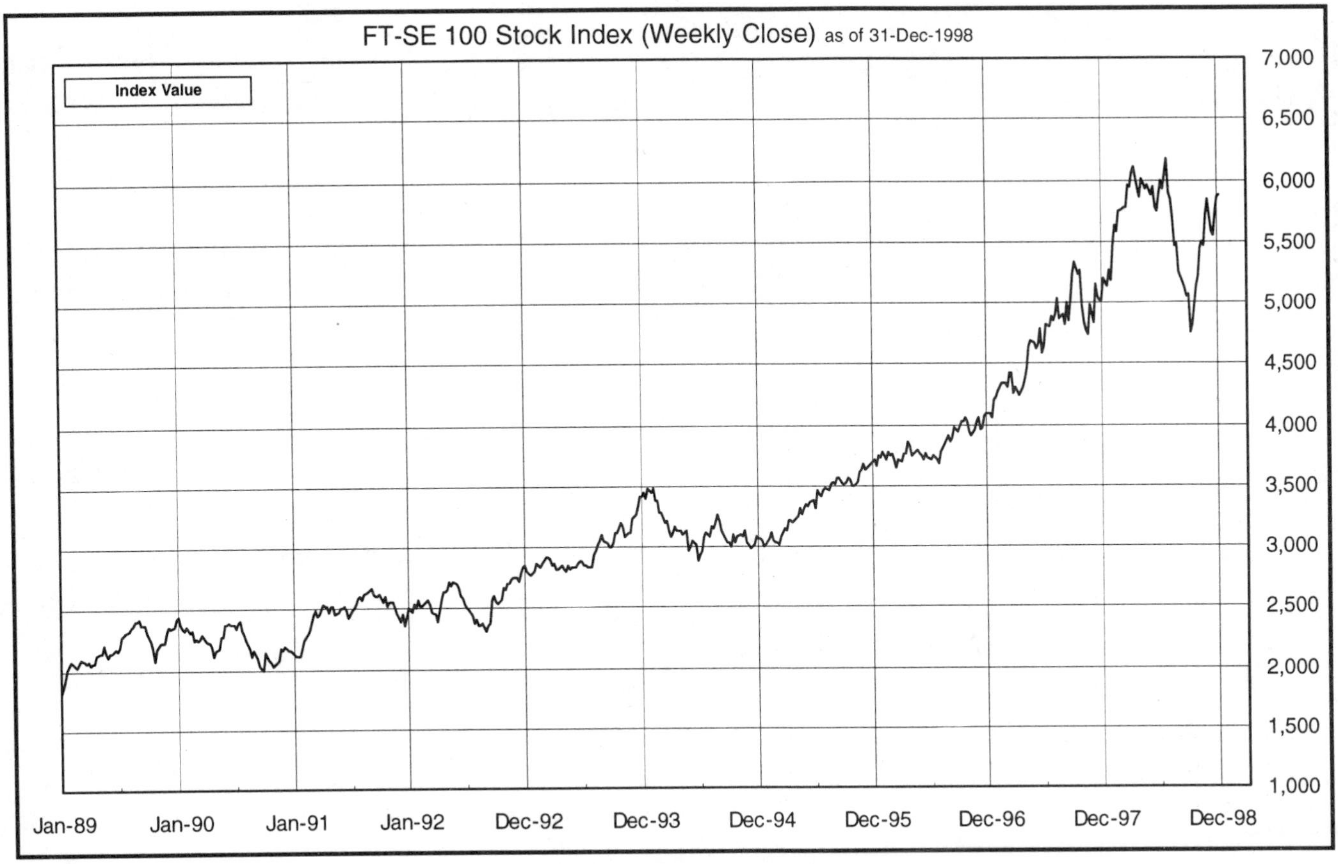

FT-SE 100 Stock Index (Weekly Close) as of 31-Dec-1998

Index Value

7,000
6,500
6,000
5,500
5,000
4,500
4,000
3,500
3,000
2,500
2,000
1,500
1,000

Jan-89 Jan-90 Jan-91 Jan-92 Dec-92 Dec-93 Dec-94 Dec-95 Dec-96 Dec-97 Dec-98

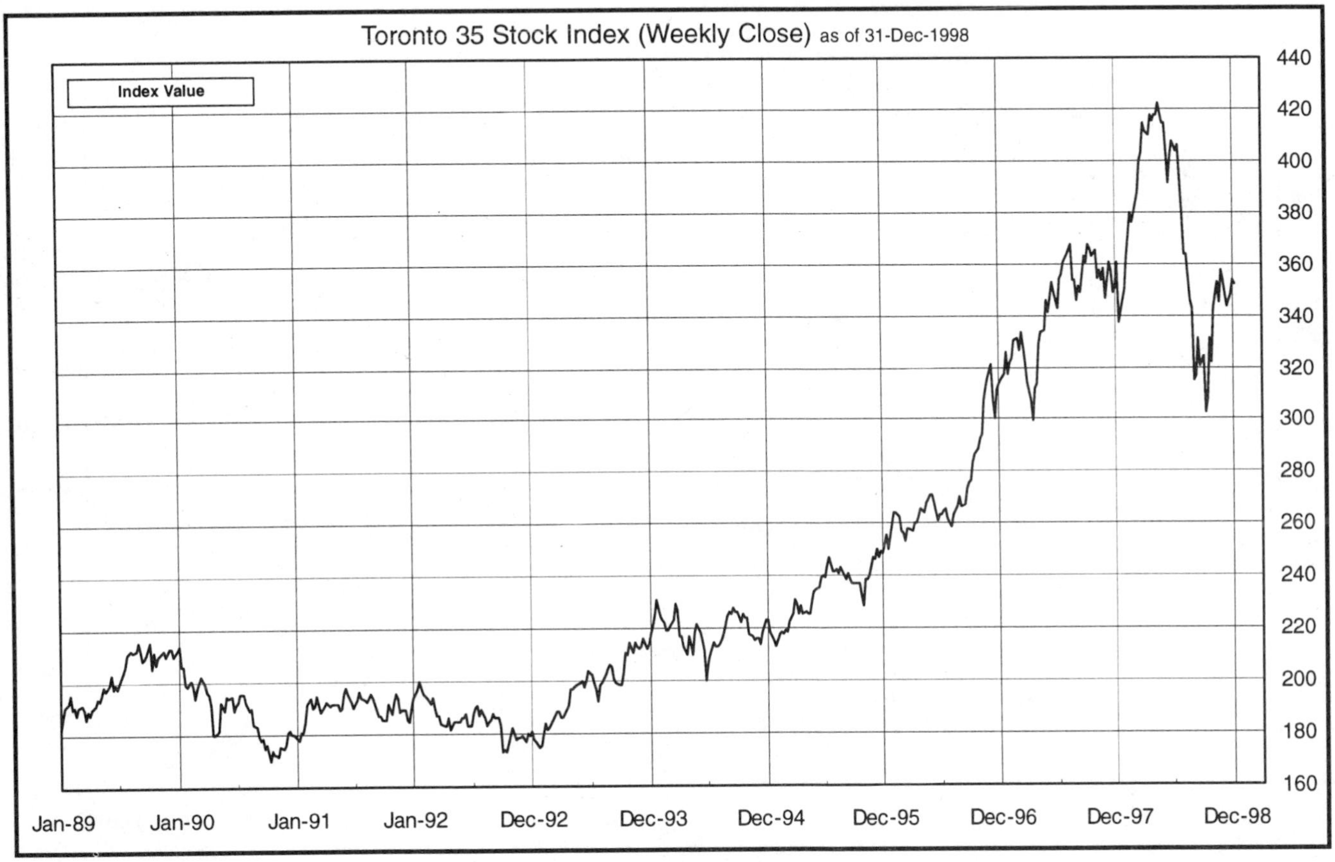

Toronto 35 Stock Index (Weekly Close) as of 31-Dec-1998

Index Value

440
420
400
380
360
340
320
300
280
260
240
220
200
180
160

Jan-89 Jan-90 Jan-91 Jan-92 Dec-92 Dec-93 Dec-94 Dec-95 Dec-96 Dec-97 Dec-98

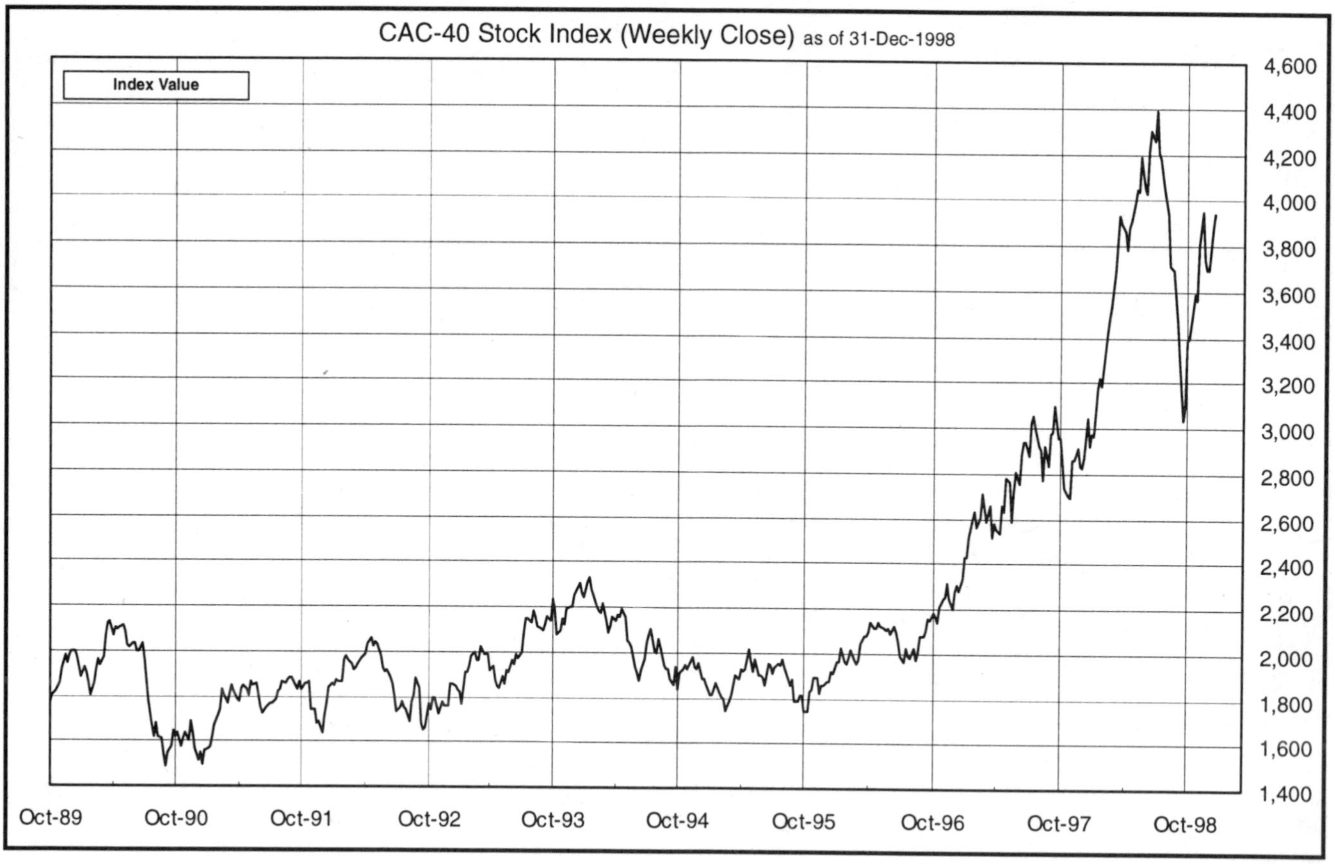

STOCK INDEX FUTURES, WORLDWIDE

CAC-40 Stock Index (Weekly Close) as of 31-Dec-1998

Index Value

4,600
4,400
4,200
4,000
3,800
3,600
3,400
3,200
3,000
2,800
2,600
2,400
2,200
2,000
1,800
1,600
1,400

Oct-89 Oct-90 Oct-91 Oct-92 Oct-93 Oct-94 Oct-95 Oct-96 Oct-97 Oct-98

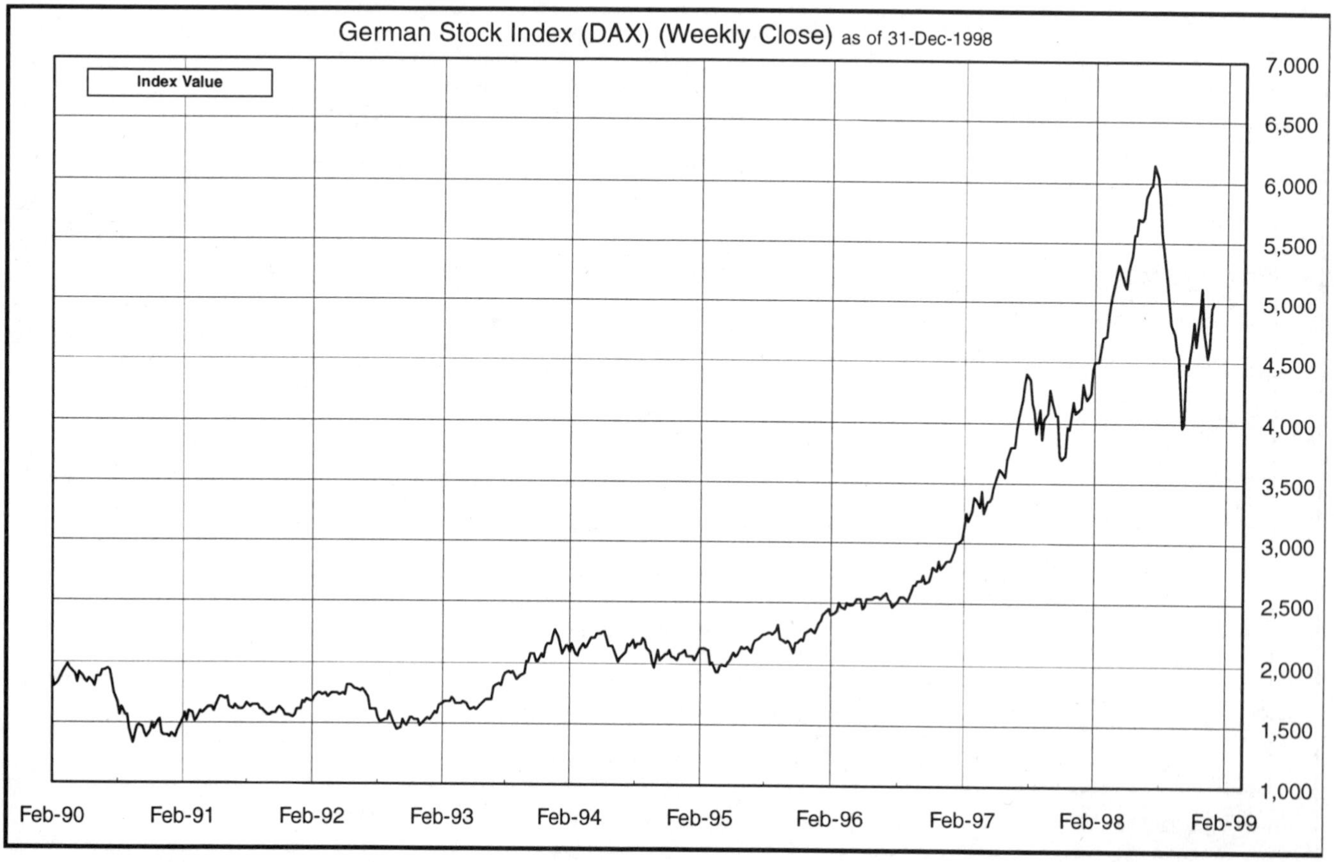

German Stock Index (DAX) (Weekly Close) as of 31-Dec-1998

Index Value

7,000
6,500
6,000
5,500
5,000
4,500
4,000
3,500
3,000
2,500
2,000
1,500
1,000

Feb-90 Feb-91 Feb-92 Feb-93 Feb-94 Feb-95 Feb-96 Feb-97 Feb-98 Feb-99

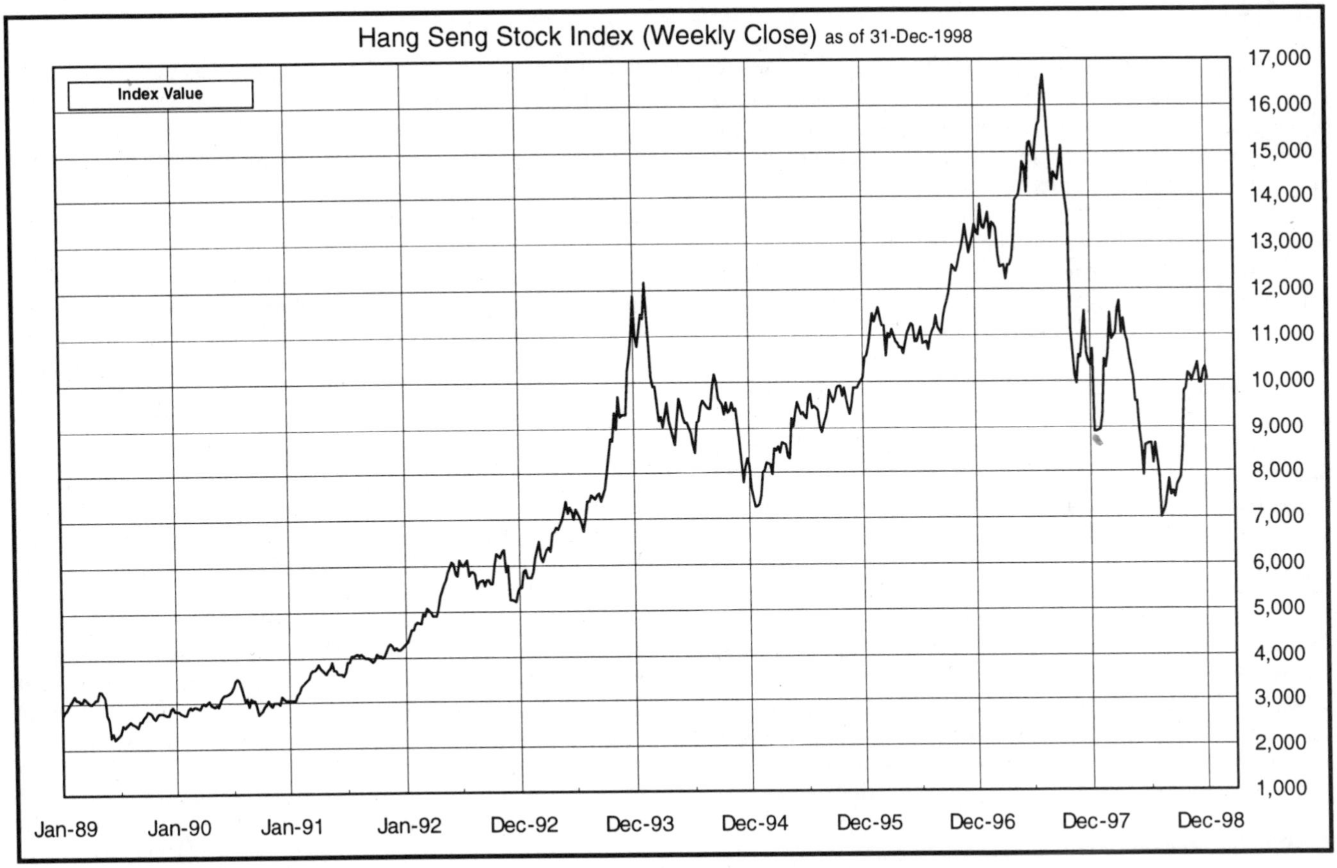

Hang Seng Stock Index (Weekly Close) as of 31-Dec-1998

Index Value

17,000
16,000
15,000
14,000
13,000
12,000
11,000
10,000
9,000
8,000
7,000
6,000
5,000
4,000
3,000
2,000
1,000

Jan-89 Jan-90 Jan-91 Jan-92 Dec-92 Dec-93 Dec-94 Dec-95 Dec-96 Dec-97 Dec-98

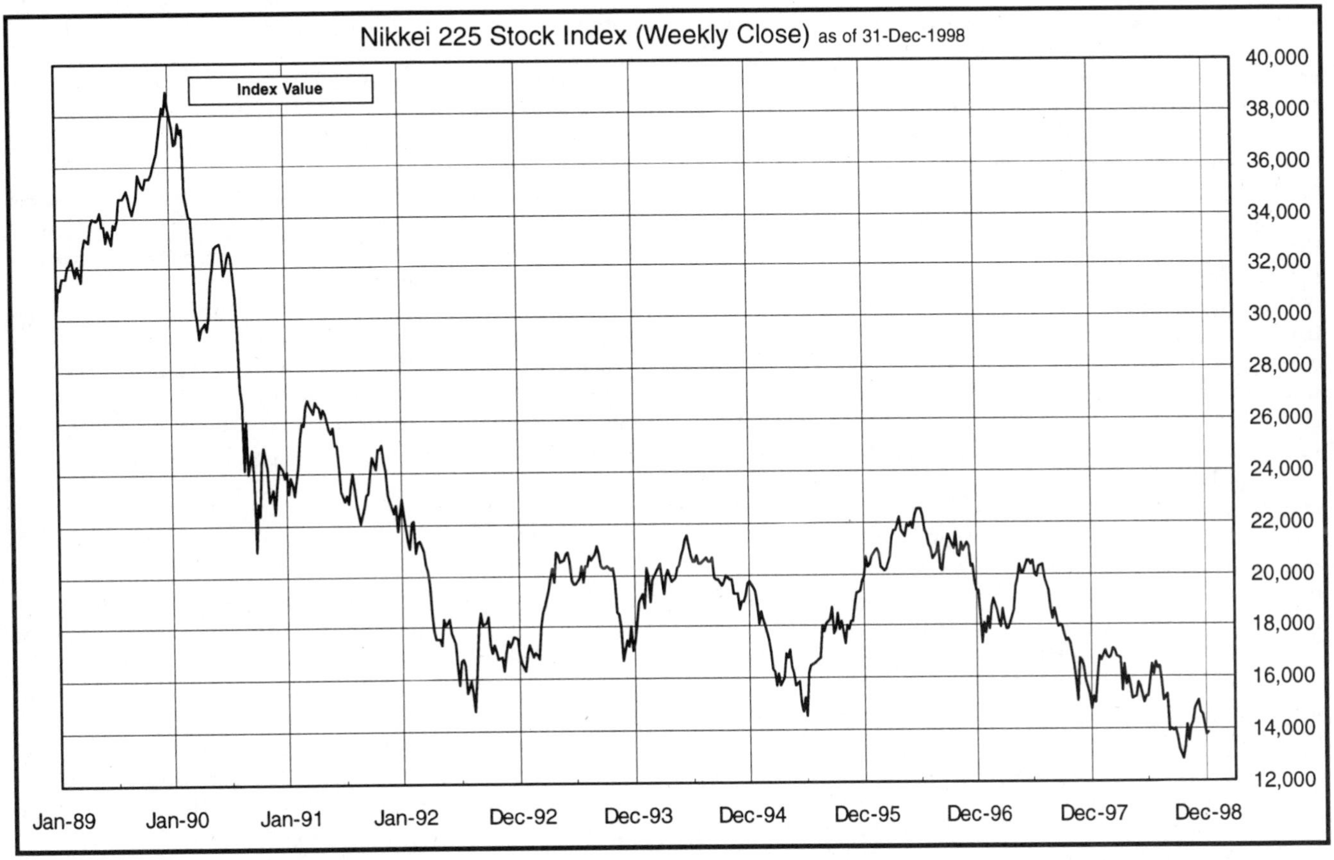

Nikkei 225 Stock Index (Weekly Close) as of 31-Dec-1998

Index Value

40,000
38,000
36,000
34,000
32,000
30,000
28,000
26,000
24,000
22,000
20,000
18,000
16,000
14,000
12,000

Jan-89 Jan-90 Jan-91 Jan-92 Dec-92 Dec-93 Dec-94 Dec-95 Dec-96 Dec-97 Dec-98

Sugar

Sugar prices trended lower in 1998, though late in the year prices appeared to be bottoming out. As 1999 started, sugar prices were at levels that were at or even below the cost of production in many countries. As such, the downside in terms of price was starting to look limited. At prices much below early 1999 levels, some sugarcane would likely be left standing in the fields. The potential for sugar prices to move higher also looked about as limited. The sugar market has seen surpluses for the last few years. World sugar production has exceeded consumption and this has resulted in an increase in world sugar stocks. As long as sugar stocks are increasing, sugar prices are not likely to move higher in any appreciable manner.

One reason for the decline in sugar prices has been the financial crises which has gripped parts of Asia. While the crises really peaked in the first half of 1998, sugar prices moved lower in response to an expected decline in consumption. Many of these Asian countries, such as Indonesia, have very large and expanding populations. Asia consumes the most sugar and use has been expanding. Annual growth in sugar use in Asia has been on the order of 3 percent. This is significant in that sugar consumption in other parts of the world is not increasing. The reason for that is slower population growth and competition from artificial sweeteners. Most of the growth in sugar consumption has been occurring in Asia. It is expected that sugar consumption in Asia will continue to increase but at a slower pace. Sugar consumption in regions like Western Europe and North America is increasing but at a very slow rate. The continuing economic uncertainty in Russia and Eastern Europe could very well result in a decline in sugar consumption. As a result of all these factors, it would appear that world sugar consumption in the 1998-99 (September-August) season will increase but the rate of increase will be slower than it has been in recent seasons. Global consumption in 1998-99 should be about 124 million tonnes (raw value).

Global consumption of sugar has been increasing though economic turbulence could slow the rate of that increase in 1998-99 and even into 1999-00. World production of sugar is much more variable and will rise and fall from season to season because of weather variability and changes in government policies. While it is possible that world sugar production in 1998-99 will decline, the fact that global sugar stocks have been increasing for the last four year will mean that sugar stocks starting the 1998-99 season were larger than the previous year. This increase will more than offset a small decline in production, if it does occur, and a minimal increase in consumption. The sugar market has been burdened by excess supplies and there is no sign that this situation will change. Countries that in recent years had been importers of sugar have produced larger crops and are now exporters. The most positive development in the current market situation is the low level of prices. This is likely to lead to some reduction in production in the coming seasons.

World production of sugar in the 1998-99 season has been variously estimated at between 126 million and 128 million tonnes (raw value). World production should continue to exceed consumption and stocks are likely to increase. Brazil has become the dominant producer of sugar in the world and is also a major exporter of sugar. The situation in Brazil is always very complicated in that part of the sugarcane crop is milled for sugar and part goes into alcohol production. If the supply of alcohol builds, more sugarcane goes to the sugar industry. Current low prices for sugar are making the outlook for the next crop difficult. The Brazilian harvest starts in May and there are ideas in the trade that production will decline. That does not necessarily mean that sugar production will decline as more sugarcane could shift from the alcohol industry over to the sugar industry. The U.S.D.A. has forecast Brazilian sugar production at 16.3 million tonnes, up 5 percent from 1997-98.

The European Union is the world's largest producer of refined sugar. Late in the season the harvesting weather turned less favorable due to heavy rains. The USDA has estimated 1998-99 European Union sugar production at 18.3 million tonnes, down 5 percent from the previous season. The sugar beet crop in Eastern Europe was poor again. A combination of poor weather and a declining infrastructure and low fuel is leading to less and less sugar beet production. The problem is most evident in Russia. In an attempt to protect the domestic sugar industry from imports which drove prices lower, the Russian government imposed import taxes on both raw and refined sugar. Since Russia is a large importer of sugar, these taxes in effect forced exporters of sugar to find new markets which added to the downward pressure on prices. In 1999, Russia is expected to import as much as four million tonnes of raw sugar. The Ukraine traditionally supplies Russia with refined sugar but the Ukrainian crop is also expected to be smaller.

In Asia, countries that had in the past been importers of sugar have either become self sufficient or have become net exporters. China is an example of a country that imported sugar in large amounts and is now close to being self sufficient. Production in 1998-99 should be a new record at 8.8 million tonnes, up 2 percent from the previous year. India is a major sugar producer. Production in 1998-99 is forecast by the U.S.D.A. to exceed 16.3 million tonnes, up almost 15 percent from 1997-98. Despite low prices, many countries that imported sugar are now exporting. Some countries are expanding sugar production. Pakistan was a net importer of sugar in 1996-97. Production in 1998-99 is expected to exceed 3.6 million tonnes, up 3 percent from 1997-98. Pakistan could export 600,000 tonnes of sugar this year.

Futures Markets

Sugar futures are traded on the Bolsa de Mercadorias & Futuros (BM&F), the Marche a Terme International de France (MATIF), Kansai Agricultural Commodities Exchange (KANEX), the Tokyo Grain Exchange (TGE), the Manila International Futures Exchange Inc. (MIFE), the London Commodity Exchange (LCE), and the New York Coffee, Sugar, and Cocoa Exchange Inc. (CSCE). Options are traded on the KANEX, the TGE, the LCE, and the CSCE.

World Production, Supply & Stocks/Consumption Ratio of Sugar In Thousands of Metric Tons (Raw Value)

Marketing Year	Beginning Stocks	Production	Imports	Total Supply	Exports	Domestic Consumption	Ending Stocks	Stocks/ Consumption Percentage
1989-90	19,395	108,772	33,179	161,346	33,179	108,709	19,458	17.9
1990-1	19,458	113,458	32,538	165,391	32,538	111,926	20,927	18.8
1991-2	20,967	116,512	30,802	168,281	30,802	113,929	23,550	20.7
1992-3	23,550	112,089	29,022	164,661	29,022	114,102	21,537	18.9
1993-4	21,537	109,787	29,753	161,077	29,753	112,801	18,523	16.4
1994-5	19,238	116,147	30,593	165,978	30,593	112,876	22,509	19.9
1995-6	22,509	122,302	34,404	179,215	34,404	118,205	26,606	22.5
1996-7	26,606	123,144	36,174	185,924	36,174	123,018	26,732	21.7
1997-8[1]	26,732	125,383	35,594	187,709	35,594	126,924	25,191	19.8
1998-9[2]	25,191	126,516	34,814	186,521	34,814	127,515	24,192	19.0

[1] Preliminary. [2] Forecast. *Source: Foreign Agricultural Service, U.S. Department of Agriculture (FAS-USDA)*

World Production of Sugar (Centrifugal Sugar-Raw Value) In Thousands of Metric Tons

Year	Australia	Brazil	China	Cuba	France	Germany	India	Indonesia	Mexico	Thailand	United States	Ukraine[3]	World Total
1989-90	3,797	7,793	5,618	8,000	4,204	4,087	12,575	2,080	3,100	3,502	6,070	5,627	108,772
1990-1	3,637	7,900	6,765	7,620	4,736	4,675	13,707	2,120	3,900	3,954	6,330	5,369	113,484
1991-2	3,192	9,200	8,492	7,030	4,413	4,250	15,249	2,250	3,500	5,062	6,627	4,178	116,512
1992-3	4,367	9,800	8,300	4,280	4,723	4,401	12,456	2,300	4,330	3,750	7,111	3,965	112,088
1993-4	4,412	9,930	6,505	4,000	4,725	4,736	11,660	2,480	3,780	3,975	6,945	4,188	109,787
1994-5	5,196	12,500	5,900	3,300	4,363	3,991	16,410	2,450	4,556	5,448	7,191	3,600	116,147
1995-6	5,049	13,700	6,686	4,450	4,564	4,159	18,225	2,090	4,660	6,223	6,686	3,800	122,302
1996-7	5,659	14,650	7,789	4,200	4,594	4,558	14,616	2,094	4,835	6,013	6,537	2,935	123,144
1997-8[1]	5,567	15,700	8,631	3,000	-----	-----	14,481	2,190	5,490	4,245	7,276	2,170	125,383
1998-9[2]	5,417	16,600	8,727	3,200	-----	-----	16,826	1,700	5,100	4,220	7,300	2,060	126,516

[1] Preliminary. [2] Forecast. [3] Formerly part of the U.S.S.R.; data not reported separately until 1989. *Source: Foreign Agricultural Service, U.S. Department of Agriculture (FAS-USDA)*

World Stocks of Centrifugal Sugar at Beginning of Marketing Year In Thousands of Metric Tons (Raw Value)

Year	Australia	Brazil	China	Cuba	France	Germany	India	Iran	Mexico	Philippines	United Kingdom	United States	World Total
1989-90	256	1,382	2,674	340	642	409	1,315	246	605	275	343	1,128	19,395
1990-1	256	1,164	1,350	475	434	330	2,376	220	750	308	300	1,111	19,458
1991-2	220	757	1,350	500	689	428	3,563	275	1,505	242	228	1,371	21,016
1992-3	194	950	2,002	500	589	340	5,245	300	910	515	281	1,340	23,602
1993-4	156	880	905	130	701	358	3,501	400	1,040	679	416	1,546	21,063
1994-5	125	455	1,168	170	784	511	2,779	400	575	412	450	1,213	19,238
1995-6	152	710	3,215	400	437	271	5,990	270	601	100	453	1,126	22,509
1996-7	101	510	2,648	400	684	331	8,455	300	714	634	457	1,354	26,606
1997-8[1]	228	860	2,784	300	-----	-----	6,979	280	634	502	-----	1,350	26,732
1998-9[2]	237	560	2,597	300	-----	-----	5,700	300	634	388	-----	1,520	25,191

[1] Preliminary. [2] Forecast. *Source: Foreign Agricultural Service, U.S. Department of Agriculture (FAS-USDA)*

Average Wholesale Price of Refined Beet Sugar[1]--Midwest Market In Cents Per Pound

Year	Jan.	Feb.	Mar.	Apr.	May	June	July	Aug.	Sept.	Oct.	Nov.	Dec.	Average
1989	28.75	29.00	29.50	29.50	29.50	29.50	29.38	29.25	29.06	28.20	29.50	31.38	29.06
1990	30.50	30.50	30.50	30.50	30.50	30.50	30.50	30.50	30.50	29.13	28.60	27.38	29.97
1991	26.88	26.50	26.50	26.13	26.00	25.75	25.50	25.50	25.00	24.94	24.60	24.50	25.65
1992	25.40	26.50	26.50	26.50	26.40	26.00	25.00	25.00	25.00	24.90	24.13	23.90	25.44
1993	23.25	23.00	23.00	23.50	23.50	23.50	25.50	27.75	27.50	27.50	27.25	26.50	25.15
1994	25.75	25.50	25.50	24.50	24.75	25.25	25.00	25.00	24.70	25.00	25.38	26.50	25.15
1995	25.50	25.50	25.50	25.50	25.13	25.10	24.75	24.75	25.50	25.75	28.13	28.85	25.83
1996	28.69	29.00	29.50	29.50	29.70	29.50	29.50	29.00	29.00	29.00	29.00	29.00	29.20
1997	29.00	29.00	28.13	28.00	28.00	27.50	27.00	26.65	26.38	24.90	25.00	25.50	27.09
1998[2]	25.50	25.50	25.50	25.50	26.00	26.00	26.00	26.00	26.50	26.90	27.00	27.00	26.12

[1] These are f.o.b. basis prices in bulk, not delivered prices. [2] Preliminary. *Source: Economic Research Service, U.S. Department of Agriculture (ERS)*

SUGAR

Average Price of World Raw Sugar[1] In Cents Per Pound

Year	Jan.	Feb.	Mar.	Apr.	May	June	July	Aug.	Sept.	Oct.	Nov.	Dec.	Average
1989	6.69	10.49	11.54	12.14	11.93	12.63	14.01	13.96	14.13	14.42	15.02	13.52	12.79
1990	14.38	14.63	15.39	15.24	14.62	12.99	11.92	10.92	11.00	9.77	10.00	9.72	12.55
1991	8.88	8.57	9.22	8.55	7.88	9.37	10.26	9.45	9.39	9.10	8.79	9.03	9.04
1992	8.43	8.06	8.22	9.53	9.62	10.52	10.30	9.78	9.28	8.66	8.54	8.15	9.09
1993	8.27	8.61	10.75	11.30	11.87	10.35	9.60	9.30	9.52	10.27	10.10	10.47	10.03
1994	10.29	10.80	11.71	11.10	11.79	12.04	11.73	12.05	12.62	12.75	13.88	14.76	12.13
1995	14.87	14.43	14.58	13.63	13.49	13.99	13.46	13.75	12.72	11.94	11.96	12.40	13.44
1996	12.57	12.97	13.07	12.43	11.94	12.54	12.83	12.33	11.87	11.65	11.29	11.38	12.24
1997	11.13	11.06	11.17	11.50	11.54	12.02	12.13	12.54	12.65	12.86	13.19	12.90	12.06
1998[2]	11.71	11.06	10.66	10.27	10.17	9.33	9.70	9.50	8.21	8.24	8.73	8.59	11.33

[1] Contract No. 11 fob stowed Caribbean port, including Brazil, bulk spot price. [2] Preliminary. *Source: Economic Research Service, U.S. Department of Agriculture (ERS-USDA)*

Average Price of Raw Sugar New York (C.I.F., Duty/Free Paid, Contract #12 & #14) In Cents Per Pound

Year	Jan.	Feb.	Mar.	Apr.	May	June	July	Aug.	Sept.	Oct.	Nov.	Dec.	Average
1989	21.88	22.07	22.12	22.30	22.45	22.99	23.56	23.57	23.50	23.14	23.24	22.84	22.81
1990	23.11	22.93	23.58	23.81	23.58	23.33	23.42	23.27	23.23	23.29	23.15	22.47	23.26
1991	21.86	21.42	21.46	21.23	21.29	21.42	21.25	21.83	22.06	21.76	21.75	21.50	21.57
1992	21.38	21.56	21.36	21.38	21.04	20.92	21.10	21.34	21.55	21.61	21.39	21.11	21.31
1993	20.76	21.16	21.56	21.76	21.36	21.42	21.89	21.85	21.97	21.80	21.87	22.00	21.62
1994	22.00	21.95	21.95	22.08	22.18	22.44	22.72	21.84	21.78	21.58	21.57	22.35	22.04
1995	22.65	22.69	22.46	22.76	23.10	23.09	24.47	23.18	23.21	22.67	22.60	22.63	22.96
1996	22.39	22.68	22.57	22.71	22.62	22.48	21.80	22.51	22.38	22.37	22.12	22.14	22.40
1997	21.88	22.07	21.81	21.79	21.70	21.62	22.04	22.21	22.30	22.27	21.90	21.93	21.96
1998[1]	21.85	21.79	21.74	22.14	22.31	22.42	22.66	22.19	21.92	21.67	21.83	22.19	22.06

[1] Preliminary. *Source: Economic Research Service, U.S. Department of Agriculture (ERS-USDA)*

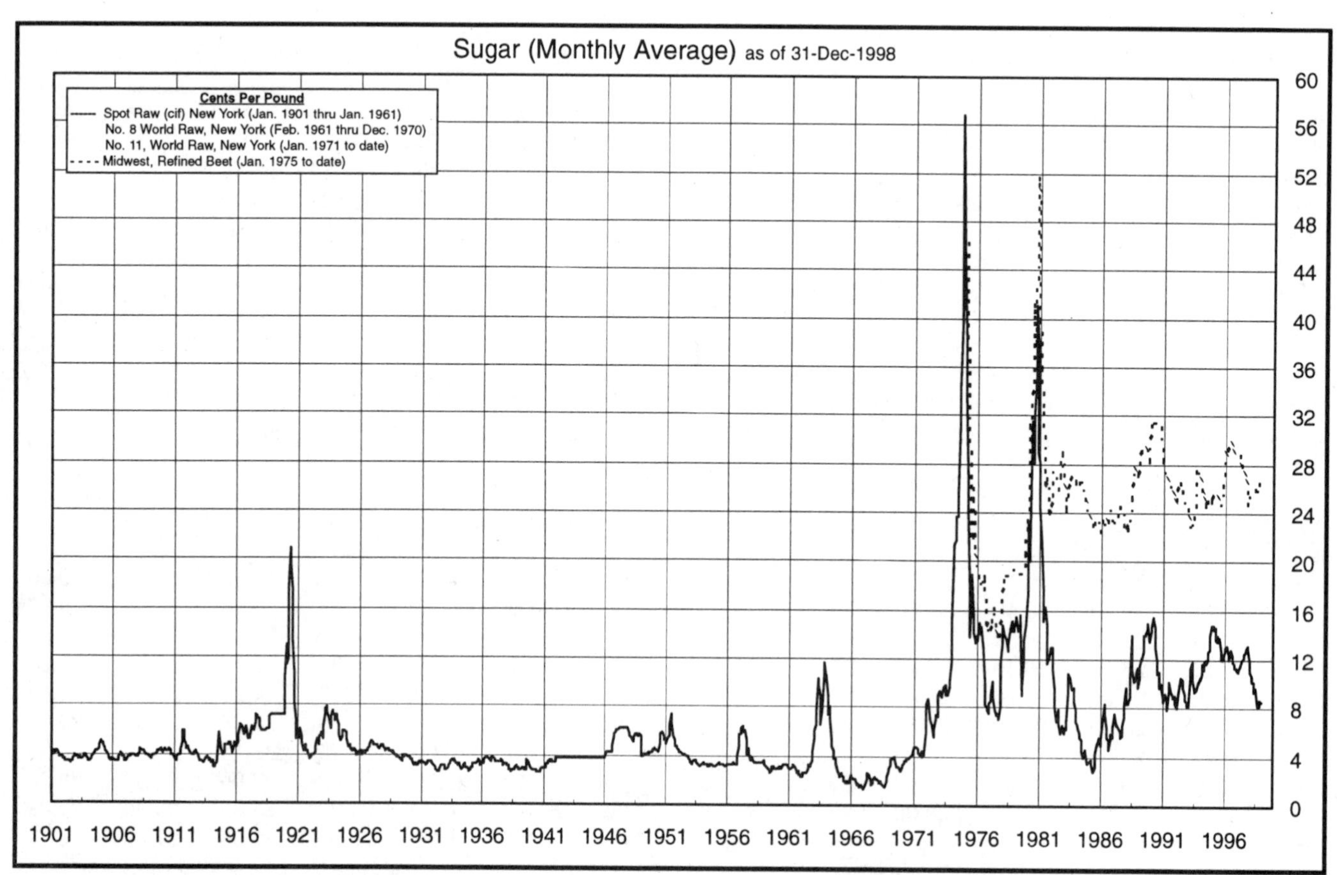

Centrifugal Sugar (Raw Value) Imported into Selected Countries In Thousands of Metric Tons

Year	Algeria	Canada	China	France	Iran	Rep. of Korea	Malaysia	Morocco	Nigeria	Russia	United Kingdom	United States	World Total
1990-1	990	1,109	1,055	343	875	1,233	900	350	480	3,580	1,143	2,619	32,558
1991-2	980	961	1,230	398	825	1,258	921	380	560	3,850	1,442	2,071	30,822
1992-3	980	1,095	506	487	780	1,233	900	408	430	3,500	1,352	1,827	29,605
1993-4	990	1,219	874	156	950	1,258	958	417	510	3,150	1,363	1,604	29,753
1994-5	990	1,020	4,110	361	800	1,345	1,030	455	460	2,700	1,261	1,664	30,593
1995-6	1,000	1,174	1,775	523	940	1,411	1,120	477	447	3,200	1,361	2,536	34,404
1996-7[1]	1,000	1,057	1,014	553	1,150	1,497	1,166	513	480	3,600	1,260	2,530	36,174
1997-8[2]	1,010	1,216	560	-----	1,150	1,450	1,280	505	560	3,800	-----	1,967	35,594
1998-9[3]	1,010	1,210	885	-----	1,150	1,490	1,340	510	560	3,660	-----	1,976	34,814

[1] Preliminary. [2] Estimate. [3] Forecast. *Source: Foreign Agricultural Service, U.S. Department of Agriculture (FAS-USDA)*

Centrifugal Sugar (Raw Value) Exported from Selected Countries In Thousands of Metric Tons

Year	Australia	Brazil	Cuba	Dominican Republic	France	Germany	Mauritius	Mexico	South Africa	Swaziland	Thailand	United Kingdom	World Total
1990-1	2,819	1,300	6,800	328	2,751	1,857	621	285	757	469	2,741	255	32,558
1991-2	2,345	1,607	6,100	344	2,682	1,557	590	50	969	474	3,657	368	30,822
1992-3	3,476	2,425	3,800	327	2,822	1,607	621	0	123	409	2,332	300	29,605
1993-4	3,663	2,861	3,300	346	2,636	1,785	590	0	27	395	2,718	410	29,753
1994-5	4,321	4,300	2,600	295	3,004	1,417	508	235	369	296	3,809	263	30,593
1995-6	4,242	5,800	3,800	325	2,735	1,180	560	587	399	307	4,537	327	34,404
1996-7[1]	4,564	5,800	3,600	364	2,730	1,430	575	750	1,056	293	4,194	388	36,174
1997-8[2]	4,570	7,200	2,300	292	-----	-----	643	1,280	1,160	272	2,900	-----	35,594
1998-9[3]	4,420	7,200	2,500	262	-----	-----	653	1,000	1,400	290	2,600	-----	34,814

[1] Preliminary. [2] Estimate. [3] Forecast. *Source: Foreign Agricultural Service, U.S. Department of Agriculture (FAS-USDA)*

Supply and Utilization of Sugar (Cane & Beet) in the United States In Thousands of Short Tons (Raw Value)

	Supply								Utilization						
	Production			Offshore Receipts									Domestic Disappearance		
Year	Cane	Beet	Total	Foreign	Territories	Total	Beginning Stocks	Total Supply	Total Use	Exports	Net Changes in Invisible Stocks	Refining Loss Adjustment	In Polyhydric Alcohol[4]	Total	Per Capita
1990-1	3,124	3,854	6,978	2,825	0	2,825	1,224	11,027	9,503	627	-86	61	8	9,503	64.6
1991-2	3,641	3,845	7,486	2,194	0	2,194	1,524	11,024	9,547	554	-13	0	11	9,547	64.4
1992-3	3,446	4,392	7,838	2,039	0	2,039	1,477	11,354	9,650	405	48	0	15	8,916	64.6
1993-4	3,565	4,090	7,655	1,772	0	1,772	1,704	11,131	9,794	454	7	0	15	9,794	66.1
1994-5	3,434	4,493	7,927	1,853	0	1,853	1,337	11,117	9,876	502	37	0	10	9,876	65.5
1995-6	3,454	3,916	7,370	2,777	0	2,777	1,241	11,388	9,896	385	-43	0	13	9,896	66.5
1996-7[1]	3,192	4,013	7,205	2,774	0	2,774	1,492	11,471	9,983	211	31	0	21	9,983	67.2
1997-8[2]	3,631	4,389	8,020	2,163	0	2,163	1,488	11,672	9,992	179	-2	0	20	9,992	67.2
1998-9[3]	3,757	4,500	8,257	2,178	0	2,178	1,679	12,114	10,200	175	0	0	20	10,200	68.1

[1] Preliminary. [2] Estimate. [3] Forecast. [4] Includes feed use. *Source: Economic Research Service, U.S. Department of Agriculture (ERS-USDA)*

Sugar Cane for Sugar & Seed and Production of Cane Sugar and Molasses in the United States

								Farm Value		Sugar Production				
			Production							Raw Value			Molasses Made	
Year	Acreage Harvested 1,000 Acres	Yield of Cane Per Havested Acre Net Tons	for Sugar (1,000 Tons)	for Seed (1,000 Tons)	Total (1,000 Tons)	Sugar Yield Per Acre Short Tons	Farm Price $ Per Ton	of Cane Used for Sugar (1,000 Dollars)	of Cane Used for Sugar & Seed (1,000 Dollars)	Total 1,000 Tons	Per Ton of Cane Lbs.	Refined Basis 1,000 Tons	Edible (1,000 Gallons)	Total[3] (1,000 Gallons)
1990	794.0	35.4	26,475	1,661	28,136	4.20	30.8	815,630	863,497	3,226	238	2,945	1,405	186,487
1991	897.0	33.7	28,960	1,292	30,252	3.95	29.0	840,194	876,479	3,497	237	3,206	1,825	193,117
1992	925.0	32.8	28,873	1,490	30,363	3.79	28.1	811,350	852,235	3,437	234	3,193	1,460	184,974
1993	924.0	32.8	29,652	1,449	31,101	3.82	28.5	846,132	886,285	3,532	235	3,351	1,480	198,167
1994	936.8	33.0	29,405	1,524	30,929	3.96	29.2	857,438	900,827	3,595	-----	3,308	-----	193,628
1995	932.3	33.0	29,155	1,641	30,796	3.90	29.5	859,604	906,956	3,489	-----	-----	-----	195,429
1996	888.9	33.1	27,687	1,777	29,464	-----	28.3	784,113	833,297	-----	-----	-----	-----	-----
1997[1]	914.0	34.7	30,003	1,706	31,709	-----	28.1	842,840	890,257	-----	-----	-----	-----	-----
1998[2]	949.5	35.5	31,881	1,836	33,717	-----	-----	-----	-----	-----	-----	-----	-----	-----

[1] Preliminary. [2] Estimate. [3] Excludes edible molasses. *Source: Economic Research Service, U.S. Department of Agriculture (ERS-USDA)*

SUGAR

U.S. Sugar Beets, Beet Sugar, Pulp & Molasses Produced from Sugar Beets and Raw Sugar Spot Prices

Year of Harvest	Acreage Planted (1,000 Acres)	Acreage Harvested (1,000 Acres)	Yield Per Harvested Acre Tons	Production 1,000 Tons	Sugar Yield Per Acre Sh. Tons	Price[3] Dollars	Farm Value $1,000	Sugar Production: Equivalent Raw Value[4] (1,000 Short Tons)	Sugar Production: Refined Basis (1,000 Short Tons)	Raw Sugar Prices: World[5] Refined #5 (Cents Per Pound)	Raw Sugar Prices: Cof., Sugar Exch. #11 World (Cents Per Pound)	Raw Sugar Prices: Cof., Sugar Exch. N.Y. Duty Paid (Cents Per Pound)	Wholesale List Price HFCS (42%) Midwest
1989	1,324	1,295	19.4	25,131	2.66	42.10	1,058,298	3,442	3,217	17.15	12.79	22.81	19.24
1990	1,400	1,377	20.0	27,513	2.79	43.00	1,182,221	3,842	3,591	17.32	12.55	23.26	19.69
1991	1,427	1,412	20.3	28,203	2.68	38.50	1,085,728	3,729	3,485	13.41	9.04	21.57	20.93
1992	1,437	1,412	20.6	29,143	3.10	41.40	1,206,480	4,386	4,099	12.39	9.09	21.31	20.70
1993	1,438	1,409	18.6	26,249	2.87	38.50	1,023,687	4,047	3,792	12.79	10.03	21.62	18.83
1994	1,476	1,443	22.1	31,853	3.17	38.80	1,234,470	4,578	4,090	15.66	12.13	22.04	20.17
1995	1,445	1,420	19.8	28,065	2.78	38.10	1,070,663	3,944	-----	17.99	13.44	22.96	15.63
1996	1,368	1,323	20.2	26,680	3.06	45.40	1,211,001	3,900	-----	16.64	12.24	22.40	14.46
1997[1]	1,459	1,428	20.9	29,886	3.00	38.80	1,160,029	-----	-----	14.33	12.06	21.96	10.70
1998[2]	1,498	1,452	22.5	32,660	-----	-----	-----	-----	-----	11.59	9.68	22.06	10.58

[1] Preliminary. [2] Estimate. [3] Includes support payments, but excludes Government sugar beet payments. [4] Refined sugar multiplies by the factor of 1.07.

Sugar Deliveries and Stocks in the United States In Thousands of Short Tons (Raw Value)

Year	Quota Allocation	Actual Imports	Deliveries by Primary Distributors: Cane Sugar Refineries	Beet Sugar Factories	Importers of Direct Consumption Sugar	Mainland Cane Sugar Mills[3]	Total Deliveries	Total Domestic Consumption	Stocks (January 1): Cane Sugar Refineries[4]	Beet Sugar Factories	Commodity Credit Corp.	Refiners' Raw	Mainland Cane Mills	Total
1989	3,093.1	2,995.8	4,764	3,449	76	6	8,295	8,952	187	1,372	0	487	1,008	3,053
1990	2,314.9	2,242.8	4,998	3,570	39	8	8,615	9,309	155	1,412	0	381	899	2,947
1991	1,526.7	1,477.0	4,786	3,713	30	11	8,540	9,470	168	1,327	0	371	812	2,729
1992	2,500.0	2,275.4	4,808	3,966	52	7	8,936	8,772	194	1,336	0	619	890	3,039
1993	[5]	[5]	4,781	4,087	52	10	9,064	9,577	183	1,640	0	507	895	3,225
1994	[5]	[5]	4,929	4,170	78	-----	9,321	9,813	218	1,696	0	438	1,160	3,512
1995	2,413.2	2,308.0	4,808	4,486	44	15	9,451	9,971	192	1,600	6	448	906	3,139
1996	2,339.1	-----	5,539	3,923	33	14	9,619	-----	195	1,383	0	334	996	2,908
1997[1]	-----	-----	5,553	3,997	27	-----	9,755	-----	196	1,520	0	323	1,156	3,195
1998[2]	-----	-----	-----	-----	-----	-----	-----	-----	212	1,535	0	322	1,308	3,377

[1] Preliminary. [2] Estimate. [3] Sugar for direct consumption only. [4] Refined. [5] Combined with 1992. *Source: Economic Research Service, U.S. Department of Agriculture (ERS-USDA)*

Sugar, Refined--Deliveries to End Users in the United States In Thousands of Short Tons

Year	Bakery & Cereal Products	Beverages	Confectionery[2]	Hotels, Restaurant & Institutions	Ice Cream & Dairy Products	Canned, Bottled & Frozen Foods	All Other Food Uses	Retail Grocers[3]	Wholesale Grocers[4]	Non-food Uses	Non-Industrial Uses	Industrial Uses	Total Deliveries
1989	1,532	215	1,187	106	426	342	637	1,026	2,051	126	3,259	4,465	7,730
1990	1,608	228	1,279	108	462	332	642	1,077	2,130	109	3,391	4,660	8,051
1991	1,632	204	1,277	100	439	331	623	1,182	2,079	88	3,469	4,594	8,063
1992	1,719	164	1,246	101	429	315	649	1,230	2,104	69	3,668	4,591	8,259
1993	1,785	158	1,292	108	424	336	725	1,235	2,075	85	3,589	4,805	8,394
1994	1,952	156	1,313	93	453	322	704	1,269	2,039	77	3,598	4,977	8,575
1995	1,905	169	1,372	103	452	279	863	1,236	2,173	64	3,701	5,103	8,804
1996	1,993	196	1,335	80	445	318	849	1,263	2,241	66	3,759	5,202	8,962
1997[1]	2,161	158	1,350	78	436	308	793	1,281	2,283	66	3,828	5,272	9,100

[1] Preliminary. [2] And related products. [3] Chain stores, supermarkets. [4] Jobbers, sugar dealers. *Source: Economic Research Service, U.S. Department of Agriculture (ERS-USDA)*

U.S. Deliveries[1] of All Sugar by Primary Distributors, by Quarters In Thousands of Short Tons (Raw Value)

Year	First Quarter	Second Quarter	Third Quarter	Fourth Quarter	Total	Year	First Quarter	Second Quarter	Third Quarter	Fourth Quarter	Total
1987	1,908	2,001	2,146	2,112	8,167	1993	2,039	2,172	2,432	2,277	8,920
1988	1,951	1,983	2,147	2,107	8,188	1994	2,121	2,265	2,532	2,260	9,177
1989	1,923	2,051	2,181	2,185	8,340	1995	2,105	2,311	2,542	2,379	9,337
1990	1,837	1,911	2,154	2,149	8,051	1996	2,191	2,355	2,519	2,445	9,511
1991	1,878	1,955	2,173	2,057	8,063	1997	2,143	2,401	2,591	2,443	9,578
1992	1,985	2,178	2,390	2,273	8,826	1998[2]	2,233	2,428	2,565		9,635

[1] Includes for domestic consumption and for export. [2] Preliminary. *Source: Economic Research Service, U.S. Department of Agriculture (ERS-USDA)*

Sunflowerseed, Meal, and Oil

1997/98 world sunflowerseed production ranked fourth among the world's major oilseed crops, although still less than 20 percent of soybeans. However, unlike soybeans for which most of the crop is crushed for meal, sunflowerseed has nearly equal amounts of meal and oil produced. The U.S. produces six percent of world sunflowerseed production, but has a larger role in world trade.

World production in 1997/98 of a near record 25 million metric tonnes was higher than expected and compares with 23.7 million in 1996/97. Argentina is the largest producer with 5.6 million tonnes in 1996/97 down from the previous year's record 5.9 million tonnes. The Russian Federation (FSU-12) remains the largest producing area--6.1 million tonnes in 1997/98 vs. 5.2 million in 1996/97; production in the E.U. in 1997/98 of 3.5 million tonnes compares with 3.9 million, respectively. Sunflowerseed is the third largest oilseed in foreign trade, 1997/98 exports of 3.7 million tonnes compares with 2.7 million in 1996/97. World stocks generally average about one million tonnes. Sunflower meal production in 1997/98 of 10 million tonnes compares with 9.9 million in 1996/97; sunflower oil of 8.8 million tonnes compares with 8.6 million, respectively; but more oil moves in foreign trade than meal.

The acreage planted to sunflowerseed production in the U.S. shows an irregular pattern, as does average yield. In the 1990's the highest acreage planted was 3.6 million acres (1994/95), for 1997/98 about 2.9 million were planted vs. 2.6 million in 1996/97. Production (September/August) in 1997/98 of 1.7 million metric tonnes compares with 1.6 million in 1996/97, and the 1990's high of 2.2 million (1994/95). The Dakotas, notably North, are the largest producing states, with about two-thirds of total production.

U.S. sunflower meal production in 1997/98 (October/September) of 417,000 metric tonnes was unchanged from a year earlier. Disappearance in 1997/98 of 422,000 tonnes was also unchanged from 1996/97, with about five percent exported. Sunflower oil production in 1997/98 of 362,000 tonnes compares with 365,000 in 1996/97. However, unlike meal, most U.S. sunflower oil production is exported; 283,000 tonnes in 1997/98 vs. 325,000 in 1996/97, with Mexico the largest buyer. Domestic oil use has recently hovered around 75,000 tonnes. The U.S. also exports sunflower seed, much of it going to the European Union. Seed exports of 177,000 tonnes in 1997/98 compare with 147,000 in 1996/97.

The 1997/98 sunflower oil price was forecast at \$507-\$573 per metric tonne vs. \$497 in 1996/97, basis average crude Minneapolis. The sunflower meal price was forecast to range from \$90-\$123 per metric tonne vs. \$136 in 1996/97, basis 28 percent protein.

Abroad, the 1996/97 average sunflowerseed oil price of \$545 per metric tonne, basis Rotterdam, compares with \$617 the year before; for protein meal the average of \$139 compares with \$151, respectively.

World Production of Sunflowerseed In Thousands of Metric Tons

Crop Year	Argentina	Bulgaria	China	France	Hungary	India	Romania	South Africa	Spain	Turkey	United States	Former U.S.S.R.	World Total
1994-5	5,900	602	1,367	2,053	664	1,204	764	352	979	740	2,194	4,516	23,927
1995-6	5,556	650	1,269	1,993	785	1,324	933	755	588	790	1,819	7,405	26,171
1996-7	5,450	530	1,420	1,996	905	1,315	1,096	530	1,138	670	1,627	404	24,635
1997-8[1]	5,600	505	1,150	1,995	640	1,250	869	562	1,373	750	1,707	258	24,127
1998-9[2]	7,000	480	1,200	1,720	740	1,350	1,000	900	1,130	675	2,100	305	26,601

[1] Preliminary. [2] Forecast. *Source: The Oil World*

Sunflowerseed Statistics in the United States In Thousands of Metric Tons

Crop Year Beginning September	Harvested Acres 1,000	Harvested Yield Per Cwt.	Farm Price \$ Per Metric Ton	Value of Production Mil. \$	Supply: Stocks, Sept. 1	Supply: Production	Supply: Imports	Supply: Total	Disappearance: Crush	Disappearance: Exports	Disappearance: Non-Oil Use & Seed	Disappearance: Total
1994-5	3,430	14.10	236	512.8	71	2,194	42	2,306	1,313	287	604	2,203
1995-6	3,368	11.90	254	457.6	103	1,819	21	1,943	915	224	598	1,737
1996-7	2,479	14.36	258	414.8	205	1,614	18	1,837	844	149	648	1,641
1997-8[1]	2,792	13.17	256	426.8	196	1,668	29	1,933	1,061	189	591	1,841
1998-9[2]	3,476	15.09	212-227	524.7	92	2,380	29	2,501	1,275	236	756	2,267

[1] Preliminary. [2] Forecast. *Source: Economic Research Service, U.S. Department of Agriculture (ERS-USDA)*

Sunflower Oil and Meal Statistics in the United States In Thousands of Metric Tons

Crop Year Beginning October	Oil Supply: Stocks, Oct. 1	Oil Supply: Production	Oil Supply: Total[3]	Oil Disappearance: Exports	Oil Disappearance: Domestic	Oil Disappearance: Total	Oil Price \$ Per Metric Ton[4]	Meal Supply: Stocks, Oct. 1	Meal Supply: Production	Meal Supply: Total[3]	Meal Disappearance: Exports	Meal Disappearance: Domestic	Meal Disappearance: Total	Meal Price \$ Per Metric Ton 28% Protein
1994-5	29	528	558	444	78	521	622	5	653	660	89	566	653	72
1995-6	37	390	428	285	76	361	560	5	458	463	25	433	458	136
1996-7	67	371	448	322	84	406	497	5	440	445	21	419	440	122
1997-8[1]	42	460	505	370	108	478	608	5	494	499	13	482	495	90
1998-9[2]	27	558	590	431	114	545	518-552	5	630	635	23	607	630	35-68

[1] Preliminary. [2] Forecast. [3] Includes imports. [4] Crude at Minneapolis. *Source: Economic Research Service, U.S. Department of Agriculture (ERS)*

Tall Oil

Tall oil is the major by-product of the kraft or sulfate processing of pinewood. Tall oil is obtained by chemically treating the cooking liquor used in pulp operations in paper manufacturing. After lumber is pulped, the resulting liquor concentrate is skimmed. These skimmings are acidified to produce crude tall oil.

Crude tall oil contains 40-50 percent fatty acids such as oleic and linoleic acids; 5-10 percent sterols, alcohols and other neutral components When distilled these resins and fatty acids are used in alkyd and synthetic resins, lubricants, adhesives, soaps and detergents, linoleum, flotation and waterproofing agents, paints, varnishes and drying oils.

The U.S. Department of Commerce, Bureau of Census, reported that U.S. tall oil production in January 1998 was 133.7 million pounds, down 1 percent from the previous month but some 12 percent higher than a year ago. In the fourth quarter of 1997, U.S. production of tall oil was 373.5 million pounds, up 7 percent from the same quarter of 1996. In the 1996-97 (Oct.-Sept.) year, U.S. production of tall oil was 1.34 billion pounds, 4 percent more than in 1995-96.

U.S. tall oil consumption in December 1997 was 88.4 million pounds, down 11 percent from the previous year and 1 percent more than the previous month. U.S. consumption of tall oil in 1997 was estimated at 1.14 billion pounds, down 3 percent from the previous year. In the last five years, U.S. consumption of tall oil has averaged 1.14 billion pounds.

U.S. stocks of tall oil on February 1, 1998 were 233.4 million pounds, up 30 percent from February 1, 1997. Stocks of crude tall oil on February 1, 1998 were 203.6 million pounds, while stocks of refined tall oil were 29.8 million pounds.

Consumption of Tall Oil in Inedible Products in The United States In Millions of Pounds

Year	Jan.	Feb.	Mar.	Apr.	May	June	July	Aug.	Sept.	Oct.	Nov.	Dec.	Total
1991	-------	249.1	-------	-------	237.3	-------	-------	223.1	-------	-------	230.5	-------	940
1992	77.8	7.5	73.2	67.6	77.8	74.8	71.5	78.4	77.1	78.9	63.8	69.2	884
1993	68.6	64.8	73.1	68.1	76.3	68.8	79.0	78.1	78.0	75.4	78.4	83.2	892
1994	117.4	98.8	124.0	118.4	115.0	118.8	106.8	114.9	119.8	113.7	101.9	113.0	1,363
1995	99.8	93.6	96.9	95.8	87.3	96.5	93.1	102.3	89.4	91.6	100.5	88.9	1,136
1996	93.1	103.4	89.2	104.1	100.5	96.6	85.4	100.7	94.9	111.5	101.4	98.8	1,180
1997	111.5	89.0	91.0	99.5	97.0	105.8	103.7	94.4	84.7	87.2	87.3	88.4	1,139
1998[1]	86.7	114.4	113.2	120.0	108.0	101.8	117.2	114.8	120.3	111.6	119.0	121.0	1,348

[1] Preliminary. *Source: Bureau of the Census, U.S. Department of Commerce*

Crude Tall Oil Production in the United States In Millions of Pounds

Crop Year	Oct.	Nov.	Dec.	Jan.	Feb.	Mar.	Apr.	May	June	July	Aug.	Sept.	Total
1991-2	-------	342.7	-------	131.4	121.5	131.2	133.2	121.9	129.8	130.6	129.9	119.7	1,372.2
1992-3	120.2	114.7	122.7	119.4	128.4	142.1	131.8	120.0	126.6	117.0	104.3	117.3	1,347.2
1993-4	107.5	120.7	124.6	127.0	115.4	148.1	131.0	119.1	109.1	108.7	110.8	117.4	1,322.0
1994-5	111.1	114.5	115.1	108.3	108.1	123.0	111.1	116.5	118.2	116.4	119.2	102.9	1,261.6
1995-6	109.8	105.2	105.2	115.5	123.3	126.9	108.9	120.3	120.3	120.5	124.9	112.9	1,281.0
1996-7	119.2	113.9	114.5	119.9	125.1	125.1	118.5	116.6	116.4	135.0	132.9	130.8	1,337.2
1997-8	122.7	115.4	135.4	137.7	126.6	127.5	132.3	131.2	131.1	132.0	120.2	121.1	1,540.6
1998-9[1]	118.4	113.4	118.5										1,401.0

[1] Preliminary. W = Withheld proprietary data. *Source: Bureau of Census, U.S. Department of Commerce*

Stocks of Tall Oil in the United States, on First of Month In Millions of Pounds

Crop Year		Oct.	Nov.	Dec.	Jan.	Feb.	Mar.	Apr.	May	June	July	Aug.	Sept.
1991-2	Crude	-------	139.1	-------	188.9	153.9	163.1	163.2	156.9	158.4	161.0	190.7	186.1
	Refined	-------	36.0	-------	35.0	35.0	35.7	36.2	13.5	16.1	15.2	15.9	28.4
1992-3	Crude	173.3	167.5	143.7	137.8	162.5	170.8	184.7	187.3	165.3	179.2	173.1	149.9
	Refined	17.4	18.1	13.8	14.1	14.0	12.6	13.7	9.4	7.7	7.3	7.5	7.2
1993-4	Crude	132.8	124.0	113.0	103.7	109.5	109.7	118.2	124.4	112.6	105.3	101.1	97.5
	Refined	7.0	7.5	8.5	10.7	13.7	13.5	13.5	12.0	10.2	9.7	11.6	10.9
1994-5	Crude	86.3	82.7	94.1	104.1	107.6	117.2	123.4	132.1	118.1	132.3	134.7	135.0
	Refined	12.0	14.4	16.3	13.5	15.4	14.1	11.7	10.8	10.2	10.0	9.9	8.9
1995-6	Crude	120.9	117.5	112.9	100.7	105.7	120.3	146.0	131.8	127.0	130.5	138.7	147.3
	Refined	10.1	11.6	7.9	6.0	7.9	9.7	8.5	10.4	8.5	6.0	6.1	7.2
1996-7	Crude	172.3	192.1	167.4	182.4	173.0	196.0	200.8	220.6	187.3	237.5	248.5	242.2
	Refined	8.3	7.0	7.5	8.9	6.5	26.5	17.4	31.7	20.9	32.0	13.2	16.6
1997-8	Crude	208.6	187.9	209.7	202.1	202.8	219.4	256.8	254.1	239.1	259.1	278.4	245.2
	Refined	32.3	25.6	34.9	21.4	30.4	17.0	14.2	13.0	13.1	15.1	14.7	15.3
1998-9[1]	Crude	268.7	219.8	200.3	197.5								
	Refined	15.1	14.9	17.0	12.5								

[1] Preliminary. *Source: Bureau of the Census, U.S. Department of Commerce*

Tallow and Greases

Production of tallow and greases is related to the number of cattle produced. Tallow finds widespread use in baking and cooking. World production of tallow and greases (edible and inedible) has averaged about 8 million tonnes in the last few years. The U.S. is by far the world's largest producer of tallow and greases. The U.S. Department of Agriculture estimated production in 1997 at 3.4 million tonnes or more than 40 percent of total world production. The next largest producer of tallow and greases is Brazil though production is only about 5 percent of the world total. Other large producers include Australia, Russia and Canada.

The U.S.D.A. estimated U.S. stocks of edible tallow at the beginning of the marketing year in October 1998 at 37 million pounds. That was down 23 percent from stocks at the start of the 1997-98 season. U.S. production of edible tallow in the 1998-99 season was estimated at 1.42 billion pounds. That represented a decline of 6 percent from production in 1997-98. Production of edible tallow since 1994-95 has averaged 1.49 billion pounds.

The U.S. imports very small amounts of edible tallow. For the 1998-99 season, imports were estimated at only 5 million pounds, up slightly from the 4 million pounds imported in 1997-98. There have been years when imports were larger. In the 1994-95 season, edible tallow imports were 18 million pounds while in 1993-94 they were 15 million.

The total supply of edible tallow in the U.S. in the 1998-99 season was projected to be 1.46 billion pounds, down 6 percent from the previous year. The recent peak for tallow supplies was in 1991-92 when they were 1.94 billion pounds.

Use of tallow is in either the domestic market or in the export sector. U.S. domestic use of tallow in 1998-99 was estimated at 1.2 billion pounds, down 6 percent from the previous season. Domestic use of tallow has averaged just over 1.2 billion pounds for several seasons. Over the last five seasons, domestic use of tallow has averaged 1.27 billion pounds.

Exports of tallow are more variable. For the 1998-99 season, exports were projected to be 215 million pounds, down 10 percent from the previous season. Exports in the 1997-98 season were as low as 181 million pounds while in 1993-94 they were as high as 316 million pounds. Over the last five season, exports of tallow have averaged 228 million pounds. Total use of tallow in the 1998-99 marketing year was estimated at 1.42 billion pounds, down 6 percent from the previous year. Over the last five seasons, use of tallow has averaged 1.49 billion pounds.

Projected ending stocks of tallow at the end of the 1998-99 season are 40 million pounds. That represents an increase of 8 percent from the previous season. Stocks of tallow over the last five seasons have averaged 42 million pounds.

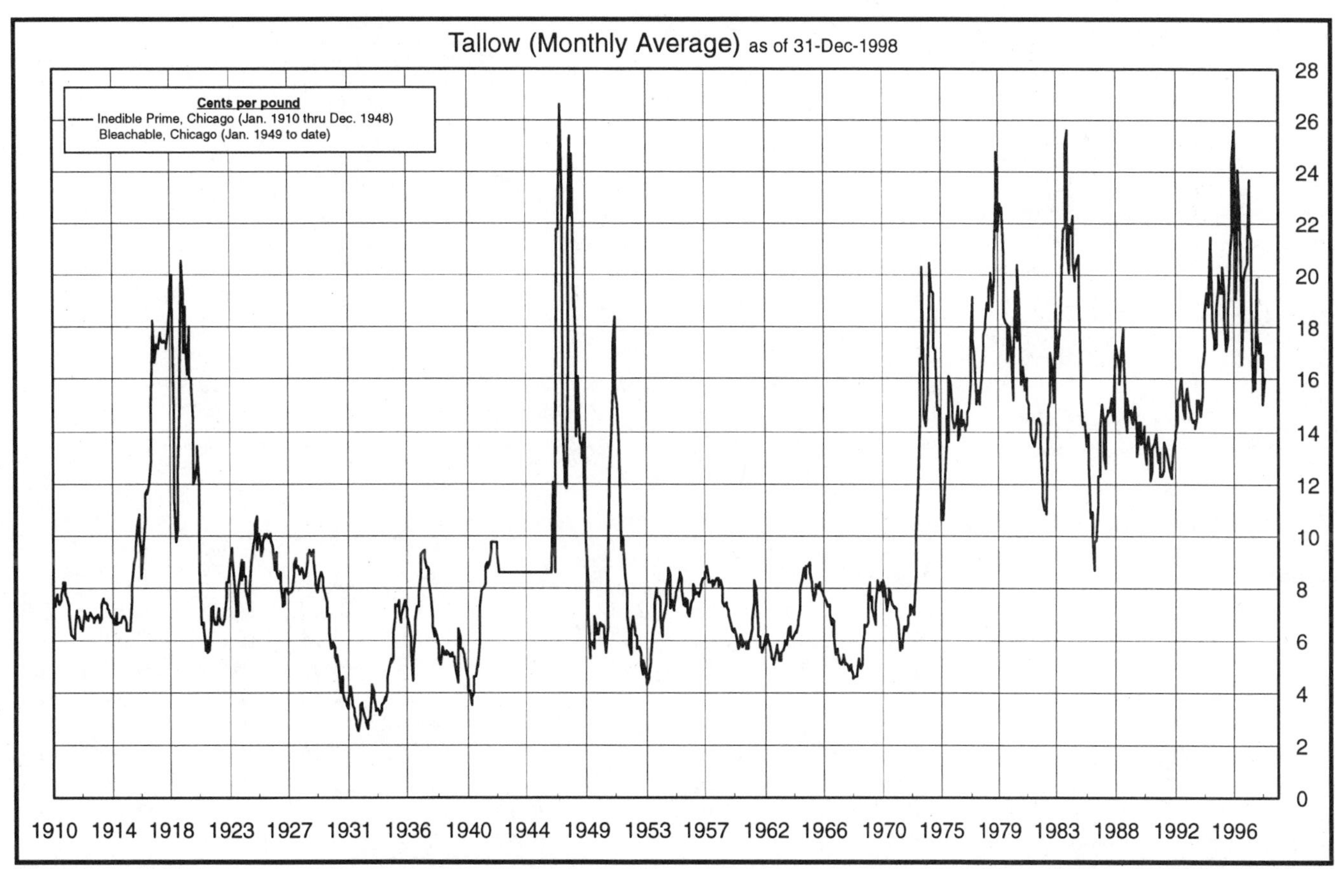

TALLOW AND GREASES

World Production of Tallow and Greases (Edible and Inedible) In Thousands of Metric Tons

Year	Argentina	Australia	Brazil	Canada	France	Germany	Rep. of Korea	Netherlands	New Zealand	Russia[4]	United Kingdom	United States	World Total
1989	278	489	272	203	179	280	60	125	133	400	207	3,212	6,614
1990	285	530	340	193	185	270	85	150	132	108	230	3,180	6,538
1991	268	472	336	212	275	197	121	150	134	106	225	3,309	6,677
1992	260	526	345	209	240	178	115	163	145	115	212	3,487	7,511
1993	250	446	350	213	206	167	120	159	135	90	215	3,851	7,716
1994	248	423	462	217	220	166	118	158	147	377	230	3,756	8,253
1995	240	397	467	242	220	168	198	161	155	400	165	3,581	8,184
1996	233	456	460	255	220	167	209	232	161	340	160	3,467	8,081
1997[1]	200	423	467	260	220	166	225	170	160	320	180	3,800	8,364
1998[2]	210	408	478	250	210	167	225	169	150	310	195	3,851	8,447

[1] Preliminary. [2] Estimate. [3] Forecast. [4] Formerly part of the U.S.S.R.; data not reported separately until 1990. *Source: Foreign Agricultural Service, U.S. Department of Agriculture (FAS-USDA)*

Salient Statistics of Tallow and Greases (Inedible) in the United States In Millions of Pounds

	Supply				Consumption			Wholesale Prices, ¢ Per Lb.	
Year	Production	Stocks Jan. 1	Total	Exports	Soap	Feed	Total	Edible, (Loose) Chicago	Inedible, Chicago No. 1
1989	5,848	399	6,247	2,679	368	1,919	3,194	15.8	14.4
1990	5,217	374	6,097	2,267	402	2,000	3,061	14.6	13.7
1991	5,759	357	6,116	1,936	392	1,748	2,949	14.3	13.3
1992	5,768	349	6,117	2,276	334	1,954	3,050	15.5	14.4
1993	6,621	309	6,930	2,117	300	1,995	3,018	16.2	14.9
1994	6,364	320	6,684	3,039	301	2,183	3,246	18.4	17.4
1995	6,481	350	6,831	2,486	264	2,071	2,334	21.4	19.2
1996	6,242	373	6,615	1,807	245	2,389	2,634	22.0	20.1
1997[1]	6,249	266	6,515	775	245	2,401	2,646	23.2	20.8
1998[2]	6,644	339	6,983	1,047	228	2,533	2,761	18.9	17.5

[1] Preliminary. [2] Estimate. *Sources: Economic Research Service, U.S. Department of Agriculture; Bureau of the Census, U.S. Department of Commerce*

Supply and Disappearance of Edible Tallow in the United States In Millions of Pounds, Rendered Basis

	Supply			Disappearance					
Year	Stocks Jan. 1	Production	Total	Domestic	Exports	Total	Direct Use	Baking or Frying Fats	Per Capita (Lbs.)
1989	48	1,167	1,215	975	202	1,177	223	752	3.9
1990	34	1,202	1,247	955	251	1,206	342	637	3.8
1991	41	1,515	1,944	1,197	333	1,530	604	460	3.9
1992	33	1,414	1,456	1,109	306	1,415	537	427	4.7
1993	41	1,499	1,556	1,204	316	1,519	700	404	4.4
1994	33	1,510	1,559	1,228	295	1,523	731	405	4.7
1995	36	1,536	1,590	1,091	279	1,548	710	374	4.1
1996	43	1,520	1,568	1,123	218	1,535	796	320	4.2
1997[1]	33	1,488	1,527	964	185	1,475	648	312	3.6
1998[2]	46	1,460	1,511	1,256	215	1,471	-----	-----	-----

[1] Preliminary. [2] Forecast. *Sources: Economic Research Service, U.S. Department of Agriculture; Bureau of the Census, U.S. Department of Commerce*

Average Wholesale Price of Tallow, Inedible, No. 1 Packers (Prime), Delivered, Chicago In Cents Per Lb.

Year	Jan.	Feb.	Mar.	Apr.	May	June	July	Aug.	Sept.	Oct.	Nov.	Dec.	Average
1989	14.90	16.00	14.86	14.60	14.70	15.10	14.48	13.52	14.13	15.25	15.50	15.50	14.88
1990	14.87	14.50	14.47	13.77	13.66	NA	13.50	10.12	12.00	13.42	14.09	14.75	13.56
1991	13.88	14.28	14.43	14.80	13.02	12.36	12.96	14.00	13.50	13.68	13.08	12.50	13.54
1992	12.25	12.63	12.68	13.25	13.75	13.98	14.75	15.42	15.25	15.94	16.75	16.13	14.40
1993	15.36	14.70	15.24	16.15	15.41	14.51	14.36	14.53	14.66	14.62	14.69	14.63	14.91
1994	15.00	15.00	15.22	15.19	15.25	15.63	16.67	18.64	19.50	19.78	20.38	22.48	17.40
1995	21.75	18.86	18.00	17.75	17.50	17.89	19.61	19.81	19.53	19.46	19.75	20.08	19.17
1996	19.45	17.00	17.03	17.54	19.37	19.50	20.98	22.40	25.98	21.05	19.65	21.63	20.13
1997	23.40	22.88	19.35	17.39	18.09	19.64	19.65	20.10	20.88	22.13	22.88	22.60	20.75
1998[1]	18.20	16.88	17.58	17.70	20.35	19.63	17.31	17.57	16.69	16.98	15.06	16.07	17.50

[1] Preliminary. *Source: Economic Research Service, U.S. Department of Agriculture (ERS-USDA)*

Tea

Tea is produced in a number of countries around the world. It is usually grown on plantations. The tea plant is an evergreen shrub which can grow 15-30 feet tall in its natural state, though on a plantation it is kept to a height of about five feet. It thrives in tropical climates with plenty of rain. It does well at higher altitudes though it can be grown at sea level. Most commercial production of tea takes place near the equator.

Tea is usually classified into three classes. The first is black tea or fermented tea; second is green tea or unfermented tea; and third is oolong tea or semifermented. All of these teas are differentiated in processing, the tea leaves used are all the same. Black tea is made by taking tea leaves and fermenting them under damp clothes, then drying the leaves until they are black. The fermentation reduces astringency and changes flavor. Green tea is steamed in a boiler with fermentation and the leaves are dried. Oolong teas are partially fermented. After drying, teas are graded with orange pekoe being the highest quality.

World production in 1996 was estimated by the Food and Agricultural Organization of the United Nations at 2.62 million metric tonnes. That represented an increase of close to 2 percent from the previous year. World production of tea has held fairly steady for several years. Between 1992 and 1996, global tea production averaged 2.58 million tonnes per year. By far the largest producer of tea in the world is India. Production in 1996 was estimated at 715,000 tonnes, unchanged from the previous year. Between 1992 and 1996, India's production of tea averaged 727,000 tonnes. India produces mostly black tea and has been putting more emphasis on producing higher quality tea. India's tea is grown principally in the Assam Valley and in the south in Kerala.

China is the next largest producer of tea with production in 1996 estimated at 609,000 tonnes, unchanged from the previous year. China's production between 1992 and 1996 averaged 602,200 tonnes per year. China has been trying to improve the quality of its tea. Green tea is produced for the domestic market while black tea is exported. Kenya is the third largest producer of tea with 1996 production of 255,000 tonnes, an increase of 4 percent from the previous year. Kenya has been gradually increasing its production of tea and it is the largest exporter of tea. Sri Lanka is the next largest producer of tea with 1996 production estimated at 246,000 tonnes, unchanged from the previous year.

About 40 percent of the world's tea production is exported. Along with production, exports have been holding steady for several years. In 1995, world exports of tea were 1.12 million tonnes, up almost 7 percent from the previous year. Kenya is the largest exporter of tea with about 19 percent of the market. Other large exporters include Sri Lanka, India and China.

The U.S. is a major importer of tea, most of which is black tea. U.S. per capita consumption of tea is just over nine gallons. The U.S. exports small amounts of tea. The U.S. Department of Commerce reported that in October 1998, exports were about 354 tonnes while in September 1998 exports were about 258 tonnes.

World Tea Production, in Major Producing Countries — In Thousands of Metric Tons

Year	Argentina	Bangladesh	China	India	Indonesia	Iran	Japan	Kenya	Malawi	Sri Lanka	Turkey	Former USSR[2]	Wprld Total
1988	44.0	43.6	545.0	700.0	133.8	55.6	89.8	164.0	40.2	228.2	166.4	118.0	2,490
1989	48.0	39.1	535.0	688.1	141.4	46.0	90.5	180.6	39.5	208.0	141.6	119.2	2,444
1990	50.0	45.9	540.0	720.3	145.2	44.0	89.9	197.0	39.1	234.1	126.7	123.2	2,528
1991	40.0	45.2	542.0	741.7	133.4	45.0	87.9	203.6	40.5	241.6	135.3	110.0	2,541
1992	43.0	46.0	580.0	704.0	163.0	55.0	92.0	188.0	28.0	179.0	144.0	57.0	2,439
1993	55.0	49.0	600.0	757.0	169.0	57.0	92.0	211.0	39.0	232.0	117.0	81.0	2,645
1994	50.0	51.0	613.0	744.0	136.0	56.0	86.0	209.0	35.0	242.0	134.0	66.0	2,615
1995	47.0	52.0	609.0	753.0	154.0	54.0	85.0	245.0	34.0	246.0	103.0	44.0	2,613
1996	47.0	48.0	617.0	780.0	159.0	62.0	89.0	257.0	37.0	258.0	115.0	38.0	2,701
1997[1]	48.0	53.0	633.0	785.0	162.0	62.0	91.0	221.0	38.0	277.0	121.0	38.0	2,734

[1] Preliminary. [2] Mostly Georgia and Azerbaijan. *Sources: Food and Agriculture Organization of the United Nations (FAO-UN)*

World Tea Exports from Producing Countries — In Metric Tons

Year	Argentina	Bangladesh	Brazil	China	India	Indonesia	Kenya	Malawi	P. New Guinea	Sri Lanka	Vietnam	Zimbabwe	World Total
1987	33,647	21,606	8,073	174,274	201,891	90,422	134,779	33,404	5,491	200,774	13,000	10,105	978,368
1988	34,258	26,187	9,686	198,289	200,956	92,687	138,201	36,961	5,834	219,710	14,800	14,190	1,039,313
1989	43,335	23,426	9,400	204,584	211,622	114,709	163,188	39,891	5,439	203,763	15,016	12,768	1,121,251
1990	45,966	26,970	7,976	195,471	209,085	110,964	169,586	43,039	5,375	215,251	24,698	11,507	1,141,026
1991	36,029	26,860	7,347	190,188	215,144	110,207	175,625	41,185	3,747	212,017	7,953	11,304	1,206,282
1992	36,530	24,990	8,211	180,834	166,359	121,243	172,053	37,056	5,638	181,259	12,967	6,088	1,130,355
1993	44,258	29,620	8,335	206,659	153,159	123,925	199,379	35,264	6,441	134,742	21,200	8,065	1,193,144
1994	43,355	29,040	8,377	184,071	150,874	84,916	176,962	38,670	3,400	115,097	23,500	9,688	1,078,460
1995[1]	41,175	26,445	7,252	169,788	158,333	79,227	258,564	32,600	4,200	178,005	18,800	9,156	1,180,002
1996[2]	35,042	26,445	3,891	173,145	132,700	101,532	260,819	36,700	6,500	218,714	13,600	11,540	1,214,584

[1] Preliminary. [2] Estimate. *Source: Food and Agriculture Organization of the United Nations (FAO-UN)*

Tin

Tin is used in the manufacture of coatings for steel containers used to preserve foods and beverages. It finds use in solder alloys, electroplating, ceramics and in plastic. The U.S. Geological Survey estimated that the major uses for tin were: cans and containers, 25 percent; electrical, 20 percent; transportation, 12 percent; construction, 10 percent; and other, 33 percent. Tin was mined in 24 countries with the top 5 accounting for about 82 percent of the total world production of 211,000 tonnes in 1997. That was 1 percent more than in 1996. China was the largest producer of mined tin in 1997 with a total of 65,000 tonnes or 7 percent less than in 1996. The next largest producer was Indonesia with 47,000 tonnes or some 22 percent more than in 1996. Peru was the next largest producer of mined tin with 27,952 tonnes. Other large producers include Brazil, Bolivia and Australia. World tin reserves are estimated to be 8 million tonnes which is considered adequate to meet future requirements. Most of the reserves are in Asia and South America.

World smelter production of tin in 1997 was estimated to be 213,000 tonnes, down 7 percent from 1996. Total primary tin production in 1997 was 196,000 tonnes while secondary smelter production was 17,500 tonnes. The major producer of smelter tin in 1997 was China with 61,000 tonnes, down 15 percent from 1996. Indonesia was the next largest producer with 40,000 tonnes, up almost 3 percent from 1997. Malaysia was the next largest producer with 35,800 tonnes. Other large producers of smelter tin include Brazil, Bolivia and the U.S. and Thailand.

In 1997, there was no domestic mine production of tin in the U.S. which marked the fourth consecutive year there has been no output. Before 1994, some small tin mines had operated. The United States is probably the world's largest producer of secondary tin. Tin metal that was recovered from new tinplate scrap and used tin cans was the only type of secondary tin available in the marketplace as free tin. Most secondary tin was produced from the various scrapped alloys of tin and recycled in those same alloy industries. Secondary tin from recycled fabricated parts was used as a major source for solder in the brass and bronze industries.

U.S. production of secondary tin in 1997 was 12,300 tonnes, up 6 percent from 1996. In July 1998, secondary production of tin was 900 tonnes, the same level as in June 1998. In the January-July 1998 period, secondary production of tin was 6,300 tonnes.

U.S. consumption of primary tin in 1997 was 37,200 tonnes, up 2 percent from 1996. Consumption of primary tin in July 1998 was 3,320 tonnes which was down 6 percent from June. In the January-July 1998 period, consumption of primary tin was 24,400 tonnes. U.S. consumption of secondary tin in 1997 was 11,000 tonnes or some 34 percent more than in 1996. In July 1998, secondary consumption of tin was 954 tonnes, down 1 percent from June. In the first seven months of 1998, consumption of secondary tin was 6,630 tonnes.

U.S. tin metal imports for consumption in 1997 were 40,600 tonnes, up 34 percent from 1996. In June 1998, imports of tin for consumption were 3,870 tonnes, down 8 percent from May 1998. In the January-June 1998 period, tin imports for consumption were 20,000 tonnes. The major suppliers were China, Peru, Indonesia, Bolivia and Brazil. U.S. exports of refined tin in 1997 were 4,660 tonnes, some 27 percent more than in 1996. In June 1998, tin metal exports were 514 tonnes, an increase of 20 percent from May. In the first half of 1998, exports of tin were 2,540 tonnes.

U.S. tinplate production in July 1998 was 144,000 tonnes, down from 175,000 tonnes in June. The July production of tinplate had a tin content of 652 tonnes. Tin contained in each metric tonne of tinplate in July 1998 was 4.5 kilograms. For all of 1997, tinplate production was 2.01 million tonnes The tin content of that production was 9,300 tonnes. The tin contained in each metric tonne of tinplate in 1997 was 4.6 kilograms. Shipments of tinplate in June 1998 were 211,000 tonnes, an increase of 9 percent from May 1998. For all of 1997, tinplate shipments were 2.48 million tonnes. Tinplate waste (waste, strips, cobbles, etc.) produced in July 1998 was 10,300 tonnes. For all of 1997, tinplate waste production was 157,000 tonnes.

In July 1998, the Defense Logistics Agency disposed of 250 tonnes of tin. In the January-July 1998 period, disposals were 1,220 tonnes.

Futures Markets

Tin futures are traded on the London Metals Exchange (LME) and on the Kuala Lumpur Commodity Exchange (KLCE). Options are traded on the LME.

World Mine Production of Tin (Contained) In Metric Tons

Year	Australia	Bolivia	Brazil	China	Indo-nesia	Malaysia	Nigeria	Peru	Portugal	Russia[3]	Thailand	United Kingdom	World Total
1988	7,009	10,504	44,102	29,500	29,590	28,866	300	4,181	81	16,000	14,225	3,454	204,654
1989	7,709	15,849	50,232	40,000	31,263	32,034	217	5,082	63	16,000	14,922	3,846	232,857
1990	7,377	17,249	39,149	42,000	30,200	28,468	192	5,134	4,780	15,000	14,635	3,400	221,000
1991	5,708	16,830	29,253	42,100	30,061	20,710	217	6,558	8,333	13,500	14,937	2,326	201,000
1992	6,609	16,516	27,000	43,800	29,400	14,339	415	10,044	6,560	15,160	11,484	2,044	191,000
1993	8,057	18,634	26,500	49,100	29,000	10,384	200	14,310	5,334	13,100	6,363	2,232	190,000
1994	7,495	16,169	16,619	54,100	30,610	6,458	278	20,275	4,332	10,460	3,926	1,922	178,000
1995	8,656	14,419	17,317	61,900	38,378	6,402	600	22,331	4,627	9,000	2,201	1,973	194,000
1996[1]	8,828	14,802	19,617	69,600	38,500	5,175	3,000	27,004	4,800	8,000	1,457	2,103	208,000
1997[2]	10,169	14,500	18,500	65,000	47,000	5,100	3,000	27,952	4,000	7,500	750	1,800	211,000

[1] Preliminary. [2] Estimate. [3] Formerly part of the U.S.S.R.; data not reported separately until 1992. *Source: U.S. Geological Survey (USGS)*

World Smelter Production of Primary Tin In Metric Tons

Year	Australia	Bolivia	Brazil	China	Indo-nesia	Japan	Malaysia	Mexico	Russia[2]	South Africa	Spain	Thailand	World Total
1988	439	5,373	41,857	29,500	28,365	846	49,945	1,812	18,500	1,377	806	14,675	215,163
1989	424	9,448	44,240	29,500	29,916	808	50,874	4,752	18,000	1,306	1,767	14,571	221,569
1990	312	12,567	37,580	35,000	30,389	816	49,067	5,004	16,000	1,140	600	15,512	246,000
1991	340	14,663	25,776	36,400	30,415	716	42,722	2,262	13,000	1,042	600	11,255	205,000
1992	240	14,393	27,000	39,600	31,915	821	45,598	2,590	15,200	592	600	10,679	194,000
1993	222	14,541	26,900	52,100	30,415	804	40,079	1,640	13,400	452	500	8,099	215,000
1994	315	15,285	20,400	67,800	31,100	706	37,990	768	11,500	43	500	7,759	217,000
1995	570	17,709	16,789	67,700	38,628	630	39,433	770	9,500	-----	500	8,243	223,000
1996	460	16,733	18,371	71,500	39,000	524	39,195	1,234	9,000	-----	150	10,981	229,000
1997[1]	605	16,100	18,500	61,000	40,000	507	35,800	1,188	6,700	-----	150	10,000	213,000

[8] Preliminary. [2] Formerly part of the U.S.S.R.; data not reported separately until 1992. *Source: U.S. Geological Survey (USGS)*

United States Foreign Trade of Tin In Metric Tons

		Imports (For Consumption)											
		Concentrates[2] (Ore)			Unwrought Tin Metal								
Year	Exports (Metal)	Total All Ore	Bolivia	Peru	Total All Metal	Bolivia	Brazil	China	Indo-nesia	Malaysia	Singa-pore	Thailand	United Kingdom
1988	1,209	2,837	923	1,914	43,493	3,926	16,213	6,223	5,334	5,317	1,342	670	1,354
1989	904	216	-----	149	33,988	4,795	10,572	4,793	5,162	2,392	456	180	391
1990	658	-----	-----	-----	33,810	8,472	6,535	4,339	4,695	3,873	40	60	227
1991	970	1	1	-----	29,102	8,912	4,489	5,281	4,425	1,751	100	-----	344
1992	1,888	-----	-----	-----	27,314	4,623	8,167	5,389	3,854	2,799	320	427	-----
1993	2,598	-----	-----	-----	33,682	8,027	11,366	4,202	5,678	846	220	-----	6
1994	2,560	-----	-----	-----	32,400	7,260	9,990	3,230	6,620	1,390	142	-----	666
1995	2,790	-----	-----	-----	33,200	6,630	8,070	5,610	7,230	3,810	40	-----	97
1996	3,670	-----	-----	-----	30,200	6,290	9,460	2,760	7,550	965	120	-----	243
1997[1]	4,660	57	-----	-----	40,600	6,680	8,610	4,710	7,610	1,640	120	600	20

[1] Preliminary. [2] Tin content. *Source: U.S. Geological Survey (USGS)*

Consumption (Total) of Tin (Pig) in the United States In Metric Tons

Year	Jan.	Feb.	Mar.	Apr.	May	June	July	Aug.	Sept.	Oct.	Nov.	Dec.	Total
1989	4,800	4,700	4,300	4,500	4,500	4,100	4,000	4,200	4,100	4,300	4,000	3,300	46,371
1990	4,000	4,000	4,200	4,100	4,200	4,100	4,100	4,300	4,100	4,100	4,200	3,900	44,363
1991	4,100	3,900	4,100	4,300	4,100	4,200	3,900	4,100	4,000	4,300	4,100	4,000	49,000
1992	3,800	3,800	3,800	3,800	3,700	3,800	3,800	3,500	3,600	3,600	3,400	3,300	45,090
1993	3,400	3,500	3,600	3,600	3,500	3,600	3,500	3,600	3,500	3,500	3,500	3,400	47,107
1994	3,500	3,700	3,700	3,600	3,600	3,700	3,500	3,400	2,500	3,600	3,600	3,400	42,700
1995	3,500	3,600	3,680	3,726	3,877	3,833	3,544	3,895	3,825	3,823	3,735	3,770	44,808
1996	3,862	3,938	3,940	3,878	3,894	3,976	3,926	3,996	3,687	3,779	3,908	3,730	48,800
1997	4,953	4,025	4,023	4,067	3,999	4,079	3,936	3,912	4,050	4,098	3,964	4,250	44,350
1998[1]	4,410	4,493	4,445	4,508	4,388	4,483	4,273	4,300	4,404	4,402	4,680		53,221

[1] Preliminary. *Source: U.S Geological Survey (USGS)*

Tin Stocks (Pig -- Industrial) in the United States, on First of Month In Metric Tons

Year	Jan.	Feb.	Mar.	Apr.	May	June	July	Aug.	Sept.	Oct.	Nov.	Dec.
1989	4,943	4,242	3,894	4,320	3,717	4,945	4,912	5,597	5,872	6,241	5,313	5,530
1990	6,072	5,975	5,824	6,401	4,959	3,298	3,792	3,592	3,836	4,762	4,819	4,829
1991	6,337	6,677	6,688	6,177	5,993	5,991	6,348	6,739	6,544	8,544	6,616	6,347
1992	3,024	3,022	3,369	2,844	2,877	2,901	2,651	3,111	3,321	3,454	3,654	3,178
1993	3,221	3,572	4,450	4,483	3,898	3,609	4,648	4,652	4,561	3,709	3,262	3,535
1994	3,651	4,635	3,775	3,967	3,471	3,470	3,825	3,027	2,891	2,980	2,844	2,908
1995	2,741	3,931	3,850	2,780	3,000	3,080	3,210	3,910	3,800	3,880	4,380	4,290
1996	4,580	6,000	5,200	4,390	4,880	5,590	5,760	5,640	4,790	4,580	4,810	6,810
1997	4,670	5,100	5,610	5,600	5,070	5,270	5,180	5,650	5,590	5,420	5,290	5,590
1998[1]	6,100	5,570	5,390	5,840	6,170	5,940	5,830	5,580	6,660	6,270	5,880	7,290

[1] Preliminary. *Source: U.S. Geological Survey (USGS)*

TIN

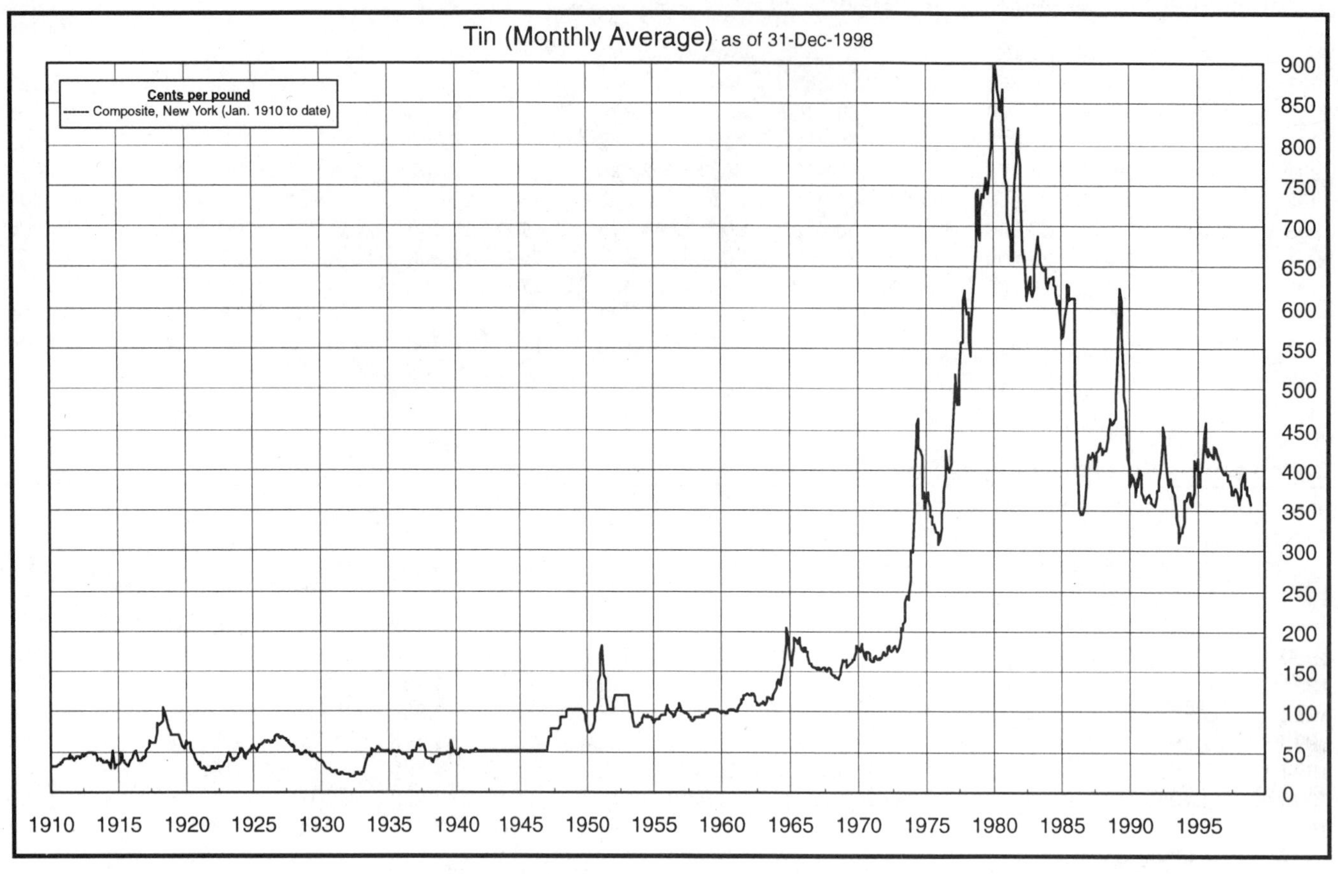

Average Price of Ex-Dock Tin in New York In Cents Per Pound

Year	Jan.	Feb.	Mar.	Apr.	May	June	July	Aug.	Sept.	Oct.	Nov.	Dec.	Average
1989	355.80	377.77	419.64	486.72	484.42	474.15	458.64	415.80	395.99	379.67	329.10	324.79	408.54
1990	317.89	296.28	302.41	308.97	307.02	295.86	288.09	287.48	279.20	296.11	292.27	261.82	295.41
1991	269.97	268.00	264.51	265.78	271.78	272.30	270.55	269.02	265.86	264.50	262.26	262.05	267.21
1992	261.30	267.79	267.52	277.20	290.05	313.07	331.10	322.19	315.66	291.60	268.54	271.76	289.81
1993	280.40	280.91	277.43	275.67	269.62	255.35	252.31	230.17	213.22	220.02	224.88	236.90	251.41
1994	249.55	267.55	261.20	258.49	277.79	282.43	276.11	265.35	279.39	292.17	325.83	346.21	281.84
1995	374.77	260.25	266.45	288.00	283.62	314.33	316.06	331.64	304.12	297.77	304.47	300.28	303.48
1996	299.55	297.45	296.68	308.49	306.71	296.20	298.47	291.30	292.13	285.11	285.87	280.61	294.88
1997	281.91	281.34	281.51	274.36	274.19	267.31	261.03	259.85	262.56	266.77	268.39	262.61	270.15
1998	249.39	252.65	262.36	271.65	280.71	284.27	284.27	270.98	260.79	259.17	261.82	251.55	265.80

Source: American Metal Market (AMM)

Average Price of Tin (Straights) in New York In Cents Per Pound

Year	Jan.	Feb.	Mar.	Apr.	May	June	July	Aug.	Sept.	Oct.	Nov.	Dec.	Average
1989	464.49	488.17	542.72	622.13	624.62	607.96	568.59	515.89	493.12	477.14	419.57	413.34	519.81
1990	403.31	380.61	387.60	394.20	389.34	376.17	367.19	390.25	380.34	399.32	394.50	372.81	386.30
1991	368.22	364.86	360.89	362.04	368.33	368.95	367.07	365.06	361.19	358.63	355.35	354.27	362.91
1992	367.89	375.70	375.25	386.88	402.70	431.63	453.05	441.89	434.02	398.27	380.41	380.89	402.38
1993	390.01	384.48	378.36	374.06	369.82	347.55	339.79	330.63	310.94	322.67	322.26	326.72	349.77
1994	334.38	362.81	361.86	363.65	371.63	372.59	360.45	353.85	362.48	371.82	411.63	401.31	369.04
1995	415.05	379.08	378.61	395.99	399.17	433.75	438.04	458.66	423.71	417.23	425.41	419.75	415.37
1996	418.68	415.65	414.71	429.34	427.24	413.65	416.63	409.12	407.79	400.25	400.65	394.46	412.35
1997	396.18	395.50	395.64	386.52	386.58	377.83	369.97	369.01	372.45	377.39	378.00	371.35	381.37
1998	356.97	359.76	370.96	381.99	392.16	397.36	377.72	380.02	368.89	366.87	370.49	357.69	373.41

Source: Wall Street Journal (WSJ)

Tin Plate Production & Tin Recovered in the United States In Metric Tons

Year	Tinplate Waste (Gross Weight)	Tinplate (All Forms) Gross Weight	Tin Content (Tonne)	Tin per Tonne of Plate (Kilograms)	Tin Metal	Bronze & Brass	Solder	Type Metal	Babbitt	Antimonial Lead	Chemical Compounds	Misc.[2]	Grand Total
	Tin Content of Tinplate Produced				Tin Recovered from Scrap by Form of Recovery								
1984	151,540	2,409,399	8,659	3.6	1,107	9,146	3,653	142	123	894	301	51	15,417
1985	146,041	2,215,042	9,321	4.2	1,302	8,045	3,565	122	88	791	186	10	14,109
1986	120,186	2,068,246	8,660	4.2	1,134	7,996	3,676	197	66	891	W	17	13,977
1987	141,842	2,302,173	10,357	4.5	1,353	10,245	3,765	66	77	623	W	30	16,159
1988	149,054	2,375,809	11,582	4.9	578	9,939	3,619	70	112	902	W	29	15,249
1989	153,542	2,263,769	11,764	5.2	569	10,305	3,225	46	116	952	W	W	15,213
1990	156,419	2,467,205	11,750	4.8	186	13,312	2,876	46	28	739	W	4	17,187
1991	166,647	2,468,769	11,482	4.7	234	11,719	W	44	24	928	W	2,705	12,949
1992	195,760	1,620,007	9,821	6.1	137	12,761	W	47	78	704	W	181	13,727
1993	196,874	1,625,132	9,945	6.0	112	10,670	W	43	51	796	W	W	11,672
1994	188,921	1,528,303	9,396	6.1	NA	NA	NA	NA	NA	NA	NA	NA	NA
1995	205,000	1,660,000	9,600	5.8	W	11,200	W	39	W	335	W	W	11,600
1996	181,100	1,551,000	9,617	6.2	W	11,400	W	37	34	171	W	W	11,600
1997[1]	157,000	2,010,000	9,300	4.6	W	12,200	W	W	W	149	W	W	12,300

[1] Preliminary. [2] Includes foil, terne metal, cable lead, and items indicated by symbol "W". W = Withheld proprietary data.
Source: U.S. Geological Survey (USGS)

Consumption of Primary and Secondary Tin in the United States In Metric Tons

Year	Net Import Reliance as a % of Apparent Consumption	Industry Stocks Jan. 1[2]	Net Receipts: Primary	Net Receipts: Secondary	Net Receipts: Scrap	Net Receipts: Total	Available Supply	Stocks Dec. 31 (Total Available Less Total Processed)	Total Processed	Consumed in Manufacturing Products
1984	74	8,063	38,813	6,110	6,791	51,714	59,777	11,145	48,632	48,315
1985	72	8,430	38,006	8,904	7,471	54,381	62,811	13,928	48,883	48,669
1986	74	9,336	35,475	11,636	6,346	53,457	62,793	18,915	43,878	43,524
1987	74	9,876	38,401	11,707	6,635	56,743	66,619	21,887	44,731	44,219
1988	78	10,217	39,421	12,472	6,707	58,600	68,817	23,586	46,232	45,602
1989	77	9,242	37,760	10,901	8,168	56,829	66,071	19,184	46,887	46,463
1990	71	13,551	38,473	9,501	6,534	54,508	68,059	22,578	45,481	45,165
1991	74	12,502	36,126	1,622	8,370	46,118	58,620	13,540	45,080	44,805
1992	80	12,038	34,327	2,279	8,412	45,018	57,056	11,669	45,387	45,120
1993	84	8,556	37,700	3,280	8,768	49,700	58,300	11,566	46,700	46,600
1994	83	9,540	35,400	4,210	4,940	44,500	54,100	11,600	42,500	42,200
1995	84	8,480	39,400	5,020	6,240	50,600	59,100	13,000	46,100	46,000
1996	83	9,300	39,200	2,750	6,140	48,100	57,300	12,500	44,900	44,700
1997[1]	85	9,100	38,900	2,360	6,010	47,300	56,400	11,900	44,500	44,300

[1] Preliminary. [2] Includes tin in transit to the U.S. *Source: U.S. Geological Survey (USGS)*

Consumption of Tin in the United States, by Finished Products In Metric Tons (Contained Tin)

Year	Tinplate[2]	Solder	Babbitt	Bronze & Brass	Tinning	Chemicals[3]	Tin Powder	Bar Tin & Anodes	White Metal	Other	Total	Total: Primary	Total: Secondary
1984	8,825	17,249	2,684	4,998	1,748	W	1,057	526	958	11,396	48,315	37,201	11,114
1985	9,321	18,621	1,488	4,330	1,511	W	976	466	937	12,100	48,669	36,524	12,145
1986	8,660	15,810	1,324	3,502	1,437	W	1,002	449	1,134	10,204	43,522	33,324	10,198
1987	10,357	15,240	1,060	3,559	1,398	W	W	703	1,175	10,704	44,219	35,620	8,599
1988	11,582	15,288	926	3,934	1,406	W	W	557	1,131	10,777	45,601	37,529	8,072
1989	11,764	16,370	794	3,693	1,505	W	711	619	1,074	9,926	46,456	36,603	9,853
1990	11,750	16,443	763	3,166	1,707	6,275	563	603	1,045	2,850	45,165	36,770	8,395
1991	11,482	16,296	941	2,896	1,465	6,564	539	436	868	3,318	44,805	35,138	9,667
1992	9,821	18,461	916	2,916	1,275	6,301	573	919	974	2,964	45,090	34,983	10,137
1993	9,650	19,000	823	3,093	1,249	6,446	608	946	789	3,927	46,600	34,600	11,900
1994	9,480	15,100	831	3,080	1,230	5,740	625	1,190	992	3,990	42,200	33,700	8,530
1995	9,670	17,700	871	2,830	1,110	7,060	W	1,200	965	4,550	46,000	35,200	10,800
1996	9,340	15,600	851	2,760	2,050	7,520	573	1,150	1,340	3,230	44,700	36,500	8,180
1997[1]	9,350	15,900	909	3,160	1,140	8,170	W	661	754	3,960	44,300	36,100	8,250

[1] Preliminary. [2] Includes small quantity of secondary pig tin and tin acquired in chemicals. [3] Including tin oxide. W = Withheld proprietary data.
Source: U.S. Geological Survey (USGS)

Titanium

Titanium has unique properties including a density that is one-half that of steel, excellent strength and immunity to corrosion. That makes it an ideal construction material for engines and air frames. Pure titanium metal is called "sponge" because of its porous cellular form. Titanium sponge is processed to form an ingot and the ingot is processed by mills to make plate sheet tubing. Due to its unique combination of high strength and light weight, titanium is finding a growing number of uses. One of the most publicized is in golf clubs. There continue to be new applications in the automotive industry where titanium parts add strength and reduce weight which increases energy efficiency. Other uses of titanium are in pollution control devices, desalination plants, chemical processing, and in tubing for power plants and oil refineries. Titanium dioxide is used in white pigments and porcelain enamels. The major producers of titanium sponge metal are the U.S., Russia, Japan and China.

U.S. production data on titanium sponge metal in the first quarter of 1998 was withheld by the U.S. Geological Survey to avoid disclosing company proprietary data. Production of titanium ingot in first quarter 1998 was 16,200 tonnes, an increase of 17 percent from first quarter 1997. For all of 1997, titanium ingot production was 58,800 tonnes. Production of titanium mill products in first quarter 1998 was 8,920 tonnes, an increase of 7 percent from 1997. For all of 1997, mill product production was 34,300 tonnes.

U.S. consumption of titanium sponge metal in the first quarter 1998 was 9,440 tonnes, up 37 percent from 1997. For all of 1997, sponge consumption was 26,400 tonnes. Consumption of titanium scrap in first quarter 1998 was 8,290 tonnes, up 25 percent from 1997. For all of 1997, titanium scrap consumption was 26,400 tonnes. Titanium ingot consumption in first quarter 1998 was 13,300 tonnes. That was an increase of 27 percent from 1997. For all of 1997, ingot consumption was 45,500 tonnes.

U.S. imports of titanium sponge in January-February 1998 were 2,500 tonnes, down 35 percent from 1997. For all of 1997, imports of sponge were 16,100 tonnes. Imports of waste and scrap in January-February 1998 were 1,520 tonnes, down 54 percent from 1997. Total imports of all titanium products in January-February 1998 were 5,450 tonnes, down 54 percent from 1997. Industry stocks of titanium metal on March 31, 1998 were 25,800 tonnes. Government stocks of titanium sponge were 33,000 tonnes.

Average Prices of Titanium in the United States

Year	Ilmenite F.O.B. Australian Ports $ Tonne	Slag, 85% TiO_2 F.O.B. Richards Bay, South Africa $ Tonne	Rutile Large Lots Bulk, F.O.B. U.S. East Coast $ Tonne	Rutile Bagged F.O.B. Australian Ports $ Tonne	Avg. Price of Grade A Titanium Sponge, F.O.B. Shipping Point	Titanium Metal Sponge	Titanium Dioxide Pigments, F.O.B. U.S. Plants: Anatase	Titanium Dioxide Pigments, F.O.B. U.S. Plants: Rutile
					Dollars Per Pound			
1988	64-77	250-275	NA	547-572	4.21	4.25-4.75	.92-.95	.95-.97
1989	67-75	275-300	540-550	553-632	5.11	4.80-5.30	1.01-1.02	1.04-1.05
1990	69-77	285-310	550-580	693-770	5.31	4.75	.99	1.01
1991	68-76	295-325	606-650	515-545	5.25	4.75	.99	.99
1992	58-62	310	510-520	380-414	3.96	3.50-4.00	.99	.92-.95
1993	61-64	330	NA	370-400	3.75	3.50-4.00	.99	.92-.95
1994	74-80	334	410-430	450-480	3.96	3.75-4.25	.94-.96	.92-.94
1995	81-85	349	550-650	650-800	4.06	4.25-4.50	.92-.96	.99-1.03
1996[1]	82-92	353	525-600	700-800	-----	4.25-4.50	1.06-1.08	1.08-1.10
1997[2]	68-81	391	500-550	650-710	-----	4.25-4.50	1.01-1.03	1.04-1.06

[1] Preliminary. [2] Estimate. NA = Not available. *Source: U.S. Geological Survey (USGS)*

Salient Statistics of Titanium in the United States In Metric Tons

Year	Titanium Dioxide Pigment: Production	Titanium Dioxide Pigment: Imports[3]	Titanium Dioxide Pigment: Apparent Consumption	Ilmenite: Imports[3]	Ilmenite: Consumption	Titanium Slag: Imports[3]	Titanium Slag: Consumption	Rutile[4]: Imports[3]	Rutile[4]: Consumption	Exports of Titanium Products: Ores & Concentrates	Exports: Scrap	Exports: Dioxide & Pigments	Exports: Ingots, Billets, Etc.
1988	926,746	185,468	991,536	394,170	679,008	434,641	300,013	231,124	352,356	9,368	5,939	118,422	2,083
1989	1,006,581	166,346	947,259	411,751	659,584	386,146	414,830	264,895	366,143	19,832	5,474	212,197	2,702
1990	978,659	147,592	925,447	345,907	688,948	373,623	390,537	274,605	369,454	18,765	5,487	202,288	2,371
1991	991,976	166,094	935,829	213,886	738,089	408,302	341,379	240,120	368,643	26,912	4,568	211,854	1,700
1992	1,137,038	169,260	999,930	294,585	684,882	537,118	539,323	317,399	460,969	34,665	2,770	270,422	1,455
1993	1,161,561	171,939	1,028,311	301,000	693,940	476,000	545,809	371,481	464,825	15,202	3,893	261,000	1,511
1994	1,250,000	176,000	1,090,000	808,000	W	472,000	583,000	332,000	510,000	19,000	4,120	313,000	1,559
1995	1,250,000	183,000	1,080,000	861,000	1,410,000	388,000	582,000	318,000	480,000	32,300	3,420	306,000	2,560
1996[1]	1,230,000	167,000	1,070,000	939,000	1,400,000	421,000	NA	324,000	398,000	15,500	3,410	292,000	3,130
1997[2]	1,340,000	194,000	1,130,000	952,000	1,520,000	-----	-----	336,000	489,000	23,800	5,500	362,000	3,860

[1] Preliminary. [2] Estimate. [3] For consumption. [4] Natural and synthetic. W = Withheld proprietary data. *Source: U.S. Geological Survey (USGS)*

World Production of Titanium Ilmenite Concentrates In Thousands of Metric Tons

Year	Australia[2]	Brazil	China	India	Malaysia	Norway	Sierra Leone	Sri Lanka	Thailand	Ukraine[3]	World Total	Titaniferous Slag[4]: Canada	Titaniferous Slag[4]: South Africa
1984	1,525	40.9	139.7	140.0	268.5	651.8	-----	102.1	-----	440	4,619	726	417
1985	1,433	76.4	140.0	143.0	314.7	735.8	-----	114.9	1.00	445	4,737	845	435
1986	1,252	75.5	140.0	140.0	414.9	803.6	-----	129.9	13.50	450	4,705	850	435
1987	1,509	169.3	140.0	140.0	509.2	852.3	5.6	128.5	27.10	455	3,937	925	650
1988	1,622	142.2	150.0	229.7	486.3	898.0	42.1	74.3	18.30	460	4,033	1,025	400
1989	1,714	144.2	150.0	240.7	533.7	929.8	62.3	101.4	16.99	460	4,353	1,040	725
1990	1,621	114.1	150.0	280.0	530.2	814.5	54.6	66.4	10.67	430	4,072	1,046	840
1991	1,381	69.1	150.0	311.5	336.3	625.0	60.4	60.9	17.08	400	3,360	701	808
1992	1,806	76.6	150.0	300.0	337.7	708.0	60.3	33.3	2.97	450	3,920	753	884
1993	1,804	90.6	155.0	320.0	279.0	713.0	62.9	76.9	20.82	450	3,990	653	892
1994	1,782	97.4	155.0	300.0	116.7	826.4	47.4	60.4	1.68	530	3,950	764	744
1995	1,980	102.1	160.0	300.0	151.7	833.2	-----	49.7	.03	359	3,970	815	990
1996	2,028	98.0	165.0	300.0	244.6	746.6	-----	62.8	-----	250	3,930	825	1,000
1997[1]	2,233	98.0	170.0	300.0	167.5	750.0	-----	19.0	-----	250	4,020	850	990

[1] Preliminary. [2] Includes leucoxene. [3] Formerly part of the U.S.S.R.; data not reported separately until 1992. [4] Approximately 10% of total production is ilmenite. Beginning in 1988, 25% of Norway's ilmenite production was used to produce slag containing 75% TiO_2. NA = Not available.
Source: U.S. Geological Survey (USGS)

World Production of Titanium Rutile Concentrates In Metric Tons

Year	Australia	Brazil	India	Sierre Leone	South Africa	Sri Lanka	Thailand	Ukraine[2]	World Total
1984	170,427	412	5,988	91,302	56,246	6,467		9,979	340,821
1985	211,615	713	6,800	80,611	55,000	8,558	110	10,000	373,407
1986	215,774	495	7,000	97,100	55,000	8,443	48	10,000	393,860
1987	246,263	324	7,000	113,300	55,000	7,200	92	10,000	439,179
1988	230,637	1,514	5,000	126,358	55,000	5,255	128	10,000	433,892
1989	243,000	2,613	9,931	128,198	60,000	5,589	150	10,000	459,331
1990	245,000	1,814	11,000	144,284	64,056	5,460	NA	9,500	481,114
1991	201,000	1,094	13,635	154,800	77,000	3,085	76	9,000	460,000
1992	183,000	1,798	10,000	148,990	84,000	2,741	281	60,000	491,000
1993	186,000	1,744	13,900	152,000	85,000	2,643	87	60,000	501,000
1994	233,000	1,911	14,000	137,000	78,000	2,410	49	80,000	546,000
1995	195,000	1,985	14,000	-----	90,000	2,697	-----	112,000	416,000
1996	180,000	2,018	14,000	-----	115,000	3,532	-----	50,000	365,000
1997[1]	235,000	2,020	15,500	-----	110,000	2,970	-----	50,000	415,000

[1] Preliminary. [2] Formerly part of the U.S.S.R.; data not reported separately until 1992. NA = Not available. *Source: U.S. Geological Survey (USGS)*

World Production of Titanium Sponge Metal & U.S. Consumption of Titanium Concentrates

	Production of Titanium (In Metric Tons) Sponge Metal[2]						U.S. Consumption of Titanium Concentrates, by Products (In Metric Tons): Ilmenite (TiO_2 Content)			Rutile (TiO_2 Content)			
Year	China	Japan	Russia[3]	United Kingdom	United States	Total	Pigments	Misc.	Total	Welding Rod Coatings	Pigments	Misc.	Total
1984	1,814	15,366	41,731	2,268	22,069	83,462	446,939	5,733	452,672	3,548	210,296	57,081	270,925
1985	1,814	15,366	42,638	1,361	21,099	82,555	430,522	5,751	436,273	4,428	217,631	37,843	259,902
1986	1,814	16,330	43,546	1,361	15,876	78,926	463,643	1,501	465,144	6,956	221,518	52,199	280,673
1987	1,814	10,074	44,453	1,361	17,849	75,298	420,099	1,648	421,747	3,781	246,448	51,309	301,538
1988	2,000	16,500	46,000	1,500	24,000	88,000	429,736	590	430,326	3,737	262,998	64,641	331,376
1989	2,000	21,000	46,000	1,500	25,225	95,725	419,329	414	419,743	3,603	271,208	71,178	345,989
1990	2,000	25,630	47,000	1,500	24,679	101,000	445,502	726	446,228	4,047	271,637	71,373	347,057
1991	2,000	18,945	20,000	2,000	13,366	56,000	476,145	495	476,640	6,931	286,741	42,200	335,872
1992	2,000	14,554	20,000	2,000	W	38,554	425,876	647	426,523	W	405,875	32,553	438,428
1993	2,000	14,400	20,000	1,000	27,938	37,000	434,097	451	434,548	W	405,784	30,223	436,007
1994	2,000	14,400	12,000	-----	29,510	33,000	W	637	W	W	460,000	18,500	478,500
1995	2,000	16,000	12,000	-----	W	35,000	1,010,000	[4]	1,010,000	W	417,000	22,300	439,300
1996	2,000	21,100	18,000	-----	W	51,000	1,010,000	[4]	1,010,000	W	341,000	24,200	365,000
1997[1]	2,000	24,100	20,000	-----	W	58,000	1,410,000	[4]	1,410,000	W	406,000	27,600	434,000

[1] Preliminary. [2] Unconsolidated metal in various forms. [3] Formerly part of the U.S.S.R.; data not reported separately until 1993. [4] Included in Pigments. NA = Not available. W = Withheld proprietary data. *Source: U.S. Geological Survey (USGS)*

Tobacco

U.S. per capita cigarette consumption is expected to decline by 2 percent in 1998. Per capita consumption of cigarettes by those 18 years or older in 1998 was estimated to be 2,350 pieces. That compares with 2,423 pieces in 1997. Cigarette consumption has been declining for several years with per capita use in 1989 at 2,945 pieces. For 1998, the amount of tobacco contained in the cigarettes was 3.9 pounds. Per capita consumption of cigarettes by those 16 years and older in 1998 was estimated at 2,261 pieces, down 3 percent from the previous year. Total U.S. consumption of cigarettes in 1998 was estimated at 470 billion pieces, down 2 percent from the previous year and some 10 percent less than in 1990.

U.S. cigarette consumption in 1998 was estimated by the U.S.D.A. at 680 billion pieces, down 6 percent from 1997. Cigarette production shows no discernible trend as production in 1989 was 677 billion pieces. Taxable cigarette production in 1998 was 470 billion pieces, close to the same as in 1997. Discount brand cigarettes were 27.5 percent of the market in 1997 compared to 28.4 percent in 1996. The proportion of low-tar and low-nicotine cigarettes increased slightly in 1997 but was still lower than the record high reached in 1981.

Cigarette consumption has declined because of changes in social acceptance as well as higher prices. Cigarette manufacturers raised prices several times in 1998. In January prices were increased by $1.25 per thousand pieces. In April prices were increased by $2.50 per thousand pieces while there was a $2.50 increase in May and a $3.00 increase in August. The manufacturers price increases raised wholesale prices by 14 percent. In late 1998, there was a settlement in the dispute between the tobacco industry and the States. One part of the agreement called for the tobacco industry to pay a settlement of $206 billion. Of that total, $2.4 billion was to be paid by the four large tobacco manufacturers with the remaining paid by cigarette users. Immediately after the settlement, some manufacturers raised prices by 45 cents a pack. Only one state increased its tax rate in 1998. On July 1, Hawaii increased its excise tax by $1.00. In 1997, six states increased cigarette taxes. Taxes for other tobacco products were increased in California and New Hampshire.

In 1998, per capita consumption of snuff was .33 pounds, an increase of 6 percent from 1997. Consumption of snuff has been trending higher. Per capita consumption by males 18 and older of large cigars and cigarillos in 1998 was 37.8, an increase of 2 percent from 1997. Cigar consumption has been trending higher. Per capita consumption of smoking tobacco in 1998 was .12 pounds, unchanged from 1996. Per capita consumption of chewing tobacco in 1998 was .64 pounds, unchanged from 1997. Both smoking tobacco and chewing tobacco consumption is trending higher.

U.S. tobacco production is forecast to be 1.54 billion pounds. This represents a 14 percent decline from the 1997 crop. Harvested acreage in 1998 was 749,000, down 15 percent from the previous season. The yield per acre was 2,048 pounds, down 7 percent from the previous year.

The 1998 flue-cured tobacco crop was estimated at 771.9 million pounds, down 26 percent from 1997. On-farm carryover was about 48.2 million pounds. Beginning stocks on July 1, 1998 were 1.25 billion pounds, up 12 percent from 1997. Flue-cured tobacco disappearance in 1997-98 was 877.7 million pounds, down 69 million pounds from 1996-97. Domestic use and exports declined and it is expected that use could decline in 1998-99 due to lower cigarette production and exports. Exports of flue-cured tobacco were at their lowest level since 1942.

The U.S. burley tobacco crop was estimated at 672.5 million pounds, up 4 percent from 1997. Despite some adverse weather, yield increased slightly. In the October 1997 to September 1998 period, domestic use of burley tobacco was expected to be 390 million pounds, down 13 percent from the same period of 1996-97. The decline was due to lower cigarette production and reduced leaf exports. In the first nine months of 1997-98, burley tobacco exports totaled 144.3 million pounds, down 27 percent from a year before. For the 1997-98 marketing year, exports should be 180 million pounds, down 14 percent from the previous year.

World production of unmanufactured tobacco in 1998 was estimated to be 6.03 million tonnes, down 16 percent from 1997. China is the world's largest producer with 2.27 million tonnes, down 26 percent from 1997. Other large producers are the U.S., India, Brazil, Turkey and Zimbabwe.

World Production of Leaf Tobacco In Metric Tons

Year	Brazil	Canada	China	Greece	India	Indo-nesia	Italy	Japan	Pakistan	Turkey	United States	Zim-babwe	World Total
1988	419,000	69,776	2,731,251	184,355	367,400	137,775	184,355	85,790	69,530	218,774	621,205	123,671	6,835,351
1989	462,000	75,573	2,830,353	197,316	492,800	146,914	197,316	74,397	71,089	269,517	620,152	135,205	7,110,889
1990	435,000	63,057	2,627,500	134,368	564,400	158,865	214,846	80,542	68,040	295,599	737,710	139,803	7,106,502
1991	422,000	78,704	3,030,700	165,650	555,900	164,850	193,296	69,897	80,806	239,405	754,949	178,107	7,563,836
1992	577,000	71,775	3,499,000	196,500	584,400	145,420	150,784	79,366	107,980	331,786	780,944	211,394	8,293,001
1993	608,000	86,094	3,451,000	148,000	580,600	152,800	135,698	67,430	105,966	338,068	731,914	235,286	8,300,069
1994	442,000	71,500	2,238,000	135,400	528,000	160,000	131,010	79,503	100,351	187,733	717,955	177,816	6,391,942
1995	398,000	79,287	2,317,700	131,875	587,100	171,400	124,492	78,212	80,917	204,900	575,380	209,042	6,354,987
1996[1]	452,000	79,287	2,900,000	131,500	562,750	177,000	136,000	66,031	80,760	229,400	688,222	207,767	7,175,429
1997[2]	545,000	79,287	2,900,000	132,000	604,500	184,300	136,000	75,600	78,320	235,400	781,949	210,580	7,513,370

[1] Preliminary. [2] Estimate. *Source: Foreign Agricultural Service, U.S. Department of Agriculture (FAS-USDA)*

Production and Consumption of Tobacco Products in the United States

Year	Cigarettes -Billions-	Cigars[3] -Millions-	Chewing Tobacco: Plug	Twist	Loose-leaf	Total	Smoking Tobacco	Snuff[4]	Consumption[5] of Per Capita[6]: Cigarettes	Cigars[3]	Cigarettes	Cigars[3]	Smoking Tobacco	Chewing Tobacco	Total Products
			Million Pounds						Number		Pounds				
1989	677.2	2,010	8.3	1.3	64.9	74.5	17.0	49.7	2,926	27.9	4.90	.46	.22	.82	5.67
1990	709.7	1,896	7.4	1.3	64.3	72.9	16.4	53.1	2,817	26.2	4.80	.43	.20	.79	5.48
1991	694.5	1,740	6.7	1.2	64.3	72.2	15.7	54.3	2,713	24.9	4.70	.41	.19	.79	5.41
1992	718.5	1,741	5.9	1.2	61.6	69.7	14.9	57.5	2,640	24.1	4.70	.40	.17	.74	5.38
1993	661.0	1,795	5.3	1.1	58.0	64.4	13.7	59.1	2,539	23.9	4.50	.39	.17	.70	5.12
1994	725.5	1,942	4.6	1.1	56.8	62.5	13.4	59.5	2,527	25.3	4.23	.41	.16	.67	4.90
1995	746.5	2,058	4.1	1.1	57.7	62.9	12.2	60.2	2,505	27.5	4.22	.45	.13	.67	4.70
1996	755.4	2,413	3.9	1.1	56.0	61.1	12.0	61.5	2,482	32.7	4.20	.54	.12	.64	4.70
1997[1]	719.6	2,424	3.5	1.0	53.7	58.1	11.4	64.3	2,423	36.9	4.10	.53	.12	.64	4.55
1998[2]	680.0	2,900	3.1	1.0	51.3	55.4	-----	66.1	2,350	37.8	3.90	.53	.12	.64	4.50

[1] Preliminary. [2] Estimate. [3] Large cigars and cigarillos. [4] Includes loose-leaf. [5] Consumption of tax-paid tobacco products. Unstemmed processing

Production of Tobacco in the United States, by States In Thousands of Pounds

Year	Florida	Georgia	Indiana	Kentucky	Maryland	North Carolina	Ohio	Pennsylvania	South Carolina	Tennessee	Virginia	Wisconsin	Total
1989	17,755	87,200	13,237	366,551	8,103	541,056	15,925	17,925	103,680	79,820	93,814	11,248	1,367,188
1990	19,044	103,845	15,050	442,253	9,656	639,639	18,915	19,780	109,905	112,218	110,269	13,346	1,626,380
1991	15,312	80,600	18,920	479,794	12,900	634,655	22,776	20,765	111,180	121,524	116,849	15,191	1,664,372
1992	19,575	100,980	18,900	524,378	11,931	609,873	21,840	20,840	112,320	146,556	111,459	13,100	1,721,671
1993	18,673	96,320	17,415	455,080	12,255	608,415	18,900	18,260	110,760	139,423	99,544	6,643	1,613,319
1994	16,575	80,660	15,265	453,687	12,750	599,853	18,360	18,360	108,100	132,289	106,092	5,866	1,582,896
1995	17,676	84,000	13,601	328,581	11,475	484,599	15,015	15,685	105,000	92,907	81,269	6,220	1,268,538
1996	20,100	113,620	14,972	395,542	10,000	585,542	12,640	16,817	117,810	109,888	103,543	5,162	1,518,704
1997	19,053	89,225	18,690	497,928	12,000	731,199	22,230	17,020	126,360	114,292	117,576	5,690	1,787,399
1998[1]	17,102	92,400	17,000	460,910	9,100	566,890	17,934	15,720	96,750	117,969	98,625	4,230	1,529,647

[1] Preliminary. *Source: Agricultural Statistics Board, U.S. Department of Agriculture (ASB-USDA)*

Salient Statistics of Tobacco in the United States

Year	Acres Harvested 1,000 Acres	Yield Per Acre Pounds	Production Million Pounds	Farm Price ¢ Lb.	Farm Value Million $	Tobacco (July-June) Exports[2]	Imports[3]	U.S. Exports of Cigarettes	Cigars & Cheroots	All Tobacco	Smoking Tobacco[4]	Stocks of Tobacco[5] Various Types: All Tobacco	Fire Cured[6]	Cigar Filler[7]	Maryland
						Million Pounds		Millions				Million Pounds			
1989	678.4	2,016	1,367	170.8	2,335	485.9	365.0	141,782	78	582	46.6	2,714	75.9	31.8	27.0
1990	732.3	2,218	1,625	173.8	2,827	487.4	415.0	164,301	72	631	58.0	2,401	70.2	26.9	19.3
1991	763.4	2,179	1,664	177.3	2,951	511.0	502.2	179,200	70	499	63.2	2,232	66.7	25.6	12.1
1992	784.4	2,195	1,722	177.7	3,059	528.8	881.0	205,600	76	574	59.1	2,280	61.6	26.7	9.4
1993	746.4	2,161	1,613	175.3	2,830	529.7	707.8	195,476	67	458	62.5	2,412	64.0	26.7	7.5
1994	671.1	2,359	1,583	177.4	2,779	442.1	537.5	220,200	75	434	77.0	2,588	69.7	24.1	8.4
1995	663.1	1,913	1,269	182.0	2,305	432.6	623.3	231,100	94	462	91.8	2,541	80.5	20.5	11.7
1996	733.1	2,072	1,519	188.2	2,854	533.1	717.2	243,900	84	486	110.4	2,225	80.2	17.9	15.0
1997	836.2	2,137	1,787	180.2	3,217	450.1	565.8	217,000	136	487	118.2	2,055	83.3	13.2	18.5
1998[1]	726.9	2,104	1,530	183.9	2,809	331.3	509.6	215,000	191		143.8				

[1] Preliminary. [2] Domestic. [3] For consumption. [4] In bulk. [5] Flue-cured and cigar wrapper, year beginning July1; for all other types, October 1. [6] Kentucky-Tennessee types 22-23. [7] Types 41-46. *Source: Economic Research Service, U.S. Department of Agriculture (ERS-USDA)*

Tobacco Production in the United States, by Types In Thousands of Pounds (Farm-Sale Weight)

Types	11-14	21	22	23	31	32	35-36	37	41	41-61	51	54	55	61
1989	808,350	2,480	18,463	7,980	482,568	17,825	6,430	104	10,725	25,512	1,256	7,648	3,600	2,283
1990	939,234	2,762	22,931	9,285	597,927	16,316	7,491	102	13,120	30,278	1,160	9,328	4,018	2,652
1991	911,887	3,563	20,620	8,704	658,181	19,920	8,776	156	13,735	32,587	1,433	9,799	5,392	2,228
1992	906,025	2,567	23,736	10,486	719,552	18,771	10,332	124	14,000	30,098	1,484	8,460	4,640	1,514
1993	886,908	1,872	26,985	12,060	633,838	18,335	11,123	104	12,180	22,094	1,694	4,690	1,953	1,577
1994	869,920	2,403	31,723	14,205	612,398	19,770	11,797	124	11,340	20,680	1,808	4,180	1,686	1,666
1995	746,616	1,540	26,609	11,041	436,343	17,935	8,488	79	9,225	19,887	2,441	4,513	1,707	2,001
1996	908,345	1,738	29,461	13,029	520,483	16,545	8,550	112	10,272	20,441	2,901	3,610	1,552	2,106
1997	1,047,438	1,968	27,952	12,342	648,633	18,240	8,196	119	10,780	22,511	3,637	4,194	1,496	2,404
1998[1]	833,037	2,400	27,750	12,695	607,994	15,370	10,244	140	9,450	20,017	3,818	3,150	1,080	2,519

[1] Preliminary. *Source: Agricultural Statistics Board, U.S. Department of Agriculture (ASB-USDA)*

TOBACCO

U.S. Exports of Unmanufactured Tobacco In Millions of Pounds (Declared Weight)

Year	Australia	Belgium-Luxem.	Denmark	France	Germany	Italy	Japan	Netherlands	Sweden	Switzerland	Thailand	United Kingdom	Total U.S. Exports
1989	6.2	12.3	13.8	4.8	75.4	17.1	105.3	43.2	8.3	10.4	15.7	18.4	485.9
1990	8.3	12.4	15.1	5.7	75.9	19.3	106.5	45.3	9.5	13.3	22.2	20.5	492.5
1991	7.7	11.0	14.8	6.5	82.8	19.9	83.1	42.8	8.3	14.8	19.5	18.9	499.3
1992	6.9	21.4	15.6	4.2	93.3	19.0	131.0	49.9	8.8	7.5	16.9	24.3	574.4
1993	5.7	12.8	15.5	4.3	52.1	7.3	124.7	38.1	8.1	6.1	17.8	20.8	458.0
1994	6.4	12.3	14.9	3.1	54.1	11.3	126.2	30.9	7.3	6.0	19.0	14.7	433.9
1995	4.8	17.9	14.6	3.9	70.7	14.8	106.9	39.2	3.0	14.4	19.0	14.2	461.8
1996	5.6	40.1	15.1	3.2	60.3	17.5	88.7	40.4	37.4	14.9	15.9	34.4	490.1
1997	4.2	39.1	15.5	7.0	72.2	18.3	80.5	30.2	5.3	11.4	21.6	18.2	488.3
1998[1]	3.7	23.6	14.7	5.7	75.3	11.3	72.4	37.5	2.6	10.1	12.1	15.4	412.9

[1] Preliminary. *Source: Economic Research Service, U.S. Department of Agriculture (ERS-USDA)*

Salient Statistics for Flue-Cured Tobacco (Types 11-14) in the United States In Millions of Pounds

Crop Year	Acres Harvested 1,000	Yield Per Acre Pounds	Marketings	Stocks July 1	Total Supply	Exports	Domestic Disappearance	Total Disappearance	Farm Price ¢ Lb.	Placed Under Gov't Loan Mil. Lb.	Price Support Level ¢ Lb.	Loan Stocks Nov. 30	Loan Stocks Uncommitted
1989-90	390.7	2,069	838	1,424	2,262	387	567	954	167.4	28.4	146.8	314.5	218.2
1990-1	416.9	2,253	920	1,308	2,228	403	609	1,012	167.3	74.4	148.8	226.4	223.8
1991-2	402.6	2,265	882	1,216	2,098	403	472	875	172.3	49.9	152.8	153.7	174.5
1992-3	401.5	2,257	901	1,223	2,124	420	509	929	172.6	81.8	156.0	223.6	129.0
1993-4	400.1	2,217	892	1,195	2,087	359	433	792	168.1	204.9	157.7	330.5	317.5
1994-5	359.5	2,420	807	1,295	2,102	346	569	915	169.8	97.7	158.3	298.5	396.5
1995-6	386.2	1,933	854	1,187	2,041	345	531	875	179.4	12.0	159.7	157.6	62.3
1996-7	422.2	2,151	897	1,166	2,064	391	556	947	183.4	1.8	160.1	181.0	.0
1997-8[1]	454.3	2,306	1,014	1,117	2,130	334	543	878	172.0	195.5	162.1		.0
1998-9[2]	384.5	2,007	800	1,226	2,053						162.8		

[1] Preliminary. [2] Estimate. *Source: Economic Research Service, U.S. Department of Agriculture (ERS-USDA)*

Salient Statistics for Burley Tobacco (Type 31) in the United States In Millions of Pounds

Crop Year	Acres Harvested 1,000	Yield Per Acre Pounds	Marketings	Stocks Oct. 1	Total Supply	Exports	Domestic Disappearance	Total Disappearance	Farm Price ¢ Lb.	Gross Sales[3]	Price Support Level ¢ Lb.	Loan Stocks Nov. 30	Loan Stocks Uncommitted
1989-90	244.4	1,975	498	963	1,461	169	446	614	167.2	398.1	153.2	314.5	91.6
1990-1	270.6	2,204	592	847	1,439	199	475	674	175.3	467.8	155.8	226.4	52.0
1991-2	312.0	2,110	657	765	1,422	209	407	616	178.8	501.5	158.4	62.3	32.8
1992-3	332.7	2,163	700	807	1,507	183	385	568	181.5	502.4	164.9	131.2	71.7
1993-4	299.7	2,115	627	939	1,566	152	400	552	181.6	492.4	168.3	178.8	141.9
1994-5	266.3	2,300	568	1,014	1,582	159	464	623	184.1	455.7	171.4	345.2	380.8
1995-6	234.2	1,863	483	959	1,441	165	386	551	185.5	321.1	172.5	212.5	50.8
1996-7	268.3	1,940	516	890	1,407	209	446	656	192.2	403.4	173.7	216.8	27.1
1997-8[1]	315.3	2,059	628	751	1,379	180	390	570	188.5	337.9	176.0		24.1
1998-9[2]	322.5	2,085	670	809	1,479						177.8		

[1] Preliminary. [2] Estimate. [3] Before Christmas holidays. *Source: Economic Research Service, U.S. Department of Agriculture (ERS-USDA)*

Exports of Tobacco from the United States (Quantity and Value) In Metric Tons

Year	Unmanufactured: Flue-Cured	Value $1,000	Burley	Value $1,000	Total	Value $1,000	Manufactured	Value $1,000
1989	120,344	782,337	47,498	327,988	220,408	1,301,173	NA	3,662,176
1990	131,155	883,155	50,262	349,561	223,413	1,441,116	NA	5,038,830
1991	115,481	776,654	61,852	441,223	226,463	1,427,630	NA	4,574,086
1992	146,100	983,478	64,481	483,743	260,526	1,650,559	58,115	4,509,395
1993	111,636	752,646	51,892	389,964	207,747	1,306,067	49,669	4,253,286
1994	107,411	749,305	49,859	380,993	196,792	1,302,744	63,837	5,367,220
1995	123,040	866,208	47,129	365,206	209,481	1,399,863	77,135	5,221,487
1996	112,797	786,473	52,202	380,012	222,316	1,390,311	83,383	5,238,340
1997[1]	116,457	832,381	56,803	454,849	221,510	1,553,314	85,734	4,956,392
1998[2]	90,800	644,797	49,322	402,475	187,287	1,302,615	------	4,517,500

[1] Preliminary. [2] Forecast. NA = Not available. *Source: Foreign Agricultural Service, U.S. Department of Agriculture (FAS-USDA)*

Tung Oil

Tung oil is derived from the seeds of the tung tree and is used as an industrial lubricant and drying agent. The tung tree is found mainly in China which produces about 75 percent of the world supply. Other major producers of tung oil include Argentina and Paraguay. While production is concentrated in a few countries, consumption of tung oil is divided among many industrialized countries. Among the major importers of tung oil are South Korea, Japan, the United States, Taiwan, the Netherlands and Germany. World imports of tung oil average around 40,000 metric tonnes per year. Prices of tung oil have shown wide variability in the past few years. The price of tung oil (imported, drums) f.o.b. New York in 1991 averaged 63 cents per pound. By 1993, the price had more than doubled to almost $1.19 per pound. By 1995 the price had fallen to 60 cents and in 1997 it was back up to almost $1.00 per pound.

The U.S.D.A. reported that in August 1998, U.S. imports of tung oil were 214 tonnes, down 39 percent from the previous month and 23 percent less than the year before. In the October-August 1997-98 period, U.S. imports of tung oil were 3,941 tonnes, a 3 percent decline from the comparable period of 1996-97. The value of U.S. tung oil imports in August 1998 was $318,000. In the October-August 1997-98 period, the value of tung oil imports was $6.49 million dollars. This compared with $6.08 million dollars in the same period of 1996-97.

World Tung Oil Trade In Metric Tons

	Imports								Exports				
Year	Germany	Hong Kong	Japan	Netherlands	South Korea	Taiwan	United States	World Total	Argentina	China	Hong Kong	Paraguay	World Total
1991	1,138	6,476	11,890	543	3,035	4,957	5,646	39,766	8,522	14,485	7,182	9,039	40,600
1992	1,036	8,509	13,326	782	3,722	6,676	4,996	44,146	5,808	20,867	8,174	4,221	40,269
1993	720	5,222	6,549	1,351	3,490	3,595	4,270	29,793	2,497	16,990	6,004	2,295	29,200
1994	912	7,843	8,628	1,663	4,294	7,454	5,401	43,082	2,415	30,582	6,476	4,603	45,182
1995	825	3,671	8,429	2,174	7,200	5,777	4,427	38,234	4,319	25,620	3,838	4,587	39,816
1996[1]	863	1,247	3,619	1,253	7,317	4,244	3,944	27,250	2,427	18,205	1,266	3,156	27,068
1997[2]	733	1,404	6,807	1,076	7,001	5,931	6,264	34,779	3,867	24,810	991	3,000	35,191

[1] Preliminary. [2] Estimate. *Source: The Oil World*

Consumption of Tung Oil in Inedible Products in the United States In Thousands of Pounds

Year	Jan.	Feb.	Mar.	Apr.	May	June	July	Aug.	Sept.	Oct.	Nov.	Dec.	Total
1992	435	459	574	498	502	694	572	705	674	873	530	790	7,306
1993	958	966	693	1,041	833	1,022	867	1,427	1,354	860	585	593	11,199
1994	608	592	635	1,408	1,558	840	861	910	480	392	660	382	9,326
1995	427	503	976	1,389	1,437	1,387	1,886	2,830	2,549	2,645	2,455	2,126	20,610
1996	1,724	1,427	1,730	1,750	1,498	1,813	2,214	2,024	1,431	2,045	1,908	2,081	21,645
1997	934	1,922	2,720	2,170	1,335	2,034	2,618	1,262	1,267	1,099	857	1,157	19,375
1998[1]	935	1,146	1,342	1,103	1,536	1,255	1,248	1,172	1,214	1,216	1,037	1,109	14,313

[1] Preliminary. *Source: Bureau of the Census, U.S. Department of Commerce*

Stocks of Tung Oil at Factories & Warehouses in the U.S., on First of Month In Thousands of Pounds

Year	Jan.	Feb.	Mar.	Apr.	May	June	July	Aug.	Sept.	Oct.	Nov.	Dec.
1992	1,608	2,421	2,439	1,605	1,323	1,540	847	1,348	2,162	1,724	2,560	3,545
1993	3,122	2,038	2,390	2,120	2,966	1,773	866	815	1,596	1,217	1,635	1,752
1994	1,551	2,053	1,507	2,049	2,091	2,591	2,148	1,562	820	2,455	1,712	1,909
1995	1,764	1,490	1,055	3,193	2,554	2,551	2,369	2,116	2,038	2,361	2,210	2,048
1996	2,013	1,635	2,232	3,018	2,386	2,532	2,641	2,381	2,670	2,525	2,459	2,834
1997	2,373	2,754	3,417	2,808	2,134	2,230	2,230	1,561	2,525	2,535	2,311	2,326
1998[1]	2,484	3,116	4,548	3,949	3,357	3,300	2,435	2,409	3,578	2,523	2,501	2,272

[1] Preliminary. *Source: Bureau of the Census, U.S. Department of Commerce*

Average Price of Tung Oil (Imported, Drums) F.O.B. in New York In Cents Per Pound

Year	Jan.	Feb.	Mar.	Apr.	May	June	July	Aug.	Sept.	Oct.	Nov.	Dec.	Average
1992	70.00	70.00	70.00	76.00	82.00	130.00	130.00	130.00	132.00	131.50	132.00	130.00	106.96
1993	130.00	130.00	130.00	130.00	117.00	130.00	130.00	130.00	107.50	100.00	94.75	93.00	118.52
1994	93.00	79.25	78.00	78.00	78.00	78.00	78.00	78.00	78.00	74.40	60.00	60.00	76.05
1995	60.00	60.00	60.00	60.00	60.00	60.00	60.00	60.00	60.00	60.00	60.00	60.00	60.00
1996	60.00	60.00	64.00	64.00	64.00	64.00	64.00	64.00	64.00	64.00	64.00	64.00	63.33
1997	74.00	92.00	92.00	103.00	103.00	103.00	103.00	108.00	110.00	110.00	110.00	110.00	101.50
1998[1]	110.00	110.00	110.00	110.00	100.00	100.00	100.00	100.00	100.00				104.44

[1] Preliminary. *Source: Economic Research Service, U.S. Department of Agriculture (ERS-USDA)*

Tungsten

Tungsten has unique high-temperature properties making it a material that has a wide range of industrial uses. It has a high melting point, high density, good corrosion resistance as well as other favorable properties. It also has excellent wear-resistance and cutting properties. Most tungsten is used to produce tungsten carbide and tungsten carbide is used in the production of cemented carbides. Cemented carbides or hardmetals are wear-resistant materials used in mining, metalworking and construction. Tungsten is used to make dies, bearings, superalloys for turbine blades as well as armor-piercing military projectiles. Tungsten metal wires, electrodes and contacts are used in electrical, heating, welding and lighting applications. Tungsten is employed in chemical processes as a catalyst, inorganic pigment and high-temperature lubricant.

The U.S. Geological Survey reported that in July 1998, U.S. reported consumption of tungsten was 259 metric tonnes. Over the first seven months of 1998, U.S. reported tungsten consumption was 3,260 tonnes while for all of 1997 it was 6,590 tonnes. U.S. tungsten imports for consumption in June 1998 were 284 tonnes. In the first half of 1998, imports for consumption were 3,049 tonnes while for all of 1997 they were 4,850 tonnes. U.S. stocks of tungsten at the end of July 1998 were 773 tonnes. At the end of 1997, tungsten stocks were 658 tonnes.

U.S. reported consumption of ferrotungsten in July 1998 was 33 tonnes (tungsten content). For the January-July 1998 period consumption of ferrotungsten was 236 tonnes while for all of 1997 it was 463 tonnes. Consumption of tungsten metal powder in July 1998 was 92 tonnes and in the first seven months of 1998 it was 813 tonnes. For 1997, tungsten metal powder consumption was 963 tonnes.

World Concentrate Production of Tungsten — In Metric Tons (Contained Tungsten[3])

Year	Australia	Austria	Bolivia	Brazil	Burma	China	Kazakhstan[4]	Mongolia	Peru	Portugal	Rep. of Korea	Russia[4]	World Total
1989	1,371	1,517	1,118	679	233	30,200	------	600	970	1,376	1,701	9,300	51,038
1990	1,086	1,378	1,014	316	443	32,000	------	500	1,536	1,410	1,361	8,800	51,900
1991	237	1,314	1,065	223	356	31,800	------	300	1,232	971	780	8,000	48,200
1992	159	1,490	851	205	531	25,000	200	260	802	1,870	247	6,500	40,400
1993	23	104	287	245	524	21,600	150	250	398	1,280	200	8,000	35,100
1994	11	------	462	270	544	27,000	200	150	259	60	------	4,000	34,300
1995	------	738	655	171	531	27,400	225	200	728	870	------	5,400	38,600
1996[1]	------	1,413	582	171	334	26,500	220	200	332	776	------	3,000	35,100
1997[2]	------	1,400	500	170	280	25,000	200	100	280	1,036	------	3,000	33,400

[1] Preliminary. [2] Estimate. [3] Conversion factors: WO_3 to W, multiply by 0.7931; 60% WO_3 to W, multiply by 0.4758. [4] Formerly part of the U.S.S.R.; data not reported separately until 1992. *Source: U.S. Geological Survey (USGS)*

Salient Statistics of Tungsten in the United States — In Metric Tons (Contained Tungsten)

			Consumption of Tungsten Products by End Uses										Stocks at End of Year	
			Steel										Concentrates	
Year	Net Import Reliance as a % Apparent Consumption	Total Consumption	Tool	Stainless & Heat Assisting	Alloy Steel[3]	Superalloys	Cutting & Wear Resistant Materials	Products Made from Metal Powder	Miscellaneous	Chemical and Ceramic	Exports	Imports for Consumption	Consumers	Producers
1990	81	5,878	342	64	74	325	4,985	2,181	464	50	139	6,420	1,077	16
1991	91	5,309	243	44	W	287	4,801	1,941	614	44	21	7,837	1,778	26
1992	86	4,313	407	52	66	25	4,211	1,309	828	W	38	2,477	702	44
1993	82	2,866	388	43	40	282	5,064	1,434	2	37	63	1,721	592	44
1994	95	3,630	529	20	19	300	5,920	1,200	W	108	44	2,960	756	44
1995	90	5,890	265	W	18	215	6,590	1,200	3,600	W	20	4,660	627	44
1996[1]	90	5,260	434	107	177	371	5,960	687	0	97	72	4,190	569	44
1997[2]	85	6,590	361	151	278	367	6,290	828	0	124	40	4,850	658	44

[1] Preliminary. [2] Estimate. [3] Other than tool. W = Withheld proprietary data. *Source: U.S. Geological Survey (USGS)*

Average Prices of Tungsten — In U.S. Dollars

Year	Jan.	Feb.	Mar.	Apr.	May	June	July	Aug.	Sept.	Oct.	Nov.	Dec.	Average
	European Market (London), 65% WO_3 Basis, C.I.F.[1] -- $ Per Metric Ton												
1994	29.94	29.94	37.71	35.38	35.38	37.09	38.10	38.10	42.03	45.36	47.63	49.56	38.85
1995	56.00	60.00	64.00	64.00	65.00	66.00	67.00	66.00	66.00	66.00	66.00	62.50	64.04
1996	56.00	54.00	56.00	57.00	57.00	57.00	53.50	50.00	50.00	47.50	45.00	48.00	52.58
1997	48.00	49.00	50.00	50.00	50.00	50.00	50.00	43.00	43.00	43.00	46.00	46.00	47.33
	U.S. Spot Quotations, 65% WO_3, Basis C.I.F., U.S. Ports (Including Duty) -- $ Per Short Ton												
1994	37.48	40.79	44.10	44.10	44.10	44.53	47.95	48.50	48.50	48.50	48.50	48.50	45.46
1995	44.00	44.00	44.00	44.00	55.00	65.00	65.00	62.50	60.00	60.00	60.00	60.00	55.29
1996	60.00	60.00	60.00	60.00	60.00	60.00	60.00	60.00	60.00	60.00	60.00	60.00	60.00
1997	60.00	60.00	60.00	60.00	60.00	60.00	60.00	60.00	60.00	55.00	50.00	50.00	57.92

[1] Combined wolframite and scheelite quoations. *Source: U.S. Geological Survey (USGS)*

Turkeys

Annual U.S. turkey production shows signs of having temporarily peaked. A record 5.48 billion pounds were produced in 1997, but production in 1998 dipped to 5.33 billion and initial estimates for 1999 call for 5.3 billion pounds. The slippage reflects smaller flock numbers; 300.6 million birds in 1997 vs. 302.7 million in 1996 with a further drop likely in 1999, although the decline in inventory has been partially checked by higher slaughter weights. North Carolina is the largest producing state, generally producing at least 50 million birds annually followed by Minnesota with about 45 million. On a world basis, the U.S. consistently produces more than half the total production, estimated at 4.6 million metric tonnes in 1998 with U.S. output at 2.4 million.

There's a strong seasonality to the turkey industry that reflects a well entrenched U.S. tradition. The industry, however, is attempting to iron out the pronounced yearend holiday seasonal demand for whole birds by marketing prepackaged turkey parts on a year round basis. The additional processing required to cut up and package turkey cuts, such as breast and legs, has increased the supply of edible trimmings, which processors sell in several forms, including mechanically deboned turkey (MDT). Foreign demand remains a promising market for MDT; also, as a relatively low-cost meat protein MDT can easily be incorporated into sausage and other meat products.

U.S. per capita ready to cook retail weight turkey consumption of 17.7 pounds in 1997 trailed initial forecasts of at least 18 plus pounds and compares with a scaled back 17.6 pounds in 1996. A further decline to 17.1 pounds is forecast for 1999. The October-December quarter traditionally accounts for more than a third of total use followed by a sharp tapering off in the January-March period. November is the highest slaughter month. Prices follow a similar pattern, peaking generally in the fourth quarter and trending lower during the first quarter, basis 8-16 pound hens in New York. Turkeys of 14-22 pound weight are classified as toms. Changes in consumer food tastes that favor poultry could yet alter turkey's seasonality.

U.S. turkey and turkey product exports in 1998 of 510 million pounds (half the world's total) compare with a record high 598 million pounds in 1996. Exports in 1999 were forecast to rise to 580 million pounds. Mexico is the largest market for U.S. turkey products, mostly shipments of lower valued MDT products that are used primarily for sausage production. The U.S. imports no turkey products.

Wholesale turkey prices, basis Eastern U.S., averaged 70.0 cents per pound in late 1998. The 1997 full year average of 58.0-63.0 cents compares with 64.90 cents in 1996. Prices for 1998 were forecast to average 60.0-64.0 cents.

Production and Consumption of Turkey Meat, by Selected Countries — In Thous. of Metric Tons (RTC)

	Production							Consumption						
	Canada	France	Germany	Italy	United Kingdom	United States	World Total	Canada	France	Germany	Italy	United Kingdom	United States	World Total
1990	129	432	145	279	223	2,048	3,600	125	315	208	272	211	1,992	3,486
1991	131	487	149	273	242	2,088	3,722	126	342	240	265	236	2,060	3,630
1992	132	558	159	269	246	2,167	3,892	129	354	272	268	228	2,072	3,732
1993	128	532	169	266	252	2,176	3,902	126	321	280	256	249	2,075	3,759
1994	133	568	183	269	253	2,239	4,040	128	330	295	245	258	2,110	3,756
1995	141	650	206	294	289	2,299	4,295	126	353	196	262	287	2,133	3,921
1996	146	671	217	315	293	2,450	4,536	123	352	220	277	298	2,225	4,162
1997	142	731	243	338	293	2,455	4,709	126	355	240	295	277	2,144	4,165
1998[1]	139	738	255	338	275	2,369	4,634	130	388	250	295	260	2,208	4,219
1999[2]	144	730	268	336	280	2,375	4,666	133	399	260	293	265	2,203	4,246

[1] Preliminary. [2] Estimate. [3] Forecast. *Source: Foreign Agricultural Service, U.S. Department of Agriculture (FAS-USDA)*

Salient Statistics of Turkeys in the United States

Year	Poults Placed[3]	Number Raised[4]	Liveweight Produced	Liveweight Price	Value of Production	Production	Beginning Stocks	Exports	Ready-to-Cook-Basis Consumption Total	Consumption Per Capita	Production Costs Feed	Production Costs Total	Wholesale Ready-to-Cook Production Costs	3-Region Weighted Average Price[5]
	In Thousands	In Thousands	Mil. Lbs.	¢ Per Lb.	Million $	Million Pounds	Million Pounds	Million Pounds	Million Pounds	Lbs.	Liveweight Basis	Liveweight Basis		
1988	261,406	242,421	5,059.1	38.6	1,957.3	3,930	266	51	3,844	15.7	24.60	38.30	64.20	60.69
1989	290,678	261,280	5,465.5	40.9	2,234.4	4,181	250	41	4,109	16.6	26.70	40.40	66.80	65.75
1990	304,863	282,450	6,029.6	39.4	2,378.6	4,567	236	54	4,390	17.6	23.40	37.10	62.60	62.35
1991	308,083	285,110	6,110.7	38.4	2,344.7	4,658	306	103	4,541	18.0	22.72	36.42	61.83	60.79
1992	307,823	288,980	6,333.8	37.7	2,387.7	4,835	264	171	4,599	18.0	23.06	36.76	62.25	60.48
1993	308,871	287,650	6,432.6	39.0	2,509.1	4,798	272	244	4,577	17.7	22.20	35.86	61.12	62.83
1994	317,468	289,025	6,332.4	40.4	2,643.8	4,937	249	280	4,652	17.8	24.00	37.70	63.40	65.90
1995	320,882	292,856	6,506.1	41.0	2,776.4	5,069	254	348	4,705	17.9	21.90	35.60	60.80	66.20
1996[1]	325,375	302,708	7,233.1	43.3	3,128.8	5,466	271	438	4,907	18.5	31.60	45.30	72.90	66.80
1997[2]	305,612	300,620	7,215.7	39.9	2,880.5	5,478	328	598	4,727	17.6	28.20	41.90	68.70	63.80

[1] Preliminary. [2] Estimate. [3] Poults placed for slaughter by hatcheries. [4] Turkeys placed August1-July 31. [5] Regions include central, eastern and western. Central region receives twice the weight of the other regions in calculating the average. *Source: Economic Research Service, U.S. Department of Agriculture*

TURKEYS

Turkey-Feed Price Ratio[1] in the United States In Pounds

Year	Jan.	Feb.	Mar.	Apr.	May	June	July	Aug.	Sept.	Oct.	Nov.	Dec.	Average
1989	4.8	5.3	5.5	5.9	6.1	6.3	6.1	6.6	6.0	6.4	6.8	6.5	6.0
1990	5.9	5.7	6.1	5.9	6.0	6.2	6.4	6.7	7.0	7.6	7.7	6.7	6.5
1991	6.0	6.3	6.4	6.5	6.7	6.9	7.2	7.1	7.0	6.5	6.4	6.5	6.6
1992	6.0	5.8	6.0	6.0	6.0	6.1	6.5	6.8	6.7	7.1	7.2	7.1	6.4
1993	6.3	6.4	6.6	6.5	6.6	6.7	6.4	6.4	6.9	7.2	6.7	6.1	6.5
1994	5.4	5.4	5.5	5.8	5.9	6.0	7.0	7.4	7.4	7.9	8.0	7.3	6.6
1995	6.7	6.4	6.5	6.4	6.3	6.3	6.0	6.3	6.4	6.3	6.5	5.7	6.3
1996	5.3	5.2	5.1	4.7	4.6	4.9	4.9	4.8	5.3	6.1	6.4	6.2	5.3
1997	5.4	5.0	5.0	5.1	5.3	5.6	6.0	5.9	6.1	6.2	6.2	5.8	5.6
1998[2]	5.4	5.2	5.4	5.7	5.8	6.1	6.5	7.6	8.1	8.3	8.3	7.7	6.7

[1] Pounds of feed equal in value to one pound of turkey, liveweight. [2] Preliminary. *Source: Economic Research Service, U.S. Department of Agriculture*

Average Price Received by Farmers for Turkeys in the United States (Liveweight) In Cents Per Pounds

Year	Jan.	Feb.	Mar.	Apr.	May	June	July	Aug.	Sept.	Oct.	Nov.	Dec.	Average
1989	35.5	38.4	40.3	42.0	43.6	43.8	41.2	40.8	36.4	38.2	40.7	39.3	40.0
1990	35.4	33.7	36.4	36.6	38.3	38.7	39.1	40.2	40.3	42.5	42.3	36.9	38.4
1991	33.6	35.1	37.0	37.6	38.3	38.7	39.1	40.1	40.2	37.0	37.0	38.1	37.7
1992	36.3	35.5	37.0	37.0	37.7	37.7	37.9	37.8	37.5	38.5	39.4	39.3	37.6
1993	35.6	35.7	37.6	37.6	37.7	37.6	38.7	39.6	41.1	43.2	42.7	40.8	39.0
1994	37.0	37.3	38.4	39.2	39.9	40.3	40.6	42.1	43.1	44.5	44.3	42.2	40.7
1995	39.3	37.2	38.3	38.3	38.4	39.3	39.6	41.9	43.6	45.2	47.3	44.0	41.0
1996	40.9	42.4	41.8	42.2	43.2	44.4	45.0	44.3	44.2	45.1	45.5	43.2	43.5
1997	38.6	36.4	37.8	39.7	41.3	41.6	41.1	41.0	41.1	41.0	41.9	38.7	40.0
1998[1]	35.5	34.0	34.6	35.7	35.4	35.9	37.5	38.8	40.2	42.8	44.0	41.1	38.0

[1] Preliminary. *Source: Economic Research Service, U.S. Department of Agriculture (ERS-USDA)*

Average Wholesale Price of Turkeys[1] (Hens, 8-16 Lbs.) in New York In Cents Per Pound

Year	Jan.	Feb.	Mar.	Apr.	May	June	July	Aug.	Sept.	Oct.	Nov.	Dec.	Average
1989	59.03	62.17	65.71	68.33	72.08	72.98	66.40	62.61	57.88	67.61	72.45	72.70	66.66
1990	55.55	55.16	58.86	59.62	61.27	62.88	63.37	66.57	68.99	76.15	73.70	56.05	63.18
1991	53.49	55.76	59.10	60.32	62.32	62.68	63.41	64.66	64.38	60.52	63.07	65.18	61.24
1992	58.74	55.00	58.77	60.00	60.03	59.46	57.02	57.80	61.02	63.92	65.57	65.14	60.21
1993	58.05	56.83	58.41	58.98	58.81	58.35	59.76	63.43	66.73	71.28	71.76	68.20	62.55
1994	60.09	59.32	60.98	61.58	63.14	64.61	65.26	66.39	68.98	73.13	74.01	70.35	65.65
1995	60.71	58.54	60.04	60.05	60.57	62.76	64.78	68.52	72.92	76.73	80.31	70.35	66.36
1996	64.60	64.65	65.07	64.82	65.39	65.85	65.66	64.94	64.16	69.09	73.58	70.05	66.49
1997	59.71	57.84	59.30	62.93	66.64	68.60	68.59	68.20	67.89	67.33	70.07	62.18	64.94
1998[2]	55.65	54.04	55.49	55.49	58.14	58.14	58.68	63.17	65.65	71.52	72.95	69.00	61.49

[1] Ready-to-cook. [2] Preliminary. *Source: Economic Research Service, U.S. Department of Agriculture (ERS-USDA)*

Certified Federally Inspected Turkey Slaughter in the U.S. (Ready-to-Cook Weights) In Millions of Pounds

Year	Jan.	Feb.	Mar.	Apr.	May	June	July	Aug.	Sept.	Oct.	Nov.	Dec.	Total
1989	254.1	248.1	301.3	268.8	356.9	388.6	360.4	430.3	385.7	422.6	423.1	334.9	4,175
1990	334.0	298.3	351.1	328.4	384.1	389.2	395.7	444.0	382.9	478.4	446.2	328.6	4,561
1991	365.6	322.0	329.7	375.8	398.2	380.7	402.2	421.8	404.8	482.0	419.2	349.9	4,652
1992	362.9	331.7	361.3	385.2	374.2	435.0	451.8	411.9	431.3	467.6	423.0	393.1	4,829
1993	354.1	322.7	382.9	391.9	378.7	446.7	419.3	426.9	436.0	451.4	461.8	375.3	4,848
1994	347.8	342.0	400.9	380.6	415.6	457.9	405.6	483.6	447.7	453.6	453.9	397.5	4,992
1995	386.3	368.9	433.1	369.6	441.4	478.4	409.1	447.3	419.5	480.2	463.0	394.4	5,091
1996	412.4	426.5	422.3	430.9	483.0	454.7	484.8	476.6	440.9	518.1	465.9	406.1	5,422
1997	439.7	389.5	399.6	448.8	465.8	481.4	488.8	453.0	457.6	510.0	450.6	457.9	5,443
1998[1]	430.5	408.0	442.0	444.7	417.5	453.3	455.8	411.0	423.9	469.9	457.1	427.7	5,241

[1] Preliminary. *Source: Economic Research Service, U.S. Department of Agriculture (ERS-USDA)*

Per Capita Consumption of Turkeys in the United States In Pounds

Year	First Quarter	Second Quarter	Third Quarter	Fourth Quarter	Total	Year	First Quarter	Second Quarter	Third Quarter	Fourth Quarter	Total
1988	3.1	3.4	3.8	5.4	15.7	1994	3.6	3.9	4.4	6.2	17.8
1989	3.2	3.2	4.2	6.0	16.6	1995	3.6	3.9	4.2	6.2	17.9
1990	3.5	3.6	4.2	6.2	17.6	1996	3.7	3.9	4.6	6.2	18.5
1991	3.7	4.0	4.1	6.4	18.0	1997	3.5	4.0	4.2	6.0	17.6
1992	3.4	3.8	4.2	6.5	18.0	1998[1]	3.9	3.9	4.2	5.9	18.0
1993	3.5	3.7	3.9	6.5	17.7	1999[2]	3.4	3.9	4.3	6.0	17.5

[1] Preliminary. [2] Estimate. *Source: Economic Research Service, U.S. Department of Agriculture (ERS-USDA)*

Storage Stocks of Turkeys (Frozen) in the United States, on First of Month In Millions of Pounds

Year	Jan.	Feb.	Mar.	Apr.	May	June	July	Aug.	Sept.	Oct.	Nov.	Dec.
1989	249.7	262.5	263.1	269.2	298.7	355.6	454.6	496.9	574.3	569.3	571.8	258.6
1990	235.9	268.4	276.3	317.9	354.9	405.6	481.3	541.7	593.1	623.6	625.1	338.4
1991	306.4	302.5	342.2	370.0	408.5	453.4	503.1	571.3	625.8	667.2	653.0	305.5
1992	264.1	325.5	354.1	392.3	430.2	486.8	580.1	662.1	684.2	734.4	714.7	320.5
1993	271.7	314.7	359.8	359.2	424.4	474.0	556.1	624.2	678.6	713.8	683.6	290.6
1994	249.1	279.8	304.8	346.5	399.1	461.4	539.2	288.1	623.4	648.6	636.2	280.7
1995	254.4	312.9	359.5	432.1	466.2	536.3	598.8	651.1	678.2	686.0	644.2	270.1
1996	271.3	339.2	423.1	445.4	514.5	587.4	679.7	718.2	723.2	721.0	658.3	347.8
1997	328.0	401.0	446.4	496.5	543.3	611.8	667.9	714.3	742.0	770.7	736.6	438.6
1998[1]	415.1	497.6	512.7	527.0	580.2	612.9	656.5	703.0	708.8	702.6	661.2	314.9

[1] Preliminary. *Source: Economic Research Service, U.S. Department of Agriculture (ERS-USDA)*

Average Retail Price[2] of Turkeys (Whole frozen) in the United States In Cents Per Pound

Year	Jan.	Feb.	Mar.	Apr.	May	June	July	Aug.	Sept.	Oct.	Nov.	Dec.	Average
1989	67.60	66.90	71.90	75.10	79.40	80.60	74.40	71.80	67.80	73.28	79.80	79.60	74.02
1990	65.20	64.60	67.30	69.40	70.10	70.10	68.70	73.60	76.60	81.90	82.30	66.40	71.35
1991	62.30	63.06	66.61	66.78	69.70	70.00	70.30	72.20	72.80	69.10	70.80	73.90	68.96
1992	67.90	65.80	68.10	68.70	69.24	69.04	65.70	68.10	69.60	72.30	74.00	74.90	69.45
1993	67.85	67.22	67.94	68.80	68.40	68.19	67.08	72.07	74.91	78.37	80.08	75.03	71.33
1994	70.30	69.40	70.60	70.90	72.00	72.58	72.77	74.75	77.32	79.89	83.33	77.34	74.27
1995	69.54	67.08	68.47	68.62	70.05	72.49	74.18	77.77	81.60	84.89	86.50	77.50	74.89
1996	103.50	104.70	106.90	101.40	104.30	104.10	104.40	108.60	106.50	107.40	98.10	102.00	104.33
1997	106.30	106.70	104.70	103.20	104.50	107.80	107.40	109.20	108.90	106.20	97.60	98.20	105.06
1998[1]	103.40	100.10	99.60	97.20	95.70	99.10	100.80	102.40	105.20	102.50	93.40	95.40	99.57

[1] Preliminary. [2] Data prior to 1996 are prices to selected retailers. *Source: Economic Research Service, U.S. Department of Agriculture (ERS-USDA)*

Turkey (Whole) Retail-to-Consumer Price Spread in the U.S. In Cents Per Pound

Year	Jan.	Feb.	Mar.	Apr.	May	June	July	Aug.	Sept.	Oct.	Nov.	Dec.	Average
1989	29.8	29.9	25.7	23.2	20.7	20.7	30.2	32.3	34.2	28.9	13.4	15.4	25.4
1990	33.7	33.7	32.1	27.7	29.8	29.7	32.1	27.8	26.7	23.7	8.8	29.6	27.9
1991	37.1	38.1	31.2	33.7	30.9	32.0	32.6	31.2	30.3	34.9	20.8	17.5	30.9
1992	28.2	29.2	27.0	29.4	29.6	29.5	33.3	32.5	31.4	27.2	15.4	18.1	27.5
1993	30.0	31.7	32.6	31.9	32.3	34.5	35.8	29.7	27.7	25.0	13.6	20.4	28.8
1994	27.5	29.7	28.1	25.1	27.1	28.8	28.7	27.6	27.1	25.5	13.9	20.3	25.8
1995	28.5	32.0	33.7	32.1	32.7	32.8	30.8	28.2	27.0	20.1	10.6	21.2	27.5
1996	30.4	30.7	33.6	28.0	29.3	28.0	27.9	32.1	30.3	28.9	18.0	26.6	28.7
1997	38.3	40.7	37.5	32.0	29.6	32.0	32.0	34.5	34.3	31.9	20.0	26.9	32.5
1998[1]	38.8	37.2	35.2	31.2	29.4	30.7	29.6	29.0	29.3	21.3	10.3	19.0	28.4

[1] Preliminary. *Source: Economic Research Service, U.S. Department of Agriculture (ERS-USDA)*

Uranium

The U.S. Energy Information Agency reported that in 1997, U.S. uranium production was 5.6 million pounds (in the form of uranium concentrate) or 2,200 metric tonnes of uranium. That represented a decline of 11 percent from the 1996 production level of 6.3 million pounds. The period of 1995-1997 saw U.S. annual production of uranium average just under 6 million pounds per year. In 1993 and 1994, production averaged 3.3 million pounds. That is in contrast to 1988 and 1989 when production averaged 13.5 million pounds per year.

In 1997, mine production of uranium was 4.7 million pounds (uranium concentrate), unchanged from 1996. Mine production fell to a low in 1992 when it was 1 million pounds. Eleven uranium concentrate production facilities operated in the U.S. in 1997. Uranium production at U.S. uranium mills accounted for 14 percent; and in-situ leaching and as a by-product of phosphate processing combined for 86 percent of concentrate production. Three mills produced uranium concentrate by processing uranium form other feed materials.

Total exploration and development expenditures in 1997 were $304 million, a substantial increase from $10.1 million in 1996. Surface drilling (exploration and development) in the U.S. was 4.9 million feet in 7,793 holes. In 1996, surface drilling was 3 million feet. U.S. uranium companies held 840,000 acres for all exploration purposes at the end of 1997. That represents a large increase in land held for exploration. The types of land acquired and held include fee land, mineral fee leases and patented and unpatented mining claims.

U.S. utilities purchased from U.S. and foreign suppliers some 42 million pounds of uranium concentrate in 1997. Fuel assemblies loaded in U.S. commercial nuclear power reactors in 1997 contained 48.7 million pounds of uranium concentrate. That was 5 percent higher than in 1996. Uranium inventories held by U.S. utilities at the end of 1997 contained 63.9 million pounds of uranium concentrate. That was 3 percent less than in 1996. U.S. utility and supplier inventories at the end of 1997 were 75.8 million pounds, down 5 percent from 1996.

U.S. uranium concentrate shipments from domestic production facilities (mills, in-situ and phosphate by-product plants) were 5.8 million pounds in 1997. That was 3 percent less than in 1996. At the end of 1997, U.S. uranium reserves of $30 per pound concentrate were 281 million pounds, down 1 percent from 1996. Reserves of $50 per pound concentrate were 931 million pounds. Underground mining reserves accounted for one-half of total reserves. New Mexico, Texas and Wyoming accounted for most of the reserves.

World Production of Uranium Oxide (U_3O_8) Concentrate In Short Tons (Uranium Content)

Year	Australia	Canada	China	Czech Rep. & Slovakia	France	Gabon	Germany	Namibia	Niger	South Africa	United States	Former U.S.S.R.	World Total
1988	4,580	15,646	-----	-----	4,377	1,194	58	4,551	3,845	5,039	6,500	-----	46,846
1989	4,752	14,855	1,039	2,989	4,183	1,157	4,961	4,000	3,874	3,810	6,919	18,849	75,264
1990	4,589	11,400	1,039	2,600	3,661	922	3,864	4,030	3,682	3,169	4,443	18,199	64,642
1991	4,909	10,609	1,039	2,340	3,204	882	1,569	3,185	3,853	2,248	3,975	13,650	53,458
1992	3,032	12,087	1,039	2,040	2,755	702	325	2,199	3,855	2,449	2,822	11,205	46,124
1993	2,949	11,990	1,300	911	2,220	769	195	2,168	3,786	2,261	2,587	10,491	43,027
1994	3,050	11,950	-----	-----	1,700	750	-----	2,500	3,800	2,250	1,950	-----	41,750
1995	4,900	13,600	-----	-----	1,250	800	-----	2,600	3,750	1,850	3,050	-----	43,050
1996[1]	6,450	15,250	-----	-----	1,200	750	-----	3,150	4,300	2,200	3,150	-----	46,650
1997[2]	7,150	15,650	-----	-----	975	600	-----	3,800	5,100	1,450	2,900	-----	46,800

[1] Preliminary. [2] Estimate. NA = Not available. *Source: American Bureau of Metal Statistics, Inc. (AMBS)*

Month-End Uranium (U_3O_8) Transaction Values[1] In Dollars Per Pound

Year	Jan.	Feb.	Mar.	Apr.	May	June	July	Aug.	Sept.	Oct.	Nov.	Dec.	Average
1988	16.85	16.65	16.55	16.45	16.10	15.80	15.45	15.00	14.50	14.40	13.30	12.50	15.30
1989	12.25	12.00	11.25	11.00	10.75	10.45	9.95	9.80	9.80	9.65	9.55	9.40	10.49
1990	9.25	9.05	8.75	8.65	8.55	8.80	9.75	10.80	11.40	10.10	9.30	9.15	9.46
1991	9.40	9.45	9.35	9.30	9.30	9.20	9.15	8.95	8.70	8.35	7.45	7.50	8.84
1992	7.55	7.80	7.95	7.90	7.85	7.80	7.75	7.85	7.95	8.40	8.55	8.75	8.01
1993[2]	8.80	8.60	8.80	9.20	8.70	8.90	8.20	8.80	9.05	8.45	8.60	8.71	8.74
1994	8.58	8.45	8.25	8.25	8.23	8.25	8.23	8.15	8.13	8.10	8.13	8.25	8.25
1995	8.30	8.45	8.65	8.78	9.18	9.48	9.50	9.83	9.83	9.83	9.95	10.05	9.32
1996	10.20	10.48	10.93	11.70	13.03	13.25	14.93	15.18	15.40	15.53	15.48	15.38	13.45
1997	15.33	15.08	14.85	14.75	14.43	10.95	10.68	10.45	10.55	10.48	10.43	10.53	12.37

[1] Transaction value is a weighted average price of recent natural uranium sales transactions, based on prices paid on transactions closed within the previous 3-month period for which delivery is scheduled within one year of the transaction date; at least 10 transactions involving a sum total of at least 2 million pounds of U_3O_8 equivalent. 2 Data beginning December 1993 represents average of Unrestricted and Restricted. *Source: American Metal Market (AMM)*

Reported Average Price Settlements for Purchases by U.S. Utilities and Domestic Suppliers In $ Per Lb.[2]

Year of Delivery	Contract Price	Market Price[1]	Price & Cost Floor	Total	Contract & Market	Year of Delivery	Contract Price	Market Price[1]	Price & Cost Floor	Total	Contract & Market
	Averages of Reported Prices						Averages of Reported Prices				
1988	28.20	16.12	33.52	21.59	26.15	1993	14.96	9.57	14.87	11.03	13.14
1989	20.87	11.48	22.50	15.42	19.56	1994	10.68	9.76	20.03	10.57	10.63
1990	17.94	9.18	19.40	11.65	15.70	1995	10.58	10.19	17.86	12.05	10.79
1991	13.94	9.04	21.84	12.62	13.66	1996	13.40	13.66	16.13	14.91	13.72
1992	13.16	8.65	18.35	13.89	13.45	1997	13.33	11.20	14.52	12.11	13.13

[1] No floor. [2] U_3O_8 equivalent. Note: Price excludes uranium delivered under litigation settlements. Price is given in year-of-delivery dollars.
Source: Energy Information Adminstration, U.S. Department of Energy (EIA-DOE)

Uranium Industry Statistics in the United States In Millions of Pounds U_3O_8

Year	Production: Mine	Production: Concent-rate	Concent-rate Ship-ments	Employment -- Person Years: Explor-ation	Mining	Milling	Pro-cessing	Total	Deliveries to U.S. Utilities[1]	Avg. Price Delivered Uranium $/lb. U_3O_8	Imports	Avg. Price Delivered Uranium Imports $/lb. U_3O_8	Exports
1988	9.5	13.130	12.791	144	849	572	576	2,141	17.6	26.15	17.0	19.03	4.3
1989	9.7	13.837	14.808	86	659	367	471	1,583	18.4	19.56	13.7	16.75	2.5
1990	5.9	8.885	12.957	73	664	304	293	1,335	20.5	15.70	26.6	12.55	2.4
1991	5.2	7.952	8.437	52	411	191	361	1,016	26.8	13.66	23.1	15.55	3.5
1992	1.0	5.645	6.853	51	219	129	283	682	23.4	13.45	45.4	11.34	20.9
1993	2.0	3.063	3.374	36	133	65	145	380	15.5	13.14	41.9	10.53	21.3
1994	2.5	3.352	6.319	41	157	105	149	980	38.3	10.40	36.6	8.95	17.7
1995	3.5	6.000	5.500	27	226	121	161	1,107	43.4	11.25	41.3	10.20	9.8
1996	4.7	6.300	6.000	27	333	155	175	1,118	47.3	14.12	45.4	13.15	11.5
1997	4.7	5.600	5.800	30	413	175	175	1,097	42.0	12.88	43.0	11.81	17.0

[1] From suppliers under domestic purchases. *Source: Energy Information Administration, U.S. Department of Energy (EIA-DOE)*

Commercial and U.S. Government Stocks of Uranium, End of Year In Millions of Pounds U_3O_8 Equivalent

Year	Utility: Natural Uranium	Utility: Enriched Uranium[1]	Domestic Supplier: Natural Uranium	Domestic Supplier: Enriched Uranium[1]	Total Commercial Stocks	DOE-Owned & USEC-Held: Natural Uranium	DOE-Owned & USEC-Held: Enriched Uranium
1990	61.5	41.2	22.0	4.4	129.1	59.8	32.8
1991	70.9	27.1	18.7	2.0	118.7	46.8	36.7
1992	66.5	25.5	19.1	6.1	117.3	45.8	23.1
1993	57.9	23.3	19.1	5.4	105.7	52.4	26.9
1994	42.4	23.0	17.4	4.1	86.9	57.2	28.0
1995	41.2	17.5	13.2	.5	72.5	82.0	28.8
1996	42.2	23.9	13.0	1.0	80.0	83.2	25.3
1997	45.9	18.1	10.3	1.7	75.8	76.5	26.4

[1] Includes amount reported as UF_6 at enrichment suppliers. DOE = Department of Energy USEC = U.S. Energy Commission.
Source: Energy Information Administration, U.S. Department of Energy (EIA-DOE)

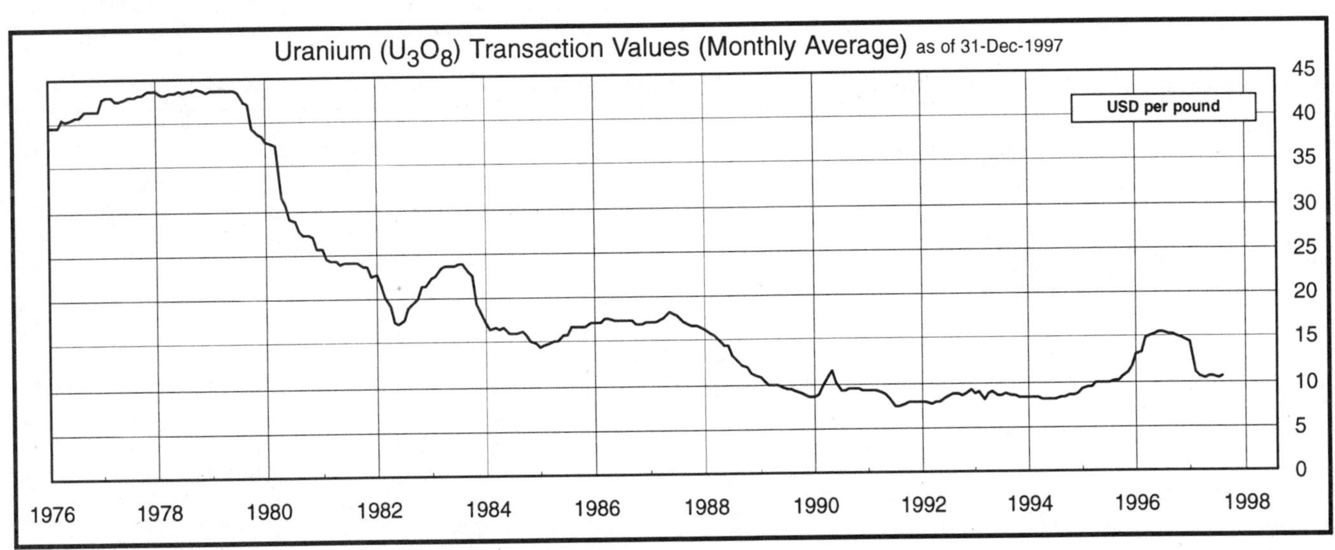

Vanadium

Vanadium is used in the production of carbon and alloy plates and steel, pipe steels and structural bars. It finds use as an oxidation catalyst and is used in tool production to provide strength and toughness. Ferrovanadium is an iron alloy used in steel. Vanadium pentoxide is used in dyeing and painting applications. Vanadium is also important in the production of aerospace titanium alloys and as a catalyst in the production of maleic anhydride and sulfuric acid. The major producers of vanadium are South Africa, China and Russia. In 1997, U.S. vanadium production was limited to that which is recovered from industrial waste streams. Vanadium is recovered from vanadium-bearing ferrophosphorus slag, iron slag, petroleum residues and spent catalysts. From these sources, vanadium pentoxide, ferrovanadium and vanadium metal are produced. The dominant use for vanadium is in metallurgical applications in which vanadium is an alloying agent with iron, steel and titanium. The major nonmetallurgical use for vanadium is as a catalyst.

U.S. consumption of ferrovanadium in July 1998 was 285,000 kilograms, contained vanadium. This was about the same as the month before. For all of 1997, consumption of ferrovanadium was 3.94 million kilograms. U.S. stocks of ferrovanadium in July 1998 were 271,000 kilograms. Stocks at the end of 1997 were 290,000 kilograms. Most data on other vanadium materials was withheld by the U.S. Geological Survey to avoid disclosing proprietary data. U.S. consumption of vanadium oxide in 1997 was 13,400 kilograms. U.S. stocks of vanadium-aluminum alloy in July 1998 were 11,600 kilograms while at the end of 1997 they were 8,330 kilograms.

U.S. consumption of vanadium materials including vanadium alloys, vanadium metal and other materials totaled 323,000 kilograms in July 1998, down 1 percent from June. For all of 1997, U.S. consumption of vanadium materials was 4.48 million kilograms. Stocks of vanadium materials in July 1998 were 291,000 kilograms.

U.S. imports of aluminum-vanadium master alloy in the first half of 1998 were 298,000 kilograms. Imports of vanadium metal including waste and scrap in the first half of 1998 were 11,200 kilograms. For all of 1997, imports were 564,000 kilograms. U.S. exports of aluminum-vanadium master alloy in January-June 1998 were 736,000 kilograms while exports of vanadium metal were 243,000 kilograms.

World Production of Vanadium   In Metric Tons (Contained Vanadium)

	From Ores, Concentrates and Slag						From Petroleum Residues, Ash, Spent Catalysts			
			Republic of South Africa							
Year	China[3]	Russia[4]	Content of Pentoxide & Vanadate Products	Content of Vanadiferous Slag Product	Total	Total[5]	Japan[6]	United States[7]	Total	World Grand Total
1988	4,500	9,600	6,330	11,300	17,631	31,731	728	2,950	3,678	35,409
1989	4,500	9,600	7,270	11,300	18,567	32,967	868	2,389	3,257	36,224
1990	4,500	9,000	7,100	10,000	17,106	33,900	700	2,308	3,008	36,900
1991	4,500	8,500	6,500	8,460	14,962	31,700	404	2,250	2,650	34,300
1992	4,700	11,000	6,300	7,730	14,033	29,900	245	1,347	1,590	31,500
1993	5,000	10,000	6,650	8,400	15,051	31,500	252	2,867	3,120	34,600
1994	5,400	11,900	6,050	9,600	16,350	34,700	252	2,740	2,990	37,700
1995	13,700	11,000	6,500	9,000	16,297	42,100	245	1,990	2,240	44,400
1996[1]	14,000	11,000	-----	-----	15,685	41,800	245	3,730	3,980	45,800
1997[2]	8,000	11,000	-----	-----	17,000	37,100	245	-----	-----	-----

[1] Preliminary. [2] Estimate. [3] In vanadiferous slag product. [4] Formerly part of the U.S.S.R.; data not reported separately until 1992. [5] Excludes U.S. production. [6] In vanadium pentoxide products. [7] In vandium pentoxide and ferrovandium products. *Source: U.S. Geological Survey (USGS)*

Salient Statistics of Vanadium in the United States   In Metric Tons (Contained Vanadium)

		Vanadium Consumption by Uses in U.S.									Exports			Imports			
Year	Consumer & Producer Stocks, Dec. 31	Tool Steel	Cast Irons	Hign Strength, Low Alloy	Stainless & Heat Resisting	Superalloys	Carbon	Full Alloy	Total	Average $ Per Lb. V_2O_5	Vanadium Pentoxide, Anhydride	Oxides & Hydroxides	Ferro-Vanadium	Ores, Slag, Residues	Vanadium Pentoxide, Anhydride	Oxides & Hydroxides	Ferro-Vanadium
1988	1,266	481	20	1,339	41	9	1,259	887	4,834	3.40	620	-----	462	2,025	219	-----	108
1989	1,736	420	18	1,225	96	38	1,103	898	4,646	6.17	1,171	1,080	399	4,210	133	106	527
1990	1,082	421	18	1,122	38	42	994	814	4,081	4.21	819	976	271	3,826	83	217	244
1991	935	242	15	919	37	14	919	739	3,293	2.85	700	1,110	94	882	133	110	420
1992	1,084	453	17	989	28	13	1,262	828	4,079	2.28	26	1,113	213	838	206	103	592
1993	900	373	21	981	33	13	1,413	789	3,973	1.45	126	895	219	1,454	70	19	1,630
1994	1,110	424	31	979	26	16	1,680	777	4,290	1.55	335	1,050	374	1,900	294	3	1,910
1995	1,100	443	40	1,070	32	20	1,870	833	4,640	4.63	229	1,010	340	2,530	547	36	1,950
1996[1]	1,070	433	W	890	22	16	1,820	1,030	4,200	3.11	241	2,670	479	2,270	485	11	1,880
1997[2]	1,000	481	W	944	20	24	1,800	908	4,730	4.54	614	385	446	2,950	711	126	1,840

[1] Preliminary. [2] Estimate. W = Withheld proprietary data. *Source: U.S. Geological Survey (USGS)*

Vegetables

U.S. production of fresh tomatoes in 1998 was estimated at 3.62 billion pounds. That represented a decline of 4 percent from 1997. U.S. imports of fresh tomatoes in 1998 were forecast at 1.8 billion pounds, an increase of 10 percent from the previous season. The total supply of fresh tomatoes in 1998 was 5.42 billion pounds, virtually unchanged from 1997. In terms of use, exports of fresh tomatoes in 1998 were estimated at 320 million pounds, a decline of 6 percent from the previous year. Domestic use of fresh tomatoes was 5.1 billion pounds, little changed from 1997. U.S. per capita use of fresh tomatoes in 1998 was 18.9 pounds, the same as in 1997.

U.S. production of fresh head lettuce in 1998 was 6.88 billion pounds, about the same as in 1997. Imports of lettuce were 40 million pounds with the total supply of lettuce in 1998 being 6.92 billion pounds. In terms of usage, U.S. lettuce exports in 1998 were 400 million pounds, up 1 percent from 1997. Domestic utilization of fresh lettuce was 6.52 billion pounds, about unchanged from 1997. U.S. per capita use of lettuce in 1998 was 24.1 pounds.

U.S. production of fresh sweet corn in 1998 was 2.27 billion pounds, about unchanged from 1997. U.S. imports of sweet corn in 1998 were 25 million pounds. In terms of use, exports of sweet corn in 1998 were 110 million pounds, down 12 percent from 1997. Domestic utilization of sweet corn was 2.19 billion pounds, up 1 percent from 1997. Per capita use of fresh sweet corn in 1998 was 8.1 pounds, the same as in 1997.

Production of fresh carrots in 1998 was 3.46 billion pounds, up almost 3 percent from 1997. Imports of fresh carrots in 1998 were 223 million pounds. Domestic use of fresh carrots was 3.44 billion pounds while exports were 240 million pounds.

Commercial and Fresh Vegetables: Indices of Prices Received by Growers in the United States

Year	Jan.	Feb.	Mar.	Apr.	May	June	July	Aug.	Sept.	Oct.	Nov.	Dec.	Annual
					Commercial[1]		1990-92 = 100						
1992	97	118	144	106	93	94	102	113	115	125	109	121	111
1993	119	125	108	164	126	100	105	109	112	95	102	124	116
1994	114	111	92	87	97	104	97	94	104	117	123	163	109
1995	120	115	147	172	155	122	98	101	117	98	98	101	120
1996	93	109	143	120	102	115	97	115	100	107	110	94	109
1997	111	105	119	113	109	116	112	124	118	146	140	133	121
1998[2]	127	120	127	156	128	108	122	111	112	140			125
						Fresh[3]	1982 = 100						
1992	117.5	154.7	147.9	99.7	89.9	81.3	85.5	114.8	115.1	149.4	108.2	133.4	116.5
1993	128.8	125.8	117.4	178.5	163.5	80.7	98.4	110.5	117.0	89.5	141.1	167.0	126.5
1994	146.3	99.3	96.1	91.4	91.2	94.9	104.8	95.7	107.1	113.8	128.1	244.7	117.8
1995	163.5	149.2	159.2	199.1	167.2	127.2	107.3	94.8	152.9	116.0	115.8	125.5	139.8
1996	133.9	119.4	202.5	155.6	108.2	96.6	108.8	97.2	91.3	106.0	131.5	99.3	120.9
1997	105.2	126.2	150.4	109.6	103.2	112.2	115.7	125.2	121.8	143.1	124.7	118.5	121.3
1998[2]	133.1	136.6	148.2	162.9	123.2	106.5	153.7	114.9	135.0	161.9	131.2	148.1	137.9

Not seasonally adjusted. [1] Includes fresh and processing vegetable. [2] Preliminary. [3] Producer Price Index (0113-02). *Source: National Agricultural Statistics Service, U.S. Department of Agriculture (NASS-USDA)*

Processed Vegetables in the United States: Producer Price Indices 1982 = 100

Year	Jan.	Feb.	Mar.	Apr.	May	June	July	Aug.	Sept.	Oct.	Nov.	Dec.	Annual
						Canned[1] (0244)							
1992	110.3	109.7	109.3	108.9	109.8	109.4	109.5	109.6	109.2	109.1	109.5	109.8	109.5
1993	110.1	109.8	109.7	109.1	108.8	109.9	111.1	109.6	110.4	111.5	112.3	112.6	110.4
1994	113.1	115.1	116.8	116.5	117.9	118.0	118.9	118.1	116.0	116.0	114.0	112.4	116.1
1995	112.6	114.3	114.7	112.9	115.6	117.5	118.2	117.5	117.6	117.8	118.4	119.6	116.4
1996	120.4	119.8	120.4	120.4	120.8	121.0	122.6	122.1	121.9	121.8	121.9	121.8	121.2
1997	121.5	121.1	120.5	120.1	119.8	119.9	119.1	119.3	119.3	120.2	120.3	120.7	120.1
1998[2]	121.2	121.9	121.8	121.8	121.9	121.9	122.0	122.0	122.6	120.2	120.7	119.7	121.5
						Frozen (0245)							
1992	116.8	116.1	116.2	116.6	116.3	115.5	115.3	115.4	116.8	116.3	117.5	118.2	116.4
1993	118.0	118.0	117.9	118.7	119.9	121.1	121.3	122.1	122.6	123.2	123.7	124.7	120.9
1994	125.5	126.1	126.1	126.4	126.9	127.0	126.4	126.4	125.2	124.9	124.7	125.0	126.0
1995	125.1	124.7	124.9	125.1	124.3	123.6	123.2	123.6	124.4	124.6	123.7	124.0	124.3
1996	125.1	124.8	124.6	124.9	125.0	125.4	125.5	125.8	126.0	125.7	125.8	126.0	125.4
1997	125.9	125.7	125.6	125.6	125.7	125.7	126.9	125.6	125.7	126.6	125.5	125.3	125.8
1998[2]	125.2	126.0	124.8	125.7	125.0	124.6	125.5	125.6	125.3	126.0	125.6	125.1	125.4

Not seasonally adjusted. [1] Includes canned vegetables and juices, including hominy and mushrooms. [2] Preliminary. *Source: Bureau of Labor Statistics, U.S. Department of Labor (BLS)*

VEGETABLES

Per Capita Use of Selected Commercially Produced Fresh and Processing Vegetables in the United States

Pounds, Farm Weight Basis

Crop	1988	1989	1990	1991	1992	1993	1994	1995	1996	1997[9]	1998[10]
Asparagus, all	1.0	1.0	1.0	1.0	1.0	1.0	.9	1.0	.9	1.0	1.0
Fresh	.6	.6	.6	.6	.6	.6	.6	.6	.6	.7	.7
Canning	.3	.3	.3	.3	.3	.3	.2	.3	.2	.2	.2
Freezing	.1	.1	.1	.1	.1	.1	.1	.1	.1	.1	.1
Snap Beans, all	6.7	7.1	6.7	7.0	7.2	7.3	7.4	6.9	7.1	6.9	7.3
Fresh	1.2	1.2	1.1	1.1	1.5	1.5	1.6	1.7	1.4	1.4	1.5
Canning	3.8	3.9	3.7	4.1	4.0	4.0	3.8	3.5	3.8	3.7	3.9
Freezing	1.7	2.0	1.9	1.8	1.7	1.8	2.0	1.7	1.9	1.8	1.9
Broccoli, all[1]	6.2	6.0	5.6	5.4	5.8	5.2	6.2	6.6	7.1	7.5	7.5
Fresh	3.8	3.8	3.4	3.1	3.4	2.9	3.9	4.0	4.5	5.2	5.1
Freezing	2.4	2.2	2.2	2.3	2.4	2.3	2.3	2.6	2.6	2.3	2.4
Carrots, all[2]	10.4	11.5	11.9	11.2	12.3	12.0	12.8	13.1	14.4	16.4	16.7
Fresh	7.1	8.1	8.3	7.7	8.3	8.2	8.7	9.0	10.1	12.5	12.7
Canning	1.0	.9	1.3	1.1	1.7	1.0	1.3	1.5	1.5	1.3	1.3
Freezing	2.3	2.5	2.3	2.4	2.3	2.8	2.8	2.6	2.8	2.6	2.7
Cauliflower, all[1]	3.1	3.1	3.0	2.6	2.5	2.4	2.2	2.0	2.0	2.0	2.1
Fresh	2.2	2.3	2.2	2.0	1.8	1.7	1.6	1.4	1.5	1.6	1.6
Freezing	.9	.8	.8	.6	.7	.7	.6	.6	.5	.4	.5
Celery, fresh	7.2	7.5	7.2	6.8	7.4	7.1	6.8	6.4	6.3	6.0	5.9
Sweet Corn, all[3]	24.9	24.4	26.3	26.4	27.8	28.0	27.6	28.8	29.3	28.5	28.2
Fresh	5.8	6.5	6.7	5.9	6.9	7.0	8.2	7.8	8.3	8.1	8.1
Canning	10.4	9.5	11.0	11.1	11.9	11.2	10.2	10.5	10.5	10.0	9.5
Freezing	8.7	8.4	8.6	9.4	9.0	9.8	9.2	10.5	10.5	10.4	10.6
Cucumbers, all	10.1	10.0	9.7	9.7	9.6	9.7	10.2	10.9	10.1	11.6	11.2
Fresh	4.8	4.8	4.7	4.6	5.0	5.3	5.5	5.7	6.0	6.3	6.1
Pickles	5.3	5.2	5.0	5.1	4.6	4.4	4.7	5.2	4.1	5.3	5.1
Melons	23.8	26.5	24.6	23.4	25.4	25.0	25.8	26.8	30.1	30.4	31.9
Watermelon	13.5	13.6	13.3	12.8	14.8	14.6	15.4	15.7	17.4	16.1	17.0
Cantaloupe	7.9	10.4	9.2	8.7	8.5	8.7	8.6	9.2	10.6	11.7	12.2
Honeydew	2.4	2.5	2.1	1.9	2.1	1.7	1.8	1.9	2.1	2.6	2.7
Lettuce, Head	27.0	28.8	27.8	26.1	25.9	24.6	24.3	22.5	23.3	24.3	24.1
Onions, all	16.2	16.4	17.1	17.3	17.6	18.5	17.5	18.9	18.8	18.8	19.0
Fresh	14.5	14.8	15.1	15.7	16.2	16.5	16.5	17.6	17.9	17.9	18.0
Green peas, all[4]	3.7	3.7	4.2	4.2	4.1	3.5	3.7	3.7	3.4	3.5	3.6
Canning	1.8	1.7	2.0	1.9	2.1	1.6	1.5	1.6	1.5	1.5	1.5
Freezing	1.9	2.0	2.2	2.3	2.0	1.9	2.2	2.1	1.9	2.0	2.1
Tomatoes, all	78.1	86.2	90.9	92.8	89.2	92.4	90.1	92.8	92.2	91.6	92.0
Fresh	16.8	16.8	15.5	15.4	15.5	16.0	16.5	17.2	18.0	18.9	18.9
Canning	61.3	69.4	75.4	77.4	73.7	76.4	73.6	75.6	74.2	72.7	73.1
Subtotal, all[8]	249.5	263.7	268.1	267.2	271.7	274.6	273.2	276.9	284.4	287.2	291.1
Fresh	135.5	142.6	138.5	134.3	141.6	141.7	146.2	146.2	155.2	161.3	163.1
Canning	91.2	98.7	107.3	109.8	108.1	108.7	103.9	106.4	104.8	102.5	103.7
Freezing	21.1	20.8	20.3	21.5	20.6	22.2	22.1	23.0	23.5	22.5	23.3
Potatoes, all	122.4	127.1	124.1	134.5	130.7	134.9	140.2	138.1	145.2	142.1	142.7
Fresh	49.6	50.0	46.8	50.4	48.6	49.3	50.3	49.2	49.9	47.9	48.1
Processing	72.8	77.1	77.3	84.1	82.1	85.6	89.9	88.9	95.3	94.2	94.6
Sweetpotatoes, all	4.1	4.1	4.6	4.0	4.3	3.9	4.7	4.5	4.6	4.6	4.6
Total, all items	386.8	404.6	407.5	417.1	418.5	424.9	430.5	431.8	446.2	446.2	450.7

[1] All production for processing broccoli and cauliflower is for freezing. [2] Industry allocation suggests that 27% of processing carrot production is for canning and 73% is for freezing. [3] On-cob basis. [4] In-shell basis. [5] Includes artichokes, brussel sprouts, eggplant, endive/excarole, garlic, radishes and spinach. [6] Includes beets, chile peppers and spinach. [7] Includes green lima beans, spinach and miscellaneous freezing vegetables. [8] Fresch, canning and freezing data do not add to the total because onions are for dehydrating are included in total. [9] Preliminary. [10] Forecast. *Source: Economic Research Service, U.S. Department of Agriculture (ERS-USDA)*

Fresh Vegetables: Average Prices Received by Growers in the United States   Dollars Per Cwt.

Year	Jan.	Feb.	Mar.	Apr.	May	June	July	Aug.	Sept.	Oct.	Nov.	Dec.	Season Average
						Broccoli							
1996	34.60	22.00	30.90	25.20	28.20	30.60	24.10	24.10	23.90	24.30	31.10	28.60	27.10
1997	36.80	27.80	25.90	24.20	23.10	30.30	27.50	23.30	31.20	40.70	27.00	30.20	29.10
1998[1]	27.80	27.00	31.40	40.50	27.10	29.60	23.30	27.60	29.20	41.10			30.46
						Carrots							
1996	12.60	13.80	15.90	15.70	12.00	11.00	10.50	14.50	12.60	12.00	16.00	17.20	13.30
1997	15.00	14.80	13.50	12.60	12.60	12.60	12.60	13.20	12.70	12.00	12.50	16.80	13.10
1998[1]	12.70	13.00	13.20	12.20	12.10	11.60	10.60	11.00	10.90	10.50			11.78
						Cauliflower							
1996	35.20	36.10	52.80	37.00	37.70	35.70	24.30	27.20	23.80	29.20	30.00	31.10	33.00
1997	29.60	33.80	32.60	27.70	20.70	31.20	38.90	23.40	34.60	46.90	27.60	28.90	31.20
1998[1]	40.00	43.20	49.30	44.50	35.50	26.40	23.20	25.30	31.30	23.00			34.17
						Celery							
1996	7.90	8.50	12.20	11.60	8.90	11.50	11.50	10.30	11.60	9.79	12.40	13.40	10.60
1997	16.20	16.20	12.30	10.50	15.40	9.89	19.30	17.00	14.30	13.40	18.40	19.10	15.10
1998[1]	11.20	11.40	16.40	13.80	15.40	12.40	10.50	10.50	10.90	11.00			12.35
						Corn, Sweet							
1996	29.90	30.20	28.90	21.90	17.50	14.00	18.90	17.40	16.70	17.90	19.40	17.70	16.90
1997	29.00	25.80	33.90	26.00	21.20	17.00	18.40	18.10	16.90	15.30	18.90	19.90	17.60
1998[1]	23.10	32.30	24.50	22.90	16.80	12.30	15.00	17.30	18.30	22.10			20.46
						Lettuce, Head							
1996	11.30	14.90	16.50	13.20	13.30	15.20	12.70	23.50	13.70	15.40	17.70	8.87	14.70
1997	14.90	9.58	13.50	15.60	10.40	14.90	17.10	22.80	22.30	34.80	29.90	21.30	17.30
19981	19.00	10.90	13.40	27.90	14.70	11.40	15.40	16.20	14.00	24.30			16.72
						Tomatoes							
1996	18.40	40.00	81.70	50.50	24.40	24.20	26.00	22.10	23.40	28.30	29.70	30.40	28.00
1997	33.50	47.30	58.80	26.30	33.40	32.60	28.60	27.30	25.20	27.40	45.40	48.80	33.00
1998[1]	47.00	48.00	33.20	36.50	34.70	27.00	40.80	20.40	27.20	44.90			35.97

[1] Preliminary. *Source: National Agricultural Statistics Service, U.S. Department of Agriculture (NASS-USDA)*

Frozen Vegetables: January 1 and July 1 Cold Storage Holdings in the U.S.   In Thousands of Pounds

Crop	1994	1995		1996		1997		1998		1999[1]
	July 1	Jan. 1	July 1	Jan. 1	July 1	Jan. 1	July 1	Jan. 1	July 1	Jan. 1
Asparagus	19,175	9,808	15,493	9,689	14,001	8,353	12,276	6,908	11,766	6,162
Lima Beans	24,093	59,440	29,783	60,208	33,350	60,696	28,015	72,221	37,659	75,469
Snap Beans	71,457	244,681	87,436	224,297	80,224	202,648	95,868	230,661	91,266	213,400
Broccoli	152,312	109,076	110,075	136,850	150,883	120,972	108,411	112,311	108,673	113,752
Brussels sprouts	20,166	30,191	18,181	18,883	9,533	16,314	7,975	19,926	7,485	18,745
Carrots	165,748	271,244	176,054	307,645	177,248	283,770	162,153	300,870	163,176	256,623
Cauliflower	40,077	77,243	49,561	65,008	38,355	54,376	32,785	58,512	38,028	5,298
Corn, Sweet[2]	119,206	485,361	199,148	498,626	215,553	494,308	203,740	532,645	228,765	673,315
Mixed vegetables	51,737	58,272	59,414	60,492	67,031	54,208	50,755	45,744	79,375	53,020
Okra	31,799	62,491	43,367	39,954	23,902	28,576	18,711	52,230	63,950	46,567
Onions	31,296	51,244	42,810	48,761	38,342	40,790	37,817	42,218	33,598	40,348
Black-eyed peas	3,159	13,157	3,145	9,994	3,529	9,795	2,952	9,344	6,654	8,039
Green peas	218,032	260,487	219,669	281,349	163,293	224,134	137,615	219,533	230,233	277,858
Peas and carrots	14,063	9,329	9,034	10,401	8,340	6,731	6,840	5,760	7,154	10,285
Spinach	120,542	70,010	100,274	68,940	86,281	46,890	104,073	67,092	10,369	69,232
Squash	53,763	64,533	39,494	57,785	44,785	58,749	48,184	75,397	64,966	70,272
Southern greens	29,194	29,993	30,079	21,659	32,363	26,936	16,681	20,771	37,660	32,765
Other vegetables	238,554	241,252	189,124	319,519	235,880	314,640	253,158	285,670	251,391	301,595
Total	1,404,373	2,288,336	1,422,141	2,390,428	1,422,893	2,185,704	1,317,049	2,303,007	1,539,168	2,317,745
Potatoes	1,099,850	1,083,747	1,116,454	1,123,744	1,057,470	1,131,642	1,271,316	1,163,547	1,316,450	1,151,294
Grand total	2,504,223	3,372,083	2,538,595	3,514,172	2,480,363	3,317,346	2,588,365	3,466,554	2,855,618	3,469,039

[1] Preliminary. [2] Cut-basis with cob corn converted to cut-basis using a factor of 0.4706. *Source: National Agricultural Statistics Service, U.S. Department of Agriculture (NASS-USDA)*

Wheat

U.S. and world wheat prices were largely on the defensive during 1998, continuing a downtrend that took hold in 1996. The persistent weakness reflects large supplies and lackluster demand, notwithstanding some increase in the latter during 1998/99.

World wheat production in 1998/99 of 591 million metric tonnes compares with the record high 1997/98 crop of 612 million tonnes. Production in the mid-1990's averaged about 540 million tonnes. Global usage in 1998/99 of a record large 602 million tonnes compares with 588 million in 1997/98 which will require about an 8 million ton draw on carryover stocks, estimated at 126 million tonnes at yearend 1998/99. Still, carryover supplies appear adequate, certainly relative to the 106 million tonnes at yearend 1995/96, the lowest since the 1970's. The 1998/98 world stocks-to-usage ratio of about 21 percent compares with almost 24 percent a year earlier.

Since the late 1980's China has been the world's largest single wheat producer with nearly 20 percent of total production, 110 million tonnes in 1998/99 vs. a record large 123 million in 1997/98. China's wheat acreage and average yield, which had been trending higher through much of the 1990's, backtracked in 1998/99 due to untimely rains during the harvest of their winter crop. China's 1998/99 domestic wheat use was forecast at a record large 116 million tonnes, marginally higher than in 1997/98. Despite the apparent supply/demand imbalance, China's 1998/99 imports of only 2 million tonnes pale relative to the mid-1990's when 15 million tonnes were imported and reflect since then a large buildup in carryover supplies, estimated at nearly 30 million tonnes for the 1998/99 marketing year, about unchanged from 1997/98. However, China's wheat inventory totals tend to be suspect as is the government's willingness to utilize carryover supplies. What seems more certain is that China's import needs are very price sensitive and world prices can quickly strengthen on talk, real or otherwise, of Chinese buying which in turn brakes their interest. Still, 1.3 million tonnes net imports are estimated for 1998/99 after allowing for exports of 700,000 tonnes.

The persistent decline during the 1990's in the former U.S.S.R.'s wheat production still shows little sign of stopping: 1998/99 production in the key republics were forecast at: Russia, 28.5 million tonnes vs. 44.2 million in 1997/98; Kazakstan at 5.5 million vs. 8.5 million and the Ukraine at 15 million vs. 18.4 million, respectively. The smaller crops largely reflect lower average yield as acreage has been fairly stable. The Russian Federation was once the world's largest importer; Russia's 1998/99 imports of only 2 million tonnes compare with 14 million tonnes early in the 1990's, the drop reflecting a chronic lack of foreign exchange and/or credit. Consumption among the Russian republics has also dropped with Russia's use estimated at 36.5 million tonnes in 1998/99 vs. 39 million in 1997/98 and more than 50 million on average early in the 1990's. The Ukraine's 1998/99 usage of 16 million tonnes compares with the early 1990's average of more than 20 million.

The 1998/99 world wheat trade is forecast at 98 million tonnes vs. the record large 100.1 million in 1997/98. Four countries generally account for about two-thirds of total exports: Argentina, Australia, Canada and the U.S. with the E.U. supplying much of the balance. The U.S., the largest exporter, is forecast to ship 29.5 million tonnes in 1998/99 vs. 28.1 million in 1997/98, and a mid-1990's average of about 33 million tonnes. Canadian 1998/99 exports were forecast at 15.5 million tonnes vs. 21.3 million in 1997/98; and E.U. exports of 17 million compare with 15.5 million, respectively. Australian exports have soared to 16.5 million tonnes in 1998/99 from a mid-1990's average of less than 10 million. Importing nations are scattered, among those taking at least 5 million tonnes in 1998/99 were Brazil, Egypt, and Japan.

The U.S. 1998 wheat crop of 2.56 billion bushels compares with 2.53 million in 1997/98. The marginal increase reflected a record high average yield--43.3 bushels per acre vs. 39.7--which more than offset a planted acreage of 66.2 million acres vs. 71 million, respectively. Winter wheat accounts for more than half of U.S. production, 1.9 billion bushels in 1998/99, about unchanged from 1997/98. Kansas is the largest producing state and North Dakota the largest spring wheat and durum producing state. The 1998/99 durum wheat crop of 141 million bushels compares with 86 million in 1997/98; other spring wheat production was put at 529 million bushels vs. 558 million.

The U.S. imports some wheat, mostly from Canada. Carryin stocks as of June 1, 1998 of 722 million bushels compare with 444 million a year earlier. The U.S. wheat supply for 1998/99 of 3.37 billion bushels, a ten year high, compares with 3.06 billion in 1997/98. Total usage in 1998/99 of 2.47 billion bushels compares with 2.34 billion in 1997/98. Exports generally account for almost half the total disappearance. Food use takes about two-thirds of domestic usage, feed about 20 percent and seed the balance. If the 1998/99 supply/demand estimates are realized, ending stocks on May 31, 1999 would rise to at least 900 million bushels, boosting the stock to use ratio to 36 percent vs. 31 percent a year earlier. This ratio is often used to forecast prices, the smaller it is the greater the likelihood for higher prices as the crop year progresses.

The 1998/99 average price received by farmers was forecast to range from $2.45 to $2.75 a bushel vs. $3.38 in 1997/98 and the 1990's high of $4.55 in 1995/96.

Futures Markets

Wheat futures and options are traded on the London Commodity Exchange (LCE), the Chicago Board of Trade (CBOT), the Kansas City Board of Trade (KCBT), the Minneapolis Grain Exchange (MGE), and the Mid America Commodity Exchange (MidAm). Feed wheat futures and options are traded on the Winnipeg Commodity Exchange (WCE).

World Production of Wheat In Thousands of Metric Tons

Crop Year	Argentina	Australia	Canada	China	France	Germany	India	Pakistan	Russia[4]	Turkey	United Kingdom	United States	World Total
1989-90	10,150	14,214	24,796	90,807	32,100	14,482	54,110	14,419	87,151	12,500	14,030	55,428	533,001
1990-1	10,900	15,066	32,098	98,229	33,600	15,242	49,850	14,429	49,596	16,000	14,000	74,292	587,995
1991-2	9,880	10,557	31,946	96,000	34,594	16,610	55,134	14,565	38,900	16,500	14,400	53,891	542,132
1992-3	9,800	16,184	29,871	101,590	32,777	15,542	55,690	15,684	46,170	15,500	14,000	67,135	561,807
1993-4	9,700	16,479	27,232	106,390	29,630	15,767	57,210	16,157	43,500	16,500	12,900	65,220	559,216
1994-5	11,300	8,903	23,122	99,300	30,550	16,480	59,840	15,212	32,100	14,700	13,314	63,167	525,196
1995-6	8,600	16,504	25,037	102,215	30,860	17,760	65,470	17,002	30,100	15,500	14,310	59,400	538,126
1996-7[1]	15,900	23,702	29,801	110,570	35,940	18,920	62,097	16,907	34,900	16,000	16,100	62,191	582,947
1997-8[2]	14,800	19,417	24,280	123,300	34,000	19,870	69,275	16,650	44,200	16,000	15,050	68,761	610,979
1998-9[3]	10,500	22,000	23,300	110,000	36,000	20,000	67,000	18,700	28,000	18,000	17,000	69,604	588,295

[1] Preliminary. [2] Estimate. [3] Forecast. [4] Formerly part of the U.S.S.R.; data not reported separately until 1990-91. *Source: Foreign Agricultural Service, U.S. Department of Agriculture (FAS-USDA)*

World Supply and Demand of Wheat In Millions of Metric Tons/Hectares

Crop Year	Area Harvested	Yield	Production	World Trade	Utilization Total	Ending Stocks	Stocks as % of Utilization
1989-90	225.8	2.36	533.2	103.9	532.7	118.9	22.3
1990-1	231.4	2.54	588.0	101.0	561.5	145.4	25.9
1991-2	222.5	2.44	542.1	110.8	554.7	132.8	23.9
1992-3	223.1	2.52	561.8	112.7	549.9	144.8	26.3
1993-4	222.3	2.52	559.2	100.2	561.9	142.1	25.3
1994-5	215.5	2.44	525.2	100.1	548.2	118.6	21.6
1995-6	219.8	2.45	538.1	98.2	550.9	105.8	19.2
1996-7[1]	231.2	2.52	582.9	100.8	577.6	111.1	19.2
1997-8[2]	229.9	2.66	611.0	100.5	585.3	136.8	23.4
1998-9[3]	225.1	2.61	588.3	97.7	601.4	123.8	20.6

[1] Preliminary. [2] Estimate. [3] Forecast. *Source: Foreign Agricultural Service, U.S. Department of Agriculture (FAS-USDA)*

Salient Statistics of Wheat in the United States

Crop Year	Planting Intentions	Acreage Harvested: Winter	Acreage Harvested: Spring	Acreage Harvested: All	Average - All Yield Per Acre	Value of Production	Foreign Trade[5]: Domestic Exports[2]	Foreign Trade[5]: Imports[3]	Per Capita[4] Consumption: Flour	Per Capita[4] Consumption: Cereal
	1,000 Acres				in Bushels	$1,000	Millions of Bushels		In Pounds	
1989-90	76,615	41,509	20,680	62,189	32.7	7,542,464	1,232.0	22.5	129.6	4.0
1990-1	77,041	49,721	19,382	69,103	39.5	7,184,427	1,069.5	36.4	135.8	4.3
1991-2	69,881	39,506	18,297	57,803	34.3	5,956,642	1,282.3	40.7	136.5	4.5
1992-3	72,219	42,123	20,638	62,761	39.3	7,978,911	1,353.6	70.0	138.3	4.7
1993-4	72,168	43,811	18,901	62,712	38.2	7,647,527	1,227.8	108.9	143.0	5.0
1994-5	70,349	41,335	20,415	61,770	37.6	7,968,237	1,188.3	91.9	144.0	5.1
1995-6	69,132	40,972	19,973	60,945	35.8	9,787,213	1,241.1	67.9	142.0	5.4
1996-7	75,105	39,574	23,245	62,819	36.3	9,782,238	1,001.4	92.3	146.0	5.4
1997-8	70,412	41,340	21,500	62,840	39.5	8,286,741	1,040.2	94.8	148.0	-----
1998-9[1]	65,871	40,126	18,876	59,002	43.2	6,931,996	1,025.0	95.0		

[1] Preliminary. [2] Includes flour milled from imported wheat. [3] Total wheat, flour & other products. [4] Civilian only. [5] Year beginning June.
Source: Economic Research Service, U.S. Department of Agriculture (ERS-USDA)

Supply and Distribution of Wheat in the United States In Millions of Bushels

Crop Year Beginning June	Supply: Stocks, June 1: On Farms	Supply: Stocks, June 1: Mills, Elevators[3]	Supply: Stocks, June 1: Total Stocks	Supply: Production	Supply: Imports[4]	Supply: Total Supply	Domestic Disappearance: Food	Domestic Disappearance: Seed	Domestic Disappearance: Feed & Residual[5]	Domestic Disappearance: Total	Exports[4]	Total Disappearance
1989-90	289.0	412.6	701.6	2,036.6	22.5	2,761.0	748.9	104.3	139.1	992.3	1,232.0	2,224.0
1990-1	212.5	324.0	536.5	2,729.8	36.4	3,303.0	789.8	92.9	482.1	1,365.1	1,069.5	2,435.0
1991-2	341.2	524.7	868.1	1,980.1	40.7	2,889.0	789.5	97.7	244.5	1,131.6	1,282.3	2,414.0
1992-3	144.6	327.2	475.0	2,466.8	70.0	3,011.8	834.8	99.1	193.6	1,127.5	1,353.6	2,481.2
1993-4	183.8	345.3	530.7	2,396.4	108.8	3,035.9	871.7	96.3	271.7	1,239.7	1,227.8	2,467.4
1994-5	175.3	393.2	568.5	2,321.0	91.9	2,981.4	852.9	89.2	344.4	1,286.5	1,188.3	2,474.8
1995-6	163.4	343.2	506.6	2,182.7	67.9	2,757.2	882.9	103.5	153.7	1,140.1	1,241.1	2,381.2
1996-7	74.6	301.4	376.0	2,277.4	92.3	2,745.7	890.8	102.3	307.6	1,300.7	1,001.4	2,302.1
1997-8[1]	154.6	289.0	443.6	2,481.5	94.8	3,019.9	916.7	92.6	248.0	1,257.2	1,040.2	2,297.4
1998-9[2]	224.2	498.3	722.5	2,550.4	95.0	3,367.9	925.0	88.0	350.0	1,363.0	1,025.0	2,388.0

[1] Preliminary. [2] Estimate. [3] Also warehouses and all off-farm storage not otherwise disignated, including flour mills. [4] Imports & exports are for wheat, including flour & other products in terms of wheat. [5] Mostly feed use. *Source: Economic Research Service, U.S. Department of Agriculture (ERS-USDA)*

WHEAT

Stocks, Production and Exports of Wheat in the United States, by Class In Millions of Bushels

Year Beginning June	Hard Spring June 1 Stocks	Hard Spring Production	Hard Spring Exports[3]	Durum[2] June 1 Stocks	Durum[2] Production	Durum[2] Exports[3]	Hard Winter June 1 Stocks	Hard Winter Production	Hard Winter Exports[3]	Soft Red Winter June 1 Stocks	Soft Red Winter Production	Soft Red Winter Exports[3]	White June 1 Stocks	White Production	White Exports[3]
1989-90	219	433	280	60	92	55	302	711	359	39	549	345	81	251	193
1990-1	155	555	201	50	122	53	215	1,196	369	32	344	230	85	313	216
1991-2	279	431	380	62	104	45	360	901	559	80	325	105	87	219	193
1992-3	131	707	438	55	100	47	194	967	464	41	427	210	54	266	195
1993-4	171	512	266	49	70	54	204	1,066	486	43	401	173	64	347	249
1994-5	201	515	292	28	97	40	227	971	422	45	434	212	67	304	222
1995-6	193	475	330	26	102	39	194	825	384	37	456	250	57	325	238
1996-7	106	631	300	25	116	38	154	759	286	35	420	140	55	352	237
1997-8	166	491	240	31	88	57	143	1,098	358	45	472	180	59	332	205
1998-9[1]	220	487	260	26	141	37	307	1,182	438	80	443	75	90	298	215

[1] Preliminary. [2] Includes "Red Durum." [3] Includes flour made from U.S. wheat & shipments to territories. [4] Estimate. *Source: Economic Research Service, U.S. Department of Agriculture (ERS-USDA)*

Seeded Acreage, Yield and Production of Wheat in the United States

Year	Seeded Acreage--1,000 Acres Winter	Other Spring	Durum	All	Yield Per Harvested Acre (Bushels) Winter	Other Spring	Durum	All	Production (1,000,000 Bushels) Winter	Other Spring	Durum	All
1989	55,091	17,733	3,791	76,615	35.0	28.8	25.1	32.7	1,454.6	489.7	92.2	2,036.6
1990	56,748	16,723	3,570	77,041	40.7	36.7	34.9	39.5	2,024.2	583.1	122.4	2,729.8
1991	51,024	15,604	3,253	69,881	34.7	33.4	32.5	34.3	1,371.6	504.6	104.0	1,980.1
1992	50,922	18,750	2,547	72,219	38.2	41.8	39.7	39.3	1,609.3	757.6	99.9	2,466.8
1993	51,587	18,340	2,241	72,168	40.2	33.7	33.6	38.2	1,760.1	565.8	70.5	2,396.4
1994	49,197	18,329	2,823	70,349	40.2	31.8	35.6	37.6	1,661.9	562.3	96.7	2,321.0
1995	48,726	17,015	3,436	69,177	39.4	30.2	30.5	35.8	1,547.3	535.9	102.3	2,185.5
1996	51,445	20,030	3,630	75,105	37.1	35.1	32.6	36.3	1,469.6	691.7	116.1	2,277.4
1997	47,985	19,117	3,310	70,412	44.6	29.9	27.6	39.5	1,845.5	548.2	87.8	2,481.5
1998[1]	46,449	15,617	3,805	65,871	46.9	34.9	37.8	43.2	1,880.6	528.7	141.1	2,550.4

[1] Preliminary. *Source: Economic Research Service, U.S. Department of Agriculture (ERS-USDA)*

Production of Winter Wheat in the United States, by State In Thousands of Bushels

Year	Colorado	Idaho	Illinois	Kansas	Missouri	Montana	Nebraska	Ohio	Oklahoma	Oregon	Texas	Washington	Total
1989	57,200	56,700	105,020	213,600	86,950	54,000	55,350	62,730	153,900	48,900	60,000	68,900	1,454,642
1990	84,150	69,000	91,200	472,000	76,000	87,500	85,500	79,650	201,600	54,600	130,200	138,600	2,024,224
1991	71,300	49,000	44,800	363,000	48,000	76,000	67,200	52,920	135,000	41,600	84,000	40,600	1,371,617
1992	70,500	55,250	62,100	363,800	64,800	65,250	55,500	59,095	168,150	42,900	129,200	102,000	1,609,284
1993	94,350	67,150	68,200	388,500	53,200	102,900	73,500	52,520	156,600	61,060	118,400	162,500	1,760,143
1994	76,500	56,880	50,400	433,200	50,400	64,750	71,400	68,440	143,100	55,680	75,400	124,200	1,661,943
1995	102,600	58,520	68,110	286,000	47,970	54,800	86,100	73,810	109,200	57,750	75,600	133,300	1,544,653
1996	70,400	68,800	41,800	255,200	48,750	61,380	73,500	51,870	93,100	58,680	75,400	164,500	1,469,618
1997	86,400	68,800	66,490	501,400	58,320	55,100	70,300	68,670	169,600	53,790	118,900	141,900	1,845,528
1998[1]	99,450	63,140	57,600	494,900	57,500	48,750	82,800	74,240	198,900	52,930	136,500	136,500	1,880,605

[1] Preliminary. *Source: Crop Reporting Board, U.S. Department of Agriculture (CRB-USDA)*

Official Winter Wheat Crop Production Reports in the United States In Thousands of Bushels

Crop Year	May 1	June 1	July 1	August 1	September 1	Current December	Final
1989-90	1,430,148	1,407,898	1,461,924	1,466,049	1,451,746	1,453,842	1,454,642
1990-1	2,091,614	2,089,234	2,035,087	2,054,287	2,036,059	----------	2,030,874
1991-2	1,495,943	1,449,418	1,361,316	1,371,946	1,372,182	----------	1,372,617
1992-3	1,618,017	1,618,017	1,573,901	1,600,931	----------	----------	1,609,284
1993-4	1,807,657	1,824,062	1,821,345	1,788,005	1,788,005	----------	1,760,143
1994-5	1,657,938	1,674,563	1,658,426	1,670,436	1,670,436	----------	1,661,043
1995-6	1,638,211	1,608,396	1,529,950	1,552,230	1,552,230	----------	1,544,653
1996-7	1,363,851	1,369,861	1,484,836	1,494,716	----------	----------	1,477,058
1997-8	1,561,470	1,603,580	1,780,554	1,855,474	----------	----------	1,882,609
1998-9[1]	1,706,784	1,743,294	1,898,719	1,914,359	----------	----------	1,887,395

[1] Preliminary. *Source: Crop Reporting Board, U.S. Department of Agriculture (CRB-USDA)*

Production of All Spring Wheat in the United States In Thousands of Bushels

	Durum Wheat						Other Spring Wheat							
Year	Arizona	Cali-fornia	Mon-tana	North Dakota	South Dakota	Total Durum	Idaho	Minne-sota	Mon-tana	North Dakota	Oregon	South Dakota	Wash-ington	Total Other
1989	7,560	8,715	6,030	66,000	2,880	92,229	34,720	96,900	85,000	174,000	4,935	45,100	41,710	489,747
1990	4,136	5,346	4,465	103,700	3,204	122,171	30,600	134,750	53,900	277,200	3,016	67,200	11,480	583,124
1991	3,705	3,360	5,907	88,350	1,675	103,957	32,660	64,170	81,600	212,350	2,300	49,000	58,000	504,565
1992	3,740	5,115	4,851	81,700	990	99,906	44,840	137,500	79,050	382,200	4,900	85,000	17,640	757,608
1993	4,500	3,800	3,534	57,970	432	70,476	43,200	69,750	99,900	274,350	3,900	54,540	15,080	565,821
1994	8,554	5,605	5,340	76,375	598	96,747	43,400	70,000	100,500	278,775	2,900	51,480	9,800	562,291
1995	8,514	6,800	7,950	77,760	896	102,280	44,800	70,400	133,000	221,400	5,928	33,600	20,470	535,658
1996	14,760	13,800	7,000	79,380	720	116,090	50,400	105,000	106,600	313,500	6,405	83,250	18,170	691,680
1997	8,010	13,680	7,540	57,860	513	87,783	45,030	75,200	118,900	210,000	6,600	63,000	23,220	548,155
1998[1]	15,120	15,750	12,040	97,350	624	141,069	39,270	78,720	108,000	211,200	4,560	59,200	20,925	528,709

[1] Preliminary. *Source: Crop Reporting Board, U.S. Department of Agriculture (CRB-USDA)*

Grindings of Wheat by Mills in the United States In Millions of Bushels (60 Pounds Each)

Year	July	Aug.	Sept.	Oct.	Nov.	Dec.	Jan.	Feb.	Mar.	Apr.	May	June	Total
1989-90	58.5	70.6	63.6	67.4	65.1	58.7	63.4	64.0	66.7	61.6	63.6	60.6	763.8
1990-1	62.3	73.2	65.7	74.9	73.9	64.3	66.7	65.2	63.2	67.6	69.9	60.9	807.8
1991-2	65.3	71.2	67.7	72.2	73.5	65.6	65.7	66.0	65.6	67.3	67.0	67.2	814.3
1992-3	70.0	77.3	71.9	77.9	71.9	65.5	68.1	70.0	76.2	72.0	69.6	67.9	858.2
1993-4	69.2	75.2	74.1	75.8	77.0	76.3	70.0	68.3	81.1	73.0	73.0	70.6	883.8
1994-5	68.9	78.7	76.3	77.9	75.9	71.1	69.0	65.2	76.9	66.6	74.7	71.9	873.1
1995-6	69.8	77.8	74.2	78.4	74.8	70.0	70.1	72.4	72.1	69.4	72.6	67.7	869.1
1996-7	73.6	77.4	75.1	82.7	73.7	71.3	69.6	66.9	70.3	73.2	72.5	72.2	878.6
1997-8	76.4	75.8	78.4	82.7	75.3	74.8	---------	217.0	---------	---------	218.1	---------	898.5
1998-9[1]	---------	226.4	---------	---------	241.1	---------	---------		---------	---------		---------	935.0

[1] Preliminary. *Source: Bureau of the Census, U.S. Department of Commerce*

Wheat Stocks in the United States In Millions of Bushels

	On Farms				Off Farms				Total Stocks			
Year	Mar. 1	June 1	Sept. 1	Dec. 1	Mar. 1	June 1	Sept. 1	Dec. 1	Mar. 1	June 1	Sept. 1	Dec. 1
1989	463.0	289.0	832.0	592.0	764.7	412.6	1,086.0	830.5	1,227.7	701.6	1,918.0	1,422.5
1990	376.0	212.5	1,000.0	763.2	567.1	324.0	1,409.5	1,144.8	943.1	536.5	2,409.5	1,909.5
1991	532.9	341.2	828.0	564.8	863.3	524.7	1,212.7	877.3	1,396.3	865.9	2,040.7	1,442.1
1992	275.6	144.6	979.4	672.0	611.7	327.2	1,128.2	918.5	887.2	471.9	2,107.6	1,590.5
1993	378.0	183.8	987.0	653.1	670.3	346.8	1,145.6	932.6	1,048.3	530.7	2,132.6	1,585.7
1994	363.2	175.3	859.8	575.6	664.8	393.2	1,209.7	920.6	1,028.0	568.5	2,069.5	1,491.1
1995	335.3	163.4	743.6	477.0	633.8	343.2	1,137.5	861.3	969.1	506.6	1,881.1	1,338.3
1996	220.6	74.6	824.5	584.2	602.9	301.4	899.7	634.7	823.5	376.0	1,724.2	1,218.8
1997	320.8	154.6	794.4	604.0	501.1	289.0	1,282.0	1,015.2	821.8	443.6	2,076.3	1,619.2
1998[1]	399.9	224.2	885.7	680.2	766.6	498.3	1,499.8	1,211.7	1,166.6	722.5	2,385.5	1,891.9

[1] Preliminary. *Source: Crop Reporting Board, U.S. Department of Agriculture (CRB-USDA)*

Wheat Supply and Distribution in Canada, Australia and Argentina In Millions of Metric Tons

	Canada (Year Beginning Aug. 1)					Australia (Year Beginning Oct. 1)					Argentina (Year Beginning Dec. 1)				
	Supply			Disappearance		Supply			Disappearance		Supply			Disappearance	
Crop Year	Stocks Aug. 1	New Crop	Total Supply	Domestic	Exports[3]	Stocks Oct. 1	New Crop	Total Supply	Domestic	Exports[3]	Stocks Dec. 1	New Crop	Total Supply	Domestic	Exports[3]
1989-90	5.0	24.8	29.8	6.5	16.9	2.6	14.2	16.8	3.0	10.8	.5	10.2	10.7	4.5	6.1
1990-1	6.4	32.1	38.5	6.5	20.5	3.0	15.1	18.1	3.5	11.7	0	10.9	10.9	4.5	4.8
1991-2	10.3	31.9	42.3	7.8	24.5	2.8	10.6	13.4	3.4	7.1	.8	9.9	10.7	4.6	5.8
1992-3	10.1	29.9	40.1	8.1	19.7	2.9	16.2	19.1	4.2	9.9	.3	9.8	10.1	4.3	5.9
1993-4	12.2	27.2	39.4	9.3	19.1	5.0	16.5	21.5	4.1	13.7	0	9.7	9.7	4.3	5.0
1994-5	11.1	23.1	34.2	7.8	20.9	3.7	8.9	12.7	3.9	6.3	.4	11.3	11.7	4.3	7.3
1995-6	5.7	25.0	30.7	7.8	16.3	2.4	16.5	18.9	4.2	13.3	.2	8.6	8.8	4.2	4.5
1996-7	6.7	29.8	36.5	8.2	19.5	1.5	23.7	25.2	3.6	19.2	.2	15.9	16.1	5.1	10.2
1997-8[1]	9.0	24.3	33.3	7.4	20.2	2.4	19.4	21.8	5.0	15.5	.8	14.8	15.6	4.9	10.0
1998-9[2]	6.0	23.3	29.3	8.2	15.0	1.3	22.0	23.3	5.3	15.0	.7	10.5	11.2	4.8	6.0

[1] Preliminary. [2] Forecast. [3] Including flour. *Source: Foreign Agricultural Service, U.S. Department of Agriculture (FAS-USDA)*

WHEAT

Quarterly Supply and Disappearance of Wheat in the United States In Millions of Bushels

Crop Year Beginning June 1	Supply				Disappearance						Ending Stocks		
					Domestic Use								
	Beginning Stocks	Production	Imports[3]	Total Supply	Food	Seed	Feed & Residual[7]	Total	Exports[3]	Total Disap-pearance	Gov't Owned[4]	Privately Owned[5]	Total Stocks
1988-9	1,261.0	1,812.2	22.6	3,095.7	725.8	103.0	150.5	979.3	1,414.9	2,394.2	190.5	511.1	701.6
June-Aug.	1,261.0	1,812.2	8.6	3,081.6	183.3	1.0	282.2	466.5	361.6	828.1	250.0	2,003.6	2,253.6
Sept.-Nov.	2,254.0	--------	6.3	2,259.8	197.3	67.0	-49.4	214.9	329.0	543.9	213.0	1,502.9	1,715.9
Dec.-Feb.	1,716.0	--------	3.7	1,719.6	173.4	3.0	-44.5	131.9	360.0	491.9	203.2	1,024.5	1,227.7
Mar.-May	1,228.0	--------	4.1	1,231.9	171.8	32.0	-37.8	166.0	364.2	530.2	190.5	511.1	701.6
1989-90	701.6	2,036.6	23.4	2,760.7	748.9	104.3	139.1	992.3	1,232.0	2,224.3	116.6	419.9	536.5
June-Aug.	701.6	2,036.6	5.9	2,744.1	190.7	1.7	264.9	457.3	368.7	826.0	167.9	1,750.1	1,918.0
Sept.-Nov.	1,918.0	--------	7.1	1,925.1	191.7	70.3	-87.8	174.2	328.6	502.8	154.5	1,268.0	1,422.5
Dec.-Feb.	1,423.0	--------	4.7	1,427.1	184.3	2.7	37.4	224.4	259.6	484.0	136.5	806.6	943.1
Mar.-May	943.1	--------	5.8	947.9	182.2	29.6	-75.4	136.4	275.1	411.5	116.6	419.9	536.5
1990-1	536.5	2,729.8	36.4	3,302.6	789.8	92.9	482.4	1,365.1	1,069.5	2,434.6	162.7	705.4	868.1
June-Aug.	536.5	2,729.8	8.0	3,274.2	194.1	1.7	399.7	595.5	267.7	863.2	104.6	2,306.5	2,411.1
Sept.-Nov.	2,409.5	--------	13.4	2,424.5	210.6	62.9	-38.3	235.2	279.4	514.6	129.9	1,780.0	1,909.9
Dec.-Feb.	1,908.0	--------	7.8	1,917.7	191.0	2.1	101.5	294.6	225.5	520.1	152.5	1,245.2	1,397.7
Mar.-May	1,396.0	--------	7.2	1,404.9	194.1	26.3	19.5	239.9	296.9	536.8	162.7	705.4	868.1
1991-2	868.1	1,980.1	40.7	2,889.0	789.5	97.2	244.5	1,131.2	1,282.3	2,413.5	152.0	323.0	475.0
June-Aug.	868.1	1,980.1	7.8	2,856.1	189.4	1.2	359.1	549.7	251.7	801.4	162.8	1,891.9	2,054.7
Sept.-Nov.	2,054.7	--------	7.3	2,062.0	213.0	62.2	-26.9	248.3	365.9	614.2	160.7	1,287.1	1,447.8
Dec.-Feb.	1,447.8	--------	10.7	1,458.5	192.9	2.4	-.5	194.8	371.7	566.5	156.9	735.1	892.0
Mar.-May	892.0	--------	14.9	906.9	194.2	31.9	-87.3	138.8	293.0	431.8	152.0	323.0	475.0
1992-3	475.0	2,466.8	70.0	3,011.8	834.3	99.1	194.2	1,127.6	1,353.6	2,481.2	150.0	380.7	530.7
June-Aug.	475.0	2,466.8	20.1	2,962.0	212.1	1.4	345.3	558.8	282.6	841.4	151.6	1,969.0	2,120.6
Sept.-Nov.	2,120.6	--------	16.4	2,137.0	218.8	63.4	-81.9	200.3	345.0	545.3	151.1	1,440.6	1,591.7
Dec.-Feb.	1,591.7	--------	17.4	1,609.1	196.7	2.6	5.2	204.5	356.3	560.8	150.4	897.9	1,048.3
Mar.-May	1,048.3	--------	16.1	1,064.4	206.7	31.7	-74.4	164.0	369.7	533.7	150.0	380.7	530.7
1993-4	530.7	2,396.4	108.8	3,035.9	871.7	96.3	271.7	1,239.7	1,227.8	2,467.4	150.3	418.2	568.5
June-Aug.	530.7	2,396.4	14.6	2,941.7	211.3	1.3	295.8	508.4	300.7	809.1	149.9	1,982.7	2,132.6
Sept.-Nov.	2,132.6	--------	30.1	2,162.7	225.3	60.9	-38.5	247.7	329.2	577.0	150.3	1,435.4	1,585.7
Dec.-Feb.	1,585.7	--------	26.9	1,612.6	211.0	2.3	39.0	252.3	332.3	584.6	150.4	877.6	1,028.0
Mar.-May	1,028.0	--------	37.2	1,065.2	224.1	31.8	-24.7	231.2	265.5	496.7	150.3	418.2	568.5
1994-5	568.5	2,321.0	92.0	2,981.4	852.5	89.2	344.9	1,286.6	1,188.3	2,474.9	142.1	364.5	506.6
June-Aug.	568.5	2,321.0	30.7	2,920.2	213.2	1.6	376.3	591.1	259.6	850.7	146.4	1,923.1	2,069.5
Sept.-Nov.	2,069.5	--------	21.4	2,090.9	229.3	61.1	-28.8	261.6	338.2	599.8	142.8	1,348.3	1,491.1
Dec.-Feb.	1,491.1	--------	17.7	1,508.8	201.5	2.2	25.6	229.3	310.4	539.7	142.3	826.8	969.1
Mar.-May	969.1	--------	22.2	991.2	208.5	24.3	-28.2	204.6	280.1	484.7	142.1	364.5	506.6
1995-6	506.6	2,182.6	67.9	2,757.1	882.9	104.1	153.0	1,139.9	1,241.1	2,381.1	118.2	257.8	376.0
June-Aug.	506.6	2,182.6	22.7	2,711.9	215.3	8.0	305.0	528.3	302.5	830.8	141.5	1,739.6	1,881.1
Sept.-Nov.	1,881.1	--------	16.3	1,897.4	232.2	64.9	-98.7	198.3	360.8	559.1	141.2	1,197.1	1,338.3
Dec.-Feb.	1,338.3	--------	11.8	1,350.0	215.8	3.0	13.3	232.1	294.5	526.6	137.5	686.0	823.5
Mar.-May	823.5	--------	17.2	840.7	219.6	28.2	-66.5	181.3	283.4	464.6	118.2	257.8	376.0
1996-7	376.0	2,277.0	92.4	2,753.5	891.4	103.1	314.0	1,308.5	1,001.4	2,309.9	93.0	350.6	443.6
June-Aug.	376.0	2,277.0	14.9	2,676.0	223.7	8.8	385.3	617.8	334.1	951.9	109.5	1,614.7	1,724.2
Sept.-Nov.	1,724.2	--------	20.7	1,744.9	233.8	60.4	-76.4	217.8	308.3	526.1	96.1	1,122.7	1,218.8
Dec.-Feb.	1,218.8	--------	27.1	1,245.9	213.1	1.8	29.9	244.8	179.3	424.1	95.3	726.5	821.8
Mar.-May	821.8	--------	29.7	851.6	220.8	32.1	-24.8	228.1	179.8	407.9	93.0	350.6	443.6
1997-8[1]	443.6	2,481.0	95.0	3,020.0	917.0	93.0	248.0	1,258.0	1,040.0	2,298.0			722.0
June-Aug.	443.6	2,481.0	23.0	2,948.0	228.0	3.0	352.0	583.0	288.0	871.0			2,076.0
Sept.-Nov.	2,076.0	--------	23.0	2,099.0	239.0	59.0	-113.0	185.0	296.0	481.0			1,619.0
Dec.-Feb.	1,619.0	--------	24.0	1,643.0	220.0	2.0	-1.0	221.0	255.0	476.0			1,167.0
Mar.-May	1,167.0	--------	26.0	1,192.0	230.0	29.0	10.0	269.0	201.0	470.0			722.0
1998-9[2]	722.0	2,550.0	95.0	3,368.0	925.0	88.0	350.0	1,363.0	1,025.0	2,388.0			980.0
June-Aug.	722.0	2,550.0	24.0	3,297.0	227.0	1.0	426.0	654.0	257.0	911.0			2,385.0
Sept.-Nov.	2,385.0	--------	24.0	2,409.0	243.0	55.0	-72.0	226.0	292.0	518.0			1,892.0

[1] Preliminary. [2] Forecast. [3] Imports & exports include flour and other products expressed in wheat equivalent. [4] Uncommitted, Government only. [5] Includes total loans. [6] Includes alcoholic beverages. *Source: Economic Research Service, U.S. Department of Agriculture (ERS-USDA)*

Wheat Government Loan Program Data in the United States   Loan Rates (Cents Per Bushel)

Crop Year Beginning June	National Average[3]	Target Rate	Farm Loan Prices: Corn Belt (Soft Red Winter)	Farm Loan Prices: Central & Southern Plains (Hard Winter)	Farm Loan Prices: Northern Plains (Spring & Durum)	Farm Loan Prices: Pacific Northwest (White)	Placed Under Loan	% of Production	Acquired by CCC Under Program	Stocks Ending May 31: Total Stocks	Total CCC Stocks	Outstanding: CCC Loans	Outstanding: Farmer-Owned Reserve	"Free"
							Millions of Bushels							
1990-1	195	400	200	194	195	206	405	14.8	90	868	163	217	14	474
1991-2	204	400	209	200	204	214	143	7.2	1	475	152	20	50	273
1992-3	221	400	232	220	221	237	240	9.8	.1	531	150	47	28	353
1993-4	245	400	251	243	245	269	258	14.7	.3	569	150	67	6	413
1994-5	258	400	253	257	258	271	231	10.0	0	507	142	64	0	365
1995-6	258	400	254	258	258	276	114	5.2	0	376	118	13	0	258
1996-7[1]	258	NA	253	257	258	271	194	8.1	0	444	93	72	0	351
1997-8[2]	258	NA					248		0	723	94	50	0	629
1998-9[2]	258	NA								980	125		0	855

[1] Preliminary. [2] Estimate. [3] The national average loan rate at the farm as a percentage of the parity-priced wheat at the beginning of the marketing year. NA = Not avaliable. *Source: Agricultural Marketing Service, U.S. Department of Agriculture (AMS-USDA)*

Exports of Wheat (Only)[2] from the United States   In Thousands of Bushels

Year	June	July	Aug.	Sept.	Oct.	Nov.	Dec.	Jan.	Feb.	Mar.	Apr.	May	Total
1990-1	88,235	80,831	93,617	107,786	84,488	76,800	56,444	66,473	91,313	112,809	88,526	81,760	1,029,072
1991-2	59,167	79,319	97,794	94,991	124,155	136,385	112,771	132,413	115,126	103,024	116,850	59,764	1,231,759
1992-3	75,045	96,382	99,290	92,723	132,232	108,235	111,389	111,584	118,607	118,782	126,845	104,540	1,295,653
1993-4	85,874	103,836	100,516	104,732	100,618	112,667	121,900	109,389	87,250	96,873	71,575	82,838	1,178,068
1994-5	73,364	66,314	103,941	117,555	101,450	107,549	104,139	93,735	97,478	98,876	85,251	75,006	1,124,658
1995-6	78,355	88,649	119,797	131,424	117,679	105,535	99,175	96,085	91,876	108,800	90,373	78,303	1,206,051
1996-7	73,715	108,437	145,840	125,910	98,302	75,245	50,979	63,431	59,039	55,936	69,821	47,640	974,295
1997-8	65,654	92,465	123,141	119,029	89,331	79,528	80,906	97,090	68,972	63,914	64,623	68,359	1,013,012
1998-9[1]	67,372	86,605	96,664	90,507	109,168	81,913							1,064,458

[1] Preliminary.. [2] Grains. *Source: Economic Research Service, U.S. Department of Agriculture (ERS-USDA)*

United States Wheat and Flour Imports and Exports   In Thousands of Bushels

Crop Year Beginning June	Imports: Wheat: Suitable for Milling	Imports: Wheat: Unfit for Human Con-sumption	Imports: Grain	Imports: Flour & Products[2]	Imports: Total	Exports: P.L . 480	Exports: Foreign Donations Sec. 416	Exports: Aid[3]	Exports: Total con-cessional	Exports: CCC Export Credit	Exports: Export Enhance-ment Program	Exports: Total U.S. Wheat Exports
			-- Wheat Equivalent ---			In Thousands of Metric Tons						
1989-90	13,548	NA	12,583	9,884	22,467	2,985	0	28	3,065	7,759	12,806	28,064
1990-1	25,540	NA	25,574	10,832	36,407	2,975	0	0	3,159	8,339	15,150	26,792
1991-2	30,924	NA	31,019	9,675	40,694	2,286	0	0	2,416	13,334	21,111	34,322
1992-3	56,859	NA	56,859	13,142	70,001	2,043	890	0	4,001	8,538	21,806	36,081
1993-4	91,287	NA	91,288	11,086	108,860	2,801	0	0	3,527	5,874	18,157	31,145
1994-5	70,561	NA	70,562	21,386	91,946	1,491	0	NA	1,948	4,202	18,073	32,088
1995-6[1]	47,753	NA	47,754	20,179	67,933	1,530	0	NA	1,530	5,581	570	33,708
1996-7[1]	71,727	NA	71,728	20,605	92,333							

[1] Preliminary. [2] Includes macaroni, semolina & similar products. [3] Shipments mostly under the Commodity Import Program, financed with foreign aid funds. NA = Not available. *Source: Economic Research Service, U.S. Department of Agriculture (ERS-USDA)*

Comparative Average Cash Wheat Prices   In Dollars Per Bushel

Crop Year Beginning June	Received by U.S. Farmers	No. 2 Soft Red Winter Chicago	No. 1 Hard Red Ordinary Protein Kansas City	No. 2 Soft Red Winter St. Louis	Minneapolis: No. 1 Dark Northern Spring 14%	Minneapolis: No. 1 Hard Amber Durum	No. 1 Soft White Portland Oregon	No. 2 Western White Pacific N.W.	No. 2 Soft White Toledo	Export Prices[2] (U.S. $ per Metric Ton): Australian Standard Wheat	Canada Vancouver No. 1 CWRS 13 1/2 %	Argentina F.O.B. B.A.	U.S. Gulf No. 2 H.W.	Rotterdam C.I.F. U.S. No. 2 Hard Winter
1990-1	2.61	2.74	2.94	2.81	3.06	3.48	3.16	2.75	2.59	144	158	107	137	164
1991-2	3.00	3.49	3.77	3.32	3.82	3.61	4.11	3.66	3.41	137	141	99	129	154
1992-3	3.24	3.49	3.67	3.54	3.91	3.88	4.11	3.69	3.18	165	177	122	152	173
1993-4	3.26	3.20	3.60	3.23	5.02	5.76	3.53	3.12	3.16	154	192	131	141	200
1994-5	3.45	3.62	3.97	3.62	4.26	5.98	4.16	3.75	3.37	162	199	NA	150	210
1995-6	4.55	4.78	5.49	4.82	5.72	7.03	5.27	4.74	4.41	198	204	178	177	221
1996-7	4.30	NQ	4.88	4.10	4.97	5.59	4.54	4.26	3.71	237	230	218	207	235
1997-8[1]	3.38	NQ	3.71	3.43	4.31	5.47	3.78			NA	181	157	143	166
1998-9[1]	2.75		3.11	2.38	3.88	4.26	2.92						120	

[1] Preliminary. [2] Calendar year. NA = Not available. *Source: Economic Research Service, U.S. Department of Agriculture (ERS-USDA)*

WHEAT

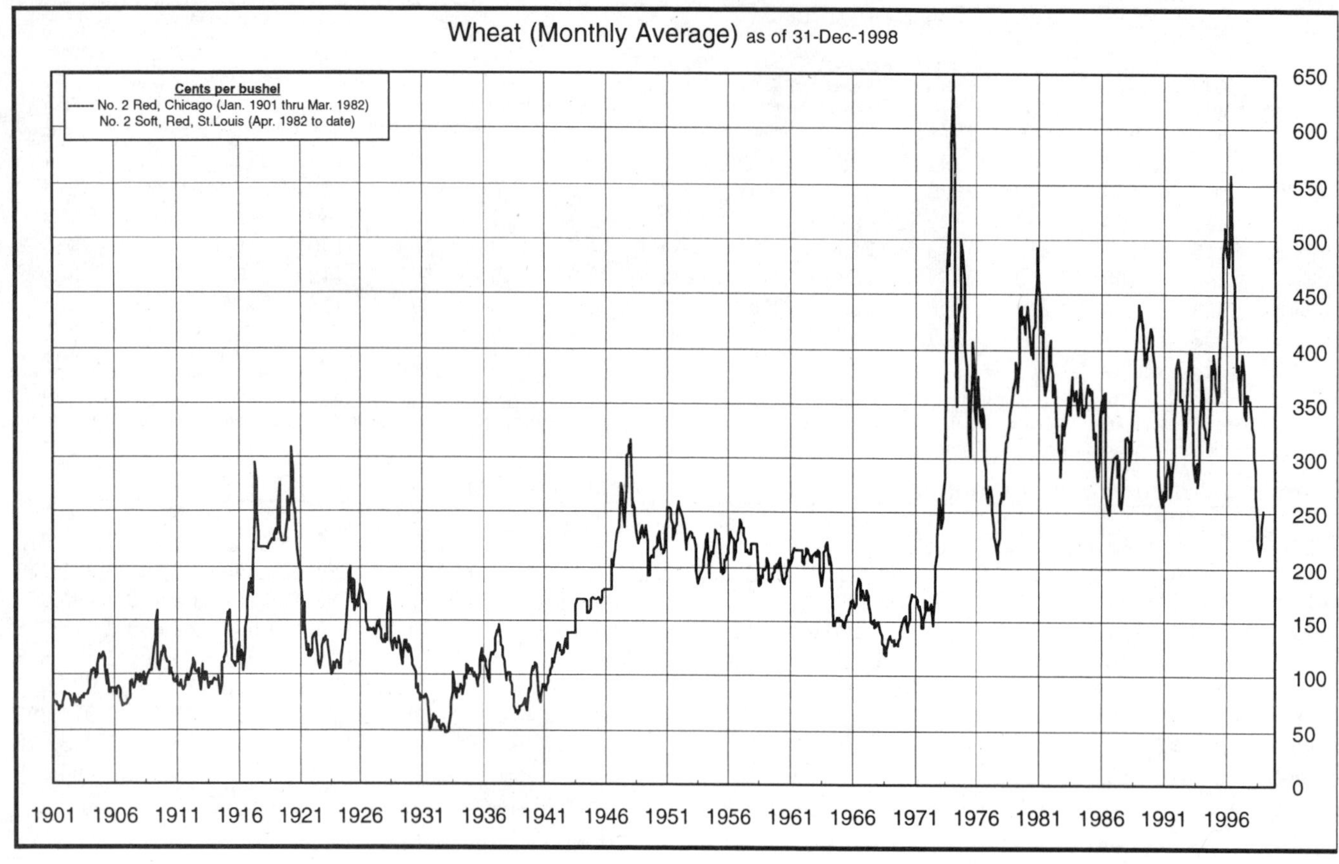

Average Price of No. 2 Soft Red Winter (30 Days) Wheat at Chicago In Dollars Per Bushel

Year	June	July	Aug.	Sept.	Oct.	Nov.	Dec.	Jan.	Feb.	Mar.	Apr.	May	Average
1988-9	3.56	3.52	3.61	3.84	4.07	4.09	4.25	4.39	4.30	4.31	4.04	4.07	4.00
1989-90	3.87	3.92	3.94	3.93	4.07	4.07	4.13	4.03	3.92	3.61	3.83	3.71	3.92
1990-1	3.26	3.04	2.83	2.62	2.62	2.41	2.52	2.50	2.53	2.76	2.80	2.83	2.73
1991-2	2.86	2.79	2.97	3.24	3.50	3.57	3.79	4.12	4.15	3.71	3.53	3.68	3.49
1992-3	3.60	3.39	3.09	3.24	3.39	3.60	3.59	3.77	3.67	3.58	3.72	3.19	3.49
1993-4	2.82	3.03	3.12	2.99	3.02	3.29	3.53	3.67	3.48	3.20	3.15	3.15	3.20
1994-5	3.21	3.14	3.34	3.63	3.97	3.85	3.99	3.88	3.74	3.49	3.51	3.64	3.62
1995-6	3.94	NQ	4.26	4.55	NQ	4.97	5.13	5.02	NQ	NQ	NQ	5.59	4.78
1996-7	4.91	4.64	4.71	4.61	NQ	NQ	NQ	NQ	NQ	NQ	NQ	NQ	4.72
1997-8[1]	NQ	NQ	NQ	NQ	NQ	NQ	NQ	NQ					

NQ = Not quoted. *Source: Economic Research Service, U.S. Department of Agriculture (ERS-USDA)*

Average Price[1] Received by Farmers for Wheat in the United States In Cents Per Bushel

Year	June	July	Aug.	Sept.	Oct.	Nov.	Dec.	Jan.	Feb.	Mar.	Apr.	May	Average[2]
1989-90	3.85	3.78	3.74	3.72	3.75	3.72	3.79	3.71	3.56	3.48	3.49	3.40	3.72
1990-1	3.08	2.79	2.58	2.46	2.43	2.39	2.40	2.42	2.42	2.53	2.60	2.65	2.61
1991-2	2.55	2.50	2.63	2.80	3.07	3.25	3.44	3.54	3.78	3.72	3.65	3.64	3.00
1992-3	3.43	3.15	3.01	3.20	3.21	3.29	3.31	3.37	3.33	3.30	3.26	3.11	3.24
1993-4	2.84	2.85	2.96	3.10	3.25	3.47	3.63	3.58	3.60	3.70	3.56	3.43	3.26
1994-5	3.21	3.04	3.25	3.57	3.76	3.75	3.74	3.69	3.61	3.52	3.48	3.66	3.45
1995-6	3.84	4.10	4.26	4.53	4.72	4.81	4.88	4.83	4.98	5.07	5.32	5.73	4.55
1996-7	5.25	4.73	4.58	4.37	4.18	4.14	4.06	4.03	3.88	3.93	4.11	4.09	4.28
1997-8	3.52	3.23	3.56	3.67	3.55	3.50	3.45	3.33	3.27	3.32	3.15	3.06	3.38
1998-9[2]	2.77	2.56	2.39	2.41	2.79	2.97	2.87	2.86					2.70

[1] Weighted average by sales. [2] Includes an allownace for unredeemed loans at average loan value. *Source: Economic Research Service, U.S. Department of Agriculture (ERS-USDA)*

Average Price of No. 1 Hard Red Winter (Ordinary Protein) Wheat in Kansas City In Dollars Per Bushel

Year	June	July	Aug.	Sept.	Oct.	Nov.	Dec.	Jan.	Feb.	Mar.	Apr.	May	Average
1989-90	4.44	4.28	4.24	4.18	4.28	4.36	4.39	4.30	4.13	4.04	4.13	3.91	4.22
1990-1	3.60	3.11	2.89	2.82	2.81	2.78	2.78	2.71	2.77	2.94	2.98	3.04	2.94
1991-2	2.99	2.91	3.10	3.31	3.64	3.76	4.06	4.66	4.51	4.33	4.02	3.90	3.77
1992-3	3.91	3.52	3.27	3.56	3.60	3.78	3.81	3.97	3.75	3.74	3.59	3.51	3.67
1993-4	3.33	3.38	3.34	3.37	3.52	3.39	4.15	4.00	3.80	3.64	3.63	3.65	3.60
1994-5	3.60	3.48	3.70	4.05	4.31	4.24	4.27	4.06	3.98	3.87	3.86	4.22	3.97
1995-6	4.72	4.98	4.76	5.00	5.28	5.34	5.51	5.40	5.67	5.63	6.60	7.02	5.49
1996-7	6.12	5.34	5.01	4.70	4.76	4.78	4.70	4.61	4.52	4.58	4.78	4.61	4.88
1997-8	4.08	3.57	3.84	3.86	3.88	3.87	3.72	3.61	3.64	3.61	3.39	3.41	3.71
1998-9[1]	3.16	3.02	2.74	2.81	3.30	3.42	3.31						3.11

Source: Economic Research Service, U.S. Department of Agriculture (ERS-USDA)

Average Price of No. 1 Dark Northern Spring (14% Protein) Wheat in Minneapolis In Dollars Per Bushel

Year	June	July	Aug.	Sept.	Oct.	Nov.	Dec.	Jan.	Feb.	Mar.	Apr.	May	Average
1989-90	4.41	4.36	4.18	4.08	4.14	4.12	4.23	4.21	4.06	3.96	4.08	4.09	4.16
1990-1	3.96	3.56	3.05	2.84	2.85	2.80	2.82	2.83	2.85	3.00	3.07	3.10	3.06
1991-2	3.04	2.94	3.10	3.21	3.68	3.78	4.11	4.36	4.56	4.36	4.28	4.44	3.82
1992-3	4.42	4.04	3.65	3.79	3.85	3.94	3.88	4.05	3.87	3.87	3.80	3.71	3.91
1993-4	3.96	4.80	4.88	4.90	5.17	5.50	5.45	5.32	5.29	4.94	4.99	5.05	5.02
1994-5	4.20	4.14	4.00	4.27	4.40	4.41	4.37	4.21	4.09	4.11	4.30	4.61	4.26
1995-6	4.89	5.52	5.06	5.27	5.52	5.63	5.80	5.62	5.82	5.81	6.53	7.14	5.72
1996-7	6.73	6.04	5.29	4.63	4.69	4.64	4.51	4.62	4.45	4.62	4.78	4.58	4.97
1997-8	4.44	4.36	4.49	4.36	4.35	4.42	4.27	4.12	4.15	4.26	4.29	4.24	4.31
1998-9[1]	4.01	3.89	3.58	3.53	4.03	4.15	3.97						3.88

Source: Economic Research Service, U.S. Department of Agriculture (ERS-USDA)

Average Wheat Farm Prices for Leading Classes in the United States In Dollars Per Bushel

Year	June	July	Aug.	Sept.	Oct.	Nov.	Dec.	Jan.	Feb.	Mar.	Apr.	May	Average
						Winter Wheat							
1990-1	3.02	2.75	2.53	2.45	2.40	2.34	2.37	2.36	2.37	2.52	2.56	2.62	2.52
1991-2[2]	2.58	2.54	2.69	2.87	3.16	3.29	3.49	3.63	3.93	3.84	3.67	3.47	3.26
1992-3	3.36	3.13	2.99	3.24	3.30	3.31	3.41	3.47	3.39	3.32	3.20	3.03	3.26
1993-4	2.72	2.76	2.83	2.88	3.00	3.21	3.43	3.41	3.36	3.26	3.24	3.17	3.11
1994-5	3.09	2.99	3.23	3.57	3.79	3.76	3.75	3.67	3.61	3.47	3.45	3.65	3.50
1995-6	3.77	4.05	4.22	4.47	4.70	4.78	4.88	4.80	5.01	5.06	5.39	5.81	4.75
1996-7	5.14	4.67	4.52	4.28	4.07	4.05	4.04	4.02	3.90	3.98	4.14	4.14	4.25
1997-8	3.42	3.16	3.39	3.47	3.42	3.31	3.25	3.16	3.16	3.15	2.94	2.90	3.23
1998-9[1]	2.68	2.48	2.25	2.32	2.66	2.78	2.67	2.71					2.57
						Durum Wheat							
1990-1	3.36	3.11	2.53	2.39	2.44	2.44	2.47	2.61	2.55	2.62	2.61	2.61	2.63
1991-2	2.55	2.44	2.24	2.36	2.62	2.68	2.75	2.98	3.34	3.24	3.33	3.40	2.82
1992-3	3.31	3.03	2.75	2.96	2.92	3.04	3.00	3.00	3.08	3.09	3.10	3.26	3.05
1993-4	3.18	3.26	3.43	3.92	4.23	4.91	4.92	4.97	5.36	5.71	5.70	4.93	4.54
1994-5	4.59	4.32	4.30	4.51	4.89	4.88	4.67	4.61	4.68	4.61	4.48	4.82	4.61
1995-6	5.20	5.29	5.33	5.87	5.80	5.78	5.75	5.66	5.72	5.73	5.63	5.62	5.62
1996-7	5.58	5.13	5.03	4.69	4.78	4.56	4.59	4.47	4.31	4.32	4.40	4.50	4.70
1997-8	4.21	4.61	5.23	5.35	5.09	5.25	5.17	5.02	4.71	4.68	4.45	4.29	4.84
1998-9[1]	3.98	3.37	3.25	3.08	3.16	3.17	3.14	3.02					3.27
						Other Spring Wheat							
1990-1	3.33	2.96	2.58	2.46	2.44	2.40	2.43	2.45	2.44	2.52	2.60	2.65	2.61
1991-2	2.57	2.49	2.56	2.76	3.03	3.26	3.44	3.56	3.83	3.79	3.82	3.86	3.25
1992-3	3.87	3.63	3.12	3.19	3.18	3.28	3.24	3.33	3.34	3.32	3.34	3.19	3.34
1993-4	3.21	3.50	3.51	3.37	3.50	3.67	3.75	3.69	3.68	3.64	3.68	3.63	3.57
1994-5	3.51	3.28	3.19	3.38	3.52	3.51	3.56	3.50	3.40	3.38	3.34	3.53	3.43
1995-6	3.78	4.26	4.19	4.27	4.45	4.61	4.72	4.66	4.81	4.88	5.21	5.67	4.63
1996-7	5.48	5.30	4.63	4.41	4.23	4.11	4.01	3.95	3.80	3.83	4.04	3.94	4.31
1997-8	3.74	3.66	3.75	3.64	3.49	3.55	3.51	3.45	3.34	3.42	3.41	3.31	3.52
1998-9[1]	3.22	3.08	2.71	2.65	3.12	3.26	3.26	3.20					3.06

[1] Preliminary. [2] Data thru 1991-2 are for Central and So. Plains (hard red winter). *Source: Agricultural Statistics Board, U.S. Department of Agriculture (ASB-USDA)*

WHEAT

Average Open Interest of Wheat Futures in Chicago   In Contracts

Year	Jan.	Feb.	Mar.	Apr.	May	June	July	Aug.	Sept.	Oct.	Nov.	Dec.
1989	66,904	63,154	64,669	61,729	60,391	69,898	67,118	65,463	61,511	52,246	52,023	54,117
1990	54,225	56,395	56,984	51,548	56,624	63,819	64,576	59,792	57,237	58,231	55,850	47,061
1991	48,597	51,520	55,922	53,668	53,030	58,997	54,946	52,283	55,220	61,257	57,679	51,845
1992	61,484	70,152	58,957	53,706	50,978	50,340	60,116	62,071	50,093	54,564	57,693	49,263
1993	50,329	47,858	44,885	48,354	51,353	55,829	58,705	64,335	58,603	61,496	62,877	50,523
1994	53,912	48,013	45,110	47,430	44,552	54,622	57,151	65,388	73,200	78,419	70,815	67,150
1995	66,715	67,768	55,973	55,612	67,875	90,208	101,351	90,800	91,505	103,987	102,475	99,422
1996	102,718	104,807	91,378	98,260	93,378	81,211	69,222	66,128	65,561	65,639	60,810	58,533
1997	63,388	71,304	76,747	85,516	84,721	83,675	92,815	105,320	104,587	108,480	101,089	90,386
1998	96,870	99,103	97,585	114,193	115,199	116,008	121,794	127,240	125,747	131,322	130,186	116,249

Source: Chicago Board of Trade (CBT)

Volume of Trading of Wheat Futures in Chicago   In Contracts

Year	Jan.	Feb.	Mar.	Apr.	May	June	July	Aug.	Sept.	Oct.	Nov.	Dec.	Total
1989	283,879	255,584	326,201	244,321	281,159	347,012	333,646	287,543	233,465	243,185	209,931	191,783	3,237,709
1990	211,769	197,397	209,873	251,823	346,922	296,337	297,182	298,383	197,304	201,589	231,845	135,846	2,876,270
1991	198,340	182,158	291,762	268,560	234,880	391,134	286,097	271,625	187,232	300,628	271,927	262,501	3,146,844
1992	366,736	460,354	318,810	236,063	290,148	303,044	304,217	283,379	250,003	220,502	257,017	188,541	3,498,814
1993	246,125	237,936	277,632	217,898	173,607	268,206	366,414	266,893	202,308	256,329	310,464	195,817	3,019,629
1994	288,321	211,703	187,617	244,544	300,324	370,135	272,492	330,758	343,548	398,041	354,975	318,173	3,620,631
1995	353,603	302,950	316,330	279,099	345,455	598,762	507,876	527,716	436,145	472,794	454,352	359,985	4,955,067
1996	628,340	510,138	455,981	660,722	531,979	512,883	452,690	345,626	305,448	362,047	359,005	261,108	5,385,967
1997	312,680	373,411	368,547	567,099	422,935	469,158	470,992	493,225	401,277	405,978	432,621	340,722	5,058,645
1998	363,511	473,114	452,186	514,557	432,167	601,149	401,508	490,242	475,766	543,680	539,488	394,201	5,681,569

Source: Chicago Board of Trade (CBT)

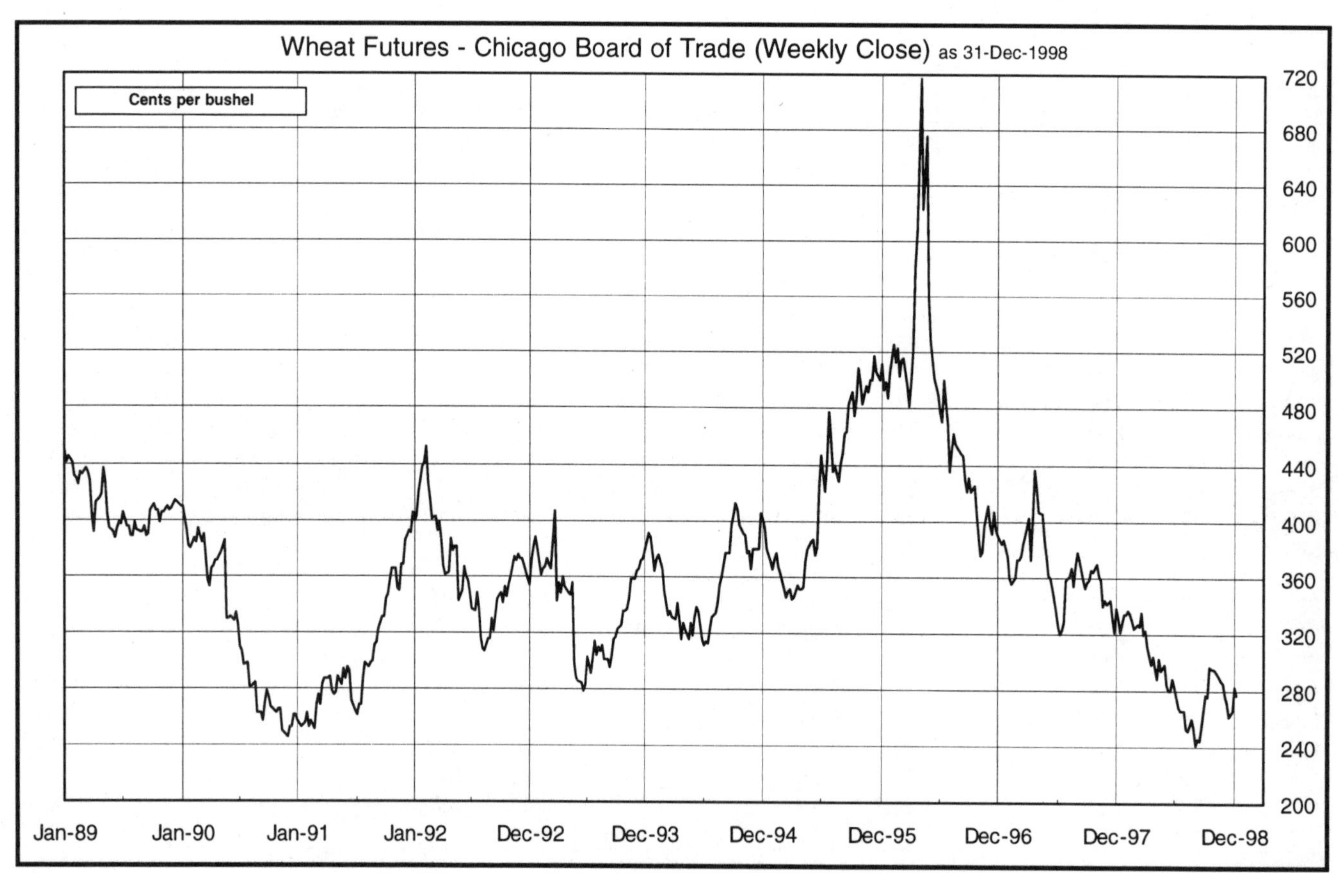

Commercial Stocks of Domestic Wheat[1] in the United States, on First of Month In Millions of Bushels

Year	July	Aug.	Sept.	Oct.	Nov.	Dec.	Jan.	Feb.	Mar.	Apr.	May	June
1989-90	130.5	171.6	211.7	211.8	196.0	180.2	164.2	150.4	127.9	109.7	87.2	77.8
1990-1	121.8	212.7	289.7	290.2	284.6	264.8	243.7	237.7	------	------	174.5	174.5
1991-2	244.8	275.5	296.9	308.2	271.0	264.8	249.8	227.0	205.2	180.7	170.9	209.1
1992-3	269.6	290.5	202.5	228.2	231.9	202.7	185.5	169.5	153.3	132.6	112.9	87.0
1993-4	102.9	145.1	171.8	194.9	199.3	174.9	169.5	168.3	162.2	143.8	127.3	111.3
1994-5	145.7	203.9	243.0	269.7	268.6	238.2	199.5	181.0	162.5	150.2	108.7	91.8
1995-6	92.3	161.7	201.1	234.3	228.3	200.2	178.7	170.8	156.6	137.7	107.6	87.2
1996-7	86.3	112.9	128.0	145.3	117.2	94.9	89.0	80.4	77.0	75.6	68.1	64.6
1997-8	80.1	186.3	235.2	268.1	258.1	231.4	196.8	178.1	170.6	158.0	146.4	145.7
1998-9	209.8	265.0	314.9	325.6	307.3	291.3	272.9	265.7	256.8			

[1] Domestic wheat in storage in public and private elevators in 39 markets and wheat afloat in vessels or barges at lake and seaboard ports, the first Saturday of the month. *Source: Livestock Division, U.S. Department of Agriculture (LD-USDA)*

Stocks of Wheat Flour Held by Mills in the United States In Thousands of Sacks (100 Pounds Each)

Year	Jan. 1	April 1	July 1	Oct. 1	Year	Jan. 1	April 1	July 1	Oct. 1
1987	5,228	4,900	5,581	5,258	1993	5,487	4,863	6,197	5,882
1988	5,858	4,508	4,822	5,303	1994	5,611	5,904	5,834	6,020
1989	4,800	4,423	5,116	5,489	1995	7,060	6,496	6,312	6,582
1990	5,207	5,072	5,818	7,980	1996	6,869	6,927	6,400	6,350
1991	8,051	5,474	8,115	6,336	1997	6,671	6,040	5,820	6,330
1992	5,660	5,210	5,841	5,864	1998[1]	6,343	6,248	6,190	7,223

[1] Preliminary. *Source: Bureau of the Census, U.S. Department of Commerce*

Average Producer Price Index of Wheat Flour (Spring[1]) June 1983 = 100

Year	Jan.	Feb.	Mar.	Apr.	May	June	July	Aug.	Sept.	Oct.	Nov.	Dec.	Average
1989	110.7	110.0	112.4	109.5	112.0	112.7	112.1	110.7	109.5	108.5	108.7	109.6	110.5
1990	109.4	109.0	106.9	108.8	107.9	106.0	99.7	93.4	92.0	91.2	89.4	89.8	100.3
1991	88.7	90.2	92.0	93.0	94.0	93.7	91.3	94.1	96.3	100.1	97.5	102.7	94.5
1992	109.7	116.4	111.5	110.3	109.2	111.0	104.9	99.6	104.1	104.4	104.7	103.5	107.4
1993	107.5	108.1	107.2	108.4	105.2	104.7	103.7	107.2	102.1	107.3	108.4	112.5	106.9
1994	111.8	110.5	108.9	107.9	109.4	106.4	100.8	101.2	109.1	112.0	110.9	111.4	108.4
1995	110.7	108.5	107.9	109.8	113.5	118.6	127.4	126.7	129.5	132.6	132.3	133.5	120.9
1996	130.4	138.0	136.6	137.6	160.1	146.8	138.0	127.0	121.5	125.7	121.7	121.4	133.7
1997	119.4	119.3	116.6	121.8	120.8	117.4	112.1	113.5	115.1	112.6	111.5	111.1	115.9
1998[2]	106.8	108.1	111.5	110.1	109.9	106.4	105.5	101.8	100.8	106.9	107.7	104.5	106.7

[1] Standard patent. [2] Preliminary. *Source: Bureau of Labor Statistics, U.S. Department of Commerce (0212-0301)*

World Wheat Flour Production (Monthly Average) In Thousands of Metric Tons

Year	Australia	France	Germany	Hungary	India	Japan	Kazakhstan	Rep. of Korea	Mexico	Poland	Russia	Turkey	United Kingdom
1989	109.0	435.6	280.0	102.2	391.3	381.8	164.0	134.5	207.0	241.1	NA	136.4	333.0
1990	114.9	442.7	218.1	102.4	394.3	387.7	163.5	134.7	209.4	150.6	NA	112.9	323.0
1991	112.7	464.8	341.1	97.7	398.0	389.8	167.8	130.4	207.3	128.6	NA	111.1	320.0
1992	113.9	465.2	327.0	106.9	400.0	389.0	161.0	129.4	223.3	167.1	449.5	112.2	320.0
1993	116.3	480.6	336.4	75.0	399.4	399.3	155.3	129.5	214.0	113.4	449.5	122.1	331.0
1994	116.9	470.8	378.8	62.9	400.0	387.2	157.0	132.6	219.8	150.5	348.0	104.9	337.0
1995	112.6	473.1	382.3	84.0	400.0	389.3	131.0	139.9	210.7	156.9	274.6	119.7	341.0
1996	123.8	-----	394.2	75.1	400.0	389.6	105.5	141.2	215.9	108.5	309.7	119.3	353.5
1997[1]	-----	-----	404.8	77.7	412.5	388.1	103.0	145.9	216.0	115.9	361.9	159.1	354.5
1998[2]	-----	-----	405.3	71.0	430.3	374.9	130.3	140.2	204.7	118.0	347.8	144.3	355.5

[1] Preliminary. [2] Estimate. NA = Not available. *Source: United Nations*

WHEAT

Production of Wheat Flour in the United States In Millions of Sacks (100 Pounds Each)

Year	July	Aug.	Sept.	Oct.	Nov.	Dec.	Jan.	Feb.	Mar.	Apr.	May	June	Total
1990-1	27.7	33.7	29.9	32.2	32.7	29.1	29.4	29.5	29.5	29.4	29.2	29.1	362.3
1991-2	29.2	31.8	30.1	32.2	32.7	29.2	29.3	29.3	29.4	30.0	29.8	29.8	363.0
1992-3	31.1	34.2	31.9	34.6	32.2	29.2	30.6	31.3	34.1	32.0	31.0	30.3	382.4
1993-4	30.7	33.3	32.9	33.5	34.0	33.8	30.9	30.2	35.9	32.3	32.2	31.1	390.8
1994-5	30.5	34.9	34.2	35.0	33.7	31.7	30.9	29.4	34.5	29.9	33.5	32.3	390.4
1995-6	31.0	34.5	33.0	35.1	33.4	31.2	31.6	32.3	32.2	31.2	33.2	30.6	389.3
1996-7	33.9	35.6	34.6	37.5	33.1	32.0	31.3	30.0	31.8	33.1	32.6	32.5	397.9
1997-8	34.0	34.3	35.1	37.2	33.8	33.5	---------	97.1	---------	---------	97.3	---------	402.4
1998-9[1]	---------	101.4	---------	---------	108.0	---------	---------		---------	---------		---------	418.9

[1] Preliminary. *Source: Bureau of the Census, U.S. Department of Commerce*

United States Wheat Flour Exports (Grain Equivalent[2]) In Thousands of Bushels

Year	June	July	Aug.	Sept.	Oct.	Nov.	Dec.	Jan.	Feb.	Mar.	Apr.	May	Total
1990-1	1,035	2,207	2,785	1,464	3,303	3,407	4,480	2,698	3,809	6,301	3,719	3,525	38,733
1991-2	5,582	5,362	4,207	3,743	1,179	2,222	3,140	2,549	5,549	4,630	3,771	4,579	46,513
1992-3	3,257	5,284	2,856	2,325	3,840	4,641	3,903	2,325	7,744	5,832	7,499	5,285	54,791
1993-4	4,408	3,793	1,811	3,642	3,840	3,416	3,170	5,838	4,390	6,099	4,198	3,368	47,973
1994-5	2,922	6,824	5,636	3,407	3,105	4,721	4,734	2,805	7,085	7,617	6,945	6,005	61,806
1995-6	2,822	5,018	7,520	2,249	2,080	1,221	3,458	808	2,537	1,230	2,415	1,830	33,188
1996-7	2,005	2,008	1,669	3,133	2,496	2,748	2,240	1,344	1,897	2,490	1,253	2,086	25,369
1997-8	1,731	2,849	1,621	3,101	2,518	1,631	3,118	1,403	2,723	1,280	1,257	925	24,157
1998-9[1]	1,971	1,740	2,027	2,914	3,812	2,354							29,636

[1] Preliminary. [2] Includes meal, groats and durum. *Source: Economic Research Service, U.S. Department of Agriculture (ERS-USDA)*

Supply and Distribution of Wheat Flour in the United States

Year	Wheat Ground 1,000 Bu.	Milfeed Production 1,000 Tons	Flour Production[3]	Flour & Product Imports[2]	Total Supply	Exports: Flour	Exports: Products[2]	Domestic Disappearance	Total Population July 1 Millions	Per Capita Disappearance Pounds
			1,000 Cwt.							
1990	788,186	6,109	354,348	3,623	357,971	18,872	273	338,826	249.9	136
1991	808,966	6,436	362,311	4,070	366,381	20,044	440	345,897	252.6	137
1992	833,339	6,707	370,829	5,037	375,866	20,711	619	354,536	255.4	139
1993	871,408	6,963	387,419	6,233	393,652	23,241	548	369,863	258.1	143
1994	884,707	7,186	392,519	9,048	401,567	24,234	733	376,599	260.7	144
1995	869,296	7,144	388,689	9,306	397,995	24,343	716	372,936	263.0	142
1996	878,070	7,042	397,776	8,847	406,623	11,003	714	394,906	265.6	149
1997[1]	885,843	6,886	404,143	9,190	408,388	11,229	1,095	396,064	267.8	148
1998[1]	902,532	7,301	403,880							

[1] Preliminary. [2] Import and exports of macaroni and noodle products (flour equivalent), reporting methods changed in 1990. [3] Commercial production of wheat flour, whole wheat, industrial and durum flour and farina reported by Bureau of the Census. *Source: Economic Research Service, U.S. Department of Agriculture (ERS-USDA)*

Wheat and Flour -- Price Relationship at Milling Centers in the United States In Dollars

Crop Year (June-May)	At Kansas City: Cost of Wheat to Produce 100 lb. Flour[1]	Wholesale Price of: Bakery Flour 100 lb. Flour[2]	Wholesale Price of: By-Products Obtained 100 lb. Flour[3]	Total Products: Actual	Total Products: Over Cost of Wheat	At Minneapolis: Cost of Wheat to Produce 100 lb. Flour[1]	Wholesale Price of: Bakery Flour 100 lb. Flour[2]	Wholesale Price of: By-Products Obtained 100 lb. Flour[3]	Total Products: Actual	Total Products: Over Cost of Wheat
1989-90	9.58	10.41	1.45	11.86	2.28	9.48	10.00	1.36	11.36	1.89
1990-1	6.86	7.78	1.29	9.07	2.21	6.98	7.73	1.21	8.94	1.96
1991-2	8.58	9.53	1.26	10.79	2.21	8.71	9.39	1.16	10.55	1.84
1992-3	8.53	9.65	1.28	10.93	2.40	8.91	10.12	1.15	11.27	2.37
1993-4	10.03	10.34	1.46	11.79	1.77	11.45	12.50	1.28	13.77	2.33
1994-5	9.25	10.50	1.21	11.71	2.46	9.71	11.01	1.04	12.05	2.34
1995-6	12.97	13.35	1.93	15.28	2.31	13.04	13.03	1.68	14.71	1.67
1996-7	11.22	11.89	1.92	13.81	2.60	11.32	11.68	1.87	13.54	2.22
1997-8 I	9.20	10.42	1.20	11.62	2.42	10.10	10.98	1.28	12.27	2.17
II	9.31	10.00	1.66	11.66	2.35	9.98	10.50	1.50	12.00	2.02
Dec.[4]	9.14	9.70	1.69	11.39	2.24	9.74	10.30	1.52	11.82	2.09
Jan.[4]	8.66	9.50	1.75	11.25	2.59	9.39	10.15	1.47	11.62	2.22

[1] Based on 73% extraction rate, cost of 2.28 bushels: at Kansas City, No. 1 hard winter, 13 % protein; and at Minneapolis, No. 1 dark northern spring, 14% protein. [2] Quoted as mid-month bakers' standard patent at Kansas City and spring standard patent at Minneapolis, bulk basis. [3] Assumed 50-50 millfeed distribution between bran and shorts or middlings, bulk basis. *Source: Agricultural Marketing Service, U.S. Department of Agriculture (AMS-USDA)*

Wool

The decline in world wool production (greasy) persisted through the 1990's with little sign of any change taking hold by the end of the decade. The decline largely reflects the steady contraction in world sheep numbers to less than one billion head in 1998 from an average of over 1.1 billion head in the late 1980's. Except for China, the sheep flock has been contracting worldwide. In Australia, the world's largest wool producer, sheep numbers fell from 163 million head in 1990/91 to about 120 million in 1998/99, and wool production (clean) from 1.5 billion pounds to about one billion, respectively. Changing worldwide consumer attitudes have also adversely affected wool demand with current fashion using more cotton and manmade fibers than wool.

New Zealand, the second largest wool producer, has seen its herd drop to 47 million head, the lowest since the 1960's. China's sheep inventory is the world's largest at 150 million head in 1998/99 vs. 120 million in the mid-1990's. Russia's sheep inventory in 1998/99 is estimated at 20 million head, a drop of 50 percent since the early 1990's. The drop is U.S. sheep numbers is not much better; the 1998 inventory of about 6.5 million head totals half the number on hand in the late 1980's. U.S. shorn wool production is insignificant; about 28 million pounds in the first half of 1998, marginally under the like 1997 period, suggesting a calendar year production of about 55 million pounds (greasy).

In line with declining production and usage foreign trade has also fallen. Australia remains the largest exporter followed by New Zealand, the two nations accounting for 75 percent of world exports. Importing nations are numerous; but China has been first since 1993/94. Japan, the U.K., Italy and France import around 200 million pounds each although Japan's wool imports were slowing even before recent economic problems. And imports into the former U.S.S.R. dropped dramatically in the 1990's. U.S. raw wool imports (clean) averaged 7.0 million pounds per month in the first half of 1998, marginally ahead of a year earlier. Australian wool accounts for most of U.S. imports. The U.S. imports wool tops with the total about 10 percent of raw wool exports. U.S. raw wool consumption in the second quarter of 1998 was 33 million pounds vs. 37 mil. in 1997.

Global wool prices are a function of origin and grade; South African wool is priced higher than Australian wool which in turn is moderately higher than New Zealand's wool. U.S. clean wool prices (56's) were under pressure in the first half of 1998 and quoted at $1.00/pound in mid-year vs. $1.50/pound a year earlier. U.S. 60's grade averaged $1.85/pound in July 1998 vs. Australian 60's at $2.10, the latter in the mid-1990's averaged near $3.00/pound.

Futures Markets

Wool futures are traded on the Sydney Futures Exchange (SFE), the Nagoya Textile Exchange, the Osaka Textile Exchange, the Tokyo Commodity Exchange (TOCOM), and the New Zealand Futures & Options Exchange Ltd. (NZFOE).

World Production of Wool In Metric Tons-Degreased

Year	Argentina	Australia	China	Kazakhstan[3]	New Zealand	Pakistan	Romania	Russia[3]	South Africa	United Kingdom	United States	Uruguay	World Total
1989	87,600	622,000	120,111	-----	302,800	34,800	20,900	284,400	46,500	52,765	21,665	60,000	2,011,693
1990	85,800	724,000	122,400	64,750	233,000	28,200	26,500	136,050	49,500	53,358	21,140	58,100	2,029,209
1991	75,400	699,000	123,000	62,640	227,000	28,900	19,196	122,700	51,000	51,055	20,830	56,500	1,953,339
1992	74,200	574,000	121,500	63,000	221,000	29,600	16,800	107,400	48,500	50,876	19,980	50,700	1,780,613
1993	58,000	557,000	122,000	56,800	193,000	30,300	15,600	95,000	45,000	48,329	18,520	49,410	1,688,806
1994	48,000	570,000	130,000	55,000	214,000	31,000	17,000	73,000	40,000	47,000	16,000	50,000	1,693,000
1995	44,000	475,000	141,000	35,000	214,000	32,000	16,000	56,000	35,000	48,000	15,000	46,000	1,512,000
1996[1]	39,000	447,000	152,000	25,000	199,000	32,000	16,000	46,000	38,000	46,000	14,000	43,000	1,449,000
1997[2]	39,000	447,000	153,000	25,000	200,000	33,000	13,000	42,000	38,000	46,000	14,000	48,000	1,450,000

[1] Preliminary. [2] Estimate. [3] Formerly part of the U.S.S.R.; data not reported separately until 1990. *Source: Food and Agriculture Organization of the*

Production of Wool Goods[1] in the United States In Millions of Yards

Year	First Quarter	Second Quarter	Third Quarter	Fourth Quarter	Total Year	Year	First Quarter	Second Quarter	Third Quarter	Fourth Quarter	Total Year
1989	48.3	50.9	40.1	37.0	176.3	1994	49.1	51.1	39.4	39.0	178.6
1990	38.0	38.7	32.6	31.4	140.7	1995	46.8	45.9	35.2	34.3	162.2
1991	38.0	48.7	41.4	41.5	169.6	1996	44.8	43.6	30.8	32.8	152.0
1992	45.7	47.2	43.9	39.5	176.3	1997	42.7	49.7	42.3	40.5	175.2
1993	48.4	48.9	43.9	42.8	184.0	1998[2]	38.6	37.5	29.5	26.2	131.8

[1] Woolen and worsted woven goods, except woven felts. [2] Preliminary. *Source: Bureau of the Census, U.S. Department of Commerce*

Consumption of Apparel Wool in the United States In Millions of Pounds--Clean Basis

Year	First Quarter	Second Quarter	Third Quarter	Fourth Quarter	Total Year	Year	First Quarter	Second Quarter	Third Quarter	Fourth Quarter	Total Year
1989	35.4	31.0	29.8	26.3	120.5	1994	36.3	35.6	32.7	34.0	138.6
1990	31.5	31.7	26.9	30.5	120.6	1995	36.3	35.5	29.4	28.1	129.3
1991	31.6	37.1	34.6	33.9	137.2	1996	39.1	36.2	27.4	26.8	129.5
1992	36.4	35.1	33.6	31.1	136.1	1997	33.1	33.8	30.6	32.8	130.4
1993	35.5	35.9	35.5	34.4	141.4	1998[2]	29.2	29.6	21.9	21.5	102.1

[1] Preliminary. *Source: Bureau of the Census, U.S. Department of Commerce*

WOOL

Salient Statistics of Wool in the United States

Year	Sheep & Lambs Shorn[4] 1,000	Weight per Fleece Lbs.	Shorn Wool Production 1,000 Lbs	Price per Lb.	Value of Production 1,000 $	--- Shorn Wool --- Support	Payment Rate	Total Wool Production	Raw Wool (Clean Content): Domestic Production	Exports Domestic Wool	Dutiable Imports for Consump.[3] 48s&Finer	Total New Supply[2]	Duty Free Imports (Not Finer than 46's)	Mill Consumption: Apparel	Carpet
						----- ¢ Per Lb. -----		----- Thousands of Pounds -----							
1989	11,314	7.89	89,220	124.0	110,537	177	53.0	89,220	47,108	1,188	77,003	152,860	29,889	120,534	14,122
1990	11,222	7.84	88,033	80.0	69,534	182	102.0	88,033	46,481	2,736	50,328	115,461	21,355	120,622	12,124
1991	11,009	7.97	87,740	55.0	47,178	188	133.0	87,740	46,327	3,867	68,242	128,916	18,166	137,187	14,352
1992	10,521	7.88	82,943	74.0	60,162	197	123.0	82,819	43,728	3,413	65,457	129,599	23,802	136,143	14,695
1993	9,976	7.77	77,535	51.0	39,077	204	153.0	77,319	40,824	2,529	76,001	138,606	21,876	141,380	15,431
1994	8,877	7.73	68,577	78.0	52,377	209	131.0	68,577	36,209	2,863	64,889	122,880	24,645	138,563	14,739
1995	8,138	7.80	63,513	104.0	64,277	212	108.0	63,513	33,535	6,042	63,781	116,313	25,039	129,299	12,667
1996	7,279	7.79	56,669	70.0	39,659			56,669	29,921	5,715	54,063	99,240	20,971	129,525	12,311
1997[1]	7,000	7.70	53,900	84.0					28,600	4,000	51,484		24,295	130,386	13,576

[1] Preliminary. [2] Production minus exports plus imports; stocks not taken into consideration. [3] Appearal wool includes all dutiable wool; carpet wool includes all duty-free wool. [4] Includes sheep shorn at commercial feeding yards. *Source: Economic Research Service, U.S. Department of Agriculture (ERS-USDA)*

Shorn Wool Prices

Year	U.S. Farm Price Shorn Wool Greasy Basis[1] ¢ per Lb.	Australian Offering Price, Clean[2]: Grade 70's Type 61	Grade 64's Type 63	Grade 64/70's Type 62	Grade 60/62's Type 64A	Grade 58's-56's 433-34	Market Indicator[3] Cents/Kg.	Graded Territory Shorn Wool, Clean Basis[4]: 64's Staple 2 3/4" & up	60's Staple 3" & up	58's Staple 3 1/4" & up	56's Staple 3 1/4" & up	54's Staple 3 1/2" & up
		----- Dollars per Pound -----						----- Dollars per Pound -----				
1989	124.0	5.82	4.21	3.86	3.44	2.81	990	3.14	2.61	2.06	2.04	1.91
1990	80.0	4.76	3.60	3.26	2.87	2.46	870	2.06	1.66	1.45	1.30	1.18
1991	55.0	3.56	2.32	2.02	1.87	1.68	627	1.58	1.31	1.14	1.03	.93
1992	74.0	2.58	2.32	2.17	2.10	1.94	557	1.81	1.61	1.47	1.35	1.23
1993	51.0	2.08	1.70	1.84	1.49	1.44	488	1.37	1.13	1.05	.99	.94
1994	78.0	3.72	2.43	3.01	1.96	1.86	547	2.12	1.50	1.26	1.27	1.21
1995	104.0	3.22	2.81	3.01	2.49	2.33	888	2.49	1.93	1.77	1.63	1.53
1996	70.0	2.81	2.34	2.54	1.96	1.84	619	1.93	1.54	1.43	1.31	1.22
1997	84.0	3.56	2.57	2.90	2.06	1.95	615	2.38	1.78	1.64	1.43	1.14

[1] Annual weighted average. [2] F.O.B. Australian Wool Corporation South Carolina warehouse in bond. [3] Index of prices of all wool sold in Australia for the crop year July-June. [4] Wool principally produced in Texas and Rocky Mountain States. *Source: Economic Research Service, U.S. Department of Agriculture*

Average Wool Prices[1]--Australian--64's, Type 62, Duty Paid--U.S. Mills In Cents Per Pound

Year	Jan.	Feb.	Mar.	Apr.	May	June	July	Aug.	Sept.	Oct.	Nov.	Dec.	Average
1989	511	484	454	429	414	403	405	410	414	417	417	420	431
1990	417	404	403	414	406	342	338	352	355	343	332	332	370
1991	334	335	209	221	271	286	NA	248	229	215	274	270	242
1992	259	270	277	264	268	246	NA	224	210	192	195	193	236
1993	186	176	170	158	179	169	167	154	153	171	175	176	170
1994	204	216	205	223	249	258	243	248	259	256	273	297	244
1995	281	297	302	302	307	308	292	284	266	236	242	237	280
1996	240	237	238	234	242	245	236	234	228	220	225	232	234
1997	234	261	254	261	279	287	NA	270	262	250	245	240	258
1998	218	225	247	205	214	179	NA	144	144	140	145	147	183

[1] Raw, clean basis. NA = Not available. *Source: Economic Research Service, U.S. Department of Agriculture (ERS-USDA)*

Average Wool Prices--Domestic[1]--Graded Territory, 64's, Staple 2 3/4 & Up--U.S. Mills In Cents Per Pound

Year	Jan.	Feb.	Mar.	Apr.	May	June	July	Aug.	Sept.	Oct.	Nov.	Dec.	Average
1989	450	438	410	375	375	365	350	350	350	350	333	300	370
1990	294	287	287	284	275	257	242	235	235	235	225	220	256
1991	217	210	163	167	203	230	230	167	156	148	148	155	158
1992	163	203	195	196	199	218	210	188	210	193	168	168	193
1993	158	148	132	127	135	140	138	140	130	129	133	133	124
1994	140	150	170	201	226	230	230	235	250	238	238	252	213
1995	245	252	265	288	295	285	261	250	235	185	208	192	247
1996	188	192	197	197	195	192	192	192	192	192	190	190	192
1997	190	190	208	228	248	255	255	255	255	255	260	260	238
1998	236	195	195	188	177	170	170	150	140	115	115	115	164

[1] Raw, shorn, clean basis. *Source: Economic Research Service, U.S. Department of Agriculture (ERS-USDA)*

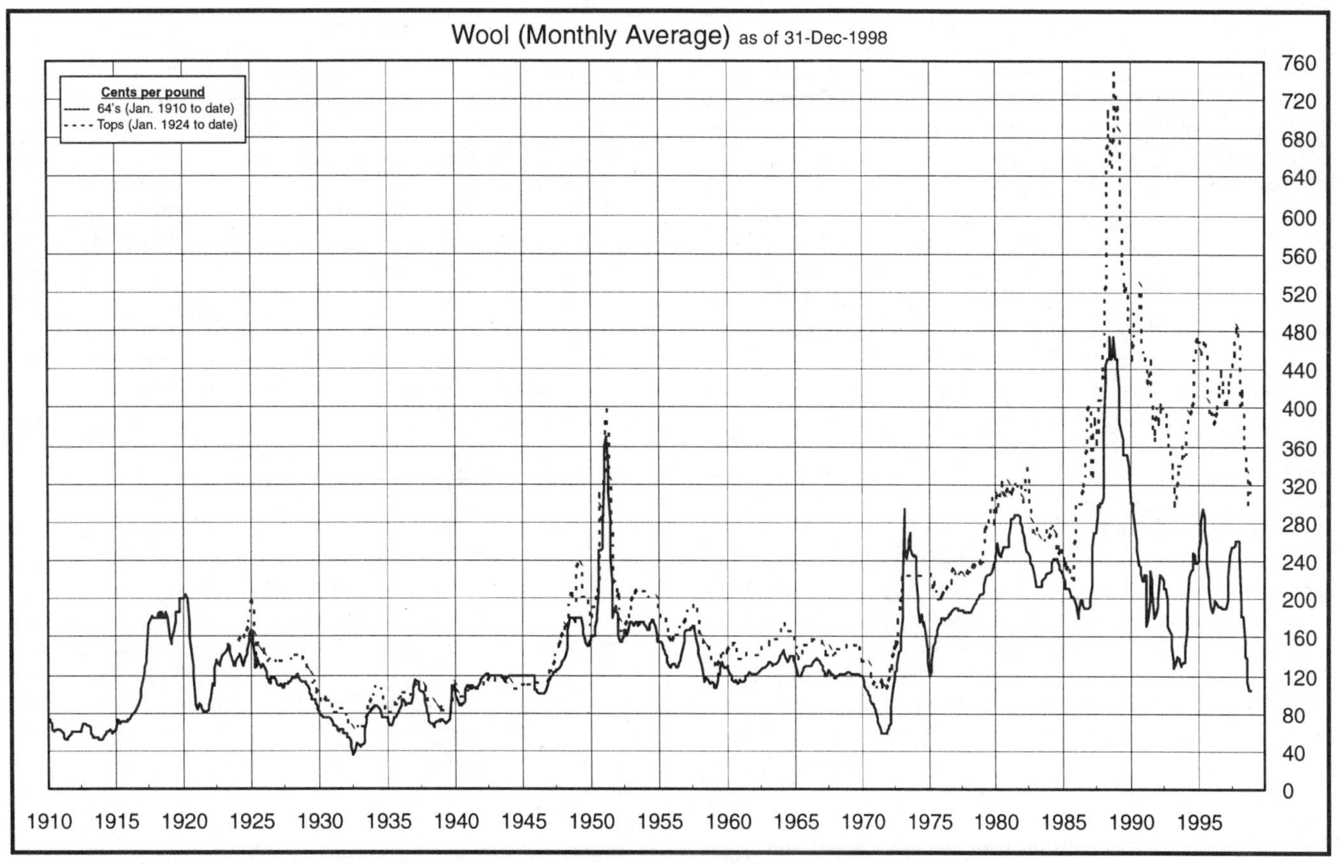

Wool: Mill Consumption, by Grades in the United States, Scoured Basis In Thousands of Pounds

	Apparel Wool[1]							
	Woolen System			Worsted System				
Year	60's & Finer	Coarser Than 60's	Total	60's & Finer	Coarser Than 60's	Total	All Total	Carpet Wool[2]
1988	23,769	20,876	44,645	54,553	17,871	72,424	117,069	15,633
1989	24,123	21,803	45,935	56,065	18,534	74,599	120,534	14,122
1990	26,173	24,941	51,114	50,630	18,878	69,508	120,622	12,124
1991	31,961	26,599	58,560	56,521	22,106	78,627	137,187	14,352
1992	33,878	25,600	59,478	58,495	18,170	76,665	136,143	14,695
1993	40,895	26,624	67,519	58,834	15,027	73,861	141,380	15,431
1994	35,960	26,038	61,998	59,599	16,966	76,565	138,563	14,739
1995	30,211	27,089	57,300	54,980	17,019	71,999	129,299	12,667
1996[3]	42,141	27,575	69,716	46,057	13,752	59,809	129,525	12,311
1997[4]	49,038	21,303	70,341	48,153	11,892	60,045	130,386	13,576

[1] Domestic & duty-paid foreign. [2] Duty-free foreign. [3] Preliminary. [4] Estimate. *Source: Economic Research Service, U.S. Department of Agriculture*

United States Imports[1] of Unmanufactured Wool (Clean Yield) In Millions of Pounds

Year	Jan.	Feb.	Mar.	Apr.	May	June	July	Aug.	Sept.	Oct.	Nov.	Dec.	Total
1989	8.7	11.3	9.0	13.1	10.3	8.3	10.0	6.9	3.9	10.4	5.1	9.8	106.9
1990	7.3	9.2	4.7	8.2	5.0	4.8	3.4	5.5	5.0	6.9	7.5	4.2	71.7
1991	10.7	6.9	5.4	5.5	7.3	8.1	9.2	7.0	4.4	7.8	5.1	9.0	86.5
1992	10.2	8.1	7.3	10.6	8.8	6.2	6.9	5.0	3.9	5.5	9.1	7.8	89.3
1993	7.8	8.7	8.5	9.3	11.0	9.6	9.7	8.7	5.7	7.7	7.2	8.4	100.3
1994	10.0	7.7	7.7	12.7	7.5	7.7	6.9	6.5	4.1	5.7	8.1	7.0	91.7
1995	10.4	7.7	10.8	6.0	11.5	5.2	7.3	7.3	4.9	7.9	7.7	4.1	90.6
1996	9.6	9.1	8.8	5.6	7.0	5.9	5.3	6.6	3.1	4.6	4.6	5.1	75.3
1997	5.1	5.8	5.8	6.6	5.8	4.2	4.9	4.2	4.8	8.5	7.3	8.6	71.5
1998[2]	8.6	5.4	7.2	7.9	5.9	5.5	5.7	4.4	3.3	7.3	4.9		72.0

[1] Data are imports for consumption. [2] Preliminary. *Source: Economic Research Service, U.S. Department of Agriculture (ERS-USDA)*

Zinc

Zinc is utilized as a protective coating for iron and steel in a process known as galvanizing. Zinc also finds use as an alloy with copper to make brass and as an alloying compound with aluminum and magnesium.

The U.S. Geological Survey reported that world mine production of zinc in 1997 was 7.46 million metric tonnes. That was down less than 1 percent from 1996. The world's largest producer of zinc in 1997 was China with 1.2 million tonnes. That was an increase of 7 percent from 1996. The next largest producer of zinc was Canada with 1.06 million tonnes, down 14 percent from 1996. The third largest producer of zinc in 1997 was Australia with output of 1.04 million tonnes, down 3 percent from 1996. Production of zinc by Peru was 865,267 tonnes, up 14 percent from 1996. The next largest producer was the U.S. with 632,000 tonnes. Other large producers in 1997 were Mexico, Kazakstan, North Korea and Spain.

World smelter production of zinc in 1997 was 7.74 million tonnes, an increase of 2 percent from 1996. Primary smelter production was 3.96 million tonnes, up almost 2 percent from 1996. Secondary smelter production was 368,000 tonnes, an increase of 3 percent from 1996. Undifferentiated world smelter production in 1997 was estimated at 3.42 million tonnes, up almost 4 percent from 1996. The largest producer of primary and secondary zinc in 1997 was China with 1.4 million tonnes in 1997, an increase of 19 percent from 1996. The next largest producer was Canada with 701,000 tonnes, down 2 percent from 1996. Japan was the next largest producer with 1997 smelter production of 650,078 tonnes, up 1 percent from 1996. Other large producers of smelter zinc include the U.S., Australia, Spain and South Korea. Total world reserves in 1997 were 190 million tonnes of contained zinc.

U.S. mine production of zinc (zinc content of concentrate) in July 1998 was 62,900 tonnes, up 9 percent from June. In the January-July 1998 period, mined zinc production was 404,000 tonnes, up 19 percent from the same period of 1997. For all of 1997, zinc mine production was 601,000 tonnes (zinc content of concentrate). Alaska produced more than one-half of U.S. output of zinc concentrate. U.S. mine production of recoverable zinc in July 1998 was 59,900 tonnes, an increase of 9 percent from June 1998. The production in January-July 1998 was 385,000 tonnes, up 18 percent from the previous year. For all of 1997, mine production of recoverable zinc was 574,000 tonnes.

U.S. smelter production of refined zinc in July 1998 was 32,100 tonnes, up 2 percent from June. In the January-July 1998 period, smelter production was 227,000 tonnes, up 2 percent from the year before. For all of 1997, smelter production was 377,000 tonnes. U.S. production of zinc oxide (gross weight) in July 1998 was 13,100 tonnes, up 5 percent from the prior month. In the first seven months of 1998, production was 88,200 tonnes, down 7 percent from 1997. For all of 1997, zinc oxide production was 164,000 tonnes.

U.S. consumption of refined zinc in July 1998 was reported to be 46,600 tonnes, down 5 percent from June. In the January-July 1998 period, consumption was 327,000 tonnes, about the same as in 1997. For all of 1997, refined zinc consumption was 558,000 tonnes. Zinc ore consumption in July 1998 was 150 tonnes. In January-July 1998 it was 1,050 tonnes while for all of 1997 it was 1,800 tonnes.

Consumption of zinc-base scrap (zinc content) in July 1998 was 8,300 tonnes, the same as in June. In the first seven months of 1998, consumption was 58,100 tonnes, the same as in 1997. For all of 1997, zinc-base scrap consumption was 99,600 tonnes. U.S. consumption of copper-base scrap (zinc content) in January-July 1998 was 98,000 tonnes vs. 168,000 tonnes for all of 1997. Total consumption of zinc in all forms in January-July 1998 was 485,000 tonnes while for all of 1997 it was 828,000 tonnes. Apparent consumption of zinc metal in January-July 1998 was 689,000 tonnes while for 1997 it was 1.26 million tonnes.

U.S. producer stocks of refined (slab) zinc at the end of July 1998 were 8,560 tonnes. Consumer stocks of refined zinc at the end of July 1998 were 56,900 tonnes. Merchant stocks of refined zinc in July 1998 were 15,800 tonnes. Shipments of zinc metal from the Government stockpile in January-July 1998 were 10,800 tonnes. For all of 1997 they were 32,300 tonnes.

Futures Markets

Zinc futures and options are traded on the London Metal Exchange (LME).

Salient Statistics of Zinc in the United States In Metric Tons

	Slab Zinc Production		Mine	Imports for Consumption		Exports		Consumption			Net Import	
Year	Primary	Secondary	Production (Recovered)	Slab Zinc	Ore (Zinc Content)	Slab Zinc	Ore (Zinc Content)	Slab Zinc	Consumed as Ore	All Classes[3]	as a % of Consumption	High-Grade, Price ¢ Per Lb.
1988	241,294	88,492	244,314	748,130	62,966	482	33,590	1,089,000	2,412	1,340,000	70	60.20
1989	260,305	97,904	275,883	711,554	40,974	5,532	78,877	1,060,000	2,107	1,311,000	61	82.02
1990	262,704	95,708	515,355	631,742	46,684	1,238	220,446	992,000	2,178	1,240,000	41	74.59
1991	253,276	124,078	517,804	549,137	45,419	1,253	381,416	933,000	2,098	1,165,000	24	52.77
1992	272,000	128,000	523,430	644,482	44,523	565	307,114	1,050,000	2,400	1,290,000	30	58.38
1993	240,000	141,000	488,374	723,563	33,093	1,410	311,278	1,120,000	2,200	1,340,000	36	46.15
1994	216,600	139,000	570,000	793,000	27,374	6,310	389,000	1,180,000	2,400	1,400,000	35	49.26
1995	232,000	131,000	614,000	856,000	10,300	3,080	424,000	1,230,000	2,400	1,460,000	35	55.83
1996[1]	226,000	140,000	598,000	827,000	15,100	1,970	425,000	1,210,000	1,400	1,450,000	33	51.11
1997[2]	227,000	140,000	605,000	876,000	49,600	3,630	461,000	1,280,000	-----	1,510,000	35	64.56

[1] Preliminary. [2] Estimate. [3] Based on apparent consumption of slab zinc plus zinc content of ores and concentrates and secondary materials used to make zinc dust and chemicals. *Source: U.S. Geological Survey (USGS)*